Political Governance in China

Political Governance in China

Edited by

Tony Saich

Daewoo Professor of International Affairs
Director, Ash Center for Democratic Governance and Innovation
Harvard University, USA

An Elgar Research Collection
Cheltenham, UK • Northampton, MA, USA

Published by
Edward Elgar Publishing Limited
The Lypiatts
15 Lansdown Road
Cheltenham
Glos GL50 2JA
UK

Edward Elgar Publishing, Inc.
William Pratt House
9 Dewey Court
Northampton
Massachusetts 01060
USA

A catalogue record for this book is available from the British Library

Library of Congress Control Number: 2014952127

MIX
Paper from responsible sources
FSC® C013056
www.fsc.org

ISBN 978 1 78195 383 9

Printed and bound in Great Britain by T.J. International Ltd, Padstow

Contents

Acknowledgements

The editor and publishers wish to thank the authors and the following publishers who have kindly given permission for the use of copyright material.

Cambridge University Press for articles: Jean C. Oi (1992), 'Fiscal Reform and the Economic Foundations of Local State Corporatism in China', *World Politics*, **45** (1), October, 99–126; Gabriella Montinola, Yingyi Qian, and Barry R. Weingast (1995), 'Federalism, Chinese Style: The Political Basis for Economic Success in China', *World Politics*, **48** (1), October, 50–81; Andrew C. Mertha (2005), 'China's "Soft" Centralization: Shifting *Tiao/Kuai* Authority Relations', *China Quarterly*, **184**, December, 791–810; Hongbin Cai and Daniel Treisman (2006), 'Did Government Decentralization Cause China's Economic Miracle?', *World Politics*, **58** (4), July, 505–35; Kellee S. Tsai (2006), 'Adaptive Informal Institutions and Endogenous Institutional Change in China', *World Politics*, **59** (1), October, 116–41; Lily L. Tsai (2007), 'Solidary Groups, Informal Accountability, and Local Public Goods Provision in Rural China', *American Political Science Review*, **101** (2), May, 355–72; Elizabeth J. Perry (2008), 'Chinese Conceptions of "Rights": From Mencius to Mao—and Now', *Perspectives on Politics*, **6** (1), March, 37–50; Yongshun Cai (2008), 'Power Structure and Regime Resilience: Contentious Politics in China', *British Journal of Political Science*, **38** (3), July, 411–32; Andrew Mertha (2009), '"Fragmented Authoritarianism 2.0": Political Pluralization in the Chinese Policy Process', *China Quarterly*, **200**, December, 995–1012; Graeme Smith (2010), 'The Hollow State: Rural Governance in China', *China Quarterly*, **203**, September, 601–18; Victor Shih, Christopher Adolph and Mingxing Liu (2012), 'Getting Ahead in the Communist Party: Explaining the Advancement of Central Committee Members in China', *American Political Science Review*, **106** (1), February, 166–87; Cheng Li (2012), 'The End of the CCP's Resilient Authoritarianism? A Tripartite Assessment of Shifting Power in China', *China Quarterly*, **211**, September, 595–623; Patricia M. Thornton (2013), 'The Advance of the Party: Transformation or Takeover of Urban Grassroots Society?', *China Quarterly*, **213**, March, 1–18; Jessica C. Teets (2013), 'Let Many Civil Societies Bloom: The Rise of Consultative Authoritarianism in China', *China Quarterly*, **213**, March, 19–38.

Fondazione Giangiacomo Feltrinelli for excerpt: Tony Saich (2002), 'The Blind Man and the Elephant: Analysing the Local State in China', in Luigi Tomba (ed.), *East Asian Capitalism: Conflicts, Growth and Crisis*, 75–99.

Johns Hopkins University Press for articles: Andrew J. Nathan (2003), 'Authoritarian Resilience', *Journal of Democracy*, **14** (1), January, 6–17; Henry S. Rowen (2007), 'When Will the Chinese People Be Free?', *Journal of Democracy*, **18** (3), July, 38–52.

John Wiley and Sons Ltd for article: Jude Howell (2006), 'Reflections on the Chinese State', *Development and Change*, **37** (2), March, 273–97.

Pacific Affairs for article: Tony Saich and Xuedong Yang (2003), 'Innovation in China's Local Governance: "Open Recommendation and Selection"', *Pacific Affairs*, **76** (2), Summer, 185–208.

Rowman and Littlefield Publishers, Inc. and Cambridge University Press for excerpt: Tony Saich (2006), 'Negotiating the State: The Development of Social Organizations in China', in Lowell Dittmer and Guoli Liu (eds), *China's Deep Reform: Domestic Politics in Transition*, Chapter 10, 285–301.

Rowman and Littlefield Publishers, Inc. and the Academy of Political Science for excerpt: Bruce J. Dickson (2006), 'Cooptation and Corporatism in China: The Logic of Party Adaptation', in Lowell Dittmer and Guoli Liu (eds), *China's Deep Reform: Domestic Politics in Transition*, Chapter 4, 119–43.

Tony Saich for his own article: (2012), 'The Quality of Governance in China: The Citizens' View', *Harvard Kennedy School, Faculty Research Working Paper Series*, RWP12-051, i, 1–41.

Sage Publications via the Copyright Clearance Center's RightsLink Service for articles: Melanie Manion (2006), 'Democracy, Community, Trust: The Impact of Elections in Rural China', *Comparative Political Studies*, **39** (3), April, 301–23; Pierre F. Landry, Deborah Davis and Shiru Wang (2010), 'Elections in Rural China: Competition Without Parties', *Comparative Political Studies*, **43** (6), June, 763–90.

Springer Science and Business Media B.V. for article: Sebastian Heilmann (2008), 'Policy Experimentation in China's Economic Rise', *Studies in Comparative International Development*, **43**, March, 1–26.

Taylor and Francis Ltd (www.taylorandfrancis.com) for articles: Gunter Schubert (2008), 'One-Party Rule and the Question of Legitimacy in Contemporary China: Preliminary Thoughts on Setting Up a New Research Agenda', *Journal of Contemporary China*, **17** (54), February, 191–204; Kevin J. O'Brien and Rongbin Han (2009), 'Path to Democracy? Assessing Village Elections in China', *Journal of Contemporary China*, **18** (60), June, 359–78; Steve Tsang (2009), 'Consultative Leninism: China's New Political Framework', *Journal of Contemporary China*, **18** (62), November, 865–80; Barry Naughton (2010), 'China's Distinctive System: Can It Be a Model for Others?', *Journal of Contemporary China*, **19** (65), June, 437–60; Kevin J. O'Brien (2011), 'Studying Chinese Politics in an Age of Specialization', *Journal of Contemporary China*, **20** (71), September, 535–41; Minglu Chen and David S.G. Goodman (2012), 'The China Model: One Country, Six Authors', *Journal of Contemporary China*, **21** (73), January, 169–85.

University of Chicago Press for articles: Elizabeth J. Perry (2007), 'Studying Chinese Politics: Farewell to Revolution?', *China Journal*, **57**, January, 1–22; Lianjiang Li (2010), 'Rights Consciousness and Rules Consciousness in Contemporary China', *China Journal*, **64**, July, 47–68.

Every effort has been made to trace all the copyright holders but if any have been inadvertently overlooked the publishers will be pleased to make the necessary arrangement at the first opportunity.

In addition the publishers wish to thank the Library of Indiana University at Bloomington, USA for its assistance in obtaining these articles.

Introduction

Tony Saich

The study of Chinese politics has evolved significantly over the last three decades. This evolution has gone hand in hand with the years of economic reform that have created a country that looks more like other developing nations and that have opened up greater research opportunities. Not only is more statistical data available but also greater use can be made of survey research, interviews, and fieldwork. This has changed the nature of research on China substantially and has meant that such study is more amenable to comparative research questions. Research projects now may include not only work with Chinese colleagues but also collaborations with 'non-China specialists' who are interested in questions of comparative development and what the study of China might contribute to this broader agenda.

Until the 1970s, research was mainly characterized as 'area studies' with one group of researchers analyzing contemporary China in terms of its historical and cultural legacies. This placed emphasis on questions of continuity and change and the extent to which traditional patterns of authority still influenced the contemporary polity. Research that was not 'Sino-centric' explored the differences between the Chinese communist experience and that of the Soviets, especially those that derived from the Chinese Communist Party's (CCP) revolutionary and cultural heritage (see, for example, Schwartz, 1951). Some tried to include the study of the Chinese Revolution in the broader field of comparative revolutions (Moore, 1966). In so far as Chinese politics were taught, certainly in the United Kingdom, it was as a sub-set of a course on comparative communist systems. This approach also dictated research themes with attempts to apply concepts developed in the study of the Soviet Union to see whether they applied, or not, to the Chinese situation (for example, Goodman, 1984). Given the paucity of materials and lack of access, most 'field' interviews were conducted with refugees in Hong Kong and where the University Services Center in Hong Kong provided an abundant collection of resources. It is true that students from many countries, with the notable exceptions of the USA and the USSR, were able to study in China from the early 1970s, although access was strictly controlled and serious fieldwork was not feasible. The academic community was relatively small, so it was possible to keep abreast of most areas of study and the field was relatively isolated from 'mainstream' political science. Reading a couple of newspapers and journals could make you an expert on almost anything to do with China. Reform tore up this cozy existence: the language changed, publications proliferated, access opened up, and academic specialization became not only possible but also necessary. This collection concentrates on political science writing that has been a product of the post-1978 reform period.

The Study of Chinese Politics

The situation outlined above has been transformed completely with fruitful engagement with questions of comparative development and the involvement of non-China specialists who bring their own comparative research questions to the empirical hunting ground of China. China has become an important area of research for those interested in questions of transitional systems, especially the relationship between an authoritarian polity and a more liberalized economy; one-party political systems; or the East Asian Developmental state. The career incentives for young scholars entering the field pushes research toward a disciplinary focus and away from what might still be thought of as traditional 'area studies.'

However, Elizabeth Perry (Chapter 1, this volume) warns of 'throwing out the baby with the bathwater.' While acknowledging the increasing engagement with comparative questions such as the development of civil society, and the role of property rights in development or democratization, she stresses how China's development experience and its revolutionary experience have still shaped outcomes. Perry notes the importance of how 'retention—and reinvention—of many elements of China's revolutionary heritage [...] have managed to fashion a surprisingly durable brand of "revolutionary authoritarianism."' As a result, she is cautious about the extent to which Soviet studies, theories about 'run-of-the-mill authoritarianism,' and the East Asian Development state are useful comparators. There is a residual impact from Maoist institutions and practices. This has highlighted relevance with the ascent to General Secretary of the CCP of Xi Jinping (in 2012), who has promoted Maoist practices such as the 'mass line' and has been sharply critical of those who completely reject the development experience under Mao Zedong.

O'Brien (Chapter 2, this volume) takes up the theme of the possible trade-offs between more traditional area studies and the discipline of political science. He notes two main trends. First, as we have noted above, there has been a growing disciplinary orientation. Second, the research focus has narrowed to very specific topics and there is hesitation to link this research to larger questions about the nature of the political system and its evolution. There has been a push not only to ignore 'Chinese exceptionalism' but also not to see it as relevant. These trends provide first-rate research but one might conclude that we are getting a good view of the individual trees but we are losing sight of the woods.

This sets a challenge for what a future research agenda might look like. Certainly, the field has been reinvigorated by integration with the disciplines and, given China's importance, this will continue to evolve. However, following the extensive period of fieldwork and the production of many excellent micro-studies, there is a need for a project of synthesizing to tell us what such research reveals about systemic evolution and what it contributes to ideas about transition and authoritarian regimes. Schubert (Chapter 3, this volume) looks at what a research agenda might comprise. He suggests that micro-research might help us shed valuable light on larger questions, in particular regime legitimacy. His article counters a prevalent view that political legitimacy is precarious, that the necessary political reforms to ameliorate this situation are not feasible, and that significant change is only a matter of time (see Chapter 32, this volume, by Rowen). His proposal is to promote a research agenda that looks at specific examples where reforms may be generating or sustaining citizen participation and regime support. Such topics might include village elections, the reform of the local people's congress, and various participatory channels. He concludes that the 'authoritarian resilience' of CCP rule may be grounded in a critical degree of overall regime legitimacy that has not been grasped by China scholars. We return to the question of 'authoritarian resilience' in the final section below.

The Nature of the Chinese Political System

The reforms have led to considerable debate and confusion about what Baum and Shevchenko (1999) call the 'state of the state' in China. Different views have been expressed in the literature about the kind of system that has evolved and this has been accompanied by discussions about whether the experiences of China's developmental model can be transferred to other developing countries. This has produced a flurry of articles that try to categorize the nature of the Chinese development model by defining its key characteristics. As one would expect, there is no unanimity on this and there has been a proliferation of terms to try to capture the evolving nature of the Chinese system.

Study of the nature of the Chinese system and its applicability to other countries was given a boost by Joshua Cooper Ramo's publication *The Beijing Consensus* (2004). This was a direct challenge to the Washington Consensus as a model for aspiring developmental states to achieve economic take-off. Based on his observations of China's development, Ramo proposed three main features. First, China had displayed a consistent commitment to 'innovation and constant experimentation.' Second, he proposed that the sustainability of development and an equitable distribution of wealth were equally as important as measuring development in terms of GDP per capita alone. Third, developing countries should pursue a 'policy of self-determination' to check the influence of foreign powers and should be especially vigilant to maintain financial sovereignty. The bottom line of Ramo's view is that an authoritarian polity and economic liberalization can coexist to produce effective development. This leads to two particular questions: is the depiction accurate and is China a model for others?

Chen and Goodman (Chapter 4, this volume), in reviewing Ramo's thesis and those of a number of other writers, suggest that their analyses propose that there is a specific model of the relationship between the state, society and the market. By contrast, they suggest that China's success is the result of unique circumstances that might be difficult to replicate elsewhere. They highlight two features of China's developmental trajectory that are important: the size and scale of its huge domestic market and, echoing Perry, the peculiarities of its own historical experiences. They highlight the use of marketization and competition, rather than privatization, as crucial elements in China's success. In addition, they view three factors as important for China's development: the rise of a substantial middle class, the level of state investment in infrastructure, and the operation of a mixed economy.

Howell (Chapter 5, this volume) analyzes China's development in light of the East Asian Development model, a view that has gained traction in the literature. Writers such as Blecher and Shue (1996) and Oi (1989; Chapter 14, this volume; 1999) have used the developmental state as applied to Japan, South Korea, and Taiwan as a starting point for their understanding of how the local state functions in China. Oi develops the notion of local state corporatism, while Blecher and Shue develop the idea of a local entrepreneurial state. Howell rejects the application of the developmental state as a satisfactory characterization of the Chinese political system. Unlike with the other successful East Asian states, she does not view the central state as the prime actor in development. Instead she sees an increasingly fragmented state structure in operation. In turn, the vacillating legitimacy of the CCP reduces the state's capacity to develop a nationwide strategy that, in turn, has led to the promotion of nationalism as a mobilizing factor. The fragmentation creates an environment where the pursuit of personal and institutional survival overrides the broader policy objectives. In place of the notion of the developmental state, she favors the descriptor of the state as 'polymorphous,' assuming multiple, complex forms that defy reduction to a unitary actor.

Given this fragmentary nature of the state, one key question that arises is what holds the system together? Tsang (Chapter 6, this volume) with his concept of 'consultative Leninism' highlights the key role the CCP plays in ensuring that the political machinery is more resilient in confronting the challenges it faces in a rapidly changing environment. He portrays this system as resilient and as not moving toward a more democratic system. It has evolved from the measures that the CCP took to save itself after the shocks produced by the student-led demonstrations of 1989 and the subsequent collapse of the communist regimes in the Soviet Union and Eastern Europe. The primary objective of the system is to ensure continued CCP rule. Reforms and other governing mechanisms will be adopted and adapted to meet this overriding priority. This has resulted in governance reforms that are intended to pre-empt moves toward democracy; new feedback loops to incorporate public opinion while, at the same time, guiding it; a more pragmatic economic management; and, importantly, the promotion of nationalism as a core belief to bolster (or even substitute for) the diminishing belief in Marxism.

One further crucial question that arises is how the Chinese system has been amended to confront the new challenges. If there has been little institutional or political reform, as some have suggested, then one might see the system as vulnerable to potential collapse. Kellee Tsai (Chapter 7, this volume) rejects the notion that the Chinese political system has resisted change and instead puts forward the idea that there has been significant change from below through the adaptation of informal institutions that have, in turn, led to amendment of formal institutions and constitutional revision. Her study shows how informal practices at the local level paved the way for legalization of the private sector, which had attracted party members into entrepreneurial activities. This was taken up by Jiang Zemin, when he was General Secretary, in his notion of the 'three represents' that was a more inclusive definition of the groups the CCP represented. The CCP was to represent the 'advanced social productive forces, the progressive course of China's advanced culture,' and the 'fundamental interests of the overwhelming majority of the people.' This paved the way for a constitutional amendment that included private sector workers as an integral part of the working class and provided the private sector with greater legitimacy in the economic sphere. She shows how adaptive informal institutions can serve a vital intermediate role in explaining the process of endogenous institutional change in the absence of 'cataclysmic events or institutional collapse.'

Naughton (Chapter 8, this volume) makes the strongest case for not viewing China's development as a model that can be easily copied by others. He acknowledges that certain aspects may be beneficial for other countries to consider but suggests that the totality of the Chinese developmental experience owes too much to conditions that cannot be replicated by others. He views three features that define China's development as unique: the size of the internal market (similar to Chen and Goodman); the shift to labor-intensive development from the earlier state-led capital intensive development; and the retention and adaptation of China's hierarchical authoritarian political system. He highlights six lessons from the development experience, all of which are important but may not be easy for others to copy in their entirety.

These include that, contrary to Washington Consensus orthodoxy, public ownership has not been abandoned and has proved 'reasonably efficient'; competition is more important than ownership; state-led investment means that it can anticipate demand; the state sector can create growth outside of the sector; and managers in the sector can be incentivized.

The Policy-Making Process

While much of the policy-making process remains a black-box, the notion that the system operates solely in a top-down fashion is clearly outdated. We know that there is a much more sophisticated interaction between different organizations at the same level and between different levels of government, but it is difficult to specify the precise nature. There are many instances of the Center issuing policy directives that are resisted or deflected by local administrations. This is reflected in two common phrases: 'The mountains are high and the Emperor is far away' (*shangao Huangdi yuan*) and 'They have their policies and we have our counter measures' (*tamen you zhengce, women you duice*). Yet, it is also the case that local experimentation has played a significant role in national policy development. We saw in the previous section how adaptive informal institutions have contributed to change in national practice. In addition, the important reforms that led to the reversion to household farming began with local experimentation in Anhui province, while the Special Economic Zones, such as in Shenzhen, have been crucial for providing a test bed for controversial labor and industrial reforms.

Thus, local experimentation is viewed by many as a key component of the policy-making process in China. This counters the view of a dominant top-down policy-making process and the more general notion of communist party-states as being extremely inflexible. Heilmann (Chapter 9, this volume) argues that '[t]he combination of decentralized experimentation with ad hoc central interference, which results in selective integration of local experiences into national policymaking, is key to understanding how a distinctive policy process has contributed to China's economic rise.' He calls this process 'experimentation under hierarchy' whereby political elites can benefit from local policy entrepreneurship. The central government then has the crucial role of scaling up the experiment and turning the specific into a more generalizable policy through national laws and regulations.

Montinola, Qian and Weingast (Chapter 10, this volume) also stress the role of the local to explain China's remarkable economic growth. Unlike many countries, they see a special type of institutionalized decentralization they refer to as 'federalism, Chinese style' that is market-preserving. They identify three consequences that follow from this decentralization. First, it fosters competition not just in product markets but also among local governments for labor and foreign capital. This encourages the kind of local experimentation that Heilmann sees as a crucial component of policy-making. Second, it provides local government with the necessary incentives to promote local economic prosperity. Third, this system provides local governments and their enterprises with protection against 'political intrusion' by the central government.

By contrast, Cai and Treisman (Chapter 11, this volume) strongly reject the notion that decentralization has been a major driver of China's economic growth. They claim that the key reforms shaping China's economic growth occurred in the late 1970s and early 1980s before significant decentralization had been introduced. They see much greater engagement of different groups of central leaders in local experimentation. Instead of decentralization, they view competition between rival factions at the center with local connections that have competing ideological predispositions. Thus, they see central leaders as more willing to promote local experimentation and being in a better position to coordinate such experimentation across regions and to implement it nationwide. Thus, they reject the notion that China's reforms have been shaped by innovative, autonomous local leaders.

Schurmann (1968) was one of the first writers to point out the problem of bureaucratic coordination in what he refers to as 'vertical' and 'dual' rule. The dominance of one rule over the other will affect the implementation of central policy and how authority is exerted. The Chinese refer to these systems as '*tiao*' (branches) and '*kuai*' (areas). Under the former, the line ministry or equivalent exerts a 'leadership relationship' over the units at the lower administrative level. This encourages vertical flow of information, commands, and incentives. '*Kuai*' refers to horizontal linkages and stresses the authority of the party branch/committee at each level. Here, the party at the corresponding level exerts the leadership relationship. The resultant system is one of dual rule as the organization at the lower level is responsible to the corresponding departments of the line ministry at the higher levels as well as to the party committee at the same level. Unger (1987) used this struggle over the tension between the two sets of rule to interpret post-1949 administrative history.

Mertha (Chapter 12, this volume) revisits this key question about lines of authority and decision-making in the Chinese political system. He claims that, in recent years, a process of recentralization to the provincial level has been taking place: what he refers to as 'soft centralization.' While the first period of reforms was characterized by the decentralization of economic and political decision-making to local governments, by the end of the 1990s there had been a partial centralization of key bureaucracies to regulate local governments and reduce 'local protectionism.' This process accompanied the evolution of the early characteristics of a regulatory state in China. This recentralization would undermine the market-preserving federalism that Montinola and colleagues see as driving China's economic growth. However, this shift of bureaucratic control from the township and county to the provincial level has produced unintended consequences that may presage further readjustments in the future.

In terms of policy-making generally, one of the most enduring theories has been that of 'fragmented authoritarianism' first proposed by Oksenberg and Lieberthal (1988; see also Lieberthal, 1992). In their view, authority below the 'very peak' of the administrative system is fragmented and disjointed in a manner that is structurally based and that has been enhanced by reform policies regarding procedures. This means that policies introduced by the center are shaped by bureaucratic agencies that have their own organizational interests and imperatives and also by the regional jurisdictions. As a result, in implementation these diverse interests are incorporated leading to 'incremental change' in the policy arena through the process of bureaucratic bargaining. Mertha (Chapter 13, this volume) then adapts this theory to look at how the authoritarian system has been responding to the increasingly diverse demands of society. While he still sees the theory as the key explanatory factor, he suggests that the policy process has become increasingly pluralized. The fragmented nature of the system allows 'space' for policy entrepreneurs to operate to influence policy formulation and implementation. In particular, he identifies three new types of policy entrepreneur: officials in agencies opposed to a given policy, journalists and editors, and NGOs.

The Nature of the Local State

As is clear from the comments above, reforms have changed the nature of the local state both in terms of its hierarchical relations but also in terms of its relationship to society. Local resources and power structures increasingly determine political outcomes. Within the same province and even within the same county, one can witness dramatically different socio-political outcomes deriving from reforms. The effective decentralization of the fiscal system, more than any other factor, accounts for this local variation. It also explains why there is such inequality in the provision of public goods and services from one administrative jurisdiction to another.

Oi (Chapter 14, this volume) was one of the first to analyze in detail how the incentives provided by fiscal reform had created the conditions for local officials to drive economic growth forward. The break-up of the collectives meant that local governments lost access to agricultural revenue, and the harder budget constraints combined with local governments obtaining the rights over any surplus drove them to look to industrial development. As a result, they became local government entrepreneurs promoting local township and village collective enterprises under what she terms 'local state corporatism.' The local leaders acted as a board of directors in deciding on the investment and distribution of revenues. She suggests that this system of incentives meant that reforms could be pushed forward, generating economic growth without them presenting any real threat to their power.

Since Oi's early work there has been a number of excellent local studies that provide various descriptions of the nature of the local state. As Saich (Chapter 15, this volume) writes, '[t]he tendency for both Chinese and Western scholars has been to dwell on the fusion of political and economic power at local government levels. This has been accompanied in Western writings with an emphasis on property rights relationships.' Financial decentralization is crucial but the resultant structures are strongly influenced by the pre-reform economic structure. Out of this approach comes a categorization of local government forms: entrepreneurial, developmental, predatory, and varieties of corporatism. Saich suggests that two other factors are important in addition to the impact of fiscal decentralization. First, there is the impact of the political contracting system that sets up clear incentives for local leaders to concentrate on certain types of work over others. Second, there is the structure of local society. The nature of the local community and the ties of local officials to that community will also have a significant impact on the nature of the local state. These factors produce a 'patchwork' of different relationships with the precise outcome 'dependent on a location's historical legacy, resource endowment, and leadership.'

Tsai (Chapter 16, this volume) explores in detail the relationship between local officials and the community. She starts with the basic question: why would officials in an authoritarian system provide more than the minimum level of public goods that would be necessary to maintain social stability? She uses the notion of solidary groups that are based on shared moral obligations and interests as ensuring that they fulfill public obligations. These organizations would include village temples and village-wide lineages. For local officials to be committed to the provision of public goods within the community, these solidary groups need to be both 'encompassing' and 'embedding.' Encompassing in Tsai's usage means that they must be open to all under the jurisdiction of the local government with the social boundaries overlapping with political boundaries. Embedding means that local officials are incorporated into the group as members. Where these conditions exist, weak formal institutions for accountability can be overcome and these unofficial norms will help local administrators to enforce their 'public obligation.'

The role of the township, the lowest formal level of government administration, has been a subject of much discussion, and some have even questioned its value, suggesting that it be abolished. This has not happened to date and is problematic as the township is a major source of employment and of patronage within the countryside. Instead, some townships are being merged and the focus of their work is shifting. With the county being developed as the fiscal center, reforms have attempted to turn township governments into 'service-oriented' agencies and away from being extractive agents of the state. This latter function was drastically reduced by the abolition of the agricultural tax in 2006. Smith (Chapter 17, this volume), in his detailed study of a county in Anhui province, shows how, in reality, the township level of government is being 'hollowed out' by pressures from above and below. From above, there are the needs to attract more investment to compensate for the loss of the agricultural tax; to meet obligations dictated by higher levels of government, enhanced by the 'soft centralization' that is taking place; and to receive inspection teams. From below, many township officials are being seconded to the villages to oversee family planning and to ensure social stability among other tasks. These trends have undermined the government's desire to see the township function as a more effective service provider.

One feature that is implicit and explicit in much of the writing about incentives for local officials in terms of job performance and promotion is the need to focus on GDP growth and local investment tasks. However, despite the prevalence of performance contracts that emphasize these targets, recent research suggests that more traditional factors of loyalty and factional allegiance may be more important, especially in terms of promotion into the CCP's leading bodies. Landry (2008), for example, concludes that exceptional economic performance has virtually no effect on the chances for internal promotion of mayors to party secretary.

Shih, Adolph and Liu (Chapter 18, this volume) in their detailed study of membership of the central committee (both full and alternate members) conclude that the cadre evaluation system and the geographic-based governing system that many have seen as causing local governments to compete with one another to produce high growth rates do not lead to promotion to higher party position. By contrast, they find that factional ties to top leaders play a more substantial role in promotion. In addition, they find that educational qualifications and provincial revenue collection are also important in terms of elite ranking. Thus, they make the important observation that 'promotion systems served the immediate needs of the regime and its leaders, rather than encompassing goals such as economic growth.' If this is true more generally, it contradicts much of the literature (including Saich above) on the incentives for prioritization of activities by local officials.

One final question remains as to how citizens view the performance of their government. Saich (Chapter 19, this volume), through his survey, shows that citizens disaggregate the state when they think about satisfaction with government performance. While they express high levels of satisfaction with the central government, this declines with each lower level of government. Thus, the township government receives the lowest satisfaction ratings; not surprising given the analysis presented by Smith (Chapter 17, this volume). However, interestingly, during the years of the survey (2003–11), satisfaction levels with the work of government have risen, perhaps showing a response to the 'people-centered' policies of the Hu Jintao–Wen Jiabao leadership. Yet, dissatisfaction with the performance of local government officials remains high with many respondents feeling that they were aloof, close to those with money, and primarily took care of their own interests. In terms of what they wanted their government to focus on, citizens wanted more attention to be paid to services that are related to alleviating the negative impacts of reforms and do not see a strong role for government in overseeing religious belief, or family planning, or being involved in attracting business and investment.

Participation and Protest

The reform program has fundamentally changed the relationship between state and society, opening new channels for participation in the political process. The conscious withdrawal of the state has led to the creation of greater space for citizen engagement and the emergence of non-governmental organizations (NGOs) to undertake services that formerly were carried out by the state agencies. However, this should be interpreted not as the emergence of a more democratic polity but rather as the liberalization of previous regime practices as the party acknowledges that it needs the input of certain kinds of knowledge from different sectors of society and that certain functions can be carried out more effectively by the NGOs. In turn, this has led to both a loosening of the party's grip over society and also the development of new mechanisms of control. The increasingly complex nature of a society in which liberalization coexists with continued party-state control has also led to the rise of new areas of conflict and the creation of new mechanisms and repertoires for dissent, as well as traditional expressions.

One of the most noticeable features of the reform period has been the rise of NGOs (social organizations). By the end of 2012, there were over 450,000 social organizations officially registered with the Ministry of Civil Affairs, while there are millions that are not registered. Saich (Chapter 20, this volume) notes that the space in which these organizations can operate has expanded, and that they now represent the varied societal interests, convey those interests into the policy-making process, and carry out vital welfare functions that the state cannot or is no longer willing to undertake. In turn, this has led the state to develop mechanisms to incorporate these organizations into the control structure of the party-state. He suggests that this has led to attempts to develop a traditional Leninist reordering of the sector with legislation seeking to mimic the composition of government departments and limit horizontal linkages. Yet, control is not absolute, and he suggests there exists a symbiotic relationship through which some of these organizations have developed strategies to negotiate a relationship that maximizes the interests of their members or that circumnavigates or deflects state intrusion. The more complex set of relationships that emerges from this process means that some organizations can have effective input into decision-making and create relationships that transcend traditional Leninist vertical controls.

The trend that Saich identifies of local governments carrying the main burden for the provision of public goods and services has intensified in recent years. The fact that often they have insufficient revenue streams has placed great pressure on them, a pressure that was compounded by the transfer of many social services from the work unit to the state and to society. This has further expanded the space for civic organizations to operate and fosters greater tolerance on the part of local authorities toward their activities and even causes them to engage in co-production. However, as Teets (Chapter 21, this volume) shows in her article and case study of Beijing and the Shining Stone Community Action, the state has sought to develop new mechanisms of indirect control. Thus, the expansion of civil society leads not necessarily to democratization but rather to better governance and enhanced citizen satisfaction. This gives support to the argument of 'resilient authoritarianism' that we look at in the final section. In addition to the need to provide public goods more effectively, Teets also points to the influence of the model of the Western regulatory state that facilitates the 'transition of governing institutions from a producer function to more of a regulatory function.' The rise of the color revolutions and the Arab Spring served as warnings, and the perceived success of the state-led development in China in response to the global financial crisis (2008–09) set limits to the expansion of the sector. Here she sees the influence of the 'New Left' thinking that has given rise to 'consultative authoritarianism.' This is distinct from corporatism in that it permits a pluralistic society to participate in policy formulation and implementation. Accompanying this is the use of multiple indirect tools of state control. This explains the possibility of civil society development under authoritarian conditions without any necessary momentum toward democratization.

Saich and Teets concentrate, as do many others, on the state response to these new organizations but Thornton (Chapter 22, this volume) suggests that the CCP itself has begun to adapt to influence this emergent societal sector. She suggests that the downsizing of government that has taken place since 1998 has resulted in an 'unprecedented advance of the Party' to fill the space that has been created. This has resulted in the CCP being able to steer civil society to serve its own objectives. While earlier writing has concentrated on government-organized NGOs, she writes of Party-organized NGOs. This suggests that the CCP, far from passively accepting state withdrawal and the rise of a more autonomous social sphere, has actively promoted new mechanisms of social governance. She looks at this phenomenon through a detailed case study of Shanghai where the party has shaped and guided the sector to meet the societal needs as defined by the regime. She estimates that the Party has engaged with and manages over 90 percent of the NGOs in Shanghai through a policy she terms selective 'absorption.' This is part of a general drive to reassert party engagement in an increasingly varied and diverse socio-economic landscape.

The most extensively covered area of citizen participation has been the development of village elections across China. With the abandonment of the communes in the early 1980s and the restoration of the administrative system of counties and townships, formal state power stopped at the township level. This meant that there was no effective governing agency at the village level and numerous reports referred to the rise in conflicts at the local level with no effective mechanism for dispute resolution. Consequently, a program of elections was proposed to elect villagers' committees to form a self-governing mechanism throughout the countryside. This has led to debate about the efficacy of the elections, the extent to which they are genuinely representative, whether they are dominated by traditional social organizations such as clans and lineages, and whether such experimentation at the grassroots level might lead to the promotion of democratic experimentation at more formal levels of the state such as the township level (Saich and Yang, Chapter 26, this volume). Do elections build trust? Who votes and why? What happens once they are elected? These are all important questions that have received attention.

Drawing on surveys conducted in 1990 and 1996, Manion (Chapter 23, this volume) looks at the extent to which the village election program has raised the level of trust that citizens feel towards their leaders. She looks not just at the impact that formal institutions of electoral democracy have in creating trust but also at the importance of informal community institutions such as lineage relationships. She concludes that greater electoral contestation and more inclusive voting procedures matter. Comparison of the two surveys reveals that broader trust has evolved with 51 percent of respondents in 1996 considering most officials not to be corrupt in comparison with just 35 percent in 1990. In addition, the survey shows that informal community institutions such as lineage relationships are also important.

Landry, Davis and Wang (Chapter 24, this volume), in their survey of a rural county in Yunnan, note that in a one-party system where some candidates can lose in the election, voters are more likely to participate. Thus, regular rejection of candidates through contested elections in an authoritarian polity can simultaneously result in strengthening the demand for accountability and loyalty to the regime. In terms of individual voter preferences, they consider a number of factors that may determine participation and discover surprisingly that neither CCP membership nor membership of the communist youth league increases turnout. In terms of income, the poorest and the wealthiest families in the villages do not see a special value in participation. Higher education only has a marginal impact but the ethnic minorities in the region were more likely to vote. In conclusion, they deem the most important factor to be the institutional character of the election, whether there was choice and whether the election was seen to be fair.

O'Brien and Han (Chapter 25, this volume) look at the important question of governing once elections have taken place. They highlight the fact that the villagers' committees have to vie both with other formal institutions and with informal ones in the countryside and that this limits their effectiveness. They note three constraints that villagers' committees face in providing democratic rule. First, in all villages there should be a party branch that constitutes the 'leadership core.' In all the villages that I have visited, it has been clear that the head of the party branch dominates and the village head defers to his (very rarely her) authority. Second, the township may exert its authority in the electoral process and may even suggest its preferred candidates for village head. As they note, where township leaders and villagers' committees disagree, the village officials will not prevail. Last but not least, there is the social network within which the villages are embedded. Clans, religious groups and criminal elements may also compromise democratic rule. This leads them to observe that changes in the 'exercise of power' have not kept up with 'access to power.'

With village elections established, some questioned whether direct elections might be raised to the township level, the lowest level of government administration. While experimentation took place in the late 1990s, it was deemed unconstitutional, but the problem has remained of how to make the township level of government more accountable. As a result, a number of alternative methods have been experimented with to evaluate township officials. Saich and Yang (Chapter 26, this volume) describe the process of 'open recommendation and selection' that was experimented with in Suining Municipality, Sichuan Province. This process used some electoral procedures to broaden the scope of participation in the selection of local leaders while retaining the Leninist concern for control and does not contravene the constitution. The article also sheds further light on the process of innovation in China. Development theory suggests that political innovation tends to occur as levels of well-being rise and markets expand. Yet, a number of significant reforms in China have occurred in poor rural areas, such as the return to household farming and the use of village elections. A situation of crisis and distance from the political center when combined with astute political leadership may serve as the catalyst for significant institutional reform.

The reforms have also seen a considerable rise in both the number and the nature of protests. Most protests have been local in nature concerning specific socio-economic grievances, while only a few have led to political unrest. In the countryside, most protests have concerned land seizures by local authorities and inadequate compensation. As noted, local authorities suffer from insufficient revenues and thus, in recent years, land seizure and subsequent transfer of usage from agricultural to development can raise significant funds, with relatively little dedicated to compensating farmers. In the urban areas, in addition to confiscation of property and resettlement, most protests concern unpaid wages or unfair dismissal. More recently, we have witnessed the rise of middle-class protests that concern lifestyle issues such as resistance to the building of polluting factories, constructing of nuclear processing plants, or other environmentally damaging projects. It has been rare for protests to address overtly political concerns and they have not been regime threatening. The exception during the reform period was the student-led demonstrations of 1989 that coincided with severe divisions within the party leadership about the future direction of reform (see Calhoun, 1994; and Saich, 1990).

Cai (Chapter 27, this volume) analyzes why the rise in protests has not undermined credibility in the regime. He notes that protest creates problems for authoritarian regimes because both making concessions and conducting repression can lead to unpredictable outcomes. He suggests that the CCP has avoided this problem by granting to local governments considerable autonomy to deal with protest. This means that the Center can avoid the blame if the local authority resorts to repression. He notes that this phenomenon of divided state power has allowed the CCP to maintain social stability despite the rise in social unrest. He credits this with creating 'state resilience' allowing the coexistence of social unrest and political stability. Rarely do central level authorities intervene.

These findings are supported by survey work outlined by Saich (Chapter 19, this volume) that discusses citizens' 'disaggregation' of the state with only 10.9 percent of respondents stating that they were 'extremely satisfied' with the performance of their local government. While the consequences of these findings may raise concerns about the quality of local governance, they confirm Cai's view that the protests are not necessarily bad news for the central government and it enjoys a relatively strong source of legitimacy. Most would appear to see the problem as lying with local policy implementation rather than with lack of the Center's will or systemic bias.

The rise in the number of protests begs the question as to whether it is possible that there might be an increase in rights awareness leading to a possible challenge to the regime's legitimacy more broadly. Li (Chapter 28, this volume) suggests that a 'rights consciousness' is indeed emerging as a result of the new forms of protest and that this could lead to a more far-reaching questioning of the state's legitimacy. Li asserts that citizens have an awareness of their existing rights and that they have developed a willingness to exercise those rights. By contrast, Perry (Chapter 29, this volume) questions the extent to which such consciousness has developed and suggests that protest has assumed more traditional forms and does not imply a nascent demand for systemic change or the emergence of 'rights consciousness.' In fact, she implies that the current forms of protest, far from undermining state legitimacy, might bolster it. She uses various examples to show that the language of protest is actually framed in that of

Mencius and Mao and that many Western observers are mistaken to see the protests as reflecting the emergence of an individual rights consciousness that we are used to in the West. This leads her to adopt the term 'rules consciousness' rather than 'rights consciousness.' She sees the protests fitting into a more traditional pattern of resistance where citizens have a legitimate right to rebel against corrupt officials, with the objective being redress of grievance or replacement of particular errant officials rather than systemic change.

Authoritarian Resilience or Democratization

The changes that have been noted above give rise to the key question of what this means for the future evolution of the Chinese political system. Following the student-led demonstrations of 1989 and the collapse of the Soviet Union and its satellite states, attention focused on the resilience of the Chinese system. As it continued to endure and indeed thrive and prosper through the 1990s, the assumption that the CCP would go the way of the Soviet Party was replaced by a search for what factors made the Chinese case different and what was the cause of its systemic resilience (Shambaugh, 2008). The question also arises as to how long this resilience might persist and whether, as in many other polities, eventually the rising incomes that reforms have created and the increasingly complex society that has evolved will lead to systemic change.

Nathan (Chapter 30, this volume) was one of the first to outline systematically why China was unlikely to join the 'third wave' of democratization (Huntington, 1991) and noted the key factors that provided the 'authoritarian resilience.' He focuses on the increasing institutionalization of the system and highlights four key features. First, leadership succession has become more bounded by norms and predictability. Both Mao Zedong and Deng Xiaoping anointed and disposed of successors as their policy preferences shifted. Second, the factional determination of promotion to leadership has been replaced by more meritocratic evaluation. This has resulted in a more professional and competent set of senior leaders. Third, the system has adapted well to the increasing complexity of administrative needs by developing greater differentiation and functional specialization of institutions. Fourth, the CCP has reacted to the increased differentiation within society and citizens' demands by developing more responsive institutions for political participation. This has meant that the reforms have led not to calls for regime change but rather to an increase in the popular perception of regime legitimacy. It gives rise to the question of whether authoritarianism might be viable 'even under conditions of advanced modernization and integration with the global economy.'

Dickson (Chapter 31, this volume) also tackles the question of whether the CCP can adapt to the outcomes that its own reforms have created, noting the important organizational adaptation that has been sponsored by the Party. In particular, he highlights the cooptation of new members and the creation of new links with organizations outside of the CCP. Developing these new linkages is important as the reforms have reduced the traditional state dependency of key groups and thus the power of the ruling party. The Party has moved to recruit new elites such as the intelligentsia and entrepreneurs in the private sector so that they will not form an opposition block outside of the existing power structure. This process has led to an interest in the concept of corporatism and its applicability to China. However, Dickson concludes that Leninism, not corporatism, still defines the Chinese political system.

The changes wrought and the rise of an urban middle class have led a number of writers to speculate on the timing of democratization in China. It is not a question of if but rather when this will occur (Gilley, 2004). Rowen (Chapter 32, this volume), using comparative work on transitional regimes related to rising well-being, suggests that by 2015 China will have moved into the partly free category as defined by Freedom House and that by 2025 it will be classified as free. His starting point is Lipset's view of the relationship between economic growth, development and democratization supported by more recent research by those such as Barro that suggests that higher incomes and higher levels of education are good indicators for a better realm of freedoms.

Finally, Li (Chapter 33, this volume) analyzes the situation as the CCP prepared the leadership transition to Xi Jinping and Li Keqiang, who could rule China until 2022–23. He suggests that the four indicators of institutionalization that Nathan identifies as underpinning 'authoritarian resilience' are unraveling. By contrast, he describes the system as 'stagnant' both conceptually and empirically, primarily because the CCP is resisting the needed democratic changes. Nepotism still trumps meritocracy. Li views the system as marked by three parallel developments: weak leaders–strong factions; weak government–strong interest groups; and weak party–strong country.

It is impossible to predict the future trajectory of the country but it is clear that China is evolving quickly and that in some ways it resembles other developing countries that are approaching a crucial point in time where decisions about the future structures need to be made. Comparative theory and experiences may be useful in helping one discern possible directions. However, as a number of authors have pointed out, the specific history, culture, and norms of China will shape the outcomes. Increasingly, writers within China and senior party figures have recognized that the development model that has worked in the past to produce such tremendous economic growth will not be viable moving forward and that changes will have to be made. In terms of the economy, the reliance on state investment and export-led growth cannot continue to produce the double-digit growth of the past. Looking forward, China will have to rely more on consumption to maintain momentum, while also trying to ensure that growth is more sustainable. At the same time, the country will have to deal with the consequences of the current growth model such as the environmental damage from pollution and rising inequality. While the leaders of the CCP have rejected what they term the Western system of division of powers, they will have to develop a political system that is more transparent and more accountable to its citizenry. This is a significant challenge and to date no single-party system has dealt with this effectively. The system of single-party rule dominating an increasingly market influenced economic system will come under increasing pressures for change and it remains to be seen whether 'authoritarian resilience' can continue to evolve or whether it proves to be a transitional step toward the emergence of a more durable system. Whether that system is democratic or not remains to be seen.

References

Baum, R. and A. Shevchenko (1999), 'The "State of the State"', in M. Goldman and R. MacFarquhar (eds), *The Paradox of China's Post-Mao Reforms* (Cambridge, MA: Harvard University Press).

Blecher, M. and V. Shue (1996), *Tethered Deer: Government and Economy in a Chinese County* (Stanford, CA: Stanford University Press).

Calhoun, C. (1994), *Neither Gods nor Emperors: Students and the Struggle for Democracy in China* (Berkeley, CA: University of California Press).

Gilley, Bruce (2004) *China's Democratic Future: How it Will Happen and Where it Will Lead* (New York, NY: Columbia University Press).

Goodman, D.S.G. (ed.) (1984), *Groups and Politics in the People's Republic of China* (Cardiff: University College Cardiff Press).

Huntington, S. (1991), *The Third Wave: Democratization in the Late Twentieth Century* (Norman, OK: University of Oklahoma Press).

Landry, Pierre F. (2008), *Decentralized Authoritarianism in China: The Communist Party's Control of Local Elites in the Post-Mao Era* (Cambridge: Cambridge University Press).

Lieberthal, K. (1992), 'Introduction: The "Fragmented Authoritarianism" Model and Its Limitations', in K. Lieberthal and D. Lampton (eds), *Bureaucracy, Politics, and Decision-Making in Post-Mao China* (Berkeley, CA: University of California Press).

Moore, B. (1966), *Social Origins of Dictatorship and Democracy: Lord and Peasant in the Making of the Modern World* (Boston, MA: Beacon Press).

Oi, J. (1989), *State and Peasant in Contemporary China: The Political Economy of Village Government* (Berkeley, CA: University of California Press).

Oi, J. (1999), *Rural China Takes Off: Institutional Foundations of Economic Reform* (Berkeley, CA: University of California Press).

Oksenberg, M. and K. Lieberthal (1988), *Policy-Making in China: Leaders, Structures and Processes* (Princeton, NJ: Princeton University Press).

Ramo, J. (2004), *The Beijing Consensus* (London: The Foreign Policy Centre).

Saich, T. (ed.) (1990), *The Chinese People's Movement: Perspectives on Spring 1989* (Armonk, NY: M.E. Sharpe, Inc.).

Schurmann, F. (1968), *Ideology and Organization in Communist China* (Berkeley, CA: University of California Press).

Schwartz, B. (1951), *Chinese Communism and the Rise of Mao* (Cambridge, MA: Harvard University Press).

Shambaugh, D. (2008), *China's Communist Party: Atrophy and Adaptation* (Washington, DC: Woodrow Wilson Center Press).

Unger, J. (1987), 'The Struggle to Dictate China's Administration: The Conflict of Branches vs Areas vs Reform', *Australian Journal of Chinese Affairs*, 18, July.

Part I
The Study of Chinese Politics

[1]

STUDYING CHINESE POLITICS: FAREWELL TO REVOLUTION?

Elizabeth J. Perry*

Nearly three decades after Mao's death and more than fifteen years after the Tiananmen uprising, China is still a Leninist Party-state. In fact, one might well argue that the prospects for fundamental political transformation look less promising today than they did in the 1980s when leaders like Hu Yaobang and Zhao Ziyang spearheaded serious, if short-lived, efforts at political reform.[1] But while political progress appears to have stalled, the Chinese economy continues to demonstrate impressive growth. Perhaps not surprisingly, then, scholarly interest in village elections and other signs of "democratization" has in recent years been somewhat eclipsed by debates about political economy: can China sustain high rates of economic growth without a clear specification of property rights, as has occurred in many formerly Communist countries?[2] Will China succumb to the scourge of crony capitalism which has hamstrung a number of

* This paper was originally prepared for presentation at the conference to celebrate the Fiftieth Anniversary of the Fairbank Center for East Asian Research at Harvard University (December 2005). I am grateful to the conference organizers, Wilt Idema and Roderick MacFarquhar, as well as to the many conference participants who raised challenging comments and suggestions.

1 On the early post-Mao experiments in political reform, see Merle Goldman, *Sowing the Seeds of Democracy in China: Political Reform in the Deng Xiaoping Era* (Cambridge: Harvard University Press, 1994); Shiping Zheng, *Party versus State in Post-1949 China: The Institutional Dilemma* (New York: Cambridge University Press, 1997). On stalled political reform, see Joseph Fewsmith, *China Since Tiananmen: The Politics of Transition* (New York: Cambridge University Press, 2001).

2 Edward S. Steinfeld, *Forging Reform in China: The Fate of State-Owned Industry* (New York: Cambridge University Press, 1998); Jean C. Oi and Andrew G. Walder (eds), *Property Rights and Economic Reform in China* (Stanford: Stanford University Press, 1999).

other developing countries?[3] Or can strong state supervision keep the Chinese economic experiment on track—even as it moves steadily toward greater privatization and market freedom?[4] The answers to these questions are far from clear, in large part because we have such limited understanding of what holds the contemporary state structure together and thus allows the political system to function as effectively as it does.[5] Moreover, there are no obvious counterparts elsewhere in the world to the situation that China currently faces.[6]

The Limits of Comparison

Although the field of Chinese politics has been greatly invigorated by its post-Mao re-engagement with comparative questions—ranging from civil society and democratization to property rights and rent-seeking—the fact is that contemporary China is not easily likened to other countries. Longstanding differences between Chinese and Soviet Communism have held major implications for the course of reform in the two countries.[7] For example, in Mao's communes, unlike Stalin's collective farms, peasants were paid in collectively determined workpoints rather than in state wages, and land ownership was vested in the production team rather than the state. This meant that, although a return to family farming was eagerly embraced by many rural Chinese as a substitute for collective workpoints, issues of land ownership and control remain highly contentious—accounting for much of the conflict and

---

3 Lu Xiaobo, *Cadres and Corruption: The Organizational Involution of the Chinese Communist Party* (Stanford: Stanford University Press, 2000); David C. Kang, *Crony Capitalism: Corruption and Development in South Korea and the Philippines* (New York: Cambridge University Press, 2002); Melanie Manion, *Corruption by Design: Building Clean Government in Mainland China and Hong Kong* (Cambridge: Harvard University Press, 2004); Yan Sun, *Corruption and Market in Contemporary China* (Ithaca: Cornell University Press, 2004).

4 A positive assessment of Chinese state capacity is Dali L. Yang, *Remaking the Chinese Leviathan: Market Transition and the Politics of Governance in China* (Stanford: Stanford University Press, 2004); a negative assessment is Wang Shaoguang, "The Problem of State Weakness", *Journal of Democracy*, Vol. 14, No. 3 (2003), pp. 36-42. On the importance of state-led economic growth in developing countries more generally, see Atul Kohli, *State-Directed Development* (New York: Cambridge University Press, 2004).

5 Michel Oksenberg noted presciently in 1999 that "such previous depictions as 'totalitarianism,' a 'Leninist party state,' 'fragmented authoritarianism,' 'soft authoritarianism' or 'bureaucratic pluralism' miss the complexity of China's state structure on the eve of the twenty first century". Michel Oksenberg, "China's Political System: Challenges of the Twenty First Century", paper prepared for the Keio University International Symposium (December 1999).

6 Andrew G. Walder observes, "The longer China continues along its current trajectory of change, the less relevant are the prior examples of collapse and regime change in Eastern Europe and the USSR". Andrew G. Walder, "The Party Elite and China's Trajectory of Change", *China: an International Journal*, Vol. 2, No. 2 (September 2004), p. 190.

7 Pei Minxin, *From Reform to Revolution: The Demise of Communism in China and the Soviet Union* (Cambridge: Harvard University Press, 1994).

violence sweeping the Chinese countryside today. But post-Mao authoritarianism also departs markedly from garden-variety authoritarian regimes where militarists gain power by means of coups d'état (rather than revolutionary mobilization) only to preside over bankrupt economies.

In some respects the "East Asian developmental state", which afforded a fruitful paradigm for the analysis of other rapidly growing economies in the region, seems a more promising framework for cross-national comparison than either Communism or run-of-the-mill authoritarianism.[8] Yet, as is often noted, China's huge size and heterogeneity render facile comparisons with Japan—let alone the "Four Little Tigers" (Taiwan, South Korea, Singapore and Hong Kong)—of limited applicability.[9]

In terms of scale and diversity, the only case roughly comparable to China is of course India—which has also launched an ambitious program of economic liberalization in recent years (beginning in the 1980s, but with particular urgency following India's severe macroeconomic crisis of 1991). Yet the very different patterns of reform in the two Asian giants remind us of their starkly divergent histories and political systems. While both countries have enjoyed impressive economic growth in recent decades,[10] on virtually every standard indicator of economic success (gross national product, per capita income, industrialization, total factor productivity, exports, capital flows, external debt and the like) China has far outpaced its neighbor. Moreover, in terms of quality-of-life measures such as literacy and life expectancy, China also notably outperforms India.

Scholars who have attempted to explain this glaring discrepancy in the two countries' socio-economic development offer contradictory assessments of the impact of their respective political systems.[11] Atul Kohli has attributed India's

---

8 Chalmers A. Johnson, *MITI and the Japanese Miracle* (Stanford: Stanford University Press, 1982); Meredith Woo-Cumings (ed.), *The Developmental State* (Ithaca: Cornell University Press, 1999); Robert Wade, *Governing the Market: Economic Theory and the Role of Government in East Asian Industrialization* (Princeton: Princeton University Press, 2004).

9 Some have therefore attempted to apply the model at the level of the local rather than the national Chinese state, see Jean C. Oi, *Rural China Takes Off: Institutional Foundations of Economic Reform* (Berkeley: University of California Press, 1999). In addition to size, however, there are other important differences between the PRC and the Four Tigers; for example, Chinese economic development has involved far greater foreign investment than was true for its East Asian neighbors. Mary Elizabeth Gallagher, *Contagious Capitalism: Globalization and the Politics of Labor in China* (Princeton: Princeton University Press, 2005), pp. 6-7; Yasheng Huang, *Selling China: Foreign Direct Investment During the Reform Era* (New York: Cambridge University Press, 2003).

10 Between 1980 and 1990, among 122 countries China's average economic growth rate was second-highest and India's was eleventh. Between 1990 and 2000, China's was again second-highest—among 140 countries—while India ranked tenth. T. N. Srinivasan, "Economic Reforms and Global Integration", in Francine Frankel and Harry Harding (eds), *The India–China Relationship* (New York: Columbia University Press, 2004), p. 236.

11 This is not surprising, inasmuch as larger cross-national studies have been unable to establish a significant correlation between either authoritarian regimes or democratic regimes and economic growth. Adam Przeworski, Michael E. Alvarez, Jose Antonio

relatively lackluster reform results to interest-group gridlock stemming from its pluralist democracy.[12] In a similar vein, T. N. Srinivasan notes that in China "the firm control held by the party made it much easier than in India to undertake and implement reforms ... the success of Chinese reforms has been in part due to China's being an authoritarian society".[13] Jean Dreze and Amartya Sen, by contrast, stress that "while India has much to learn from China in the field of economic and social policy, the lessons do not include any overwhelming merit of its more authoritarian system".[14] Jagdish Bhagwati, characterizing India as "the model that couldn't", argues nonetheless that "authoritarianism seems to be neither a necessary nor a sufficient condition for rapid growth".[15]

Yet the fact remains that it was during the height of Chinese authoritarianism—the Maoist era—that the foundations of contemporary growth were laid. Following upon a successful revolution that had been waged and won in the countryside, Mao and his comrades devoted unprecedented attention to the peasantry. That attention definitely had its dark side—as the horrendous Great Leap famine (following the introduction of rural communes) attested. Despite its peasant revolution, China suffered what economist Nicholas Lardy characterizes as a "puzzling" undervaluation of agriculture for most of the Maoist period. The result was chronic poverty for millions of rural dwellers.[16] Even so, Mao's revolutionary regime must also be credited with important gains in improving the quality of life for much of its populace. Deeply flawed as the Chinese effort certainly was, the contrast with India is nonetheless stark. Bhagwati notes that, in comparison to China, "the Indian planners underestimated the productive role of better health, nutrition, and education and hence underspent on them".[17] As Dreze and Sen acknowledge, "the larger success of the Chinese efforts at social progress has been, to a great extent, the result of the stronger political commitment of its leadership to eliminating poverty and deprivation".[18] Rhoads Murphey, writing at the end of the Maoist period, attributed China's relative success (*vis-à-vis* India) in improving rural living standards to "the government's commitment to this idea, and the power of central planning there, backed up by a revolutionary ideology and drawing on the immense force of a uniquely

---

Cheibub and Fernando Limonqi, *Democracy and Development* (New York: Cambridge University Press, 2000).

12 Atul Kohli, *Democracy and Discontent: India's Growing Crisis of Governability* (Cambridge: Cambridge University Press, 1990).

13 T. N. Srinivasan, "Economic Reforms", pp. 245, 259.

14 Jean Dreze and Amartya Sen, *India: Economic Development and Social Opportunity* (New York: Oxford University Press, 1995), p. 85.

15 Jagdish Bhagwati, *India in Transition: Freeing the Economy* (New York: Oxford University Press, 1993), pp. 20-21.

16 Nicholas R. Lardy, *Agriculture in Modern China's Economic Development* (New York: Cambridge University Press, 1983).

17 Jagdish Bhagwati, *India in Transition*, p. 36.

18 Jean Dreze and Amartya Sen, *India*, pp. 85-86.

mobilized population".[19] Without the PRC's investment during the 1950s–70s in rudimentary health care, education and infrastructure, all of which Mao personally championed as an expression of his revolutionary agenda and which he implemented (to varying degrees) through a series of mass campaigns, China's subsequent economic gains appear inconceivable.[20] As John Fairbank observed at the outset of the reform era, "This rural industrialization bears the stamp of Chairman Mao … Tarnished or not, his monument is in the countryside".[21]

Bringing the Revolution Back In

The prevalent claim today that the Chinese revolutionary tradition is "fading as the country is set to become one of the major economic powers of the twenty-first century",[22] may therefore be open to qualification. One might argue instead that China's stunning economic strides in the reform era can only be understood against the background of a revolutionary history that remains highly salient in many respects. To be sure, China's weakly articulated legal and financial institutions (closely linked to its revolutionary past) may in time pose insuperable barriers to continued economic vitality. Regardless of whether China's political system eventually proves to be a fetter on economic development, a number of elements of China's revolutionary legacy have facilitated recent gains. Despite valiant philosophical efforts to bid "farewell to revolution", [23] China's revolutionary past has not yet been relegated to the dustbin of history. As Fairbank cautioned during the height of Deng Xiaoping's reform effort, "China for all its spectacular modernization still faces the problems and perils of the social revolution …"[24]

The Chinese revolutionary tradition cannot be equated simply with Soviet-style Communism, important as the Soviet example (with its Leninist Party-state and command economy) assuredly was. Mao's techniques of mass mobilization, born in revolutionary struggle but adapted to the tasks of post-revolutionary rule,

---

19 Rhoads Murphey, *The Fading of the Maoist Vision: City and Country in China's Development* (New York: Methuen, 1980), pp. 54-55.

20 On Mao's stated commitment to these goals, see Stuart Schram (ed.), *Chairman Mao Talks to the People: Talks and Letters, 1956-1971* (New York: Pantheon, 1974), pp. 197-233; on the implementation via mass campaigns, see Michel C. Oksenberg, *Policy Formulation in China: The Case of the 1957–1958 Water Conservancy Campaign* (Columbia University PhD dissertation, 1969) and Charles P. Cell, *Revolution at Work: Mobilization Campaigns in China* (New York: Academic Press, 1977).

21 John King Fairbank, *The United States and China*, 4th ed. (Cambridge: Harvard University Press, 1979), p. 449.

22 Proposal for conference to celebrate the fiftieth anniversary of the Fairbank Center for East Asian Research, Harvard University (December 2005).

23 Li Zehou and Liu Zaifu, *Gaobie geming: huiwang ershishiji Zhongguo* (Farewell to Revolution: Looking Back on Twentieth-Century China) (Hong Kong: Tiandi Book Company, 1997).

24 John King Fairbank, *The Great Chinese Revolution, 1800-1985* (New York: Harper and Row, 1986), p. 351.

lie at the heart of Chinese exceptionalism. Distinctions between Chinese and Russian variants of Communism, noted by Benjamin Schwartz more than half a century ago,[25] help to make sense of China's current situation—which differs both from that of other post-Communist countries and from other developing countries, including India. Any serious study of the Chinese revolution and its aftermath, as Schwartz discovered, leads to an appreciation of the distinctions between Chinese and Soviet Communism—not to mention the even greater differences with countries that experienced neither social revolution nor Communism.[26]

The curious paradox whereby certain elements of China's revolutionary inheritance have actually furthered the stunningly successful implementation of market reforms has yet to be fully explored or explained by students of Chinese politics. To be sure, specific features of China's "economic miracle" have been linked to Maoist precedents. In particular, the initial dynamism of township and village enterprises was often attributed to legacies of the collective era such as commune and brigade enterprises and the continuing influence of cadre control.[27] But while many scholars have plumbed the origins of (sometimes short-lived) local economic formations, few have tried to elucidate the defining elements of the larger political system within which such experiments have occurred. Taking a page from students of Latin America and Eastern Europe, China specialists routinely invoke the concept of "regime transition", despite the fact that the post-Mao period of PRC history has already lasted longer than the Maoist era that preceded it. Whether or not current political conditions persist for many more years, their distinguishing features are surely as worthy of careful attention and analysis as a previous generation of China scholars once showered upon the Maoist political system.[28]

---

25 Benjamin I. Schwartz, *Chinese Communism and the Rise of Mao* (Cambridge: Harvard University Press, 1951).

26 The opening of the Soviet archives in recent years has rekindled old debates about the extent to which the Chinese revolution simply replicated the Russian exemplar. For a partisan view that insists upon Soviet direction over virtually all aspects of the Chinese revolution, see Alexander Pantsov, *The Bolsheviks and the Chinese Revolution, 1919-1927* (Richmond: Curzon, 2000); a more balanced picture which argues for considerable autonomy and innovation on the part of the Chinese is presented in S. A. Smith, *A Road is Made: Communism in Shanghai, 1920-27* (Richmond: Curzon, 2000).

27 Jean C. Oi, *Rural China Takes Off*; Susan H. Whiting, *Power and Wealth in Rural China: The Political Economy of Institutional Change* (New York: Cambridge University Press, 2001).

28 A recent effort to explain élite dynamics under Mao (and Deng) in game-theoretic terms is Huang Jing, *Factionalism in Chinese Communist Politics* (New York: Cambridge University Press, 2000). For a textbook overview of both Maoist and post-Mao systems, see Kenneth Lieberthal, *Governing China: From Revolution Through Reform*, 2nd ed. (New York: W. W. Norton, 2004). General essays on the topic by several political scientists can be found in Jonathan Unger (ed.), *The Nature of Chinese Politics: From Mao to Jiang* (Armonk: M. E. Sharpe, 2002).

If it is "transitional", how has the current regime held onto power for three decades now, weathering a series of potentially destabilizing leadership successions (Mao to Hua to Deng to Jiang to Hu) while presiding over what may well be the fastest sustained economic and socio–cultural transformation that any nation has ever undergone? A large part of the complex answer to this question lies in the retention—and reinvention—of many elements of China's revolutionary heritage. In moving from Maoist Communism to post-Mao authoritarianism, China has not simply jettisoned its revolutionary past as it "transits" toward a democratic future. Rather, a succession of post-Mao leaders have managed to fashion a surprisingly durable brand of "revolutionary authoritarianism" capable of withstanding challenges, including grievous and growing social and spatial inequalities, which would surely have undone less hardy regimes. The achievement is even more impressive when we remember that the geographical entity we now think of as "China" is of fairly recent vintage, a product of Qing imperial expansion that was reunited by first Nationalist and then Communist revolutionary armies.[29]

As Andrew Nathan confesses in a recent *mea culpa*, "After the Tiananmen crisis … many China specialists and democracy theorists—myself among them—expected the regime to fall to democratization's 'third wave.' Instead, the regime has reconsolidated itself".[30] Nathan proceeds to detail the ways in which the post-Mao state has managed to institutionalize the elite succession process so as to overcome factionalist tendencies and thereby avoid the political crisis that many had once presumed to be its inevitable fate. Recognizing that political stability hinges on social support (or at the very least social acquiescence) as well as on state institutionalization, Nathan concedes that "there is much evidence from both quantitative and qualitative studies to suggest that … the regime as a whole continues to enjoy high levels of acceptance".[31] To explain this puzzling degree of popularity for a government responsible for the Tiananmen massacre, Nathan points to the impact of various "input institutions"—local elections, letters-and-visits departments, people's congresses, administrative litigation, mass media—that "enable citizens to pursue grievances without creating the potential to threaten the regime as a whole".[32]

Other explanations for the remarkable survival of China's non-democratic polity focus on particular social forces. Drawing upon an influential social science literature that stresses either the bourgeoisie or industrial labor as the

---

29 On Qing expansion, see Peter Perdue, *China Marches West: The Qing Conquest of Central Eurasia* (Cambridge: Harvard University Press, 2005). On the fragility of China's geographical, political and cultural unity, see James E. Sheridan, *China in Disintegration* (New York: Free Press, 1975); and Edward Friedman, *National Identity and Democratic Prospects in Socialist China* (Armonk: M.E. Sharpe, 1995).

30 Andrew J. Nathan, "Authoritarian Resilience", *Journal of Democracy*, Vol. 14, No. 1 (2003), p. 6.

31 Andrew J. Nathan, "Authoritarian Resilience", p. 13.

32 Andrew J. Nathan, "Authoritarian Resilience", pp.14-15.

vanguard of democratization,[33] China scholars have observed that neither the rising class of entrepreneurs nor the declining class of state workers is pressing actively for political reform. Bound to the Party-state through a web of policies and institutions, the Chinese "bourgeoisie" expresses more interest in political stability than in political reform.[34] Indeed, a substantial portion of private entrepreneurs, welcomed by Jiang Zemin's inclusiveness, have recently joined the Communist Party itself.[35] And although state workers, pensioners and laid-off and migrant laborers have all launched dramatic protests in recent years, their criticisms have tended more to evince nostalgia for the Maoist past than enthusiasm for liberal democracy.[36] Divided by region, generation and workplace conditions, aggrieved workers have been unable to form a united labor movement to press for improved labor standards—let alone a political movement to challenge the state.[37]

Revealing as these analyses are, their focus on the interests and inclinations of social forces seems inadequate as an overall explanation for China's "delayed democratization".[38] Neither attitude surveys of enterprising business people nor

---

33 On the bourgeoisie, see Barrington Moore, Jr., *Social Origins of Dictatorship and Democracy* (Boston: Beacon, 1966); on the working class, see Dietrich Rueschemeyer, Evelyn Huber Stephens and John D. Stephens, *Capitalist Development and Democracy* (Chicago: University of Chicago Press, 1992); on both, see Ruth Berins Collier, *Paths Toward Democracy* (New York: Cambridge University Press, 1999).

34 Dorothy J. Solinger, "Urban Entrepreneurs and the State", in Arthur Lewis Rosenbaum (ed.), *State and Society in China: The Consequences of Reform* (Boulder: Westview, 1992), pp. 121-41; Margaret M. Pearson, *China's New Business Elite: The Political Consequences of Economic Reform* (Berkeley: University of California Press, 1997).

35 Bruce J. Dickson, *Red Capitalists in China: The Party, Private Entrepreneurs, and Prospects for Political Change* (New York: Cambridge University Press, 2003); Kellee S. Tsai, *Capitalism without Democracy: The Politics of Private Sector Development in China* (forthcoming).

36 Ching Kwan Lee, "The Revenge of History: Collective Memories and Labor Protests in Northeastern China", *Ethnography*, Vol. 1, No. 2 (December 2000), pp. 217-37, and "From the Specter of Mao to the Spirit of the Law: Labor Insurgency in China", *Theory and Society*, Vol. 31 (April 2002), pp. 189-228; Chen Feng, "Subsistence Crisis, Managerial Corruption and Labor Protests in China", *The China Journal*, No. 44 (July 2000), pp. 41-63; William Hurst and Kevin J. O'Brien, "China's Contentious Pensioners", *The China Quarterly*, No. 170 (June 2002), pp. 345-60; Cai Yongshun, "The Resistance of Chinese Laid-off Workers in the Reform Period", *The China Quarterly*, No. 170 (June 2002), pp. 327-44.

37 Ching Kwan Lee, "Pathways of Labour Insurgency", in Elizabeth J. Perry and Mark Selden (eds), *Chinese Society: Change, Conflict and Resistance*, 2nd edition (London: Routledge, 2000), pp. 71-92.

38 Mary Gallagher has proposed that the way in which foreign direct investment took place in China—occurring before the advent of fundamental SOE reform or massive privatization—worked to "delay democracy" by fragmenting and forestalling potential political opposition, as enterprises and workers alike were forced to compete for capital and jobs. Mary E. Gallagher, "Reform and Openness: Why China's Economic Reforms Have Delayed Democracy", *World Politics*, Vol. 54, No. 3 (2002), pp. 339-72.

interviews with restive workers are likely to shed as much light on the likelihood of regime change as a sober assessment of the techniques of rule perfected by the Chinese Communist state.

One key explanation for the survival of the PRC lies in the continuing strength of the Chinese Communist Party, especially its ability to recruit, monitor and reward the political élite.[39] Barry Naughton and Dali Yang point out that "China has retained a core element of central control: the *nomenklatura* system of personnel management" and argue that "this nomenklatura personnel system is the most important institution reinforcing national unity".[40] In differentiating the Chinese trajectory from that of failed Communist states, Andrew Walder observes that "China's Party hierarchy has survived unchanged".[41] For Walder, cohesion among the top political leadership, state cadres and party members at large is the glue that holds the system together.[42] While the *composition* of the political elite has changed dramatically since Mao's day (reflecting, among other things, an exponential growth in its educational credentials), its organizational *structure* has remained remarkably stable.[43]

Crucial as these élite dynamics are, the regime's future survival also rests upon its capacity to curb and channel potentially threatening social forces. Nathan's discussion of "authoritarian resilience" is a valuable step in the direction of understanding state–society relations in the current period, but his conclusion that "China has made a transition from totalitarianism to a classic authoritarian regime"[44] seems to underestimate the numerous continuities from the Maoist to the post-Mao period. As many have pointed out, the term "totalitarianism" does not capture the extent to which Mao's polity made room for social involvement.[45] Thanks to its Maoist heritage, moreover, China's *revolutionary* authoritarianism is in some respects also quite unlike "a classic

---

39 Kjeld Erik Brødsgaard, "Management of Party Cadres in China", in Kjeld Erick Brødsgaard and Zheng Yongnian (eds), *Bringing the Party Back In: How China is Governed* (Singapore: Eastern Universities Press, 2004), pp. 57-91.

40 Barry J. Naughton and Dali L. Yang (eds), *Holding China Together: Diversity and National Integration in the Post-Deng Era* (New York: Cambridge University Press, 2004), p. 9. On the importance of the *nomenklatura* system during the 1980s, see Yasheng Huang, *Inflation and Investment Controls in China: The Political Economy of Central-Local Relations During the Reform Era* (New York: Cambridge University Press, 1996).

41 Andrew G. Walder, "The Party Elite", p. 194.

42 Andrew G. Walder, "The Party Elite", p.195-97.

43 Hong Yung Lee, *From Revolutionary Cadres to Party Technocrats in Socialist China* (Berkeley: University of California Press, 1991); Melanie Manion, *Retirement of Revolutionaries in China* (Princeton: Princeton University Press, 1993).

44 Andrew J. Nathan, "Authoritarian Resilience", p. 16.

45 Critiques of the totalitarian model as a characterization of Mao's China include Vivienne Shue, *The Reach of the State: Sketches of the Chinese Body Politic* (Stanford: Stanford University Press, 1988) and Andrew G. Walder, *Communist Neo-Traditionalism* (Berkeley: University of California Press, 1986).

authoritarian regime". Although authoritarian regimes display considerable variation, Juan Linz notes that they generally share in common "the characteristic of low and limited political mobilization".[46] Sidney Tarrow elaborates,

> That authoritarian states discourage popular politics is implicit in their very definition. In particular, they suppress the sustained interaction of collective actors and authorities that is the hallmark of social movements ... Repressive states depress collective action of a conventional and confrontational sort, but leave themselves open to unobtrusive mobilization.[47]

Like other authoritarian societies, the PRC has certainly witnessed the development of a "hidden transcript" of unobtrusive dissent.[48] But Communist China parts company with classic authoritarianism in having periodically encouraged—indeed compelled—its citizens to express their private criticisms publicly in the form of big-character-posters, struggle sessions, denunciation meetings, demonstrations and the like. The Cultural Revolution was the most dramatic, but not the last, expression of this state-sponsored effort at stimulating and shaping confrontational politics.

"Revolutionary Authoritarianism": From Divide and Conquer to Divide and Rule

The post-Mao leadership, following the example set by the Great Helmsman, has proven adept at the art of creating coalitions with, and cleavages among, key social elements as a means of stimulating popular political involvement so as to bolster its own political hegemony. This core feature of China's revolutionary authoritarianism reflects hard-won lessons learned in the course of decades of life-or-death struggles. As Chen Yung-fa details in his insightful study of the wartime base areas, the Chinese Communists' methods of revolutionary mobilization (and de-mobilization) comprised a remarkably flexible and highly effective strategy, perfected over many years of trial-and-error practice in diverse geographical settings.[49] Despite all the calls for nationalism and national unity issued by Mao and his comrades during the War of Resistance against Japan, their real recipe for revolutionary success lay in identifying and intensifying domestic tensions in a manner that enhanced the power of the emerging Communist Party-state. A wide variety of social contradictions were reinterpreted as "class struggles" that required CCP intervention and direction. Chen aptly characterized the Communists' approach as one of "controlled polarization".[50]

---

46 Juan J. Linz, *Totalitarian and Authoritarian Regimes* (Boulder: Lynn Reinner, 2000), p. 269.

47 Sidney Tarrow, *Power in Movement: Social Movements, Collective Action and Politics* (New York: Cambridge University Press, 1994), pp. 92-93.

48 James C. Scott, *Domination and the Arts of Resistance: Hidden Transcripts* (New Haven: Yale University Press, 1990).

49 Chen Yung-fa, *Making Revolution: The Communist Movement in Eastern and Central China, 1937-1945* (Berkeley: University of California Press, 1986).

50 Chen Yung-fa, "Making Revolution", p. 11.

The history of state–society relations under the PRC is largely the application of this revolutionary lesson to the task of regime consolidation. Nationalistic rhetoric continued to be tempered by a politics of division. As Chen observes, "there was no sharp break between wartime and postwar Chinese communism".[51] A strategy of divide-and-conquer was adapted to one of divide-and-rule. The key institutions of the Maoist era such as work units (*danwei*) which isolated the industrial labor force, people's communes (*renmin gongshe*) that enforced rural self-sufficiency, job allocations (*fenpei*) that rendered intellectuals dependent upon state favor, labor insurance (*laobao*) that bestowed generous welfare benefits upon permanent workers at state-owned enterprises while leaving the majority of the workforce unprotected, personnel dossiers (*dang'an*) which marked citizens with "good" or "bad" political records, household registrations (*hukou*) that separated urban and rural dwellers, class labels (*jieji chengfen*) that categorized people into "five kinds of red" (*hong wulei*) and "five kinds of black" (*hei wulei*) —all served to divide society and foster subservience to the state.[52]

Contrary to what some have suggested, this social fragmentation and dependence on the state did not amount to a "totalitarianism" that robbed the Chinese populace of a capacity for protest—quite the opposite.[53] Just as "controlled polarization", waged under the unifying banner of nationalism, facilitated a peasant revolution of staggering size and scope, so it also provided the framework for the huge mass movements for which the People's Republic of China has been renowned.[54] Participants in mass criticisms and demonstrations of various sorts routinely organized themselves along officially prescribed lines. Even in the post-Mao "democracy movement" of 1989, often characterized as the

---

51 Chen Yung-fa, "Making Revolution", p. 517. Similarly, Edward Friedman refers to Mao's style of rule as "war communism". See Edward Friedman, *National Identity*, pp. 208-09.

52 For the operations of these institutions in the Maoist era, see William L. Parish and Martin King Whyte, *Village and Family in Contemporary China* (Chicago: University of Chicago Press, 1978); Martin King Whyte and William L. Parish, *Urban Life in Contemporary* China (Chicago: University of Chicago Press, 1984); Richard C. Kraus, *Class Conflict in Chinese Socialism* (New York: Columbia University Press, 1981); Andrew G. Walder, *Communist Neo-Traditionalism*; T. J. Cheng and Mark Selden, "The Origins and Social Consequences of China's Hukou System", *The China Quarterly*, No. 139 (September 1994), pp. 644-68; Lu Xiaobo and Elizabeth J. Perry (eds), *Danwei: The Changing Chinese Workplace in Historical and Comparative Perspective* (Armonk: M. E. Sharpe, 1997).

53 Elaboration of this argument can be found in Elizabeth J. Perry, "Shanghai's Strike Wave of 1957", *The China Quarterly*, No. 137 (March 1994), pp. 1-27; and Elizabeth J. Perry and Li Xun, *Proletarian Power: Shanghai in the Cultural Revolution* (Boulder: Westview Press, 1997).

54 Mao's effort to reconcile the ideological vision of nationalism with the instrumental tactics of polarization can be seen in his 1938 essay, "The Role of the Chinese Communist Party in the National War", in *Selected Readings from the Works of Mao Tsetung* (Peking: Foreign Languages Press, 1971), pp. 138-59. On mass campaigns in the PRC, see Gordon A. Bennett, *Yundong: Mass Campaigns in Chinese Communist Leadership* (Berkeley: University of California Center for Chinese Studies, 1976).

most "autonomous" of contemporary Chinese demonstrations, protesters marched through Tiananmen Square behind banners announcing their state-designated units (for example, the Capital Iron and Steel Works, or the Propaganda Department of the Central Committee). This reliance upon state-supplied organizations and identities permitted rapid mobilization (and de-mobilization) at the same time as it undercut the potential for collective protest to escalate into a fundamental challenge to the state.

Although Maoist institutions have undergone substantial transformation in the reform era, earlier practices retain significant residual power.[55] Today urban registrations may be purchased by the well-to-do as well as inherited, but they remain a crucial means for gaining access to educational opportunity. Jobs are now often procured via market mechanisms rather than by state fiat, yet personnel dossiers continue to play a role in promotions, sensitive assignments, and the like. The changing operations of these Maoist institutions, along with the emergence of new organizations, such as "homeowners' associations" (*yezhu hui*) and "communities" (*shequ*) to replace residents' committees, demand our careful attention and analysis if we are to understand the multiple means, coercive as well as cooptative, by which the Chinese state manages to hold its restive citizenry in check.

It is worth reiterating that these mechanisms have never prevented the Chinese populace from demonstrating an impressive appetite for contentious politics—whether in Mao's day or today.[56] Mao himself of course inspired a good deal of just such activity through the purposeful stirring up of popular contradictions and criticisms. In the post-Mao era as well, central leaders have sometimes (implicitly if not explicitly) encouraged ordinary people to take to the streets as a means of furthering élite agendas.[57] Although social groups often respond to state-initiated opportunities by airing complaints that exceed official bounds, both the mobilization and the de-mobilization of mass movements proceed along state-designated occupational and territorial lines and thus reinforce social cleavages in favor of state control.[58]

In every decade since the founding of the PRC, state power has appeared to have been challenged: during the Hundred Flowers Campaign of 1956–57, the

---

55 Dorothy J. Solinger, *Contesting Citizenship in Urban China* (Berkeley: University of California Press, 1999).

56 Elizabeth J. Perry, "To Rebel is Justified: Cultural Revolution Influences on Contemporary Chinese Protest", in Kam-yee Law (ed.), *Beyond Purge and Holocaust: The Chinese Cultural Revolution Reconsidered* (Palgrave Press, 2003), pp. 262-81.

57 Notable examples include Deng Xiaoping and the Democracy Wall movement of 1978–79; Hu Yaobang and the student protests of 1986–87; Zhao Ziyang and the Tiananmen unrest of 1989; Hu Jintao and anti-Japanese demonstrations in 1999 and later. See Elizabeth J. Perry, *Challenging the Mandate of Heaven: Social Protest and State Power in China* (Armonk: M. E. Sharpe, 2002), Introduction, pp. ix-xxxii.

58 Sebastian Heilmann, "The Social Context of Mobilization in China: Factions, Work Units and Activists During the 1976 April Fifth Movement", *China Information*, No. 8 (Winter 1993-94), pp. 1-19.

Cultural Revolution of 1966-69, the Democracy Wall Movement of 1978–79, the Tiananmen uprising of 1989 and the Falun Gong demonstrations of 1999. But in each case the central leadership (while invoking the rhetoric of national unity) has adroitly applied the techniques of divide and rule. Public security forces, augmented by military units if necessary, work to ensure that various social groups—especially workers and intellectuals—do not join hands.[59] During the Hundred Flowers movement, the massive strikes that swept through China's factories remained isolated from the big-character-poster campaign being waged on university campuses. That summer the suppression of the Anti-Rightist Campaign (directed by Deng Xiaoping) applied different criminal "hats" to worker and student activists—symbolizing their distinctive political status. Although the early weeks of the Cultural Revolution saw student Red Guards take their struggles to the factories, within a few months they were prohibited from such activities; and eventually the tide was reversed as propaganda teams of workers, often accompanied by PLA soldiers, moved into the schools to restore order. A decade later, the harsh fifteen-year sentence meted out to Democracy Wall activist Wei Jingsheng in 1979 reflected his embodiment of dual worker and intellectual status more than his incendiary calls for a "fifth modernization" of democratic freedoms. In 1989, the very different punishments suffered by students and workers active in the protests again illustrates the Deng Xiaoping regime's divide and rule strategy (student leaders were detained and then released while worker leaders were often executed).

Long segregated into separate state-created categories, citizens themselves are often inclined to accept these divisions as a normal part of the political order. Consider the following incident. In the winter of 1986–87, large-scale student demonstrations broke out in Shanghai after police brutality during a concert by an American rock group. During the concert, several college students who had responded enthusiastically to the performers' invitation to dance in the aisles were hauled outdoors and beaten. Fellow students, and then workers, poured into the streets to protest against the police action. On orders from Jiang Zemin, then mayor of Shanghai, barricades were erected at People's Square to prevent workers from entering the ranks of the student protesters. Only those with valid student IDs were permitted inside the police cordon. Workers massed just outside the barricades, tossing in bread and cigarettes and shouting "Younger brothers, your elder brothers support you!" To defuse this potentially explosive situation, Jiang Zemin went in person to the university of the students who had been roughed up to deliver an apology on behalf of the city government. He explained to the tense all-campus assembly that the police had mistaken the *students* for *workers*, which was the reason they had reacted so harshly. Even more surprising in this self-proclaimed "workers' state" was the fact that the professors and

---

[59] On the mechanics of state suppression, see Murray Scot Tanner, *Chinese Government Responses to Rising Social Unrest* (Santa Monica: Rand, 2005); Timothy Brook, *Quelling the People: The Military Suppression of the Beijing Democracy Movement* (Stanford: Stanford University Press, 1998).

students in attendance reported that they found nothing inappropriate in the mayor's explanation.[60]

Jiang Zemin's skillful deployment of the familiar strategy of divide and rule won him the attention of Deng Xiaoping. After being tapped for central leadership during the 1989 protests, Jiang put these techniques to effective use in responding to a wide range of potential challenges. His regime dealt extremely harshly with movements (such as the China Democracy Party and Falun Gong) that boasted a socially and regionally diverse membership but showed considerable leniency toward conflicts that were more homogeneous in composition and locale. Indeed, Jiang's government even endorsed and encouraged some single-issue protests (for example, the student demonstrations against the US bombing of China's Belgrade embassy in the spring of 1999).[61]

While Jiang Zemin relied upon familiar revolutionary methods of "controlled polarization" to tame social forces, the inclusive ideology that he attempted to formulate (and to propagate through a series of Maoist-style ideological campaigns) reinforced the official stress on national unity. Jiang's *Three Represents*—by which the Communist Party is supposed to serve as the representative of "advanced productive forces, advanced culture, and the interests of the overwhelming majority of the people"—was an effort to update Mao's "mass line". Moreover, as Jiang's own rise to the pinnacle of power was tied to the state's verdict on the 1989 protest movement as a "counter-revolutionary rebellion", his scope for ideological innovation was limited.

Jiang Zemin's much-publicized campaign against Falun Gong resorted to divisive revolutionary rhetoric by branding the "evil cult" as "counter-revolutionary".[62] Jiang's successor as General-Secretary of the Chinese Communist Party, Hu Jintao, has also repeatedly summoned revolutionary symbolism in justifying his party's claim to rule. On a visit to the site of the former Jiangxi Soviet in the summer of 2003, Hu enjoined officials at all levels of the party to "carry on the revolutionary tradition". As Hu put it, "Comrade Mao Zedong and other revolutionaries of the elder generation not only made

---

60 Interviews in Shanghai, January 1987. That workers and intellectuals continue to experience markedly different treatment at the hands of state authorities (and in the eyes of the public) was demonstrated graphically by the infamous Sun Zhigang case in 2003. Sun, a university graduate who was traveling without identification papers, was arrested when the police mistook him for a migrant laborer. After Sun was beaten to death while in police custody, the media, intellectual commentators and state officials all made much of the fact that a university graduate had been treated so terribly. Had Sun been an uneducated migrant worker, as the police originally suspected, his brutal death would surely not have elicited the same public outcry. A detailed discussion of the media coverage of this case can be found in a forthcoming book by Zhao Yuezhi, to whom I am grateful for this interpretation.

61 Jeffrey N. Wasserstrom, "The Year of Living Anxiously: China's 1999", *Dissent* (Spring 2002); Elizabeth J. Perry, *Challenging the Mandate of Heaven*, Introduction.

62 *Notice on Various Issues Regarding Identifying and Banning of Cultic Organizations* (Beijing: Ministry of Public Security of The People's Republic of China, 2000), reprinted in "Religion and Public Security in China, 1999-2002", *Chinese Law and Government*, Vol. 36, No. 2 (2003).

historical achievements by realizing national independence and liberation, but also bequeathed to us precious spiritual wealth". A front-page article in *People's Daily* elaborated on Hu's remarks: "such revolutionary spirit and tradition, which were fostered through arduous struggles, provide strength for overcoming difficulties and risks of all kinds in our way forward".[63] Hu's subsequent slogan of "building a harmonious society" has not displaced the recourse to revolutionary mobilization techniques.

The 2003 battle waged against SARS was a telling example of how the new leadership adapted Maoist tactics to cope with contemporary challenges. In what Hu Jintao dubbed the "People's War against SARS", neighborhood committees were charged with enforcing strict sanitation standards within their jurisdictions. Activists (some dressed as that *passé* paragon of Maoist virtues, Lei Feng) went from door to door to ensure that the public adhered to the government's guidelines.[64] Reminiscent of public health campaigns in Mao's day (such as the campaign against schistosomiasis or the campaign against the Four Pests), the anti-SARS effort attested to the continuing capacity of the regime to mobilize its citizenry behind state-initiated projects.

Slogans recalled the patriotic battle cries of an earlier era: "Activate the whole Party, mobilize the entire populace, win the war of annihilation against SARS!"; "Enlarge the national spirit, unite with one heart to battle SARS!" Despite the calls for unity, the tactics were draconian: tens of thousands of people were forcibly placed under strict quarantine; countless civet cats, chickens and other possible disease-carriers were slaughtered with little concern for the consequences, and so on.[65] Those who succumbed to the disease were designated "national heroes" and "martyrs", and their survivors became eligible to receive the same state-conferred benefits (free schooling, generous medical insurance and the like) that this exalted status had long conferred on the dependents of "revolutionary martyrs".[66] While the PRC's response to SARS was understandably criticized by some policy analysts for its "out-dated mode of

---

63 *Renmin ribao* (People's Daily) (3 September 2003).

64 "President Hu Jintao Calls for a 'People's War' Against SARS", *Xinhua Report* (Tianjin: 1 May, 2003), translated in *Chinese Law and Government* (July/August 2003), p. 44; Joseph Kahn, "The SARS Epidemic", *New York Times* (25 April 2003); Elisabeth Rosenthal, "SARS Makes Beijing Combat an Old but Unsanitary Habit", *New York Times* (28 May 2003).

65 Over 30,000 people were quarantined with official government approval, but many others were placed under unauthorized quarantine by their local neighborhood committees. On the official process, see Xinghuo Pang, Zhonghan Zhu, Fujie Xu, Jiyong Guo, Xiaohong Gong, Donglei Liu, Zejun Liu, Daniel P. Chin and Daniel R. Feikin, "Evaluation of Control Measures Implemented in the SARS Outbreak in Beijing, 2003", *Journal of the American Medical Association*, Vol. 290, No. 24 (24/31 December 2003), pp. 3215-221; for the unofficial situation, see Taru Salmenkari, "SARS Prevention Campaign and the Limits of Media Mobilization", unpublished paper.

66 *Renmin ribao* (People's Daily), 4, 14, 29 and 30 July 2003.

crisis management", [67] in retrospect the effort to resuscitate seemingly anachronistic campaign methods for new purposes appears to have been quite successful. Joan Kaufman, highlighting the Chinese government's ability "to detain and isolate citizens", observes that the resort to Maoist-style public campaigns "was precisely what was required to put in place the series of preventive measures that broke the chain of transmission".[68] A summary article in the *Journal of the American Medical Association* concludes approvingly that "the multiple control measures implemented in Beijing likely led to the rapid resolution of the SARS outbreak".[69]

The current PRC leadership is not content simply to make instrumental use of Maoist mobilization tactics. It also tries actively to instill a sense of revolutionary continuity among officials and ordinary people alike. Following Hu Jintao's visit to Jiangxi, a branch of the Central Party School was opened at the site of Mao's first rural revolutionary base area in the Jinggangshan highlands, so that cadres could reconnect with their revolutionary roots (while "roughing it" at one of the two three-star hotels located within the spacious party school compound!).[70] For ordinary citizens, "red tourism" (*hongse lüyou*) to the sacred sites of Mao's revolution is being vigorously promoted as a means both of improving the party's public image (by showcasing its past struggles and sacrifices) and as a vehicle for pumping much needed revenues into what remain some of the poorest regions of the countryside.

With such state-promoted glorification of the revolutionary tradition, it is not surprising that contemporary protesters should attempt to capitalize on this "precious spiritual wealth" to further their own purposes. At the Anyuan coal mine in Jiangxi, where in 1922 Mao Zedong, Li Lisan and Liu Shaoqi had organized the first working-class branch of the Chinese Communist Party and instigated the first successful industrial strike under CCP direction, retired miners in 2004 called attention to that history: "During the years of revolutionary struggle, Anyuan workers suffered and sacrificed for the sake of the Chinese revolution … Under the reforms, thanks to the exertions of our generation of miners, the enterprise has profited and prospered and yet we have not enjoyed the fruits of reform. Our wages have been cut and our pensions are very, very meager".[71]

---

67 Tony Saich, "Is SARS China's Chernobyl or Much Ado About Nothing?" in Arthur Kleinman and James L. Watson (eds), *SARS in China: Prelude to Pandemic?* (Stanford: Stanford University Press, 2006), p. 89.

68 Joan Kaufman, "SARS and China's Health-Care Response: Better to be Both Red and Expert!" in Arthur Kleinman and James L. Watson (eds), "SARS in China", pp. 66-67.

69 Xinghuo Pang *et al.*, "Evaluation of Control Measures", p. 3221.

70 Visit to Jinggangshan, Jiangxi, in summer 2005.

71 *Laodong tiaojian zui cha, gongzuo zui jianku, zui weixian, dui guojia he qiye gongxian zui da de pingkuang tuixiu zhigong tuixiu yanglaojin dixia* (The Dwindling Pensions of Retired Pingxiang Miners Whose Labor Conditions Were the Worst, Whose Work Was the Most Difficult and Dangerous, Yet Whose Contribution to Country and Enterprise Was the Greatest), unpublished protest manifesto (Anyuan, Jiangxi, 2004).

Today's protesters draw not only rhetorical but also practical inspiration from revolutionary precedents. Faced with the threat of bankruptcy triggered by post-Mao industrial policies, disgruntled workers have once again been organizing militia units to protect their factories—in conscious imitation of the revolutionary exemplar.[72] But this time they hope to "liberate" their workplaces from forced closures by the Party. Political scientist Feng Chen reports on a recent scene at a Shanghai plastics factory:

> As some workers proudly describe it, their action of defending the factory is similar to that of their predecessors on the eve of the Communist takeover in 1949 when pro-Communist workers formed "worker guard teams" [*gongren jiuchadui*] to protect factories from sabotage by the Guomindang. Ironically, however, the workers are now using the same method to ward off capitalistic takeovers endorsed by a party-state that still labels itself socialist.[73]

Similar confrontations, pitting "revolutionary" workers against "reformist" government authorities, have taken place in many other parts of the country as well. Despite the use of revolutionary nomenclature and symbolism, such labor protests are not proto-revolutionary movements poised to topple the state. Rather, aggrieved workers draw creatively upon the language and legacy of the Communist revolution in an effort to shame the Party-state into living up to the promises of its own "revolutionary tradition".

The Consequences of Revolutionary Authoritarianism

The tendency for protesters to take cues from officially approved symbols of authority can be found in any polity, but is especially pronounced in authoritarian systems where the state exercises a virtual monopoly over political discourse. In such contexts, the clever appropriation and inversion of officially sanctioned slogans and practices is a prominent feature of (often unobtrusive) protest behavior.[74] Under the revolutionary authoritarianism of the PRC, where mass mobilization has been a hallmark of state–society relations, the practice of "waving the red flag to oppose the red flag" has been honed to a high—and often highly ironic—art form.[75] Sebastian Heilmann observed this phenomenon among workers seeking wage hikes and improved workplace conditions during the Cultural Revolution:

---

72 For the revolutionary history of the worker pickets, see Elizabeth J. Perry, *Patrolling the Revolution: Worker Militias, Citizenship and the Modern Chinese State* (Lanham: Rowman and Littlefield, 2006).

73 Feng Chen, "Industrial Restructuring and Workers' Resistance in China", *Modern China*, Vol. 29, No. 2 (April 2003), p. 250. In the countryside as well, there are reports of unruly militias challenging state authority. See, for example, *China Focus*, Vol. 6, No. 9 (1 September 1998), p. 4.

74 James C. Scott, *Domination and the Arts of Resistance*.

75 Patricia M. Thornton, "Framing Dissent in Contemporary China: Irony, Ambiguity and Metonymy", *The China Quarterly*, No. 171 (September 2002), pp. 661-81.

> In most cases, angry workers skillfully made use of official campaign slogans to camouflage their "economistic" interests. Officially approved slogans like "Down With the Capitalist Roaders" were deliberately used as a means of confronting an unresponsive leadership ... Under the cloak of rebellion against "revisionist" forces, diverse groups of workers used the opportunity to complain about specific grievances in their respective work units and about economic hardship.[76]

The turmoil of the Cultural Revolution originated in part from Mao Zedong's effort to stem the tide of "revisionism" by cultivating "revolutionary successors" among the younger generation. Although student Red Guards (and other social groups) strayed far from Mao's vision of proper revolutionary activity, they were nonetheless constrained by the fact that their "revolution" had been launched by the Chairman of the Communist Party himself.

Once Mao was gone, it became commonplace among students of Chinese politics to suggest that contemporary popular protest exhibits a degree of spontaneity and independence that marks it as qualitatively different from the mobilized movements of Mao's day. Despite the pivotal role of Deng Xiaoping in first encouraging and then suppressing the Democracy Wall movement of 1978–79, foreign observers hailed it as an unprecedented expression of citizen-based pressures for democratization.[77] A decade later, the Tiananmen uprising of 1989 led many scholars to express excitement about what they saw as a fundamental break with previous campaign-style modes of popular involvement. Andrew Walder described participation in the Tiananmen uprising of 1989 as "something new on the political scene: massive, independent, popular protests. The old mode of regimentation and elite-sponsored turbulence has been broken, and Chinese politics appears to have entered a new era".[78] Similarly, Wang Shaoguang argued that "the protest movement of 1989 marked a turning point of changing class relations ... the working class in China is no longer a pillar of continuity but a force for change".[79] The notion of a qualitative transformation was picked up by general comparativists as well. Jack Goldstone wrote of 1989 that "unlike other confrontations that involved mainly intellectuals, such as the

---

76 Sebastian Heilmann, "Turning Away from the Cultural Revolution: Political Grass-Roots Activism in the Mid-Seventies", Center for Pacific Asia Studies at Stockholm University, *Occasional Paper*, No. 28 (September 1996), pp. 11-13.

77 James D. Seymour (ed.), *The Fifth Modernization: China's Human Rights Movement, 1978-79* (Stanfordville: Human Rights Publishing Group, 1980); John Fraser, *The Chinese: Portrait of a People* (New York: Summit, 1980); David S. G. Goodman, *Beijing Street Voices: The Poetry and Politics of China's Democracy Movement* (London: Marion Boyars, 1981). A more nuanced assessment can be found in Andrew J. Nathan, *Chinese Democracy* (Berkeley: University of California Press, 1985).

78 Andrew G. Walder, "Urban Industrial Workers: Some Observations on the 1980s", in Arthur Lewis Rosenbaum (ed.), *State and Society in China: The Consequences of Reform* (Boulder: Westview, 1994), p. 104.

79 Wang Shaoguang, "Deng Xiaoping's Reform and the Chinese Workers' Participation in the Protest Movement of 1989", *Research in Political Economy*, Vol. 13 (1992), pp. 163-97.

Hundred Flowers Movement, or other events that were in some sense orchestrated by the regime, such as the Cultural Revolution, Tiananmen marked the first time that intellectuals and popular elements acted independently to challenge the regime".[80]

More than fifteen years after Tiananmen, however, it is increasingly difficult to regard that confrontation as having signaled a dramatic turning point in state–society relations. Sober reflections on the activities of Tiananmen protesters—including retrospectives by some of the principals themselves—question the extent to which their behavior in the spring of 1989 constituted a genuine rupture with earlier modes of protest. As Tiananmen activist Liu Xiaobo conceded in a bitterly impassioned essay entitled "That Holy Word: 'Revolution'",

> Most of the resources and methods we made use of to mobilize the masses were ones that the Communist Party itself had used many times before ... As soon as we began our revolution, we became extremely conceited—just as if we had reverted to the time of the Cultural Revolution and felt ourselves to be the most revolutionary. As soon as we joined the 1989 protest movement, we considered ourselves to be the most democratic. After all, had we not fasted for democracy and devoted ourselves to it and made sacrifices for it? ... Our voice became the only truth. We felt as though we possessed absolute power.[81]

Liu's reflections are a stinging indictment of the Tiananmen protest as an undemocratic movement that unwittingly recreated many of the core features of Chinese Communist revolutionary culture. The searing experience of the state-orchestrated Cultural Revolution in particular, according to Liu Xiaobo, continued to inhibit the development of a genuinely democratic perspective.

Despite its bloody suppression, the 1989 uprising did not end popular protest in China, and many scholars continue to see the signs of an imminent breakthrough in state–society relations in the most recent ferment. Kevin O'Brien and Li Lianjiang see the tendency of restive farmers to cite official government regulations and policies in justifying their (sometimes unruly) behavior as "rightful resistance" and argue that it reflects a growing sense of "citizenship rights" among ordinary Chinese.[82] David Zweig also detects an emerging "rights conscious peasantry".[83] Pei Minxin, discussing the impact of rapid economic

---

80 Jack A. Goldstone, "Analyzing Rebellion and Revolution: A Reply to the Critics", *Contention* (1994), pp. 177-98.

81 Liu Xiaobo, "That Holy Word, 'Revolution'", in Jeffrey N. Wasserstrom and Elizabeth J. Perry (eds), *Popular Protest and Political Culture in Modern China*, 2nd edition (Boulder: Westview, 1994), pp. 315, 318.

82 Kevin O'Brien and Li Lianjiang, *Rightful Resistance in the Chinese Countryside* (New York: Cambridge University Press, 2006). For a more cautious assessment of contemporary rural protest, noting the continuities with peasant unrest in previous periods of Chinese history, see Thomas P. Bernstein and Xiaobo Lu, *Taxation without Representation in Contemporary Rural China* (New York: Cambridge University Press, 2003).

83 David Zweig, "To the Courts or to the Barricades: Can New Political Institutions Manage Rural Conflict?", in Elizabeth Perry and Mark Selden (eds), *Chinese Society*, p. 132.

development as well as the implementation of legal reforms such as the Administrative Litigation Law, notes a "rising rights consciousness" within Chinese society at large. Summing up the history of the reform era with an eye toward the future, Pei predicts that "China's incipient opposition is likely to become more resilient, sophisticated and adept in challenging the regime as the conditions for democratic resistance further improve".[84] Merle Goldman argues that "by the century's end the sense of rights consciousness ... had spread ... beyond intellectual and elite circles ... to the population at large ... [T]he transition from comrade to citizen in the People's Republic of China has begun".[85] This optimistic outlook pervades much of the journalistic reporting on China as well; a recent *Business Week* article, for example, speaks glowingly of "a new labor-rights revolution sweeping China".[86]

Such arguments about the growth of Chinese social power, fueled by newfound conceptions of citizenship, dovetail with a prevalent view of the post-Mao state as a pale shadow of its predecessor—sapped of both the desire and the capacity fully to control society at large. David Shambaugh observes: "If one of the hallmarks of the Maoist state was the penetration of society, then the Dengist state was noticeable for its withdrawal. The organizational mechanisms of state penetration and manipulation were substantially reduced or dismantled altogether".[87] Ding Xueliang characterizes the post-Mao state as gripped by a legitimacy crisis that and a "gradual functional and organizational decay of the massive party-state machinery".[88] The result, Pei Minxin concludes, is "the erosion of state capacity in China".[89]

I am skeptical both of such accounts of state withdrawal or weakness and of claims of a new and growing awareness of rights-based citizenship in contemporary China. It is true that protesters today routinely invoke the language of "rights" in pressing their demands, as is only to be expected in the light of widespread government propaganda promoting the importance of such state-conferred "rights".[90] Bookstores these days are stocked with pamphlets detailing

---

84 Pei Minxin, "Rights and Resistance", in Elizabeth Perry and Mark Selden (eds), *Chinese Society*, pp. 40-43; see also Pei Minxin, "Citizens v. Mandarins: Administrative Litigation in China", *The China Quarterly*, No. 152 (December 1997), pp. 832-62.

85 Merle Goldman, *From Comrade to Citizen: The Struggle for Political Rights in China* (Cambridge: Harvard University Press, 2005), pp. 222-23.

86 Dexter Roberts, "Waking Up to Their Rights", *Business Week* (22/29 August 2005), p. 123.

87 David Shambaugh, "The Chinese State in the Post-Mao Era", in David Shambaugh (ed.), *The Modern Chinese State* (Cambridge: Cambridge University Press, 2000), p. 183.

88 X. L. Ding, *The Decline of Communism in China* (New York: Cambridge University Press, 1994), p. 200.

89 Pei Minxin, *China's Trapped Transition: The Limits of Developmental Autocracy* (Cambridge: Harvard University Press, 2006)

90 There is, of course, a serious issue about the meaning of the Chinese term *quanli* ("rights"). Stephen C. Angle delineates what he characterizes as "a distinctive Chinese discourse about

government laws, policies and regulations; the air waves are filled by radio talk shows that advise listeners on how to ensure that regulations are enforced and contracts are fulfilled; newspapers are replete with legal advice columns for aggrieved citizens; and so on.[91] But post-Mao state proclamations heralding "reform" and "legal rights" bear a certain parallelism to Maoist state propaganda harping on "revolution" and "class struggle". Just as protesters during the Maoist era borrowed the then hegemonic language of *class* in pressing their demands, so protesters today adopt the currently hegemonic language of *rights* in framing their grievances. This phenomenon, in my view, is "rules consciousness" rather than "rights consciousness".[92] Instead of indicating some novel expression of proto-democratic citizenship or state vulnerability, the continuing adherence to rules consciousness seems to me to reflect a seasoned sensitivity on the part of ordinary Chinese to (changing yet still powerful) top-down signals emanating from the state.[93]

Revolutionary authoritarianism demands active engagement (rather than "exit") by society, in a manner authorized by the state. People are encouraged to express "voice" as well as "loyalty",[94] so long as they play by the official rules of the game. For these reasons, although protest in Communist China has been more frequent and widespread than in other authoritarian settings, ultimately it has proven less politically destabilizing. Precisely because protest in the PRC is both routine and officially circumscribed, once the top leadership decides upon a course of repression most of the populace is quick to fall into step. The crackdown on Tiananmen protesters in 1989 or Falun Gong demonstrators a decade later was after all a familiar drill harking back to the Anti-Rightist Campaign of 1957, the military suppression of Cultural Revolution mass activism in 1968, the clearing of Tiananmen Square in April 1976 and the clampdown on

---

rights" in his illuminating book, *Human Rights and Chinese Thought* (New York: Cambridge University Press, 2002).

91 On the limited scope of these legal reforms, see Stanley Lubman, *Bird in a Cage: Legal Reform in China after Mao* (Stanford: Stanford University Press, 1999).

92 In a related vein, the German Sinologist Harro Von Senger noted some years ago: "In the PRC statutory law thus does not serve the function of an autonomous force for shaping the social order, independent of the CCP Party norms. It serves rather as a vehicle for making casuistic elaborations to Party norms and their translation into guiding principles which are compulsory for all citizens of the PRC". Harro Von Senger, "Recent Developments in the Relations between State and Party Norms in the People's Republic of China", in Stuart R. Schram (ed.), *The Scope of State Power in China* (New York: St. Martin's Press, 1989), p. 207.

93 Su Shaozhi remarks ruefully that "Chinese society has long been characterized by state worship". See his "Problems of Democratic Reform in China", in Edward Friedman (ed.), *The Politics of Democratization: Generalizing East Asian Experiences* (Boulder: Westview Press, 1994), p. 223. Examples of "rules conscious" protests in the Maoist era can be found in Elizabeth J. Perry, "Shanghai's Strike Wave", and Elizabeth J. Perry and Li Xun, *Protetarian Power*.

94 Albert O. Hirschman, *Exit, Voice and Loyalty: Responses to Decline in Firms, Organizations and States* (Cambridge: Harvard University Press, 1970).

Democracy Wall in 1979. In China, unlike Eastern Europe or the former Soviet Union, both leaders and ordinary citizens know how to put the genie of mass protest back into the bottle of state socialism.

One might well ask whether this is only a temporary situation, now that educated engineers rather than experienced revolutionaries occupy Zhongnanhai. [95] Has the revolutionary tradition lost its intrinsic *value* for contemporary Chinese, rulers and ruled alike, much as Joseph Levenson argued was the fate of the Confucian tradition a century ago?[96] Will today's Communist reformers find it as impossible to cling to their discredited traditions as the Qing self-strengtheners once did? Just as the abolition of the Confucian examinations was a clear acknowledgment of bureaucratic weakness and moral bankruptcy in 1905, the CCP's resort to an open-door policy that welcomes even capitalists into Party is a clear acknowledgment of its own moribund condition.

It is entirely possible that the engineers responsible for running the train of Chinese Communism will soon discover that they cannot proceed full steam ahead along an outmoded set of rails. Advanced economic development may indeed demand new political arrangements that afford far greater autonomy to legal institutions and civil society. Without a willingness on the part of its leadership to risk the consequences of such a political transformation, the PRC could devolve into a run-of-the-mill authoritarianism that dispenses with both the ideological and the organizational features of its revolutionary past. Even if this "transition" to stable authoritarianism should occur (as some suggest it already has),[97] we would still be well advised to cast a more discerning eye back upon the past quarter-century. Tarnished as the extraordinary, and quite unanticipated, accomplishments of the post-Mao polity may be, their explanation nevertheless presents a major challenge to the field of Chinese politics. That challenge, I would submit, cannot be fully met by comparisons with other countries (whether post-Communist, "classic" authoritarian or developmental), nor by recourse to general theories of regime transition and democratization.[98] For better *and* worse, China has yet to bid farewell to revolution.

---

95 On the changing of the élite guard, see Li Cheng, *China's Leaders: The New Generation* (Lanham: Rowman and Littlefield, 2001).

96 Joseph R. Levenson, *Confucian China and Its Modern Fate: A Trilogy* (Berkeley: University of California Press, 1968).

97 In addition to Andrew J. Nathan, "Authoritarian Resilience", see also Cheng Chen, "Institutional Legitimacy of an Authoritarian State: China in the Mirror of Eastern Europe", *Problems of Post-Communism*, Vol. 52, No. 4 (July/August 2005), pp. 3-13.

98 It may be significant, however, that all of the other remaining Communist regimes—Cuba, North Korea, Vietnam and Laos—share with China a legacy of nationalistic rural revolution.

[2]

Journal of Contemporary China (2011), **20**(71), September, 535–541 Routledge Taylor & Francis Group

Studying Chinese Politics in an Age of Specialization

KEVIN J. O'BRIEN*

The relationship between area studies and political science is fraught with tradeoffs. In particular, a danger exists that the field of Chinese politics is being hollowed out because (a) there are many islands of highly specialized research with few bridges between them; and (b) more and more Chinese politics scholars are engaged in debates in which the 'other side' is no longer a China scholar but instead a colleague in the discipline. At a time when China's economic growth and prominence in world affairs have generated remarkable interest inside and outside the academy, few scholars are willing to take a stab at characterizing the polity or addressing other, equally large questions. Further thought is needed about the 'terms of enlistment' for China scholars in political science, in an era when ever more-focused studies and greater participation in disciplinary debates have become the norm.

In American academia, two trends in the study of Chinese politics have intensified of late. The first is a growing disciplinary orientation, especially among younger scholars. Although it remains as vibrant as any area study in political science, the field of Chinese politics is being integrated into the examination of comparative politics (and international relations) to an extent unseen before. Second, researchers on Chinese politics tend to choose relatively narrow topics and display some hesitancy to link what they have discovered to larger questions about how the political system operates. Instead of making grand statements, they burrow into a topic and stick to close-to-the-ground generalizations about what it might mean for China.

As a result of this disciplinary and topical specialization, researchers are more deeply embedded in political science than was common a generation ago,[1] and

*Kevin J. O'Brien is Alann P. Bedford Professor of Asian Studies and Professor of Political Science at the University of California, Berkeley. His books include *Reform without Liberalization* (Cambridge, 1990, 2008), *Engaging the Law in China* (Stanford, 2005), *Rightful Resistance in Rural China* (Cambridge, 2006), *Popular Protest in China* (Harvard, 2008), and *Grassroots Elections in China* (Routledge, 2011). He can be reached by email at kobrien@berkeley.edu. The author is grateful to Lianjiang Li and Rachel Stern for comments on an earlier draft.

1. Lowell Dittmer and William Hurst, 'Analysis in limbo: contemporary Chinese politics amid the maturation of reform', *Issues & Studies* 38(4) and 39(1), (December 2002/March 2003), pp. 11–48; Richard Baum, 'Studies of Chinese politics in the United States', in Robert Ash, David Shambaugh and Seiichiro Takagi, eds, *China Watching: Perspectives from Europe, Japan and the United States* (London: Routledge, 2007); Bjørn Alpermann, 'Political science research in China: making the most of diversity', *Journal of Chinese Political Science* 14(4), (December 2009), pp. 343–356; Allen Carlsen, Mary Gallagher, Kenneth Lieberthal and Melanie Manion, eds, *Chinese Politics: New Sources, Methods, and Field Strategies* (New York: Cambridge University Press, 2010).

ISSN 1067-0564 print/ 1469-9400 online/11/710535-7 © 2011 Taylor & Francis
DOI: 10.1080/10670564.2011.587157

findings are more solid than ever, but we cohere less as a group engaged in the enterprise of understanding Chinese politics broadly construed.[2] This change is perhaps not of great issue for individual scholars, most of whom have either adjusted to it or are actively working to bring it about; it has, however, led to a certain hollowing out of the field of Chinese politics.

Disciplinary specialization

A hole at the center of the field became apparent while updating the syllabus for my graduate seminar on Chinese politics. For over a decade I had arranged weekly readings around a series of debates: memorable tussles over the reach of the state, neotraditionalism, the role of *guanxi*, peasant power, civil society, corporatism, and so on. But by the mid-2000s this structure was no longer tenable and I switched to a string of exemplary new books. Why? The old debates had largely exhausted themselves and there were few new ones to take their place. Yes, some lively areas of contention remain on issues such as state capacity and nationalism,[3] but most current debates are somewhat polemical,[4] narrow-gauge,[5] or marked by agreement as much as disagreement.[6] Could this be because we are in accord on the big questions about

2. On losing track of 'the bigger picture', see Baum, 'Studies of Chinese politics in the United States', p. 161, and Michel Oksenberg, quoted in Jean-Pierre Cabestan, 'Studies of Chinese politics in Europe', in Ash *et al.*, eds, *China Watching*, p. 121; also see Harry Harding, 'The evolution of American scholarship on contemporary China', in David Shambaugh, ed., *American Studies of Contemporary China* (Armonk, NY: M.E. Sharpe, 1993). On 'overspecialization', see Cabestan, 'Studies of Chinese politics in Europe', p. 99, and Alpermann, 'Political science research in China', p. 351.

3. On state capacity, see Wang Shaoguang and Hu Angang, *The Chinese Economy in Crisis: State Capacity and Tax Reform* (Armonk, NY: M.E. Sharpe, 2001), and Barry J. Naughton and Dali L. Yang, eds, *Holding China Together: Diversity and National Integration in the Post-Deng Era* (New York: Cambridge University Press, 2004). On nationalism, see Peter Hays Gries, *China's New Nationalism: Pride, Politics, and Diplomacy* (Berkeley, CA: University of California Press, 2004), and Suisheng Zhao, *A Nation-State by Construction: Dynamics of Modern Chinese Nationalism* (Stanford, CA: Stanford University Press, 2004).

4. On democratization versus stagnation, see Bruce Gilley, *China's Democratic Future: How it Will Happen and Where it Will Lead* (New York: Columbia University Press, 2004), and Minxin Pei, *China's Trapped Transition: The Limits of Developmental Autocracy* (Cambridge, MA: Harvard University Press, 2006).

5. Valuable examples include: on voter turnout, Tianjian Shi, 'Voting and nonvoting in China: voting behavior in plebiscitary and limited choice elections', *Journal of Politics* 61(4), (November 1999), pp. 1115–1139, and Jie Chen and Yang Zhong, 'Why do people vote in semicompetitive elections in China?', *Journal of Politics* 64(1), (February 2002), pp. 178–197; on property rights and township and village enterprises, Jean C. Oi, *Rural China Takes Off: Institutional Foundations of Economic Reform* (Berkeley, CA: University of California Press, 1999), and Susan H. Whiting, *Power and Wealth in Rural China: The Political Economy of Institutional Change* (New York: Cambridge University Press, 2001); on local people's congresses, Ming Xia, *The People's Congresses and Governance in China: Toward a Network Mode of Governance* (London: Routledge, 2008), and Young Nam Cho, *Local People's Congresses in China: Development and Transition* (New York: Cambridge University Press, 2009); and on intellectual property protection, Martin Dimitrov, *Piracy and the State: The Politics of Intellectual Property Rights in China* (New York: Cambridge University Press, 2009), and Andrew C. Mertha, *The Politics of Piracy: Intellectual Property in Contemporary China* (Ithaca, NY: Cornell University Press, 2005). The numerous mini-debates among analysts of villages elections can also be placed in this category; see Kevin J. O'Brien and Suisheng Zhao, eds, *Grassroots Elections in China* (London: Routledge, 2011).

6. On contemporary protesters and their rules or rights consciousness, see Elizabeth J. Perry, 'A new rights consciousness?', *Journal of Democracy* 20(3), (July 2009), pp. 17–20; Elizabeth J. Perry, 'Chinese conceptions of "rights": from Mencius to Mao—and now', *Perspectives on Politics* 6(1), (March 2008), pp. 37–50; Lianjiang Li, 'Rights consciousness and rules consciousness in contemporary China', *China Journal* 64, (July 2010), pp. 47–68; Peter L. Lorentzen and Suzanne E. Scoggins, 'Rising rights consciousness: undermining or undergirding China's stability?', unpublished paper, (8 December 2010), available at: http://papers.ssrn.com/sol3/papers.cfm?abstract_id = 1722352.

Chinese politics at a moment when authoritarian resilience has become the consensus view, or is it more likely that we are not talking with each other as much, not meeting as often in area studies journals to hash things out, but instead aiming to engage disciplinary colleagues who focus on social capital or popular contention or corruption or political trust or production chains or the policymaking process in other countries? Our target readers, in other words, increasingly include comparativists and international relations scholars as well as China studies colleagues, and we often put our primary effort into delighting this new audience with the significance of our findings for theory or conceptual clarity rather than highlighting what they mean for understanding Chinese politics.[7]

Growing disciplinary orientation is not surprising for many reasons. To begin with, career incentives point in this direction. Chinese politics faculty at most American universities are evaluated in a way that privileges 'hits' in political science journals, even at a time when leading China studies journals continue to score high on the citation charts and rival the most prestigious disciplinary outlets for impact. The tendency to favor disciplinary publication is less strongly felt elsewhere, but in the United States salary increases, promotion, and mobility often depend on visibility in the discipline more than visibility among other China scholars.[8] This is especially so in highly quantitative departments and formal modeling shops, but it is also the case in more qualitative departments and at universities that host area studies centers. This incentive structure affects faculty and is internalized by graduate students, who quickly notice which of their classmates are considered stars and often conclude that bringing knowledge from China to a disciplinary audience is the path to a marketable dissertation, a good first job, and rapid advancement.

But it is more than securing a position or tenure or career-mindedness that has drawn students of Chinese politics into closer contact with political science. Many of us do not want to be exotic zoo animals confined to an area studies pen.[9] We wish to speak to disciplinary colleagues much as sociologists, for example, have for some time.[10] Survey researchers have led the way into mainstream political science, but Chinese politics experts of all stripes are designing articles for *The American Political Science Review* or *World Politics*, or seeking to gain an acceptance in *Comparative Politics* or *Comparative Political Studies* or more specialized disciplinary outlets. This makes sense at a time when reform and opening up have made China look more familiar to those who study

7. Examples include Kevin J. O'Brien and Lianjiang Li, *Rightful Resistance in Rural China* (New York: Cambridge University Press, 2006), and the chapters in Kevin J. O'Brien, ed., *Popular Protest in China* (Cambridge, MA: Harvard University Press, 2008). Some of the contributions to Carlsen *et al.*, *Chinese Politics*, also reflect this impulse.

8. Nearly 20 years ago, Lucian W. Pye ['Social science theories in search of Chinese realities', *China Quarterly* 132, (December 1992), p. 1161] wrote: 'It is not enough to hold the respect of other area specialists. Tenure depends upon the judgment of those who guard the standards of each discipline'.

9. For similar thinking among political scientists who focus on Southeast Asia, see Erik Martinez Kuhonta, Dan Slater and Tuong Vu, 'Introduction: the contributions of Southeast Asian political studies', in Erik Martinez Kuhonta, Dan Slater and Tuong Vu, eds, *Southeast Asia in Political Science: Theory, Region, and Qualitative Analysis* (Stanford, CA: Stanford University Press, 2008).

10. Andrew Walder and Victor Nee are prime examples from the senior generation, Ethan Michelson and Xueguang Zhou more recently. On reasons why sociologists and economists of China have found it easier to 'transcend the perennial divide between area studies and social science', see Andrew G. Walder, 'The transformation of contemporary China studies, 1977–2002', in David L. Szanton, ed., *The Politics of Knowledge: Area Studies and the Disciplines* (Berkeley, CA: University of California Press, 2004), p. 322.

other countries. Researchers on Chinese politics have much to say to political scientists who examine the political economy of development, the role private entrepreneurs play in political change, the effects of foreign direct investment, policy implementation, regulation, the rule of law, citizenship, legitimacy, popular support, property rights and many other topics. There is much low-hanging fruit to be harvested from the China case[11] and perhaps the time has come to put Chinese exceptionalism aside permanently and to associate ourselves not with a single country but with problems than can be studied in that country. This has already happened to a large extent for most area studies within political science: why should we be holdouts?

Topical specialization

Topical specialization also has unmistakable benefits and is a natural development, given the avalanche of information now available on Chinese politics. No one can begin to read everything that appears online or in the academic and popular press, and even trying to keep up with news filters and postings on listservs is a challenge. If depth is to be achieved in our research, some division of labor is inevitable and desirable.

Very fine-grained studies are also a result of field work opportunities that have opened up over the last 30 years. Particularly at the local level, researchers can go (nearly) everywhere and study (nearly) everything.[12] This had led to a flourishing of empirical investigations that explore political dynamics in single (or a small number of) settings. Much of lasting value has been learned by homing in on individual pieces of the puzzle of Chinese politics. This research strategy has also made China scholars more like other area specialists in political science and even natural scientists. Students of American politics, for example, have long ago learned to live with a high degree of topical specialization and clear lines have been drawn between what scholars, journalists, and pundits do. Natural scientists, for their part, tend to be even more specialized and have proliferated subfields at a swift rate.[13] Nearly all academics are less conversant with subfields some distance from their own than was true in the past. Perhaps we are simply witnessing the maturing of the study of Chinese politics in an era when it no longer makes sense (or is feasible) to be an expert on more than a few aspects of political life in China. If this is so, specialization is the path to progress.

Islands of research

Advantages aside, disciplinary and topical specialization also have some troubling implications. First, narrow topics make it difficult for those who study other aspects

11. For a defense of this research strategy, see Kevin J. O'Brien, 'Discovery, research (re)design and theory building', in Maria Heimer and Stig Thøgersen, eds, *Doing Fieldwork in China* (Honolulu, HI: University of Hawaii Press, 2006).

12. For vigorous disagreement, see James Mann, *The China Fantasy: How Our Leaders Explain Away Chinese Repression* (New York: Viking, 2007); and Carsten A. Holz, 'Have China scholars all been bought?', *Far Eastern Economic Review* 170(3), (April 2007), pp. 36–40. There remain of course some 'forbidden zones', including significant parts of, for example, ethnic politics and elite politics. For a balanced treatment of fieldwork opportunities and constraints, see Heimer and Thøgersen, eds, *Doing Fieldwork in China*.

13. For growing signs of this in the social sciences, see the 20 subfields (and over 600 sub-subfields) into which research on economics is divided in the *Journal of Economic Literature* classification system [see http://www.aeaweb.org/journal/jel_class_system.php (accessed 22 January 2010)].

of Chinese politics to place the best new research and to figure out what it all adds up to.[14] Topical specialization produces high resolution pieces of a puzzle, but little sense of how the pieces fit together and no boxcover that illustrates what the puzzle depicts.[15] At a time when China's economic growth and prominence in world affairs have generated extraordinary interest inside and outside the academy, relatively few of us are willing to take a stab at characterizing the polity or addressing other equally large questions.[16] When policymakers, citizens, and other scholars need maps of Chinese politics more than ever, we offer less insight than we might about what connects scattered islands of research.[17]

Disciplinary specialization also has some worrisome consequences, including discouraging interdisciplinary, China-centered discussion. Most of the debates I taught in my Chinese politics seminar involved Sinologists across the social sciences. These exchanges become less likely when immersion in political science is expected from sociologists or economists or anthropologists, who are understandably focused on their own discipline and China's role in it. Disciplinary specialization inevitably cuts off experts on Chinese politics from non-political scientists, journalists, and other China watchers who are more interested in China than in political science. It creates new islands of research, fenced off by disciplinary jargon and parochial concerns, which can inhibit interdisciplinary work and hamper efforts to develop a holistic understanding of Chinese politics, economics and society. In Alpermann's words, 'what looks like "integration" from a disciplinary perspective can be seen as "fragmentation" from the vantage point of China area studies'.[18]

Disciplinary specialization hives us off from other China scholars and also from each other. These days, experts on Chinese politics seem to discuss less as a group and share less common knowledge. This encourages agreement or, more precisely, deference to specialized knowledge, largely because there is not enough engagement to disagree or to appreciate fully what is at stake. Leaning toward political science makes researchers less visible to other students of Chinese politics who do not follow or find great relevance in some disciplinary debates. These debates may be pivotal in political science, but that does not make them so for China. The old debates that structured my syllabus had China scholars on both sides and exploring and

14. 'As we learn more about the minutiae of life in China, it is becoming more difficult to comprehend the broad patterns of change and structure' (Harding, 'The evolution of American scholarship on contemporary China', pp. 32–33).

15. On the jigsaw puzzle metaphor, and the need to assemble pieces into a full picture, see Elizabeth J. Perry, 'Trends in the study of Chinese politics: state–society relations', *China Quarterly* 139, (September 1994), pp. 712–713.

16. Exceptions, on the nature of China's authoritarianism, include Andrew C. Mertha, '"Fragmented authoritarianism 2.0": political pluralization in the policy process', *China Quarterly* 200, (December 2009), pp. 995–1012; Pierre Landry, *Decentralized Authoritarianism in China: The Communist Party's Control of Local Elites in the Post-Mao Era* (New York: Cambridge University Press, 2008); and Teresa Wright, *Accepting Authoritarianism: State–Society Relations in China's Reform Era* (Stanford, CA: Stanford University Press, 2010). For a time, not long ago, when there were arguably too many characterizations of the Chinese state, see Richard Baum and Alexei Shevchenko, 'The "state of the state"', in Merle Goldman and Roderick MacFarquhar, eds, *The Paradox of China's Post-Mao Reforms* (Cambridge, MA: Harvard University Press, 1999).

17. On, for example, the 'gap between studies of [China's] political economy and studies of contentious politics', see Sidney Tarrow, 'The new contentious politics in China: poor and blank or rich and complex?', in O'Brien, ed., *Popular Protest in China*, p. 6.

18. Alpermann, 'Political science research on China', p. 352. While lauding 'falling barriers between the area and the disciplines', Walder ('The transformation of contemporary China studies', pp. 337, 338) also sees fragmentation, as China scholars become 'more insulated in their respective disciplines, their work increasingly inaccessible to those without specialized training'.

adjudicating them touched on issues that virtually all researchers on Chinese politics agreed were important. In the new disciplinary debates, the 'other side' is often unknown to many China scholars and what the received wisdom maintains is clearly not the case in China. This creates a potential for theoretical and conceptual payoffs that are indecipherable or not overly revealing to students of Chinese politics: findings that are slightly disappointing, or obvious, or of abiding interest primarily to those who know little about China.

Finally, disciplinary and topical specialization affect teaching, in particular training the next generation of researchers on Chinese politics. My current graduate seminar does not add up especially well, generating mainly prosaic conclusions such as China is globalizing, international actors play a growing role in domestic politics, and it is helpful to disaggregate the state.[19] It is also challenging to place a title above each week's assignments: to summarize what large issues have been addressed and how the readings relate to each other. Composing broad, overarching questions about China for the East Asian Politics Ph.D. exam has likewise become more difficult. In fact, I still return to and encourage anxious test-takers to consult my 2005 syllabus, which laid out a more organized and coherent field, packed with what seemed to be enduring questions and debates. Sharp graduate students have of course noticed the empty space at the center of the field, and more of them are designing dissertations that tackle questions drawn from political science (or other social sciences) rather than China studies. This promises further hollowing out of the field, as the next generation of researchers looks outward, toward interlocutors who are not fellow China scholars. This will bring much to political science, but also means missed opportunities in an era when so many want and need to know about China for its own sake.

Terms of enlistment

It is possible that the gains from disciplinary and topical specialization outweigh the costs. Chinese politics as a whole is too much to keep up with, especially for non-resident scholars; engagement with comparativists and international relations experts does bring knowledge about China to political science and reduces the paradigmatic role that European and American experiences still enjoy on too many questions. Students of Chinese politics, moreover, do not face a one-time, either–or choice between allegiance to China studies or the discipline. As Emmerson aptly put it: 'a career is not a snapshot but a film'. Researchers can, across time and in different works, address distinct audiences and identify more or less with area studies or disciplinary colleagues.[20]

Contemporary political science also allows for mixed and shifting loyalties. Since the heat in the area studies debate died down in the early 2000s, we less frequently

19. The conclusion nearly every week is: 'China is in transition, it is a moving target, a political hybrid that is unfamiliar and difficult to get our arms around'. With the reform era now longer than the Maoist era, this is unsatisfying. I am beginning to worry that for my entire career, from my first day of graduate school in 1979, we will be saying 'China is in transition'.

20. Donald K. Emmerson, 'Southeast Asia in political science: terms of enlistment', in Kuhonta *et al.*, eds, *Southeast Asia in Political Science*, p. 305.

hear statements like: 'I have long regarded area programs as a problem for political science' or 'The idea of having a political science specialist for every piece of international real estate may soon seem as arcane as having a specialist for every planet in an astronomy department'.[21] Instead, we are more likely to be told there is 'no necessarily fatal tension between studying an area and doing political science' or, as three young Southeast Asianists concluded, there can be 'a synergy between region and discipline' and a 'complementary and mutually reinforcing relationship' between area studies and political science.[22]

Still, there are questions about what the 'terms of enlistment'[23] should be for China scholars in political science. In my view, it would be a mistake to follow the example of the discipline of economics, where country-based studies are uncommon and area specialists are marginalized; nor would it be advisable to heed Yang Zhong's call for students of Chinese politics to revive the search for a science of comparative politics that has little use for country names.[24] It may even be unwise to emulate the field of European politics, where many Europeanists have come to identify with political scientists who study the same topic (e.g. federalism, legislatures, political economy) or problem (e.g. multilevel governance, democratic transition, immigration) over area studies colleagues who conduct research on the same piece of 'real estate'.

There are many reasons to produce country specialists on China. First, social science theories come and go but China will last. It is a sad truth that much social science knowledge disappears with little trace, because it is ignored or falls out of fashion and is supplanted by the next big thing. This is much less likely for China. Second, mainstreaming the study of Chinese politics may at times be wrong-headed or premature, if it springs from a belief that China is more familiar than it is. Using theories and concepts from political science to interpret protest or voting behavior or elections or bureaucracy may place findings from China in a Procrustean bed that slices off what matters most. Third, interest in Chinese politics is high. A large and growing demand for informed, broad-gauged, country-based analysis exists, both inside and outside the classroom. If scholars do not address this need, and instead limit themselves to ever more-focused studies and intramural disciplinary debates, others will step into the breach.

21. Robert H. Bates, 'Letter from the president: area studies and the discipline', *APSA-CP* 7(1), (Winter 1996), pp. 1–2; David D. Laitin, 'Letter from the incoming president', *APSA-CP* 4(2), (Summer 1993), pp. 3, 18.

22. Emmerson, 'Southeast Asia in political science', p. 305; and Kuhonta *et al.*, 'Introduction', pp. 2, 3.

23. Emmerson, 'Southeast Asia in political science', p. 304.

24. Yang Zhong, 'The logic of comparative politics and the development of political science in China', *Journal of Chinese Political Science* 14(4), (December 2009), pp. 335–342.

Journal of Contemporary China (2008), **17**(54), February, 191–204 Routledge Taylor & Francis Group

One-Party Rule and the Question of Legitimacy in Contemporary China: preliminary thoughts on setting up a new research agenda

GUNTER SCHUBERT*

Most scholarly research takes for granted that political legitimacy in contemporary China is precarious and that the current regime suffers from a legitimacy crisis only superficially covered by economic development and nationalism. Political reform—branded as zhengzhi tizhi gaige*—is not considered viable and usually discredited as too limited and manipulated by the Communist Party as to deserve its name. Consequently, the impact of these reforms on the current regime's legitimacy is under-researched, arguably blinding us for a better understanding of its resilience. This article argues for taking seriously the possibility of* zhengzhi tizhi gaige *engendering critical degrees of political legitimacy for the current regime. It proposes a new research agenda of micro-political research which should thoroughly address the relationship between different reform measures and the public's responses to them.*

> A conundrum about legitimacy is that most people sense what it is, but its most expected causes and results both correlate only loosely with it insofar as attitude surveys or elections can measure it. This understandably makes behavioural researchers nervous. Yet social science can use information from expressed normative intentions, as well as from conduct. Relying on the hope that a researcher can understand the consciousness of the people being studied is an unsure way to draw conclusions—but so is its alternative, relying only on direct observations of behaviour and testing them against hypotheses that neglect ideas not constructed by the researcher.[1]

I. Introduction

It seems to be established wisdom in the Western *academe* that Communist one-party rule in present-day China is historically anachronistic and suffers from a governance

*Gunter Schubert, Ph.D., is Chair Professor of Greater China Studies at the Institute of Chinese and Korean Studies, University of Tuebingen, Germany. His research focuses on political and social developments in Greater China, local governance reform in the PRC, cross-Strait relations, Chinese and Taiwanese nationalism and East Asian regionalism. He can be reached at gunter.schubert@uni-tuebingen.de.

1. Lynn T. White, 'Introduction—dimensions of legitimacy', in Lynn T. White, ed., *Legitimacy: Ambiguities of Political Success or Failure in East and Southeast Asia* (New Jersey *et al.*: World Scientific, 2005), p. 26.

ISSN 1067-0564 print/ 1469-9400 online/08/540191–14 © 2008 Taylor & Francis
DOI: 10.1080/10670560701693153

and legitimacy crisis that is deepening. Regime change will therefore happen—albeit slowly—and is only a matter of time.[2] Most observers find that the effects of economic and social change driven by market reform have caused serious cleavages within Chinese society in the form of rising income disparities, regional development imbalances, deficits in the provision of public goods (e.g. social security, environmental protection), and growing unemployment. Moreover, the party-state is assumed to be constantly challenged by rural and urban protests against cadre corruption and the unlawful behaviour of officials. It is therefore generally believed in the West that the current regime's political legitimacy has since long evaporated and cannot be regained by reforming one-party rule.

The Communist leadership, for its part, does not deny the problems caused by China's market transformation. It has therefore engaged in a continuous process of ideological adaptation since the early reform era, which has culminated in the adoption of 'the very important thoughts of the Three Represents' and—most recently—in the concept of a 'harmonious socialist society'. Within this normative framework, private entrepreneurs have been incorporated into the 'workers' category and accepted as regular party members. At the same time, the Hu-Wen leadership has promised to energetically enhance the quality of 'government for the people', especially by developing a 'socialist rule-of-law system'. Further efforts in this vein include the promotion of political structural reform (*zhengzhi tizhi gaige*), which mainly aims at implementing professional standards of cadre recruitment and management, new modes of direct political and social participation at the local level (e.g. village and urban neighbourhood elections, a refined petition system, etc.), more autonomy for the People's Congresses, as well as new mechanisms of public control over government agencies (e.g. via the introduction of public hearing systems), and intra-party democracy.[3] It is the declared aim of the Party to bring about more efficiency, accountability, transparency, reliability, and trust in the state–society relationship without changing the basic parameters of one-party rule.

Although rising numbers of social protests are reported throughout the country and cadre corruption continues to be rampant, non-democratic China has also seen surprisingly high degrees of interpersonal trust and overall regime support on the part of its citizens over the last 15 years (see below). This observation may support, although arguably, the assumption that the Communist Party's endeavours to generate legitimacy through a mix of nationalism, economic performance,

2. Cf. Minxin Pei, 'China's governance crisis', *Foreign Affairs*, (September–October 2002), pp. 96–106; Bruce Gilley, *China's Democratic Future* (New York: Columbia University Press, 2004); Yongnian Zheng, *Will China Become Democratic? Elite, Class and Regime Transition* (Singapore: Eastern Universities Press, 1998); Yongnian Zheng, 'The party, class, and democracy in China', in Kjeld Erik Brodsgaard and Yongnian Zheng, eds, *The Chinese Communist Party in Reform* (New York: Routledge, 2006), pp. 231–260; Willy Wo-Lap Lam, *Chinese Politics in the Hu Jintao Era. New Leaders, New Challenges* (Armonk, NY: M.E. Sharpe, 2006). Some scholars have been more careful by accentuating the obstacles to democratic transition in China. However, they do not seriously consider the current regime to be capable of generating political legitimacy over time. Cf. Suisheng Zhao, *China and Democracy. The Prospect for a Democratic China* (New York: Routledge, 2000).

3. Cf. Thomas Heberer and Gunter Schubert, eds, 'The State of Political Reform in Contemporary China', *ASIEN*, no. 99, Special Edition, (April 2006); Yiu-chung Wong, *From Deng Xiaoping to Jiang Zemin. Two Decades of Political Reform in the People's Republic of China* (Lanham, MD: University Press of America, 2005); Zengke He, *Zhongguo zhengzhi tizhi gaige yanjiu* [*Studying China's Political Structural Reform*] (Beijing: Zhongyang bianyi, 2004).

technocratic governance and limited political reform (including a more legally based system)—while successfully claiming to be the only viable force in the country capable of guaranteeing social and political stability—have paid off and can explain what has been called the regime's 'authoritarian resilience'.[4] Whilst most observers believe that this resilience is only temporary and cannot stave off the ultimate demise of 'Socialism with Chinese Characteristics', there seems to be a growing inclination among some native as well as Western China scholars to test the hypothesis that one-party rule in China can indeed become more *democratic* and, consequently, more stable in the future.

As obtaining convincing empirical substantiation of the 'legitimacy hypothesis' is impeded in the absence of democratic elections at all levels of the political system, which would allow the people to voice their judgment on Communist one-party rule in the most direct manner, it is argued here that the diagnosis of a deepening legitimacy crisis simply due to the lack of such elections is unconvincing. On the contrary, the 'resilience' of the current regime might provide considerable evidence that it does in fact have much leeway to cope with the challenges and contradictions that 'Market Leninism' produces. It is therefore my central argument (or hypothesis) that—at least for the time being—the Chinese political system is able to generate significant degrees of regime legitimacy by adapting rather successfully to a changing domestic and international environment.[5]

Although neither democratic nor fully accountable to the people, no informed scholar would contest that the Communist regime has become *more* open and *more* accountable, even *more* democratic, during the last decade with the implementation of the various legal and political reforms mentioned above.[6] At present, an organizational alternative to the Communist Party is not in sight, and to many Western observers the majority of the Chinese people would like the Party to remain in power to ensure political stability. If we additionally factor in that the regime's overall economic performance is still good, and that it has won China unprecedented 'Great Power' status in the international arena, the perspective of a rather strong and enduring 'party-state democracy'[7] becomes more real than it may appear at first glance. Even if such a regime type runs counter to our beliefs, the 'legitimacy hypothesis' could at least be useful in a counterfactual sense: the Chinese political system might be much better understood by looking at its capacity to generate political legitimacy and, hence, stability, rather than focusing on its numerous problems and structural weaknesses caused by market transformation and societal

4. Andrew Nathan, 'Authoritarian resilience', *Journal of Democracy* 9(1), 2003, pp. 6–17.

5. I therefore question Minxin Pei's argument that the Communist Party is able to maintain (temporarily) its political supremacy first and foremost through the implementation of successful strategies of 'illiberal adaptation' and 'selective repression', cf. Minxin Pei, *China's Trapped Transition: The Limits of Developmental Autocracy* (Cambridge, MA: Harvard University Press, 2006), p. 81. Whilst I do not completely discredit Pei's stance, my argument is mainly concerned with a different perspective on China's transition process which privileges a micropolitical over a macropolitical view and takes issue with the image of an illegitimate regime, if only for the sake of triggering a debate on the substance and plausibility of the points made thus far to explain the current regime's 'authoritarian resilience'.

6. See e.g. the recent collection of articles in Suisheng Zhao, ed., *Debating Political Reform in China: Rule of Law vs. Democratization* (Armonk, NY: M.E. Sharpe, 2006).

7. Brantly Womack, 'Democracy and the governing party (执政党): a theoretical perspective', *Journal of Chinese Political Science* 10(1), (April 2005), pp. 23–42.

change, as most China scholars usually do.[8] The unquestioned truth of an illegitimate regime in China that informs so much scholarly research should not simply be taken for granted.

II. Watching out for regime legitimacy in contemporary China

If we hypothesize on the capacity of the Chinese political system to generate legitimacy, how is this legitimacy produced and where does it become manifest? In the absence of nation-wide democratic elections, could we possibly identify 'zones of legitimacy' in present-day authoritarian China in which the people do express—actively or passively—their accordance with the regime in terms of ideology (moral values), structure (institutional order), and roles of authority (quality of personnel), as laid out in David Easton's approach to regime legitimacy?[9] To answer this question, we need to conceptualize regime legitimacy as the net sum of those 'partial legitimacies' of moral values, institutional order and roles of authority which are generated in different spaces, as well as at different administrative layers and by different personal relationships within the Chinese political system. At the same time, it is held that deficits in legitimacy which might occur at one point within this system can be compensated by gains in legitimacy at another point, resulting in overall regime support (and system stability). This holds true as long as a certain critical level of overall legitimacy (and trust) is maintained. Regime legitimacy must therefore be aggregated from a complex array of empirical phenomena. Consequently, it is first of all necessary to *dis*aggregate the Chinese political system (or state) and look at the potential 'zones of legitimacy' at different spatial, administrative and personal levels in order to assess the Communist regime's overall legitimacy, i.e. the people's belief in the normative validity and appropriateness of the current political order. This implies foremost a distinction between the central and the local state. Apart from taking into account economic performance, nationalist zeal, and the promise to deliver stability as those factors usually believed to produce legitimacy for one-party rule in China,[10] potential zones of legitimacy-building within the political system may be identified in each dimension of the Eastonian concept—ideological, structural, and personal (see Table 1).

As regards ideological legitimacy, i.e. the people's moral consent to the regime and its values, the Communist Party has taken remarkable steps in recent years to broaden its

8. E.g. Gilley, *China's Democratic Future*; Yongnian Zheng, *Will China Become More Democractic? Elite, Class and Regime Transition* (Singapore: Eastern Universities Press, 2004); Pei, *Trapped Transition*; Larry Diamond, 'The rule of law as transition to democracy in China', in Zhao, ed., *Debating Political Reform in China*, pp. 79–90.

9. See David Easton, *A Systems Analysis of Political Life* (New York: Wiley, 1965; reprint, Chicago: University of Chicago Press, 1979) pp. 282–286 (page citations refer to the reprint edition). In Easton's political system theory, legitimacy and trust are the two dimensions of diffuse support of a political order. Whilst (belief in) legitimacy refers to ideology, structure and authority in the above-mentioned sense, trust refers to some common good—'the interest of realm, the public, common, or national interest, the general good and public welfare, or the good of ... [our people]' (p. 312)—and is not conditioned upon institutionalized control over authority. I consider Easton's theory still to offer the most sophisticated approach to the 'legitimacy conundrum', because it encourages a multi-dimensional research programme for the empirical investigation of people's ideas and opinions in different contexts; it further does not reduce legitimacy to a single and abstract explanatory variable such as 'economic performance', which is only too often treated as self-evident by China scholars.

10. Vivienne Shue, 'Legitimacy crisis in China?', in Peter Hays Gries and Stanley Rosen, eds, *State and Society in 21st-Century China: Crisis, Contention, and Legitimation* (New York: Routledge, 2004), pp. 24–49.

Table 1. An Eastonian approach to legitimacy-building in non-democratic China

Sources of legitimacy	'Zone of legitimacy'
Ideology (moral legitimacy)	• Initiating ideological change and support, e.g. by – introducing the 'Three Represents' and co-opting new elites – transforming the CCP into a 'governing party' – establishing the concept of a 'Harmonious Society', i.e. – setting up a new social contract between the rich and the poor • Implementing 'socialist rule of law', thereby – achieving (more) legal accountability of cadres – combating cadre corruption (more) effectively • Extending political participation and strengthening democratic surveillance, e.g. by – granting more power and autonomy to the People's Congresses – implementing direct elections at the local level (villages committees and urban neighborhood committees, village party secretaries)
Structure	• Enhancing the quality of government, e.g. by – professionalizing cadre recruitment and management – providing better public services and administration • Promoting intra-party reform by – institutionalizing more participation and transparency for party members and the public concerning intra-party decision-making
Personal authority	• Enhancing trust in (local) officials, e.g. by – enhancing accountability through direct and (new modes of) indirect elections – extending and improving the petition system – revising the cadre evaluation system

support base in the Chinese society and to become a 'governing party' (*zhizhengdang*) instead of a class-based party.[11] With the introduction of the 'Three Represents'[12] to both internal party discourse and the general public, it was not necessarily Jiang Zemin's primary aim to leave a theoretical legacy that would garner him an 'immortal' status. More importantly, the official admission of private entrepreneurs and modern professionals to the party membership as representatives of the new 'advanced

11. As it is stated at the beginning of its revised Charter, 'the Communist Party of China is the vanguard both of the Chinese working class and of the Chinese people and the Chinese nation. It is the core of leadership for the cause of socialism with Chinese characteristics and represents the development trend of China's advanced productive forces, the orientation of China's advanced culture and the fundamental interests of the overwhelming majority of the Chinese people'. Consequently, the CP has not abandoned its working class profile, though this is now relativized by its equal and explicit concern for *all* Chinese.

12. According to the 'Three Represents', the Communist Party should represent the development trend of advanced productive forces, the orientation of advanced culture, and the fundamental interests of the overwhelming majority of the people in China.

productive forces' served to underline the CP's resolve to adjust its ideology wherever necessary to push forward with marketization and economic development. Jiang Zemin's approach was certainly elitist and unequivocally directed at those rising segments within Chinese society that would prove to be critical for the regime's survival. But it also demonstrated the Party's will to reward entrepreneurial success, professional expertise, and 'unideological' pragmatism by turning these attributes into cornerstones of 'Socialism with Chinese characteristics'. For Jiang, the 'Three Represents' stood for the Party's theoretical innovativeness and continuous adaptability to ever-changing circumstances and challenges in the real world—aspects that were correctly identified by Jiang Zemin as critical for securing regime legitimacy.[13] As a net result of their introduction and 'canonization', these added ideological elements may have forged a new path to bring about increased intra-party coherence, as it is now much more in tune with the expectations of the young and modern elites who are striving for party membership in elevated numbers.

Certainly enough, Jiang's zeal for ideological revisions met with widespread dissatisfaction and resistance among party traditionalists. Under Hu Jintao, the 'Three Represents' have therefore been reinterpreted in more popular terms as aiding in the construction of a 'harmonious socialist society' and bridging the gap between those who normally stand on opposite sides in a market economy—private entrepreneurs and high salaried professionals on one side, workers and peasants on the other. Whilst such 'theorizing' sounds quite opportunistic from a Western point of view, the Chinese government's new focus on social and economic equality may indeed help the Party even more to regain critical support from those whom it has alienated since the reform course started to produce rising levels of inequality. To put the implicit hypothesis in a nutshell: under the non-negotiable condition of one-party rule, a people's party is more legitimate in present-day China than a class-based party; and a party with social-democratic (even Confucianist) concerns is more legitimate than a party declaring that it is fine for some to get rich first.

On the *structural* level, Chinese legal reforms have probably done the most to generate legitimacy for the current regime. Although the PRC's human rights record remains highly problematic, the harsh treatment of regime critics and political dissidents taken as undeniable facts alone reveals little about the people's attitudes on the changes in China's legal system in recent years. Surely, there is much well-founded criticism that the 'socialist rule of law' has not attained (and cannot attain) the quality of a genuine *rule of law*.[14] But at the same time, it cannot be denied that the new laws and regulations have made officials more accountable and granted citizens more rights, not least of all in the realm of China's notorious criminal law. It is therefore essential to determine on a broad scale how the people evaluate the regime's attempt to strengthen China's legal system, as well as the protection of their rights as they affect their everyday lives.

13. Cf. Heike Holbig, *Ideological Reform and Political Legitimacy in China: Challenges in the Post-Jiang Era* (Hamburg: GIGA Working Papers No. 18, February 2006), available at: www.giga-hamburg.de/content/publikationen/pdf/wp18_holbig.pdf.

14. Stanley Lubman, 'Bird in a cage: Chinese law reform after twenty years', *Northwestern Journal of International Law and Business* 20(3), (Spring 2000), pp. 383–423; Randall P. Peerenboom, *China's Long March Toward the Rule of Law* (Cambridge: Cambridge University Press, 2005).

Moreover, no systematic assessment has been made so far regarding the response of the people to the Communist leadership's efforts to enhance the autonomy and substantiate the function of democratic surveillance of the People's Congress System. This has been attempted by introducing new modes of candidate selection and of strengthening the Congresses' constitutional basis, which is usually compromised by the Party's heavy interference in both candidate nomination and the law-making process.[15] Although there are no genuine multi-party elections in China for People's Congresses and the direct ballot at the township and county levels prescribed by the constitution is still closely monitored by the Party, experiments with public hearing systems to provide more independent input for congressional decisions[16] and observable tendencies of deputies and Congress sub-committees seeking more functional independence may point at a newly forming self-consciousness of China's law-makers and at relative gains of power for the Congresses on all administrative levels. This may give the regime more credit on the part of the people (and their representatives) in the future. Up to now, however, there has not been any study that has systematically dealt with the public's thinking on these matters.

In relation to local governance reforms, which have gained special prominence in the Communist Party's drive for *zhengzhi tizhi gaige*, the nation-wide introduction of direct village elections,[17] some experiments with the 'recommendation and public selection' of township heads[18] and new modes of political and social participation in China's urban communities (*shequ*)[19] may have produced new regime legitimacy in the local state. Village elections in particular have come a long way before achieving their current state of sound institutionalization in many parts of China. Whilst many problems remain concerning implementation quality, the relationship between elected VCs and village party branches, the interference of township authorities in the electoral process and post-election village governance, and—most notoriously—law-violating local cadres who ignore, and even scorn the peasants' democratic empowerment, a general consensus nevertheless exists among most scholars both in

15. Murray S. Tanner, *The Politics of Lawmaking in China* (Stanford: Stanford University Press, 1999); Jean-Pierre Cabestan, 'More power to the People's Congresses? Parliaments and parliamentarism in the People's Republic of China', *ASIEN*, no. 99, Special Edition: 'The State of Political Reform in Contemporary China', (April 2006), pp. 42–69.

16. While there are not yet any established rules on legislative hearings, the provinces of Anhui and Guangdong and the cities of Shenzhen, Shenyang, and Shijiazhuang, for instance, have all held public hearings on draft legislation in recent years. Insufficient information is available at this stage to indicate the level of impact that public opinion has on draft legislation—and on how this affects the legitimacy of the law-making process in the eyes of ordinary Chinese. This should be researched by China scholars in the future.

17. Lianjiang Li and Kevin J. O'Brien, 'The struggle over village elections', in Merle Goldman and Roderick MacFarquhar, eds, *The Paradox of China's Post-Mao Reform* (Cambridge, MA: Harvard University Press, 1999), pp. 129–144; Kevin J. O'Brien and Lianjiang Li, 'Accommodating "democracy" in a one-party-state: introducing village elections in China', *China Quarterly* no. 162, Special Issue: 'Elections and Democracy in Greater China', (June 2000), pp. 465–489.

18. Lianjiang Li, 'The politics of introducing direct township elections in China', *China Quarterly* no. 171, (September 2002), pp. 704–723; Tony Saich and Xuedong Yang, 'Township elections in China: extending democracy or institutional innovation', *China Report* 39(4), (Fall 2003), pp. 477–497.

19. Robert Benewick, Irene Tong and Jude Howell, 'Self-governance and community: a preliminary comparison between villagers' committees and urban community councils', *China Information* 18(1), (March 2004), pp. 11–28; James Derleth and Daniel R. Koldyk, 'The Shequ experiment: grassroots political reform in urban China', *Journal of Contemporary China* 13(41), (November 2004), pp. 747–777.

China and the West that village elections have obtained a meaningful status in terms of direct political participation and are now perceived as such by most people in the countryside.

In those places where they operate well, peasant–cadre relations have been horizontalized to some extent, and overall cadre accountability has been enhanced. Certainly enough, rising numbers of peasant protests in recent years point to serious problems and strained peasant–cadre relations in the countryside. Nevertheless, protest does not always imply the erosion of public identification with and support for the political system as a whole. Much of the peasants' anger is directed at law-violating cadres who are accused of working against the centre. The centre, for its part, is often assumed to be benevolent to the 'common people', or at least accredited the benefit of the doubt.[20] Consequently, conflict at the local level does not necessarily translate into overall regime delegitimization. Apart from this, too little is known about the extent of political legitimacy in those places where local governance works well and 'noiselessly' (see below). Gains in legitimacy here may translate into overall regime legitimacy, pointing at a possible 'bridging effect' that has not been investigated systematically in the China studies field so far.

Another zone of potential legitimacy-building is the broad area of cadre quality enhancement and public service reform which is left largely unexamined by China scholars. The CP's efforts to professionalize cadre management, e.g. through the introduction of a national civil service system based on transparent regulations of recruitment and evaluation, have mostly been received with scepticism by China scholars.[21] However, cadre management reforms may have done comparatively well at the local level. For example, many efforts have been made in China's urban neighbourhoods and communities (*shequ*) in recent years to recruit young and well-educated cadres and provide them with more service-oriented training. This is part of a broader effort to create new *shequ* identities in urban China through a mixture of greater social and political participation (including direct elections of neighbourhood committees), increased administrative autonomy within the *shequ*, improved welfare services, and a refurbished, i.e. more amicable relationship between the people and the local cadres.[22] While these measures do certainly highlight the regime's objective of regaining control over urban society, it would be interesting to explore their outcomes in terms of whether they entail heightened (or decreased) regime legitimacy for the local state.

Finally, 'intra-party democracy' as one of the regime's more recent initiatives to drive forward *zhengzhi tizhi gaige* should also be discussed in terms of legitimacy-building. Ordinary party members shall be empowered to exert more influence on the selection of leading cadres and on the formulation of party and public policies. Party congresses at all levels should convene more regularly, while intra-party

---

20. Lianjiang Li, 'Political trust in rural China', *Modern China* 30(2), (April 2004), pp. 228–258.

21. Bill K. P. Chou, 'Civil service reform in China, 1993–2001: a case of implementation failure', *China: An International Journal* 2(2), (September 2004), pp. 210–234.

22. Linda Wong and Bernard Poon, 'From serving neighbors to recontrolling urban society', *China Information* 19(3), (2005), pp. 413–442.

decision-making is to become more transparent and accountable.[23] A true empowerment of the party rank-and-file could entail more public input into the party machinery and make the Party more attractive for the young and better educated—the so-called 'middle class' usually declared as the harbinger of regime change in 'classical' democratization theory. Besides their own support for the current regime, these elites might be most effective in helping the Party to remain in touch with societal change and the expectations of the people. Therefore, intra-party democracy has the potential to contribute positively to legitimacy-building within the current regime and should not be disregarded by China scholars.

On the *personal* level, the quality of the relationship between the people and the cadres in the local state—in both rural and urban China—is decisive for the regime's political legitimacy. The direct election—or more circumscribed selection—of public officials in the villages, townships and urban communities; more legal leeway to engage in *shangfang*; and new cadre evaluation criteria that place a special emphasis on lawful behaviour and cadre responsiveness to public demands—these are a number of ongoing experiments that may enhance trust in local officials, thereby strengthening the regime's legitimacy. Although most reports draw a picture of the upheaval in China's countryside and big cities due to rampant cadre corruption as well as a general arbitrariness on the part of these officials, empirical research has shown that successful local governance reform can result in greater stability and new regime legitimacy (see below). Real accountability of cadres and genuine choice for the people may indeed do the trick, even in the absence of competitive multi-party elections.

This all may sound apologetic or, at least, empirically thin. However, it is contended here that at least for the purpose of stimulating the debate on political reform and legitimacy in contemporary China and encouraging more systematic research on this issue, the Party's efforts of *zhengzhi tizhi gaige* should not be ignored but properly assessed to determine more precisely the extent of the people's support for the current regime. By taking steps in this direction, the 'resilience' of Communist one-party rule may find new and more convincing explanations that go beyond those which refer exclusively to the regime's promise of stability and 'truth, benevolence, and glory',[24] or the rather simplistic contention that all would depend on the economy.

III. Researching political legitimacy in contemporary China

How does the research on political legitimacy undertaken thus far by scholars in the China studies field stack up? A look at the literature shows that this issue has hardly been addressed up until the present. This is especially true with regard to the legitimacy-building potential of China's *zhengzhi tizhi gaige*, which has yet to be

23. See *Building of Political Democracy in China*, a government White Paper published in December 2005, available at: http://www.china-un.ch/eng/bjzl/t225536.htm; and 'Important measures for developing inner Party democracy and safeguarding Party members' rights', *People's Daily*, (26 October 2004). For some empirical examples, see Baogang He, 'Intra-party democracy. A revisionist perspective from below', in Brodsgaard and Zheng, eds, *The Chinese Communist Party in Reform*, pp. 192–209.

24. Shue, 'Legitimacy crisis in China?'.

thoroughly investigated by China scholars. One of the reasons for this fact is 'the problem of proving legitimacy from observable behaviour alone'.[25] As a matter of fact, research on legitimacy poses serious methodological pitfalls, not to mention considerable practical problems. To begin with, legitimacy is a 'soft' category within the social sciences, prone to change over time and difficult to operationalize for quantitative or qualitative research.[26] How Chinese people think about the normative validity of the current political order in which they live can only be investigated—apart from theoretical and historical reflection[27]—by macro-quantitative or micro-qualitative research. Both approaches suffer from the suspicion that in an authoritarian environment, people do not say what they think, even if this danger has diminished considerably in the course of China's reform process, given the degree of social pluralization that it has produced. Moreover, the micro-political approach is particularly sensitive, as it aims at investigating the political awareness of the people and their (specific and diffuse) regime support in a local context where serious 'legitimacy gaps' caused by illegal cadre behaviour and dysfunctional political institutions—if they are exposed—would seriously endanger the careers of local officials. Legitimacy as an object of scientific analysis is therefore seldom researched 'on the ground', even by Chinese scholars.[28]

Macro-quantitative analysis of regime legitimacy has primarily been conducted—albeit often indirectly—with the help of the World Values Surveys and some other nation-wide data sets.[29] For instance, Tang Wenfang has found high levels of interpersonal trust in contemporary China despite low levels of political freedom. He attributes the former to 'a combination of close family ties and lively informal social interaction'.[30] While Tang points at the fact that there is no correlation between the degree of interpersonal trust and the probability of democracy, he also holds that trust can be related to higher levels of faith in 'political and social institutions that perform universal functions, such as national security, welfare, crime control, business practices, and so on. Trust can therefore increase support for the political system in democratic as

25. White, 'Introduction', p. 2.

26. 'Legitimacy varies over time. It is not something that a regime just has or lacks. It is not wholly created by either old traditions or new agents—but it is created, not natural' (*Ibid.*, p. 28).

27. See e.g. Jungmin Seo, 'Nationalism and the problem of political legitimacy in China', in White, ed., *Legitimacy*, pp. 141–182; and Yongnian Zheng and Fook Lye Liang, 'Political legitimacy in reform China: between economic performance and democratization', in White, ed., *Legitimacy*, pp. 183–214, provide good examples for these 'conventional' approaches.

28. In a provocative essay published in the April 2007 edition of the *Far Eastern Economic Review* titled 'Have China scholars all been bought?', Carsten Holz claimed that the work of contemporary China scholars is heavily compromised by their opportunism and career thinking. They do not dare to question the legitimacy of the current regime in China and pretend to be dealing with a 'normal' country instead of a 'mafia state', as Holz maintains China should be regarded. From that perspective, any approach that takes the current regime's legitimacy-building capabilities seriously sanctifies Communist authoritarianism and exposes an unacceptable political amorality. Whilst Holz makes some strong points for substantiating his reproaches, his judgment is issued from a moral pedestal and, as it seems to me, not overly informed by sound empirical knowledge of how the political system operates and what Chinese people think on the ground. As scholars who do not want to be bought we should not be afraid of asking questions that may sound as if we have been bought.

29. See Shiping Hua, ed., *Chinese Political Culture, 1989–2000* (Armonk, NY: M.E. Sharpe, 2001); Jie Chen, *Popular Political Support in Urban China* (Stanford: Stanford University Press, 2004); Wenfang Tang, *Public Opinion and Political Change in China* (Stanford: Stanford University Press, 2005); Zhengxu Wang, 'Political trust in China: forms and causes', in Tang, *Public Opinion and Political Change in China*, pp. 113–139.

30. Tang, *Public Opinion and Political Change in China*, p. 111.

well as non-democratic countries'.[31] It operates, as Tang notes, the same way in both systems where it may or may not promote democratic values and citizen participation. This implies that any measure to elevate the level of interpersonal trust may bring about more regime legitimacy in China—a significant point when looking at the CP's efforts to institutionalize political reforms, especially in the realm of local governance.

In the same study explicitly focusing on the issue of regime legitimacy, Tang found that the Chinese government enjoyed much support in urban China, as

> by 1999, support for China's single-party structure was relatively high. Neither Western-style democracy nor indeed any kind of coherent ideology seemed to capture the respondents' aspirations. Most people, especially administrators and managers, seemed to instead want a pragmatic government capable of delivering economic results.[32]

However, as the author emphasizes, the regime enjoys only conditional support and legitimacy, as 'one-quarter of urban Chinese want to change the single-party system and launch democratization, and more than half of them demand more democratic rights and government accountability'.[33] Whilst these findings, which show that regime legitimacy is highly dependent on the public's perception of the government's economic reform policies, neatly reflect the mainstream viewpoint on current support levels for one-party rule in China, the effects on regime legitimacy produced by *zhengzhi tizhi gaige* do not make it onto Tang's agenda. Consequently, the author may be right as far as he takes his argument; still, he may not go far enough. I argue that this is roughly applicable to the whole China studies field.

Micro-qualitative research on Chinese village elections has, however, produced at least a few insights into the 'legitimacy conundrum'. Contrary to the impression evoked by countless recent reports on rural unrest and upheaval, China's 'grassroots democracy' does not always belie the authorities' claim that it has delivered increased cadre accountability, social stability and political efficacy for peasants. For instance, in a recent study based on survey data gathered in 2000 in Jiangsu province, Chen Jie found relatively high degrees of popular support for village self-government (including direct village elections).[34] Apparently, peasants in Jiangsu assess this system positively for providing more opportunities to participate in and influence local politics. Chen found a striking difference between the peasants' evaluation of the incumbent authorities on the one hand and of the institutional order of village self-government on the other: whilst they were far from being enthralled by the policy performance of their local cadres, peasants were more positive concerning village elections, management transparency and public participation *per se*, which are central pillars of the current system of village self-government. This may imply that peasants tend to lend diffuse support to the current political order (at least on the local level),[35]

31. *Ibid.*, p. 114.
32. *Ibid.*, p. 76.
33. *Ibid.*
34. Jie Chen, 'Popular support for village self-government in China', *Asian Survey* 45(6), (November/December 2005), pp. 865–885.
35. See also Li, 'Political trust in rural China'.

but are more reluctant in terms of specific support for local officials who are responsible for implementing and supervising village self-government.[36]

My own field work in different Chinese villages conducted in the provinces of Jilin and Jiangxi, and in Shenzhen Special Economic Zone from 2002 to 2005, on the contrary, found much *specific* support for local cadres. Especially in Jilin's model Lishu county, where *haixuan* elections for village committee members were introduced in the early 1990s, I found surprising degrees of trust in local officials on the part of the peasants. The direct ballot had given them a feeling of political empowerment, whilst the cadres seemed to have accepted village elections as a check on their performance, with lawful electoral implementation serving as an evaluation criterion on a par with their contributions to economic development and social stability in the locality. It is *rational* trust that characterizes the peasant–cadre relationship in Lishu: as long as the cadres credibly support and work for direct village elections and transparent village self-government, they retain the peasants' trust and are not voted out of office. Consequently, the low turnover of village cadres is not a sign of insignificant political participation or electoral manipulation but, to the contrary, of a rather successful consolidation and re-legitimation of established power in the village.[37]

The fact that Lishu is a model county which has been under close scrutiny by central authorities does not constitute a viable argument against the validity of the phenomenon at hand. Apparently, local cadres in Lishu 'discovered' the 1987 experimental Organic Law on Villager Committees as a means to reinstate their legitimacy and to spur economic development. Their early success was later praised by the central government in Beijing as a confirmation of the rationale to implement direct elections in the countryside: the experiment seemed to work well for all parties concerned. Lishu proved that limited political participation can produce increased stability and greater cadre legitimacy, strengthening the regime in the local state and, presumably, on the national level as well by transferring the credit of positive local experiences to the party state. Although village elections and village self-government do not operate well in many parts of China today, the main point to be made is that those areas where they actually do should also be closely monitored—an area of focus that is conspicuously lacking in the China studies field so far.

To sum up, research on political legitimacy in contemporary China is still too scant to make any generalized assumptions. The few studies touching upon this issue do suggest, however, that a new research agenda pinpointing the significance of specific and diffuse regime support and the 'belief in legitimacy', in David Easton's terms, might present a valuable path to developing a better understanding of the contemporary dynamics within the multi-layered Chinese political system and of its future course. The next step should therefore be to set up an alternative research agenda for a systematic exploration

36. However, Chen Jie also made it clear that 'the majority of rural residents were still ambivalent about both the leaders and the current state of self-government in their villages', relativizing the degree of diffuse support for the institution of village self-government to some extent; Chen, 'Popular support for village self-government in China', p. 884.

37. Susanne Brandtstädter and Gunter Schubert, 'Democratic thought and practice in rural China', *Democratization* 12(5), (December 2005), pp. 801–819; Gunter Schubert, 'Authority, trust and legitimacy in the PRC (in German)', *China aktuell* 35(2), (March/April 2006), pp. 5–39; Gunter Schubert and Chen Xuelian, 'Village elections in contemporary China: new spaces for generating regime legitimacy? Experiences from Lishu county' (in Chinese) (forthcoming in China Perspectives 2007/3).

of the different 'zones of legitimacy' outlined above, focusing on the responses to *zhengzhi tizhi gaige* from the people and those who are of critical importance for the survival of the regime: the cadre bureaucracy. This is especially important at the local state level where the CP's endeavours to achieve a top-down implementation of political reforms have been repeatedly met with independent initiatives from below,[38] resulting in a complex political reality that is not yet sufficiently understood by China scholars. *Macro-quantitative research* should address 'legitimacy' more explicitly in its efforts to interpret broad data sets like the World Values Surveys and similar records. However, the most promising trajectory to understand political legitimacy in contemporary China lies in more micro-political and qualitative research on those issues that are most sensitive to the state–society relationship, including:

- the long-term impact of village elections on the political awareness of peasants and local cadres as well as on peasant–cadre relations;
- the consequences of administrative restructuring and new modes of social and political participation in China's urban communities;
- the relevance of reforming China's Local People's Congresses in terms of public responsiveness;
- the role of local cadres (especially at the county and township levels) as influential agents of development and political brokers (transmitters) in the ongoing transformation process;[39]
- the effects of local governance reform in the public service sector; and
- the success of China's legal reforms and their reception by the populace.

Needless to say, macro-quantitative research would profit from a combined approach with such micro-qualitative studies to provide a comprehensive picture of how people view their cadres and their institutions, and how they relate this to their expectations of a political order that they believe is just and right. The cadres' perspectives on these issues should also be taken into account, since they figure as important middlemen between the central state and the local populace and are therefore essential producers of regime legitimacy.

IV. Concluding remarks

It has been hypothesized in this article that the 'authoritarian resilience' of Communist one-party rule may be grounded on a critical degree of overall regime legitimacy that has not yet been grasped by China scholars. Political legitimacy in China is usually understood as the net outcome of the CP regime's economic performance, nationalist politics, and the Chinese people's conservative preference for stability over uncertainty, an alleged result of the introduction of multi-party democracy. The possibility of China's *zhengzhi tizhi gaige* creating meaningful 'zones of legitimacy' within the current political system has hardly been addressed to

38. See, for example, Lisheng Dong, 'Direct township elections in China: latest developments and prospects', *Journal of Contemporary China* 15(48), (August 2006), pp. 503–515.

39. Together with Professor Thomas Heberer, University of Duisburg-Essen (Germany), I have now set up a project to investigate local township and county cadres as 'strategic groups' in the process of administrative and financial reform in China's vast countryside.

this point by systematic empirical research. Consequently, China's political system has remained a 'black box' in terms of its capacity to adapt to changing external conditions and of how this adaptation exactly functions. This is not only to be attributed to methodological or practical problems. There is also too little belief in the possibility that one-party rule in China does not only depend on steady economic gains for the majority of the population, but could also be based on limited political reforms which make the regime *more* (though not fully) accountable and *more* democratic without fundamentally questioning the current political order. However, future research should give this possibility some credit. Even if one does not believe that one-party rule is sustainable in a 'marketized' China, one might get a better understanding of the regime's longevity by taking the 'legitimacy hypothesis' seriously. We must begin to link it to studies particularly concerned with public responses to the current regime's drive for *zhengzhi tizhi gaige*. This implies both macro-quantitative and micro-political approaches to the whole range of political, legal and administrative reforms that have been pursued in rural and urban China throughout the last two decades. Only if we have a better understanding of how the people judge the CP regime on the ideological, structural and personal level can we get a better idea of how 'resilient' this regime really is.

Part II
The Nature of the Chinese Political System

[4]

Journal of Contemporary China (2012), **21**(73), January, 169–185

The China Model: one country, six authors

MINGLU CHEN and DAVID S. G. GOODMAN*

The rapid economic development of the People's Republic of China has not only been spectacular since 1978 but also suggests that there is a specific China Model of the relationship between the state, society and the market. In particular, this model would seem to have particular application to the less developed economies of the world. Certainly the emergence of a Beijing Consensus to replace the democratic capitalist Washington Consensus of the 1990s would seem to suggest the purchase that China's rise has brought in many parts of the world. An examination of six prominent different accounts of China's growing economic and political importance suggests that there are distinct limits to the conceptualisation of China's development in terms of a model, though there may be lessons about the interaction of public and private to be learnt more widely.

The China Model is the phrase now widely employed or alluded to in describing the substantial and sustained economic growth and development of the People's Republic of China (PRC) since the end of 1978, and the political consequences of that growth and development. This China Model, in its international context, is also sometimes referred to as the Beijing Consensus, in contrast to the earlier Washington Consensus—based on democratic capitalism and distinctly neoliberal development policies—that dominated the 1990s.[1] Whatever descriptive label is employed, there is a fairly widespread assumption, not simply that the PRC has had a specific recipe for development, but that other countries may copy its model, or at the very least learn lessons from its experience.

In many ways the economic growth of the PRC since 1978 seems to have directly challenged theories of economic development. One key challenge to theories of modernisation is that the PRC's experience seems to suggest that authoritarian politics and economic liberalisation can co-exist. Certainly in many ways from the standpoint of 1978 the most remarkable feature of the PRC's development does seem to have been not simply the continuation of Chinese Communist Party (CCP) rule but its

* Minglu Chen and David S. G. Goodman are both in the Department of Government and International Relations and the China Studies Centre, the University of Sydney. This article is based on the Keynote Address delivered to the Conference of the Consejo de Estudios Latinoamericanos de Asia y de Oceanía [Council for Latin American Studies in Asia and Oceania] at the University of Guadalajara, 22 November 2010. The authors can be reached by email at minglu.chen@sydney.edu.au or david.goodman@sydney.edu.au.

1. The Beijing Consensus was developed as an idea first in a booklet by Joshua Cooper Ramo, *The Beijing Consensus* (London: The Foreign Policy Centre, May 2004).

ISSN 1067-0564 print/ 1469-9400 online/12/730169-17 © 2012 Taylor & Francis
http://dx.doi.org/10.1080/10670564.2012.627672

adaptability. This has even led some commentators to argue that China's democratic centralism is not only 'decent' but at least as preferable as liberal democracy as a system of governance.[2]

The defying of received wisdom attends appreciation of much of the PRC's economic development. A growth rate of 9–10% per annum for over 30 years with little if any hyper-inflation would have seemed unlikely 30 years ago. Indeed, when the goal of doubling and redoubling the PRC's GDP by the year 2000 was first announced in 1978, it was greeted with extreme scepticism by academic economists outside the PRC specialising in analysis of the Chinese economy. It was regarded as a desirable but unattainable aspiration.[3] In the event, this goal was achieved in 1995. A pattern of development and sceptical response has characterised much of the economy's subsequent development at both the macro- and micro-economic levels. For the last ten years for example, external voices have warned about the real estate bubble that is about to burst.[4] The PRC's recent stimulus package and attempts to obviate the possible adverse impact of the global financial crisis, particularly through the development of a high speed rail network, have been greeted with not a little derision by external commentators,[5] and yet failure has not resulted, nor even a hiatus in development, though there is always the danger of hubris in making such a statement.

Both the success of economic growth and the apparent challenges to received wisdom about economic development have led to the possibility that China offers a different path to modernisation. This is essentially the intellectual origin of the search for a China Model. It is a powerful trope, especially given the economic development problems of the first decade of the twenty-first century. To quote Ramo, writing even before the global financial crisis of 2008

> The Beijing Consensus offers hope for the world. After the collapse of the Washington Consensus, the breakdown of WTO talks, the implosion of Argentina's economy, much of the world was uncertain what a new paradigm for development ought to look like.[6]

The problem comes when there is an attempt to develop this basic idea further. The degree of purchase obtained by the China Model rests on the extent to which China's experience is seen to be presenting an alternative path that others may follow, and not simply seen to be *suis generis.* An examination of the arguments presented by six authors concerned with explaining and accounting for the PRC's economic success and its political consequences—Joseph Cooper Ramo, Giovanni Arrgihi, Martin Jacques, Stefan Halper, Suisheng Zhao and Barry Naughton—in recent publications suggests that there is very little evidence that there is a replicable China Model in that sense. The development of the PRC since 1978 is rather the result of unique circumstances, though of course there may still be lessons that others may also learn from this experience, always bearing in mind that there are costs as well as benefits in certain practices and processes.

2. Stephen C. Angle, 'Decent democratic centralism', *Political Theory* 33(4), (August 2005), pp. 518–546.
3. See the statements in *The China Quarterly's* Chronicle and Documentation, March 1979.
4. See, for example: David Pierson, 'In China real estate fever is rising', *Los Angeles Times*, (26 April 2010).
5. See, for example: 'Stealing the airlines' business', *The Economist*, (12 February 2010); and 'High-speed rail on fast track to nowhere', *South China Morning Post*, (6 July 2010).
6. Ramo, *The Beijing Consensus*, p. 60.

The search for consensus

The notion that there might be a China Model is very seductive. The PRC has had spectacular growth rates for 30 years and has transformed the country. The Beijing Olympics and Shanghai Expo, not to mention the national-level universities, have demonstrated not only that China has reached a level of wealth and technical competence that can increasingly match the more developed countries of the world, but also that it is possible for a less developed country to become one of the wealthiest. The economy is now the second largest in the world and almost every other country (Mexico and Canada are notable exceptions) has the PRC as their largest trade partner.

Of course, the picture of success is not complete. There remain pockets of horrendous poverty in China and inequality has grown significantly. The average annual real disposable income of rural residents remains only 3,587 Chinese *yuan* (US$564) a year compared to the average for urban residents of 11,759 Chinese *yuan* (US$1,849). Disregarding the limited applicability of the Gini coefficient as a measure of inequality, China's has increased from 0.22 in 1978 to 0.49 in 2009.[7] Nonetheless, even a casual observer cannot fail to notice that the PRC has become the manufacturing workshop to the world, that the prospects for continued growth are good, and that wealth generation has delivered benefits individually and collectively, domestically and internationally.

It is, then, no surprise to find that journalists, public intellectuals and academics have all tried to identify a China Model. There has been a widespread attempt to highlight the key characteristics of the PRC's development whose collective results are almost amusing in their lack of agreement on the dimensions of the China Model. To take some examples: the China Model is inherently neoliberalist, says David Harvey.[8] The China Model is the very antithesis of neoliberalist capitalism, says Giovanni Arrighi.[9] The China Model combines economic reform with no political change, says Martin Jacques.[10] The China Model would not have been sustainable, says Suisheng Zhao, without political reform alongside the economic restructuring that has taken place.[11] The China Model is based on privatisation above all else, argues Steven Halper.[12] The China Model is often mistaken for privatisation, says Barry Naughton, stressing instead the roles that both private and public play in successful economic development.[13]

This lack of agreement is a useful starting point for attempting understanding. Before considering the various interpretations and explications of the China Model it is, though, as well to bear three considerations in mind. The first is to be aware of the

7. The 2007 statistics on income are from: 'China's GDP grows annual average of 9.67% from 1978 to 2006', *Xinhua* [*New China News Agency*], (6 May 2007). US$1 = 6.7 Chinese *yuan*. A Gini coefficient of 0.40 is usually regarded as a presentiment of social tension.

8. David Harvey, *A Brief History of Neoliberalism* (New York: Oxford University Press, 2007), ch. 4.

9. Giovanni Arrighi, *Adam Smith in Beijing: Lineages of the Twenty-First Century* (London: Verso, 2007).

10. Martin Jacques, *When China Rules the World: The Rise of the Middle Kingdom and the End of the Western World* (London: Allen Lane, 2009), p. 12.

11. Suisheng Zhao, 'The China Model: can it replace the Western model of modernization?', *Journal of Contemporary China* 19(65), (June 2010), p. 424.

12. Stefan Halper, *The Beijing Consensus: How China's Authoritarian Model Will Dominate the Twenty-First Century* (New York: Basic Books, 2010), pp. 11 and 209.

13. Barry Naughton, 'China's distinctive system: can it be a model for others?', *Journal of Contemporary China* 19(65), (June 2010), p. 451.

ideological dimension of the discussion. The Cold War may have been resolved more than 20 years ago but the views expressed by many of the authors involved in discussion of the China Model have their roots in those much earlier debates. Halper's embrace of American capitalism and its superiority is very much on parade. Arrighi, Harvey and Jacques make little secret of their distaste for the same American capitalism. The second consideration is the necessary danger of essentialising China, and especially reading backwards from the present to earlier periods in China's development. For example, Jacques is completely correct to regard China as a continent rather than a simple nation-state, but misled when he attributes to the earlier Empires the characteristics of a nation-state, such as borders.[14] Similarly, Arrighi's description of the Southern Song Dynasty (1127–1279) as a 'nation state' with a 'national market' does seem to be going too far as an exercise in comparative history.[15] Ramo's assumption that Mandarin, a language of twentieth century construction, was spoken throughout the Empire[16] in earlier dynasties, is as interesting as Braudel's much earlier observation that the Chinese were vegetarian.[17] Thirdly, there is an evolutionary process to the analysis being presented, with the most recent publications building on and debating the issues with other earlier-published authors. For this reason, the different views of the China Model will be examined in the order that they appeared in print.

Joseph Cooper Ramo

One of the first current incarnations of the China Model was Joseph Cooper Ramo's pamphlet on *The Beijing Consensus*.[18] Ramo's argument is mainly concerned with the international political impact of China's growth since 1978 rather than concentrating on the details of the dynamics of the development itself, though necessarily he provides explanation of that kind in the process. The emergence of the Beijing Consensus is set in the global economic failures at the end of the 1990s and 'the collapse of the Washington Consensus'. In Ramo's words

> The essential ideas of what is happening in China—innovation, asymmetry, a focus on equality, the exploration of new ideas of citizenship—are appealing to nations that have ambitions for development and security but have seen hundreds of years of failure of development models that rely too much on developed nations for assistance.[19]

The Beijing Consensus in this interpretation has three key characteristics: innovation-based development; economic success measured not by per capita GDP growth but by its sustainability and level of equality; and a strong principle of self-determination for China and for other countries in their dealings with the United States. There can be little doubt that the weight of emphasis here is on the third characteristic. Ramo explicates clearly the appeal of the PRC to many of the less developed countries of the world. There is opposition to the Washington Consensus

14. Jacques, *When China Rules the World*, p. 12.
15. Arrighi, *Adam Smith in Beijing*, p. 321.
16. Ramo, *The Beijing Consensus*, p. 31.
17. Fernand Braudel, *A History of Civilizations* (London: Penguin, 1995), p. 187.
18. Ramo, *The Beijing Consensus*.
19. *Ibid.*, p. 60.

and in particular resistance to Washington itself. There is the possibility that each country can enter the various processes of globalisation on its own terms and not be subject to direction from the East Coast of the USA. In the same spirit, there is also an emphasis on countries not interfering in the domestic affairs of others, stressed by the PRC as an infringement of sovereignty. The PRC exercises influence by example, not by weaponry, and there is a ready acceptance by other countries of its increased economic impact through trade, investment and aid. This increased international influence has helped the PRC to develop the asymmetric capability to counter the USA, through what is often described as 'soft power'. As might be expected, this third point and its view of the world has been taken up widely in the PRC itself.[20]

The first two points in Ramo's description of the Beijing Consensus are more concerned with the domestic dynamics of change, and both require some further substantiation. On the surface, the PRC's development has been little concerned with innovation. Indeed, one of the common criticisms made by external economists is that much of the PRC economy has been developed by managers and those in charge of resources engaging in rent-seeking activity rather than developing new ideas and new technologies. This is not Ramo's point at all. His argument is, that as a late developer, the PRC does not need to go through earlier stages and can simply import the most up-to-date technology *ab initio*.[21] Similarly, the claim that the PRC is not driven by GDP growth targets seems a little strange in a system where local officials have incentive schemes that include GDP growth targets as essential key performance indicators.[22] Here Ramo's point is in danger of being lost in his rhetoric: growth is important but the CCP also places a premium on total factor productivity and is capable, as it has shown since 2005, of pulling back the emphasis on economic growth as such in order to meet alternative goals of improving (and increasing spending on) welfare.[23]

Giovanni Arrighi

Giovanni Arrighi also has global concerns that underwrite his account of China's rise. *Adam Smith in Beijing*[24] is revisionist history on a grand scale, focussing on East Asia but concerned ultimately with US foreign policy. While he does not consider the impact of China's rise on the less developed world in the way that Ramo does, he is concerned with the failings, as he sees them, of the USA's foreign policy, which he criticises for its involvement in the Middle East, not on moral grounds, but because it has meant that the US government's attention has focussed disproportionately on that region.

In the context of understanding the China Model, Arrighi's contribution comes from the attempt to decouple Adam Smith from neoliberalism and to argue that Smith

20. See, for example: Cai Tuo, *Quanqiuhua yu zhengzhide zhuanxing* [*Globalization and Political Transformation*] (Beijing: Peking University Press, 2007).

21. Ramo, *The Beijing Consensus*, p. 11.

22. SASAC, *Provisional Methods for Assessing Performance of Responsible Managers of Central Enterprises*, (30 December 2006), available at: http://www.sasac.gov.cn/gzjg/yjkh/200701310039.htm.

23. Jane Duckett and Beatriz Carrillo, eds, *China's Changing Welfare Mix* (Abingdon: Routledge, 2011).

24. Arrighi, *Adam Smith in Beijing*.

would not only recognise but would also praise the Chinese alternative to American capitalism:

> ... the failure of the Project for a New American Century and the success of Chinese economic development, taken jointly, have made the realization of Smith's vision of a world-market society based on greater equality among the world's civilizations more likely than ever it was in the almost two and half centuries since the publication of *The Wealth of Nations*.[25]

Arrighi's argument challenges the neoliberal interpretation of globalising capital. Through a re-examination of the works of Adam Smith and Marx and a discussion of the 'great divergence' between the European and East Asian patterns of economic development during the nineteenth century, Arrighi identifies an East Asian tradition of the non-capitalist market economy. He takes a long-term perspective on China's development, arguing that in the Ming Dynasty (1368–1644) as well as the Qing Dynasty (1644–1911), the economy was one best characterised as merchant capitalism. It is this market economy that Arrighi highlights as an explanation of China's economic history since 1850, including its spectacular growth during the last three decades. At the heart of this distinction between market and capitalist economies is the question of the relationship of labour to production. Where the East Asian market economy tradition is labour intensive, the capitalist tradition of Europe and North America expropriates the labour of the direct producer.

Unlike those who emphasise the development of a private sector in the PRC as a defining feature of the economy under reform, Arrighi argues that

> deregulation and privatization have been far more selective, and have proceeded at a far slower pace, than in countries that have followed neoliberal prescriptions. Indeed, the key reform has not been privatization but the exposure of state-owned enterprises to competition with one another, with foreign corporations, and, above all, with a mixed bag of newly created private, semi-private and community-owned enterprises.[26]

Where neoliberalism demands the state withdraws from direct government management of the economy, in Arrighi's view the government's role in the economy in the PRC has far from disappeared. On the contrary, Arrighi argues that government action has been crucial in establishing and encouraging export-oriented industrialisation, especially but not exclusively through the creation of export democratic zones in the Pearl River Delta and the Yangtze River Delta. Government has also played a crucial role in encouraging foreign investment, and in general in reinforcing the development of a 'self-centred national economy, informally protected by language, customs, institutions, and networks accessible to outsiders only through local intermediaries'.

Martin Jacques

Martin Jacques in *When China Rules the World*[27] similarly approaches China's rise of the last three decades and possible future, especially its interaction with the rest of

25. *Ibid.*, p. 8.
26. *Ibid.*, p. 356.
27. Jacques, *When China Rules the World.*

the world, from a long-term sense of history. In his view, China cannot be judged in the same way as other countries:

> The mainstream Western attitude has held that in its fundaments, the world will be relatively unchanged by China's rise. This is based on three key assumptions: that China's challenge will be primarily economic in nature; that in due course China will become a typical Western nation; and that the international system will remain broadly as it is now, with China acquiescing in the status quo and becoming a compliant member of the international community. Each of these assumptions is misconceived. The rise of China will change the world in the most profound ways ... It is inconceivable, however, that China will become a Western-style nation in the manner to which we are accustomed. China is the product of a history and culture which has little or nothing in common with that of the West.[28]

Jacques identifies several key differences from his examination of China's history that set its current and most likely future development apart from that of the rest of the world. The starting point is that China should be seen as a 'civilization-state' rather than a nation-state, not least because of its scale and sense of history. This, of course, is not a new approach to the study of China by any means, reflecting the sinological analyses of the mid-twentieth century.[29] In the past, China's relations with other parts of the world were governed not through a system of military domination, but through the political symbiosis of a tributary system. Jacques suggests that this is the likely future too, in ways that resonate with Ramo's description of the PRC's development of asymmetric capability in countering the influence of the USA.

Clearly the size and scale of China do make for significant difference and Jacques makes much of this.[30] The PRC covers a large range of cultures and social practices. The most obvious examples of this are the non-Chinese peoples of the PRC, the Zhuang, Tibetans, Uighurs, Mongols and altogether 55 nationalities other than the Chinese; however, as Jacques also points out, the Chinese parts of China also differ greatly in languages, cultures, social relationships and even patterns of economic development. Scale and size also matter in the ways in which China has a vast domestic market. Like the USA and possibly India, while it may prefer its social and economic interaction with the rest of the world, it does not need them that much. As with the USA, China could be a self-sufficient economy.

Scale and size also bequeath to the Chinese an attitude to race and ethnicity that differentiates it from the rest of the world. This difference in the appreciation of 'the other' is at once both more tolerant of social variety and more insistent on acceptance of conformity, or at least the need for conformity. This is, of course, one reason for another key difference—China remains an authoritarian and unaccountable polity. Jacques does not say so explicitly, but it seems likely from his analysis that this too can be read into the future.

28. *Ibid.*, pp. 12–13.

29. See, for example: Joseph Levenson, 'The province, the nation and the world: the problem of Chinese identity', in Albert Feuerwerker, Rhoads Murphey and Mary C. Wright, eds, *Approaches to Modern Chinese History* (University of California Press, 1967), pp. 268–288.

30. Jacques, *When China Rules the World*, p. 227.

Three final key differences outlined by Jacques refer to the process of development itself. One is the speed of transformation, which has clearly been surprisingly fast. During the Great Leap Forward (1958–1960), the PRC adopted a slogan to 'Catch up and overtake Britain's industrial revolution in 15 years: make every one of our days equivalent to ten of theirs'. Development during the last three decades has come closer to that goal than ever was the case during the late 1950s. In describing this speed of transformation, Jacques comes close to letting his rhetoric speed ahead too: 'Chinese modernity ... is distinguished by the speed of the country's transformation. It combines, in a way quite different from the Western experience of modernity, the past and the future at one and the same time in the present'.[31] The second developmental observation is that while China remains Communist, this is clearly not a European or Soviet Union style experience of Communism.[32] The third observation is that China will somewhat paradoxically remain a developed and a developing country for some time to come, not least again because of the PRC's size and scale.

Stefan Halper

Stefan Halper's version of *The Beijing Consensus*[33] is radically different, not least because it identifies China as a threat, the major challenge to the USA's hegemony, that has to be beaten back.

> Beijing does present a clear and gathering threat to Washington, but the terms of the challenge remain unformed in the public mind, and, indeed, in policy circles. Eschewing confrontation, China's true challenge arises in a separate realm, namely, Beijing's transformative, leading role in the rise of a Chinese brand of capitalism and a Chinese conception of the international community, both opposed to and substantially different from their Western version. In a global battle between different visions of the future and different versions of capitalism, China is the protagonist. As traditional hubs of Western power—like the International Monetary Fund and the World Bank—are circumvented and undermined by readily available Chinese capital, these new non-Western champions of the free market are *beating the West at its own game*.[34]

Unlike any of the authors previously discussed, Halper sees in China's rise the triumph of liberal market reform. His argument is further that *pace* Ramo, the attractiveness of China lies precisely in its rampant capitalism which permits developing countries to follow economic growth without abiding by 'the Western conditions of financial engagement'. This is by way of being Halper's main criticism of China. Liberal market reform has permitted the PRC to deliver

> sufficient economic opportunities, and higher living standards, to persuade the populace that the future held a better quality of life. In a country the size of China, this policy has only been made possible through private businesses and economies of scale, which can guarantee a sufficient number of jobs for the millions leaving state-owned enterprises and Communist social safety nets. Stability at home, therefore, depends on feeding the beats of high-rate economic growth, year upon year. In turn, this means ready access to foreign

31. *Ibid.*, p. 425.
32. *Ibid.*, p. 427.
33. Halper, *The Beijing Consensus.*
34. *Ibid.*, p. 11.

> resources and markets—sufficient to keep the factory belts moving and their produce flying off the shelves. This means Africa for access to oil, iron ore, copper, zinc, lead, tin, and uranium. It means Latin America for access to soybeans, steel and more oil. It means contracts to sustain the global turnover for fast-growing telecommunications and construction giants. It means access to consumer markets from Europe to South Asia for the endless flow of Chinese textiles, shoes, clothing, electrical appliances, household wares, and office equipment.[35]

But, according to Halper, this neo-imperialist vision has also meant that the PRC has needed to seek out

> every possible business partner the world has to offer, no matter where they sit on the spectrum between dictator or democrat ... China does business with the good, the bad, and the ugly—as long as they pay ... Beijing has worked hard in the last decade to become an alternative source of aid, trade, loans, and investment to any state that falls below Western standards of good governance. Not only are Western observers offended by the deeds and the dictatorships that this policy helps to sustain, but we are also apparently powerless to do anything about it.[36]

The solution for Halper is for the USA to campaign more effectively internationally. In his words: 'China's greatest fear is American ideas'.[37]

Suisheng Zhao

Suisheng Zhao takes a more academic and considerably more dispassionate approach to the question of the China Model.[38] He challenges head-on the oft-cited assumption that the China Model is liberal economic reform with no political change. Instead he queries exactly the extent of free market operation and the extent of authoritarianism. In both cases he argues that neither exists in such black and white terms: shades of grey dominate.

In terms of a free market economy, Zhao points out that China lacks many of the institutions and structures usually associated with a free market. There are still no independent courts. Though the political and legal system now acknowledges property rights, they may not always be enforceable. Governance is not noticeably or consistently transparent and there is no right or exercise of free information. The state still plays a major economic role through its control over strategic sectors of the economy and strategic industries—utilities, transport, communications, media, finance.[39]

In Zhao's view, the China Model is a twenty-first century version of the East Asian Developmental State[40] with three major characteristics: economic pragmatism and agency; developmental state behaviour; and state control of ideas:

35. *Ibid.*, pp. 209–210.
36. *Ibid.*, p. 209.
37. *Ibid.*, p. 208.
38. Suisheng Zhao, 'The China Model', pp. 419–436.
39. *Ibid.*, p. 422.
40. Robert Wade, *Governing the Market: Economic Theory and the Role of Government in East Asian Industrialization* (Princeton, NJ: Princeton University Press, 1990); Meredith Woo-Cummings, *The Developmental State* (New York: Cornell University Press, 1999).

> What makes the Chinese model unique is that the communist regime has safeguarded its own policy space as to when, where and how to adopt Western ideas. In particular, while the Chinese state has adopted most of the basic principles of the Washington Consensus, especially its emphasis on the role of the market, entrepreneurship, globalization and international trade, it rejected or modified the liberal aspects that would greatly reduce the role of the state. For example, while the state gradually opened the domestic economy to international competition, it has maintained protection to key sectors and infant industries.[41]

At the same time, Zhao is quite insistent that there has also been political reform, but political reform that also fits within the developmental state approach. There has not been the introduction of a liberal democracy but in a managed top-down way there has been the institutionalisation of the leadership system; the effort to make the government more responsive to an increasingly plural society; an improvement in citizens' constitutional rights; and the transformation of the CCP from a revolutionary to a ruling party. These markers of change are clearly significant for a political system that was previously, during the Mao-dominated years of China's politics, highly personalist and arbitrary, not just for leading cadres, but also for individual citizens. Deng Xiaoping is often lauded as the harbinger of spectacular economic growth but his main contribution to the reform era was the restoration of the CCP's internal democracy and the push to restore the PRC's wider legitimacy.[42]

In Zhao's interpretation of the China Model, this approach to development makes the PRC fairly attractive to other countries, especially those in the developing world. It appears non-ideological, favours both economic growth and social stability, and preserves an authoritarian regime's ruling position. The PRC is also attractive because it emphasises a non-interventionist and value-free stance in its dealings with other countries; and this too in an era when 'The West' is considerably less attractive because of the latter's intervention in Iraq.[43]

Barry Naughton

The final expression of the China Model to be discussed here actually denies that there is any such thing. Barry Naughton,[44] in his attempt to characterise the PRC's developmental experience over the last 30 years, argues that so much of what has happened there cannot be replicated anywhere else there is no point in talking about a model at all.[45] He identifies three features of that experience which are unique. These are the scale of China and the possibilities offered by a large internal market; the emergence of new industry based on labour intensive development after a period of state socialism based on capital intensive development; and the maintenance and restructuring of China's hierarchical authoritarian system.

Naughton begins by criticising those views of China's developmental experience that have emphasised its pragmatism and flexibility (and particularly the work of

41. Suisheng Zhao, 'The China Model', p. 424.
42. David S. G. Goodman, 'The Chinese political order after Mao: "socialist democracy" and the exercise of state power', *Political Studies* 33(2), (June 1985), pp. 218–235.
43. Suisheng Zhao, 'The China Model', p. 431.
44. Naughton, 'China's distinctive system', pp. 437–460.
45. *Ibid.*, p. 439.

Joseph Cooper Ramo), arguing that these characteristics are not sufficient to explain the PRC's success. As he points out, many other countries have been pragmatic and flexible in approaching development but have still failed to achieve spectacularly high growth rates. Rather, Naughton emphasises the extent to which the PRC has a mixed economy with a three-tier enterprise system consisting of large, central-government firms; hybrid local and foreign firms; and small-scale capitalism.[46] It is the dynamic between the public and private sectors, under the management of the Party-state, that in his view has brought success.

Nonetheless, Naughton highlights six aspects of the PRC's economic development that he sees as crucial to the successes achieved to date and which can each be taken as a possible lesson to others. The first is that public ownership has not been abandoned and has proved itself 'reasonably efficient'. Indeed, the PRC now has a mixed industrial system. It remains a market-based developmental system where private firms dominate in the sectors where competition is encouraged, but government ownership dominates industries regarded as strategically important for economic development or social stability: transport, energy, pharmaceuticals, finance, communications, mining. It is a balanced as well as a mixed system, where Party-state direction monitors and may change the balance.[47]

The second is that competition is encouraged in all sectors except those designated as strategic and remains more important than ownership. Naughton gives the example of the restructured telecommunications industry in China where three companies, albeit still state-owned companies, replaced the former state monopoly. He contrasts the quality of service produced with Mexico, where weak regulation and a lack of competition has produced high prices, poor service, and the world's richest man.[48]

The commitment to competition in a large national market makes a difference, argues Naughton:

> In contrast to smaller economies, China's political system is forced to acknowledge multiple interest groups and contenders for power. Chinese leaders act as if their hold on power is always somewhat tenuous, and depends on good economic performance. There are always multiple candidates waiting in the wings, ready to step up to the demands of power. The contrast is great with a political system which is capable of being united in the interest of a single, narrowly defined clique, as in the case of Marcos in the Philippines. Highly ineffective policies and extreme corruption typically lead to serious challenges to individual leaders. China is not less prone to bad policy or corruption than other countries, but the degree of both is arguably held in check by the challenge of political competition.[49]

The third highlighted feature is that public ownership is used to exploit market power and to generate revenues for investment and public goods' creation. Naughton emphasises the developmental state aspects of the PRC's economy in ways that

46. Arthur Kroeber, 'Rising China and the liberal West', *China Economic Quarterly*, (March 2008); Dieter Ernst and Barry Naughton, 'China's emerging industrial economy: insights from the IT industry', in Christopher A. McNally, ed., *China's Emergent Political Economy: Capitalism in the Dragon's Lair* (New York: Routledge, 2008), pp. 39–50.

47. Naughton, 'China's distinctive system', p. 442.

48. *Ibid.*, p. 445.

49. *Ibid.*, p. 445.

reinforce Zhao's approach. He notes the rising profits of state-owned enterprises, especially during the last five years, and far from being alarmed by this, argues that it reinforces the Party-state's ability to manage the structuring of the economy, especially its management of competition and its ability to ensure that competition is maintained.

Naughton fourthly emphasises the importance of a strategy of investment-led growth. Unlike in a highly privatised or idealised neoliberal economy, it is seen as desirable to invest ahead of demand and create capacity that can be used later. This too is part of the government management of structuring the economy. At the same time it is important for growing the middle class base of support for the future of the regime. Investment ahead of demand for example has created the infrastructure in roads, rail and air for increased people and goods movement. The only limit to such pre-investment must be that it goes to increase productivity.[50]

The fifth highlighted feature of economic development is that the state sector has been, and remains, able to create growth and revenue opportunities outside the state sector. Once again there is not simply a mix of the public and the private but also a directed attempt at balance in development. The private contributes to the public in terms of taxation but it may also benefit through investment.

The final aspect of the PRC's economic development highlighted by Naughton as a possible lesson is that managers of state-owned enterprises are subject to market forces despite their position in non-competitive (for the most part) enterprises. Their incentives to better economic performance come from tying their remuneration to their company's performance in maximising asset value, efficiency and performance, in a system established by the state body responsible for overseeing state-owned enterprises. These comments lead Naughton inevitably to the observation that:

> It cannot be said that China has had no political reform; rather, the political reforms that have taken place have created a newly effective authoritarian hierarchy. The result is a system in which market incentives and administrative supervision and surveillance are both unusually strong. The system is pulled taut. Officials and managers have lots of authority and strong temptations, but they are also subject to strong surveillance and draconian punishments.[51]

This observation also supports Zhao's comments on the developmental state and political reform.

Explaining success

There are necessary differences in these various approaches to explaining the success of China's development during the last three decades, not least because of different initial standpoints and concerns. All the same, examining these different accounts highlights the structures and dynamic elements that account for China's developmental experience during the last three decades. The comparison also highlights remarkably clearly that despite the rhetoric with which people speak of 'the China Model' there is, as Barry Naughton points outs, little chance of replicability: there is not, in that sense, a 'model'.

50. *Ibid.*, p. 451.
51. *Ibid.*, p. 457.

There are two unique circumstances that form the foundations on which the PRC's developmental success has been based: its size and scale; and the history of its developmental trajectory.

One of the most important unique features of China's success is the size and scale of the country, and for that matter the economy. Much has been made of China's growth and its status as the second largest aggregate economy (by PPP). The growth and achievements are spectacular. At the same time, having the largest population in the world does mean that China has always been a large economy, and that the impact of fairly small changes in individual income may be magnified in terms of the aggregate economy. It was the world's largest aggregate economy until 1830 and only ceased to be so when industrialisation meant that GDP per capita in Europe and North America grew disproportionately. Even so, from 1830 to 1978 when China's economic growth was low, China never slipped below being the fourth largest economy in the world.[52] One consequence then, is that government expenditure can then grow quite considerably assuming the state's extractive power.

The scale of China also helps explain the apparent challenge to theory that follows from 30 years with an annual growth rate of 9–10%, with relatively little inflation. Of course there have, at times, been inflationary pressures, and as in other economies these have been mediated through interest rate management. In China's case though, the notion of a national growth rate masks the lack of an integrated economy, or perhaps more accurately the slow pace of economic integration for China's economic regions. There are 13 poorly integrated economic regions, with communications still difficult north to south, and even to some extent east to west, despite the two large river systems (the Yellow River in the north, the Yangtze River in the south).[53] This lack of integration explains, for example, China's need to import coal despite having the Ordos, the world's largest and best quality coalfield in the north, statistically able to meet all national needs. A national average annual growth rate of 10% per annum masks a process in which first one economic region (centred on Guangdong) grew at rates well in excess of the national average for a few years, to be followed by others in turn expanding at similarly rapid rates.

China's size and continental scale means too that it has a vast domestic market that to date has been little developed. Development has been concentrated for the most part on the eastern seaboard, where the initial export-oriented industries of the reform era were located. The opening up of the interior is an obvious and long-standing challenge[54] with the prospect that China may ape the developed countries of the world and generate a larger proportion of world GDP than its share of world population.[55]

52. Angus Maddison, *Chinese Economic Performance in the Long Run 960–2030 AD* (Paris: OECD Publishing, Development Centre Studies, 2007).

53. C. W. Kenneth Keng, 'China's future economic regionalization', *Journal of Contemporary China* 10(29), (November 2001), pp. 587–611.

54. David S. G. Goodman, ed., *China's Campaign to 'Open Up the West': National, Provincial and Local Perspectives* (Cambridge: Cambridge University Press, 2004).

55. In 2003 the PRC produced about 15.1% of world GDP with 20.5% of world population. This contrasts with the USA that produced 20.6% of world GDP from 4.6% of world population; and Europe that produced 21.1% of world GDP from 8.2% of world population. Source: Maddison, *Chinese Economic Performance in the Long Run 960–2030 AD*.

The structures for this were put in place at a fairly early stage of the PRC's reform development with the introduction of fiscal federalism.[56]

The second unique set of circumstances in the PRC's economic success results from the trajectory of its development both before and after 1978. There is a developmental aspect to the PRC's economic experience of reform that is often overlooked. Reform proceeded tentatively immediately after 1978 and economic growth required a number of kick-starts before moving in its current direction. Equally as important, the reform era was not written on a blank sheet of paper. As Naughton details, 30 years of state socialism before 1978 bequeathed both the structures of a modernising state, and considerable slack in economic capacity. Development had been capital intensive and inefficient in terms of productivity. The PRC's experience before 1978 also resulted in a unified and centralised political system. A crucial legacy for the reform era has been a hierarchical and authoritarian system.

The history of reform's evolution after 1978 also needs to be kept firmly in mind. While commentators outside China are fond of referring to the flexibility and pragmatism that seems to characterise the PRC's development experience, they sometimes miss the dynamics of policy experimentation that occur. There is considerable local autonomy but it too is subject to the Party-state's monitoring and approval. Contrast the experiments conducted in Shenzhen to establish a special economic zone in the early 1980s,[57] with those to establish 'big society, small government' in Hainan in 1988, when the latter achieved provincial status.[58] Shenzhen has been a run-away success from the Party-state's point of view, with the policy of special economic zones spreading and developing to much of China. The experiments in Hainan on the other hand led nowhere and were brought to an end by Beijing. The CCP, and the Party-state more generally, have shown themselves to be tremendous learning organisations. This need not be a unique feature of development in the PRC, though one suspects that when coupled with the continuation and enhancement of its hierarchical authoritarianism—which is necessary in order to maintain organisational discipline—there would be few countries able to emulate this aspect of reform.

Clearly the role of the CCP has been central to the PRC's development during the last three decades, and not simply because it has restored its own political order and created a new stability. As Bruce Dickson makes clear, in the process the CCP has also created a strategic alliance with the new entrepreneurs whose emergence it has encouraged: cadres have become businessmen and entrepreneurs have been co-opted in various ways into the Party-state.[59]

The pace of reform, though sustained, has not been even. This is not too surprising. The politics of Cultural Revolution left many scars so that individuals—in both leadership positions and at the base of the social hierarchy—were sometimes loathe to use their initiative or to act differently, as they were now being asked to do. The

56. G. Montinola, Y. Qian and B. R. Weingast, 'Federalism, Chinese style—the political basis for economic success in China', *World Politics* 48, (October 1995), p. 50.

57. Ezra F. Vogel, *One Step Ahead in China: Guangdong under Reform* (Cambridge, MA: Harvard University Press, 1989).

58. Feng Chongyi and David S. G. Goodman, *China's Hainan Province: Economic Development and Investment Environment* (University of Western Australia Press, 1995).

59. Bruce J. Dickson, *Wealth into Power: The Communist Party's Embrace of China's Private Sector* (Cambridge: Cambridge University Press, 2008), p. 238.

CCP itself has, at times, been anxious about how to proceed, as in 1978–1979 once a decision to reform had been taken; in 1989 as popular protest seemed to get out of hand; and in 1992 when faced by sudden apparent self-doubt. Economic reform started in the countryside and only came to urban China in and after 1984. Global interactions have certainly played their role in this unevenness as China has become more economically integrated with the rest of the world.

One of these was the important role played by the Chinese diaspora in the early years of reform. Much was made in the 1980s of China's increased integration with the region and the global economy. The vehicle of this integration was often overseas Chinese, who though now resident in other countries, were prepared to work with their former 'home place' for mutual benefit. Speaking the same language, understanding local customs and practices, and above all able to deliver introductions and connections to local notables and economic leaders, they played a vital role particularly at that time in China's economic development.

In similar vein there is an evolutionary aspect to the pattern of economic growth. Initially this started out, as already noted, in the south, in Guangdong and Fujian Provinces and particularly their special economic zones, with the focus on the development of export-oriented production. In those areas, clothing, textiles and light industry production lines have gradually been replaced by higher technology activities, with the original industries moving north and inland. At the same time, by 2000 though export-oriented production continued to be a substantial proportion of the economy (about 32% in that year) and continued to grow, it had ceased to be the provider of the largest annual increase in GDP. That place has been taken by real estate development, and more recently by growth in consumption.[60]

Possible lessons

Alongside these unique features of China's developmental experience, there are other aspects that may be of wider interest. An obvious starting point is the introduction of marketisation and competition, though not privatisation even if it is often used as a short-hand for the former. The distinction between marketisation and privatisation is important for two reasons in explaining the success of China's economic development.

The first is that privatisation implies ownership relationships that could not be applied to the PRC until the legal recognition of property rights in 2006 and the introduction of insolvency legislation in 2008, and even then remains more complex than might immediately seem to be the case. While state and collective sector assets may have been assigned away from the original company responsible for their development, it has been rare for their ownership, as opposed to control over their use and disposal, to pass to individuals. Moreover, while there have been private enterprises since 1984, for the most part these enterprises have been structurally confined to the small-scale, deprived of access to land, labour and resources in order to grow. A significant feature of the growth of the PRC economy has been the development of the collective local government sector, which has become the home

60. Cary Huang, 'Domestic consumption now top mainland growth driver', *South China Morning Post*, (16 January 2010); Capital Economics, *China Economics Update*, (27 May 2010); Jonathan Anderson, 'Is China export-led ?', *UBS Investment Research Asian Focus*, (27 September 2007).

for restructured state-owned enterprise subordinate companies, restructured collective enterprises, and once private enterprises that wish to continue developing. In these circumstances, control and management of resources is more important than ownership.[61]

The second reason for not describing change in terms of privatisation is that this suggests the withdrawal of state management of the economy. While it is clearly the case that economic enterprise management is no longer a function of government departments, the state retains a central role in economic management that extends way beyond the macro-economic controls exercised by nation-states acting as regulators. In the case of the PRC, there is still a large state-owned enterprise industrial sector. Numbers are uncertain but there are about 155 central government state-owned enterprises, and about 143,000 in total subject to all levels of jurisdiction. State-owned enterprises may be, but are not necessarily, share-based. Those that are in designated strategic industries—transport, energy, mining, pharmaceuticals, finance—cannot go bankrupt. Moreover, the state retains its role in strategic economic planning, not least by monitoring and adjusting the public–private balance in the mixed economy. The state ensures and manages competition to a high degree.

It is clear that the principle of the sanctity of market forces has been introduced into the public sector, as well as necessarily private enterprise. State-owned enterprises are required to operate within the market, and as already noted, their managers are judged by their performance in that regard. Competition and its maintenance is an essential part of the PRC development strategy. Alongside marketisation this has meant that there has been a high degree of both governmental decentralisation and local autonomy in enterprise management, which are also significant markers of China's recent developmental experience. The PRC now has a world-high 70% of total governmental expenditure managed by sub-central jurisdictions[62] and enterprise management is judged on results, whether in state-owned or private enterprises, or any of the extensive varieties of hybrid public–private companies.[63]

One corollary of this introduction of market forces has been the growth of a consumer society and a significant increase in the middle classes. While attention almost necessarily focuses on the emergence of the super rich in the PRC's reform era, the continuing and substantial growth in the numbers of the middle classes may be of considerably more long-term significance for the PRC. The PRC certainly had middle classes before; professionals and managers were essential to the modernising project of state socialism. Now, however, with the growth of economic, professional and technological activities of all kinds, the middle classes have continued to expand still further. These middle classes increasingly have more real disposable income which now goes towards house purchase and development, education, as well as more lifestyle choices including leisure time activities: activities and expenditure which are seen by both the middle classes and the Party-state as creating a community of interest. Official sources estimate that the middle classes (defined in income terms)

61. David S. G. Goodman, 'Why China has no new middle class: cadres, managers and entrepreneurs', in David S. G. Goodman, ed., *The New Rich in China: Future Rulers, Present Lives* (London: Routledge, 2008), p. 29.

62. Pierre F. Landry, *Decentralized Authoritarianism in China: The Communist Party's Control of Local Elites in the Post-Mao Era* (Cambridge: Cambridge University Press, 2008), p. 3.

63. Dickson, *Wealth into Power*, pp. 40–41.

currently constitute about 8% of the population (those earning more than 60,000 *yuan* a year) but estimate that the middle classes will grow to 20% of the population by 2020.[64]

The developmental challenge

The applicability of the lessons learnt from the PRC's developmental experience during the last three decades to other countries has to be limited. Few have experienced state socialism and a ruling Communist Party for 30 years. On the other hand, there are three specific improvements that might be drawn from China's recent experience, which, especially if taken together, are more than a little reminiscent of an earlier period of social democracy in Europe. One is the development of a substantial middle class, not simply as a matter of economic expansion but also as part of a state project to establish a social base. The second is state investment in infrastructure, borne out of concerns about the negative impact of the global financial crisis but embraced *inter alia* as an instrument to counter the previously disappearing welfare provision. The third, and possibly the single most important aspect of the PRC's development that reminds the observer of European social democracy, is the state's operation of a mixed economy. This is an economy that runs on a public–private mix, with the Party-state keeping a firm hand on the tiller to ensure what it considers to be the appropriate balance to that relationship. State-owned and private enterprises have different roles to play in the developing economy, as do the range of hybrid enterprises that come from their interaction.

These domestic conditions apart, it is of course not hard to see the appeal of the idea of the China Model to many of the lesser developed countries of the world. China has maintained stable government and become an international economic force within four decades of having been close to being a pariah state. It has also become more of an independent voice in international affairs, especially independent of the USA. In the process too it has tapped into a dominant discourse of modern nationalism: there has been a cultural shift designed to restore place in the world.[65] The test of this appeal can be seen in the case of Mexico: all but in a trade war with the PRC for much of the last decade, their political relationship remains very close in international relations.[66]

64. Goodman, ed., *The New Rich in China*.

65. See, for example, the views of the Brazilian Ambassador to the PRC, Luiz Augusto de Castro Neves, 'Zhongguo de chuqi: Baxi (huo Lading Meizhou) guanjiao' ['China's rise seen from a Brazilian (and perhaps a Latin American) perspective'], *Lading Meizhou Yanjiu* [*Journal of Latin American Studies*] 29(2), (April 2007), p. 9.

66. Beatriz Carrillo, Minglu Chen and David S. G. Goodman, 'Beyond asymmetry: cooperation, conflict and globalisation in Mexico–China relations', *The Pacific Review* 24(4), (September 2011), pp. 421–438.

[5]

Reflections on the Chinese State

Jude Howell

ABSTRACT

This article examines critically the application of the developmental state concept to China. A conjuncture of specific political, socio-economic and institutional processes, both internal and external, undermines the case for China as a developmental state. Against a back-drop of intensifying global economic competition, intense rivalry between local economic actors for markets, resources and foreign investment not only produces contradictory developmental outcomes but also undermines the political and administrative capacity for fundamental social and economic transformation. The Chinese state is best understood as polymorphous, assuming multiple, complex forms and behaviours across time and space, and defying reduction to a unitary actor.

INTRODUCTION

The concept of the developmental state surfaced in the early 1980s in development studies as a rival explanation for the rapid economic growth of the Four Little Tigers (Singapore, Hong Kong, Taiwan and South Korea). It thereby challenged the dominant neo-liberal account that the market was the prime variable behind the miraculous success of these economies and fuelled further normative debates around the relative roles of the market and state in economic development. The concept was further refined to capture the alternative developmental trajectories of 'Third World' socialist states such as China, North Korea and Vietnam, and a distinction was made between capitalist development states and socialist development states.

With the collapse of socialist regimes in Eastern Europe and the former Soviet Union in the late 1980s the politico-economic context within which the developmental state was framed and debated changed radically. The end of the Cold War and mounting concern about the developmental consequences of neo-liberal economic policies allowed for a reassessment of the role of the state in economic development. By the mid-1990s international institutions such as the World Bank were already acknowledging the

I am very grateful for the useful and detailed comments of two anonymous reviewers on an earlier draft of this article.

Development and Change 37(2): 273–297 (2006). © Institute of Social Studies 2006. Published by Blackwell Publishing, 9600 Garsington Road, Oxford OX4 2DQ, UK and 350 Main St., Malden, MA 02148, USA

significant role the state had played in the economic success of the Four Little Tigers. This in turn led to a growing interest in 'effective states' and 'good governance', a concern that was soon mirrored in aid programmes and analyses of development processes. However, the expectations that 'good governance' should be democratic and observant of human rights simultaneously challenged the notion of the developmental state, which in practice had proved to be authoritarian, often repressive of civil society, and less than respectful of civil and political human rights. The intensification of global trade and capital flows from the 1980s onwards led some scholars, such as Cerny (1997, 2000), to question the potential of nation-states to steer national economic development and the possibility therefore of developmental states. Despite the challenges posed by the good governance agenda and globalization, the concept of the developmental state continues to be advanced and adapted,[1] both as an empirically observed phenomenon and as a normative ideal of state–market relations. Adrian Leftwich (1996, 1998), for example, has opened up a debate around democratic and non-democratic developmental states, while the late Gordon White revised his concept of a socialist developmental state to take account of market reforms in China.

This article explores the relevance of the developmental state concept to China against the backdrop of a high degree of economic decentralization and intensifying global competition. The intense rivalry between local economic actors for markets, resources, and foreign investment not only produces contradictory developmental outcomes — on the one hand, economic growth and rising average annual per capita incomes, and on the other hand exploitative working conditions, environmental degradation and increasing inequality — but also undermines the political and administrative capacity for fundamental social and economic transformation. The article starts by reviewing the concept of the developmental state, examining its application to China and the emergence of alternative notions such as the entrepreneurial and corporatist state. It suggests that this proliferation of terms to capture the changing character of the state in post-Mao China masks a deeper process of state fragmentation that fosters contradictory and complex patterns of state behaviour.[2] The conjuncture of specific political, socio-economic and institutional processes, both internal and external, undermine the case for China as a developmental state. Like Brazil and India, China lies between the two categories of predatory and developmental, displaying elements of efficiency and inefficiency, of control and chaos, of relative autonomy and clientelism, of neo-liberalism and neo-corporatism.

1. See, for example, the edited volume by Woo-Cummings (1999).
2. Kenneth Lieberthal (1992, 1995) highlighted the issue of state fragmentation by coining the term 'fragmented authoritarianism', capturing thereby the classic bureaucratic matrix problem of competing horizontal (*kuai*) and vertical (*tiao*) lines of authority.

The Chinese state is best understood as polymorphous, assuming multiple, complex forms and behaviours across time and space, and defying any definition which reduces it to a single actor.

CHALLENGES TO THE DEVELOPMENTAL STATE

It was within the context of the Cold War and a sharply polarized debate about the respective roles of the state and market in the economy that the concept of the developmental state gained intellectual currency in the late 1970s and 1980s. While neo-liberal economists such as Balassa et al. (1982), Lal (1983), Little (1982) and Westphal (1978) attributed the economic successes of the Four Little Tigers to unconstrained market forces, others such as Amsden (1989) and Wade (1988) underlined the strategic role of the state in guiding the processes of industrialization and modernization. In doing so they reinforced the earlier findings of Chalmers Johnson's research on Japan, which pointed to the pivotal role of the state in economic development (Johnson, 1982). By the early 1990s even the World Bank (1997: 21), once a staunch advocate of free markets and minimal states, had to admit to the significant contribution of the state to the high growth rates and rising living standards of these East Asian states.

Like many concepts which have gained popularity, the notion of the developmental state, too, has become vulnerable to semantic overload, ideological appropriation and empirical amorphousness. Moreover, the concept is inevitably contested, given the subjective, historical and contextual understanding of what constitutes development. Given this conceptual ambiguity, it is important to clarify our definition of the developmental state by indicating both what it is and what it is not. The developmental state must first be distinguished from any particular economic measures and policies, such as protectionist measures, or state macro-management of the economy through control of interest rates, or state-owned production enterprises. Such state actions do not add up to a developmental state, which in contrast constitutes a particular historical, political and institutional formation, with defined normative goals, and a capacity to bring about fundamental change.

The ideal-typical developmental state has the following key features: first, it has a political and policy elite committed to economic growth and transformation, with the power, authority and legitimacy to promote a developmental agenda. Often motivated by strong nationalist sentiments, such elites strive to modernize their countries, raise economic living standards and bridge the technological gap. Second, complementing such a development-focused elite is a competent, authoritative state administration, particularly in the economic sphere, with the technical and managerial capacity to guide and steer economic and social development, such as MITI (the Ministry of International Trade and Industry) in Japan or the

Economic Planning Board in South Korea. Both the political and policy elite and state institutions in general are relatively autonomous from particular vested interests, allowing them to stand above the demands of specific social groups, whether defined by class, ethnicity or region, to shape policy for a broader, national interest.

Third, developmental states tend to have weak civil societies, poor civil and political rights records and repressive political regimes — although Adrian Leftwich has opened this up for debate by drawing a distinction between democratic developmental states such as Botswana, Malaysia and Singapore, and non-democratic developmental states, such as China, South Korea (1960–87) and Taiwan (up till the mid-1980s).[3] Finally, developmental states are defined not only by their normative agendas, their political and institutional structures, and state–society relations, but also by their achieved outcomes. Developmental states deliver rapid economic growth as well as general well-being, measured in terms of social indicators such as literacy, health status, life expectancy and per capita income. Taking the Human Development Index as a broader measure of achievement than merely economic growth, the performance of developmental states is striking. Contrary to neo-liberal assertions that the benefits of growth will eventually trickle down to the poor, developmental states demonstrate a capacity to combine economic growth with a good dose of redistribution.[4]

Whilst the concept of the developmental state was advanced initially to distinguish different routes to and models of capitalist development, White (1984; see also White and Wade, 1988) extended it to describe a particular type of state socialist development. The key features of the socialist developmental state are the virtual elimination of private industrial capital, all-pervasive controls over the economy, and a state that, at least initially, represents the interests of a revolutionary coalition (White, 1984: 103). Given the centrality of the capitalist economy to the definition of the developmental state, it can be convincingly argued that pre-reform China and other state socialist regimes do not by definition belong. By capturing

---

3. By juxtaposing the two concepts of democratization and development, Leftwich (1996: 281) challenges the normative paradigm prevailing since the late 1980s in development and political studies that democratization is a vital ingredient for development, rather than merely an end-result, and avoids the conceptual paralysis introduced by conflating the two processes.
4. There are numerous variants on this description of the developmental state. Weiss (2000), for example, similarly lists the importance of developmental elites and insulated bureaucracies, but does not mention the repressive nature of state–society relations, or the authoritarian character of the political system. Wade (1988: 38) notes that neither business associations nor trade unions played any significant role in policy formulation in South Korea and Japan. Furthermore, authors differ as to which countries can be classified as developmental states (see Leftwich, 1996; Weiss, 2000: 22–4). Moreover, apart from White and Wade (1988), most discussions of the developmental state have focused on its capitalist variants.

the term, however, scholars such as White were endeavouring to demonstrate, in an ideologically-charged political and intellectual environment, that there were alternatives both to the neo-liberal capitalist path and non-developmental, predatory state formations such as Zaire under Mobutu or Haiti under the Duvaliers.

The concept of the developmental state has been challenged in two respects in the 1990s. First is the argument that global economic integration undermines the power of nation-states to govern their economies, and hence the room for manoeuvre of a developmental state.[5] Cerny (1997, 2000), for example, argues that it has become more difficult for a state to be developmental or strategic in the context of increasing global competition, pressures from a diversity of state and transnational actors, and heightened contestation of what constitutes a 'public good'. Increasing involvement in global economic and political processes erodes the political autonomy and policy capacity of the developmental state.[6] Cerny contends that with the spread of neo-liberalism in the 1980s, the classic competition state[7] — namely, the developmental state[8] — is giving way to a new orthodox state model — namely, the neo-liberal state.

However, this view of globalization and neo-liberalism as undermining the autonomy and sovereignty of the nation-state is contested. For example, Weiss (2000) counters the neo-liberal story of international convergence[9] by arguing that external factors have been far less significant than domestic political and institutional factors in processes of state adaptation. Developmental states, rather than being dismantled, have instead shifted gear from 'catching up' to 'continuous upgrading', as illustrated by Taiwan and South Korea.

The second challenge to the developmental state concept from the 1990s onwards is the normative agenda of 'good governance' flowing from international financial institutions, development agencies and Western governments. The effects of the good governance agenda are probably more directly experienced in aid-dependent countries such as Mozambique, Bangladesh or Uganda, than, say, China or Brazil. However, this is not to say that other international factors, such as transnational companies, global

5. See Weiss (2000) for a detailed discussion of the neo-liberal argument.
6. A similar argument is made more generally for all states, including advanced liberal democracies (Held, 1993: 23–8; Luckham, 1998: 307, 316).
7. Cerny defines the competition state as a state which pursues marketization with the goal of making the domestic economy internationally competitive.
8. For Cerny the developmental or strategic state is a sub-type of competition state, which stands in contrast to the welfare state.
9. Cerny's (1997: 268) picture of the declining room for manoeuvre for the developmental state is more nuanced than a neo-liberal image of international convergence. Cerny argues that there are processes of convergence and divergence as states differ in their vulnerability to international pressures, in their capacity for strategic action and their relative strengths and weaknesses in achieving international competitiveness.

trade agreements, environmental treaties, human rights conventions and membership of international agencies, do not also place increasing political pressure on less aid-dependent states to liberalize their political regimes. Current demands for good governance in the South implicitly challenge the argument that authoritarian governance may be an essential requirement for rapid economic growth, making the normative ideal of the developmental state much harder to defend.

While this article endorses the position that increased global economic integration in the post-Cold War context undermines the developmental capacity of nation-states, it goes on to propose, in contrast to Cerny, another alternative to the neo-liberal or neo-corporatist models, namely, the polymorphous state. While developmental elites may strive to pursue strategic agendas, the necessity to compete globally coupled with the fierce nature of that competition pushes states into dysfunctional patterns of behaviour that undermine their political, institutional and administrative capacity to effect fundamental social transformation. In other words different regional parts of the state and different sectors of the state compete with each other and other economic actors for markets and resources, placing the pursuit of profit over and above broader economic and social considerations. This in turn leads to sub-optimal developmental outcomes such as disregard for the environment, exploitation of labour, uneven development and the weakening capacity of central actors to shape national economic development. At the same time specific domestic processes of political, institutional and socio-economic change exacerbate these tendencies. This affects whether a developmental state can continuously upgrade, as Weiss argues, or whether the market tail wags the developmental dog, undermining the ability of political and policy elites to steer a developmental course. The outcome is a polymorphous state that reveals contradictory features of developmentalism and predation, rivalry and unity, autonomy and clientelism, efficiency and inefficiency, across time and space. The next section will look more closely at the application of the concept of the developmental state to China and the emergence of alternative ways of conceptualizing the state.

CONCEPTUALIZING THE CHINESE STATE

Several scholars have deployed the concept of the 'developmental state' to describe the Chinese state in both the pre-reform and reform periods and to explain China's developmental successes. Despite the shift away from economic planning towards market reform, the concept of the developmental state has been retained, revised and refined to take account of the changing politico-economic circumstances. Furthermore, new conceptualizations of the state in the reform period have emerged, such as the 'entrepreneurial state', the 'corporatist state', 'the regulatory state', 'the dual developmental state', 'the market-facilitating state' and less complimentary terms such as the 'rent-seeking state'.[10] In this section we argue that this multiplicity of terms reflects less the perspectives of different schools of political economy, and more observed empirical changes in local states, their relations to the economy and society, and to the central state. The multiplicity of terms highlights the fragmentation of policy-making (Lieberthal, 1992, 1995), the diverse effects of economic rivalism (Montinola et al., 1995: 65–66), and the growing complexity of state structures and processes in the context of global integration, interest pluralization and decentralization.[11]

Gordon White was the first scholar to develop the concept of a socialist development state, which he contrasted to capitalist development states such as Taiwan and South Korea (White, 1984; White and Wade, 1988). He distinguished between 'mature' socialist developmental states such as China and North Korea, and more recently established, proto-industrializing socialist states on the periphery such as Nicaragua, Angola and Mozambique, with Cuba and Vietnam lying in between (White, 1984: 111–14). In his later work, White took account of the far-reaching changes in China's economy, and in particular the switch from pervasive to parametric regulation, decentralization and marketization (White and Wade, 1988). For White, China in the first decade of the reform period was an example par excellence of a 'socialist guided market' and a reformist (socialist) developmental state. Though China's reformist leadership had embraced markets, China remained a 'socialist' developmental state because, unlike Taiwan and South Korea, guidance of the market took place 'within a socialist integument' (White and Wade, 1988: 19). As will be seen later, this reformist version of the socialist developmental state has become increasingly problematic as ideology loses its potency and political reform drags its heels behind market reforms.

Regardless of whether China could be classified as a sub-type of socialist developmental state in the pre-reform period, scholars such as Marc Blecher, Vivienne Shue and Jean Oi have found sufficient mileage in the concept of the developmental state to deploy it in their analyses of particular local state formations.[12] Not only have they refined further the concept of the developmental state, drawing upon detailed studies of county governments in Hebei and Sichuan provinces, but they have also introduced new terms such as the 'entrepreneurial', 'regulatory' (Shue, 1995), and 'local corporatist' state to

10. For a useful analysis of rent-seeking in China see Wedeman (2003). On the market-facilitating state see Howell (1993) and on the dual developmental state see Ming (2000).
11. Baum and Shevchenko (1999: 344–6), in their excellent review of the changing nature of the state, develop a matrix of four modes of local state, namely, entrepreneurial, corporatist, developmental and predatory, and attribute these developments to marketization and decentralization of fiscal and administrative authority.
12. Whiting (2001), Bernstein and Lu (2003) and Unger and Chan (1999) also make use of the developmental state concept as an entry-point into discussing the state.

capture observed changes in local state formations. By focusing on the county level, Blecher (1991) and Blecher and Shue (1996) extend the application of the concept beyond the abstract macro level, thereby departing from previous work on the developmental state, both generally and in China. They use the term 'developmental state' to describe the commitment of county officials to use local resources and to apply their administrative discretion for the purpose of local economic growth and balanced local economic development (Blecher and Shue, 1996: 1, 209–14). Shulu county leaders drew upon the considerable latitude in the relationships amongst county institutions and between higher-level authorities and the villages and townships below them. With this flexibility they seized opportunities to pursue local economic developmental goals both in the last decade of the Mao era and the first decade of Dengist reforms. Blecher and Shue (ibid.: 42) attribute this developmentalism to a combination of ideological and historical factors, that in turn underpin a deep-seated resistance to entrepreneurial profit-making either for self-gain or on the part of state institutions.

As well as pioneering detailed empirical studies of the local developmental state, Blecher and Shue also introduce the idea of the 'entrepreneurial state' to describe the behaviour of Guanghan county government. Compared with the developmental state, such a state is oriented towards profit-seeking. Rather than focusing on an enabling environment for independent economic enterprises, the entrepreneurial state itself becomes an economic player, engaging in production, creating new enterprises, procuring finance and competing for business. Whilst in the developmental state of Shulu County, officials channelled resources to public goods such as a new park, workers' cultural palace and theatre, in Guanghan county individual bureaux in the entrepreneurial state used profits for their own purposes, updating their fleet of cars and constructing ostentatious, shiny government buildings (Blecher, 1991: 288).

Inspired by the idea of the developmental state, Jean Oi advances the notion of a local 'corporatist state' as a type of 'decentralized developmental state' (Oi, 1995: 1139).[13] In this variation, local government officials at village, township and county levels promote local economic development by supporting local collective rural industrial enterprises through the provision of information, access to materials and technology, and through the redistribution of resources from wealthier enterprises to start-up ventures or to less successful village enterprises that nevertheless absorb surplus local labour (ibid.: 1139–40).[14] In the local corporatist state model local government officials become 'fully-fledged economic actors' (ibid.: 1137), 'entrepreneurs' (Oi, 1992: 124), intervening in key investment decisions, especially at village level, to promote local political and economic interests.

---

13. For a recent critique of the local corporatist state concept see Sargeson and Zhang (1999).
14. Unlike the developmental local state in Xinji County, Hebei province, described by Blecher, government cadres are not engaged in developing infrastructural projects so much as providing information and access.

In doing so, state officials are driven not just by profit motives but also by considerations of employment provision, unlike in the entrepreneurial state of Guanghan County described by Blecher and Shue.

Oi (1995: 1139) also uses the term 'entrepreneurial developmental state' to distinguish the depth of government officials' involvement in market research, product development and technology acquisition from that of 'the usual provision of bureaucratic service'. In this sense Oi's concept of the entrepreneurial developmental state is in fact akin to Blecher's developmental state in Xinji County, Hebei province. Not much would be lost if we were to replace the notion of 'entrepreneurship' or 'entrepreneurial local officials' with 'dynamic planners' or 'dynamic developmental actors'. Oi's 'local state corporatism' thus describes more the activities of a dynamic local government, intervening in the market and selectively allocating resources to enterprises, for the purpose of local economic interests, than an 'entrepreneurial local government', seeking opportunities for individual self-gain or for departmental expansion, as described by Blecher in Guanghan county. Moreover, Oi's use of the metaphor of a 'large, multi-level corporation' to describe the county government makes the term 'corporate state' more appropriate than 'corporatist', the latter referring to a specific system of interest representation, usually contrasted with pluralism.

These county-level studies point not only to the emergence of entrepreneurial state behaviour, but also to the diversification of state forms through processes of decentralization and marketization and through local policy traditions (Berstein and Lu, 2003: 8; Segal and Thun, 2001). This trend towards state entrepreneurialism is highlighted further in the fine work of Jane Duckett (1998) on the real estate management and urban commerce sectors of Tianjin city government. In this local entrepreneurial state individual bureaux engage directly in profit-seeking and risk-taking business, by creating new business ventures, investing bureaucratic funds, and competing with other bureaux. The profits are used to maintain the bureaux by covering administrative and salary costs and the costs of bureaux activities such as repairing public buildings and housing.

Duckett's version of the entrepreneurial state differs to Blecher's in that individual bureaux use the profits for collective bureaux purposes (such as salary costs, carrying out bureaux tasks), whilst in Blecher's model profits are used for the political and economic interests of the individual bureaux (such as upgrading the fleet of cars). However, although Duckett emphasizes that the prime motive of the bureaux is the pursuit of profits, she also acknowledges that in the case of the commerce departments in Tianjin, which were under threat of closure, a strong motive for establishing new enterprises was the redeployment of staff. This seems to undermine the case for including the commerce departments in Tianjin as an example of the entrepreneurial state. At the very least it seems necessary to distinguish two types of entrepreneurial state: one which engages in business for the purpose of expanding bureaucratic economic and political interests, that is, 'pro-active bureaucratic entrepreneurialism'; and one which pursues business activities as a transitional measure in the face of imminent closure and state restructuring, that is, 'defensive bureaucratic entrepreneurialism'. Nevertheless, the entrepreneurial state, as outlined by Blecher and Duckett, is a different creature to the developmental state, which assumes a collective vision of, and commitment to, development amongst the political leadership, a degree of state co-ordination of economic development, whether through pervasive or parametric measures, and a unified state which acts in the overall interests of society.

To sum up, the local case studies of Blecher and Shue, Duckett, and Oi have pushed the boundaries of discussion around the developmental state beyond a narrow focus on the central state to the local level. By coining the term 'entrepreneurial state', Blecher also implicitly challenges uniform, aggregate descriptions of the Chinese state, which in the context of increased decentralization and the growing complexity of local administrative and political structures and processes, have become much harder to sustain. Furthermore, both Blecher and Duckett's studies demonstrate that distinct models can co-exist within the same locality.[15]

As a result of these and other studies (such as Edin, 2000; Saich, 2002; Whiting, 2001), a more complex picture has emerged of an increasingly fragmented state structure, with growing variation in leadership styles, opportunities and economic dynamism. The profusion of competing terms to describe the Chinese state in the reform period, such as 'developmental', 'entrepreneurial', 'corporatist', 'market-facilitating', 'regulatory', 'rent-seeking', reflect not merely alternative explanations of state behaviours arising out of different normative and intellectual starting-points, but, more significantly, highlight deeper problems of fragmentation in governance processes in a context of rapid economic and institutional change and heightened global integration. The next section will examine in greater depth why the multi-chequered landscape of state formations and behaviours renders the conceptualization of China as 'a developmental state' less tenable.

POLYMORPHOUS, BUT NOT DEVELOPMENTAL

At first glance it might seem odd to suggest that China cannot be a developmental state. For the past two decades China has enjoyed staggering growth rates, averaging around 8 per cent over this period, and living standards have generally risen. Absolute poverty levels have fallen dramatically, from 490 million people living on less than $1 per day in 1981 to 88 million in 2003. The rhetoric of Party leaders embraces ideas of development, growth and stability. Even though the route to development is distinct from the

15. Saich (2002) suggests that there are different local state formations and socio-political outcomes across counties in the same province and that local states can be predatory and developmental at the same time.

developmental ambitions espoused by Mao and his followers, there is nevertheless a strong drive for development, read as economic growth, amongst the top leadership, and reiterated by the new Party leadership under Hu Jintao. Indeed the concept of 'scientific development' and 'people-centred development' (*yi ren wei ben*) introduced at the 3rd Plenary session of the 16th Chinese Communist Party Central Committee marks not only a commitment to economic development but also a shift away from a unitary focus on growth to a 'balanced' approach which takes into account environmental and equity issues.[16] Moreover the continued authoritarianism of the Chinese Party-state echoes the political tendencies of other successful East Asian late-comers.

Nevertheless there are a number of reasons why the concept of the developmental state is less applicable to China, and why China, like Brazil and India, lies between the two poles of a developmental and a predatory state. First, the standard definition of a developmental state assumes the central state to be the prime actor. All accounts of developmental states focus their analyses on central policy elites, particularly in the economic domain. Such an approach removes from view the politics of local governments and their relations to the centre, presumably because it is assumed that they are inconsequential to the realization of central objectives and/or that they will automatically comply with directives from above.

However, with its continental proportions, the high degree of decentralization in China makes it increasingly difficult to conceptualize the state as a homogeneous actor, and therefore able to ensure the internal coherence that is a vital ingredient of the developmental state. Unable to steer growth from the centre, the Chinese government from the early 1980s onwards gradually decentralized information, policy powers and authority to local governments (Chung, 1995). Local governments can retain a greater portion of their revenues and mobilize resources outside of the budget through foreign investment, foreign loans and various administrative fees, and are thus less dependent on the central state (Whiting, 2001), especially in the relatively prosperous cities and provinces of China such as Guangdong, Shanghai and Tianjin. The drawback of this strategy, which Montinola et al. (1995) describe as 'market-preserving federalism'[17] is that it has become much

16. For reports on Premier Wen Jiabao's speech on this concept at the Party School in February 2004, see Xinhua News Agency, Beijing, 29 February 2004 and 4 March 2004, and *Renmin Ribao*, 18 March 2004, as well as the comments by Hu Angang (a highly influential economist) on a new development strategy (Zhongguo Xinwen She News Agency, Beijing, 2 March 2004).

17. The key features of market-preserving federalism are a hierarchy of governments with a specified range of authority: local governments enjoy authority over the economy; the national government guarantees a common market and mobility of factors and goods across regions; there is limited revenue-sharing and a hard-budget constraint; and durability of these institutional arrangements (Montinola et al., 1995: 55). For a critique of this idea see Bernstein and Lu (2003: 249).

harder for the central government to enforce national policy, to direct national economic development in a coherent way (Bernstein and Lu, 2003; Breslin, 1996; Yang and Wei, 1996; Zweig, 2002: 12), and to redistribute resources across regions and social groups (Baum and Shevchenko, 1999; Park et al., 1996). In her insightful study of informal financing in China, Tsai (2004), for example, describes vividly the divergent attitudes of local governments to the private sector, ranging from encouragement and collaboration to hostility and obstruction. By highlighting the ability of local governments to subvert central regulatory policies, she underlines the variability in local government responses to informal financing.

Second, in standard accounts of the developmental state, a key ingredient driving central policy and political elites is a sense of nationalism, which they in turn mobilize to galvanize broader societal support for developmental plans. While nationalist appeals have had some resonance in the reform period, particularly with the waning potency of socialist ideology and in key moments of national crisis such as the NATO bombing of the Chinese embassy in the former Yugoslavia, local government officials in the context of significant decentralization are driven more by local and sometimes personal interests than by abstract nationalist notions. Localism has indeed been a highly potent driver behind local economic development in some parts of China (Segal and Thun, 2001; Yang and Wei, 1996). Indeed Ming (2000) uses the concept of a 'dual developmental state' to capture the developmental ambitions of the central policy elite and provincial governments. But it can also be in tension with centrally-driven national economic ambitions such as shaping the national economy around regional comparative advantages or the strategic development of particular industries and sectors (Lu, 1997; Unger and Chan, 1996; Zweig, 2002). Without effective central levers of control and redistribution, heightened localism fuels intense rivalry (Blecher and Shue, 2001; Wedeman, 2003), resulting in unbalanced and uneven development (Park et al., 1996; Wong, 1991, 1992).[18] Such imbalances are already manifest in the widening disparities between both geographic regions — especially between East and West China, and between mountains and plains areas within regions — and socio-economic groups such as laid-off workers, Chinese managers in foreign companies, and successful private entrepreneurs (Wang and Hu, 1999; Yang, 1997).[19] As reflected in the Decision of the Chinese Communist Party (CCP) on Strengthening the Party's ability to Govern, passed by the Fourth Plenum

18. A common sub-optimal outcome in the reform period has been local protectionism and subsequent duplication of production. Breslin (1996: 696) refers to the local erection of tariffs and quotas to keep out products from other provinces so as to maximize sales within provinces.
19. According to the National Bureau of Statistics, China's gini coefficient rose from 0.3 in 1978 to 0.46 in 2003 (Xinhua News Agency, Beijing, 1 March 2004).

of the 16th Central Committee in autumn 2004, socio-economic disparities and central–local relations loom large amongst the concerns of central leaders.[20]

Third, the vacillating legitimacy[21] of the Party, as underscored by the rise of social protests (Cai, 2002; Chen, 2000; Hurst and O'Brien, 2002; O'Brien, 2004), the greater trust of farmers in central versus local leaders (Bernstein and Lu, 2003: 247) and the related problems of ideology (Cheng, 2001; Dickson, 2003; Lieberthal, 1995) and Party discipline (Lieberthal, 1995: 179–80; Lu, 1997) have compounded the difficulties for the central government in asserting its will on subordinate parts of the state and steering a coherent nationwide trajectory of economic development. Throughout the reform period the CCP has struggled to maintain its legitimacy in the wake of the catastrophic and deeply divisive effects of the Cultural Revolution, the calamitous outcome of the 1989 Democracy Movement and the pervasive problems of corruption at all levels. Party leaders have increasingly staked the legitimacy of their rule upon their ability to maintain a stable environment for promoting economic growth and prosperity (Shue, 2004: 28–9, 41),[22] as piecemeal attempts to rework ideology have proved unconvincing. The revolutionary fervour that mobilized a visionary project of social transformation and legitimized the Party-state in the pre-reform period has been replaced by an individualistic, consumerist vision contingent upon rapid economic growth, with potentially devastating environmental consequences.[23]

The global spread of the internet, greater access to information and ideas from the outside, and greater contestation of what constitutes the good life, have made it much harder for the political elite to mobilize people around a hegemonic developmental project. The diversification of interests and a more informed and demanding society as a result of both market reforms and global integration make it more difficult to impose a unitary and binding vision of development. Although divisions among the political elite are less fundamental than in the early years of reform, when elite

20. This decision outlined the key six relationships which needed to be handled appropriately (see Xinhua New Agency, Beijing, 17 October 2004).
21. On the changing sources of legitimacy of the CCP in the reform period, see Shambaugh (2001). On differences in legitimacy enjoyed by central and local governments, see the work of Bernstein and Lu (2003), Li and O'Brien (1996, 1997) and O'Brien (2002).
22. I am grateful to an anonymous reviewer for drawing my attention to Vivenne Shue's (2004) insightful chapter on legitimacy, where she makes a cogent critique of the reductionist view that Chinese leaders stake their legitimacy on their economic achievements.
23. The head of the UN environment programme, Klaus Toepfer, warned of the unsustainability of China's ambitious plans to expand its economy fourfold over the next twenty years. Taking the example of cars, Toepfer estimated that if China were to have the same density of private cars as Germany, the world would run out of metal and oil (Watts and Morris, 2003).

struggles around the path to development led to stops and starts in the reform process and a lack of coherence in national strategy (Howell, 1993; Shirk, 1993), political differences among top leaders regarding the desirable route to development are likely to sharpen over the next decade as the negative effects of rapid economic growth become more visible. In particular the key axes of tension will lie around the need to restructure the economy to remain globally competitive, whilst also maintaining social stability; between letting a few get rich quick first and the idea of egalitarianism;[24] and between the pace of economic and political reform. Higher standards of living and the distributional issues accompanying rapid economic growth will make it much harder, as Peter Evans (1992: 165) suggests in the case of South Korea, for the Party to mobilize people around a national project based solely on its contribution to economic growth. Moreover, as Huff et al. (2001: 717) argue, the legitimacy of developmental states hinges not only on economic performance but also on growth that is 'widely shared among the population', and as in the cases of Singapore and South Korea, substantial state investment in health and education systems. In China the decline of the health system, particularly in rural areas (and as most recently evidenced in relation to SARS), as well as low public investment in education point to the uneven distribution of the fruits of growth, providing an undercurrent of tension in efforts to legitimize the regime around economic performance.

Added to this is the persisting problem of corruption within Party and government ranks (Lu, 2000). This creates two sets of problems for a developmental Leninist elite: first, it undermines any attempts to create a more effective, meritocratic and capable administration — a key element of a developmental state. Although numerous policies have been introduced over the last decade to promote selective meritocratic recruitment to the bureaucracy, government and Party are still closely fused. Party membership continues to be an important criterion for advancement in the administration and government bureaucrats remain beholden to Party leadership. Second, along with the decline in the mobilizing force of socialist ideology, the problem of corruption reflects, and reinforces, the weakening of Party discipline, an essential part of a socialist developmental state machine, and particularly important in the context of deep decentralization. Without Party discipline, the central Party/state battles against the odds to steer a comprehensive development course. The fraying of the 'socialist integument' thus eats away at the central core of the socialist (reformist) developmental state described by White.

24. Indicative of the concern about rising inequality are the results of an internal survey of 107 leading local Party officials conducted by the Central Party School, which revealed that 44 per cent viewed the income gap as the most serious problem affecting social development (*South China Morning Post* website, 30 November 2004).

Fourth, though streamlining and rationalization of state structures is intended to foster a more efficient and effective state administration, it also inadvertently places the pursuit of personal and institutional survival over and above broader policy objectives.[25] When local government department leaders are preoccupied with securing salaries for their staff and protecting staff positions in the face of restructuring and downsizing, any grander goals of local or even national development are likely to take second place to the more immediate imperatives of survival. Observed entrepreneurship in such instances may be a misnomer, reflecting a desperate struggle to ride the tide rather than a coherent strategy of fostering local economic development. Intra-state profit-seeking undermines the competence and authority of state administration. Whilst at central and provincial levels of the state administration, the emphasis in the reform period on expertise and competence over political credentials has led to a more technocratic and able administration, there is nevertheless considerable variation at lower levels, especially in poor areas and at county level and below. China continues to lack the kind of expertise that fuelled Japan's MITI, Korea's Economic Planning Board or Taiwan's Council on Economic Planning and Development. The influence of economic think-tanks and committees has been subject to political winds, the demise of the Economic Reform Institute after Tiananmen being a case in point. The 'pockets of efficiency' identified by Evans (1992: 171) in Brazil thus fall prey to vacillations in elite politics in China, thereby undermining the corporate coherence of the administration.

Fifth, in a developmental state the administration is not only competent and authoritative, but is also relatively autonomous of particular interests. Evans (1992) put forward the idea of 'embedded autonomy' to capture the workings of the South Korean and Japanese developmental state.[26] He argues that informal networks both within the state and between the state and business elites, as well as the relative autonomy of organizations such as the MITI in the case of Japan, are crucial for the effectiveness of a developmental state. Social ties amongst government officials and between officials and business elites, based on shared educational backgrounds and social experiences, work effectively to foster a process of industrialization. In other contexts such informal ties have tended to foster clientelistic predation rather than developmental outcomes. In the case of reformist China, there are several reasons why personalized ties between government officials and business elites do not produce developmental outcomes and undermine the case for casting China as a developmental state. This relates

25. For example, in 2004 the Ministry of Civil Affairs merged 864 towns and villages leading to 56,400 cadre redundancies (*South China Morning Post* website, 17 November 2004).

26. 'It is an autonomy embedded in a concrete set of social ties which bind the state to society and provide institutionalised channels for the continual negotiation and renegotiation of goals and policies' (Evans, 1992: 163).

to the history of state–private capital relations in communist China, personalistic clientelism and the organization of capital.

In the first three decades of Communist China relations between the Party/state and domestic capital were severely strained and the social status of private entrepreneurs was low. With the opening up of China from 1978 onwards the Party/state has stimulated the expansion of both the domestic and foreign private sector. There is some evidence that the social standing of entrepreneurs and their awareness of a shared identity have increased since the mid-1990s (Dickson, 2003: 163; Heberer, 2003a). At the central level successful entrepreneurs are sometimes courted for their views on economic policy. Moreover an elite core has influenced legislation relevant to its interests through participation as deputies in the National People's Congress, through Party connections, and through strategic manipulation of key corporatist institutions such as the Association of Industry and Commerce (Heberer, 2003b).

Despite Jiang Zemin's speech on 21 July 2001, when he opened the Party door to private entrepreneurs,[27] there is still considerable diversity in the attitudes of local governments to the private sector and to particular types of private capital, as described finely by Tsai (2004). Though Heberer (2003b) makes a compelling case for a positive embedded autonomy that is founded on the relationship of a core entrepreneurial elite to the central state, he also concedes that relations at the local level are often seriously strained by combinations of predation, corruption and overzealous regulation, undermining the perceived legitimacy of local states (ibid.: 12). As a result of the deep, historically-rooted mutual suspicion between the Party and private entrepreneurship, it will take some time before the kind of positive 'embedded autonomy' observed by Evans in the cases of South Korea and Japan emerges in China. Even though the children and relatives of top Party leaders have extensive business interests at home and abroad, such links, with their overtones of corruption, undermine rather than preserve the relative autonomy of the Party-state.

There is a further reason why state–business relations in China do not approximate the embeddedness described by Evans as conducive to positive developmental outcomes. The new business elites do not in general share the same educational and cultural experiences of state officials.[28] Informal networks based on Party membership provide the primary cement for key leaders in the bureaucracy, yet business people have until very recently

27. The preservation of Party power is also an important motive here. By co-opting business leaders, the Party can pre-empt the formation of an alternative site of political power centred on an economic elite.
28. Dickson (2003) distinguishes those entrepreneurs who have left Party/government positions to enter the private sector from those of different social backgrounds. He also argues that those Party members who have entered the private sector gradually lose their connections with the Party (ibid.: 44–5).

been excluded from the Party. The lack of strong informal and formal ties between government bureaucrats and business elites as pertained in Japan (Evans, 1992: 154) militates against the forging of a common project around national industrial development. Despite numerous strategies and plans by central and provincial governments to develop the Special Economic Zones in Fujian and Guangdong provinces as sites for the transfer of advanced technology from the West, the bulk of foreign investment in these areas has stemmed from Overseas Chinese capital engaged in small-scale, short-term, labour-intensive export-oriented assembly and processing (Howell, 1993; Hsing, 1998). Although the state has, over time, created a broad legislative and regulatory framework to facilitate the development of market forces, unlike Taiwan and South Korea, the Chinese state has not been able to realize its intentions in highly selective intervention in the accumulation of industrial capital (Zweig, 2002). The persistent suspicion between private capital and government intentions (Dickson, 2003: 107–14, 161–2) undermines the ability of the state to build credibility in government policy and thus establish a reputation as developmental that Huff et al. (2001) and Grabowski (1994) identify as an important ingredient of a successful developmental state. This, however, may change as more entrepreneurs take up the offer of Party membership and as highly, overseas-educated business and management scholars return to the country.

Added to this, entrepreneurs seeking resources and information from government officials develop personalized, clientelistic relations with individual cadres (Wank, 1996). To the extent that corruption sets in — that is, bribes are given for securing contracts and so on — then developmental priorities come second place to individual economic gain (Saich, 2002; Sargeson and Zhang, 1999). Such clientelistic relations undermine the insulation needed for government officials to remain above the demands of particular social groups and therefore get in the way of officials steering a developmental course. In the absence of strong intra-Party discipline, the potential 'corporate coherence' (Evans, 1992: 163) that Party-based informal networks might produce render the bureaucracy vulnerable to personalistic interests (Fewsmith, 2001: 89–90). Moreover, to the extent that the state itself becomes a source of economic rents and bureaucrats compete to purchase promotions and positions, as described in fine detail by John Burns (2003), then reforms intended to clean and technocratize the bureaucracy become ever elusive. As the interests of local government officials and local capital converge around localistic and/or personalistic goals of money-making, all-inclusive ideological claims such as the Three Representations appear vacuous and highlight the problems of legitimacy.

A further factor contributing to the lack of embedded autonomy in China relates to the weak organization by capital. Although there are national and local level associations of business people such as chambers of commerce and the China Entrepreneurs' Association (Nevitt, 1997; Pearson, 1994; Unger, 1996; Unger and Chan, 1996), capital is still not well organized.

This becomes evident when local states try to establish collective bargaining processes. Local trades union officials and government cadres find that they often have no representative organization to bargain with.[29] The weak level of organization of capital relates more broadly both to the historically specific development of state–capital relations in post-Liberation China and to the lack of well institutionalized structures of interest intermediation that reflect the growing diversification of socio-economic interests in the reform era. The constant tension within the Party/state between retaining a controlling hand over more independent organizing and stimulating its growth for purposes such as welfare reform and market regulation, continues to inhibit the development of predictable, institutionalized arrangements for the aggregation and articulation of interests. The history of state–business relations in post-Liberation China, the weak organization of capital and the absence of Party organization in most private firms (Dickson, 2003: 15) make it difficult for the Party/state to harness the necessary information about the market and ensure that private capital can be guided towards sectors prioritized in industrial policies.

The final factor contributing to the emergence of hyper-rivalistic local state behaviour in China is intensified global economic integration in a post-Cold War scenario.[30] Competition between local governments for foreign trade and investment has on the one hand promoted local economic growth and prosperity, but on the other hand undermined the capacity of the central government to direct national economic development, and in particular to address growing popular dissatisfaction with rising inequality.[31] Problems of duplication of production have been reported from the late 1980s in the Special Economic Zones and have worsened as more cities and towns in China have opened up to foreign investment.[32] Local governments increasingly undercut each other in the preferential policies and incentives they offer foreign investors (Zweig, 2002: 269), as seen in the shift in foreign investment from Shenzhen to Dongguan in the early 1990s. In his study of cultural industries in China, Keane (2003) notes how transnational corporations exploit the competition between regions for business to their competitive advantage. Decentralization may increase the incentives to local

29. Comment made by a local trade unionist at a workshop on WTO, Labour Relations and Trade Unions held in October 2002 in Beijing.
30. See Zweig (2002) for an excellent account of China's internationalization, and also Moore (2000, 2002) and Economy and Oksenberg (1999).
31. In his excellent review of research on central–provincial relations, Chung (1995: 506–7) points to the undermining effects on central government of expanding local–international nexuses. On regional competition and protectionism see Breslin (1996: 696), Montinola et al. (1995: 65–66), and Unger and Chan (1996: 114).
32. In August 2004 Ma Kai, minister of State Development and Reform Commission, in his report to the 11th session of the 10th National People's Congress Standing Committee, drew attention to the mounting problem of 'blind investment' and 'low-level expansion' (Xinhua News Agency, 26 August 2004).

governments and market actors, but against a backdrop of intensifying global competition, finding a balance between national and local power and between conflicting objectives such as growth and equality becomes increasingly strained.[33]

If we accept for the moment this extension of the idea of the developmental state, what remains of the socialist developmental state is an increasingly isolated central policy elite faced with formidable implementational constraints — wavering legitimacy of the Party amongst some sectors of society; weak administrative and political capacity, especially at the lower levels in poor regions; diverse and contradictory links with private capital, ranging from clientelism and predation to collaboration and support; and increasing subjection to the vacillations of a global economy. The state in China is subject to fragmenting, eroding and hyper-rivalistic pressures — fragmenting because power and authority are diffused amongst a diversity of territorial and socio-economic actors, an outcome of decentralization and marketization; eroding because of the gradual decay of the class-based, Leninist Party machine and its institutional infrastructure; and hyper-rivalistic because parts of the state are locked in competition with each other — sectorally and regionally — and with other nation-states in the world. These pressures in turn lead to an increasingly complex tapestry of local state formations, exhibiting overlapping and contradictory features of developmentalism and predation; of relative autonomy and clientelism; of efficiency and inefficiency; of regulation and anarchy; of facilitation of and excessive interference in the private sector.

CONCLUSION

Scholars such as Cerny (2000) argue that the intensification of global trade and capital flows in the post-Cold War era makes it much harder for developmentally-oriented political elites to steer national economic development. In these circumstances the idea of the developmental state is giving way to the neo-liberal state, although a neo-corporatist state might point to a middle road. In the case of China the high degree of economic decentralization and subsequent jurisdictional competition against a background of intense global competition has contributed to a diversity of policies, economic outcomes and development strategies across provinces. What emerges is not a developmental state or a neo-liberal state but a polymorphous state with

33. Saich (2002) counters the market–federalist argument that enhanced local competition provides an incentive to foster local economic development. Instead he argues that this leads to the maximization of short-term revenue at the expense of longer-term distributional needs. Qian and Weingast (1997: 89) acknowledge the risk of economic federalism leading to increased inequality but link this to the absence of central policies of redistribution.

a complex mix of local state formations, policies and economies. A polymorphous state displays both contradictory features and processes such as autonomy and clientelism, developmentalism and predation, control and chaos, as well as contradictory outcomes such as rapid economic growth and a general rise in average per capita income against rising income inequalities, uneven geographical development, exploitative working conditions and environmental degradation.

It might seem odd, even counter-intuitive, to suggest that China is not a developmental state. The Chinese state at central and provincial levels has indeed played a role in facilitating the development of market forces, through political rhetoric, legislative and regulatory changes, and incentives to export-oriented production and foreign investment. Increasing market competition at home and abroad through the decentralization of economic power and authority to lower levels of government has undoubtedly had positive developmental outcomes such as rapid economic growth, a reduction in absolute poverty and a rise in living standards for urban middle classes. However, to deduce that China is a developmental state because it has achieved rapid economic growth is not only tautological, but also detracts attention away from other possible explanations of its economic miracle. China's economic success, understood as rapid economic growth and rising per capita incomes, has as much to do with its large pool of cheap labour, its continental size economy, its high degree of economic decentralization, and a seemingly insatiable global demand for cheap manufactured goods, as with the strategic intervention of the central state.

There is also a darker side to China's development trajectory. Increased decentralization, fragmentation of policy-making, and marketization have fuelled intense rivalry between local states, within state structures, and between China and other nations for markets and resources. Different regional and sectoral parts of the state compete with each other and with different economic actors for resources and market access, privileging the pursuit of profit over other broader economic, national and social goals. This intense rivalry leads to unpredictable outcomes, such as uneven and unequal development, environmental degradation and exploitative conditions of employment that are tolerated because of the hegemony of global competitiveness. Although the goals of modernization, consumerism, urbanization and greater global integration espoused by China's political elite may resonate with broad sections of Chinese society, the increasingly transparent contradictions between these aspirations and the lived realities of more vulnerable groups such as unemployed and laid-off workers, rural migrants and struggling farmers in resource-poor areas weaken the mobilizing potency of this vision.

The question remains whether China's polymorphous state is a 'transitional' phenomenon that will settle down into a distinctive neo-liberal or neo-corporatist state, or even mature towards a more orthodox developmental state. For the latter to occur would require the central state to restore its grip over policy implementation at the local level. Whilst a dose of recentralization might potentially strengthen the capacity of central government to redistribute resources, such action would also jeopardize the global competitiveness of local economic actors, which is premised on a good deal of economic autonomy and vested interests that local governments are unlikely to be willing to cede. Given that local level authorities have historically often distorted central directives to suit their particularistic needs and given the institutional durability of economic decentralization (Montinola et al., 1995: 69–70), such an outcome is unlikely, unless there were a crisis situation such as a war or national catastrophe that would legitimize a very strong central hand. Moreover, the ideal-type of developmental state may no longer be the appropriate model for addressing the new challenges facing the regime, such as the pluralization of societal demands, rising inequality, increasing external economic, cultural and political pressures. The neo-liberal trajectory also seems remote, given the reluctance of the Communist Party to liberalize the political system.

The polymorphous state is thus likely to be more than a brief, transitional phenomenon. Nevertheless the central government will be under constant pressure to address the question of inequality as growing dissatisfaction with social and regional inequality becomes increasingly manifested in protests across China and is perceived to threaten stability. Balancing national and local interests within a context of intensifying global competition will be crucial to how the Chinese government handles issues of social and regional inequality whilst at the same time maintaining growth and social stability.

REFERENCES

Amsden, Alice H. (1989) *Asia's Next Giant: South Korea and Late Industrialisation*. New York: Oxford University Press.

Balassa, B. in association with J. Berlinski et al. (1982) *Development Strategies in Semi-industrial Economics*. Baltimore, MD: Johns Hopkins University Press for the World Bank.

Baum, Richard and Alexei Shevchenko (1999) 'The "State of the State"', in Merle Goldman and Roderick Macfarquhar (eds) *The Paradox of China's Post-Mao Reforms*, pp. 333–60. Cambridge, MA: Harvard University Press.

Bernstein, Thomas and Xiaobo Lu (2003) *Taxation without Representation in Contemporary Rural China*. Cambridge: Cambridge University Press.

Blecher, M. (1991) 'Development State, Entrepreneurial State: The Political Economy of Socialist Reform in Xinji Municipality and Guanghan County', in Gordon White (ed.) *The Chinese State in the Era of Economic Reform: The Road to Crisis*, pp. 265–94. Basingstoke: Macmillan.

Blecher, Marc and Vivienne Shue (1996) *Tethered Deer: Government and Economy in a Chinese County*. Stanford, CA: Stanford University Press.

Blecher, Marc and Vivenne Shue (2001) 'Into Leather: State-Led Development and the Private Sector in Xinji', *The China Quarterly* 166: 368–93.

Breslin, Shaun (1996) 'China: Developmental State or Dysfunctional Development', *Third World Quarterly* 17(4): 689–706.

Burns, John (2003) 'Governance and Civil Service Reform', in Jude Howell (ed.) *Governance in China*, pp. 37–57. Lanham, MD: Rowman & Littlefield Publishers.

Cai Yongshun (2002) 'The Resistance of Chinese Laid-off Workers in the Reform Period', *The China Quarterly* 170: 327–44.

Cerny, Philip G. (1997) 'Paradoxes of the Competition State: The Dynamics of Political Globalisation', *Government and Opposition* 32(2): 251–74.

Cerny, Philip G. (2000) 'Structuring the Political Arena: Public Goods, States and Governance in a Globalising World', in R. Palan (ed.) *Global Political Economy: Contemporary Theories*, pp. 21–35. London: Routledge.

Chen Feng (2000) 'Subsistence Crises, Managerial Corruption and Labour Protests in China', *The China Journal* 44: 41–63.

Cheng Li (2001) *China's Leaders: The New Generation*. Lanham, MD: Rowman & Littlefield.

Chung, Jae Ho (1995) 'Studies of Central–Provincial Relations in the People's Republic of China: A Mid-Term Appraisal', *The China Quarterly* 142: 487–508.

Dickson, Bruce J. (2003) *Red Capitalists in China. The Party, Private Entrepreneurs and Prospects for Political Change*. Cambridge: Cambridge University Press.

Duckett, Jane (1998) *The Entrepreneurial State in China. Real Estate and Commerce Departments in Reform Era Tianjin*. London: Routledge.

Economy, Elizabeth and Michael Oksenberg (1999) 'Introduction: China Joins the World', in E. Economy and M. Oksenberg (eds) *China Joins the World: Progress and Prospects*, pp. 1–41. New York: Council on Foreign Relations Press.

Edin, Maria (2000) *Market Forces and Communist Power: Local Political Institutions and Economic Development in China*. Uppsala: Uppsala University.

Evans, Peter (1992) 'The State as Problem and Solution: Embedded Autonomy and Structural Change', in S. Haggard and R. R. Kaufman (eds) *The Politics of Economic Adjustment*, pp. 139–81. Princeton, NJ: Princeton University Press.

Fewsmith, Josesph (2001) 'The New Shape of Elite Politics', *The China Journal* 45: 83–94.

Grabowski, Richard (1994) 'The Successful Developmental State: Where does it Come From?', *World Development* 22(3): 413–22.

Heberer, Thomas (2003a) 'Entrepreneurs in China and Vietnam as Strategic Players in Social and Political Change', *The Journal of Communist Studies and Transition Politics* 19(1): 64–79.

Heberer, Thomas (2003b) 'Strategic Groups and State Capacity: The Case of the Private Entrepreneurs', *China Perspectives* 46 (March–April): 4–14.

Held, David (1993) 'Democracy: From City-States to a Cosmopolitan Order', in David Held (ed.) *Prospects for Democracy: North South East West*, pp. 13–52. Cambridge: Polity Press.

Howell, Jude (1993) *China Opens its Doors: The Politics of Economic Transition*. Boulder, CO: Lynne Rienner Inc.

Hsing, You-tien (1998) *Making Capitalism in China: The Taiwan Connection*. Oxford: Oxford University Press.

Huff, W. G., G. Dewit and C. Oughton (2001) 'Credibility and Reputation Building in the Developmental State: A Model with East Asian Applications', *World Development* 29(4): 711–24.

Hurst, W. and Kevin O'Brien (2002) 'China's Contentious Pensioners', *The China Quarterly* 170: 345–60.

Johnson, Chalmers (1982) *MITI and the Japanese Miracle: The Growth of Industrial Policy, 1925–1975*. Stanford, CA: Stanford University Press.

Keane, Michael (2003) 'Bringing Culture Back In', in Jude Howell (ed.) *Governance in China*, pp. 77–97. New York: Rowman & Littlefield Publishers.

Lal, Deepak (1983) *The Poverty of 'Development Economics'*. Hobart Paperback 16. London: Institute of Economic Affairs.

Leftwich, Adrian (1996) 'Two Cheers for Democracy? Democracy and the Developmental State', in Adrian Leftwich (ed.) *Democracy and Development*, pp. 279–96. Cambridge: Polity Press.

Leftwich, Adrian (1998) 'Forms of the Democratic Developmental State', in M. Robinson and G. White (eds) *The Democratic Developmental State*, pp. 52–83. Oxford: Oxford University Press.

Li Lianjiang and K. J. O'Brien (1996) 'Villagers and Popular Resistance in Contemporary China', *Modern China* 22(1): 28–61.

Li Lianjiang and K. J. O'Brien (1997) 'The Struggle over Village Elections', in Roderick MacFarquhar and Merle Goldman (eds) *The Paradox of China's Reforms*, pp. 129–44. Cambridge, MA: Harvard University Press.

Lieberthal, Kenneth (1992) 'The "Fragmented Authoritarianism" Model and its Limitations', in K. Lieberthal and David M. Lampton (eds) *Bureaucracy, Politics and Decision Making in Post-Mao China*, pp. 1–30. Berkeley and Los Angeles, CA: University of California Press.

Lieberthal, Kenneth (1995) *Governing China. From Revolution through Reform*. New York and London: W. W. Norton and Company, Inc.

Little, I. M. D. (1982) *Economic Development: Theory, Policy and International Relations*. New York: Basic Books.

Lu, Xiaobo (1997) 'The Politics of Peasant Burden in Reform China', *The Journal of Peasant Studies* 25(1): 113–38.

Lu, Xiaobo (2000) *Cadres and Corruption. The Organisational Involution of the Chinese Communist Party*. Stanford, CA: Stanford University Press.

Luckham, Robin (1998) 'Are there Alternatives to Liberal Democracy?', in M. Robinson and G. White (eds) *The Democratic Developmental State: Politics and Institutional Design*, pp. 306–42. Oxford: Oxford University Press.

Ming Xia (2000) *The Dual Developmental State: Development Strategy and Institutional Arrangements*. Brookfield,VT: Ashgate.

Montinola, Gabriella, Qian Yingyi and B. R. Weingast (1995) 'Federalism, Chinese Style: The Political Basis for Economic Success', *World Politics* 48(1): 50–81.

Moore, Thomas G. (2000) 'China and Globalization', in Samuel S. Kim (ed.) *East Asia and Globalization*, pp. 105–31. Lanham, MD: Rowman & Littlefield.

Moore, Thomas G. (2002) *China in the World Market: Chinese Industry and International Sources of Reform in the Post Mao Era*. Cambridge: Cambridge University Press.

Nevitt, C. E. (1997) 'Private Business Associations in China: Evidence of Civil Society or Local State Power', *The China Journal* 36: 25–43.

O'Brien, Kevin J. (2002) 'Collective Action in the Chinese Countryside', *The China Journal* 48: 139–54.

O'Brien, Kevin J. (2004) 'Neither Transgressive nor Contained: Boundary-Spanning Contention in China', in P. H. Gries and S. Rosen (eds) *State and Society in 21st Century China: Crisis, Contention and Legitimation*, pp. 105–22. New York and London: RoutledgeCurzon.

Oi, Jean (1992) 'Fiscal Reform and the Economic Foundations of Local State Corporatism in China', *World Politics* 45(2): 99–126.

Oi, Jean (1995) 'The Role of the Local State in China's Transitional Economy', *The China Quarterly* 144: 1132–49.

Park, Albert, Scott Rozelle, Christine Wong and Changqing Ren (1996) 'Distributional Consequences of Reforming Local Public Finance', *The China Quarterly* 147: 751–78.

Pearson, Margaret M. (1994) 'The Janus Face of Business Associations in China: Socialist Corporatism in Foreign Enterprises', *The Australian Journal of Chinese Affairs* 31: 25–46.

Qian Yingyi and B. R. Weingast (1997) 'Federalism as a Commitment to Preserving Market Incentives', *The Journal of Economic Perspectives* 11(4): 83–92.

Saich, Anthony (2002) 'The Blind Man and the Elephant: Analysing the Local State in China', in Luigi Tomba (ed.) *On the Roots of Growth and Crisis: Capitalism, State and Society in East Asia*, pp. 75–99. Milan: Annale Feltrinelli.

Sargeson, Sally and Jian Zhang (1999) 'Reassessing the Role of the Local State: A Case-Study of Local Government Interventions in Property Rights Reform in a Hangzhou District', *The China Journal* 42: 77–99.

Segal, Adam and Eric Thun (2001) 'Thinking Globally, Acting Locally: Local Governments, Industrial Sectors, and Development in China', *Politics and Society* 29(4): 557–88.
Shambaugh, David (2001) 'The Dynamics of Elite Politics During the Jiang Era', *The China Quarterly* 45: 101–12.
Shirk, Susan (1993) *The Political Logic of Economic Reform in China* Berkeley, CA: University of California Press
Shue, Vivienne (1995) 'State Sprawl: The Regulatory State and Social Life in a Small Chinese City', in Deborah S. Davis, Richard Kraus, Barry Naughton and Elizabeth J. Perry (eds) *Urban Spaces in Contemporary China*, pp. 90–112. Cambridge: Cambridge University Press and Woodrow Wilson Center Press.
Shue, Vivienne (2004) 'Legitimacy Crisis in China?', in P. H. Gries and S. Rosen (eds) *State and Society in 21st Century China: Crisis, Contention and Legitimation*, pp. 24–49. New York and London: RoutledgeCurzon.
Tsai, Kellee S. (2004) *Back-Alley Banking. Private Entrepreneurs in China.* Ithaca, NY, and London: Cornell University Press.
Unger, Jonathan (1996) '"Bridges": Private Business, the Chinese Government and the Rise of New Associations', *The China Quarterly* 147: 795–820.
Unger, Jonathan and Anita Chan (1996) 'Corporatism in China: A Developmental State in an East Asian Context', in P. F. Bowles, B. L. McCormick and J. Unger (eds) *China After Socialism. In the Footsteps of Eastern Europe or East Asia?*, pp. 95–129. Armonk, NY: M. E. Sharpe, Inc.
Unger, Jonathan and Anita Chan (1999) 'Inheritors of the Boom: Private Enterprise and the Role of Local Government in a Rural South China Township', *China Journal* 42: 45–74.
Wade, Robert (1988) 'State Intervention in "Outward-looking" Development: Neoclassical Theory and Taiwanese Practice', in G. White (ed.) *Developmental States in East Asia*, pp. 30–67. Basingstoke: Macmillan Press.
Wang Shaoguang and Hu Angang (1999) *The Political Economy of Uneven Development.* Armonk, NY: M. E. Sharpe, Inc.
Wank, David (1996) 'The Institutional Process of Market Clientelism: Guanxi and Private Business in a South China City', *The China Quarterly* 147: 820–38.
Watts, Jonathan and Steven Morris (2003) 'On China's Menu: 260 Billion Eggs and World's Fish Catch', *The Guardian* 18 July: 13.
Wedeman, Andrew H. (2003) *From Mao to Market. Rent Seeking, Local Protectionism, and Marketisation in China.* Cambridge: Cambridge University Press.
Weiss, Linda (2000) 'Developmental States in Transition: Adapting, Dismantling, Innovating, not "Normalising"', *The Pacific Review* 13(1): 21–55.
Westphal, L. E. (1978) 'The Republic of Korea's Experience with Export-Led Industrial Development', *World Development* 6(3): 347–82.
White, Gordon (1984) 'Developmental States and Socialist Industrialisation in the Third World', *Journal of Development Studies* 21(1): 97–120.
White, Gordon and Robert Wade (1988) 'Developmental States and Markets in East Asia: An Introduction', in G. White (ed.) *Developmental States in East Asia*, pp. 1–29. Basingstoke: Macmillan Press.
Whiting, Susan H. (2001) *Power and Wealth in Rural China. The Political Economy of Institutional Change.* New York: Cambridge University Press.
Wong, Christine (1991) 'Central Local Relations in an Era of Fiscal Decline: The Paradox of Fiscal Decentralisation in Post-Mao China', *The China Quarterly* 128: 691–714.
Wong, Christine (1992) 'Fiscal Reform and Local Industrialisation: The Problematic Sequencing of Reform in Post-Mao China', *Modern China* 18(2): 197–227.
Woo-Cumings, Meredith (ed.) (1999) *The Developmental State.* Ithaca, NY, and London: Cornell University Press.
World Bank (1997) *World Bank Development Report 1997. The State in a Changing World.* Oxford: Oxford University Press.

Yang Dali (1997) *Beyond Beijing: Liberalisation and the Regions in China.* New York: Routledge.
Yang Dali and Houkai Wei (1996) 'Rising Sectionalism in China', *Journal of International Affairs* 49(2): 456–77.
Zweig, David (2002) *Internationalizing China. Domestic Interests and Global Linkages.* Ithaca, NY, and London: Cornell University Press.

Jude Howell is Professor and Director of the Centre for Civil Society, London School of Economics and Political Science, Houghton Street, London WC2 2AE, UK. Her recent books include *Governance in China* (Rowman & Littlefield, 2003) and *Gender and Civil Society* (with Diane Mulligan, Routledge, 2004). She has published widely on civil society and development in general, and civil society, labour relations, gender and governance in China. Her current research includes projects on female political participation, trade union reform and civil society in China.

[6]

Journal of Contemporary China (2009), **18**(62), November, 865–880 Routledge Taylor & Francis Group

Consultative Leninism: China's new political framework

STEVE TSANG*

This paper puts forward the concept of consultative Leninism to describe the political system that has taken shape in China after the death of Deng Xiaoping. It argues that the Communist Party has made its essentially Leninist political machinery more resilient in confronting the huge social and political challenges that the current global financial crisis may unleash in China by incorporating consultative elements. Consultative Leninism has five defining characteristics: an obsessive focus upon staying in power; continuous governance reform designed to pre-empt public demands for democratization; sustained efforts to enhance the Party's capacity to elicit, respond to and direct changing public opinion; pragmatism in economic and financial management; and the promotion of nationalism in place of Communism.

China has been undergoing great changes—so much so that someone who visited it once, in 1978 when the post-Mao reforms started under Deng Xiaoping, will wonder if one has gone to the wrong country if one returns again in 2008, three decades later. The changes are not limited to the infrastructure, urban skyline and availability of consumer goods and services in shops. They are noticeable in how people live their life, conduct business transactions, settle business disputes in courts, make their living, travel around the country and beyond, interact with foreigners, access information and converse among themselves about politics. China under Hu Jintao may not be a superpower that can challenge the United States of America as an equal, but it stands tall as a rapidly rising power that the developed world cannot ignore and the developing world looks up to in admiration, if not for a non-democratic development model. The risk that it would follow the steps of other former Communist states and collapse, as was deemed a serious prospect at the start of the 1990s, has now been largely dismissed.

The Chinese leadership after the death of Deng Xiaoping in 1997 has become increasingly confident. It now seeks and experiments with a development model that

* Steve Tsang is Professorial Fellow and University Reader in Politics at St Antony's College, Oxford University. He previously served as Dean of the College and Director of its Asian Studies Centre. He is the author of five books and the editor or co-editor of 11 others. His most recent books are: *Taiwan and the International Community* (ed.) (Oxford: Peter Lang, 2008); *Intelligence and Human Rights in the Era of Global Terrorism* (ed.) (Stanford, CA: Stanford Security Studies, 2008); and *Governing Hong Kong* (London: I.B. Tauris, 2007).

ISSN 1067-0564 print/ 1469-9400 online/09/620865-16 © 2009 Taylor & Francis
DOI: 10.1080/10670560903174705

is married to a political system distinctly different from liberal democracy.[1] Under Hu Jintao the Communist Party is promoting a sense of national pride that uses terminology borrowed from the Confucian past to highlight the 'Chinese character' of its development model without giving up the basic Leninist nature of the political system. In spite of the fact that real and significant changes have taken place in the political arena, the Communist Party still vehemently rejects democracy. 'Chinese democracy' as interpreted and implemented under the Communist Party does not tolerate any scope for it to lose power.

Communism effectively ceased being the state ideology in China sometime between the Tiananmen protests of 1989 and the collapse of Communism in Eastern Europe and the Soviet Union in the following two years. Its Leninist political system has, however, been kept though modified significantly. Since then the Communist Party has imposed what amounts to a social contract on the people of China. In a nutshell, the Party delivers stability, order, rapid growth and general improvement to the living conditions of the people in return for its continued dominance of government and politics. The 'general improvement in living conditions' includes not only economic prosperity but a larger scope for individual freedom and improved government responsiveness to public demands.

This new political set up can best be described as consultative Leninism, a system that blends together the Leninist instrument of control with innovations from other sources. It has five defining characteristics:

- the Communist Party is obsessively focused on staying in power, for which maintaining stability in the country and pre-emptively eliminating threats to its political supremacy are deemed essential;
- a focus on governance reform both within the Party and in the state apparatus in order to pre-empt public demands for democratization;
- a commitment to enhance the Party's capacity to elicit, respond to and direct changing public opinion;
- a commitment to sustain rapid growth and economic development by whatever means and, where the party leadership deems politically expedient, regardless of its previous ideological commitment to Communism; and
- the promotion of a brand of nationalism that integrates a sense of national pride in a tightly guided narrative of China's history and its civilization with the greatness of the People's Republic under the leadership of the Party.

Supremacy of the Party

Even though Communism is no longer the ultimate goal for development, the Communist Party keeps its Leninist structure and organizational principles and remains totally dedicated to staying in power. It is anti-democratic in nature and relies on the Party as the principal instrument to exercise control over the state institutions. This is notwithstanding the Party's formal commitment to 'democracy'—for which the Party requires electoral outcomes to be predictable and guaranteed to be 'correct'.

1. Pan Wei, 'Genyu Xinfang fanzhan zhengzhi guannian jingzheng', *Huanqiu Shibao*, (28 January 2008), reproduced in http://www.chinaelections.org/NewsInfo.asp?NewsID=122158 (last accessed 3 June 2008).

The mechanism that delivers this is the principle of democratic centralism and its Maoist variant known as 'from the masses and to the masses'. In essence this means the Party must go to the masses or 'patriotic citizens' to collect and collate ideas from them, then organize and otherwise add new input to produce a coherent and constructive set of policies and then take them back to the masses, educate and otherwise induce the masses to embrace such ideas as their own.[2] When the Communist Party refers to 'democracy' this is the meaning it has in mind.

Indeed, the leading role and position of the Party remains enshrined in the Constitution of the People's Republic of China (PRC) as the basic principle that underpins the political system.[3] This is the only one of the 'four cardinal principles' that Deng Xiaoping put forth at the start of the reform period that are still being strictly upheld.[4] As the 'vanguard party' and 'guardian of the people', the Party not only maintains its long-standing repressive capacities but also devises and implements a development model that seeks to deliver growth, employment, stability, order, prosperity and improved governance for the ordinary people.

Under Jiang Zemin this approach was described in terms of 'the Three Represents', a concept articulated in July 2001. Jiang proclaimed that

> The whole Party must always maintain the spirit of advancing with the times and constantly extend Marxist theory into new realms ... give top priority to development in governing and invigorating the country and constantly break new ground and open up a new prospect in the modernization drive ... [and] improve its Party building in a spirit of reform and constantly inject new vitality into itself.[5]

Jiang did not spell out clearly his formulation except the fundamental importance of upholding the leading role of the Party with a new requirement. It was to broaden the basis of the Party from an alliance of workers and peasants to include the culturally advanced and economically vibrant elements of society. The private space in which individuals could seek work or personal fulfilment without engaging in activities the Party deemed threatening to its supremacy was enlarged.

Since Hu Jintao took over from Jiang the concept of 'the Three Represents' has been gradually replaced by a policy of promoting a socialist harmonious society. Hu's formula stipulates that 'a harmonious society should feature democracy, the rule of law, equity, justice, sincerity, amity and vitality' in order to produce 'lasting stability and unity'.[6] The general trend in enlarging the private space for

2. Tony Saich, *Governance and Politics of China*, 2nd enlarged edn (Basingstoke: Palgrave Macmillan, 2004), p. 44. The concept of 'the masses' is essentially a Maoist concept. The nearest meaning to such a term is 'patriotic' citizens, with the Communist Party holding the right to define what 'patriotic' means. The issue of patriotism is examined further towards the end of this paper.

3. *Constitution of the People's Republic of China*, (4 December 1982), available at: http://english.people.com.cn/constitution/constitution.html (last accessed 16 May 2008).

4. The four cardinal principles are: '(1) We must keep to the socialist road. (2) We must uphold the dictatorship of the proletariat. (3) We must uphold the leadership of the Communist Party. (4) We must uphold Marxism–Leninism and Mao Zedong Thought'. They were first formally articulated by Deng on 30 March 1979. Deng Xiaoping, *Deng Xiaoping Wenxuan (1975–1982)* (Hong Kong: Sanlian shudian, 1983), pp. 150–151.

5. 'Three Represents', (26 June 1996), available at: http://english.cpc.people.com.cn/66739/4521344.html (last accessed 16 May 2008).

6. 'Building harmonious society crucial for China's progress: Hu', (27 June 2005), available at: http://english.people.com.cn/200506/27/eng20050627_192495.html (last accessed 16 May 2008).

individuals to engage in many different kinds of activities continued, as long as such expansion does not make the Party feel its monopoly of power is being challenged.

Whether it is put in the language of Jiang or Hu, the fundamental principle is for the Party to adapt in order to improve its capacity to stay in power. This is to be achieved, when the general conditions in the country are benign, by the Party dominated government machinery delivering improvements in governance, reaching out to the general public, redressing public grievances and improving living conditions. This is meant to evolve into a political model that pre-empts popular demand for liberal democracy and sustains a benevolent and efficient one party system that practises democratic centralism. In so doing the Communist Party retains its Leninist character and structure. This implies maintaining the capacity and the political will to use whatever means it deems necessary to stay in power should this policy fail to achieve its desired result and the Party's political supremacy is challenged. Consultative Leninism seeks to use small-scale repression and, where practicable, inducements to adroitly eliminate or neutralize challenges to the Party as soon as such challenges are detected in order to pre-empt or reduce the need to resort to dramatic large-scale repression.

Good governance with Chinese characteristics

The definition of 'good governance with Chinese characteristics' is one that needs to be treated carefully. The 'Chineseness' in this formulation should not be confused with traditional Chinese culture. The traditional Chinese concept of 'the ideal government ... is one which is efficient, fair, honest and paternalistic, yet non-intrusive vis-à-vis the life of the ordinary people'.[7] This contradicts the basic nature of the Communist Party as a Leninist institution, which is about pro-actively leading and directing development in the country and mobilizing the general population to follow its lead.

In defining good governance with Chinese characteristics the Communist Party looks back into both its own relatively short history and China's long history for inspiration. It also examines ideas and experience from outside of China as it constructs an alternative model to democratization that is suited to the 'special conditions of China'. An important set of lessons it learned are the causes that led to the collapse of Communism in the Soviet Union and Eastern Europe.[8] It has further examined the experience of the 'Asian tiger economies' under authoritarian rule, particularly that of Singapore.[9] The final product is, however, what the Communist Party chooses to put together regardless of their origins, which it labels as a distinctly modern Chinese approach.

7. Steve Tsang, ed., *A Documentary History of Hong Kong: Government and Politics* (Hong Kong: Hong Kong University Press, 1995), p. 5.

8. Joseph Fewsmith, *China since Tiananmen: The Politics of Transition* (Cambridge: Cambridge University Press, 2001), pp. 52–53.

9. Chen Feng, 'Xinjiapo Remin Xindongdang minzhu shehuizhuyi mowu jichi jiejian yiyi', *Guoji Gongyun Shi Yanjiu* no. 1, (1993), pp. 5–10.

The chosen instrument to deliver good governance is the Communist Party itself.[10] It is an instrument that requires constant reform and updating. The Party seeks to do so by broadening

> its membership base, promoting a new generation of leaders, reformulating its ideological content, appealing to nationalist impulses in society, strengthening its organizational apparatus throughout the country, and opening the channels of discourse within the party and between the party–state and society.[11]

Such an approach, which is reinforced by increasing institutionalization and merit based promotion, has made its brand of authoritarianism resilient.

More specifically the Party has introduced reforms in the political arena aimed at enhancing its own capacity and that of the state to govern effectively. It should be emphasized that such reforms are not meant to be political changes in the direction of democratization but administrative and other changes intended to pre-empt the need for democratization.[12] The Party uses 'a mix of measures to shore up popular support, resolve local protests, and incorporate the beneficiaries of economic reform into the political system'.[13] Reforms, including anti-corruption drives, are deemed necessary to enhance positively its governance capacity. At the same time the Party also 'forcefully represses efforts to challenge its authority and monopoly on political power and organization'.[14]

The biggest difference between Hu Jintao and his predecessor Jiang Zemin's approach lies in the former's tendency to revitalize selectively some of the Maoist ideas or practices as a means to enhance the capacity of the Party. They include, for example, putting greater emphasis on reviving the principle of democratic centralism,[15] as well as making a public commitment to redress the neglect and abuse faced by the rural population, who had been left behind in the rush towards fastest possible growth under Jiang. This suggests a stronger recognition that the Party must deliver social justice in order to pre-empt discontent in the countryside from developing into a major source of instability.[16] Hu publicly advocates that the government should 'provide improved public services for the country's citizens'.[17] He takes the view that 'the biggest danger to the Party ... has been losing touch with the masses' and the Party leadership must therefore 'focus on the core issue of the inextricable link between the Party and the masses'.[18] His approach also

10. 'Zhonggong zhongyang guanyu goujian shehuizhuyi hexie shehui ruogan zhongda wenti de jueding', *Xinhuanet*, (18 October 2006), available at: http://news.xinhuanet.com/politics/2006-10/18/content_5218639.htm (accessed 7 August 2007).

11. David Shambaugh, *China's Communist Party: Atrophy and Adaptation* (Washington, DC: Woodrow Wilson Center Press, 2008), p. 9.

12. Tan Xianmin and Xiao Guangrong, *Zhongguo Gongchandang zhizheng guilu tansuo* (Changsha: Hunan Remin chubanshe, 2001), pp. 215–216.

13. Bruce Dickson, 'Populist authoritarianism: China's domestic political scebe', conference paper dated 23 May 2005, quoted in Shambaugh, *China's Communist Party*, p. 37.

14. *Ibid.*

15. Wang Yang, *Xin shiqi Dang de ganbu zhidu jianshe* (Beijing: Zhonggong dangshi chubanshe, 2006), p. 354.

16. Shambaugh, *China's Communist Party*, pp. 114–115.

17. 'Hu: building a government "by the people, for the people"', *Xinhua*, (25 February 2008), available at: http://www.chinaelections.net/newsinfo.asp?newsid=15816 (last accessed 11 February 2009).

18. Quoted in Andrew J. Nathan and Bruce Gilley, eds, *China's New Rulers: The Secret Files* (London: Granta Books, 2002), pp. 193–194.

reflects awareness of how effective some of the Maoist mobilization and propaganda methods were, and a preparedness to revive some of them.

Building a consultative Leninist infrastructure

The Party has chosen institutionalization as a means to make Chinese politics less volatile. The most important success in this connexion was the peaceful and relatively uneventful transfer of power from Jiang's 'third generation' leadership to Hu's 'fourth generation' leaders in 2002–2003. This is a significant landmark as all previously anointed successors, from Liu Shaoqi to Zhao Ziyang ended their careers in dramatic and in most cases tragic circumstances. If, as looks likely, the pattern set by Hu's succession to Jiang is sustained this will make the politics of succession nearly predictable, even if this involves considerable horse-trading behind the scenes. The old practice of the paramount leader anointing a successor is being replaced by a new one, which is at the early stage of being institutionalized.[19] It involves the existing top leadership collectively choosing their successors and placing them in apprenticeship for five years before ascending to the top offices, as General Secretary of the Party and Premier of the state. The handing over of power may not be democratic but it is becoming structured, stable and basically predictable—indeed, much more predictable than possible in a genuine democratic system.

Greater institutionalization also means increasing importance being put on enforcing the law and containing corruption. In sharp contrast to the Maoist era when the law was reduced to irrelevance, the Communist Party has resorted to rule by law.[20] Whereas the judicial system was a shambles three decades ago, China now has roughly 200,000 judges, 160,000 prosecutors, and 150,000 registered lawyers at work to improve the quality of justice administered. To be sure the Party and its top leadership remain above the law and there is no indication that they are individually or collectively willing to subject themselves to the law, but it does occasionally allow one of their own to face the force of the law where it is in the interest of the current top leadership for this to happen.

What is being put in place is not the rule of law, essential for democracy to function properly and flourish, but rule by law. This means that in cases with no wider political implications, the law is increasingly being upheld and the Communist Party seeks to govern through the enforcement of the law rather than in spite of the law.[21]

The improvements in the criminal justice system mean substantial reduction in cases of human rights abuse even though dissidents and political activists are treated no less harshly than under Deng. Substantial improvements came during Xiao Yang's tenure as President of the Supreme People's Court (1998–2008), as Xiao focused on improving training and standards of judicial personnel in order to reduce gross abuses that used to be endemic in the criminal justice system.[22] Although this did not

19. In the case of Deng Xiaoping, apart from anointing Hu Yaobang and Zhao Ziyang before 1989, he also anointed Jiang Zemin and Jiang's successor, Hu Jintao. With the passing of Deng, strongman politics, and with it the prospect of the top leader anointing his own successor, appears to have ended in the PRC.

20. Chen Yonghong, *Lun Xianzheng yu Zhengzhi Wenming* (Beijing: Renmin chubanshe, 2006), pp. 195–196.

21. Stanley Lubman, 'Looking for law in China', *Columbian Journal of Asian Law* 20(1), (Fall 2006), pp. 6–7.

22. 'Zuigao Renmin Fayuan Gongzuo Baogao', (22 March 2008), available at: http://news.xinhuanet.com/newscenter/2008-03/22/content_7837838_1.htm (last accessed 10 February 2009).

eliminate or even significantly reduce political interference into the judicial system its resultant improvement in the administration of justice in criminal cases was valuable in enhancing the credibility of the regime and thus the Party's governance capacity.

As far as corruption is concerned the Party recognizes the importance of tackling it, but the Party cannot stamp out bureaucratic corruption as China lacks the necessary institutional checks and balances against corruption as well as the rule of law. Unchecked power corrupts. Nevertheless, and despite considerable public scepticism, for a population used to systemic corruption and abuse of power, the periodic high profile attempts to contain the ills of corruption still go a little way to rectifying the credibility deficit of the government and the Party.

The ascendance of the 'third' and 'fourth generation' leaders has brought about another major change from the past, when the top positions were held almost exclusively by revolutionary cadres. This generational change meant technocrats replaced the revolutionary cadres holding all the top offices by the time Jiang became the genuine core of the third generation leadership in 1997. The technocrats have a different outlook from the 'old revolutionaries'.[23] They recognize that none of them can really take over Deng Xiaoping's mantle as the paramount leader.[24] They cannot justify their hold on power by their revolutionary pedigree as founders of the PRC or veterans of 'the revolutionary war' or of the Long March. Instead they must do so by demonstrating their competence and political skills in keeping others in line.

This has led to a greater acceptance of the idea of a meritocracy based on expert knowledge in government or in other relevant fields including the political astuteness required to operate successfully in a modified Leninist system. Since the legitimacy of Communist Party rule after 1989 has been based in part on a *de facto* social contract that the people will acquiesce to the continuation of the Party's monopoly of power as long as the Party delivers continuous improvements in living conditions, improving the governing capacity of the Party is vital. The other element that sustains this *de facto* social contract, namely that the Party's political dominance should not be challenged as it has the will and the means to use force to suppress any such attempt, also requires a strengthening of the administrative capacity of the Party. With the technocrats lacking the standing that Deng Xiaoping enjoyed in the armed forces which enabled him to deploy the army to stage the crackdown in June 1989 despite the initial public articulation of reservation within the military establishment, their rise to power provides a strong incentive to pre-empt a crisis that will necessitate a similar military crackdown. Since the technocrats cannot count on the military to repress popular unrest in the way that Deng could, they have less scope to ignore public opinions.

The Party has also sought to enhance governance capacity by recruiting and promoting on merit.[25] This does not spell the end of privileges or relevance of family background. The so-called Princelings faction—or, the grouping of senior cadres who are descendants of leaders of the revolution—has not visibly suffered. Instead many senior cadres of 'princeling' background have benefited from this

23. Zheng Yongnian, *Jiang–Zhu zhixia de Zhongguo* (Hong Kong: Taipingyang shiji chubanshe, 2000), p. 12.
24. Susan Shirk, *China: Fragile Superpower* (New York: Oxford University Press, 2007), p. 46.
25. Shambaugh, *China's Communist Party*, pp. 142–143.

new emphasis. They have privileged upbringings, career backgrounds and family connections that enable them to build up the necessary technical competence, personal network and political skills to operate successfully within the Party. This puts them in good positions to gain promotion on the basis of merit or achievement. The elevation at the 17th Party Congress (2007) of Xi Jinping to become the unofficial heir apparent to Hu Jintao illustrates nicely the Party's emphasis on meritocracy in action. The promotion of Xi, a 'princeling', despite Hu's personal preference for anointing 'non-princeling' Li Keqiang, has widely been attributed to two factors. They are the economic success of two coastal provinces where Xi served as party secretary and wide acceptance of him within the Party establishment.[26] The latter quality counts as a 'merit' as the capacity to garner support or at least neutralize opposition within the establishment is an important requirement to function effectively in consultative Leninism. By adopting a system that enables the more able administrators and political operators to rise more quickly, the Party ensures that its upper echelons are filled by individuals who are most able to work effectively within the existing political system.

While consultative Leninism is meant to pre-empt democratization, ironically its adoption also involves the introduction of some changes that are commonly seen in democratization. They include not only expanding good governance practices but also allowing for a greater scope for civil liberties and for political participation. In terms of greater political participation the most important general elections in China are not those for the National People's Congress but for the Communist Party's national congress. At the 17th Party Congress, held in October 2007, the party leadership allowed 15% of nominees to fail to get elected.[27] The Chinese government has also experimented with township level elections since the turn of the century on the basis of experimentation with village level elections introduced since the 1980s.[28] Admittedly such developments do not amount to genuine democratic exercises as the Party can and does secure its desired electoral outcomes, but they do enlarge the scope for election.[29]

The Communist Party has also made a point in consulting more individuals and organizations outside of the Party than before. Important gestures underlining the Party and the government's commitment to do so range from reaffirming the right of existing consultative institutions to criticize specific government policies to the use of the Internet as an opinion forum, to allowing greater scope for civil society to operate.[30] Indeed, the Party revived the Chinese People's Consultative Political Conference (CPPCC) as an institution of consultation. Non-Communist parties that

26. Melinda Liu and Jonathan Ansfield, 'A princeling of the people', *Newsweek*, (5 November 2007), available at: http://www.newsweek.com/id/62256 (accessed 28 May 2008).

27. John L. Thornton, 'Long time coming: prospect for democracy in China', *Foreign Affairs* 87(1), (January/February 2008), pp. 8–9.

28. Tianjian Shi, 'Economic development and village elections in rural China', in Suisheng Zhao, ed., *China and Democracy: Reconsidering the Prospects for a Democratic China* (New York: Routledge, 2000), pp. 244–246.

29. Deliberative and incremental steps in increasing the element of election are part of democratization. In the case of Taiwan, for example, local elections from the 1950s onwards helped the democratization process once the Kuomintang authoritarian regime under Chiang Ching-kuo accepted the need to democratize in the late 1980s, even though such elections in the 1950s were not particularly democratic or meaningful at the time.

30. For enlarging the scope for civil society, see discussions below regarding the rescue and relief efforts during the Sichuan earthquake of 2008.

are represented at the CPPCC are now encouraged to articulate their views and 'discuss directly with the central government leaders'.[31] Non-Communist individuals of considerable personal achievement, such as Chen Zhu and Wan Gang, have also been co-opted to join the central government as Minister of Health and Minister of Science and Technology, respectively. Although the last represented primarily the application of a classic United Front idea to 'show the trust of the CPC Central Committee [had] in people from outside the Party', it was a significant step in strengthening the non-exclusive element of consultative Leninism.[32]

As to the Internet, which can be an important instrument for undermining authoritarian regimes, the Chinese authorities not only monitor and control it vigorously but also adopt it as an instrument for consultation. Starting in 2007 the State Council has committed itself experimentally to use its official website to collect opinions on draft laws and regulations. Even top leaders prefer to project an image that they can be accessible via the Internet. Premier Wen Jiabao maintains a presence on Facebook.[33] Even Hu Jintao publicly got online to conduct discussions in the *Renmin Ribao*'s 'strong country forum' in 2008.[34]

In building up a consultative Leninist system, Hu has left his personal marks. He is both politically astute and decisive though he remains highly cautious. As the top leader he appears to have learned a key lesson from the political infightings in the run-up to the Tiananmen protests of 1989. It is that by acting decisively and in unity the Party can reduce the risk of popular challenges getting out of hand, which happened in 1989 as internal divisions at the top became public knowledge after the Party failed to act quickly and decisively at the start of the protests.[35]

The swift and effectively choreographed responses to the Sichuan earthquake of May 2008 suggest Hu and the top leadership had learned this lesson well. They were able to react quickly and collectively. Hu further seized the moment to strengthen the state and the Party's capacity to reach out to the general population and win over their support. In so doing it demonstrated consultative Leninism working at its best.

By dispatching Premier Wen Jiabao to the disaster scene while he retained supreme control in Beijing, Hu projected the image that the government cared and the top leadership worked closely together. It focused public attention on the efforts being led by the top leadership and directed media coverage to showcase the rescue efforts rather than the sufferings of the victims.[36] It distracted attention, even of the international media, from raising obvious questions about China's less than perfect rescue operation. The Chinese government's decision not to permit foreign rescue

31. 'Greater role ahead for non-communist parties', *China Daily*, (7 March 2008), available at: http://www.chinaelections.net/newsinfo.asp?newsid=16175 (last accessed 11 February 2009).

32. 'CCP taps talents outside the Party', *Xinhua*, (29 June 2007), available at: http://www.chinaelections.net/newsinfo.asp?newsid=4331 (last accessed 11 February 2009).

33. Wen's Facebook page is available at: http://en-gb.facebook.com/pages/-Wen-Jia-bao/13823116911 (last accessed 12 February 2009).

34. 'Online chat with Hu Jintao', *Danwei*, (20 June 2008), available at: http://www.danwei.org/internet/president_hu_jintao_talks_to_n.php (last assessed 11 February 2009).

35. Andrew Nathan and Perry Link, eds, *The Tiananmen Papers* (London: Little Brown and Company, 2001), p. xxxvi.

36. Richard Spencer, 'China orders journalists to end negative quake coverage', *The Sunday Telegraph*, (8 June 2008), available at: http://www.telegraph.co.uk/news/worldnews/asia/china/2091084/China-earthquake–journalists-orderered–to-end-negative-quake-coverage.html (accessed 9 June 2008).

teams to go to Sichuan immediately after the scale of the earthquake was known meant irreplaceable time for rescuing victims from collapsed buildings was lost. In the end the first external or foreign rescue teams were allowed to reach the scene of the earthquake on day four, when experience elsewhere established that by then relatively few survivors trapped in collapsed buildings or buried under rubble could be pulled out alive. Whatever the government's considerations were for such a decision, the adroit management of the public image of the rescue operations allowed the importance of this specific inhumane decision to go largely unnoticed.

By seizing the moral high ground promptly and turning public reactions to the disaster into a nationalist response, Hu's government made it possible to win wide praise and support from the country generally and to deflect the inevitable criticisms on specific failings in the rescue and relief operation. Where such criticisms could not be silenced, they were directed against the inadequate performance of lower level officials in Sichuan and thus avoided criticism being directed against the overall performance of the central government or the Party. This effective use of propaganda to shape public opinion helps to sustain their positive image and moral authority which, in turn, reinforces their governance capacity and legitimacy.

In addition, by beaming images of 'Grandpa Wen' at the front of the disaster zone, the Chinese government reached out to the general public nationwide in a paternalistic way. Through its well-oiled propaganda machine it created a heroic image of the government led by Premier Wen, ably assisted by soldiers of the People's Liberation Army, saving victims of a natural disaster in the front line and under the overall leadership of General Secretary Hu. Thus, even in a situation where public opinions were being formed and changed quickly, the Party leadership seized the moment to control, shape and direct public opinion.

This further enabled the Party to claim credit unobtrusively for galvanizing the country to respond proudly as a nation, once the outpouring of sympathy nationwide turned into self-organized non-government organization (NGO)-based efforts to help the victims. With its moral authority affirmed, the Party was able to require NGOs to co-operate without appearing overly heavy-handed.

This shows an important improvement in governance capacity as the Party allowed a much larger scope than usual for NGOs to take civic actions at a time of a major natural disaster, but it also reveals the existence of a strategy for the Party–state to play a leadership role in directing the efforts of NGOs. The approach Hu has adopted is to treat civil society like a bird in a cage. The Party or the state is prepared to enlarge the cage as it sees fit but a cage is nonetheless maintained. This is to ensure that civil society can have sufficient scope to operate in the non-critical realm while its ambition to extend its scope to the critical realm is contained so that the development of civil society cannot pose a threat to the continuation of Party rule.

Economic pragmatism

Since the start of the reform period under Deng Xiaoping in 1978, pragmatism has generally been the catch phrase for managing China's economy, but it took time for the old command economy to be transformed and for the mentality of policy makers to adjust. The 'bird cage approach' for managing the economy, as explained by party elder Chen Yun, was clearly applied in the earlier half of the reform period. In this conception the economy was the bird and the scope for it to develop was the cage and the Party was willing to enlarge the cage as long as the performance of the bird justified it, but the Party could and did reduce the cage when required.

By the time Deng died, in 1997, transformation from the old command economy had basically been completed. With the economy substantially modernized, much new infrastructure already built, a generation educated in modern management and other skills required to service a modern economy, the Party leadership increasingly allowed greater scope for the economy to develop, particularly after the potential contagion effect of the Asian Financial Crisis passed. In the last decade major debates among economic and financial policy makers have no longer been about whether the economy should be primarily a socialist or a market one but about what would be most effective policy to secure sustained and sustainable rapid growth.

Indeed, China's economy is neither a free market nor a command economy. It is a mixed one where private capital now has huge scope to invest in almost whatever it deems the most profitable lines of manufacturing or service provision. It is also one where state or publicly owned enterprises enjoy great privileges and government patronage, and are still subject to government direction. In a nutshell the Party leadership has enlarged the bird cage so much that the bird largely developed without finding itself seriously constrained by the cage most of the time; but the cage has not been removed.

As the Chinese economy slows down significantly, as it has started to do in the last quarter of 2008, the Party leadership takes a tighter control over economic policies and economic and financial developments. This is not a matter of reducing the size of the cage for any ideological based reason as much as a matter of ensuring the economic slowdown will not turn into a major source of social and political instability. In working out its strategy to limit the impact of the global economic downturn, the Party leadership will consult China's best economists in think tanks and in academia as well as corporate leaders, and engage in dialogues with major foreign governments and corporate partners, but the Leninist nature of the regime will also assert itself. As far as the Party is concerned, it consults not because of recognition of the intrinsic value of consultation but because it sees consultation as useful in enabling the Leninist system to retain control and come out of an impending crisis stronger.

Nationalism as the new ideology

The last defining feature of consultative Leninism is the promotion of nationalism as the new ideological force that binds the country together under the leadership of the Party. After Communism in effect ceased being the state ideology, the Communist Party had to put in place a new ideological framework. This was in part a reaction to the events in Eastern Europe and the Soviet Union as the Chinese establishment feared social and national disintegration following 'the decline of the traditional ideology'.[37] It was also because the Party intended to pre-empt Western values and beliefs from captivating Chinese citizens living in an ideological void.[38] In any event, the provision of an ideological binding force was needed to enable the Leninist system to function effectively.

The choice of nationalism as the new though informal state ideology is meant to enhance the Communist Party's capacity to stay in power in two mutually reinforcing ways. It is to provide a new ideological basis for legitimacy on the one hand and to serve as a new rallying force to develop a national aspiration around the leadership of the Party on the other. After the cleavages created between the Party and the ordinary people by the Tiananmen Massacre, the top leaders found nationalism 'the most reliable claim to the Chinese people's loyalty and the only important value shared by the regime and its critics'.[39] They thus 'moved quickly to position themselves as the defenders of China's national pride' and unity.[40] Few Chinese citizens in fact know the history of their country well but they have all been indoctrinated in the greatness of China's long civilization and unity, as well as the iniquity of the 'century of humiliation' when China suffered from Western imperialism after 1838.[41] The historical narrative chosen is outwardly a 'pan-Chinese' one, but in reality it is a Han-centric view of the history of greater China, in which minorities like Tibetans and Uighurs are written into Chinese history as Mongolians and Manchurians have been incorporated. Any ethnic group thus 'honoured' by their inclusion into China's history will be deemed traitorous should they try to assert their own national identity and separate historical narratives. The nationalism thus promoted is essentially xenophobic in nature, which encourages the Chinese people to identify with a rising China under the leadership of the Communist Party in juxtaposition against the West that is portrayed as uncomfortable with China's resurgence and historic unity.[42]

More specifically, the Party has launched an extensive propaganda and educational campaign to indoctrinate the people in patriotism. It is one that requires the citizens of the PRC to participate in affirming 'the rightness and acceptability of the state, its values, policies and agencies'.[43] The core of this campaign is to emphasize 'how China's unique national conditions make it unsuitable to adopt Western style liberal democracy' and how China's existing political system helps to 'maintain political stability, a prerequisite for rapid economic development'.[44] By '[r]einforcing China's national confidence and turning past humiliation and current weakness into a driving

37. Zheng Yongnian, *Discovering Chinese Nationalism in China: Modernization, Identity, and International Relations* (Cambridge: Cambridge University Press, 1999), p. 51.

38. Chen Shaoming, 'Minzu zhuyi: Fuxing zhi dao', *Dong Fang* no. 2, (1996), p. 74.

39. Zhao Suisheng, 'China's pragmatic nationalism: is it manageable?', *The Washington Quarterly* 29(1), (Winter 2005–2006), p. 134.

40. *Ibid.*

41. Yuan Weishi, 'Xiandaihua yu lishi jiaokeshu', (11 January 2006), available at: http://edu.people.com.cn/GB/1055/4016350.html (last accessed 16 May 2008).

42. The large public outburst of nationalism when the Olympic torch relay outside of China met with large scale public protests in April 2008 confirms the xenophobic nature of China's new nationalism. This is addressed later in this essay. For a strong representation of some Chinese nationalists' frustrations, see 'My friends, what do you want from us?', *China Digital Times*, (12 April 2008), available at: http://chinadigitaltimes.net/2008/04/my-friends-what-do-you-want-from-us/ (last accessed 16 May 2008).

43. David Kelly, 'Citizen movements and China's public intellectuals in the Hu–Wen era', *Pacific Affairs* 79(2), (Summer 2006), p. 201.

44. Zhao, 'China's pragmatic nationalism', p. 135.

force for China's modernization' the Party has turned nationalism into 'an effective instrument for enhancing [its] legitimacy'.[45] The intention is to instil in the mind of the Chinese people a sense of pride in China and its development that is inseparable from the leadership of the Party or a strong feeling of 'my government right or wrong'.

The success of this nationalist indoctrination campaign manifested itself dramatically in 2008, the year the Communist Party had intended to launch the rebranded modern China on the occasion of the Beijing Olympics. The force of nationalism, however, could not be contained until the Olympics as was originally planned. The nationalists asserted themselves internationally when the Olympic torch relay outside of China generated unfavourable foreign comments and reactions in April. The negative foreign reactions were directed immediately at the way the Chinese authorities organized the relay, which was heavily guarded by elite members of the People's Armed Police dressed as torch attendants. More generally most Western critics of the PRC were concerned with its support for the repressive military junta in Burma and for protecting the extremely brutal Sudanese regime's conduct in Darfur, and related them, however loosely, to the PRC government's demands over policing against pro-Tibetan demonstrators in Western cities.

Chinese nationalists reacted angrily and strongly against those who demonstrated in foreign cities where the torch passed against specific Chinese government policies, particularly that on Tibet.[46] They readily ignored the fact that the criticisms of Chinese support for the Burmese junta and Sudanese regime were against specific policies of the Chinese government and not anti-Chinese. Equally they dismissed out of hand the fact that by sending elite police officers who often told the local police how the torch should be guarded during the overseas relay, Chinese authorities were interfering with the domestic affairs of the host countries concerned. The large number of Chinese citizens who responded so nationalistically showed that they preferred to choose to 'side with the government when foreigners criticize it, believing that, no matter how corrupt [or misguided] the government is, foreigners have no right to make unwarranted remarks about China and its people'.[47]

The Party's adoption of nationalism also dramatically enhanced its governance capacity in the aftermath of the Sichuan earthquake of May 2008. By adopting a nationalist approach to the rescue operation and holding back entry of foreign teams from reaching the scene, the Chinese government ensured that nearly all survivors were saved by Chinese rescue workers. The heroism of the rescue operations by the Chinese nation was used to galvanize a countrywide movement to rally around the Party's leadership in the subsequent relief efforts, even though generous foreign aid and donations were readily accepted. Thus, however well or poorly the Party might have actually performed on the ground, and whether bureaucratic corruption and other policy failures were responsible for the collapse of a disproportionately large number of school buildings, the Party still emerged from it stronger than before. Just as the astute management of propaganda after the earthquake ensured a positive

45. *Ibid.*

46. Austin Ramzy, 'China's view of the Olympic torch war', *Time*, (9 April 2008), available at: http://www.time.com/time/printout/0,8816,1729169,00.html (last accessed 10 April 2008).

47. Zhao, 'China's pragmatic nationalism', p. 136.

image of the Party being projected, the long standing indoctrination of nationalism produced a people 'willing to dissociate their leaders in Beijing from the local officials they blame'.[48] The Chinese government might not be able to silence all grieving parents but it could divert their anger from the central government to specific individuals or departments at the local level and reduce the negative impact on its own credibility.[49] Galvanizing the nation to focus on the 'heroic' rescue operations of the People's Liberation Army apparently personally superintended by Premier Wen, was key to this success.

Conclusions

Consultative Leninism has given China arguably as resilient a political system as it can have without democracy to face the challenges of the major economic slowdown triggered by the global financial crisis. The resilience is rooted in the ruthless repressive capacity inherent in what remains an essentially Leninist political machinery. It is strengthened by incorporating various consultative elements. By modernizing the regime's capabilities to monitor and direct public opinion and instil a sense of patriotic duty on its citizens to support the government, the Party has significantly increased its ability to deflect public discontent away from itself. By enhancing its capacity to detect challenges as they emerge and remove most of them, either by co-optation or by low level repression, before they become major threats to the system, consultative Leninism only needs to resort to large-scale repression very sparingly. This implies reduced exposure to risks that can destabilize or break the system in a fundamental way.

Consultative Leninism is not a system that was specifically designed to replace the Maoist or Dengist political edifice. It evolved out of measures the Communist Party took to confront and contain the challenges posed by the Tiananmen movement of 1989 and the subsequent collapse of Communism in Eastern Europe and the Soviet Union. The original impetus for change in the political arena was the Communist Party's concern over its own hold on power in China.

Once this threat came to pass in the late 1990s and China found itself on track for very fast growth, the Communist Party leadership gained in confidence. The post-Deng political setup, which I describe as consultative Leninism, became accepted in the last few years as a sustainable political system for China as it appeared capable of sustaining not just itself but also the rise or re-emergence of China as a great power of the first league. As the Chinese establishment felt it had developed a sustainable political system to support rapid growth, it lost interest in the Singaporean approach, an earlier favourite, as a possible model for China. This new found confidence among Chinese leaders has been reinforced by the existence of a China fever in the twenty-first century, as a world infatuated with China offers general recognition of and praise for its post-Deng achievements.

48. Tom Mitchell and Mure Dickie, '"Just emperor" in Beijing escapes blame', *The Financial Times*, (30 May 2008), p. 5.

49. Mark Magnier, 'China tightens media limits loosened after earthquake', *Los Angeles Times*, (5 June 2008), available at: http://www.latimes.com/news/nationworld/world/la-fg-rollback5-2008jun05,0,4764776.story (accessed 6 June 2008).

Consultative Leninism is not a static system but one that continues to evolve, as inherent in its requirements is the need for the Communist Party to adapt to the changing environment in order to stay in power and direct China's development, but its basic structure and governing dynamics have taken shape. It is the incorporation of consultative elements to enhance the Communist Party's basically Leninist institution to react and respond to new challenges and to monitor and to direct public opinion. Consultative Leninism uses whatever means at its disposal to maintain stability, order and economic growth, and it seeks to minimize the need to use harsh repressive means in a large scale but it also at the same time keeps such capacity readily available for use. Indeed, a hallmark of consultative Leninism under Hu Jintao is the Party's readiness to nip in the bud any challenge to the political supremacy of the Party as soon as such a challenge is detected. To maintain this capacity the Party needs to collect and collate constantly the changing mood and opinions in the country at large. Indeed, doing so is essential for the Party to pre-empt nationalism from asserting itself so much that it may tie the hands of the Party leadership in dealing with a major great power such as the United States of America or Japan in some future and as yet undefined crisis.

In general terms, consultative Leninism consolidates the Communist Party gains in confidence and competence. As it does so it allows greater scope than previously for experimentation in finding ways to enable China to develop without moving towards democracy. Corporatist ideas are taken on board where they appear to work. A larger sphere is allowed for civil society to operate as long as the Party feels confident that it can keep civil society in line when and where required. Reinvigoration of specific Maoist or highly modified Confucian ideas has also been adopted where the Party believes they can enhance its ability to govern or improve its moral authority, but the bottom line remains unchanged—the dominance of the Party, even if intra-party reforms, such as greater 'inner party democracy', may appear to make the top leader more responsive to others than his predecessors. Indeed, the increased scope for debate among party leaders is one of the means through which the Communist Party enhances consultative Leninism and improves on its development model.

Resilient as it is, consultative Leninism suffers from a major inherent problem. It is that the Communist Party needs to get its policies on the economy, the politics and the society right most of the time—a very tall order in the long term. The built-in safety valve to ensure a major policy or economic failure that may have significant negative impact on people's living conditions that exists in a democracy—a change of government via the ballot box—does not exist in this model. Its primary systemic 'safety valve' is nationalism. This raises the prospect that in order to divert public frustration and anger away from itself during a crisis the Communist Party is likely to channel them against foreign powers or capitalists and blame them for turning a benign international environment into a hostile one for China. What is also inherent in this model is that the Party will assert its Leninist nature at the expense of its consultative elements if the country should face a sustained crisis against which the Party appears helpless. Repression and tightening of control are the default options for ensuring regime survival when the Party feels it is under threat.

How well consultative Leninism will fare in the very long term remains unknown, as the PRC has not faced any real crisis since 1992 after the aftershocks of the 1989 protests and the subsequent collapse of Communism in Eastern Europe and the Soviet Union. Its first real test may come in 2009–2010 if the economic slowdown should turn out to be deep and sustained, trigger a groundswell of social movements and unrest, and cause a split at the top of the leadership. By transforming the political system into consultative Leninism, the Communist Party leadership has prepared itself as well as possible without the benefits of a democratic system in confronting the pending challenges. The resilience of consultative Leninism is likely to enable China under the Communist Party leadership to get through the challenges unleashed by the major economic slowdown by a combination of enhanced governance capacity, direction of public opinion, economic pragmatism and use of repressive means, provided the central leadership can stay united.

[7]

ADAPTIVE INFORMAL INSTITUTIONS AND ENDOGENOUS INSTITUTIONAL CHANGE IN CHINA

By KELLEE S. TSAI*

SHORTLY after the third wave of democratization, Francis Fukuyama's "The End of History" and Lucian Pye's "Political Science and the Crisis of Authoritarianism" became oft-quoted readings for political scientists, alongside the existing core of regime transition literature.[1] For a brief moment, it seemed as if it were just a matter of time before the remaining authoritarian regimes experienced democratic transitions. By the late 1990s and early 2000s, however, these teleological accounts had given way to a spate of nuanced, typological analyses concerning "democracy with adjectives" and "hybrid regimes."[2] The rise of "illiberal democracy" and "competitive authoritarianism" created an intermediate category of regimes that fell short of meeting classic definitions of either liberal democracy or authoritarianism.[3] It is in this

* A National Science Foundation grant (INT-0107326) provided funding for the research in this article. While many people have commented on the larger project, I would like to thank Eva Bellin, Mark Blyth, Chen Guangjin, Bruce Dickson, Richard Doner, Stephan Haggard, Scott Kennedy, Andrew Nathan, Kevin O'Brien, Margaret Pearson, Ben Ross Schneider, Aseema Sinha, Dorothy Solinger, Sidney Tarrow, three anonymous readers, and audiences at the annual meetings of the American Political Science Association and at Columbia University, Cornell University, Harvard University, Indiana University, Johns Hopkins University, the University of Havana, the University of North Carolina-Chapel Hill, and the University of Pennsylvania for more recent and detailed input. They are, of course, absolved of responsibility for any inadequacies.

[1] Francis Fukuyama, "The End of History?" *National Interest* 16 (Summer 1989); Samuel P. Huntington, *The Third Wave: Democratization in the Late Twentieth Century* (Norman: University of Oklahoma Press, 1991); Guillermo O'Donnell and Philippe C. Schmitter, *Transitions from Authoritarian Rule: Tentative Conclusions about Uncertain Democracies* (Baltimore: Johns Hopkins University Press, 1986); and Lucian Pye, "Political Science and the Crisis of Authoritarianism," *American Political Science Review* 84 (March 1990).

[2] David Collier and Steven Levitsky, "Democracy with Adjectives: Conceptual Innovation in Comparative Research," *World Politics* 49 (April 1997); and Larry Diamond, "Thinking about Hybrid Regimes," *Journal of Democracy* 13 (April 2002).

[3] Steven Levitsky and Lucan Way, "The Rise of Competitive Authoritarianism," *Journal of Democracy* 13 (April 2002); Michael McFaul, "The Fourth Wave of Democracy *and* Dictatorship: Noncooperative Transitions in the Postcommunist World," *World Politics* 54 (January 2002); and Fareed Zakaria, "The Rise of Illiberal Democracy," *Foreign Affairs* (November–December 1997).

World Politics 59 (October 2006), 116–41

context that various scholars have criticized the transition paradigm for being misleading, even "fundamentally flawed," calling instead for a focus on "what is happening politically."[4]

Following this recommendation, this article examines the most populous nontransition case in the world, the People's Republic of China (PRC). Although China shows no signs of making a transition to democracy, the country's political economy has experienced substantial structural and institutional changes relating to the development of the private sector. Whereas in 1977 China did not even keep official statistics on private firms because they were illegal and negligible in number, by 2005 there were 29.3 million private businesses, employing over 200 million people and accounting for 49.7 percent of the GDP.[5] Classic structural explanations of political change might expect a growing capitalist class to make liberalizing demands in the spirit of "no taxation without representation."[6] This raises a fundamental puzzle: even though China's private entrepreneurs are not mobilizing politically, much less agitating for democracy,[7] major reforms in China's formal institutions have enhanced the private sector's political legitimacy and economic security. In a complete reversal of its founding principles, the Chinese Communist Party now welcomes capitalists and, at least on paper, the PRC constitution protects private property rights. How can this be explained? I argue that adaptive informal institutions can serve a vital intermediate role in explaining the process of endogenous institutional change.

Without denying the proximate causal role of elite politics and decisions, this article contends that under certain circumstances, the etiology of formal institutional change lies in the informal coping strategies devised by local actors to evade the restrictions of formal institutions. The argument starts from the premise that formal institutions

[4] Thomas Carothers, "The End of the Transition Paradigm," *Journal of Democracy* 13 (January 2002), 18; Howard J. Wiarda, "Southern Europe, Eastern Europe, and Comparative Politics: 'Transitology' and the Need for New Theory," *East European Politics and Societies* 15 (September 2001), 486; cf. Valerie Bunce, "Rethinking Recent Democratization: Lessons from the Postcommunist Experience," *World Politics* 55 (January 2003).

[5] *China Daily*, December 14, 2005. A 2006 report issued by the Chinese Academy of Social Sciences estimated that in five years the nonstate sector would account for three-quarters of China's GDP and 70 percent of the country's firms would be privately owned. See *China Daily*, September 22, 2006.

[6] Barrington Moore, Jr., *Social Origins of Dictatorship and Democracy: Lord and Peasant in the Making of the Modern World* (Boston: Beacon Press, 1966).

[7] Bruce J. Dickson, *Red Capitalists in China: The Party, Private Entrepreneurs, and Prospects for Political Change* (New York: Cambridge University Press, 2003); Margaret M. Pearson, *China's New Business Elite: The Political Consequences of Economic Reform* (Berkeley: University of California Press, 1997); and Kellee S. Tsai, *Capitalism without Democracy: The Private Sector in Contemporary China* (Ithaca, N.Y.: Cornell University Press, 2007).

comprise a myriad of constraints and opportunities that may motivate everyday actors to devise novel operating arrangements that are not officially sanctioned. With repetition and diffusion, these informal coping strategies may take on an institutional reality of their own. In contrast to deep-rooted, "primordial" informal institutions, which tend to resist change, the resulting norms and practices can be called *adaptive* informal institutions because they represent creative responses to formal institutional environments that actors find too constraining. Widespread use of adaptive informal institutions may then motivate—and, indeed, enable—political elites to reform the original formal institutions. Examining the life cycle of adaptive informal institutions can thus demonstrate how some formal institutions manage to undergo significant transformations in the absence of external intervention, crisis conditions, or societal demands. Relatedly, focusing on the emergence and impact of adaptive informal institutions can reveal the processes through which apparently incremental reforms yield radical change.

To illustrate this iterative logic, the article examines the dynamics of private sector development in China since the late 1970s by focusing on three institutional spaces in which major changes have occurred: first, the official policy adjustments that sanctioned the revival of China's private sector; second, the incorporation of capitalists into the Chinese Communist Party (CCP); and as a complementary institutional effect of the first two changes, third, the amendments to the PRC constitution that formally recognized and protected private property. Taken together, these three cases represent dramatic transformations in the most important formal institutions in the country, namely, economic policy orientation, the party, and the state. They also show that even in nondemocratic contexts, the etiology of formal institutional change may lie in the informal coping strategies devised by local actors to evade the restrictions of formal institutions. To be sure, reform-oriented elites in Beijing were instrumental in making the official decisions to reform the Communist Party and the PRC constitution. But this article proposes that the accumulation of informal interactions between local state and economic actors provided both the impetus and the legitimizing basis for these key reforms. When viewed from this perspective, the remarkable institutional changes promoting private sector development become less puzzling. Ultimately, both the designers and enforcers of China's formal institutions have proven to be flexible, and even responsive, to the actors driving the country's economic growth—private entrepreneurs.

The article proceeds as follows. The first section shows how explanations for endogenous institutional change derived from advanced industrial democracies may be extended to elucidate the processes of institutional innovation in nondemocratic contexts, including contemporary China. I propose that the emergence and incorporation of adaptive informal institutions are key processes in a broader sequence of endogenous institutional change. The article then examines three empirical cases to illustrate how adaptive informal institutions underlying private sector development have stimulated sequential changes in China's formal institutions. The conclusion reflects upon the theoretical implications of the argument.

Explaining Endogenous Institutional Change

Although revolutions, economic crises, wars, natural disasters, and foreign intervention/occupation provide a readily identifiable context for major institutional transformations, the literature on historical institutionalism and American political development offers various typological concepts for describing institutional change during "normal" periods. The notion of "reactive sequences" draws attention to the manner in which certain events may produce backlash effects.[8] Institutional "layering" focuses on the potential for different types of institutions either to conflict with one another or to coexist in a synthetic manner.[9] Relatedly, "institutional conversion" refers to the use of institutions in ways that deviate from their intended purpose.[10] Building on these concepts, I examined the informal coping strategies inspired by the formal institutional environment and identified a key, yet typically overlooked dimension in endogenous accounts of institutional development. This is not to say that all informal interactions are causally relevant in explaining formal institutional change. Rather, it suggests that under the political circumstances such as those found in reform-era China, extensive reliance on adaptive informal institutions may foreshadow the possibility of institutional reforms that bridge the gap between official regulations and everyday practices. Institutional change is possible in the absence of cataclysmic events or institutional collapse.

[8] James Mahoney, "Path Dependence in Historical Sociology," *Theory and Society* 29 (August 2000).

[9] Robert C. Lieberman, "Ideas, Institutions, and Political Order: Explaining Political Change," *American Political Science Review* 96 (December 2002), 703.

[10] Kathleen Thelen, *How Institutions Evolve: The Political Economy of Skills in Germany, Britain, the United States, and Japan* (New York: Cambridge University Press, 2004). This notion of organizational appropriation may be traced back to Selznick's classic study of the Tennessee Valley Authority; Philip P. Selznick, *TVA and the Grass Roots* (Berkeley: University of California Press, 1949).

Path Dependence and Sequencing

The sequencing approach to institutional development typically focuses on the self-reinforcing dynamics of path dependency and institutional continuity.[11] As Douglass North explains: "Path dependence comes from the increasing returns mechanisms that reinforce the direction once on a given path."[12] But path dependence does not preclude change over time. In particular, Paul Pierson distinguishes between "self-reinforcing event sequences" and "non-reinforcing event sequences" in path-dependent arguments. A common expression of a self-reinforcing event sequence is evidenced when certain political actors consolidate power during an early formative period and end up promoting institutions and rules that enable them to maintain their authority over time.[13] By contrast, in "non-reinforcing event sequences," or what James Mahoney calls "reactive sequences," certain events occur in reaction to earlier events, and these propel subsequent developments along an alternative trajectory.[14] As in self-reinforcing event sequences, events that occur earlier in a particular sequence can have a much greater impact on the final outcome of events than later events—but as Pierson points out, "not necessarily by inducing further movement in the same direction. Indeed, the route might matter precisely because it sets the stage for a particular kind of reaction in some other direction."[15]

The concept of reactive sequences is fruitful for appreciating the potentially nonlinear trajectory of institutional development. That is, short of authoritarian breakdown, it is plausible that significant changes could nevertheless occur within the apparent limits of the existing political system. Some institutions may elicit responses that undermine the dynamics of institutional reproduction and reinforcement.[16] This raises the question of when reinforcing processes are likely to shift to reactive ones, a question addressed in terms of the notions of institutional layering and friction, discussed next.

[11] Brian Arthur, *Increasing Returns and Path Dependence in the Economy* (Ann Arbor: University of Michigan Press, 1994); Paul David, "Clio and the Economics of QWERTY," *American Economic Review* 75 (May 1985); and cf. Paul Pierson, "Increasing Returns, Path Dependence, and the Study of Politics," *American Political Science Review* 94 (June 2000).

[12] Douglass C. North, *Institutions, Institutional Change, and Economic Performance* (New York: Cambridge University Press, 1990).

[13] Paul Pierson, "Not Just What, but *When:* Timing and Sequence in Political Processes," *Studies in American Political Development* 14 (Spring 2000), 77.

[14] Mahoney (fn. 8).

[15] Pierson (fn. 13), 84.

[16] On self-reinforcing versus self-undermining institutions, see Avner Greif and David Laitin, "A Theory of Endogenous Institutional Change," *American Political Science Review* 98 (November 2004).

Institutional Layering and Friction

The second category of explanations for endogenous institutional change emphasizes institutional layering and complexity as a product of multiple sources of human action. "Layering" refers to the fact that most institutional environments comprise a variety of institutions, some of which may have inconsistent or competing objectives. Thus, the reality of multilayered institutional contexts limits the degree of coherence that particular formal institutions (for example, the United States Congress) may have at any given point.[17] As for the potential timing of endogenous institutional change, Robert Lieberman hypothesizes that "significant extraordinary political change" is more likely when there is "friction among multiple political orders."[18] In other words, the impetus for institutional change may emerge out of conflicts occurring in otherwise stable patterns of politics. And the "causal mechanism linking structural friction and political change is the reformulation of the incentives and opportunities for individual political action that friction produces."[19] Due to this friction among various institutional layers, actors may establish adaptive patterns that are simultaneously new, yet familiar.

The transformative potential of multilayered institutional environments is also apparent in the PRC. Even though China has a unitary rather than a federal political system, political scientists have described its regime type as "fragmented authoritarianism" because the vertical bureaucratic entities are structurally prone to conflict with horizontal levels of territorial-based governmental administration.[20] Meanwhile, its policy-making process has been characterized as "protracted, disjointed, and incremental."[21] We will see in the forthcoming examples that the growth of the private sector in a transitional economy has brought about its share of intrabureaucratic and central-local conflicts, as various political actors have grafted new institutions onto socialist-era

[17] Karen Orren and Stephen Skowronek, "Beyond the Iconography of Order: Notes for a 'New Institutionalism,'" in Lawrence C. Dodd and Calvin Jillson, eds., *The Dynamics of American Politics: Approaches and Interpretations* (Boulder, Colo.: Westview Press, 1994); and Eric Schickler, *Disjointed Pluralism: Institutional Innovation and the Development of the U.S. Congress* (Princeton: Princeton University Press, 1994).

[18] Lieberman (fn. 9).

[19] Ibid., 704. On political entrepreneurs as key sources of endogenous institutional change, see Adam Sheingate, "Political Entrepreneurship, Institutional Change, and American Political Development," *Studies in American Political Development* 17 (Fall 2003).

[20] Kenneth G. Lieberthal and David M. Lampton, eds., *Bureaucracy, Politics, and Decision-Making in Post-Mao China* (Berkeley: University of California Press, 1992).

[21] Kenneth G. Lieberthal and Michael Oksenberg, *Policy Making in China: Leaders, Structures, and Processes* (Princeton: Princeton University Press, 1988).

ones, while subnational officials have adapted national policies to local conditions. In short, the concepts of layering and friction in explaining endogenous institutional change are well suited for analyzing political dynamics in China's complex bureaucratic and administrative context.

A related phenomenon within the layering approach to institutional development is what Kathleen Thelen calls "institutional conversion," meaning the use of existing institutions for new or alternative purposes.[22] In contrast to the self-reinforcing view of institutions, this perspective recognizes that even when the formal attributes of institutions remain in place, their substantive roles may change quite dramatically. Moreover, Thelen's analysis demonstrates that "more subtle and smaller-scale changes in 'settled' rather than 'unsettled' times are also worthy of our attention, as, over time, they can cumulate into significant institutional transformation."[23] The empirical cases in this article provide additional examples of how institutional conversion can result from endogenous processes of economic and social change during normal times.[24]

In sum, the sequencing, layering, and conversion approaches portray institutional development in an evolutionary manner, while emphasizing its politically contested processes and potentially discontinuous consequences. The next section builds upon these insights by showing how the study of adaptive informal institutions may contribute to identifying the origins of institutional flexibility.

The Role of Adaptive Informal Institutions in a Relational Approach

Theoretically, this article makes two complementary suggestions for furthering our understanding of institutional development—first, adaptive informal institutions may play an analytically meaningful role in explaining endogenous institutional change; and second, the causal process underlying endogenous institutional change is relational, meaning that it derives from interactions among various grassroots actors. When combined with the concepts of reactive sequences and institutional layering, these contentions provide a more compelling explanation for endogenous institutional change in China than the conventional theories reviewed above.

[22] Thelen (fn. 10).

[23] Ibid., 292.

[24] In the Chinese context, X. L. Ding refers to a similar phenomenon as "institutional amphibiousness." Ding, "Institutional Amphibiousness and the Transition from Communism: The Case of China," *British Journal of Political Science* 24, no. 3 (1994).

The case of China demonstrates that even in nondemocratic settings where formal institutions appear to be imposed in top-down fashion rather than subject to popular suffrage, everyday actors may quietly appropriate formal institutions to serve their own ends. This is most likely to occur when there is a gap between the original intentions of formal institutions and the perceived needs and interests of local actors. At the same time, local state agents may collaborate with ordinary people by intentionally misinterpreting the formal institutions that they are supposed to uphold. Such bureaucratic deviance is more likely to be found in situations (1) where different formal institutions have conflicting mandates (a situation that facilitates ignoring one set of rules in order to comply with another); (2) where policy implementation is relatively decentralized; and (3) where local officials have convergent interests with local citizens in a particular policy area (for example, promoting local economic growth, hiding revenues from higher levels of government, protecting local industry, bending rules to attract external investment, and so on). In turn, these collaborative interactions may generate adaptive informal institutions that provide a powerful demonstration effect and prompt policy elites to transform key attributes of the official political and economic orders. Institutions depend on human interaction for their survival and transformation. They are not simply imposed and enforced by state agents and other proprietors of formal institutions. The analytical basis and implications of these claims are clarified below.

The Formal Origins of Adaptive Informal Institutions

The cliché that rules are meant to be broken may indulge latent rebellious sensibilities, but the argument advanced here starts from the assumption that rules are meant to be observed, enforced, and followed. This view of formal institutions resonates with that of sociological institutionalism, which views them as being behaviorally prescriptive and normative: institutions tell actors how they should or should not act.[25] Formal institutions are intended to provide a certain element of predictability and stability to human interactions. Given this assumption, certain outcomes should predictably follow from certain institutions. Even complex multilayered institutional environments can be modeled elegantly to yield convincing explanations for why counterintuitive be-

[25] Walter W. Powell and Paul J. DiMaggio, eds., *The New Institutionalism in Organizational Analysis* (Chicago: University of Chicago Press, 1991).

haviors or policy choices occur.[26] However, formal institutions do not always function as intended: unintended consequences can flow from formal institutions and cases of institutional failure abound throughout the world. This reality, in turn, has inspired entire research agendas devoted to explaining the gap between intended and unintended institutional outcomes.

It is in this context that institutionalists have paid greater attention to "softer variables," such as ideas, norms, and culture[27]—or what others might call informal institutions. The underlying rationale for turning to less formal variables is relatively straightforward. If formal institutions are expected to produce X outcome, but Y occurs instead, then the noise must stem from exogenous informal variables. The analytic shortcoming of this reasoning is that informal institutions effectively become residual variables that are expected to bear the explanatory slack whenever formal institutions can no longer account for the variation in outcomes. And more typically, informal institutions are blamed for inhibiting the normal functioning of formal institutions. Cultural explanations for why certain countries are neither more developed nor more democratic are often cited as cogent examples of how informal institutions may undermine formal ones.[28] As Douglass North explains, in certain contexts "the formal rules change, but the informal constraints do not. In consequence, there develops an ongoing tension between informal constraints and the new formal rules," which may be attributed to "the deep-seated cultural inheritance that underlies many informal constraints."[29]

This observation leaves us with the analytic conflation of informal constraints, informal institutions, and cultural inheritance—and the vague impression that all three compromise the intended functions of formal institutions. The tendency for explanations to privilege informal institutions only when formal ones have failed at their prescribed tasks ironically demonstrates the normative power that scholars reflexively ascribe to formal institutions. Formal institutions implicitly represent the baseline from which we evaluate the desirability of various

[26] George Tsebelis, *Nested Games: Rational Choice in Comparative Politics* (Berkeley: University of California Press, 1990).

[27] Robert Bates, "Contra Contractarianism: Some Reflections on New Institutionalism," *Politics and Society* 16 (September 1988); Sheri Berman, "Ideas, Norms, and Culture in Political Analysis (Review Article)," *Comparative Politics* 33 (January 2001); and Mark Blyth, "Any More Bright Ideas? (Review Article)," *Comparative Politics* 29 (1997).

[28] For example, Lawrence E. Harrison and Samuel P. Huntington, eds., *Culture Matters: How Values Shape Human Progress* (New York: Basic Books, 2000).

[29] North (fn. 12), 91.

outcomes. More recently, however, efforts have been made to theorize directly about the causal impact of informal institutions. Gretchen Helmke and Steven Levitsky, in particular, have proposed a typology for classifying the relationship between formal and informal institutions, such that they may be complementary, accommodating, competing, or substitutive.[30] The typology represents a helpful first step in clarifying the nature and function of informal institutions relative to formal ones, but it does not develop a theory about the processes by which informal institutions emerge and change or are formalized. And indeed, a large part of the challenge in inserting informal institutions into causal explanations is determining where to place them temporally, given that almost no society is completely devoid of some semblance of formal institutions.

For the purposes of capturing the causal effects of informal institutions at a more manageable intermediate stage, this article thus brackets the "deep-seated cultural inheritance" underlying informal institutions and starts with the blank slate of formal institutions, which I define as rules, regulations, policies, and procedures that are promulgated and meant to be enforced by entities and agents generally recognized as being official.[31] As in my earlier work, this study regards formal institutions as being both constraining and enabling.[32] On the one hand, formal institutions limit the range of officially permissible behavior. On the other hand, multilayered institutional environments offer transformative possibilities; in particular, formal institutional contexts with overlapping jurisdiction and inconsistent or unrealistic mandates provide opportunities for actors to adjust, ignore, or evade discrete portions of formal institutions.

Initially, many of these adaptive responses may appear to be idiosyncratic or isolated. However, over time they may evolve into "adaptive informal institutions," which I define as regularized patterns of interaction that emerge as adaptive responses to the constraints and opportunities of formal institutions, that violate or transcend the scope

[30] Helmke and Levitsky, "Informal Institutions and Comparative Politics," *Perspectives on Politics* 2 (December 2004). Five types of informal institutions are identified in Hans-Joachim Lauth, "Informal Institutions and Democracy," *Democratization* 7 (Winter 2000).

[31] This definition draws from Helmke and Levitsky (fn. 30, 727) but also includes public policies because they typically have institutional consequences. Pierson suggests: "[I]t makes good sense to think of public policies as important institutions. For the individuals and social organizations that make up civil society, public policies are clearly very central rules governing their interactions"; Paul Pierson, *Politics in Time: History, Institutions, and Social Analysis* (Princeton: Princeton University Press, 2004), 165.

[32] Kellee S. Tsai, *Back-Alley Banking: Private Entrepreneurs in China* (Ithaca, N.Y.: Cornell University Press, 2002).

of formal institutions, and that are widely practiced. In order for this intermediate stage of institutional adaptation to develop, at least the base-level guardians of formal institutions need to be complicit in allowing the institutional distortions to occur, over and over again. As such, adaptive informal institutions are more likely to arise and thrive in localities where the enforcers of formal institutions and the creators of informal adaptations have convergent interests. By definition, this means that while local state and nonstate actors benefit mutually from the resulting adaptive informal institutions, those arrangements transgress existing formal institutional mandates. This is the first part of my argument in a longer sequence explaining endogenous institutional development.

The second part concerns what happens after adaptive informal institutions emerge. At the most basic level, the proliferation of adaptive informal institutions may undermine the legitimacy of formal institutions. The relevance of institutions, whether formal or informal, depends on their capacity to guide human perceptions and practices. But do the enforcers of formal institutions discipline, ignore, or incorporate the actors sustaining adaptive informal institutions? The answer to this question is historically and nationally contingent. In the case of China, adaptive informal institutions that threaten to undermine social stability or to compromise the CCP's political monopoly are likely to provoke official censure. Official tolerance for mass mobilization and political dissent remains limited. Meanwhile, crackdowns on adaptive informal institutions in the economic realm are most likely to occur during political campaigns against corruption and at other times when there is heightened political sensitivity to local deviations from national mandates.[33] But if the law enforcers themselves are party to the offending activities, then efforts to curb them are unlikely to be sustainable beyond those priority moments.

Beyond China, we may expect that when adaptive informal institutions constitute flagrant forms of criminal activity, they will elicit the attention of law-enforcement entities. Yet even the definition of "flagrant" criminal behavior is contextually variable. In some cases, embezzlement of state assets would constitute flagrant criminal activity, but under other circumstances, asset stripping of public enterprises by managers and workers might be so common that it fails to trigger

[33] For example, distinct cycles of crackdowns on local financial institutions such as trust and investment companies were apparent and corresponded with the broader policy reform cycles through the late 1990s, when Zhu Rongji was premier. Correspondence with Yi-feng Tao, November 10, 2006.

strong official reactions. For the present purposes, I will simply define flagrant forms of criminal activity as illegal practices that are readily discernible and have immediate social costs that would be difficult to cover up. An example of this would be Ponzi schemes: by the time they collapse, they have usually entangled large numbers of enraged people.[34] Another example would be violation of food and drug safety standards, which endangers lives and motivates regulatory development.[35]

In contrast, adaptive informal institutions that merely stretch the limits of formal institutions or create new patterns of interaction not explicitly governed by formal institutions may endure and even thrive unencumbered for some length of time. The adaptive practices discussed in this article fall into these quasi-legal and extralegal gray areas. They are institutions that arise in a context where some local political and economic actors face incentives to promote private sector development but where formal institutions at the national level lag in adjusting to new businesses and their associated externalities.

This focus on the origins and effects of adaptive informal institutions resonates with the logics of nonreinforcing event sequences and structural friction found in the multiple institutional layers of historical institutionalism and American political development. When adaptive informal institutions arise in response to the dissonance between existing formal institutions and the operational preferences of actors, adaptive informal institutions start to redirect and undermine the previously self-enforcing formal institutions.[36] In this narrative, the use of preexisting formal institutions as the analytical baseline against which actors devise coping strategies is important. Indeed, the formal-informal-formal sequence represents the core of the argument. The next section illustrates this contention more concretely with three instances of major institutional changes relating to private sector development in China.

The Political Economy of Adaptive Informal Institutions in Reform-Era China

As historical institutionalists have pointed out, most institutions do not exist in isolation from one another. Instead, instances of "institutional coupling" may be observed among clusters of institutions that are

[34] Mitchell Zuckoff, *Ponzi's Scheme: The True Story of a Financial Legend* (New York: Random House, 2005).

[35] Waikeung Tam and Dali Yang, "Food Safety and the Development of Regulatory Institutions in China," *Asian Perspective* 29, no. 4 (2005).

[36] Cf. Greif and Laitin (fn. 16).

mutually dependent.[37] The following cases of institutional transformations relating to private sector development in China should be viewed in this light. Certain changes in formal institutions may be traced to particular informal practices and adaptive informal institutions. In turn, the resulting changes in formal institutions facilitate complementary adjustments in other formal institutions. Specifically, the examples below show how informal practices at the ground level paved the way for legalization of the private sector, which attracted the participation of party members in entrepreneurial activities. The rise of "red capitalists" then influenced the formal incorporation of capitalists into the CCP. In turn, the preceding adaptive informal institutions enabled reform-oriented elites to justify revisions to the PRC constitution that recognize the existence and contribution of the private economy.

Red Hat Disguises and Private Sector Development

In contemporary China "wearing a red hat" (*dai hongmaozi*) refers to the practice of registering a business as a collective enterprise when it is really privately managed and owned. A related disguise is paying a state-owned enterprise for use of its name in running a private business; those are called "hang-on" enterprises (*guahu qiye*) because they are registered as appendages to established government operations. Red hat operations emerged as an adaptive informal institution during the first decade of economic reform, when private enterprises with more than eight employees (*siying qiye*) were not legally permitted.[38] Therefore, until 1988, China's private sector technically consisted of only "individual households" (*getihu*) with fewer than eight employees.[39] In reality, however, many of the collective enterprises were larger private businesses wearing red hats.[40] One entrepreneur I interviewed in Huizhou, Guangdong, for instance, explained that he was able to open a sizable piglet store as early as 1978 because he ran it under the auspices of the local township's communal supply shop.[41] Another entrepreneur in Nanjing, Jiangsu, proudly recounted that in 1982 she was able to run

[37] Pierson (fn. 31), 224–27.

[38] The eight-employee limit has an ideological rationale: in *Das Kapital* (1867), Marx indicated that capitalist producers with more than eight employees were exploitative and surplus accumulating, while those with fewer than eight workers were nonexploitative household producing units.

[39] For more detail, see Susan Young, *Private Business and Economic Reform in China* (Armonk, N.Y.: M. E. Sharpe, 1995).

[40] Barry Naughton, "Institutional Innovation and Privatization from Below," *American Economic Review, Papers and Proceedings* 84 (May 1994).

[41] Author interview with anonymous entrepreneur, Huizhou, Guangdong, October 16, 2002. As part of a larger project, I conducted interviews with more than three hundred Chinese entrepreneurs and officials over the course of 2001 to 2005. A list of interviewees is available in Tsai (fn. 7).

a large and lucrative clothing business as a collective enterprise, while running the same business as a private one would have been "impossible."[42] By the time private enterprises were permitted, an estimated half a million businesses were already using the red hat disguise. And in certain localities, it was commonly known that between 90 and 95 percent of registered collective enterprises wore red hats.[43]

After the 1988 regulations permitting private enterprises—and the politically rooted economic downturn of 1989–92 following the Tiananmen Square crisis—the private sector boomed. Between 1990 and 2000, the average annual growth rate in the number of registered private businesses was 32.8 percent, the number of people employed in the private sector grew at an average annual rate of 29.2 percent, their registered capitalization grew at 65.1 percent, their value added to the GDP grew at 58.7 percent, and their volume of retail sales grew at a rate of 70.2 percent.[44] In the interim a network of formal institutions governing the private sector had developed throughout the country.

On the most superficial level, it is tempting to attribute China's rapid private sector development to official policies and institutions regulating the nonstate economy. I would argue, however, that China's formal institutions have presented local state and economic actors with more of a constraining than a permissive environment for private capital accumulation—and key to our purposes here, local actors have exercised agency in manipulating formal institutions to their advantage.

Throughout the 1980s and most of the 1990s, private entrepreneurs experienced not only a social stigma but also political persecution for being profit oriented. There was considerable political uncertainty about the trajectory of economic reform, and private entrepreneurs were publicly criticized during the national campaigns against "spiritual pollution" in 1983–84 and against "bourgeois liberalization" in 1987. On a day-to-day basis, entrepreneurs were also subjected to arbitrary treatment by tax collectors and harassment by other bureaucrats. By contrast, state and collective enterprises received favorable treatment relative to private ones in terms of tax breaks, bank loans, and use of land. Those were the operating realities that business owners faced beneath the impressive statistics.

Why, then, were entrepreneurs willing to enter and stay in business? As suggested above, one way for entrepreneurs to avoid social and political

[42] Author interview with anonymous entrepreneur, Nanjing, Jiangsu, October 10, 2002.

[43] Kristin Parris, "Local Initiative and National Reform: The Wenzhou Model of Development," *China Quarterly* 134 (June 1993).

[44] *Zhongguo tongji nianjian* (China Statistical Yearbook) (various years).

ostracism was to wear a red hat. This adaptive strategy was so widespread that "wearing a red hat" became (and remains) a common term in everyday discourse. The practice became institutionalized as a standard, albeit informal, operating practice for private entrepreneurs.[45] Yet the actual process through which this occurred was not simply a case of entrepreneurs deceiving local bureaucrats; instead, the actions of agents were collaborative and reflexively strategic. Most local cadres knew exactly what they were doing when they accepted, or perhaps extracted, a registration fee from a local entrepreneur to run a collective enterprise. Due to fiscal decentralization and the hardening of local budget constraints, cadres in many rural localities had a vested interest in allowing profitable businesses to operate and contribute to local revenues regardless of their true ownership status.[46] As a result, hundreds of thousands of both state and nonstate actors were complicit in popularizing the red hat phenomenon. Meanwhile, China's collective sector flourished and represented the basis of rapid rural industrialization.[47]

In the spirit of Deng Xiaoping's dictum to focus on practical results rather than ideology, when central-level elites realized that so many collectives were really private enterprises, it was futile—and indeed, impractical—to insist on limiting the private economy to household producing units with fewer than eight employees. Although conservative or "leftist" political elites would have preferred to restrict the nonstate sector, both the popularity and economic effectiveness of wearing a red hat gave reformers concrete evidence and, thus, political support for expanding the scope of China's nascent private economy. Influential scholars, such as Yu Guangyuan and Xue Muqiao from the Chinese Academy of Social Sciences, drew on their observations of local empirical realities to help reformist leaders reach a consensus about the appropriate next steps in China's reform process. During a pivotal academic and policy meeting held in Beijing in 1986, they reasoned that since China was still in the initial stage of socialism, the following points were applicable: (1) it would be impossible to avoid private sector development; (2) the advantages of developing the private economy

[45] On local variation in the use of red hat strategies and development of private property rights, see Jean Oi and Andrew G. Walder, eds., *Property Rights and Economic Reform in China* (Stanford, Calif.: Stanford University Press, 1999); and Susan H. Whiting, *Power and Wealth in Rural China* (New York: Cambridge University Press, 2001).

[46] By the same token, Whiting (fn. 45) points out that local officials and entrepreneurs "shared a common interest in the security of shareholding cooperatives" as legitimate collective enterprises in localities that were dominated by genuine collective enterprises, as well as localities that were dominated by private businesses (pp. 163–64).

[47] Jean C. Oi, *Rural China Takes Off: Institutional Foundations of Economic Reform* (Berkeley: University of California Press, 1999).

would outweigh the disadvantages; and (3) the private sector could still be subject to state guidance and control under a socialist system.[48]

Broad-based agreement on these key points about China's "initial stage of socialism" paved the way for shifts in the official guiding principles and policies of the party-state. On the party side, at the 13th National Congress of the CCP in 1987, Premier Zhao Ziyang announced that "cooperative, individual and private sectors of the economy in both urban and rural areas should all be encouraged to expand. . . . [W]e must formulate policies and enact laws governing the private sector as soon as possible, in order to protect its legitimate interest."[49] Following the party's lead, on the state side, the National People's Congress passed a constitutional amendment accepting Zhao's proposal in April 1988, and two months later the PRC State Council issued regulations governing "private enterprises" with eight or more employees. In an acknowledgment that these regulations were really post hoc sanctioning of ground-level realities, official publications disclosed that by then China already had 225,000 private enterprises employing 3.6 million employees with an average of 16 employees per business—that is, twice the number of workers that individual private businesses were permitted to employ.[50]

In sum, the practice of wearing a red hat is an example of how an adaptive informal institution contributed to the institutional conversion of a formal regulation, the collective registration status. Camouflaging the true ownership structure of a business rendered the formal distinction in nomenclature between collective and private enterprises virtually meaningless. By the same token, as an adaptive informal institution, the red hat practice also became an increasingly prominent institutional layer in China's once-limited field of corporate organizational types. Instead of displacing the collective sector, red hat enterprises represented an additional form of collective enterprise; this innovative layer not only expanded the institutional space in which private businesses operated but also created a politically acceptable rationale for devising a more transparent registration status for larger private enterprises. In this case, the impetus for institutional change stemmed from two strains of "structural friction" in China's political economy—first, there was tension between preexisting institutions that privileged the collective

[48] Author correspondence with anonymous government researcher, Chinese Academy of Social Sciences, Beijing, November 19, 2006.

[49] *Beijing Review*, November 9–15, 1987, cited in Rashid Malik, *Chinese Entrepreneurs in the Economic Development of China* (Westport: Praeger, 1997), 15.

[50] *Beijing Review* (July 18–24, 1988), 6, cited in Malik (fn. 49).

sector and policies that sanctioned limited development of the private sector; and second, there was an inconsistency between fiscal reforms that enabled rural localities to retain more revenues and national restrictions on larger private enterprises. Both state and economic actors coped with these institutional incongruencies by popularizing the adaptive informal institution of wearing a red hat. The economic success and widespread use of this adaptive informal institution then provided reformers with the requisite evidence that expanding the scope of the private sector would enhance China's productive forces during the initial stage of socialism. As we will see below, ultimately, the adaptive informal institution of wearing a red hat not only influenced the legalization of private enterprises with more than eight employees but also provided the basis for subsequent institutional changes in the CCP and state constitution.

The Chinese Communist Party's Incorporation of Capitalists

The first generation of profit-oriented business operators in post-Mao China generally came from two different backgrounds. The "individual entrepreneurs" (*getihu*) consisted of street peddlers, itinerant vendors, and small retail business owners who subsisted on the fringes of the socialist-era economy and did not have the benefits of state employment. The popular perception of *getihu* was that they were criminals and social outcasts who lacked alternative employment options; hence, they experienced considerable political and social discrimination. In reality, however, most were simply underemployed farmers who no longer had to work in collectives.

At the other extreme, the other strata of society active in commerce were "cadre entrepreneurs" and "red capitalists" who used their privileged political status to run businesses indirectly or help others run red hat operations. Even though CCP members were not allowed to operate private businesses, it was apparent throughout the 1980s and 1990s that many were active participants in the nonstate sector. Indeed, official surveys reveal an increasing proportion of self-identified CCP members among private entrepreneurs over time, such that only 7 percent of business owners admitted to being party members in 1991, but by 2003 over one-third admitted to being party members.[51] It is reasonable to assume that the earlier official figures underestimate the true proportion of party members in the private sector due to the po-

[51] China State Administration for Industry and Commerce (SAIC), *Zhongguo siying jingji nianjian* (China Private Economy Yearbook) (various years).

litico-ideological sensitivity concerning the appropriate relationship between the CCP and "market socialism with Chinese characteristics." For many years, the uneasy coexistence or "friction" between China's official socialist ideology and the reality of private sector development accounted for the simultaneous growth of business owners among party members—and the underreporting of party members in official surveys of private entrepreneurs.

On the CCP's eightieth anniversary on July 1, 2001, however, then General Secretary Jiang Zemin gave a landmark speech widely interpreted as inviting private entrepreneurs to join the party. Although the rationale was weaved into Jiang Zemin's "Theory of the Three Represents," which was supposed to represent the theoretical extension of Marxism-Leninism, Mao Zedong Thought, and Deng Xiaoping Theory, it actually made the controversial recommendation that the party should represent "the most advanced forces of production, the most advanced cultural forces, and the interests of the overwhelming majority of people." The CCP had launched a mass-media campaign publicizing the Three Represents leading up to the anniversary, but it was the July 1 speech, followed by the 16th Party Congress in late 2002, that clarified the implication of the "theory," that is, that the CCP should not discriminate against private entrepreneurs and should in fact embrace them because they are contributing (the most) to China's economic development. A number of the party's old guard disapproved of the sharp ideological turn advocated by Jiang and his supporters. Even online chat rooms and message boards filled with colorful, passionately argued objections to the selling out of the CCP.[52]

As such, it is remarkable that the CCP agreed to change—and indeed, reverse—its former ideological depiction of capitalists as exploitative "class enemies." Bruce Dickson suggests that allowing private entrepreneurs into the party was a strategic decision to incorporate a growing and increasingly wealthy portion of Chinese society.[53] It was an effort to preempt autonomous political organization on the part of private business owners. While this interpretation of the party's decision makes sense, I would add that the underlying causal mechanisms leading to this decision were rooted in the growing power of the informal rules of the game that had evolved over the first two decades of economic reform. Party members were already active in the private sector well

[52] For example, "Deng Liqun, Others, Criticize Jiang Zemin for Agreeing to Admit Capitalists into the CPC," originally posted on http://www.renminbao.com on July 20, 2001, translated text from FBIS-China, July 28, 2001.

[53] Dickson (fn. 7).

before private entrepreneurs were formally permitted to join the party. But how was this possible, given that China remains an authoritarian regime dominated by a Leninist party?

As discussed, the adaptive informal institution of wearing a red hat offered Communist Party members an ideologically appropriate cover for participating in for-profit activities. This, in turn, led to the adaptive practice of being a "red capitalist" (*hong zibenjia*). Because private entrepreneurs were explicitly banned from joining the party after 1989, wearing a red hat became a safer way for party members to run large businesses. And local party cadres were willing to look the other way because red capitalists often contributed more to the local economy than did ordinary entrepreneurs. For illustrative purposes, consider the experience of a furniture manufacturer in rural Hebei province.[54] After earning his bachelor's degree from the local Communist Party school, Mr. Hong (pseudonym) worked as a high-ranking manager in a state-owned enterprise for more than a dozen years. By the time he was thirty-six years old in 1991, however, Mr. Hong was ready for a big change. He had harbored dreams of running his own business for a while but knew that it would "look bad" if a party member entered the private sector. To avoid political trouble, he registered his furniture factory as a collective enterprise. Given that Mr. Hong was well regarded in his locality, he had little difficulty negotiating with the local bureaucracy for the right to wear a red hat. In fact, I met Mr. Hong through local officials who introduced him as "an upstanding red capitalist." Besides being an economically successful party member, Mr. Hong serves as a deputy in the local People's Congress and serves as the vice director of the local chamber of commerce. Mr. Hong is hardly the typical business owner, but local government hosts selected him, despite his wearing a red hat, as an interviewee because they were proud of his local commercial and political stature.

By the early 2000s the spread of red capitalists presented the party with the critical dilemma of whether to condemn their economic activities or embrace them: 19.8 percent of entrepreneurs surveyed by official entities in 2000 indicated that they were already CCP members.[55] Should such a large percentage of business owners remain politically marginalized? After consulting with provincial and subprovincial officials throughout China, the party's core leadership decided that it was in the interest of continued economic growth, as well as party re-

[54] Author interview with anonymous entrepreneur, Liangfeng, Hebei, August 20, 2002.
[55] SAIC, *Private Economy Yearbook* (2005).

juvenation and survival, to legitimize the existing red capitalists and co-opt other private entrepreneurs.[56] Shortly after the party lifted the ban on cultivating capitalist members, a party theoretician explained, "If our Party doesn't build more branches [under the circumstances of rapid growth in the nonpublic economic organizations], then other social forces will attract those people. If the Party doesn't open up its organizations [to private entrepreneurs], then other organizations will hold activities for them."[57] The report further highlighted the relative underrepresentation of business owners in the party: "[B]y the end of 2002 there were 2.1 million Party members in non-public economic organizations, which accounts for only around two percent of the total membership, and over 80 percent of foreign-invested enterprises and private enterprises do not have Party members."[58]

Within a relatively short period of time, the party line shifted from banning capitalists to welcoming them. Such a policy reversal would have been difficult to justify in the absence of preexisting grassroots deviations from the party line. Wearing a red hat enabled party members to become red capitalists, with the result that the occupational composition of the party was changed from within. As employees of the party-state began running their own businesses, albeit disguised as collective ventures, the party's ban on private entrepreneurs became increasingly unrealistic, if not anachronistic. Although Jiang Zemin is generally credited (or blamed) for allowing capitalists into the party, the decision was not the impulsive act of a dictator. The decision did not occur in a societal void, as evidenced by the series of discussions with local officials throughout the country. And at a deeper causal level, all of the informal coping strategies that both state and nonstate actors had reproduced in their daily interactions took on an institutional reality of their own, thereby challenging national leaders to adapt preexisting formal institutions to assimilate these hitherto informal practices. The cumulative effects of this dynamic can also be seen in revisions to the PRC constitution that have become increasingly favorable toward the private sector.

[56] These consultations "took place over a period of perhaps two years." Joseph Fewsmith, "Rethinking the Role of the CCP: Explicating Jiang Zemin's Party Anniversary Speech," *China Leadership Monitor* 1 (Winter 2002), 3.

[57] Li Yan, "Qieshi jiaqiang fei gongyouzhi jingji zhuzhi dangjian gongzuo buduan guangda dang de gongzuo de fugai mian," in SAIC, *Zhongguo siying jingji nianjian 2002–2004* (China Private Economy Yearbook) (Beijing: Zhonghua gongshang lianhe chubanshe, 2005), 107.

[58] Ibid., 108.

Private Sector–Friendly Revisions to the PRC Constitution

Revisions to the PRC Constitution have generally lagged behind developments in practice. Of the various constitutional changes that have occurred since 1982, the first two revisions represent reactive formalization of local practices and realities. Meanwhile, the most recent revision puts forth an ambitious objective that was inspired by the two adaptive informal institutions discussed above—the wearing of a red hat and the proliferation of red capitalists. Of all the institutional changes discussed thus far, the following sequence of constitutional revisions illustrates most organically the article's argument about the causal mechanisms underlying endogenous dynamics of formal institutional change.

First, as mentioned earlier, in 1988 the First Session of the Seventh NPC added a paragraph to Article 11 that "permits the private sector of the economy to exist and develop within the limits prescribed by law." The paragraph also stated, "The private sector of the economy is a complement to the socialist economy." This new section provided the legal basis for allowing "private enterprises" (*siying qiye*) with more than eight employees to operate, while indicating that the private sector would still be subject to state control, as indicated in the final clause of the paragraph: "The state protects the lawful rights and interests of the private sector of the economy, and exercises guidance, supervision, and control over the private sector of the economy." This formal recognition of larger private businesses trailed ground-level practices, as ambitious entrepreneurs were already scaling up in the guise of collective enterprises, but going forward, legal recognition of private enterprises also rendered the adaptive informal institution of red hat disguises less necessary.

Second, in 1999 the Second Session of the Ninth NPC amended the aforementioned paragraph in Article 11 to say, "Individual, private and other non-public economies that exist within the limits prescribed by law are major components of the socialist market economy." The 1999 revisions also included a statement indicating, "The People's Republic of China governs the country according to law and makes it a socialist country ruled by law." The combination of elevating the nonstate sector to a "major component" of the economy and introducing the notion that the country is governed by the rule of law signaled a more legitimate and secure status for the private sector. The reason these amendments may not appear to be ground breaking is because, once again, the constitutional revisions followed changes that were already taking place in the Chinese economy. By 1999 spontaneous "privatization" or restructuring (*gaizhi*) of collective enterprises had already been occurring in rural China for five years.[59] Due to various local innovations in property rights structures, the nonstate sector was already a "major component" of the economy by the time the constitution acknowledged it.

Third, in 2004 the Second Session of the Tenth NPC made the more radical revision of encouraging private sector development and protecting private property rights under the constitution. Article 11 was changed again to stipulate:

> The state protects the lawful rights and interests of the private sector of the economy, including individual and private businesses. The state encourages, supports and guides the development of the private sector, and exercises supervision and administration over the sector according to law.

And Article 13 introduced the following: "The lawful private property of citizens shall not be encroached upon." Meanwhile, the Theory of the Three Represents—which makes the controversial claim that the party represents the "most advanced forces of production" (that is, private entrepreneurs)—was incorporated into state ideology alongside "Marxism, Leninism, Mao Zedong Thought and the Theories of Deng Xiaoping." Since the 16th Party Congress in 2002 had incorporated upholding the Three Represents into the CCP's mission statement, it was not surprising that the state constitution would be similarly amended.

Unlike the first two amendments discussed above, however, the constitutional stipulation that private property rights would be protected should be viewed as an objective rather than post hoc recognition of ground-level realities. Although certain adaptive informal institutions enable economic actors to engage in contractual exchanges as if they were guaranteed by a formal legal system of private property rights,[60] the rise of serious disputes concerning asset ownership demonstrates that such arrangements are not immune to government intervention/expropriation. This is a risk that all adaptive informal institutions face, of course, but the point here is that because the most recent constitutional revisions have more complex systemic implications for China's political economy, lags in actual implementation should be expected. Formal protection of private property rights requires strengthening the

[59] As Whiting (fn. 45) points out, privatization of collectives was the result of changes in the fiscal system, the cadre evaluation system, and the national political economic environment. Furthermore, by 1999 the selling off of small and medium-size state-owned enterprises, announced at the 15th Party Congress in 1997, was gaining momentum.

[60] Oi and Walder (fn. 45).

institutions that support the rule of law.[61] As Yu An, a Tsinghua University law professor who served on the constitution's drafting committee, commented:

> Some revised articles are an acknowledgement of the current situation, while others are new stipulations. That means adjustments should be made to existing laws, or new laws should be implemented. . . . The Constitution itself can hardly regulate the particular behavior of the government and the people. Without significant adjustment of current common laws, the impact of the constitutional revision may be greatly reduced.[62]

In the interim, various adaptive informal institutions will continue to serve as self-enforcing substitutes for property rights.

Although the series of constitutional revisions relating to the private sector appears to be a linear progression of increasing official recognition and legal protection of its interests, there was nothing automatic or predetermined about the development of various formal institutions to support the private sector. In the context of evolving property rights regimes in rural China, Susan Whiting observes, "[E]ven dramatic change occurs incrementally. The presence of complementarities among institutions and policies means that singular changes interact to bring about more fundamental changes in the incentives and constraints in the institutional environment."[63] I would add that in the case of China's constitutional revisions, the "singular changes" are rooted in the informal adaptive strategies of grassroots actors.

Given the opacity of China's political system, it is challenging to prove with definitive data that the spread of adaptive informal institutions used by private entrepreneurs directly influenced the various constitutional amendments. Based on published sources, as well as field interviews with government officials, elite intellectuals, and private entrepreneurs, however, we may infer the plausibility of the counterfactual to my argument. That is, in the absence of the adaptive informal institutions discussed above, it is unlikely that reform-oriented elites would have found the pro–private sector constitutional amendments either desirable or feasible. Both the economic success of private businesses and the popularity of private entrepreneurship among party members offered reformers evidence (against "leftist" or conservative

[61] Donald Clarke, Peter Murrell, and Susan Whiting, "The Role of Law in China's Economic Development," The George Washington University Law School Public Law and Legal Theory Working Paper no. 187 (2006).

[62] Yu An, cited in "Constitutional Revision Requires Law Adjustment," *China Business Weekly*, March 8, 2004.

[63] Whiting (fn. 45), 299.

leaders) that enhancing the scope of the private sector would be in the country's political and economic interest. Indeed, various legal scholars were already pushing for the protection of private property rights during the drafting meetings of the 1999 constitutional revision, but their recommendations were shelved due to opposition by more conservative party members.[64] Only after the party came to terms with red capitalist members in 2002 was it politically possible to revisit the earlier constitutional proposals to protect private property.

While there was still internal debate over the inclusion of protecting private property in the consultative processes leading up to the 2004 constitutional revision, by 2003 and early 2004 proponents of private property rights were able to build their case by implying that there was societal support for constitutional revision along those lines. Even though private entrepreneurs themselves never mobilized from below to lobby for constitutional protection of their assets, reformers strategically solicited input from the official mass association representing private entrepreneurs, the All-China Federation of Industry and Commerce (ACFIC, *gongshang lian*). In practice, state-sponsored mass associations in Leninist systems usually serve to transmit official policy to constituent members in a state corporatist fashion, but they are also meant in principle to represent the interests of its members. As such, during the earlier rounds of constitutional revision, ACFIC was charged with convening small-scale forums with entrepreneurs throughout the country to gather their opinions about the upcoming constitutional revisions.[65] Prior to the 2004 revision, however, the official narrative of the process is that ACFIC initiated the consultative discussions with entrepreneurs and that it played an important role in advocating constitutional protection of private property.[66] In other words, reformers gave ACFIC credit for representing the voice of private entrepreneurs and pushing for the private property clause to create a stronger political case for revising the constitution along the lines that they had been hoping for at least five years earlier. In reality, private entrepreneurs themselves were remarkably absent from the actual process, but the cumulative effect of their adaptive informal institutions and the changes that they engendered in formal institutions governing the private sector enabled reformers to justify further protections on their behalf. The

[64] Lian Xisheng, former vice chair of the China Constitution Society, cited in "Amendments Protect Private Property," *China Business Weekly*, January 4, 2004.

[65] Author correspondence with Scott Kennedy, University of Indiana-Bloomington, November 2, 2006.

[66] Author correspondence with anonymous government researcher, Chinese Academy of Social Sciences, Beijing, November 12, 2006.

causal mechanisms were indirect, informal, incremental, and fundamentally political.

Conclusion

How can we explain major institutional changes when they occur in the absence of external shocks, domestic crises, or societal demands? Recent literature on institutional development is effective in describing different manifestations of endogenous institutional change, but the causal mechanisms in these accounts remain vague, especially when it comes to change in nondemocratic regimes. This article thus builds upon the notions of institutional sequencing, layering, and conversion in historical institutionalism by proposing the following: first, that the causal mechanism for institutional change depends on interactions between various state and nonstate actors; and second, that adaptive informal institutions may play an important role in endogenous accounts of such change. Specifically, adaptive informal institutions may emerge out of the collaborative coping strategies of state and nonstate actors when they find formal institutions too constraining. In the case of reform-era China, the contextual conditions that are conducive to the emergence of adaptive informal institutions include conflicting mandates among different formal institutions, a bureaucratic structure with a certain degree of decentralization in policy implementation, and policy areas in which local state and nonstate actors have convergent interests. Over time the diffusion of adaptive informal institutions facilitates substantial transformations in formal institutions by providing elites with political support for introducing key reforms. This reactive sequence of institutional change can occur even in authoritarian regimes where political institutions are not necessarily expected to be responsive to grassroots interactions.

Furthermore, a central component of my argument is that this apparent political "responsiveness" occurs through indirect means. Private entrepreneurs as a group have not lobbied directly for protection of their property rights or for membership in the Chinese Communist Party.[67] Instead, people from different social backgrounds entered the private sector as a self-help strategy to enhance their material welfare and in the process appeared to party-state elites as an increasingly important constituency. In the course of their daily interactions with one

[67] Business owners lobby for narrower, sector-specific issues such as setting industry standards and prices. Scott Kennedy, *The Business of Lobbying in China* (Cambridge: Harvard University Press, 2005).

another and with local staff of the party-state, business owners have had a structural impact on the direction of formal institutional reforms. Therefore, even though the regime has pursued policies that imply a strategy of corporatist inclusion of private capital, this article suggests that the causal mechanism underlying these preemptive corporatist efforts lies in the cumulative effect of informal interactions at the local level rather than in purely economic or social pressures.

Ultimately, the ability of the nominally socialist regime to accommodate private sector development is only one expression of the broader transformation that has occurred in China's institutional context. Although the PRC is still an authoritarian regime, the nature of its political economy has changed so dramatically that China scholars have felt compelled to qualify its categorical nomenclature with various adjectives to distinguish it from the party-state of the 1950s and 1960s.[68] Rather than worrying about whether contemporary China is now a bureaucratic-authoritarian regime or a capitalist developmental state, however, greater attention should be paid to the causal mechanisms and processes underlying the regime's institutional resilience. Informal interactions and informal institutions may represent an important, yet typically overlooked part of the story.

Indeed, beyond the case of China there is comparative analytic value in viewing adaptive informal institutions as vehicles for change in formal institutions. Attending to the rise of informal adaptive responses expands the scope of those factors that we typically deem to be relevant in political analysis. Local innovations, evasive tactics, and other extralegal practices often seem distant from the hallowed ranks of political elites and their associated formal political institutions. The concept of adaptive informal institutions brings them a little closer. Sporadic acts of noncompliance or random criminality are not at issue. By contrast, strategic responses that are repeated, widespread, systematically reproduced, and therefore "institutionalized" through informal praxis generally attract official attention in some form or other. Determining when and whether adaptive informal institutions will have such catalytic effects is politically contingent and requires empirical study of both the high politics *and* the apparently apolitical low politics of grassroots adaptations to formal institutions.

[68] Richard Baum and Alexei Shevchenko, "The State of the State," in Merle Goldman and Roderick MacFarquar, eds., *The Paradox of Post-Mao Reforms* (Cambridge: Harvard Contemporary China Series, 1999).

Journal of Contemporary China (2010), **19**(65), June, 437–460

Routledge
Taylor & Francis Group

China's Distinctive System: can it be a model for others?

BARRY NAUGHTON*

The idea of the 'Beijing Consensus' does not accurately describe what has happened in China, nor does it represent a consensus among Chinese economists and policy-makers. This article presents six distinctive features of China's economic development, and argues that while each provides important lessons, none are easily copied by other developing countries. The intertwining of state and market in China is at the root of China's most distinctive developmental features. However, the specific character of the Chinese system and the way in which government and business relations have been structured cannot be readily replicated in other countries.

The term 'Beijing Consensus' is an oxymoron, which is why it is appealing. The term manages to suggest both that orthodoxy is being shattered, and that around the corner, in the next *hutong*, a new set of pragmatic guidelines are about to take shape. This sense of dynamism tickles our interest, while also distracting us from the more precise meaning of the terms. After all, 'consensus' signifies that understanding is held universally, while 'Beijing' stands for what is probably the most unusual political-economic regime in the world. A Beijing Consensus can exist only if the unusual experiences of 'Beijing' turn out to illuminate the broad principles that shape effective development policy around the world. In current popular usage, 'Beijing Consensus' implies that a common understanding is coming together, but based on an exceptional case. This is possible, of course, but in order to achieve the level of a paradoxical truth—as opposed to a simple logical contradiction—its proponents would need to demonstrate (a) why the distinctive approaches of Chinese policy-makers were the key to China's remarkable rapid growth; and (b) why those distinctive approaches are also applicable to other, dramatically different, contexts. So far, nobody has come anywhere close to demonstrating either one of these propositions.

When John Williamson coined the term 'Washington Consensus' in 1988, his intention was to describe the unexpected emergence of a rare degree of unanimity among economists giving policy advice, particularly those economists affiliated with

*Barry Naughton is the So Kwanlok Chair of Chinese and International Affairs at the Graduate School of International Relations and Pacific Studies at the University of California, San Diego, where he has been a professor since 1988. Professor Naughton has published extensively on the Chinese economy, with a focus on four interrelated areas: economic transition; industry and technology; foreign trade; and Chinese political economy. His most recent book is *The Chinese Economy: Transitions and Growth*, a comprehensive survey of the Chinese economy that was published by MIT Press in 2007. The paper was originally presented to the 6th International Symposium of the Center for China–US Cooperation, *'Washington Consensus' versus 'Beijing Consensus': Sustainability of China's Development Model*, Denver, CO, 30–31 May 2008.

ISSN 1067-0564 print/ 1469-9400 online/10/650437-24 © 2010 Taylor & Francis
DOI: 10.1080/10670561003666079

the major multi-lateral financial institutions based in Washington, DC. His original emphasis was not so much on the strength of the consensus, but rather on the fact that a consensus existed at all. The natural state of policy advisers, no doubt, is disagreement and debate, so it was unusual that Williamson could actually identify and list what he subsequently called the 'lowest common denominator' of Washington policy advice.[1] Williamson's original consensus, then, was 'in Washington', and not 'of Washington'. This was meaningful because so much power and influence is concentrated in Washington, and the term achieved immediate polemic resonance because it acknowledged the concentration of power in Washington while also suggesting the reign of orthodoxy and closed minds. By contrast, it is not really meaningful to speak of a consensus 'in Beijing', because Beijing economists disagree on many fundamental issues. Even if you could list a series of propositions on which Beijing economists did agree, this would only be 'a' Beijing Consensus, and not 'the' Beijing Consensus. Moreover, there are no significant institutions that propagate the viewpoints of Beijing economists on a global stage.

Instead, the dawning recognition that China had done well economically *without* following the Washington Consensus contributed to the erosion of the Washington Consensus style of economic policy prescription-writing, which may now be headed for collapse in the wake of the US and global financial crisis. This reversal of fortunes has given Beijing policy-makers increased confidence in their own approach and increased their willingness to pursue and defend policies that correspond to their own conception of development *and* their own interests; but these shifts hardly constitute a 'Beijing Consensus'. It is no doubt true that power and influence are shifting. 'Washington is declining and the Washington consensus is crumbling, while Beijing is rising and ... ' and it is tempting to fill in the dots with a 'rising Beijing consensus'. However, it would be strange indeed if one consensus were to be quickly replaced by another consensus, or one orthodoxy by another. The fact that so many are tempted by an obviously faulty syllogism shows that the 'Beijing Consensus' is a concept that draws its power from its key position in a whole system of interacting concepts: as the polar opposite of the Washington Consensus, the term expresses compactly the collapse of the Washington Consensus *and* the success of the Chinese growth experience *and* the rising role of China in the world today. As such, it can attract to itself a huge cluster of heterogeneous and not-necessarily-consistent meanings.

Indeed, even before we attempt to go from the particularity of Chinese development practices to a potentially generalizable Chinese development model, we must confront the uniqueness of China's basic starting conditions. Anyone can write a long list of unique things about China, but there are three unique initial conditions of fundamental importance:

(a) China's size implies that it has (and had) a large potential internal market, which fosters competition and attracts foreign interest and investment. Among

1. John Williamson, 'What Washington means by policy reform', in John Williamson, ed., *Latin American Readjustment: How Much has Happened?* (Washington, DC: Institute for International Economics, 1989). See also Williamson's retrospective discussion: John Williamson, 'What should the World Bank think about the Washington Consensus?', *The World Bank Research Observer* 15(2), (August 2000), pp. 251–264, available at: http://www-wds.worldbank.org/external/default/WDSContentServer/IW3P/IB/2000/11/10/000094946_00102705411757/Rendered/PDF/multi_page.pdf.

developing economies, only the US (in the nineteenth century), or India (in the twenty-first) has had a similar initial size advantage.

(b) China, with its labor-abundant economy, had been following a capital-intensive socialist development strategy. During this period, China had already been investing in human resources, and its relatively healthy and well-trained labor force *increased* its comparative advantage in labor-intensive activities, but it had obstinately refrained from benefiting from its comparative advantage in labor-intensive activities. When China finally shifted into a labor-intensive development strategy, the results were explosive.

(c) China as a transitional economy retained and rebuilt a hierarchical authoritarian political system which it actively deployed in the new market economy environment.

Each of these features on its own is potentially important and unique enough to disqualify Chinese experience from easy generalization; put together, they guarantee China's uniqueness. Simply put, nobody else is so big, possesses such a unique comparative advantage, or operates a remotely similar political system. We must ask whether commentators who discuss the 'Beijing Consensus' show any awareness of these basic features of China's situation.

In fact, most discussions of the Beijing Consensus or Chinese model skip right over these fundamental features, and sometimes seem to be unaware of them. As a result, much of the discussion of a 'Beijing Consensus' has little or no content. A whole school of thought asserts that the essence of the China model is flexibility and pragmatism.[2] Adherents of such an approach like to quote comments like this one by Justin Lin: 'I think that China does not follow a model. We need to change policy all the time'.[3] Deng Xiaoping made a number of comments that suggested that adaptability and flexibility were the keys to success, and he is almost invariably credited with coining the term 'crossing the river by groping for stepping stones', although in fact he never said it.[4] So the model may simply mean 'Stay flexible', which is pretty good advice. Consider this comparable quote: 'We don't have a bureaucratic system like the French or the Germans. We're just opportunistic future-grabbers'. The evocative description actually comes from an Irish civil servant describing that country's successful economic experience.[5] Also surprisingly content-free are those approaches that see the key feature of the Beijing Consensus as being the combination of government political control and a market economy.

2. David Pilling, 'China's "warp-speed" industrial revolution', *Financial Times* [London], (17 December 2008), available at: http://www.ft.com/cms/s/0/db443b20-cc5b-11dd-9c43-000077b07658.html; see also 'China's reforms: the second Long March', *The Economist*, (11 December 2008), available at: http://www.economist.com/world/asia/displayStory.cfm?story_id = 12758848&source = most_commented.

3. Andrew Batson, 'Lin urges flexibility in fighting poverty', *Wall Street Journal*, (29 February 2008), p. A10.

4. Both Pilling and *The Economist* attribute the 'crossing the river' phrase to Deng Xiaoping. As readers of this journal are probably aware, Chen Yun used this term in 1980 to emphasize the importance of caution in reforms. Justin Lin, since June 2008 the Chief Economist of the World Bank—the first Chief Economist from a developing country—has clearly and repeatedly argued that the fundamental root of China's development success has been the shift toward a 'comparative advantage following' strategy of labor-intensive development. See Justin Lin, Fang Cai and Zhou Li, *The China Miracle: Development Strategy and Economic Reform* (Hong Kong: Chinese University Press, 1996).

5. Roy F. Foster, *Luck and the Irish: A Brief History of Change from 1970* (New York: Oxford University Press, 2008).

Usually denounced as iniquitous,[6] a surprising number of commentators see it as positive. They view China's authoritarian government as decisive and responsive, quick to cut through obstacles in pursuit of their vision of the future. China's willingness to run rough-shod over local property rights is often contrasted (positively) with India's slower and more labyrinthine system. The Chinese government is 'rapid in its implementation of changes to spur economic development'.[7] The most frequently cited work of all is probably the 2004 work by Ramo, a Fauvist canvas of bright smears of description that holds together only because the artist is willing to abandon verisimilitude.[8] Ramo appears to champion the Chinese government's dynamic agenda-setting, but it's hard to be sure which specific actions he approves of, if any. Almost never do these appraisals present persuasive accounts of what China's authoritarian system can and cannot achieve in practice.

This is peculiar: the core 'lessons' of those advocating a 'Beijing Consensus' seem to be to avoid dogmatism; avoid applying abstract policy principles that ignore local differences; and then act decisively in pursuit of whatever the local situation dictates. If this is right, one would expect to see that work in the spirit of this 'consensus' emphasizes fine-grained empirical work that captures the peculiarities of the Chinese experience, but this, alas, is precisely what is lacking in the existing literature. This is the initial paradox of the 'Beijing Consensus' returning with renewed force: those who most eagerly proclaim consensus are the most impatient to gloss over the details, but the truth of the 'Beijing Consensus', if any, lies in those details.

In the following, I propose to work within this relatively large gap in the literature. I will describe clearly some of the specific institutional features that characterize the Chinese industrial system. To be sure, these are not 'details', they are fundamental features of the entire system of industrial organization; but they are individual policies and institutional features, the building blocks out of which a complete description of the Chinese development model will (later) be built, and not a description in themselves of the Chinese development model. This distinctive industrial system can legitimately be considered a variant of 'capitalism', because most of the agents, even when state-owned, are driven to maximize profit. Moreover, the discussion below often emphasizes the role of state-ownership, so it is important to stress at the outset that the system as a whole is firmly founded on a market economy system, and this is, of course, crucial to Chinese economic success. I will then advance six 'conjectures'. In fact, each of these is first an assertion, and then a conjecture. First, I assert that the particular feature is so significant and so entwined with others aspects of China's development policy, that it must be part of China's development model. That is, it is inconceivable that we would ever successfully define a set of Chinese policies that created China's spectacular economic success that *didn't* include this feature. Then, I conjecture that this policy is a plausible

6. Ian Buruma, 'China's dark triumph', *Los Angeles Times*, (13 January 2008); Rowan Callick, 'The China model', *The American*, (November–December 2007), available at: http://www.american.com/archive/2007/november-december-magazine-contents/the-china-model/.

7. Patrick Arippol, 'WI Harper—strategic crossroads', *Stanford Graduate School of Business Case E-257*, (6 June 2007), p. 14.

8. Joshua Cooper Ramo, *The Beijing Consensus* (London: The Foreign Policy Centre, May 2004), available at: http://fpc.org.uk/fsblob/244.pdf.

candidate for recommendation to other dissimilar developing countries. I discuss this conjecture and find, in general, the difference of initial conditions between China and other countries, particularly the three basic conditions listed above, limit the applicability of these policies and institutions. We can still learn lessons from each of these features, of course, but we should be wary of the idea that there is a Chinese development model that can be directly applied to other countries, that is, that there is any Beijing Consensus.

The Chinese industrial system: six conjectures

After decades of restless change, the Chinese industrial system has settled into a relatively stable configuration during the first decade of the twenty-first century. The creation of SASAC (the State Asset Supervision and Administration Commission) in 2003 is a convenient milestone to date the beginning of the current system. SASAC's establishment did not mark any rupture with previous policy, to be sure, but it did provide a formal structure where one had been lacking, and created a bureaucratic interest that articulates policies and projects a more-or-less coherent vision of the future. A key feature of the current system has been the working out of a division of the industrial system into three different segments that work reasonably well together, and do not impinge on each other too much. Ernst and Naughton called this a three-tier system consisting of large, central-government firms; hybrid local and foreign firms; and small-scale capitalism. Kroeber draws the dividing line slightly differently, distinguishing more conventionally between state, private and foreign-invested, but he also stresses the association between ownership and industrial specialization, and concludes: 'All three ownership sectors perform their assigned roles reasonably effectively, and while their shares of output may vary, the basic tripartite structure of the economy is unlikely to change much in the coming decade'.[9] The Chinese reform process has settled down into a system in which state ownership has an important role.

The Chinese development model—whatever the precise content—has been first and foremost a strategy to facilitate China's rapid industrialization. For 30 years, successive waves of industrial reform have been launched in the effort to secure a workable management system. Given the recent stabilization of the industrial system—in what remains the fastest-growing economy in the world—it is worth making some observations about what this means for other developing economies. Moreover, as I will demonstrate, the features of China's industrial system are strongly inter-related, so it makes sense to consider them as a package. In the following, I advance six 'conjectures'. These are statements that I conjecture might mature into 'lessons' of the Chinese experience following debate, discussion, reformulation and verification.

9. Arthur Kroeber, 'Rising China and the liberal West', *China Economic Quarterly*, (March 2008), p. 33; cf. Dieter Ernst and Barry Naughton, 'China's emerging industrial economy: insights from the IT industry', in Christopher A. McNally, ed., *China's Emergent Political Economy: Capitalism in the Dragon's Lair* (New York: Routledge, 2008), pp. 39–50.

Conjecture 1: Public ownership can be reasonably efficient, and the 'mixed economy' is a decent model of industrial organization, after all

Privatization was one of the cardinal principles of the Washington Consensus, and advocates of the Washington Consensus did not put significant bounds on the scope of their advice to privatize. They urged developing countries to take advantage of new techniques of regulation to privatize even industries with natural monopoly features, substituting regulation for direct government ownership. China has not followed this advice. To be sure, there has been massive *de facto* privatization of Chinese industry. Township and village enterprises started out publicly owned and are today almost entirely private. In cities, competitive industrial sectors—defined as sectors where no obvious entry barriers, natural monopolies or national security considerations prevent full reliance on a competitive market solution—have long since been dominated by private firms. However, government ownership has continued and been upgraded in virtually all those sectors that for whatever reason are not completely competitive: utilities (electricity, water); transport; telecommunications; oil and natural gas; and military industries. Moreover, government ownership has not been rigorously withdrawn even from competitive industrial sectors. A handful of technologically advanced firms have been retained by the central government to serve as technological pioneers and 'national champions', such as Baoshan in steel, or the main heavy industrial equipment firms. Local governments also own and operate their versions of these firms: 'local champions', we should call them. Finally, the central government has retained ownership of the specialized construction firms that were run by the industrial ministries—although the ministries themselves are gone—and coordinates these firms in ambitious construction initiatives. In other words, China's industrial system has settled down into a 'mixed economy' model where competitive sectors are primarily private, but government ownership plays the dominant role in non-competitive sectors and a subsidiary role in several other sectors. This system seems to be working reasonably well. Perhaps the 'mixed economy' is a decent model of industrial organization after all.

Why 'after all'? Because over the past 30 years, the move away from government ownership has been broad-based and remarkably consistent, such that it is not easily blamed on mistaken policy advice from multi-lateral financial institutions, or on the imposition of neo-liberal orthodoxy on diverse local conditions. Privatization has been carried out in France as well as Argentina, while only the latter was arguably under the thrall of IMF economists. The fact is that the evidence showing that privatization leads to efficiency gains is quite strong.[10] Moreover, advocates of privatization in competitive sectors have an additional extremely strong argument encapsulated in a simple question: why would you have public ownership in a competitive market where private ownership works perfectly well? All it can do, it would seem, is lower efficiency and divert scarce public sector management talent away from other pressing concerns.

10. An introduction to this extensive literature is provided by William Megginson and Jeffry M. Netter, 'From state to market: a survey of empirical studies on privatization', *Journal of Economic Literature* 39, (2001), pp. 321–389.

Furthermore, the current Chinese industrial model looks an awful lot like 'developmental socialism' as practiced in the 1950s to the 1970s in a whole host of developing countries, including prominently Egypt and India. In that model, the state would take control of the 'commanding heights' of the economy, while leaving the rest to native entrepreneurs. The government would thus be able to achieve certain vaguely defined social goals, while also protecting national security and preventing foreign dominance of the economy. But 'developmental socialism' has been pretty much universally dismissed as a dismal failure. More tellingly, most countries that practiced developmental socialism in the past have moved away from it, including the pre-eminent practitioners of the past, Egypt and India, and they have been rewarded with growth acceleration. In and of itself, China's example is hardly going to overwhelm the hard-won experience of many other economies.

Therefore, China's development model is not an argument against privatization *per se*. Rather, the conjecture that emerges from the Chinese experience is that public ownership by itself is not debilitating. Perhaps—further conjecture—the key features of developmental socialism that condemned it to failure were the closed economy model (import substitution strategy), combined with the extensive administrative controls placed over what was nominally the private, market-oriented sector. India's 'license Raj' is the most important example, because it is universally recognized. Everybody who examined India's regulatory regime during the 1980s was surprised that the economy could grow at all, given the large number of rules whose purpose was to prevent entry, investment and expansion of production.

Rather, the Chinese experience suggests that when governments are trying to deal with market failures, the costs of public ownership may be acceptable. Governments might legitimately seek to restrain monopoly power; foster technological creativity; and protect national security. Economists argue that regulation is first-best, since it combines the efficiencies of private ownership with selective government intervention that achieve public goals. This is true, but it overlooks the fact that all existing regulatory agencies are themselves second-best, and that few governments in developing countries really have the capability to create and run effective regulatory institutions. Government ownership is clearly second- or third-best, but it may be an acceptable real world outcome. Indeed, in the wake of the global financial crisis, many countries are finding the government ownership stake in their economy expanding, as bailed-out firms fall into government receivership. The government objective of maintaining macroeconomic stability has unwittingly been implemented through public ownership. The Chinese 'development model' suggests that countries might be advised to get comfortable with this new reality and invest some administrative resources into running government firms well. Diverse causes and objectives lead to public ownership, and developing countries don't always need to feel that privatization is a priority objective. Perhaps the mixed economy is a decent model of industrial organization, after all. While the general argument *for* public ownership is still feeble, the argument *against* it is weaker, given recent Chinese experience. However, the confidence with which we can recommend this direction to other developing economies depends on the next conjecture.

Conjecture 2: Competition is (still) more important than ownership

Why 'still'? The conjecture that competition was more important than privatization was made long ago in the specific context of early transitional economies.[11] As a matter of priority, it was then argued, the focus on privatization was both costly and misguided, because it was far more important to focus on the creation of competition as a driver of behavioral change and improved efficiency. Under centrally planned economies, market demand was ignored. As a result, in hundreds of different markets, a new entrant would be rewarded for simply matching assortment and variety to the consumer's needs. The Chinese experience with TVEs proved this point, embodied by the pioneering merchants of Wenzhou who became wealthy selling Chinese consumers, for a few pennies, buttons in the colors, sizes and variety they wanted. However, this was an 'early stage' lesson that was not necessarily applicable to the 'later stage' economic conditions that apply once socialism's chronic neglect of market demand and resultant shortage economy disappears.

In fact, Conjecture 2 appears to be robust in a new context. The previous conjecture spoke about government ownership, but it is essential that this is government ownership in the context of market competition. China's policy-makers have built some competition into all the sectors in which state ownership is prominent. In the central government monopoly sectors there are always at least two firms competing (for example, three in telecom: China Mobile, Unicom, and China Telecom). Firms have been split into competitors even in defense industries, where the government is the only real customer, as in armaments (the North Industries Group Corporation and the South Industries Group Corporation) and, until recently, the aircraft industry. More radically, sectors like civil aviation are structured as a dominant-player oligopoly along with a competitive fringe: central government-run Air China, China Southern and China Eastern have to contend with Hainan Air, Dragonair, and a few other scrappy players that keep them on their toes. To be sure, this is a far cry from free and fair competition, and should rather be called 'limited and managed' competition. Nevertheless, it appears to be sufficient to strip away the promise of a quiet life from state firm managers, and force them to improve their performance and results. It is difficult to imagine the survival of the Chinese state sector without the incentive effects of this competition.

Again, the Chinese approach can be contrasted with the 'Washington Consensus' approach. Managed competition would be anathema to the Washington Consensus policy package. One of the key advantages of privatizing and then regulating, in this view, is precisely that the government would *not* impose its preconceptions about market structure on a domestic industry. It is quite possible that large efficiency gains can be achieved by radically different business models and industry structure, which can only emerge if government stops managing the market directly. This is a strong argument, but it is weakened by the difficulty of establishing a strong regulator who can achieve public objectives *and* maintain a light touch on the market itself. Indeed, China does have market regulators.

11. One example is the piece I wrote with John McMillan at the very beginning of the 1990s: John McMillan and Barry Naughton, 'How to reform a planned economy: lessons from China', *Oxford Review of Economic Policy* 8(1), (Spring 1992).

For example, there is an Electricity Regulatory Commission and the CAAC regulates airlines, but these regulatory agencies have remained in the shadow of the powerful—formerly bureaucratic—interests that directly run the large companies. Without doubt, China has failed to create a capable, arm's length regulatory apparatus, but in this respect, the Chinese experience may actually be the more typical one. The Washington Consensus prescription for an authoritative and independent regulatory agency may be first-best, but it is also virtually unattainable. Regulatory independence requires not only a strong legal framework, but also resources of expertise and influence that permit the gradual establishment of credibility. The outcomes in China were typical of ineffective or failed regulatory solutions in developing countries. The difference in China is that the failure of the independent regulatory agencies was to some extent offset by continuing state ownership in the context of vigorous competition. China's telecom outcome, for example, is better than that in Mexico, where weak regulation and a single private firm with a dominant position has produced the world's richest man (Carlos Slim), and some of the consumer's highest prices.

Competition is surely one of the key driving forces of Chinese success. It is strongly correlated with size, since China's regional markets are generally open to product competition from numerous other locales. The importance of China's size in generating inter-regional competition has long been recognized by analysts of China. It lies behind Qian Yingyi's classic analyses of the 'M-shaped hierarchy' and 'market-preserving fiscal federalism'. If we search for the least common denominator among many analyses, we find that they come back to the simple fact that China has managed to foster a profoundly competitive national market. Though Chinese leaders are not ideologically committed to competition, they are deeply allergic to monopoly positions in markets. Chinese leaders from Chen Yun to Zhu Rongji have displayed sensitivity to the delusions and damage a powerful actor can do in a situation where he has a monopoly and is unconstrained by competitive threats. As a result, many Chinese leaders have moved in practice to prevent the emergence of too much market power.

A broader question is whether China's size also provides a degree of political competition, even within the hierarchical authoritarian system. In contrast to smaller economies, China's political system is forced to acknowledge multiple interest groups and contenders for power. Chinese leaders act as if their hold on power is always somewhat tenuous, and depends on good economic performance. There are always multiple candidates waiting in the wings, ready to step up to the demands of power. The contrast is great with a political system which is capable of being united in the interest of a single, narrowly defined clique, as in the case of Marcos in the Philippines. Highly ineffective policies and extreme corruption typically lead to serious challenges to individual leaders. China is not less prone to bad policy or corruption than other countries, but the degree of both is arguably held in check by the challenge of political competition.

Conjecture 3: Public ownership can be used to exploit market power and generate revenues for investment and public goods' creation

This conjecture is in tension with the preceding point. While some competition prevents the exploitation of the monopoly position, the limitation of competition ensures large oligopolistic profits. In general, we expect an association between the number of competitors in a market and the level of profit: the fewer the players, the larger the profits. A single market participant—a pure monopoly—will generate the highest total level of profits; an oligopoly of only two or three participants will generate the next largest profit; and so forth, up to a market with 'many' players where all excess profits will be competed away. Such a theoretical generalization depends on the reaction function hypothesized to the competition's behavior. If market participants elect to fight a war of attrition, the generalization will not hold.

Chinese experience confirms that oligopolistic markets are more profitable. As Chinese market structure has stabilized, and the Chinese economy has boomed, profitability of large, state-owned firms has soared. When managers become 'too competitive'—threatening sectoral profitability by aggressive competition and price-cutting—government personnel managers have intervened to re-shuffle managers among competing firms. This gives the managers a fresh perspective, dampening their enthusiasm for unbridled competition, and reminding them that the government is the ultimate owner of all the competing oligopolists. For example, in November 2004, the Chinese government rotated the top managers of the three telecom firms such that each new top manager had come from a competing firm. The telecom firms got the message, and aggressive price-cutting came to an end. Thus, Chinese policy-makers seem to have been able to structure markets to bring in some competition, but also to maintain overall profitability at high levels.

Certainly, the profitability of Chinese state-owned firms has increased dramatically and consistently since its low-point in 1995–1997. As Figure 1 shows, through to 2007, state-firm profitability soared, as is evident in two overlapping but distinct definitions. Profit of all state-owned industry (including central and local firms, as well as joint stock companies in which any level of government has the controlling share) increased sharply from 2003 to 2007, jumping from 2.8% to 4.2% of GDP.[12] Over the same period, profits of central SASAC firms (which excludes local industrial SOEs but includes centrally-run communications, transport and service firms) grew even faster from 2.2% to 4.0% of GDP.[13] This is a very different reality from the financially crippled state sector of the mid-to-late 1990s.

To be sure, changes in profitability of the Chinese state sector are due to multiple factors, not just to government market structuring. During the late 1990s, China closed down thousands of loss-making firms, raising overall profitability by dramatically cutting losses. After 2002, the global rise in natural resource prices combined with the export surge following WTO membership to create a cyclical boom in the Chinese economy that contributed to soaring profitability. The dramatic

12. National Bureau of Statistics, *2009 Statistical Abstract* [*Zhongguo Tongji Zhaiyao 2009*] (Beijing: Zhongguo Tongji, 2009), p. 141 and earlier issues.

13. The State Asset Supervision and Administration Commission (SASAC) regularly updates total profitability on its website. For 2008 final data, see SASAC, *General Operating Conditions of Central Enterprises in 2008*, available at: http://www.sasac.gov.cn/n1180/n1566/n258203/n258329/6649463.html.

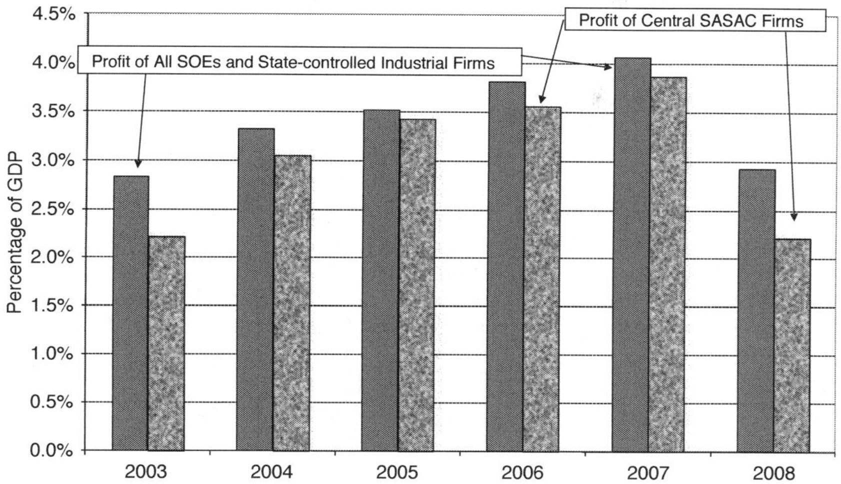

Figure 1. Profits of state industry and central SASAC firms.

drop in 2008 profits, in turn, was due primarily to the impact of the global financial crisis. The seriousness of the 2008 decline probably indicates that a portion of the surge in profits to 2007 was unsustainable, part of a global cyclical phenomenon to which Chinese state firms were highly exposed. The Chinese government has the ability to structure competition, but not the ability to block or reverse overall market trends. Indeed, it is crucial that this market structuring capability is *limited*: it is founded on the basis of the competitive market economy described in the previous section. Otherwise, excess government control would strangle the market operations upon which Chinese economic success is based. For China to reap the advantages of a market economy it must be subject to the discipline as well.

Despite the large drop in profits in 2008, it is already clear that these partially-protected state-owned oligopolists were well-positioned to weather the global financial crisis. In all countries, governments provided aid to firms that experienced remarkably sudden deterioration in their balance sheets. Government aid, not surprisingly, goes first to firms that are well-connected to governments and politicians. The same is of course true in China as well. By early 2009, China's SASAC was already injecting funds into the state-run airlines and electricity companies. SASAC was able to move quickly because it had a moderate sum of money drawn from the state firms under its control.[14] During 2009, a flood of money went from state-owned banks into investment projects, and disproportionately into the large state-owned firms, which found economic stability much earlier than their private, free market counterparts. Clearly, the ability to structure market competition can potentially be an advantage in the face of economic crisis, but it can also lead to new pitfalls, especially if it convinces politicians to tilt too far in favor of government

14. Zhou Limin, 'SASAC will inject about 10 billion RMB; electric firms make the "gift list"', *Zhongguo Jingjingbao*, (17 January 2009), available at: http://news.cb.com.cn/?action-viewnews-itemid-3639.

firms. In fact, structured competition is a precarious balancing act, one that requires a healthy respect for the market, combined with a willingness to tilt the scales in favor of the public interest.

Precisely because structuring competition involves such a delicate balance of competing objectives, there should be reasonable doubts about the ability of other countries to replicate China's experience. Once again, size matters. China's huge marketplace provides room for two or three big state-owned players, with room left over for foreign firms or innovative domestic hybrid firms in defined niches. Few other countries will have such a capacious domestic market. Lacking the huge competitive potential of China's market, efforts to structure competition are much more likely to degenerate into simple patronage and protection. For smaller economies, the commitment to openness is likely to be more black-and-white, with less ability than China has to discriminate among sectors and degrees of openness. What difference does the overall level of profitability of Chinese state firms make? Profitability matters because state firm profits, combined with reviving budgetary revenues, kept investment high and fueled the recent boom of the Chinese economy. This leads to the next conjecture.

Conjecture 4: A strategy of investment-led growth is essential. Therefore, it is acceptable to invest out ahead of demand, creating capacity that is only gradually utilized

Williamson's list of Washington Consensus items from 1989 includes the recommendation that government should focus on infrastructure investment and basic social services, so it is not entirely fair to say that the Washington Consensus neglected infrastructure investment. However, the single area in which Chinese economic policy has diverged most consistently from the advice given to China by the International Monetary Fund or the World Bank has been in the area of investment. Economists from the international financial organizations have repeatedly warned the Chinese government that it was investing too much in the aggregate, and investing in inefficient or perhaps unnecessary projects that would turn out to have low rates of return. State-owned financial institutions were identified as the institutions facilitating frivolous and wasteful investments. The Chinese government, in practice, has consistently ignored these recommendations. In the mid-1990s, when the discussion began, China was investing around 32–33% of its GDP in new fixed assets. By 2004, China was investing 40% and more of its GDP. To be sure, the Chinese government has recently committed to a greater consumption share of GDP and a 'more balanced' growth pattern. However, in practice, the Chinese government is extremely reluctant to take measures that would seriously lead to a reduction in the relative share of investment in the economy. Instead, in specific policy decisions, the Chinese government repeatedly displays a preference for high levels of investment. For example, recent changes in the way the value-added tax is computed encourage investment by treating investment-related outlays the same as the purchase of inputs for current production, making both of them deductible from income for the purpose of calculating value-added taxes. When it came time to stimulate the economy in the face of the global financial crisis, China moved quickly to pump up investment, and belatedly to try to shore up consumption. The commitment to 'balance' is lukewarm and conditional; the commitment to ample investment is fundamental and ongoing.

One of the most striking ways the Chinese government has encouraged investment is through the simple expedient of allowing Chinese SOEs to retain their after-tax profits. This policy, adopted quietly in 1994 in the context of overall fiscal reform, gives state firms strong incentives to increase profits, and few alternate uses of the profits created. Paying out too much of the profits in bonuses or managerial compensation can get a state-run firm in trouble; expanding the business through re-investment is the best, if not the only, alternative. This policy obviously interacts with the policy of structured competition described in the previous section. For 14 years, from 1994 to 2007, China's investment rate soared as SOEs returned to profitability. Flush with retained funds, China's state firms poured money into expansion and new investment projects.

The policy allowing firms to retain all after-tax profits was slightly modified toward the end of 2007. During 2008, the first full year of the new policies, most state firms were required to remit 5% of their after-tax profits to SASAC, the instrument of the government's ownership. In a few monopoly sectors, firms were required to remit 10% of after-tax profits.[15] Obviously, this policy could have been used to slow investment (although a reduction in the corporate tax rate at the same time essentially restored state firm profit levels), but in an ironic twist, the arrival of the global financial crisis meant that SASAC ended up re-injecting these funds into the state firms under its control. This was the source of the financial aid described in the previous section. Thus, even this modest step to tame the growth of retained funds in the government corporate sector ended up reinforcing China's obsession with investment.

Yet what seems clear is that China's incredible growth in the 2000 decade has retrospectively validated this high investment policy. Project after project that seemed at inception to be superfluous and wasteful now hums along as part of China's booming economy. Without doubt, there has been overshooting: even by Chinese standards, the over 40% investment rates after 2004 are likely to prove too high, and China is already running into serious difficulties as a result of this super-high investment policy. Nevertheless, it is hard to imagine a crash so devastating that it will wipe out the benefits of GDP growth above 10% for five years. Even a superficial familiarity with China reveals the remarkable speed with which China has built the infrastructure for a modern, middle-income economy. Indeed, one of the challenges facing Chinese policy-makers in the face of the 2008–2009 financial crisis has been that high investment rates have created such an impressive infrastructure that it is not immediately apparent what glaring unfulfilled needs planners should rush to fill in order to prop up the economy. China's road network has gone from non-existent to impressive; airports and harbors are adequate; and electricity generation facilities

15. Barry Naughton, 'Claiming profit for the state: SASAC and the capital management budget', *China Leadership Monitor* no. 18, (Spring 2006), available at: http://media.hoover.org/documents/CLM18BN.pdf; Barry Naughton, 'SASAC and rising corporate power', *China Leadership Monitor* no. 24, (Winter 2008), available at: http://media.hoover.org/documents/CLM24BN.pdf.

sufficient to meet needs. This is a challenge many developing countries would be delighted to face.

A good way to look at the Chinese experience in this respect is through the contrast with India. China's high investment rate is one of the key characteristics that differentiate it from India. China consistently builds infrastructure out ahead of demand; India only slowly builds infrastructure as bottlenecks develop. As a result, the return to an individual infrastructure investment in India is very high—probably much higher than in China—since by the time a project is built, it has become a response to clear demand and produces immediate and enormous saving. Individual infrastructure investment decisions are probably made more efficiently in India, because they are based on such clear demand signals, but the Indian policy imposes large costs on other economic actors as they cope with bottlenecks and delays throughout the economy. Overall, the Chinese approach is better.

The obvious importance of China's sustained investment effort has been one of the crucial facts leading to the collapse of the Washington Consensus, and causing a wider acceptance of stronger government involvement.[16] The report of the Commission on Growth and Development—often called the 'Spence Report' after its chairman Michael Spence—was a multi-national effort convened to re-establish and articulate a degree of consensus about growth policy. The report concluded that governments needed to take the lead in formulating a vision of future growth and mobilizing investment in support of the vision.[17] The Spence group is quite mainstream, so it might be fair to say that in this respect the Chinese 'model' has triumphed, and that there is an emerging agreement in favor of greater government involvement in guiding and fostering investment.

However, such a conclusion would be slightly premature. In fact, the need for a government-led investment effort was once part of the oldest orthodoxy in the field of development economics. During the 1950s and the 1960s, the need for developing countries to raise their investment effort—perhaps even to the level of a 'Big Push'—was the main thrust of development advice. It was also the prime justification for involvement by the World Bank and developed country donors. But the record of those programs was extremely mixed: indeed, this is what led originally to the shift to the 'Washington Consensus' in the 1980s. The problem comes because there is no agreement about what mechanisms are most likely to increase investment while maintaining a modicum of efficiency. Taxation imposes costs on the economy, even in fair and efficient tax systems. Reliance on either foreign investment or foreign aid presents serious problems. The Chinese answer, in practice, is rooted in the importance of the government and the state-owned sector in the economy. The Chinese approach has been to privilege the state sector: structured market competition, retained funds, and limited investment alternatives all lead to firms

16. Dani Rodrik has incorporated this 'Chinese' lesson into a broader framework which stresses the need to first go through a process of 'growth diagnostics'. If the diagnostic indicates that a weak investment effort is the key obstacle to development, then a country should give priority to clearing away obstacles to investment, including having the government take the leading role in some situations. See Dani Rodrik, *One Economics, Many Recipes: Globalization, Institutions, and Economic Growth* (Princeton, NJ: Princeton University Press, 2007).

17. Commission on Growth and Development, *The Growth Report: Strategies for Sustained Growth and Inclusive Development* (Washington, DC: World Bank, 2008), pp. 34–37, available at: http://www.growthcommission.org/index.php?option = com_content&task = view&id = 96&Itemid = 169.

oriented toward investment-driven expansion. Similarly, government officials are given incentives that are strongly tilted toward investment and development (discussed later). The Chinese experience indicates that this approach works. Empowering big publicly-owned corporations and government officials contributes to growth. It also inevitably means that average citizens have less voice and command a comparatively smaller share of society's resources.

Other developing countries have this option as well, and many have chosen to exercise it in the last several years. However, the outcomes are likely to be dramatically different in different political systems. Powerful firms in most developing countries are likely to be run by cronies of political leaders without much oversight. China at least has a system of oversight, but it is most certainly not a democratic system of oversight. Nor, since it is based on the Communist Party, is it a system that most developing economies are likely to emulate. In the meantime, the lesson for developing countries is incomplete: governments should take the lead in stimulating investment, but we cannot give them much guidance on which instruments they can choose. All we can advise is that the broad sweep of daily economic policy-making decisions should all be informed by the need to encourage productive investment. Other than this, each country must choose instruments from the idiosyncratic opportunities available to them in context.

Conjecture 5: For a growth-oriented polity, the state sector may be used aggressively to create growth (and revenue) opportunities outside the state sector

Typical Washington Consensus advice on institutions and investments is that, as much as possible, projects should pay for themselves. The twin emphases on budget discipline and protecting well-defined property rights together have typically led to advice that state-sponsored projects should be self-supporting through user's fees. As much as possible, there should be a dis-entangling of public and private interests. While China certainly has plenty of 'user's fees' for various facilities, China hasn't respected the dividing line between public and private very well. The Chinese government often invests in ways that create spill-over benefits for private parties.

Indeed, the intertwining of private and public interests has been one of the most consistent and striking features throughout China's reform process. A wide spectrum of activity fits into this generalization. At one extreme, township and village enterprises, constituted as publicly-owned firms, in some parts of China worked to generate entrepreneurial activities that benefited everyone in their local community. At another extreme, well-connected individuals channel profits into the pockets of their cronies. This complex mix of different forms of public/private interest coordination can be condemned as corruption or praised as pragmatism. Whatever one's judgment, the one robust generalization is that, since the beginning of the reform period, Chinese policy-makers have almost never attempted to prevent parties benefiting from government policies 'unfairly' or because they were not worthy. In other words, China really has followed Deng Xiaoping's dictum that it's alright for some people to get rich first. The result has been policies that do not try too scrupulously to collect the benefits of growth or investment. Actual policy has been rather permissive about who benefits.

This is the broader perspective within which to evaluate China's infrastructure investment strategy, discussed in the previous section. In the Indian approach, infrastructure investment is efficient, but extra costs are put on the private sector. In the Chinese approach, infrastructure investment is less efficient, but part of the higher cost of infrastructure investments is implicitly a subsidy to other economic actors. The Chinese state provides infrastructure services that are not (yet) economically justified and private actors take advantage of the opportunities created. Of course, well-connected insiders may be especially well positioned to take advantage of the opportunity. As long as this occurs in the context of continuing economic growth, the government is not overly scrupulous. Indeed, in various ways, the Chinese state sector subsidizes huge swathes of the economy, with cheap land deals and tax breaks for favored sectors and innovation. This approach seems to work better than an attempt to capture the benefits from each investment decision.

This conjecture seems eminently transferrable to other developing economies. Indeed, Taiwan may actually have been the pioneer in this kind of policy-making. In Taiwan's promotion of high technology industry in the 1980s, the government poured money into industrial research, and then looked favorably upon individuals commercializing the fruits of public investment. In the case of the most successful of these spin-offs of public investment—the Taiwan Semiconductor Manufacturing Company (TSMC)—the government not only provided the initial research support, it also took a 48% stake in the company when it was first listed in 1987.[18] This example of entangled public and private interest provided a model for Beijing, and may provide a general lesson. If the government takes the lead in generating growth and driving investment, it will inevitably create spill-over benefits for many private parties. This creates both political and economic opportunities for governments. A relaxed attitude may be superior to investing administrative resources into the difficult task of insuring a fair distribution of the benefits.

Conjecture 6: Managers of publicly-owned corporations can be motivated by tying their compensation to their company's performance in maximizing asset value

The stress on privatization in the Washington Consensus unavoidably means that relatively little attention has been given to the question of how best to motivate public firm managers. In the meantime, China has been muddling through to a reasonably effective way to tie managerial compensation to firm performance. China's stock market still lacks many of the desirable features of a developed-country equity market, and so it is not very effective as a tool for automatically generating managerial incentives through fractional ownership or stock options. However, growth of a stock market appears to help managers and owners think in terms of the assets of a business having a market-set value. As those conceptions take root, they can be portaged over to the state sector, and made part of the incentive system.

At the central level, SASAC has put a great deal of emphasis on strengthening managerial incentives. Its primary tool for doing this is through three-year

18. Chintay Shih, Kung Wang and Yi-ling Wei, 'Hsinchu, Taiwan: Asia's pioneering high-tech park', in Henry S. Rowan, Marguerite Gong Hancock and William F. Miller, eds, *Making IT: The Rise of Asia in High Tech* (Stanford, CA: Stanford University Press, 2007), pp. 101–122 at p. 116.

performance contracts. Nearly all SASAC firms signed these in 2004, and again in 2007. The contracts outline annual and three year targets. In the annual target, profit plays the dominant role. A 100-point scale is established, of which 30 points go for profit in relation to an agreed target; and 40 points for the rate of return on equity, scaled to sectoral averages. (A further 30 points are available for sector-specific targets.) Thus, the firm can have a big impact on their score by economizing on net equity, and leveraging a smaller amount of assets. The trade-off between profit maximization and asset minimization is carried through in the three-year targets, which include the growth of total capital value and the growth of aggregate revenues. The final element of the third-year target is the summation of the annual profit results, so that some of the reward for short-term profit maximization is held back until it is verified that short-term and long-term outcomes are consistent. These targets do a reasonable job of striking the balance between efficiency and growth, profit and value.

In order to convert the targets into effect incentives, SASAC scores performance on a 100-point scale, and then assigns grades A–E to firms and their managers. Managerial salaries depend on the grade: incentive payments range from three times base salary (for A + managers) down to zero (for those who get an E). In 2005, half of the SASAC firms got Bs, and one-sixth got As. Four firms got Ds, for failing to meet profit targets, and two firms received an E, for falsifying records. The names of firms were publicized.[19] Thus, the impressive performance of central SOEs over the last five years may be partially attributed to a fairly appropriate incentive structure. While certainly not perfect, the incentive system is a practical and workable creation. It balances material rewards and public reputation. It establishes the idea that the long-run objective of a public manager ought to be to maximize the value of the public's assets. It creates strong incentives for short-term profit maximization, without creating too-strong incentives that would erode long-term value. It is a strong second-best, in a world in which first-best outcomes are rare.

The Chinese experience with managerial compensation is probably applicable in many developing countries. The important pre-requisite is that countries decide that they have a functioning public enterprise sector that will continue to be with them for the immediately foreseeable future. In that case, the proper motivation of public sector managers immediately assumes critical importance. The link with the five previous sections is evident: the combination of state ownership and a market economy can be made to work. It will not be the optimum system, but it can avoid failure and contribute to long-run economic goals. In order for this to happen, though, continuous adjustment and adaptation must be put into the different parts of the economic system, not least of which is managerial compensation.

19. SASAC, *Provisional Methods for Assessing Performance of Responsible Managers of Central Enterprises*, (30 December 2006), available at: http://www.sasac.gov.cn/gzjg/yjkh/200701310039.htm; SASAC, *Results of 2005 Performance Assessment for Central Enterprises*, available at: http://www.sasac.gov.cn/gzjg/yjkh/200608220155.htm. In 2005, two firms had their grades lowered for safety or environmental violations (PetroChina and the Railroad Construction company), and another eight firms lost points for safety or financial infractions.

The broader applicability of the Chinese approach

The preceding sections have looked at specific features of the Chinese industrial system, highlighting those that are most distinctive and also most fundamental to the performance of that system. They have in common that they all describe a far larger and more activist role for the government in the economy that is contemplated in the Washington Consensus. Indeed, taking the lowest common denominator, we could say that in the Chinese development model 'government ownership and government investment play a strong role in the economy'. This is a rather obvious, but still important fact, and it has been appropriately emphasized by those seeking to break away from the old Washington Consensus. Thus, a key tenet of the new 'Spence report', referred to above, is that government should play a stronger role in orienting the economy and stimulating investment, though not necessarily through direct state ownership, about which it is largely silent. So perhaps it is fair to characterize the Chinese development model as one in which 'government ownership and investment play a strong role in the economy, but in a pragmatic and flexible way'.

Once again, we are likely to feel that this characterization, fair as it is, simply doesn't go far enough. For one thing, it doesn't make clear what role, if any, the government is playing in actually steering the economy to specific outcomes. Planning is ubiquitous in China, with seemingly every government organization having long-range targets and objectives; yet we will search in vain for a unified vision of the development of the economy that in any way predicts specific outcomes. The 11th Five Year Plan called unambiguously for a more 'balanced' economy with greater attention to consumption and the quality of life, but this did nothing whatsoever to predict the actual economic outcomes that were observed between 2005 and 2008. The economy is clearly not 'planned' in this overall sense, so it must be that the planning exercises are part of the adaptation of individual government agencies and firms to the continuously evolving signals of the market economy.[20] It remains to be determined how much success the government actually has achieved in its specific initiatives to develop specific sectors, foster new technologies, and upgrade the economy.

Furthermore, saying that the government plays a strong role in the Chinese economy does nothing to distinguish China from numerous other developing economies where government has played a similarly strong role in the economy, even approaching issues in a way that seemed to be pragmatic and flexible, but ended up being disastrous. We don't need to descend to the horror stories such as Myanmar and Zimbabwe to recognize that government involvement in developing economies has typically brought as much negative as positive impact. Indeed, one of the milestone achievements of economics during the 1970s and 1980s was the explicit recognition that 'government failure' was at least as important as 'market failure' in understanding why economies performed poorly. In the preceding part of this paper it has been shown that there is an association in China between intrusive government policies and rapid economic growth, but this is not really adequate.

20. In this sense, 'planning' must be closely related to 'experimentation', even though the two are usually thought of as being polar opposites. See the line of argument developed by Sebastian Heilmann, 'Policy experimentation in China's economic rise', *Studies in Comparative International Development* 43(1), (March 2008), pp. 1–26.

It is also necessary to ask *how* China was able to avoid some of the most debilitating aspects of government failure.

When we phrase the question in this way, we quickly encounter what is by far the most distinctive feature of the Chinese development model. China possesses an authoritarian political system which has evolved over the course of 30 years in conjunction with the development of a market economy. The features of that authoritarian system have been adapted to strengthen it, and to reduce agency loss, and it has been focused on economic objectives. The result, through three decades of tinkering and adjustment, is a system that is quite good at avoiding catastrophic outcomes, but one that is also tied to a contingent and highly peculiar set of political circumstances. China has reduced government failure in the same way that it has marketized: through a gradual process of trial and error, but that gradual process has not been random or accidental. Rather, the hierarchical system has been steadily tuned, pruned, focused and rebuilt in order to keep it functioning in the pursuit of economic growth.

The role of government in the contemporary Chinese economy evolved out of a situation in which governmental control was pervasive, under socialist planning. This fact is obvious, but its significance is rarely considered. In the transition process, it was impossible for government to 'get out of the way' as the Washington Consensus urged. Rather, governmental institutions had to be completely remade. China's approach, in essence, was that government bodies should be 're-purposed' and then 'incentivized'. The argument for re-purposing was sensible and strong. Reasonably well functioning organizations possessed pools of valuable organizational and human capital, that should be used, not discarded, in transition.[21] Moreover, existing organizations are also interest groups that may block growth if they are not co-opted into the new growth environment. Therefore, organizations should be re-purposed if it is possible.

Alongside the 're-purposing' went the 'incentivization' of government. China has provided powerful incentives to government officials during the process of marketization, and it means that incentives are highly aligned in support of economic growth. Cadres are subject to annual evaluations, in which they can score up to 100 points, of which more than 70 are awarded for outcomes that are directly linked to economic growth. Annual bonuses and promotion depend on the scores. Moreover, the relatively permissive attitude to community enrichment alluded to above means that local officials who generate growth are, to a certain extent, free to reward associates and build patronage networks. Moreover, officials face an overall incentive environment that is highly asymmetric: when undertaking investment, for example, risks are largely socialized, while decision-makers can share in and distribute some of the benefits of success. Penalties for misguided and wasteful development schemes are virtually nil, while rewards on the upside are substantial. By the time the flaws in a local leader's ambitious schemes are revealed, he will have been promoted out of the district.

21. This important point was emphasized by Joseph Stiglitz, 'Whither reform? Ten years of the transition', *Annual World Bank Conference on Development Economics*, Washington, DC, 1999.

This type of incentivized hierarchical system might have been a recipe for disaster. Soft budget constraints, misguided and wasteful projects and pervasive corruption would follow from such an incentive environment. Of course, all those things are evident in the Chinese context, but they seem also to be restrained by the monitoring effect of the authoritarian hierarchy operated by the Communist Party. Indeed, there appears to be a complementarity between authoritarianism and high-powered incentives within official organizations. Elsewhere I have argued that such a complementarity exists in a different sense: when the free market has been introduced in an authoritarian context, the hierarchy will survive only if incentives for compliance to the hierarchy are strengthened.[22] In China, the top of the hierarchy responded to the emergence of new market opportunities by reinforcing incentives within the hierarchy. Otherwise, the hierarchy would have been hit with a cascade of defections and collapsed, as it did in Russia. Such a collapse would presumably have been debilitating for economic growth.

Complementarity exists in another sense as well. The authoritarian hierarchy creates an unusually strong and pervasive system of monitoring that allows the system to continue functioning despite the incentives for corruption and personal enrichment. We can speculate that this would be true for at least three reasons. First, most obviously, the Communist Party through its control and evaluation of personnel provides an additional, particularly intrusive, means of monitoring behavior. Communist Party oversight makes it possible to draw distinctions between different types of behavior with a precision not possible in most systems. While this ability is undermined by corruption within the monitoring agencies, it still represents a capability which will be foreign in most developing societies. Second, the authoritarian structure is capable of drawing particularly sharp lines between areas of activity, so that it can make certain fields or sectors off-limits, while throwing other areas open for competition. Since the system has direct command-and-control capabilities, it does not need to be bothered by the search for a consistent rule that can be applied across fields. Third, and finally, the Communist Party has the obvious ability to use its own hierarchical command relations to reinforce, or even replace, the nominal rules and incentives of these newly repurposed institutions. Indeed, sometimes the institutions themselves are actually shells, set up perhaps for legitimate reasons of gaining experience or soliciting public input, while the Communist Party continues to make decisions behind the scenes.

For example, in the Chinese state-run enterprise sector, the Communist Party reinforces, or sometimes pre-empts, the emergent formal institutions of corporate governance. Thus, SASAC nominally exercises the government's role as owner of state firms, but the Communist Party continues to make the most important personnel decisions. Indeed, the largest central SOEs are so important that we even have the unusual case of an openly published directive that specifies that appointment of the top three managers in 50-some enterprises nominally under the SASAC will be made directly by the Organization Department of the Central

22. Barry Naughton, 'Hierarchy and the market economy: how has political hierarchy shaped China's transition to a market economy?', in Janos Kornai and Yingyi Qian, eds, *Market and Socialism Reconsidered* (London: Macmillan, for the International Economic Association, 2008).

Committee of the Party.[23] More generally, the Party Committee lies at the center of a network of interacting organizations that hold ultimate authority in the state-run corporate sector.[24] Ordinarily, the Party chooses to exercise power in the background, especially when the foreground institutions are functioning well, but in the event of a mishap, the direct control relationship can always be resumed. This is particularly useful in a situation where nascent regulatory institutions are imperfect, not arm's length, and sometimes incapable of performing their function. In these cases, the hierarchy simply makes rulings directly, especially through personnel decisions.[25] This capability gives China's institutional innovations and organization re-purposings a robustness that is not available to most other developing economies.

China's reform period has seen a strengthening both of incentives and of hierarchy. The hierarchical system that runs China has been renovated, professionalized, regularized and strengthened. It cannot be said that China has had no political reform; rather, the political reforms that have taken place have created a newly effective authoritarian hierarchy. The result is a system in which market incentives and administrative supervision and surveillance are *both* unusually strong. The system is pulled taut. Officials and managers have lots of authority and strong temptations, but they are also subject to strong surveillance and draconian punishments. Since an authoritarian hierarchy with these characteristics is likely to remain fairly unique to China, it suggests that Chinese experience is not likely to be highly generalizable.

Conclusion: sustainability and evolution

The Chinese system will continue to evolve, since it faces rapidly changing conditions and has already 'learned' the need to evolve continuously. The immediate impact of the global financial crisis will be to reinforce the system's current form and postpone further changes. This is because the quick responsiveness and option of direct control that the current system provides will be prized in the current crisis environment. But after the world emerges from crisis, the Chinese development model will face major changes because of two aspects of economic and social change. First, China will soon reach a turning point of economic growth, in which it will cease being a pure follower economy dominated by industrialization and the transition from rural to urban. Second, the sheer size and sophistication of China's economy will require further adaptation of the system's key parameters.

23. Communist Party of China, 'Party center notification on a few matters relating to the establishment of State Council SASAC', (24 March 2003), in *2004 Zhongguo Guoyou Zichan Jiandu Guanli Nianjian* [*China State-owned Assets Supervision and Management Yearbook*] (Beijing: Zhongguo Jingji, 2004), p. 99.

24. This relationship is described very clearly in Christopher McNally, 'Strange bedfellows: Communist Party institutions in the corporate governance of Chinese state holding corporations', *Business and Politics* 4(1), (2002), pp. 91–115.

25. An interesting case of this occurred at the end of 2007, when China Eastern Airlines tried to bring in Singapore Airlines as a strategic investor. The proposal was eventually defeated by a vote of minority shareholders, who had to approve it according to corporate governance provisions of the listed vehicles in Hong Kong and Shanghai. But the key decisions were actually made behind the scenes when the chairman of China Air—which vigorously opposed the proposal—was promoted to be head of the nominal regulatory agency CAAC. Such a promotion could only have been decided by the Politburo Standing Committee (see Naughton, 'SASAC and rising corporate power').

BARRY NAUGHTON

China has been able to cut many corners in the development process because of its status as a follower country. The essence of rapid growth has been moving labor expeditiously from the backward agricultural sector and into the modern and semi-modern industrial and service sectors, and in doing so China has been able to mimic the process of forerunner economies both in the West and in East Asia. Pointing this out should not be taken as playing down the Chinese achievement. After all, *every* developing country could make much the same statement, yet it is still a difficult task, and China has succeeded at it by making the transformation more rapidly and more thoroughly than any other economy. But the specific Chinese approach was developed in response to those specific challenges. It was relatively easy to know what infrastructure needed to be built—which highways, which ports—once planners had confidence in the growth trajectory. Moreover, the growth potential was clearly high, as long as investment momentum could be sustained to bring people out of agriculture, house them in cities, and equip them with the machinery needed for a new occupation.

This phase of China's development is almost over. By the end of 2007, only 40% of China's labor force was still in agriculture. The agricultural labor force is declining in absolute terms—almost 75 million people left the farms between 2002 and 2007—and even more in relative terms. To be sure, this process is not over, and indeed, it went temporarily into reverse in the wake of the global financial crisis, but already the Chinese countryside has been transformed. Agriculture is increasingly the province of older farmers: most of the young people have already left the villages. The era of mass movement out of agriculture will soon be coming to an end. As this occurs, the need will be less to create infrastructure pell-mell, and more to improve the efficiency and creativity of existing sectors. The current Chinese complex of institutions and strategies is much better suited for the earlier task than for the coming task. The Chinese economy is approaching a structural turning point.

As China approaches this turning point, the government also finds itself managing an economy dramatically different in scale from anything it has dealt with before. The state-run oligopolists are becoming global-scale giants. Other sectors are expanding rapidly with private firms vastly out-growing residual state firms. In one version of the future, each of the remaining state firms would be reorganized into a transparent joint stock company, and floated on the stock market. The markets would be better able to value these corporations and judge the relative effectiveness and promise of different managerial teams. The state would then turn over some or all of its ownership stake to competing wealth managers, including sovereign wealth funds, pension funds and perhaps investment banks, and open the door to a more thorough restructuring of managerial incentives in the companies themselves. State ownership would no longer be exercised primarily through SASAC, and SASAC would turn into one of several social asset-holders, whose performance and compensation would be benchmarked against other asset managers.

But for the system to move in this direction, the Communist Party has to acquiesce in a qualitative redefinition of its function. The Party would have to agree that 'one share, one vote' really means that appointments to the Board of Directors, and ultimately appointments of managers, are determined by weighted alliances of different shareholders, and not just by the Party speaking for the dominant government shareholder. Such a move is entirely conceivable, but it would also be unprecedented. If the Chinese corporate sector were to take this step, it implies that we would continue to see important government actors, but more diverse, and in a relatively highly marketized environment.

It is worth bringing out the contrast with Japan during the peak years of Japan's industrial policy (1960s–1970s). Japan's market was much less open to foreign trade and, even more crucially, Japan was essentially closed to foreign investment, in sharp contrast to China today. The result, when combined with Japan's small geographic extent, was that policy-makers could rely primarily on direct administrative guidance and the ability of bureaucrats to compel 'concertation' among a limited group of large corporations. This kind of informal consultation is only barely possible in China today, because of its vast extent and diversity. As a result, China is already more market-driven and less active in shaping specific industrial outcomes than Japan was during the heyday of industrial policy, even though state ownership looms so much larger in China today. The Chinese state sector is likely to continue to evolve in this distinctive direction, towards a model that is more open and more 'financial' than was the case in Japan. Even though the government does not hesitate to intervene, and certainly puts its thumb on the scales from time to time, the end result is that markets absorb the impact of government intervention and transmit it as prices and other kinds of market information.

There is without doubt a world-wide movement intellectually away from the mis-placed certainties of market fundamentalism and the Washington Consensus. At the same time, there is an equally evident movement towards governments resuming an activist and interventionist role in the economy, at least in developing countries. The association between these two doubtless inter-twined movements allows us to say that the Washington Consensus is being replaced by different views of the world, yet this initial movement is itself a primarily pragmatic adaptation to circumstance, rather than the adoption of a new set of principles. We see this in, for example, the rise of Sovereign Wealth Funds, which emerged in response to under-valued currencies and the surge in natural resource prices, and which have been accorded broader legitimacy because of the need for new investment funds in the wake of the global financial crisis. And we see it in a willingness of governments to re-engage with specific initiatives to spur development activity within the context of global markets. A nice index of this is the apparent decision by the Japanese government to resume funding commercial aircraft development. Back in 1973, in the twilight of the Japanese government's period of 'industrial policy', the government pulled the plug on its subsidies to a commercial aircraft development and production consortium led by Mitsubishi, widely seen as a fiasco. In 2008, Japan's Ministry of Economy, Trade and Industry announced it was once again prepared to fund a third of the US$1.5 billion development costs for a 70–90 seat regional jet to be produced by, yes, Mitsubishi Heavy Industries.[26] Surely, there could be no better indicator that the pendulum has swung.

Yet, it is premature to speak of a consensus. Indeed, the contrary is true. There is a startling lack of consensus among economists about what the main principles and

26. Jonathan Soble, 'Japan set to build passenger jets with ANA order', *Financial Times*, (28 March 2008), p. 22.

lessons are. The attempts by those such as the Spence Commission to define a new consensus are to be welcomed, and their definition is certainly superior to that of the Washington Consensus, but their new 'consensus' looks an awful lot like the old development consensus of the aid agencies of the 1950s and 1960s. That similarity shouldn't lead us to reject or denigrate their findings. After all, reaffirming old truths can be just as positive as discovering new truths, but it does mean that the specificity of the Chinese experience needs to be harnessed to a more intellectually focused problem. What have we learned since the 1960s that will allow us to sidestep some of the pitfalls of the 1950s and 1960s developmental approach? What was specific to the Chinese approach that allowed China to avoid some of the many problems that were predicted for it? To what extent was the Chinese success tied up with its maintenance of a hierarchical and authoritarian order? Only after we have been able to address those questions with greater confidence will we be able to speak about a Beijing Consensus.

Part III
The Policy-Making Process

[9]

St Comp Int Dev (2008) 43:1–26
DOI 10.1007/s12116-007-9014-4

Policy Experimentation in China's Economic Rise

Sebastian Heilmann

Published online: 27 December 2007

Abstract Policy experimentation is frequently highlighted as a potent means to facilitate institutional innovation, and avoid reformist leaps in the dark by injecting bottom-up initiative and local knowledge into the national policy process. Yet experimentation remains a surprisingly vague concept in the debate over variants of economic governance. This article contributes to the study of experiment-based policymaking by examining the distinctive tools, processes, and effects of experimental programs in major domains of China's economic reform. China's experience attests to the potency of experimentation in bringing about transformative change, even in a rigid authoritarian, bureaucratic environment, and regardless of strong political opposition. Large-scale experimentation stimulated policy learning and economic expansion effectively in those sectors in which political elites could benefit from supporting new types of private and transnational entrepreneurial activity. Conversely, experimental programs largely failed in generating an effective provision of social goods which would require a combination of active societal supervision and strict central government enforcement to make it work. Though the impact of reform experiments varies between policy domains, China's experimentation-based policy process has been essential to redefining basic policy parameters. At the heart of this process, we find a pattern of central–local interaction in generating policy—"experimentation under hierarchy"—which constitutes a notable addition to the repertoires of governance that have been tried for achieving economic transformation.

The research for this article was supported by the German National Research Foundation and the Fairbank Center for East Asian Research at Harvard University. The author is especially indebted to Elizabeth Perry, Steven Goldstein, Rolf Langhammer, Dani Rodrik, Victor Shih, Ezra Vogel, and Rudolf Wagner for their encouragement and comments. Nancy Hearst made a crucial contribution by bringing precious sources from the Fairbank Center's library to my attention that I otherwise would have overlooked.

S. Heilmann (✉)
Trier University, Politikwissenschaft, 54296 Trier, Germany
e-mail: Heilmann@uni-trier.de

Introduction

Thanks to the institutional turn that has taken place in development studies over the last two decades, we now understand much better the impact of diverse institutional arrangements on economic growth. However, institutionalist research has not produced many concrete answers to one crucial challenge: how to facilitate institutional change despite massive inertia and opposition that block structural reform and inhibit economic development in many political economies, without trying to impose foreign blueprints and thereby ignoring the intricacies of local conditions (Evans 2004, 2005). A critical undercurrent within the institutional turn, represented for instance by Peter Evans and Dani Rodrik, has consistently stressed that it is not enough to understand and propagandize the institutional prerequisites and international "best practices" for economic growth and good governance. We need to identify political and administrative processes that help to mobilize bottom-up initiative, stimulate institutional experimentation, and feed viable local experience into national policymaking. As Charles Lindblom (1979, p 521) bluntly notes, the real challenge of policymaking lies in "smuggling" changes into often uninviting and resistant political economies.

This article attempts to contribute to the study of policy processes that can bring about administrative, legislative, and economic institutional innovation—even in the context of a rigid authoritarian-bureaucratic environment and regardless of strong political opposition. The focus will not be *what* institutions have to be established to fulfil certain tasks from a predictive functionalist perspective. Instead, I will concentrate on *how* existing, and initially deficient, institutions can be put to work, transformed, or replaced for economic and social development in an open-ended process of institutional innovation that is based on locally generated solutions rather than on imported policy recipes.

One country that potentially can provide important lessons on this is China. Judged by Evans' (2004, p 30) emphasis on the need to "expand the range of institutional strategies explored," China has advanced the farthest among the large emerging countries in achieving such an objective in the economic realm. During the last three decades, China's political economy has proven to be highly innovative in finding policies and institutions to master the complex challenges of large-scale economic change while avoiding systemic breakdown. Mukand and Rodrik (2005) move the Chinese experience, together with that of India, to the center of their analysis and stress the unorthodox policies, regulatory practices, and unclarified property rights regime that have accompanied the strong economic growth. China's economic transition has been facilitated by an unusual adaptive capacity that, according to North (1990, p 80–81; 2005, p 154), entails an institutional structure that, despite ubiquitous uncertainties, enables it to try out alternative approaches to overcome long-standing impediments to economic development, tackle newly emerging challenges, and grasp opportunities when they open up. That this was possible in the Chinese context is unexpected since, throughout the course of its economic reform, China's policymakers and administrators have had to work with the institutions of a Communist party-state—an institutional context that has proven to be extremely inflexible in almost every other place where this type of polity has existed (Bunce 1999).

I argue that a distinctive policy cycle, experimentation under hierarchy, is the key to understanding the emergence of an unexpectedly adaptive authoritarianism in

China. Though ambitious central state planning, grand technocratic modernization schemes, and megaprojects have never disappeared from the Chinese policy agenda, an entrenched process of experimentation that precedes the enactment of many national policies has served as a powerful correcting mechanism.

First, I propose a definition of transformative experimentation that helps to understand why this approach to reform differs fundamentally from conventional policymaking and is not confined to mere incremental change. Next, I examine the specific tools and processes that facilitated experimentalism in China. Then I turn to case studies of experimentation in crucial economic reform domains that, although sharing the same basic processual patterns, reveal very different political dynamics and innovative effects, due to a starkly varying constellation of actors, interests, and risks that promote or inhibit change in different policy subsystems. The following section synthesizes the insights that China's experience gives on the interrelation between policy learning and rent-seeking in experimentation. In the conclusion, I discuss the applicability of the experimental approach to reform-making in other political economies.

Policy Experimentation as a Distinct Mode of Governance

Several prominent scholars have pointed to policy experimentation as an effective mechanism that may help to find out what works on the ground, induce behavioral changes, and produce institutional innovations that are conducive to entrepreneurialism, investment, and economic growth (Hayek 1978; North 1990; Roland 2000; Mukand and Rodrik 2005). Though the importance of experimentation is frequently highlighted, it remains a surprisingly ill-defined and vague concept. In a lax usage, experimentation often just paraphrases the cycles of policy reversals and policy re-prioritization that are characteristic of all political systems if established policies come to be seen as failing, too costly, or politically risky. Experimentation in a stricter definition, as used in here, implies a policy process in which experimenting units try out a variety of methods and processes to find imaginative solutions to predefined tasks or to new challenges that emerge during experimental activity. Policy experimentation is not equivalent to freewheeling trial and error or spontaneous policy diffusion. It is a purposeful and coordinated activity geared to producing novel policy options that are injected into official policymaking and then replicated on a larger scale, or even formally incorporated into national law.

In more technical terms, experimentation aims "to inform policy by using experiments with direct interventions and control groups instead of observational studies or theoretical analyses" (Mosteller 2006, pp 487, 496). If experimentation is designed and evaluated by social scientists as part of government-sponsored pilot programs, it is usually limited to narrowly defined trial measures and preselected target groups. It often is confined to the fine-tuning of implementation technicalities (such as testing the suitability of a new social security card in a pilot site), but only very rarely to substantive policy formulation (such as the extent, focus, or budgeting of social policies) that are the object of complex bargaining processes in which tactical political considerations weigh much heavier than outside expertise (Jowell 2003).

In contrast, the transformative policy experimentation laid out in this article is much more comprehensive and ambitious since it strives to alter economic and administrative behavior and institutions. Such experimentation also opens up entirely new market segments and establishes new types of corporate organization, thereby regularly moving beyond the originally defined test groups and procedures and involving policymakers on different levels of the political system. Mosteller (2006, pp 479, 480, 492–496) sees such "reorganization experiments" as the most difficult to carry out because they depend on a chain of complex interrelations, may require a great deal of time and resources, tend to provoke stiff political opposition, have to deal with ongoing contextual changes, and are subject to political-administrative interference and changes of the rules of the game in the middle of the experimental process. Transformative experimentation usually comes in the shape of demonstration projects taking place in a politically realistic—i.e., fluid, disturbed, and contested—context that escapes strict scientific controls, but can give a fuller view of the workings of novel policies and their impact on major social, market, or administrative actors.

Policy experimentation in this variant constitutes a distinct mode of governance that differs in one fundamental way from standard assumptions about policymaking. The conventional model of the policy process that is widely taken for granted by jurists, economists, and political scientists holds that policy analysis, formulation, and embodiment in legislation *precede* implementation. Policy experimentation, as presented in this study, means innovating through implementation first, and drafting universal laws and regulations later.

At first sight, policy experimentation displays commonalities with what Lindblom (1959, 1979) characterizes as the incremental method of successive limited comparisons in making public policy: the exploratory, reversible character of policymaking and the prior reduction of political antagonisms by avoiding drastic change at the outset. Yet, under certain conditions identified in the following analysis, experimentation can transcend incrementalist tinkering with existing practices and lead to drastic policy departures and transformative change marked by the emergence of new configurations of actors, interests, institutions, ideologies, and goals.

The pursuit of extensive, continuous, and loosely institutionalized experimentation can be understood as a crucial policy mechanism in China's economic rise. Several students of China's political economy have already emphasized the importance of experimentation in facilitating institutional innovation and economic efficiency gains (Rawski 1995; Cao et al. 1999; Roland 2000; Qian 2003). However, the specific origins, tools, processes, and effects of experimentation in major domains of economic reform have largely been unstudied. Chinese policymakers and their advisors, in public statements and in interviews conducted for this study, tend to explain the pervasive use of experimental programs as a product of reform entrepreneurship, either as a controlled "scientific" generation of novel policies or as a way to pioneer policy change in circumvention of political and bureaucratic constraints. In social science explanations, Chinese-style policy experimentation is treated either as a product of specific structural preconditions that allowed for sectoral and spatial gradualism (see Roland 2000), as an outcome of administrative decentralization and jurisdictional competition (see Montinola et al. 1995; Yang 1997), or as a second-best approach forced onto reformists by the need to broaden their base of political support while avoiding ideological controversies and keeping factional rivals at bay (see Shirk 1994; Woo 1999; Cai and Treisman 2006).

Each of these explanations captures important individual aspects of China's economic reform policy. Taking a broader view that includes the entire policy cycle, the processes that are at the heart of large-scale experimentation in China do not easily fit into standard assumptions of central-local interaction and policy implementation that are based largely on the experiences of democratic and federalist systems in advanced political economies where constitutional government produces vertical checks and balances. In the hierarchical setting of China's party-state, the causal relationship that underlies central-local interaction in experimentation is different. In China, proceeding from experimental programs to national policy is shaped by a policy terminology and methodology that stem from the formative revolution-era experience of the Chinese Communist Party, which legitimated developing policy by "proceeding from point to surface" and implementing policy "in accordance with local circumstances" (Heilmann 2008). The pattern of experimental governance that we find in China's party-state, experimentation under hierarchy, has distinctive foundations and is not identical with what is treated conventionally under sweeping headings such as decentralization or federalism. Though hands-on experimentation is delegated to local officials, China's central government plays an indispensable role in scaling up and generalizing local innovations, thereby providing coordination to the reform process. This approach to experimentation resembles the modes of social program replication that have been discussed in the development community (see Wazir and Oudenhoven 1998), in particular, the approach of "staged replication," which moves from local pilot testing through implementation in a broader selection of demonstration sites to universal replication. In contrast to the experience of other countries, including India, where the "corpses of pilot projects litter the development field" (Pyle 1980, pp 123, 124), Chinese-style experimentation managed to transform many pilot projects into full-scale operational programs that cover a broad policy spectrum ranging from economic regulation to organizational reforms within the Communist Party.

Tools of Experimentation

In democratic polities, policy experimentation comes as mostly small-scale explorative pilot projects, as pioneering legislation by individual states in federal systems ("states as laboratories"), as experimental or sunset clauses incorporated into formal legislation, or, very rarely, as a special dispensation for local administrative districts to be exempt from certain provisions of national law (see Morand 1993; Greenberg et al. 2003; Hummel 2003). The approach in China's party-state is very different. Experimentation comes in three main forms as (1) experimental regulation (provisional rules made for trial implementation), (2) "experimental points" (model demonstrations and pilot projects in a specific policy domain), and (3) "experimental zones" (local jurisdictions with broad discretionary powers).

Experimental Regulation

An examination of regulations dealing with the economy (including health services and social insurance reform) during the first two decades of China's economic

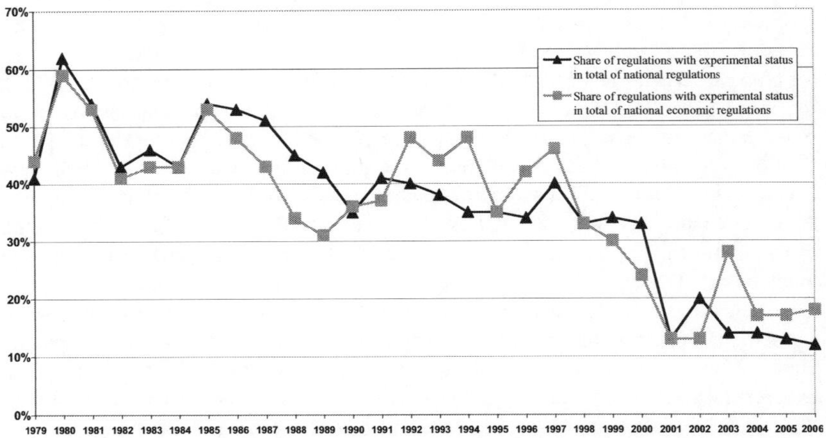

Database: Beijing University Law School, http://vip.chinalawinfo.com/Newlaw2002/chl, as of August 15, 2007. Based on an analysis of ordinances, stipulations, and measures issued in the name of the State Council and ministerial-level central government organs that are marked in their title as "provisional," "experimental" or as regulating "experimental points/zones." Regulatory documents with a lesser legal and administrative status (classified as "normative documents," *guifanxing wenjian*), are not included in this quantitative analysis.

Fig. 1 Experimental regulation in China, 1979–2006

reforms shows that throughout this period, well above 30% of the total were marked in their titles as provisional or experimental or as regulating experimental points and zones (see Fig. 1). In 1985, the national legislature made a formal decision, giving the central government the power to formulate interim regulations concerning economic structural reform. Since then, the government has made full use of this prerogative and issued thousands of economic regulations, bypassing the legislative bodies. Corne (2002, p 382) points to a proliferation of experimental regulations in China's economic policymaking, characterizing it as "a form of 'quasi-law,'" that is, revised and finalized by formal legislation only after sufficient experience has been obtained during the trial period. Since 1997, the share of experimental economic legislation has declined, due to the growing overall institutionalization of economic administration and World Trade Organization (WTO)-driven harmonization with international regulatory standards. From 2001 to 2006, the share of experimental economic regulation has fluctuated between a bottom of 13% (2001, 2002), and an extraordinary peak of 28% in 2003, when rural and welfare experimentation were pushed energetically by a just installed new leadership. From 2004 the share remained almost constant at 17% to 18%. Considering that the main burden for policy experimentation was formally delegated to regional governments in 1998, the share of experimental regulations issued by the central government since then remains significant. Clearly, the increasing comprehensiveness of economic legislation and the impact of the WTO have reduced, but not terminated, the role of experimental legislation in policy innovation. Although experimental regulations have lost the quantitatively striking importance they enjoyed in the 1980s and 1990s, they are particularly important in certain policy domains, such as rural and welfare reform, that draw strong attention from top policymakers. In actuality, the distribution of reformist ambition over the spectre of policy domains can still be derived from the concentration of experimental regulation in individual sectors.

Experimental Points

Even more pervasive than formal experimental regulation is the use of a particularly Chinese governance technique in preparing, testing, and revising policies and regulations: "experimental points" or "proceeding from point to surface." The term experimental point indicates experimentation with new policies or institutions limited to a certain policy area or economic sector and carried out in limited experimental units. Most major reform initiatives in post-Mao China were prepared and tried out by means of experimental points before they were universalized in national regulations. At the end of the 1980s, the experimental point method became fully institutionalized at the central government level. Within the National Commission for Economic Structural Reform, a high-level Bureau for Comprehensive Planning and Experimental Points was established in 1988. This bureau, in existence until 1998, was charged with guiding and coordinating the various departmental and local experimental points in economic reform, as well as with drafting related economic regulations. When the bureau was overwhelmed by the administrative complexity and political controversies inherent in this task, experimental point work was officially delegated to the regional governments in 1998 (Zhongyang zhengfu jigou 1998, pp 466–469). However, individual central government bodies continued to coordinate experimental point work to promote major national reform initiatives. General implementation guidelines are issued for every experimental point that is authorized by the central government. Initially, these guidelines were vague, simply establishing guiding thoughts and general demands. In recent years, provisions regarding the establishment, objectives, and legal embedding of individual experimental points have become much more elaborate. A series of recently designated experimental points dealing with rural reforms, for example, has been established by issuing a formal State Council circular for each pilot program (*Yearbook* 2005, pp 50–54, 90–92). Between 2003 and 2006, a total of 138 experimental point programs coordinated by 31 ministerial-level State Council organs, can be documented, with a special focus on rural economic and societal policies, financial regulation, social security, health care, and education. Each of these experiments was implemented in several locations concurrently. Notwithstanding the overall regularization of legislative procedures since the mid-1990s, experimental points continue to be emphasized by national ministries as indispensable in optimizing the implementation of national policies.

Experimental Zones

Whereas experimental points in a narrow sense involve testing specific measures in a specific policy area only, experimental zones are geographical units and jurisdictions that are provided by the central authorities with broad discretionary powers, for example, to streamline the economic bureaucracy or to promote foreign investment and thereby generate or test new policy approaches (State Council General Office 1992, foreword). Every new reform push was marked with the establishment of a new batch of special zones (see Table 1), "creating a new system alongside, or in the interstices of, the existing one" that served as a test ground for entire new sets of unorthodox policies and institutions (Naughton 2007, pp 406–408). The internationally best-known examples of this reform approach are China's special economic zones, which were also authorized to draft and to enact their own legislation. The Shenzhen Special Economic Zone (SEZ), due to its proximity to Hong Kong, turned out to be the most active laboratory of such legislation. It issued more than 400 pieces of economic regulation from 1979 to 1990, and exerted a strong influence on national economic legislation with regard to foreign trade and investment (Zhang 2003, pp 140, 141). The SEZ experiments are characterized by testing in a Chinese context controversial policies that often were inspired by experience in neighboring East Asian or Western advanced economies. The actual content of many major experimental policies pioneered in the SEZs, for example, those dealing with land auctions, wholly foreign-owned companies, or labor market liberalization by far exceeded the reform limitations, which then still applied to the rest of China. Thus, SEZs were distinct from conventional experimental points that remained fully integrated in the domestic economy and were subject to stiffer political constraints.

Due to China's deep integration into the international economy, constraints on experimental policy solutions have been growing. The rules of the WTO have placed restrictions on experimental regulations in the special economic zones (Wu 2004). China's national legislature has taken an increasingly critical stance toward government experimentation that bypasses formal legislation. The Chinese Communist Party itself emphasizes law-based policy implementation more. Despite these recent constraints, institutional and policy experimentation continues to be employed vigorously in China. The government's ambitious plan to create a "new socialist countryside" has become a new field of intensive decentralized experimentation. In the 2000–2007 period, a stupendous variety of experimental point programs and

Table 1 Major types of experimental zones designated by China's central government

Major types of experimental zones	Number
1. Special Economic Zones (from 1979)	5
2. Cities with status as "experimental point for comprehensive reform" (from 1981)	72
3. Economic and technological development zones (from 1984)	54
4. Coastal economic development zones (from 1985)	7
5. Experimental zones for rural reform (from 1987)	30
6. Experimental zone for developing the commodity economy (Wenzhou 1987–1989)	1
7. High-tech industrial development zones (from 1988)	53
8. Investment zones for Taiwanese investors (from 1989)	4
9. Shanghai Pudong new zone (1990)	1
10. Bonded zones (special customs regulation) (from 1990)	15
11. Border-area economic cooperation zones (from 1992)	14
12. "Experimental zones for comprehensive coordinated reform" (from 2005)	2
13. "Experimental zones for coordinated and balanced development between urban and rural areas" (from 2007)	2

Data as of July 2007. Data compiled from: State Council General Office 1992; Yearbook, 1989ff. Homepages of the Ministry of Agriculture/Research Center for Rural Reform (http://www.rcre.cn), State Council Taiwan Affairs Office (http://www.gwytb.gov.cn)

point-to-surface replication efforts have dealt with pressing rural issues such as the marketing of rural products (from 2000), reduction of taxes and levies (2000–2004), land management (2001–2004), cooperative health care (since 2003) and rural credit cooperatives (since 2003). Experimental programs resulted in major policy change regarding the abolishment of entire categories of rural taxes and levies and the introduction of central government co-funding of rural health services. Beyond rural reforms, in 2005 and 2006, two "experimental zones for comprehensive coordinated reform" in Shanghai and Tianjin have been designated by the central government to take on the issue of institutional complementarities between economic, social, and administrative development. Experimental policy tools continue to be used for pioneering reforms that belong to the top of the policy agenda.

The Experimentation-Based Policy Cycle

In rule-of-law systems, the principle of law-based administration virtually rules out discretionary and experimental administrative measures before enacting laws and regulations. One striking feature of the legislation-centered policy process in liberal democracies is that the potential impact of policies under deliberation must be largely assessed beforehand, without first being able to refine novel policies through implementation in experimental sites. Even the much quoted state-level policy innovation in federalist systems ("laboratories of federalism") firmly rests on issuing laws and regulations, rarely on pre-legislation administrative experiments.

Conversely, discretionary experimentation through implementation *in advance* of legislation plays a crucial role in China's policy cycle. The analytical model depicted in Fig. 2 synthesizes common features that can be identified across the different domains of reform experimentation and also lie at the heart of the policy cases examined in the ensuing sections of this article. The processual patterns differ starkly from standard models of the policy cycle in their content and sequence.

As can be expected in an authoritarian party-state, initiation of experimental programs from inside the government is by far the most frequent starting point of policy experimentation. Based on the findings obtained in a series of interviews with senior officials who have been in charge of experimental point work over the last three decades, most experimental efforts are set off by local policymakers who, to tackle pressing problems in their jurisdiction and at the same time pursue personal career and material interests, seek the informal backing of their pilot efforts by higher-level policy patrons. Contacts are usually taken up during inspection tours of senior leaders to the localities or through secretaries, advisors, and researchers that serve as go-betweens for policymakers on different administrative levels. Encouragement and protection extended by senior leaders to local experimenters, a mechanism of informal "policy hedging," is a major determinant of pioneering behavior on the local level since unhedged individual initiative can be either risky careerwise or simply futile in China's polity. Even in cases such as rural decollectivization and private business growth, in which popular entrepreneurialism at the outset triggered local policy adjustments, the informal rules of policy hedging and senior patronage turned out to be decisive in legitimating, defending, and scaling up local experiments. In a hierarchical system, bottom-up experimentation goes nowhere without higher-level patrons or advocates

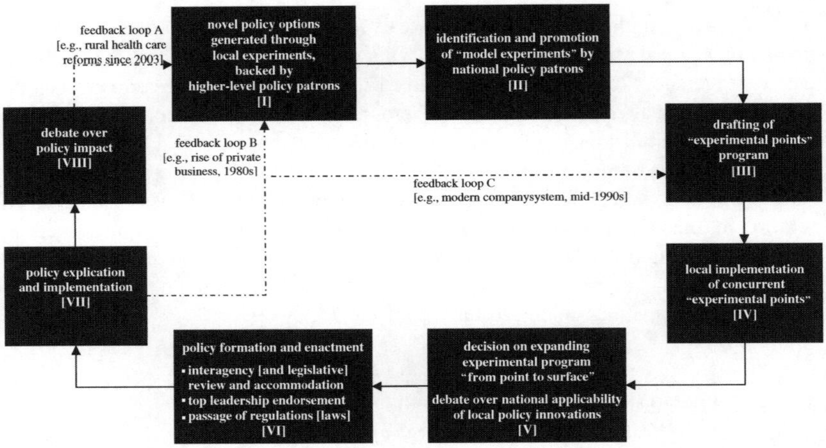

Fig. 2 China's experimentation-based policy cycle

who are indispensable in propagating and rolling out locally generated policy innovations. In essence, as the case studies will demonstrate, distinguishing between bottom-up ("spontaneous") and top-down ("mobilization-style") initiation of experimentation is nearly meaningless since there is a strong element of both, local initiative and central sponsorship, in the initial stages of major experimental efforts. Neither works without the other. The dynamics of the experimental process rest precisely on this interplay (Fig. 2; I).

After the results and means of local experimentation have been endorsed by a powerful policymaker as a model for others, veritable campaigns to broaden support for the new policy option are initiated by top-level policy advocates and their followers. Policy advisors and researchers are typically asked to make systematic studies that take into account domestic and foreign experience. Foreign experts from economically advanced countries and international organizations are invited to contribute to policy intelligence and to drafting concrete proposals (Fig. 2; II). If positive results of local experiments and potential benefits of policy innovation can be successfully communicated among the policymaking community, and if other top-level decisionmakers join the policy initiative, national guidelines for piloting in a larger number of "experimental points" will be formulated. This action leads to an intensification of lobbying efforts by local officials who strive to obtain official "experimental point" status to gain access to central preferential treatment and to improve their career prospects (Fig. 2; III).

The central government authorizes the jurisdictions that have been selected as official experimental points to try out new policy solutions. The center also selectively extends generous subsidies (at least to the end of the 1990s) and discretionary powers to the designated pilot projects that are obliged to report regularly to higher-up authorities (Fig. 2; IV). Inspectors are sent in to conduct official evaluations. Feedback and consultation between national policymakers and local experimenters are facilitated during official conferences that deal with the lessons learned from local experiments. Policymakers identify successful innovations produced by the experimental units. These innovations become the subject of internal and often also public debate. If several major national policymakers support the "model experience" of specific experimental points and agree to "proceed from point to surface," a new wave of piloting based on the "model experiment" is extended to a much larger number of local jurisdictions. Simultaneous emulation campaigns are started, which frequently trigger a veritable policy tourism, with hundreds of outside delegations converging on the sites of officially designated "model experiments" (Fig. 2; V).

National policymakers order the drafting of formal government regulations or laws and give detailed directives to the drafting group. Then a complex process of interministerial review and accommodation commences, which is similar to bureaucratic regulation-making in most other polities. Top national policymakers can still stall the new policy initiative. If none of them raises and organizes energetic opposition, the new policy will be accepted by the Politburo and the State Council and imposed nationwide through central party directives, government regulations, or law (Fig. 2; VI). Yet, the adoption of new regulations or laws is not the end of the policy process since the ensuing explication and implementation of policy (Fig. 2; VII) may yield an immediate next round of experimentation, as indicated by the feedback loops B and C. Those government regulations that are marked as "provisional" and "experimental" in their title expressly invite efforts at policy modification through implementation. Feedback loop A, through which a new round of experimentation is initiated in response to the impact of new policies (Fig. 2; VIII) is the standard feedback mechanism. All three basic types of feedback processes are found in the case studies presented below.

It is the distinctive interaction of generating national and local policy that is essential for continuing the experimental policy cycle. We find the hands-on experimenters in local governments, not in the central government whose role is focused on filtering out generalizable models and policy lessons that can be derived from local experience. Centrifugal forces that naturally come up in such a policy process are contained by the hierarchical nature of the Communist Party's system of top-down cadre appointments including all important leading positions in the polity and state-controlled parts of the economy. Due to its segmented character, policy experimentation prevents collective action by local governments that, instead of collaborating in demanding all-out decentralization, lobby the central government for individual concessions (Zweig 2002, p 52). The atomistic character of intrastate lobbying essentially bolsters the political authority of the center.

In their study of central-local interaction in China's reform process, Cao et al. (1999, pp 124, 125) draw analogies with federalism but miss the central role of higher-level policymakers in granting local experiments a go-ahead through nonintervention, informal patronage, or public advocacy. In a hierarchical system of official appointments, the authority of higher levels is a fact and must be taken into account even by the boldest local-level pioneers of reform. The "federalism, Chinese style" approach suggests that hierarchical governance has been replaced by administrative decentralization, jurisdictional competition, and central-local bargaining. Although these factors play an important role in central-local interactions and local governments clearly feel more confident and secure today in making local policies, none of these changes has eliminated the weight of hierarchy and ad hoc central interference in China's political economy.

As an organizational approach, the Chinese "point-to-surface" approach in policy development is devised to ensure local initiative while maintaining ultimate hierarchical control (Shue 1980, p 88). Since this method is decidedly open with regard to the means of reform, it naturally leads to decentralized initiatives that cannot be anticipated by the center. In the process of policy conception, implementation, and revision, governments at various levels thereby become participants, sometimes leaders, and sometimes followers of reform initiatives. The entire policy process must be conceptualized as an oscillating multilevel interaction rather than as a dichotomized process of centralization vs. decentralization.

The Impact of Experimentation in Major Policy Domains

The pervasive use of special tools and patterns of experimentation substantiates the importance of unorthodox policy mechanisms in China's approach to economic reform but it does not tell us much about the actual interests behind and effects resulting from experimental regulations, points, or zones in the policy process. To clarify the functions and effects of experimentation in China's economic transformation, we must take a closer look at crucial contested domains of reform-era policymaking.

As the discipline of policy studies has amply demonstrated, policymaking is "taking place in policy domain-specific subsystems, which operate more or less independently of one another in a parallel fashion" (Adam and Kriesi 2007, p 129). Thus the specific configuration of institutions, actors, interests, ideas, issues, and risks in a policy subsystem determines the chances and outcome of generating and revising policy. Moreover, policy subsystems tend to reveal durable patterns of interaction, which undergo major changes if systemic or sectoral crises destroy core elements of the old configuration or, less dramatically, if new actors with differing interests and ideologies manage to enter the subsystem and modify the customary rules of the game.

Table 2, to classify major domains of China's economic reform according to their dynamics of experimentation, is structured along two key variables: (1) newly emerging economic actors and their opportunities for interest articulation in national

Table 2 Patterns of experimentation in crucial domains of economic reform

	Denial and delay of new actors' entrance to national policymaking	Entrance of new actors to national policymaking
Extensive policy risks in experimentation	*restructuring of state-owned enterprises (1978 to mid-1990s)* incentivized bureaucratic experimentation results in policy repertoire tinkering	*liberalization of foreign investment and trade (1992–2000)* central policy pushes trigger runaway local experimentation
Limited policy risks in experimentation	*toleration and promotion of private business (1978–2004)* low-key local experimentation sets off successive national policy adjustments	*introduction and regulation of stock exchanges (1990–2005)* technocratic grand experimentation allows policy repertoire extension

policymaking, and (2) the policy risk attached to experimentation, which shall be narrowly defined as the extent of uncertainty among national policymakers about the impact of experimentation on core properties of the political economy (state control and dominant position of state enterprises) and on essential systemic outputs (economic growth and social stability).

Political macroconditions that were particularly volatile in the first phase of economic reform (1978–1991) clearly had an immediate impact on all policy subsystems scrutinized here. Before the 1992 breakthrough, economic policy was strongly contested and "reforms seemed to advance strongly in certain years and retreat in other years" (Naughton 2007, p 97). In spite of the changing "macro-climate" in China's polity, the four policy subsystems studied here (state-owned enterprises, private business, foreign trade and investment, and stock markets) reveal "microclimates" that diverged considerably from overall policy moods. Each policy subsystem worked according to a distinct logic of policymaking. Yet policy change through experimentation played a crucial role in each of them.

The following case studies cannot do justice to the entire sequence and intricacies of reform measures in the respective policy domains. They focus instead on the factors that help to understand the contribution of experimentation to facilitating policy change: configurations of policy actors, risk perceptions, conflict ("factionalism") and consensus among national policymakers, the interplay between local initiative and central auspices, and the type and extent of policy renewal ranging from instrument tinkering to strategic departures.

Policy Tinkering in a Closed Subsystem: State-Owned Enterprises

From 1978 to the mid-1990s, reforms at the core of China's socialist economy, the state-owned enterprise (SOE) sector, took place in a virtually closed policy subsystem, dominated by powerful entrenched state bureaucratic and enterprise actors with strong vested interests and shored up by official ideological adherence to state control over strategic economic assets. Under such restrictive conditions, policy experimentation was confined to tinkering with a policy repertoire that continued to be based on bureaucratic instruments and incentives for making SOE management

Table 3 "Experimental point" programs in China's state sector, 1978–1997

"Experimental point" programs	Duration
Delegation of greater autonomy to enterprises	1978–1980
Delivery of contract profit to the state	1981–1982
Substitution of profit with taxes	1983–1986
Transformation of SOEs into shareholding companies	1984–1997
Bankruptcy regulation	1984–1997
Preparation of national SOE law	1984–1988
SOE responsibility contracts	1987–1993
Establishment of enterprise groups	1991–1997
Modern company system (formal corporatization of large SOEs)	1994–1997

Source: *Yearbook*, 1988ff

less wasteful. SOE managers and their patrons in industrial bureaus continued to be successful in lobbying top policymakers to refrain from exposing SOEs to harder budget constraints. These factors worked to delay the entrance of new actors and new regulatory frameworks to the national policymaking arena for almost two decades until the subsystem was forced open by mounting financial crisis perceptions and the imposition of a new policy paradigm that aimed at "grasping the big, releasing the small SOEs."

Experimental programs of the 1980s (see Table 3), designed as a response to chronic SOE deficits, were mostly oriented to improving the performance (less waste, better products, less state subsidies) of SOEs by giving additional incentives and decision-making powers to SOE managers, albeit without transforming the bureaucratic institutional set-up outside of the companies (Steinfeld 1998). But reformist experimentation met with strong reservations among parts of the policy-making community, industrial bureaucracies, and in the national legislature. In effect, SOE restructuring that went beyond bureaucratic incentive changes and aimed at full-scale corporate reorganization turned out to be unachievable (Tanner 1999. pp 167–205).

In the mid-1990s, an ambitious new attempt to transform SOE operations was undertaken with the "modern company system" (MCS) experimental program. Confronted with an accelerating accumulation of debts in the state sector, top policymakers agreed on the need for a thorough SOE restructuring. As a result, a new Company Law was passed in 1993, which envisaged the transformation of SOEs in modern business entities with transparent structures of corporate governance, while still shunning the privatization of state assets. Policy implementation was then based on "post-law experimentation" (see Fig. 2, feedback loop C): MCS experiments were designed for smoothing the implementation of a reformist national law. Experimental points established between 1994 and 1997 revealed how tacit resistance from SOE managers and their supervisory agencies produced a heavily bureaucratized design for experimentation and consequently meager results. An evaluation of MCS implementation in the 100 centrally supervised experimental companies at the end of 1996 concluded that "almost no experimental enterprise had achieved the minimum standards of a modern corporation" (Wu 2005, p 155; *Yearbook* 1995, pp 138–141, 1996, pp 222–226). Overall, the MCS program appeared heavily inhibited and clumsy in comparison to pioneering experimentation that was possible in more open policy subsystems.

Policy tinkering in SOE reform helped to contain political and ideological controversies, but allowed only incremental change. By the mid-1990s, SOE management had moved away from the rigid administrative coordination of earlier times, but was still dominated by the socialist legacy of soft budget constraints. The closed and sluggish policy regime in China's state sector was finally broken up as a response to mounting financial risks that were perceived as an immediate threat under the impression of the Asian Financial Crisis. From 1997 on, China's central policymakers moved beyond incremental reform and adopted a package of transformative policies to turn SOEs around, including large-scale mergers, management and employee buyouts, takeover of small SOEs by private investors, the inclusion of foreign strategic partners, closures, mass layoffs, and exposure to international competition through WTO accession.

Successive Policy Adjustments in a Curbed Subsystem: Private Business

From 1978 to 2004, the promotion of private business took place in a curbed policy subsystem. For ideological reasons, private business was one of the least acceptable emerging elements of China's reforming socialist economy and, at the outset, it was tolerated only as a marginal, temporary, and controlled supplement, which would not be allowed to disrupt the public sector and therefore did not pose a major policy risk (Young 1995, pp 13–14; Naughton 2007, p 95). The lack of official recognition severely restricted articulating private sector demands at the level of national policymaking until the mid-1990s. Locally, business interests were curbed by officials who first obstructed the emergence, then learned quickly to extract new resources (most importantly taxes, fees, kickbacks, and employment) from private companies. Private business underwent a gradual political ascent starting locally and progressing from a "dependent clientelism" to varying patterns of "symbiotic clientelism" in which private business people managed to further their interests through collusive relations with local officials who had a strong interest in opening up a new source of levies that were not subject to central control (Wank 1995). In the early stages of reform, central-state policy toward the private sector was confined to vague policy statements that had to be "stretched" by local governments to justify their ideologically dubious experimentation with private business. Therefore, policy change in this reform domain was driven by unregulated, low-key, yet broad-based, bottom-up initiative. We find a sequence of "unpublicized experimentation, followed by a general 'in principle' approval, then by ratification and specific regulations" only after the new type of economic activity was already widespread and flourishing locally (Young 1995, pp 9, 10, 16).

Moving beyond low-key local experimentation, reformist central policymakers undertook one prominent initiative for elevating a powerhouse of self-propelled private business development to a national model when they designated the coastal Wenzhou District an "experimental zone for developing the commodity economy" in late 1986. After obtaining the official label of an "experimental zone," the local government pioneered in formulating China's first regulations on joint stock cooperative firms and nonstate financial institutes, both ideologically contested institutional innovations that attracted much national publicity for about 2 years. Reformist policymakers and their advisors used the Wenzhou experimental zone for demonstrating the potential advantages of private business growth and questioning the official adherence to public enterprise dominance. The debate of the Wenzhou pattern of private sector development served to prepare the ground for new national regulations and a constitutional amendment in 1987 and 1988, which improved the legal standing of private firms. The Wenzhou experiments had a major impact on national policy debate until the political winds blowing from Beijing changed drastically in 1989 and terminated de facto the official legitimation of the "experimental zone" (Parris 1991).

Local policymaking in relation to the emerging private sector generally was strongly discretionary. Myriad provisional regulations and temporary permits were extended to private businesses. One crucial informal institutional innovation utilized by local governments across China was the registration of private companies as "collective" enterprises to conceal the true extent of the private sector and avoid the political pitfalls involved in the open promotion of nonsocialist businesses. This transitional institutional arrangement was tacitly tolerated by central policymakers for most of the 1980s and 1990s, and came under heavy political fire only briefly in the ideologically charged 1989–1991 years. Pretending to belong to the socialist "collective" economy was crucial to the private sector's spectacular, yet concealed, growth until the mid-1990s when most entrepreneurs began to feel safe enough to stage their public "coming out" and register officially as private businesses. Local experience with promoting and regulating private business provided the basis for successive national policy adjustments between 1987 and 2004. Official access to the *national* policy arena was obtained from the mid-1990s through the reactivation of the Federation of Industry and Commerce that had represented the private sector in the 1950s, but had been mostly dormant since then. However, private enterprise and private property did not enjoy full legal protection until 2004, when the state constitution eventually guaranteed them a credible legal and political status.

The ascent of China's private sector is a remarkable example of how bottom-up experimentation could promote gradual, yet transformative change of policy parameters and priorities in a politically curbed subsystem over time. From the central government's view, a problematic legacy of locally driven policy innovation lies in the entrenchment of collusive networks between local officials and entrepreneurs that continue to pose a challenge to unified national regulation and taxation of the private sector.

Policy Departures in a Cracked-Open Subsystem: Foreign Investment and Trade

As opposed to the 1978–1991 period when foreign opening and in particular the SEZs had been the subject of major political controversy, the promotion of foreign trade and investment thereafter took place in a policy subsystem that was effectively cracked open by the vehement reformist initiative that Deng Xiaoping launched in early 1992. Consequently, China's integration into the world economy became driven by a drastic policy departure consisting of redefinitions of the goals, instruments, and rules guiding foreign economic relations. Economic opening was officially extended from the coastal regions to all of China (Yang 1997, pp 54, 55), thereby accepting extensive risks inherent in downgrading central state control over the external economy and in inviting powerful foreign investors and companies. Ideological debate and factional rivalry that had accompanied market-oriented reforms in the 1980s were effectively silenced by Deng's injunction to stop discussing economic reforms in rigid antagonistic (socialist vs. capitalist) categories. The shockwave of the Soviet Union's disintegration contributed to elite consent as much as the fierce reformist determination displayed by Deng.

The ambitious central policy packages formulated in 1992–1993 called for "breakthroughs" in transforming the economic system into an internationally competitive "socialist market economy," and amounted to a comprehensive overhaul of economic strategy. This forceful central policy push signaled a strategic opportunity for policy entrepreneurs and was immediately understood locally. The pushes in reform in 1992–1993 triggered runaway "policy grabs" and spontaneous experimentation by local officials who were eager to benefit from the new dynamism in transnational economic exchanges. Local policymakers started to lobby and compete fiercely for establishing special trade and development zones and obtaining preferential conditions, which were extended selectively to such zones by the central government for boosting foreign trade and investment. In securing policy privileges, formal bureaucratic application procedures proved to be much less important than the support of individual national policymakers who could serve as advocates for the establishment of particular zones (Zweig 2002, pp 82–84). Since many local policymakers did not wait for proper approval to establish special zones, the central government undertook several retrenchments, forcing the closure of illicit zones that consumed huge public investment funds and offered generous tax breaks to investors without considering the effects on macroeconomic stability, which the central government struggled to maintain.

During the post-1992 policy rush, economic exchange with the outside world was transformed from a supportive measure of reform to a core pillar for China's modernization. The proliferation of special trade and development zones broadened support among local officials for market-oriented reform (Shirk 1994, p 42). Since the special zones provided foreign trade opportunities to countless domestic firms, which conducted their transactions through the zones, their function exceeded that of a local experimental site and became crucial to the rise of new foreign trade-oriented actors across China's domestic economy (Yang 1997, pp 48, 49).

The preferential policies, bestowed by the central government on trade and development zones, provided economic incentives. The policies also allowed much room for experimenting with novel administrative and business practices, as well as generating new policies and regulations (Chung 1999, pp 106, 111), while most other jurisdictions would still have to play by the established rules. This "segmented deregulation" created a policy regime in which central decisionmakers, not market forces, determined "which localities had a comparative advantage in foreign and domestic trade" (Zweig 2002, p 50). From an economic perspective, this approach created severe distortions and opportunities for rent-seeking. But viewed from the angle of policy reform, segmented deregulation was highly conducive to reorienting policymakers and administrators toward foreign trade and investment.

Joint central-local initiative achieved the post-1992 policy departure in China's foreign economic relations. Central policymaking determined the speed and extent of deregulation, but the keen competition for preferential policies from localities exerted new types of pressures on central policymakers. Remarkably, China's economic opening before WTO accession was "accomplished not by liberalization but by a series of administrative arrangements that achieved a bureaucratic consensus and accommodated the individual incentives of central and local political officials" (Shirk 1994, p 55). The post-1992 policy rush prepared the ground for the next, much more formalized, treaty- and law-based policy departure in 2001 when WTO accession deepened and liberalized China's participation in world trade and investment flows.

Policy Repertoire Extension in an Alien Subsystem: The Stock Market

In the construction and regulation of stock exchanges in Shanghai and Shenzhen since 1990, we find rare constellations of a policy subsystem that represents a radically alien element in China's political economy. The stock market had to be "squeezed into an economy still based on state planning and the absence of private ownership" (Walter and Howie 2006, p 4). Insiders from China's newly emerging financial industry, using their excellent connections to top national policymakers, had launched the policy initiative to establish stock exchanges in a socialist economy on an experimental basis. Limited experiments with issuing and trading shares had already been approved by the central government and undertaken locally during the 1980s. Remarkably, giving stock exchanges a hand in financing and restructuring enterprises was judged as a low-risk initiative, and therefore supported even by otherwise staunch sceptics of capitalist methods since this experiment was designed to open new channels for SOE financing without relinquishing state control over the listed entities (Green 2004, pp 61, 62). Operating under this basic political constraint, financial reformists managed to insert a new set of policy instruments—stock exchanges with their accompanying institutions and organizations—into a political economy that lacked a credible legal definition and protection of private property and equity rights. The introduction of stock exchanges represents technocratic grand experimentation that produced an odd combination of state control over most listed assets with the volatile dynamics of equity trade and speculation.

While the Shanghai and Shenzhen stock exchanges were under the supervision of the respective municipal governments in the early to mid-1990s, national regulatory institutions were only gradually established from 1993 to 1997. After 1997, responding to a series of shocking domestic scandals and to the challenge of the Asian Financial Crisis, the central government brought the stock exchanges under its control, affirmed their legitimate role in a socialist market economy, and made them serve the purposes of national industrial policy and SOE restructuring.

Stock market history in China overall is marked by a series of experimental schemes. Most important are the repackaging of SOEs into listed shareholding companies (early 1990s), selected transfers of legal person shares to new owners (1992), Hong Kong listings of SOEs (1993), the creation of "national champions" (from the second half of the1990s), and several attempts at reducing the holdings of state shares (1999, 2001, and 2005). The two stock exchanges were classified as "experimental points" from 1990 to 1997.

The novel set of policy instruments that was introduced through the stock market experiments has brought much less substantive change to the Chinese economy than might be expected. The stock market has remained dominated by government agencies and government-linked companies that are eager to raise capital by going public, but share a uniform interest in inhibiting the access and ascent of private corporate competitors. Politically well-connected companies continue to dominate the market, and since market growth has been given priority most of the time over strict regulation and supervision, the officially sought-after benefits of the shareholding experiment (better corporate governance, greater competitiveness, etc.) have largely remained unattainable (Walter and Howie 2006, pp 130, 166). Overall, the fundamental policy parameters guiding the stock market experiment from the beginning have not been transformed. The exchanges were not designed to become a vehicle of privatization but to raise capital for government-linked companies. Whether the institutions and practices of stock markets can be credibly adapted to China's corporate world, which is dominated by state actors and shaped by constant political interference, remains an unresolved issue.

Limits to Elite-Sponsored Experimentation: Social Goods and Societal Participation

In these case studies of major economic reform domains, initiatives from inside government played a predominant role in starting experimentation, as expected in an authoritarian polity. Yet outside initiation—that is, bringing policy issues to the national agenda through social demands and public criticism—has become more prevalent in China's recent reform experience.

The Chinese practice of elite-sponsored experimentation, geared toward opening new channels for profit-seeking *and* rent-seeking opportunities, does not work toward solving the problems of those segments of society that are left behind in economic growth, and do not have the economic status and means to influence administrative discretion in their favor. A systematic dilemma of providing social goods in developing political economies is that decentralization, due to collusive rent-seeking between local political and economic elites, may work to the detriments of weaker segments of the population (Duflo et al. 2006). Remarkable for an authoritarian polity and clearly influenced by international assistance, official experimental programs, aimed at improving the provision of social and public goods, have been complemented by more systematic societal consultation since the mid-1990s. Developments in the intensely disputed fields of rural health care and land management illustrate this phenonomen.

As a side-effect of rural decollectivization and marketization, the Maoist basic cooperative medical scheme, which had been effective in preventing epidemics and raising life expectancy in the countryside, had collapsed almost totally by the early 1990s. By 2003, about 80% of the rural population did not have health insurance anymore. Since the late 1980s, various local pilot programs in rural health care reform were endorsed by the central government and carried out with continuous involvement of international governmental and nongovernmental organizations. Yet none of the pilot efforts was scaled up to a national reform program (Liu et al. 1999; World Bank 2005). Rural health reform was only pushed to the top of the national policy agenda when the Severe acute respiratory syndrome (SARS) epidemic in 2003 triggered massive public criticism, which resulted in government statements that the official approach to privatize health care in the countryside had been a failure (Wang 2006, pp 92, 93). Public outrage over SARS led to a change of the policy paradigm. Central state co-funding of a "new cooperative medical scheme" became the basis of large-scale experimental programs that have been undertaken in 300 of China's more than 2,000 counties since 2003, and is supposed to be rolled out to all counties by 2010. An innovative feature of several pilot programs lies in making local health providers and administrators accountable and health expenses transparent by giving popular representatives seats in supervisory boards. Though all tested variants of the new medical scheme leave many expenses uncovered and therefore will only bring partial solutions, health care has been pushed so swiftly to the top of the policymaking agenda due to a new intensity of public involvement and societal pressure on policymakers.

Regarding land management, in the context of rapid industrial and real-estate development in formerly agricultural areas, abusive requisition of land and standards of compensation have become an intensely contested policy issue since the end of the 1990s. This has led to local protests, petition movements and public debate about better regulation. After a new law on land management issued in 1998 had failed to resolve the massive ongoing conflicts in this domain, the central government sponsored and evaluated several rounds of local experimental programs (Ministry of Land and Resources 2004) and issued a series of trial regulations on transfer of tenure rights and fair compensation in 2005 and 2006. Continuing public protests were the driving force behind these extensive efforts to revise official policy.

The tensions, conflicts, and abuses inherent in the policy domains of rural health care and land management have not been settled. But popular voice and peasant interests have been legitimized as an integral part of policymaking by the new variant of consultation-based experimentation. Since 2004, new government guidelines for "administration in accordance with the law" institutionalized the role of public scrutiny as a regular element of drafting legislation (Horsley 2007). State-sponsored experimentation that seeks societal input has complemented policymaking but not transformed it. Societal input is still ad hoc and selective, and civil society organizations do not play a significant or even institutionalized role. While agenda-setting has become more open to public demands, the policy process overall is still controlled by government decisionmakers. Therefore, as officials and foreign advisors involved in years of experimental point work stated: In China, "efforts to effect change must focus on mobilizing powerful officials… to allow experimentation to proceed. A major challenge for scaling up program reform in China is to build innovation from within the government, which remains the main actor in service delivery and policy formulation" (Kaufman et al. 2006, p 18).

Herein is a core dilemma of policy experimentation in China's current political system: experimental programs that do not immediately benefit the interest of local elites have a very slim chance of success. The negligence in dealing with rural health care before the SARS crisis makes this clear. Only when public outrage pushed health system reform to the top of the national agenda and societal consultation became an integral element of the policy process, experimentation started to generate reform schemes that promised to be more viable.

The crucial importance of bottom-up initiative to policy experimentation is also manifest in economic reform. Experimentation resulted in transformative change only in those domains in which new social actors, in particular private entrepreneurs and transnational investors, were involved most actively and worked to redefine the entrenched rules of the game and power configurations. The emergence of new profit-seeking entrepreneurs was promoted by political-administrative actors who found many new opportunities for dividend-collecting (a variant of rent-seeking that is compatible with economic growth, see Wedeman 1997; Khan and Jomo 2000) in the rapidly growing private and transnational economic activities. The interplay between profit-seeking and dividend-collecting behavior made policy experimentation and institutional innovation in private business and foreign economic relations so forceful. In policy domains that remained under the control of vested state interests and in which state actors tended to lock in partial reforms, as in SOE management (from 1978 to mid-1990s) or stock market regulation (1990–2005), extensive experimentation produced incremental innovation at best.

Policy Learning and Rent-Seeking

China's economic reforms and the policy processes that facilitated them clearly cannot be reduced to being policymakers' rational response to inefficiencies in the economic system (Shirk 1994, p 5). For policymakers who wanted to change how the economy was run, experimentation turned out to be a good way to deal with *uncertainty* (the inability to predict the precise impact of specific reforms in a rapidly changing economic context) and *ambiguity* (the ambivalence, vagueness or even confusion in policymakers' thinking about their policy priorities). From setting policy objectives to selecting model experiments and identifying generalizable policy options, experimentation has always been an intensely politicized process driven by tactical opportunism, personal rivalries, clashes of interests and ideologies, ad hoc crisis management, or strategic consensus-building.

In the political logic of economic reform, policy experimentation minimized beforehand political resistance and political risks. In cases of success, it maximized political support and political gains retrospectively (see Lau et al. 2000, pp 121, 122). Forceful policymakers such as Zhu Rongji (China's preeminent economic leader from 1992 to 2002) utilized experimental point programs for ultimately preparing radical policy shifts in the guise of incremental measures, thereby reducing reform risks while increasing the "controllability" of reforms (Liu et al. 2006, p 281). Zhu applied experimental schemes to smuggle changes into the system and to achieve objectives that would have been politically obstructed if revealed more explicitly beforehand (see Lindblom 1979). Policy experimentation thus reduced the frictions and delays characteristic of top-level consensus-building and interagency accommodation, and helped to avoid protracted policy deadlock.

Generally, decentralized experimentation minimized the risks and the costs to central policymakers by placing the burden on local governments and providing welcome scapegoats in cases of failure. Locally produced policy innovations were taken up by reformist policymakers eager to bolster their political standing and keep rivals at bay by godfathering local models that could demonstrate the success and the superiority of their policy preferences. Local reform efforts that did not fulfil these highly contextual and tactical political exigencies did not reach the national policy agenda, as the example of experimental point work in rural health care up to 2003 illustrates. On the other hand, active godfathering of individual reform exemplars by central policymakers could produce fake models that yielded wasteful policies and were propagated for years until revealed to be unsustainable (see Steinfeld 1998, pp 165–224). Since local experimenters tend to do everything possible to overstate the positive results of pilot projects in their jurisdictions, ill-conceived and impracticable experiments often were detected only when they were being spread "from point to surface." Experiments that got stuck at this stage were rarely publicly terminated in a clear-cut way, but more often just abandoned silently after having already created considerable social or budgetary costs (e.g., experiments with transforming the structure and functions of local governments in the 1980s, with decentralized pension funds in the 1990s, or recently, with restructuring myriad public services institutions). Failing local experiments could be costly, but they were certainly much less costly than a failing national policy. Since 1978, "proceeding from point to surface"—i.e., testing local experimental findings in more jurisdictions before entering into national policy formulation—has been effective as a practical litmus test for novel reform approaches and has prevented the national disasters that were characteristic of several major economic policy initiatives of the 1957–1978 period (see Heilmann 2008).

Significantly, reform-era experimentation did not stop at the search for individual models and policy solutions. In society at large and among policymakers in particular, the experiments with rural markets, private business, and foreign investment stimulated comprehensive collective learning processes that resulted in serial, and cumulatively radical, redefinitions of policy parameters for economic activity. Experimentation prepared the ground for major policy breakthroughs by unspectacularly furthering dispersed institutional and policy changes, initiating learning processes and ideological reorientation among policymakers, undermining entrenched interests, and providing test runs for innovative administrative and business practices. Experimentation over time fundamentally transformed the economic policy context for local and central decisionmakers. In combination with transnational push factors such as the Asian Financial Crisis and WTO negotiations, experimentation also provided the policy planks for reform departures in 1997 (SOE reform) and 2001 (foreign trade liberalization) that included drastic reorganizations of China's economic administration. Protracted policy learning was helped immensely by the massive growth in private and transnational economic activity, which lessened the pressure for immediate structural reform in the public sector and thereby provided policymakers with an unusually opportune environment for long-term adaptation.

One of the most controversial aspects of policy experimentation is how much it promotes rent-seeking. Beyond a doubt, generating new sources of income for local elites has been a key driving force behind experimentation. However, this cannot be simply equated with wasteful or predatory rent-seeking since the material and career interests of local officials became an effective catalyst for entrepreneurship and innovation in many policy areas. In accordance with the logic of dividend-collecting, experimental programs that were seen as conducive to economic growth and generating income within a particular jurisdiction were vigorously pursued by local officials. This incentive structure facilitated the emergence of new profit-seeking entrepreneurship, new administrative practices, and new types of economic organization that frequently turned out to be highly productive in the rapidly changing context of China's political economy. From this perspective, experiments in economic policy generated diffuse benefits that unleashed the energies of local-level institutional and policy entrepreneurs, and facilitated a broad realignment of interests among China's administrators in accordance with the economic growth imperative set by the national leadership.

China's record of policy experimentation is a key to understand how it was possible to create a series of transitional institutions that were mostly not optimal by market-economy standards but often had efficiency-enhancing and Pareto-improving effects (predominantly in the 1978–1994 period of reforms) or Kaldor-improving effects (predominantly since about 1994 and particularly in the state sector), and were therefore politically acceptable, even to initial reform opponents (Lin et al. 2003, p 327). Neoclassically oriented Chinese economists tend to reject the use of experimental points in generating policy as an anachronistic instrument of an administrative state, which is incompatible with creating the "level playing field" for competition in a market economy and which blocks the market-driven creation of reform solutions (Pan 1995; Li 1997). Such a critique appears to be detached from the realities of China's political economy. The omnipresence of state agencies in the economy cannot be theorized away, but renders the administrative involvement, guidance, and accommodation inevitable during economic restructuring. For China's policymakers, the economic inefficiencies that are seen as inherent in experimentation by neoclassical economic theory, in practice, constitute a "necessary transaction cost" (Oi and Han 2006, p 21) to maintain political control and social stability under conditions of rapid economic change.

Conclusion

Compared to the standards of legal consistency and political and administrative accountability, which are part of policy implementation and which constrain open-ended experimentation under democratic rule of law, the Chinese practice of experimentation must be seen as arbitrary and volatile. Yet the unexpected capacity of the Chinese party-state to find innovative solutions to long-standing or newly emerging challenges in economic development rests on the broad-based entrepreneurship, adaptation, and learning facilitated by experimentation under hierarchy. The combination of decentralized experimentation with ad hoc central interference, which results in selective integration of local experiences into national policy-making, is a key to understanding how a distinctive policy process has contributed to China's economic rise.

Limitations of experimentation are obvious in improving the provision of social and public goods, such as access to basic health care and credible protection of land tenure rights in rural areas or environmental protection. Providing these goods requires a combination of societal interest articulation and imposition of national policy priorities that goes against the short-term interests of most local elites, and is therefore not easily reconciled with the entrenched mode of economic experimentation.

Can China's experiment-based policy process provide lessons for other political economies in overcoming impediments to institutional change? China's experience strongly points to the potency of tapping local knowledge, mobilizing bottom-up initiative, and embracing decentralized policy generation as a contrasting approach to the imposition of international "best practices" regularly proposed by foreign economic advisors (e.g., Meyer 2007). Moreover, it demonstrates that applying static standards of legislative consistency to the utterly fluid context of transitional economies can be detrimental to policy learning and institutional adaptation. It is questionable whether, in a context of rapid economic change, "deftly tailored regulations" really increase certainty for market participants and encourage rational market behavior (Corne 2002, p 375). On the contrary, by conducting extensive experimentation in advance of formal legislation, it may be possible to avoid many of the leaps in the dark that are inherent risks in rash national legislation (Jevons 1904, p 9).

In addition, China's case explains how complex the relationship between policy entrepreneurship and rent-seeking can be. Policy experimentation was shown to provide effective incentives for administrative and economic actors to embrace new types of both profit-seeking and rent-seeking behavior. Since changing the basic incentives for policymakers and administrators is the precondition for motivating reforms, it appears indispensable to let local officials derive dividends from entrepreneurial activities and growth in their jurisdictions. However, a symbiotic relationship between officials and entrepreneurs that is conducive to economic growth is likely only in a stable political environment in which actors can afford to take a longer-term perspective, not a grab-and-run view, of their interests in the local economy.

The effectiveness of experimentation in China has rested on special institutional prerequisites (the Communist Party's unitary, hierarchical organization and the Maoist legacy of a cellular economic administration), narrowly defined policy imperatives (growth by any means), particular actor constellations (policymakers who are not subject to electoral cycles or democratic competition and who are unified in their commitment to economic modernization, yet argue over the priorities, parameters, and methods of reform) and particular actor expectations. Whereas most policymakers, administrators, interest groups and citizens in advanced political economies tend to view experimental policy departures as risky, destabilizing and threatening to their stakes in the status quo, political actors in a less advanced, yet rapidly growing economy with a successful reform record, such as China, tend to display more confidence in the benefits that policy change may bring.

Experimentation can innovate policy only as long as the dynamism of growth expectations is intact and newly emerging interest groups feel comfortable in a fluid policy environment. As soon as expectations and interests begin to shift in defense of the status quo or in favor of redistribution, experimentation becomes subject to increasing limitations from both the demand and the supply side: interest groups and citizens come to ask for universal and irreversible regulation; domestic and transnational economic actors come to demand equal legal protection; and policymakers come to see experiments as a political risk that can be avoided by legislative incrementalism. A hardening of political and legal constraints on policy experiments is the result. In most political economies, this mechanism works against extensive experimentation, despite the many obvious advantages it would entail for institutional adaptation. China's party-state, which has demonstrated for almost three decades the potency of experiment-based economic governance—but has begun to narrow the range of experimental activity in recent years—will hardly escape this logic.

References

Adam S, and Kriesi H. The network approach. In: Sabatier PA, editor. Theories of the policy process. 2nd ed. Westview: Boulder; 2007. p. 129–54.

Bunce V. Subversive institutions: the design and the destruction of socialism and the state. New York: Cambridge University Press; 1999.

Cai H, and Treisman D. Did government decentralization cause China's economic miracle. World Polit 2006;58:505–35(July).

Cao Y, Qian Y, and Weingast B. From federalism, Chinese style to privatization, Chinese style. Econ Transit 1999;7(1):103–31.

Chung JH. Preferential policies, municipal leadership, and development strategies. In: Chung J, editor. Cities in China: recipes for economic development in the reform era. London: Routledge; 1999. p. 105–40.

Corne PH. Creation and application of law in the PRC. Am J Comp Law 2002;50:369–443.
Duflo E, Fischer G, and Chattopadhyay R. Efficiency and rent-seeking in local government: evidence from randomized policy experiments in India. Paper presented at the Harvard Institute of Quantitative Social Science; December 2006.
Evans P. Development as institutional change: the pitfalls of monocropping and the potentials of deliberation. Stud Comp Int Dev 2004;38(4):30–52. (Winter).
Evans P. The challenges of the 'institutional turn': interdisciplinary opportunities in development theory. In: Nee V, Swedberg R, editors. Sociology of capitalist institutions. Princeton: Princeton University Press; 2005. p. 90–116.
Green S. The development of China's stock market, 1984–2002: equity politics and market institutions. London: RoutledgeCurzon; 2004.
Greenberg DH, Linksz D, and Mandell M. Social experimentation and public policymaking. Washington, DC: Urban Institute; 2003.
Hayek FA. The constitution of liberty. Chicago: University of Chicago Press; 1978.
Heilmann S. From local experiments to national policy: the origins of China's distinctive policy process. China J 2008;59. (January 2008).
Horsley JP. The rule of law in China: incremental progress. In: China: the balance sheet in 2007 and beyond. Washington, DC: Center for Strategic and International Studies; 2007. p. 93–108.
Hummel K. Recht der behördlichen Regelungsexperimente [Law of experiments in administrative regulation]. Berlin: Duncker and Humblot; 2003.
Jevons WS. [1880]. Experimental Legislation. Hitchin: Garden City; 1904.
Jowell R. Trying it out: the role of 'pilots' in policy-making. London: Government Chief Social Researcher's Office; 2003.
Kaufman J, Zhang E, and Xie Z. Quality of care in China: scaling up a pilot project into a national reform program. Stud Fam Plann 2006;37(1):17–28.
Khan MH and Jomo KS, editors. Rents, rent-seeking and economic development. Cambridge: Cambridge University Press; 2000.
Lau LJ, Qian Y, and Roland G. Reform without losers: an interpretation of China's dual-track approach to transition. J Polit Econ 2000;108(1):120–43.
Li S. Li Shuguang jianyi quxiao gaige shidian [Li Shuguang proposes to abolish experimental points of reform]. Jinrong xinxi cankao 1997;5:32.
Lin JY, Fang C, and Zhou L. The China miracle: development strategy and economic reform. Hong Kong: Chinese University Press; 2003.
Lindblom CE. The science of muddling through. Pub Admin Rev 1959;19(2):79–88. (Spring).
Lindblom CE. Still muddling, not yet through. Pub Admin Rev 1979;39(6):517–26. (November–December).
Liu Y, Hsiao WC, and Eggleston K. Equity in health and health care: the Chinese experience. Soc Sci Med 1999;49(10):1349–56. (November).
Liu Z, Wang S, and Huang Z. Lun gonggong guanli shijian zhong de 'shidian' fangfa [On the piloting method in public management practice]. Dongbei daxue xuebao 2006;8(4):280–83. (July).
Meyer, MW. Notes on China's second economic transition. Paper presented at the China Institute for Policy Studies, Beijing, January 27; 2007.
Ministry of Land and Resources. 2004. "Wenbu tuijin zhengdi gaige" [Advance the reform of [compensation for] land expropriations with steady steps]. June 25, 2004. At http://www.mlr.gov.cn/pub/gtzyb/gtzygl/tdzy/gdbh/t20040625 _13553.htm. Accessed March 15, 2006).
Montinola G, Yingyi Q, and Weingast B. Federalism, Chinese style: the political basis for economic success in China. World Politics 1995;48:50–81. (October).
Morand CA, editor. *Évaluation législative et lois expérimentales* [Legislative evaluation and experimental laws]. Aix-en-Provence: Presse Universitaires d'Aix-Marseille; 1993.
Mosteller F. Selected papers of Frederick Mosteller.New York: Springer; 2006.
Mukand SW, and Rodrik D. In search of the Holy Grail: policy convergence, experimentation, and economic performance. Am Econ Rev 2005;95(1):374–83.
Naughton B. The Chinese economy: transitions and growth. Cambridge: MIT; 2007.
North DC. Institutions, institutional change and economic performance. Cambridge: Cambridge University Press; 1990.
North DC. Understanding the process of economic change. Princeton: Princeton University Press; 2005.
Oi JC and Han C. Political and institutional complementarities: the evolution of corporate restructuring in China, unpublished manuscript, Stanford University; 2006.
Pan X. Gaige shidian cheng bai bian" [Discussing success and failure of experimental points for reform]. Fazhan 1995. (2):26–9.

Parris KD. Local society and the state: the Wenzhou model and the making of the private sector in China [unpublished dissertation]. Indiana University; 1991.
Pyle DF. From pilot project to operational program in India: The problems of transition. In: Grindle MS, editor. Politics and policy implementation in the third world. Princeton: Princeton University Press; 1980. p. 123–44.
Qian Y. How reform worked in China. In: Rodrik D, editor. In search of prosperity: analytic narratives on economic growth. Princeton: Princeton University Press; 2003. p. 297–333.
Rawski TG. Implications of China's reform experience. Chin Q 1995. (144):1150–73.
Roland G. Transition and economics: politics, markets, and firms. Cambridge: MIT; 2000.
Shirk SL. How China opened its door. Washington, DC: Brookings; 1994.
Shue V. Peasant China in transition: the dynamics of development toward socialism, 1949–1956. Berkeley: University of California Press; 1980.
State Council General Office, editor. *Zhongguo jingji gaige kaifang shiyanqu* [China's experimental zones for economic reform and opening]. Beijing: China Youth; 1992.
Steinfeld ES. Forging reform in China: the fate of state-owned industry. NY: Cambridge University Press; 1998.
Tanner MS. The politics of lawmaking in post-Mao China. Oxford: Clarendon; 1999.
Walter CE, and Howie FJT. Privatizing China: inside China's stock markets. Singapore: Wiley; 2006.
Wank DL. Bureaucratic patronage and private business: changing networks of power in urban China. In: Walder AG, editor. The waning of the communist state: economic origins of political decline in China and Hungary. Berkeley: University of California Press; 1995. p. 153–83.
Wang S. Zhongguo gonggong zhengce yicheng shezhi de moshi [Patterns of public policy agenda-setting in China]. Zhongguo shehui kexue [Social Science in China] 2006;5:86–99.
Wazir R, and van Oudenhoven N. Increasing the coverage of social programmes. International Soc Sci J 1998. 145–54. (UNESCO) (155) (March).
Wedeman A. Looters, rent-scrapers, and dividend-collectors: the political economy of corruption in Zaire, South Korea, and the Philippines. J Dev Areas 1997;31(4):457–78.
Woo WT. The real reasons for China's Growth. Chin J 1999;41:115–37. (January).
World Bank. 2005. "Rural Health in China." China Rural Health Analytical and Advisory Activities, *Briefing Note* 6 (May).
Wu J. Understanding and interpreting chinese economic reform. Mason: Thomson; 2005.
Wu X. Chuangxin: Jingji tequ lifa de guihun [Innovation: the heart and soul of legislation in the Special Economic Zone]. Hainan renda 2004;1:30–1. (Hainan People's Congress).
Yang D. Beyond Beijing: liberalization and the regions in China. London: Routledge; 1997.
Yearbook of Economic Structural Reform in China (Zhongguo jingji tizhi gaige nianjian). Beijing: Financial and economics. 1988ff.
Young S. Private business and economic reform in China. Armonk: Sharpe; 1995.
Zhang J. Bianfa moshi yu zhengzhi wendingxing [The mode of legal reform and political stability]. Zhongguo shehui kexue 2003;1:137–50.
Zhongyang zhengfu jigou [Organs of the central government]. Beijing: Reform Press, 1998.
Zweig D. Internationalizing China: domestic interests and global linkages. Ithaca: Cornell University Press; 2002.

Sebastian Heilmann is professor of comparative government and the political economy of China at Trier University, Germany. He is the author (in German) of *The Politics of Economic Reform in China and Russia* (2000), *The Political System of the PRC* (2002, updated editions 2004 and 2008), and co-editor of *The Politics of Financial Market Regulation* (forthcoming).

[10]

FEDERALISM, CHINESE STYLE
The Political Basis for Economic Success in China

By GABRIELLA MONTINOLA, YINGYI QIAN, and BARRY R. WEINGAST*

I. Introduction

THE remarkable success of China's economic reforms—fostering economic growth averaging 9 percent per year over the past fifteen years—seems to defy conventional wisdom. Consider the following:

—Economic reform appears to have been successfully pursued without any political reform.

—The central government seems to retain considerable political discretion, including the ability to reverse suddenly the reform process or to impose onerous exactions on successful enterprises.

—Finally, there have been few attempts to provide the central feature of private markets, a system of secure private-property rights. Nor has an attempt been made to develop a commercial law (for example, property and contract law) or an independent court system for adjudication.

Each of these factors bodes ill for economic reform. Without political reform, economic returns remain at the mercy of political predation. Political discretion, in turn, implies that there are no impediments to the government reversing the reforms. In this context, leadership turnover would allow the new government not only to reverse the reforms, but also to confiscate considerable wealth and to punish those who were successful under the reforms. Alternatively, problems may

* The authors gratefully acknowledge the helpful conversations of Masahiko Aoki, Nina Halpern, Anne Krueger, John Litwack, Ronald McKinnon, Paul Milgrom, Ramon Myers, Douglass North, Jean Oi, Gérard Roland, Susan Shirk, and Dorothy Solinger; and the research assistance of Jiahua Che. This paper was prepared under a cooperative agreement between the Institute for Policy Reform (IPR) and the Agency for International Development (AID), Cooperative Agreement No. PDC-0095-A-00-1126-00. Qian's research was also supported by the Research Incentive Fund from the Office of Technology Licensing (OTL) at Stanford University. Views expressed in this paper are those of the authors and not necessarily those of IPR, AID, or Stanford.

World Politics 48 (October 1995), 50–81

occur during unexpectedly hard times. With severe budget problems and a population clamoring for "solutions, now," the immediate need for revenue produces powerful pressure for a partial or wholesale reversal of the reforms. This type of discretion typically kills the prospects of any reform program.[1] Because economic agents know in advance that political discretion affords no protection for their economic success, they are unlikely to put their effort and wealth into undertakings that put them at risk, and hence the reforms will fail. These problems are seemingly further exacerbated in China by the lack of a system of private-property rights—a clear, necessary condition for a successful market system. All these factors point toward poor performance for Chinese economic reform.

The actual performance of the Chinese reforms provides a striking contrast to these expectations. Over the past fifteen years, China's performance potentially parallels that of the other high-growth East Asian economies. The juxtaposition of the conventional wisdom with experience demands an explanation.

The purpose of this paper is to provide such an explanation. We argue that the problem with the conventional wisdom is severalfold. First, it provides too narrow a definition of political reform. Second, although it asks the right question about political discretion, the inappropriate definition of political reform leads it to the wrong conclusion. Third, though much is wrong with the system of property rights in China, looking for a system of such rights as exists in the West has confused many analysts. Rights are not as secure in China as they could be, and the absence of a law of property and contracts along with a judicial system to enforce it remains a significant lacuna in the reform process. Yet, property rights are not completely insecure and without political foundation. Indeed, political reform in China has placed considerable limits on the discretion of the central government. These limits, in turn, provide the beginnings of a strong and credible political foundation for many market-oriented enterprises throughout the successful regions of China.

To understand the basis for these claims, we begin with the notion

[1] See Ronald I. McKinnon, "Financial Control in the Transition from Classical Socialism to a Market Economy," *Journal of Economic Perspectives* 5, (1991); Douglass C. North, *Structure and Change in Economic History* (New York: Cambridge University Press, 1981); idem, *Institutions, Institutional Change, and Economic Performance* (New York: Cambridge University Press, 1990); Hilton Root, "The Environment for Investment: Institutional Reform for a Market Economy," Country Report, no. 11 (Iris Center, University of Maryland, 1993); Barry R. Weingast, "The Economic Role of Political Institutions: Market-Preserving Federalism and Economic Growth," *Journal of Law, Economics, and Organization* 11 (Spring 1995).

of political reform. In the common parlance, political reform focuses on democratization and, hence, the separation of the Chinese Communist Party (CCP) from the state.[2] On this important component of reform, China has made little progress. Nearly all the formal aspects of democracy are absent, notably, individual rights of free speech and political participation, a viable system of competition for political office, and a set of constitutional limits on the state. As democracy is one of the central aspects of political freedom, China's record speaks for itself.

Yet, democratization does not encompass all aspects of political reform. So what has changed? We emphasize three principal factors. First, not only has political decentralization enhanced the powers of local government, but it has also altered central-local government relations in several critical ways that are difficult, though not impossible, to reverse.[3] Second, a major shift in ideology underpins the reforms, with the CCP moving from a dogmatic emphasis on the Maoist version of Marxism-Leninism to a pragmatic, market-oriented approach. Although the rhetoric of socialism has been retained (for example, the recent emphasis on the "socialist market economy"), the staunch antimarket, anti-private initiative, anti-private gain focus has been removed. Third, China has for the first time under the communists opened its economy.

In our view, these changes have resulted in a new political system that we characterize as *federalism, Chinese style*. This system, in turn, provides considerable political protection for China's reforms, including limits on the central government. Viewed from the perspective of the individual, this system differs considerably from federalisms in the developed West.[4] Viewed from the perspective of the political relationships among the different levels of government, China's political decentralization shares much in common with Western federalisms. The modern Chinese system includes a division of authority between the central and local governments. The latter have primary control over

[2] Katherine Hartford, "Socialist Agriculture Is Dead; Long Live Socialist Agriculture! Organizational Transformation in China," in E. Perry and C. Wong, eds., *The Political Economy of Reform in Post-Mao China* (Cambridge: Council on East Asian Studies/Harvard University, 1985); T. Saich, "Much Ado about Nothing: Party Reform in the 1980s," in Gordon White, ed., *The Chinese State in the Era of Economic Reform* (London: Macmillan Professional and Academic, 1991).

[3] Susan L. Shirk, *The Political Logic of Economic Reform in China* (Berkeley and Los Angeles: University of California Press, 1993).

[4] Federalism in the West is nearly always associated with political freedom and the protection of individual rights. See Weingast (fn. 1) for details of these federalisms, including a discussion of how federalism provided the important political foundations for the impressive growth of England in the eighteenth century and the United States in the nineteenth century.

economic matters within their jurisdictions. Critically, there is an important degree of political durability built into the system.

As we argue, the Chinese system provides a partial basis for a special kind of federalism called *market-preserving federalism.*[5] Central to the success of market-preserving federalism is the element of political durability built into the arrangements, meaning that the decentralization of power is not merely at the discretion of the central political authorities. And here, conventional wisdom's focus on the relationship between the national government and the individual results in erroneous judgments, for this focus ignores the relationship between the central authorities and the provincial and lower governments. The latter relationships have not only changed dramatically, but have done so in ways that are difficult to undo. They thus provide a degree of commitment.

Nonetheless, the new economy is not without its limitations. An understanding of how China's current system differs from a more complete system of market-preserving federalism provides some guide to both its current problems and solutions to them. First, China lacks an adequate mechanism for policing the internal common market. This absence explains in part why many local governments have focused on trade barriers and aggressive antimarket policies within their jurisdiction. Second, political decentralization has yet to be institutionalized to ensure its long-term stability. A third problem is the absence of private-property rights and a commercial law, as many have noted. These limitations should not be seen as economically debilitating; rather they should be seen as problems that need to be addressed in the near future.

This paper proceeds as follows. The next section discusses the theory of federalism and is divided into two parts. The first examines the necessary political foundations of market-preserving federalism, while the second examines the economic consequences of federalism. Sections III and IV turn to federalism, Chinese style, paralleling the two parts of Section II. Section III discusses whether and how the conditions of market-preserving federalism hold in China. Section IV reveals the remarkable parallel between the predicted effects of market-preserving federalism and China's decentralization. This approach also helps order the seemingly chaotic variety of behavior in the different provinces and localities. Much of this variation, especially the trends in

[5] Weingast (fn. 1); see also Ronald I. McKinnon, "Market-Preserving Fiscal Federalism" (Working paper, Department of Economics, Stanford University, 1994).

behavior, policy, and economic outcomes, is as predicted by the theory of federalism. Several imperfections of the system are also noted. Our conclusions follow in Section V.

II. The Theory of Market-Preserving Federalism

Political Foundations of Market-Preserving Federalism

A fundamental dilemma faces a government attempting to build and protect markets: it must not only be strong enough to enforce the legal rights and rules necessary to maintain the economy, but it must also be strong enough to commit itself credibly to honoring such rules.[6] In the absence of credible limits on governmental behavior, nothing prevents the government from taking away wealth from the citizens for its own purposes. This behavior may take many forms: an outright confiscation of wealth, onerous taxation, or inflationary financing by printing money. The absence of a credible commitment, in turn, adversely affects the "positive incentives" of economic agents. Because rational actors understand that this political environment reduces their economic benefits *ex post*, they will withhold their efforts, investments, and information *ex ante*, thus jeopardizing economic growth.

Another form of the lack of commitment can be seen in a government that is unable to impose a "hard budget constraint" on itself and other economic agents.[7] In this case, the government continues to bail out or subsidize troubled institutions and agents.[8] Lack of commitment fails to provide "negative incentives" to economic institutions and agents, who rationally distort their efforts, typically leading to wasteful investment and low productivity. Put simply, the soft budget constraint eliminates the need for sensible planning, since mistakes are not costly to the decision makers.[9]

Reputation is often held as an important mechanism to achieve credible commitment, but it alone is hardly sufficient. Political institutions are also necessary because, in the appropriate form, they provide for a balance of power that can make commitment credible.[10] One set of po-

[6] North (fn. 1); Weingast (fn. 1).

[7] Janos Kornai, *Economics of Shortage* (Amsterdam: North-Holland, 1980).

[8] Although the most pervasive forms of the soft budget constraint are observed in the centrally planned economy where the government controls nearly everything, the problem occurs in all modern economies. Indeed, the exploding savings-and-loan problem in the United States resulted from a version of this problem. So, too, is the rampant inflation typical of many Latin American regimes.

[9] McKinnon (fn. 5).

[10] Weingast (fn. 1).

litical institutions that play this role are those surrounding federalism.

Understanding the implications of federalism requires a clear notion of how it is sustained, that is, of its political foundations. Most studies simply take federalism as an exogenously specified system, focusing on its effects. For the purposes of studying the consequences of federalism in the developed West (for example, in Switzerland or the United States), this often involves no great loss. For the purposes of implementing and perfecting a new system of federalism, however, an appreciation of its political foundations proves essential.

The fundamental feature of federalism is decentralization; however, not all systems of decentralization are federal. To understand federalism, we must identify its principal characteristics. As a special type of federalism, *market-preserving federalism* encompasses a set of conditions that governs the allocation of authorities and responsibilities among different levels of government:

F1. A *hierarchy* of governments with a *delineated scope of authority* (for example, between the national and subnational governments) exists so that each government is autonomous within its own sphere of authority.

F2. The subnational governments have primary *authority over the economy* within their jurisdictions.

F3. The national government has the authority to police the *common market* and to ensure the mobility of goods and factors across subgovernment jurisdictions.

F4. Revenue sharing among governments is limited and borrowing by governments is constrained so that all governments face *hard budget constraints.*

F5. The allocation of authority and responsibility has an *institutionalized degree of durability* so that it cannot be altered by the national government either unilaterally or under the pressures from subnational governments.

These conditions represent an ideal type of institutional arrangement of a market-preserving federalism. The purpose of these institutions is, in part, to limit the degree to which a political system can encroach on markets.[11]

Condition 1 contains the defining characteristic of federalism. But formalized decentralization alone does not generate federalism's market-preserving qualities. These require the addition of conditions 2–5.

From the perspective of preserving market incentives, the authority of the national government over markets is limited to policing the common market across regions (condition 3) and providing national public goods, which should not be left to the subnational level governments (for example, monetary policy).

[11] McKinnon (fn. 5); Weingast (fn. 1).

The institutional arrangements of federalism recognize a critical difference between the national government and the subnational governments: there is only one of the former but many of the latter. The natural limits on the discretionary authority of the subnational level governments are induced by competition among jurisdictions. But this competition is beneficial only if there are no trade barriers and the entire nation becomes a common market (condition 3). Without condition 3, each subnational government would become something of a de facto "national government" in its jurisdiction, and its discretionary authority over the economy again would limit its ability to make a credible commitment. Condition 2 thus enhances the effects of condition 3. If decentralization remained at the discretion of the national government, the latter could intervene in the economy first by using its discretion (in the absence of condition 2) to compromise the system of federalism and then to intervene.

The constraint of condition 4 has two parts, one for fiscal revenue transfers between levels of governments, and one for borrowing through the financial system. The hard budget constraint in the fiscal channel limits revenue sharing and equalization among governments, especially through soft grants. The hard budget constraint in the financial channel restricts open-ended access to capital markets, especially borrowing from the central bank. Condition 4 applies to both the national government and the subnational governments. A hard budget constraint for the latter is necessary because it directly ties local revenue to local economic prosperity. A local government's financial problems remain its own, providing important incentives for local officials to oversee and ensure their government's fiscal health. If, in contrast, local governments were readily bailed out of their financial problems, they would have considerably fewer incentives to worry about the consequences of their choices. The constraint on the national government is necessary in part because a soft budget constraint would allow it to use monetary discretion to get around the limits on its authority.

Condition 5 provides for credible commitment to the federal system and thus for limits on the national government's discretionary authority. Not only must there be decentralization, but that decentralization must not be under the discretionary control of the national government. Condition 5 addresses the enforcement problem and is critically important. It is also likely, however, that an individual country, due to its own unique history and complicated social conditions, may require a different arrangement.

Market-preserving federalism's balance of power between the national and subnational governments is superior to either a complete centralization with a unitary government or a complete decentralization with each region an independent state. Under complete centralization or decentralization, the national government's authority is not limited through internal institutional arrangements; hence a potential danger exists for the discretionary authority to encroach on markets.

Before turning to the economic implications of market-preserving federalism, we pause to discuss the relationship between the conditions underlying market-preserving federalism and various systems of federalism throughout the world. Our approach shows that whether a nation calls itself federal—"de jure federalism"—is irrelevant.[12] What matters is whether the various conditions hold. Many de jure federalisms are nothing like market-preserving federalisms, for example, in Argentina, Brazil, and India. In these cases, conditions 2 and 5, and often condition 4, fail. The failure of conditions 2 and 5 implies that the political discretion and authority retained by the central government in these systems greatly compromises their market-preserving qualities. As discussed later in this section, these conditions are a necessary component of federalism's market-preserving qualities.

The contrast between market-preserving federalism and the decentralization of the former Soviet Union is also instructive. The Soviet system was characterized by administrative decentralization without authority. Lower governments were largely administrative units of the central government with little autonomous political power, let alone power over their local economies. The center also carefully controlled factor mobility. Hence, all but condition 1 failed in that system.[13]

In sum, though many forms of political decentralization exist, only a narrow subset is characterized by market-preserving federalism.

The Economic Effects of Market-Preserving Federalism

The most important implication of market-preserving federalism is the induced competition among jurisdictions,[14] which produces a number of salutary effects. First, no government has a monopoly of regulatory authority over the entire economy. Any subnational government that

[12] See Oliver Williamson, "The Institutions and Governance of Economic Development and Reform" (Working paper, University of California, Berkeley, 1994).

[13] In contrast, eighteenth-century England was characterized by market-preserving federalism, although the English did not call their system federal. See Weingast (fn. 1).

[14] This section summarizes an extensive literature in economics, including the classic work of Tiebout and Oates. For a review of this literature see Daniel Rubinfeld, "Economics of the Local Public Sector," in A. J. Auerbach and M. Feldstein, eds., *Handbook of Public Economics*, vol. 2, (New York: Elsevier, 1987).

seeks to use its authority for purposes of monopolization or other political ends is at a considerable disadvantage because it cannot impose its will on the entire economy. When a particular jurisdiction imposes an onerous restriction on its firms, the latter face a competitive disadvantage relative to competing firms from other jurisdictions that are not bound by the restriction. Producers outside the particular jurisdiction are not bound by these rules, and, hence, their costs will be lower and they will outsell those firms bound by the restriction.

Second, competition among jurisdictions extends to factors of production, such as capital and labor. Jurisdictions are thus induced to provide a hospitable environment for factors, typically through the provision of local, public goods, such as establishing a basis for secure rights of factor owners, the provision of infrastructure, utilities, access to markets, and so on. Those jurisdictions that fail to provide these goods find that factors move to other jurisdictions. Local economic activity and tax revenue decline as a consequence.

Third, the hard budget constraint implies that local governments can go bankrupt. This provides them with incentives for proper fiscal management.[15] Local enterprises, local politicians, and citizens in particular areas hardly want their government to spend more money than is prudent. Bankruptcy would greatly hinder the ability of local governments to finance needed public goods, such as those needed to attract foreign capital and lower business costs.

Finally, market-preserving federalism provides the political foundations for markets.[16] By placing the authority over markets in the hands of lower governments, it fosters local economic prosperity. By keeping the central government out of this activity, it prevents massive intervention of political goals that distort markets for other purposes. Once established, markets are difficult to alter since national political forces are deflected from this issue and, at the local level, it is hard for a group with any particular goal to capture the lion's share of the local governments. In turn, the implication is that some governments are always likely to retain their promarket focus. Market-preserving federalism, therefore, diminishes the prevalence of rent-seeking and patronage systems. The latter can only survive in areas with political protection from market forces, a phenomenon that market-preserving federalism is designed to eliminate.

Predictions following the inception of market-preserving federalism. Following the imposition of a system of federalism, we should observe a

[15] McKinnon (fn. 5).

[16] Weingast (fn. 1).

diversity of policy choices and experiments. People in different political jurisdictions are likely to have markedly different interests, expectations, and capabilities. We should, therefore, observe that they choose a range of policies to promote their goals.

As the results of these experiments and policies become known, individuals and policymakers will update their expectations about the effects of various policies. Thus, decentralization under market-preserving federalism results in an important degree of feedback, which would not be present under a unitary system that imposes a single national experiment over all regions.

Competition among jurisdictions provides incentives to replace poorly chosen strategies with variants of strategies that appear to succeed elsewhere. To the extent that some jurisdictions are better at promoting markets, generating wealth, and caring for the needs of their citizens, their policies are likely to be imitated by others that have been less successful. Still, we do not expect the appearance of uniformity among jurisdictions for several reasons. First, individuals and firms will sort themselves into jurisdictions, to the extent, for example, that they require different types of public goods. Second, resources and access to markets imply that a variety of economic and political differences will survive.[17] Finally, individuals are likely to vary in their tastes for public goods, as well as in their ability to pay for them.

Predictions when market-preserving federalism remains incomplete. The set of predictions just noted will vary in systematic ways if particular components of market-preserving federalism are missing. We discuss the implications of two limitations on market-preserving federalism. The first concerns the absence of a common market, allowing individual jurisdictions to erect trade barriers. The principal difference is that the common market is highly unlikely to be sustained without explicit protection from the central authorities.[18] This implies that some areas, particularly those not likely to perform well under competition with jurisdictions, are likely to erect trade barriers to firms and products from other areas. A federalism of this sort (which is only incompletely mar-

[17] See, for example, Paul Krugman, *Geography and Trade* (Cambridge: MIT Press, 1991).

[18] For example, the common market in the United States in the early nineteenth century could not have been sustained without vigilant policing by the Supreme Court. Policing the market against encroachments by state governments proved a major use of the Court's constitutional powers. These cases reveal the remarkable diversity and cleverness of the states in their efforts to erect such barriers. See Barry R. Weingast, "The Political Foundations of the Antebellum American Economy (Working paper, Hoover Institution, Stanford University, 1993). Similarly, such barriers are a major reason underlying the movement for economic and political union in Europe. See G. Garrett, "The International Cooperation and Institutional Choice: The European Community's Internal Market," *International Organization* 46 (Spring 1992).

ket-preserving) will produce seemingly contradictory results. Some areas will promote markets while others will closely control their economy, especially from influence outside the jurisdiction.

We also expect this juxtaposition to be more pronounced in jurisdictions just after a system of federalism is imposed than in a more mature system, especially in an economy like China's with only limited experience with markets. Limited exposure to markets naturally generates suspicion of them and of their potential dependence on outsiders. The feedback provided by multiple jurisdictions that conduct independent experiments is important for the next stage. As the market grows in those areas that commit themselves to it, the tendency of other jurisdictions toward protectionism will diminish. The experience with markets will reveal new information about how they allow local governments to provide for the needs of citizens. Even in the presence of strong trade barriers, fiscal pressures will push insulated areas to substitute market mechanisms for those activities that have been demonstrated elsewhere to be superior providers of particular goods and services. Nonetheless, some regions may never foster markets.

The second explicit limit on market-preserving federalism concerns the absence of centralized control over the monetary system. To the extent that the authority over credit, for example, is not centralized, but remains, at least in part, at the discretion of lower governments, several problems are likely to emerge. The most obvious is inflation as each government overgrazes the "commons," causing too much growth in the money supply. The second problem is a consequence of the first. Decentralized access to credit under these circumstances also softens the hard budget constraint, as governments that increase their exposure can always borrow more in the short run. This induces moral hazard—for example, too much borrowing to finance too many investments, many of which would not be financed were it not for access to credit in this manner.

III. Federalism, Chinese Style

The decentralization in China differs from Western federalism in several important respects. First, the latter virtually always roots federalism in an explicit system for protecting individual rights. Second, Western federalism typically has strong, explicit constitutional foundations. Third, it is almost always associated with political freedom, representation, and democratization. None of these factors are present in China. Notice, however, that as defined above, market-preserving federalism in no way depends on these factors. Instead, it depends on the political relationships among levels of government, with no reference to an explicit or constitutional basis or its promotion of individual rights and political freedom.

In this section, we present evidence from China on each of the five conditions, both positive and negative, underlying market-preserving federalism. As we show, with some important qualifications, the conditions are satisfied.

The differences between Western and Chinese federalism noted above constitute the first aspect of federalism, Chinese style. The second aspect concerns the specific nature of the institutional changes of decentralization underpinning the reforms, the increased reliance on markets, and openness to the outside world. Perhaps the most significant steps toward reform taken by the Chinese central government were its decentralization of authority from the central to local governments and, to a lesser degree, the state-owned enterprises. The idea of decentralization in China is not new—it experienced two previous waves of "administrative decentralization," the Great Leap Forward in 1958 and the Cultural Revolution in 1970. Decentralization in the 1980s differed, however, in that it is combined with financial incentives, reliance on market mechanisms, increased control for lower governments over their economies, and a new openness to international markets. These features generate far-reaching consequences for political institutions and economic performance.[19]

Decentralization of Authority

Even before the current economic reform began in 1979, a large number of state-owned industrial enterprises in both light and heavy industries were controlled by local governments rather than the central government. In 1978 the share of industrial output of state-owned enterprises controlled by the central government was less than one-half of the national total.[20] In the early 1980s, as a result of the reforms, many state-owned enterprises controlled by the central government were delegated to local governments. By 1985 state-owned industrial enterprises controlled by the central government accounted for only 20

[19] See Yingyi Qian and Chenggang Xu, "Why China's Economic Reforms Differ: The M-form Hierarchy and Entry/Expansion of the Non-State Sector," *Economics of Transition* (June 1993). Qian and Xu provide a detailed analysis of how and why this happened in China, offering an institutional explanation of differences between economic reforms in China and in Eastern Europe and the Soviet Union.

[20] Christine Wong, "Between Plan and Market: The Role of the Local Sector in Post-Mao China," *Journal of Comparative Economics* (September 1987).

percent of the total industrial output from such enterprises at or above township level. At the same time, provincial and city governments controlled 45 percent, county governments 9 percent, and the rest came from township enterprises.[21]

Unlike previous decentralizations, which were carried out within the framework of central planning, provincial and local governments under the market-oriented reforms enjoyed a wide range of authority within the market environment. More and more foreign capital, for example, flowed into firms and projects that were not controlled by the central government. The total foreign investment in China increased from $4.5 billion in 1985 to $19.2 billion in 1992 (among the largest investors were Hong Kong, Taiwan, U.S., and Japan). At the same time, the share of foreign investment administered by provinces (rather than ministries of the central government) increased from 35 percent in 1985 to 68 percent in 1992.[22]

Many reform policies were also delegated to provinces and local governments. For example, China did not liberalize prices in one stroke. The dual price system was a common practice in China in the 1980s, with one planned price and another market price. A little known fact is that, for many goods, moving from a dual price system to a single price system was not carried out solely by the central government, but also by local governments. Decisions about prices were largely delegated to lower-level governments. (Exceptions to this generalization are some nationally important goods, like energy and transportation services.) Many governments have extended their authority to pursue reform to liberalize the prices. With grain prices, which had been under the control of the central government, Guangdong took the lead in liberalization in 1992, and many other provinces have since followed suit.

Decentralization of authority is particularly associated with the establishment of special economic zones, coastal open cities, and development zones. In 1979 China established four special economic zones: Shenzhen; Zhuhai; Shantou, adjacent to Hong Kong in Guangdong Province; and Xiamen, in Fujian Province across the Taiwan strait.[23] Subsequently, Guangdong and Fujian gained substantial autonomy in developing their regions when the central government granted them authority to pursue reform "one step ahead." Not only did these areas enjoy lower tax rates, but they gained more authority over economic de-

[21] Qian and Xu (fn. 19).

[22] See *China Statistical Yearbook* (various years).

[23] Hainan was added as the largest special economic zone when it was organized as a separate province in 1988.

velopment. For example, they have the authority to approve foreign investment projects up to $30 million, while other regions' authority remain much lower.

In 1984 the central government declared fourteen coastal cities as "coastal open cities," conveying to them new authority that paralleled power granted earlier only to special economic zones. In the early 1990s treatment of special economic zones was extended to various inland regions. For example, some inland cities along the Yangtze River and cities bordering Russia obtained similar authority as the coastal cities. Furthermore, many inland cities, which did not qualify for these special treatments as a whole, established numerous "development zones" inside their regions to enjoy part of the tax benefits and autonomy.

Fiscal Incentives: The Fiscal Contracting System

Starting in 1980, China implemented a fiscal revenue-sharing system between any two adjacent levels of governments.[24] Although schemes vary across both regions and time, the basic idea is that a lower-level regional government contracts with the upper-level regional government on the total amount (or share) of tax and profit revenue (negative values imply a reverse flow of subsidies) to be remitted for the next several years; the lower-level government keeps the rest. This system was maintained until the end of 1993, and a new fiscal system was introduced in the beginning of 1994.

Consider fiscal contracting schemes between the central and provincial governments (lower-level fiscal contracting is similar). In the first step, revenue income in each province is divided between "central fixed revenue," all of which is remitted to the center, and "local revenue," which is subject to sharing. In the second step, a particular formula of sharing is determined. There were six basic types of sharing schemes for the thirty provinces and five cities during 1988–93.[25]

1. Fixed sharing: a fixed proportion is remitted to the center (three provinces/cities);

[24] See, for example, Jean Oi, "Fiscal Reform and the Economic Foundations of Local State Corporatism in China," *World Politics* 45 (October 1992); Michael Oksenberg and James Tong, "The Evolution of Central-Provincial Fiscal Relations in China, 1971–1984: The Formal System," *China Quarterly* (March 1991); and, Christine Wong, "Fiscal Reform and Local Industrialization," *Modern China* 18 (April 1992).

[25] The five cities are below the provincial level but have independent budget agreements with the center. The list is based on: Roy Bahl and Christine Wallich, "Intergovernmental Fiscal Relations in China" (Working papers, Country Economics Department, World Bank, WPS 863 1992); Christine Wong, "Central-Local Relations in an Era of Fiscal Decline: The Paradox of Fiscal Decentralization in Post-Mao China," *China Quarterly* 128 (December 1991); idem (fn. 20).

2. Incremental sharing: a certain proportion is retained up to a quota, and then a higher proportion is retained in excess of the quota (three provinces/cities);

3. Sharing up to a limit with growth adjustment: the localities retain a specified proportion that is within a specific percentage of revenue from the previous year, and then retain all above that quota (ten provinces/cities);

4. Fixed quota delivery: a specified, nominal amount is remitted to the center (three provinces/cities);

5. Fixed quota with growth adjustment: the fixed amount remitted to the center is increased at a contracted rate (two provinces/cities);

6. Fixed subsidies (fourteen provinces/cities).

The importance of these new fiscal arrangements is that they induce a strong positive relationship between local revenue and local economic prosperity for all provinces and cities, thus providing local officials with an incentive to foster that prosperity. Schemes 4 to 6, which cover nineteen out of thirty-five provinces or cities, at the margin allow local governments to retain 100 percent of local revenues. Scheme 3, which covers another ten provinces and cities, has the same effect when the increased revenue limits for sharing are not a binding constraint. Even in scheme 2, the marginal remittance rate is regressive.

The fiscal contracting in budgetary revenue described above is only one aspect of fiscal decentralization; the other is the expansion of the so-called extra-budgetary funds (certain categories of revenues collected by the local governments and ministries, including some retained profits of state-owned enterprises). In the early 1990s the extra-budgetary revenue reached about the same level as budgetary revenue. Unlike the budgetary revenue, which is subject to sharing with the higher governments, the extra-budgetary revenue is wholly retained by the local government. Moreover, the local government has complete authority over the determination of taxes or fees that fall into the categories of extra budget. The decentralized nature of extra-budgetary revenues also increases local government security from predation by the central government, as such revenues are easier to hide from the higher governments. These funds are especially valuable to local governments as their use is more flexible than budgetary revenues.

By way of summary, these changes provide for substantial independence of the governments in China, from the provincial to the township, which ensures that governments in each region assume primary responsibility for economic development in that region. Hence, these governments possess both significant fiscal autonomy from the central government and considerable independent authority over their economies.

Notice the striking contrast between this system and that of the former communist system, including the former Soviet Union and Eastern Europe. In the latter, the central authorities retained the discretionary authority to the profits "earned" by producers, typically using this authority both to take resources from those firms with positive earnings and to bail out those with negative earnings. This discretionary redistribution was described in the Soviet Union by the Russian word *uravnilovka*, which translates as "equalization" or "leveling off."[26]

The Common Market Condition

In contrast to the decentralizations accompanying the Great Leap Forward and the Cultural Revolution, decentralization in the current reform is associated with increasing marketization. The development of good and factor mobility across regions is considerable but remains imperfect. On the one hand, there are clear signs of increased factor mobility over time, as evidenced by the huge "floating migrant" population and the foreign-capital inflow. On the other hand, decentralization has increased the incentives as well as the range of political means for local governments to erect trade barriers, resulting in the so-called dukedom economies phenomenon, which has worried the central government and economists. This form of protectionism has occurred most often in the markets of high profit-margin manufacturing goods (such as automobiles, tobacco products, and alcohol) and raw materials in short supply (such as cotton, silkworm cocoons, tobacco, and aluminum).

The imperfect common market implies that some areas have used their political freedom to maintain considerable trade barriers.[27] We offer two examples. First, consider automobile assembly. The total production of automobiles in China was around 1.2 million in 1992, despite the fact that it had more than 126 assembly factories with an average production of 10,000 units.[28] Almost all provinces have their own automobile factory. Such an inefficient scale can be maintained

[26] For discussion of the Russian case, see John Litwack, "Discretionary Behavior and Soviet Economic Reform," *Soviet Studies* (March 1991); and idem, "Legality and Market Reform in Soviet-Type Economies," *Journal of Economic Perspectives* 5, no. 4 (1991).

[27] See Wong (fn. 24). In a recent comprehensive study of China's internal market, the World Bank concluded that "despite considerable progress in the substitution of allocation by the price mechanism, markets for both goods and factors of production (capital, labor and foreign exchange) are still regionally fragmented. . . . Links with the overseas exterior appear to have been easier to develop than links with other provinces, both in terms of the mobility of goods and some factors, particularly capital investment. There has been some tendency for individual provinces to behave as separate countries, rather than as parts of a single large country. *China: Internal Market Development and Regulation* (Washington, D.C.: World Bank, Country Operation Division, China and Mongolia Department, 1993).

[28] *People's Daily*, October 11, 1993, overseas edition, p. 2.

only in the presence of substantial government protection: tariffs at the national level and various trade barriers at the regional level.[29]

Second, in 1985 Jiangxi Province liberalized hog procurement.[30] As a result of the large demand from rich neighboring provinces such as Guangdong and Fujian, hog prices increased rapidly. To maintain the welfare of its urban constituents, the local governments of Jiangxi attempted to keep the urban retail pork price of local government-owned food companies at a low level. The local governments thus spent a large amount of their budgets on subsidizing hog sales in local cities. As it was more profitable for rural households to sell hogs to neighboring rich provinces where hog prices were much higher, hogs were exported out of the region. At the end of 1985, the Jiangxi provincial government reacted to this situation (in which the "Jiangxinese raise hogs and Cantonese consume pork") by establishing tax offices on the provincial border. Their purpose was to develop a so-called hog development fund derived from hog sales out of the region. Since this fund actually could be captured by any level of authorities that charged it, many county and even township governments in Jiangxi set up tax offices. In response, hog production decreased dramatically.[31]

As these examples suggest, the imperfect policing of the common market allows local governments to insulate themselves from competition by erecting trade barriers. These barriers also allow the emergence of corruption. In insulated regions beyond the reach of the central government, local officials can take advantage of their power for personal gain. In the presence of open competition, this type of corruption is harder to sustain because of market pressure.

The Hard Budget Constraint Condition

At all levels of government, fiscal budget constraints are relatively hard due to the declining tax revenues and the limited intergovernmental budgetary transfers under the fiscal revenue sharing schemes. The one exception is the state banking system, which has become the most significant source of the soft budget constraint for governments at or above the county level.

China's state banking system features a central bank supervising four major specialized state banks. The banking institutions in China

[29] For example, it is reported that one provincial government instructed its automobile registration department to refuse to issue license plates to unauthorized automobiles produced outside the province.

[30] C. Wang, "Hog Production Problems in Jiangxi Province," *Economic Study* (May 1988).

[31] Though the details differ, this pattern was repeated in 1986 and 1987.

evolved from the planning era in which the central bank and each of the four specialized banks established a branch in every province, municipality, and county. Under regional decentralization, the regional governments at provincial, municipality, and county levels also gained great influence over credit decisions through the regional branches of the central bank and specialized banks. The local bank branches were under the "dual subordination" principle (*shuangchong lingdao*): they were subordinated to the banking hierarchy as well as to the local government. As reform proceeded, the latter carried more weight. *Ex ante*, the local governments were directly involved in the credit-plan formulation and might impose loans on specialized banks. *Ex post*, the local governments had the authority to decide whether the enterprise should pay back the loan.

The absence of a unified monetary system has allowed local governments access to credit in a way that has expanded the money supply. When all local governments behave in this manner, the result is inflation. Yet not one of them has an incentive to stop; each province claims that overheating is caused by the other provinces, not by itself. This has the structure of the "tragedy of the commons" and is the main reason that the monetary system is a national public good: it must be controlled by a single authority, and, best, by a national one.[32]

THE CASE FOR TOWNSHIP AND VILLAGE GOVERNMENTS

Central, prefecture, municipal, and county governments all have full authority in the Chinese governmental hierarchy to regulate the market through administrative methods. But township and village governments have very limited authority. Historically, their responsibility was confined to agriculture and rural governance, and they had no control over state-owned enterprises (SOEs) and no access to the state banking system. These institutional constraints have made the township and village governments somewhat different from the higher level governments: township and village governments operate under a hard budget constraint and without trade barriers. Both conditions were somewhat relaxed, however, for higher level governments in China. In this sense, the Chinese federalism seems to better approximate a market-preserving one at the township and village levels than at higher levels.

One result of China's reform is the spectacular growth of the market in the flourishing sector of township-village enterprises (TVEs), which

[32] This conclusion is standard in the fiscal federalism literature. See, for example, Wallace Oates, *Fiscal Federalism* (New York: Harcourt Brace Jovanovich, 1972).

are owned by township and village communities and controlled by township and village governments.[33] By the end of 1993, TVEs produced 30 percent of the total industrial output in China. This remarkable success of TVEs can be understood from the incentives facing these firms. First, the structure of these firms affords residual claim rights (in essence, the rights to profits) to township and village governments. Second, two forms of limits are imposed upon the township and village governments and their firms. The first limit is that these governments do not have the authority to enact protectionist policies. They cannot use political means to protect their firms, for example, by erecting trade barriers to keep out competition. The second limit is a hard budget constraint. Not only may they go bankrupt, but the local governments, in contrast to the central government that can print money, cannot endlessly bail them out. In 1989, for example, about three million TVEs went bankrupt or were taken over by other TVEs. In the same year almost all loss-making state-owned enterprises were bailed out by the state.[34] Furthermore, total credit going to the TVE sector was no more than 8 percent of the total outstanding loans, despite the fact that this sector produced more than 25 percent of total industrial output at the time.[35] Although both TVEs and SOEs are "owned" by governments, their incentives and hence their behavior are far different.[36]

Durability and Irreversibility of Federalism, Chinese Style

Decentralization began with the delegation of considerable economic authority to local governments. These governments assumed primary authority over economic matters within their jurisdiction. We have also suggested that the reforms have provided considerable limits on the discretion of the central government. They are also often associated

[33] A burgeoning literature studies this topic. See, for example, William Byrd and Qingsong Lin, eds., *China's Rural Industry: Structure, Development and Reform* (Oxford: Oxford University Press, 1990); Victor Nee and Su Sijin, "Institutional Change and Economic Growth in China: The View from the Villages," *Journal of Asian Studies* 49 (1990); Oi (fn. 24); Qian and Xu (fn. 19); Martin Weitzman and Chenggang Xu, "Chinese Township-Village Enterprises as Vaguely Defined Cooperatives," *Journal of Comparative Economics* (April 1994); Chun Chang and Yijiang Wang, "The Nature of the Township Enterprise," *Journal of Comparative Economics* (December 1994); Andrew Walder, "The Varieties of Public Enterprises in China: An Institutional Analysis" (Manuscript, Harvard University, 1994); Jiahua Che and Yingyi Qian, "Boundaries of the Firm and Governance: Understanding China's Township-Village Enterprise" (Manuscript, Stanford University, 1994).

[34] *People's Daily*, March 23, 1990, overseas edition.

[35] *Almanac of China's Finance and Banking*. Beijing: China's Financial Publishing House, 1992.

[36] This topic is further explored in Yingyi Qian and Barry R. Weingast, "Institutions, State Activism, and the Role of Government in Economic Development" in Masahiko Aoki, Masahiro Okuno-Fujiwara, and Hyung-Ki Kim, eds., *The Role of Government in East Asian Economies: Comparative Institutional Analysis* (New York: Oxford University Press, forthcoming).

with the emergence of strong regional economic powers, such as Guangdong Province. These limits seem to endow the reforms with a degree of durability, making reversal more costly, if not impossible. Three events after the Tiananmen Square uprising in 1989 demonstrate these conclusions.

1. *After Tiananmen Square, 1989–1991.* The single best indication of the linkage between durability of reform and decentralization concerns the events following Tiananmen Square, especially between 1989 and 1991 under the austerity program. During that period, the conservatives gained the most political, ideological, and military power for a possible reversal. Li Peng tried to recentralize investment and financial powers but failed. The governor of Guangdong refused to cooperate and many other governors followed.[37] This, however, is only part of the story. This incident suggests the striking new power of local governments to shape decisions by the central government. On several previous occasions when the economy faced difficulties (for example, in 1962 and 1981), Chen Yun, an advocate for central planning, succeeded in compelling the provincial governments to "help the central government overcome the difficulties," that is, to turn over more revenue to the central budget. The contrast between this situation and Li Peng's failed attempt illustrates our point: the limits on the discretion of the central government provides for the durability of reforms.

Five considerations support this claim. First, by this time, the price of recentralization had increased. In order to recentralize, the central government would have to undertake substantial new obligations by providing social safety-net expenditures. A major retrenchment would increase the regime's financial obligations while the economy would shrink as firms, successful under markets, withered. This raises immediate financial problems: how would these obligations be financed? Fiscal problems of this magnitude raise the specter of the former Soviet Union's failure, surely a possibility to be avoided. Further, a major retrenchment would risk considerable social problems.

Second, some regions have already accumulated sufficient wealth in ways that do not allow the central government to easily confiscate the revenue because the regional governments followed a strategy of "storing wealth in people and in enterprises." The regional governments also have greater vested interest in continuing the reform.[38]

[37] Shirk (fn. 3).

[38] Paralleling these problems is the substantially diminished reach of the central planning system. Put simply, the central government no longer has the administrative apparatus to monitor and plan the economy as necessary under the older system.

Third, incentive structures within the government and the Party have altered considerably. In advanced regions, many officials no longer care to be promoted to posts in the higher level government.[39] This is because, at a lower level of the government, the more autonomy the officials enjoy, which also translates into higher financial benefits. This contrasts strikingly with the earlier period in which climbing up the Party ladder was desired by most individuals. Thus, in Guangdong Province today, township officials do not want to be promoted to the county level, municipal officials do not want to be promoted to the provincial level, and provincial officials do not want to be promoted to the central government.

This difference reflects an important change in political incentives. Local political officials are now far less beholden to the central authorities. In the past, central authorities retained a variety of incentives to control the behavior of lower officials: fiscal control of local government operations allowed them to manipulate local decision making, and individuals were promoted for appropriate behavior and punished for behavior deemed inappropriate. Each of these incentives has been weakened under the current arrangements. Although the central government retains control over the army and over the appointment and dismissal of high-level personnel, the power of these tools is weaker than when they were combined with the more microlevel incentives employed during previous eras.

Fourth, the fall of socialism in Eastern Europe and the former Soviet Union has had an important impact on China. China's immediate reaction to the collapse of these communist regimes was recentralization, but the Chinese government soon realized that its legitimacy could only be sustained by economic growth. A reversal of the reforms that cut off access to international markets would result in significant shrinking of domestic production and unemployment, thus dramatically increasing the demands on the central government. An outright reversal of the reforms would greatly expand the central government's fiscal commitments while dramatically contracting the economy, putting the regime at risk. Complementing this financial incentive is the economic stake due to openness to the international market, in particular, pressure from the booming East Asian neighbors. Further, the sheer growth of the market economy makes the imposition of a new round of central control of the economy difficult, if only because the central government no longer retains the capacity to monitor the vast new economy.

[39] Shirk (fn. 3).

A final aspect of the reforms, as often claimed, is that a majority of Chinese people seem to have gained economically under the reforms, including farmers, workers, and even most bureaucrats. A widespread feeing that reforms have left people better off places a constraint on any attempt to reverse reforms.

2. *Deng's southern tour, 1992.* The above evidence suggests that the reforms were not reversed after the Tiananmen Square incident in part because of the increased political power of local governments. Amid the political deadlock within the central government at the end of 1991, Deng Xiaoping made his now famous southern tour to the province of Guangdong. Among his stops were several special economic zones. Using the regional support for continued reforms, Deng's visit tipped the political balance of the central government. This resulted in the central government's official declaration in October 1992 to build a "socialist market economy."[40] Ending the deadlock revealed two interrelated elements about the security of the reforms. First, it indicated that the immediate threat to the reforms after Tiananmen had failed. Second, the failure of the retrenchment revealed that the reforms were protected by a degree of durability.

3. *Rationalization and institutionalization, 1993–94.* Further evidence for the durability of the reforms and decentralization is provided by the recent controversies over recentralization.

In the transition from a planned to a market economy, certain types of overshooting in decentralization have not been avoided. Several problems have thus emerged from the lack of central authority, raising calls for a recentralization. The crucial question is: will the central government use the occasion for centralization and reversal to the old system, or will it have to justify its action as an integrated part of more reforms, that is, a process of rationalization of market institutions? We provide two examples below indicating the latter path.

In the first half of 1993 the economy seemed to become "overheated," reflecting problems of macroeconomic imbalance similar to those experienced in 1988. This caused instability in the foreign-exchange market. At first the government attempted to control the exchange rate through administrative methods by imposing a ceiling, but this failed. The market exchange rate was later stabilized in July 1993 when the central bank sold dollars rather than imposing ceilings. This intervention was followed soon by the implementation of foreign-exchange reform on January 1, 1994, which unified the previous official

[40] It should be noted that reforms in many southern regions went ahead despite actions from the central government during the period from 1989 to 1991.

and market rates and essentially achieved trade-account convertibility.

Second, amid the continuing decline of central government revenue as a proportion of GDP from 31 percent in 1978 to 15 percent in 1992 (within-budget consolidated revenue), the call for an increase of government revenue comes together with a proposal for enacting a more formal system of fiscal federalism, which was implemented in January 1994. The new fiscal system, which resembles that of the United States, established a two-tier tax-administration system (national and local) that separates taxes into national, local, and shared taxes. It also simplifies tax rates and makes them more uniform. Furthermore, rule-based transfer formulas are being studied for possible implementation in the future. The reason for such a shift toward a formal fiscal federalism is that it appears impossible (prohibitively costly) to collect more revenue through methods of centralization, and fiscal federalism is the only alternative that will satisfy both central and local governments. Importantly, it holds the promise of resolving the problems of an overly weak government without removing the beneficial effects of the decentralization. A direct recentralization, in contrast, would threaten to remove this essential political component underlying the success of the economic reforms.

Summary. A range of factors contributes to the durability of the reforms, limiting the discretion of the central government to attempt a reversal. First, as a result of the reforms, new, rival power centers have emerged in China. Local governments, particularly those in areas with the largest growth, now have substantial independent sources of revenue, authority, and political support. Second, although local officials are still appointed and dismissed by the central government, their authority is implied and enhanced by their access to and control of local information and resources (for example, in the case of extra-budgetary revenue). Third, the gradual decline of the personal authority of national leaders and the rise of local governments have weakened the reach of the Chinese Communist Party into the lower levels of government; many lower government officials now bestow their loyalty on localities, not the central government. Fourth, as the private market economy has expanded, the ability of the central government to monitor and control local economic behavior has weakened enormously. Finally, as noted above, any attempt by the center at economic retrenchment would strain its financial capacity, raising the specter of the fall of the Soviet Union.

These changes endow the economic reforms with a degree of political durability. Each serves to raise the costs of a recentralization of political authority and an economic retrenchment, although this effect was often unintended. The short-lived attempt at recentralization following Tiananmen Square is consistent with this logic, as are the recent institutional and tax changes reflecting an attempt to correct for overshooting in decentralization. Our argument does not imply that a retrenchment is impossible, but that it would be costly and might fail, thus making it less likely.

IV. The Effects of Federalism, Chinese Style

The economic approach to market-preserving federalism outlined in Section II yields predictions about economic performance following the onset of federalism. We now turn to investigate some of the varied economic response to federalism, Chinese style, over the past fifteen years.[41]

Economic policy-making by provincial and local governments reveals a wide range of behavior over the past fifteen years. Many areas initially chose to remain unchanged. Others sought to reinforce the status quo. Still others, of course, chose the path of reform. Moreover, this pattern of policy choice has not remained stationary but has changed over time, in part reflecting the emerging evidence about the consequences of the different policies. Competition among jurisdictions is evident in many forms.

Competition among Jurisdictions: Experimentation, Learning, and Imitation

Following the predictions of the economic approach to federalism, jurisdictions in China initially chose different policies. As the results became known, some of those with inferior policies adopted the superior ones. First, failed experiments were discarded while successful ones were expanded and imitated. Second, there has emerged a large range of seemingly puzzling results that appears inconsistent with marketization. Many governments pursue strikingly interventionist policies, for example, by erecting trade barriers and preventing competition from firms from neighboring provinces. Moreover, there are widespread reports of overcompetition. How do we make sense of all this? The following series of cases reveal patterns consistent with the theory developed above.

[41] Additional evidence is provided by Steve Lewis, "Marketization and Government Credibility in Shanghai: Federalist and Corporatist Perspectives" (Manuscript, Washington University, 1994).

1. *Heilongjiang's "Project 383."*[42] Bordering Russia, Heilongjiang is China's most northeastern province, and a conservative one. In an effort to demonstrate their dedication to the old system, Heilongjiang's officials announced "Project 383" in 1989. This policy was designed to achieve a significant reduction in the rate of price increases (from 17 percent in the previous year to 13 percent) for the 383 goods in the official basket used to calculate the inflation index. The policy proved very costly and was criticized by the government—for example, members of the financial bureaucracy—and the public. The contrast with Guangdong was apparent to all. Guangdong had freed prices on the same set of goods, and, due to reforms, prices had fallen. Guangdong's policies had thus achieved the same results but without significant financial participation by the government. Reports from economists suggest that Project 383 has been abandoned.

This episode represents an important instance of the learning that takes place during the experimental process. Given its goals and expectations, Heilongjiang initiated Project 383. It decided that the project was a failure, not because the province changed its goals, but because market methods had proved more effective.

2. *Two prefectures.* The process of choosing different strategies followed by the comparison of results and the adoption of the superior strategy occurred in two similar prefectures just across the provincial border, Shaoguan in Guangdong and Binzhou in Hunan.[43] When reform was first adopted in Guangdong in 1980, many commodity prices in Guangdong rose above those in Binzhou since the reform was not carried out in Hunan. As a result, resources from Binzhou flowed to Guangdong. The Binzhou government set up tax offices on the border in an attempt to stop this outflow. These attempts did not bring prosperity to Binzhou. Years later when the people in Binzhou compared themselves with their neighbor, Shaoguan, they found that, although both had similar initial economic conditions, Shaoguan had significantly benefited from economic reform in Guangdong. People in Binzhou urged the government to undertake reform.

In 1988 the central government allowed Binzhou to adopt some reform measures. This enabled Binzhou to enjoy the benefits of opening markets to Guangdong. The prefecture government withdrew all its tax offices along the border with Guangdong. Soon the adjacent areas between Binzhou and Guangdong prospered, and interregional trade

[42] "Heilongjiang Province Implements Project 383 to Control Prices," *Price Theory and Practice* (July 1990).

[43] *Economic Daily*, November 25, 1991.

reached a record level. Importantly, the Binzhou government obtained far more tax revenue from these businesses than from those border tax offices.[44]

3. *Coordinating labor flows.*[45] China's floating labor population, estimated variously between 60 and 100 million workers, is so large that it can overwhelm the ability of local governments to provide basic services, such as water, food, sewage, transportation, security, and housing.[46] In part, due to the congestion caused by these migrants, several provinces have begun to manage and coordinate these flows.[47] For example, in early 1992, Guangdong, Hunan, Guangxi, and Sichuan established an interregional labor coordination center to help coordinate labor movements among these four provinces. Under the new regulations, migrant workers in Guangdong must obtain approval from labor-management organizations of their home province. Guangdong, in turn, agrees to provide labor-demand information to the other three provinces.

A comparison of labor flow into Guangdong and Shanghai reveals the effect of these organizations. For both areas, the labor inflow of 1993 was the largest in history. Yet the two regions responded very differently. In Guangdong, transportation was much more reliable than in previous years. The crime rate dropped sharply compared with the same period (spring) of the previous year. Many firms provided their own transportation for workers hired from other regions. Likewise some local governments of other provinces also provided transportation for workers from their regions. In contrast, large numbers of migrants flowed into Shanghai trying to find work in the recently established Pudong Developmental Zone. The development zone only needed approximately 500,000 to 600,000 workers. But the labor arriving in Shanghai on the two days of January 31 and February 1 more than doubled this figure. Many people were detained in the train station or on the streets. On January 31, the Shanghai municipal government sent

[44] Stories of this type can be replicated manyfold. As an additional example, we note the comparison of Nanyang and Xiangfan, two cities in Henan and Hubei provinces, respectively. The latter made much faster progress, and when this was reported in the *Economic Daily* in 1984, the former designed a new set of developmental programs to learn from and imitate the advanced regions. Five years later, Nanyang was ranked as one of the best among middle and small size cities within the nation (*Economic Daily*, December 6, 1991).

[45] *Economic Daily*, May 15, 1991, and July 4, 1992; *Outlook*, February 22, 1993.

[46] See, for example, Dorothy Solinger, "The Floating Population as a Form of Civil Society" (Paper presented at the forty-third annual meeting of the Association for Asian Studies, New Orleans, La., April 11–14, 1991).

[47] Undoubtedly there are other factors underlying these policies, for example, keeping the benefits of local services (such as education) for local residents. Moreover, under other circumstances, these mechanisms could be used to cartelize labor markets, or for other political purposes.

an emergency request to neighboring provinces asking them to stop labor flowing to Shanghai. In the meantime, Shanghai started to deport those migrants who could not find jobs.

The difference between these two regions occurred in part because Guangdong had experienced the large amount of labor inflow much earlier than Shanghai. Therefore, Guangdong and its neighboring provinces have learned much more about the markets and what they can do about it. The market capacity appears to have reached a sufficient scale in Guangdong so that organized labor markets will pay off.

Competition among Jurisdictions: Factor Mobility

Beyond experimentation and imitation discussed above, there is a more explicit type of competition for resources, particularly labor and foreign capital. Here, too, localities with more efficient economies outcompete less efficient ones.

1. *Organized labor export and capital import in Sichuan Province.* Evidence of labor mobility is striking. Although many restrictions remain on migration, the floating labor pool is enormous by any standard.[48] Labor moves from areas of surplus to areas of need. An interesting story concerns labor export from Sichuan province.[49] Total labor exported from this province has reached 3 million per year. Remittances from migrants have totaled as much as 3–5 billion yuan annually, accounting for 10 percent of net farmer income in the province. Provincial authorities have attached great importance to labor export. The vice governor of Sichuan province pointed out that labor export has become an important means of developing backward local economies. It requires less capital and yields quick and high returns. Individuals leave with nothing and return with what is, by local standards, a fortune. Their annual incomes are largely higher than 1000 yuan, and some have assets over 1 million. They bring back capital to invest in the local economies, promoting the local economy and township-village enterprises.

To foster the process of labor export and capital import, the Sichuan provincial government established a labor development office headed by the vice governor. Different levels of local government authorities established organizations that are responsible for managing labor exports and the provision of training to improve skills. Some counties established county-township-village hierarchical labor service systems, providing auditing, monitoring services, and coordination with tax bureau and financial institutions.

[48] Solinger (fn. 46).

[49] *Financial Times* (China), March 9, 1993; *People's Daily*, January 2, 1993.

2. *Competition for foreign capital.* There is also considerable competition among regions—provinces, townships, cities, special economic zones, and developmental zones—for foreign capital. Two of the main ingredients in this competition are: first, the laws, regulations, and taxes that promote economic development, including secure property rights and private returns (known as the "software"); and second, infrastructure (such as transportation and port facilities) and access to markets (known as the "hardware"). There are now over one thousand zones designed to attract foreign capital. There is considerable evidence that foreign capital flows toward those areas where a high return is likely.

As noted in Section III, not only has foreign investment increased, but the share of regional control also has increased dramatically. Closely related is another recent trend that might be termed "development zone" fever.[50] Under the efforts of several levels of local authorities, development zones mushroomed in the 1990s. According to the national bureau of land regulation, in 1991 there were only 117 development zones for the entire country. For 1992, it estimated the number to be 2,700.[51] In some cases, the cause for this development zone fever is that local governments try to attract foreign investment or business (so-called "building a nest to attract the phoenix"). In other cases, it is related to the emerging real-estate business, which is extremely profitable in China. This fever, however, does not automatically turn on the flow of foreign investment. In many instances, there are not complementary, well-established facilities and other conditions that suit large amounts of capital investment. This puts pressure on the local governments to further improve infrastructure and complementary facilities.

Dynamics of Competition among Jurisdictions: Trends and Momentum

As discussed above, successful aspects of reform and marketization are being imitated in many areas in China. The divergence in success and prosperity of seemingly similar towns, cities, and regions encourages those who struggle to copy those who thrive. Competition for factors implies that the various levels of government must provide secure promises to maintain reform and encourage investment.

Shaanxi's learning from and imitating Guangdong's system of opening trade illustrates the trend in imitation of the successful areas.[52] The

[50] *People's Daily,* January 30, 1993; *South Weekend,* March 5, 1993; *Guangming Daily,* June 29, 1993.

[51] Among the new development zones, only ninety-five are approved by the various departments of the central government. Most development zones were established by different local authorities, from provincial governments down to township governments.

[52] *Financial Times* (China), April 1, 1992.

governor of Shaanxi province observed that the reason that Guangdong province achieved fast economic growth was that its markets were open and interregional trade was not blockaded. Shaanxi, in contrast, maintained considerable trade barriers, including large numbers of tax offices across its different counties and prefectures. In 1991 the provincial government released its control over 125 commodity prices and withdrew 12,289 tax offices. The commodity trade soon flourished. In the second half of 1991, the business tax of commerce increased by 20.1 percent over the same period of 1990. The central government attached great importance to Shaanxi's experience. The state council made copies of Shaanxi government's documents about its reform policy and sent them to other provincial governments. Many provinces, such as Gansu, Yunnan, Sichuan, Henan, Jilin, Ningxia, and Jiangsu, responded earnestly. Before long, Jiangsu established a "market guidance and coordination council"; Guizhou organized a "coordination team for market circulation reform." Many provinces have now incorporated the development of a market system into their socioeconomic development plans.

As part of this effort, authorities from various regions are actively studying the political and economic arrangements within the most successful regions. For example, in 1991 Jiangsu province sent a group of seventy-three government officials to the southern part of Shaanxi province, which is a very poor area.[53] This was the first cross-province exchange of government officials. After one year, they helped many counties, organizations, and firms in that area establish cooperative connections with those in Jiangsu province. Due to their efforts, the southern part of Shaanxi has attracted more than two hundred projects, including more than ten million yuan and a range of different types of personnel from other regions. These officials also helped to train over twenty-two hundred local personnel; they provided information to local firms; and they helped promote the firms' sales on international markets. The official exchange enabled the rich province of Jiangsu to develop markets and resources in Shaanxi province.

Summary

This section indicates that a range of behavior under the reforms is consistent with the predictions of market-preserving federalism. Experimentation, learning, and adaptation all follow from the inception of local political freedom over the economy. Local governments com-

[53] *Economic Information Daily*, May 3, 1992.

pete with one another for factors and in the international market for exports.

The illustrations provided in this section do not prove our hypothesis, for they are not a representative sample of behavior. They nonetheless provide a sufficient basis to establish the plausibility of our contentions.

V. Conclusions

An economic system faces a fundamental dilemma: not only does it depend on the political system for specifying and enforcing property rights and contracts, but it also depends on the political system to protect the market from political encroachment. The developed economies of the West learned to mitigate this problem long ago, and, for many purposes, economists can ignore them. But the same cannot be said for developing countries, particularly those with long histories of unconstrained government.

The central hypothesis of this paper is that the form of decentralization inherent in the reforms in China—what we have called "federalism, Chinese style"—provides an important set of limits on the behavior of all levels of government. By design, decentralization directly limits the central government's control over the economy. It also induces competition among local governments, serving both to constrain their behavior and to provide them with a range of positive incentives to foster local economic prosperity.

The constraints of federalism, Chinese style, are especially important for China for a second reason. The other forms of credible limits on government typical of the developed West, notably, popular elections and a separation of power, appear not to be politically feasible for China at this time. Consequently, federalism may be one of the few ways in which a large, nondemocratic state can provide credible limits on its behavior. The discussion in Sections III and IV reveals that a substantial range of economic behavior exhibited in China is consistent with our central hypothesis. These case studies illustrate the range of experimentation, learning, and imitation that has occurred in many areas of China. The observation of the results of particular experiments provides information to all provinces, not just the one conducting the experiment. These observations have changed expectations nationwide. Yes, many individuals have gotten rich, as some had warned, but so too have many province, township, and village governments. This unexpected but striking fiscal power has played a significant role in the comparisons across jurisdictions, as several of the above cases illustrate. The remarkable ability of the reforms to generate resources for many local governments has had substantial consequences. Not only did this allow them to provide for the welfare of its residents, often far better than nearby areas that had fought marketization, but it helped change the minds of many who were initially skeptical of reform.

The results of experiments have thus proved critical to the recent history of China, underscoring the importance of the federalism with its institutionally created *absence* of a single government with monopoly control over the economy. When there is only one government and it claims that the market would fail to provide for citizens and social needs, who can credibly claim otherwise, especially in the presence of the obvious initial costs of marketization? In contrast, if many regions can choose policies for themselves, all can compare the results, including those which do not wish to initiate reform policies. The successive comparisons over the past fifteen years, in combination with other factors, such as the conservatives' failure in 1989-92, underpin the new push toward markets over much of China.

Our explanation overlaps with and departs from Shirk's important work. Like Shirk, we emphasize decentralization and the incentives of local governments in the success of economic reform.[54] In comparison to our argument, Shirk places greater weight on the political organization of local governments and their control over the economy, arguing that local political officials should be viewed as creating systems of patronage and loyalty. We believe that there is considerable truth in Shirk's assertion. Because the approval of officials is necessary for enterprises, and because their protection is part of the maintenance of enterprise property rights and contracts, local governments play a more central role in the economy than local governments in Western Europe or the United States.

Nonetheless, Shirk's argument about particularism and patronage requires qualification. As stated, it applies in broad form to the patronage systems common in Latin America and Africa. Yet those economies have performed, respectively, poorly and abysmally. Missing from Shirk's approach is an explanation of the limits on the degree of

[54] Shirk's more extensive discussions allow her to treat a much wider range of topics central to the success of reforms for example, the importance of gradualism, the initial role of agrarian reform, and the political mechanisms underpinning reform within the central government. See Shirk (fn. 3); and idem, *How China Opened Its Door* (Washington, D.C.: Brookings Institution, 1994). Our analysis also has much in common with Oi's recent work. See Oi (fn. 24); and idem, *Rural China Takes Off: Incentives for Industrialization* (Berkeley: University of California Press, forthcoming).

economic extraction of local governments in China, without which there would be no spectacular economic success.

Our approach suggests an answer: the system of federalism and the inherent jurisdictional competition places striking limits on this system of patronage and political spoils. So too does competition on the international market. Were particularism and patronage in a particular locality to place onerous restrictions or burdens on these firms, they simply could not succeed in international competition. China's striking economic success suggests that local government particularism differs significantly from that in Latin America and Africa. These issues deserve further research.

Before concluding, we would like to discuss briefly some of the limits of our analysis. First, the evidence provided in Sections III and IV is intended to demonstrate the plausibility of our approach; it does not represent a systematic empirical test. The latter would require further analysis and more systematic data from an appropriately constructed sample of provinces, but no such data is available at this time. Second, although our approach does not rely on arguments about Chinese culture, we do not imply that Chinese culture is irrelevant. Undoubtedly culture is central to the ability of individuals and groups who have taken advantage of new opportunities under reform. Our argument emphasizes that Chinese economic success reflects, in part, institutional changes. A more complete approach would show how to integrate our institutional analysis with the relevant aspects of Chinese culture.

China's transition toward a market system is at a critical moment. The success of the past fifteen years of reform is a tremendous asset, not only in terms of economic benefits achieved, but also in terms of political institutions restructured. On the other hand, the institutional foundation underpinning a secure market system in China is far from rationalized and secure. We have discussed problems that arise from too weak a central government: internal trade barriers and soft budget constraints of various levels of government are just two phenomena that reflect such a problem. It is fortunate for China's economic success that both are less a problem for the township and village levels of government of China. There are, however, problems from a central government that is too strong, and this is the danger of recentralization per se. Without further institutional constraints, a financially independent central government would pose potential dangers to the reform's progress over the past fifteen years, especially if run by leaders far less favorable to the reforms than Deng Xiaoping.

[11]

DID GOVERNMENT DECENTRALIZATION CAUSE CHINA'S ECONOMIC MIRACLE?

By HONGBIN CAI and DANIEL TREISMAN*

I. INTRODUCTION

WHAT roles have political and fiscal decentralization played in China's economic reforms and in the remarkable development they fostered? Since the late 1970s China has liberalized most prices, decollectivized agriculture, and integrated into world markets. These changes fueled an unprecedented period of growth that increased GDP per capita from $674 in 1978 to $5,085 in 2004 (in PPP-adjusted 2000 dollars).[1] Scholars have attributed this economic miracle to many causes—recovery from the Cultural Revolution, initial underdevelopment, and a rich diaspora, to name a few. But some suggest the country's decentralized structures of government and public finance played an important part.[2]

* We thank Richard Baum, Thomas Bernstein, Bo Li, Dorothy Solinger, James Tong, Dali Yang, and Li-An Zhou for comments and suggestions.

[1] Based on the International Comparison Program, as reported in the World Bank's *World Development Indicators Database*. In non-PPP adjusted 2000 U.S. dollars, the increase was from $153 to $1,162.

[2] For instance, Qian and Weingast assert that "the critical component of China's market-oriented reform, which began in 1979, is decentralization"; Yingyi Qian and Barry R. Weingast, "China's Transition to Markets: Market-Preserving Federalism, Chinese Style," *Journal of Policy Reform* 1 (1996). Montinola, Qian, and Weingast characterize China's reform-era political system as "market-preserving federalism" and see in this various economic benefits; Gabriella Montinola, Yingyi Qian, and Barry R. Weingast, "Federalism, Chinese Style: The Political Basis for Economic Success in China," *World Politics* 48 (October 1995). Qian and Roland argue that "one of the most distinct features of China's transition has been associated with devolution of authority from the central to local levels of government"; Yingyi Qian and Gérard Roland, "Federalism and the Soft Budget Constraint," *American Economic Review* 88 (December 1998), 1156. Other articles that link the success of economic reforms to political decentralization include Ping Chen, "China's Challenge to Economic Orthodoxy: Asian Reform as an Evolutionary, Self-Organizing Process," *China Economic Review* 4, no. 2 (1993); and Chenggang Xu and Juzhong Zhuang, "Why China Grew: The Role of Decentralization," in Peter Boone, Stanislaw Gomulka, and Richard Layard, eds., *Emerging from Communism: Lessons from Russia, China, and Eastern Europe* (Cambridge: MIT Press, 1998). Adherents note that decentralization can have costs—increased inequality, policy externalities, the creation of local "dukedom" economies—but argue that in China

World Politics 58 (July 2006), 505–35

Those who link the success of China's reforms to decentralization make five main arguments. First, some focus on the prereform economy's cellular organization. Rather than a specialized, nationwide hierarchy, China's economy consisted of parallel, diversified provincial economies. This situation reduced dislocations and stimulated competition when markets were introduced. Second, some believe political decentralization encouraged local reform experiments that allowed new ideas to percolate up from the grass roots. Third, some argue decentralization created political checks on the central authorities, limiting predation and convincing investors that reforms would last. Fourth, some suggest fiscal decentralization gave local officials strong incentives to stimulate economic growth. Finally, some contend decentralization helped harden budget constraints on enterprises, forcing them to restructure.

In this article, we challenge the claim that decentralization had much to do with the success of China's reforms and its dramatic growth. Grassroots initiatives did, of course, occur, and considerable administrative decentralization took place in the the mid-1980s. But the key reforms that reshaped China's economy began in the late 1970s and early 1980s, before any significant decentralization had occurred. In fact, China's authoritarian centralization helped speed the geographical spread of policies found to work well. Provincial governors were not then—and still are not—a reliable check on central abuses, and they certainly do not guarantee property rights. The most cited case of a governor resisting Beijing actually ended in victory for the center: he was removed and his successor was forced to accept Beijing's preferred policy. Fiscal decentralization cannot explain improved performance because any beneficial effect of larger local revenue shares was offset by the sharp decline in the fraction of GDP collected as taxes and available for sharing. Nor can fiscal decentralization have hardened state enterprises' budget constraints because these did not harden. In fact, loss-making enterprises multiplied in the era of decentralization and rapid growth, and the state banks virtually went bankrupt bailing them out. Budget constraints only hardened after *central* fiscal and monetary policy was tightened. To be clear, day-to-day control over various economic activities did pass to subnational officials during the 1980s, subject to ultimate review from above. However, local discre-

these were outweighed by the benefits; Qian and Weingast (fn. 2), 3. Blanchard and Shleifer make the more nuanced claim that fiscal decentralization helped in China, but only because it was combined with political *centralization*; Olivier Blanchard and Andrei Shleifer, "Federalism with and without Political Centralization: China versus Russia," *IMF Staff Papers* 48 (December 2001).

tion had both positive and negative effects; from the evidence, it is not clear which dominated.[3]

If decentralization does not explain why China's leaders adopted growth-promoting market reforms, where does the explanation lie? We propose another view of politics in post-Mao China. The driving force behind reform, we argue, was not pressures from or initiatives of autonomous local officials but competition at the center between rival factions with different ideological predispositions and local connections. Faction leaders sought supremacy within the party by demonstrating the effectiveness of their chosen policies across the chessboard of China's territorial administration. Local officials were linked to these factions and sought to impress higher-ups with suggestions and sometimes spontaneous—even illegal—initiatives. This view, which actually coincides with many traditional understandings of Chinese politics, can explain the temporal pattern of reform, which ebbed and flowed with shifts in the factional balance of power rather than with changes in decentralization.[4] It also explains why reforms continued and economic performance did not deteriorate in the 1990s despite a shift toward recentralization.

II. Centralization and Decentralization

Decentralization means different things to different people.[5] Based on examination of common usage, we distinguish three types. *Administrative decentralization* occurs when national authorities permit their subnational agents to make certain policy decisions, subject to review

[3] For a discussion of some dysfunctional behaviors caused by decentralization, see Andrew H. Wedeman, *From Mao to Market: Rent Seeking, Local Protectionism, and Marketization in China* (New York: Cambridge University Press, 2003).

[4] For one similar view, see Joseph Fewsmith, *Dilemmas of Reform in China: Political Conflict and Economic Debate* (Armonk, N.Y.: M. E.Sharpe, 1994). For a few of the many works that emphasize the role of factions in Chinese politics, see Andrew J. Nathan, "A Factionalism Model for CCP Politics," *China Quarterly* 53 (January–March 1973); Dorothy Solinger, "Politics in Yunnan Province in the Decade of Disorder: Elite Factional Strategies and Central-Local Relations, 1967–1980," *China Quarterly* 92 (December 1982); Richard Baum, *Burying Mao: Chinese Politics in the Age of Deng Xiaoping* (Princeton: Princeton University Press, 1994); Lowell Dittmer and Yu-Shan Wu, "The Modernization of Factionalism in Chinese Politics," *World Politics* 47 (July 1995); and Jing Huang, *Factionalism in Chinese Communist Politics* (New York: Cambridge University Press, 2000). We concur with those who see factions as fluid, evolving as the focus of competition changes, and having policy preferences as well as material interests. Since the early 1990s all major factions have accepted the goal of marketization, so this is no longer a point of contention; they differ in their personnel networks, sectoral and regional connections, and commitment to income redistribution. The main point here is that the key axis of competition ran vertically, dividing members of different factions at each level of the state hierarchy, rather than horizontally, pitting a coalition of local officials against their central counterparts.

[5] For recent discussions, see Jonathan Rodden, "Comparative Federalism and Decentralization: On Meaning and Measurement," *Comparative Politics* 36 (July 2004); and Robert D. Ebel and Serdar Yilmaz, *On the Measurement and Impact of Fiscal Decentralization* (Washington, D.C.: World Bank, 2002).

and possible veto from above. *Political decentralization* can mean either or both of two things. First, a system is more politically decentralized if subnational governments have the right to make certain policy decisions *not* subject to being overruled by higher levels. Second, a system is more politically decentralized if subnational officials are chosen by local residents rather than by higher officials. *Fiscal decentralization* is used in various ways, so we will try to interpret the meaning implied by each of the arguments we examine. We use *government decentralization* to include any or all of these three types of decentralization.

Applying these definitions, we consider China to have been highly centralized, both administratively and politically, in 1978. During the 1980s the country became much more administratively decentralized. Administrative decentralization peaked around 1988–89, followed by some recentralization in the 1990s. Politically, the system has remained highly centralized throughout. Although in the 1980s subnational officials came to make an increasing share of decisions, especially on economic matters, central authorities could always overrule them or take back authority delegated downward (as they did in various ways during the 1990s). As for appointments, from the late 1980s village officials have been locally elected. In practice, all other subnational appointments have been made by—or at least have been subject to the approval of—higher authorities, with the center exercising ultimate control. In 1984 the party central committee delegated the right to make and review appointments of subprovincial officials to provincial party committees; but in 1990 these appointments were again brought under central control.[6] The Chinese regime remains, in Andrew Nathan's words, "a centralized, unitary system in which power at lower levels derives from grants by the center."[7]

Although these definitions seem to be reasonable and also correspond to common usage, our critique in subsequent sections does not depend on them. Our position is not that the arguments we challenge fail only because of our definitions of administrative and political decentralization: we contend that they fail under their proponents' own definitions. We examine these arguments on their own terms, focusing on the definitions authors explicitly adopt or those implied by the arguments themselves. The one possible exception is the argument about the cellular organization of the Chinese economy in Section III; we

[6] John P. Burns, "Strengthening Central CCP Control of Leadership Selection: The 1990 Nomenklatura," *China Quarterly* 138 (June 1994).

[7] Andrew J. Nathan, "Authoritarian Resilience: China's Changing of the Guard," *Journal of Democracy* 14 (January 2003), 13. We list important changes in the division of powers between center and localities in a longer version of the paper on Treisman's Web site at www.polisci.ucla.edu/faculty/treisman/.

find this internally consistent and plausible but contend it has nothing to do with political or administrative decentralization under *any* definition. Thus, we differ with the authors we discuss not on questions of semantics but on judgments of logic and evidence.

Two points require clarification. First, in Chinese debates, decentralization is sometimes given a far broader meaning, encompassing both devolution of political authority and economic liberalization.[8] "Decentralization" is often translated as *fenquan*, which means the abdication of planning powers by the government. Clearly, if decentralization *means* economic liberalization, decentralization cannot explain why economic liberalization occurred. Consistent with Western discussions, we focus on government decentralization. We distinguish all types of decentralization from a mere weakening of the central state apparatus. A common perception in China is that the central authorities' ability to control economic life has decreased since 1978.[9] However, powers "lost" by Beijing are not necessarily gained by local governments. The increasing complexity of the Chinese economy and society as the country modernizes has made monitoring and control by any level of government less comprehensive.

Second, analysts sometimes equate the occurrence of grassroots policy initiatives with political or administrative decentralization. That local officials innovate without prior instructions is itself taken as evidence that the political system is decentralized. There are two problems with this. First, it leads to circularity. If local innovation is itself an indicator of decentralization, decentralization cannot explain innovation. Second, grassroots initiatives clearly can occur in states universally considered centralized. Even under Stalin's totalitarian rule, Soviet enterprise managers experimented spontaneously, hoping to be rewarded for success and fearing failure if they stuck to the rules. In 1934, for instance, managers at the Menzhinskii Aviation Firm started paying premiums for high-quality production, in clear violation of instructions. In 1935 executives at the Stalingrad Dzerzhinskii Tractor Plant "drew up a plan for the total reorganization of the plant and its production, and presented the plan in the national industrial press." In 1937, at the height of the purges, the Moscow Kuibyshev Electrical Plant

[8] Deng, for instance, in his famous December 1978 speech, "Emancipate the Mind, Seek Truth from Facts and Unite as One in Looking to the Future," advocated devolving more decision-making power to the "various localities, enterprises and production teams," running together what in the West would be thought of as political decentralization and economic liberalization; Deng, People's Daily Online, *Selected Works of Deng Xiaoping*, http://english.people.com.cn/dengxp/.

[9] Of course, distance has always facilitated noncompliance, as suggested by the old Chinese saying, "Qiang zai wai jun ming you suo bu shou" (When the emperor is far away, a general does not obey all his orders).

nevertheless "decided on its own to revise premium systems in order to give timeworkers greater incentives."[10] To our knowledge, no one has suggested such practices rendered the Stalinist system politically or administratively decentralized. If, by contrast, one defines China in 1978 as decentralized *because* local officials innovated, then decentralization does, of course, explain reform—but in an uninteresting way.

III. The M-Form Economy

Qian and Xu and Xu and Zhuang argue that China's economy as of 1978 was structured in a way particularly conducive to marketization, at least as compared with its northern communist neighbor.[11] In the Soviet Union regional economies were mutually dependent, specialized units that played different roles in the national division of labor and were coordinated by central planners. In China, by contrast, provincial economies were more self-sufficient and internally diversified. Fearing military invasion, Mao encouraged local self-sufficiency and devolved much planning and administration to provincial cadres.[12] Thus in the USSR, single plants often supplied the entire market, whereas in China parallel enterprises in different provinces produced similar goods. Using the vocabulary of Chandler and Williamson, Qian and Xu compare the Chinese economy to a multidivisional (M-form) organization and the Soviet Union to a unitary (U-form) organization.[13]

This inherited economic structure helped China as markets replaced planning. Since provinces and counties within them had relatively diversified economies, competition could emerge between rival producers of the same goods. Deliberate redundancy left the system less vulnerable to shocks by reducing the cost of transitional disorganization and the risk of disruption when Beijing conducted localized experiments. Finally, M-form structure enabled central leaders to use yardstick competition to evaluate the relative performance of local officials.[14]

[10] See David Granick, *Management of the Industrial Firm in the USSR: A Study in Soviet Economic Planning* (New York: Columbia University Press, 1954), 112–16 and 133. Granick suggests this was common practice in the Stalinist 1930s: "It is in the plants that grass-roots ideas originate; they may later be taken up by higher bodies and spread to all industries or they may be condemned in official instructions. Nevertheless, it is here that they get their first test and hearing."

[11] Yingyi Qian and Chenggang Xu, "Why China's Economic Reforms Differ: The M-Form Hierarchy and Entry/Expansion of the Non-State Sector," *Economics of Transition* 1 (June 1993); Xu and Zhuang (fn. 2).

[12] Qian and Weingast (fn. 2).

[13] Alfred J. Chandler, *Strategy and Structure* (New York: Doubleday, 1962); Oliver Williamson, *Markets and Hierarchies* (New York: Free Press, 1975); Qian and Xu (fn. 11).

[14] Eric Maskin, Yingyi Qian, and Chenggang Xu, "Incentives, Information, and Organizational Form," *Review of Economic Studies* 67 (April 2000).

These arguments are quite compelling. However, they have nothing to do with political, administrative, or fiscal decentralization. They concern China's economic structure at the start of transition—specifically, its lower industrial concentration and geographical specialization than the Soviet Union's. Low industrial concentration and diversified regional economies help make market systems more competitive and resilient. But this is true regardless of how political authority and fiscal resources are shared between levels of government. The purported benefits of the M-form economy—competition among enterprises, alternative suppliers, less risky local experiments—would help just as much in a politically centralized market economy as in a politically decentralized one. Yardstick competition can be used to evaluate local agents' performance whether the principals are local voters or central leaders. Market liberalization in an M-form economy like that of China may indeed be less disruptive than in a U-form economy like that of the Soviet Union. But it does not follow that decentralization outperforms centralization in either system. To make this case, some other argument is needed.

IV. Local Policy Experiments

China's political or administrative decentralization is often said to have stimulated spontaneous local experiments that grew into nationwide reforms. Cao, Qian, and Weingast, paraphrasing Justice Louis Brandeis's famous remark, note that China has relied on "the 'laboratory of the local governments' to pursue reform."[15] Xu and Zhuang see China's reform strategy as distinctive in its success "in using local experiments and in adopting the 'bottom-up' approach."[16] The lesson China's experience teaches, write Montinola, Qian, and Weingast, is that "experimentation, learning, and adaptation all follow from the inception of local political freedom over the economy."[17]

Three sets of local experiments are usually singled out. First, Chinese agriculture was transformed by the introduction of the "household responsibility system" (HRS). This apparently began when in 1978 peasants in drought-stricken Fengyang County, Anhui Province, divided their team's land into separate plots for individual households to farm. Seeing the rise in grain yields, the higher authorities embraced the scheme and extended it to other provinces.

[15] Yuanzheng Cao, Yingyi Qian, and Barry R. Weingast, "From Federalism, Chinese Style to Privatization, Chinese Style," *Economics of Transition* 7, no. 1 (1999), 123–24.

[16] Xu and Zhuang (fn. 2), 194.

[17] Montinola, Qian, and Weingast (fn. 2), 78.

By 1986 almost all China's peasants had adopted the HRS.[18] Second, four "special economic zones" (SEZs) were established in 1979 in Guangdong and Fujian Provinces. These zones were allowed low tax and tariff rates and flexible investment rules to encourage high-technology exports. Their success fueled the proliferation of other privileged zones—"coastal open areas," "coastal open cities," "economic and technological development zones," "hi-tech development zones," "border open cities," and so on—totaling about three thousand by 1993.[19] Third, parallel experiments with different profit-retention schemes in state-owned enterprises (SOEs) were begun in 1978 in the provinces of Sichuan and Hubei, followed by experiments in other locations. These led ultimately to the replacement of profit remittances by taxes in SOEs in 1986.

These three sets of experiments laid the foundations for China's economic transformation. The HRS decollectivized Chinese agriculture and, along with higher procurement prices, prompted increases in agricultural productivity of more than 6 percent a year in the early 1980s (see Figure 1). The SEZs began China's integration into the world economy. Exports grew from $10 billlion in 1978 to $593 billion in 2004. The state enterprise reforms had a less clear effect. They may have helped secure moderate productivity growth in 1984–88, although the highest growth in this period was in collective enterprises. In the 1990s both state-owned and collective enterprises lost ground to the rapidly growing private sector, which has fueled the expansion of the last fifteen years (see Figure 2). But the SOE reforms started the process of converting these into market corporations, leading ultimately to their privatization in the late 1990s, after attempts to make them profitable failed.[20]

Were these experiments the result of political or administrative decentralization? We dispute this for three reasons. First, the theory that political decentralization should stimulate policy innovation is open to serious question. Second, even if decentralization did encourage experiments, this could not explain China's success because the most important reforms were introduced when China was still highly centralized. Third,

[18] Jae Ho Chung, *Central Control and Local Discretion in China: Leadership and Implementation during Post-Mao Decollectivization* (New York: Oxford University Press, 2000), 77. For details from Fengyang County, see William Hinton, *The Great Reversal: The Privatization of China, 1978–1989* (New York: Monthly Review Press, 1990), 48–73.

[19] Jae Ho Chung, "Reappraising Central-Local Relations in Deng's China: Decentralization, Dilemmas of Control, and Diluted Effects of Reform," in Bruce J. Dickson, ed., *Remaking the Chinese State: Strategies, Society, and Security* (New York: Routledge, 2001), 58.

[20] The accuracy of Chinese GDP statistics after 1998 has been disputed; see, for example, Thomas Rawski, "What Is Happening to China's GDP Statistics?" *China Economic Review* 12, no. 4 (2001). Some consider official growth rates to be exaggerated. By contrast, a national economic census in 2005 concluded GDP had been underreported largely due to inadequate measurement of the service sector.

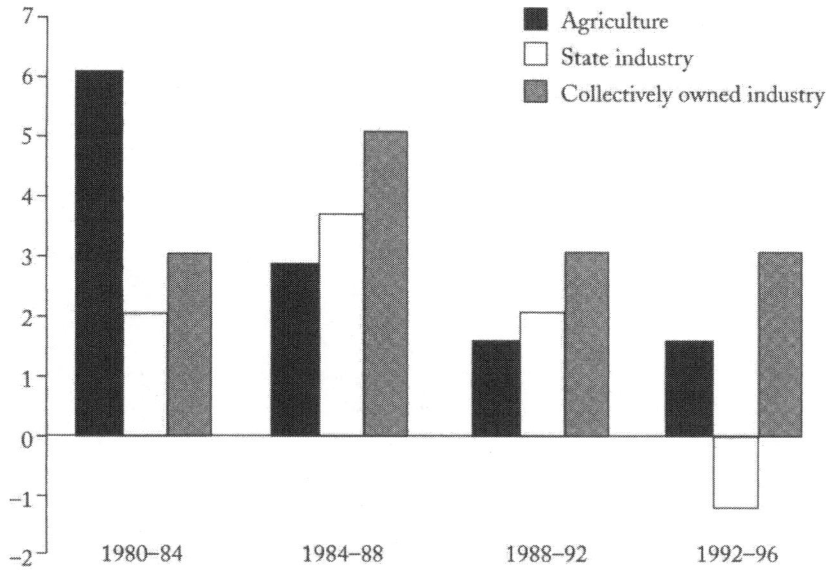

FIGURE 1
TOTAL FACTOR PRODUCTIVITY GROWTH
(% PER YEAR)

SOURCE: Gary H. Jefferson, Thomas Rawski, Wang Li, and Zheng Yuxin, "Ownership, Productivity Change, and Financial Performance in Chinese Industry," *Journal of Comparative Economics* 28 (December 2000).

the speed with which effective local policies were identified, evaluated, and extended, often against the resistance of conservative local cadres, actually owed much to China's political and administrative *centralization.*

Taking these points in order, there are several reasons to doubt the common intuition that decentralization stimulates policy innovation. First, local experiments generate positive informational externalities. Discoveries from one region can be usefully applied in others. Local leaders will care less about such spillovers than will a national leader, whose jurisdiction encompasses the whole country.[21] Second, the risk for a local official experimenting in his unit is greater than that for a central government experimenting in one of the country's many districts.[22] Together, these factors suggest central leaders should generally

[21] Susan Rose-Ackerman, "Risk Taking and Reelection: Does Federalism Promote Innovation?" *Journal of Legal Studies* 9 (June 1980).

[22] Hongbin Cai and Daniel Treisman, "Political Decentralization and Policy Experimentation" (Manuscript, Department of Political Science, UCLA, 2005).

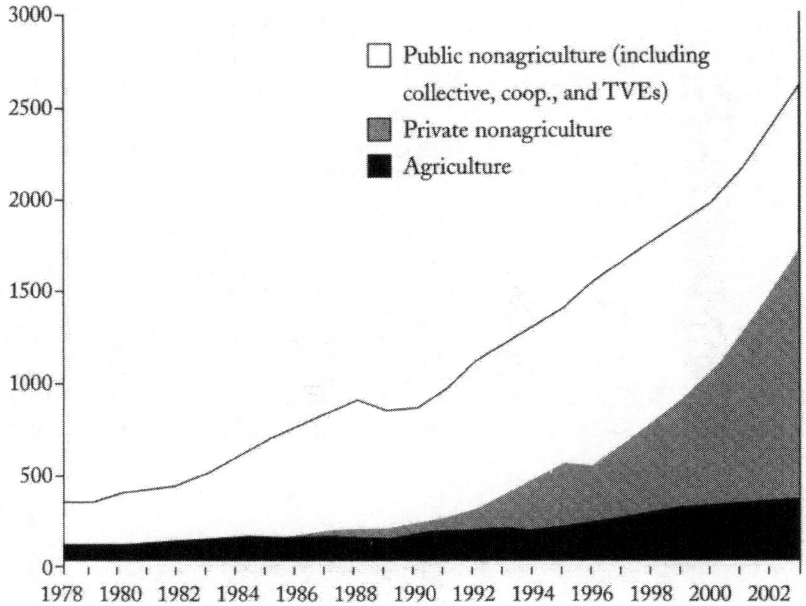

FIGURE 2
REAL OUTPUT
(BILLION 1978 YUAN)

SOURCE: Robert Dekle and Guillaume Vandenbroucke, "Whither Chinese Growth? A Sectoral Growth Accounting Approach" (Manuscript, USC, Department of Economics, 2006).

be *more* eager to introduce local experiments than their local counterparts. Central leaders should also be better able or motivated to coordinate experiments across regions and rapidly exploit discoveries nationwide.[23] China's experience contains evidence of each of these effects.[24]

Even if a stronger logic linked decentralization to experimentation, this could not explain China's experience. The three most significant, trailblazing experiments occurred at a time when China's political and administrative systems were highly centralized. As of 1978 China was one of the most centralized countries in the world—a communist autocracy in which local cadres not only were not free to set policies but also

[23] Ibid.

[24] A vast body of literature in industrial organization explores how the degree of administrative decentralization and the arrangement of responsibilities within a hierarchy may affect innovation and productive efficiency under different conditions. For two examples, see Raaj K. Sah and Joseph E. Stiglitz, "The Architecture of Economic Systems: Hierarchies and Polyarchies," *American Economic Review* 76 (September 1986); and Patrick Bolton and Joseph Farrell, "Decentralization, Duplication, and Delay," *Journal of Political Economy* 98 (August 1990).

knew they could go to jail for trying to do so. In Section II we defined "political decentralization" as the local selection of local officials or the right of local officials to decide policies without being overruled. As of the late 1970s neither of these applied. Until village elections began in the late 1980s, appointment of all subnational officials—even if formally local—was controlled by higher levels. As for choosing policies, one can judge how free local officials felt from the precautions some took. The production team leader implicated in the Fengyang peasants' scheme reportedly agreed only after the peasants pledged to raise his children until age eighteen if he should be imprisoned.[25]

A 1978 editorial in the *People's Daily* cataloged an impressive list of fears that kept most local officials from innovating: "The fear of being labeled as a 'capitulationist'; the fear of being dismissed from one's post; the fear of being expelled from the party; the fear of being divorced by one's wife; the fear of serving a prison term; and the fear of being beheaded."[26] Repression was less extreme than during the Cultural Revolution, but officials knew nevertheless that in the past initiative had been punished as often as rewarded. In fact, reforms similar to the HRS had been introduced several times under Mao, but "each such attempt had been ruthlessly criticized"; the official who backed the first such reform, in Zhejiang Province in the 1950s, was later "named a 'rightist element,' expelled from the party, and sent down (*xia fang*) for labor."[27] "Decentralism" was traditionally labeled a serious breach of discipline. As late as 1985 party secretary Hu Yaobang felt the need to reassure local officials that, although they might be fired for committing this "mistake," at least they would "normally not be deprived of their material privileges, nor would their family members and relatives be discriminated against."[28] The local risk taking of peasants in Anhui and elsewhere is actually remarkable evidence of their desperation and enterprise despite a history of Leninist political centralization.[29]

Even those who believe political decentralization stimulated reform apparently agree that China was highly centralized as of 1978–81, at least in comparison with noncommunist countries. In a series of articles, Qian and Weingast trace the success of reforms in China to a

[25] Chung (fn. 18), 90; Fewsmith (fn. 4), 28.

[26] *People's Daily*, December 7, 1978, quoted in Chung (fn. 18), 41.

[27] Fewsmith (fn. 4), 23–24.

[28] Sen Lin, "A New Pattern of Decentralization in China: The Increase of Provincial Powers in Economic Legislation," *China Information* 7 (Winter 1992–93), 31.

[29] The memory of the catastrophic famine of 1958–61 may also have emboldened peasants; see Dali L. Yang, *Calamity and Reform in China: State, Rural Society, and Institutional Change since the Great Leap Famine* (Stanford, Calif.: Stanford Univesity Press, 1996).

kind of federalism in which local governments have "primary *authority over the economy* within their jurisdictions" and "the allocation of authority and responsibility has an *institutionalized degree of durability* so that it cannot be altered by the national government."[30] However, according to Qian and Weingast it was only in 1984–88 that "federalism, Chinese style, took shape." As of the late 1970s the most one could say was that China was administratively and economically "decentralized in comparison with economies of the Soviet Union and Eastern Europe"—compared, that is, with other communist dictatorships.[31]

Among communist countries, it is true China's economic administration was relatively decentralized after 1978. For the next decade, one could contrast China's successes with the reform failures of the more centralized USSR. However, by late 1989 political decentralization in the Soviet Union had clearly outstripped that in China. The Baltic republics were racing toward independence, and by early 1991 Gorbachev was trying to save the Soviet Union as a loose confederation. After its partly free regional elections in 1990, Russia was also more politically decentralized than China, with economic policies diverging in the regions. If decentralization explains why reforms worked better in China than the Soviet Union in the 1980s, it cannot explain why China fared better than Russia in the 1990s. The opposite should have occurred.

Examined closely, China's "local" experiments were not always as local as might appear. Central authorities were often deeply involved, if not from the start then from soon after. And central involvement clearly helped, speeding the spread of useful discoveries, reducing redundancy, and overcoming resistance to reform. The Fengyang peasants apparently acted spontaneously. But higher-level reformers promoted the model vigorously. Hu Yaobang and Zhao Ziyang toured sluggish provinces, scolding their leaders, and teams were sent to expose and "rectify" foot-dragging cadres.[32] The Heilongjiang party leader, who resisted the HRS, was removed.[33] The Sichuan SOE experiments, although sometimes portrayed as a spontaneous initiative of Zhao Ziyang, then provincial party chief, were one of a centrally coordinated set of pilot schemes. Lee, who analyzed a number of these, contends that those in

[30] Qian and Weingast (fn. 2), 6, italics in original.

[31] Ibid., 13, 15.

[32] John P. Burns, "Local Cadre Accommodation to the 'Responsibility System' in Rural China," *Pacific Affairs* 58 (Winter 1985), 619–21.

[33] Fewsmith (fn. 4), 125. Demand from the population was also important in the spread of the HRS; Xiaopeng Luo, "Rural Reform and the Rise of Localism," in Jia Hao and Zhimin Lin, eds., *Changing Central-Local Relations in China: Reform and State Capacity* (Boulder, Colo.: Westview Press, 1994).

Sichuan were authorized in advance by the State Economic Commission and other State Council ministries.[34] Central ministries monitored and reviewed the schemes, codified them in five policy documents, and ordered similar experiments in Beijing, Tianjin, and Shanghai.[35]

If the SEZs were an experiment, they were clearly an experiment of the central authorities. Initial authorization came in a July 1979 State Council directive.[36] Deng claimed leaders of Guangdong Province—two old comrades of his—suggested the idea, but without Deng's support nothing would have come of it, and their slowness to implement the reforms casts doubt on the enthusiasm of these two old-timers.[37] Frustrated with their delays, Deng replaced them in late 1980 with more committed reformers.[38] Similarly, in Fujian the leaders were replaced in the early 1980s for their delay in building the Xiamen SEZ. First secretary Liao "distinguished himself by his lack of enthusiasm for reform."[39] Deng sent a more dynamic ally instead. The zones' host provinces helped work out implementation; but central authorities regulated this process, set guidelines, monitored the results, and authorized extensions.[40]

Central control also shows in the way SEZ locations were chosen. To reduce political and economic risk, they were placed in relatively sparsely populated, underdeveloped provinces. Fujian "had no international airport, and its major ports and railroad system were inadequate for moving large volumes of freight and passengers."[41] Guangdong also "suffered from the lack of a strong industrial base as well as insufficient infrastructural facilities."[42] In 1988 an additional SEZ was sited on the island of Hainan, in part because "leaders of the CCP believed that Hainan was expendable."[43]

[34] Peter Nan-shong Lee, "Enterprise Autonomy Policy in Post-Mao China: A Case Study of Policy-Making, 1978–83," *China Quarterly* 105 (March 1986), 57.

[35] Fewsmith (fn. 4), 74; Lee (fn. 34); Barry Naughton, "False Starts and Second Wind: Financial Reforms in China's Industrial System," in Elizabeth Perry and Christine Wong, eds., *The Political Economy of Reform in Post-Mao China* (Cambridge: Harvard University Press, 1985).

[36] Clyde D. Stoltenberg, "China's Special Economic Zones: Their Development and Prospects," *Asian Survey* 24 (June 1984), 639.

[37] Barry Naughton, "Deng Xiaoping: The Economist," *China Quarterly* 135 (September 1993), 509.

[38] Peter T. Y. Cheung, "The Guangdong Advantage: Provincial Leadership and Strategy toward Resource Allocation since 1979," in Peter Cheung, Jae Ho Chung, and Zhimin Lin, eds., *Provincial Strategies of Economic Reform in Post-Mao China: Leadership, Politics, and Implementation* (Armonk, N.Y.: M. E. Sharpe, 1998).

[39] Shawn Shieh, "Provincial Leadership and the Implementation of Foreign Economic Reforms in Fujian Province," in Cheung, Chung, and Lin (fn. 38), 309.

[40] Stoltenberg (fn. 36), 640-41.

[41] Shieh (fn. 39), 305.

[42] Cheung (fn. 38), 122.

[43] Chongyi Feng and David S. G. Goodman, "Hainan: Communal Politics and the Struggle for Identity," in David S. G. Goodman, ed., *China's Provinces in Reform: Class, Community, and Political Culture* (New York: Routledge, 1997), 61–62.

Only after the idea was tested in the periphery was it extended to the less "expendable" Shanghai. Although grassroots initiatives played a part in these reforms, their design and geographical spread owed much to the authoritarian centralization of Chinese politics.

Local experiments continued in some areas as economic administration was decentralized in the mid-1980s. The privatization of small state-owned enterprises and of housing began with local experiments. It is hard to measure whether the frequency of experiments increased over time; however, the HRS, SEZs, and SOEs in the late 1970s certainly show that decentralization was not necessary for major local policy innovations. As before, some of the later "local" experiments actually began with a lot of central input. For instance, local experiments began in housing privatization in Zhengzhou, Changzhou, Siping and Shashi, and then Yantai in the mid-1980s; they were pilot projects designed and authorized by central authorities.[44]

In sum, most of the experiments that shaped China's reforms were not initiated by innovative, autonomous local leaders in defiance of an ideologically blinkered center. Most are better seen as gambits in a game played between competing factions centered in Beijing. Vertically structured, pro- and antireform factions spanned the state's many tiers. Most often, experiments began in provinces where Deng had strong supporters—Anhui (Wan Li), Sichuan (Zhao Ziyang), Guangdong (Yang Shangkun)—and spread fastest where Deng had allies. Until 1981 the HRS spread fastest "in the provinces like Anhui, Fujian, Gansu, Guangdong, Guangxi, Guizhou, Henan, and Inner Mongolia where Deng's forces dominated, or in the remote areas like Ningxia and Yunnan."[45] When feeling secure, Deng and his allies replaced conservative local leaders with their own men, who then engaged in more "local" experiments.[46] Decentralization was selective and aimed at circumventing Deng's central opponents. As reforms proved effective, Deng promoted provincial supporters such as Zhao and Wan Li to Beijing, from where they could direct reform nationwide. Other Deng allies at the center (Hu Yaobang and Song Renqiong) protected local reformers from party discipline and ideological attacks in the national press.[47] Grassroots initiatives were certainly important, but the main battlefront ran not between between center and regions but rather through the heart of Beijing.[48]

[44] Ya Ping Wang and Alan Murie, "The Process of Commercialization of Urban Housing in China," *Urban Studies* 33, no. 6 (1996).

[45] Huang (fn. 4), 371–75.

[46] For instance, in 1985 Beijing sent Liang Buting, a protégé of Hu Yaobang, to serve as party secretary and inject "reformist spirit" into the conservative province of Shandong; Chung (fn. 18), 133.

[47] Huang (fn. 4), 375.

[48] For a similar view, see Solinger (fn. 4).

V. Resisting Central Abuses

One argument for decentralization is that powerful local governments can entrench liberal economic policies by coordinating to resist predatory central interventions. Qian and Weingast contend that China's provincial governors have defended economic reform against central hard-liners. They point to the reformist governor of Guangdong, Ye Xuanping, who opposed attempts by Premier Li Peng in 1988–90 to recentralize budget revenues: "In China, . . . the central government tried to reverse local political authority underpinning market-oriented reform in the aftermath of Tiananmen Square in 1989. Led by the governor of Guangdong, the governors of many provinces resisted so that the central government eventually backed down."[49]

This incident is worth examining. In 1988–90 conservative party leaders sought to rein in inflationary pressures and increase central revenues. Li Peng and his allies wished to replace the fiscal contracting system with one in which tax revenues would be more evenly shared. At several meetings in 1989–90 Ye, sometimes supported by other governors, criticized this. At one conference of provincial governors, his speech was reportedly greeted with "wild applause."[50] This might have seemed a serious challenge, coming from a popular provincial politician and the son of one of the country's military leaders. Marshal Ye Jianying, Ye Xuanping's father, was one of the founders of communist China. In 1977 he had orchestrated the coup that deposed the Gang of Four, making possible Deng's return.[51]

This did not stop Beijing from removing Ye Xuanping the following year, along with the Guangdong party secretary, whose term was ending.[52] Two more junior officials, also reformist but more deferential, were appointed. In late 1993 the tax-contracting system Ye favored was replaced by Li Peng's preferred arrangement. Provincial governments no longer collected tax for the center, and their share was cut drastically, although they received compensatory transfers. In preparation, the center also removed the Jiangsu party chief, and other regional officials were "dumped for rubbing up Beijing the

[49] Yingyi Qian and Barry R. Weingast, "Federalism as a Commitment to Preserving Market Incentives," *Journal of Economic Perspectives* 11 (Autumn 1997), 90; see also Montinola, Qian, and Weingast (fn. 2); and Susan Shirk, *The Political Logic of Economic Reform in China* (Berkeley: University of California Press, 1993), chap. 9.

[50] Frank Gibney, Jr., "China's Renegade Province," *Newsweek International*, February 17, 1990, 35.

[51] Yumin Sheng, "Governing Economic Openness: Provincial Level Evidence from China, 1977–2002" (Manuscript, Yale University, 2004), 11; Baum (fn. 4), 39–47.

[52] Ye was reassigned to a ceremonial post in Beijing.

wrong way."[53] To underline Beijing's victory, Zhu Rongji even praised Guangdong's leaders for serving as a "model for submission by the part to the whole."[54] Ye's resistance had delayed Li's plans a little. But as an effort to block central interventions, it seems a rather limited success.

In fact, it is not clear the image of center-region conflict accurately captures what was going on. Ye's "provincial rebellion" may actually have been instigated from Beijing. Deng feared Li Peng's retrenchment would slow growth and undermine his achievements. Shortly before the 1990 meeting at which Ye challenged Li, Deng reportedly sent his old friend President Yang Shangkun to tell Ye that Deng would support resistance to Li.[55] Li's hesitations in responding may also have had as much to do with central politics as provincial pressure. In the post-Tiananmen uncertainty, Li knew too vigorous an attack on the pioneering provinces might provoke a counterattack from central reformers and very possibly from Deng himself.

Central authorities had little trouble removing regional leaders on many other occasions. The average tenure of provincial leaders declined in the 1980s, as cadres were more quickly rotated, promoted, or demoted.[56] Between 1991 and mid-1994 more than ten thousand officials at different levels were moved around, and in late 1994 and early 1995 Beijing reshuffled the leaders of more than half the provinces and major cities.[57] In 1994, while touring Heilongjiang, Vice Premier Zhu Rongji dismissed party boss Sun Weiben on the spot.[58]

Beijing did have temporary difficulty dislodging some recalcitrant governors (as occurred with Ye). But this was not because provincial officials operated some corporate defense mechanism or coordinated to protest violations of some implicit constitution. Rather, individual governors exploited their vertical networks, enlisting protection of powerful patrons at the center.[59] Ye had excellent connections in the party via his father. As a child, he had camped out in the caves of Yan'an along with Mao, Deng, and the other early communists. His appointment in 1985 showed Deng's commitment to reform in

[53] Willy Wo-Lap Lam, "Plenum's Push for Growth Masks a Power Scramble," *South China Morning Post*, November 20, 1993, 11, quoted in Dali L. Yang, *Beyond Beijing: Liberalization and the Regions in China* (New York: Routledge, 1997), 103.

[54] Yang (fn. 53), 104.

[55] Joseph Fewsmith, *China since Tiananmen: The Politics of Transition* (New York: Cambridge University Press, 2001), 42.

[56] Yasheng Huang, "The Post-Deng Era: Why China Will Not Collapse," *Foreign Policy* 99 (Summer 1995).

[57] Willy Wo-Lap Lam, *The Era of Jiang Zemin* (New York: Prentice Hall, 1999), 216–17.

[58] Ibid.

[59] Huang (fn. 56), 61.

Guangdong.[60] This complicated Li Peng's task but did not save the Guangdong leadership.

China's economic reforms have acquired credibility over time. This reflects the sheer number of citizens and firms with a stake in their continuation and the increasing complexity of the economy, which makes restoration of tight state control hard to imagine. Provincial governors are important players in Beijing politics, as they almost always have been. But the historical record to date does not support the claim that the governors can reliably coordinate to limit central interventions.

VI. Fiscal Decentralization and Incentives

Some scholars argue that fiscal decentralization gave Chinese local officials strong incentives to promote economic growth, which contributed to high growth nationwide.[61] By fiscal decentralization, they mean assigning local governments a large share of marginal revenues from profit or income taxes. From 1980 the central authorities began signing fiscal contracts with provincial governments over the division of tax revenues. Jin, Qian, and Weingast report that over time these gave provinces ever larger shares of marginal revenues, while becoming increasingly credible.[62] By 1989 more than two-thirds of provinces had the right to keep all marginal revenues. These scholars argue that letting local officials retain a larger share of marginal revenues should give them stronger incentives to "grow" the tax base by building infrastructure and reducing regulation and bribery. Jin, Qian, and Weingast examined a panel of twenty-nine provinces during 1980–92 and found that higher marginal retention rates were associated with faster employment growth in nonstate enterprises and faster reform in state-owned enterprises.

One might argue about whether assigning high marginal retention rates to local governments is a kind of fiscal decentralization at all. It does not require the allocation of any significant decision-making rights or fiscal resources to local governments. It is quite possible

[60] Peter T. Y. Cheung, "Changing Relations between the Central Government and Guangdong," in Y. M. Yeung and David K. Y. Chu, eds., *Guangdong: Survey of a Province Undergoing Rapid Change* (Hong Kong: Chinese University Press, 1998), 27.

[61] Hehui Jin, Yingyi Qian, and Barry R. Weingast, "Regional Decentralization and Fiscal Incentives: Federalism, Chinese Style," *Journal of Public Economics* 89 (September 2005); Ekaterina V. Zhuravskaya, "Incentives to Provide Local Public Goods: Fiscal Federalism, Russian Style," *Journal of Public Economics* 76 (June 2000); Yingyi Qian, "How Reform Worked in China," in Dani Rodrik, ed., *In Search of Prosperity: Analytical Narratives on Economic Growth* (Princeton: Princeton University Press, 2003).

[62] Jin, Qian, and Weingast (fn. 61).

for local governments to retain 100 percent of revenues at the margin but still get only a tiny share of *total* locally generated revenues. Jin, Qian, and Weingast try controlling for provinces' shares of total tax revenues—a more common measure of fiscal decentralization—but find these are not associated with faster economic reform. In fact, the argument seems more aptly characterized as one about high-powered agency contracts. Such contracts can be useful in all types of regimes where agents have the ability to shirk.

Nevertheless, accepting the authors' definitions, is the argument compelling? A more specific reason exists to doubt its application to China. Formally, such arguments assume provincial officials maximize an objective function like the following:

$$U = rstY(e) - C(e), \tag{1}$$

where Y is the provincial tax base, which increases with provincial government effort, e; C is the cost of exerting effort, also increasing in e; t is the expected effective tax rate; s is the proportion of tax revenues that is shared between governments; and r is the province's marginal share in shared revenues.[63] Given standard assumptions that Y is concave and C convex, the provincial government's optimal effort increases with rst. If s and t are fixed, then optimal effort must also increase with r. This is the claim about incentives in China. As r rose in the 1980s, this should have increased local officials' incentives to support business and thereby generate higher output.

But in this case s and t were anything but fixed.[64] First, s fell in the 1980s as the central authorities changed the rules to increase their revenues. Under fiscal contracting, before revenues were shared, certain "central fixed revenues" were reserved for the center. These included customs duties, some taxes, and remittances or profit taxes paid by the center's "own" state-owned enterprises.[65] During the 1980s the central government increased the scope of central fixed revenues, shrinking the pool available for sharing. Consequently, s fell from about 85 percent of total budget revenues to about 60 percent.[66] At the same time, total budget revenues as a share of GDP, which might serve as a proxy for the

[63] For a similar formalization, see Jin, Qian, and Weingast (fn. 61).

[64] Another problem with this argument is that it ignores the central government's potential to either support or impede economic activity; see Daniel Treisman, "Fiscal Decentralization, Governance, and Economic Performance: A Reconsideration," *Economics and Politics* 18 (July 2006).

[65] Christine Wong, Christopher Heady, and Wing T. Woo, *Fiscal Management and Economic Reform in the People's Republic of China* (New York: Oxford University Press, 1995), 86–87.

[66] Ibid., 90; see Table 1.

effective tax rate, *t*, were also falling. Total budget revenues fell from about 28 percent of GDP in 1979 to about 16 percent in 1990, depleted by tax evasion, decline of the old state enterprises, and difficulties collecting from the new nonstate sector. (The tax rate, *t*, is the expected—not actual—rate, so one might argue that only the formal rate matters. However, the steady drop in collections was obvious to officials and must have influenced their expectations.)

We estimated the marginal retention rate, *r*, for twenty-nine provinces in 1980–90, based on their existing fiscal contracts. Our measure of the average *r* for these years is close to that presented by Jin, Qian, and Weingast in their Figure 1.[67] This increased from around 68 percent in 1980 to a little below 90 percent in 1990. However, the increase in *r* was probably more than offset by simultaneous decreases in *s* and *t* (see Table 1). We estimate that the product *rst* fell from about 15 to about 8 percent. If these figures are approximately right, incentives to stimulate the economy weakened in the average province rather than improving. Although fiscal incentives might explain why growth was faster in some provinces than in others, it is unclear—given the fall in shared revenues as a fraction of GDP—how such incentives could explain rapid growth nationwide.

In another sense, the argument about marginal retention rates may miss the point. Throughout this period, local governments could set up various extrabudgetary and "off-budget" funds, all revenues of which they generally got to keep. Local governments usually had "complete authority over determination of tax rates and the amount of fees that fall into the categories of extra budget."[68] Subnational extrabudgetary fund revenues equaled 70 percent of subnational budget revenues in 1995 and 47 percent in 2002. On several occasions central authorities tried to regain control over such flows, but with limited success. For instance, from January 1983 Beijing imposed a 10 percent tax on extrabudgetary revenues, a figure later increased to 15 percent.[69] Such efforts prompted local governments to move money into off-budget funds, completely outside formal control.[70] Revenue from fees, most of which were paid into local off-budget funds, was estimated at 413 billion RMB in 1996, more than half the country's total budgetary revenues.[71]

[67] Jin, Qian, and Weingast (fn. 61).

[68] Qian and Weingast (fn. 2), 17.

[69] See Oksenberg and Tong (in sources to Table 1), 28.

[70] Xin-Qiao Ping, "Fiscal Decentralization in Chinese Economic Reform" (Manuscript, China Center for Economic Research, Peking University, 2000).

[71] Ibid., 21.

TABLE 1
ESTIMATING FISCAL INCENTIVES, CHINA
(1979–90)

	Estimated Marginal Retention Rate (Average for 29 Provinces) *r*	*Estimated Percentage of Tax Revenues That Was Shared* *s*	*Total Government Revenues as Percentage of* GDP *t*	*rst*
1979		85.7	28.4	
1980	68.2	84.0	25.7	14.7
1981	69.4	79.4	24.2	13.3
1982	78.1	77.0	22.9	13.8
1983	78.3	70.2	23.0	12.6
1984	78.3	65.1	22.9	11.7
1985	82.2	62.1	22.4	11.4
1986	84.7	59.5	20.8	10.5
1987	85.1	61.7	18.4	9.7
1988	88.7	60.2	15.8	8.4
1989	88.7	62.5	15.8	8.8
1990	88.7	58.7	15.8	8.2

SOURCES: Marginal retention rates estimated from Roy Bahl and Christine Wallich, *Intergovernmental Fiscal Relations in China* (Washington, D.C.: World Bank, 1992); Wong, Heady, and Woo (fn. 65); Michel Oksenberg and James Tong, "The Evolution of Central-Provincial Fiscal Relations in China, 1971–1984: The Formal System," *China Quarterly* 125 (March 1991); and Roy Bahl, *Fiscal Policy in China: Taxation and Intergovernmental Fiscal Relations* (San Francisco, Calif.: The 1990 Institute, 1999), figure for 1984 extrapolated from 1983. Percentage of tax revenues shared estimated from figures in Bert Hofman, "An Analysis of Chinese Fiscal Data over the Reform Period," *China Economic Review* 4, no. 2 (1993); we subtracted "central fixed revenue" from total budgetary revenue. Total government revenues and GDP from *China Statistical Yearbook* (2001, 2005).

Thus, both before and after the decentralizing reforms of the 1980s, local governments could collect revenues they did not have to share with anyone. If residual claimancy creates incentives to support growth, these incentives existed both before and after the introduction of fiscal contracts.[72] Increases in subnational governments' marginal retention rate for taxes might encourage subnational governments to shift revenues from extrabudgetary or off-budget funds into the formal tax system. It should also reduce incentives for local governments to help enterprises underreport output to evade taxes that would have to be shared with Beijing. This could increase reported output, but it is not clear why local governments would be more supportive of economic activity than they were before.

[72] Loosely regulated local extrabudgetary funds also existed in Russia in the 1990s, a country Jin, Qian, and Weingast (fn. 61) suggest grew more slowly because of poor fiscal incentives.

A final problem with the fiscal incentives argument is that it is inconsistent with experience after 1993. The tax reform implemented in 1994 replaced a system of fiscal contracts with high regional retention rates with one in which the largest tax, the VAT, was shared between provinces and the center, with the provinces retaining only 25 percent. Other taxes were assigned entirely to one level or the other, but their bases often overlapped. If local governments supported the growth of local businesses, for instance, they would get to keep 100 percent of additional business tax receipts, but would get only 25 percent of additional VAT and none of any additional export taxes generated. This must have significantly weakened local incentives. Worse still, a complicated system of compensatory transfers made it hard to tell what the net retention rates actually were. In the early years, according to Wang, "no one knew what constituted real central revenue or local revenue."[73] Yet there was no observable decline in the willingness of local governments to support local business after 1994. Although the fluctuations of the business cycle complicate comparisons and although dwindling opportunities for reallocating labor were reducing potential growth, the average growth rate in the seven years after the reform (1994–2000) was 8.1 percent, exactly the same as that for the seven years before it (1987–93). The OECD estimates that in the period 1993–98, increases in productivity added 3.4 percentage points to annual growth, compared with 1.7 percentage points in 1988–93 and 2.4 points in 1983–88. Increases in capital also added more to growth in the later period.[74]

An alternative explanation would attribute local officials' increasing efforts to promote growth precisely to the system's enduring centralization. Subnational officials in China undergo detailed performance reviews by their superiors and are rewarded or penalized based on their success in achieving specific targets.[75] Promotions, demotions, and job-related benefits all depend on such reviews, which have become increasingly formal. Criteria have varied over time. Under Mao, promotion depended in part on ideological conformity. But as reformers came to dominate in the 1980s, targets focused increasingly on economics.[76] As of the mid-1990s, the system for evaluating provincial leaders assigned 60 out of 100 points to targets related to economic performance.[77] This

[73] Shaoguang Wang, "China's 1994 Fiscal Reform: An Initial Assessment," *Asian Survey* 37 (September 1997), 805.

[74] OECD, *OECD Economic Surveys: China* (Paris: OECD, 2005), 32.

[75] Kai-yuen Tsui and Youqiang Wang, "Between Separate Stoves and a Single Menu: Fiscal Decentralization in China," *China Quarterly* 177 (May 2004), 71–90.

[76] More recently, criteria have included environmental protection and worker safety.

[77] Tsui and Wang (fn. 75), 77.

is clear in the results. Li and Zhou examined top officials in twenty-eight provinces in 1979–95 and found promotions were significantly more likely—and demotions less likely—in provinces with higher growth.[78] Similarly, Maskin, Qian, and Xu found provincial officials were more often promoted to the party's Central Committee if the relative growth rate of their province increased.[79] Career concerns create strong incentives to improve economic performance. They explain better than fiscal factors why the rise of market reformers in Beijing led to reforms and growth in the provinces, continuing after 1994.

VI. Hard Budget Constraints

Qian and Roland argue that, when capital is mobile, decentralizing fiscal authority can harden budget constraints on state enterprises.[80] They present a model in which enterprises lobby local—but not central—governments for aid. Local governments must divide their budget between building infrastructure—which increases local profitability and so helps attract capital—and bailing out insolvent firms. Since reducing infrastructure investments prompts an outflow of capital, local governments face a higher opportunity cost of spending on bailouts than a central government would (assuming capital is less mobile across national than regional borders). Thus, local governments should be less eager than a central government to provide subsidies. Qian and Roland contend that such effects have hardened budget constraints on SOEs in China.

Although the argument is elegant, it is not clear it establishes that fiscal decentralization contributed to better economic performance in China, for two reasons. First, even if competition for capital hardened budget constraints on some state enterprises, it simultaneously softened them for those, whether private or state-owned, that partnered with external—especially foreign—investors. Second, there is little evidence that decentralization and competition for capital did harden budget constraints on state-owned enterprises. On the contrary, they appear to have softened. Financial discipline was tightened in the late 1990s. But this reflected a reimposition of controls by the *central* government, not an increase in political or fiscal decentralization.

[78] Hongbin Li and Li-An Zhou, "Political Turnover and Economic Performance: The Incentive Role of Personnel Control in China," *Journal of Public Economics* 89 (September 2005).

[79] Maskin, Qian, and Xu (fn. 14).

[80] Yingyi Qian and Gérard Roland, "The Soft Budget Constraint in China," *Japan and the World Economy* 8 (June 1996); Qian and Roland (fn. 2).

To take these points in turn, local governments can compete for mobile capital in various ways. Building infrastructure is only one of them, and it is not always the most cost effective. Investors may be lured to a region precisely by the local government's promises of soft credit, subsidies, or tax breaks. Provincial and municipal governments in China have made such offers quite explicit. The Jiangsu government pledged in a 1986 regulation that "problems concerning the funding of the investment of the Chinese party to a foreign investment enterprise will be fully resolved. . . . The various banks with which a foreign investment enterprise has opened an account will give priority when formulating loan targets to guaranteeing availability of working capital loans and short-term working funds for the foreign investment enterprise." Qinhuangdao Municipal Government promised its development company would "be responsible for and partially or wholly handle the loans for short-term working funds needed for production and distribution, as well as for other needed credit of enterprises with foreign investment." Xiamen, Heilongjiang, Guangdong and many other units have made similar commitments.[81] Foreign investors are often required to partner with a Chinese SOE, whose budget constraints are softened by such privileges.

Subnational governments have often pressured local banks and state bank branches to fund favored firms. A 1987 survey found most nonperforming state bank loans had been made "under pressure from local governments."[82] Until the late 1990s local governments helped appoint and promote the directors of local state bank branches.[83] Bank employees relied on local governments for water, electricity, housing, and schooling for their children.[84] Local governments also held shares in many joint equity and commercial banks and continued to meddle in their operations.[85]

Provincial governments have often guaranteed foreign loans, explicitly or implicitly. Some set up financial trust companies to channel government-guaranteed loans to local projects. Many were in infrastruc-

[81] For details, see www.novexcn.com/sev regs jiangsu encor for.html, www.novexcn.com/qinhuangdao perf treat for.html, www.novexcn.com/imp forinvest inves xiamen.html, www.novexcn.com/encou for inv heilongjiang.html, and www.novexcn.com/guangdo im prov encor f in.html (accessed March 2, 2006).

[82] Shaoguang Wang, "Central-Local Fiscal Politics in China," in Hao and Lin (fn. 33), 100.

[83] OECD (fn. 74), 170.

[84] Jing Jin and Heng-fu Zou, "Soft-Budget Constraints and Local Government in China," in Jonathan Rodden, Gunnar Eskeland, and Jennie Litvack, eds., *Fiscal Decentralization and the Challenge of Hard Budget Constraints* (Cambridge: MIT Press, 2003).

[85] Y. C. Richard Wong and M. L. Sonia Wong, "Competition in China's Domestic Banking Industry," *Cato Journal* 21 (Spring–Summer 2001).

ture, consistent with Qian and Roland's argument, but other loans went to unpromising state enterprises, often connected to officials. By 1999 China had 242 financial trust companies.[86] One, the Guangdong International Trust and Investment Corporation (GITIC), suffered a spectacular bankruptcy in 1999, having amassed a $1.8 billion net debt.[87] Provincial officials had promised a bailout just months before.[88] Besides local roads and telecommunications, GITIC had invested in state-controlled enterprises manufacturing cement, glass, soft drinks, beer, and motorcycles. It lent about $82 million to one fabric manufacturer in Maoming, Guangdong, which later closed, defaulting on the entire loan.[89] Rather than disciplining local officials, foreign investment often served as a screen behind which local officials could—sometimes corruptly—direct state funds to favored firms.

The second problem with this argument is that fiscal and administrative decentralization in the 1980s did not coincide with any noticeable hardening of state enterprise budget constraints. Some economic decision-making authority was devolved to subnational governments in the mid-1980s just as competition for foreign capital was developing. One might therefore expect to see budget constraints harden in this period. Government subsidies to loss-making state enterprises did drop as a percentage of GDP (see Table 2.) But this source of soft finance was merely replaced by others. In part, loss-making enterprises kept afloat by accumulating arrears to suppliers, workers, or public utilities.[90] However, the most important source of funds was bank loans. Bank credit more than doubled as a share of GDP between 1978 and 1998, from 50 percent to an estimated 108 percent.[91] Most went to state enterprises, which by 1996 were paying less than one-third of the interest due.[92] Despite overstating profits—for instance, by counting unpaid interest on nonperforming loans as income—the state banks reported sharply falling profitability. Data on nonperforming loans have been available

[86] Jonathan Sprague, "Beyond Bankruptcy: The Gitic Failure Puts Foreign Lenders on Alert," *Asiaweek*, January 29, 1999.

[87] Ibid. Similar, although smaller, cases occurred in Guangzhou and Dalian; see Kyodo News International, *Asian Economic News*, June 26, 2000.

[88] *Washington Post*, January 12, 1999, A14.

[89] Jiachun Fang, *Jinrong Tuoguan Jingdian Anli Yanju* (Studies of classical cases in financial trust) (Beijing: Economic Science Publisher, 2002).

[90] Harry G. Boardman, "The Chinese State as Corporate Shareholder," *Finance and Development* 36 (September 1999).

[91] Nicholas Lardy, "The Challenge of Bank Restructuring in China," in Bank for International Settlements, *Strengthening the Banking Systems in China: Issues and Experience* (Basel, Switzerland: Bank for International Settlements, 1999), 20.

[92] Nicholas Lardy, "The Case of China" (Manuscript, Brookings Institution, Washington D.C., 2000), 24; Boardman (fn. 90).

TABLE 2
STATE SUBSIDIES TO LOSS-MAKING STATE-OWNED ENTERPRISES

	Total		*of Which*	
	Billion RMB	% GDP	*Central Billion* RMB	*Local Billion* RMB
1985	50.7	5.7		
1986	32.5	3.2		
1987	37.6	3.1		
1988	44.6	3.0		
1989	59.9	3.5	22.7	37.1
1990	57.9	3.1	21.0	36.9
1991	51.0	2.4	23.6	27.4
1992	44.5	1.7	16.8	27.7
1993	41.1	1.2	10.2	30.9
1994	36.6	0.8	5.8	30.9
1995	32.8	0.6	5.9	26.9
1996	33.7	0.5	7.2	26.6
1997	36.8	0.5	9.6	27.3
1998	33.3	0.4	7.5	25.9
1999	29.0	0.4	5.2	23.8
2000	27.9	0.3	4.9	23.0
2001	30.0	0.3	3.8	26.2
2002	26.0	0.2	4.6	21.4
2003	22.6	0.2	3.2	19.4
2004	21.8	0.2	3.6	18.2

SOURCES: *China Statistical Yearbook* (2001, 2004, 2005); *Finance Statistical Yearbook of China* (1993, 1999, 2004).

only sporadically. When they are, they are not always comparable (the method of classification changed in 2003) and are believed to greatly understate the problem.[93] Announcements by monetary officials suggest the rate of nonperforming loans was high and increasing in the 1990s, reaching more than one-third of the value of outstanding loans in 1999 (see Table 3). The rate began to decrease only after the central government intervened to clean up banks' balance sheets, as discussed below.

If budget constraints were hardening, one might expect a decrease over time in the proportion of loss-making enterprises (since losses must be financed by subsidies or borrowing).[94] This does not seem to have occurred. Directly comparable data for the entire period since 1978

[93] Lardy (fn. 91), 30.
[94] One might expect a temporary increase if discipline were increasing, but if the proportion continues to rise year after year, some source of financing must be covering the losses.

TABLE 3
NONPERFORMING LOANS OF THE FOUR MAIN STATE BANKS

	Old Classification		*5-Category Classification*	
	% of Total Loans	*Bn $ U.S.*	*% of Total Loans*	*Bn $ U.S.*
1994	20			
1995	21.4	79		
1996	24.0	111		
1997	28.4	179		
1998	32.2	239		
1999	34.0	266		
2000	29.2	224		
2001	25.4	213		
2002	21.4	206		
2003	16.9	192	20.4	232
2004			15.6	190

SOURCES: Lardy (fn. 92), 19, for 1994; OECD (fn. 74), 146, for new classification 2003–4; Ping Xie, "The Problem of Non-Performing Loans in the Chinese Banking Industry," *Contemporary Bankers* (May 2004), for other years. Converted to dollars using official exchange rate, average for period, from World Bank, *World Development Indicators* (various years).

were not available, but Table 4 shows the trends in two closely related series. The share of loss-making state-owned industrial enterprises did fall between 1976 and 1985. But then it rose dramatically, from 9.6 percent in 1985 to 47.4 percent in 1998. Total losses increased by more than thirty times, from 2.7 billion to 85 billion RMB. In 1996 the state-owned enterprise sector as a whole was in the red. Budget constraints do appear to have tightened somewhat in the late 1990s. Between 1998 and 2000 the share of loss-making state-owned or state-controlled industrial enterprises fell from 40.6 to 34.1 percent, before stabilizing at about 35 percent. Did this reflect increasing competitive pressures on local governments as capital mobility intensified?

In fact, there is a simpler explanation. The central government intervened to reimpose control over state bank local branches and tighten credit administratively. In late 1998 the People's Bank of China replaced its provincial branches with nine regional offices. Local governments lost influence over appointments of bank personnel, now chosen and monitored by a vertical party committee system. Premier Zhu Rongji ordered state banks either to cut wages of managers who authorized bad loans or to fire them.[95] Simultaneously, Beijing launched a mas-

[95] Victor Shih, "Dealing with Non-Performing Loans: Political Constraints and Financial Policies in China" (Manuscript, Northwestern University, Department of Political Science, 2005), 17–18.

TABLE 4
LOSS-MAKING AMONG STATE ENTERPRISES IN CHINESE INDUSTRY
(1975–2004)

	Share of State Industrial Production Enterprises That Are Loss Making (%)	*Losses of Loss-Making State Industrial Production Enterprises (100m Yuan)*	*Share of State and State-Controlled Industrial Enterprises That Are Loss Making (%)*	*Losses of Loss-Making State and State-Controlled Industrial Enterprises (100m Yuan)*
1975	31.4	52.0		
1976	37.2	72.5		
1977	27.4	57.5		
1978	23.9	44.3		
1979	23.4	36.9		
1980	22.4	31.9		
1981	27.7	42.4		
1982	25.1	42.7		
1983	14.6	28.6		
1984	10.5	22.9		
1985	9.6	27.1		
1986	13.4	47.1		
1987	12.8	50.7		
1988	10.7	71.3		
1989	15.9	128.0		
1990	30.3	278.8		
1991	28.0	300.2		
1992	22.7	300.1		
1993	29.8	281.7		
1994	32.6	273.8		
1995	33.3	364.8		
1996	37.5	501.4		
1997	43.9	607.2		
1998	47.4	850.2	40.6	1150.7
1999			39.2	966.7
2000			34.1	704.3
2001			36.0	752.2
2002			36.1	668.5
2003			35.2	680.0
2004			35.0	669.5

SOURCES: For 1975–98, *Finance Statistics Yearbook of China* (1999); for 1998–2004, *Statistics Yearbook of China* (2005).

sive bailout, creating four asset-management companies to take over bad loans and providing 2,295 billion RMB ($277 billion) in emergency funds between 1998 and 2005.[96] Some provincial investment companies were forced into bankruptcy.

Even local government subsidies to loss-making enterprises fell much more slowly than central ones (see Table 2), although this partly reflects the transfer of some unprofitable central enterprises to local control. Thus, harder budget constraints could be attributed more plausibly to *centralization* of authority in China, the continuing ability of Beijing to dictate subnational economic policy. Any additional effect of interregional capital competition is difficult to detect.

In fairness, Qian and Roland explicitly acknowledge most of these points. A key condition for fiscal competition to work in their model is that local governments cannot increase the money supply. They recognize this was not true during the period of fiscal decentralization in the 1980s, and they accept that budget constraints did not harden until the late 1990s. They even associate this hardening with Beijing's recentralization of monetary policy.They nevertheless conclude that "China benefited greatly from regional decentralization in its first 15 years of reforms, and the Chinese experience shows that decentralization of fiscal authority has helped in advancing the reform."[97] It is this conclusion that we question.

VIII. Conclusion

China's remarkable growth coincided with a decentralization of practical decision making on various economic matters in the 1980s, followed by some recentralization in the 1990s. It occurred in a system in which a large share of expenditure and tax collection took place at subnational levels. Some scholars believe decentralization facilitated market reforms and catalyzed the country's economic development. Although sophisticated and thought-provoking arguments along these lines have been developed and are quite widely accepted both in China and in the West, they are ultimately not convincing.

Decentralization could not have stimulated the main policy experiments that shaped China's reforms because these experiments began in the late 1970s and early 1980s, before any significant political or administrative decentralization occurred. China was, at that time, a hi-

[96] OECD (fn. 74), 43.

[97] Qian and Roland (fn. 80), 222.

erarchical Leninist autocracy. Considerable administrative decentralization occurred later, but it did not create a credible check on central economic interventions; Beijing remained fully able to fire disobedient provincial governors and impose its policies. Provincial governors who managed to delay central policies did so via vertical ties to central patrons rather than by mobilizing horizontal organizations of governors or coordinating a common response. (We are not aware of any significant cases of such coordination.) Improved local fiscal incentives in the 1980s cannot explain higher growth because the increase in the provincial share of marginal revenues was offset by rapid shrinking of the fiscal pie as a share of GDP. Nor could fiscal decentralization have hardened budget constraints on state enterprises because budget constraints did not harden until fiscal authority was recentralized. The relative economic self-sufficiency of China's provinces may have rendered them less vulnerable to disruption. But this is a fact about the country's inherited economic structure, not one about political, administrative, or fiscal decentralization.

Local actors were of course important in the story of Chinese reforms.[98] But they were important as actors in a game directed from Beijing. The driving force was not political pressure from subnational officials, spontaneous innovation by them, or competition among them to attract capital. It was competition between ideologically different *central* political factions, whose leaders sought to win support within the party by demonstrating the effectiveness of their favored policies. Central factions enlisted the aid of sympathizers at all levels and built vertical networks. Grassroots initiatives, both of reformers and of antireformers, aimed to win the initiator favor and promotions from the relevant faction leaders. Deng and his associates repeatedly promoted provincial reformers to central positions—not just Zhao Ziyang and Wan Li but also, later, Li Ruihuan and Zhu Rongji—and Deng sent trusted lieutenants to stimulate reforms in lagging areas. In short, this was the kind of competition between vertical teams one would expect in a centralized, multitier system.

Administrative decentralization coincided with reform in the 1980s, in part because decentralization was itself a reform promoted by Deng and his supporters, in part because Deng sought to circumvent opposition at the center by empowering his allies in the provinces. But economic reforms continued in the 1990s, accelerating in some areas, despite a shift toward recentralization of control and revenues. Table 5 shows our es-

[98] For an interpretation of agricultural reforms that emphasizes local initiatives, see Yang (fn. 29).

timates of trends in administrative decentralization, economic reforms, and the strength of proreform factions at the center during the first two decades of reform.[99] Although this exercise obviously involves some subjectivity, we found a great deal of scholarly consensus about the timing of economic reform and the history of factional politics. While the ups and downs of the central proreform faction correlate quite closely with the ebbs and flows of economic reform, there is no clear correlation between reform and the degree of administrative decentralization.

We do not mean to suggest that centralization always leads to reform and rapid growth. Obviously this is not the case, as China's history from 1945 to 1978 demonstrates. It was quite possible proreform factions would lose or win only temporary victories, as had happened before. Nor did all the central reformers' choices reflect an even-handed commitment to liberalization and growth: they played favorites, supporting some units, such as Guangdong and later Shanghai, at the expense of others.[100] Since 1992, when the goal of marketization was essentially accepted by all, factional lines have reflected less fundamental divisions—geographical or institutional loyalties, personal ties, and more muted conflicts over the balance between liberalization and income redistribution.[101] Nevertheless, factional competition continues to influence central politics and policy, as illustrated by the greater emphasis on developing inland provinces since the more populist faction of Hu Jintao overtook the Shanghai-centered network of Jiang Zemin.

Understanding the role of political and fiscal decentralization in China's reforms is important because the country's experience is often taken as an example for other countries. Those who praise China's gradualist, incremental approach often associate this with decentralization.[102] Decentralization is sometimes presented as almost a functional equivalent of privatization, an alternative to more fundamental reform of property rights,[103] or as a source of pluralism—perhaps accountability—even in the absence of democracy. If one accepts that decentralization had little to do with the success of China's reforms, one must seek other explanations for the country's performance.

[99] The specific events on which these classifications are based, along with the sources, are listed in a longer version of the paper on Treisman's Web site at www.polisci.ucla.edu/faculty/treisman/.

[100] On the case of Wuhan, see Dorothy Solinger, "Despite Decentralization: Disadvantages, Dependence and Ongoing Central Power in the Inland—The Case of Wuhan," *China Quarterly* 145 (March 1996).

[101] This is, of course, a matter of degree. Personal connections were always important in shaping the support group of the usually pragmatic Deng.

[102] Chen (fn. 2).

[103] For example, Qian and Roland (fn. 2), 1156.

TABLE 5
DECENTRALIZATION, FACTIONAL COMPETITION, AND ECONOMIC REFORMS IN CHINA
(1978–98)

	1978	1979	1980	1981	1982	1983	1984	1985	1986	1987	1988	1989	1990	1991	1992	1993	1994	1995	1996	1997	1998
Administrative decentralization	centralized			gradually becoming more administratively decentralized								recentralizing[a]						stabilized at intermediate level of decentralization[a]			
Factional competition	reformers, protected by Deng, competing with Hua Guofeng faction			reformers (Hu, Zhao) increasingly dominant, but conservatives fight back with "spiritual pollution" campaign			reformers dominant, but conservative opposition growing, Deng increasingly concerned about political instability, 1986–88					Tiananmen; conservatives (Li Peng) dominant, Deng in background			Deng returns—tour of South—fights back against Li Peng, gets Zhu promoted, then gradually passes power to Jiang			Jiang consolidating power, triangulating between Zhu and Li Peng, increasingly supporting Zhu and reform			
Economic reforms	first experimental reforms in agriculture, SOEs, SEZs				reforms slower		reforms accelerate again					reforms slow down			renewal and continuation of reforms: privatization, external opening, support of private enterprise, banking system reform						
Strongest ec. reform momentum	■	■	■				■	■		■					■	■	■				■

SOURCES: For detailed sources, see longer version of the paper at www.polisci.ucla.edu/faculty/treisman/, appendix.

[a]There is some question about how to characterize the year-to-year changes in the degree of centralization in the 1990s. Administrative reforms in 1993–94 had some decentralizing consequences. Lam (fn. 57) characterizes the 1995–98 period as one of "aggressive efforts" by the center to claw back powers, albeit with only partial success. However, there is agreement that the 1990s witnessed a trend toward recentralization compared to the late 1980s.

[12]

China's "Soft" Centralization: Shifting *Tiao/Kuai* Authority Relations*

Andrew C. Mertha

ABSTRACT This article analyses China's recent attempts to counter "local protectionism" and establish standardization in policy implementation and enforcement by centralizing a growing number of its regulatory bureaucracies up to the provincial level (what I refer to as "soft" centralization). In this article, I argue that Beijing's experiment with soft centralization, while successful to some extent, has nevertheless fallen short of its goals and that thus far this transformation remains imperfect and incomplete. The institutional cleavages and fragmentation that so often give rise to corruption and other pathologies of the state appear to have shifted from horizontal, geographic lines to vertical, functional ones. Moreover, the principal beneficiaries of this shift to centralized management are the provinces, not Beijing, as the institutional mechanisms of personnel and budgetary resource allocations are concentrated at the provincial level. Although this has curbed localism to a degree by transferring power from local governments to the newly centralized bureaucracies, it has also contributed to a situation in which newly-strengthened provinces may play a key role in the emergence of a sort of perverse federalism.

Within the past quarter of a century China's former command economy has morphed into one largely governed by the market. China has become integrated into the world economy, and the living standards of many of its citizens have risen dramatically. During this time, China's leaders have experimented with two radically different structural approaches towards managing the economy. The first has marked the reform path since 1978: the decentralization of economic and political decision-making to local governments in order to establish the conditions necessary for markets to take root.

The second, more recent, approach is in many ways the opposite of the first: the partial centralization of a number of key bureaucracies in order to regulate and discipline local government agents in their management of the economy and the implementation of policy more generally. Under this "centralized management" (*chuizhi guanli*) system, individual offices

* This research was made possible by a Roland Grimm Fellowship and a Weidenbaum Small Grant from the Murray Weidenbaum Centre, both at Washington University in St Louis. The article is based on interviews and archival research in China in 1999 and during the summers of 2002 and 2003. Because sources agreed to be interviewed anonymously, I indicate interviews by number. The first two digits indicate the year and the two letters indicate the location (BJ for Beijing, CD for Chengdu, CQ for Chongqing, GY for Guiyang, GZ for Guangzhou and SH for Shanghai). I thank Kjeld Erik Brødsgaard, Bruce Dickson, Pierre Landry, Gary Miller, Daniel O'Neill, Susan Whiting and Dali Yang for comments on earlier drafts, and Kenneth Lieberthal and Nicholas Lardy for feedback on an early presentation which marked the beginning of this research. I am solely responsible for any errors that remain.

within these bureaucracies are no longer beholden to superiors within local governments (*kuai*); rather, they are directly controlled by their functional administrative superiors (*tiao*) and have only a consultative relationship with their former local government bosses. This centralization, moreover, does not appear to be a temporary measure like the macroeconomic adjustments and retrenchment undertaken to cool the overheating economy.[1] Centralization establishes new economic and political incentives that guide officials' behaviour. It creates new winners and provides them with benefits they are unlikely to relinquish voluntarily. Finally, it forges new institutional arrangements that are likely to endure far into the future.

I refer to this as "soft centralization" because, although these bureaucracies are centralized from the township/county to the provincial level, they remain decentralized between the centre and the province (that is, governing the relations between the provincial bureaucratic offices and the provincial governments). In this article, I argue that Beijing's experiment with soft centralization, while successful to some degree, has nevertheless fallen short in its goals and that thus far this transformation remains imperfect and incomplete. The institutional cleavages and fragmentation that so often give rise to corruption and other pathologies of the state appear to have shifted from horizontal, geographic lines to vertical, functional ones. Moreover, the principal beneficiaries of this shift to centralized management are the provinces, not Beijing, as the institutional mechanisms of personnel and budgetary resource allocations are concentrated at the provincial level. Although this has curbed localism to a degree, by transferring power from local governments to the newly centralized bureaucracies, it has also contributed to a situation in which newly strengthened provinces may play a key role in the emergence of a sort of perverse federalism.

The sections below introduce the goals of centralization and the actual bureaucracies that have been centralized since 1998. I discuss the tools that have been used to effect these changes. I then analyse the initial outcomes of soft centralization and discuss their substantive and conceptual significance, particularly with regard to a strengthening of the provinces and a blurring of administrative and jurisdictional lines of authority at lower administrative levels.

Goals: Combating Local Protectionism and Establishing Standardization

Chinese officials point to local protectionism as the target and a greater degree of standardization of policy implementation and enforcement in China as the goal of soft centralization. "Local protectionism" (*difang baohu zhuyi*) is a difficult term to pin down conceptually and even more difficult to establish empirically in China. Conceptually, it can have a

1. See Richard Baum, *Burying Mao: Chinese Politics in the Age of Deng Xiaoping* (Princeton, NJ: Princeton University Press, 1994).

number of different meanings. It can refer to trade barriers that reduce the sale of goods between localities, thereby preventing the growth of significant scale economies. In this definition, local protectionism represents a barrier to the creation of an efficient, integrated national economy from a mosaic of balkanized local markets that establish unfair barriers to entry, engage in illegal production and sales, or both. Others attach a broader definition, in which local protectionism refers to the adaptation and mutation of national laws and regulations to suit the interests of local officials and which are at a variance with the initial intent of Beijing. Indeed, the term has been applied so loosely that for some there is little if any distinction between "local protectionism" and "corruption."

Empirically, there is some debate over the extent of local protectionism as well as its overall effects on the economy. While there are countless pieces of anecdotal evidence (the Chinese press is full of such stories), there has thus far been little *systematic* analysis of the problem. Moreover, as Naughton and others have found, local protectionism has little, if any, effect on cross-border trade when aggregated to the provincial level.[2] Nevertheless, what is important is that it has been widely *perceived* as a genuine problem by the authorities in Beijing. Moreover, because the conventional wisdom in China is that local protectionism is rampant, it is useful as a political tool to mobilize individuals and agencies against those that might resist the changes to the status quo brought about by soft centralization.

If the target of soft centralization is local protectionism, the goal is to establish a degree of standardization in policy implementation and enforcement. In the case of foreign investment, for example, local governments often offer preferential policies – such as low (or no) taxes, tax refund schemes, or liberalizing remittance of hard currency to investing firms – to potential investors. The problem is that these local governments do not have the legal authority to do this; responsibility for enacting these types of laws and regulations rests with the national government. As a response to these phenomena, the national government wants to standardize policy enforcement throughout China, and centralization is theoretically an effective method of achieving this.[3]

Currently, there are three broad categories of organizations that are either already centralized or which are being considered for centralization: administrative regulation, financial regulation and commodities

2. Barry Naughton, "How much can regional integration do to unify China's markets?" in Nicholas C. Hope, Dennis Tao Young and Mu Yang Li (eds.), *How Far Across the River? Chinese Policy Reform at the Millennium* (Stanford, CA: Stanford University Press, 2003, pp. 204–232). Still others, like Wedeman, argue that local protectionism was actually *beneficial* to China's economic reform, particularly with regard to China's movement away from price subsidies. Andrew Wedeman, *From Mao to Market: Rent Seeking, Local Protectionism, and Marketization in China* (New York: Cambridge University Press, 2004).

3. Interview 02CD06, 18 July 2002; and interview 03BJ03, 9 March 2003.

management.[4] Why have these particular sectors been selected? Interviews with local officials confirm that their bureaucracies were chosen specifically because of their vital role in China's economic development.[5] Administrative regulatory bureaucracies are key actors in monitoring the economy and standardizing commercial practices throughout China. The centralization of financial services is an attempt to help it withstand the competition to which it will be exposed under the World Trade Organization (WTO). Finally, the centralization of commodities is intended to target their unregulated production and sale and rationalize China's distribution networks and related infrastructure.

Commercial and Regulatory Agencies

Beginning in late 1998, the Administration for Industry and Commerce (AIC) was ordered to alter its authority relations from a decentralized (*kuai*-based) structure to a centralized (*tiao*-based) one. The functions of the AIC shifted from a focus on micro-level (local market and small individual retailers) to macro-level market supervision (the socialist market writ large). Geographic/jurisdictional areas were also enlarged. Moreover, the AIC changed its focus to supervision and was forced to give up its own enterprises. It was told to establish strict qualifications to ensure the professionalism and incorruptibility of its officials.[6]

In March of the following year, Beijing decided to apply centralized management to the sub-provincial level units of the Quality Technology Supervision bureaucracy (QTSB).[7] These changes were identical to those at the AIC, with the exception that the QTSB was ordered to focus less at the retail level and more on the wholesale level in the production chain.[8]

In June 2000, the State Council approved a drug supervision system reform plan that stipulated the provision of centralized management below the provincial level[9] led by the Pharmaceutical Supervision Management Bureau. This bureaucracy is responsible for supervision of all

4. Wang Dingqi, " 'Tiao guan bumen' ye yao jieshou renda jiandu" ("Vertically-managed units should also accept supervision from people's congresses"), http://zgrdxw.peopledaily.com.cn/gb/paper7/9/class000 700001/hwz160811.htm.

5. Earlier attempts at centralization in 1994–95 of the taxation bureau provided a blueprint for changing these other bureaucracies, which began around 1999–2000.

6. "Gaige gongshang xingzheng guanli tizhi sheng yi xia jiguan shixing chuizhi guanli" ("Reform the Administration for Industry and Commerce regulatory system by using vertical management below the provincial level"), http://202.99.23.245/zdxw/21/981201/A114.html.

7. "Dang zhongyang guowuyuan jueding zhiliang jishu jiandu guanli tizhi shishi zhongda gaige – sheng yi xia zhiliang jishu jiandu xitong shixing chuizhi guanli" ("Party centre and State Council decide to reform management of the quality and technology supervision system – implement vertical management below the provincial level in the quality technical supervision system"), *Renmin ribao* (*People's Daily*), 27 March 1999.

8. "Zhiliang jishu jiandu zhineng zhize" ("Functions of quality technical supervision"), http://www.hn315.gov.cn/gov/znzz.htm.

9. *Ibid.*

stages of production, distribution, sales and use of pharmaceuticals and medical equipment. The goals of this centralization include abolishing local standards and implementing uniform national ones, increasing the supervision and regulation of the pharmaceuticals market, enlarging the definition of "counterfeit" drugs, and raising the penalties for counterfeiting.[10]

Financial Services

The China Securities Supervision Commission (CSSC) was established in 1993. In July 1999, the "Securities Regulations" were enacted and two months later, the CSSC Stock Issuing Approval Committee was established. In 1999, the CSSC applied for centralized management in order to establish a uniform securities supervision system with adequate supervision and monitoring over securities and futures markets as well as to improve the quality of market information and thus market stability.[11] At present, securities supervision offices (as well as some of the securities-related responsibilities of the People's Bank of China, PBOC) are now under the direct centralized management of the CSSC. It has also consolidated a potentially destabilizing futures market after centralized management was applied to futures markets in 1998. The number of exchanges for futures was reduced to three (Shanghai, Dalian and Zhengzhou) and registered futures companies were scaled back to 180.[12]

The PBOC reinforced this commitment to centralized management by establishing nine large regional branches on 1 January 1999 and abolishing the 31 provincial branches. This reform, based on a pilot programme in Shanghai, seeks to enhance the effectiveness of the central branch's currency policy decision-making and supervision over financing. The PBOC now applies centralized management to commercial banks and credit organizations that are agents for managing state reserves.[13]

The China Construction Bank has established its own centrally managed auditing departments in Guangzhou, Xi'an, Wuhan, Beijing, Nanjing, Dalian, Shanghai and Chengdu,[14] each of which has independent

10. "Guanyu yaopin guanli fa lifa zongzhi de jueding" ("Decision regarding the tenets of pharmaceutical laws"), http://www.sda.gov.cn/webportal/portal.po?UID = DWV1_WOU1D_URL_68212&TOC = COLUMN_68212&OBJ = 71786).

11. "Zhongguo zhengjianhui 'san ding' fang'an huo pizhun" ("China Securities Commission 'three fixes' plan approved"), http://61.129.103.17/overview/publication/company/98/s981156.htm.

12. "Hua tiaozhan wei jiyu, yi guifan cu fazhan – tan wo guo qihuo shichang de xianzhuang yu weilai" ("Make opportunities out of challenges, promote the development of criteria"), http://www.czce.com.cn/Publish/research/200206/3310.asp.

13. "Dai Xianglong hangzhang da jizhe wen" ("Bank director general Dai Xianglong responds to reporters' questions"), http://www.china.org.cn/ch-xinwen/content/news/PressConferences/990127–2.htm.

14. "Jianxing sheli 8 da shenji fenbu" ("Construction bank establishing eight auditing departments"), http://www. sfnews.sh.cn/epublish/gb/paper9/146/class000900002/hwz12292.htm.

vertical-based authority relations with the higher-level Auditing Department. An "auditor-in-chief" in each of the first-tier branches is in charge of the all the auditing that goes on in that particular branch office. Second-tier branches and those below now submit to the superior first-tier branch, while county-level auditing offices are in the process of being abolished.

Finally, the life insurance sector is also experimenting with centralized management. A life insurance fund was created at the provincial level in 1992 and municipal-level governments were required to contribute a specified amount to it. However, because those life insurance agencies were subject to local government interference, the actual funding was not uniformly regulated.[15] The introduction of centralized management is intended to help resolve these problems.[16]

Regulation and Management of Goods and Commodities

The developments sketched out above have also extended into some of the institutions charged with managing goods and commodities, including the management of electricity and grain. Local protectionism was blamed by central authorities for causing widespread inter-provincial electricity market barriers, resulting in suboptimal allocation and utilization of scarce electricity resources.[17] At around the same time these other developments were taking place, the State Council Development Research Centre submitted a report suggesting that China establish an "Electricity Supervision Commission." Subsequent electricity regulation reforms have been based on this report.[18] The main functions of the Electricity Supervision Commission, an office directly below the State Council, include drafting nationwide supervision regulations, establishing electricity permit regimes, and supervising inter-regional electricity transactions. Regional agencies are charged with enforcing these national regulations as well as regulating electricity businesses that are inter-provincial but which stay within the larger region. The provincial level agencies' functions and duties are to supervise and regulate the electricity business within the province.[19]

On 10 March 1998, the First Plenum of the Ninth National People's Congress approved the "Decision on Reform of the Structure of the State Council," which placed the State Grain Reserves Bureau under the jurisdiction of the State Planning and Development Commission.

15. "Touxi chuizhi guanli" ("The anatomy of vertical management"), http://www.clssn.com/qqhg/2001/06/14/shbz 4b20010614.htm.

16. *Ibid.*

17. "Guowuyuan fazhan yanjiu zhongxin: jianyi sheli 'dianjianhui' " ("The State Council Development Research Centre: suggestions on establishing an 'Electrical Supervision Commission' "), http://www.sp.com.cn/newsp/ggzl/gdgs 04291. htm.

18. *Ibid.*

19. *Ibid.*

Then Premier Zhu Rongji announced five reform projects, one of which was grain circulation. A "Notice on Transferring Property to Central Grain Reserves Warehouses under Central Control" mandated that in 1998, 20 billion kilogram storage capacity warehouses would be transferred to the central grain reserves system (Zhu Rongji also mandated the construction of 50 billion kilogram storage capacity warehouses to be placed under direct central control within the framework of centralized management).[20] In August of that year, local management companies and offices under centralized management by the State Grain Reserves Bureau were established in Beijing, Shanghai, Shenyang, Zhengzhou, Chengdu, Xi'an, Harbin, Wuhan, Changsha and Urumqi.[21]

The Parameters of Centralization: Tiao and Kuai

Chinese administrative units generally distinguish between two types of political relationships: those governed by binding orders, and those based on non-binding instructions. Any political unit in China has the second type of relationship with any number of other units. But it has the first type of relationship with only one, its direct "superior." A relationship based upon such binding orders is referred to as "leadership relations" or *lingdao guanxi* (the other type is based on "professional relations" or *yewu guanxi*). In China's largely decentralized political system, leadership relations are often not with administrative superiors (described by the Chinese as "leadership along a 'line'," or *tiaoshang lingdao*), but *with local governments at the same administrative level* (or "leadership across a 'piece'," *kuaishang lingdao*).[22] In theory, "line" administration ensures that higher-level government decrees are implemented smoothly and uniformly. "Piece-" or *kuai*-based leadership relations help local governments achieve a degree of independence from external influence, enhance sensitivity to local conditions in the policy process, and facilitate co-ordination between functional departments (see Figure 1).

The next section describes the means through which the transformation of a *kuai*-based set of authority relations to one based on centralized management takes place. It is largely through personnel/budgetary allocations (*bianzhi*), cadre recruitment and allocation (*nomenklatura*), and revenue collection.

20. "Zhonghua liangwang" ("China grain net, timeline of major events – 1998"), http://www.cngrain.com/Publish/data/200110/58424.asp.

21. "Jianli wanshan zhongyang chubei liang chuizhi guanli tizhi" ("Establish and improve vertical management in central grain reserves"), http://www.cngrain.com/Publish/data/200105/32176.htm.

22. Kenneth Lieberthal and Michel Oksenberg, *Policy Making in China: Leaders, Structures, and Processes* (Princeton, NJ: Princeton University Press, 1988), pp. 148–49.

Figure 1: **Before and After "Soft Centralization" (the Case of the SAIC/AIC)**

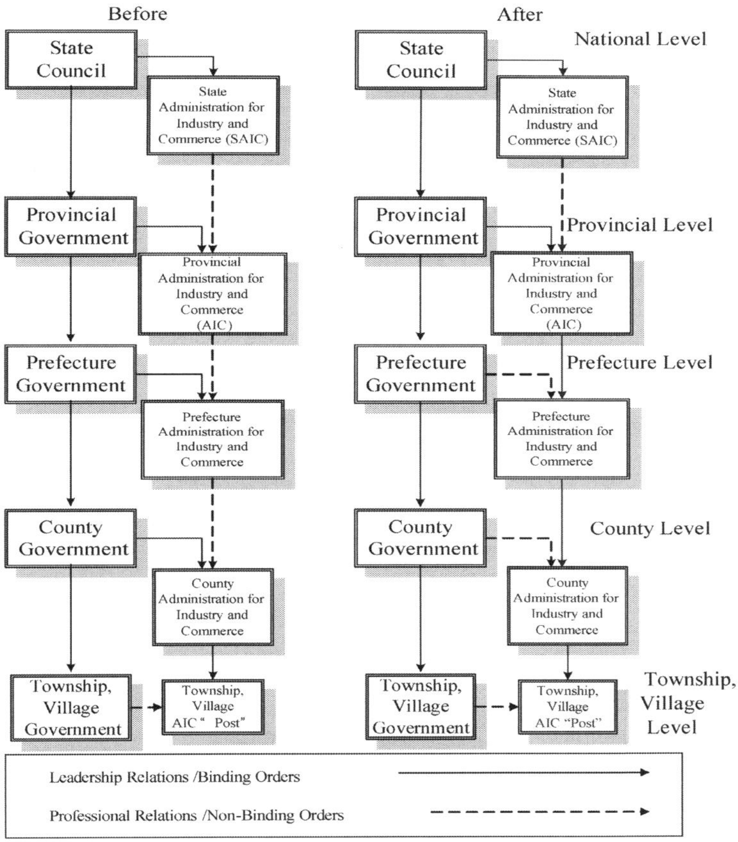

The Mechanics of Soft Centralization: Bianzhi, Nomenklatura and Fee Collection

Soft centralization and bianzhi.[23] Perhaps the most important mechanism of this centralization is the shift in the allocation of *bianzhi*.[24] Authority over the quantity of personnel appointments and budgetary outlays at the national level is held by the Commission on the

23. The most thorough discussion of *bianzhi* can be found in Kjeld Erik Brødsgaard, "Institutional reform and the *bianzhi* system in China," *The China Quarterly,* No. 170 (June 2002), pp. 361–386.

24. Brødsgaard defines *bianzhi* as "the authorized number of personnel (the number of established posts) in a[n] … administrative organ, a service organization or a working unit" (*ibid.* p. 364). I refer to *bianzhi* as the authorized allocation for personnel, and, by extension, basic budgetary revenues. This system in which budgets are grounded in personnel (and not the other way around) is akin to that of the USSR. It is the reverse of conventional bureaucracies, in which personnel numbers are based on budgets.

Composition of Government Organizations (CCGO, *jigou bianzhi weiyuanhui* or *bianwei*). The CCGO is an extremely powerful body because of its ability to allocate the number of personnel, and, by extension, the level of budgetary appropriation to government units throughout the system (although such power is far from absolute, as local offices have ways of exceeding their *bianzhi* numbers – *chaobian* – and they also bargain and lobby extensively with the *bianwei*). The number is centrally mandated. However, the provincial-level CCGO has the power to distribute this aggregate figure as it wishes among the various government offices within the provincial level. The number of personnel allocated to each unit is an indication of the unit's importance in the eyes of the provincial CCGO. For decentralized bureaucracies, this procedure is repeated, with some variation, all the way down to the county (there is no CCGO below the county level).[25]

Soft centralization takes these decision-making responsibilities away from the CCGO below the provincial level and transfers them to *within* the provincial-level functional bureaucracy in question. For example, the personnel and budgetary flows within the recently centralized Quality Technical Supervision bureaucracy are as follows. The provincial *bianwei* gives the lump-sum *bianzhi* figure to the provincial QTSB and the money is released from the provincial Finance Bureau. The provincial QTSB then slices up this aggregate figure in a manner that it sees fit (with consultations with lower-level QTSBs). The provincial QTSB still depends on the provincial government, which sets the constraints for the overall size of the QTSB *xitong* within each province (*bianzhi* allocations from the provincial QTSB to the sub-provincial QTSB are based upon the level of economic development, population size, degree of technical development and so on). These estimates are made in conjunction with the budget estimates by the sub-provincial offices. The county QTSB gives its estimate to the prefecture-level QTSB which reviews it and sends it on to the provincial QTSB. The provincial QSTB makes its decision and then gives the money to the prefecture-level QTSB for its own use, while the prefecture-level QTSB remits the money earmarked for the county QTSB to the latter.[26] It is important to note that under soft centralization, at the provincial level, the QTSB has decentralized leadership relations with the provincial government, so the latter effectively, albeit indirectly, controls the aggregate *bianzhi* for the entire QTSB bureaucracy at and below the provincial level.

Soft centralization and nomenklatura. Also significant is the shift in the allocation of *nomenklatura* appointments within these newly centralized bureaucracies.[27] Broadly speaking, *nomenklatura* appointments of the

25. At the township and village levels, personnel allocations (but not the lump-sum figure, which is decided upon by the county CCGO) are determined by the township and village governments. This number is generally very small, and there are no specialized village- or township-level CCGO (Interview 99CD06, 1 July 1999).

26. Interview 03GY01, 19 July 2003.

27. For a discussion on the distinction between *bianzhi* and *nomenklatura*, see Brødsgaard, "Institutional reform," pp. 363–66.

highest-ranking cadres in any political unit (from a ministry all the way down to a state enterprise at the county level and below) are controlled by the Chinese Communist Party (CCP), primarily, although not exclusively, by the CCP Organization Department. Different organs at the same administrative level might have a different number of positions on the CCP's *nomenklatura* list, depending on the CCP's interest in controlling the unit in question.[28] There have been changes in the cadre appointment system in the past. In the mid-1980s, for example, the system was decentralized to some degree through the introduction of the "one-level down" appointment mechanism and by the shift of central-level appointment authority from the Central Committee to the "Party core groups" (*dangzu*) within a particular ministry.[29]

Centralization adds to this shift in *nomenklatura* appointments. Under the *kuai* system, leading cadres were generally chosen by the Organization Department office at the corresponding administrative level (that is, the leading cadres at the county-level Bureau X would be chosen by the CCP Organization Department at the county level).[30] Since centralization, leading cadres at the sub-provincial level (the director and the deputy director at the district/county levels) are now chosen by the Party core group at the provincial-level bureau. In other words, the national level of the Communist Party still retains the monopoly on appointing leading government and Party cadres at all levels of the system. However, with centralized management, cadres are chosen by the Party apparatus that is contained *within these bureaucracies*, and not by the "external" local organization departments.[31]

Again, using the QTSB as an example, before centralized management, the Party committee (*dangwei*) at the same administrative level (the county *dangwei* for leadership in the county-level bureau QTSB) would choose the leadership. Under centralized management, the provincial QTSB Party core group evaluates candidates for leadership at the prefecture level and the QTSB Party core group at the prefecture level evaluates the candidates for leadership at the county level. However, the QTSB Party core group at the provincial level must vet the leading cadre (the QTSB director) at the county level (the county-level deputy director is only vetted up to the prefecture level). Moreover, for county-level cadres, the Organization Department of the county-level Party committee participates in this process, and for prefecture-level cadres, the Organization Department of the prefecture-level Party committee participates in this process ("dual leadership"/*shuangchong lingdao*).[32]

28. John Burns, "China's *nomeklatura* system," *Problems of Communism*, Vol. 36 (1986), pp. 36–51.

29. Kenneth Lieberthal, *Governing China: From Revolution through Reform* (2nd ed.) (New York: Norton), pp. 234–36.

30. Local-level organization departments had non-binding, professional (*yewu*) relations with their administrative superiors and had binding, leadership (*lingdao*) relations with the Party committee at the same administrative level. Burns, "China's *nomenklatura* system," p. 41.

31. Interview 02CQ02, 10 July 2002; and interview 02GY02, 24 July 2002.

32. Interview 03GY01, 19 July 2003.

Soft centralization and remittances. Standardization of fee collection is an important goal of centralization. Along this dimension, the General Administration of Customs is the model: 20 per cent of the national budget is derived from customs remittances. Although officials have glossed over the fact that customs remains one of the more corrupt bureaucracies at the local level, the political logic here is that a centralized customs bureaucracy brings in a substantial amount of revenue.[33]

Under a decentralized system, a local unit receives its minimal base budget through its *bianzhi* allocations, decided upon by the local government. It can appeal for additional funds both to the local government (through the finance bureau at the same administrative level) and to the unit's functional superior at the next level up the administrative hierarchy. In addition, with regard to fines, fees and other extra-budgetary revenues, these units can either keep them "in house" (*zishou zizhi*) or make arrangements with the local finance bureau to gain access to them when necessary.[34]

This new system is called "two distinct avenues of fee collection" (*shouzhi liangtiao xian*).[35] In the past, fines were collected by the local administrative enforcement agencies which then were *supposed* to transfer them to the finance bureau at the same administrative level (but often did not). In the current system, the administrative enforcement agency is not even supposed to *see* the money. Instead, it issues a notice that sets a date by which the remitter must make payment. The fee remitter goes to the bank and remits the payment to a special account that is in the name of the enforcement agency but is actually managed and controlled by the finance bureau at the same administrative level. The bank issues a receipt to the fee remitter who then presents it to the original administrative enforcement agency to show that payment has been made (see Figure 2). If the offending party does not pay, the matter is referred to the administrative agency's enforcement arm, the investigation team (*jicha dui*).[36]

There are problems with this new rubric. Because of disincentives and because there is no exogenous control mechanism, there is nothing to prevent administrative enforcement agencies from demanding an on-the-spot cash payout instead of issuing a notice to the offender under *shouzhi liangtiao xian*. Complicating the notion of local governmental non-interference with centrally managed units is local governments' physical proximity to the units no longer officially directly under their control. Transaction costs are often lower when entering into arrangements with a unit's own county government than with that unit's administrative

33. Interview 03BJ03, 9 March 2003.

34. Interview 02GZ01 (telephone interview with Guangzhou source from Guiyang), 25 July 2002.

35. It should be noted that this system of *shouzhi liangtiao xian*, while facilitating vertical management (in theory at least), is nevertheless an independent policy. That is to say, bureaucratic units that operate under *shouzhi liangtiao xian* need not be vertically-managed units. I thank Dali Yang for this observation.

36. Interview 02SH12, 5 July 2002; interview 02SH13, 5 July 2002; interview 02GY02, 24 July 2002; and interview 02GY03A, 25 July 2002.

Figure 2: ***Zishou Zizhi* versus *Shouzhi Liangtiao Xian* (Provincial and Prefecture Levels)**

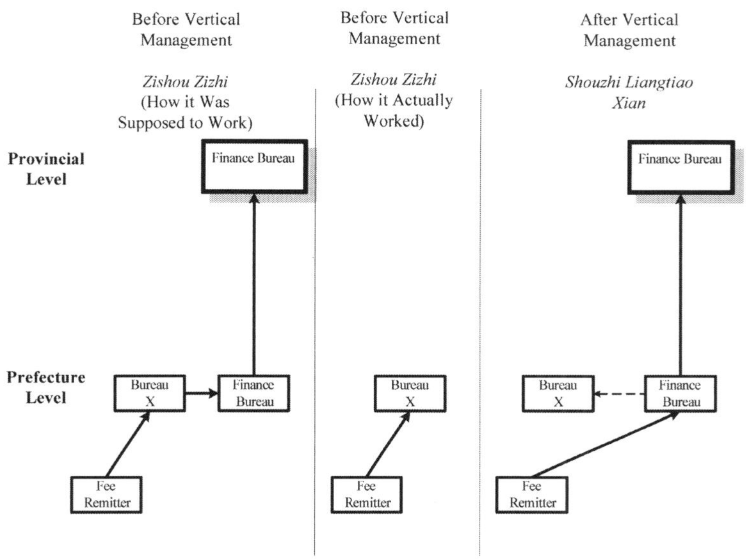

superior at the municipal or provincial level. Moreover, extra-budgetary revenues can, and are, provided by the local government, which can use them to buy back some degree of the influence it has lost under centralization.

Outcomes and Unintended Consequences

Empowering the provinces. One important question is who has gained as a result of centralized management? One set of winners are those provincial-level bureaus of the "softly" centralized bureaucracies. These officials have witnessed a dramatic increase in their leverage vis-à-vis their administrative subordinates within their own *xitong*, particularly through their ability to control personnel and budgetary flows. *Bianzhi* becomes the responsibility of the newly centralized bureaucracy – and not the local government – from the provincial level down. This represents a potentially significant loss of leverage on the part of local governments over these bureaucracies, as the local governments can no longer directly control personnel, budgetary and other related arrangements.

Provincial governments (the generalists within the provincial government offices) are arguably even larger beneficiaries of these reforms. Because bureaucracies under soft centralization are decentralized at the provincial level, all the newly centralized bureaucracies continue to be under the direct authority of the provincial government. Of course, even under decentralization, provincial-level governments can influence prefecture- and county-level governments. One difference is that then the "implementation biases" by sub-provincial governments can go in myriad directions and take many different forms. If a provincial-level government enforces a decision through a softly centralized bureaucracy, it still encounters an *organizational* bias as the policy decision passes through that bureaucracy to be implemented, but such an outcome is theoretically far easier to anticipate (and thus pre-empt) than would be the case with the multidimensional biases of sub-provincial governments under decentralized leadership relations.

It should also be noted that across the bureaucracies analysed in this article, centralization follows slightly different trajectories and is based on various blueprints (or experiments), and the province is not always the clear winner (as in the case of the PBOC and some aspects of the centralization of grain management). Put differently, some centralized bureaucracies are more firmly under the control of provincial-level authorities than others. Specifically, the regulatory bureaucracies remain more tightly under provincial control than those for financial services and commodities. Moreover, even within the latter two cases, some provinces seem to be doing better than others, given their location as regional "hubs" (in both the cases of the PBOC and grain management, Shaanxi, Hubei, Shanghai and Sichuan have benefited relative to other provinces). But in absolute terms provincial-level control of that bureaucracy *within the province* has increased in all these bureaucracies.

As far as the "losers" are concerned, those who have suffered the most appear to be the sub-provincial governments, who lose direct control over these bureaucracies and find it more difficult to manipulate provincial-level directives. One AIC official said that he received orders to "refrain from gloating" over the newly enhanced powers of his bureaucracy, especially when in the presence of lower-level government officials.[37] Moreover, the formal authority relations and procedural parameters between local government organs (people's congresses) and these newly centralized bureaucracies is anything but clear, as argued below.

But insofar as politics can be separated from policy, on the former dimension ("politics"), Beijing is also on the losing end, even if the policy is deemed successful. Although in theory soft centralization reduces considerably the principal-agent and other collective action-related problems by reducing the number of "gatekeeper agents" to the relatively manageable number of 31 provincial-level actors (although this point is itself debatable), the goals of provincial-level authorities are rarely the same as those of their counterparts in Beijing. Centralization may simply transfer local malfeasance and concentrate it at the provincial level.[38]

Of course, the spin that provincial-level authorities place on soft centralization is markedly different from that discussed above. When

37. Interview 99GY03, 14 June 1999.
38. Interview 02GZ01, 25 July 2002.

asked why centralization only extends below the provincial level, these officials claim that soft centralization is a natural compromise in which Beijing can rein in local excesses, but provincial control allows for a degree of sensitivity for local conditions in the implementation of national policy (to avoid the problems of hyper-centralization of the First Five-Year Plan model, 1953–57).[39] However, this upbeat assessment stands in marked contrast to some of the unintended consequences of soft centralization.

Vertical protectionism? In the most general sense, centrally managed units are economic law enforcement agencies, fund management institutions or commodities co-ordination bureaucracies. The directors at the apex – most notably at the provincial level – of the centralized bureaucracies have a tremendous amount of power, specifically (but not exclusively) over cadre appointments and finance. Without supervisory checks and balances from the local governments, corruption from *within* the centralized system is difficult to avoid.[40] Centrally managed units are usually geographically distant from their functional and administrative superiors, and therefore difficult to supervise. In the opinion of one observer, it is easy for centrally managed units to establish "father–son relationships": when the higher level unit discovers a problem, it might be less inclined to be overly strict with its subordinate unit.[41]

Some have argued that although the enforcement of commercial laws is not a new problem, since the institution of centralized management, such as in the Administration for Industry and Commerce, it has actually worsened. Relations with local governments, the former superiors of AIC units in the area, have deteriorated; in some cases, their interests are diametrically opposed. In these cases, the local governments do not provide the support necessary for AIC work.[42]

Moreover, the police, procuratorial organs and judicial departments remain largely decentralized – regulated through spatial/geographic division of territory – and even though they may have the power to supervise centrally managed units physically within their jurisdictions, they usually do not provide serious checks because of their "preoccupation with local concerns."[43] Or, given the concentration of power on leading cadres of centrally managed units at certain administrative levels (the province), there may be a considerable disincentive to supervise or otherwise cross them.[44]

39. Interview 02CD03, 12 July 2002.

40. Ye Xiaoping, " 'Tiao tiao' shei lai jiandu?" ("Who will supervise vertical/*tiao* management?"), http:// www.people.com.cn/GB/channel7/35/20001218/353454.html.

41. *Ibid.*

42. Wu Fan, "Chui guan hou gongshang ban'an de zhang'ai ji duice" ("Handling obstacles and countermeasures after vertical management in industry and commerce"), *Zhongguo gongshang guanli yanjiu* (June 2001), pp. 56–58.

43. *Ibid.*

44. "Cong quanli yihua kan jinrong fubai" ("From influence to corruption in finance"), http://www.hubce. edu.cn/jwc/jwc5/messages/8965.html.

Dubbed by some as virtual "separatist regimes," centralized institutions risk becoming independent entities in themselves. Personnel are no longer exchanged through normal channels with the local governments: personnel in centralized units do not move to local governments, and local governments do not move people to centrally managed systems (except through a breach as a result of a power grab or through unofficial "exchanges of interest").[45] Some county-level officials in Sichuan told me that once a unit becomes centralized, it is expected to move out of the common building complex that houses other (non-centralized) county-level government offices.[46] Perhaps to add insult to injury, sometimes the income of personnel in centrally managed units is not modulated to be commensurate with income and consumption levels of those non-centralized government offices in the same regions, arousing resentment.[47]

Relationship with local people's congresses. Under centralized management, units are not created and managed by, or responsible to, the corresponding local people's congresses. This raises a number of issues. First, centrally managed units are far from immune to corruption, but the people's congresses are powerless to stop them (this is nothing new, but with centralized management an enhanced degree of such a power imbalance is enshrined as policy). Secondly, it creates a procedural glitch in that it is unclear whether or not the work of these centrally managed units is approved or even reported on by the local people's congress in the latter's work reports.[48] More to the point, national and local laws stipulate that local people's congresses have supervision power over the administrative departments within the locality. At the very least, centrally managed units are "blind spots" for the local people's congresses[49]; at most they question the very durability of recent improvements in the people's congress system.[50]

The debate is rife with empirical examples of such "contradictions." In Pinggang town, Jiangcheng district, Yangjiang municipality, Guangdong province, the Number Two Market was prevented from opening (it attempted to do so no less than three times) by the local AIC office. The local people's congress deemed the AIC actions to be in violation of the law, but after more than three years, it has been unable to do anything about it; it has been "blindsided" by the centrally managed AIC.[51] In

45. Zhang Liming, "Zhongguo xingzheng jigou piping" ("Criticism of China's administrative organizations"), http://www.xslx.com/htm/mzfz/gjzz/2002–9–25–10043.htm.

46. Interview 03XJ01/1–6, 17 July 2003.

47. Zhang Liming, "Criticism of China's administrative organizations."

48. Wang Dingqi, "Vertically-managed units should also accept supervision from people's congresses."

49. Shen Luhu, "Renda jiandu wu mangqu."

50. Yin Zhongqin, "Difang renda pingyi: zai hansuo zhong qianjin" ("Local people's congress criticism: advancing the inquiry"), http://www.npcnews.com.cn/gb/paper8/6/class000800001/hwz170514.htm.

51. "Yi fazhi shi guanjian zai yu yange zhifa" ("Act according to the law, strictly enforcing the law"), http://www.yjfazhi.gov.cn/ab3htm.

Henan, law enforcement has become disjointed: it is extremely difficult to enforce the law within the jurisdiction of centrally managed units. Although the local people's congresses have the right to supervise law enforcement, they lack means with regard to centralized units. The results have been pockets in which there is a vacuum in law enforcement.[52]

Lack of local co-ordination. The lack of uniformity, the crisscrossing and intersecting responsibilities and jurisdictions, and the lack of co-ordination that results, have made the emerging system akin to one in which some of the worst parts of localism have been combined with the bureaucratic inefficiencies endemic to planned markets.[53] There are contradictions between the central government policy of centralized management and how it is actually financed at the local level. Because personnel, finance and remittances are all subject to centralized management, financing at the local level for these responsibilities has dried up (and, as noted above, there is an increase in the demand by these local governments for extrabudgetary revenues).[54]

There are several other problems associated with the transition. The first concerns shortfalls in funding. Before the introduction of *shouzhi liangtiao xian*, budgetary allocations came from the finance bureaus, fines and fee collections. Income and expenditure were not separated (*zishou zizhi*). As a result, AIC units competed for cases because of the positive financial incentives in doing so. Now there is no such incentive to engage in proactive and (positively) aggressive behaviour. In addition, this has robbed the AICs in poorer regions of direct control over especially precious resources.[55]

In other cases, the local governments have maintained the upper hand. According to one AIC official, although local AICs are nominally centrally managed, in fact the transformation is only half complete. Some aspects of personnel appointments are still unclear, but the extra personnel necessary for law enforcement work is squarely under the control of local governments, which are reluctant to penalize those commercial operations that provide jobs, money and social stability to

52. Yang Qingshan, "Lun dangqian jiceng zhifa yu jiandu gongzuo cunzai de wenji ji duice" ("Discussion of current problems and countermeasures in local level law enforcement and supervision work"), http://zgrdxw.peopledaily.com.cn/gb/paper8/5/class000800001/hwz165418.htm.

53. "Xiao cheng zhen xingzheng tizhi yingchuangxin" ("Small city and town administrative systems should take the initiative to create something new"), http://www.hnjmw.gov.cn/jmw.nsf/0/FFEA86A8CA9166 B948256A40002F2B59?opendocument.

54. Bu He, Qi Qinghai and Lin Yongcai, "Fangfan he huajie xian xiang caizheng fenqian de duice yu yanjiu" ("Research and countermeasures for preventing and dissolving county and village financial risks"), http://www.wuhai.gov.cn/whsczj/2003dcyj11.htm.

55. Li Yafei, "Gongshang xingzheng chuizhi lingdao tizhi queli hou zhifa lidu he nandu yanjiu" ("Study on law enforcement following the establishment of vertical management in the administration for industry and commerce system"), *Zhongguo gongshang guanli yanjiu* (September 2001), pp. 31–33.

their jurisdictions. He likened this situation to "mixing fresh air with coal gas" (*meiqi chan kongqi*).[56]

The experience of the Shaoxing county QTSB illustrates how even within the context of centralized management, local governments can effectively isolate the QTSB units in their areas and prevent the latter from enforcing the law. In June 2001, the Shaoxing QTSB found a local clothing manufacturer, Buxinsheng, to be making counterfeit shirts and ordered the manufacturer to pay a fine of 31,000 RMB. Buxinsheng sued the QTSB, and the court, which was under the control of the local government, ruled in favour of Buxinsheng, citing that "the facts are not clear, there is insufficient evidence, and that the QTSB Supervision Department went beyond its scope." In December, the Shaoxing Intermediate People's Court struck down the lower court ruling, after the case gained sufficient international interest (the French company Givenchy, an interested party, made its displeasure known to the State Council and to the Zhejiang provincial government). The above success notwithstanding, the lack of certainty that the QTSB can enforce its own mandate without being taken to court, coupled with the expenditure of time and other resources spent on the litigation process, undermines the QTSB's ability to do its job, even under the structure of centralized management.[57]

There are two other ways in which local governments have resisted centralized management. The first concerns how they view these former subordinate agencies. Often, their thinking is along the lines of "these are no longer 'my people,' so I do not have to take such good care of them in the future," according to one QTSB official.[58] Secondly, there is an "eating in separate kitchens" (*fenzao chifan*) situation with regard to the flow of budgetary revenues. Before centralized management, the local (municipal or county) finance bureaus would send money up to the provincial-level Finance Bureau and then receive their allotment from the provincial Finance Bureau. The latter would transfer funds to the provincial-level QSTB and the city or county finance bureaus would transfer funds to the city- or county-level QTSB. However, what can – and does – happen is that in the "after centralized management" environment, the sub-provincial government might push the finance bureau at the same administrative level to remit less than it should to the provincial Finance Bureau.[59]

The case of the Pharmaceutical Supervision Management bureaucracy (PSMB) is even more poignant. Although experiencing many of the same co-ordination problems as the AIC and the QTSB, the PSMB seems to

56. Cheng Gang, "Fushun 'meiqi chan kongqi' shijian zai bao xinwen" ("News on Fushun 'mixing fresh air with coal gas' "), http://stock.163.com/editor/011210/011210_70584.html.
57. Cui Lijin, "Kua guo zhi jia shouduan fanxin, zhifa bumen zaoyu ganga" ("Transnational counterfeiters adopt new methods, law enforcement departments faced embarrassment"), http://www.zj.xinhuanet. com/gazetteer/clj/page/clj_r2002080807.htm.
58. Interview 03GY01, 19 July 2003.
59. *Ibid.* and interview 03CD01, 14 July 2003.

be suffering from an even greater shortage of operating funds, particularly those necessary to establish municipal- and county-level offices. This transformation was also plagued by a sluggish separation of administration and enterprise (*zheng qi fenkai*) as well as a lack of unified standards governing the layout of the new system at the local level. One PSMB official said that while his department had many responsibilities, his office had very little money to accomplish them.[60] Indeed, funding is so problematic that local governments end up finding themselves responsible for some portion of the local PSMB budget[61]: municipal and county governments have been called upon to provide the conditions necessary for the normal operation of local *centrally managed* PSMBs. These include office- and law enforcement-related equipment and guaranteed funding for normal operation of drug supervision work.[62] One lament taken from the minutes of a finance work committee meeting was that "drug supervision personnel have no place to work ... there is inadequate equipment for law enforcement ... no transportation or communication tools and equipment for gathering evidence."[63]

Conclusion: Implications of China's Soft Centralization

The foregoing provides a basic sketch of some of the more opaque but important changes that are taking place in the Chinese government today, and it suggests several implications for the continued evolution of the Chinese state. The first is that these moves signal the beginning of an important shift in the structure of the reform-era state in terms of managing central–local relations and economic development. If the first 20 years of economic reform in China can be defined by the degree of decentralization that unfolded, we are entering a brand new phase of economic management, regulation and control. It would be overstating the case to say that local governments are being forced to give up the freedoms they have grown to expect. Nevertheless, these adjustments signal a dramatic change by bumping up the locus of management to a smaller number of provincial-level offices for these bureaucracies,

60. Interview 02CD09, 19 July 2002.

61. Zheng Xiaoyu, "Renzhen guanche 'san ge daibiao' zhongyao sixiang, jiakuai tuijin yaopin jiandu guanli tixi gaige" ("Earnestly carry through the important thought of the 'three represents' step up and advance the reform of the pharmaceutical supervision management system – speech by Pharmaceutical Supervision Management Bureau eirector Zheng Xiaoyu"), 29 August 2001, http://www.sda.gov.cn/webportal/portal.po?UID = DWV1_WOUID_URL_4241&TOC = COLUMN_4241&OBJ = 20793.

62. Shao Mingli, "Bawo quanju zashi gongzuo nuli wancheng jinnian de gexiang gongzuo renwu" ("With all bureaus plunge into and carry out hard work and complete this year's tasks – speech by Pharmaceutical Supervision Management Bureau deputy director Shao Mingli"), 31 August 2001, http://www.sda.gov.cn/webportal/portal.po?UID = DWV1_WOUID_URL_4241&TOC = COLUMN_4241&OBJ = 20795.

63. "Quanguo yaopin jiandu guanli xitong caiwu gongzuo zuotanhui huiyi jiyao" ("Minutes of the national pharmaceutical supervision management system finance work meeting, 8 April 2001"), http://www.sda.gov.cn/webportal/portal.po?UID = DWV1_WOUID_URL_4241&TOC = COLUMN_4241& OBJ = 20789.

concentrating power at the provincial level and within these discrete bureaucracies, and insulating them from interference (but also from more positive dimensions in their interactions with their former local government hosts). The initial institutional arrangements have been completed; the evolution of the informal networks critical to policy implementation and enforcement around these new institutional arrangements is already beginning.

What is the impact of these changes on the debate on decentralization? The ability of the central government to enact the changes – even if the most direct beneficiaries are the provincial and not the national-level authorities – calls into question the notion of "durability" of market-protecting federalism. That Beijing can recast so dramatically such fundamental authority relationships as those governing personnel, budgets and property rights from a *kuai*-based decentralized system to a *tiao*-based centralized one demonstrates its power and ability to effect significant unilateral change on its economic reform programme and undermines durability claims. This disputes the market-protecting federalism claim that "each government is autonomous within its own sphere of authority."[64] Given that the direct control of these bureaucracies – including those operating within their jurisdiction – is no longer exercised by local governments, it seems that local government powers have certainly been deflated. Moreover, insofar as these bureaucracies are crucial to the management of local economic development and commercial activity, the authority of sub-provincial governments over the economy within their jurisdictions has eroded.

A second implication concerns the centralization of these bureaucracies and the impact this will have on China's evolving legal system. China is unique in that it has both a legal and a separate administrative structure to handle the resolution of disputes. One might assume that this increases the effectiveness of adjudication and enforcement of dispute settlements. The reality is quite different. These two systems are often in conflict with one another as their jurisdictional and economic interests clash. Insofar as the new centralization strengthens these bureaucracies, it makes them even more formidable competitors and can further undermine the smooth transition towards greater legal and judicial power, particularly concerning enforcement. This is especially true with regard to the uncertain authority relationship between centrally managed administrative units and local people's congresses.

Finally, this glimpse into China's administrative centralization is also interesting conceptually because it provides an example of substantial domestic structural change to enable China to meet its

64. Gabriella Montinola, Yingqi Qian and Barry Weingast, "Federalism, Chinese style: the political basis for economic success in China," *World Politics*, Vol. 48, No. 1 (October 1995), pp. 50–81; Steven Lewis, "Marketization and government credibility in Shanghai: federalist and local corporatist explanations," in David Weimer (ed.), *The Political Economy of Property Rights: Institutional Change and Credibility in the Reform of Centrally Planned Economies* (New York: Cambridge University Press, 1997), pp. 259–287.

international commitments, particularly those of the WTO. It is relatively easy to harmonize laws and regulations, particularly in an authoritarian country such as China. It is quite another to undertake such fundamental institutional change in the service of meeting international obligations. As such, the foregoing problems and challenges notwithstanding, China's administrative centralization may be interpreted as demonstrating credible commitment to implementing its WTO obligations. How, or whether, China is actually able to do so will depend on the durability of these more recent institutional changes.

[13]

"Fragmented Authoritarianism 2.0": Political Pluralization in the Chinese Policy Process*

Andrew Mertha

ABSTRACT Traditional analyses of political liberalization in China focus on elections or other facets of democratization. But they cannot account for the fact that although China remains authoritarian, it is nevertheless responsive to the increasingly diverse demands of Chinese society. I argue that the rules of the policy-making process are still captured by the fragmented authoritarianism framework, but that the process has become increasingly pluralized: barriers to entry have been lowered, at least for certain actors (hitherto peripheral officials, non-governmental organizations and the media) identified here as "policy entrepreneurs." With policy change as the variable of interest, I compare three cases of hydropower policy outcomes. I argue that policy entrepreneurs' ability to frame the issue effectively explains variation in hydropower policy outcomes. I then extend these findings to an unlikely policy area, international trade, specifically, the 2001–06 Sino-EU trade talks over child-resistant lighter safety regulations.

In 2007, the Chinese media and blogosphere were abuzz with the story of Chongqing's "nail house" (*dingzi hu* 钉子户). Its occupant, Wu Ping 吴苹, refused to give up rights of return on her property when she was offered what she considered insufficient compensation from developers who wanted to build a luxury apartment complex. Wu and her husband held out for three years until their house, perched on a lone column of land surrounded by the excavation site, was finally demolished in April 2007. Wu's "nail-like" tenacity transformed her into a folk hero for many, displacing tired, officially sanctioned models like Lei Feng 雷锋, whose similarly hardware-evocative "spirit of the screw" (*luosiding jingshen* 螺丝钉精神) – in which people were urged to follow Lei's example of being anonymous, rust-free screws in the great revolutionary machine – seemed

* I would like to thank Sebastian Heilmann, Lianjiang Li, William Lowry, Dorothy Solinger, Patricia Thornton and Fei-Ling Wang for comments on earlier drafts. I am also grateful to Ka Ho Matthew Wong for his first-rate research assistance. All remaining errors are mine. Earlier versions were presented at the American Political Science Association Annual Meeting in Chicago, 1 September 2007 and at the International Studies Association Annual Meeting in New York City, 17 February 2009.

 doi:10.1017/S0305741009990592

996 *The China Quarterly*, 200, December 2009, pp. 995–1012

hopelessly out-of-date. The media coverage suggested a new, unofficial "model citizen": ordinary individuals like Wu Ping who were willing to hold the state accountable in protecting the private property of its citizens.

While the drama of the Chongqing nail house captured the attention of the Chinese public and the world, a quieter but far more systematic and potentially wider-ranging development has also been unfolding: the increasing pluralization of the policy-making process in authoritarian China. That is, otherwise marginalized officials, non-governmental organizations and activists of all stripes have managed to wriggle their way into the policy-making process and even help shape policy outcomes. They have succeeded in part because they have understood and accepted the general rules of the game of policy making under the rubric of "fragmented authoritarianism."[1]

The "fragmented authoritarianism" framework, first proposed in 1988, has remained the most durable heuristic through which to study Chinese politics. It asserts that policy made at the centre becomes increasingly malleable to the parochial organizational and political goals of various vertical agencies and spatial regions charged with enforcing that policy. Outcomes are shaped by the incorporation of interests of the implementation agencies into the policy itself. Fragmented authoritarianism thus explains the policy arena as being governed by incremental change via bureaucratic bargaining.

This article suggests that previously-excluded members of the policy-making process in China – officials only peripherally connected to the policy in question, the media, non-governmental organizations and individual activists – have successfully entered the political process precisely by adopting strategies necessary to work within the structural and procedural constraints of the fragmented authoritarianism framework. The point of entry is through the agency slack that results from the inability of institutions to adapt sufficiently to rapid socio-economic change, the aggressive lobbying of pressure groups or the changing expectations of the citizenry. These spaces are fertile ground for policy change; that is, if the right set of elements is in place.

Policy Entrepreneurs

The most important of these elements are "policy entrepreneurs." John Kingdon defines policy entrepreneurs as "advocates for proposals or for the prominence of an idea" and describes their defining characteristic as "their willingness to invest their resources – time, energy, reputation, and sometimes money – in the hope of a future return … [including] in the form of policies of which they approve."[2] A fragmented political system allows policy entrepreneurs a key resource

1 Kenneth Lieberthal and Michel Oksenberg, *Policy Making in China: Leaders, Structures, and Processes* (Princeton, NJ: Princeton University Press, 1988).

2 John W. Kingdon, *Agendas, Alternatives, and Public Policies*, 2nd ed. (New York: HarperCollins, 1995), pp. 122–23.

necessary to compete in such a way within the policy process: the existence of the "spaces" necessary for them to operate without being snuffed out by the coercive apparatus of the state. Territorial, jurisdictional and other political cleavages provide comparatively fertile ground for various contending interested parties to push their agendas and to arrive at compromises that better reflect their own parochial or institutional goals, which is exactly the method employed by policy entrepreneurs in China. In other words, the political dynamics captured in the fragmented authoritarianism framework provide policy entrepreneurs with a road map, a playbook by which they can pursue their policy goals. They adopt the strategies that traditional actors in China have used for decades to pursue their agendas and institutional mandates.

There are three new types of policy entrepreneurs in China that figure prominently in the analysis to follow. The first are officials within Chinese government agencies opposed to a given policy, often because of official organizational mandates. These officials are able to voice their opposition in part because their policy portfolios give them a degree of political cover (for example, officials in seismological bureaus can articulate the negative geological effects of a hydropower station proposal without fear of reprisal). Conversely, by refraining from pursuing their organizational mandates, these units run the risk of being seen as weak or even irrelevant, a potentially deadly label in the current era of administrative downsizing and bureaucratic fat-cutting.[3]

A second category of policy entrepreneurs, journalists and editors, is emerging in a gradually evolving and expanding liberal media environment. Although it is important to avoid overstating the growing parameters of acceptable discourse in China, newspapers, magazines and television broadcasts have provided a platform for journalists to pursue stories that match their own growing progressive interests and agendas. This in turn has been reinforced by the Chinese media being increasingly required to generate their own budgetary revenue. As a result, they must rely on advertising, which depends upon circulation and readership.[4] Towards this end, there has been a dramatic increase in the proportion of tabloid journalism that, in addition to racy sex stories, cover government injustice, civil protest and the like.

One particularly important node of the media's power is the close relationship the media shares with the third type of policy entrepreneur, individuals within Chinese non-governmental organizations (NGOs). The successes of NGOs in Chinese politics can be partially explained by the fact that a large percentage of their officers and staff members were trained as journalists or editors, giving them especially close access to the media. NGOs are a critical set of actors that define the contours of policy entrepreneurship in China. There are

3 Dali Yang, *Remaking the Chinese Leviathan: Market Transition and the Politics of Governance in China* (Stanford, CA: Stanford University Press, 2004); and *Zhongyang zhengfu zuzhi jigou* (*Central Government Organizations*) (Beijing: Gaige chubanshe, 1998).

4 Daniel C. Lynch, *After the Propaganda State: Media, Politics, and "Thought Work" in Reformed China* (Stanford, CA: Stanford University Press, 1999).

998 *The China Quarterly*, 200, December 2009, pp. 995–1012

somewhere between 300,000 and a million NGOs in China today. Michael Büsgen argues that NGOs in China are different from those which helped bring about regime change in the Soviet Union and Eastern Europe because the former must work *within* the Leninist party state and avoid even the appearance of threatening the structural status quo.[5] The almost seamless interface between the two groups allows Chinese NGOs to play a more significant role in the political process than might otherwise be the case.

Issue Frames

Policy entrepreneurs interpret events using often-existing ideas in new ways with the goal of recruiting potential supporters. This is done through "articulation" and "amplification." By articulating how an issue is described, entrepreneurs link together and assemble events in order to establish a natural and persuasive narrative, offering a fresh, alternative perspective on the issue in question.[6] They pick symbols that can be packaged in such a way as to offer a different point of view by which to understand and appreciate events, objects and situations.[7] In addition to articulating the issue, policy entrepreneurs amplify it by identifying its core components and boiling them down into a portable narrative, which they can shop around to potential supporters. These narratives often depend upon deliberate references to historical antecedents, metaphors, analogies and images.[8]

The concept of framing is important because it suggests a number of dimensions not captured in the current literature on policy making in China. First, it shows a degree of authority within the Chinese media in their ability to report critically on issues that would have been unthinkable a decade or more ago. It also underscores media sophistication in providing stories that are couched in terms that undermine Beijing's ability to maintain its monopoly on spin. Third, it reveals the role of NGO leaders in spearheading this media assault. Fourth, it also demonstrates the intimate contact between the media, government leaders in Beijing, government officials in the localities and activists throughout

5 Michael Büsgen, "NGOs and the search for Chinese civil society: environmental non-governmental organizations in the Nujiang Campaign," Master's thesis, Institute for Social Studies, Graduate School of Development Studies, The Hague, Netherlands, 2005, pp. 2–3.

6 John A. Noakes and Hank Johnson, "Frames of protest: a road map to a perspective," in Johnson and Noakes (eds.), *Frames of Protest: Social Movements and the Framing Perspective* (Lanham, MD: Rowman and Littlefield, 2005), p. 8.

7 *Ibid.* See also William A. Gamson, "Political discourse and collective action," *International Journal of Social Movements, Conflict, and Change*, No. 1 (1988), pp. 219–44.

8 Hanspeter Kriesi and Dominique Wistler, "The impact of social movements on political institutions: a comparison of the introduction of direct legislation in Switzerland and the United States," in Marco Giugni, Doug McAdam and Charles Tilly (eds.), *How Social Movements Matter* (Minneapolis: University of Minnesota Press, 2002), pp. 42–65; Sidney Tarrow, *Power in Movement: Social Movements and Contentious Politics* (New York: Cambridge University Press, 1998); and Elizabeth J. Perry, *Challenging the Mandate of Heaven: Social Protest and State Power in China* (Armonk, NY: M.E. Sharpe, 2001).

the system. Moreover, this has affected the policy-*making* process, not simply the *implementation* of policy already agreed upon in Beijing.

Finally, it provides the foot-in-the-door necessary to "expand the sphere of political conflict," in Schattschneider's classic phrase,[9] by transforming hitherto irrelevant actors not traditionally associated with the policy (but who are now relevant because of the oppositional issue frame cast by the initial policy entrepreneurs) into allies. In the Dujiangyan 都江堰/Yangliuhu 杨柳湖 controversy summarized below, it was only after the issue frame of "economically developing the west" (*xibu da kaifa* 西部大开发) was supplanted by "protect China's cultural heritage" (in this case a 2,000-year-old irrigation project predating the Qin dynasty) that the Cultural Relics Bureau, and by extension, the Ministry of Culture, could legitimately enter the bureaucratic tug-of-war.

In China, "state framing,"[10] which I do not distinguish conceptually from official propaganda, has met with mixed success in the reform era. The age of infallibility of Mao Zedong Thought died out before Mao himself did,[11] and the reform era has been marked by a degree of scepticism about official ideological exhortations. As a result, there is variation in the success of "official" state framing. Some types of framing appear to be quite strong – such as the shift of *falun gong* 法轮功 from a "sporting club" to a somewhat suspicious homegrown spiritual society to its current conception as a poisonous cult[12] – and are backed up by the state's coercive apparatus. Similarly, one is likely to find very little deviation from the government "line" on contentious issues like Taiwan and Tibet. Others, such as the official welcoming of capitalists into the Chinese Communist Party under the larger rubric of "The Three Represents" (*sange daibiao* 三个代表) have drawn scorn from both citizens and, privately, many officials.

But what is central here is the *unofficial* framing that has taken place in China and how it has shaped the policy processes in the past few years. There has been some scholarship on the role of framing in Chinese politics, but it tended to focus on the mass protests of 1989,[13] a set of events that is largely unique and unlikely to be replicated while the current regime remains in power. As such, it is not particularly helpful in allowing us to draw wider generalizations. By contrast, I am looking at how framing by policy entrepreneurs has begun to shape the political debate on all sides of contentious and substantively important issue areas in China today.

9 E.E. Schattschneider, *The Semisovereign People: A Realist's View of Democracy in America* (New York: Holt, Rinehart and Winston, 1960).

10 John A. Noakes, "Official frames in social movement theory: the FBI, HUAC, and the communist threat in Hollywood," in Johnson and Noakes, *Frames of Protest*, pp. 89–111.

11 Frederick C. Teiwes and Warren Sun, *The End of the Maoist Era: Chinese Politics During the Twilight of the Cultural Revolution, 1972-1976* (Armonk, NY: M.E. Sharpe, 2007).

12 David A. Palmer, *Qigong Fever: Body, Science, and Utopia in China* (New York: Columbia University Press, 2007).

13 See, *inter alia*, Zuo Jiping and Robert D. Benford, "Mobilization processes and the 1989 Chinese democracy movement," *Sociological Quarterly*, No. 36 (1995), pp. 131–56.

1000 *The China Quarterly*, 200, December 2009, pp. 995–1012

Differences from the Democratization and Contentious Politics Literature

Others have argued that the Chinese state may be just as fragmented as it was in the 1980s – perhaps even more so – but not as authoritarian as it was a decade ago. However, even though scholars begin from this premise, they tend to ignore the more prosaic dimension of the policy process, focusing instead on scenarios of regime change, state–society relations and electoral mechanisms.

Recent literature on democratization in China tends to focus on one of two dynamic processes: elite-driven change and grassroots efforts. Bruce Gilley ventures that democratization is likely to be elite-initiated in the form of a rational response to a "multiple metastatic dysfunction." But Gilley assumes that elite-level democratization at the national level would necessarily lead to replication of such events at local levels throughout China. Much of the top-down variant of democratization is flawed because democratization imposed on local governments from on high in Beijing is not really democracy at all.[14]

The literature on the mechanisms of democracy in China, particularly those works focusing on township and village elections, does not explicitly provide any guidance to how its conclusions can translate into meaningful policy outcomes. It concentrates on process, and insofar as it looks at outcomes, the focus is on the role of elections in strengthening the Chinese Communist Party. This leaves us with two bookends, each of which fails to capture an important dynamic: the pluralization of the Chinese political process.[15] Other strands of recent scholarship focus on the fact that while state capacity has eroded to the extent that organized protest is increasingly becoming a political reality in China, the state's coercive power remains strong enough to resist the demands of many of these protests, rendering the latter more symbolic than substantive.

The State Security Bureau has released figures, now widely cited, of 58,000 protests in 2003, 74,000 in 2004 and 87,000 in 2005.[16] There has been some scholarly debate over the significance of these data. Some argue that the numbers are relatively trivial when considered relative to China's overall population, or that only a few protests are large-scale organized demonstrations as we might imagine them in the West, leaving the majority quite small and therefore insignificant.[17] Others contend that protesters are hindered by the fragmentation of the workforce, the poor prospects for workers disenfranchised by reform, the strong deterrent measures facing potential protest leaders, and the patterns of strategically dismantling state-owned enterprises to minimize social instability (or, rather, to

14 Bruce Gilley, *China's Democratic Future: How It Will Happen and Where It Will Lead* (New York: Columbia University Press, 2004).

15 Melanie F. Manion, "The electoral connection in the Chinese countryside," *The American Political Science Review*, Vol. 90, No. 4 (1996), pp. 736–48; and M. Kent Jennings, "Political pluralization in the Chinese countryside," *The American Political Science Review*, Vol. 91, No. 2 (1997), pp. 361–72.

16 Joseph Kahn, "Pace and scope of protest in China accelerated in '05," *The New York Times*, 20 January 2006.

17 Pierre F. Landry and Tong Yanqi, "Disputing the authoritarian state in China," paper presented at the annual meeting of the American Political Science Association, Washington, DC, 1 September 2005.

isolate into smaller groups those laid-off workers who would be most likely to lead a protest).[18]

Another group of scholars has focused on the process of the protests themselves and how protesters can come away with something, even if they lose. In their work on "rightful resistance," O'Brien and Li argue:

> Rightful resistance is a form of popular contention that operates near the boundary of authorized channels, employs the rhetoric and commitments of the powerful to curb the exercise of power, hinges on locating and exploiting divisions within the state, and relies on mobilizing support from the wider public. In particular, rightful resistance entails the innovative use of laws, policies, and other officially promoted values to defy disloyal political and economic elites.[19]

In the cases presented here, opponents to state policy are not simply content with *resisting* policies that affect them directly; they seek to *change* the substance of broader policies. Their principal targets are not merely those local officials whose corruption and other malfeasance run counter to legal and other norms. Rather, policy entrepreneurs' focus is on entering in and working within the policy process to achieve their principal policy-related goals.

Before going further, it is worth asking what is making China become less authoritarian. First, the institutions that arose during the pre-reform era have adapted to the issues facing China today only imperfectly. The problems these bureaucracies face are arguably more fast-moving and complex than had been the case under Mao. The 1998 government downsizing, as well as the proliferation of leadership small groups (*lingdao xiaozu* 领导小组) and the erosion of the outer membranes of traditional *xitong* 系统, all attest to this. The state has responded by delegating responsibilities to economic, social and other types of actors (whether NGOs, *shiye danwei* 事业单位, or other non-state or quasi-state hybrids) under the rubric of "small state large society" (*xiao zhengfu da shehui* 小政府大社会).[20] Second, there seems to be a gradual recognition by state actors that as information becomes more accessible in China as a whole, experts who are versed or literate in such information are useful, and the state actors (who do not possess the same skills) therefore seek out such expertise. Finally, there is a reinforcing effect whereby success breeds more success: once policy entrepreneurs are allowed to participate and their efforts contribute to an outcome they deem successful without drawing prohibitive sanctions, they set a precedent and are (cautiously) emboldened. Even the partial success of the Nu River 怒江

18 Cai Yongshun, *State and Laid-Off Workers in Reform China: The Silence and Collective Action of the Retrenched* (London: Routledge, 2005); Ching Kwan Lee, "From the specter of Mao to the spirit of the law: labor insurgency in China," *Theory and Society*, Vol. 31, No. 2 (2002), pp. 189–228; William Hurst and Kevin J. O'Brien, "China's contentious pensioners," *The China Quarterly*, No. 170 (2002), pp. 345–60; and William Hurst, "Understanding contentious collective action by Chinese laid-off workers: the importance of regional political economy," *Studies in Comparative International Development*, Vol. 39, No. 2 (2004), pp. 94–120.

19 Kevin J. O'Brien and Lianjiang Li, *Rightful Resistance in Rural China* (New York: Cambridge University Press, 2006), p. 2.

20 "*Xiao zhengfu da shehui*" *de lilun yu shijian: Hainan zhengshi tizhi yu shehui tizhi gaige yanjiu* (*Theory and Practice of "Small Government, Big Society": The Study of the Reform of Hainan's Governing and Social Systems*) (Beijing: Shehui kexue wenxuan chubanshe, 1998).

1002 The China Quarterly, 200, December 2009, pp. 995–1012

controversy described below almost certainly influenced the process and the initial outcome of the most recent debate over the damming of Tiger Leaping Gorge (*Hutiaoxia* 虎跳峡). Certainly other recent work on protests in China suggests a parallel with the notion of official state institutions or actors that are nevertheless critical allies of the opposition. As Perry and Selden write: "While local officials frequently crack down on popular resistance, in numerous cases their leadership is instrumental in shaping, legitimating and articulating the demands of social movements, and in some cases in networking with state officials on behalf of local interests."[21]

Policy Entrepreneurship and Issue Framing in Hydropower Politics[22]

The Nu River remains one of two undammed rivers in China. It is located in a remote stretch of western Yunnan province that hugs the contours of its border with Myanmar. The stunning beauty of the surrounding Three Parallel Rivers (*San jiang bingliu* 三江并流) region led to its designation on 3 July 2003 as a UNESCO World Heritage site. However, during the negotiations, the Yunnan provincial government had pushed for a clause that states that the "World Heritage" designation only comes into effect at an altitude of 2,000 metres.[23] This curiosity was explained by the nearly simultaneous announcement that a gargantuan hydropower project involving 13 major hydropower stations would be built along the Nu River as well as along other parts of the Three Parallel Rivers area.

Almost as soon as it was announced, opposition began to mount. In the spring of 2003, there was a meeting in the provincial capital Kunming to discuss the Nu River Project (NRP) which was attended by experts from Beijing and Yunnan. Local experts all supported the project, while their national-level counterparts from Qinghua University and the Chinese Academy of the Social Sciences expressed doubts or opposed the project outright. The views of the experts that supported the NRP were carried in the local newspapers; the views of the opponents were not. There was no firm conclusion at the close of the meeting.

At the same time, a television programme, *Newsprobe* (*Xinwen diaocha* 新闻调查), broadcast an exposé that included interviews with Yunnan watershed activist Yu Xiaogang 于晓刚 and local officials in Nujiang prefecture. The interviewers

21 Elizabeth J. Perry and Mark Selden (eds.), *Chinese Society: Change, Conflict, and Resistance*, 2nd ed. (New York: RoutledgeCurzon, 2000), p. 11.

22 The 80 or so interviews for the hydropower section of the article were conducted in Beijing, Sichuan, Yunnan and Guizhou from 2004 to 2007. The 12 interviews on the child-resistant lighter case were conducted in Wenzhou and Beijing in 2006 and 2007 (with follow-up in 2008). Interviews are indicated by code: the first two digits indicate the year, the middle letters indicate the location (Beijing is "BJ," Kunming is "KM" and Wenzhou is "WZ"), and the last two digits indicate the overall interview sequence for a given locale (with A, B, C etc. indicating the number – if more than one – of interviews with a given source).

23 Tashi Tsering, "Policy implications of current dam projects on Drichu, the Upper Yangtze River," http://www.tibetjustice.org/enviro/Harvard_paper_drichu.pdf (accessed 22 December 2008; Interview 06BJ02, 10 March 2006).

asked the local officials some very basic questions about the NRP. The officials betrayed an almost complete ignorance beyond the most general aspects of the project, underscoring the lack of information that was extended to local officials and somewhat undermining the credibility of their unqualified support for the project. Before this, prefecture-level people's congresses and political consultative conference meetings had placed the NRP on the conference agenda. After the *Newsprobe* broadcast the project was dropped from the schedule.[24]

Beijing-based environmental activist Wang Yongchen 汪永晨 learned about the NRP on 16 August 2003. The person who notified Wang asked if she could provide a list of dam experts and other scholars familiar with the Nu River who might be able to pass on information-cum-ammunition to the State Environmental Protection Administration (SEPA) for a forthcoming meeting between SEPA and the National Development and Reform Commission. Wang provided the contact information for Yunnan University professor He Daming 何大明.

In the first week of September, He presented his opposition to the NRP at the "Nu River Valley Hydropower Development and Ecological Environmental Protection Issue Expert Forum" organized by SEPA in Beijing and attended by more than 70 experts. He was the first scholar and the only local expert who opposed the Nu River development. Although He was a single, isolated voice, his opinion quickly caught on and snowballed dramatically, even though the content was characterized as an "internal" discussion.[25]

On 25 October, the NGO Green Earth Volunteers organized a petition in which 62 people from science, culture and arts, journalism, and folk environmental protection fields signed their opposition to the NRP at the "Second Meeting of the China Environment and Culture Promotion Society." This petition was publicized through the media, and elicited widespread public reaction opposing the NRP.

The first local activist to take on a leadership role was Yu Xiaogang through his own NGO, Green Watershed. On 1 October he began his own survey of the Nu River valley. Yu's goal was to obtain an unbiased understanding of the situation and to advise the Yunnan provincial government as a disinterested NGO. But he also had an agenda. Yu had spent much time and energy monitoring the effects of the Manwan 漫湾 Dam along the Lancang River 澜沧江 and anticipated many of the same problems encountered there – an adverse impact on resettled people, landslides and other negative environmental effects – to be present along the NRP. Yu had hoped to meet SEPA officials who had come to survey the Nu River at the same time, but they abruptly revised their itinerary and returned to Kunming.

In November, the venue of the debate shifted to Beijing, specifically in the form of the "Third Meeting of China and the United States Environment

24 Interview 04KM07, 24 August 2004.
25 Interview 04BJ02, 2 August 2004; and Interview 05KM03C, 20 July 2005.

1004 *The China Quarterly*, 200, December 2009, pp. 995–1012

Forum." There were a number of NGOs in attendance. Wang Yongchen's group, Green Earth Volunteers, and some others successfully pushed for a discussion of the Nu River, despite unsuccessful appeals to UNESCO's Beijing office to take action. Debate was heated. The significance of the meeting was that it led to a diffusion of opposition to the NRP throughout China's NGO network.

At around the same time, the "World Rivers and People Opposed to Dams" meeting was held in Thailand. Among the participants were Wang Yongchen, representatives of the NGO Friends of Nature, activist and *China Youth Daily* editor Zhang Kejia 张可佳, and Yu Xiaogang. At this meeting, NGOs from over 60 countries signed a document in the name of the meeting calling for protection of the Nu River and sent it to UNESCO. UNESCO replied by stating that it was paying close attention to the NRP. Over 80 NGOs in Thailand also sent a letter to China's Ambassador in Thailand on the Nu River issue. Meanwhile, the NRP debate was percolating up to the national level.

The National Environmental Impact Assessment Law came into force on 1 December 2003. Significantly, it did not have a "grandfather" clause. In August 2003, barely a month after the Three Rivers region was declared a World Heritage site and just at the time that Wang Yongchen found out about the NRP, the National Development and Reform Commission convened a meeting to examine the "Nu River Middle and Lower Reaches Hydraulic Planning Report." It was approved in two days. Bolstered by this momentum, the Huadian Group 中国华电集团公司, the state-run company responsible for the NRP, rushed to get its proposal approved by the State Council before the Environmental Impact Assessment Law came into effect, thus freeing them of the constraints of the law. The proposal itself contained no provisions on the impact of the NRP on the environment.

The bare-bones proposal, combined with the speed at which Huadian sought to push it through the State Council approval process, raised the suspicions of some, especially at SEPA. Mou Guangfeng 牟广丰, the vice-director of the Environmental Impact Assessment Office and director of SEPA's Supervision Department, in particular, was troubled by this. Mou, described by *Southern Weekend* (*Nanfang zhoumou* 南方周末) as "a lone voice in the wilderness," sought the assistance of Wang Yongchen.[26] According to the report, Wang recalled later that she encouraged the SEPA official, who was feeling isolated and powerless by saying: "SEPA must stand firm and never give up."

Mou suggested mobilizing experts on the Nu River to help mount a campaign. Through a massive effort by groups such as Green Earth Volunteers and the Yunnan-based Green Watershed, scholars, experts, citizens, and sections of the media rallied to the Nu River cause. For example, Shen Xiaohui 沈孝辉, a senior researcher at the State Forestry Bureau, succeeded in submitting a petition letter to the National People's Congress and the Chinese People's Political Consultative

26 Interview 05BJ02, 4 July 2005.

Conference with the help of Liang Congjie 梁从诫, a CPPCC member and founder of the Beijing-based Friends of Nature group.[27]

Mou's opposition – on top of a broad base of support from the media, NGOs and (privately) some local officials – was able to halt Huadian's momentum, and delayed the process indefinitely, certainly beyond the critical date of 1 December.[28] It also helped motivate others to signal their disapproval of the project, and these concerns made it all the way up to the desk of Premier Wen Jiabao 温家宝.

On 18 February 2004, Wen stated that "such a large hydropower station project that draws high social attention, and has environmental controversy, should be cautiously studied, and scientifically decided."[29] This effectively suspended the NRP. On 9 April 2004, Wen's decision was carried by *The New York Times*.[30] Over the course of the next three years, the Nu River issue would be hotly debated at all levels of government and in multiple policy circles. Although at the time of writing the outcome remains uncertain, there are clear indications that whatever policy is eventually adopted in the Nu River case, the policy entrepreneurship analysed above will have played a major role.

The Nu River Case in a Broader Context: Variation in Policy Outcomes

In order to put the Nu River case into proper context, it is useful to discuss two other instances in which the outcomes were markedly different, even though they took place at roughly the same time and in the same general area of China's south-west. In August 2003, the Sichuan provincial government cancelled the Yangliuhu hydropower project as a result of opposition from a group of policy entrepreneurs. The opposition was able to transform successfully the government's claim that a dam at the site of the 2,000-year-old Dujiangyan Irrigation Project would help bring electricity and much-needed economic development to the interior. This issue frame was supplanted by the notion that the project would destroy one of China's most important cultural heritage icons. Local officials were able to mobilize activists within the media, including such official state-run publications as *China Youth Daily*, to publicize the issue newly framed in terms of China's lost cultural heritage. The story grew as almost 200 media

27 Deng Jie, "Environmental protection's new power is growing," *Southern Weekend* (cited in *Three Gorges Probe*), 27 December 2005.

28 It is rumoured that a secretary to Premier Wen Jiabao has close connections to "somebody in the environmental community" and this has made it easier to get such issues on the table at the State Council (Interview 04BJ03, 3 August 2004).

29 Cao Haidong, "Nujiang de minjian baowei zhan" ("The NGO battle over protection of the Nu River"), *Jingji* (*Economics*) May 2004.

30 Jim Yardley, "China's Premier orders halt to a dam project threatening a lost Eden," *The New York Times*, 9 April 2004.

1006 The China Quarterly, 200, December 2009, pp. 995–1012

outlets descended on Dujiangyan, and the widespread public outcry was instrumental in halting the project.[31]

The third case, Pubugou 瀑布沟, stands in sharp contrast to the other two. Unhappiness with the proposed Pubugou hydropower dam project in Hanyuan county 汉源县 – particularly with the terms of financial compensation to the resettlers – began in 2001 but erupted in protest four years later when between 50,000 and 100,000 local residents occupied the dam site. Ultimately the outcome was only to delay the beginning of the construction of the dam by a year, and the protests were followed by an almost complete news blackout and police crackdown. Opponents were unable to provide an alternative issue frame to that of developing the western part of China, while the government was able to inject its own revised issue frame of the need to maintain social stability. Any remaining opposition was quickly silenced.[32]

The outcome of these three cases is summarized in Table 1. Variation across the two upper cells depends on the dominance of the issue frame in question. In the case of Yangliuhu (the upper-left cell) the oppositional issue frame achieved an almost insurmountable dominance. That is, opposition framed in terms of cultural heritage issues was extremely effective in grabbing the attention of a large audience, transcending other circumstances that might otherwise mitigate the frame's effect.

In the Nu River case (the upper-right cell) policy entrepreneurship was extremely high, but on both sides of the issue. Thus, the oppositional frame of environmental protection never achieved the degree of salience that the cultural heritage frame evoked at Dujiangyan did. As a result, an otherwise "objective" scientific debate over the effects of economic development on the environment quickly became politicized. In such an environment, oppositional issue frames competed with one another rather than privileging any particular side.

The bottom-right cell illustrates the outcome when neither policy entrepreneurship nor oppositional issue frame dominance was present. Although Hanyuan residents were originally approached by journalists and their issues taken on by some local officials, their claims to be relocated became toxic once they erupted into open protest. Opposition framed around compensation seemed to have forced local government agencies to dig in their heels.[33]

The fact that these events took place at roughly the same time, in the same region and focused on the same policy areas makes possible a structured comparison across the three cases. Arguably there is a high degree of internal validity.

31 Andrew Mertha, *China's Water Warriors: Citizen Action and Policy Change* (Ithaca, NY: Cornell University Press, 2008), ch. 3.

32 *Ibid.* ch. 4.

33 Given my contention that policy entrepreneurs are a necessary condition for oppositional issue frames to emerge, the outcome in the lower left-hand cell is at odds with my above argument. That is, framing does not simply arise out of nowhere. Nevertheless, one could argue that because of the political climate in the late 1980s and early 1990s – a time when I would argue that political pluralization of the type I describe here simply did not exist – domestically and particularly internationally, oppositional issue frames against the Three Gorges Dam achieved some degree of dominance through media reports and discourse.

Table 1: **Outcomes of Three Hydropower Cases**

		Dominance of oppositional issue frame	
		High	Low
Policy entrepreneurship	High	*Yangliuhu* (complete victory of the anti-hydropower forces)	*The Nu River* (partial victory of the anti-hydropower forces)
	Low	—	*Pubugou* (complete failure of the anti-hydropower forces)

However, such a research design is poorly suited to support larger, more generalizable claims. That is, we can only speculate about the degree to which these cases are illustrative of the policy process in areas outside that of hydropower. The next section addresses this shortcoming.

Extending the Argument to Other Policy Areas

In order to achieve greater leverage with a limited amount of data, I employ the use of a critical or "crucial" case.[34] That is, if it can be demonstrated that the phenomenon described above can be found in a policy area where there is a decreased likelihood that it will arise, we can make some tentative generalizations about the argument with a bit more confidence. One arena where policy entrepreneurs might be expected to have little, if any, effect is international trade. International trade is, by definition, foreign policy, and as such it should be relatively immune to tinkering and undue influence by any single individual, particularly if that individual falls outside the formal government apparatus.

In contrast to hydropower, which can be said to encompass important symbolic and substantive arguments on all sides (that is, hydropower itself is an important issue, but so are those embraced by the opposition: cultural heritage, biodiversity, human ecology), the case below is one where policy entrepreneurs representing a tiny industry (cigarette lighters) that was not in any way favoured by the authorities in Beijing were able to leverage the entire trade policy agenda in favour of the arcane issue of child safety regulations. As a further difference, the policy entrepreneur in the case, Huang Fajing 黄发静, was motivated by economic self-interest and not by a larger activist movement.

These two distinct policy areas – hydropower and international trade – suggest that it is the political context in China and not the attributes of a certain policy area that make policy entrepreneur-led change possible. They also suggest a greater likelihood of the transportability of these changing processes to other, unrelated policy areas.

34 Arendt Lijphart, "Comparative politics and the comparative method," *The American Political Science Review*, No. 65 (1971), pp. 682–93.

1008 The China Quarterly, 200, December 2009, pp. 995–1012

International Trade and Child Safety Regulations

Factories in Wenzhou municipality began producing lighters in the late 1980s. In 1991, Huang Fajing established the Rifeng Corporation 温州市日丰打火机有限公司. Far from cornering the market, Huang faced an environment of intense competition. In 1993, Wenzhou boasted 2,000 lighter manufacturers (assembling from parts made by local companies) and lighter component factories. These companies were largely family operations run from people's homes. The family patriarch was usually the boss, and the employees included brothers, sisters and cousins. The average size of these operations was between four and five people (the shift from cottage industries to factories began in earnest in 1994, when technical expertise also began to take off). Because of the inevitable problems of quality control that arose from such an environment of unbridled competition, the Wenzhou government established an office to inspect and evaluate each factory, and if the factory and its products were not up to standard they were denied a licence. This brought the number of lighter and lighter-part factories down to around 300.

At the end of 1992, the Wenzhou Lighter Industry Association (WLIA) was established. This body was able to rein in the collective action problem so that quality grew and Wenzhou could begin developing its own designs for lighters. In addition, the WLIA began a programme to protect industry from unfair competition, under which each association member is compelled to sign an affidavit to accept association rulings when applying for product design rights (de facto patents). The designs are evaluated and published in local newspapers for comment. If nobody opposes the new design within five days, the "patent" is granted. As a result, there is an IPR/patent mechanism *completely within the industry association*. If there is a case of infringement, the association handles it.[35] The WLIA was one of the first associations to do this, but it is now increasingly a common feature of industry associations.

However, in 1994, international developments stretched the WLIA's abilities to protect its members to breaking point. The United States was instituting a standard that required lighters valued at US$2 or less to adopt child-resistant properties. This took the Wenzhou lighter industry, which was still in its infancy, completely by surprise. As a result of the passage of this law, export volume in Wenzhou dropped 70 per cent in one month. Huang resolved that he would not be caught off guard by such exogenous shocks again.[36]

His vigilance was tested in 2001. Huang was advised by the president of the European Lighter Importers Association, Klaus Troeber, that the European Union (EU) was planning to establish a child safety standard. Although this came as a shock to the Chinese manufacturers, these developments had already been going on within the EU for several years. In 1998, four years after the

35 Of course, this has not been without controversy, as the local government offices charged with protecting IPR have cried foul that these industry associations are moving on to their turf.

36 Interview 06WZ06, 11 December 2006.

adoption of the regulations in the United States, the European Commission issued a mandate to the European Standardization Organization to develop a European standard for lighters covering child-resistance (CR) requirements, which were to take into account the US standards. The Chinese saw no meaningful difference in the language between the two sets of regulations except that the proposed EU standards had substituted a €2 threshold instead of the $2 threshold in the US regulations.

The proposed standards were part of the EU–China negotiations over China's World Trade Organization (WTO) accession package.[37] But when Huang sought assistance from Chinese officials he was rebuffed. Appealing to the Economics and Trade Commission and the Quality Examination Supervision and Quarantine Bureau at the (Wenzhou) municipal and national levels, the response was the same: lighters were simply not a strategically important part of China's economic trajectory.

Faced with this situation, Huang took matters into his own hands by putting together a conference on the topic of child safety regulations. He personally invited 17 lighter factory owners plus local and national media. By paying for the event himself, he was able to go beyond official government talking points. The meeting was entitled the "Wenzhou Study Meeting of Common Interests to Resist the Proposed EU CR law" (*Wenzhou yanjiu tongren dizhi Oumeng CR fa'an yantaohui* 温州研究同仁抵制欧盟 CR 法案研讨会). The title was a clever device that evoked two long-running political, mutually-reinforcing themes. First, the phrase "*dizhi*" invokes the boycotting of Japanese goods (*dizhi Rihuo* 抵制日货). By injecting this phrase, Huang was better able to animate this issue in the eyes of his audience. In addition, and perhaps less directly, he was able to evoke the national meta-narrative of China's "century of humiliation" (*bainian guochi* 百年国耻),[38] inspired by an outside power yet again trying to prevent China from benefiting from, and thus being able to take its rightful place within, the global free trading system. Huang reframed the issue from a dry technical dispute to another, contemporary chapter of the long history of China being disadvantaged by the West. At the time, "WTO fever" was running high in China and any story on the WTO seemed to find a media outlet. This story in particular – that is, "the EU is violating its own WTO rules" – was irresistible to the media, which made up a large part of the conference participants and dutifully reported on the issue.

In the months that followed, Huang Fajing wrote a number of reports for various Chinese media sources which were widely distributed. Some even reached internal government news sources, the *neibu cankao ziliao* 内部参考资料. Indeed, when asked about this issue during the annual Bo'an Forum, then Premier Zhu Rongji stated that he was already aware of it.[39]

37 *Ibid.*
38 Peter Hays Gries, *China's New Nationalism: Pride, Politics, and Diplomacy* (Berkeley: University of California Press, 2004).
39 Interview 07WZ04, 8 August 2007.

1010 *The China Quarterly*, 200, December 2009, pp. 995–1012

At the same time, the serendipity of shared interests was being forged. The Fair Trade Bureau (*Jinchukou gongping maoyi ju* 进出口公平贸易局) (FTB) of the Ministry of Commerce was established in November 2001, immediately after China's accession to the WTO. The charge of the FTB is to remedy trade barriers, including specifically responding to and initiating anti-dumping procedures. There is a "trade barriers division," *maoyi bilei diaocha chu* 贸易壁垒调查处 – although "trade" has since been dropped from the title to expand its scope to include investment – which handles foreign trade barriers, as distinct from "foreign allegations of Chinese trade barriers." The latter are handled by various government bureaus, depending on the nature of the actual allegations, with most handled somewhere else within the Ministry of Commerce.

The CR lighter case reached the FTB in January 2002, before the bureau had been fully established. Indeed, between November 2001 and January 2002, the FTB's primary focus was the administrative issues necessary to set up the office, centred on informing others that it actually existed.

In addition to Huang's guerilla-like efforts, the CR issue was also percolating up through another channel: vice-premier and former trade negotiator Wu Yi 吴仪 was on a fact-finding trip that took her to several cities in Zhejiang province. While in Wenzhou, she met members of the local lighter association who informed her about their situation. Immediately thereafter, several top-ranking officials of the FTB went to Wenzhou. Since the FTB was fishing around for a case to begin its work, it embraced the CR issue and began collecting detailed information about the case.[40]

Things on the European side were moving apace. The voluntary standard (EN 13869) was adopted in 2002,[41] but this was regarded as suboptimal by many in the EU. This provided an opportunity for the Chinese side to try to influence the decision to move it closer to Beijing's ideal point. In the spring of 2002, another delegation led by the deputy director-general of the FTB (and including Huang Fajing) went to Europe to discuss the issue with the EU authorities.[42]

On 21 March 2003, an official body was established, which eventually became known as the *Zhongguo zhengfu lianhe daibiaotuan* (中国政府联合代表团), including four people from government (from the FTB) and three from industry, including Huang Fajing. The group embarked on a tour of six EU countries. These efforts were reported in the European media, including the local Chinese media in Europe. In China the impact was even greater. "Almost everybody in

40 Interview 07BJ02, 13 August 2007; and Interview 06WZ06, 11 December 2006.

41 In the EU, lighters are subject to the general safety requirement of the General Product Safety Directive 2001/95/EC (GPSD). However, this Directive does not include specific criteria for lighters (or any other products). In order to assist businesses and national market surveillance authorities, the GPSD allows for the referencing of European standards in the Official Journal of the EU, thereby conferring presumption of conformity with the GPSD for those products complying with such standards. For lighters, the EN ISO 9994 standard is referenced but this standard only includes general safety specifications for lighters and does not set out CR requirements. With the adoption of EN 13869 by CEN in 2002, such CR requirements were in place but the standard was not applied by industry, nor was it enforced by the national authorities (which in the EU have the sole responsibility to undertake market surveillance).

42 Communication with EU Official, 9 December 2008.

China" was aware of what was going on, according to Huang, who added, "if the people know, so does the government."[43]

In 2004, 2005 and 2006, Beijing sent an ever-growing set of delegations to the EU, visiting an increasing number of countries. These delegations included representatives from the FTB, Wenzhou and Ningbo lighter businesses, European importers of Chinese lighters, representatives from the Wenzhou government, and, of course, Huang Fajing. Over time, the two sides became increasingly sympathetic to the concerns of the other side. Bringing the situation full circle, in late 2006 the Ministry of Commerce sponsored a panel discussion in Wenzhou on lighter child safety standards, with Huang as one of the organizers.[44]

The European Commission was still trying to ameliorate what it saw as an imperfect situation,[45] ultimately proposing that EU member states adopt a specific Commission Decision under Article 13 of the General Product Safety Directive to ban non-CR and novelty lighters.[46] Although the language of the standard includes the €2 threshold, the Decision contains technical parameters to distinguish between lighters in or outside its scope, as EU member states felt that lighter safety should not be linked to the cost of a product. In essence, the €2 standard was rendered toothless. This was seen as a significant victory for the Chinese side because they saw that their concerns had been incorporated into the Decision.[47]

Huang Fajing's role as a policy entrepreneur was absolutely critical to this process. He began as an "interested party" and co-ordinated these activities to get key Chinese officials to go to Europe to discuss these issues, particularly from the Ministry of Commerce's Fair Trade Bureau. He has interacted with the EU Health and Consumer Protection Directorate, the EU CEM, EU member health directorates, and EU manufacturers and producers. Huang himself was honoured as one of China Central Television's "Men of the Year" in 2003,[48] and in late 2007 a feature film was released in China documenting his travails, entitled *Brilliance in Europe* (*Dianliang Ouzhou* 点亮欧洲).[49] Finally, this has also emboldened other Wenzhou-based industries, particularly eyeglass and leather shoe manufacturers, to get involved in EU anti-dumping cases.

43 Interview 07WZ04, 8 August 2007.

44 http://zscq.hn.gov.cn/popbase.asp?id=676, accessed 22 December 2008.

45 A 2002 study on the effectiveness of the initial 1994 US legislation reported a 60% reduction in fires, injuries and deaths caused by children under five as a result of the enforcement of CR requirements for lighters alone. An average of 100 lives had been saved in the US every year since 1995 because of the introduction of CR requirements.

46 This Decision (2006/502/EC) is temporary, valid for one year and has to be renewed annually. These temporary Decisions are still in place and the Commission has given a second mandate to CEN to revise EN 13869, with the aim of publishing its reference in the Official Journal and subsequently stopping extending the Decisions, which are not intended as a permanent measure. The revision of EN 13869 aims, amongst other things, to bring the definition of lighters covered by its scope in line with that of the Decision.

47 Communication with EU Official, 9 December 2008.

48 http://www.88088.com/wzpp/sjmr/2008/0909/328927.shtml, accessed 22 December 2008.

49 http://www.mtime.com/movie/76184/plots.html, accessed 22 December 2008. The film is based in part on Huang Fajing's story, but there has been some artistic licence to incorporate a love story and other fictionalized events.

1012 *The China Quarterly*, 200, December 2009, pp. 995–1012

Conclusion

As the above cases suggest, an increasing number of non-traditional – and increasingly non-state – policy entrepreneurs have been able to enter and significantly shape the policy process in China. Political fragmentation provides fissures in which one of the most important aspects of power – information – is jealously guarded. Such an environment decreases the amount of information available, thus increasing its value. Previously unavailable information has a much greater impact than it might in a situation in which it was freely available all along. The leaking of information by local agencies to journalists, combined with journalists' own instincts (and increasingly, mandate) for information-gathering, takes on a significant degree of political importance.

Second, as Lieberthal asserts, is "the encouragement given to many organs to become increasingly self-supporting through bureaucratic entrepreneurship," a dynamic that has also "strengthened the tendency of bureaucratic units to work vigorously to promote and protect their own interests in the policy-making process."[50] The behaviour of the Fair Trade Bureau in the lighter case and the State Environmental Protection Administration are particularly illuminating examples of this.

Although we should be modest in what we expect as far as political liberalization is concerned, an absolutely critical component of politics – the barriers to entry into the political process – arguably separates liberal political regimes from illiberal ones, and these barriers have been demonstrably lowered in China as these cases suggest. One may object to this conceptualization of policy entrepreneurs as overly strategic, but all that the characterization really means is that these individuals have learned how to prevail – or at least compete – in the rough-and-tumble world of Chinese politics without losing their normative and often strongly held personal policy goals.

In a sense, this means that the pluralization of the policy process in China provides both less and more influence on policy than would certain forms of democratization. On the one hand, meaningful elections, the mechanism on which many definitions of democracy depend, do not exist in China (village and township elections notwithstanding). On the other hand, the role of the opponents in these policy debates is as direct and firmly embedded within the political process as is the case in many democratic regimes. Of course, one must be careful in taking this implication too far; rather, the more appropriate claim here is that while the fragmented authoritarianism framework continues to define the major contours of the policy-making process in China, the playing field is becoming increasingly crowded.

50 Kenneth G. Lieberthal, "Introduction: the 'fragmented authoritarianism' model and its limitations," in Lieberthal and David M. Lampton (eds.), *Bureaucracy, Politics, and Decision Making in Post-Mao China* (Berkeley: University of California Press, 1992), p. 9.

Part IV
The Nature of the Local State

[14]

FISCAL REFORM AND THE ECONOMIC FOUNDATIONS OF LOCAL STATE CORPORATISM IN CHINA

By JEAN C. OI*

WHILE clearly lagging behind the Eastern bloc countries and the former Soviet Union in political reform, China is arguably the most successful of the socialist states in implementing economic reform. Real GNP grew at an average annual rate of 10.4 percent from 1980 to 1988 compared with only 6.4 percent during 1965–80; total GNP grew more than twofold between 1978 and 1988. During 1978–88 per capita GNP doubled in real terms.[1] The most impressive strides were in the rural economy. Calculated on the basis of comparable prices, total agricultural output value increased by an average annual rate of 6.04 percent between 1978 and 1990. Output value of rural collective enterprises increased 26.7 percent for that same twelve-year period. Per capita net income among peasants increased from 133.57 to 629.79 yuan, with an average annual increase of 41.4 yuan, as compared with only a 3.2 yuan increase on average for the previous twenty-eight years.[2]

* An earlier draft of the present paper was presented at the Program in Agrarian Studies, Colloquium Series for the Spring Term 1992, at Yale University, New Haven, February 28, 1992, and at the Meeting of the Public Choice Society, New Orleans, March 20–22, 1992. For their comments on earlier drafts of this paper, I would like to thank the members of these seminars and Houchang Chehabi, Jorge Dominguez, Frances Hagopian, Roderick MacFarquhar, Charles Sabel, James Scott, Kamal Sheel, Kenneth Shepsle, Ashutosh Varshney, Andrew Walder, Barry Weingast, and Jennifer Widner. Research was supported by the Committee on Scholarly Communication with the People's Republic of China and by Harvard University. The National Fellows Program of The Hoover Institution provided support for writing an earlier draft of this paper.

[1] Kang Chen, Gary Jefferson, and Inderjit Singh, "Lessons from China's Economic Reform," *Journal of Comparative Economics* 16 (June 1992).

[2] Zhang Hongyu, "China's Land System Transformation and Adjustment of Agricultural Structure: Reviewing China's Rural Reform and Development since 1978," *Liaowang Overseas Edition* 47 (November 25, 1991), 16–17, translated in *FBIS-CHI-91-241*, December 16, 1991, pp. 52–54. The most impressive growth in agriculture was prior to 1985. For a useful economic overview of the impact of the reforms on agriculture, see Terry Sicular, "China's Agricultural Policy during the Reform Period," in Joint Economic Committee, Congress of the United States, *China's Economic Dilemmas in the 1990s: The Problems of Reforms, Modernization, and Interdependence* (Washington, D.C.: Government Printing Office, 1991), 1:340–64. After 1985 the most dynamic growth was in rural industry.

World Politics 45 (October 1992), 99–126

Far from standing in the way of change, local officials have spearheaded the reform drive. What explains their response to national reform initiatives? Bureaucratic change is a function of whether "net incentive effects upon key officials are positive or negative, and to what degree."[3] In China the necessary incentives were provided by fiscal reform. This article seeks to illuminate how this institutional change caused local officials in a socialist system to pursue rapid rural industrial growth.[4]

North and Weingast have pointed to the importance of secure property rights for economic development.[5] The discussion has been limited to a large extent to market economies, with a focus on individuals as entrepreneurs—those who own and operate the firms within a market economy. The importance of this principle underlies the felt need in formerly socialist countries such as Poland to privatize. There is, however, no inherent reason why only individuals, as distinct from governments, can be entrepreneurs. Similarly, there is no inherent reason why secure property rights will be an effective incentive only if they are assigned to individuals.

Growth will result as long as there are secure property rights for *some* organized unit and sufficient incentives for that unit to pursue growth. The impressive growth of collective rural industrial output between 1978 and 1988 is in large measure a result of local government entrepreneurship. Fiscal reform has assigned local governments property rights over increased income and has created strong incentives for local officials to pursue *local* economic development. In the process local governments have taken on many characteristics of a business corporation, with officials acting as the equivalent of a board of directors.[6] This merger of state and economy characterizes a new institutional development that I label *local state corporatism*.

I want to make clear that "corporatism" as used here differs from its use in previous studies. By local state corporatism I refer to the workings of a *local* government that coordinates economic enterprises in its terri-

[3] Anthony Downs, *Inside Bureaucracy* (Boston: Little, Brown, 1967), 201.

[4] On institutions and the incentives within them that shape economic and political behavior, see James G. March and Johan P. Olsen, *Rediscovering Institutions: The Organizational Basis of Politics* (New York: Free Press, 1989).

[5] Douglass C. North and Barry R. Weingast, "Constitutions and Commitment: The Evolution of Institutions Governing Public Choice in Seventeenth-Century England," *Journal of Economic History* 49 (December 1989).

[6] I present a preliminary version of this argument in Oi, "The Chinese Village, Inc.," in Bruce Reynolds, ed., *Chinese Economic Policy* (New York: Paragon House Press, 1988). Others have drawn a similar analogy between local government and business entities. See, e.g., articles in William Byrd and Lin Qingsong, eds., *China's Rural Industry: Structure, Development, and Reform* (New York: Oxford University Press, 1990).

tory as if it were a diversified business corporation. I am not concerned with the role of the central state in the vertical integration of interests within society as a whole.[7] Whereas the central state set the reform process in motion and provided localities with the incentives and the leeway to develop economically, it is *local* government that has determined the outcome of reform in China. Hence, my designation *local state* corporatism.

Local state corporatism suggests a loosening of central control in a Leninist system, but it does not refer to a process that some have labeled the reemergence of civil society.[8] My argument also contradicts, or at least greatly qualifies, theories of market transition that posit a corrosive effect of markets upon the power of local officials.[9] Local state corporatism is similarly difficult to square with the view that market reform is destroying the cellular, or honeycomb, nature of Chinese rural society and allowing for greater penetration by the central state.[10] On the con-

[7] Schmitter, for example, defines corporatism "as a system of interest representation in which the constituent units are organized into a limited number of singular, compulsory, noncompetitive, hierarchically ordered and functionally differentiated categories, recognized or licensed (if not created) by the state and granted a deliberate representational monopoly within their respective categories in exchange for observing certain controls on their selections of leaders and articulation of demands and supports" (pp. 94–95). See Philippe C. Schmitter, "Still the Century of Corporatism?" reprinted in Fredrick B. Pike and Thomas Strich, eds., *The New Corporatism: Social-Political Structures in the Iberian World* (Notre Dame, Ind.: University of Notre Dame Press, 1974). Joseph Fewsmith uses a version of Schmitter's understanding of corporatism to describe China during the Republican period. See Fewsmith, *Party, State, and Local Elites in Republican China: Merchant Organizations and Politics in Shanghai, 1890–1930* (Honolulu: University of Hawaii Press, 1985). Alfred Stepan provides one of the most useful general treatments of corporatism. See Stepan, *The State and Society: Peru in Comparative Perspective* (Princeton: Princeton University Press, 1978), esp. pt. 1. Stepan uses corporatism to refer to "a particular set of policies and institutional arrangements for structuring interest representation. . . . In return for such prerogatives and monopolies the state claims the right to monitor representational groups by a variety of mechanisms so as to discourage the expression of 'narrow' class-based, conflictual demands. Many . . . have used such corporatist policies for structuring interest representation" (p. 46).

[8] This link is explicit in David Ost's treatment of Solidarity as an example of societal corporatism. See Ost, "Towards a Corporatist Solution in Eastern Europe: The Case of Poland," *Eastern European Politics and Societies* 3 (Winter 1989). A similar link to civil society is pursued in the writings on China, although with many more reservations. See, e.g., Anita Chan, "Revolution or Corporatism? Chinese Workers in Search of a Solution" (Paper presented at the conference Toward the Year 2000: Socioeconomic Trends and Consequences in China, Asia Research Centre, Murdoch University, Western Australia, January 29–31, 1992); Mayfair Yang, "Between State and Society: The Construction of Corporateness in a Chinese Socialist Factory," *Australian Journal of Chinese Affairs* 22 (July 1989); Peter Lee, "The Chinese Industrial State in Historical Perspective: From Totalitarianism to Corporatism," in Brantly Womack, ed., *Contemporary Chinese Politics in Historical Perspective* (Cambridge: Cambridge University Press, 1991); and Margaret Pearson, "The Janus Face of Business Associations in China: Socialist Corporatism in Foreign Enterprises" (Manuscript, Dartmouth College, 1992).

[9] Victor Nee, "A Theory of Market Transition: From Redistribution to Markets in State Socialism," *American Sociological Review* 54 (October 1989).

[10] Vivienne Shue, *The Reach of the State: Sketches of the Chinese Body Politic* (Stanford, Calif.: Stanford University Press, 1988).

trary, this analysis highlights the coexistence of a strong local officialdom and public enterprise with a thriving market economy and a weakened central state.

This paper shows how fiscal reforms have provided incentives for local government officials to pursue economic, especially industrial, development. I limit my discussion to an examination of local government at the county, township, and village levels—the lowest levels of government and those most directly involved in rural industrialization. First, I describe the ways that fiscal reforms changed the rules for the disposition of locally collected revenues. Second, I analyze the interests and incentives that these new rules have created. Third, I show why local governments chose to pursue rural industrialization. Finally, I examine how local governments plan and coordinate economic activity to maximize local interests. In the conclusion I consider some broader implications of local state corporatism for China's political future.

The analysis is based on interviews conducted with rural officials in China and on published Chinese sources. I conducted 222 interviews,[11] the bulk of which were with officials at the county, township, and village levels and with managers of industrial enterprises owned by local government. A smaller number were with officials at the prefectural and provincial levels in Shandong. They include interviews at finance and tax bureaus, banks, material supply bureaus, township industry management bureaus, agriculture bureaus, grain bureaus, science and technology commissions, bureaus for the administration of industry and commerce, commerce bureaus, and economic and planning commissions. I also interviewed county magistrates and county first party secretaries, township and village heads, party secretaries, and accountants, plus officials of organizations such as savings and loan cooperatives, supply and marketing cooperatives, and grain stations, and, finally, private entrepreneurs.

I. The Fiscal Reforms and Rights to Revenue Flows

As part of the effort to reform the economy, the Chinese leadership began instituting fiscal reforms in the early 1980s. The major objectives were to make localities fiscally self-sufficient, to reduce the central state's own fiscal burden, and to provide incentives for local authorities to pro-

[11] The interviews were done in 1986, 1988, 1990, and 1991. I conducted fieldwork in three primary research sites: two counties in Shandong province and one county outside Tianjin. I also conducted interviews in a few counties and villages in Liaoning and Sichuan provinces. Most interviews lasted two to three hours. A few of the interviews were with scholars working on related topics at various research institutes and with national-level officials in Beijing.

mote economic development. The most important of the fiscal reforms was a tax responsibility system for each administrative level down to the township.[12] By the mid-1980s provinces, municipalities, prefectures, counties, and townships were subject to a bottom-up revenue-sharing system that required localities to submit only a portion of their revenues to the upper levels and then allowed them to retain all, or at least most, of the remainder. Localities became independent fiscal entities that had both responsibility for local expenditures and the unprecedented right to use the revenue that they retained.[13]

Fiscal Contracting

Revenue sharing was formalized in fiscal contracts signed between the central state and each of its provinces, between each province and its prefectures, between each prefecture and its counties, and between each county and its townships.[14] Some places use an overall ratio, such as 70:30, where the locality keeps 70 percent and 30 percent is sent to the next higher level. In other cases the locality pays a set quota to the next higher level, but once that quota is met, the locality retains all or at least the bulk of the remaining tax revenues. Unlike previous revenue-sharing arrangements that changed annually, these contracts run from three to five years.

Whether a locality shares its revenue with the higher levels is determined by a complex calculation of fixed expenditures, fixed receipts, fixed payment upward, and fixed subsidy. The fixed expenditure is the amount that the higher authorities recognize as the minimum essential

[12] For a useful summary of the evolution of fiscal policies and variations in the formal system, see Michel Oksenberg and James Tong, "The Evolution of Central-Provincial Fiscal Relations in China, 1971–1984: The Formal System," *China Quarterly* 125 (March 1991); and James Tong, "Fiscal Reform, Elite Turnover and Central-Provincial Relations in Post-Mao China," in *Australian Journal of Chinese Affairs* 22 (July 1989); Christine Wong, "Fiscal Reform and Local Industrialization: The Problematic Sequencing of Reform in Post-Mao China," *Modern China* 18 (April 1992); and idem, "Central-Local Relations in an Era of Fiscal Decline: The Paradox of Fiscal Decentralization in Post-Mao China," *China Quarterly* 128 (December 1991). See also Audrey Donnithorne, *Centre-Provincial Economic Relations in China* (Canberra: Contemporary China Centre, Australian National University, 1981). For more specific treatment of the tax reform in Shanghai, see Lynn T. White III, *Shanghai Shanghaied? Uneven Taxes in Reform China*, Centre of Asian Studies Occasional Papers and Monographs, no. 84 (Hong Kong: University of Hong Kong, 1989). See also Shaoguang Wang, "From Revolution to Involution: State Capacity, Local Power, and [Un]governability in China" (Manuscript, Yale University, n.d.).

[13] The changes during the prereform fiscal system are numerous. On the early periods up until 1960, see Audrey Donnithorne, *China's Economic System* (London: George Allen and Unwin, 1967); on the later period, see Wong (fn. 12, 1992).

[14] Tong (fn. 12) notes in his survey of the tax reforms that there is tremendous variation. Not all areas have instituted the tax responsibility system to the township. The specifics of the tax responsibility system are too diverse and complex to detail here in full.

budget items of local governments. The level at which the fixed expenditure is pegged determines how much a locality will pay to the upper levels or the amount of subsidy it will receive. The fixed expenditure includes the base salary of state cadres on the local government's payroll[15] and basic services, such as education and health. The amounts are based on past expenditures, with some provision for increases based on population. The fixed expenditure is then compared with the fixed receipts, the tax collection quota set for the locality. Not all provinces, prefectures, counties, or townships pay revenue to the next higher level. A locality makes a fixed payment upward to the next higher administrative level only if the tax revenues are greater than the fixed revenues. At each level from the province to the township there are some units that cannot generate sufficient revenues to cover expenditures.[16] And if the fixed receipts are less than the fixed expenditures, then that difference becomes the fixed subsidy for an area. The fixed subsidy is the subsistence ceiling for poor areas. If expenditures and receipts are equal, then a locality neither pays revenue to the upper level nor receives a subsidy. In one Shandong county of seventeen townships, ten were deficit and therefore received subsidies from the county, and the other seven paid taxes to the county.[17]

The system is very effective in promoting local government entrepreneurship because not all revenue collected by a locality is subject to revenue sharing. Only certain taxes collected by localities are subject to share contracts. The most important of these, the taxes on state and collective industries, constitute the core of the locality's "within-budget revenues" (*yusuannei zijin*).[18] Most of the other revenue that a locality collects is considered its "extrabudgetary revenues" (*yusuanwai zijin*).[19] This latter category includes (1) all those taxes that have been designated "local taxes," including the slaughter tax, the individual income adjustment tax, and the tax on private enterprise, and (2) nontax revenues, such as the various fees and surcharges collected by local government.[20] Most of

[15] Some cadres who work for local government are not considered state cadres. They are paid not from the official budget but from extrabudgetary funds.

[16] Based on a report by China's minister of finance, Wong (fn. 12, 1991) writes that in 1989 localities remitted a total of 44.7 billion yuan to the central budget while receiving central subsidies of 56.3 billion yuan (p. 698).

[17] China Interview 52290.

[18] The other major items that make up the within-budget revenues include the agricultural tax and the profits from state-run enterprises within the locality. China Interview 8891.

[19] In addition, there are some taxes designated as "central" taxes. These similarly are not subject to revenue sharing. Central taxes are the sole property of the central state. Localities collect but receive nothing from central taxes, such as those on government commercial agencies like banks and the post office.

[20] For the details, see Oi, "Private and Local State Entrepreneurship: The Shandong Case" (Paper presented at the annual meeting of the Association for Asian Studies, Washington, D.C., April 2–5, 1992).

these local taxes have remained fairly inconsequential as revenue sources. Since the tax designations were drawn, however, the tax on private enterprises has become a very lucrative source of income for localities, a reflection of the dramatic growth of the private sector in the 1980s. Taxes on the private sector accounted for close to a quarter of all taxes collected in one Shandong county in 1990.[21]

Extrabudgetary funds existed at various times during the Maoist period, and as in the current period they consisted of minor taxes and surcharges. The fiscal reforms greatly altered both the size of these funds and the rights of localities to use these funds: before the reforms were enacted, all use of extrabudgetary funds by a locality was subject to prior upper-level approval. Now localities have license to use these funds as they wish. Furthermore, the amount of these funds has grown enormously. During the Maoist period these funds reportedly constituted from about "1%–2% of revenue collection in rich provinces and no more than 5% for most provinces."[22] During the reforms, between 1978 and 1988, there has been an estimated sixfold nationwide increase in extrabudgetary revenues.[23] In 1989 the total extrabudgetary funds were 91.2 percent of within-budget revenues.[24] In some townships the sum of extrabudgetary revenues now *exceeds* the within-budget revenues. It is very difficult to know precisely how much such revenues any locality might have. In addition to the reported extrabudgetary funds held by local governments as an administrative entity (such as a county or township), by specific bureaus within a county, and by enterprises, there are also hidden extrabudgetary funds.

In the following section I examine the within-budget taxes to show why so much revenue remains within the localities. In a later section I describe the nontax revenues extracted by and retained by local governments. Table 1 is a list of the major taxes and nontax levies taken by local governments.

Within-Budget Tax Revenues

Taxes on industry constitute the bulk of the revenue that localities share with the upper levels. In the aftermath of the reforms, state-owned industry remains the largest contributor of tax revenues to local government, but the share of total taxes contributed by state-owned enterprises

[21] China Interview 81391.

[22] Wong (fn. 12, 1992), 205.

[23] On Kit Tam, "Fiscal Policy Issues in China" (Manuscript, University of New South Wales, Canberra, July 1990).

[24] *China Statistical Yearbook 1990* (New York: Praeger, 1991), 223.

TABLE 1
WITHIN-BUDGET TAXES AND EXTRABUDGETARY REVENUES FROM TOWNSHIP AND VILLAGE ENTERPRISES

Within-Budget Taxes	*Extrabudgetary Revenues*
1. Income tax	1. Local taxes
2. Circulation tax/industrial-commercial tax	2. Nontax levies
—product tax	—contracted profits
—value-added tax	quota
—turnover/business tax	over quota
	—management fee
	—ad hoc charges

is decreasing.[25] At the same time taxes on rural collective industry continue to grow in importance for local treasuries. Between 1978 and 1990 the tax from township and village enterprises increased nationally from 2.2 billion to 27.55 billion yuan (see Table 2). Taxes on both state and collective rural enterprises fall into two major categories: tax on profits and tax on sales.

TAX ON PROFITS

The enterprise income tax (*suode shui*) was billed as the means by which the state would receive revenue but still provide incentives for enterprises to be more efficient and profitable. Because the income tax is levied only on profits, it might more properly be called a profits tax. It is based on an eight-grade progressive scale, with the rates ranging from a low of 10 percent to a high of 55 percent on profits. The rate for the large enterprises (that is, those with profits over 200,000 yuan) is 55 percent.

In practice, income tax comprises only about a quarter of total industrial taxes nationally.[26] The income tax rates are not negotiable, but the tax an enterprise pays can be reduced by inflating costs, thus decreasing profits. What can be written off as costs is largely at the discretion of the local officials charged with assessing the tax. In a semiplanned economy such as China's, "profits" and "costs" are subjective categories affected by factors beyond the control of a factory manager. In addition, institutional arrangements routinely allow the profit base to be reduced. For example, until the rule change of the late 1980s, income tax was commonly reduced by allowing enterprises to deduct loan payments from

[25] See Wong (fn. 12, 1991); and Barry Naughton, "Implications of the State Monopoly over Industry and Its Relaxation," *Modern China* 18 (January 1992).

[26] In 1988 it was 25.3% of total industrial taxes. *Zhongguo tongji nianjian 1989* (Beijing: Zhongguo tongji chubanshe, 1989), 240.

TABLE 2
COLLECTIVE, TOWNSHIP, AND VILLAGE ENTERPRISES, 1978–90[a]

Category	*Unit*	*1978*	*1980*	*1985*	*1986*	*1987*	*1988*	*1989*	*1990*
Enterprises	million	1.52	1.43	1.57	1.52	1.58	1.59	1.54	1.45
Workers	million	28.27	30	41.52	43.92	47.18	48.94	47.2	45.92
As % of rural labors	%	9.5	9.4	11.2	11.6	12.1	12.21	11.53	10.93
Output Value	billion yuan	49.3	65.69	198.78	245.87	323.74	436.27	485.56	542.92
As % of rural output	%	21.2	23.5	43	47.7	34.32	34.81	33.53	32.67
Income	billion yuan	43.15	59.61	182.74	222.36	293.41	423.22	482.16	521.86
Taxes	billion yuan	2.2	2.57	10.86	13.73	16.81	23.65	27.25	27.55
Net Profit	billion yuan	8.81	11.84	17.13	16.1	18.78	25.92	24.01	23.27

SOURCES: *Xiangzhen qiye nianjian 1978–1987* (Beijing: Nongye chubanshe, 1989), 569; and *Zhongguo tongji nianjian 1991* (Beijing: Zhongguo tongji chubanshe, 1991), 315–78.

[a] Figures for 1978 and 1980 refer to all categories of rural enterprises. Figures for 1985 to 1990 refer only to collectively owned township and village enterprises.

income before assessing the tax. In addition, there are areas that grant across-the-board cuts as standard practice; some provinces are particularly generous in this regard. In the eastern province of Zhejiang, for example, if the applicable tax rate is above 30 percent, then the amount taxed at the higher rate is cut in half. In the southern province of Guangdong, if the rate is above 20 percent, the tax levy above that level is cut in half.[27] My interviews reveal that a number of established township and village enterprises either had never paid income tax or were just about to be assessed income tax for the first time in 1988.

National regulations allow favorable treatment for township and village enterprises with regard to the collection of income tax, but whether the central state intended to provide the deep discounts described above is questionable. National regulations exempt new enterprises from income tax on their first year of business; some localities have extended the exemption to two or three years. In addition, local authorities confer a favorable tax status on enterprises that meet any of a long list of conditions.[28] To mention just a few, exemptions are granted to factories that serve agriculture, hire the handicapped, or are located in the designated old revolutionary base areas. Existing factories that start a new product line receive a tax holiday on the profit from that production.

TAX ON SALES OR VALUE ADDED

Local governments also derive revenue from enterprises through a second category of taxes based on production, income, or sales, irrespective of profits. These taxes are sometimes loosely termed circulation taxes (*liuzhuan shui*) or the industrial-commercial taxes (*gongshang shui*). The primary ones include the product (*chanpin*), value-added (*zengzhi*), and turnover/business (*yingye*) taxes (see Table 1).

Together these levies comprise the bulk of township and village enterprise taxes; nationally for 1988 they yielded almost three-quarters of the total taxes on township and village enterprises.[29] For example, one large Shandong village factory had total gross profits of 376,000 yuan for

[27] He Xian, "Woguo xiangzhen qiye shouru fenpei wenti," *Zhongguo nongcun jingji* 3 (March 21, 1988), 34.

[28] See *Xiangzhen qiye nianjian 1978–1987* (Beijing: Nongye chubanshe, 1989), 270, for an official list of exemptions. Setting up factories for the disabled and therefore earning tax-free status was pursued in two of the Shandong villages that I investigated.

[29] *Zhongguo tongji nianjian 1989* (fn. 26), 240. These proportions were similarly reflected in my field research. China Interview 6688. Andrew Walder also found that second category taxes on *state*-owned enterprises located at the county level contributed more to the local treasury than did the income tax. See Walder, "County Finance and Local Industry: A View from Zouping County, Shandong" (Paper presented at the Jackson School of International Studies, University of Washington, Seattle, February 15, 1990).

1987–88. It paid a total of 146,000 yuan in taxes, or 38.8 percent of total profits. But of this amount only 36,000 yuan was income tax; the remaining 110,000 yuan, or 75.3 percent, was sales and other taxes. When one compares the industrial-commercial tax with the agricultural tax, the logic of pursuing industry is obvious. In one township the industrial-commercial taxes yielded almost twice the agricultural tax—485,000 yuan as compared with 260,000 yuan.[30]

Second-category taxes are more strictly enforced and collected than the income tax.[31] Yet, as in state industry, there seems to be room for reductions and exemptions.[32] For example, in a highly industrialized Shandong village, taxes as a percentage of total village enterprise income decreased over time. Tax breaks, especially for new enterprises, explain some of the decrease. Thus, in the last few years this village developed a number of new enterprises, the income from which is eligible for various tax holidays. The village has also been able to reduce its tax base with the arrangement that allows for repaying loans before taxes. Similar tax breaks were enjoyed by a county outside Tianjin. In 1987 the county collected 59.30 million yuan in taxes, but almost half as much, 26.65 million yuan, was given in tax breaks.[33] In a Shandong county the amount given in tax breaks from 1987 to 1990 averaged close to 7 million yuan per year. In 1990, for example, 39.2 million yuan was collected in taxes, but 5.3 million was given in reductions or exemptions.[34]

Extrabudgetary Nontax Revenues

Localities can collect a minimum of taxes to satisfy tax quotas and provide a sufficient base for local expenses, but they need not assess national taxes in the predatory fashion that some might expect of a government in fiscal need.[35] A locality need not lose revenue by not collecting the maximum amount in taxes. Which level of government receives what income and how much through nontax levies depends on whether an enterprise is owned by a township or a village. Village-owned enterprises pay no nontax levies to the township.

[30] China Interview 21688.

[31] He Xian (fn. 27).

[32] On the state urban sector, see Andrew Walder, "Local Bargaining Relationships and Urban Industrial Finance," in Kenneth G. Lieberthal and David M. Lampton, eds., *Bureaucracy, Politics, and Decision Making in Post-Mao China* (Berkeley: University of California Press, 1992).

[33] China Interview 8888.

[34] China Interviews 52290 and 81391.

[35] Margaret Levi, among others who have highlighted the predatory nature of states, tends to focus on taxation policies. See Levi, *Of Rule and Revenue* (Berkeley: University of California Press, 1988).

Up to this point I have referred to local governments as a single entity, but in reality, even though the government may be seen as a corporate entity, within the corporation there are diverse interests competing for limited resources. Hence, it is useful to distinguish between a township government and the specific agencies within the government, particularly the economic commission. This distinction may seem overly technical, but in interviews local government officials and factory managers were careful to distinguish between the two. All within the township government have an interest in developing industry, all look to the profits from industry, but different parts of the government are responsible for different expenses. The township government as a whole is responsible for all aspects of the township and all of its various economic interests and welfare needs. The township economic commission is under the township government, but it is also a subordinate organ of the county-level township enterprise management bureau. It is specifically responsible for collectively owned enterprises. Money paid to the economic commission is more likely to be used exclusively for township and perhaps for village enterprises. In most townships, the township collective enterprises pay the bulk of the nontax levies to the economic commission, not to the township government.[36]

BEFORE-TAX LEVIES

The one levy that is paid directly to the township government is a set percentage of a township enterprise's gross income before any taxes are deducted. National regulations stipulate 10 percent, but the precise amount in some cases is higher, sometimes reaching 20 percent. While the amounts vary, all townships seem to require this payment. Some areas levy an additional amount, an "aid agriculture, aid sidelines fund" before taxes.[37]

AFTER-TAX LEVIES

Most of the after-tax levies are paid to either the township or the village, depending on the level of ownership. Because each level of government, but not individual enterprises, has property rights to after-tax profits, townships and villages use after-tax levies as a second source of revenue.

[36] Again, there seem to be regional variations. But in the majority of my cases profits are paid to the economic commission.

[37] He Xian (fn. 27) provided no details, but I assume that the sidelines refer to such activities as pig raising done by households. Around Shanghai, this is an additional 10%. In the same region there is yet a third levy, this one on workers in the enterprises, that goes toward the "aid agriculture, aid sidelines fund." He Xian (fn. 27).

At the township level, township-owned enterprises are under the supervision of the township economic commission, which collects revenue from its enterprises in two ways. First, it gets a management fee of 1 percent of total sales. This is one of the few sources of nontax levies that the township shares.[38] A percentage (50–70 percent) of this goes to the county township enterprise management bureau.[39] Second, the economic commission receives rent from factory managers who contract to use the collectively owned enterprises. This is the contracted profits stipulated under the responsibility system, consisting of quota profits and over-quota profits. Quota profits are those that a factory has contracted to meet; over-quota profits are those above that target.

National regulations stipulate that township governments are to limit themselves to no more than 20 percent of an enterprise's total after-tax profits. However, in practice, the actual share taken by economic commissions is higher. In one county outside Tianjin, for example, the economic commission took 40 percent of the quota profit and 30 percent of the over-quota profit. The way that local officials justified this in terms of national regulations reflected their view of the economy as a corporate entity. Since the funds were used for the unified management of the enterprises in the township as a whole, they explained, some of the money would eventually be returned to the enterprises.[40]

On top of the standard fees and levies, such as the management fee and contracted profit, there are a variety of other local ad hoc levies on enterprises designed to meet shortfalls in local revenue. Because the levies are taken on a need basis, these enterprises have been dubbed the "cash registers" of local government. Those who most often take such funds are the economic commissions that directly control the enterprises. Heads of economic commissions in a number of localities freely admit that they take profits from rich enterprises whenever they need extra funds. And those who deny using such practices are all aware of the practice and places that use it. This "borrowing" is most commonly done when the economic commission needs to pay off debts incurred by one of its enterprises or to expand production in one of its enterprises. One

[38] This also varies. In one county, which contains one of the richest and one of the most industrialized villages in China, the economic commission took only .6% of sales as a management fee.

[39] There are indications that this amount is not always forwarded.

[40] China Interview 8688. As a result of national regulations the amount taken by some economic commissions has apparently been reduced in the last couple of years. According to one county official of a township enterprise management bureau in Shandong, before 1985 the township economic commission took as much as 40–50% of total after tax-profits. China Interview 53188.

township economic commission took over 3 million yuan for these purposes between 1986 and 1988.[41]

At the village level, too, village factories (like township enterprises) must turn over the contracted after-tax profits. The amounts vary considerably: some pay a set percentage of profits, others a fixed levy. In the more developed villages, factories pay the village enterprise management committee a management fee of 1 percent of total income. In some highly industrialized villages, enterprises also pay an assortment of other fees and "voluntary contributions" as needed by the village (see Table 3). And as in the case of townships, villages simply take profits from well-off factories as the need arises. The nontax levies on village enterprises may seem less complex, but compared with township enterprises in terms of amounts taken out, they are on the high end of the continuum. In one village about 70 percent of enterprise profits either were taken out in taxes or turned over to the village as profits and fees.[42]

Because of the small size of village governments and the overwhelming power of the party secretary, it matters little if the profits and fees are paid to the enterprise management committee or to the village government. At the village level they are one and the same. More than any of the other levels, the village economy is the closest to that of a small corporation, where profits from one sector are freely used to support other sectors.[43]

TABLE 3
TYPES OF NONTAX LEVIES ON VILLAGE-OWNED ENTERPRISES

1. Contracted Profits
2. Management fee
3. Other Fees for
old age pension
culture-education
benefits
building fund
land use
4. Voluntary contributions
(ad hoc payments, sometimes requested as donations, and given as needed)

[41] China Interview 71988.

[42] China Interview 6488.

[43] For further documentation on this, see Oi, "The Fate of the Collective after the Commune," in Deborah Davis and Ezra Vogel, eds., *Chinese Society on the Eve of Tiananmen: The Impact of Reform*, Contemporary China Series, no. 7 (Cambridge: Council on East Asian Studies, Harvard University, 1990).

II. Institutional Interests and Incentives for Local Economic Growth

Budget constraints make it imperative for all local officials who have political ambitions, however modest, to try to expand revenue-generating sources.[44] This applies to those from whom the state requires payment of revenues, to those from whom it requires no revenue payments, and to those to whom it makes subsidy payments. County-level finance officials are quick to point out that the fixed subsidies are barely sufficient to maintain a functioning township government. There is no slack for the improvement of services; there is no room for bureaucratic growth. The number of bureaucratic positions for which the fixed subsidies will pay is set.[45] The upper levels do not provide additional funds to localities as expenditures increase. The fact that some have not succeeded in developing their local economy is due not to the lack of incentives but to other constraints, such as a locality's lack of resource endowments or the incompetence of its officials.[46]

How hard local governments work to increase revenues is tied to secure rights to increased revenues, however. Knowledge that they would be the direct beneficiary of increased revenues at a minimum fixed rate for three to five years was critical in prompting local governments to respond enthusiastically to the incentives embedded in the revenue-sharing system. Before localities had such assurances there had been few incentives to be entrepreneurial. Local finance officials have criticized the tax-sharing systems in effect in the early 1980s as offering them little incentive to work harder. Not only did localities have to meet tax quotas set by the upper levels, but they also had to turn over all surplus profits.[47] Such sentiments are reminiscent of the complaints by peasants under the Maoist system: they had little incentive to produce more grain because

[44] For the purposes of this analysis I am assuming that cadres are noncorrupt. Obviously, some are. But corruption is not a very useful explanation and would leave unexplained the impressive growth that has taken place in China's rural economy. Moreover, rapid economic growth does not preclude the improved well-being of those local officials. One must also keep in mind that the new budget constraints imposed by the fiscal reforms compel local officials to keep their own greed in check and use the profits and revenues from local enterprises to fund local expenditures and for reinvestment. The rapid growth in China's rural economy, particularly the 25-plus percent growth rate in rural industrial output, suggests that officials have used these funds to promote further growth, not just to line their pockets.

[45] On the growth of local governments, see Tyrene White, "Political Reform and Rural Government," in Davis and Vogel (fn. 43); and idem, "Below Bureaucracy: The Burden of Being a Village under the Local State" (Paper presented at the annual meeting of the Association for Asian Studies, Chicago, April 5–8, 1990).

[46] Byrd and Lin (fn. 6) examine reasons why some areas have not successfully developed rural industry.

[47] China Interview 52290.

they knew that increased production had no positive effect on the amount of their grain rations.[48] The principle that "what is important is not what is taken out, but what is left"[49] holds at least as much for taxes as for grain.

To ensure that all local officials do their utmost to develop rural enterprises, officials at each higher level of government set quotas for the subordinate level. The bonus pay of officials becomes linked to the performance of township enterprises in meeting profit and production quotas. The prefecture docks the county, and the county docks the bonus of township-level officials if the enterprises for which they are responsible fail to meet the quotas set by the county.[50] The township can affect the bonus that village officials take, but its control is less complete. But village-level officials have their own incentive to promote village industries actively since their salaries are directly tied to the total income of the village. The system is structured so that local officials have a double incentive to promote rural industry: growth allows them to benefit economically as individuals, without resort to corruption, and it allows them to alleviate the budget constraints that make their jobs difficult. Both their personal economic well-being and the financial health of the local economy are tied to successful economic development.

The most problematic aspect of the fiscal reforms for local government is the revenue sharing and assessment of within-budget taxes. The interest of local governments with regard to taxes is colored by the conflicting role that officials are expected to play. On the one hand, if local government pursues its interests as a corporation, it will try to maximize its profits and pay as little tax as possible to the central state. The rather lax assessment of the income tax is one manifestation of this tendency. On the other hand, local government cannot behave simply as a corporation intent on maximizing profits; local government is also the agent of the central state charged with tax collection, and it must meet the tax quotas agreed upon in the fiscal contracts signed with the higher levels. These tensions inhere in the broader problem faced by all local officials—having to represent both central and local interests, while watching out for their own political interests.[51] The solution that allows local governments to meet their responsibility to the upper levels and also

[48] For an elaboration of this point, see Oi, *State and Peasant in Contemporary China: The Political Economy of Village Government* (Berkeley: University of California Press, 1989).

[49] James C. Scott, *The Moral Economy of the Peasant: Rebellion and Subsistence in Southeast Asia* (New Haven: Yale University Press, 1976).

[50] China Interview 21688.

[51] I discuss how this tension was resolved by Maoist cadres in Oi (fn. 48).

increase local revenues lies in the extraction of nontax revenues and collection of those taxes designated as local.

III. Fiscal Reform and the Rise of Rural Industry

The problem faced by local governments was how best to generate revenues. Decollectivization eliminated agriculture as a viable source of needed revenue. After the institution of the responsibility system that made the household the unit of production and accounting, local governments, especially at the village and to a lesser extent at the township levels, lost legitimate access to all income from agriculture, except for a percentage of the nominal agricultural tax. Income from the sale of agricultural products went to the household.

The combination of decollectivization and revenue sharing forced local officials to make careful calculations of the benefits and costs of the different sectors of the rural economy. The smaller return on funds invested and the limited access that local officials had to income from agriculture, especially grain production, made agriculture the least desirable investment option.[52] Once the diversification of the rural economy was encouraged, local officials diverted resources and energies from agriculture to more profitable enterprises. One possible source was to promote the development of the private sector and gain revenues through taxation.[53] That, as I noted above, can be quite lucrative for local coffers. However, because of the political taint still associated with private enterprise and the shifting political winds at the center toward private entrepreneurs, that route is taken cautiously.[54] The most lucrative and least problematic strategy politically was the development of rural collective enterprises (*xiangzhen qiye*).[55]

Not only did rural collective enterprises provide a solution (applauded by the national leadership) to the surplus labor problem that arose from decollectivization,[56] but they were also increasingly lucra-

[52] For a more detailed discussion of the diverse effects of the fiscal reforms on agriculture, see Oi, "Chinese Agriculture: Modernization, But at What Costs?" in Thomas Robinson and Zhiling Lin, eds., *The Chinese and Their Future: Beijing, Taipei, and Hong Kong* (Lanham, Md.: University Press of America, 1992).

[53] I examine this option in Oi (fn. 20).

[54] The exception is in places like Wenzhou, which is famous for its private businesses.

[55] The term *rural enterprises* includes various types of ventures, from factories to food stalls, that range from collective to private owned. The largest and economically most significant of the enterprises in terms of output value, number of people employed, and taxes paid are those owned by local government, either the township or village. Unless otherwise noted, the discussion in this article is limited to collectively owned enterprises.

[56] The percentage of the rural labor force engaged in all types of rural enterprises rose

tive.[57] Beginning as a small part of the rural economy in 1980, by 1987 industry had already surpassed agriculture nationally as the dominant source of rural income.[58] For the twelve-year period from 1978 to 1990 the output value of these collective enterprises increased by 26.7 percent.[59] By the end of 1991 rural industry was producing 50 percent of total industrial output, equal to that of the state-owned industrial sector.

As the legal owner of these enterprises, local governments could legitimately extract nontax levies—the various fees and ad hoc surcharges described above. Revenue from rural collective enterprises has been the source of funds for public services, welfare, and subsidies to other, less profitable, sectors of the economy, such as agriculture, in addition to serving as the base for industrial expansion. Localities that have rural industry can provide services and are most likely to be strong effective governments; those that do not are most likely to be weak and ineffective governments.

Given the fiscal importance of rural industry, it is not surprising that it has mushroomed throughout rural China, in particular, rural industry owned by village governments. By 1988, 46.6 percent of all counties in China had rural industry with output value in excess of 100 million yuan.[60] Township and village enterprises total around 1.5 million. Table 2 provides a twelve-year overview of the development of these enterprises. In absolute numbers they are only a minor portion of the more than eighteen million enterprises in the countryside, but they are the most important in terms of the amount of revenue and output value generated.[61]

The local variations and the ad hoc levies also make it difficult to determine precisely how much of enterprise revenues any township government and its economic commission take. A national study of township governments found a tremendous range in what they took from their enterprises: from the bulk of enterprise profits to a small portion to little more than the management fee (see Table 4).[62] The amount turned

from 9.5% in 1978 to 22.1% in 1990. The proportion is even higher in areas with developed rural industries. Zhang Hongyu (fn. 2).

[57] See Byrd and Lin (fn. 6) for detailed studies of rural enterprises based on survey data. See also Christine P. W. Wong, "Interpreting Rural Industrial Growth in the Post-Mao Period," *Modern China* 14 (January 1988); and Oi (fn. 43).

[58] *Zhongguo tongji nianjian 1988* (Beijing: Zhongguo tongji chubanshe, 1988), 214.

[59] Zhang Hongyu (fn. 2).

[60] *Zhongguo nongye nianjian 1989* (Beijing: Nongye chubanshe, 1989), 20.

[61] The others are private or joint-stock enterprises.

[62] He Xian (fn. 27).

TABLE 4
REGIONAL DIFFERENCES IN AFTER-TAX PROFITS PAID TO TOWNSHIP AND VILLAGE GOVERNMENTS

Proportion Paid	*Example*	*% of Profits Paid to Government*
1. Large	Beijing,	56.99
	Shanghai	71.67
2. Small	Jiangsu,	30.00
	Zhejiang,	30.00
	Hebei	30.00
3. Minimal	Zhejiang (Wenzhou)	management fee

SOURCE: He Xian (fn. 27), 34.

TABLE 5
DIVISION OF TOWNSHIP AND VILLAGE ENTERPRISE PROFITS, 1984–87

Year	*Income Tax as % of Total Profits*	*% of After-Tax Profits Taken by Government*
1984	24.8	52.17
1986	—	40.78
1987	21.7	39.1

SOURCE: *Xiangzhen qiye nianjian 1978–1987* (fn. 28), 270.

over was correlated with the extent to which government was involved in investment and development of production. Unfortunately, the study does not tell us which method is the most common. It is important to note that the "small" amount is still 30 percent of after-tax profits.[63] Aggregate statistics suggest, however, that the percentage of such profits going to government may be decreasing. Comparing 1984, 1986, and 1987, the amount of after-tax profits paid to either township or village governments has decreased from 52.17 percent to only 39.1 percent (see Table 5).[64]

Regardless of the precise amounts, overall revenues from enterprises at the township, and particularly at the village, level are controlled either directly or indirectly by local officials. Profits that are not extracted are strictly regulated. Rules stipulate *how* retained profits must be used—this holds for township as well as village enterprises, and there is a formula that sets strict limits on the amount that can be used for workers' benefits and bonuses; the bulk of profits must be used for reinvestment.

[63] Ibid.
[64] *Xiangzhen qiye nianjian 1978–1987* (fn. 28), 270.

IV. The Sinews of Local State Corporatism

Some might read the above statistics on high rates of extraction as evidence that local officials are corrupt and bleed the collective enterprises under their control—behavior that could be seen as confirmation of the predatory nature of states. But one should go further, to examine how this income is used rather than simply accepting this behavior as rent seeking. A framework that would account for both the heavy local extractions and the significant growth of China's rural economy is to analyze local government as a corporation: it takes profits from its factories to pay for expenditures and for reinvestment.

The extraction of profits from enterprises is one of the most important mechanisms for allowing local governments to operate as a corporation. As the holders of rights over income flows, local governments can decide as a corporation how to use profits from its various enterprises and how to redistribute income.[65] But a successful corporation also needs other means to control the operation of its enterprises. Among the most important of these are the selection of management personnel, control over the allocation of scarce production inputs, provision of services, and control of investment and credit decisions. Much of the infrastructure for exercising government direction remains from the Maoist period. Let me now turn to an examination of the levers of government control.

Factory Management

Contracting or leasing of enterprises to individuals rather than privatization facilitates local government intervention and control. Decollectivization leased ("contracted") but did not sell collectively owned factories to private individuals under the *contract responsibility system.*[66] Furthermore, factory managers who contract to operate factories do not have the same degree of autonomy as do peasants who contract to farm collectively owned land. In practice, the contract responsibility system has only decentralized the day-to-day management of collectively owned enterprises and provided incentives for factory managers to be efficient and increase production—they receive bonuses if they overfulfill their quotas. But beyond that, the lessee is nothing more than an employee of

[65] See Oi (fn. 43) for a more detailed discussion of how this income keeps the village together as a "collective" by providing the necessary funds to pay for welfare and public services and to support agriculture, as well as for reinvestment in industry.

[66] An exception seems to be Fujian, where Nee and Su indicate that they were sold. See Victor Nee and Su Sijin, "Institutional Change and Economic Growth in China: The View from the Villages," *Journal of Asian Studies* 49 (February 1990).

the corporation; he has no rights to dictate the disposition of enterprise profits. That role remains with local government.

The contract responsibility system charges factory managers with the burden of running the factory efficiently and profitably—but with only limited control over factors of production. Those who lease collective factories are dependent on higher executive management (that is, the local officials who are sometimes, concurrently, the chairmen of the village's industrial corporation) to make key decisions. Where the factory manager may make suggestions about personnel, development, investment, and product line, the implementation of these changes and programs requires official approval. Factory managers who make good suggestions or happen to run the factories targeted for development or expansion may receive large bonuses, but the engine for change and development is local government.

Resource Allocation

Ideally, all the divisions within the corporation should receive assistance, but rarely do corporate resources offer such undifferentiated support. During the Maoist period all enterprises received some subsidies, but the fiscal reforms mandate that local governments make inequitable treatment of enterprises a matter of policy. The unofficial favoritism of the Maoist period has now been formalized, and new criteria are applied to determine who will receive preferential treatment: resources and breaks are directed to those enterprises that can generate the most benefit for the corporate good.[67]

The strategy of selective support of certain enterprises is reminiscent of Japan's administrative guidance.[68] Preferential allocation of key production inputs and bureaucratic support provides certain enterprises with the most favorable environment for growth. To this end local governments have begun to rank enterprises. Moreover, they let it be known that certain enterprises are considered especially important and therefore worthy of special treatment.

The rating of enterprises is yet to be firmly institutionalized, however. Political pressure and personal connections may still lead to preferential access, but banks and bureaus are increasingly allocating resources and providing assistance based on the merit of an enterprise or its potential to generate revenues. One way that local governments have tried to in-

[67] The corporate good is defined more broadly than narrow economic interest and profits. It may include social as well as ideological interests.

[68] Chalmers A. Johnson, *MITI and the Japanese Miracle: The Growth of Industrial Policy, 1925–1975* (Stanford, Calif.: Stanford University Press, 1982).

stitutionalize this preferential treatment is to rate firms on the basis of past performance, with a firm's rating determining the level of services and assistance it receives from the government and its affiliated institutions. Sometimes the ratings are done within specific bureaus. For example, the material supply bureaus have industries that are supplied first and have the best chance of getting the lowest-price inputs; these are designated key points (*zhongdian*). The rural industry management bureau working with the science and technology commission provides technical assistance to those units that they assess as the most promising.

There are two types of selective allocation. The first is privileged access to those inputs that are supplied to localities under the central allocation system, that is, the plan, which still exists. These are items that are rationed and for which the prices are lowest. For inputs such as steel and cement, the quantities allocated to rural areas are severely restricted. Officials have little discretion with regard to these production materials, as they are usually earmarked for specific enterprises that are producing for the plan. The most that a locality can hope for is access to state-supplied goods that are sold at higher than rationed prices but at lower than market prices.

The second, more common form is privileged access to inputs that are not rationed but are simply scarce. This would include, for example, fuel oil, supply of electricity, and raw materials. This privileged access is to goods that are secured and sold at *market* prices. Like the privileged access that comes from using connections and going through the back door, common not only in China but in all communist systems, what is being given is not necessarily a cheaper price but the opportunity to be first in line to buy the best of the available items at the posted prices. In the Chinese rural industrial context this means being able to buy the one ton of steel that the material supply bureau was able to procure at a favorable market price. It might also mean the opportunity to be hooked up to the special electric generator the township has installed to provide uninterrupted power to its most important industries. Plant shutdown because of power shortage is one of the major problems faced by factories in both urban and rural areas.[69]

Bureaucratic Services

In addition to supplying production materials, local governments also promote certain enterprises by providing bureaucratic services. These include help in securing licenses, certification and prizes for products, and tax breaks. As one might expect, agencies that are essential to rural en-

[69] Some factories regularly work in the middle of the night when the supply of electricity is more reliable

terprises, such as the science and technology commission and the township industry management bureau, expend large amounts of time and energy intervening with key agencies at the higher levels on behalf of local industry to acquire technology, materials, funding, and so on. They often personally accompany factory managers to the higher-level bureaus. The daily routine of leading cadres at the county-level township industry management bureau is filled with trips to the prefecture, even to Beijing, on behalf of specific enterprises.

Local state corporatist systems are noted for their ability to mobilize not just one but all agencies and bureaus within local government to nurture selective township and village enterprises. Moreover, these agencies provide services well outside of their administrative domain. For example, the county tax bureau not only collects taxes and gives tax breaks, but it also helps enterprises train accountants and find scarce technical personnel, one of the most pressing problems facing rural industry. Agencies use their connections to influence other agencies to bend the rules in favor of an enterprise. County tax bureaus, for example, lobby banks on behalf of local enterprises. To encourage a bank to give a risky loan, the tax bureau agrees to allow an enterprise to repay the bank loan before taxes are assessed.

In addition to providing routine and extraordinary service to selective enterprises, various agencies—including the tax bureau, the finance bureau, and the science and technology commission—have funds that they loan directly to enterprises. Banks are still the major source of credit, though it is possible to bypass this complicated official credit system. The local government bureaus have amassed pots of money from which they can unilaterally give no- or low-interest loans to help industries. The amounts are not large, but they can make a difference, particularly if a factory needs circulating capital to purchase raw materials. These local government sources of funding become critical when the upper levels decide to rein in growth by cutting credit, as they did in 1988–89.[70]

Investment and Credit

Control of investment and credit decisions is one of the most effective levers used by local governments to shape the course of development. Much of their ability to control investment is related to the amount of available credit in a given locality. Like an enterprise in a market economy, a Chinese rural enterprise goes to a bank to get loans. However,

[70] See Oi, "Fiscal Reform, Central Directives, and Local Autonomy in Rural China" (Paper presented at the annual meeting of the American Political Science Association, Washington, D.C., August 29–September 1, 1991).

unlike banks in a market economy, banks in China are not fully commercial operations. The amount that local banks can lend is determined by quotas set by the upper-level banks. The bank hierarchy allocates set amounts of funds to individual branches. Only recently have local banks been able to lend additional amounts based on their own deposits.[71]

Local governments exert further control, because in China a rural enterprise needs a guarantor to secure a loan; its own property is not sufficient collateral. The township economic commission often serves as the guarantor for township enterprises. Regardless of whom a factory manager secures as a guarantor, the banks are hesitant to make a capital investment loan of any size unless the local officials approve and support the project. For any major investment undertaking, it is the local officials who personally mobilize funds through the use of personal and professional connections. The head of the economic commission, the party secretary of a township, and the county head use their influence to persuade bank officials of the merit of favored projects. Sometimes tax officials, either on their own or at the urging of a county leader, will try to persuade bank officials to release a loan, by offering to allow loan repayments before taxes are assessed.

In recent years enterprises have been given credit ratings. County officials rate enterprises annually to determine the fixed capital credit as well as the financial services that each is eligible to receive at the local bank or savings cooperative. This further identifies for the banks those enterprises deemed important and creditworthy by local officials. These enterprises are then accorded the quickest approval for loans within their prescribed credit limit.

Local officials also promote local industry by allowing semiprivate credit institutions to operate. These sources of credit have only limited funds, but in periods of tight credit, such as 1988–89, they provide a critical avenue for bypassing regulations aimed at constraining growth.[72] Local officials usually do not serve on the boards of these credit institutions, but their tacit support is important for their continued operation.

V. Implications

The successful role of local governments in China's development points to the need to specify further the existing theories about the relationship

[71] For a more detailed discussion of bank reforms, see On Kit Tam, "Prospects for Reforming China's Financial System" (Paper presented at the Conference on China's Reforms and Economic Growth, Australian National University, Canberra, November 11–14, 1991).

[72] Oi (fn. 70).

between economic growth, property rights, and government intervention. In this study I have shown that individuals need not have property rights over enterprise profits for economic growth to occur. Given the large number of formerly socialist systems attempting market reform and economic development, the Chinese model may stand as a less radical but viable alternative to privatization. Furthermore, the Chinese case raises questions about the adequacy of rent-seeking theories of the state to capture the role of extracted revenues when the local state is the entrepreneur and redistributive orientations hold sway.

The economic outcome of local state corporatism in China is a thriving rural economy with an industrial sector that now rivals state-owned industry in production value and factor productivity. Some economists have questioned the economic efficiency and value of rural industrialization. Critics stress that because growth in China's reform economy has been driven by the fiscal needs of individual local governments rather than by a nationally coordinated effort, rural enterprise may be profitable locally, but they may be redundant if viewed nationally.[73] Nonetheless, the rise of rural collective industry has created market competition and reduced the role of the central state in dictating patterns of economic growth. In the short run localities might subsidize enterprises simply to generate sales and product taxes, which are unrelated to profits, and to employ increasing numbers of surplus laborers from agriculture.[74] Over the long run, however, severe budget constraints will cause local officials to change product lines or close inefficient rural industries. Certainly, rural enterprises have shortcomings, but some economists have begun to consider them as the necessary competition to make state enterprises more efficient.[75] In the short run the problem for the central state is that state industry can no longer show a high rate of profits, which in turn reduces revenues to the central government.[76]

The Chinese case also demonstrates that the introduction of markets has not resulted in a proportionate decrease in the role of local government. Authors who originally stressed the transformative effects of markets now emphasize the ways in which rural governments are like local corporations.[77] A distinguishing characteristic of local state corporatism

[73] See Wong (fn. 12, 1991 and 1992).

[74] Walder (fn. 29) has found the same phenomena operating with regard to the state-owned factories at the county level.

[75] Chen, Jefferson, and Singh (fn. 1).

[76] See Naughton (fn. 25).

[77] Compare Nee (fn. 9) with Victor Nee, "Organizational Dynamics of Market Transition: Hybrid Forms, Property Rights, and Mixed Economy in China," *Administrative Science Quarterly* 37 (March 1992).

is that markets are a key part of the local economy but government coordination and intervention continue. Most of the materials used by the rural enterprises are secured through the market; but ability to pay is necessary but not necessarily sufficient for access. Local officials have assumed new roles as entrepreneurs, selectively allocating scarce resources to shape patterns of local economic growth.

Moreover, the combination of the fiscal reforms and market competition has reinforced rather than broken down the cellular nature of rural society in a number of respects. Although there certainly is more mobility, opportunity, and trade across "cells," there is strong parochialism. Rural industrial development has made possible substantial redistribution of income and the provision of greater services and benefits than was ever possible under the Maoist system, but provision is limited to registered members of the community. The benefits given to outside workers in village-run collective enterprises are less than those given to workers from the village. The growing protectionist sentiment is evident in the unwillingness of local grain stores to sell low-priced, subsidized grain to any urban residents holding valid grain-ration coupons other than to those registered in the locality. In the past localities routinely complied with national regulations stipulating that anyone holding valid coupons should be sold subsidized grain. These regulations still hold, but budget constraints have made it too costly for localities to spend their valuable subsidies on outsiders.

Up to this point, I have focused on the economic importance of local state corporatism, but its importance goes beyond the economy. Local state corporatism may provide China with an alternative to the pains of privatization and regime collapse experienced by the Eastern bloc countries and the Soviet Union. Local state corporatism has provided China with a relatively nonthreatening alternative economic system that allows for strong local state intervention. Communist party officials can play a leading economic as well as political role. In most of the localities where I have done fieldwork, it is the local party bosses—the first party secretaries of the county, township, or village—who are at the helm of the drive for economic development. Party secretaries are involved most intimately with the development of rural collective industry, leaving other matters to their subordinates or to their counterparts in the administrative portion of government. This is especially so in villages, where the village party secretary oversees industry while the village head is responsible for agriculture. Many a village party secretary also serves as the chairman of the board of directors of the village industrial corporation, the body established in some villages to oversee village industry. It is perhaps this aspect of local state corporatism that best explains why local officials in China, unlike those in the Soviet Union, have embraced rather than resisted economic reforms. For Chinese local officials, both party and nonparty, the reforms could be achieved without any real threat to their power.

No simple, direct correlation exists between decollectivization, market reform, and the power of local officials in China. The Chinese experience has shown that some local governments have been weakened by the reforms, whereas others have been strengthened. The key variable seems to be the sources of income in a village, specifically the degree of local industrialization after the adoption of the household-responsibility system. Local governments that control only an agricultural, particularly a grain-based, economy are left with few options other than to levy ad hoc surcharges and various other fees and penalties, which the Chinese press often refers to as "increasing the peasant burden." Local governments that have continued to be strong and effective have developed nonagricultural sources of income that accrue directly to local government. The higher the level of industrialization, the more likely that local government will act in a corporate manner to intervene, extract, and redistribute income.[78] Carrying out economic reform and pursuing growth hold the potential of strengthening, not weakening, local official power.

Local state corporatism is also a path of least resistance because it allows China, a country socialized in the doctrines of Marxism-Leninism Mao Zedong Thought, to maintain its old values. As I have elaborated on elsewhere,[79] the income from rural industry has allowed local governments to redistribute substantial amounts of money to its members in the form of various subsidies, including grain subsidies and subsidies for education, health care, old-age pensions, and housing. In addition, local state corporatism allows local officials to be not just businessmen but also overseers of community well-being. And furthermore, it allows local officials to take social need into consideration when making economic decisions; the profitability of an enterprise may not be the most important factor in determining whether it will remain in operation. The need to employ the surplus labor released by decollectivization may make it eco-

[78] Writing shortly after the reforms started, Kathleen Hartford points to the general need for cadres to increase their control over finances if they are to keep the collective alive and their power strong. See Hartford, "Socialist Agricultural Is Dead: Long Live Socialist Agriculture! Organizational Transformations in Rural China," in Elizabeth J. Perry and Christine Wong, eds., *The Political Economy of Reform in Post-Mao China*, Contemporary China Series, no. 2 (Cambridge: Council on East Asian Studies, Harvard University, 1985).

[79] Oi (fn. 43).

nomically rational for villages to keep open an unprofitable factory.[80] One can wonder how efficient this growth will be over the long term, but at least in the medium term the emergence of local state corporatism allows the redistribution of income to remain an established and viable part of economic life in China's rural communities.

Local state corporatism holds the most threatening consequences for central-local relations.[81] The issue is how the pursuit of local interests conflicts with larger national concerns. Withholding of income and manipulation of tax revenues are only two examples of how the fiscal reforms have colored the way that central directives are implemented at the local level. More generally, the fiscal reforms have given local authorities access to and the ability to increase their resource endowments, to be used however they wish, regardless of constraints imposed by the center. The Chinese reforms have invigorated the economy, but the success of local state corporatism may in the long run force the emergence of something akin to a federal system that more clearly recognizes the rights and power of localities.

[80] China Interview 8691.

[81] See Oi (fn. 70).

[15]

The Blind Man and the Elephant: Analysing the Local State in China[1]

Tony Saich

1. Introduction

The economic reforms launched by the Chinese Communist Party (CCP) from the late-1970s have transformed the Chinese polity in far-reaching ways and have produced a number of unforeseen outcomes. There has been a progressive decline in direct state control over the economy, with powers devolved from state agencies to enterprises, a decrease in the use of mandatory planning mechanisms and a concomitant increase in the use of market forces to guide distribution and increasingly production choices. Local governments have been accorded greater control over local economic activity and the redistribution of economic rewards.

The economic changes have redefined the social structure and are changing the distribution of power between the local state and both higher level authorities and society have altered the principles on which society is organised and the ways in which it interacts with the state apparatus. Chinese society has become more complex as a result in terms of both structure and attitudes and at the same time has become more fluid and dynamic than at any time since the early 1950s. There is greater social and geographical mobility and horizontal interaction and integration have developed as the vertical and cellular boundaries of the traditional Leninist system have become more porous. While the central leadership rejects political reform that will challenge the CCP's dominant role and denounce the 'western separation of powers', there have been significant changes in the way China is governed and these are most pronounced at the local level. Important in guiding this process has been the conscious decentralisation of certain decision-making powers, the *de facto* fiscal decentralisation and the decline in the political centre's moral authority and financial capacity. State revenues only amounted to 14.2 per cent of GDP (Gross Domestic Product) in 1999, down from 36 per cent in 1978 and had dropped as low as 11 per cent. This has severely restricted the state's redistributive capacity

[1] I would like to thank the participants at the UCLA workshop 'Mapping the Local State in China' (8-9 June 2001) for the discussion that stimulated and refined a number of ideas presented here.

and has meant that local governments have been largely left to their own devices to raise the necessary funds. The relative decline in state revenues has created pressures at all levels and in all Chinese government agencies to meet recurrent costs from the locally generated revenues. This means that local resources and power structures determine increasingly political outcomes. Within the same province and even in adjacent counties one can see radically different socio-political outcomes deriving from the reforms. While debates about the nature of the national state have operated within a relatively limited spectrum of perspectives, there has been a profusion of definitions about the nature of local state in China. Some have seen reforms resulting in a decline in the role of the state but as is argued below the situation is rather more complex. The most important outcome has been a structuring of the state and a redistribution of power within the state sector. This chapter seeks to explain the variation and what the consequences have been.

First, it is necessary to outline what 'local' is taken to mean in this chapter. The level of analysis is at government administrative levels below the provincial level, primarily counties, municipalities and townships. While the village is not formally a level of government administration, it is included especially in terms of its relationship with the township. It is especially important to understand the interactions between these levels. In addition the local state at the county and township level are made up of multiple functional agencies, the interactions between which, both vertically and horizontally, are important for understanding local dynamics and outcomes. The nature of this organisational structure is such that its study is different from the field of local government study of centre-local government relations as normally defined. This is despite the fact that local governments in China enjoy little *de jure* legislative power. In the 1980s there were very few studies of these levels of the local state and most of those available tended to be of easily accessible coastal areas or within Guangdong province.[2] This has changed in the 1990s and we are now fortunate to have an extensive literature on a variety of local administrations conducted by Chinese and Western scholars. This is not to deny the importance of the province as a unit of analysis but the provincial governments are more heavily constrained than the lower levels of the administrative hierarchy.[3]

[2] See, for example, A. Chan, R. Madsen and J. Unger, *Chen Village*, (Berkeley: University of California Press, 1984); and E. Vogel, *One Step Ahead in China: Guangdong Under Reform*, (Cambridge, MA: Harvard UP, 1989).

[3] For good overviews of the changing nature of provincial government see D.S.G. Goodman, ed., *China's Provinces in Reform: Class, Community and Political Culture*, (New York: Routledge, 1997); P.T.Y. Cheung, Jae-Ho Chung and Zhimin Lin, eds, *Provincial Strategies of Economic Reform in Post-Mao China: Leadership, Politics, and Implementation*, (Armonk: M.E. Sharpe, 1998); and H. Hendrischke and Chongyi Feng, eds, *The Political Economy of China's Provinces: Comparative and Competitive Advantage*, (New York: Routledge, 1999). For an alarmist view that the reforms will strengthen the centripetal forces within China and might even led to a break-up of the nation-state see: J.F. William, *The Tyranny of History: The Roots of China's Crisis*, (London: Allen Lane, 1992); G. Segal, 'China's Changing Shape', *Foreign Affairs*, 73, 3 (May/June, 1994). For a more sober view that highlights the political control the centre retains over the province see Yasheng Huang, 'Why China Will not Collapse', *Foreign Policy*, 99 (Summer 1995), and 'Central-Local Relations in China during the Reform Era: The Economic and Institutional Dimension', *World Development*, 24, 4 (April 1996).

We begin by trying to get the financial picture straight as this has been determinant for most analysis. In the second part we review the different analyses to date that have been based primarily on the economic relationship between the local state and the economy. We then introduce two further important explanatory variables, the political contracting system and the structure of local society that have received less attention to date.

2. The Fiscal System and Its Consequences

The most important factor for our study has been the *de facto* decentralisation of powers away from central government agencies to those at lower levels, especially the effective decentralisation of the fiscal system. This more than any other factor accounts for local variation. Before the most recent fiscal reforms, only about one quarter of all state expenditures occurred at the central level and the major responsibility for financing infrastructure and providing social welfare occurs at the local level. Much research has seen the decline of state revenue as a percentage of GDP as a clear sign of decline in state capacity. This may be true for the central state but if one adds in the revenues that the local governments gather from a variety of resources, the percentage has not changed much over the last thirty years. There has not so much been a decline in the extractive capacity of the state under reforms but rather a realignment between the centre and the localities with the localities controlling far greater amounts of revenue than previously.[4] This realignment has had a significant impact on the nature of local government in China. By 1992, the central government's share of revenue was almost 39 per cent, having declined from 51 per cent in 1980, while collection had risen to 28 per cent from 20 per cent, and expenditure had dropped from 51 per cent to 31 per cent.[5]

The structure of the fiscal contracting system that was institutionalised in 1988 gave local governments a powerful incentive to encourage economic expansion but limited the centre's capacity to benefit sufficiently from this expansion.[6] These reforms transformed a province-collecting, centre-spending fiscal regime to an essentially self-financing regime for both the centre and the provinces.[7] Provinces collected and spent up to 70 per cent of budgetary revenues and while the provincial role for collection had declined in comparison with the Mao years, it had increased for expenditures.

Shaoguang Wang and Angang Hu cover the extreme regional inequalities that have been a product of reforms, *The Political Economy of Uneven Development: The Case of China*, (Armonk: M.E. Sharpe, 1999).

[4] Dali Yang, 'Reform and the Restructuring of Central-Local Relations', in D.S.G. Goodman and G. Segal, eds, *China Deconstructs: Politics, Trade and Regionalism*, (New York: Routledge, 1994), especially pp. 61 and 64.

[5] Le-Yin Zhang, 'Chinese Central-Provincial Fiscal Relationships, Budgetary Decline and the Impact of the 1994 Fiscal Reform: An Evaluation', *The China Quarterly*, 157 (March 1999) 120.

[6] Yang, 'Reform and Restructuring', p. 74.

[7] Zhang, 'Chinese Central-Provincial Fiscal Relationships', p. 121.

Government revenue as presented in Chinese statistics is comprised of two major components: the unitary budget and the extra-budgetary funds (EBF) for both the central and the local governments. The unitary budget comprises taxes, fees and revenues collected by state financial offices and subject to formal budgeting by the centre. The Ministry of Finance provides the central supervisory role together with the local authorities.[8] The EBF cover officially sanctioned charges such as surcharges from taxes and public utilities, road maintenance fees and incomes from enterprises run by various administrative agencies. The EBF, while reported to higher administrative levels, are, to all intents and purposes, only subject to control and oversight by the local authorities (county or township). The local financial bureau manages to fund accordingly the plans of the local administration.

Not surprisingly, it is difficult to calculate what the real value of the EBF is and one official review reported that the real amount for 1995 was probably 1.6 times that recorded in official statistics. Christine Wong has estimated that the EBF amount to 12 per cent of GDP, compared to an official budget of 14 per cent.[9] These officially sanctioned EBF do not include the various revenues collected locally without central authorisation: often referred to as self-raised funds (*zichou zijin*).[10] If one adds these extra establishment funds that by their very nature do not turn up in the statistics, the total sum of revenues available were the same in the early 1990s as at the start of the reforms; 39.5 per cent as compared with 40 per cent.[11] This means that those observers who have suggested that there has been a major decline in the state's extractive capacity have relied on the official budgetary revenue and this has indeed declined by almost 60 per cent (but not in absolute terms as the economy has been growing at a rapid rate). The alarmism that some have sounded about the decline of state capacity in this sense is unwarranted. What is important is the changing nature of the centre-local fiscal relationship and the changing role and importance of the different funds as controlled by the centre and the localities.

This is of vital importance for understanding the incentives for the local state. One inheritance of the Soviet fiscal system has been that the local government has always provided the provision of basic public goods, with very few exceptions. Apart from nationally designated poor counties that receive transfers and those that receive such transfers from the province, localities are by and large on their own to raise funds. Two factors have exacerbated this situation increasing local state concern with revenue generation. First, despite fiscal decentralisation the central government has retained control over the policy agenda. While the accounts of localities avoiding or deflecting central policy are many, the centre still sets many tasks that must be carried out and imposes burdens to be met.[12] Second,

[8] A. Wedeman, 'Budgets, Extra-Budgets, and Small Treasuries: Illegal Monies and Local Autonomy in China', *Journal of Contemporary China*, 9, 25 (November 2000) 498.

[9] Presentation by C. Wong at the workshop on 'Mapping the Local State in Reform-Era China', Los Angeles, 8-9 June 2000.

[10] For township revenue sources see Xueju Li, Zhenyao Wang and Jinsu Tang, eds, *Zhongguo xiangzhen zhengquan de xianzhuang yu gaige* [The Current Situation and Reform of Chinese Township and Village Regimes], (Beijing: Zhongguo shehui chubanshe, 1985) pp. 35-6.

[11] Zhang, 'Chinese Central-Provincial Fiscal Relationships', p. 123.

[12] There is the much quoted phrase of local officials *'tamen you zhengce, women you duice'* [they have their policies and we have our counter measures].

the 1994 financial reforms affected the relationship. The intention was to raise the ratio of the budget to GDP and the ratio of centrally collected revenue to total budget revenue.[13] The centre hoped to raise its share of state revenue to at least 60 per cent with 40 per cent as central expenditure and 20 per cent as transfer grants to local governments. This required clarifying the division of spending responsibility, how taxes would be divided between the centre and the localities and how to divide the administration for the collection of local taxes. This restructuring has indeed been successful with the share of centrally collected revenue rising from 22 per cent in 1993 to 56.5 per cent by 1997.[14] For the first quarter of 1997, the growth rate of centrally collected revenue was reported to be on a par with that of locally collected revenue, thus overcoming the initial tendency of the localities only to collect for themselves. The centre's share of budgetary revenues grew from 2.8 per cent of GDP to 6.2 per cent in 1998.[15]

Once a fee collected by a local government is reclassified as a tax, it is subject to revenue sharing agreements with higher level administrations. Thus, local governments still have a major incentive to concentrate on the EBF part of their revenue stream and the other non-sanctioned fees and levies. These are the funds that the localities can use to finance their own requirements, including their own salaries and related administrative costs. Particularly important, as we shall discuss in more detail below, is the management of local enterprises that can provide revenue to the local government and the use of other state assets such as land to rent out for commercial activities. In fact, rather than frowning on commercial activity, local governments are positively encouraged to use state assets to raise funds to cover their management and operational costs.

This structure has serious consequences for the nature of local government. Some have worried that it has led to an unhealthy rise in the power of the regions[16] and certainly there are legitimate concerns about the consequences of the significant regional inequality that has been an integral part of the reform strategy.[17] By contrast others have interpreted the trend in a positive light arguing that what is developing is 'federalism, Chinese style'.[18] In this latter view, local governments have primary control over behaviour, policy and economic outcomes with each autonomous in its own sphere of authority. They credit this with placing limits on central control and providing richer localities with substantial independent sources of revenue, authority, and political support. At the same time the emergent system induces competition among local governments, serving not only to constrain their behaviour but also to provide

[13] Zhang, 'Chinese Central-Provincial Fiscal Relationships', p. 131.

[14] *Ibid.*

[15] Jae-Ho Chung, 'Regional Disparities, Policy Choices and State Capacity in China', *China Perspectives*, 31 (September-October 2000) 46.

[16] See, for example, Shaoguang Wang, 'The Rise of the Regions: Fiscal Reform and the Decline of Central State Capacity in China', in A.G. Walder, ed., *The Waning of the Communist State: Economic Origins of Political Decline in China and Hungary*, (Berkeley: University of California Press, 1995) pp. 87-113; and Yang Zhong, 'Withering Governmental Power in China?', *Communist and Post-Communist Studies*, 29, 4 (December 1996) 364.

[17] Wang and Hu, *The Political Economy of Uneven Development*.

[18] G. Montinola, Y. Qian and B. Weingast, 'Federalism, Chinese Style: The Political Basis for Economic Success in China', *World Politics*, 48, 1 (October 1995) 50-81.

them with a range of positive incentives to foster local economic prosperity. However, the problems or advantages do not arise from the decline in the fiscal capacity of the state as a whole but rather from how revenues are collected and controlled. Given the mess that the centre has often made in directing the national economy, perhaps it is just as well that its capacity is curtailed. However, there is no guarantee that the local state will pursue development strategies that are any more rational or beneficial to their populations.

One general imperative that emerges and cuts across more economically developed and more resource constrained localities is that the need to derive one's own sources of revenue has become more acute. The resultant fiscal inequalities that arise from this system have led to an enormous inequality in the provision of public goods and services. At the same time, popular expectations and those of higher administrative levels about the range and kinds of services that they should provide have not declined. As a result the tendency is for the financial pressures to lead to the preference for a development plan that maximises short-term revenue over longer-term needs and for distributional and welfare priorities to be disfavoured. The main concern at the national and at the local level has been on how to increase revenues rather than on what the role of good government should be. A rethink of the kinds of work in which the government should be engaged, its relationship to the local community, and the acceptance that many functions previously managed by the state in the field of social welfare and asset development will have to be taken on by local communities themselves has been shunned.

The 1994 reforms have heightened the tendency to seek off-budget revenues as they require local counties to hand-over 75 per cent of value added taxes but they have increased obligations. This has led, for example, to the local Chaoyang branch (Beijing) of the fire brigade using its privileged access to high pressure water to operating a car wash out of the fire station and the Qianmen police station (Beijing) to purchase a Sichuan restaurant to be able to generate funds to pay off informers. It has also had more perverse effects with local governments running prostitution rackets through their hotels and Karaoke bars, doctors relying on kick-backs from pharmaceutical concerns and nature reserves struggling to restrain poaching by villagers only to turn around and contract out extraction to logging, fishing or mining concerns.

The most pressing need is to meet the wage bill and cover entertainment allowances and to cover vehicle costs for local officials. Together these items compromise the overwhelming majority of expenditures for local administrations and they seem to have risen significantly under reforms. Indeed a number of reformers have argued that the quickest way to cut down the demonstrations that come from the illegal levies and fines is to cut the number of government employees, a message that Premier Zhu Rongji has taken to heart. One recent national survey showed that in a medium-sized county with a population of around half a million and with 5000 administrative staff, financial revenues cover 60 per cent of the salaries. Thirty per cent of the salaries had to be raised by themselves and ten per cent from direct fines on farmers. The situation is even worse at the township level (40 000 population with 100 staff). Here 35 per cent collect their salary directly from farmers.[19] Even so, many local administrations have great difficulty in meeting salary bills. One village I visited only had money for administrative expenses. In central and west China and even Shandong, some townships have not paid their officials for nine months.[20]

In particular the financial pressures have led to a policy to expand township and village enterprises as a first priority as these are seen as the most stable sources for local income. This is the case irrespective of whether the locality concerned is relatively wealthy or poor. In addition to the change in fiscal stimulus, decollectivisation and the return to a household based farming system removed agriculture as a source of viable financing for local governments.[21] It has led many inland counties to try to ape the coastal areas in setting up similar kinds of industries irrespective of considerations of whether there is the necessary skilled labour force, a sufficient infrastructure and a market for the product itself. Local leaders have also developed strategies for hiding revenues from the higher level authorities. In Liaoning some US$ 4 million in electricity fees was kept away from provincial coffers by county governments, for example. The province sold the electricity to the counties at 0.3 cents but the county sold it to consumers for 1.25 cents.[22]

These phenomena are even more noticeable in the poorer areas. As Albert Park and his colleagues have noted 'heightened pressures on revenue-starved local governments may lead to over investment in revenue generating industrial enterprises, encouraged bureaucratic predation of enterprise resources and regional protectionism, and diverted attention away from long-term development strategies.'[23] Their conclusions were based on research in a county without a financial surplus situated in Shaanxi province. The province itself has consistently run fiscal deficits exceeding 20 per cent of expenditures making local governments increasingly self-reliant in terms of meeting expenditure responsibilities. Deficit provinces and counties have also suffered from the decline in the fiscal transfers from the central state, something that the 1994 reforms were designed to reverse.

The use of extra-budget funds and the self-raised funds (*zichou zijin*) has clearly been increasing. This financial reality is not only perpetuating but also exacerbating existing inequalities between and within regions. In poor and remote communities where marketisation has barely begun and where the scope of economic activities will always remain limited, local treasuries have little recourse other than the elimination of services. In many poorer parts of China, rural medical health schemes have been wiped out and the access to schooling has been drastically reduced.

[19] Guo Wei, 'Jiakuai xianxiang jigou gaige, cong yuantou shang jianqing nongmin fudan' [Speed Up Organisational Structure Reform at the County and Township Level and Reduce the Farmers' Burdens from the Very Beginning], *Liaowang* [Outlook Weekly], 43 (26 October 1998) 34-5.

[20] Interview, September 2000.

[21] J. Chun Oi, 'Fiscal Reform and the Economic Foundations of Local State Corporatism in China', *World Politics*, 45, 1 (October 1992) 115.

[22] Interview with provincial-level official, November 1999.

[23] A. Park *et al.*, 'Distributional Consequences of Reforming Local Public Finance in China', *The China Quarterly*, 147 (September 1996) 751-2.

Increasingly, many poor regions rely on extra budgetary revenues for even the reduced services they can provide and evidence suggests that this is increasing. According to Huang Yasheng, in 1991 extra budgetary expenditures for education were around 15 per cent of budget expenditures as compared with 8 per cent in 1979.[24] Guizhou province derives fully 80 per cent of its educational funding from such sources.[25] Park and his colleagues calculated that in Shaanxi 86 and 89 per cent respectively of provincial consolidated revenues and expenditures were from extra budgetary funds. It is precisely this kind of funding that is most vulnerable in an economic downturn.[26]

In the poorer counties, even EBFs are scarce and local administrations are dependent on the self-raised funds to cover costs. These are fees derived from the township and village levels and usually fall outside of auditing scrutiny by higher levels. They are often referred to as the three arbitraries (*sanluan*): arbitrary taxation (*luan shoufei*), arbitrary fines (*luan fakuan*) and arbitrary expropriation (*luan tanpai*).[27]

The reforms and the financial pressures have led to both the variation in service provision and even eradication of services in poorer areas and attempts to reorganise the state at the local level to cut-back the number of staff on salary. One particular feature of the determination of township government is by population and geographic size. No consideration was paid to the township's financial and economic conditions. This would mean that, before the most recent attempts at administrative reform, the number of government agencies in a poor township could be the same as in an affluent one. Naturally this has meant that the poorer a township, the greater the pressure to extract fees from the farmers. This has caused some to suggest a shift to the size of governmental apparatus being determined by financial capacity with essential government agencies funded in poorer areas through financial transfers.[28]

Combined with the rising income inequality, the financial pressures on the local state in China are accounting for the huge variation in the provision of public goods and services during the transition. As the World Bank has shown, access to health and education services was still widely available in the 1980s but became more dependent on incomes in the 1990s.[29] In 1998 22.2 per cent of those in high-income areas were covered by cooperative medical facilities but only one to three per cent in poorer areas were covered.[30]

The focus on cost recovery has hampered poorer areas from providing good facilities and the capacity for richer areas to invest more in educa-

[24] Yasheng Huang, 'Fiscal Reforms and Political Institutions', *Problems of Post-Communism*, 48, 1 (January/February 2001).

[25] Discussion with provincial vice governor, May 1997.

[26] Park *et al.*, 'Distributional Consequences', p. 767.

[27] Wedeman, 'Budgets, Extra-Budgets and Small Treasuries', p. 490.

[28] Su Nie, 'Xiangzhen zhengfu xingzheng tizhi gaige maichu zhongyao yibu' [An Important Step of Administrative System Reform of Township Government], *Liaowang* [Outlook Weekly], 25 (October 2000) 24.

[29] World Bank, *Sharing Rising Incomes: Disparities in China* (Washington, DC: The World Bank, 1997) p. 23.

[30] Ling Zhu, 'Shei lai wei nongmin kanbing chiyao tigong shehui baozhang' [Who Can Provide the Farmers with Medical Services], *Liaowang*, 16 (17 April 2000) 41-3.

tion, health and infrastructure means that the inequalities will increase further over time. For example, while a strong logic for the establishment of the village committees might have been to enforce state policy, those in richer areas actually preside over quickly growing revenues. Even those in poor areas have the fees they collect and, when market price is above state price for grain, the differential to expend. While villagers' committees in poorer areas might be more concerned with how to raise the revenues to cover basic welfare requirements, richer villages preside over an extensive income from local enterprises and make decisions that concern village investment in road building, hospital development and so on. According to John Dearlove, in the early 1990s in Fujian, committees had revenues for public expenditure that amounted to 44 per cent of total *per capita* village income.[31] In Guankou village Henan, the committee presides over 13 companies ranging from building materials to processing agricultural products to a 1000 head pig farm. This has enabled the committee to avoid illegal levies and fines and have one agricultural tax for all. In addition, funds cover all road-building costs and it was able to build a two-story 100-bed hospital. Even in the poorer nearby Fanghsan village 350 000 yuan had been invested for road repair and relieving farmers from forced unpaid labour.[32]

The impact for poor rural households is particularly dramatic. Here the example of healthcare provision is used. With the loss of the prepaid collective medical system with the disbanding of the communes in the early 1980s, some 90 per cent of rural households have to pay directly for almost all of the health services used.[33] From 1981 health care facilities were instructed that they should cover recurrent costs, with the exception of staff, from user charges and by the mid-1980s preventive care facilities were also charging on a fee-for-service basis.[34] Coverage in the collective system has dropped dramatically, from almost 80 per cent in 1979 to only 2 per cent in 1987 before improving to around 10 per cent by the mid-1990s. Thus in terms of national health spending, while the collective schemes accounted for 20 per cent in 1978, by 1993 they only accounted for 2 per cent.[35] As the World Bank concluded in its 1996 report, 'the downturn in China's health performance relative to its income level coincided with agricultural reform that reduced the ability of the village to tax the peasants.'[36]

The basic problem of healthcare delivery derives from the change of the ownership structure of village networks and the nature of the incentive system that has arisen from these changes.[37] With medical facilities there has been a growth in private medical provision and a shift away from pre-

[31] J. Dearlove, 'Village Politics', in R. Benewick and P. Wingrove, eds, *China in the 1990s*, (Houndmills: Macmillan Press, 1995) pp. 126-7.

[32] Interviews with village officials, June 1996.

[33] World Bank, *Financing Health Care: Issues and Options for China*, (Washington, DC: The World Bank, 1997) p. 47.

[34] Shanlian Hu and Minghe Jiang, 'The People's Republic of China', in D.H. Brooks and Myo Thant, eds, *Social Sector Issues in Transitional Economies of Asia*, (Oxford: Oxford UP, 1998) p. 192.

[35] United Nations Development Programme [UNDP], *China: Human Development Report: Human Development and Poverty Alleviation 1997*, (Beijing: UNDP, 1998) p. 37.

[36] World Bank, *Country Report: China*, (Washington, DC: The World Bank, 1996) p. 127.

[37] UNDP, *China*, pp. 36 and 38.

ventive medical care to fee-for-service with local governments in poor areas less able to provide adequate support. This increases the financial burden on the rural household. The choice in the poor areas is stark if major illness strikes. Either wait and die or run up economic burdens that would take decades to pay off.

Zhu Rongji's policy to trim the bureaucracy does not leave the local state untouched but reforms are more difficult to implement. While provincial level cuts were pursued in 1999, those for the county and township levels were delayed and were only just beginning on 2000-2001 because fears of instability with lay-offs from SOEs were already beginning to take a toll. The government estimates that around 60 per cent of county level staff are effectively redundant.[38] If this is true, redundancy at the township level must be even higher. The objective at all non-central levels of government is to reduce those on salary from 5.18 million, plus another 300 000 who are also paid by the government, by 2.5 million. In part the savings will go to boost salaries for those who remain; salaries are expected to be raised by 30 per cent. Many complain that if the numbers are not cut as expected, highly likely, the result will be increased expenditures for local governments and that this could well result in more levies on the farmers to cover the salary hikes.

While in many poor areas the state's presence is still overbearing, there are examples from wealthier areas of the local state trying to reduce its bureaucracy and interference in society while increasing accountability. For example, in Qindu district, in Xianyang next to the major Northwest city of Xi'an, local officials have decided that the government system is too large for the local economy. District party and government offices are to be fused and they expect to reduce the number of officials by 50 per cent. The restructuring of the local government reflects the changing economic structure of the district. The district has undertaken a major programme of industrial overhaul shedding its state-owned enterprise (SOE) sector and encouraging the private sector to expand. By 1998, of the 57 SOEs and collective enterprises (29 SOEs) under the district's control, 56 had undergone ownership 'transformation'. According to the Party Secretary, this had transformed the government's relationship with the enterprises from that of a 'parent' to a market-based one and was accompanied by a major restructuring of local government organs. Thus, for example, the Economics and Trade Bureau (*jingmao ju*) had been dissolved as the 22 enterprises under its control had dwindled to just one. Its residual functions had been taken over by a Comprehensive Economic Management Bureau (*zonghe jingji guanliju*) that covers all economic work, except agriculture, with a total staff of only seven or eight people. Given the importance of the non-state sector of the economy, a Private Economy Development Bureau (*siying jingji fazhan ju*) had been set up together with a Township and Village Enterprise Bureau (*xiangzhen qiye ju*). These changes, the party secretary reckoned had reduced the number of agencies by 25 per cent and the staff on payroll by 20.8 per cent putting it on the way to meeting the 50 per cent cut demanded by Premier Zhu.[39]

[38] *South China Morning Post*, (23 August 1999), Internet edition.
[39] Interviews and Qindu CCP Committee, 1999.

3. Interpretations of the Local State

With most problems having to be solved *in situ*, local resources and their distribution concern the majority of people's lives. While most observers agree that the economic powers of the local state have been enhanced through control over local industry and EBFs, there has been considerable disagreement about the emerging relationship between the local state and society.

The tendency for both Chinese and Western scholars has been to dwell on the fusion of political and economic power at local government levels. This has been accompanied in Western writings with an emphasis on property rights relationships. In this approach the local state is catalogued in terms of the property rights relationships that evolve from the financial decentralisation and the strategies that are taken to deal with this. The resultant structures are 'path dependent' on the economic structure that existed on the eve of reform.[40] Out of this approach comes a categorisation of local government forms: entrepreneurial, developmental, predatory, and varieties of corporatism. Before outlining these various approaches it is worth pointing out they may not be exclusionary categories. Not only might multiple models of state-society relations be operating at the same time in different administrative jurisdictions but also even within one locale different agencies might display tendencies toward developmentalism and predatory behaviour at the same time.[41] Further, we are dealing with a very fluid situation and what initially may appear as an example of a predatory local state may evolve over time into one of social partnership later. In those areas where the legacy from the commune era has been significant collective-run industry or where township and village enterprises have expanded rapidly, the local state is seen as dominating local society.[42] Especially in such areas where there is little large-scale enterprise (TVEs) that might prevent local officials from dominating the local economy so effectively, the likely outcome is liable to be corporatist. Walder in his study of Zouping county (Shandong) notes that it is impossible to explain the rapid economic development without taking note of the economic role played by local government officials. In his view, Zouping resembles an industrial corporation where revenue generation is paramount and the entire local government operates as a firm in a competitive environment.[43]

These ideas have been examined most extensively by Jean Oi with her use of 'local state corporatism' to explain the process of explosive rural eco-

[40] For an interesting overview of the literature see A. Shevchenko, 'Mapping Local State-Society Patterns', background paper prepared for 'Mapping the Local State in Reform-Era China'.

[41] See Tak-Wing Ngo, 'Developmental Imperative and Spoliatory Politics: A Comparative Study of Mainland China, Taiwan and Hong Kong', in this volume.

[42] J. Unger and A. Chan, 'Inheritors of the Boom: Private Enterprise and the Role of Local Government in a Rural South China Township', *The China Journal*, 42 (July 1999).

[43] A.G. Walder, 'Zouping in Perspective', in A.G. Walder, ed., *Zouping in Transition: The Process of Reform in Rural North China*, (Cambridge, MA: Harvard UP, 1998) pp. 16-23. On his idea of local governments as firms see 'Local Governments as Industrial Firms: An Organizational Analysis of China's Transitional Economy', *The American Journal of Sociology*, 101, 2 (September 1995) 263-301, and 'The County Government as an Industrial Corporation', in Walder, ed., *Zouping in Transition*, pp. 62-85.

nomic growth that took off in the 1980s and continued into the 1990s in areas such as Southern Jiangsu and Shandong.[44] Such areas have a legacy of collective-run industries that formed the basis for the township and village enterprise development. Oi shows how the change in incentives allowed local communist officials to play the key role in fostering this growth through local government entrepreneurship. The loss of agricultural revenue from decollectivisation combined with hardened budget constraints, while granting local governments greater rights over any surplus, were crucial. This meant that for those leaders willing to take up the challenge there was a major opportunity to develop the rural industrial economy. In Oi's view 'collectively-owned industrial enterprises served better both the political and the economic interests of local cadres during the initial stages of reform.'[45] In this process, conforming to Walder's suggestion, local officials acted like a board of directors in their management of village affairs.

A number of other writers have taken up similar themes in looking at the local state as developmental or entrepreneurial while there have been criticisms of 'corporatism' as an adequate explanatory mechanism. Marc Blecher in his study of Guanghan county, Sichuan province, noted a tendency for local governments to be entrepreneurial because of the effects of the need for revenue generation. Basically local governments went into business with various agencies at the county-level going into business to raise revenues and to provide employment opportunities for those who might be shaken off the government payroll.[46] A study of real estate and commerce government agencies in Tianjin by Jane Duckett found a similar tendency for government agencies to set up and run their own businesses.[47] The clear objective of these agencies is to turn a profit and it may not necessarily be for the broader developmental goals of the community over which they preside.

[44] For her most recent statement see J. Chun Oi, *Rural China Takes Off: Institutional Foundations of Economic Reform*, (Berkeley: University of California Press, 1999). For earlier iterations see 'Fiscal Reform and the Economic Foundations of Local State Corporatism in China', *World Politics*, 45, 1 (October 1992), and 'The Evolution of Local State Corporatism', in Walder, ed., *Zouping in Transition*, pp. 35-62. For others who have used a similar approach see J. Kai-Sing Kung's study of Wuxi, 'The Evolution of Property Rights in Village Enterprises: The Case of Wuxi County', in J. Chun Oi and A.G. Walder, eds, *Property Rights and Economic Reform in China*, (Stanford: Stanford UP, 1999) pp. 95-120; and the work by Nan Lin on China's 'richest' village, Daqiuzhuang, near Tianjin: Nan Lin and Chih-Jou Jay Chen, 'Local Elite as Officials and Owners: Shareholding and Property Rights in Daqiuzhuang', *ibid.*, pp. 145-70, and N. Lin and Xiaolan Ye, 'Chinese Rural Enterprises in Transformation: The End of the Beginning', *Issues and Studies*, 34, 11/12 (November/December 1998) 1-28. Lin has noted a variant on local state corporatism that is based on the strong clientalist ties that existed in his study area: see Nan Lin, 'Local Market Socialism: Local Corporatism in Action in Rural China', *Theory and Society*, 24 (1995) 301-54. Gregory Ruf in his study of Meishan County in Sichuan noted strong clientalist pressures that reduced societal influence on local government. See G. Ruf, *Cadres and Kin, Making a Socialist Village in West China, 1921-1991*, (Stanford: Stanford UP, 1998).

[45] Oi, *Rural China Takes Off*, p. 11.

[46] M. Blecher, 'Developmental State, Entrepreneurial State: The Political Economy of Socialist Reform in Xinji Municipality and Guanghan County', in G. White, ed., *The Chinese State in the Era of Economic Reform. The Road to Crisis*, (Houndmills: Macmillan Press, 1991) pp. 265-91.

[47] J. Duckett, *The Entrepreneurial State in China. Real Estate and Commerce Departments in the Reform Era Tianjin*, (London: Routledge, 1998).

By contrast Blecher in his work with Vivienne Shue on Xinji municipality (Hebei, formerly Shulu county) has suggested that the local state has been more developmental than entrepreneurial.[48] For them the distinction with the entrepreneurial local state is that official action is intended to promote the local economy by providing a good physical environment, the access to capital, and to provide linkage to external markets or important agencies. Unlike the entrepreneurial and corporate models the local officials do not get involved in economic activities directly but are more concerned with producing an enabling environment. The local government did not seek to maximise profits for the government but rather to expand 'developmental horizons'.[49] Blecher and Shue following the 'path dependence' school trace this tendency toward developmentalism to the legacy of the Maoist period. Prime explanatory factors were the continuity of leadership across the two periods and that there was a 'poor context for entrepreneurship' causing the local leadership to develop a broad based comprehensive development plan.

However, as noted above, the resources available to the local state vary enormously and this affects the nature of entrepreneurialism. Local leaders with no industrial base have either had to build one, often with disastrous results, or have been predatory. Even in the more economically developed areas, the nature of the local state can be more predatory than developmental or entrepreneurial. Sargeson and Zhang's study challenges Oi's and Walder's findings even for more developed areas on the basis of their work in a sub-district of Hangzhou, capital of Zhejiang province.[50] They question the general applicability of the assertion that local governments with strong property rights have acted as entrepreneurs fostering economic development and meeting social demands through the development of collective industries. Their study shows that local government officials put their own objectives above not only the aims of the central government but also above those of the local community. They assert that the notion of 'local state corporatism' mistakenly 'conflates the interests of local governments, individual officials and the members of local communities, and also fails to consider the broader implication of concentrating property and power in the hands of lower-level governments and officials'. With the lack of accountability the local community is excluded from the decision-making process and has no choice other than to go along with the decisions of the 'board of directors' whether they benefit the local community or not.

Jian Zhang presents a similarly critical view of the 'Southern Jiangsu' model (*Sunan moshi*) in a study of township and village enterprises in Kunshan. Zhang notes that the government is always supreme and seeks to control everything appointing the enterprise managers, determining the production quotas and investment levels. Decision-making powers of the enterprise are curtailed in favour of those of the local state. 'Market orien-

[48] M. Blecher and V. Shue, *Tethered Deer. Government and Economy in a Chinese County*, (Stanford: Stanford UP, 1996).

[49] Blecher, 'Developmental State', p. 270.

[50] S. Sargeson and Jian Zhang, 'Re-assessing the Role of the Local State: A Case Study of Local Government Interventions in Property Rights Reform in a Hangzhou District', *The China Journal*, 42 (July 1999) 77-99.

tation' is replaced by 'government orientation'. In the author's view this situation led to ownership reforms that began earnestly in 1996.[51]

To try to redress this problem a series of pilot reforms have been undertaken in Anhui province among others. In general, the township and village government is not allowed to become involved in investment and business activities as an owner of the collective economy. Instead the local administrations can only invest in the development of public goods such as transportation, water and electricity, education and basic agricultural facilities.[52] However, it is unclear where the revenue would come from for such activities without the enterprise revenues and myriad of fees.

With the promotion of share-holding in the latter part of the 1990s, it has become clear that local officials in a number of areas have used their official positions to acquire the major benefits for themselves, families and associates. Lin and Chen in their study of Daqiuzhuang reveal the networks between the local officials operating in a more predatory manner.[53] They show how the shareholding system has been exploited to transfer the local enterprises into private hands. As one local official in southern Jiangsu commented to me on hearing Premier Zhu's bold reform plan of March 1998, 'one last chance to get rich'. In one village I visited in May 1999 near Wuxi, Jiangsu province, the three key members of the party committee ran the village's major businesses. They complained that the pittance they received for party work (300 yuan a month) was no incentive. What was an incentive, however, was that they had used their positions of power to gain majority shareholding in the enterprises. One survey by Chinese researchers concluded that most village cadres only did the job for economic benefit, while 90 per cent of villagers refused to be village team heads as the salaries were too low and often could not be paid anyway.[54]

These observations run counter to the idea of a 'market transition' proposed by Victor Nee. Nee claims that the new opportunities in the local economy have provided individuals with control over financial and other resources independent of local cadre power. This has reduced the capacity for bureaucratic redistribution and the horizontal ties of 'market capital' have strengthened at the expense of the vertical ties of 'political capital'.[55] Much research and those who favour corporatist outcomes conjecture that the power of local officials has been enhanced by increased control over resources for distribution to those within their jurisdiction. Chinese researchers under Xu Yong have argued that despite the village elections, the

[51] Jian Zhang , 'Dui Sunan xiangzhen qiye gaizhi de kaocha – Laizi Kunshan de baogao' [Survey on the Restructuring of Township and Village Enterprises in Southern Jiangsu – Report from Kunshan], *Jingji shehui tizhi bijiao yanjiu* [Comparative Economic and Social Systems], 4 (1998) 56-62. For a similarly critical view of the anti-market nature of Southern Jiangsu see Renshou Zhang, 'Yanhai nongcun jingji fazhan moshi yu quyu wenhua bijiao yanjiu' [Comparative Study of the Economic Development Pattern and Regional Culture in the Rural Coastal Areas], *Jingji shehui tizhi bijiao yanjiu*, 2 (1995) 46-50.

[52] Su Nie, 'An Important Step of Administrative System Reform'.

[53] Lin and Chen, 'Local Elite as Officials and Owners'.

[54] Li, Wang and Tang, *The Current Situation and Reform*, p. 32.

[55] See, for example, V. Nee, 'A Theory of Market Transition: From Redistribution to Markets in State Socialism', *American Sociological Review*, 54, 5 (1989) 663-81, and 'Organizational Dynamics of Market Transition: Hybrid Forms, Property Rights, and Mixed Economy in China', *Administrative Science Quarterly*, 37 (1992) 1-27.

head of the villagers' committee acts as much as an agent of the state as a representative of the villagers.[56] Certainly the widespread practice of buying and selling of official posts suggests that much can be earned from them. Sayings such as the following have become commonplace in the countryside: 'if you bribe your superior 10 to 20 000 yuan, you have just checked in. If you offer him 30 to 40 000 yuan, you have registered for promotion. If you give him 80 to 100 000, you will get promoted.'[57]

In addition to challenges to 'corporatism' as an effective concept to describe these local states, one must bear in mind that we are also dealing with a system that is very fluid. Recent research, including that of Oi herself, suggests that the Southern Jiangsu area is going under significant changes that call 'local state corporatism' into question. In addition to the shareholding system mentioned above, it is clear that competition for the TVEs has increased and that local governments are under harder budget constraints. This has meant that, in addition to 'privatising' profitable enterprises, there is greater pressure for the local state to get rid of those that are not profitable or are unlikely to remain profitable in the foreseeable future. This is blurring the distinctions between those local states with a larger private sector and those that had a primarily corporatist structure.[58] Research by Park and Shen on 15 counties in Jiangsu and Zhejiang reveals a massive trend toward privatisation. In 1994 only 92 of the 415 enterprises surveyed were private, but by 1997 the total was 231 and it has risen since.[59]

Predatory practices have usually been identified with resource-deficient localities or those that are dependent on one product.[60] The work of Guo in Jinguan township in Northwest Yunnan reveals this, although its predation is mediated somewhat by the fact that the township receives limited subsidies for being both a minority and poor designated county.[61]

[56] Yong Xu, 'Use Village Self-Governance to Promote the Administration of Village Level Public Finances', paper delivered at the Conference to Mark the Tenth Anniversary of the Organic Law on Village Self-Governance (Beijing: n. p., 1995), and Hou'an Zhang and Yong Xu, *Zhongguo nongcun zhengzhi wending yu fazhan* [The Stabilisation and Development of Chinese Village Politics], (Wuhan: Wuhan chubanshe, 1995).

[57] Jingben Rong *et al.*, *Cong yalixing tizhi xiang minzhu hezuo tizhi de zhuanbian* [The Transformation from a Pressurised System to a Democratic Cooperative System], (Beijing: Zhongyang bianyi chubanshe, 1998) p. 315.

[58] J. Chun Oi, 'The Evolution of Local State Corporatism', in Walder, ed., *Zouping in Transition*, pp. 35-61. See also S.H. Whiting, 'The Regional Evolution of Ownership Forms: Shareholding Cooperatives and Rural Industry in Shanghai and Wenzhou', in Oi and Walder, *Property Rights and Economic Reform in China*, pp. 171-200.

[59] A. Park and Minggao Shen, 'Joint Liability Lending and the Rise and Fall of China's Township and Village Enterprises', unpublished paper, 2000.

[60] However, it is worth noting that where there are no local resources, the leadership of the village may be non-existent in terms of predation or any other activity and the villagers may despise local leaders. O'Brien has written on the existence of 'paralysed' local governments while Wang in his study of a village in Honghu county, Hebei, describes an environment within which local officials cannot make ends meet and are rejected by the local community. K. O'Brien, 'Implementing Political Reform in China's Villages', *Australian Journal of Chinese Affairs*, 32 (July 1994) 33-60, and Xiaotao Wang, 'The Politics of Village Elections: The Case of North Village', *Issues and Studies*, 35, 6 (November/December 1999) 167-85.

[61] Xiaolin Guo, 'The Role of Local Government in Creating Property Rights: A Comparison of Two Townships in Northwest Yunnan', in Oi and Walder, eds, *Property Rights and Economic Reform in China*, pp. 71-99. A more obviously predatory community is that stud-

It is a poor township where the local administration forced the farmers to plant tobacco. This generated revenue for the township government because of a good revenue-sharing agreement with the county-level government. For the province as a whole the tobacco industry provides 70 per cent of the revenues. Since 1991, the local county has obliged 11 of the 18 townships to grow tobacco and only excluded those in the mountainous areas where the conditions were clearly not conducive. Not surprisingly the farmers were unhappy as the tobacco took land away from their capacity to grow rice and they earned less from tobacco. The county government derives enormous revenues, however, as it operates a sales monopoly and has the highest agricultural tax at 38 per cent. To buy compliance of the township authorities, the county signed a revenue-sharing agreement that allowed the township to keep two-thirds of the tobacco revenue. This cosy agreement ran into problems at the end of 1993 when a bad harvest combined with the government's harsh extraction policy to cause public protests. Compulsory tobacco production was abandoned in 1994 but Guo surmises that this was because of the general 1994 fiscal reform that adjusted the sharing of tobacco revenues between higher and lower levels of government. When the county reintroduced the tobacco quota in 1996, there was no coercion, with the result that only 10 per cent of the quota was met.[62]

The predatory nature of local leadership is reflected in the popular use of phrases such as *wuzi dengke* and the complaint by locals that they are required to provide cadres the best housing, the prettiest women in the village to marry, and the fattest pigs to slaughter for the celebration.[63] *Wuzi dengke* traditionally had a positive meaning in Imperial times with a father whose five sons all passed the examinations to become officials.[64] In Republican China it became a term to criticise the abuses of Nationalist officials, and it has been revived to describe the predatory habits of local rural officials.

The picture is different again in areas with a high degree of privatisation. Unger and Chan in their work on Xiqiao township in Guangdong, not far from Hong Kong, show how the criteria for success in private enterprise and public office are beginning to converge.[65] The local township government does not need to levy any general taxes on village households and has been strongly in favour of local private business. As they conclude, this experience counters the general writing on local government in two significant ways.[66] First, local officials do not give priority to publicly owned industry over the private sector and secondly they do not insist on relationships in which private enterprises are subordinate to and depen-

ied by Jieh-Min Wu in Xinzheng village in Henan where local officials interventions into land distribution with the objective of consolidating land to promote industrial growth led to a decline in village incomes. Jieh-Min Wu, 'State Polity and *Guanxi* Network Adaptation in China: Local Bureaucratic Rent-Seeking', in Si-Ming Li and Wing-Shing Tang, eds, *China's Regions, Policy, and Economy: A Study of Spatial Transformation in the Post-Reform Era*, (Hong Kong: The Chinese UP, 2000) pp. 309-47.

[62] Guo, 'The Role of Local Government in Creating Property Rights', p. 77, ftn. 16.

[63] Thus, many villagers with whom I spoke did not like the policy of cadre rotation.

[64] The *wuzi* stand for gold, silver, houses, cars, and women.

[65] Unger and Chan, 'Inheritors of the Boom', pp. 45-74.

[66] *Ibid.*, p. 73.

dent on them. Zhang Renshou confirms these findings with his research on Wenzhou in Zhejiang province where private business is highly developed.[67] Zhang found that the enterprises were guided by the market and the local administrations did not interfere with their production of business activities.[68]

However, in other areas, the development of a private sector has not necessarily led to less dependence on officials for getting things done. David Wank's work in the Special Economic Zone of Xiamen has revealed what he terms 'symbiotic clientalism' between local government officials and entrepreneurs.[69] Whereas good relations with officials have evolved from the networks that can allow for profits to be made to one where officials provide security, they remain important players in entrepreneurs' lives. The protection that officials provide results in economic rewards for them or in employment opportunities for themselves or for family members.[70]

Empirical research thus questions the viability of one model to describe the nature of the local government in China. China is a patchwork of different relationships, each of which is negotiated through a complex interaction between branches of government at the same level, above and below and between the agencies of the local government and society. The precise outcome will be dependent on a location's historical legacy, resource endowment, and leadership. The main general imperative that emerges that cuts across more economically developed and more resource constrained localities is the need to derive revenue and this has become more acute with the *de facto* fiscal decentralisation that has taken place. This has been dealt with extensively above and underpins those analyses that argue from a property rights perspective and privilege an analysis based on the role of the local state in the economy. The next two sections deal with two factors that have received less emphasis in recent writings: the political contracting system and the structure of the local society and the degree of community organisation or homogeneity or heterogeneity. Many local officials may well be party members but they are also members of the local community and with the moderate increase in local accountability through village elections and transparency regulations they have to take this seriously.

[67] Zhang, 'Comparative Study of the Economic Development Pattern'.

[68] See also the work of Whiting on Wenzhou who sees an increase in the bargaining power of the private sector *vis-à-vis* local officials. S.H. Whiting, 'The Regional Evolution of Ownership Forms', and Id., *Power and Wealth in China's Rural Industry: The Political Economy of Institutional Change*, (New York: Cambridge UP, 1999).

[69] D. Wank, 'Private Business, Bureaucracy, and Political Alliance in a Chinese City', *Australian Journal of Chinese Affairs*, 33 (January 1995) 55-71, and *Commodifying Communism: Business, Trust and Politics in a Chinese City*, (New York: Cambridge UP, 1999).

[70] Other works with similar findings are Bruun's study of an urban district in Western Chengdu and Unger's study of private business associations in Beijing. See O. Bruun, 'Political Hierarchy and Private Entrepreneurship in a Chinese Neighbourhood', in Walder, ed., *The Waning of the Communist State*, pp. 184-212. For a contrasting study that stresses that connections will become less important with development is D. Guthrie, *Dragon in a Three-Piece Suit: The Emergence of Capitalism in China*, (Princeton: Princeton UP, 1999).

4. The Political Contracting System

We need to understand far more about the political demands that are placed on local officials by their superior agencies to complete our picture of the forces that are shaping the state at the local level. In some areas reforms have clearly led to local officials enjoying greater financial freedom from higher levels and afforded them less dependence on higher level approval for career advancement and economic reward. However, as Christopher Nevitt notes, the vertical chain of career advancement is more a concern for those at municipal and provincial leadership than for those at lower levels.[71] Yet it is clear that even those officials working at the county and township level have to be cognisant of the demands that the higher levels of administrative leadership place on them.

The work of Maria Edin, Susan Whiting, and that of a group of researchers under the Compilation and Translation Bureau of the Central Committee have argued persuasively that we need to shift attention from a pure political economy approach that views state agents as revenue maximisers and to pay more attention to the political incentives generated by the cadre responsibility system and the political contraction system and the performance contracts (*gangwei mubiao zerenshu*) that local governments and officials have to sign.[72]

These performance contracts do not discourage economic development, far from it, but make it clear that this is just one part of a complex set of tasks that local officials are required to carry out including maintaining social order, delivering taxes to higher levels of government, and maintaining birth control quotas. There are multiple principle-agent relationships that operate between the levels of local government and they need to be understood better in order to improve analysis of the local state, its functioning and the incentive structure for local officials.

The precise nature of the contracts varies across time and place but they do set out performance expectations that provide the basis for official evaluation. The system originated in the late-1980s and became more formalised through the 1990s. Thus, in Mi county (later Xinmi City) the first countywide implementation of the cadre responsibility system was launched in March 1988. This, with the contracts for accomplishing rural work for 1988, was signed between the county party committee and the county government on one side and the secretaries of the party committees of the townships and the leaders of the townships on the other.[73] Each county will set out performance contracts for the mayors and party secretaries of the townships under their jurisdiction to sign. Then contracts are signed between the towns and townships and the functional departments under their jurisdiction and then finally between the heads of these functional departments and their work personnel. Work personnel are often required to make a financial

[71] C.E. Nevitt, 'Private Business Associations in China: Evidence of Civil Society or Local State Power?', *The China Journal*, 36 (July 1996) 39-40.

[72] M. Edin, *Market Forces and Communist Power: Local Political Institutions and Economic Development in China*, (Uppsala: Uppsala UP, 2000); Whiting, *Power and Wealth in Rural China*; and Jingben Rong *et al.*, *The Transformation from a Pressurised System.*

[73] *Ibid.*, pp. 276-7.

deposit when they sign their contract and this will only be returned if they accomplish their tasks.[74]

One problem arising from this system is the weakening of the capacity for comprehensive development by township governments. One set of Chinese researchers has even referred to the responsibilities of the townships being 'dismembered' by the county. Most government agencies at the township level actually receive the contracts from the county and this undermines the township's capacity to coordinate the work of their functional agencies as the administrative power in the township region does not belong to the township.[75] Other have pointed out the weak position of the township government with it lacking not only power but also the necessary finances to carry out its mandates.[76] With the various agencies under the direction of the county, township governments have little to no power to decide personnel arrangements, financial revenue and expenditures and the allocation of materials to the county branches in the township. For example in Laiwu (Shandong province), only five staff in 28 township government offices were under the leadership of the township government. This had led some to dub the township government as a 'big title' (*paizi xiang*), 'many responsibilities' (*zeren da*), 'with little power' (*quanli xiao*) and 'difficult to deal with' (*banshi nan*).[77]

Contracting produces the same kind of relationship between the township and the village where village organisations become politicised and an extended branch of the township government at the village level.[78] One village leader felt that all 'so-called village autonomy' meant that 'leaders in the village do not receive salaries and they do not demand expenses from the township government.'[79] In terms of tasks to be completed, village leaders are said to see family planning, collecting fees and grains from farmers and conscription as administrative responsibilities, meaning that they are contracted from above. However, Hu sees the current relationship between the townships and villages today as significantly different from that of the commune and production brigades in the past. The contracts cannot be implemented solely through administrative fiat but rather the township must use material resources to exert control effectively. Village committees will fulfil the tasks mainly to get help and assistance from the township. This is even more important in the poorer areas where financial appropria-

[74] *Ibid.*, p. 277.

[75] Li, Wang and Tang, *The Current Situation and Reform of Power*, p. 5.

[76] Ziqiang Duan, 'Xiangzhang zui pa tizhi bu shun chulu zai yu dangzheng qihe – Beijing Changping xian xiang zhen jigou shezhi qingzhuang diaocha baogao' [Head of the Township Is Afraid of a Systemic Conflict. Resolution Lies in the Integration of Party and Government – An Investigative Report of Township Structure in Changping County Beijing], in Li, Wang and Tang, *The Current Situation and Reform*, p. 12.

[77] Junliang Dai *et al.*, *Zhongguo xiangzhen zhengquan jianshe gailun* [Outline of Township and Village Government], (Beijing: Renmin chubanshe, 1991) pp. 115-16.

[78] Xuedong Yang, 'Liyi fenhua he baohu–xiandaihua yu shichang jincheng zhong de Zhongyuan nongcun' [Disintegration and Protection of Benefits: Zhongyuan Countryside in the Process of Modernisation and Marketisation], *Zhongguo shehui kexue jikan* [Chinese Social Sciences Quarterly], (Spring 2000) 18.

[79] Rong Hu, 'Cunmin weiyuanhui de zizhi jiqi yu xiangzhen zhengfu de guanxi' [Village Committee Autonomy and its Relationship to the Township and Village Government], *Ershiyi shiji* [Twenty First Century], 50 (December 1998) 133-40.

tions can be crucial. This relationship is different from that between the township and the county as township officials are appointed by the county and will be dependent on the county for good approvals that will allow for promotion. For the most part village leaders will stay in the village and, where they are implemented, will be elected through village elections.

The resultant system that comes from this contracting arrangement the Translation Bureau researchers refer to as a 'pressurised system' (*yalixing tizhi*). This they define as the 'management mode of dividing up tasks and the system of conducting assessment by giving material awards adopted by the political organisation at the county or township level in order to develop the economy and attain the targets set by the higher authorities'.[80] Essentially the party and administrative organisations at the county level divides up the tasks and sets the targets for the organisation and individuals at the lower levels and requires them to accomplish them within a prescribed period of time. There are usually one, three and five year contracts. The higher level makes its decision on political and economic rewards and penalties for organisations and individuals at the lower levels according to how well they have accomplished these tasks.[81]

The targets are divided into a mixture of priority, hard and soft targets. The priority targets are set nation-wide and usually are more political or policy-oriented in nature. They would include, for example, the maintenance of social order, most recently including the eradication of the influence of *Falun gong* practitioners, and of course meeting the targets for family planning quotas. The hard targets concern primarily economic ones set by the county for the township and would include meeting tax revenues and meeting certain levels of growth. In particular it is the requirement of counties to catch up with and outperform other counties and this is reflected in the target set for lower levels. This will mean setting economic targets that exceed those of the national or provincial plans and particular attention is taken to set targets that will enable a particular county to overtake other potential rivals. These are often encapsulated in formulaic slogans. Thus, Mi county (Henan, now Xinmi municipality) in 1995 set a target of 'catching up' with Gongyi county in total economic strength, overtake Xinxiang in *per capita* income, learn from Zhanjiagang, and rank among the national top 100 counties during the Ninth Five-Year plan period (1996-2000). The soft targets tend to relate to questions of social development such as health and education provision and the concern for environmental protection. Clearly meeting the hard and priority targets are the most important as failure to meet them will mean that the rest of the work for the entire period will be discounted and there will be no promotions, titles or economic rewards distributed.

This system produces a number of perverse outcomes and explains why officials will often pursue unpopular policies with such zeal. One survey of 89 villages in Fuquan county (Guizhou province) found that village leaders spent 80 per cent of their energy and 70 per cent of their time on

[80] *Ibid.*, pp. 269-70.

[81] It is rare to use financial penalties for officials at the township level as their salaries are considered too low. However, a failure to meet priority targets will lead to demerits on file, possible transfer and certainly to future financial gains forgone.

'the most disliked' administrative affairs.[82] Not only is the contract focused on quantitative targets but also on the speed of completion of the task. This means that less attention is paid to quality of the finished product, as this is not rewarded sufficiently. This contributes to the shoddy and dangerous buildings and infrastructure that has accompanied China's urban and rural building boom.

The number of functions that a local administration is expected to carry out has not declined with the reforms in many areas and this creates significant budgetary pressures on the local governments. This means that local governments tend to accumulate projects that will bring in funds either through the running of enterprises or those that can be used to derive fund allocations from higher administrative levels. By contrast projects that have a slow turn around time in terms of producing profits or that are not a priority or hard target will be neglected.

This can be seen from the example of development in Xinmi municipality. The drive for development led first to an emphasis on expansion of township and village enterprises in the 1980s and, second, to a wave of government agencies setting up businesses following Deng Xiaoping's Southern tour in 1992. Of eight functional departments of the Xinmi government, they all had their own companies and factories. In fact the municipal party committee made the number of economic entities managed an important criterion for assessing the work of party and government organs. The easy atmosphere for getting lending if one was an official in 1992 fuelled this process further. As a result in 1995 Xinmi's revenue reached its highest levels with 228 million yuan, an increase of 76.8 per cent over 1994. This has produced noticeable benefits in terms of investment in physical and social infrastructure and in terms of *per capita* income growth. However, the government still actually ran a deficit. With the 1994 tax reforms for revenue sharing a greater percentage had to be handed over to higher levels and the incentive to collect taxes declined and the reforms also made the losses of the SOEs visible within the financial system. At the same time the tasks were growing and the government's administrative costs were expanding. They amounted to 137 per cent of the annual budget in 1994 although this was brought down to 99.8 per cent in 1995. As a result expenditures exceeded the budget in all years.

With the emphasis on launching industrial projects, implementing family planning targets and the development of townships, as this increases government financial allocations, agriculture has been neglected. Agricultural support funds in Xinmi fell in both absolute terms and relative terms from 1991 to 1995, from 5.794 million yuan (12.4 per cent of total budgetary expenditures) to 3.7 million (2.8 per cent). The financing for agricultural investment came exclusively from agricultural taxes paid in grain.

The political contracting system also provides perverse outcomes for officials and lower level governments dealing with evaluation of performance. For example, there is great pressure to juggle the statistics that are

[82] Xueju Li, *Zhongguo chengxiang jiceng zhengquan jianshe gongzuo yanjiu* [A Study of Urban and Rural Grass-Roots Regimes], (Beijing: Zhongguo shehui chubanshe, 1994).

reported upwards to fit with the targets that have been set and even to report figures that exceed the targets set. This distorted reporting is best combined with a strategy of cultivation of good social and political networks with those higher levels of government that will be engaged in the evaluation. This is especially important if key targets are going to be missed. The resultant system and incentives would suggest that political and vertical networks are more important than the 'market transition' proponents would suggest.

5. **Social Structure**

The literature to date has also paid less attention to the influence that social structure has on the nature of the local state. This is relevant both in terms of how the newly emerging economic elites are accommodating with existing political power and how social structures interact and modify the behaviour of government officials. The former is relevant to all levels of the local government whereas the latter is most applicable at the basic levels of administration, for example at the village level. The latter may also affect the township but this would require further research.

Research in a number of areas has revealed the fusion of official interest with that of business and this has clearly impacted on the management of the local state. The work of Ray Yep and others has revealed how the rise of business interests and their influence directly and indirectly on local governments has begun to influence the provision of public goods and services and public policy more broadly.[83] The access to privileged loans is one clear indication of this but also local business elites have been able to influence key decisions on infrastructure spending and to influence land redistribution practices. Sally Sargeson has shown how new business elites have been able to use local industry and commercial bureaux and the labour bureau to hold back rising labour demands for better working conditions and wages.[84]

Even within jurisdictions that fit the developmental model, there are longer-term trends at work that will present future challenges. Blecher and Shue talk of the emergence of a new petty bourgeoisie and a new *haute bourgeoisie* as a conscious creation of the local state officials in Xinji.[85] While the officials have remained separate from this new stratum and have not engaged in the same self-enriching practices as those elsewhere, support from this new bourgeoisie can only be conditional on further close co-operation with the officials and a policy framework that is beneficial to their interests. Accommodation at the local level may be occurring but at the national level the party is still finding it difficult to find a justifiable level of acceptance of this newly emerging class. The non-state sector of the

[83] R. Yep, 'The Limitations of Corporatism for Understanding Reforming China', *Journal of Contemporary China*, 9, 25 (2000) 547-66.

[84] S. Sargeson, *Reworking China's Proletariat*, (Houndmills: Macmillan, 1999).

[85] M. Blecher and V. Shue, 'Into Leather: State-Led Development and the Private Sector in Xinji', *The China Quarterly*, 166 (June 2001) 368-93.

economy has received progressively better status in party and state documents but this has still not translated into a sufficient shift in practice such as lending to the sector from the state controlled banks. By contrast with local accommodation to this new bourgeoisie, other new strata created by the reforms, such as migrants, have been excluded, on the whole, from local state power.[86]

As noted above popular expectation of the kinds of services that local authorities should provide has not declined and there is continual pressure on the need to raise revenue. This is a particular problem at the village level where authorities are not allowed to collect taxes but while they can have an extensive array of financial obligation for the provision of public goods and services. This makes them dependent on higher level authorities for funding or solely reliant on the sources they can extract from the local community.[87]

This does not have to result in predation on local villagers, although clearly there are many examples of where it does.[88] Those who have worked on the Southern Jiangsu area have noted many instances where collectively raised funds have been used for the development of social welfare.[89] However, the mechanisms that local officials will use to implement policies and to raise funds will depend not only on the level of economic prosperity but also on the nature of the community and their ties to it. From visits to various rural communities through the 1990s, it appeared to me that the local administration tended to be less coercive in their approaches to revenue generation where there was a high degree of village solidarity. This might comprise dominance of the village by one specific clan or lineage or where the temple association dominates matters of reciprocity. In a number of villages that I visited in Sichuan and Yunnan temples had become not just points for worship but the focal community points for reciprocity and exchange.

These impressionistic ideas are supported by more systematic research being carried out by Lily Tsai and some Chinese researchers. Tsai's preliminary findings conclude that in some areas social capital substitutes for governmental performance and officials allow social institutions to take over the provision of public goods. She cites the example of the village temple council in Haican peninsula (Fujian province), among others, that has taken over all road building.[90] In the Catholic Duan village in North China, the church organised the villagers to construct a road rather than the local authorities. It was said that even if the village authorities had the money no

[86] On the question of migrants see D.J. Solinger, *Contesting Citizenship in Urban China: Peasant Migrants, the State, and the Logic of the Market*, (Berkeley: University of California Press, 1999), and Id., 'Economic Informalisation by Fiat: China's New Growth Strategy as Solution or Crisis?', in this volume.

[87] L. West, 'Provision of Public Services in Rural PRC', in C. Wong, ed., *Financing Local Government in the People's Republic of China*, (Hong Kong: Oxford UP, 1997).

[88] See Xiaobo Lü, 'The Politics of Peasant Burden in Reform China', *The Journal of Peasant Studies*, 25, 1 (1997) 113-38.

[89] Oi, *Rural China Takes Off*, *passim*.

[90] L. Lee Tsai, 'Strategies of Rule or Ruin? Governance and Public Goods Provision in Rural China', paper presented at the 2001 Annual Meeting of the Association for Asian Studies, March 2001, p. 16.

one would listen to them but, by contrast, none would refuse the church.[91] As a result of this and other examples the researcher, Wu Fei, has concluded that local religious elites have become a strong group. In his view, the penetration of state power in these communities depends not only on village officials but also on the cooperation of the local elite. In fact, he concludes 'the reputation of village officials is markedly lower than that of the local religious elite.'[92]

In a study of Qiaoxia village (Jiangxi province), Zheng Yiping reveals a complex relationship between clan organisation and village authorities. Zheng claims that the village committee is still responsible for carrying out party policy, production, grain and fees' collection, enforcing family planning and overseeing the schools. The clan, however, dominated in property disputes and controlled all religious affairs even to the extent that the village authorities had to donate money and materials for such activities.[93]

These alternatives for mobilising community resources are especially important, as the incentives to encourage village officials, village elections notwithstanding, to provide public goods are weak. Certainly there is no direct incentive for township officials to invest in village infrastructure. Thus, while they might finance a road to link the village to the township, they are unlikely to invest in improving communications within the village. The use of township funds will go to meeting the obligations laid down by the county level government.[94]

6. Concluding Comments

Part of the solution of the dilemma to the need for revenue generation and the mobilisation of community resources depends on a two-fold strategy. First, there is clearly the need to increase the tax base of the government, a solution explored by the World Bank and favoured by the Chinese central government. However, this is only part of the solution and the obsession with revenue raising not only produces the perverse outcomes outlined above but also deflects from a serious consideration of the role of government, the kinds of work in which it should be involved, its relationship to the local community, and the acceptance that many functions previously managed by the local state in the field of social welfare and asset development will have to be dealt with not only by national investment but also by the local communities themselves. A thoughtful review of this issue is

[91] Fei Wu, 'Zhongguo nongcun shehui de zongjiao – Huabei mouxiang nongcun tianzhujiao huodong kaocha' [Religion in Rural Society – Investigation into Catholic Activities in a Certain County in North China], *Zhanlüe yu guanli* [Strategy and Management], 4 (1997) 54-62.

[92] *Ibid.*, 56 and 62.

[93] Yiping Zheng, 'Yingxiang cunji zhili de zhuyao yinsu fenxi – Jiangxi sheng Qiaoxia cun diaocha' [An Analysis of the Main Factors Influencing the Management of Village Autonomous Organisations – An Investigative Report from Qiaoxia Village, Jiangxi Province], *Zhongguo nongye jingji* [China's Rural Economy], 9 (1997) 47-52.

[94] Yongshun Cai, 'Between State and Peasant: Local Cadres and Statistical Reporting in Rural China', *The China Quarterly*, 162 (June 2000) 801-2.

preferable to the practice of setting up enterprises just to raise revenue without consideration of long-term developmental needs or squeezing the rural poor through levies and fees as is often favoured by local authorities.

The study of the local state in China is a rapidly developing field and has been prey to a diverse set of interpretations. As Richard Baum and Alexei Shevchenko have noted, there is considerable ideological confusion about the 'state of the state', including the local state, in China.[95] This chapter has argued that this is not surprising given that we are dealing with multiple types operating across different geographic jurisdictions and that we are dealing with a very fluid situation in which these local forms are evolving as circumstances change. Looking to the future we need to conduct more research that compares the local state in China both vertically across different regions and across different functional bureaux within one jurisdiction. In addition we need to think about change across time, not only within the reform period but also looking at how the Maoist legacy has affected reform period development and to look further back to see how the local state in the Republican era dealt with the same issues. There is little to suggest in the above that we are seeing the 'withering away' of the local state in China. Rather we are seeing a changing locus in state power and numerous attempts at local state-building to accommodate the demands of reform.

The conceptual tools we have developed to date have been on the whole unsatisfactory. To a large extent we have been trying to fit Chinese empirical pegs into Western theoretical holes. The resultant taxonomy has been useful but it is not enough. In many cases, even local states that appear to fit the model for 'local state corporatism' may turn out to be predatory and developmental at the same time. We need to pay more attention to disaggregating the interests of the state at the local level both in terms of different functional bureaux and in terms of the interrelationship between different government agencies at different levels horizontally and vertically and to society at large in terms of responsiveness. This will move us toward more open-ended explanations rather than the clear-cut ones that social scientists prefer. We should not prematurely close down the range of options available for interpretation through a process of imposing order and logic. Each specific local state is the process of complex negotiation and we need to develop explanations that allow for the shifting complexities of the current system and the institutional fluidity, ambiguity and messiness that operate at all levels in China and that are most pronounced at the local level. This does not negate the need for comparison but will provide a more reliable base for such comparison. Once we have completed this work we can begin to ask key questions about what kinds of local states are the best at performing which kinds of functions and providing what kinds of service.

95 R. Baum and A. Shevchenko, 'The "State of the State"', in M. Goldman and R. MacFarquhar, eds, *The Paradox of China's Post-Mao Reforms*, (Cambridge, MA: Harvard UP, 1999) pp. 333-60.

[16]

American Political Science Review Vol. 101, No. 2 May 2007

DOI: 10.1017.S0003055407070153

Solidary Groups, Informal Accountability, and Local Public Goods Provision in Rural China

LILY L. TSAI *Massachusetts Institute of Technology*

Why would government officials in authoritarian and transitional systems where formal democratic and bureaucratic institutions of accountability are often weak ever provide more than the minimum level of public goods needed to maintain social stability? Findings from a unique combination of in-depth case study research and an original survey of 316 villages in rural China indicate that even when formal accountability is weak, local officials can be subject to unofficial rules and norms that establish and enforce their public obligations. These informal institutions of accountability can be provided by encompassing and embedding solidary groups. Villages where these types of groups exist are more likely to have better local governmental public goods provision than villages without these solidary groups, all other things being equal.

Formal institutions of accountability are often weak in developing countries (Bardhan 2002). States in these countries often lack strong bureaucratic institutions for controlling corruption and making sure that lower level officials are doing their jobs. Democratic institutions such as elections that allow citizens to hold local officials accountable may be weak and unreliable or even nonexistent. Yet in these countries some local officials still perform better than others. Under these conditions, how do citizens make government officials organize and fund the public goods and services that they want and need?

This question is important for practical, political, and theoretical reasons. Practically speaking, people everywhere need their governments to provide roads, education, clean water, and other public goods and services that they have trouble producing on their own. The provision of these basic public goods and services matters deeply for the quality of people's lives everywhere. Politically, how effectively governments provide these goods and services has an enormous impact on their legitimacy. Many of the developing countries in Asia, Africa, and Latin America that struggle the most to provide basic public goods are also the countries struggling the most to build effective states and maintain regime stability.

This question is also important from a theoretical perspective. Existing explanations of governmental performance and variation in governmental public goods provision have focused primarily on the role of strong democratic and bureaucratic institutions. Theories of institutional design argue that the key to good government is providing formal democratic institutions and devolving power to local levels so that citizens can monitor and sanction officials effectively (e.g., Dahl 1971; O'Donnell 1996; Rose-Ackerman 2005; Seabright 1996). Theories of civil society and social capital argue that voluntary associations, interest groups, and associational activity can improve governmental performance in democratic systems (Boix and Posner 1998; Edwards and Foley 1998; Ehrenberg 1999; Putnam 1993). In consolidated democracies where formal institutions ensure the incorporation of citizen demands into the policymaking process, autonomous associations and interest groups can help citizens voice their demands more effectively. Other studies suggest that democratic institutions may not be necessary for good governmental public goods provision, but these arguments still rely on the existence of effective and coherent formal state institutions. Peter Evans (1995), for example, argues that developmental states differ from predatory states in two ways. First, developmental states generate bureaucracies with corporate coherence and strong bureaucratic institutions of internal accountability. Second, developmental states are "embedded" in the sense that the state forges informal connections with powerful business interests. Corporate solidarity enables the state to resist sliding into patron–client relationships with societal interests. Wai Fung Lam (1997) finds that irrigation governance in Taiwan is effective because strong community norms work in tandem with formal bureaucratic administration.

But what about governmental public goods provision in countries which lack strong democratic and bureaucratic institutions of accountability? Public goods provision is often much more of a problem, both practically and politically, in developing countries with nondemocratic or transitional systems. How do we account for variation in local governmental performance and public goods provision in these systems?

Lily L. Tsai is Assistant Professor, Department of Political Science, Massachusetts Institute of Technology, 77 Massachusetts Avenue, E53-425, Cambridge, MA 02139 (l_tsai@mit.edu).

I am indebted to Elizabeth Perry, Grzegorz Ekiert, Robert Putnam, and Theda Skocpol for their invaluable advice and support at various stages of the project. Earlier versions of this paper benefited greatly from comments provided by Edward Young, Adam Berinsky, Melani Cammett, Andrea Campbell, Mary Gallagher, John Gerring, Frances Hagopian, David Laitin, Chappell Lawson, Devra Moehler, Daniel Posner, Susan Rose-Ackerman, James Scott, Tianjian Shi, participants of the World Bank Seminar Series on the Political Economy of Governance Reform, the China Research Seminar at Oxford University, the Democracy, Governance, and Identity Workshop at the University of Michigan, and six anonymous reviewers. Nathan Cisneros and William Tilden provided valuable editorial assistance.

A MODEL OF INFORMAL GOVERNMENTAL ACCOUNTABILITY

Public goods provision is always associated with a collective action problem. Everyone has an incentive to free ride on the efforts of everyone else. Most models of public goods provision focus on the collective action problem. Alesina, Baqir, and Easterly (1999) argue that public goods provision is poorer in ethnically diverse areas because different ethnic groups have different preferences or tastes for particular public services, thus making any collective decision difficult. Elinor Ostrom (1990) finds that well-designed community social institutions can help overcome obstacles to collective action. Robert Putnam (1993, 2000) argues that dense social networks and norms of trust can make people more likely to cooperate with each other.

But these models do not explicitly address the additional problem associated with *governmental* public goods provision—the provision of public goods and services by the government—in systems with weak formal democratic and bureaucratic institutions: the problem of *accountability*. In these systems overcoming the collective action problem among citizens is not sufficient to guarantee that the government will provide public goods responsibly. Once public funds are in the hands of government officials, how can citizens make sure that officials use these funds to pave roads, build schools, and invest in local public projects? How can citizens have leverage over government officials in the absence of strong formal institutions?

I propose a model of informal governmental accountability. Even when formal governmental accountability is weak, local officials may still have a strong incentive to provide public goods when citizens award them moral standing for doing so. Like other types of prestige, moral standing is "the esteem, respect, or approval that is granted by an individual or a collectivity for performances or qualities they consider above the average" (Goode 1979, 7). In the case of moral standing, esteem or respect is granted for above-average performance of actions considered morally good. Those specific standards and actions vary. Moral standing can be a powerful incentive. It not only makes people feel good about themselves, but also it can translate into economic and social advancement. Local officials with higher moral standing may also find it easier to elicit citizen compliance with state policies. Moral standing can be an invaluable resource for accomplishing a variety of political, social, and economic objectives.

When are people more likely to reward officials with moral standing for providing public goods and services? First, citizens and officials must share a set of criteria for moral behavior. At minimum, these criteria include the principle that contributing to the good of the group deserves moral approval. Without this criterion, the group would not last very long. Second, opportunities must exist for publicizing behavior that meets these shared standards. The more citizens believe that officials really do share the group's obligations and standards and the more citizens know about whether officials actually behave according to these standards, the more likely they are to award officials moral standing. Like all forms of prestige, moral standing is dependent on the "verbal information disseminated in the community relating news and approval of an individual's activities" (Riches 1984, 235).

I argue that people are more likely to use moral standing to reward local officials for good public goods provision when there are local *solidary groups*—groups based on shared moral obligations as well as shared interests. To provide informal institutions that enable citizens to hold local officials accountable for public goods provision, solidary groups must have two particular structural characteristics. First, they must be *encompassing*, or open to everyone under the local government's jurisdiction. In localities with encompassing solidary groups, social boundaries overlap with political boundaries. Examples of encompassing solidary groups might include citizens' groups that monitor town planning decisions in the United States, parish churches in nineteenth-century England (Morris 2001), and village *harambees* or self-help organizations in Kenya (Miguel 1999). Second, solidary groups must be *embedding* in that they incorporate local officials into the group as members. Not all encompassing solidary groups are embedding. English parish churches are often embedding because local officials are likely to attend church services and identify as members of the congregation. In contrast citizen watchdog organizations in the United States, which are designed to monitor and challenge government, may encompass a particular town or municipality but are unlikely to embed officials into the group as members.

In localities with encompassing and embedding solidary groups, citizens and officials are more likely to share a common set of ethical standards and moral obligations. Members of clans, churches, fraternal organizations, and other solidary groups have strong obligations to the collective. In solidary groups members are judged according to the group's standards of what constitutes a good person and a good member. Members of church congregations thus feel compelled to contribute something when the donation basket is passed around. Members of clans are expected to and commended for siding with fellow members in disputes with outsiders. Group activities and dense social networks also provide ample opportunities for individual members to publicize their exemplary behavior. For moral standing to be conferred on an individual, both the individual's actions and acceptance of shared standards have to be "common knowledge" (Chwe 2003). Churches ask for volunteers to help with church activities immediately after services when the congregation is still assembled. In rural China lineage members are expected to attend group rituals of respect for shared ancestors. These collective gatherings help publicize who is deserving of moral standing in the community.

When the boundaries of a solidary group overlap with the administrative boundaries of the local government, embedded officials have a strong *social* obligation to contribute to the good of the group. Because in this case the group and the public are the same, officials in localities with encompassing and embedding solidary groups can earn moral standing for providing public goods (and suffer severe social sanctions for not doing so). Officials in localities with encompassing and embedding solidary groups thus have an extra incentive to provide public goods and services to their jurisdiction.

RESEARCH DESIGN

Contemporary rural China provides an ideal setting to examine the factors that affect the quality of local governance because of the tremendous variation in the performance of village governments.[1] As in many countries, the Chinese state has decentralized primary responsibility for the provision of basic public goods and services to local governments. During the period of this study (1999–2002), village government officials in China were expected to fund and organize the construction of all roads, drainage systems, irrigation works, primary school facilities, and sanitation and trash disposal *within* the village primarily through resources available within the village (see Wong 1997), although this may change with recent rural tax reforms and fiscal recentralization. Some village governments provide their citizens with outstanding public goods and services; other village governments provide nothing at all. Examining variation in governmental provision of public goods within the same country also allows us to hold constant macro-conditions such as political ideology, national policy, and regime type while particular factors that existing theories suggest as important for governance and public goods provision are allowed to vary.

To study this problem, in 2001, I surveyed 316 villages and carried out a set of detailed case studies in rural China. After two months of preliminary research in seven different provinces across the country and eight months of in-depth fieldwork in one set of villages in the southern province of Fujian, I designed a survey to examine the impact of formal and informal institutions on village governmental public goods provision. The four provinces for the survey—Shanxi, Hebei, Jiangxi, and Fujian—were chosen to reflect differences in levels of economic development as well as regional differences between north and south China in terrain, institutional history, and social organization. Shanxi and Hebei are neighboring provinces in the north, but Shanxi is in the interior and less developed. Jiangxi and Fujian are neighboring provinces in the south, but Jiangxi is in the interior and less developed. Within each province, two counties were selected to vary in model county status for village democratic reforms (model counties employ more administrative resources and pressure to implement village democratic reforms) but to have similar economic and geographic characteristics. The original rationale for this selection strategy was to be able to use model county status as an instrument for identifying the impact of village democratic reforms which may be endogenous to the model, but in this paper, the implementation of village democratic reforms is included as a control rather than studied as the main variable of interest.

To conduct this survey, I visited each of the eight counties and presented references from Chinese academics and researchers to the county government. After obtaining permission to carry out research in the county, I selected eight townships through a random stratified sampling procedure (with stratification by official income per capita). A county official then accompanied me and my research team of Chinese university student enumerators to each of the townships where I then selected five villages in each township through a similar procedure (again with stratification by official income per capita). In townships with fewer than five villages, all the villages were surveyed. Townships with less than five villages account for the sample of 316 villages (as opposed to 320 villages). Each township government then contacted the village governments in their jurisdiction to notify them that a couple of students would be visiting them to do academic research. The combination of official approval from the local government and our obvious status as students helped secure the willing cooperation of our respondents. In each of the sampled villages, enumerators interviewed one or, in most cases, more than one village official in order to fill out village-level survey questionnaires about village conditions. In all cases, enumerators also used village documents to corroborate interviewee responses. Survey respondents showed a high level of frankness about even potentially sensitive topics such as economic indicators and the implementation of village democratic reforms. This level of comfort can be largely credited to the highly skilled administration of the survey by the student enumerators, most of whom had grown up in villages themselves and were pursuing degrees in agricultural economics, rural sociology, and related disciplines.[2]

THE IMPORTANCE OF SOLIDARY GROUPS

Before we go on to the findings from analysis of the quantitative data, this section draws on data from in-depth case studies to illustrate how encompassing and embedding solidary groups, such as village temples and village-wide lineages, can provide incentives for local officials to provide public goods and services. When solidary groups are both encompassing and embedding, officials who provide public services to the local administrative unit (such as a ward, a town, or a village)

[1] Although the central government officially refers to village governments as "self-governing organizations," village governments are widely considered part of the state apparatus by higher level officials, village officials, and citizens themselves. Village governments collect state taxes, enforce state directives such as the birth control policy, and provide village public goods and services.

[2] When asked, for example, for the village's "official" income per capita and "real" income per capita, only 14%, in fact, reported the same figures. Village officials were also comfortable reporting interference—even by themselves personally—in the preelection process, even though such interference goes against official state regulations, as well as failure on their part to implement officially required procedures for voting and the operation of villagers' representative assemblies.

are also fulfilling collective obligations to the solidary group. Complying with group norms of collective responsibility enables them to acquire moral standing among all their constituents since, in this case, local administrative boundaries coincide with social boundaries.

Imagine the mayor of a small town in the United States with only one church. Church suppers and picnics are a major part of the town's social life, and the church hall might in fact be the only place that people can rent for social gatherings. Even if not everyone goes to church regularly, everyone sees the church as representative of the town community. In this kind of small town, if the mayor does something exemplary like bringing down the crime rate by strengthening the police force, the minister might very well mention his good work in front of the congregation during his Sunday sermon. Getting commended by the minister during services can give the mayor a measure of moral and social standing in addition to whatever he might already possess as a public official or social elite. The mayor benefits personally from this increased standing. People stop him on the street to praise his work, storekeepers treat him with more deference, the bank is willing to give him a bigger mortgage, and his children receive more attention at school. Increased moral standing may also make his mayoral tasks easier to carry out. When he tries to implement a difficult state policy—a new requirement, for example, that students of a different ethnic group be bused into the town school—additional standing can help him elicit compliance from his constituents. Moral standing can make citizens more likely to trust that the mayor is right and defer to his judgment on whether the policy should be implemented. A local official with sufficient moral standing may also be more able to persuade leaders of the community solidary group to use their own moral authority to win over particularly stubborn opponents of the policy.

Solidary Groups in Rural China

Village Temples. In the Chinese context, an analogous example would be the case of West Gate, a village of about 3900 people in the coastal province of Fujian. Over five months in 2000 and 2001, I visited West Gate weekly to talk with villagers and observe village politics. West Gate's equivalent of our hypothetical town church is the village temple community council. The temple council organizes a multitude of religious and community activities for the village. As with temple groups in many other villages, West Gate's temple council evolved out of an informal group of villagers who decided, after the start of liberalization in the late 1970s, to try to rebuild village temples destroyed during the Cultural Revolution. Unlike larger, official Buddhist temples, these small village temples are a part of Chinese folk religion and house deities that people consider the guardians of their specific village. During festival holidays, village temples organize parades, opera performances, and other ritual festivities. Villagers have clear obligations to contribute to and participate in these activities because these collective activities represent group tributes to the village's guardian deities. Village residents are expected to make donations to help fund these activities. The names of donors and the amount they donated are posted publicly on the temple wall. Village temples are an important symbol of the village community. They provide strong institutions enforcing each member's responsibility to contribute to the collective good and numerous opportunities for publicizing whether members have fulfilled their responsibilities.

West Gate's 12 village officials—who, as with most village officials in China, come from within the village—try hard to be upstanding members of the village temple group. Party secretary Sun was one of the two top donors to a recent temple reconstruction project, having donated 2,000 yuan or about the same as the national annual per capita rural income. In 1996 when the district government directed all its villages to set up senior citizens' associations, West Gate's officials agreed to call the temple community council (which had been operating since the 1980s) the village senior citizens' association, thereby giving it an extra layer of legitimacy. Because the Communist Party discourages "superstitious" activities, village officials refrain from taking leadership positions in the temple, but as ordinary members of the temple group, they diligently fulfill their obligations to contribute to the good of the group.

These obligations make West Gate's officials very responsive to citizen demands for public goods and services. In exchange, the temple gives the village officials a good name or, as the temple council head notes, "half of the spotlight." Council members also help officials mobilize villagers to attend meetings convened by the village government, convince villagers to give rights-of-way for the construction of a public drainage channel, and monitor the state ban on firecrackers during festivals.

The temple community council in West Gate has a positive effect on local governmental public goods provision because it is both encompassing and embedding. If it were not encompassing, officials would only be able to gain moral standing among some of the villagers. If it were not embedding, officials would not be able to gain any moral standing at all. The moral standing conferred by the temple community council gives an incentive for officials to provide public services, which formal state institutions do not provide.

The importance of having both structural characteristics becomes even clearer when we compare village temples to the other types of solidary groups most common in rural China—village churches and lineages.

Village Churches. The necessity of embedding local officials is clear if we compare temple groups like the one in West Gate to village churches. Extensive case study and interview data indicated that village temple groups typically embed village officials in their activities, but village churches do not. The state permits Catholic and Protestant churches, but in contrast to its tolerance of village folk temples, it considers churches to have high subversive potential and regulates them closely. Party members are thus prohibited from participating in church activities. Unlike village temples that developed indigenously, are inherently limited to the immediate locality overseen by the village guardian deity, and have a history of reinforcing the authority of the state,[3] Christian churches were started in the nineteenth century by missionaries aligned closely with foreign governments seeking to open China to trade by setting up areas of extraterritoriality and weakening the state (Esherick 1987; Latourette 1929; Madsen 1998). The state thus not only associates Christianity with threats to its sovereignty but with events like the Taiping Rebellion in which Christianity provided the basis for mobilizing vast numbers of people across localities against the state (Spence 1996). The state therefore requires all churches to be registered with the state Religious Affairs Bureau and tries hard to limit the scope of a church to the local community.

The example of South Bend, a village located in the northern province of Hebei, illustrates how village churches fail to have the same positive impact on village governmental public goods provision that village temples do. South Bend's church is easily the grandest building for miles. Mass is held daily when the state-authorized priest is in town and weekly when he is traveling around the county serving the eight other state-registered congregations. Just about everyone in the village identifies himself or herself as Christian, and at any given service about one-third of the village is in attendance. A church management committee of four male villagers appointed by the priest oversees the maintenance of the church building, materials for church activities and services, and donations from the congregation, which total about three thousand yuan per year (about $375, U.S.), an amount that exceeds the tax revenue the village government is able to extract.

The Party secretary of South Bend says that he believes in God but calls himself a bad disciple because he is a Party member and Party members are not allowed to believe in religion. He complains bitterly about his lack of authority among villagers whom he says do not trust him because he never goes to church. Instead, he says, the church management committee makes all the important decisions in the village. South Bend's village Party secretary is unable to benefit from the moral standing that the church can confer because the state does not allow him to participate as a member. Relative to the village officials in West Gate, South Bend's Party secretary has far less incentive to organize public projects. Village government funds are spent instead on the wages of village officials, and the village government does not fund or organize public services. Villagers do not listen to the village Party secretary, and there is a high level of tax evasion.

[3] Local guardian deities are seen as officials in a celestial bureaucracy that mirrored the earthly imperial bureaucracy. Just as earthly government officials are assigned responsibility for a particular district or jurisdiction, officials in the celestial bureaucracy also take responsibility for a particular district or jurisdiction (Wolf 1974).

As we can see, South Bend's church does not have a positive impact on village governmental performance. It sets clear standards for exemplary behavior and the conferral of moral standing and offers opportunities for members to show that they follow these standards, but village officials cannot take advantage of these opportunities or participate in these institutions.

Although the church does not improve public goods provision by the village government, it does, however, itself provide some public goods for the village. In 1997 the church obtained a grant from the state Religious Affairs Bureau to replace the church's roof. This grant bypassed the village government and went directly to the church. The church diverted 20,000 yuan from this grant to buy concrete and organized villagers to volunteer their labor so the village's main road could be paved.

Encompassing solidary groups which are not embedding, like South Bend's village church, may be able to enforce norms of collective obligation among their members but cannot extend these norms to local officials. They may be able to organize collective projects themselves but are far less able to hold government officials responsible for organizing these projects. All other things being equal, the hypothetical small-town mayor who does not belong to the town church is unlikely to be commended by the pastor during services and thus has less of an incentive to provide public services than the small-town mayor who does belong to the town church. In fact, as we see in South Bend, members of encompassing solidary groups may actually hold officials in low regard precisely because they are not embedded in the group. One could argue that in democratic systems low regard for government officials can be healthy and motivate citizens to monitor officials more closely. In these systems closer monitoring can improve governmental performance because democratic institutions such as elections enable them to sanction officials who perform poorly. Thus encompassing groups that are not embedding may have a positive impact on local governance in democratic systems. But in places which lack democratic institutions, autonomous civil society groups or solidary groups that are not embedding have much less direct impact on governmental performance. Low regard of government officials may increase their monitoring, but without well-implemented elections or legal guarantees, citizens may not be able to remove or punish officials if they detect misconduct. These groups thus cannot provide informal institutions to hold officials accountable for providing public services—although they may be able to provide public services *instead of* the local government.

Lineage Groups. The third type of solidary group commonly found in rural China is based on lineage solidarity. Like village temple groups and village churches, lineage groups inculcate a sense of obligation to the group, but in this case obligation is based on concepts of family and shared patrilineal descent rather than on religious beliefs. Interviews with villagers and officials in all four provinces of the study indicated that like temples, lineage groups almost always embed village officials in their institutions. In contrast to churches, the Party is noncommittal about lineage activity. Village officials almost always take part in their lineage's activities. In fact, in places where lineage groups already exist, choosing not to participate would be like choosing to be disowned and ostracized.

Unlike temples and churches, which typically have boundaries co-extensive with local administrative boundaries, lineage groups vary widely in their scale and overlap with administrative boundaries. When a lineage group encompasses everyone in the village, and membership in the lineage means the same as membership in the village, lineages function in a way similar to temple groups. But when the social boundaries of lineage groups do not map onto the administrative boundaries of the village, villagers may be fragmented into subvillage groups. The members of a subvillage lineage also feel obligations to their group, but in this case, group obligations are narrower than public obligations to the village community. Subvillage lineage groups can confer moral standing on their group members, but this standing may only carry weight with the group members and not with the rest of the village. Village officials who are embedded in subvillage lineage groups may still try to organize projects, but these projects are likely to favor their group rather than benefit the village as a whole.

We can see how important it is for solidary groups to be encompassing by comparing the two cases of Li Settlement and Pan Settlement. Li Settlement, a village in the southern province of Jiangxi, has an active village-wide lineage group that exerts moral authority over the entire village. Village officials helped to renovate the village auditorium into a village-wide ancestral hall which contains a communal spirit tablet to represent the deceased elders of all the villagers rather than the many individual spirit tablets that ancestral halls usually house. Officials in Li Settlement demonstrate their commitment to the lineage and the village by participating in lineage rituals and organizing public projects. They choose to work out of their homes rather than use public funds to construct a government office building. To pave the main village road, officials used their personal connections with higher level officials to secure a bank loan of 90,000 yuan (about $11,000, U.S.). They then held a lineage banquet to solicit donations from lineage members, but only after they had built up their credibility and standing by showing that they themselves were willing to invest their reputations and resources to fulfill their obligations to the lineage. Village officials in Li Settlement feel proud of the work they have done for the village and seem to genuinely feel an obligation to work for the good of the community.

Pan Settlement, on the other hand, is a village in the northern province of Hebei which has three distinct subvillage lineage groups which they refer to as "gates." According to local history, Pan Settlement was established by people who were forced by the imperial state during the Ming dynasty (1368–1644) to relocate to this area. The settlers divided the village into three groups—the east gate, the west gate, and the central gate. For decades, east gate villagers have been rivals with west gate villagers. Throughout the Maoist period, east gate villagers were dominant, and one of their members was the village Party secretary. In the 1990s, however, west gate villagers gained control of the village government, and now all three village officials are members of the west gate group. After failing to win back power in the 1997 elections, east gate villagers printed small white cards with the message "Oppose the village officials" and scattered them all over the village. East gate villagers accuse the village officials from the west gate of wining and dining guests, pocketing money from the sale of village land, and illegally favoring their fellow west gate villagers when renting out land and other public assets. Tensions between the subvillage groups have had a negative impact on village governance. Village officials cannot organize public projects on the same scale as neighboring villages. East gate villagers publicly berate the village officials from the west gate group for the birth control program even though they know it is actually the central government that sets the policy.

When officials are embedded in solidary groups which are not encompassing, such as Pan Settlement's west gate subvillage lineage group, they may still have strong incentives to contribute to the good of the group. In this case, however, the good of the group will not be synonymous with the public good, and any services provided by officials are likely to favor the particular group to which they belong.

The aforementioned case studies illustrate how encompassing and embedding solidary groups, such as village temples and village-wide lineages, can provide incentives for local officials to provide public goods and services. Solidary groups that are not encompassing and embedding, such as village churches and subvillage lineages, cannot provide the same incentives for governmental public goods provision, although they may use their solidarity and group norms to organize collective projects that do not involve the local government or benefit the village community as a whole. Are these patterns generalizable beyond a few cases? The next section analyzes survey data from 316 villages to answer this question.

DATA ANALYSIS AND MEASUREMENT

The main hypothesis of this article is: *in places with weak formal institutions of accountability, localities with encompassing and embedding solidary groups are likely to have better local governmental public goods provision than localities without these groups, all other things being equal.* This hypothesis does not exclude the possibility that under conditions of strong formal bureaucratic and/or democratic institutions, encompassing and embedding groups might also have a positive impact on local governmental public goods provision or that other kinds of groups might have a positive impact through other mechanisms. Nor does it exclude the possibility that other factors have an impact on

TABLE 1. Descriptive Statistics

	Mean	Standard Deviation	Number of Observations
Measures of Public Goods Provision			
2000 total village government expenditure on public projects per capita (yuan)	66.76	192.42	312
Existence of paved roads (1 = yes, 0 = no)	0.5	0.5	316
Existence of paved paths (1 = yes, 0 = no)	0.13	0.33	312
Percentage of classrooms unusable in rain	0.11	0.29	310
Average age of school building (years)	27.26	18.26	309
Existence of running water (1 = yes, 0 = no)	0.47	0.5	316
Measures of Village Temple Groups			
Existence of a temple manager (1 = yes, 0 = no)	0.14	0.35	311
Proportion households in temple reconstruction	0.09	0.29	313
Existence of temple activities at the start of the Communist period (1 = yes, 0 = no)	0.46	0.50	287
Measures of Village Church Groups			
Existence of an active church pastor (1 = yes, 0 = no)	0.07	0.25	316
Existence of church reconstruction project (1 = yes, 0 = no)	0.04	0.21	316
Measures of Village Lineage Groups			
Existence of a single active lineage hall (1 = yes, 0 = no)	0.07	0.26	315
Existence of multiple active lineage halls (1 = yes, 0 = no)	0.07	0.26	315
Surname fragmentation index	0.5	0.26	312
Strength of Formal State Institutions			
Index for implementation of preelection institutions	0	1.63	299
Index for implementation of voting institutions	0	1.27	312
Index for implementation of villagers' representative assemblies	0	1.29	285
Party membership of village head (1 = yes, 0 = no)	0.69	0.46	316
Percentage of village officials with Party membership	0.74	0.19	313
Bureaucratic targets for public projects (1 = yes, 0 = no)	0.44	0.5	316
Model county status (1 = yes, 0 = no)	0.49	0.50	316
Percentage of village government revenue from subsidies allocated by higher levels in 1997	0.13	0.29	303
Economic Controls			
1997 village govt assets (yuan)	42644	393067	311
1997 village tax revenue per capita (yuan)	21.85	27.37	306
1997 income per capita (yuan)	1481.36	1130.07	308
Existence of village enterprises in 1995	0.51	0.50	316
Existence of small-scale entrepreneurs (*getihu*) in 1995	0.84	0.37	316
Geographic and Demographic Controls			
County dummies	—	—	316
Village population	1240.1	981.42	315
Village terrain (1 = flat, 0 = not flat)	0.36	0.48	316
Distance from county seat (km)	26.45	20.97	316
Number of natural villages	3.9	4.53	316

governmental public goods provision, or that other factors or types of social groups may have a positive impact on nongovernmental public goods provision. This paper simply suggests that all other things being equal, solidary groups with these two structural characteristics have a positive impact on local governmental public goods provision.

Measuring the Dependent Variable

To measure local governmental public goods provision, the dependent variable, we look at both village government investment as well as objective measures of specific basic public goods—roads, school facilities, and running water infrastructure (see Table 1 for descriptive statistics). I chose these measures for three reasons. First, these measures are relevant and comparable across a wide variety of regions. Roads, primary school facilities, and water infrastructure are the public goods most often needed and demanded by villagers. Second, at the time of this study these public goods were usually the sole responsibility of the village government (unlike, e.g., electricity infrastructure which was usually funded and constructed in large part by county-level bureaus). Third, all of these measures reflect governmental public goods provision in relatively recent years. Although most solidary groups were started in the late 1970s and early 1980s, public goods such as paved roads and running water were not provided until much later in the reform period. As of 1985, for example, more than a third of China's

TABLE 2. Expected Impact of Solidary Groups in Rural China

	Encompassing	Embedding	Good Village Governmental Public Goods Provision?
[redacted]			
Village churches	Yes	No	No
[redacted]			
Subvillage lineages	No	Yes	No

villages were not connected to the road system at all, to say nothing of roads within the village (Benziger 1993).

A total of six measures for village governmental public goods provision are used: per capita village government expenditure on public projects in 2000, the existence of paved village roads; the existence of paved village paths, the proportion of village classrooms usable in rainy weather, the newness of the village school building (this measure was converted from the age of the school building so that a higher number indicates a newer building), and the existence of running water. Looking solely at any one of these indicators would not allow us to compare the performance of different village governments. If we looked only at the quality of school facilities as an indicator of village public goods provision, we would wrongly assume that a village government focusing investment on running water infrastructure was performing poorly. Using multiple indicators of governmental public goods provision acknowledges the fact that different places have different needs and preferences.

Measuring the Explanatory Variable

To demonstrate the plausibility of this hypothesis, the paper derives its observable implications for the four kinds of solidary groups most common in rural China: village temples, village churches, village-wide lineage groups, and subvillage lineage groups. Although the survey data do not provide direct measures of embeddedness, case study and interview data with villagers and officials from dozens of villages from both the four provinces in the survey and the three other provinces visited during preliminary fieldwork indicate that village temples and lineages are usually both embedding. In contrast, none of the interviewees had ever come across or heard of an embedding village community church. If the hypothesis is correct, we should then expect village temples and village-wide lineages to have positive effects on local governmental public goods provision. In contrast, village churches and subvillage lineages, which are not both encompassing and embedding, should not have these positive effects. Table 2 compares the structural characteristics of these four solidary groups and their expected impacts on local governmental public goods provision.

Two measures are used for village temple groups: the existence of a formal temple manager (a dichotomous variable) and the percentage of households participating in village temple reconstruction projects since the beginning of the reform period by donating money, materials, or labor. In some villages, temple activities are impromptu affairs organized informally by an *ad hoc* group of villagers. In other places, a temple manager, sometimes overseeing a temple council, organizes community activities. Temple reconstruction projects are one of the most common temple activities, and the percentage of households that can be mobilized to participate in these projects is a good measure of the group's authority. Fourteen percent of villages reported that they had a village temple manager. The average proportion of households participating in temple reconstruction across all villages in the sample (including the ones that did not have temples or engage in temple reconstruction) was 9%, but among the 58 villages reporting temple reconstruction projects, the average percentage of households participating was 58%.

Two dichotomous variables are used for village church groups: the existence of a state-approved Protestant minister or Catholic priest who organizes church services and activities and the existence of a church that has been renovated or rebuilt in the reform period. Seven percent of villages reported that they had a church with a priest organizing services and activities, and 4% reported that the church had organized a reconstruction project since decollectivization.

The clearest and most easily observed indication of organized lineage group activities is the existence of an ancestral hall with ancestor spirit tablets. These tablets are thought to contain the spirits of the deceased and are the focus of collective rituals on holidays. Fourteen percent of villages in the survey reported ancestral halls with spirit tablets. Village-wide lineage groups are measured by a dichotomous variable that is coded one when a village reported the existence of one and only one ancestral hall with spirit tablets. Subvillage groups are measured by a dichotomous variable that is coded one when the village reported multiple ancestral halls with spirit tablets. Using these measures, 7% of villages reported the existence of a village-wide lineage group, and another 7% reported the existence of multiple subvillage lineage groups.

Control Variables

To identify the effects of these solidary groups accurately, the analyses control for three sets of factors that may also have an effect on village public goods provision.

Geographic and Demographic Controls. The first set consists of geographic and demographic controls. Dummy variables for the eight counties from which the villages were randomly sampled are included. Distance from the county seat, village terrain, the number of natural villages (a proxy for spatial dispersion of village residents), and village population in 2000 were also included to control for variation in demand for specific public goods as well as variation in costs for comparable goods. Demand for public goods provision should be higher in villages with larger populations and in villages that are closer to urban areas. The cost of constructing roads, schools, and water infrastructure should be higher in villages that are located far from the county seat or in mountainous terrain. Running water infrastructure should also be more costly to construct in villages with multiple "natural villages" or scattered residential settlements.

Economic Controls. As the level of economic development rises, it seems reasonable to suppose that public goods and services will improve because more resources are available for investment in public goods or because demand for public goods increases. Economic factors controlling for variation in level of economic development and the amount of resources available to the village government are thus also included. These measures include 1997 village income per capita, 1997 village government assets, and 1997 village government tax revenue per capita. Economic data from 1997 are used instead of data from 2000, to avoid simultaneity bias. Demand for roads, schools, and infrastructure is also likely to increase with higher levels of industrial and commercial activity. The analysis thus also controls for the existence of village enterprises in 1995 and the existence of small-scale household enterprises (*getihu*) in 1995.

Democratic and Bureaucratic Institutions. The analyses also control for a third set of factors—formal institutions of accountability—which existing theories identify as central to governmental performance. To control for top-down institutions that enable higher level officials to supervise lower level officials, the analyses include measures of Party and bureaucratic institutional strength—a dummy variable for the elected village head's Party membership; the percentage of village officials who are members of the Party; and a dummy variable for villages where officials sign performance contracts including public project targets with higher level officials.

In addition to formal top-down institutions of accountability, the analyses also control for the effects of bottom-up democratic institutions. Since the late 1980s, grassroots democratic reforms have been implemented at the village level. These reforms entail direct elections for village officials and the establishment of deliberative villagers' representative assemblies. To control for the effects of these reforms, I include an index measuring the implementation of preelection procedures, an index of the implementation of voting procedures, and an index of the implementation of villagers' representative assemblies. For each of these three indices, principal components analysis was used to create an index out of a battery of survey questions (see Appendix A for details on the construction of these indices).

Estimation

I estimate the effects of different types of village solidary groups on village public goods provision using the following model:

$$Y_i^k = a^k + X_i\beta^k + \tau^k SG_i^k + \mu_i^k. \qquad \textbf{(1)}$$

In this model, Y_i^k is the public goods provision outcome measure, where k may denote village government investment, existence of paved roads, access to running water, or another provision outcome. X_i is a vector of socioeconomic, geographic, and institutional controls. SG_i denotes a particular solidary group measure (which can either be the existence of a temple manager, the percentage of households engaged in temple reconstruction, the existence of a minister or priest who organizes church activities, the existence of a church reconstruction project, the existence of a single ancestral hall with spirit tablets, or the existence of multiple ancestral halls with spirit tablets), where i denotes a village. The hypothesis can be restated as $H_0 : \tau^k = 0$, jointly for all outcomes k. Rejecting this hypothesis means that the particular solidary group being measured has a significant effect on public goods provision outcomes.

For each solidary group measure, this analysis uses seemingly unrelated regression (SUR) which estimates a system of six equations (one equation for each of the six public goods provision outcomes) and allows the errors in different equations to be correlated (see Miguel 2004). Because each measure of public goods provision is regressed on the same set of explanatory variables, the coefficients and standard errors produced by SUR are identical to those produced by ordinary least squares regression (OLS). Using SUR to look simultaneously at multiple measures of village governmental public goods has a number of advantages over combining these measures into a single index of governmental public goods provision. In developing countries such as China where resources are scarce, citizens and officials often have to make difficult choices about how to spend public funds. Few villages are able to fund roads *and* school buildings *and* water infrastructure. Having a paved road often makes it *less* likely that a village will have running water. Thus, intercorrelations among the public goods provision measures are low, and the measures do not scale together. (A table of intercorrelations can be viewed online at [http://web.mit.edu/polisci/faculty/L.Tsai.html]. Using SUR to look simultaneously at multiple measures of village governmental public goods provision allows for the possibility that different places prioritize different goods. The SUR software routine produces the covariances between estimators from different equations which allows us to test joint hypotheses involving parameters in different equations (Wooldridge 2002).

This paper presents the results when missing data are multiply imputed using the EMis algorithm developed by King et al. (2001) although *results of the analysis*

TABLE 3. Solidary Groups and Village Governmental Public Goods Provision in Rural China: Multivariate Regressions with Geographic, Demographic, Economic, and Institutional Controls (SUR)

Solidary Group Measures	Per Capita Investment	Existence of Paved Roads	Existence of Paved Paths	Percentage of Classrooms Usable in Rain	Newness of School	Existence of Running Water	H0: B = 0, p-value (SUR)
Village Temples							
Model 1a							
Existence of a temple manager	39.16 (39.08)	0.11 (0.084)	0.096 (0.057)	0.13* (0.055)	0.97 (3.13)	0.090 (0.069)	0.086*
Model 1b							
Percentage of households engaging in temple reconstruction projects	44.21 (50.79)	0.083 (0.12)	−0.023 (0.081)	0.22** (0.079)	−3.51 (4.43)	0.12 (0.099)	0.083*
Village Churches							
Model 2a							
Existence of an active village pastor	−60.58 (43.27)	0.10 (0.10)	−0.053 (0.069)	−0.25*** (0.066)	2.81 (3.79)	0.034 (0.084)	0.0048***
Model 2b							
Existence of church reconstruction projects	−69.89 (51.55)	0.28* (0.12)	−0.12 (0.083)	−0.26*** (0.079)	5.51 (4.46)	0.14 (0.10)	0.0002***
Lineage Groups							
Model 3							
Existence of a single ancestral hall with spirit tablets	66.28 (46.29)	0.25* (0.11)	0.094 (0.074)	−0.042 (0.072)	1.18 (4.09)	0.019 (0.090)	0.22
Existence of multiple ancestral halls with spirit tablets	−56.77 (43.80)	−0.13 (0.10)	0.11 (0.070)	−0.035 (0.068)	−5.35 (3.86)	−0.0059 (0.085)	0.13

Note: Control variables: Distance from county town; number of natural villages; village terrain; village population; 1997 income per capita; 1997 government assets; 1997 village tax revenue per capita; Party membership of village head; percentage of village officials in Party; existence of bureaucratic targets for public projects; index for implementation of pre-election institutions; index for implementation of voting institutions; index for implementation of villagers' representative assemblies; county dummies. These estimates are not reported (available on request). N = 316 villages. Missing data multiply imputed. Figures in cells are seemingly unrelated regression coefficients. Standard errors in parentheses. *p = 0.10; **p = 0.05; ***p = 0.01.The hypothesis that the coefficient estimates on each term is equal to zero across the six outcomes in the table is tested using SUR in the final column.

were similar regardless of whether missing data were deleted listwise or multiply imputed. This paper presents the results when missing data are multiply imputed for several reasons. First, listwise deletion generally resulted in *larger* coefficient estimates and more statistically significant results. The paper thus presents the more conservative estimates produced when missing data are multiply imputed. But as we can see from the estimates presented in Tables 3 and 4, even the more conservative coefficient estimates produced when multiple imputation is used provide substantial support for the paper's main argument. Second, listwise deletion results in a large loss of information. We can see from Table 1 that missing data for any individual variable is less than 10%. But when listwise deletion is used, about one-quarter of the observations are deleted because of the large number of controls in the analysis. For each missing item, five values were imputed to create five completed datasets. All the variables used in the analysis were included in the imputation model to help predict the missing values. Imputed values were created from the imputation model in the same way that values are simulated from a regression. Higher uncertainty about the value of a missing cell is reflected in higher variation across the five imputed values.

Table 3 presents the multivariate SUR estimates for the effects of different solidary groups on village governmental public goods provision when we control for geographic, demographic, economic, and institutional factors and missing data are multiply imputed using the process described above.[4] These results strongly support the hypothesis that localities with encompassing and embedding solidary groups are likely to have better local governmental public goods provision than localities without these groups. For each model, SUR estimated a system of six equations, one for each of the six public goods provision outcomes listed across the top of the table. In each model, each of the six public goods provision outcomes was regressed on the same solidary group measure or measures and the same array of controls. (Because of space constraints, the coefficient estimates on the controls are not shown here, but they can be viewed online at [http://web.mit.edu/polisci/faculty/L.Tsai.html].)

As we can see, village temple groups have a substantial positive impact on village public goods provision. Model 1a in Table 3 shows that the estimated relationship between village public goods provision and village temple groups as measured by the existence of a temple manager is positive for all six public goods outcomes and statistically significantly different

[4] Heteroskedasticity-robust standard errors are not reported because Stata and Clarify, a program for combining multiply imputed datasets for analysis, do not support seemingly unrelated regression with Huber robust standard errors. When listwise deletion is used, seemingly unrelated regression with robust standard errors generally results in similar standard errors.

from zero for paths and classrooms. In addition, the estimated effect of a temple manager on roads and water, though not statistically significant, has relatively low levels of uncertainty. The magnitude of this positive effect is sizable for all of the outcomes except newness of school. Although the standard errors for the individual estimates are relatively large, we can be reasonably confident that temple managers do in fact have a positive effect on village governmental public goods provision in general because such effects exist for multiple measures of village governmental public goods provision. We can also reject the null hypothesis that the coefficient estimate on village temple manager jointly across public goods provision outcomes is equal to zero at a 90% confidence level (p-value = 0.086 as shown in the last column of the table). This finding is supported by the estimates in Model 1b in which village temple groups are measured by the percentage of households engaging in temple reconstruction, although these results are more mixed. The estimated effect of village temple groups as measured by temple reconstruction is positive for four of the public goods provision outcomes (investment, roads, classrooms, and running water) and statistically significant for classrooms. The estimated effect of temple groups is negative for two of the public goods provision outcomes (paths and newness of school building), but the levels of uncertainty about these estimates were quite high, especially for paths. Using SUR we can reject the hypothesis that the coefficient estimate on temple reconstruction is equal to zero jointly across all the public goods provision outcomes at a 90% confidence level (p-value = 0.083).[5]

These results suggest that village temple groups, which are both encompassing and embedding, have a positive impact on village governmental public goods provision. But how do we know that *both* of these structural characteristics are necessary? We look next at the impact of village church groups that have only one of these characteristics—they are encompassing but not embedding. The results of Models 2a and 2b in Table 3 do not indicate that village churches have a positive impact on village governmental public goods provision.[6] Model 2a shows that the estimated relationship between village public goods provision and an active church as measured by the existence of an active village pastor who organizes church services or activities is negative for three outcomes (investment, paths, and classrooms) and statistically significant for classrooms.[7] The estimated relationship is positive but statistically insignificant for three outcomes (roads, the newness of the school building, and running water). Similar results are obtained when the existence of village church groups is measured by the existence of a church reconstruction project since liberalization began in the late 1970s. The estimated relationship between village public goods provision and this measure of churches is again negative for three outcomes (investment, paths, and classrooms) and statistically significant for classrooms. The estimated relationship is positive for three outcomes (roads, newness of school, and running water) and statistically significant for roads. Because only 7% of villages had active church pastors, these results are not conclusive. These estimates suggest, however, that village churches may have a *negative* impact on village government investment in public projects but a *positive* impact on some public goods such as roads. These estimates are thus consistent with what we saw in the case of South Bend where the church did not help hold village officials accountable for public goods provision but did organize a road project *in lieu of the local government.*

So temples—solidary groups that are both encompassing and embedding—seem to have a positive impact on village governmental public goods provision while churches—solidary groups that are only encompassing—do not. Models of public goods provision which focus on overcoming collective action problems through community norms, social capital, or ethnic homogeneity cannot account for this finding because, as we see in the village case studies, community norms and identity are strong in both villages with encompassing churches and villages with encompassing temples.

But perhaps being encompassing is not actually what is important. The positive effect of temple groups could simply be due to the fact that they are embedding, whereas churches are not. Or temple groups could be special not because of their structural characteristics but because of something about the content of their religious beliefs or the specific values they hold.

To examine these possibilities, we now turn to groups with a different basis for solidarity—lineage groups. In contrast to village temples that emphasize religious obligations to guardian deities who protect a particular geographical locale, lineage groups in rural China are based on a belief in shared ancestry and obligations due to kinship. Lineages tend to embed village officials, but not all of them encompass the entire village. Lineage group boundaries can be village-wide and overlap with village administrative boundaries, or they can be subvillage and fragment villagers into different lineage groups. If the structural hypothesis is correct—that is, both structural characteristics are necessary and the basis for solidarity does not matter—village-wide lineage groups that are both encompassing and embedding should have a positive impact on village public goods provision whereas subvillage lineage groups should not have a positive impact.

Model 3 in Table 3 estimates the impact of village-wide lineage groups and subvillage lineage groups on village public goods provision. SUR analysis suggests that village-wide lineage groups, like village temple groups, have a generally positive impact on village

[5] The findings remain similar for a model regressing public goods provision outcomes on a temple groups index created through principal components analysis of the two measures of temple groups.

[6] Again, the results are very similar for a model regressing public goods provision outcomes on an index for church groups created through principal components combining the two measures of church groups.

[7] Including the control variables changes the sign of the coefficient estimates on two outcomes (paths and water) from positive to negative.

public goods provision. The standard errors on the individual coefficient estimates were relatively large, but the estimated effect was positive for five of the six public goods provision measures (investment, roads, paths, newness of school building, and water) and statistically significant for roads. In addition, the estimated effect of village-wide lineage groups on investment and paths, though not statistically significant, had comparatively low levels of uncertainty. Moreover, the magnitude of the estimated positive effects on investment, roads, and paths was relatively large. The estimated effect was negative for classrooms usable in rain, but the level of uncertainty for this estimate as very high and the magnitude of the effect was very small. Although the effect of village-wide lineage groups jointly across the six outcomes is not significant by conventional statistical standards, it remains substantively important (p-value = 0.22). An alternative SUR analysis with heteroskedasticity-robust standard errors and listwise deletion of missing data indicates that village-wide lineage groups have a statistically significant effect jointly across public goods outcomes at a 95% confidence level (p-value = 0.04).

Not surprisingly, subvillage lineage groups as measured by the existence of multiple ancestral halls with spirit tablets do not have a positive impact on village governmental public goods provision. The coefficient estimates on the existence of multiple ancestral halls was negative and statistically insignificant for all of the public goods provision except paths. Villagers frequently reported that leftover concrete from repairs and renovations to village ancestral halls was often used to pave adjacent footpaths, which may help to account for this relationship. The coefficient estimate on paths was positive and close to statistically significant, but the coefficient estimate on per capita government investment in public projects was negative. There was some uncertainty about the magnitude of this estimated effect on investment, but it seems reasonable to conclude that if subvillage lineage groups do have an effect on government investment in public projects, it is probably not a positive one. Thus, we can surmise that although subvillage lineage groups may have a positive impact on village paths, they do not have a positive impact on village *governmental* public goods provision.

In sum, results from seemingly unrelated regression analysis are consistent with the hypothesis that solidary groups that are both encompassing and embedding have a positive impact on village governmental public goods provision. Village temples and village-wide lineages—the two solidary groups in the Chinese context which are encompassing and embedding—both had a positive effect on government investment in public goods provision as well as the provision of actual public goods. Findings from bivariate SUR regression and logit models for the existence of paved roads, the existence of paved paths, and the existence of running water (dichotomous dependent variables) are not shown but are similar to the multivariate SUR estimates, and in many cases provide even stronger support for the hypothesis that localities with encompassing and embedding groups are likely to have better village governmental public goods provision than localities without these groups. (These results can be currently viewed online at [http://web.mit.edu/polisci/faculty/L.Tsai.html]).

But what if the existence of these groups is an effect of good public goods provision rather than a cause? To examine this possibility, I used two-stage least-squares instrumental variables (IV) estimation to estimate the impact of village temples and village-wide lineage groups. Two-stage least squares can potentially estimate the effect of an endogenous variable accurately if we can identify a variable that only affects governmental public goods provision through its effect on the solidary group in question. For village temples, I use the existence of temple activity before 1949 to instrument for the current existence of a temple manager. Because of the nearly complete eradication of community temples and collective temple activities and the radical social upheaval during the Maoist period (Madsen 1984; Ruf 1998), it is unlikely that a history of precommunist temple activity has influenced the current performance of village governments in any way except by making the current existence of temple groups more likely by providing a familiar template for newly organizing social groups. A history of precommunist temple activity would not be a valid instrument if there are unchanging village characteristics that produce both temple activity and public goods provision. To reduce this possibility, the analysis includes as many controls as possible for village characteristics. For village-wide lineage groups, a simple index of surname fragmentation was used to instrument for the current existence of village-wide lineage groups. In the Chinese context, surname patterns make a good instrument for the current existence of village-wide lineage groups because they were largely determined exogenously in the precommunist period by imperial land settlement policies and natural disasters. These patterns were then frozen during the Maoist period when the state instituted strict policies against internal migration (Solinger 1999). There is no guarantee that villages in which the vast majority of households share the same surname will definitely establish an active village-wide lineage group. But surname patterns and the existence of village-wide lineage groups are likely to be correlated because the possibility of a village-wide lineage groups requires that a village be dominated by one surname group.

Due to space constraints, the results from IV estimation are not shown here, but results from IV estimation also indicated that the estimated effects of village temples and village-wide lineage groups on village governmental public goods provision are positive. (These results can be viewed online at [http://web.mit.edu/polisci/faculty/L.Tsai.html].) In fact, the coefficient estimates produced by two-stage least squares were generally larger in magnitude than the estimates produced by seemingly unrelated regression. Hausman tests indicated, moreover, that instrumental variables estimation was not necessarily warranted, because the differences between the IV estimates and the OLS estimates (which are the same as SUR estimates in this case) were not different enough to suggest that OLS estimates were inconsistent and that village temples and village-wide lineage groups were endogenous.

So as we can see, even when we control for level of economic development, variation in bureaucratic and democratic institutions, and differences in the demand for particular goods or the cost of particular goods due to variation in location, geography and size, encompassing and embedding solidary groups have a significant positive effect on village governmental public goods provision.

To get a sense of the impact of encompassing and embedding groups in more concrete terms, we can compare the mean level or likelihood of different public goods in an average village with a temple manager to an average village without a temple manager (an average village being one where all the control variables are set at their means). The mean per capita investment in an average village with a temple manager was 99 yuan (about $12, U.S.), which was substantially higher than the mean per capita investment in an average village without a temple manager, 61 yuan. The uncertainty around these estimates was somewhat high, but the fact that the provision of actual road, school, and water facilities also increased in villages with temple managers gives us more confidence in the positive relationship estimated between village temple groups and village governmental public goods provision. The probability that the average village with a temple manager has a paved road, for example, was 59%, whereas the probability that the average village without a temple manager has a paved road drops to 49%. The probability of running water in the average village with a temple manager was 55% whereas the probability of running water in a village without a temple manager was 46%.

To get a substantive idea of the actual impact of village-wide lineage groups, we can also compare the mean level or likelihood of different public goods in an average village with a village-wide lineage group as indicated by a single functioning ancestral hall, an average village with multiple subvillage lineage groups, and an average village without any lineage groups at all. The mean per capita investment for an average village with a single functioning ancestral hall was 132 yuan (about $17, U.S.), double that of an average village without any ancestral halls, although the uncertainty around these estimates was somewhat high. The difference in the probability of paved roads, however, was far more certain. The probability of paved roads in an average village with a single functioning ancestral hall is 75%, whereas the probability in an average village without a single functioning ancestral hall is only 49%. Because their 95% confidence intervals do not overlap, we can be quite certain that villages with village-wide lineage groups perform differently than villages without these groups. The average village with a village-wide lineage group had a 49% probability of running water, whereas the average village with multiple subvillage lineage groups had a 47% probability.

Data from the survey are consistent with the hypothesis that encompassing and embedding solidary groups (village temples and village-wide lineages) have a substantial positive effect on village governmental public goods provision. In contrast, solidary groups which do not have both of these structural characteristics (village churches and subvillage lineages) do not have a positive effect on local governmental public goods provision. These findings remain the same even when the effects of all four kinds of solidary groups are estimated in the same model. Model 4 in Table 4 includes all the control variables and measures for all four types of solidary groups. Even after controlling for the effects of churches and lineage groups, the estimated relationship among village temple groups as measured by the existence of a temple manager is positive for all the public goods provision measures and statistically significant for paths and classrooms. Although the estimated effect is not statistically significant for roads and water, uncertainty about these estimates are also relatively low. Similarly, the estimated relationship between village governmental public goods provision and village-wide lineage groups as measured by the existence of a single ancestral hall was positive for five out of six public goods provision outcomes and statistically significant for roads. Although the estimated effect is not statistically significant for investment and paths, uncertainty about these estimates was relatively low and the magnitude of the effects was relatively large. The estimated effect on classrooms was negative, but the uncertainty of this estimate was very high, and the magnitude of the effect was very small.

OTHER EXPLANATORY FACTORS

Contrary to what we might hope, local governments do not necessarily improve public goods and services a great deal as economic development and government resources increase. Resources matter but so does how they are used. We can see in Table 4 that the estimated relationship between village public goods provision and 1997 income per capita in Model 4 was positive for five outcomes (investment, roads, paths, school age, and water) and statistically significant for roads. The magnitude of this effect, however, was relatively small for investment and roads and very small for paths, newness of school, and water. When all other variables were held at their means, an increase from the 25th percentile to the 75th percentile in 1997 income per capita was only associated with a 6-yuan increase in investment, a 4% increase in the probability of paved roads, and a 2% increase in the probability of paved paths. The level of government assets also lacked an impact of any sizable magnitude on the six public goods provision outcomes. Higher tax revenue per capita was associated with less, not more, investment in village public projects and had little impact on any of the other public goods provision measures.

There was some indication, however, that more industrialization and a larger nonagricultural sector were

TABLE 4. Solidary Groups and Village Governmental Public Goods Provision in Rural China: All Four Solidary Groups in Same Model with All Controls (SUR)

Solidary Group Measures	Per Capita Investment	Existence of Paved Roads	Existence of Paved Paths	Percentage of Classrooms Usable in Rain	Newness of School	Existence of Running Water	H0: B = 0, p-value (SUR)
Village Temples							
Model 4							
Existence of a temple manager	37.52	0.093	0.098	0.14*	0.70	0.089	0.062*
	(38.24)	(0.082)	(0.056)	(0.053)	(3.12)	(0.069)	
Village Churches							
Existence of an active village pastor	−59.78	0.11	−0.083	−0.26***	3.66	0.031	0.0023***
	(43.61)	(0.10)	(0.070)	(0.067)	(3.83)	(0.086)	
Village-wide Lineages							
Existence of one and only one ancestral hall with spirit tablets	71.09	0.24*	0.098	−0.019	0.72	0.011	0.2664
	(46.44)	(0.11)	(0.074)	(0.070)	(4.10)	(0.091)	
Subvillage Lineages							
Existence of multiple ancestral halls with spirit tablets	−45.34	−0.15	0.13	0.013	−5.98	−0.0093	0.0986*
	(44.25)	(0.10)	(0.071)	(0.067)	(3.91)	(0.086)	
Control Variables							
Distance from county town	−0.42	−0.0057***	−0.0023*	0.00015	0.077	−0.0018	
	(0.61)	(0.0014)	(0.00098)	(0.00095)	(0.055)	(0.0012)	
Number of natural villages	−0.99	−0.0054	−0.0045	0.0084	0.14	−0.0053	
	(3.075)	(0.0071)	(0.0048)	(0.0046)	(0.27)	(0.0060)	
Village terrain	−0.50	0.065	−0.024	−0.0093	−1.68	0.0082	
	(33.88)	(0.078)	(0.053)	(0.051)	(2.95)	(0.066)	
Village population	−0.015	0.000028	0.000035*	0.0000039	−0.0011	0.000016	
	(0.011)	(0.000025)	(0.000017)	(0.000017)	(0.00097)	(0.000022)	
1997 income per capita (thousands of yuan)	0.0071	0.000048*	0.000026	0.0000083	0.00052	−0.00000043	
	(0.010)	(0.000023)	(0.000016)	(0.000015)	(0.00088)	(0.000019)	
1997 government assets (thousands of yuan)	−0.000010	0.000000075	−0.000000000017	−0.000000012	−0.00000013	0.00000014**	
	(0.000027)	(0.000000063)	(0.000000044)	(0.000000042)	(0.0000025)	(0.000000054)	
1997 tax revenue per capita	−0.45	0.00089	−0.0013	−0.00061	−0.0045	0.00094	
	(0.45)	(0.0010)	(0.00069)	(0.00067)	(0.040)	(0.00086)	
Existence of village enterprises in 1995	−4.78	0.027	0.059	0.016	−1.30	0.061	
	(21.82)	(0.050)	(0.034)	(0.033)	(1.93)	(0.042)	
Existence of small-scale entrepreneurs (*getihu*) in 1995	−5.45	0.059	0.065	−0.0086	−7.29**	0.017	
	(29.16)	(0.067)	(0.048)	(0.045)	(2.62)	(0.057)	
Party membership of village head	15.78	0.021	−0.035	−0.0011	2.68	0.022	
	(25.36)	(0.057)	(0.039)	(0.038)	(2.25)	(0.049)	
Percentage of village officials in Party	20.56	0.14	0.031	0.038	2.59	0.11	
	(66.37)	(0.15)	(0.10)	(0.099)	(5.76)	(0.13)	
Existence of bureaucratic targets for public projects	44.99*	−0.076	−0.039	0.044	1.54	−0.020	
	(22.54)	(0.051)	(0.035)	(0.033)	(1.93)	(0.043)	
Percentage of village government revenue from subsidies allocated by higher levels in 1997	63.35	0.093	−0.10	−0.095	−0.16	0.21*	
	(46.85)	(0.11)	(0.074)	(0.075)	(4.37)	(0.092)	

(*continued overleaf*)

TABLE 4. Continued

Solidary Group Measures	Per Capita Investment	Existence of Paved Roads	Existence of Paved Paths	Percentage of Classrooms Usable in Rain	Newness of School	Existence of Running Water	H0: B = 0, p-value (SUR)
Index for the implementation of preelection institutions	4.73	−0.012	0.015	0.020	−0.70	0.018	
	(6.68)	(0.017)	(0.011)	(0.011)	(0.69)	(0.014)	
Index for the implementation of voting institutions	7.67	0.017	0.017	−0.00084	0.97	−0.0083	
	(10.09)	(0.023)	(0.016)	(0.015)	(0.89)	(0.020)	
Index for the implementation of villagers' representative assemblies	11.00	0.014	0.017	0.021	−0.16	−0.010	
	(8.35)	(0.019)	(0.013)	(0.016)	(0.77)	(0.016)	
County dummies	Yes	Yes	Yes	Yes	Yes	Yes	
Constant term	34.55	0.33*	0.038	0.84***	54.54***	0.71***	
	(63.10)	(0.14)	(0.099)	(0.098)	(5.54)	(0.12)	

Note: N = 316 villages. Missing data multiply imputed. Figures in cells are seemingly unrelated regression coefficients. Standard errors in parentheses. *p = 0.10; **p = 0.05; ***p = 0.01. The hypothesis that the coefficient estimates on each term is equal to zero across the six outcomes in the table is tested using SUR in the final column. R-squared values are not available when missing data is multiply imputed, but when missing data is deleted listwise, the R-squared values are 0.15 for per capita investment, 0.30 for paved roads, 0.28 for paved paths, 0.12 for classrooms, 0.33 for newness of school building, and 0.53 for running water.

associated with better public goods, although not with more village government investment in public projects. The estimated effect of the existence of village enterprises in 1995 was positive and statistically significant or close to significant for the probability of paved paths and running water. The estimated effect of the existence of small-scale entrepreneurs in 1995 was positive and statistically significant or close to significant for the probability of paved roads and paved paths.

Generally speaking, bureaucratic institutions of top-down control and democratic institutions did not seem to have sizable positive effects on village governmental public goods provision, although there was some evidence that villages that received more subsidies from higher levels were more likely to have better village governmental public goods provision. We can see in Table 4 that the estimated effect of subsidies from higher levels was positive and statistically significant or close to significant for investment, roads, and water. The estimated effect, however, on paths, classrooms, and school building was negative and close to statistically significant for paths and classrooms.

We can also see in Table 4 that neither of the two measures for formal Party institutions had any clear effect. Coefficient estimates on Party membership of village head and the percentage of village officials in the Party were statistically insignificant and generally small or modest in magnitude. Previous studies of bureaucratic performance contracts at the township level have found that contracts have a substantial impact on cadre behavior (Bernstein and Lu 2003; Edin 2003), but at the village level, we can see that bureaucratic performance contracts did not have a consistently positive effect on governmental public goods provision. Performance contracts had a positive impact on three of the public goods provision measures and a negative impact on the other three. The estimated positive effect on investment was statistically significant. These results suggest that performance contracts have a sizable impact on government investment in public projects but that this increase in investment is not accompanied by similarly large increases in the provision of actual public goods and services.

Why might performance contracts be correlated with higher government investment but not with better village public goods? One possible reason is that performance contracts rely on simple measures of village government performance such as investment without further monitoring whether village officials actually improve roads and schools when they increase spending. These findings also suggest that investment in education facilities may, at the same time, channel funds away from rural roads and water infrastructure. Other studies have found that top-down bureaucratic performance contracts may actually be counterproductive to local governance by encouraging investment in "vanity" public projects like new government office buildings or giving local officials excuses to raise local taxes (Bernstein and Lu 2003).

Contrary to what theories of democracy might predict, the estimated effects of the implementation of democratic institutions on village governmental public goods provision were very small and in general statistically insignificant. The estimated effect of the implementation of preelection institutions was only statistically significant for one outcome, the percentage of classrooms usable in rain, but the magnitude of this effect was very small. For an increase from the 25th percentile to the 75th percentile in terms of implementation of preelection institutions, the average percentage of classrooms usable in rain increased only 3%. The estimated effect of the implementation of voting procedures such as secret ballot and regulated proxy voting was statistically insignificant and of a very small magnitude for all six public goods provision outcomes. The estimated effect of the implementation of villagers' representative assemblies was also statistically insignificant for all six public goods provision outcomes, although the level of uncertainty was relatively low for investment, paths, and classrooms. The magnitude of these effects was small to modest. For an increase from the 25th percentile to the 75th percentile in terms of implementation of villagers' representative assemblies, the mean per capita investment in public projects increased 20 yuan, the mean probability of paved paths increased 3%, and the mean percentage of classrooms usable in rain increased 4%. Results remained similar when the implementation of democratic institutions were measured in different ways. There was still no indication that democratic institutions had a clear positive effect on village government investment and village governmental public goods provision when the provision measures were regressed on additive scores for the implementation of preelection institutions, voting institutions, and villagers' representative assemblies. Nor was there any indication that democratic institutions had a clear positive effect on village governmental public goods provision when the provision measures were regressed on a single additive score summing all of the dichotomous measures for preelection, voting, and villagers' representative assembly institutions.

Findings in the previous section suggested that solidary groups with certain structural characteristics could encourage local officials to provide public goods and services even without democracy. These findings suggest that the implementation of elections does not guarantee good governmental performance, especially when other democratic institutions are weak.[8] One problem is that the implementation of village elections has done little to inform citizens about what officials are doing on a day-to-day basis. By the time villagers discover that a corrupt or inept official has drained the public coffers, they may be able to vote him out of office but they cannot necessarily get the money back. As Dali Yang and Fubing Su (2001) have noted, higher levels must institute independent accounting offices and statistical agencies to guarantee public access to information. Another problem is that in many places, the rewards of village office have diminished. In more developed localities, people may do better by becoming private entrepreneurs. Although holding public office may allow private entrepreneurs to extend their political and business connections, private entrepreneurs who become village officials rarely have a long-term time horizon for planning public projects. In poorer localities, the salaries and pensions offered to officials may be important incentives, but it is often in these places that local governments lack sufficient funds to pay salaries on time.[9]

CONCLUSION

The results presented in this paper suggest that when formal institutions of accountability are weak, citizens can still make government officials organize and fund the public goods that they want and need when they have the right kind of social groups. Solidary groups that are structured so that they overlap and mesh with government structures can provide local government officials with important incentives to provide the public goods and services that citizens demand even when democratic or bureaucratic institutions do not work effectively. By participating in encompassing solidary groups and fulfilling obligations to work for the good of the group, local officials can earn access to the moral authority conferred by these groups, which can be invaluable for pursuing their personal interests and for carrying out state tasks. Solidary groups which are not both encompassing and embedding may still be able to mobilize their members and provide some public goods and services themselves—but they are less able to hold the government responsible for providing these goods and services.

What general lessons can we draw from the experience of rural China? First, economic development is not necessarily correlated with political or institutional development. Good governance may foster economic growth and industrialization, but it is not clear that the converse is true. The evolution of state institutions in different places (even in the same country) does not simply vary in the speed of change; they do not all follow the same trajectory of institutional development.

Second, we need to differentiate between different types of social groups and social capital and to theorize about how they are correlated with particular political and economic outcomes. What the "right" kind of social group is depends on what result we are interested in. This study shows that distinguishing between different types of social groups can reveal that groups with different structural characteristics have very different effects on governmental performance. It also suggests that we need to pay more attention to important *interaction* effects between social structures and state structures.

[8] Others have also discussed the differences between democracy and accountability (see, e.g., Przeworski et al. 1999).

[9] These issues may also help account for the lack of a statistically significant or substantively important interaction term between the existence of an encompassing group (a dichotomous measure coded one when the village had at least one temple group, village church, or village-wide lineage; and zero otherwise) and an index of the implementation of village democratic reforms.

Third, the right kind of social group for governmental performance and public goods provision in authoritarian and transitional systems are not necessarily the ones that increase trust or are autonomous from the state. Without formal institutions that incorporate citizen participation in the policymaking process, it is not clear how much of an impact social organizations which help citizens voice their opinions and develop organizational skills can have. Under these conditions, solidary groups that incorporate agents of the state and offer moral standing as an incentive to contribute to the public good can provide informal institutions of accountability that substitute for formal ones.

In sum, solidary groups and informal institutions can be very beneficial to local governmental performance in transitional systems where formal institutions are weak. In democratic systems, explicit rules about how to change the rules give the system flexibility. In authoritarian and transitional systems, informality and informal institutions can provide this flexibility, sometimes at a lower cost to the state than the building of formal institutions to carry out the same functions. It may be that informal institutions can help stabilize states indefinitely, and what we think of as "transitional" systems are not really transitional at all.

But there may also be serious drawbacks to relying on solidary groups to provide informal institutions of accountability. This kind of informal system may also be difficult to "scale up" and may only work at local levels for towns and villages. In cities or at the national level, encompassing and embedding solidary groups may be both less relevant and less likely to exist. More importantly, this kind of informal system helps citizens obtain more public goods and services that they would otherwise get without this kind of informal system—but perhaps not as much as they would get if there was a system of formal accountability to make sure that higher levels of government also contributed resources and took responsibility for providing local public goods. By relieving pressure on the state in the short term, this kind of informal system may help to forestall reforms to the formal institutional system that would be more beneficial to both citizens and the state in the long term.

APPENDIX A

To measure the implementation of preelection institutions, the survey asked about interference by higher level township officials, the village Party organization, and incumbent village officials in the nomination of primary election candidates, the nomination of final candidates, and the selection of the election administration committee. For each of these nine questions, a dichotomous variable was created. Principal components analysis was then used to construct an index out of these nine items measuring the implementation of preelection institutions.

To measure the implementation of voting institutions, the survey asked the following seven questions: whether the results of elections were announced immediately after polls closed; whether there were more candidates than offices; whether ballots were counted publicly; whether secret ballot was used; whether candidates gave campaign speeches; whether proxy voting was regulated; and whether the ballot box was fixed in a designated polling place rather than brought around to each household, which increases the chances of fraud. Again, I used principal components analysis to create a index reflecting the implementation of voting procedures.

To measure the implementation of villagers' representative assemblies (VRAs), the survey asked whether the village had implemented the following seven institutions: competition for VRA seats, election through secret ballot, formal regulations on when the VRA was supposed to be convened, formal power of the VRA to recall the village head, formal power to inspect village expenditures; formal power to audit village accounts, and whether the VRA had vetoed a village government decision in the past year. Based on these seven measures, I constructed an index measuring VRA implementation using principal components analysis.

REFERENCES

Alesina, Alberto, Reza Baqir, and William Easterly. November 1999. "Public Goods and Ethnic Divisions." *The Quarterly Journal of Economics* 114 (4): 1243–84.

Bardhan, Pranab. Fall 2002. "Decentralization of Governance and Development." *Journal of Economic Perspectives* 16 (4): 185–205.

Benziger, Vincent. Spring 1993. "China's Rural Road System During the Reform Period." *China Economic Review* 4 (1): 1–17.

Bernstein, Thomas P., and Xiaobo Lu. 2003. *Taxation Without Representation in Contemporary Rural China*. Cambridge: Cambridge University Press.

Boix, Carles, and Daniel Posner. October 1998. "Social Capital: Explaining its Origins and Effects on Governmental Performance." *British Journal of Political Science* 28 (4): 686–93.

Chwe, Michael. 2003. *Rational Ritual: Culture, Coordination, and Common Knowledge*. Princeton: Princeton University Press.

Dahl, Robert. 1971. Polyarchy: *Participation and Opposition*. New Haven: Yale University Press.

Edin, Maria. March 2003. "Remaking the Communist Party-State: The Cadre Responsibility System at the Local Level in China." *China: An International Journal* 1 (1): 1–15.

Edwards, Bob, and Michael W. Foley. September 1998. "Social Capital and Civil Society Beyond Putnam." *The American Behavioral Scientist* 42 (1): 124–40.

Ehrenberg, John. 1999. *Civil Society: The Critical History of an Idea*. New York: New York University Press.

Esherick, Joseph. 1987. *The Origins of the Boxer Uprising*. Berkeley: University of California Press.

Evans, Peter. 1995. *Embedded Autonomy: States and Industrial Transformation*. Princeton: Princeton University Press.

Goode, William J. 1979. *The Celebration of Heroes: Prestige as a Control System*. Berkeley: University of California Press.

King, Gary, James Honaker, Anne Joseph, and Kenneth Scheve. March 2001. "Analyzing Incomplete Political Science Data: An Alternative Algorithm for Multiple Imputation." *American Political Science Review* 95 (1): 49–69.

Latourette, Kenneth Scott. 1929. *A History of Christian Missions in China*. New York: Macmillan.

Lam, Wai Fung. 1997. "Institutional Design of Public Agencies and Co-production." In *State-Society Synergy: Government and Social Capital in Development*. Berkeley: University of California Press.

Madsen, Richard. 1998. *China's Catholics: Tragedy and Hope in an Emerging Civil Society*. Berkeley: University of California Press.

Madsen, Richard. 1984. *Morality and Power in a Chinese Village*. Berkeley: University of California Press.

Miguel, Edward. April 2004. "Tribe or Nation? Nation Building and Public Goods in Kenya versus Tanzania." *World Politics* 56: 327–62.

Miguel, Edward. June 1999. "Ethnic Diversity, Mobility, and School Funding: Theory and Evidence from Kenya." Development Economics Discussion Paper Series No. 14.

Morris, Robert. 2001. "Structure, Culture, and Society in British Towns." In *The Cambridge Urban History of Britain, Vol. III*, ed. Martin Daunton. Cambridge: Cambridge University Press.

O'Donnell, Guillermo. April 1996. "Illusions about Consolidation." *Journal of Democracy* 7 (2): 55–69.

Ostrom, Elinor. 1990. *Governing the Commons: The Evolution of Institutions for Collective Action*. Cambridge: Cambridge University Press.

Putnam, Robert. 1993. *Making Democracy Work: Civic Traditions in Modern Italy*. Princeton: Princeton University Press.

Putnam, Robert. 2000. *Bowling Alone: The Collapse and Revival of American Community*. New York: Simon and Schuster.

Riches, David. June 1984. "Hunting, Herding, and Potlatching: Towards a Sociological Account of Prestige." *Man* 19 (2): 234–51.

Rose-Ackerman, Susan. 2005. *From Elections to Democracy: Building Accountable Government in Hungary and Poland*. Cambridge: Cambridge University Press.

Ruf, Gregory A. 1998. *Cadres and Kin: Making a Socialist Village in West China, 1921–1991*, Stanford: Stanford University Press.

Seabright, Paul. January 1996. "Accountability and Decentralization in Government: An Incomplete Contracts Model." *European Economic Review* 40 (1): 1–202.

Solinger, Dorothy. 1999. *Contesting Citizenship in Urban China: Peasant Migrants, the State, and the Logic of the Market*. Berkeley: University of California Press.

Spence, Jonathan. 1996. *God's Chinese Son: The Taiping Heavenly Kingdom of Hong Xiuquan*. London: Harper Collins.

Wolf, Arthur. 1974. *Gods, Ghosts, and Ancestors*, Stanford: Stanford University Press.

Wong, Christine. June 1997. "Rural Public Finance." In *Financing Local Government in the People's Republic of China*, ed. Christine Wong. Hong Kong: Oxford University Press.

Wooldridge, Jeffrey M. 2002. *Econometric Analysis of Cross-Section and Panel Data*. Cambridge: MIT Press.

Yang, Dali, and Fubing Su. September 2001. "Elections, Governance, and Accountability in Rural China." Paper presented at the International Symposium on Villager Self-Government and Rural Social Development in China, Beijing.

[17]

The Hollow State: Rural Governance in China

Graeme Smith*

ABSTRACT Over the last decade, rural township governments have been subjected to intensive streamlining and rationalization programmes. This article examines which ongoing reforms and processes are causing township governments to become "hollow shells," and explores the effects of "hollowing out" on township government leaders, staff and rural residents. While the aim of local government reform was to transform extractive township governments into "service-oriented" agencies, this article finds that the current logic of rural governance has produced township governments which are squeezed from above and below. From above, township leaders face the political imperatives of inspections, annual assessments, the need to attract industrial investment and an ongoing process of "soft centralization" by higher levels of government. From below, township staff are drawn out to the villages to enforce family planning policies and maintain social stability. Unprecedented numbers are working as "sent-down cadres" in villages where their capacity to deliver services has been weakened by village amalgamations and the lifting of agricultural taxes and fees. Despite significant boosts to rural health and education investment, rural residents still face a level of government that regards them as problems to be dealt with, rather than citizens to be served.

Increasing attention has been paid to the phenomenon of rural township governments being "hollowed out" in the wake of rural taxation reforms,[1] but there is a lack of detailed ethnographic information on the effects of this phenomenon. This article is a detailed study of the lowest formal level of the Chinese state at the township level. Its starting point is the perspective of township government officials and ordinary staff themselves. I explore how township governments have become hollow administrative shells and the specific processes which are the basis for this "hollowing out," and examine the implications for local

* Australian National University. Email: graeme.smith@anu.edu.au

1 See esp. John James Kennedy, "From the tax-for-fee reform to the abolition of agricultural taxes: the impact on township governments in north-west China," *The China Quarterly*, No. 189 (2007), pp. 43–59; and Linda Chelan Li, "Working for the peasants? Strategic interactions and unintended consequences in China's rural tax reform," *The China Journal*, No. 57 (2007), pp. 90–106.

© The China Quarterly, 2010 doi:10.1017/S0305741010000615

602 The China Quarterly, 203, September 2010, pp. 601–618

government in rural China. Nearly all studies in the Western literature have tended to focus on either county or village governments with few examining the inner workings of township governments, thus leaving the lowest level of formal administration as something of a lacuna in China studies. In this article, taking a county in central China's rural heartland as my case study, I examine how the local state functions at the township level, using surveys and extensive interviews with county officials, township government workers, village cadres and ordinary rural residents.

Previous authors have accurately described township governments as hollow "administrative shells," unable to provide basic services in the wake of tax-for-fee reform during the 1990s and the abolition of agricultural taxes in 2006. However, the mechanisms of hollowing out have not been fully elucidated. This article argues that it is not just a consequence of the tax-for-fee reforms, but rather is constantly reinforced by the revenue-raising and political imperatives faced by township leaders, exacerbated by recent administrative reforms.

The first section details pressures from the county level in the form of higher-level inspections, the pressure to attract investment and the "soft centralization"[2] of township agencies. These pressures are hollowing township governments from above by drawing township leaders and the most talented staff away from their bailiwicks, thus transforming township governments into service agencies for county leaders. The second section describes hollowing from below. In the past, township governments guided village work, but with village governments starved of revenue following the abolition of agricultural taxes in 2006 and the ranks of village cadres depleted by village amalgamations, township government workers are now undertaking tasks that were formerly shouldered by villages. Unprecedented numbers of township staff are working as "sent-down" village cadres to enforce the key political imperatives of family planning and social stability. I draw conclusions on how this hollowing process changes the nature of the local state, and how this affects attempts to transform township governments into service-oriented agencies.

This article is a result of extensive fieldwork conducted in 16 townships in a relatively well-off county in Anhui province, referred to as Benghai.[3] Anhui was chosen because it was the pioneer in both tax-for-fee reforms during the 1990s. The county boasts a range of agricultural products in keeping with its varied geography. Its GDP per capita in 2010 was slightly higher than the provincial average because of the presence of many successful rural industries. When agricultural taxes were abolished in 2006 the impact on government revenue was negligible, as agricultural taxes had accounted for less than 10 per cent of the county's taxes.

2 Andrew Mertha, "China's 'soft' centralization: shifting *tiao/kuai* authority relations," *The China Quarterly*, No. 184 (2005), pp. 791–810.

3 Due to the need to protect sources, Benghai is a pseudonym.

From 2004 to 2008, I spent 21 months in Benghai county, working within the county government on poverty alleviation projects related to agriculture, education and forestry. As a result, I worked closely with township and county government officials on a daily basis, allowing me to obtain information beyond the scope of formal interviews. Surveys of 286 farm households in five different townships were conducted with research teams in 2004, 2005 and 2008 to obtain background information on rural residents' experiences of taxation, land use, village amalgamations and interaction with local cadres.

A survey of 95 township government staff in all 16 townships was conducted with the assistance of the Ministry of Agriculture between January and March 2006. Extensive follow-up interviews with township staff and ordinary farmers also took place. Interviews were conducted either at my residence in the county seat or at the residences of interviewees. These provided a more nuanced picture of their behaviour, allowed them to frame and discuss issues in their own terms and to construct their own narratives of experiences with the local government. Interviews were also conducted with academics, officials and businesspeople in the prefectural capital, as well as Hefei, Beijing and Sichuan.

In addition to this ethnography, I draw upon the work of three Chinese researchers who examine the day-to-day workings of township governments. Zhao Shukai 赵树凯, from the State Council's Development Research Centre, surveyed 20 township governments in ten different provinces, spending a considerable time in each township and inviting all the township Party secretaries to Beijing for in-depth discussions.[4] Gu Wenfeng 谷文峰, a sociologist, was posted by the Henan provincial government to a township in Hebi prefecture, and detailed his experiences during two years as a township Party secretary.[5] The renowned political sociologist from the "Central China School" of rural studies, Wu Yi 吴毅, spent a year with the cadres of a township in central China.[6]

Hollowed from Above

In this section, I argue that township governments in central China have been hollowed out from above by three imperatives: the need to attract investment to compensate for lost revenue and meet the political imperatives set by county and provincial governments; the need to receive inspection teams from higher levels of government; and "soft centralization" of township bureaus, which are placed under county or provincial government control.

4 Zhao Shukai, "Rural governance in the midst of underfunding, deception, and mistrust," in Andrew Kipnis and Graeme Smith (eds.), *Chinese Sociology & Anthropology*, No. 39 (2007).

5 Gu Wenfeng, *Feichang zishu: yi ge xiangzhen shuji de meng yu teng* (*Extraordinary Accounts: the Hopes and Troubles of a Township Party Secretary*) (Beijing: Xinhua chubanshe, 2006).

6 Wu Yi, *Xiao zhen xuanxiao: yi ge xiangzhen zhengzhi yunzuo de yanyi yu chanshi* (*Uproar in a Small Town: Interpretation of a Township's Political Operation*) (Beijing: Sanlian shudian, 2007).

604 *The China Quarterly*, 203, September 2010, pp. 601–618

Attracting investment

What functions does the township government serve, and how do ordinary township government staff perceive the priorities of the local state? To address these questions, I asked township staff what, to them, were the main tasks of the township government, compared to 1999, the height of the Jiang era, and the 1980s. The figure represents the percentage of staff who saw the task as a major (in the top five of ten tasks) priority of the township government during the specified time period. Items which score more than 50 per cent in this category are major priorities and are highlighted in bold in Table 1.

Table 1 suggests that national Party policies (panel b) now have more influence on Benghai's township governments than during the Jiang Zemin era, when the pressure from higher levels of government to collect taxes (panel j) was paramount.[7] However, the third-ranked item in 2006, attracting investment (panel g), is a priority of provincial and sub-provincial Party leaders, and has repeatedly been criticized by national Party leaders.

Even the most impoverished townships are devoting resources and staff towards attracting investment. In one remote township, 16 of the 55 formally employed staff were members of the investment working group, including staff from 13 different bureaus, as well as the township Party secretary, the township head and a deputy Party secretary.[8] Wealthier townships produce glossy investment guide books which describe projects that are seeking investment, and detail the tax and land incentives available to prospective investors. Typically, a tax-free period of three years is offered, as well as low land rental rates (as little as one yuan per square metre, or even free for a certain period). Most townships had set up agencies specifically to solicit investment, but ultimate responsibility lay with the township head and the Party secretary.

Chinese scholars have questioned the value of each province, prefecture, county, township and even village competing to offer the most attractive package to investors.[9] Setting quotas for attracting investment encourages township officials to falsify reports and force local businesses to register as "outside" or, better yet, "foreign" investors.[10] Funds that could be used to provide services for rural residents are instead spent on entertaining prospective investors. This situation is

7 For an account of how township governments adapted to higher-level pressure to collect taxes during the reform period, see Tian Yi and Zhao Xu, *Ta xiang zhi shui* (*Township Taxes*) (Beijing: Zhongxin chubanshe, 2008).

8 It is near impossible to know how many staff are on the payroll of a township government. Gu estimated that 69 cadres were on his official payroll, but 124 drew a salary (or 150 if laid-off and retired staff were included): Gu Wenfeng, *Extraordinary Accounts*, p. 145.

9 See esp. Zhao Shukai, "Rural governance," pp. 68–73; Wu Licai and Zhu Hongxuan, "Xiangzhen gaige: xiangzhen ganbu de suo si suo xiang – dui Hubei sheng xiangzhen ganbu de wenjuan diaocha" ("Township reform: what township cadres think – a survey of Hubei province"), *Zhongguo nongcun jingji* (*China Rural Economy*), No. 11 (2005), p. 64.

10 Contrast this with Kellee Tsai's description of Chinese businesses registering as foreign-invested enterprises to enhance their status and thus reduce interference from local government. Kellee S. Tsai, *Capitalism without Democracy* (Ithica: Cornell University Press, 2007), pp. 183–88. In Benghai, local cadres pressure businesses to register outside the county to enhance their personal political prospects.

Table 1: **Priorities of Township Governments (%)**

Task	2006	1999	1980s
a) Tasks assigned by higher levels of government	**51**	**75**	**75**
b) National Party guiding principles and policies	**76**	**58**	**63**
c) Farmers' economic and political rights	46	9	3
d) Agricultural technology extension, information and public services	**54**	23	24
e) Developing culture, education and health	32	19	33
f) Public works and infrastructure, e.g. rural roads and irrigation	**50**	35	32
g) Attracting investment	**74**	19	5
h) Ensuring public stability	38	39	**53**
i) Family planning	**86**	**99**	**71**
j) Collecting tax	0	**95**	**92**

Source:
Author's survey, 2006, N = 95.

unlikely to change, unless the revenue incentives and assessment criteria faced by provincial and sub-provincial authorities are altered.[11] Many ordinary township staff wondered about the practicability of the policy. In the words of a township cadre who ran his own agricultural supplies business on the side:

> What sorts of companies can we attract to a township like ours? We're an hour's drive from the county seat. Get serious. Profitable businesses will look for somewhere close to the big markets, with good transport and communications, somewhere like Hangzhou or Shanghai. So we land the industries no one else wants, big polluters, unprofitable industries.

This activity is driven by a series of political and economic incentives that are common to all provinces in central China. A township Party secretary from Suxian county in Henan admitted to spending two-thirds of the year "chasing the cash" in eight different provinces.[12] Through meetings and the content of the townships' annual assessments, county leaders make it clear to township leaders that attracting investment is the surest way for them to earn promotion to a good county bureau and reap personal financial rewards. Attracting industrial investment also offers future revenue sources, which is why township governments tend to waive conveyancing fees.[13] Because of the possibility for enrichment and travel, powerful agencies, such as the police, rural credit co-operatives and the finance bureau, tend to be over-represented in working groups for attracting investment. But quick-witted and well-connected staff are also poached from township agencies, meaning that staff left behind in the township tend to be the least talented.

11 This is common elsewhere in Anhui. My attempt to survey township staff in Wuhu county came to an abrupt end when it emerged that less than 10% of staff could be located. Their colleagues had all left the county to seek investors.

12 Liang Peng, *Jiceng ganbu zhaoshang yinzi: nongmin xin liang* (*Making the Farmers' Blood Run Cold: Local Cadres Attracting Investment*), China Elections and Governance website, 13 December 2005, http://www.chinaelections.org/NewsInfo.asp?NewsID=43318, accessed 2 July 2009.

13 Such is not the case with commercial and residential property developments. See Tao Ran, Su Fubing, Liu Mingxing and Cao Guangzhong, "Leasing and local public finance in China's regional development: evidence from prefecture-level cities," *Urban Studies*, forthcoming.

606 The China Quarterly, 203, September 2010, pp. 601–618

The emphasis on attracting investment has increased this tendency for squandering limited township funds on food and drink.[14] County documents contain detailed instructions on what sort of food should be served at banquets, strict expenditure limits (no more than 90 yuan per table for village cadres, less than 120 yuan for county leaders) and a ban on drinking at lunchtime.[15] These restrictions, however, are all waived if attracting investment is the purpose of the meal. I was widely viewed as a potential "investor" and hence was a sought-after lunch guest.

Inspections

Gu Wenfeng describes the everyday frustrations arising from the township government's lack of agency in its dealings with county and prefectural leaders:

> The county has cadres who are industrious; others less so. Some cadres have no idea how to fill up their day. They'll read the smallest advertisements in the paper several times over. A newspaper and a cup of tea, that's a day's labour. But when they get fed up, it's time for an inspection of "grassroots work." They'll happily go for a tour, or perhaps score some points [on the annual assessment] by calling a meeting. They loaf around, eating and drinking for a few days, picking up "souvenirs." When the higher-level organs carry out their work, do they ever consider whether it has the slightest economic or social benefit?
>
> As far as township cadres are concerned, I tell them to focus on results, don't worry about process. If there are petitions [by farmers to higher levels], no matter the reason, blame lies with the township. If the higher levels make work arrangements, it doesn't matter if they are relevant; tasks have to be completed otherwise criticism is swift. Regardless of funding, when you're required to accomplish something it must be done. As far as higher levels are concerned, convene a meeting, write a memorandum, issue a document and then carry out inspections. That's it. But down in the township, no matter what the circumstances, no matter what difficulties you face, the task has to be completed – no one is going to do it for you, or take responsibility.[16]

As Gu notes, the large number of staff at the county level increases the frequency of inspections, forcing township leaders to take staff away from their real jobs, a situation frequently described by interviewees as "not attending to one's proper duties" (*bu wu zheng ye* 不务正业). From a macro-perspective, the township government is effectively hollowed from within as staff and township leaders are forced to leave their posts to attend to the priority of the day. Inspections by higher levels served to remind township staff that their main duty is carrying out "key work." The head of one township agency observed:

> The township leadership's work is basically about coping with all the inspections by the higher-ups, there's no thought of taking the lead in developing the region. Grassroots cadres need to be liberated from endless inspections and placed under the direct management of the county level. Then we won't all be dragged into work stemming from the "one-strike rejection."[17]

14 See also Gu Wenfeng, *Extraordinary Accounts*, pp. 146–49; Wu Yi, *Uproar in a Small Town*, pp. 577–81.

15 X Town Cadre Management System (Jiguan ganbu guanli zhidu), 2008.

16 Gu Wenfeng, *Extraordinary Accounts*, pp. 101–02.

17 The "one-strike rejection" (*yi piao foujue*) is applied to government tasks that have the highest priority, most consistently family planning and preventing social unrest. Failure to complete such tasks means that (at least in theory) all other achievements by the township government are annulled. See also Maria Edin, "State capacity and local agent control in China: CCP cadre management from a township

At the beginning of each year, all staff are divided up into work groups, often attending to tasks unrelated to their actual skills. One township had over 30 such groups in 2008, with the Party secretary acting as the chair on 14 of them.

To satisfy the requirements of higher-level inspection teams, phantom agencies are created by township leaders. These "hanging sign work units" (*gua paizi danwei* 挂牌子单位) have no personnel assigned to them on a full-time basis. When there is an inspection, the agencies for the "new socialist countryside," industry and trade, and ecology all bustle with activity. Reports will be furnished to demonstrate achievements and if necessary, an inspection tour to a carefully selected site will be arranged. As soon as the inspection team leaves, these agencies revert to what they really are: freshly painted black and white signs. Such subterfuge is common at all levels of government. Wu Yi quotes the head of a township family planning office[18]:

> All higher-level inspections of family planning work are random; you don't know which village or which hamlet they'll visit, so there's a degree of surprise. But within the space of four to five days, we're able to coach every target household in every hamlet at least once, letting them know the contents and tricks of the inspection, so really there's no surprise.

He estimates that villages experience at least six family planning inspections annually (two from each of the prefecture, county and township), in addition to continuous surveillance by village cadres and the designated "family planning worker" in each hamlet.[19] Thus, all target households are versed in coping with inspections.

Constant inspections were also a drain on township finances. In Benghai county, "entertainment expenses" ranked as the largest item of township government expenditure after salaries. Some townships have been more successful than others in reducing the burden of such expenses. One township close to the county seat had accumulated a debt of seven million yuan, and all interviewees cited "hosting guests" (*jiedai* 接待) as the main contributing factor. A large amount spent on entertainment, however, does not in itself indicate profligacy on the part of township leaders. As one county official explained, "it just means that the higher-ups like to dine there" (*shangmian ai chi* 上面爱吃). Wealthier townships see more inspection teams and thus run up larger debts. As a township leader explained to Zhao Shukai, remote townships "are rarely inspected by various higher-level departments and so have less to spend on entertainment."[20] He found that township leaders spent an average of 100 to 150 days per year on reception activities (one spent 300 days), and the expenses incurred from

footnote continued

perspective," *The China Quarterly*, No. 173 (2003), pp. 35–52; Zhao Shukai, "Rural governance," pp. 64–73; and Graeme Smith, "Political machinations in a rural county" *The China Journal*, No. 62 (2009), pp. 50–53.

18 Wu Yi, *Uproar in a Small Town*, p. 585.

19 *Ibid.* p. 590. See also Zhao Shukai, "Rural governance," pp. 23–25.

20 Zhao Shukai, "Rural governance," p. 39.

608 The China Quarterly, 203, September 2010, pp. 601–618

"karaoke singing, sauna sessions and mahjong" accounted for between 5 and 10 per cent of fiscal income.[21]

Many township staff expressed the view that the main problem faced by township governments wasn't that they were overstaffed, but rather the capricious behaviour of leading cadres and the institutional dynamics of township government.[22] In particular, they were exasperated that political machinations continued to trump government functions. As one noted: "We need to come out of this miasma of complex documents and targets set by higher levels, give up playing games on paper (*wenzi youxi* 文字游戏), and actually start providing services for ordinary people." A proliferation of documents meant that the township leaders were often bemused over how to govern. If an issue was receiving national attention, different higher-level bureaus would issue different documents, leading to "document wars" (*wenzhang douzheng* 文章斗争). The bureaus of forestry, agriculture and environmental protection were constantly at odds. In large part, the work of deputy township leaders was travelling to the county seat to settle these conflicts.

Township staff were quizzed as to whether they had any confidence in the direction township reform was taking, and what sort of reform of township government they felt was the best course. The results shown in Table 2 indicate a low level (18 per cent) of confidence in the current reform process.

The most widely accepted strategy for reform was to make the township an agency of the county government. In the view of many respondents, this reflected the existing balance of power between the townships and the county,[23] and was the most effective way to cut out the middlemen – township Party leaders. As one noted: "Most professional work carried out by township agencies is directed by county departments. If the township government itself simply becomes a county agency, everyone can go about their work more effectively, and unnecessary friction between the township and county will be alleviated." Another argued: "With improvements in transportation and communications, this [model] suits current economic conditions, and reduces the capacity of township leaders to abuse their power and connive for personal gain." Zhao Shukai found that although this would amount to removal of their own authority, this was the opinion of half of the 20 township Party secretaries he interviewed. One Party secretary from Hunan explained: "The township governments just cannot cope with all the inspections from above. [They] are like firefighters with no definite duties … all cadres are required to work together on all matters. Dismantling township governments will have no great effect on ordinary people. The biggest problem is where to put the township cadres."[24]

21 *Ibid.* pp. 21–25.

22 This echoes Linda Chelan Li, "Embedded institutionalization: sustaining rural tax reform in China," *The Pacific Review*, Vol. 19, No. 1 (2006), pp. 63–84. Li's arguments on the primary need for behavioural change among officials hold true for township governments in Benghai. At the county level, however, overstaffing is rampant, and is a major reason for cadre non-performance.

23 Kennedy, "From the tax-for-fee reform to the abolition of agricultural taxes," p. 45.

24 Zhao Shukai, "Rural governance," pp. 31–32.

Table 2: **Attitudes towards Township Government Structural Reform (%)**

Level of confidence in current reforms	
Confident	18
Unsure	67
No confidence	15
Best course for reform	
No need for change	31
County-level agency	39
Abolish township government	5
Take away some functions from the township	15
Other	9

Source:
Author's survey, 2006. N = 95.

Soft centralization: differentiated experiences within township governments

Andrew Mertha described the shifting of township or county agencies to provincial control as "soft centralization." A parallel trend has seen agencies previously controlled by township governments placed under the control of the county. The crucial distinction is whether the corresponding bureau at the county level has "leadership relations" (*lingdao guanxi* 领导关系) with the township bureau, or whether it only has "professional relations" (*yewu guanxi* 业务关系). Those which are under leadership relations and are thus controlled by their line bureau at the county level or above are referred to as "vertical agencies" (*chuizhi danwei* 垂直单位). Those with only professional relations to their line bureau are effectively controlled by township leaders, and are called "devolved work units" (*xiafang danwei* 下放单位).

Mertha observed that the first bureaus to undergo "soft centralization" to the provincial level were those associated with "administrative regulation, financial regulation and commodities management … because of their vital role in China's economic development."[25] From the perspective of township leaders, the equation is simpler. Bureaus with "money and power" (*you qian you quan* 有钱有权) are claimed by higher levels of government, while those with neither money nor power, derogatively known as "clear water agencies" (*qing shui yamen* 清水衙门), are left under the control of township leaders.

To see whether the management status of an agency influenced its rank in the eyes of ordinary township government staff, respondents were presented with an open-response question (each township has different agencies, so a list would have been incomplete) as to which six township agencies enjoyed the best working conditions and salaries (*daiyu zui hao* 待遇最好). Table 3 shows the top ten township agencies in Benghai county, where only the lowest-ranked agency, the agricultural extension station, is under full township government control.

25 Mertha, "China's 'soft' centralization," pp. 793–94.

610 The China Quarterly, 203, September 2010, pp. 601–618

Apart from vertical control, the most consistent thread between township agencies with superior working conditions is the ability to levy and – to differing extents – retain fees and fines to cover salaries, general office expenses and "entertainment." While vertical agencies are physically located in a township, the township Party and government organs in theory have no formal authority to control the leaders or even the staff of these agencies.

However, the independence of vertical agencies is not absolute. Their staff live and work in the township, and are subject to informal pressures. As an example, the rural credit co-operatives answer to the province, but township leaders, particularly the township Party secretary, exercise discretion over who can receive substantial loans. Similarly, if the township government opts to divert funds earmarked for flood relief, the finance and civil affairs agencies can be pressed to comply with little danger. The head of a township land management agency, which on paper answers to the county, explained the pressure to ignore the malfeasance of township leaders: "I have two wives. I should obey my first wife, but relatively speaking she's far away. My second wife is right here and nags me endlessly, so she usually gets what she wants." The heads of compliant agencies benefit financially, and the working conditions of these agencies will improve. The lack of funding for township governments has meant that embezzling earmarked project funds has gained acceptance among township government leaders and staff as a morally legitimate way to maintain working conditions.[26] The practice is known as "knocking down the east wall to prop up the west wall" (*chai dong qiang bu xi qiang* 拆东墙补西墙).

While wealthy vertical agencies often attempted to separate themselves physically from the township government, creating "separatist regimes,"[27] devolved agencies were unable to resist the opposite pressure from township leaders. The lack of physical boundaries between devolved agencies in many townships was striking. In one township, five different agencies shared one small room with only three desks: the agricultural extension station, the agricultural economic management station, the social insurance organization, the poverty alleviation office, and the broadcasting and culture station. Such an arrangement encouraged a collective approach to township government work. Whether collecting tax arrears, preparing for a family planning inspection or promoting the "new socialist countryside," township leaders preferred "all hands on deck." In the devolved agencies, professional boundaries were rarely respected.

Some staff in devolved agencies felt that the township leaders themselves were in an untenable position, that the proliferation of documents, meetings, inspections and other tasks received from higher levels made it difficult for the township

26 See Gu Wenfeng, *Extraordinary Accounts*, pp. 151–53; and Ray Yep, "Can 'tax-for-fee' reform reduce rural tension in China? The process, progress and limitations," *The China Quarterly*, No. 177 (2004), pp. 44–45.

27 See Mertha, "China's 'soft' centralization," pp. 804–05.

Table 3: **Township Agencies with the Best Working Conditions**

Agencies		**Mentioned by (%)**	**Management**
Finance	*caizheng suo* 财政所	100	County
Party and government	*dangzheng ban* 党政办	71	N/A
Family planning	*jisheng ban* 计生办	65	County/township
Local tax	*dishui ban* 地税办	29	Province
Police	*paichu suo* 派出所	26	County
Land	*tuguan suo* 土管所	26	County
Industry and commerce	*gongshang ju* 工商局	23	Province
Education	*jiaoyu ban* 教育办	21	County/township
Civil affairs	*minzheng ban* 民政办	16	County/township
Agricultural extension	*nongji zhan* 农技站	11	Township

Source:
Author's survey, 2006, N = 95; author's Interviews, 2004–08.

government to provide meaningful services to farmers. As one agricultural extension station head explained:

> The township government is overrun with countless difficult issues (*qian tou wan xu* 千头万绪), simply far too many to complete, so the township leaders usually have no time for agricultural extension work. That's not to say that they never will. Take last year as an example. The county pressured them to promote tea and bamboo processing, and suddenly I had their attention. But if there is the slightest let up in pressure from above, the township leaders disappear. It becomes a choice: they can pay it attention, or not. For the moment, the county is attentive, asking "How many demonstrations have you carried out? How much mountainous land has been reclaimed? What acreage of new tea plantations has been established?" County officials come to inspect, make reports, issue documents.[28] So the township leaders pay attention. But otherwise nothing will happen, and there's no way they'd ever think about looking for new responsibilities. Without extreme pressure from above, they're numb and indifferent (*wu qi wu li* 无气无力).

This picture of township government officials bewildered by the number of higher level inspections and assessments matches that outlined by a State Council research team.[29]

Many interviewees felt that they had effectively become an extension of the township Party branch, responding to the priorities of township Party leaders, which tended to change according to the political wind of the day. Interviewees explained that the effect of this chaotic work schedule was "numbness" (*mamu* 麻木). Unable to work according to Weberian "calculable rules and 'without regard for persons',"[30] many township staff in devolved agencies, while nominally under the full control of the township leaders, paradoxically become harder to mobilize than staff in vertical agencies. With little prospect of promotion or recognition, and limited agency over their daily work, they shirk their duties.[31]

28 Several sources in the county government estimated that the average township would receive at least 1,000 documents per year from higher levels.

29 Duan Yingbi and Hongyuan Song (eds.), *Zhongguo nongcun gaige zhongda zhengce wenti yanjiu baogao* (*A Research Report on the Major Policy Problems of Reform in Rural China*) (Beijing: Zhongguo caizheng jingji chubanshe, 2004), p. 57.

30 Max Weber, *Economy and Society*, 2 vols. (Berkeley: University of California Press, 1978), p. 975.

31 Zhao Shukai, "Rural governance," pp. 70–73.

612 The China Quarterly, 203, September 2010, pp. 601–618

Not all personnel within devolved agencies were keen to return to higher-level control, however, as past experience had taught them that weak county-level agencies were unable to provide financial security.[32] The township agricultural economy station is rumoured to be returning to line management later in 2009, and many staff were uneasy about this development. As one explained:

> We don't want to return to being a vertical agency (*gui tiao* 归条), because we don't want to be run by the county agricultural committee. Our wages and subsidies [for meals and transport] are guaranteed by the finance bureau, but if we go back to line management, there's no way the higher-ups will pay for our subsidies. Nor will the township government pay, because you're no longer managed by them.

While township staff tended to refer to "township leaders" as a whole, this group was sharply divided in terms of which interests it served. Township Party secretaries and township heads, selected by the county standing committee, were as a rule chosen as "a pair" and would generally work together to further their political interests. Rather than residing in their township, as was the norm during the 1980s and 1990s, township Party secretaries usually live in the county seat and commute to the township when required. However, older deputy township leaders who saw little prospect of promotion to the county level owe less fealty to the county leadership, and often lobbied against projects initiated at the county level or above, or acted to protect their own network of local business interests.

With township leaders frustrated, focused on their future careers, and spending large amounts of the year outside the township attending meetings or entertaining potential investors, a power vacuum has emerged in many townships. The office managers (*bangongshi zhuren* 办公室主任) who head the township administrative offices control access to the Party secretary, and thus wield disproportionate influence. They co-ordinate township government staff during the long periods when township leaders are away. While most township government agencies (apart from family planning, finance and the police) are usually deserted, one office manager has eight staff working under him, including a driver. Like their counterparts at the county level, their authority derives from the ill-defined limits of their powers. Many new township Party secretaries appoint their own office manager, usually a trusted personal friend whom they previously relied upon while working in the county government.

Faced with resistance from staff in vertical agencies which no longer answer to them, frustrated by unmotivated staff in devolved agencies, and pressured from above by county leaders and an endless stream of inspections, township leaders also often felt they weren't able to do real work. "Soft centralization" may have succeeded in shifting the locus of power upwards to the county and provincial levels, but the goal of building a more modern and compliant bureaucracy at the township level seems elusive. While the abolition of agricultural taxes in 2006

32 Mertha, "China's 'soft' centralization," pp. 806–08.

means that the township government has lost much of its traditional extractive function, centralization has weakened the cohesiveness of the township bureaucracy.

Hollowed from Below: Sent-Down Cadres and Family Planning

Sent-down cadres

In addition to a core staff of three to five native village cadres (Party secretary/village head, deputy Party secretary/village head, village clerk, women's cadre), villages usually contain several cadres from the county and township governments. Allocating staff to villages is usually the first item of business for a new township government, and lobbying of township leaders by staff to be sent to a "good" village is intense. This practice of cadres from higher levels being responsible for a given village was a crucial aspect of the county government's efforts to control and monitor village governments,[33] and had the effect of drawing a large number of staff out of the township government. For younger township cadres, working as a sent-down cadre enhances their prospects of promotion. However, being assigned to a village with many "problem households" (*dingzi hu* 钉子户) can severely harm their political prospects, as they face a system of financial and political punishment for any disturbances in their allocated village. This has led to infighting among township cadres during the period leading up to a change in township leaders.

One administrative village that I visited had six sent-down cadres (one from the county industrial and commercial bureau, five from the township), outnumbering the five regular village cadres, and most villages have at least three township cadres. Commonly, managing a village is either accepted as a "task" (*renwu* 任务) or resented as a waste of both the villagers' time and their own. As one former township cadre explained:

> Back in 2005, I was about to be sent down to a village, but I got out just in time [to a post in the county government]. I'd worked in the township government for more than ten years, so there was no way I wanted to be sent down, I'd still be stuck working there now. It would have been almost impossible to escape at my age. They call it "training" (*duanlian* 锻炼), but township government work is in the villages, dealing with the peasants. After such a long time, you know the villages inside out, there are no mysteries. What training? It's meaningless.

Many county government officials admitted that the practice was not just an effort to reassert control over village governments, but also a direct result of pressure to streamline township governments.

33 Another development with a similar impact was the combining of the posts of village Party secretary and (formerly elected) village head, referred to as "taking the load on one shoulder" (*yi jian tiao*). This had been implemented in 60% of Benghai's administrative villages, meaning that nearly two-thirds of village leaders were effectively appointed by township governments. This is in keeping with developments elsewhere in China, and has had the unintended consequence of increasing intra-village tensions between clans. See Gu Wenfeng, *Extraordinary Accounts*, pp. 176–78.

614 The China Quarterly, 203, September 2010, pp. 601–618

There are regional variations. One village head from Liaoning province told me that in his area they would not tolerate sent-down cadres because villagers saw them as an infringement of the village's sphere of self-governance.[34] At the other end of the spectrum, another researcher in northern Anhui found that practically all township cadres, with the exception of the township Party secretary and the township head, were working as sent-down cadres.[35] Provincial sources suggest that from 2000, as streamlining reforms were undertaken in earnest, the number of sent-down cadres increased.[36] The county government had also amassed cadres from the central, provincial and prefectural governments.[37]

Zhao Shukai suggests that sent-down cadres are required in two types of villages: those that have been selected as showcase model villages for inspections by higher levels of government (the "new socialist countryside" programme has proved a boon to these already privileged villages), and those where there have been disturbances or signs of an emerging crisis.[38] However, in Benghai the practice is routine for *all* administrative villages, and the number of sent-down cadres in a village increases with proximity to the county seat. Asked whether there were many meetings attended by village leaders in the township, one cadre declared: "There's no need. Every village has several township cadres staying in it. If the upper levels have any fresh instructions, we just inform those cadres." The number of cadres sent down from the townships was so numerous that they were divided into three different categories, according to rank: senior cadres, ordinary cadres and family planning liaison personnel.

In addition to sending out a substantial proportion of their staff, township leaders routinely interfere in village elections, often playing "moral politics."[39] Few village cadres were sacked without a well-publicized reason. One village Party secretary was axed for his perceived corruption in managing a village-run coal-brick factory during the 1990s, while a village head was removed after being involved in protracted divorce proceedings. Villagers concurred that if he could not run his own family, he was unfit to manage the village. Replacements for "failed" village leaders invariably had a strong backer in the township government, usually a well-placed relative.

The salaries of village cadres in Benghai are now paid entirely from the township government budget, rather than drawing income from village enterprises or from a percentage of collected taxes. In Benghai county, village governments are now effectively outposts of township governments, and largely respond to the

34 Author's interview, Beijing, April 2006.
35 See Man, *Sent-Down Cadres and Village Self Governance.*
36 Author's interviews, Anhui Academy of Social Sciences, November 2008.
37 Smith, "Political machinations," pp. 35–38.
38 Zhao Shukai, "Xiang cun guanxi: zai kongzhi zhong tuojie" ("Township–village relations: dislocated control"), *Huazhong shifan daxue xuebao* (*Journal of Huazhong University*), Vol. 44, No. 5 (2005), p. 4.
39 Hok Bun Ku, *Moral Politics in a South China Village: Responsibility, Reciprocity, and Resistance* (Lanham: Rowman & Littlefield, 2003).

priorities of their superiors in the township.[40] He who pays the piper calls the tune, and in Benghai county the tune in the villages is family planning.

Family planning

As well as the amount of tax collected (which ceased to be an important criterion in 2006), one aspect of government work has remained paramount for assessing the performance of townships since the 1980s: family planning. Indicators for success in implementing family planning policies have grown more complex over time, which partly explains why this now occupies township and village governments' time and resources. A county notice states how many points each task will be worth in the sent-down cadres' annual assessments (Table 4).

The "one-strike rejection policy" is attached to family planning targets in the township government's annual assessment and in the individual assessments of sent-down cadres, and reinforced by regular inspections by higher levels of government. One direct consequence is that township agencies are hollowed out from within by pressure to divert resources to family planning. To illustrate this, I provide information on the staffing situation within the agricultural extension stations of Benghai's 16 townships. These surveys revealed that a majority of township agricultural extension agents spent most of their time on tasks unrelated to extension work. Indeed, many went through 2005 without doing a single day of extension work. The main agency they worked for was the family planning office. The breakdown of Benghai's township extension agents in terms of their actual workplaces is shown in Table 5.

Table 5 indicates that in 2005 only 26 per cent of Benghai's agricultural extension workers actually worked as extension agents, with an equal number working for the family planning office. Given that sent-down village cadres have been shown to spend most of their time on family planning work, at least 37 per cent of extension agents were devoting all or most of their time to implementing family planning policy. An equal number had been transferred to the townships' family planning agencies, with the remainder working in the villages or in other township agencies which were deemed to be current priorities. This phenomenon of "not doing one's real job" (*wu bu zheng ye* 务不正业) was common to all township government agencies.

The figure of 26 per cent working as extension agents is almost certainly an overestimate. Many held "concurrent posts" (*jianzhi* 兼职) making it difficult to determine whether their main work was agricultural extension or the duties associated with their "concurrent post." Where possible, these extension agents were asked what the bulk of their work entailed, but where it was not possible

40 There are caveats to this. If a village is home to an influential cadre from a higher level of government, the township can, to an extent, be bypassed by the village government, particularly in attracting investment.

Table 4: **Assessment Criteria for Sent-down Village Cadres**

Assessment criteria	Points
Family planning	30
Ecological support (agriculture, forestry, irrigation, technical training, establishing agribusinesses)	15
Public stability (law and order, petitions, safe work practices)	10
Establishing grassroots organizations	5
Establishing basic infrastructure	5
Finance and agricultural economic work	5
Creating civilization (propaganda work, public health, markets)	4
Cadre work style	4
Developing the collective and private economy	4
Poverty alleviation	4

Notes:

Notice on the methods for implementing point-scoring assessments of sent down village cadres, Town Y, 2006.

Items scoring three points or less: transitional work, militia training, attracting investment, land management, civil administration, education, record keeping and social security.

to interview them it was assumed that their main task was agricultural extension. Even staff who were officially "full-time" (*zhuanzhi* 专职) extension agents often admitted that they did little or no extension work. The head of one extension station, who was annually awarded the title of "excellent" (*youxiu* 优秀) by the county agricultural committee, admitted that since 2001 (when township extension stations were devolved) he was lucky to spend more than 30 days each year doing his job.

Village cadres made little pretence that their work involved much beyond family planning. Male cadres often joked that the women's cadre (in charge of

Table 5: **Actual Work Units of Township Agricultural Workers**

Agency/station		%
Agricultural extension	*nongji zhan* 农技站	26
Family planning	*jisheng ban* 计生办	26
Sent-down village cadres	*xiapai cunji ganbu* 下派干部	11
Social insurance	*shehui baoxian zu* 社会保险组	9
Township government office	*xiangzhen zhengfu bangongshi* 乡镇政府办公室	7
Party and government	*dang zheng ban* 党政办	3
Agricultural supply business	*nongzi chuangshou* 农资创收	2
Industrial estate management committee	*gongyuan qu guanli weiyuanhui* 公园区管理委员会	2
Industry and commerce	*gongmao ban* 工贸办	2
Urban planning	*chengzhen guihua ban* 城镇规划办	1
Urbanization and civilization	*chengjian wenming ban* 城建文明办	1
Residential area	*shequ* 社区	1
Projects and investment	*zhaoshang ban* 招商办	1
Ecology	*shengtai ban* 生态办	1

Source:

Author's survey, 2006, N = 135.

family planning) was the only one with a real job, and that the other village cadres were just her assistants. In one internal note listing the allocation of tasks among the newly elected cadres of a relatively wealthy village, family planning was mentioned eight times, far more frequently than other priorities, such as "compiling personnel files" (twice), "public stability" (once) and "creating spiritual civilization" (once). The emphasis on family planning was confirmed in this village's budget. The main listed expenditure items for 2005 were two trips to track down pregnant women who had fled the county. The only listed item of income was 25,000 yuan from the township government,[41] but the real figures for entertainment expenses are never listed, nor are salaries. By 2008, like many villages in Benghai, the village had been forced to hire an additional staff member to work on family planning.

Conclusions

What does the view from the inside tell us about the nature of the local state in rural townships? Most of the actors are making the best of what is often quite a poor hand. Township Party secretaries and younger sent-down village Party secretaries from the county are typically hard-working, doing their best to extract visible results that will impress their superiors in the county government, which they hope will lead to promotion to a better remunerated and less taxing post. As leading cadres see their future in the county, the county government enjoys considerable control over the priorities of township governments.

With higher levels of government placing pressure on them to cut costs and streamline staff, and an increasing number of bureaus placed outside their formal control as vertical agencies, township Party leaders have responded by tightening their control over devolved agencies and villages, sending out their surplus cadres to ensure that village cadres enforce the key tasks of family planning and social stability, and ensuring that "their" candidates control the activities of village governments. Concurrently, the most able township cadres are leaving their posts to spend ever-increasing amounts of time outside the province in the hope of securing industrial investment, satisfying both the political imperatives of the annual assessments system, and the revenue imperatives of county and township governments. While during the 1980s and 1990s the township Party secretary could readily be found in the township government compound, the day-to-day running of hollowed-out township governments is now left to office managers and the least-talented staff.

41 There are still many ways by which village cadres can squeeze extra revenue from their constituents to cover their entertainment expenses. With the increased social security coverage, village cadres can use their discretionary control to extract revenue from the poorest rural residents. If villagers refuse to "give back" a percentage of the minimum living allowance (set at 860 yuan per year in 2008), cadres will direct the funds elsewhere.

Such hollowed-out organizations are unable to play an active role in rural communities, and there are ingredients in the current structure of rural governance that are anathema to service provision, and will undermine attempts to transform township governments into "service-oriented" agencies. Without a move away from the practice of administrative coercion, and the "one-strike rejection" that gives rise to it, the local state will continue to view farmers as problems, rather than as clients or citizens.

[18]

American Political Science Review Vol. 106, No. 1 February 2012
doi:10.1017/S0003055411000566

Getting Ahead in the Communist Party: Explaining the Advancement of Central Committee Members in China

VICTOR SHIH *Northwestern University*
CHRISTOPHER ADOLPH *University of Washington*
MINGXING LIU *Peking University*

Spectacular economic growth in China suggests the ruling Chinese Communist Party (CCP) has somehow gotten it right. A key hypothesis in both economics and political science is that the CCP's cadre evaluation system, combined with China's geography-based governing logic, has motivated local administrators to compete with one another to generate high growth. We raise a number of theoretical and empirical challenges to this claim. Using a new biographical database of Central Committee members, a previously overlooked feature of CCP reporting, and a novel Bayesian method that can estimate individual-level correlates of partially observed ranks, we find no evidence that strong growth performance was rewarded with higher party ranks at any of the postreform party congresses. Instead, factional ties with various top leaders, educational qualifications, and provincial revenue collection played substantial roles in elite ranking, suggesting that promotion systems served the immediate needs of the regime and its leaders, rather than encompassing goals such as economic growth.

Ever since Weber ([1921] 1958) distinguished rational bureaucracy staffed by impersonal, meritocratically selected technocrats from patriarchical management by loyal partisans, scholars have explored the underlying logics driving government organizations. Today Weber's distinction matters nowhere more than in China, where an authoritarian regime governs nearly a fifth of the world's people. Thirty years of spectacular economic performance has prompted a sizable political science and economics literature linking the bureaucracy of the Chinese Communist Party (CCP) to China's economic success. Though the link seems natural, there are good theoretical and empirical reasons to question whether yardstick competition among local officials really caused China's spectacular growth. Theoretically, a performance-based promotion system in the top echelon of the party requires a relatively unified and far-horizoned leadership that would systematically promote officials with the strongest performance (Olson 1993; Olson and McGuire 1996). Yet theories of authoritarian politics and China scholarship suggest that the top leadership in China is as much preoccupied with internal struggle as with achieving regime-wide objectives like economic growth (Bueno de Mesquita et al. 2003; MacFarquhar and Schoenhals 2006; Nathan 1973; Svolik 2009; Tullock 1987). As such, it is far from clear that CCP cadre management institutions were directly responsible for China's economic performance.

Empirical work on the growth incentive embedded in CCP institutions shows cases where cadre evaluation appeared to encourage strong performance by county and township level officials (Edin 2003; Whiting 2004). Yet systematic tests of whether provincial administrators in high-growth regions were awarded with promotions look only at provincial officials, instead of the Central Committee power elite in the CCP, and measure only promotion in state bureaucratic ranks instead of the more important party ranking (Chen, Li, and Zhou 2005; Li and Zhou 2005; Maskin, Qian, and Xu 2000). And no qualitative or quantitative work addresses the potential selection bias that would arise if politically connected officials could influence the location of their next appointments to claim credit for preexisting growth trends.

This study departs from previous studies in five important ways. First, instead of providing yet another test of the growth impact of CCP institutions, we draw from the broader political economy literature on authoritarian regimes to derive a wider range of hypotheses on the factors that help cadres obtain higher positions in the party hierarchy. Second, instead of examining only the fortune of local administrators, we examine every full and alternate member of the CCP Central Committee through five party congresses from 1982 to 2002. Third, we make use of the CCP's own reports of elections to the Alternate Central Committee (ACC) and a new biographical database of Central Committee (CC) and ACC members to place the entire CCP power elite along a continuum in terms of their status *within the ruling party*. Fourth, we analyze the pattern of ranks within the Politburo Standing Committee (PSC), the Politburo, the CC, and the ACC using a novel Bayesian model of ranks that can estimate the individual-level correlates of rank even in rank data that are only partially observed. Finally, we purge the effects of

Victor Shih is Associate Professor, Department of Political Science, Northwestern University, 601 University Place, Evanston, IL 60208 (vshih@northwestern.edu).

Christopher Adolph is Assistant Professor, Department of Political Science and Center for Statistics and the Social Sciences, University of Washington, 101 Gowen Hall, Box 353530, Seattle, WA 98195 (cadolph@uw.edu).

Mingxing Liu is Associate Professor, China Institute for Educational Finance Research, Peking University, Beijing 100871, China (liumingxing72@gmail.com)

The authors are grateful for helpful comments and advice from Dali Yang, Dingxing Zhao, and other members of the University of Chicago East Asia Colloquium, as well as Jennifer Amyx, Santiago Lopez Cariboni, Frances Rosenbluth, and Susan Whiting. All mistakes are our own. Replication data and R packages for analysis (partialrank) and visualization (tile) are available at faculty.washington.edu/cadolph

any selection bias in appointment using a suite of estimates of preappointment expected provincial economic growth. In this manner, we are able to discern whether expected and unexpected economic performance had any impact on the party ranking of senior cadres throughout the reform period.

When we examine the entire CCP elite, we find no evidence that exceptional economic growth influenced ranking in the party hierarchy. This finding is robust even when we decompose economic performance into expected and unexpected growth and when we use broader measures of economic performance. We find that educational qualifications strongly (and provincial revenue collection and minority representation weakly) bolstered cadres' ranking in some of the party congresses since 1982. Women faced significant disadvantages in three of the five congresses we examine. Most important, factional ties with various top leaders, as well as princeling status, boosted the chance of climbing higher in the CCP upper echelons through much of the reform period. In sum, CCP cadre management institutions were used by top leaders to maintain cadres' human capital, coopt ethnic minorities, and raise revenue collection, all of which directly provided immediate payoffs to the regime. Our findings suggest that senior party leaders did not bolster public goods provision through yardstick competiton among provincial officials, but they did use promotion institutions to cultivate factions. These findings are consistent with the claim of Bueno de Mesquita et al. (2003) that authoritarian regimes tend to deliver private goods to a relatively narrow winning coalition rather than to society at large.

MERITOCRATIC BUREAUCRACY AND ECONOMIC OUTCOMES

Since Weber made the distinction between bureaucracy and patrimonialism, political scientists have argued that government bureaucracies fall into either the meritocratic, impersonal type or the corrupt, clientelist type (Evans 1995; Frye and Shleifer 1997; Schneider 1993; Weber [1921] 1958). Explanations for why bureaucracies develop in disparate ways range from social capital (Putnam, Leonardi, and Nanetti 1993), to the level of external threat (Kang 2002), to colonial legacies (Acemoglu, Johnson, and Robinson 2000). In turn, bureaucratic types are thought to explain complex economic outcomes. Thus, when market enhancing policies are implemented or when growth is high, some scholars attribute this to a meritocratic bureaucracy (Evans 1995; Schneider and Maxfield 1997).

In contemporary social science, the tendency to infer bureaucratic meritocracy from high growth is perhaps strongest in the study of China. Spectacular growth in the past three decades has motivated scholars to develop a variety of explanations of China's success, ranging from a proreform leadership (Fewsmith 1994; Shirk 1993), to de facto federalism (Qian, Weingast, and Montinola 1995), to labor market mobility (Lin 1992; Sachs et al. 1994).

Scholars have also looked to the efficiency or the institutional configuration of the Chinese bureaucracy as explanations of China's rapid growth. Unlike the Soviet Union, which had a unitary system of governance, the primary organizational principle in China was geography-based, thus giving rise to a multidivisional form (M-form) bureaucracy. Some claim the M-form bureaucracy, coupled with an extensive cadre evaluation system, provided strong incentives for regional administrators to compete with each other to generate high economic growth, in order to win promotion in the ruling CCP (Chen, Li, and Zhou 2005; Li and Zhou 2005; Maskin, Qian, and Xu 2000). This body of literature presents mixed evidence that the top two provincial officials (governors and party secretaries) in the reform period were typically rewarded with promotions for realizing better economic performance than their predecessors or their peers (Chen, Li, and Zhou 2005; Li and Zhou 2005; Tao et al. 2010).

In addition to the quantitative findings, a larger qualitative literature on the evolution of the cadre evaluation system also seems to support the view of a performance-based elite promotion system in China. After the founding of the People's Republic of China, the CCP introduced formal methods of evaluating cadres, which were formally linked to their promotion. As Burns (1989) puts it, the cadre management system centered on "lists of leading positions, over which party units exercise the power to make appointments and dismissals; lists of reserves or candidates for these positions; and institutions and processes for making the appropriate personnel changes." The Central Organization Department emerged as the key human resource manager of the CCP, although senior-level promotions were ultimately decided by members of the Politburo (Nathan and Gilley 2002).

During his reign, Mao focused on ensuring the survival of the CCP regime according to his vision. Thus, he promoted cadres who shared or at least were willing to go along with his radical vision of society (Lee 1991). After reform began in 1978, education credentials came to play a prominent role in the advancement of lower level cadres, and older cadres were strongly encouraged to retire (Cui 2003; Landry 2008; Manion 1993; Walder, Li, and Treiman 2000). Furthermore, the post-Mao leadership formalized a system of scoring junior and senior cadres, which served to keep track of their administrative performance on a series of "soft" and "hard" targets. Hard targets reflected core tasks crucial to the regime, including economic growth, fiscal collection, and maintaining stability, whereas soft targets included recruiting party members and propaganda work. Shortfalls on the soft targets could be outweighed by impressive performance in key areas. However, failing to fulfill hard targets led either to low overall scores or to mandatory administrative punishment (*yipiao foujue*), a powerful tool in the CCP's arsenal for political control (Edin 2003). The existence of a comprehensive system for scoring officials on their policy performance seems to suggest that the Chinese elite was motivated by the scoring system to perform well (Edin 2003; Landry 2008; Whiting 2004).

However, on both theoretical and empirical grounds, there are strong reasons to be skeptical of an easy linkage between a formal system of cadre evaluation and economic growth in China. Theoretically, linking a limited set of policy or economic outcomes with bureaucratic characteristics may result in a false causal inference. For one thing, bureaucratic characteristics tend to be time-invariant, whereas policy and growth outcomes change frequently over time. Moreover, seemingly reform policies can mask underlying corruption or inefficiencies. In Pinochet's Chile, for example, liberalization policies implemented by the "Chicago Boys" also allowed favored conglomerates to borrow heavily overseas to buy up prized financial assets, laying the groundwork for the financial crisis in the early 1980s (Haggard and Maxfield 1996; Silva 1996). The empirical findings on corruption also cast doubt on the linkage between bureaucratic characteristics and economic outcomes. Except in extreme cases, high growth generally is not harmed by a moderate degree of corruption (Svensson 2005).

Although meritocratic criteria may influence elite ranking in China, concluding that economic performance is the *dominant* criterion driving elite ranking goes too far. A merit or performance dominant bureaucracy assumes that the Chinese regime is unified and far-horizoned, and thus is motivated to maximize performance and long-term output (Olson and McGuire 1996). But leaders of nondemocratic regimes face constant threats of dethronement from mass uprisings or coups by regime insiders (Tullock 1987; Wintrobe 1998). Thus, autocratic rulers likely place a greater priority on maintaining short-term state capacity and buying the support of winning coalitions than on providing broadly encompassing goods such as economic growth (Bueno de Mesquita et al. 2003; Gandhi and Przeworski 2006). China has witnessed its share of large-scale uprisings and intense political struggle at the top. Even after the chaotic Cultural Revolution, the top leader of the CCP was twice removed from power by irregular means.[1] Besides the Tiananmen protests in 1989, China also dealt with a series of large-scale protests motivated by ethnic and economic grievances in recent years (Pei 2006). Huang (1996) and Sheng (2007) argue that the conflict of interest between central and local governments compels the center to use its appointment control to obtain preferred outcomes, thus implicitly forgoing the appointment of the most capable officials. Because top Chinese leaders must address urgent concerns of stability and retaining office on a daily basis, we expect that the CCP often uses the personnel management system to promote these immediate goals, while neglecting more encompassing objectives like growth or fairness.

If political survival is a main concern, the top leader of a regime may shape policies, including the appointment of subordinates, to serve that end. One elite faction may pursue policies purely to undermine a rival faction, thus risking overall regime stability (Ramseyer and Rosenbluth 1998). Instead of expending resources to prevent a general uprising, leaders seeking to thwart an elite challenger may devote those resources to monitoring or cultivating the loyalty of senior officials (Svolik 2005). And instead of promoting officials with the strongest performance record, rival leaders may promote untalented but loyal followers to prevent a coup or to raise their relative standing (Easter 1996; Egorov and Sonin 2011; Nathan 1973). In other cases, an insecure leader may shuffle or promote officials simply to prevent an alliance between ambitious local officials and the populace (Debs 2007).

Empirically, the literature linking China's cadre evaluation system and growth produces highly ambiguous and problematic results. First, the qualitative literature provides an in-depth description of the cadre evaluation system, which suggests a causal link between cadre evaluation and growth. However, the existence of an evaluation system as such does not prove a causal link. Furthermore, quantitative studies of city and county officials do not find much evidence for growth-based promotions (Guo 2007; Landry 2008). At the city level, for example, Landry (2008) finds that exceptional economic performance has almost no effect on the most likely internal promotion of mayors, to the position of party secretary.

Quantitative studies on provincial officials provide some evidence that exceptional economic growth in a province is correlated with the promotion of the top two officials in a province (Chen, Li, and Zhou 2005; Li and Zhou 2005; Maskin, Qian, and Xu 2000). These studies present a number of empirical shortcomings, however. First, they focus only on provincial officials, leaving out the majority of the party elite, who served in the central party apparatus, the army, and the central economic bureaucracy. A comprehensive analysis of elite incentive should include all full and alternate members of the CC, who make up the bulk of the power elite in the CCP (Kung and Chen 2011; Shirk 1993). Measures of promotion are often poor: Li and Zhou (2005) define promotion as movement to a ministerial position or higher, but in the state bureaucracy, movement from provincial governorship to a ministerial position is horizontal, as provinces and ministries have the same bureaucratic rank. To measure whether such a rotation constituted a promotion, it is more useful to see whether a person's party rank improved, a clearer sign of advancement.

Methodologically, no previous study of elite promotion has taken into account the potential for selection bias (Chen, Li, and Zhou 2005; Guo 2007; Landry 2008; Li and Zhou 2005; Maskin, Qian, and Xu 2000). Aspiring provincial governors and party secretaries may perceive certain provinces as strong economic performers prior to a rotation, and may use political connections to engineer their appointments to claim credit. Under strategic appointment, observed correlation between exceptional growth and advancement might have been caused by strong political connections, rather than by economic performance per se.

[1] For example, party secretary Hu Yaobang was removed from power at the infamous "party life meeting" at Deng Xiaoping's house in early 1987. See Deng (2005).

HYPOTHESES

There are good theoretical and empirical reasons to doubt whether economic performance was the dominant factor driving elite advancement, despite China's geography-based administrative system and elaborate cadre evaluation system. Instead of only testing the impact of economic performance on elite ranking, we draw on the political economy literature on authoritarianism to derive two different sets of hypotheses. If we assumed that China was a unified regime with a long time horizon, we would expect performance, merit, and representation to play the dominant role in elite ranking. However, theories of elite power struggle in authoritarian regimes suggest that factional affiliation and princeling ties may play an important role in CCP elite ranking.

If the top leadership in China were unified and had a long time-horizon, it would have had a "sufficiently encompassing interest" in generating long-term growth and in developing tax collection capacity in an optimal way (Olson and McGuire 1996). Furthermore, to prevent large-scale collective action threatening the regime, a unified Chinese leadership would have combined repression with limited redistribution of its resources or greater representation for certain groups (Acemoglu and Robinson 2006; Desai, Olofsgard, and Yousef 2009; Gandhi and Przeworski 2006; Olson and McGuire 1996; Wintrobe 1998). To accomplish these ends, a unified CCP regime would have promoted officials with a talent for generating growth, collecting taxes, and repressing dissent so that "no matter how strong a candidate's factional backing, he cannot be promoted without a record of administrative achievement" (Nathan and Gilley 2002). From this understanding of elite ranking in China, we derive the following hypotheses:

Hypothesis R1. *More educated cadres win higher rank than less educated cadres.*

Hypothesis R2. *Regional administrators who generate more economic growth or raise living standards are rewarded with high ranking in the Central Committee.*

Hypothesis R3. *Regional administrators who produce higher growth in fiscal revenue win higher rank.*

Hypothesis R4. *Officials with more experience in the CCP gain higher rank because they have accumulated more administrative experience.*

Finally, ensuring female and minority representation in the higher reaches of the party may enhance the regime's legitimacy. Furthermore, minority representation may enhance stability by coopting potentially restive minority groups into the system (Dreyer 1976, 113). Thus a unified authoritarian regime might systematically promote women and minorities.

Hypothesis R5. *Being female or a member of an ethnic minority confers an advantage in the competition for high rank.*

If a regime experiences concealed or overt power struggles at the top, faction-based promotion predominates. In factional politics, loyalty counts more than skills or performance on core tasks such as growth, revenue collection, and stability. Skills may even be a liability. Egorov and Sonin (2005) provide a convincing theoretical argument that dictators facing the threat of a coup will not always choose the most competent advisors: Clever subordinates may be too good at figuring out the expected payoffs of betraying the dictator; less capable officials are more loyal. Bueno de Mesquita et al. (2003) also argue that autocrats find ways to channel resources to their supporters, including promoting them to senior regime positions. In a similar vein, China scholars long have postulated that Chinese leaders built networks of loyal followers to mitigate the fundamental uncertainty in elite politics (Dittmer 1995; Nathan 1973; Pye 1980, 1992). These factional networks bound the interests of followers to their patrons through the distribution of economic resources and offices (Nathan 1973; Nathan and Tsai 1995; Shih 2008a).

When a factional patron comes under attack, followers remain loyal because they expect large payoffs for protecting the patron, who in turn promotes followers to the upper echelons of the regime. If elite political struggles loomed large in the minds of top CCP leaders, then followers' records of loyalty would have been more important criteria for promotion than economic performance. When the factional logic dominates, individual leaders promote close allies rather than the most capable individuals, even if these appointments lead to the underprovision of regime-wide public goods such as economic growth. In this case, ambitious officials face incentives to signal their loyalty to factional patrons, instead of performing tasks for the regime (Shih 2008*b*). However, even when confronted with intense elite struggle, authoritarian leaders may still prioritize tax collection capacity, to finance both private goods for regime supporters and the regime's repressive capacity (Acemoglu and Robinson 2006; Bueno de Mesquita et al. 2003).

The main implication of the factional view of Chinese politics is the following factional hypothesis:

Hypothesis F1. *Followers of the top leaders of the party, including the faction members of Mao Zedong, Deng Xiaoping, Zhao Ziyang, Hu Yaobang, Jiang Zemin, and Hu Jintao, are ranked higher than other officials when their respective patrons are in power.*

In testing this hypothesis, we consider only the followers of the de facto or de jure leaders of the party because as the most powerful leaders, they had the strongest incentive to avoid factional politics and to ensure high regime performance. Thus, if factional politics was not pervasive, we would not expect the highest officials in the regime to rank CC members according to factional considerations.

A related hypothesis concerns the children of senior officials, or "princelings," who entered the CCP elite. Although their parents were never their direct superiors, other senior officials might expect to win some advantage from the families of princelings by promoting them. But helping princelings does not make sense in the context of a unified leadership, because princeling status per se does not help further regime goals. To the extent that CCP elites were divided and were tempted to draw on princeling resources, we expect the following.

Hypothesis F2. *Children of senior officials should be ranked higher than other officials.*

DATA

We test our hypotheses on data measuring elite ranks within the CCP. Our dependent variable is the rank ordering of officials in the upper echelon of the Chinese Communist Party, for the 12th through 16th Party Congresses (1982–2007), a difficult quantity to measure. This (still imperfect) metric of pecking order improves on existing measures, which limit analysis to provincial officials. In this section we outline what we do know about these ranks; in the next, we explain how to use ranks we know well to infer ranks we observe imprecisely, a useful strategy for exploring the distribution of political power in authoritarian regimes.

The ranking of CCP elites in the CC took place roughly once every five years at the National Party Congress. Formally, this ranking comprised three different processes, but fundamentally, all three steps reflect a single ranking highly coordinated by the PSC. Starting at the 12th Party Congress in 1982, delegates received ballots with more names than there were seats in the Central Committee. Delegates then voted for the candidates by placing checks next to their names, and delegates could check as many names as there were seats in the Central Committee. Candidates were accepted into the CC in the order of their vote totals, with the lowest-vote receipients eliminated (Organizational Division of the Central Organization Department 2001). Alternate members of the CC were also elected in this way. The elected CC then voted the Politburo, the PSC, and the party secretary general into office. In this final round of voting, there were as many candidates as there were seats, and CC members without exception voted everyone on the ballot into offce.

Although congressional delegates ostensibly voted freely, all the party congresses were tightly monitored and controlled by the party secretary general and members of the Politburo. To begin, the chairman or the party secretary general sent early signals to the rest of the political elite on who should or should not be on the list of CC candidates (Li 2007). As the congresses approached, candidates for the CC, the ACC, and the Politburo were chosen by leadership groups, which included the serving PSC and a few powerful retired cadres handpicked by the party secretary general (Organizational Division of the Central Organization Department 2001).

The selected candidates then underwent a vetting procedure carried out by the Central Organization Department, which also took instructions from the party secretary general and other members of the Politburo (Cui 2003; Nathan and Gilley 2002). When the delegates finally arrived in Beijing to vote, they were isolated from each other and received strict voting instructions from the party secretary general and other members of the Politburo on how to vote (Deng 2005; Li 2007). In the famous case of Deng Liqun's surprising elimination from the 13th CC, it turns out that the party secretary general at the time, Zhao Ziyang, sent cadres to the provinces prior to the congress to instruct delegates not to vote for him (Deng 2005).

Because of extensive intervention from PSC members, where one landed on the party pecking order largely reflected the priorities of the top leadership, which could change dramatically over time. Periodic appearance of "helicopters," or officials who obtained rapid promotion from the ACC to the Politburo, further suggests that elite ranking at the Party Congress was a single exercise of elite reshuffling closely guided by the party secretary general and the Politburo, rather than three autonomous processes. At the end of a congress, highly ranked officials typically enjoyed much more formal and informal power for the subsequent five years, whereas those who were not selected even as ACC members missed being in the power center of the CCP (Kung and Chen 2011).

We note that there is broad agreement on a set of tiers, with the PSC and the Politburo at the top, followed by the full members of the CC, and then the alternate members of the CC (Kung and Chen 2011; Lieberthal 2004). In particular, we treat as top-ranked the party secretary general (who sets the agenda in the PSC) and the chairman of the Central Military Commission (CMC), who were usually the same person. Next came the members of the PSC, who voted on every major issue confronting the regime—and whose relative political status was implied by the order of their names in public announcements.[2] Following in descending order of political power are the vice chairmen and members of the CMC (who controlled large segments of the armed forces), the Politburo (composed of regional party secretaries of major provinces, several vice premiers of the State Council, and senior military leaders), and a handful of alternate members of the Politburo. Next come the vast majority of the Central Committee who were not members of the higher party organs, whose members' individual ranks were not precisely known, beyond the general importance of these tiers.

Finally, a key to our ranking strategy lies at the bottom of this hierarchy. Beneath full members of the CC lie the ACC members, who failed to win election to higher tiers at the party congress; for example, ACC members tended to be provincial governors rather than the more powerful regional party secretaries. Starting with the Eighth Party Congress, the official press announced ACC members in the order of votes received

[2] For example, at the August 1966 11th Plenum, Liu Shaoqi fell from number 2 in the PSC to the last position in the PSC in the *People's Daily*. See MacFarquhar and Schoenhals (2006).

from delegates (the vote totals themselves remained secret). Because detailed instructions were given to delegates when they voted on the ACC slate, the votes received by ACC members should reflect the priorities of the top leadership in ranking cadres. This underexploited data on a large body of individuals contains a wealth of information about the factors influencing the ranking of all top officials. We will show in the next section how these data help us impute ranks for the entire hierarchy.

We combine our rank data with covariates measuring the characteristics of the members of the ACC, the CC, the Politburo, and the PSC. Most of these variables are drawn from a new biographical data set of Central Committee members developed by Shih, Shan, and Liu (2008). This database contains all CC and ACC members from the first party congress in 1921 to the sixteenth party congress in 2002, and follows the structure for political biographical data developed by Adolph (n.d.) in his work on the career trajectories of central bankers. Shih, Shan, and Liu collect and record nearly every state, party, and military position held by CC members throughout their careers, rather than just positions held by CC members at the time they served in the CC. Using start and end years for each position held, they reconstruct complete career histories for each member of the ACC, the CC, the Politburo, and the PSC as they stood at the start of each party congress.[3] They also collect demographic variables including birth year, gender, year of induction into the party, education, ethnicity, and princeling status.

These biographical data allow us to test whether education, performance, or factional affiliations are responsible for party rank. Basic demographic information captures merit criteria such as level of education, as well as representation criteria such as gender and minority status. We assume that factional ties occur between officials and leaders with shared birthplaces, as well as officials and leaders who overlapped in educational institutions or work units (Lieberthal and Oksenberg 1988, 156).[4] If any such coincidence occur between a CC or ACC member and a top leader, we code that member as having a factional tie to that leader.

We also combine the CC database with provincial economic data to calculate the relative economic performance of provincial administrators (governors and party secretaries) who were also CC or ACC members (China Data Online 2005). In the five party congresses under consideration, provincial administrators made up between 14 and 20% of all CC members. We consider the fraction of provincial CC members to be both large from a substantive point of view, and sufficient to estimate whether provincial economic performance was rewarded with party advancement. Although we are only able to test the economic performance hypothesis on the provincial administrators in the pool, Maskin, Qian, and Xu (2000) argue that China's success hinged on competition among provincial administrators, whose economic performance could be more readily observed than that of cadres in the central bureaucracy. If superior performance by provincial administrators did not lead to political rewards in the party, we doubt that nonprovincial officials received such rewards either.

We focus mainly on growth in GDP and fiscal revenue, but collect 22 other measures of performance for use in robustness analyses. We assume that each member of the CC hierarchy who was also a provincial party secretary or governor is judged based on the performance of his province in the five years between party congresses. In constructing our performance measures, we must solve two further problems. First, because competition for party rank is zero-sum, only officials who outperform their peers should advance. Thus we create *relative* performance scores that subtract rest-of-China performance from each province's growth rate. Second, provincial officials should not receive credit for growth trends determined before they took office. Thus, we subtract preappointment expected performance from each province's growth rate. The resulting variable measures the performance improvement in each province under its current leadership, relative to other provincial leaders. We create performance scores of this type for GDP growth, fiscal revenue growth, and other indicators of provincial performance. For example, the province of an official with a GDP growth score of +2 beat preappointment growth expectations by two percent *more* than the average province in China. Members of the ACC or CC who were not regional administrators in the five years prior to a party congress receive neutral performance scores of zero.[5]

Estimating expected provincial performance is also the key to dealing with selection bias. Although high-flying officials might manuever themselves into provinces with strong growth prospects, or be sent to turn problem provinces around, we can purge these and other selection effects from our performance measures if we accurately model expectations of provincial performance on the eve of appointment. Party leaders doling out performance rewards share our problem of isolating the innovations in growth due to provincial leaders, rather than provincial trends or China-wide shocks. Because we cannot be certain how historical leaders solved this problem, we propose three strategies, and check whether any of them provide evidence of yardstick competition. The first strategy is the simplest: We subtract the growth rate in the preappointment year from growth during an official's

[3] To accurately capture CC members' careers, Shih, Shan, and Liu (2008) assign a four-digit number to each position in the CCP bureaucracy from 1949 to 2002. The first three digits denote the political organ to which this position belongs, and the last digit represents the level of the position. The score 3021, for example, breaks down to 302, which stands for the General Political Department of the People's Liberation Army (PLA), and the final digit, 1, which denotes the highest level in that department, the Department Chief.

[4] For overlapping work experience, we identify an official as being in a leader's faction if the official worked in the same work unit as the leader for over a year, *and* was within two administrative steps of him.

[5] Our results are not sensitive to the assignment of an arbitrary score to nonadministrators: A robustness check shows the same results if we also include in the model a dummy variable for officials with no observed regional economic performance.

tenure, attributing the change to the official's efforts. We use this performance measure in our baseline models. As an alternative, we employ standard time series methods to forecast growth over officials' tenures using only preappointment data. We create forecasts using both the workhorse AR(1) model and the AIC-minimizing ARMA(p, q) model. We use these sharper estimates of expected growth in robustness checks that allow both sophisticated judgment of performance by party leaders and complex patterns of strategic appointment of provincial officials.[6] See the supplemental Online Appendix (available at http://www.journals.cambridge.org/psr2012004) for further details.

METHODS

Modeling the ranking of members of the CCP Central Committee—or any other partially observed ranking of political actors, whether the members of a legislature, a bureaucracy, or some other organization—challenges political scientists' inferential toolkit. Despite the omnipresence of hierarchy in politics, these problem have not yet been noted or solved.

Rank Data Problems

Political rank data pose three problems for quantitative-analysis-as-usual: Rank data are interdependent, require context to interpret, and are typically incomplete.

Interdependence. Virtually all regression models in political science assume that observations are identically and independently distributed (iid). Rank observations are intrinsically interdependent: Only one member can rank first, only one can rank second, and so on. Direct inference on ranks using conventional methods will thus be invalid, giving incorrect standard errors.

Context. In general, observed and counterfactual ranks are meaningful only in context. Without context, the "first-ranked swimmer" could mean anything; the "first-ranked swimmer in the Olympics" and the "first-ranked swimmer in my neighborhood" usually represent very different levels of ability. Context matters even when we know the underlying strength of individuals giving rise to their ranking: The ranking boost provided by an increase in latent strength depends on the competition posed by higher-ranked individuals.

Contextual ranks complicate interpretation of estimated regression relationships. Frequentist inference (e.g., the use of t-tests and p-values to reject null hypotheses) assumes that estimated relationships are representative of a broader pattern that could be replicated in other random samples. The collection of these imagined datasets forms a "superpopulation" from which we construct confidence intervals and significance tests. Rank data constrain us to a finite population perspective: What we learn about the impact of a covariate on rank in one year's congress tells us little about its effect on rank within a different set of members in another year (Gelman et al. 2003).

Although conventional hypothesis testing makes little sense for a rank data model, Bayesian confidence intervals are still valid, as they do not depend on the existence of any data beyond the sample analyzed. Moreover, the confidence intervals we obtain for our results are the best we will ever get—because there will never again be another 14th Party Congress, there is no possibility of finding "more data" to produce more precise estimates of its hierachical structure.

Incomplete Ranks—Ties and Tiers. An ideal rank dataset records a unique rank for each member, but such detailed ranks are seldom available. Rank data may be incomplete, or partially observed, in two ways. First, there may be "ties," defined as cases where the rankers' measurements could not distinguish the (presumably different) latent strength of two or more consecutively-ranked individuals. In an ordered list of ranked objects that omits numerical ranks, such ties may hide anywhere in the dataset, leading to measurment error if rank is treated as identical to order. Our method of constructing ACC ranks is vulnerable to ties, and these potential ties must be accounted in our model.

A broader version of this problem arises when the ranks for a large "tier" of individuals are known to political actors, but concealed from the analyst. Figure 1 illustrates the relationship between tiers and ranks using a hypothetical dataset of eight individuals. Although the ranks of the three highest and two lowest members are known exactly, the fourth through sixth ranks form a tier within which individuals' relative ranks are unknown. Discarding these cases altogether, however, would waste valuable information, because the upper and lower bounds of the tier tell us that these middle individuals rank below 1, 2, and 3 and above 7 and 8. Although we can only specify the exact rank of five out of eight observations, we can correctly identify the higher-ranking individual in 25 of the 28 possible pairwise comparisons. The best analytic strategies for rank data will find ways to include this relative rank information.

The observed ranks of members of the ACC, CC, Politburo, and PSC show essentially the same pattern as the smaller dataset shown in Figure 1. We know the ranks of ACC members and PSC members, but all we can say about the CC is that their ranks lie somewhere in the middle. Surprisingly, this simple observation about CC members unlocks essential information for inferring the relationship between the characteristics of party members and their political power, but we will not be able to examine this hidden trove of data using off-the-shelf quantitative methods.

[6] Even if actual Chinese leaders did not use ARMA models to judge their subordinates' performance, experience in macroeconomic forecasting suggests that these models perform at least as well as more data- and knowledge-intensive methods often used in the 1960s–1980s, and may thus serve as shortcuts to estimating how sophisticated political actors of that period may have formed their expectations (Diebold 2000).

FIGURE 1. Observed Ranks, Missing Ranks, and Tiers

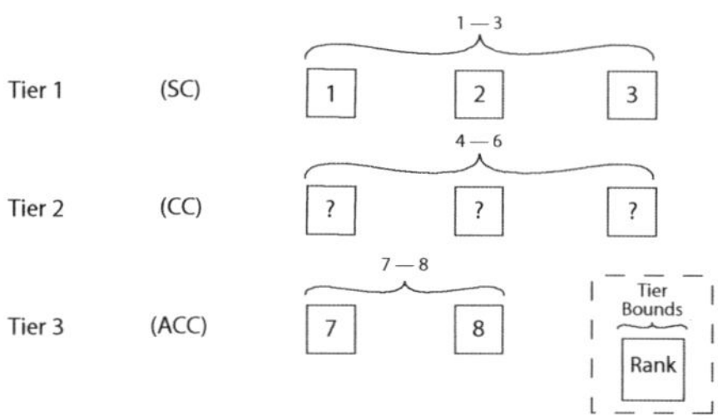

Note: In this hypothetical dataset, the ranks of the top three individuals (who occupy the top tier, or the PSC) and the ranks of the bottom three individuals (who occupy the lowest tier, or the ACC) are known precisely. The ranks of the middle three individuals are unknown, but still bounded by the rank of their tier, the CC.

Flawed Analytic Strategies

Three seemingly appropriate methods from the political science toolkit—linear regression, censored regression, and ordered probit—either assume properties that rank data clearly violate or ignore useful information contained in the ranks. Even though ranks take on unique and interdependent integer values, least-squares regression inappropriately assumes that ranks are iid Normal, computes incorrect standard errors, and predicts impossible ranks. Because linear regression requires us to listwise delete any observations with imprecisely observed ranks, we also lose information captured by the bounds on those ranks, which is statistically inefficient and a possible source of bias (King et al. 2001).

Censored regression (or tobit) models a Normally distributed outcome that is observed when it falls in certain ranges, but censored elsewhere (Schnedler 2005). This avoids bias and inefficiency from deleting partially observed cases, but because censored regression also assumes ranks are iid Normal, its standard errors are still biased. And neither censored nor linear regression protects against measurement error from miscoding tied ranks.

If we abandoned our analysis of the rank-level data, we might focus on estimating the probability of an individual appearing in a given tier using ordered probit. Ordered probit does not assume ranks are Normal, and mitigates (but does not eliminate) the dependence of observations. But it exacts a large cost for these improvements, throwing out even more of the observed data than linear regression, and adding a new parameter to estimate for each uniquely identified tier, so that estimation becomes harder the more we know. To analyze partial ranks without violating model assumptions or discarding data, we look beyond the usual suspects, and develop statistical models calibrated to the unusual properties of rank data.

A Bayesian Model of Partially Observed Ranks

To understand the relative power of Chinese Communist officials, we propose and apply a Bayesian model of partially observed ranks with three advantages over conventional methods. First, we allow interdependence of ranks through the rank likelihood (Hoff 2008). Second, we generalize this approach to allow for partial observation of ranks, preserving all the information available in our data—a step we expect will be critical for most applications of the method to political data. Finally, we interpret our results in the context of each rank dataset: Rather than assume there is a "superpopulation" from which each party congress is a random sample, Bayesian methods let us treat each party congress as sui generis, thus quantifying the magnitude and uncertainty of effects of covariates on ranks in historical context.

We denote the rank of each individual $i \in 1, \dots, n$ as a unique integer $y_i \in 1, \dots, n$. Lower values of y_i represent *higher* ranks; i.e., $y = 1$ indicates the highest-ranked individual, and $y = n$ the lowest. Each individual lies within a tier, or range of ranks, which is known even if y_i is missing. Our model of y_i rests on three assumptions:

Assumption 1. *Each ranked member has a unique latent strength* y_i^*.

Assumption 2. *Higher latent strength entails better expected rank:* $y_i^* > y_j^* \Leftrightarrow {}_i \text{ outranks }_j \Leftrightarrow y_i < y_j$.

Assumption 3. *Latent strengths are iid Normal.*

To examine the relationship between ranks and observable covariates, we parameterize the latent strength y_i^* using a linear model, which for identification has no constant and unit variance:

$$y_i^* \sim \text{Normal}(\mu_i, 1)$$
$$\mu_i = \beta_1 x_{1i} + \beta_2 x_{2i} + \dots \beta_p x_{pi}. \quad \textbf{(1)}$$

For convenience, we refer to the random component of latent strength as $\alpha_i = y_i^* - \mu_i$; we interpret α_i as representing the unmeasured political talent and good or bad fortune of official i.

The model relies on the notion that if we could only observe latent strength directly, a simple linear regression would be sufficient to understand its conditional expectation. We link partially observed ranks to latent strengths through a set of bounds around each rank, denoted $\{y_i^{\text{lower}}, y_i^{\text{upper}}\}$. For a given observation, there are three possible kinds of bounds. From most to least informative, these are

Bound Type 1. *Rank known exactly:* $y_i^{\text{lower}} = y_i = y_i^{\text{upper}}$.

Bound Type 2. *Rank known up to a potential tie with an adjacent ranked individual:* $y_i^{\text{lower}} = y_i^{\text{upper}} + d$, *where* $d + 1$ *indicates the number of ranks included in the tie.*

TABLE 1. Goodness of Fit

	Party Congress				
	12th	13th	14th	15th	16th
All observations (N)	410	285	320	342	356
Fully observed (N_{full})	141	114	135	157	166
Partially observed (N_{part})	269	171	185	185	190
Completely unobserved (N_{miss})	0	0	0	0	0
Percent fully observed ($100 \times N_{\text{full}}/N$)	34.4	40.0	42.2	45.9	46.6
Percent of variance explained	29.5	46.5	40.4	47.6	34.7
Percent prediction error of known ranks ($\sqrt{\text{MSE}}$)	31.1	26.6	26.4	25.1	25.5
Percent of tiers correctly predicted	65.6	66.3	75.3	69.6	71.6
Bayesian information criterion	532.3	447.6	403.2	468.0	396.0

Setting $d = 1$ discounts the observed difference in rank between any two immediately adjacent ranked individuals as potential measurement error, but assumes that two individuals separated by two ranks or more must have correspondingly ordered latent strengths.

Bound Type 3. *Rank known up to a tier:* $y_i^{\text{lower}} < y_i < y_i^{\text{upper}}$*, where* y_i^{lower} *is set to the lower bound of the tier, and* y_i^{upper} *is set to the upper bounds of the tier.*

In our application, we treat the ranks of (most) members of the PSC as known exactly (Type 1), members of the CC as known only within the tier bounds of the CC (Type 3), and members of the ACC as known up to a potential tie, as a check on the possibility that two adjacently ranked members of the ACC actually won the same number of votes (Type 2).[7]

With bounds in hand for each ranked individual, we form a rank likelihood model around Assumptions 1, 2, and 3. Rank likelihoods capture the probability, conditional on covariates, that a given individual falls between the next higher and next lower ranked observations, and make no distributional assumptions about the ranks themselves (Hoff 2008; Pettitt 1982). Rank likelihood models do not require an independence assumption, accept even partially observed ranks, and require sophisticated Markov chain Monte Carlo (MCMC) methods to estimate. Full details regarding model parameterization, priors, and estimation procedures can be found in the Appendix.

Estimating and Fitting the Model

We estimated the model on the members of each party congress *separately*, without any pooling of parameter values across years, to allow the nature of political competition in each Party Congress to vary freely.[8] Each model controls for contemporaneous faction affiliations, relative changes in economic and revenue performance, educational attainment, gender, minority status, age, and party tenure. We report the goodness of fit for our baseline specifications in Table 1.[9] First, we compute the percentage of variance in latent political strength explained by the measured covariates (analogous to R^2 in linear regression). Second, we present the average error in percentiles when the fully observed ranks are predicted using only the measured covariates. Third, we calculate the percentage of all individuals classified in the correct tier based on their observed characteristics. Finally, we report the Bayesian information criterion (BIC) for each model (Spiegelhalter et al. 2002). As the BIC weighs the explanatory benefit of additional covariates against the cost of added model complexity, it serves as our preferred tie-breaker among substantively similar models, and it supported the set of controls employed here. Even though a majority of ranks were observed only partially in each party congress, the models fit well, explaining at least one-third and as much as one-half of the variance in latent strength, correctly predicting tiers for at least two-thirds of officials, and predicting members with exactly known ranks with as little as 25% error. Nevertheless, there remains a substantial chunk of variance left over, suggesting significant opportunities for further research.

Interpretation of Results

As usual for a regression model, substantive interest centers on calculating conditional expectations and first differences for carefully chosen counterfactual values of the model covariates. Because the rank benefit of any covariate depends not only on a given individual's

[7] The analyses reported in this paper assume $d = 1$; runs with higher d yielded substantively identical results and slightly wider confidence intervals.

[8] We leave the problem of temporal interdependence in party ranks to future work. A time-series version of the rank-data model would make more efficient use of the available data, but would also need to deal with a number of thorny issues, including the fact that the membership of elite bodies changes in each period.

[9] For each estimated model, we ran three parallel MCMC chains, discarding the first 5,000 iterations, and sampling every 10th iteration thereafter through 5,000 more iterations. All diagnostics suggest rapid convergence: Chains mixed well after the burn-in period, and $\hat{R}$ values were generally below 1.1.

characteristics, but also on the competition, we must also supply the hypothetical rivals for our hypothetical ranked individual. Usually, it makes sense to insert our hypothetical individual into a historical ranked body. As an example of a properly formed conditional expectation, we might ask what rank to expect for an otherwise average official with a college degree in the 15th Party Congress. A proper first difference, on the other hand, would ask how many percentiles in rank an average official would gain in the 15th Party Congress by earning a college degree. The Appendix gives further details on calculating these quantities.

FINDINGS

Overall, our findings do not suggest any linkage between growth performance of regional administrators who were also ACC, CC, or Politburo members and their *party* ranking in the CCP. However, some regime-strengthening factors, such as education and, to a lesser extent, fiscal performance and minority status, had positive impacts on ranking in the party elite. At the same time, there is considerable evidence that factional affiliation played a large role in political advancement.

Because the raw parameters estimated in our models are on a latent scale of no direct interest, and because we estimate five separate models, each with numerous covariates, it is easiest to explore our results through graphical summaries. These graphics show either the expected ranks of members with differing characteristics (for the 16th Party Congress see Figure 2; for other years, see the supplemental Online Appendix), or the expected change in rank associated with a change in one covariate, all else equal (Figures 3 and 4). To guide readers through our results, we first explore how different factors affected expected elite ranking at the most recent party congress for which we had data, the 16th Party Congress (2002). Then we take a broader view, and examine how the impact of these factors has waxed or waned between the 12th Party Congress and the 16th. Finally, we consider a broad range of alternative specifications to confirm the robustness of our findings.

Getting Ahead at the 16th Party Congress (2002–07)

Figure 2 lists the correlates of CCP rank in the 16th Party Congress in order from the biggest hinderances to the greatest advantages. The dotted vertical line marks the expected rank of a member with average values of all covariates. Black circles show the expected rank of members with the characteristics listed at left. The thin horizontal lines give 95 percent Bayesian confidence intervals; the thicker horizontal lines are single standard error bars. Also plotted to the left and right of the main estimates are gray diamonds showing the expected rank of members with the given characteristics *and* a random effect (or unmeasured political ability) one standard deviation below or above the mean, respectively. Thus the right gray diamond shows the rank we expect for a particularly talented or fortunate politician who has a high value of the listed covariate and otherwise average *observed* characteristics. These gray diamonds show the magnitude of the unmeasured effects not captured by the model, and also reveal how our modeled covariates provide a crucial boost or barrier for even extremely powerful elites—note, for example, the plight of skilled or lucky politicians who lack an education (banished to the ACC), or extremely talented or fortunate observationally average older members (potential Politburo material).

So how do our hypotheses fare in the 16th Party Congress? We start with our meritocratic regime hypotheses, which held that education, growth, revenue performance, and experience should be favored, along with broad representation of women and ethnic minorities. On face, education had a strong effect, as college graduates and graduate degree holders outranked high school graduates and dropouts by as much as 25 percentiles in party rank. Of course, by the 16th Party Congress, education was such a necessary condition for advancement that only 2% of members lacked a college degree. Despite a scramble to obtain graduate degrees among Chinese officials, having a graduate degree did not provide any additional advantage for an official's ranking at the 16th Party Congress.

Contra Maskin, Qian, and Xu (2000), Li, and Zhou (2005), and Chen, Li and Zhou (2005), we find little effect of growth performance on the prospects of local administrators who were ACC or CC members. At the 16th Party Congress, and controlling for revenue growth and political connections, relative provincial GDP growth provided no advantage to the expected ranking of an official. In this same party congress, collecting more taxes relative to the other provinces provided only a tiny, statistically uncertain boost to one's ranking [95% CI: −6.6, 11.5].

We find contrasting results for women and ethnic minorities. At the 16th Party Congress, a woman with otherwise average characteristics was expected to rank over 15 percentile points [95% CI: −1.3, −29.8] below a similar man. Even an exceptionally talented or fortunate woman with a high random effect was expected to rank more than a decile behind a similarly exceptional male official. Not surprisingly, in the 16th Party Congress only 4 of over 100 full CC members were women. Minorities, in contrast, appear to suffer no disadvantage, and may even have seen a slight benefit (3.9 percentiles) from a deliberate policy of promotion, though this effect was far from precisely estimated [95% CI: −9.8, 17.3]. A skilled or lucky minority official with a high random effect could reasonably expect to rise nearly to the 90th percentile, as did Hui Liangyu, an ethnic Hui in the Politburo.

Finally, years of experience in the CCP seemed to give elites an advantage in obtaining a higher rank. Here, we distinguish the effect of experience within the party from that of age itself. The model's estimates for the effect of age are ambiguous: No other variable had such a large average effect, but neither did any

FIGURE 2. Formal Selection Criteria and Rank in the 16th Party Congress: Estimated Relationships

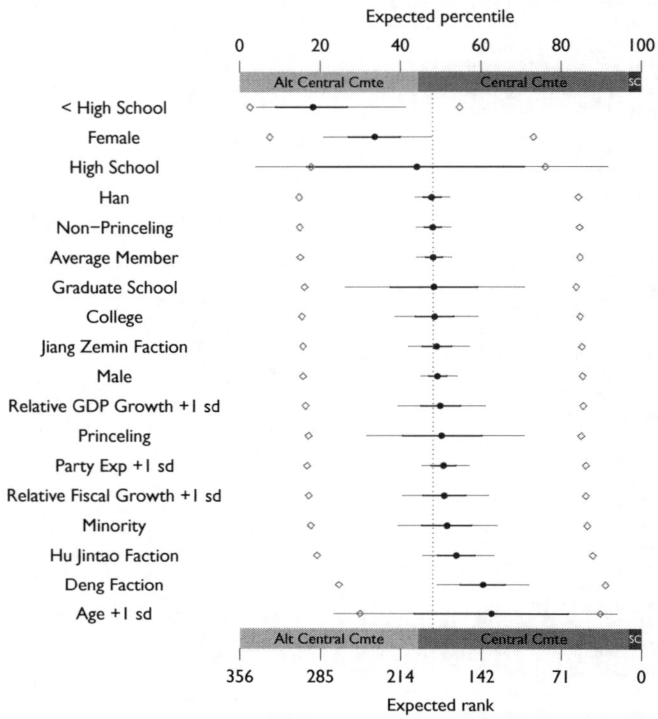

Note: For each row of the plot, we set the indicated covariate at one (for binary covariates) or the mean plus one standard deviation (for continuous covariates), and hold all other variables at their means. The black circles indicate expected rank for an individual with these observed covariates and an average random effect (or degree of unmeasured political ability). Gray diamonds show expected ranks for members with random effects one standard deviation above or below the mean. Thick horizontal lines mark 67% Bayesian confidence intervals and thin horizontal lines indicate 95% Bayesian confidence intervals. The dotted vertical line shows the expected rank of a member with the average covariates. The light gray region indicates the actual ranks of ACC members, the medium gray region shows the CC, and the dark gray region the ranks of the Standing Committee.

other variable have so imprecisely estimated an effect (indeed, no matter which specification we chose, the confidence interval for age remained stubbornly wide). First, age exerted the greatest positive impact on the expected rank of an official at the 16th Party Congress. Even controlling for age, however, we find that experience, measured as the share of an official's adult life spent in the party, also exerted a positive effect on one's ranking, albeit also with a wide confidence interval.

Did elite conflict and factionalism play a role in influencing elite ranking? For the 16th Party Congress, we examine the effect of being in the same faction as departing Party Secretary Jiang Zemin, incoming Party Secretary Hu Jintao, and deceased veteran Deng Xiaoping. Even in 2002, five years after Deng's passing, members of Deng's faction—some 12% of the CC and ACC who still had historical ties with Deng—had average ranks 14 percentile points higher [95% CI: 2.5, 25.8] than the average member, whereas members of Hu Jintao's Communist Youth League faction were expected to rank about seven percentiles above the average member [95% CI: −2.3, 17.7]. Surprisingly, CC and ACC members with ties to Jiang Zemin ranked the same as the average member, a pattern held over from the 14th and 15th Party Congresses. This puzzle can be explained, in part, by Jiang's vigorous promotion of close allies and supporters possessing little administrative experience or personal political resources. Even with Jiang's assistance, the best these individuals could do was to rank at the bottom among ACC members.[10]

[10] Some famous examples include Jiang's secretary Jia Ting'an and his bodyguard You Xigui, who ranked at the bottom of the ACC list. See Zhang (2002).

FIGURE 3. The Effects of Factional Ties, Performance, Demography, and Education on Political Rank: Estimated First Differences over Time

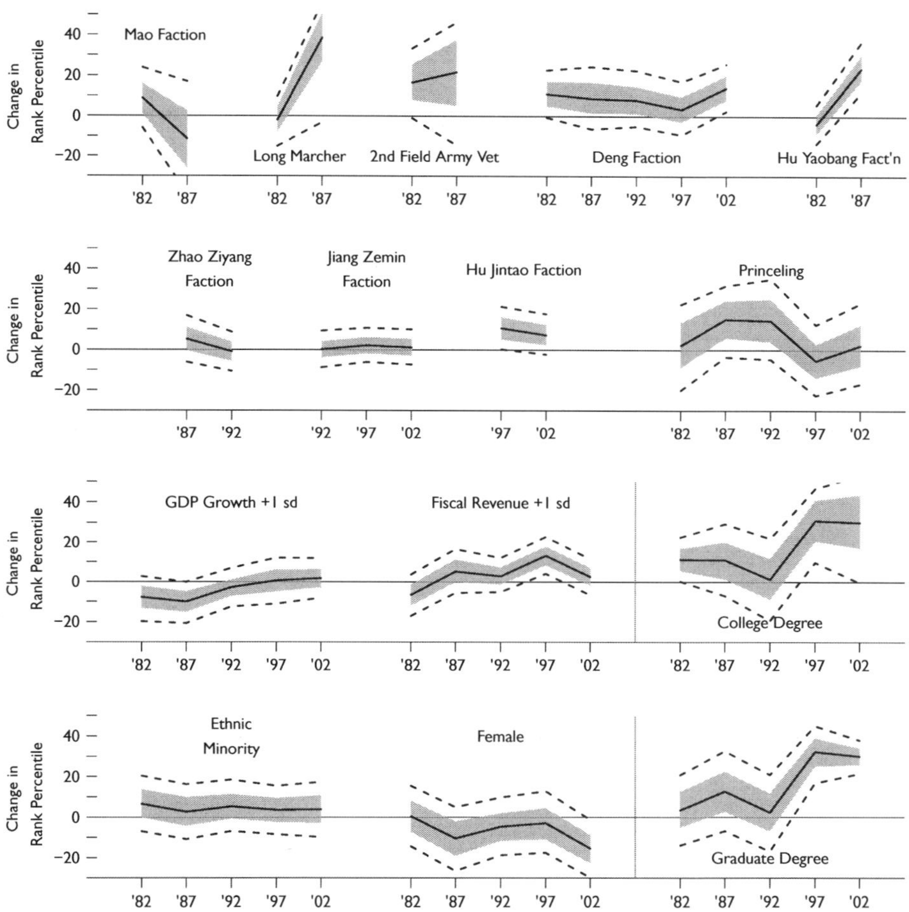

Note: Each plot shows the estimated change in rank percentile for a member with otherwise average measured and unmeasured characteristics, but a higher value for the listed covariate. For performance measures, we estimate the impact on rank of performance 1 standard deviation above the mean. For education variables, we show the difference in rank associated with a switch from less than high school to the listed degree. All other covariates are binary, so we estimate the effect on rank of switching from a 0 to 1. Shaded regions show 67% Bayesian confidence intervals, and dashed lines mark 95% Bayesian confidence intervals.

Finally, holding their educational advantages constant, princelings at the 16th Party Congress differed little from other Central Committee members [+2.2 rank percentiles; 95%: −16.9, 23.0]. All else being equal, the princeling advantage was not apparent at the 16th Party Congress.

In examining ranking at the 16th Party Congress, we find that economic performance did not matter. Obtaining a college education had become an unambiguous prerequisite for membership in the CC elite by 2002. Accumulating more experience in the CCP likewise may have provided officials with a boost in their ranking. However, performance-based criteria such as tax collection exerted only modestly positive effects on one's ranking. Departing from the expectations of a broadly representative regime, women faced distinct disadvantages in seeking high rank, although minorities enjoyed a slight advantage. Meanwhile, factional affiliation with Hu Jintao and Deng Xiaoping allowed connected officials who were average in other respects to rank significantly higher than their peers. In this core indicator, factional considerations continued to matter in 2002.

Getting Ahead in the Reform Era: Changes over Time

To understand how the struggle for power in the CCP has evolved over the reform period, we review our results for the 12th through 16th Party Congresses, covariate by covariate. We take up the results in three parts, first examining the performance and merit hypotheses, then focusing on how factional or princeling ties emerged as determinants of political rank, and concluding with a closer look at the interaction effects of age and party experience.

We start, in Figure 3, with the effects of education. These plots reveal that even at the beginning of the reform era, a college or graduate degree boosted party rank. At the 13th Party Congress in 1987, education continued to exert a positive effect on ranking. However, educational level beyond high school did not affect ranking at the 1992 14th Party Congress. In the aftermath of the 1989 Tiananmen Square Massacre, the party was preoccupied with punishing those who had failed to take a hard line and rewarding those who had helped the party survive the crisis. Over half of the CC was replaced at the 14th Party Congress (Gilley 1998). The benefits of education grew dramatically after 1992. By 2002, college was an unambiguous prerequisite for entry into the top of the elite, setting off a scramble for degrees that appears to have reached a point of diminishing returns, as graduate education produced no added advantage beyond a college degree at the 15th and 16th Party Congresses. All one can say is that the education advantage became more certain when one obtained a graduate degree relative to an official who only completed college, as shown by the narrower confidence interval for graduate degree holders in recent years.

Members of ethnic minorities held a steady but slight and imprecisely estimated advantage throughout the reform period, perhaps because of the party's "united front" policies, which sought to maintain stability and legitimacy through minority representation in the CCP elite (Mackerras 2003, 21). Women faced no disadvantage versus men at the 12th Party Congress in 1982, but were systematically lower-ranked for most of the remaining party congresses. What explains the relatively fair treatment of women at the 12th Party Congress and its subsequent decline? Perhaps female Long March veterans, still politically active at the 12th Party Congress, worked to promote women in the ACC and CC. In 1982 Deng Yinchao (Zhou Enlai's wife), Deng Jinliu, Cai Chang, Li Zheng, and Kang Keqing all exerted considerable influence on CC ranks, either through the Central Advisory Commission or from behind the scenes. By the late 1980s and early 1990s, these veterans had retired from active politics, leaving few senior women officials to lobby for the promotion of new female cadres. In the 1990s, only a small handful of "strong women" emerged in the political scene, such as Chen Muhua and Wu Yi, but they were the exceptions to an increasingly male-dominated elite body. This trend suggests that fairness and representation considerations were low priorities in the ranking of high-level officials in the CCP.

Turning to performance measures, we find growth performance exerted a decisively negative influence on CC ranking from the beginning of the reform period until the 15th Party Congress in 1997. From 1982 to 1992, provincial officials with above average growth performance could expect to be ranked 3 to 10 percentiles *lower* than average performers. From 1997 onwards, officials from high-growth regions enjoyed neither an advantage nor a disadvantage vis-à-vis officials from average-growth regions. Relying on more detailed, party-based ranks, which do not treat lateral bureaucratic rotations as promotion, we thus cast doubt on the notion that regional growth was propelled by the prospect of promotion (Blanchard and Schleifer 2000), and on the findings of Li and Zhou (2005), Maskin, Qian, and Xu (2000), and Chen, Li, and Zhou (2005).

Indeed, the historical record suggests that party secretaries of provinces deemed politically important were automatically inducted into the Politburo, regardless of the province's economic performance. For example, at the 16th Party Congress, party secretaries from economic dynamos such as Guangdong and Shanghai won seats in the Politburo, but party secretaries of mediocre growth performers such as Hubei and Tianjin also gained entry into the body. At the same time, the serving party secretaries of Zhejiang and Jiangsu, which typically had high growth, were never inducted into the Politburo. Our findings also lend support to Huang (1996), who finds that highly ranked regional leaders had an incentive to stifle growth through reducing investment because they did not want to violate the center's macroeconomic control measures.

The picture for fiscal performance is more nuanced. In contrast to economic performance, which benefits society as a whole, tax collection delivers funds directly to Beijing, helping political leaders fulfill various objectives. In 1994, Beijing centralized China's fiscal system, and we see some benefit in rank from exceptional revenue collection over the period 1992–97 during the 15th Party Congress in 1997. As Beijing struggled to ensure that local officials complied with the new fiscal system (Chen 2005), these new incentives were unsurprising. The need to reward local officials for tax collection seemed to have diminished somewhat by the 16th Party Congress in 2002.

Our findings on the effect of factional ties and princeling relationships throughout the reform period suggest that top Chinese leaders consistently sought to promote faction members already in the political elite to higher ranks. Although members of Chairman Mao's residual faction at first were not discriminated against in elite ranking, by the 13th Party Congress, after the demotion of Mao's designated successor Hua Guofeng, Maoists saw their standing fall by an average of 11.5 percentiles compared with non-Maoists, though the effect is very poorly estimated [95% CI: −39.0, 17.0]. Many Maoists were forced out of the CC and ACC in the 13th Party Congress, and their representation in the CC and ACC declined from 16% to 6% (see the Appendix).

ACC and CC members with historical ties to Deng Xiaoping enjoyed positive and substantial rank advantages through most of the reform period, even through the 15th Party Congress, immediately following Deng's death. This effect holds even controlling for a potential confounder, Deng's command of the Second Field Army during the Chinese Civil War (1945–1949), which produced many senior officials. Even when we partial out Deng allies from the Second Field Army, his other followers did well at the 12th and 13th Party Congress.

The two party secretaries of the 1980s, Hu Yaobang and Zhao Ziyang, exerted different effects on the ranks of faction followers. Hu Yaobang followers made up some 41% of the 12th Party Congress, which may explain why being a Hu follower did not produce extra rank advantages in 1982. At the 13th Party Congress in 1987, some of Hu's followers were forced to step down (like Hu before them), reducing the faction to 25% of the CC and ACC. The survivors enjoyed a 20% rank advantage over non-Hu Yaobang followers, perhaps as a result of a selection effect: With the weakest Hu followers weeded out, the stronger survivors may have been better suited to retain their rank.

In contrast, although Zhao followers made up roughly one-fourth of the CC and ACC body at both the 13th and 14th Party Congresses, they held no particular rank advantage in either. Jiang followers, who made up 17% and 20% of the CC and ACC at the 15th PC and 16th Party Congresses, are similarly neutrally ranked. This appears to contradict tales of Jiang forcefully filling the PSC and Central Committee with his own followers (Lam 1994, 1999; Zhang 2002). But just as Jiang tried to promote many of his key followers, including Huang Ju, Zeng Qinghong, and Jia Qinglin, into key positions in the Politburo Standing Committee, he also tried to appoint members of his household staff with little administrative experience into alternate central committee seats. These Jiang supporters were consistently among the lowest vote recipients on the ACC list. Indeed, we see Jiang's faction clustered into two types—one at the top of the elite rank hierarchy and one at the bottom. The net effect of a Jiang factional tie as zero is thus somewhat misleading. Without Jiang's help, many in his inner circle would not have been qualified to even enter the bottom of the Communist elite, so his influence arguably raised the rank of both clusters.

Factionalism persists in recent Chinese politics. We find that members of Hu Jintao's Communist Youth League (CYL) faction enjoyed a distinct rank advantage of 7 to 10 percentiles at both the 15th and 16th Party Congresses, all else equal. To be sure, Youth League members were cultivated in the 1980s to take high offices in the 1990s, and many of them indeed entered the elite CC/ACC bodies in the late 1990s. However, once they entered the ACC, ties with Hu Jintao, who had served as the party secretary of the Communist Youth League, pulled them further upward into the CC and higher.[11]

Finally, children of senior officials, or "princelings," held substantial rank advantages at the 13th and 14th Party Congress, all else equal, though the effect has declined since the 15th PC. Although in many cases the parents of these princelings have retired or died, political leaders in China still found it useful to promote these princelings over the average member. The princeling advantage stood out particularly in the 13th and 14th Congress, when Deng Pufang, Yu Zhengsheng, Li Peng, and Xi Jinping were propelled into the upper reaches of the CC or even into the Politburo over revolutionary veterans despite being notably young. From the late 1990s on, however, relatively young Communist Youth Leaguers were also getting promoted into the higher ranks, and the princeling advantage no longer seemed as strong. Nevertheless, future study of the 17th Party Congress may well find a revival of the princeling advantage, as the cohort of princelings who had entered high politics in the late 1980s and early 1990s reached the apex of the CCP.

We turn now to the important but complex interaction of each official's age and party tenure, which we control for using both a simple measure of the years an official spent in the CCP as a fraction of his total years lived, as well as dummy variables for specific revolution cohorts.[12] In each of our models, age—not party tenure—is the more potent determinant of rank. However, even though our estimates partial out the effects of age and tenure, in real data these concepts can never be fully separated (e.g., in 2002, there were no 40-year-olds who joined the CCP in the 1930s). To show how age and tenure reinforce one another, we calculate from the model posterior the expected rank for a range of observed combinations of age and date of party entry; we plot the results by party congress in Figure 4. The graphs trace out "cohort lines" showing the effect of age on rank for officials who joined the party in the same year; for each party congress, we plot a cohort line for members at the 25th, 50th, and 75th percentiles of party tenure. The upward slope of the lines reflects the strong, positive association between age and political rank and the degree of spread between the lines shows the effect of party experience.

[11] We only identify CYL members as Hu followers if they worked within two administrative steps of Hu Jintao during his career.

[12] We thus dummy out the pre-Long March (–1935), Anti-Japanese War (1936–1945), and Civil War (1946–1949) cohorts separately, as suggested by improved BIC scores.

FIGURE 4. The Interactive Effect of Age and Party Tenure on Rank by Party Congress: Estimated First Differences

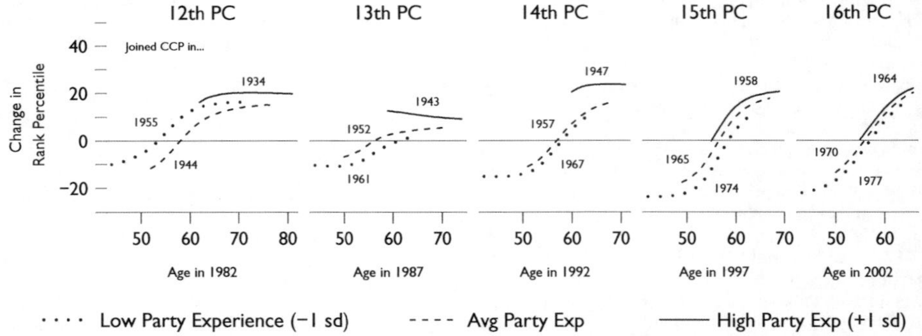

Note: Plots display the estimated change in rank percentile associated with switching from the average age to the age shown on the horizontal axis. A separate line traces out the effects of age for early, average, and late CCP joiners. All other covariates are held at their means. To avoid extrapolation, each line is limited to show only counterfactuals drawn from inside the convex hull (King and Zeng 2006).

Two main findings emerge from Figure 4. First, the rank benefits of age are strong—indeed, stronger than any other measured covariate—and have grown stronger in recent party congresses. To guard against selection bias (as only unusually powerful officials can maintain their positions in the CC past the mandatory retirement age of 65), we reran each model with a control for the retirement threshold, and the overall age effect persisted strongly. We conclude, then, that age mostly reflects the accumulation of political capital over time.

Second, the rank benefits of party tenure and revolutionary experience loom large in early reform party congresses, but diminished greatly over time. At the 12th Party Congress, CC members from the Long March cohort on average placed above the 60th percentile, much higher than the expected ranking of the later Anti-Japanese War and Civil War cohorts. Unique efforts in the 12th Party Congress to promote young officials meant that some members of the post-1950 cohort ranked higher than revolutionary veterans and even some Long Marchers. In all other party Congresses, greater party seniority brought about higher ranks. At the 13th and 14th Party Congresses, revolutionary veterans on average ranked around the 60th percentile, whereas at the 15th Party Congress, revolutionary veterans ranked around the 75th percentile, but by 2002, all revolutionaries had retired from the CC, and party experience diminished as a determinant of rank.

The overall impression of Figure 4 is that the significance of age has risen whereas the impact of years in the party has faded. Nevertheless, their large combined effect suggests an "up-or-out" system for the CCP elite, as officials who endured years of intraparty political struggle were very likely to accumulate the political experience and capital needed to advance through the party ranks.

Robustness of Results

We find no relationship between growth performance and party ranking, and a strong relationship between factional ties and rank. Because these findings are debated both for China and for the broader field of authoritarian politics, we conduct additional robustness tests to raise our confidence in the results. In particular, we drop the assumption that the order of votes received for the ACC measures political strength, consider more specific measures of factional affiliation to protect against measurement error, add controls for educational institutions and fields of study, add broader measures of economic performance in case political ranks are awarded holistically, and finally, exploit our provincial performance data to mitigate selection bias. Because the details of these tests could fill a second article, we relegate discussion of theory, measurement, design, and ancillary results to the supplemental Online Appendix. Here, we focus on the consistency of our estimated results for the impact of faction, performance, and education on expected party rank.

Figure 5 displays results for all robustness checks overlapped. The similarity of these results to each other and the baseline estimates is striking, and the few deviations worthy of note.

Our first robustness check is the toughest, because it discards much potentially useful information. We now treat the ranks of ACC members as missing, and allow the rank data model to impute ACC ranks along with CC ranks and other parameters. Remarkably, there is enough information in the tier bounds on the ACC and CC to estimate our models, and for every party

FIGURE 5. The Effects of Factional Ties, Performance, Demography, and Education on Political Rank: Robustness Checks

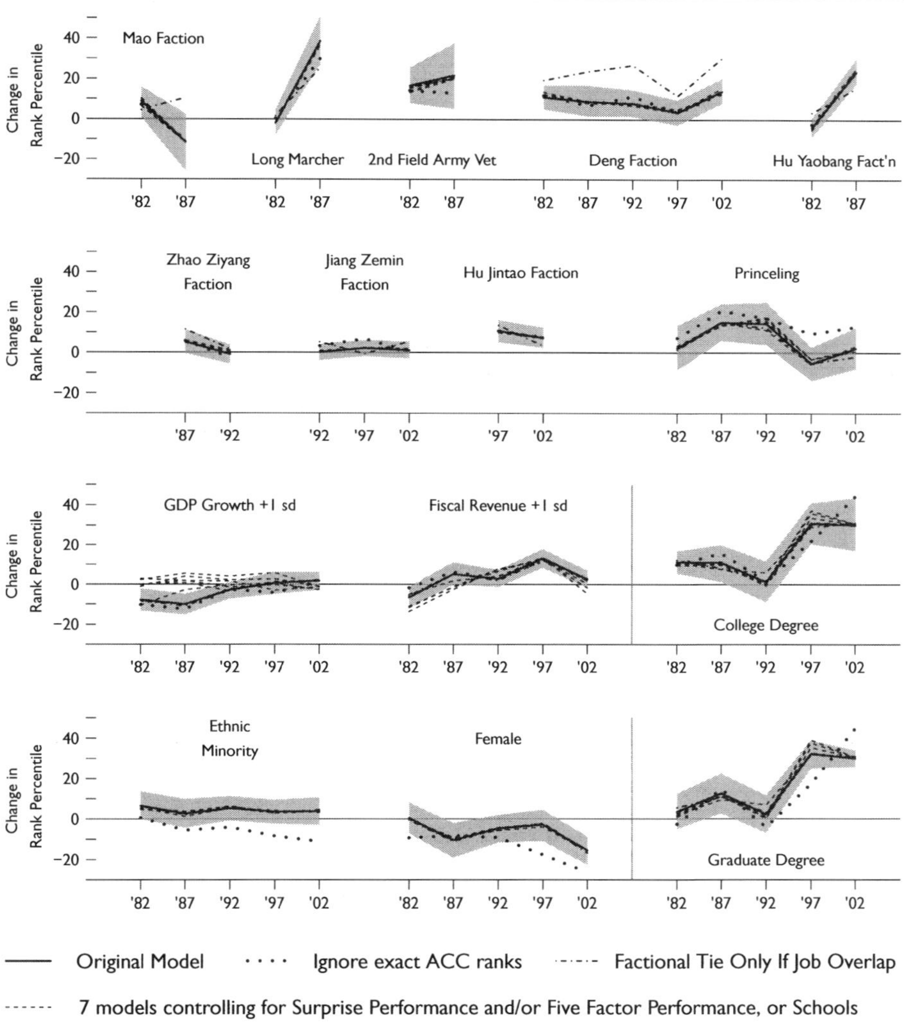

Note: As in Figure 3, each plot shows the estimated change in rank percentile for a member with otherwise average measured and unmeasured characteristics, but a higher value for the listed covariate. Estimates from nine different specifications join the original model. Shaded regions show 67% Bayesian confidence intervals for the original models. See the supplemental Online Appendix (available at http://www.journals.cambridge.org/psr2012004) for confidence intervals for other models.

congress, the new, more conservative results agree remarkably well with the baseline models on the effects of factions, performance, and education (see the dotted lines in Figure 5). Our main conclusions no longer depend on whether ACC votes are informative, as they do not enter the model. The principal change in the results is that minorities and women both fare poorly, which we take as evidence of a glass ceiling. It is apparently easier for women and minorities to rise in the ACC ranks than it is for them to leave the ACC for higher tiers.

Our factional tie measures are also vulnerable to measurement error. Designed to be sensitive to affiliations hinted at by shared birthplaces, school ties, and shared work environments, our baseline measures may include false positives because of coincidences of birth and school attendance. A more specific measure counts only cases where an official worked closely with the faction leader in one of China's hundreds of ministerial and vice-ministerial work units or state-owned enterprises. Substituting these measures leaves most estimates of faction unchanged, and strengthens results for Mao and Deng, perhaps by zeroing in on core faction members or by excluding marginal members (see the dashed–dotted lines in Figure 5). As a further check against spurious factional results, we confirm that our factional measures also explain considerably more variance in rank than randomly generated factional variables do (see the supplemental Online Appendix for details).

As our remaining robustness checks all agree so closely with each other and with the original model as to be mostly indistinguishable, Figure 5 plots them all as dashed lines. The first such test allows for the possibility that not all college and graduate degrees are equal, and adds to the model controls for the origin of each official's highest university degree (whether from the Central Party School or abroad) and for fields of study (either natural science or social science/administration/law). The average effect of education is unchanged, as is the impact of faction and performance covariates, whereas the effects of degree origins and fields of study vary over time (see the supplemental Online Appendix).

We perform two tests of our findings on performance. In the first, we consider the possibility that GDP growth is too narrow a yardstick, and substitute a set of five orthogonal factors of performance summarizing 24 provincial performance variables. For this model, the quantity plotted under "GDP Growth" in Figure 5 is the effect on rank of the largest factor from our factor analysis, which loads heavily on growth in industrial output, retail sales, gross capital investment, and, of course, GDP itself. Even with this broader measure, we still find no evidence of incentives for growth. Nor do we see any correlation between higher party rank and improvement in the other factors: urban and rural standards of living, social service provision, and employment (see the supplemental Online Appendix for factor analysis details and full results).

In our final test, we return to the problem of selection bias. Our baseline measures of GDP growth provide some protection against selection effects by subtracting preappointment growth rates in each province. Still, better preappointment forecasts—such as AR(1) or ARMA(p, q) forecasts from historical data—should offer more protection against selection bias, and more closely capture the kind of performance most relevant for political rewards. In our remaining robustness checks, also shown as dashed lines in Figure 5, we isolate the surprising performance of provincial officials left over after removing expected growth, as forecast from preappointment data by either an AR(1) model or by the best available ARMA(p, q) model. We use the same forecasting techniques to isolate surprising performance on the five latent performance factors. Across all four of these robustness checks, the rewards to unexpected economic growth hover near zero, whereas the rank effects of factional ties, education, and demographics remain unchanged.

We consider the breadth and consistency of these results to be a strong refutation of the widespread claim that Chinese leaders advance based on yardstick competition. There is no hint that higher provincial growth leads to political advancement: not for officials who perform well compared to the past performance of their own province, not for officials who beat their peers' performance in other provinces, not for officials who perform well on a broad range of factors, and not even for officials who beat the specific expectations one could form of their likely performance on appointment. Factional ties, on the other hand, appear to be strong predictors of party rank no matter what the specification of the model.

CONCLUSIONS

In this study, we use a novel Bayesian model of rank to estimate the impact of covariates on elite ranking within the ruling Chinese Communist Party. Guided by the literature on comparative authoritarianism, we derive hypotheses about covariates that may drive elite ranking in China. The empirical results show that the existing theoretical literature on authoritarian regimes predicts ideal types that, in reality, coexist in the same regime. Communist institutions in China worked well enough to make college education a prerequisite of entry into the upper echelon. The regime also systematically favored ethnic minorities, probably to enhance stability. Finally, when a centralized fiscal system was first implemented in the mid-1990s, the CCP used the cadre evaluation system to ensure that provincial leaders cooperated with central tax officials in maximizing revenue for the central government. Consistent with the predictions of Bueno de Mesquita et al. (2003), the CCP regime deployed the cadre evaluation system to ensure basic state functions, stability, and fiscal income, all of which were necessary to deliver private goods to the ruling elite.

Chinese leaders, however, did not apply the cadre management system to encourage growth. To be sure, the system assigned scores to cadres' growth performance, but we find no evidence that provincial officials who generated higher-than-average growth or higher than expected growth were rewarded with higher party ranks in any year and on any measure. Given our findings, one can no longer argue that China enjoyed spectacular growth *because* of promotion incentives embedded in the political system. To be sure, officials had some incentive to be educated, which increased human capital in the regime. After the beginning of the reform, provincial administrators certainly did not have an incentive to reduce growth in their jurisdictions and may even have seen growth performance as a way to earn promotion. However, there were other (formal and informal) paths upward that were more effective. In terms of formal performance criteria, raising revenue collection, at least in the 1990s, earned advancement. Chinese leaders also did not promote gender fairness at the elite level through the cadre management system, thus allowing systematic discrimination against women to persist.

CCP cadre management institutions also delivered promotions to followers of senior party leaders. First, ties with Deng Xiaoping, Hu Yaobang, or Hu Jintao while they were in power elevated officials in the party hierarchy. Even though these leaders were the nominal and de facto heads of the party, they still engaged in factional politics. In fact, the literature suggests that leaders were able to stay in power *because* they engaged in factional politics instead of selecting the most capable officials (Egorov and Sonin 2011; MacFarquhar and Schoenhals 2006; Pye 1992). Princelings also held distinct advantages in some party congresses, again suggesting that senior CCP leaders favored promoting members of their support coalitions.

China's growth in the past 30 years has been spectacular, but the precise source of this growth remains highly contested. The findings of this paper suggest that the CCP's cadre management system did not directly lead to China's growth. The findings, however, are consistent with the argument that crucial policies enacted in the 1980s, including the household responsibility system, labor mobility, price reform, and the welcoming of foreign direct investment, paved a strong foundation for three decades of growth (Huang 2008; Naughton 1996; Sachs et al. 1994; Shirk 1993). Although Chinese leaders enacted them on an experimental basis, these early policies produced strong momentum for growth that lasted for decades. Furthermore, by encouraging cadres to deliver short-term benefits to the regime, party institutions delivered several crucial conditions for economic growth, including relatively low inflation, a well-financed central authority, and political stability (Huang 1996; Shih 2008a). Without these basic conditions, growth in China likely would have been much lower. The challenge for China going forward is to uncover institutional mechanisms that counteract the natural tendency of political institutions to deliver private goods in the form of rent-seeking opportunities to the support coalitions of senior leaders.

In future research, instead of static evaluation of regimes as "meritocratic" or "clientelistic," scholars should focus on mechanisms that shift a regime's priorities toward public good provision, rather than delivering private goods to a small elite. Exogenous shocks, such as inter-state wars, worldwide depression, and exogenously driven inflation, may change the relative balance of power and degree of elite rivalry, which in turn may alter promotion incentives, and ultimately affect policy outcomes. Outside events may also shift the policy priority of top leaders, leading to adjustments in promotion criteria. For example, the collapse of the Soviet Union motivated China to centralize its fiscal system. Our findings suggest that when faced with the challenge of bolstering central fiscal resources, the leadership placed a heavier emphasis on tax collection when ranking officials at the 15th Party Congress. Following the research of Ramseyer and Rosenbluth (1998) and Boix and Svolik (2010), more work should inquire into the expected behavior of authoritarian regimes under different degrees and types of internal rivalry induced by external shocks.

APPENDIX

This Appendix provides details for the estimation and interpretation of the Bayesian model of partially observed rank data introduced in the main text.

Markov Chain Monte Carlo Rank Likelihood Estimation

Rank likelihood estimation is sometimes used to avoid the strong distributional assumptions used in maximum likelihood models, and is especially useful for inference in models where the response is only known up to a rank (Pettitt 1982). Whereas the maximum likelihood estimate of β maximizes the probability of obtaining the observed response y_i given its assumed probability distribution and the covariates, the rank likelihood estimate maximizes the probability that the observed response falls between the next higher and next lower ranked individuals, given the covariates, but without any assumption that y_i follows a particular distribution (Hoff 2008). Rank likelihood allows us to directly include (even partial) rank information in the likelihood, but requires Markov chain Monte Carlo (MCMC) methods to estimate.

As usual with MCMC, our goal is to initiate a random walk through the parameter space which eventually converges to the correct posterior distribution, so that we can simply sample from the Markov chain to calculate estimates and confidence intervals of our quantities of interest (Gelman and Hill 2007). MCMC estimation of the Bayesian partial rank model proceeds using a combination of the Gibbs sampler and Metropolis–Hastings algorithms. We set diffuse Normal priors over the β parameters and then construct several Markov chains using the following four-step procedure, iterating over steps 3 and 4 m times to produce each chain:[13]

[13] Using priors over β is an optional step that makes the model Bayesian, but is not strictly required to apply the rank likelihood approach. Including diffuse priors made no substantive difference in our results for the party congress data.

1. ***Initialize the latent strengths***, y^*_{i0}**:** Draw, for all members of the party congress, a random feasible rank. A set of feasible ranks must respect all tier bounds and tie restrictions, and use each possible rank only once.
2. ***Initialize*** $\boldsymbol{\beta}_0$**:** Using the starting values y^*_{i0} and the covariate data $\mathbf{x}_i$, compute the starting values of the parameters by least squares. Then compute $\mu_{i0} = \mathbf{x}_i\boldsymbol{\beta}_0$.
3. ***Update the latent strengths***, y^*_{im}**:** Using the $\boldsymbol{\mu}_{m-1}$'s from the previous iteration, for a randomly chosen i, draw a new latent strength y^*_{im} somewhere above the highest latent strength of individuals known to rank below i, but below the lowest latent strength of individuals known to outrank i. Continue drawing until each individual has an updated latent strength.

   Formally, draw y^*_{im} within $[\ell^*_{im}, u^*_{im}]$, where

$$\begin{aligned}&\text{lowest known higher latent strength, } u^*_{im}\\ &= \min\left(y^*_{km} : y^{\text{upper}}_{im} < y^{\text{lower}}_{km}\right)\\ &\text{highest known lower latent strength, } \ell^*_{im}\\ &= \max\left(y^*_{jm} : y^{\text{upper}}_{jm} < y^{\text{lower}}_{im}\right). \qquad \textbf{(2)}\end{aligned}$$

   By default, draw each new y^*_{im} using the Gibbs sampler. To perform a single Gibbs draw from y^*_{im}, sample a single probability w_{im} from the interval implied by the tier bounds,

$$w_{im} \sim \text{Uniform}\left(\int_{-\infty}^{\ell^*_{im}} \text{Normal}\left(\mu_{i,m-1}, 1\right), \int_{-\infty}^{u^*_{im}} \text{Normal}\left(\mu_{i,m-1}, 1\right)\right). \qquad \textbf{(3)}$$

   Then y^*_{im} is simply the quantile of the standard Normal distribution corresponding to w_{im}.

   The Gibbs sampler can run into computational difficulties when computing Normal cumulative distribution functions if, for a given observation i and MCMC iteration m, the expected value of the distribution of latent strengths $\mu_{i,m-1}$ lies far outside the bounds $\{\ell^*_{im}, u^*_{im}\}$. In those cases, we employ instead the slower Metropolis–Hastings algorithm (of which Gibbs is a special case), for which we need only draw new candidate values of y^*_{im} from the appropriate proposal distribution:

$$y^*_{im} \text{ candidate} \sim \text{Truncated Normal}\left(\mu_{i,m-1}, \sigma^2, \ell^*_{im}, u^*_{im}\right). \qquad \textbf{(4)}$$

   As usual, candidates for y^*_{im} replace the older values $y^*_{i,m-1}$ based on a Metropolis–Hastings acceptance probability. To speed up convergence, tune σ^2 to achieve an acceptance rate close to 40% (Gelman et al., 2003).
4. ***Update*** $\boldsymbol{\beta}_m$**:** Using the updated latent strengths y^*_{im} and the covariate data $\mathbf{x}_i$, compute the updated parameters by least squares. Then compute $\mu_{im} = \mathbf{x}_i\boldsymbol{\beta}_m$.

After an intial burn-in, iterate the Markov chains until all y^*_i's and β's appear to have converged to stable distributions, and then sample the posterior distributions of the latent stengths and parameters from the chains. For convenience, one can also sample the posterior distribution of each individual's unmeasured component of latent strength, α_i.

Interpretation of Results

We interpret the model using conditional expectations and first differences for counterfactual scenarios as recommended by King, Tomz, and Wittenberg (2000), with the important caveat that we must also condition on the historical context against which any counterfactual individual is ranked:

Conditional Expectations. Conditional expectations in a rank model must condition not only on the hypothetical characteristics $\mathbf{x}_c$ of a new member c, but also on the characteristics $\mathbf{x}_i$ of all the observed members in the party congress the new member might outrank.[14] To calculate these conditional expected ranks, we draw sets of the parameters $\tilde{\boldsymbol{\beta}}$ from the converged MCMC chains. For each draw h, we calculate a single conditional expectation of the new member's rank,

$$\mathrm{E}\left(\tilde{y}_{ch}|\mathbf{x}_c, \mathbf{x}_i, \tilde{\boldsymbol{\beta}}_h, \tilde{\alpha}_{ih}\right) = \text{rank}\left(\mathbf{x}_c\tilde{\boldsymbol{\beta}}_h; \mathbf{x}_i\tilde{\boldsymbol{\beta}}_h + \tilde{\alpha}_{ih}\right), \qquad \textbf{(5)}$$

where rank$(a;b)$ indicates the rank of object a within the set b.[15] We summarize the posterior distribution of $\mathrm{E}\left(y_c|\mathbf{x}_c, \mathbf{x}_i, \tilde{\boldsymbol{\beta}}, \tilde{\alpha}_i\right)$ using the mean and 95% interval of our h draws. Finally, to facilitate comparison across party congresses, we transform the expected ranks to a percentile scale.[16]

First Differences. As in linear regression models, we are interested in how changing a covariate from $\mathbf{x}^{\text{old}}_c$ to $\mathbf{x}^{\text{new}}_c$ shifts the expected rank for a hypothetical individual. Although this "first difference" is simply β for linear regression, in the Bayesian partial rank model, as in many non-linear models, we must calculate it from the model parameters. To calculate a first difference for the Bayesian partial rank model, we draw a vector of $\tilde{\boldsymbol{\beta}}$'s from the model posterior, and subtract the rank for the baseline scenario from the rank for the new scenario:

$$\begin{aligned}&\mathrm{E}\left(\tilde{y}^{\text{new}}_{ch} - \tilde{y}^{\text{old}}_{ch}|\mathbf{x}^{\text{new}}_c, \mathbf{x}^{\text{old}}_c, \mathbf{x}_i, \tilde{\boldsymbol{\beta}}_h, \tilde{\alpha}_{ih}\right)\\ &= \text{rank}\left(\mathbf{x}^{\text{new}}_c\tilde{\boldsymbol{\beta}}_h; \mathbf{x}_i\tilde{\boldsymbol{\beta}}_h + \tilde{\alpha}_{ih}\right) - \text{rank}\left(\mathbf{x}^{\text{old}}_c\tilde{\boldsymbol{\beta}}_h; \mathbf{x}_i\tilde{\boldsymbol{\beta}}_h + \tilde{\alpha}_{ih}\right). \qquad \textbf{(6)}\end{aligned}$$

As before, we summarize the distribution of first differences with their mean and 95% confidence interval, and convert these to a percentile scale for ease of comparison across years and covariates.

Implementation

A complete suite of tools for inference and interpretation of the Bayesian partial rank model is available in the R package partialrank.[17] Monte Carlo experiments across

[14] If $\mathbf{x}_c$ is set to the value for an observed individual, this procedure calculates a fitted value for that observation.

[15] We could instead produce predicted ranks—counterfactuals that reflect not only the uncertainty in our estimates of $\boldsymbol{\beta}$, but also the uncertainty introduced by letting the hypothetical member c have a random degree of unmeasured strength α_c—by calculating

$$\text{Predicted}\left(\tilde{y}_{ch}|\mathbf{x}_c, \mathbf{x}_i, \tilde{\boldsymbol{\beta}}_h, \tilde{\alpha}_{ch}, \tilde{\alpha}_{ih}\right) = \text{rank}\left(\mathbf{x}_c\tilde{\boldsymbol{\beta}}_h + \tilde{\alpha}_{ch}; \mathbf{x}_i\tilde{\boldsymbol{\beta}}_h + \tilde{\alpha}_{ih}\right),$$

where $\tilde{\alpha}_{ch}$ is a randomly chosen $\tilde{\alpha}_{ih}$. The same algorithm can be used, mutatis mutandis, to create predicted first differences.

[16] Because low-rank numbers correspond to high percentiles, and vice versa, we calculate expected rank percentiles as $100 \times (n - \mathrm{E}(y_c|\mathbf{x}_c, \mathbf{x}_i, \tilde{\boldsymbol{\beta}}, \tilde{\alpha}_i))/n$.

[17] Available at faculty.washington.edu/cadolph/software.

a range of hypothetical rank data sets of varied size and degrees of partial observation show that the model meets or exceeds the performance of linear regression, censored regression, and ordered probit in terms of bias, mean squared error, and coverage of confidence intervals (Adolph 2011).

TABLE 2. Summary Statistics for Model Covariates

	Party Congress				
	12th	13th	14th	15th	16th
Female	0.06	0.07	0.07	0.07	0.07
Minority	0.09	0.11	0.11	0.11	0.10
Age at party congress	59.59	56.15	56.90	56.60	56.09
	(8.03)	(6.55)	(6.17)	(5.78)	(5.32)
Party experience	0.66	0.62	0.60	0.56	0.56
	(0.10)	(0.11)	(0.13)	(0.12)	(0.1)
Year joined party	1942.13	1951.60	1957.32	1964.78	1970.52
	(9.44)	(8.97)	(9.90)	(9.08)	(6.97)
CCP since 1935[a]	0.22	—	—	—	—
CCP since 1945[a]	0.42	0.23	0.10	—	—
CCP since 1949[a]	0.13	0.26	0.19	0.05	—
Less than high school	0.17	0.06	0.03	0.01	0.01
High school	0.24	0.15	0.10	0.04	0.01
College	0.55	0.71	0.77	0.78	0.69
Graduate degree	0.04	0.08	0.11	0.17	0.29
Mao faction	0.16	0.06	—	—	—
Long Marcher	0.17	0.01	—	—	—
2nd Field Army veteran	0.06	0.01	—	—	—
Chen Yun faction	0.26	—	—	—	—
Ye Jianying faction	0.23	—	—	—	—
Deng faction	0.27	0.14	0.12	0.11	0.12
Hu Yaobang faction	0.41	0.25	—	—	—
Zhao Ziyang faction	—	0.28	0.26	—	—
Jiang Zemin faction	—	—	0.32	0.28	0.25
Hu Jintao faction	—	—	—	0.17	0.20
Princeling	0.02	0.05	0.04	0.04	0.04
Relative GDP growth[b]	−1.52	−2.12	−0.92	0.03	0.02
	(4.8)	(5.83)	(7.34)	(3.6)	(2.41)
Relative revenue growth[b]	15.82	28.12	13.92	6.14	0.91
	(9.44)	(164.59)	(73.55)	(46.18)	(7.13)

Note: Entries are the observed means for each covariate in each model, by party congress. For continuous variables, the standard deviation is included in parentheses. [a]CCP since 1935, CCP since 1945, and CCP since 1949 are coded 1 for members who joined the CCP before 1935, between 1935 and 1945, and between 1945 and 1949, respectively. However, if CCP by 1935 is omitted from the model, CCP by 1945 then includes all members who joined before 1945, and so on. [b]Relative GDP growth and Relative revenue growth are measured as the difference between the average annual percent growth in GDP (or revenue) in the province governed by the individual and the corresponding population-weighted average annual percent growth in GDP (or revenue) across all other provinces. The GDP and revenue figures in this table reflect means and averages for members who were provincial governors or party secretaries only.

REFERENCES

Acemoglu, Daron, Simon Johnson, and James Robinson. 2000. "The Colonial Origins of Comparative Development: An Empirical Investigation." NBER Working Paper No. 7771. Cambridge, MA: National Bureau of Economic Research.

Acemoglu, Daron, and James A. Robinson. 2006. *Economic Origins of Dictatorship and Democracy*. Cambridge: Cambridge University Press.

Adolph, Christopher. 2011. "Small Sample Properties of Partial-rank Data Estimators." Seattle: University of Washington. faculty.washington.edu/cadolph (accessed October 6, 2011).

Adolph, Christopher. N.d. *The Myth of Neutrality: Bankers, Bureaucrats, and Central Bank Politics*. Cambridge: Cambridge University Press.

Blanchard, Olivier, and Andrei Schleifer. 2000. "Federalism with and without Political Centralization: China versus Russia." NBER Working Paper No. 7616. Cambridge, MA: National Bureau of Economic Research.

Boix, Carles, and Milan Svolik. 2010. "The Foundation of Limited Authoritarian Government: Institutions and Power-sharing in Dictatorships." Working Paper. Princeton University.

Bueno de Mesquita, Bruce, Alastair Smith, Randolph Siverson, and James D. Morrow. 2003. *The Logic of Political Survival*. Cambridge, MA: MIT Press.

Burns, John P. 1989. *The Chinese Communist Party's Nomenklatura System: A Documentary Study of Party Control of Leadership Selection, 1979–1984*. Armonk, NY: M.E. Sharpe.

Chen, J. 2005. *Guoshi yishu [Remembering State Affairs]*. Beijing: CCP Party History Publisher.

Chen, Ye, Hongbin Li, and Li-An Zhou. 2005. "Relative Performance Evaluation and the Turnover of Provincial Leaders in China." *Economic Letters* 88 (3): 421–25.

China Data Online. 2005. "China Yearly Macro-economic Statistics." Ann Arbor, MI: China Data Center.

Cui, Wunian. 2003. *Wode 83 ge yue [My 83 Months]*. Hong Kong: Ko Man Publishing Co.

Debs, Alexandre. 2007. The Wheel of Fortune: Agency Problems in Dictatorships. Rochester, NY: University of Rochester.

Deng, Liqun. 2005. *Shi'erge chunqiu: 1975–1987 [Twelve Springs and Autumns: 1975–1987]*. Hong Kong: Boszhi Publisher.

Desai, R. M., A. Olofsgard, and Tarik Yousef 2009. "The Logic of Authoritarian Bargains." *Economics & Politics* 21 (1): 93–125.

Diebold, Francis X. 2000. "The Past, Present, and Future of Macroeconomic Forecasting." *Journal of Economic Perspectives* 12 (1): 175–92.

Dittmer, Lowell. 1995. "Chinese Informal Politics." *China Journal* 34: 1–34

Dreyer, June Teufel. 1976. *China's Forty Millions: Minority Nationalities and National Integration in the People's Republic of China*. Cambridge, MA: Harvard University Press.

Easter, Gerald. 1996. "Personal Networks and Postrevolutionary State Building: Soviet Russia Reexamined." *World Politics* 48 (4): 551–78.

Edin, Maria. 2003. "State Capacity and Local Agent Control in China: CCP Cadre Management from a Township Perspective." *China Quarterly* 173: 35–52.

Egorov, Georgy, and Konstantin Sonin. 2011. "Dictators and their Viziers: Endogenizing the Loyalty-competence trade-off. Journal of European Economic Association. 9 (5): 903–13.

Evans, Peter B. 1995. *Embedded Autonomy: States and Industrial Transformation*. Princeton, NJ: Princeton University Press.

Fewsmith, Joseph. 1994. *Dilemmas of Reform in China: Political Conflict and Economic Debate*. Armonk, NY: M.E. Sharpe.

Frye, Timothy, and Andrei Shleifer. 1997. "The Invisible Hand and the Grabbing Hand." *American Economic Review* 87 (2): 354–58.

Gandhi, Jennifer, and Adam Przeworski. 2006. "Cooperation, Cooptation, and Rebellion under Dictatorships." *Economics & Politics* 18 (1): 1–26.

Gelman, Andrew, John B. Carlin, Hal S. Stern, and Donald B. Rubin. 2003. *Bayesian Data Analysis*. 2nd ed. Boca Raton, FL: Chopman and Hall/CRC Press.

Gelman, Andrew, and Jennifer Hill. 2007. *Data Analysis Using Regression and Multilevel/Hierarchical Models*. Cambridge: Cambridge University Press.

Gilley, Bruce. 1998. *Tiger on the Brink: Jiang Zemin and China's New Elite*. Berkeley: University of California Press.

Guo, Gang. 2007. "Retrospective Economic Accountability under Authoritarianism: Evidence from China." *Political Research Quarterly* 60: 378–90.

Haggard, Stephan, and Sylvia Maxfield. 1996. The Political Economy of Financial Internationalization in the Developing World. In *Internationalization and Domestic Politics*, eds. R. Keohane, and H. Milner. New York: Cambridge University Press.

Hoff, Peter. 2008. "Rank Likelihood Estimation for Continuous and Discrete Data." *ISBA Bulletin*, 8–10.

Huang, Yasheng. 1996. *Inflation and Investment Controls in China: The Political Economy of Central–Local Relations during the Reform Era*. Cambridge: Cambridge University Press.

Huang, Yasheng. 2008. *Capitalism with Chinese Characteristics: Entrepreneurship and the State*. Cambridge: Cambridge University Press.

Kang, David C. 2002. *Crony Capitalism: Corruption and Development in South Korea and the Philippines*. Cambridge: Cambridge University Press.

King, Gary, James Honaker, Anne Joseph, and Kenneth Scheve. 2001. "Analyzing Incomplete Political Science Data: An Alternative Algorithm for Multiple Imputation." *American Political Science Review* 95 (1): 49–69.

King, Gary, Michael Tomz, and Jason Wittenberg. 2000. "Making the Most of Statistical Analyses: Improving Interpretation and Presentation." *American Journal of Political Science* 44 (2): 347–61.

King, Gary, and Langche Zeng. 2006. "The Dangers of Extreme Counterfactuals." *Political Analysis* 14 (2): 131–59.

Kung, James Kai-Sing, and Shuo Chen. 2011. "The Tragedy of the *Nomenklatura*: Career Incentives and Political Radicalism during China's Great Leap Famine." *American Political Science Review* 105 (1): 27–45.

Lam, Willy Wo-Lap. 1994. "Jiang Faction Stages Its Surrogate Coup." *South China Morning Post* October 5.

Lam, Willy Wo-Lap. 1999. *The Era of Jiang Zemin*. New York: Simon and Schuster.

Landry, Pierre F. 2008. *Decentralized Authoritarianism in China: The Communist Party's Control of Local Elites in the Post-Mao Era*. Cambridge: Cambridge University Press.

Lee, Hong Yung. 1991. *From Revolutionary Cadres to Party Technocrats in Socialist China*. Berkeley: University of California Press.

Li, Hongbin, and Li-An Zhou. 2005. "Political Turnover and Economic Performance: The Incentive Role of Personnel Control in China." *Journal of Public Economics* 89 (9/10): 1743–62.

Li, Junru. 2007. *Zhongguo gongchandang lici quanguo daibiao dahui yanjiu [Studies of the Past Party Congresses of the Chinese Communist Party]*. Beijing: Dongfang Publisher.

Lieberthal, Kenneth. 2004. *Governing China: From Revolution through Reform*. 2nd ed. New York: W. W. Norton.

Lieberthal, Kenneth, and Michel Oksenberg. 1988. *Policy Making in China: Leaders, Structures, and Processes*. Princeton, NJ: Princeton University Press.

Lin, Justin Yifu. 1992. "Rural Reforms and Agricultural Growth in China." *American Economic Review* 82 (1): 34–51.

MacFarquhar, Roderick, and Michael Schoenhals. 2006. *Mao's Last Revolution*. Cambridge, MA: Belknap Press.

Mackerras, Colin. 2003. *China's Ethnic Minorities and Globalisation*. London: Routledge Curzon.

Manion, Melanie. 1993. *Retirement of Revolutionaries in China: Public Policies, Social Norms, Private Interests*. Princeton, NJ: Princeton University Press.

Maskin, Eric, Yingyi Qian, and Chenggang Xu. 2000. "Incentives, Information, and Organizational Form." *Review of Economic Studies* 67 (2): 359–78.

Nathan, Andrew. 1973. "A Factionalism Model for CCP Politics." *China Quarterly* 53: 33–66.

Nathan, Andrew, and Bruce Gilley. 2002. *China's New Rulers: The Secret Files*. New York: New York Review of Books.

Nathan, Andrew J., and Kellee S. Tsai. 1995. "Factionalism: A New Institutionalist Restatement." *China Journal* 34: 157–92.

Naughton, Barry. 1996. *Growing out of the Plan: Chinese Economic Reform 1978–1993*. New York: Cambridge University Press.

Olson, Mancur. 1993. "Dictatorship, Democracy, and Development." *American Political Science Review* 87 (3): 567–76.
Olson, Mancur, and Martin McGuire. 1996. "The Economics of Autocracy and Majority Rule: The Invisible Hand and the Use of Force." *Journal of Economic Literature* 34 (March): 72–96.
Organizational Division of the Central Organization Department. 2001. *Dang zuzhi xuanju gongzuo shouce [Handbook of Party Election Work]*. Beijing: Party Building Reading Material Publisher.
Pei, Minxin. 2006. *China's Trapped Transition: The Limits of Developmental Autocracy*. Cambridge, MA: Harvard University Press.
Pettitt, A. N. 1982. "Inference for the Linear Model Using a Likelihood Based on Ranks." *Journal of the Royal Statistical Society, Series B* 44: 234–43.
Putnam, Robert D., Robert Leonardi, and Raffaella Nanetti. 1993. *Making Democracy Work: Civic Traditions in Modern Italy*. Princeton, NJ: Princeton University Press.
Pye, Lucian. 1980. *The Dynamics of Factions and Consensus in Chinese Politics*. Santa Monica, CA: Rand Corporation.
Pye, Lucian. 1992. *The Spirit of Chinese Politics*. Cambridge, MA: Harvard University Press.
Qian, Yingyi, Barry Weingast, and Gabriella Montinola. 1995. "Federalism, Chinese Style: The Political Basis for Economic Success in China." *World Politics* 48 (1): 50–81.
Ramseyer, J. Mark, and Frances McCall Rosenbluth. 1998. *The Politics of Oligarchy: Institutional Choice in Imperial Japan*. Cambridge: Cambridge University Press.
Sachs, Jeffrey, Wing Thye Woo, Stanley Fischer, and Gordon Hughes. 1994. "Structural Factors in the Economic Reforms of China, Eastern Europe, and the Former Soviet Union." *Economic Policy* 9 (18): 102–45.
Schnedler, Wendelin. 2005. "Likelihood Estimation for Censored Random Vectors." *Econometric Reviews* 24 (2): 195–217.
Schneider, Ben Ross. 1993. "The Career Connection: A Comparative Analysis of Bureaucratic Preferences and Insulation." *Comparative Politics* 25 (3): 331–50.
Schneider, Ben Ross, and Sylvia Maxfield. 1997. "Business and the State in Developing Countries." In *Business and the State in Developing Countries*, ed. B. R. Schneider, and S. Maxfield. Ithaca, NY: Cornell University Press.
Sheng, Yumin. 2007. "Global Market Integration and Central Political Control: Foreign Trade and Intergovernmental Relations in China." *Comparative Political Studies* 40 (4): 405–34.
Shih, Victor. 2008a. *Factions and Finance in China: Elite Politics and Inflation*. New York: Cambridge University Press.
Shih, Victor. 2008b. "Nauseating" Displays of Loyalty: Monitoring the Factional Bargain Through Ideological Campaigns in China." *Journal of Politics* 70 (4): 1177–92.
Shih, Victor, Wei Shan, and Mingxing Liu. 2008. "Biographical Data of Central Committe Members: First to Sixteenth Party Congress" [Dataset]. Northwestern University.
Shirk, Susan. 1993. *The Political Logic of Economic Reform in China*. Berkeley, CA: University of California Press.
Silva, Eduardo. 1996. "From Dictatorship to Democracy: The Business–State Nexus in Chile's Economic Transformation, 1975–1994." *Comparative Politics* 28 (3): 299–320.
Spiegelhalter, D. J., N. G. Best, B. P. Carlin, and A. van der Linde. 2002. "Bayesian Measures of Model Complexity and Fit." *Journal of the Royal Statistical Society B* 64: 583–639.
Svensson, Jakob. 2005. "Eight Questions about Corruption." *Journal of Economic Perspectives* 3: 19–42.
Svolik, Milan. 2009. "Power-sharing and Leadership Dynamics in Authoritarian Regimes." American Journal of Political Science. 53 (2): 177–94.
Tao, Ran, Fubing Su, Xi Lu, and Yuming Zhu. 2010. "Jingji zengzhang nenggou dailai pushengma? [Can Economic Performance Bring about Promotion?]" *Guanli shijie [Management World]* 12: 13–27.
Tullock, Gordon. 1987. *Autocracy*. Boston: Kluwer Academic.
Walder, Andrew G., Bobai Li, and Donald J. Treiman. 2000. "In a State Socialist Regime: Dual Career Paths into the Urban Chinese Elite, 1949–1996." *American Sociological Review* 65 (2): 191–209.
Weber, Max. [1921] 1958. "Characteristics of Bureaucracy." In *From Max Weber: Essays in Sociology*, ed. H. H. Gerth, and C. W. Mills. New York: Oxford University Press.
Whiting, Susan H. 2004. "The Cadre Evaluation System at the Grass Roots: The Paradox of Party Rule." In *Holding China Together: Diversity and National Integration in the post-Deng Era*, ed. D. L. Yang, and B. Naughton. New York: Cambridge University Press, 101–19.
Wintrobe, Ronald. 1998. *The Political Economy of Dictatorship*. Cambridge: Cambridge University Press.
Zhang, Liang. 2002. "Trilogy by Zhang Liang: 'Part One—Deng Xiaoping's Magnanimity, Jiang Zemin's Pettiness.'" *Hsin pao*, November 27.

[19]

HARVARD Kennedy School
JOHN F. KENNEDY SCHOOL OF GOVERNMENT

The Quality of Governance in China: The Citizens' View

Faculty Research Working Paper Series

Tony Saich

Harvard Kennedy School

November 2012
RWP12-051

Draft: Not to quoted without author's permission

The Quality of Governance in China: The Citizens' View

Tony Saich

Harvard Kennedy School

Paper Prepared for Sonoma Workshop

The Quality of Governance in China

Organized by Francis Fukuyama

October 2012

The government of General Secretary Hu Jintao and Premier Wen Jiabao (2002-2012) has placed an emphasis on improving the quality of governance and service delivery, especially for those who have not benefitted so well from, or who have been disadvantaged by the reform program to date. This emphasis is encapsulated in populist slogans such as "putting people first" (*yiren weiben*) and "building a harmonious society" (*goujian hexie shehui*). At a systemic level, the Chinese Communist Party (CCP) has declared that it is no longer a "revolutionary" but rather a "ruling party" that needs to modernize and adjust its systems of management (CCP Central Committee 2005). Reforms have attempted to improve the quality of expert and even citizen input into the decision-making process and evaluation of local officials, and to improve the functioning of government agencies. Other reforms have sought to boost "inner-party democracy" but all measures stop short of providing institutionalized mechanisms for feedback and any notion of open, competitive politics.

Despite these reforms, one could argue that many of China's core problems arise from deficiencies in governance. The system is riddled with corruption, a sure sign of poor governance, with officials abusing official position for personal gain and with the sale of government positions undermining the notion of promotion based on meritocratic principles. Many, if not most, of the local protests are caused by the improper or illegal actions of local officials. This includes the poor implementation of good national regulation at the local level (leading to environmental pollution or sale of substandard products), the illegal transfer of land that dispossesses or undercompensates farmers, and restricting access to public goods and services.

In comparative terms, China's indicators are not too bad with the exception of "voice and accountability". According to the World Bank's Governance Indicators (Kaufmann, Kraay and Mastruzzi 2010 and web access http://info.worldbank.org/governance/wgi/sc_chart.asp), China's governing performance has not varied significantly since 1996 when the project began. Four of the six indicators rank in the 50th to 75th percentile. The exceptions are government effectiveness (60.7 in 2011) and voice and accountability (4.7 in 2011). Compared with other large developing countries and those with similar income levels, China's evaluation is favorable. However, as China strives in economic terms to emulate the "tiger economies" of East Asia and others that have escaped the "middle-income trap", China still has a long way to go to improve its governance indicators (see **Table One**). Institutions lag behind economic growth and may become a drag on further growth. One could argue, of course, that the causality is unclear and that it is the rising incomes that lead to a need for improved governance rather than better government performance yielding higher per capita incomes.

Despite the lack of formal channels for citizen voice and accountability, citizens' views and popular pressure are increasingly impacting on policy-makers. This can range from the pressure of ultra-nationalist groups on and off-line, to the rise of protests against local abuses of power to the increased use of social media to express views and spread "unofficial" news. Unlike during the pre-reform era, citizens are more willing and able to stake claims against the state in order to obtain better service from their government. The paternalism of the Maoist state retains a strong influence down to the present day but the "infantilization" of society is harder to maintain. It is difficult for the current leadership to maintain the view that their citizens are children who do not know what is in their best interests. Representation has usually meant presuming knowledge of individual and societal interest and therefore being empowered to take all important decisions on their behalf (Saich, forthcoming). However, increasingly citizens have different expectations of their government expecting it to provide them with the necessary resources to make better individual choices and to provide effective protection against the vicissitudes of the market.

The spread of new social media has expanded greatly "voice" for citizens and the CCP has invested heavily in policing and shaping the online messages (Yang 2009 and Fallows 2011). However, new social media provides a major challenge to a party that is used to traditional media controls and censorship, with hierarchy of information access that provides the basis for the exchange of secrets that can be traded for power and wealth. The danger is that a system of information control becomes dysfunctional leading to distrust of official media and online rumor is given greater credibility (Saich 2006). In our 2011 survey, 65.2 percent of respondents expressed relative or extreme confidence in news transmitted on Sina Weibo, China's twitter equivalent, only a few percentage points lower than the Edelman annual global survey found for the media in China (73 percent, trustbarometer2012in fographic.pdf).[1] Sina Weibo was also seen by 56.7 percent as playing a role in combating corruption in the future and 36.6 percent definitely saw it as a medium for exposing corruption when it occurred. A further 46.7 percent noted that they might use Weibo to expose a corrupt action.

At the present time, these lacunae do not necessarily present insuperable problems for the CCP. It does not appear that a majority of citizens see the problems as systemic and our surveys suggest that the abuses are seen as local aberration rather than the consequence of central policy intent. The *Qiu Ju* mentality remains strong.[2] Second, government institutions have been remarkably flexible in accommodating new challenges and groups. The Chinese state is a "negotiated" one where each entity negotiates space and its relationship to others (see Saich 2000 and Saich and Hu forthcoming). For those entities that are successful in this negotiation, it allows them not only to survive but also often to prosper by using the facilities of the state to pursue their own objectives. Of course, some organizations are crushed while there is always the fear of state capture by vested interests. This has been argued most strongly for the capture of local government by Minxin Pei (2006) and recently there has been growing discussion of capture of national decision-making by vested interests. This is not necessarily an efficient mechanism for governing but it does provide a safety valve and a process for inclusion.

The main question is whether China's citizens are sufficiently satisfied to reduce potential challenges to CCP rule. It is reasonable to assume that if a significant percentage of citizens are more satisfied with government performance and the provision of public goods, the government will have a greater capacity for policy experimentation and enjoy a residual trust that may help them survive policy errors. Various writers have posited the relationship between citizen confidence in government and the capacity to implement laws and policies and reduce the need for coercion (see Hetherington 1998 and Warren 1999)

This paper asks three sets of questions. The first set asks about the general levels of satisfaction with government across different levels. Second, we ask about how citizens view the performance of local officials in dealing with the public and in implementing policy. Third, we look at the level of satisfaction with the provision of a number of specific goods and services, with a more in-depth look at dealing with corruption. In particular, it compares responses between those who live in major cities, small towns and townships, and villages. The findings are based on a survey that was conducted together with Horizon Market Research Company in the fall of 2003, 2004, 2005, 2007, 2009 and 2011. The survey is a purposive stratified survey ranging from 3,800 to 4,150 respondents selected from three administrative levels: city, town and village (for details see **Appendix One**). It is not a nationwide probability sample but comprises a number of sites selected on the basis of three variables: geographic location, average per capita income and population.[3] Seven cities (eight from 2005) were selected together with seven townships and eight villages. Within each of the cities respondents were selected randomly through the household registration lists using the KISH method (Kish 1949 and *Survey Sampling* 1965). At the township and village levels because of the large average size of families, respondents were selected randomly through the closest birthday method. In terms of coverage, the surveys exclude two groups. They do not cover the migrant populations in the major cities, which make up significant percentages (in 2011, 35.9 percent of Beijing's population and 36.4 percent of Shanghai's), nor do they include China's autonomous regions as these have somewhat different policies for public goods provision. However, some data concerning rural migrants drawn from the 2008 China Comprehensive Social Conditions Survey (*Zhongguo shehui zonghe zhuangkuang diaocha*) is included below.

One advantage is that the survey does allow us to compare resident attitudes in cities, towns *and* villages within the sample.[4] Since the 1950s when the Chinese state created a dual rural-urban society enforced through the household registration system (*hukou*), the two populations have been subject to quite distinct systems for the provision of public goods and services with more generous benefits for urban residents, especially those who were state sector employees. Reforms have loosened these divisions rendering urban and rural more integrated than at any time since the early 1950s. There has been little research that compares satisfaction across the urban-rural divide. Certainly, urban residents receive better service but does this lead them to be more satisfied? The uncertainties that reforms have brought and the removal of some benefits may have caused a rise in dissatisfaction. By contrast, rural inhabitants have experienced a major collapse in collectively provided goods and services that the leadership has tried to repair in recent years. Across the board, not only does place of household registration matter but also level of income in terms of access to important goods such as education and healthcare. With rising migration, rural residents have learned more about conditions in the urban areas and this might lead to increased frustration with their lot. Are different government services perceived differently dependent on whether one lives in a major city, a town or the village and does this affect what residents expect from their local government? Such questions allow us to speculate on the long-term stability of CCP-rule as it is reasonable to presume that widespread deep dissatisfaction will undermine regime support.[5]

The Mountains are High and the emperor is far Away: Disaggregating the State

Rather than contemplating extensive reform of the Leninist system, General Secretary Hu has placed emphasis on improving the quality of local officials and trying to inspire in them a moral notion of what it means to be a "good communist." This draws on a selective reading of China's Confucian heritage and its application by former head of state Liu Shaoqi (1939), something for which he was roundly condemned during the Cultural Revolution. The Hu-Wen leadership has supported this by introducing policy measures to provide basic safety nets for Chinese society and to integrate migrants into urban services more effectively.

With respect to general satisfaction levels, there are two main findings. The 2011 survey confirms those of earlier years that respondents "disaggregate" the state and while they express high levels of satisfaction with the Central Government, satisfaction declines with each lower level of government. This view is confirmed by other surveys that have been conducted (Li and O'Brien 1996, Li 2004 and Li 2012).

Tianjin Shi's national survey (2001) found that citizens who might be wary of local governments may still trust the Central Government. A survey by Zhang Houan and his colleagues from Central China Normal University on trust in different levels of the party apparatus carried out between 1999 and 2001 shows a similar tendency (cited in Li 2012, p. 109),[6] as does the China Survey for 2008.[7] Our survey shows that this trend holds steady throughout the Hu-Wen administration. The findings imply that the disaggregation of the state with a benevolent center and an obstructionist local authority that many have observed in rural China also applies to urban China.

In 2011, 91.8 percent of respondents were either relatively or extremely satisfied with the work of Central Government (37.3 percent were extremely satisfied) but this dropped progressively to 63.8 percent at the local level (10.9 percent extremely satisfied) (see **Table Two**). This trend maps fairly closely with the China Survey 2008 on trust in leaders at different levels. In 2008, 44.6 percent had high level of trust in central leaders (37.3 percent extremely satisfied in our 2011 survey); 24.3 percent in provincial leaders (28.4 percent in 2011) and 17.1 percent in county/town leaders (14.6 percent in 2011). The fact that satisfaction declines as one gets closer to the people is problematic as local governments provide most public services and carry the heaviest financial burden, especially at the county and township level. The Maoist slogan of "self-reliance" reinforced the idea that each administration should minimize "dependence" on support from higher levels of government and this continued throughout the reform era. This has resulted in sub-national expenditures of 80 percent as a share of total public spending, a very high figure,[8] and one that has risen from 52.6 percent when reforms began in 1978. This means that local governments are engaged in strategies to increase transfers from the central government or the next higher level of government or have to find ways to increase their own revenue base to meet their obligations. Sub-national levels of government provide 98.9 percent of spending on education, 98.4 percent on health, 94 percent on safety nets, and 98 percent on environmental protection (http:www.stats.gov.cn/tjs/ndsj/2010/indexeh.htm). Local government finances in rural areas have become even tighter since the government converted all fees into the single agricultural tax in 2002 and then abolished the tax entirely in 2006.

The county level administration is being developed into the fiscal center for the rural areas and it is eclipsing the township. This expansion of responsibility has been conducted under the slogan of "taking the county as the lead" (*yixian weizhu*); spending at the county-level now accounts for about one-quarter of all public expenditures. Most important was the decision in 2001 to shift the fiscal responsibility for teachers' salaries to the county from the township (*People's Daily*, June 14, 2001). The number of respondents extremely satisfied with the performance of county government is just 14.6 percent, with a further 57.2 relatively satisfied. In part this may be related to lack of information. For example, only 8.2 percent of residents knew the name of the county magistrate.

The decline in level of satisfaction holds constant no matter where the respondent lives. Thus we find the phenomenon of declining satisfaction with government performance other scholars have documented throughout rural China, holds true for urban China while the rise in dissatisfaction is not so acute. At the lowest levels of government, satisfaction was relatively constant with the highest level of satisfaction among those living in small towns (68.7 percent extremely or relatively satisfied), 63.9 percent for those in major cities and 62 percent in the villages (see **Table Three**). This was a change from previous years where satisfaction of those living in the municipalities was the highest. Those living in the villages had the highest response rate for those extremely satisfied with the Central Government (45.2 percent), perhaps attesting to recognition of the measures introduced by Hu and Wen to improve the lot of rural communities.[9] By contrast, only 26.6 percent of those living in major municipalities were extremely satisfied with the work of the Central Government.

The second major finding is that, on the whole the level of satisfaction with the work of government has risen across the board since the Hu-Wen administration began, rising to a peak in 2009 before dropping back slightly in 2011. A number of factors caused 2009 to represent a peak. The Summer Olympics and the 60th anniversary of the founding of the People's Republic gave the government an opportunity to promote its global role and national achievements. The national government was also able to use the tragedy of the Wenchuan Earthquake to promote a positive view of its role as did its quick response to the 2008 financial crisis that resulted in a major stimulus package that significantly moderated the impact in China. However, by 2011 some of these positive effects had worn off and urban residents were affected by high housing prices, and all were affected by higher inflation and concerns about things such as food safety.[10] The poor handling of the July 2011 Wenzhou high-speed rail crash might also have had a negative impact. The Edelman Trust barometer showed a drop in 2011 from 88 to 75 percent.

Satisfaction with the Central Government has remained consistently high (86.1 percent relatively or extremely satisfied in 2003 and 91.8 percent in 2011) while for the lowest levels of government it has risen from 43.6 percent to 63.8 percent. If we rank the responses from four to one for extremely satisfied to extremely dissatisfied, then the satisfaction index for Central Government rose from 3.16 in 2003 to a high of 3.41 in 2009 before dropping back to 3.30 in 2011. For township and village government and street committees it has risen consistently from 2.32 to 2.71 (see **Table Four**). The highest and lowest income groups tend to be those that are most satisfied. This would suggest that those with the highest income feel that they have done well under the current system and thus are relatively satisfied with the way that the government does it work. That there is higher satisfaction levels among the lowest income group suggests that they see central policy intent as being supportive of their interests.

While the consequences of these findings may raise concerns about the quality of local governance, they are not necessarily bad news for the Central government. The lower levels of satisfaction might be a potential indicator of social instability but the survey suggests that for our sample at least, citizens do not see the problems as lying with the Central government. This accords with the findings of others that while demonstrations, strikes and unrest may be daily occurrences in rural and urban China, the Central government retains a strong source of legitimacy.

Many would appear to see the problem with local policy implementation rather than with lack of the Center's will or systemic bias. In fact, the incentives for local governments to follow central directives in areas such as environmental and social policy are weak, while there is intense pressure on them to generate revenue often through non-sanctioned fees and levies.[11] However, this set of perceptions holds out the possibility that residents will continue to remonstrate against local officials seeing their actions as justified by central policy intent. In addition, the leadership can draw some comfort from the fact that satisfaction levels have risen over time. The second set of questions turns to look at how citizens view the character of their local officials and whose interests they think they serve.

Serving the People or Serving Themselves: Satisfaction with the Performance of Local Government and Officials

Protests against the unjust actions of local agents of the state have become commonplace in contemporary China and have reached a wider audience through the use of new social media. As noted above, many local protesters appeal to the higher levels of government to rectify local abuse and feel that their demands are justified under national policy. One might expect that there is a greater chance for demonstration and unrest if citizens' opinions about local officials are negative, viewing them as acting in their own interests rather than in those of the people they are supposed to serve. To analyze this, we asked two sets of questions. The first covers the attitude of local officials and their competency; the second asked in whose interests citizens thought officials acted in carrying out their work.

Again we see the same two trends with lower evaluation of the quality of officials at the local level than at higher levels of government but the general assessment rising since 2003 (once more with the peak year being 2009). We asked respondents whether they thought the attitude of local officials when implementing policy was cool and indifferent or warm and friendly and whether they thought that local officials were very knowledgeable (competent) or stupid (incompetent) (see **Tables Five and Six**). In 2011, the view that local officials were very knowledgeable was held by 69.4 percent of respondents, up from 50.8 percent in 2003 but down from a peak of 74.8 percent in 2009. Not surprisingly, the favorable percentage was highest for those living in major cities (82.1 percent) dropping to 60.4 percent in the towns and townships but rising to 65.6 percent for those living in villages. Similarly, there was an increase among those who thought that local officials were bureaucratic in nature rather than caring for the people. In the surveys up until 2005, a majority of respondents felt that local officials were bureaucratic in behavior but by 2011, 41.4 percent of respondents had this view as opposed to 46.1 percent who thought that they cared about people when carrying out their work.

The stress on "putting people first" and attempts to encourage local governments to be more responsive and take care of those in need seems to be having a limited effect. We asked six pairs of questions comparing government behavior that corresponded to concern for ordinary people or bureaucratic behavior (see **Table Seven**). Although dissatisfaction remains relatively high and satisfaction relatively low all the indicators have improved in this category from 2003 to 2011. However, it should still cause concern, as irrespective of place of residence, large percentages feel that the behavior of local officials is bureaucratic rather then being helpful to the concerns of ordinary people. By 2011, the only two pairs where a majority for the perception of bureaucratic behavior prevailed were for officials trying to get closer to those with money and getting closer to their superiors. However, the difference was considerably lower than in 2003. In 2003, all the categories had a majority that saw local government and its official behavior as bureaucratic and self-serving. These results should not be surprising given the results of a survey by Chen Wensheng on the way key township officials allocated their time. Of their time, only 2 percent was spent on serving the people, while 22 percent was spent on receiving higher level officials, 9 percent on economic development and 17 percent on family planning.[12]

Perception of the attitude of officials in municipalities was the most favorable. In all six categories there were majorities for behavior that could be seen as showing concern for ordinary people, whereas in towns and townships and the villages, under 50 percent shared this view for all categories. In the villages, only 39 percent and 38.7 percent respectively thought that the local officials brought benefits to ordinary people and had the mentality of taking care of ordinary people. In fact, in all categories except for bringing benefits to ordinary people, villagers ranked the attitude of their local officials the worst. Interestingly, given the emphasis on eradicating illegal fees and levies and only raising funds in line with the law, support for the view that fees were indeed raised legally dropped in all three residencies in 2011 even to below the level of support in 2007. In the municipalities only 62 percent held this view down from a high of 70.8 percent in 2009, in the towns and townships, it was 47.5 percent down from 64.3 percent and in the villages it was 49 percent down from 64.3 percent. There have been widespread demonstrations and complaints, especially in rural China about the imposition of illegal fees and levies in order for local officials to raise funds to cover their salaries and expenses or to fund their often ill-thought out development plans. It would appear that despite the attempts to stamp out this behavior the practice still lingers and is even prevalent in municipalities and towns.

This sets a challenge for the new leadership that will succeed Hu and Wen. Despite improvement, the policy attempts to promote the image of the government as close to the people and concerned about their needs still has some way to go to be translated into practice at the local level. It is not necessarily the case that frustration with local government will turn into criticism and disillusionment with Central government. However, continued suspicion of local officials' intent might lead to broader dissatisfaction with the Central government if the Center is seen as incapable or unwilling to bring local governments into line with policy intention.

What Quality Services do Citizens Expect Their Government to Provide?

The last set of questions deals with the kinds of services that citizens want local government to provide and their satisfaction with the quality service provision. As noted above, it is the local government that is the main provider of goods and services in both urban and rural China. In particular, since the abolition of agricultural taxes, there has been considerable attention paid to the continued role of township administrations with policy attempting to transform them from extractive to "service-oriented" agencies. However, the result of various reforms has been to "hollow-out" township administrations leaving much of the service provision to the county/district or the village in the rural areas.[13]

One important legacy of the Maoist years was the notion of "self-reliance" meaning that local levels of administration should minimize its dependence on higher levels of government. Subsequent tax-sharing reforms in 1993-94 and the abolition of the agricultural tax in 2006 have added to the fiscal pressure on local governments that still carry the greatest burden for financing infrastructure and providing social welfare. Consequently, a major imperative for local governments is to raise revenues either by seeking transfers from above, hence the large budget for wining and dining,[14] or by extracting finances from the community, hence the large number of protests and demonstrations.

An added burden for local governments has been the new mandates from the Central government to expand pension schemes and the minimum living support schemes, provide free rural elementary education, and to integrate migrants into urban support schemes. These are laudable goals but these mandates are only partially supported by central transfers and the burden on local governments have meant that, on occasion, services have actually been cut or officials have sought ways to deflect the full impact of the policies. In the countryside, policy has been to merge or cut the number of townships and since 1985 the number has halved. However, these mergers have led to the elimination of accessible services since the schools and clinics may be closed in those townships that lose their administrative status. This is a particular problem where the distances are large and populations are scattered, such as in Tibet. In addition, the county still assigns each township a tax quota thus often compounding misguided development strategies that put pressure on them to develop the non-agricultural economy. Calculations vary but it is clear that township debt is significant. More recently, reforms have included county management of township finances and also direct provincial management of county financial management (*sheng guan xian*). The intention is to reduce fiscal management from five levels of government to three.[15]

To date, the main approaches for dealing with inadequate revenues have been two-fold. The World Bank and the Chinese government have proposed improving the revenue stream and thinking about better mechanisms for financial redistribution. Second, there have been a number of proposals for restructuring township government and shifting the financial center in the countryside to the county. In addition to the mergers noted above, there have been experiments to consolidate all the agencies into three to five service centers and transform the non-social service agencies into market-oriented enterprises with services outsourced to them. The management of these agencies could then be assigned to the county level government. It is hope that such reforms would move township government out of extensive engagement and interference in farmers' lives and allow them to concentrate on providing public goods and maintaining public order.[16]

This supports the view that there needs to be a thorough re-think of the role of government in providing services and what kinds of partnerships can be formed to meet policy objectives. A better understanding of how citizens view government, what kind of services they expect and how they prioritize them will help clarify thinking about this changing role of government. Rather than focusing exclusively on the supply side, it would be beneficial to consider the demand side, more specifically what citizens think about the provision of specific public goods by local government and how they prioritize different needs.

The questions relating to satisfaction with the provision of specific public services reveal some interesting insights that are helpful for thinking about what local government could concentrate on to improve satisfaction levels. Generally, there has not been significant variation in terms of those services that the respondents were most satisfied with and those with which they expressed the greatest dissatisfaction. We ranked the responses from four as extremely satisfied to one for extremely dissatisfied. The overall satisfaction index has risen from 2.54 to 2.82 in 2011 but it has dropped below the levels of 2009 and 2007. It is also worth noticing that across all categories for all the years, only nine services have received a satisfaction rating of three or above.[17] Water and electricity provision (3.09) topped the satisfaction list in 2011, displacing family planning (3.05) that had been the top service in each previous survey going back to 2003. The fact that family planning regularly receives the highest rating requires further investigation. When follow-up questions were asked, respondents said that they knew it was a Central government priority and that there was no point in being critical of the service. However, as we shall see below they did not think that it was an important area of work for the government to be engaged in.

The other three categories of work that citizens were most satisfied with were: road and bridge construction (2.93), the practice of religious belief (2.92), and the management of elementary and secondary schools (2.92). When we followed up to ask about satisfaction with government policy on religious belief, especially in major cities, it appeared that high satisfaction levels had more to do with the fact that it was not important to most people and thus they were relatively satisfied. These services tend to be ones that the old planning system was good at delivering and monitoring but do not relate to the new challenges brought about by reforms. There was some variation depending on where one lived but the top two in all places of residence were the same: water and electricity provision and family planning (see **Table Eight**). In villages, medical insurance was placed fifth, presumably reflecting the expansion of the new cooperative health insurance scheme that the Hu-Wen leadership has pushed.

The five areas of public goods provision that the respondents were the least satisfied with in 2011 were: combatting corruption (2.37), unemployment insurance (2.65), employment creation (2.67), helping families in hardship (2.69), and land management (2.74). By contrast, these are all needs or problems that have been created by the negative impacts of the reform program and for the most part are very much household based (see **Table Nine**). Combatting corruption has always been the area of government work that caused most citizen dissatisfaction and in 2003, employment creation, unemployment insurance and helping families in hardship were also in the bottom five. There was some variation depending on place of residence. While combatting corruption ranked worst irrespective of residency and employment creation, helping families in hardship and unemployment insurance featured across all locales, land management was cited in the cities, tax management in the towns and the attraction of commerce and capital in the villages.

Li Peilin (2010) provides some data for comparison based on the China Comprehensive Survey of Social Conditions. He reports on migrant workers satisfaction with a number of public services provided by local government that allow broad comparison with our findings. Overall, in 2008 migrants were slightly less satisfied with public service provision (58.4 percent relatively or extremely satisfied) than with workers in small towns (59.8 percent) and villagers (62.7 percent). This marked a shift from the 2006 survey when migrant workers' satisfaction was higher. The services in 2008 that they were least satisfied with were: the provision of cheap rentals and economically suitable housing for middle and lower income individuals (46.1 percent), environmental protection and pollution control (46.5 percent) and honesty when performing official duties and combatting corruption (48.1 percent). Satisfaction with environmental protection saw a significant drop from 57.5 percent in 2006. Those public services that received the most favorable ratings were: the provision of quality basic education (75.5 percent), good provision of medical and health services (70.1 percent) and cracking down on criminal activity and the maintenance of social order (64.6 percent). Provision of medical services saw a rise from 59.3 percent in 2006.

To analyze our survey results further we designed a simple matrix that correlated the level of importance citizens attached to certain services with the level of satisfaction with local government service provision. This is an attempt to understand those areas of government service citizens approved of and which frustrated them. The five areas of work that citizens felt government should pay most attention to were: combatting corruption (3.43), medical insurance (3.43), social order (3.36), unemployment insurance (3.32) and employment creation (3.3). The five areas that citizens felt deserved the least government attention were: religious belief (2.84), family planning (3.12), attracting business and investment (3.14), tax management (3.15), and cultural and educational facilities (3.15). Again we see a correlation between citizens wanting government to pay attention to services that are related to the impact of reforms and do not see a strong role for government in overseeing religious belief, family planning and for governments to be involved in attracting business and investment.

Thus, when we apply the matrix we get a list that is much more closely related to the social and economic problems faced by households that are a result of the reform program. In 2011, areas identified where government work is unsatisfactory and that urgently need more attention are: combatting corruption, unemployment insurance, employment creation, helping families in hardship, medical insurance, environmental management, environmental health, land management, drugs and medical services, and traffic management (see **Table Ten**). Since the surveys began environmental concerns have risen up the agenda for respondents. Those services that respondents feel are important and where the government pays sufficient attention are: social order, water and electricity provision, road and bridge construction and middle and elementary school management. It is noticeable that family planning and religious belief fall in the quadrant where respondents feel that government do not need to pay too much attention to it.

The general trends are the same but there is some interesting variation between the views of those living in cities, towns and villages. All see combatting corruption and employment creation as important and not receiving enough attention from government. The most satisfied with government service would appear to be those living in the villages as nine of the services fall in the category of high importance and high satisfaction, whereas for those in cities only one does so (water and electricity provision). Not surprisingly, land management is an area of work that villagers want government to pay more attention to. Those living in the cities would appear either to have more gripes or expect better service delivery as they identify no less than fifteen services as being important and requiring greater government attention. By contrast, those in towns and villages only identify five. The healthcare reforms seem to have had an impact in the villages as this is now seen as a service that is important but that the government is paying attention to, unlike in previous surveys.

Concern with corruption is clearly a major problem for all categories of respondents. It is worth looking at in more detail as high levels of corruption are a problem of governance and a symptom that something has gone wrong in the management of the state. Given the regular exposure in the press of spectacular cases of corruption it is not surprising that this is a major concern. It is also a phenomenon that eats its way into everyday life as citizens have to pay for access to goods and services that the government should be providing. The pursuit of economic riches without genuine marketization and democratization and where power remains hierarchically structured with information dependent on position and party membership lies behind the corrupt activities of government officials. In our 2011 survey, only 2.6 percent thought that government and its officials were extremely honest (up from 1.2 percent in 2007), while 8.4 percent thought them extremely dishonest (up from 5.2 percent in 2007) (see **Table Eleven**). The feeling that government and officials are relatively or extremely honest was higher for those in cities (42 percent) than in towns (29 percent) or villages (33.9 percent). All of those showed a considerable decline from 2009. Low-income families had the most negative view of government honesty. The main causes of corrupt activity identified by respondents were with economic management (40.3 percent), construction projects (29 percent), within public security and justice systems (29 percent) and financial and commercial circles (28.3 percent). The least corrupt areas of work were seen to be the armed police and military (2.6 percent) and telecommunications (2.4 percent). Most respondents would probably have little contact with the armed police or the military.

Given the attitude of respondents, it is not surprising that they are pessimistic about the government's capability to deal with corruption. 38.2 percent felt that government work and dedication to eradicating corruption was relatively small or extremely small (an increase of 10.3 percent over 2009). There is a greater sense among city dwellers that government is dedicated to combatting corruption (62.5 percent) and less so in the villages (54 percent). Only 3.1 percent of respondents thought that government work to combat corruption was extremely effective (a further 32.4 percent thought it was relatively strong). Again the impression is worse in villages than in the cities. In the villages only 2.3 percent thought the work was extremely strong and 5.2 percent in the cities and 2.4 percent in the towns. Last but not least, only 6.4 percent of respondents had a strong belief that government work to improve corruption would improve and only 57.4 percent had some belief.

Concluding Comments

The new leadership that will take power through late-2012 and 2013 will inherit a mixed situation. There is clearly much dissatisfaction with the performance of local government and its officials and very few have faith that the government can deal effectively with the problem of corruption. Yet, there is still good will towards the Central government that is not identified with the problems that are seen to blight the performance of those levels of government closer to the people. The surveys confirm the view of others that Chinese citizens do "disaggregate" the state and would appear to retain faith in the central government. In addition, the satisfaction with all levels of government has risen since we began the surveys in 2003. This may give the Central leadership some cushion if it makes policy errors in the future. However, as we have seen in the recent past seemingly stable authoritarian regimes can unravel quickly and citizen frustration can spill out onto the streets. Recently in China this frustration has been restricted to protests against local abuses of power.

Despite improving indicators, there remain substantial percentages of respondents who view the behavior of local officials as bureaucratic and self-centered. They clearly do not feel that the slogan of "putting people first" has become the modus operandi for local officials. Neither do respondents have much faith that the government can cure the problems of corruption and they feel that their work in this area is ineffective. What is also clear is that citizens want government to help resolve the challenges that have arisen during the transition to a more market-influenced economy. Rather than supporting blanket services, they seem most concerned that government help with the household-based socio-economic challenges such as employment creation and unemployment insurance.

It will be interesting to see whether the new leadership will continue the approach of Hu and Wen in rejecting substantive political reform in favor of marginal improvements to make the current system function more effectively. As noted, our survey suggests that citizens feel that local officials are not very effective in promoting the interests of ordinary folk but are quite adept at pursuing their own interests and sucking up to those with money and power. It will be a significant challenge for the new leadership to bring about significant improvement in those areas of public service citizens deem most important without increasing transparency and accountability in local government.

Appendix One: The Surveys[1]

The findings and analysis of the survey are based on the results of a purposive stratified survey of between 3,800 and 4,100 (3,850 in 2001). Respondents, aged between 16 and 60, were selected from three administrative levels: city, town, and village. The respondents were aged between 18 and 60 in the cities and town and 18 and 60 in the villages. At the city level, eight sites were chosen based on their geographic location, average per capita income, and population.[2] The sites varied in all three variables, representing lower-middle income, middle income, and upper income individuals, as well as western, eastern, northern and southern populations of China. Within the cities respondents were randomly selected through the household registration lists using the KISH method.[3] At the town and village levels because of the large average size of families, respondents were selected randomly through the closest birthday method. No fewer than 250, 150, and 100 respondents were identified for each city (2000 total), town (1050 total), and village (800 total), respectively. Consequently, the sample has an urban bias, resulting in respondents with higher age ranges and, in some cases, higher income levels than the corresponding regional averages. In the analysis stage, the results were weighted to compensate for both urban bias and relative population size. Thus, for cities, the final weight for cities in terms of weighting for urban was 0.5008 while that for the villages was 2.6487. With the exception of those in the age range of 16 to 19, the demographic profile mirrors reasonably well the national range.

The survey forms contained around 50 questions, with slight distinctions for the rural and urban to address minor discrepancies in income measurements and employment responses. Interviewers recorded multiple choice, binary, and free-response answers. Care was taken to record respondent demographic data when

[1] Unless otherwise stated the details for all the surveys are the same. All surveys were conducted in the Fall.

[2] In 2003 and 2004 only seven cities were included but in 2005 Nantong was added.

[3] Household area sampling according to a 'face sheet' or table with fractional representation of each adult Kish (1949).

available, such as profession, gender, age, household registration, educational attainment, employment status, private/public enterprise or NGO employee, income range, etc. Professional staff trained and employed by Horizon Research Group conducted all interviews. The response rate was around 80 percent for each year.

The sample, by design, does not include migrants or the majority of ethnic minorities living in China. Using the household registration system does not capture migrant communities. Also, the purpose of this article is to compare the levels of satisfaction with local government and certain public goods and services of those living in urban and rural China. In some cases, migrants lack legal access to public goods and services and their responses therefore create bias in the survey findings. Similarly, ethnic minorities residing in autonomous regions live under varying policy frameworks, rendering a comparison of government performance between regions difficult at best and misleading at worst.

The questionnaire was conducted in the two Municipalities of Beijing and Shanghai and the five cities of Guangzhou, Wuhan, Chengdu, Shenyang and Xi'an, with Nantong (Jiangsu) added in 2005. Seven small towns (county level cities) were covered: Zhuji in Shaoxing (Zhejiang, village--Fengqiao), Changle in Fuzhou (Fujian, village--Changxian), Beining in Jinzhou (Liaoning, village--Zhongan), Xinji in Shijiazhuang (Hebei, village--Xinji), Linxiang in Yueyang (Hunan, village--Zhanqiao), Pengzhou in Chengdu (Sichuan, village—Li'an), and Xingping in Xianyang (Shaanxi, viallage--Pan). In addition, the village of Feng Shuling under the jurisdiction of Wuhan (Hubei) was selected to make eight villages in total.

Bibliography

Chen, Jie (2004) *Popular Political Support in Urban China* (Stanford: Woodrow Wilson Center Press and Stanford University Press).

Chen, Wensheng (2010) "Hou nongyeshui shidai xianzhen zhengfu de zhineng dingwei yanjiu" (Research on the Definition of the Functions of Township Government in the Period of Post Rural Taxes), July 5, http://www.zgxcfx.com/Article_Show.asp?ArtilceID=25823.

Chinese Communist Party Central Committee (2005) "Resolution of the Fourth Plenum of the Sixteenth Central Committee of the Chinese Communist Party," *Xinhua News Agency* Domestic Service, September 26.

Evans, Michael (2012) "China Says Trust in Government is Rising, But Shaky," http://asiancorrespondent.com/88826/china-says-trust-in-government-is-rising-but-shaky/ September 5.

Fallows, James (2011) "Arab Spring, Chinese Winter," *Atlantic Magazine*, September.

Hetherington, Mark J. (1998) "The Political Relevance of Political Trust," *American Political Science Review*, Vol. 92, No. 4, pp. 791-808.

Kaufmann, Daniel, Kraay, Aart, and Mastruzzi, Massimo, 2010. "The Worldwide Governance Indicators: Methodology and Analytical Issues," *Policy Research Working Paper Series*, 5430 (the World Bank).

Kish, Leslie (1949) "A Procedure for Objective Respondent Selection within the Household," *Journal of the American Statistical Association*, Vol.44, No.247, September, pp. 380-387.

Li, Lianjiang (2004), "Political Trust in Rural China," *Modern China*, Vol. 30, No. 2, April 2004, pp. 228-258.

Li, Lianjiang (2011) "Distrust in Government leaders, Demand for Leadership Change, and Preference for Popular elections in Rural China," *Political Behavior*, 332, pp. 291-311.

Li, Lianjiang (2012) "Chaxu zhengfu xinren" (Difference in Trust in Government), Ershiyi shijie yuekan (Twenty-First Century Monthly), June, pp. 108-14.

Li, Lianjiang and Kevin O'Brien (1996) "Villagers and Popular Resistance in Contemporary China," *Modern China*, Vol. 22, No.1, January, pp. 28-61.

Li, Peilin (2010) " Jinnianlai nongmingongde jingji zhuangkuang he shehui taidu" (The Economic Conditions and Social Attitude of Rural Migrant Workers in Recent Years), *Zhongguo shehui kexue* (China Social Sciences), No.1, pp. 119-31.

Liu, Shaoqi (1939) "How to Be a Good Communist," English language version in *Selected works of Liu Shaoqi*, vol.1 (Beijing: Foreign Languages Press, 1984).

Manion, Melanie (1994) "Survey Research in the Study of Contemporary China: Learning from Local Samples," *The China Quarterly*, No. 139 (September 1994), pp. 741-765.

Pei, Minxin (2006) *China's Trapped Transition. The Limits of Developmental Autocracy* (Cambridge, MA: Harvard University Press).

Saich, Tony (2000) "Negotiating the State: The Development of Social Organizations in China," *The ChinaQuarterly*, No. 161 (March).

Saich, Tony (2002) "The Blind Man and the Elephant: Analysing the Local State in China," in Luigi Tomba (ed.), *East Asian Capitalism. Conflicts, Growth and Crisis* (Milan: Fondazione Giangiacomo Feltrinelli, 2002), pp. 75-100

Saich, Tony (2006) "SARS: China's Chernobyl or Much Ado About Nothing," in Arthur Kleinman and James Watson (eds.) *SARS in China: Economic, Political and Social Consequences* (Stanford: Stanford University Press).

Saich, Tony (2007) "Citizen's Perceptions of Governance in Rural and Urban China," *Journal of Chinese Political Science*, Vol. 12, No. 1, pp. 1-28.

Saich, Tony (2008) *Providing Public Goods in Transitional China* (New York: Palgrave Macmillan).

Saich, Tony (2011a) *Governance and Politics of China* (Basingstoke: Palgrave McMillan).

Saich, Tony (2011b) "Chinese Governance Seen Through the People's Eyes," *East Asia Forum*, July.

Saich, Tony (forthcoming) "Political Representation in China," in Chris Ogden (ed.), *Routledge Handbook China's Governance and Domestic Politics* (Routledge).

Saich, Tony and Biliang Hu (forthcoming) *Chinese Villager, Global Market: New Collectives and Rural Development* (New York: Palgrave McMillan).

Shi, Tianjin (2001) "Cultural Values and Political Trust: A Comparison of the People's Republic of China and Taiwan," *Comparative Politics*, Vol. 33, No. 4, pp. 401-419.

Smith, Graeme (2010) "The Hollow State: Rural Governance in China," in *The China Quarterly*, No. 203, September, pp. 601-18.

Survey Sampling (New York: John Wiley and Sons, 1965).

Tian, John Q. (2009) "Reorganizing Rural Public Finance: Reforms and Consequences," *Journal of Current Chinese Affairs*, No. 4, pp. 145-71.

Warren, Mark (1999) *Democracy and Trust* (New York: Cambridge University Press,).

Yang, Guobin (2009) *The Power of the Internet: Citizen Activism Online* (New York: Columbia University Press).

Zhao, Shukai (2007) "The Accountability of Township Governments," *Chinese Sociology and Anthropology*, Vol. 39, No.2, pp. 64-73.

Endnotes

[1] Personal observation would suggest lower confidence in official media but admittedly this is among educated elites in major cities.

[2] This is Zhang Yimou's 1992 movie that traces the attempts by a woman to seek redress of grievance for herself and her husband. Having been mistreated by the village head, she moves to ever higher levels of government to seek retribution for local abuse, all to no avail.

[3] For the limitations and uses of non-random samples in the context of China see Melanie Manion 1994. Manion demonstrates how much can be gleaned about a larger Chinese population from surveys that sample in non-randomly selected localities. In particular, one can use such surveys to discuss relationships between variables. However, it should be noted that the descriptive results do not permit generalizations to be made about the population of China as a whole. For further details on the methodology of this survey see Appendix One.

[4] On rural China see, for example, Lianjiang Li (2004), for urban China see Jie Chen (2004). For the levels of trust in government see Lianjiang Li (2011 and 2012). Earlier articles that have drawn on the surveys include Saich 2007, 2011a and 2011b)

[5] Chen (2004) in his study of Beijing drawing on three surveys from 1995 to 1999 uses David Easton's distinction between diffuse and specific support. He finds that diffuse support was moderately high, although it had declined over the period. This implies that the system still enjoys a basic legitimacy. By contrast, specific support in terms of evaluation of particular policy areas was low. Our sample survey allows us to look at the area of specific support for government performance in general and with respect to the provision of certain particular public goods.

[6] Of the respondents, 80.7 percent had a very high or relatively high level of trust in the Party central committee but only 35.2 percent had the same trust in the village party branch and 53.1 in the party committee at the county level.

[7] This asks about the degree of trust in leaders at three different levels (central, provincial and county or town). Those with extreme or relative trust in the leaders amounted to 85.1 percent of respondents for central leaders but only 67.1 percent for leaders from the county and town level (cited in Li 2012, p. 110).

[8] The figure for 2009 is from http://www.stats.gov.cn/tjs/ndj/2010/indexeh.htm. This figure has been rising in recent years despite Hu Jintao's and Wen Jiabao's increase in government support for welfare and education in the countryside as much of the obligation falls on local governments. This percentage is higher than

other countries in the region: for example in Vietnam it is 48 percent, Indonesia 32 percent, and Thailand 10 percent (Mountfield and Wong, 2005, p. 86).

[9] The leadership under Hu and Wen recognized that some of the problems of social development would not be solved by growth alone. This realization led to the development of a more coherent policy framework based on identification of vulnerable groups that were then provided with targeted support. Policy began to shift from the provision of short-term safety nets to developing a more integrated, comprehensive system. Policy sought to provide greater guarantees to China's rural population and to integrate the growing numbers of migrants into welfare structures away from their homes. Thus, since 2002, experimentation with rural pensions was stepped up, since 2003 there has been a major push to extend coverage of the rural cooperative medical insurance; in 2006 agricultural taxes were finally abolished; in 2007 rural residents no longer were required to pay miscellaneous school fees and free compulsory education was introduced for rural children; and in 2007 the leadership pledged to extend minimum living support payments across rural China. For details see Saich 2008.

[10] A survey by Tsinghua University and *Xiaokang* magazine on trust in government also showed a rising trend. While the level of trust had been 60.5 percent in 2006, it had risen to 67.8 percent in 2012. In contrast with our survey, it shows trust rising each year. Evans 2012.

[11] On the issue of incentives for local governments see Saich 2002.

[12] In addition, 32 percent was spent on meetings and 15 percent on work evaluation. Chen Wensheng 2010.

[13] For an excellent article looking at this trend see Smith 2010.

[14] Zhao Shukai estimates that township leaders spent an average of 100 to 150 days per year on receiving other officials and that the cost of "karaoke singing, sauna sessions and mahjong" accounted for some 5 to 10 percent of the township's fiscal income. Zhao 20007.

[15] John Q. Tian 2009.

[16] It is not surprising that in our 2005 survey when we asked whether there were too many government agencies, 61 percent of villagers said that they should be reduced. Fully 87 percent of respondents in the urban areas said that the number of officials should be cut. The preference was to cut those agencies that were seen as most intrusive in citizens' lives and those that they had little knowledge about.

[17] These were family planning from 2005 to 2011, water and electricity provision from 2007 to 2011, tax management in 2009, and road and bridge construction in 2009.

Table One: World Bank Governance Indicators/Income per Capita (PPP)

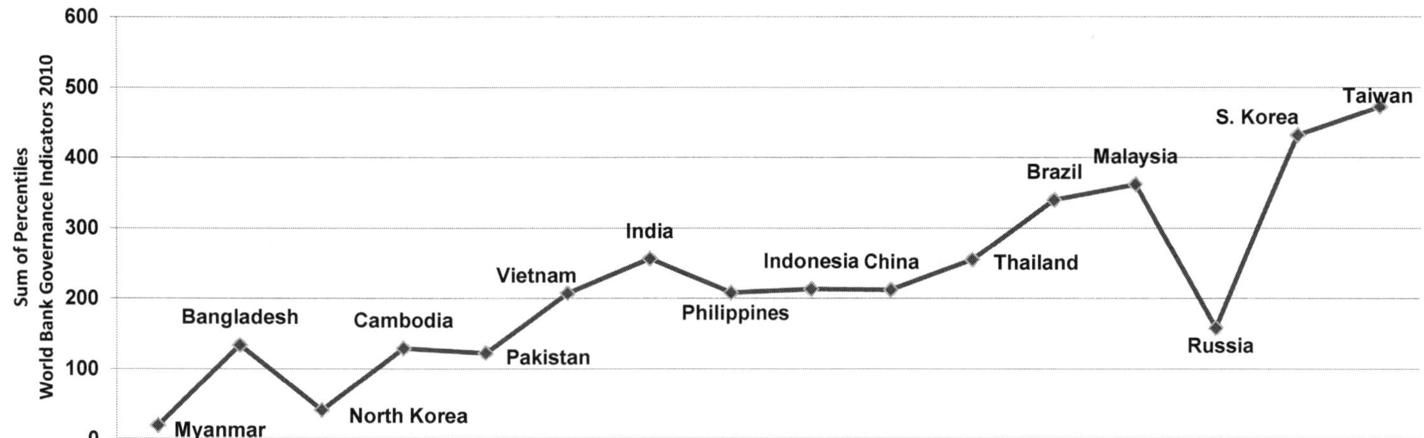

2010 Income per capita	Myanmar	Bangladesh	North Korea	Cambodia	Pakistan	Vietnam	India	Philippines	Indonesia	China	Thailand	Brazil	Malaysia	Russia	S. Korea	Taiwan
	$1,250	$1,600	$1,800	$2,100	$2,800	$3,130	$3,340	$3,740	$4,400	$7,520	$9,200	$11,240	$14,670	$15,840	$29,840	$35,230

My thanks to David Dapice for this table.

Table Two: Percentage of Citizens who are Extremely or Relatively Satisfied with Government Performance

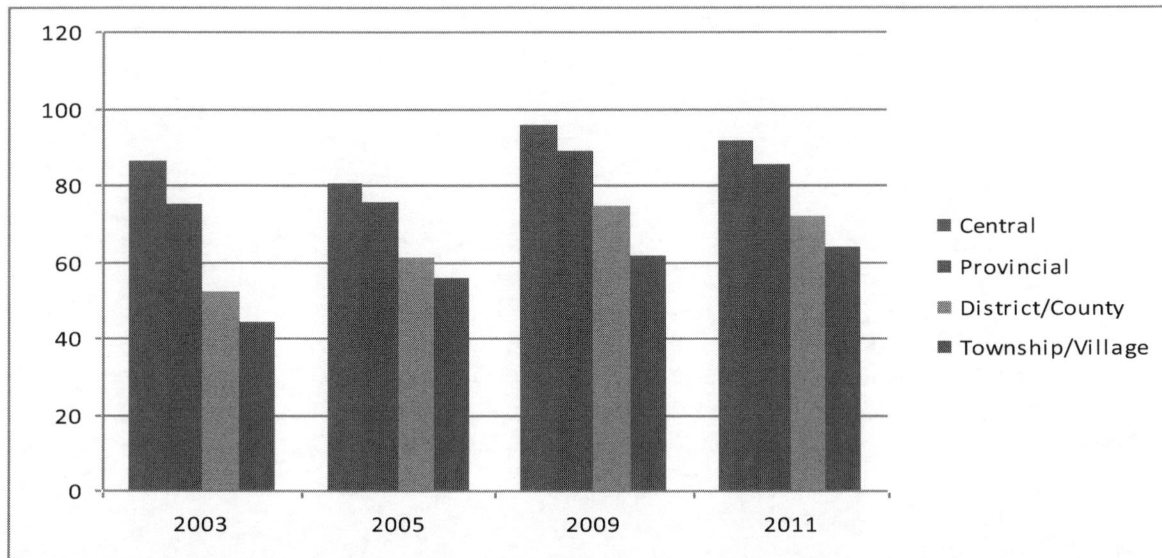

Source: Author's surveys, 2003-2011

Table Three: Satisfaction Levels with the Performance of Township And Administrative Village Government or Sub-Distract Office--2011

	City		Small Town		Village	
	Number	%	Number	%	Number	%
Extremely Dissatisfied	69	5.8%	37	4.9%	152	6.8%
Relatively Dissatisfied	332	27.9%	172	23.0%	617	27.7%
Relatively Satisfied	640	53.7%	439	58.4%	1,127	50.6%
Extremely satisfied	122	10.2%	78	10.3%	254	11.4%
No Answer	2	0.1%	1	0.1%	3	0.1%
Unclear	27	2.3%	25	3.3%	74	3.3%

Source: Author's survey 2011

Table Four: Citizens' Satisfaction Level With Government Work 2003 to 2011

Government Level	Satisfacion	2003	2004	2005	2007	2009	2011
Central	Level	3.16	3.11	3.11	3.32	3.41	3.30
	Change	----	-2%	0%	7%	3%	-3%
Provincial or equivalent	Level	2.89	2.97	3.01	3.18	3.23	3.15
	Change	----	3%	1%	6%	2%	-2%
District or County	Level	2.54	2.72	2.76	2.89	2.88	2.86
	Change	----	7%	1%	5%	0%	-1%
Village/Township or Sub-District Office	Level	2.32	2.57	2.6	2.65	2.65	2.71
	Change	----	11%	1%	2%	0%	2%

Source: Author's surveys 2003-2011

Table Five: Citizens' Assessment of the Character of Local Government and Their Subordinate Agencies When Executing Policy

	2003	2004	2005	2007	2009	2011
Warm/Friendly	39.1	37.2	47.2	62.4	60.1	61.1
Cool/Indifferent	38.9	37.9	32.1	26.7	28.7	26.4
No response	1.3	1.1	0.9	1.7	3.3	2
Unclear	20.7	23.8	19.8	9.2	7.8	10.5
Total	**100**	**100**	**100**	**100**	**100**	**100**
Competent	50.8	47.5	59.6	69.3	74.8	69.4
Incompetent	21.5	21.7	14.4	16.7	9.2	15.4
No response	1.8	1.6	1.4	2.0	4.6	2.9
Unclear	26.0	29.2	24.5	12.1	11.4	12.3
Total	**100**	**100**	**100**	**100**	**100**	**100**

Source: Authors' surveys 2003-2011

Table Six: Citizens' Assessment of the Character of Local Government and Their Subordinate Agencies When Executing Policy By Place of Residence

	Cities				Small Towns				Villages			
	2005	2007	2009	2011	2005	2007	2009	2011	2005	2007	2009	2011
Warm	60.7	72.2	73.3	72.0	40.2	59.8	60.7	52.0	43.6	59.4	54.1	58.3
Cold	23.8	22.4	21	20.7	31.1	33.5	30.1	34.3	35.4	26.9	31.6	26.9
No response	1.2	1.3	2.5	1.0	1. 0	1.1	3.7	2.5	0.8	1.9	3.6	2.3
Unclear	14.3	4.1	3.3	6.4	27.6	5.6	5.5	11.2	20.2	11.8	10.7	12.5
Total	**100**	**100**	**100**	**100**	**100**	**100**	**100**	**100**	**100**	**100**	**100**	**100**
Competent	72.5	82.3	83.6	82.1	53.2	75.6	75.4	60.4	56.3	63.0	70.7	65.6
Incompetent	9.9	11.2	10.8	11.2	13.1	11.1	9.7	25.9	16.4	20.0	8.3	14.2
No response	1.9	1.3	1.8	2.1	2.0	2.3	4.8	4.0	1.1	2.2	5.8	2.9
Unclear	16.0	5.2	3.8	4.6	31.7	11.0	10.1	9.7	26.2	14.8	15.2	17.4
Total	**100**	**100**	**100**	**100**	**100**	**100**	**100**	**100**	**100**	**100**	**100**	**100**

Source: Authors' survey 2003-2011

Table Seven: Citizens' Perception of the Attitude of Local Government and Their Subordinate Agencies, 2003-2011

	Bureaucratic Behavior				**Concern for Ordinary People**		
	2003	2009	2011		2003	2009	2011
Stand high above the people	48.2	39.4	42.2	Method of helping ordinary people	30.9	46.8	47.3
Close to those with money	50.1	43.9	44.6	Care about ordinary people with hardships	28.1	44.2	44.0
Move close to superior leaders	54.0	49.4	45.8	Have the idea of taking care of ordinary people	24.5	39.4	43.0
Act in Line with Slogans	51.2	37.4	42.5	Resolve real problems	26.3	45.6	47.1

(*continued overleaf*)

(continued)

Primarily take care of own interests	49.8	40.3	41.6	Bring benefits to ordinary people	23.7	45.6	42.5
Arbitrarily collect fees	41.3	17.6	31.6	Collect fees in accordance with the law	31.7	65.9	52.4

Source: Author's survey 2003-2011

Table Eight: Top Five Pubic Services Ratings According to Place of Residence, 2011

Cities		Small Towns		Villages	
Public Service	Rating	Public Service	Rating	Public Service	Rating
Water and electricity supply	3.14	Water and electricity supply	3.00	Water and electricity supply	3.09
Family planning	3.07	Family planning	2.99	Family planning	3.06
Road and bridge construction	2.98	Middle/elementary school man.	2.97	Social order	2.98
Religious belief	2.96	Road and bridge construction	2.94	Middle/elementary school man.	2.95
Cultural/educational facilities	2.93	Cultural/educational facilities	2.94	Medial insurance	2.94

Source: Author's survey 2011

Table Nine: Lowest Ranked Public Services According to Place of Residence, 2011

Cities		Small Towns		Villages	
Public Service	Rating	Public Service	Rating	Public Service	Rating
Help for hardship families	2.73	Tax management	2.78	Attraction of commerce and capital	2.68
Employment creation	2.70	Help for hardship families	2.70	Help for hardship families	2.67
Unemployment insurance	2.69	Unemployment insurance	2.67	Employment creation	2.66
Land management	2.68	Employment creation	2.65	Unemployment insurance	2.63
Combatting corruption	2.44	Combatting corruption	2.30	Combatting corruption	2.35

Source: Author's survey 2011

Table Ten: Satisfaction with Public Services and Citizens' Perception of Importance of Such Work by Government, 2011

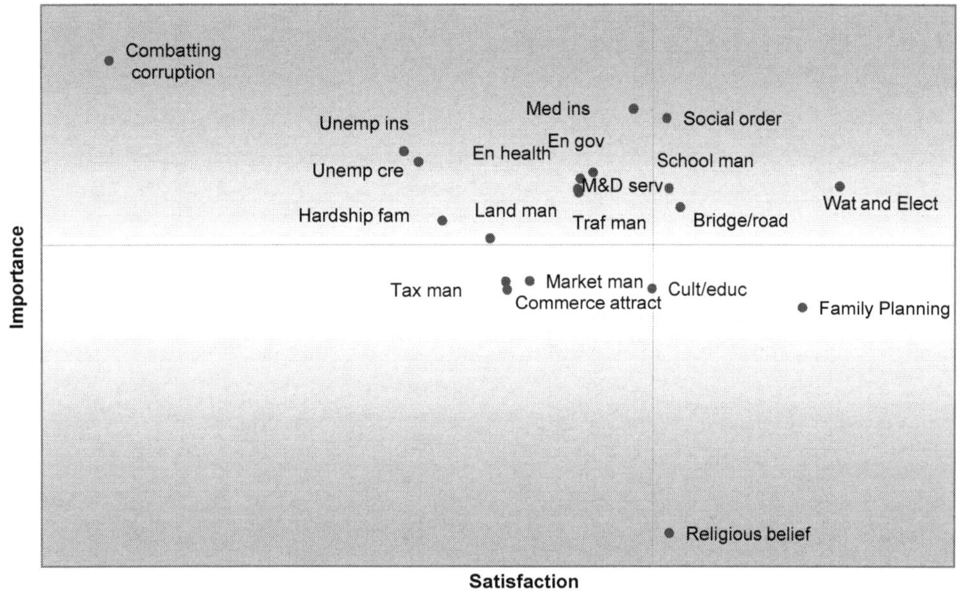

Source: Author's survey 2011
Unemp ins = unemployment insurance; unemp cre = unemployment creation; med ins = medical insurance; en gov = environmental governance; en health = environmental health; school man = middle and elementary school management; wat and elect =water and electricity provision; M&D serv = medical and drug services; hardship fam = help for families in hardship;

land man = land management; traf man = traffic management; bridge/road = bridge and road construction; traf man =traffic management; cult/educ =cultural and educational facilities; commerce attract = attraction of commerce and investment.

Table Eleven: Citizens' Evaluation of the Honesty of Government and Government Officials

	2007	2009	2011
Extremely dishonest	5.2	6.0	8.4
Not too dishonest	41.6	42.8	46.8
Relatively honest	40.1	41.2	32.8
Extremely honest	1.2	1.5	2.6
No response	0.9	0.8	0.6
Unclear	11.1	7.8	8.8
Total	**100.0**	**100.0**	**100.0**

Source: Author's surveys 2007-2011

Part V
Participation and Protest

[20]

10

Negotiating the State

The Development of Social Organizations in China

Tony Saich

One notable feature of the reform program sponsored by the Chinese Communist Party (CCP) has been the expansion of social organizations.[1] With greater social space created by the reforms and with the state unable or unwilling to carry the same wide range of services and functions as before, social organizations with varying degrees of autonomy from the party-state structures have been set up. They have been allowed or have created an increased organizational sphere and social space in which to operate, and to represent social interests, and to convey those interests into the policy-making process. They not only liaise between state and society but also fulfill vital welfare functions that would otherwise go unserved.

Most analyses of the resultant state–society relationship have concentrated on the capacity of party and state organizations to organize and compartmentalize society to frustrate genuine organizational pluralism. The focus has been on top-down control and the binding of organizations into various forms of state patronage. Thus, many analysts have eschewed the idea of an extant civil society in China, although some point to its possible emergence, and instead have provided various tunes on the theme of corporatism to explain state–society relations. This line of analysis seeks to explain how the pluralizing socioeconomic changes induced by market reforms coexist with the continued dominance of the party-state.[2] The opening up of social space can be examined while explaining continued party-state control through indirect mechanisms of coordination and cooptation.

However, exclusive focus on "state-dominant" theories, and even the more "society-informed" concepts of social corporatism or a state-led civil society, risk obscuring the dynamics of change in China and the capacity of the coopted groups to influence the policy-making process or to pursue the interests of their members.[3] First, while the state appears to exert extensive formal control, its capacity to realize this control is increasingly limited. There is a significant gap between rhetoric and practice and between the expressed intent of the party-state authorities, a system that is itself deeply conflicted, and what can actually be enforced for any significant period of time throughout the entire country. Second, such a focus can neglect the benefits the "subordinate" organizations and their members derive from the institutional arrangements. The interrelationships are symbiotic rather than unidirectional. Third, these relationships are symbiotic because social organizations have devised strategies to negotiate with the state a relationship that maximizes their members' interests or that circumvents or deflects state intrusion.

A study of the social organization sector sheds light on these aspects and the complex interplay between the party-state and society.[4] Structures and regulations exist to bind these organizations to state patronage and control their activities. However, social practice reveals a pattern of negotiation that minimizes state penetration and allows such organizations to reconfigure the relationship with the state in more beneficial terms that can allow for policy input or pursuit of members' interests and organizational goals. This chapter reviews the state's strategy for a traditional Leninist reordering of the sector and the strategies of negotiation, evasion, or feigned compliance of the social organizations, and concludes with some comments on the nature of state–society relations in contemporary China.

LENINIST STRATEGIES FOR CONTROL

The social organizations that have been established run across the whole spectrum from the China Family Planning Association, which was set up by the government Family Planning Commission to receive foreign donor funding, to a group such as Friends of Nature that operates as freely as one can in the field of environmental education. Naturally the further one moves along the spectrum of party-state sponsorship toward autonomy, the more vulnerable the group is in terms of administrative interference.

By the end of 2002, there were some 133,357 registered social organizations, defined as community entities composed of a certain social group with common intention, desires, and interests.[5] This is an 18 percent drop from the 1996 high of 184,821 social organizations, of which 1,845 were national-level organizations (1,712 in 1998).[6] This drop was caused by an extensive review of registered organizations in the late 1990s that led many to lose their official registration. In addition, there are 700,000 civilian nonprofit institutions, which are set up by enterprises, social groups, or individuals to provide nonprofit social services.[7] This article is concerned with the smaller group of organizations.

While there is an increasing acceptance of the social organization sector and its further development, senior CCP leaders have made it clear that this is no free-for-all for society to organize itself to articulate its interests. Rather they prefer that the sector be developed within a highly restrictive legislative and organizational framework that ensures CCP and state control. The reasons for this are twofold: the party's Leninist organizational predisposition and the current phase of reforms that will shrink the role of the state in people's lives even further.

Since the 1980s the state has tried to influence key groups in society by binding them into organizations that become dependent on patronage. To head off potential mass opposition, the state will attempt to extend its organization, coordination, and supervision of as much of the population as possible. This is evident in the strategies for control over the social organizations. This move by the state from insulation from society to integration within it can be interpreted as an attempt to prevent a plurality of definitions arising by revising the structure of the regime and the state's relationship to society. In this sense, the state moves to accommodate the increasingly wide range of articulate audiences to thwart or limit the possibility of political–ideological definitions arising. However, it imports varied social interests into the state and, of course, the party. It opens up the party and state to greater influence from society than before and imports fault lines of conflict in society into the state and party.

The natural Leninist tendency to thwart organizational plurality is compounded by the fear of potential for social unrest and the opposition that the reforms have created. There has been a consistent fear that social organizations might become covers for groups engaging in political activities or to represent the interests of disgruntled workers and/or peasants. The phenomenon of Solidarity in Poland remains a very powerful image to many of China's leaders as they grapple with the far-reaching economic reforms and this was reinforced by the fall of Suharto in Indonesia following street demonstrations. Throughout China, a number of underground workers groups have sprung up with names such as the Antihunger League and the Antiunemployment Group. Strikes, go-slows, sit-ins, and rural unrest have become a feature of daily life. Finally, the senior leadership was shocked by the sudden appearance of some 10,000 supporters of the Falun Gong who surrounded the party headquarters in Zhongnanhai and woke up senior leaders for the potential of such faith-based movements to inspire loyalty.[8] This concern and the humiliation that senior leaders felt at being caught by surprise led to the draconian crackdown on the organization, its ban, and the subsequent campaign to discredit the organization. Some senior leaders fear that the vagueness of previous legislation and its lax implementation have allowed suspect groups to register at sporting or cultural events to escape detection and some officially registered groups are said to have linked with dissident and underground religious movements.

Reforms have reduced the intrusive role of the state and have created far greater sponsor social differentiation. With individuals taking greater responsibility for finding their own work and housing, having more individual responsibility for social security and pensions, and becoming consumers in an increasingly marketized economy, they will wish to have a greater political voice, accountability over officialdom, and develop new organizations to fulfill their desires and objectives.

Essentially the CCP is left with a fundamental dilemma. Continued rapid economic growth is deemed vital to party survival but this will entail further layoffs, downsizing of the government bureaucracy, and the shedding of more government functions. This creates the need to expand the social organization sector to take on these functions on behalf of society or the likelihood of social instability and unrest will increase. Pluralism of service delivery is now a fact of life with voluntary organizations supplementing the state in providing basic services and with private institutions in health and education expanding. With many local governments strapped for cash, the nongovernmental organization (NGO) sector is taking on many functions that are being shed. At the same time, however, the party's Leninist predisposition makes it wary, at best, and hostile, at worst, to any organization that functions outside of its direct or indirect control.

Recognition of the necessity of the further development of social organizations received a boost at the Fifteenth Party Congress (1997) and the sector has slowly consolidated since. In his speech to the Fifteenth Party Congress, Jiang Zemin stressed the need to "cultivate and develop" what he termed "social intermediary organizations" as the reforms progressed.[9] Jiang recognized that the key to unlocking the problem of state enterprise reform was the provision of adequate social security coverage, especially for pensions, and restructuring medical and unemployment insurance. The shift of these burdens away from state-run enterprises inevitably requires an expansion of the social organization sector.

The plan for restructuring the State Council that was passed at the First Session of the Ninth Congress (1998) stated that many functions appropriated by government organs be given back to society and handled by new social intermediary organizations. The plan mentioned several times the important role that such organizations could play and Luo Gan, then State Councilor and secretary general of the State Council, complained that the government had taken on too much work that could be handled better by social intermediary organizations. This would allow the government to concentrate better on its core functions.[10]

Subsequently, more ground has been marked out for such organizations to develop. In a major departure from past practice, the current ten-year plan for poverty alleviation explicitly states that NGOs be brought on board to help implement government development projects in poor areas.[11] This trend has been continued under the new leadership of General Secretary Hu Jintao and Premier Wen Jiabao, especially in light of their concern to help those who have not benefited so well from the reforms. In 2004, Premier Wen Jiabao vowed to turn over responsibility for more activities the government should not be engaged in to enterprises, NGOs, and intermediary organizations.[12]

Recognition of the need to expand the sector brought back to the fore the need to tighten regulation.[13] As a result, officials were instructed to push ahead quickly to complete the Regulations on the Registration and Management of Social Organizations, and the State Council approved them in September 1998. The speed took many observers by surprise as severe differences of opinion about the level of control by the state over social organizations had held up the drafting process. The slow progress was also hampered by the fact that noneconomic regulation is not usually accorded high priority in the legislative process.

The regulations provide a clear example of the attempt to incorporate social organizations more closely with existing party-state structures.[14] There are several key features of the legislation that are important for a traditional Leninist reordering of the social organization sector. First, all social organizations must find a professional management unit *(yewu zhuguan danwei)* that will act as the sponsor, and is usually referred to as the sponsoring unit *(guakao danwei)* or "mother-in-law" in Chinese. After finding the sponsor and gaining its approval, the paperwork for the social organization is sent to the Ministry of Civil Affairs or its relevant department (referred to in the regulations as the registration management agency, *dengji guanli jiguan*). This sets up a two-tier registration system where affiliation precedes registration. In comparison with the 1989 provisional regulations, the regulations specified for the first time the role of the sponsoring institution and also raised the requirements, time, and steps necessary for registration.[15] The fact that the 1989 regulations did not outline the details of the duties of the sponsor meant that many social organizations operated in practice with no or minimal interference from the sponsor. The sponsor is expected to examine whether the social organization corresponds to an actual need and will not overlap with other organizations and that its members have the capacity to run the organization. In addition, the sponsor should ensure that the social organization abides by the law and the sponsor is held responsible for the actions of the social organization. Prior to the application to begin preparatory work, the sponsor is responsible for all reviews of the work and it is the responsibility of the sponsor to apply to the relevant department of the Ministry of Civil Affairs for registering the social organization to carry out preparatory work (Articles 9, 10, and 28).

If rejected at any stage, there is no right of appeal and it remains unclear that if a potential sponsor rejects an application, the social organization is free to look for another sponsoring organization. However, in practice, rejection by one organ makes it very difficult to seek approval from another. For example, in the social sciences only the Chinese Academy of Social Sciences may register organizations. However, the academy has been swamped with applicants and does not have the time to review them properly. This leads to insiders having the best chance of registration, while many others will be rejected. Once rejected by the academy it is virtually impossible to find another sponsoring organization. This is what happened to the Chinese Union of Economic Societies that was rejected by the academy for, essentially, reasons of internal academy politics. Each subsequent sponsor it approached rejected it on the grounds that the academy was entrusted to sponsor organizations in the field of social sciences. As a result, the union continued its activities on an informal basis.[16]

This need for a sponsoring organization and its role was the key bone of contention in the drafting of the new regulations and it has remained so since. Reformers proposed eliminating the sponsoring agency and simply requiring registration directly with the Ministry of Civil Affairs. Those who wish to loosen controls have used utilitarian arguments to gain support across the various ministries. They have argued that the sponsorship system forms a burden that costs much time, cannot be maintained properly, and probably would only detect a problem after an organization was found by the police or security authorities to have stepped out of line.[17] They have argued quite simply that the sponsors do not have the capacity to deal with the obligations. This kind of argumentation was persuasive to many ministries and potential sponsor agencies. As a result, an earlier draft that was submitted to the State Council for review abolished the need for the sponsoring organization proposing that social organizations just register with the relevant department of the Ministry of Civil Affairs directly. However, powerful figures such as Luo Gan, were opposed to any relaxation of controls. On seeing the draft, Luo is said to have become very angry and declared that the purpose of the new regulations was to tighten not loosen control over social organizations.[18]

Disagreement has rumbled on and in October 2004 the deputy head of the NGO registration service center under the Ministry of Civil Affairs stated that direct registration would come eventually. This has been a consistent position of the Ministry's in part because of their better understanding of social realities but also because it would strengthen their institutional position. However, they are a relatively weak player and have been consistently overruled by senior party officials in the State Council. The latest example is with the drafting of the Regulations for Registration and Management of Foundations (June 2004). Earlier drafts excluded the need for an intermediary government sponsor but again this was finally rejected.[19]

Secondly, "similar" organizations are not allowed to coexist at the various administrative levels. Thus there cannot be two national calligraphy associations or two national charity federations. This helps control representation to a smaller number of manageable units and has been used to deny registration for some groups. It ensures that the mass organizations such as the All-China Women's Federation and the All-China Federation of Trade Unions enjoy monopoly representation and cannot be challenged by independent groups seeking to represent the interests of women and workers. Conversely, some groups have rejected taking on such a monopoly of representation. For example, Liang Congjie and his Friends of Nature group after waiting ten months on their request for registration received a reply from the National Environment Protection Agency that it could only register if it would take on the responsibility for representing the interests of all the Chinese people sharing environmental concerns. Liang felt this too ambitious a goal and declined. He registered instead as a secondary organization in 1994 with the Academy of Chinese Culture where he is a professor and vice president.[20] It was established as a national level membership group.

Third, social organizations must register with the appropriate civil affairs department from the county level up. This makes it impossible for local groups to enroll members from different areas, thus limiting the potential for the spread of grassroots organizations that could develop national or horizontal representation. Thus, the China Charities Federation, the Ministry of Civil Affairs' own "social organization" for welfare had in 1998 fifty-nine local charity organizations as its institutional members but all are registered separately at the respective governmental levels.[21]

The regulations expressly prohibit national organizations from establishing any kind of regional branch (Article 19). Also, organization names are to reflect the activities and nature of the organization. Names that include China (Zhongguo or Zhonghua) or All-China (Quanguo) can only be approved in accordance with state regulations while under no circumstances can a locally registered social organization use such names (Article 10).

The total intent of this legislation is to mimic the compartmentalization of government departments and limit horizontal linkage. This favors those groups with close government ties and discourages bottom-up initiatives. It keeps people with different opinions on the same issue from setting up "opposing" interest groups. Other aspects of the regulations further hamper bottom-up initiatives or those by the disadvantaged and poorer sectors of society. The need to have substantial assets and the paperwork necessary to register will make it difficult for those groups that lack good connections and a relatively sophisticated organizational apparatus. This preference for large organizations and those close to government is also seen in the Public Welfare Donations Law (September 1999) and the Regulations of Foundations (June 2004).

In addition to the application of the regulations, the state has other means beyond cooptation to attempt control.[22] For groups the state sees as a threat or does not wish to see develop further it has adopted a number of tactics beyond cooptation. The first is outright repression and declaring the group illegal. This has been the case for a number of religious groups and those that appear to have a more political intent. However, groups closed down are not restricted to those engaged in political activities or establishing independent labor organizations. Over the years a number of organizations providing social welfare to groups not officially recognized as having needs have been shut down. For example, in 1993 a discussion club for homosexual men was shut down when its coordinator, Wang Yan, lost his job at the Ministry of Health. He was sacked for allegedly "advocating homosexuality and human rights" and the closure of the discussion group reflects official hostility to the issue of homosexuality in China.[23] Decisions can be idiosyncratic. In 1996, the first home for battered women that had been set up in Shanghai was closed down. One of the prime reasons was that it was improper for an individual to run such an institution rather than the government. The shelter had been set up with funding from a local businessman as an undertaking of his business enterprise. This shows the ambivalence of authorities to the role of both individuals and business in social welfare undertakings.[24] The local government did not take over responsibility for looking after the battered women.

In addition, a Public Security Bureau circular from the beginning of 1997 suggests that a number of administrative measures can be used to stop certain organizations from functioning effectively. The circular proposes three measures: have the sponsoring organization remove its support (this happened to the Women's Hotline in Beijing); pull them up on financial regulations (as with various groups in Shanghai); and identify key members and transfer them to state jobs where they will be too busy to engage in the work of the social organization (this was tried with the leadership of the *Rural Women Knowing All* group).

Finally, the CCP has reactivated the use of party cells within nonparty organizations to try to ensure control and monitoring. In early 1998, an internal circular called for the establishment of party cells in all social organizations and the strengthening of party work in those where a cell already existed. In fact, this circular was only a reminder of party policy. According to the CCP constitution, a cell should be established in all those organizations that have three or more members (Article 29). Where there are not enough members to establish a party cell, individual members are to link to the party cell or group of the sponsoring organization. Even where there is a party cell it is subordinated to the Party Committee of the sponsoring unit and will report to it and receive instructions and direction from it.

STRATEGIES OF NEGOTIATION AND CIRCUMVENTION

The capacity of social organizations to evade such tight strictures and negotiate more beneficial relations with the state derives from two main factors. The first is the declining state capacity to implement policy consistently. The second is the strategies that the social organizations use either to evade control or to turn the relationship of state sponsorship more to their own advantage.

The state lacks the financial and human resources to implement policy effectively. Government revenue as a percentage of GDP declined to 10.78 percent in 1994 before reviving somewhat to 18 percent in 2002. At the same time "off-budget" revenues have been increasing and form a significant part of local government revenues. Successful resolution lies not only in increasing the tax base of the government, a solution explored by the World Bank and favored by the Chinese central government, or squeezing the rural poor through levies and fees, a strategy favored by many local authorities, but also a rethinking of the kinds of work in which the government should be engaged, its relationship to the local community, and acceptance that many functions previously managed by the local state in the field of social welfare and asset development will have to be taken on by the local communities themselves. In poor and remote communities where marketization has barely begun and where the scope of economic activities will always remain limited, local treasuries have little recourse other than the elimination of services. In general, the decision has been taken to downsize government, and social organizations set up by government departments are seen as a key provider of employment for laid-off government bureaucrats. The financial allocations to these newly formed social organizations will be reduced by one-third each year so that they will be financially independent of the originating government department after three years. Inevitably over time these organizations will develop an identity independent of the state and will become increasingly dependent on society and the business sector for funding.

Even where there is better fiscal buoyancy and a commitment to implement controls, it is questionable how consistently and for how long they can be applied. Human resources are scarce. For example, in the late 1990s the All-China Women's Federation was responsible for some 3,500 social organizations dealing with women's affairs. It seems inconceivable that they have the labor power to discharge their duties responsibly.

One of the most popular strategies for evasion was for a social organization to register as a business under the relevant industrial and commercial bureau. Registration as a business operation required a minimal management structure with a high degree of autonomy. However, the 1998 regulations closed off this method of registration as a commercial entity for social organizations as a commercial entity.[25] While the route of business registration has, in theory, been closed off, the most effective way for social organizations to evade restrictions has not. This method is to register as a "secondary organization." In this case, the organization only needs to secure approval from the agency that has accepted to bring it under its supervision. The organization merely deposits a file at the appropriate administrative level of civil affairs but this organ is not involved in monitoring, or auditing the group and does not require its host agency to submit any reports. Institutions of higher learning are the most popular choice given their generally more open and liberal leaderships. Organizations range from the university's own research centers that can operate more independently of direct Education Ministry scrutiny to centers that provide services to the public at large. An example of the latter is a walk-in legal services clinic for the disadvantaged based in Wuhan. In fact, it was the Hubei Civil Affairs Department that suggested this form of registration to the Center claiming it would "make things easier." Such organizations can simply withdraw into the shell of the university if the atmosphere becomes harsher or less accommodating.[26]

Another method is to register as a subsidiary organization within an essentially dormant social organization. An example of this is a very active family and sexual advice center in Beijing that operates under the moribund China Association of Social Workers. A more political example is that of Chen Ziming and Wang Juntao in the 1980s who were able to weave their way through the system to establish both an influential research institute and newspaper. The Beijing Social and Economic Sciences Institute had a strong political agenda and attained a high degree of financial and intellectual autonomy.[27] Administratively, the Institute was registered to the Talents Exchange Center of the State Science and Technology Commission and had been set up by Chen Ziming's sister in November 1986.[28] To obscure the activities of the institute, Chen and his colleagues then set up a number of subsidiary companies and cultural academic organizations. Activities were often conducted under these other organizations. In March 1988, the institute was able to take over a newspaper, the *Economics Weekly*. This newspaper had been founded in January 1982 and was the official newspaper of the Chinese Union of Economics Societies, representing 418 economic entities with over a million individual members.[29] After the takeover Chen Ziming acted as manager and Wang Juntao as deputy editor in chief. It became one of the most lively pro-reform publications in China.

Other groups do not bother with this burrowing strategy but simply do not register at all but organize an informal group. While technically illegal, there are many "clubs," "salons," and "forums" throughout urban China. In rural China, there has been the revival of traditional philanthropic practices that revolve around clans, kinship, and local place association.[30] Paradoxically, the more complex registration becomes, the more organizations are likely simply not to register. Obviously, it is impossible to know how many organizations are operating illegally but a 1996 report suggests around 20,000. This report cites other surveys from 1994 that suggest that Anhui had over 800 "illegal social organizations" and Hubei over 600, while in June 1995 only 13 of some 100 foundations in Yunnan were properly registered with the People's Bank of China.[31]

Last but not least, because this is still a system where personal relationships overlay the formal structures, some groups have been able to use their connections to register directly with civil affairs departments or have been able to receive the patronage of a sponsoring organization even if the proposed activities do not fit readily within its domain.[32] This is particularly prevalent at the local level and it is difficult to see the Regulations changing customary practice.

Many social organizations have also been effective in negotiating the state to influence the policy-making process or at least to bring key issues to the public domain. Three examples are noted here. The first is that of the China Family Planning Association, an organization set up by the State Family Planning Commission to operate as its NGO, what is referred to as a government-organized NGO (GONGO). The second is that of Friends of Nature, an environmental NGO that operates almost as freely as one can in this field. The third is a group of women activists gathered around the magazine *Rural Women Knowing All (Nongjia nu)*.

The China Family Planning Association has provided significant input into state policy innovation. It provides an interesting example of the extent to which GONGOs function in the traditional Leninist "transmission belt" framework and to what extent, by operating at one remove from government, they can open up social space and provide policy innovation. The association was set up by the State Family Planning Commission to bring in international funding from which the commission was blocked, in part by the hostility of the U.S. Congress, and to be a member of organizations such as the International Planned Parenthood Federation. While it is charged with promoting official family planning policy, the Association has become sensitized through its international contacts and grassroots policy experimentation to the needs of women and the inadequacies of the current methods of policy implementation. The association, particularly its local branches, has run a number of innovative projects on problems to do with sex education for young people, income generation for women, and public health education, and raising women's awareness about their rights. Through its pilot programs, the association has affected the government's approach to family planning and conducted experiments to shift from a target-driven, quota-based system of family planning to one that is more client driven, offering choice of contraception combined with education. This is reflected in the launch by the State Family Planning Commission in 1995 of experimentation in five rural counties with an approach to family planning called Improving Quality of Care. This project and its subsequent expansion have emphasized reorientation toward a reproductive, more client-centered family planning program.[33] In addition, the commission has not always been able to control the association entirely and the latter has begun to develop its own organizational identity and ethos. Attempts by the commission to place its own officials in key posts within the association have been resisted and have not always been successful.

Broadly speaking, those groups working in the field of education and environment have been permitted or have negotiated relatively freer space. Elizabeth Knup has noted with respect to managing environmental problems "it is here that rapid economic development—seen as desirable and essential—conflicts directly with other social needs which it finds difficult to address efficiently on its own."[34] Friends of Nature provides a good example of how effective an organization can be when it is run by an energetic, charismatic individual who has a powerful vision of what they wish to achieve. The fact that this individual is Liang Congjie, grandson of Liang Qichao, and has been a member of the Chinese People's Political Consultative Conference obviously helps.

Liang has been able to use his talents, connections, and political skill to steer Friends of Nature through a number of successes. In particular, his group was involved with the attempts to protect the habitat of the golden monkey that was being hacked away by illegal loggers in Yunnan. This was an issue that caught the attention of young people in Beijing and provided the possibility for Friends of Nature to engage in policy advocacy. Students at the forestry academy in Beijing and at other campuses began to hold candlelight vigils for the monkeys. This greatly worried not only the Beijing municipal authorities but also some central leaders. They were worried that the students' peaceful, candlelit vigils might turn to something more sinister but, at the same time, knew they could hardly break up the actions.[35] Friends of Nature began to mobilize public support for the monkey's cause and its members wrote letters and petitions to central leaders while mobilizing friends in the media to publicize the monkey's plight. The combination of social mobilization, media spotlight, and central leaders' fear of student action caused them to adopt decisions to reinforce the ban on illegal logging. Friends of Nature managed to extract a decision from the local authorities to ban the activities to preserve the golden monkey's habitat.[36]

The group of women activists gathered around the magazine *Rural Women Know-*

ing All has undertaken work ranging from sexual health of rural women, to hotlines for migrant women, to raising concerns about the high levels of suicide among young rural women. The effectiveness of this group comes not only from the social commitment of its members but also because a number of the key figures are senior members of the All-China Women's Federation. The key figure in the group is one of the chief editors of the *China Women's Daily (Zhongguo funu bao)*, the official organ of the federation. This has meant that the group can use the infrastructure and staff of the federation to publish their own journal specifically targeted at rural women and to ensure that important policy issues are taken up in the official newspaper. This means that such issues are immediately in the domain of key policy makers with respect to issues concerning women.

CONCLUSION

The examples given above reveal the increasing complexity of the relationship between state and society under the reforms and defy easy categorization. The problem of definition is compounded by the fact that we are trying to analyze a moving target, a state, and society in transition. We are dealing not only with the dynamics of the interaction and how this has changed over time but also with the changes within the state sector and society. What appears in one place or at one time as a predatory local state may evolve into one of social partnership later. We are also dealing with a country where multiple models of state–society relations may be operating at the same time. It is clear that the local state apparatus in Wenzhou, Zhejiang, with its privatized economy and multiple intermediary organizations operates in quite a different way from a neo-Maoist showcase on the North China plain that stresses collective and state organization. As Baum and Shevchenko have pointed out, there is considerable ideological confusion concerning the analysis of the state in China.[37] One can add that a field of study that was seriously undertheorized and parasitic in terms of the theory used is now seriously overtheorized and has begun to strain the imagination of creative word play.

As the example of social organizations shows, while social space has opened up, the state has continued to retain a great deal of its organizational power and has moved to dominate the space and reorganize the newly emergent organizations. Clearly, from these examples, China is far from creating a civil society as conventionally defined. Analyses that rely on some variant of corporatism capture well the top-down nature of control in the system and how citizens are integrated into vertical structures where elites will represent their perceived interests.

However, such explanations risk both obscuring important elements of change and oversimplifying the complexities of the dynamics and interaction. It can mean that researchers pay less attention to the benefits the subordinate organizations and their members derive. What are the attractions and benefits of participation or at least acquiescence with this process? The discussion of social organizations reveals that they can have considerable impact on the policy-making process, indeed more than if they were to try to create an organization with complete operational autonomy from the party-state. The interrelationships are symbiotic. Even for the more autonomous organizations, it would be foolish not to have strong party-state links. Those with close government links often play a more direct role in policy formulation than their counterparts in many other countries as they do not have to compete in social space with other NGOs for dominance and access to the government's ear on relevant policy issues.

Each social organization in China has negotiated with the state its own niche that derives from a complex interaction of institutional, economic, and individual factors. In some cases, the outcome may be a close "embedded" relationship with the state.[38] In others it may entail formal compliance while operating strategies of evasion and circumnavigation of the state. As the political scientist Kevin O'Brien has suggested, coopted groups become embedded over time in the system and through this process they acquire viability and legitimacy.[39] This study of social organizations suggests that it is not mere expediency that causes new social formations or organizations to tie their fortunes to the existing state structures, especially at the local level, but it is strategically optimal for them. It can enable them to manipulate the official and semiofficial institutions to their own advantage.

The study of social organizations also reveals the tensions inherent in a traditional Leninist party culture under the current development strategy. Many organizations have developed strategies to evade party and state controls and to turn the traditional "transmission belt" function to their own advantage. In addition, with the emphasis on economic development, and the shift in the party's fundamental legitimacy to its capacity to deliver the economic goods, the objectives of party and state are not always synonymous. The party needs to effect its policy intent through both mobilization of party members and organizations at all levels and the implementation and enforcement by state organs. Local governments in pursuit of local developmental goals may take policy options that at best conflict with party policy and at worst run counter to it. The party cannot count on state organs for automatic policy support. A good example is with the privatization of state-owned enterprises that is rife at the local level but is deeply contested at the center. Also, local governments will approve social organizations or other nonstate bodies that contribute to the local economy and well-being. This is irrespective of formal regulatory requirements. With a membership of around 60 million, the party itself is deeply conflicted over fundamental policy issues and visions of the future. This causes a tension between the party's traditional Leninist vanguard role and its other roles as an integrating mechanism and development agency. Last but not least it must be remembered that the party is made up of members who also form a part of the local community. Is the local party secretary who is also a shaman loyal to the party, the locality, his beliefs, or all of them? Does he import his social values into the party and if so to what effect, or are they discreet spheres of activity?[40]

Focusing on vertical integration and lines of administrative control while ignoring the way in which the relationship is negotiated ignores important horizontal relationships in society. As government downsizes further, citizens have greater responsibility for their own welfare, and more functions will be devolved to national and especially local social organizations, people will look more to the local provider of goods than the central party and state directives and regulations. This will become more important as the wealthy business class is given greater freedom over how they choose to dispose of their money.

As the historian Timothy Brook has noted, emphasis on the vertical "minimizes the capabilities and opportunities that people exercise regularly to communicate horizontally and form cooperative bodies."[41] He suggests that we should be more aware of "auto-organization" as a more cooperative principle of social integration at the local level. Certainly many new social organizations and loose groups are not registering with the authorities and local religious and traditional belief groups are flourishing. In the urban areas, native place is the main organizing principle for the migrant communities, many of which have set up their own governing and welfare structures outside of the state.[42]

Social scientists tend to dislike open-ended theories and seek to close down the range of options available for interpretation through a process of imposing order and logic. The notion of negotiating the state tries to do justice to the complexities of social reality in China. In the field of state–society relations, we need to develop explanations that allow for the shifting complexities of the current system and the institutional fluidity, ambiguity, and messiness that operates at all levels in China and that is most pronounced at the local level.

NOTES

I would like to thank Professor Richard Baum and Professor David Apter, for their comments on an earlier draft of this chapter, as well as two anonymous reviewers.

1. A literal translation of the Chinese term *shehui tuanti* is preferred here to the more usual English usage of nongovernmental organization (NGO). This includes both the more autonomous organizations and those set up by state agencies specifically to carry out social welfare functions. While NGO is used by some inside the community, it is clear that the restrictions surrounding their autonomy of action mean that in formal terms they are quite distinct from NGOs in the West. China has followed a number of other Asian countries in adopting restrictive legislation to control and shrink the social space available for such organizations.

2. See Richard Baum and Alexei Shevchenko, "The 'State of the State,'" in Merle Goldman and Roderick MacFarquhar, eds., *The Paradox of Reform of China's Post-Mao Reforms* (Cambridge, MA: Harvard University Press, 1999), 348. For one of the most extensive reviews of the potential for the emergence of civil society that is relevant to this chapter, see Gordon White, Jude Howell, and Shang Xiaoyuan, *In Search of Civil Society: Market Reform and Social Change in Contemporary China* (Oxford: Clarendon, 1996). For one of the most

enthusiastic Chinese accounts of the emergence of civil society, see Deng Zhenglai and Ding Yuejiang, "Building Civil Society in China," in *Zhongguo shehui kexue jikan* [Chinese Social Sciences Quarterly] 1 (1992). For an excellent analysis that uses corporatism, see Jonathan Unger and Anita Chan, "Corporatism in China: A Developmental State in an East Asian Context," in Barrett McCormick and Jonathan Unger, *China after Socialism: In the Footsteps of Eastern Europe or East Asia?* (Armonk, NY: Sharpe, 1996), 95–129.

3. The distinction between state and social corporatism is made in Philippe C. Schmitter, "Still the Century of Corporatism?" in Frederick B. Pike and Thomas Stritch, eds., *The New Corporatism* (Notre Dame, IN: University of Notre Dame Press, 1974). For an initial review of its application to China, see Yijiang Ding, "Corporatism and Civil Society in China: An Overview of the Debate in Recent Years," *China Information*, Spring 1998, 44–67. For the seeming contradiction in terms of a state-led civil society, see B. Michael Frolic, "State-led Civil Society," in Timothy Brook and B. Michael Frolic, eds., *Civil Society in China* (Armonk, NY: Sharpe, 1997).

4. The role of the CCP in analyzing state–society relations provides a complicating factor. Many writers choose the appellation "party-state" to circumvent this problem of analysis. Reforms have led to a more complex relationship, especially at the local level. This issue is returned to in the conclusion.

5. Ministry of Civil Affairs, *Zhongguo minzheng tongji nianjian 2003* [China civil affairs statistical yearbook] (Beijing: China Statistical Press, 2003), 132. Examples include professional associations, academic societies, research associations, and foundations.

6. Ministry of Civil Affairs, *Zhongguo minzheng tongji nianjian 2003*, 159.

7. Deng Guosheng, "New Environment for Development of NGOs in China," in NGO Research Center, ed., *The 500 NGOs in China* (Beijing: United Nations Center for Regional Development, 2002), 26. This category includes private schools, hospitals, community service centers, vocational training centers, research institutes, and recreational facilities. As of 2002 there were 1,268 registered foundations (Ministry of Civil Affairs, p. 160). The State Council adopted new regulations for social organizations on September 25, 1998, and new regulations for foundations came into effect in June 2004.

8. This provides an interesting example, as the Falun Gong was originally registered with the official China Qi Gong Science Research Society. The society decided that it was a Buddhist sect and consequently deregistered the organization in February 1997. Thus it had no linkage to the Ministry of Civil Affairs. Its members mobilized when an article critical of the group was published in Tianjin and when the rumor spread that the group would be declared illegal. Among its members were many senior retired cadres, especially from the military, and many women who believe that the exercise regime of the group will enhance their health.

9. Jiang Zemin, "Hold High the Great Banner of Deng Xiaoping Theory for an All Round Advancement of the Cause of Building Socialism with Chinese Characteristics into the Twenty-first Century," *Beijing Review*, October 6–12, 1997, 10–33. Neither journalistic nor academic reviews of the congress and Jiang's speech have paid attention to his comments on "social intermediary organizations."

10. Luo Gan, "Explanations on Plan for Institutional Restructuring of the State Council Delivered at the First Session of the Ninth People's Congress on 6 March 1998," *Ta Kung Pao*, March 7, 1998, B1–2, translated in FBIS-CHI 98-068, March 9, 1998.

11. State Council, "The Development-Oriented Poverty Reduction Programme for Rural China," Xinhua News Agency, October 15, 2001.

12. *China Daily*, March 13–14, 2004.

13. This formed part of a succession of attempts to reassert party and state control over business, society, and the localities that began after Jiang Zemin's speech entitled "More Talk about Politics" in October 1995. These attempts intensified in late 1996 after the Sixth Plenum of the Fourteenth CCP Central Committee adopted the resolution on the need to build a "socialist spiritual civilization."

14. These regulations retain the essential features of the provisional regulations adopted in 1989 after the student-led demonstrations but are more extensive and imply an attempt to control not only activities but also the number of social organizations. The initial response from foreign journalists and human rights organizations was uniformly critical of the controls these regulations place on the sector. See, for example, Human Rights in China, "Bound and Gagged: Freedom of Association in China Further Curtailed under New Regulations," November 13, 1998; Sophia Woodman, "Less Dressed Up as More? Promoting Non-Profit Organizations by Regulating Away Freedom of Association," *China Perspectives* 22 (1999): 17–27. Although the regulations clearly err on the side of state control, they also mark a significant step forward in terms of official recognition that the sector will play in China's future development. On their indispensability to future development, see the comments of Wei Jianxing, then member of the Standing Committee of the Politburo, to a State Council meeting on the new regulations held in November 1998. "Work Conference on Strengthening the Management of NGOs and Supporting Social Stability," *Xinhua*, Domestic Chinese Service, November 23, 1998.

15. The length of time before a social organization can actually carry out activities has been increased from thirty to ninety days.

16. Retired researcher from the Institute of Marxism-Leninism, Mao Zedong Thought, interview, summer 1996.

17. Senior Ministry of Civil Affairs, interview, October 1996.

18. Interview with senior officials from the Ministry of Civil Affairs involved in the legislative drafting process, September 1997.

19. Ministry of Civil Affairs official, interview, October 2004.

20. Liang Congjie, interview, April 1996.

21. Discussion with federation leaders, April 1998.

22. The state has decided to rely on administrative regulations issued by the State Council rather than a law passed by the National People's Congress. This gives the authorities greater flexibility in implementation and avoids an open-ended discussion of the role of this sector. This point is well made by Woodman, "Less Dressed Up as More?" 18.

23. Interviews with relevant personnel, October 1994.

24. Other reasons cited included unspecified "financial irregularities" and foreign and domestic media attention. Interviews in Shanghai, April 1996, and Human Rights in China, *China*, 19.

25. See also the related regulations "Minban feiqiye danwei dengji guanli zanxing tiaoli" [Provisional regulations on the registration and management of people-run non-enterprise units], in *Renmin ribao* (People's Daily), November 9, 1998.

26. Michaela Raab, *Non-Governmental Social Development Groups in China*, Ford Foundation Report, February 1997, p. 26.

27. The sources for this account are Gu Xin, "The Structural Transformation of the Intellectual Public Sphere in Communist China (1979–1989) (Ph.D. diss., University of Leiden,

1997); Merle Goldman, *Sowing the Seeds of Democracy in China: Political Reform in the Deng Xiaoping Era* (Cambridge, MA: Harvard University Press, 1994); Min Qi, discussions with author, 1995 and 1996.

28. Goldman, *Sowing the Seeds*, 66–77.

29. For the details of the takeover, see Gu Xin, *Structural Transformation*, 129–134.

30. Lily Tsai, "Cadres, Temple and Lineage Institutions, and Governance in Rural China," *China Journal*, July 2002.

31. Qi Hong, *Zhongguo shehui tuanti xianzhuang ji falu tiaozheng kuangjia* [The current situation and legal readjustment and framework for Chinese social organizations] (mimeo, 1996).

32. I have come across numerous examples of this in Beijing and Shanghai.

33. In 1997, four urban districts were added and one more rural county. Current estimates suggest that since 1997 over three hundred counties and districts have been selected as provincial pilots. *The Quality Project. Improving Quality of Care and Client Orientation in Reproductive Health/Family Planning Services in China* (Beijing: Ford Foundation, 1999), 7.

34. Elizabeth Knup, "Environmental NGOs in China: An Overview," *China Environment Series* (n.d.), 10.

35. Party secretaries at the institutions of higher education were instructed to monitor the situation carefully and resolve it swiftly.

36. See also Knup, "Environmental NGOs," 12; Seth Dunn, "Taking a Green Leap Forward," *Amicus Journal*, Winter 1997, 12–14.

37. Baum and Shevchenko, "State of the State," 333–334.

38. For use of the term "embedded," see Peter Evans, *Embedded Autonomy: States and Industrial Transformation* (Princeton, NJ: Princeton University Press, 1995).

39. Kevin J. O'Brien, "Chinese People's Congresses and Legislative Embeddedness," *Comparative Political Studies*, April 1994,101.

40. For an analysis of some of the inherent tensions in a Leninist regime, see Ken Jowitt, *New World Disorder: The Leninist Extinction* (Berkeley: University of California Press, 1992).

41. Timothy Brook, "Auto-Organization in Chinese Society," in Brook and Frolic eds., *Civil Society in China*, 23.

42. Xiang Biao, "How to Create a Visible 'Non-State Space' through Migration and Marketized Traditional Networks: An Account of a Migrant Community in China" (paper delivered to the International Conference on Chinese Rural Labor Force Migration, Beijing, June 1996).

[21]

Let Many Civil Societies Bloom: The Rise of Consultative Authoritarianism in China

Jessica C. Teets*

Abstract

In this article, I analyse civil society development in China using examples from Beijing to demonstrate the causal role of local officials' ideas about these groups during the last 20 years. I argue that the decentralization of public welfare and the linkage of promotion to the delivery of these goods supported the idea of local government–civil society collaboration. This idea was undermined by international examples of civil society opposing authoritarianism and the strength of the state-led development model after the 2008 economic crisis. I find growing convergence on a new model of state–society relationship that I call "consultative authoritarianism," which encourages the simultaneous expansion of a fairly autonomous civil society *and* the development of more indirect tools of state control. This model challenges the conventional wisdom that an operationally autonomous civil society cannot exist inside authoritarian regimes and that the presence of civil society is an indicator of democratization.

Keywords: China; civil society; authoritarian politics; policy learning

---

The associational revolution that began in the early 1990s in China introduced the idea of a relatively autonomous civil society, departing from traditional forms of social organizations such as kinship groups and corporatist federations.[1] In this article, I analyse the state–civil society relationships that developed over these last two decades, interwoven with examples from Beijing to explore the motivations prompting government officials to allow the expansion of civil society. I use examples from Beijing due to its status as both the capital of China and a distinct city-province, which means that local officials are exposed to national and international pressures in ways not experienced by cadres in other provinces; it thus serves as both a mirror and microcosm of national political trends. I argue that local officials' ideas about civil society play a causal role in determining the evolving relationship between the local state and groups: specifically, that both "strategic" ideas, such as the material benefits and disadvantages of group activity, and "modular" ideas, derived from successful

* Middlebury College. Email: jteets@middlebury.edu.

1 Wang and He 2004; this term is derived from Salamon 1994.

 doi:10.1017/S0305741012001269 First published online 23 January 2013

international and domestic state–society models, influence the current development of a "consultative authoritarianism" model in Beijing.[2]

Through fieldwork in Beijing and over one hundred interviews in four other provinces beginning in 2006, I find that the "strategic" idea of civil society assistance with the delivery of public goods and the "modular" idea of a "small state–big society" derived from Western regulatory states together have created positive feedback for the idea of local government collaboration with civil society groups. As I explore in the case study of Shining Stone (*Canyu shi* 灿雨石), decentralization of public welfare to the local government and the linkage of promotion to the delivery of these goods generated a strategic idea of civil society development benefiting the career advancement of local cadres. Additionally, this strategic idea was supported by the regulatory state model, such as seen in the US, of a large public welfare role for social groups and a regulatory role for the local state.[3]

However, during the same period competing "strategic" and "modular" ideas undermined this cooperative relationship and advocated more of a confrontational relationship. The "strategic" idea of civil society challenging social stability – the maintenance of which is a vital component of cadre promotion – was formed both from domestic experiences and from the international examples of civil society opposing authoritarian regimes, such as the colour revolutions in the former Soviet Republics and more recently the Arab Spring protests. Moreover, this more confrontational relationship outcome was also supported by the increasing popularity of the "modular" idea of state-led development after the successful Olympics in China, which contrasted with the rocky Asian Games in India, and strong economic growth in China during the global economic crisis, which contrasted with economic decline in the US.

This feedback undermined but did not destroy cadres' idea of a collaborative relationship with civil society. In fact, these contradictory ideas interacted to encourage convergence on a new model of state–society relationship in Beijing, which I call "consultative authoritarianism," that encourages the simultaneous expansion of a fairly autonomous civil society and the development of indirect tools of state control. This model is being used in Beijing as a "social management" pilot and increasingly appears to be the model for a new proposed national law regulating the development and activity of civil society.[4] National ideational convergence on this model of consultative authoritarianism challenges the conventional wisdom that an operationally autonomous civil society cannot exist inside an authoritarian regime, and also that the presence of civil society is an indicator of a process of democratization. In fact, as I illustrate in this article, the expansion of civil society in China is not leading to a process of democratization

2 I do not have the space to discuss ideational models; one of the best overviews is Blyth 1997. Additionally, due to space constraints I only examine the influence of cadres' ideas here, but in other publications also include those of group leaders.

3 Lian 2010.

4 Chen 2011.

but rather to better governance under the conditions of authoritarianism, which in turn is increasing citizen satisfaction with the regime.[5]

The Associational Revolution in China

Chinese civil society has grown dramatically since the early 1990s in the number of registered groups and their participants, from about 400 registered groups in 1986 to over 400,000 by 2006. In fact, despite crackdowns on organized social groups during the 1989 Tiananmen protests and again with the 1998 *falun gong* protests, civil society has grown even more dramatically and diversified its activities since the mid-1990s. Most scholars believe the number of active groups far exceeds the 400,000 registered groups reported by the ministry of civil affairs in 2006, with some estimates as high as eight million registered and unregistered groups.[6] While both foreign and domestic groups have proliferated, the government does not provide separate figures for registered foreign groups. In 1995, Jude Howell suggested that 15 international nongovernmental organizations (INGOs) existed in China, including Médecins Sans Frontières, the US Peace Corps, Oxfam Hong Kong, and Save the Children.[7] More recently, Hsia and White estimate that at least 50 registered organizations have a long-term presence in China, and approximately 150 international NGOs lack permanent registration but fund development work in China through local partners.[8]

Domestic groups are comprised of social organizations (*shehui tuanti* 社会团体), popular groups (*minjian zuzhi* 民间组织) and non-profit groups (*feiyingli zuzhi* 非营利组织) mostly engaged in service delivery and community development. Although the numbers of groups and participants are increasing, most grassroots organizations are understaffed, with 72 per cent having fewer than ten staff and insufficient volunteers.[9] These capacity problems are exacerbated by the lack of funding sources – domestic sources due to regulations restricting fund raising and international sources because most international funding goes to larger, more established groups or Chinese branches of INGOs.[10] Surveys of civil society in China reveal the rapid growth of these organizations in sheer numbers, participation and diversity of issue areas; however, groups face significant challenges with capacity issues and mostly operate at the local level, with only 6 per cent of surveyed groups conducting interprovincial activities.[11]

In addition to concerns about the capacity of this emergent civil society in China, questions likewise have been raised about this emergent civil society's autonomy from the state. The majority of analyses conducted in the 1990s

5 Others have argued that China is improving governance not democratizing. See Nathan 2003.
6 Wang and He 2004.
7 Howell 1995.
8 Hsia and White 2002.
9 Xiong and Qin 2008.
10 Simon 2009.
11 Xiong and Qin 2008.

22 The China Quarterly, 213, March 2013, pp. 19–38

concluded that these associations were not fully autonomous from the state, and operated as a corporatist extension of the state apparatus.[12] In fact, in 1996 an official in the ministry of civil affairs estimated that less than 50 per cent of groups were self-organized, self-supported and self-governed.[13] More recent analyses of Chinese civil society still debate the level of autonomy; however, they reveal more independence among both government-organized groups and grassroots groups.[14] As Yiyi Lu finds, most groups independently locate funding sources, hire staff and run programmes.[15] This debate also occurs inside civil society, and is likewise often expressed in a more nuanced fashion as a continuum of autonomy outcomes rather than a dichotomous category. For example, a group leader contended that he must balance cooperating with the government in return for access to the policy process, with the risk of losing this access if he criticized government actions.[16] Although this is still a contentious debate in the existing literature, many scholars, including myself, argue that over the last decade increasing group activity and professionalization have given rise to a sector comprised of both grassroots and government-organized groups that help deliver goods and participate in policy decisions at the local level, or possess what Wang calls "operational autonomy."[17] While civil society autonomy is not the main focus of this analysis, it clearly is a part of the overall state–group relationship outcome that I seek to explain. Thus, in the rest of this article, I explore how cadres' "strategic" and "modular" ideas of civil society influence the current state–society relationship outcome of "consultative authoritarianism," beginning with the ideas that support a more collaborative relationship with autonomous groups.

Motivating State–Society Cooperation: Decentralization of Public Goods Provision

My contention that a relatively autonomous civil society is emerging in China raises the question of why local officials allow such an expansion in an authoritarian state. In contrast to most of the literature which posits the expansion of civil society as an indicator or precursor of democratization, I argue that the decentralization of public goods and linking of the provision of these goods to promotion generated the "strategic" idea among local officials that civil society expansion might benefit them, which was further supported by the regulatory state–society model provided by Western industrial states.[18]

12 Brook and Frolic 1997; Chamberlain 1993.
13 Ma 2002.
14 Howell and Pearce 2002; Saich 2000.
15 Lu 2007.
16 Interview with director of grassroots group, Beijing, July 2007.
17 Wang 2006.
18 Diamond 1994.

Beginning in the 1980s, the central state increasingly decentralized fiscal policy to local governments under the slogan of "cooking in separate kitchens" (*fenzao chifan* 分灶吃饭). The central government transferred to local governments the primary responsibility for the provision of public goods such as education, health care, infrastructure and social security programmes like unemployment insurance. Consequently, the Chinese fiscal system is highly decentralized, with the central government accounting for only 30 per cent of total budgetary expenditures, and the remaining 70 per cent distributed among four sub-national levels.[19] In comparison, sub-national governments account on average for only 14 per cent of total budgetary expenditures in developing countries, and 32 per cent in developed countries. As Christine Wong notes, this model of decentralization is even more notable because China is one of the only countries in the world to assign responsibility for providing vital social services such as social security, basic education, health care and public safety to local governments.[20]

Decentralization gave local government limited political devolution alongside more significant administrative and economic devolution, and was intended to increase the ability of local governments to regulate local markets and provide public services to society.[21] However, local governments do not possess the necessary fiscal autonomy to meet these unfunded mandates. The central government restricts the ability to tax local populations and to secure bonds or loans through fiscal budget laws, so local governments cannot issue debt and should not run fiscal deficits. Nevertheless, with the demands on local governments increasing while fiscal transfers from the central government remain low, most provinces operate a budget deficit, tax illegally, or borrow using special financial vehicles to fund social programmes through extra-budgetary revenue.[22] This gap between responsibilities and funding represents one mechanism motivating local governments to view an emerging civil society as a source of potential partners in securing international funding and innovative models to bridge the resource gap and solve welfare provision problems.

The experience of decentralization in China has led to the creation of unfunded mandates and high levels of local debt.[23] In addition to this resource gap, the linkage of public goods provision to promotion further motivates local officials to cooperate with civil society to deliver public services. The target management responsibility system (*gangwei mubiao guanli zerenzhi* 岗位目标管理责任制) prioritizes economic targets like public goods provision to evaluate cadre performance and determine promotions and pay. Although there is debate over which performance criteria actually result in promotion, the two most important goals are economic development and social order.[24] When the work-unit system

19 Park et al. 1996.
20 *Ibid.*
21 Qian and Weingast 1996.
22 Li 2006; Wong 2007.
23 Frazier 2010; Cai and Treisman 2002.
24 Whiting 2001; Landry 2003.

24 The China Quarterly, 213, March 2013, pp. 19–38

of welfare disintegrated, social intermediaries became necessary to provide health and other welfare services.[25] As a senior official in the ministry of civil affairs succinctly explained, "The government cannot totally manage health, culture, social welfare and education. In the future China will have a big society and a small government. Social organizations will play a big role."[26] According to interviewed local officials, this pressure to provide public goods motivated collaboration with civil society because officials could access international funding and resources to further their promotion goals and increase welfare in the local community, and if the collaboration appeared to lead to unrest, they could simply shut down the whole project.[27] As one official explained, partnering with these groups opened up a new line of finance with little risk, unlike common extra-budgetary channels such as increasing fees and taxes or selling land, both of which create social protest.[28]

The decentralization of public goods provision corresponded with an increase in international funding sources for civil society groups. Beginning in the early 1990s, international funding agencies and INGOs began to work in China, often explicitly excluding local governments and funding grassroots groups.[29] The World Bank and other international funding agencies, such as the Ford Foundation, wanted to fund development through more bottom-up initiatives.[30] Together this environment created limited space for the legitimate functioning of civil society groups in service delivery as well as raising the capacity among these groups to undertake expanded projects in the poorest areas. As one group member explained, "my organization's role is service delivery – providing services that the government cannot provide. While government investment in health is increasing, the majority goes to the cities – with 80 per cent of the funding serving 20 per cent of the population."[31] In order to take advantage of this new funding stream, local officials partnered with existing groups or supported the creation of new groups, as I later illustrate with the Shining Stone case.[32]

Motivating State–Society Cooperation: the Regulatory State Model

In addition to this "strategic" idea of collaborating with groups to provide public goods, the Western regulatory state model supported this type of cooperation. Beginning in 1979 with the initiation of economic reform, elites engaged in a national debate over developing a regulatory state. The regulatory-state model consists of transitioning governing institutions from a producer function to

25 Howell 2004, 144.
26 Howell 1995, 10.
27 Over 100 interviews conducted by the author with academics, officials, and civil society leaders in Beijing, Yunnan, Jiangsu and Sichuan provinces between 2006 and 2010.
28 Interview with retired health bureau (*weisheng ju*) cadre, Yunnan, May 2007.
29 Mathews 1997; Salamon and Anheier 1996.
30 Sanyal 1994.
31 Interview with founder of health-care association, Simao, Yunnan, February 2007.
32 Foster 2001.

more of a regulatory function, similar to advanced industrial models found in the West. Many Party leaders, like Deng Xiaoping 邓小平 and Jiang Zemin 江泽民, believed that economic reform required restructuring state institutions designed to *produce* market goods to become institutions designed to *regulate* a combination of state-owned and private firms producing market goods. This idea of a regulatory state dominated local policy in Beijing, as well as nationally, during the first 20 years of economic reform. Reforms were initiated that consisted of developing regulatory institutions and policies, building a professional and technocratic civil servant corps, decentralizing fiscal and public welfare functions to lower levels of government, and expanding the private sector composed of both firms and civil-society organizations.[33] As Wen Jiabao 温家宝 – another proponent of this regulatory-state model – asserts, as the state withdraws from its former responsibilities, civil society develops to mediate problems associated with development and globalization.[34]

The regulatory-state model patterned after advanced industrial economies such as the US and Germany supports this idea of a collaborative role for civil society, where the state provides a supportive legal and fiscal structure, and groups provide public goods, mediate social unrest and promote good governance. For example, in addition to a tax-exempt status, the US government supplies approximately 56 per cent of civil society groups' funding, and the German government supplies 65 per cent.[35] The US and Germany, as developed capitalist states, represent examples of China's potential future that many policy makers use to discuss how the state, society and economy might evolve over time.[36] However, while this collaborative state–society model might be the ultimate goal, the methods of transition and process of reform are debated between advocates of the regulatory state and New Left (*xin zuopai* 新左派) models.[37]

Throughout the reform era, officials proceeded with economic restructuring by "crossing the river by groping for stepping stones" (*mozhe shitou guo he* 摸着石头过河), which implies that change occurs by moving slowly from one stage to another after recalibrating the strategy to adjust for any negative effects. Officials also apply this approach to political reform, especially the development of civil society, by encouraging civil society groups to solve social problems without threatening Party hegemony. For example, Wen Jiabao recently called on Shenzhen to serve as a pilot for political reform, and in response local government officials initiated a system of contracting the provision of public goods out to civil society groups.[38] As illustrated in the following case study, both

33 See Dali Yang (2004) for a comprehensive overview of administrative reforms.
34 Sibin Wang 2011.
35 Salamon 1996.
36 I first heard this during a civil society conference at Peking University's Civil Society Research Center, 15 January 2007, and then again at a staff research meeting at Tsinghua University's NGO Research Center, 2 June 2008.
37 Li 2010.
38 See Wen Jiabao and Hu Jintao's speeches about piloting political reform in Shenzhen (quoted in Lee 2010).

"strategic" and "modular" ideas influenced local officials in Beijing to collaborate with civil society groups to provide public goods.

State–Society Collaboration in Beijing: The Case of Shining Stone Community Action

Beijing is unique in that it serves as both a provincial and national capital; however, the local government in Beijing is organized in a similar fashion to other provinces, with a four-level municipal government, local Party authority held by the Beijing Party secretary, and authority over 16 urban and suburban districts and two rural counties. Beijing is one of the most developed cities in China, with 26 *Fortune* Global 500 companies. This rapid development and urbanization creates a multitude of challenges, such as strained social-welfare provision and a large migrant population without access to basic social services. The registered population of Beijing consists of those holding a permanent residence permit (*hukou* 户口) or a temporary residence permit; as of February 2010, the combined population of permanent and non-permanent residents exceeded 22 million, with the latter category numbering eight to nine million.[39] In addition to the difficulty in developing new affordable models to provide these services to residents, a large number of migrant workers (*min gong* 民工) live in Beijing without official residence permits of either kind, which limits access to social services for the migrants and their children. This large population places pressure on Beijing's local government to provide social welfare services such as compulsory education, health care, unemployment benefits, pensions and elder care services.

Beijing is divided administratively into districts (*qu* 区), supervised by street affairs offices (*jiedao banshichu* 街道办事处) responsible for residents' committees (*jumin weiyuanhui* 居民委员会) in communities of approximately 2,000 households. Most residents' committees have six or seven staff members appointed by the street affairs office who have developed various service delivery models as part of the "community construction" initiative. This initiative was established by the central government to encourage local governments to adapt to the rapid changes in service delivery in urban China – including both the influx of rural economic migrants and the wide service gaps left by the collapse of the work-unit model. While Beijing is a wealthy city-province, officials lacked models for service delivery that were not linked to state-owned enterprises, traditional practices of elder care by families, and stable migration practices governed by the hukou system.

This difficulty in creating new service delivery models is illustrated by surveys from the Horizon Research Group for 2003 to 2005, which revealed that the majority of Beijing residents are not satisfied with government service, primarily due to an overly bureaucratic approach to welfare, and a "one size fits all" model that does not actually address existing problems.[40] In response to these problems

39 *China Daily* 2010.
40 Saich 2007.

providing social-welfare services to vulnerable communities in Beijing, domestic and international groups initiated projects to provide many of these services. Local officials allowed the proliferation of these projects at the lowest levels of administration in order to test innovative international models piloted by the groups, and this successful collaboration reinforced the idea of civil society mediating social problems, as advocated by the advanced industrial state model.

One of these groups, Shining Stone Community Action (SSCA), uses a community-participation model to deliver services to migrant communities in the Beijing suburbs, and contends that public participation in China's municipal affairs will increase citizen satisfaction as the government involves citizens in the provision of social services as partners of the local government, thereby giving them some influence in selecting types of services.[41] The founder of Shining Stone, Song Qinghua 宋庆华, joined one of China's original NGOs, Global Village of Beijing, in 1997 to encourage recycling. Five years later, Song formed Shining Stone Community Action, registering it initially as a consulting company due to difficulty receiving permission to register as a civil society group. The group's aim is to develop urban community capacity to sustain participatory governance, and it has received a number of international grants to operate these projects. For example, Shining Stone initiated training programmes for street affairs office staff in Beijing with a grant from the Ford Foundation in 2002. After working in Beijing for seven years, the group was allowed to register as nonprofit in 2009, and currently has seven full-time staff.

Addressing service delivery to the growing migrant population in Beijing, Shining Stone partnered with the Qingyuan 清源 street office to initiate a pilot project in 2007. This office supervises 28 neighbourhoods with a total of 110,000 registered residents and 20,000 migrant workers. Each neighbourhood has its own residents' committee responsible for household registration, public safety, enforcement of the one-child policy, and services for the elderly, disabled and unemployed. SSCA worked with the residents' committees to train government officials and residents in participative methods and project management skills.[42] Next, using these skills, the participants jointly identified services that were needed and designed a pilot programme to create participatory mechanisms to solve future problems cooperatively. The Qingyuan street office funded promising projects that were suggested by participants, such as a training centre for migrants employed as domestic helpers and a cultural association run by the participating residents and members of the residents' committees. These SSCA-proposed projects assist the residents' committees in meeting the social innovation requirement, outlined by the municipal government, of each committee implementing at least one such civic project by 2010. Many of the projects implemented with Shining Stone assistance address service-delivery problems with either elderly or migrant residents, such as library and kindergarten

41 Shining Stone Community Action website, www.communityaction.org.cn.
42 Geisselmann and Warmer 2009.

28 The China Quarterly, 213, March 2013, pp. 19–38

programmes for migrant children, community dinners where pensioners can buy a meal for less than one yuan, and training courses for migrants in urban skills such as learning how to use ATM machines.

In the past, urban and community development was strictly controlled by the local government without the participation of community members. However, after the collapse of the former model of welfare delivery, municipal officials are uncertain how to adopt new models of service delivery without being overwhelmed by citizen dissatisfaction as soon as they open channels for participation.[43] Additionally, local officials and residents lack practical experience with policy participation. Shining Stone's pilot programmes in Beijing help local officials manage the transition from former service delivery models to a new participatory model based on practices in advanced industrial states, without generating a flood of social unrest and public grievances.[44] Through its extensive training programmes, SSCA promotes a new understanding of the roles of both state and civil-society actors. According to this model of service delivery, local officials no longer provide all necessary services or use a "one-size" plan, but instead fund and supervise projects proposed and run cooperatively by residents and committees. This collaboration allows committees and community leaders to help the local state mediate between various interests, and does not treat participation as "mass mobilization" in the way that previous models calling for public participation did. In this way, Shining Stone's pilot programme in Qingyuan created positive collaborative experiences for local officials and a model for other communities to follow, both of which reinforce the idea of civil society partnering with the state to mediate social problems.

In addition to creating a stable path for transition to new social welfare models, Shining Stone's projects in Beijing improve local governance, which also positively reinforces the idea of collaborating with civil society. For example, as the Horizon surveys found, many residents view the residents' committees and street offices as intervening in their private affairs and acting in an arbitrary manner with little concern for their needs. The committees often do not investigate diverse needs across communities and use the same programmes in communities with different needs, leading to non-cooperation and occasional outbreaks of protest on the part of displeased residents. As SSCA's founder notes, uniform welfare provision presupposes that every neighbourhood has identical needs, yet this is simply incorrect.[45] For example, she finds that in contrast to poorer areas, families in richer neighbourhoods have books at home so library use is negligible, thus government funding would be better spent meeting needs identified by the residents rather than providing a library in every community.

Services identified and provided by residents after deliberation with committees and street offices offer better local governance because residents, being

43 Interview with ministry of civil affairs official, Beijing, January 2007.
44 Interview with Beijing municipal representative, Beijing, June 2010.
45 Young and Qian 2006.

directly affected by welfare provision, stress quality and efficiency and understand the local context and needs. As Song finds, "The other day the staff in one neighbourhood were discussing how, when they have to announce a new decision or policy, if they just put up posters (*tongzhi* 通知) to communicate this, people always criticize and complain. But if they hold a meeting to explain and discuss changes with the community, people usually see the point and are supportive, and there is less conflict."[46] In addition to satisfied citizens, local officials gain recognition from supervisors through "innovation awards" that many provincial governments award to encourage policy innovation at lower levels. These innovations can then be tested and disseminated by provincial leaders. For example, in Beijing, one district official who partnered with Shining Stone in order to develop a new model for integrating migrant families into their new communities won an "innovation in governance" award with a cash reward and recognition from the municipal government.[47] This experience reinforces officials' idea of civil society partnering with the local state to mediate development and globalization problems, such as urbanization.

Shining Stone's successful collaboration with street offices and residents' committees in Beijing supports the regulatory-state model whereby civil society assists the state in mitigating social problems through innovation difficult for the state to achieve without public participation. Song argues that collaboration has changed many officials' ideas of service delivery and more broadly of the role of civil society from the early 1990s: "Some people at the very top understand the need for this, but local government is more generally populated by bureaucrats operating on remote control. Many Chinese officials have their own idea of citizen participation: "We decide, you participate."[48] After the first pilot projects in Beijing in 2002, Shining Stone's model of service delivery spread to other provinces. Throughout 2003, the group trained cadres and community workers across 26 urban communities in Beijing and 22 in Wuhan with funding support from the Ford Foundation, and then trained local officials in Tianjin, Nanjing, and Shanghai with funding from the ministry of civil affairs. In late 2006, Shining Stone secured funding from Oxfam Hong Kong to support a programme to help migrant communities develop a plan for future development in Chengdu, Nanchang and Ningbo.

As illustrated in this brief case study, the participatory model of service coordination advocated by Shining Stone improves community welfare provision in Beijing, and creates a new model of service delivery. This new model is based on state–society co-production of public goods, and as discussed further in the conclusion, has quickly been adopted by other local governments.[49] However, as I discuss in the following section, both the strategic and modular ideas supporting state–society collaboration were challenged by competing ideas of

46 *Ibid.*
47 Interview with staff member of Shining Stone, Beijing, June 2008.
48 Young and Qian 2006.
49 Jing and Savas 2009.

30 The China Quarterly, 213, March 2013, pp. 19–38

civil society as a threat to single-party rule and the success of a state-led model in the wake of the global economic crisis and the colour revolutions in the post-Soviet Republics.

Undermining State–Society Cooperation: Stability Maintenance and Colour Revolutions

As illustrated by the Shining Stone case, collaboration with civil society helps local officials solve development issues and improve governance; however, officials must balance these benefits with social stability concerns. The target management responsibility system prioritizes *both* economic development and social order goals for officials. Concerns with social stability, or perceived anti-state activities, permeate the Party leadership and all levels of government in Beijing. Statistics illustrate growing numbers of "mass incidents" such as demonstrations, protests and riots throughout the 2000s – totaling 87,000 in 2006, an increase of 6.6 per cent from 2005.[50] Since 2008, central government officials have expressed rising concern about protests in the minority areas of both Tibet and Xinjiang in western China, and local officials in Beijing worry about the possibility that growing income gaps and unemployment among the migrant population and recent college graduates might trigger increasing unrest.[51] In fact, the most recent national budget showed more spending on "stability maintenance" than any other category, including public goods, and equivalent to national defence.[52] Thus social stability is the paramount goal of the Party leadership, with "instability" broadly defined as social unrest which might threaten economic development and the Party's political hegemony.[53]

The ability of civil society organizations to mobilize citizen action against the state is well understood in Beijing after the colour revolutions and the Arab Spring, and local officials must balance the benefits of partnership with concerns about social mobilization and instability. The confrontational role played by civil society groups in the colour revolutions during the 2000s reinforces desire for more state control over group activity. As Deyong Yin notes, a constant concern of the Chinese government is that NGOs supported by governments of Western countries may subvert the rule of the Chinese Communist Party through "peaceful transformation"; this concern encourages officials to pay particular attention to groups with funding from overseas foundations or foreign NGOs, to prevent a colour revolution in China.[54] As one staff member of a Beijing group noted, "After the colour revolutions government officials have frequently visited our office and invited me to have tea to discuss the goals and strategies of the group."[55] She

50 Tanner 2004.
51 Ford 2009.
52 Tsinghua University report, cited in *New York Times* 2010.
53 Interview with faculty member of Central Party School, Beijing, June 2007.
54 Yin 2009.
55 Interview with staff member of domestic NGO, Beijing, February 2007.

contends that the colour revolutions led local officials to attempt to learn about all unregistered groups' "intentions and organizational structure."[56] With increasing unemployment in both migrant and recent graduate populations in Beijing, local officials fear the ability of civil society groups to mobilize and link these populations, as seen in the youth movements during the colour revolutions. In fact, President Hu Jintao issued a joint declaration with President Putin where he stated that the imposition of "alien models of social and political systems" was deemed "inadmissible," and suggested that the Belarusian strategy of crushing potential social mobilization was the way to maintain stability.[57] Most recently, the Beijing government responded to suggestions in online chat rooms that there be a "Jasmine Revolution" modeled after the Arab Spring protests by closing several civil society groups, arresting known dissidents and physically repressing any large gatherings in the city.[58] This response illustrates the "strategic" idea held by many officials that civil society is not a partner and in fact may mobilize society to oppose an authoritarian regime, which challenges the idea that the local state should collaborate with these groups to coproduce goods.

Undermining State–Society Cooperation: the Successful State-Led Model

In addition to fears of instability, the successful 2008 Beijing Olympics and weathering of the global economic crisis generated feedback undermining the idea of collaborating with civil society. In fact, the ability of local officials to hold the Olympics despite international and domestic "disruptions," and to maintain strong economic growth despite a global economic crisis, increased the prominence of ideas that imagined a larger, more active state role than under the regulatory-state idea, which was delegitimized by the decline in the US economy during the economic crisis. Since 2008, many officials have discussed the "rise" of China and "decline" of the US as evidence of the superiority of a state-led model.[59] In Beijing, the local economy was not as tied to exports as the coastal cities in the south, and thus felt less of a manufacturing impact. Instead it suffered the decline of the construction sector and hiring freezes by multi-national corporations, which disproportionately affected migrants and recent college graduates. After central and local officials implemented a stimulus package, Beijing experienced a surge in consumer sales and a slow resurgence in building. In fact, local GDP increased by 10 per cent in 2009. In response to these successes on the part of state leadership, the New Left idea of the superiority of a state-led model challenged the hegemony of the regulatory-state idea.[60]

56 *Ibid.*
57 *TASS* 2005.
58 Jacobs 2011.
59 Jisi Wang 2011.
60 Mishra 2006.

New Left ideology is characterized by an emphasis on the state's power to redress the problems of injustice and other negative effects of privatization, marketization and globalization. Following the Marxist tradition, New Left theorists believe that the capitalist mode of production is grounded in exploitation, and that a civil society developed under capitalism is simply a vehicle for ensuring the dominance of capitalist interest groups.[61] Thus, the New Left advocates the development of new state-controlled mechanisms for participation, and distrusts current civil society in China as representing dominant capitalist interests at the expense of social justice. However, New Left ideas differ from Maoist ideology, where civil society was incorporated into the state, in instead promoting state guidance of fairly independent civil society to help the state meet goals coupled with strict controls on groups that attempt to promote special interests or pursue a role outside of the one envisioned by the state. In fact, the head of the ministry of civil affairs policy office recently published an article calling for state guidance of autonomous groups to avoid the "bad" civil society seen in many Western countries.[62]

While New Left ideas were gaining in popularity, the perceived failure of the US-style regulatory model has greatly undermined neoliberal reformers in China who would like to see a more complete dismantling of the state-owned sector and rise of non-state actors such as civil society.[63] The rising influence of the New Left in the "harmonious society" policies adopted in 2005 illustrates the ideational challenge to the regulatory-state ideas of the 1990s.[64] Thus, events in the last decade undermined the idea of civil society as a partner advocated by both the Western regulatory-state model and successful collaboration experiences such as with Shining Stone. The interaction of these conflicting ideas created a new state–civil society model which simultaneously allows for the expansion of relatively autonomous groups *and* the development of indirect state control mechanisms.

The Rise of "Consultative Authoritarianism"

These strategic and modular ideas influenced the development of a new model of state–society relationship, what I call "consultative authoritarianism," which merges the regulatory-state idea of a relatively autonomous civil society collaborating with the state to solve social problems with the New Left idea of state guidance of groups to protect society from narrow interest groups and social instability. This model is characterized by two main aspects – a pluralistic society participating in policy formation and implementation, and the use of multiple indirect tools of state control. As I explain below, while the goals of this

61 Hui Wang 2001, 185.
62 Zhou 2011.
63 Bo and Chen 2009.
64 Huang 2011; He Li 2010.

consultative authoritarianism are the same, the social pluralism and differentiated state control present in this model distinguish it from earlier corporatist models.

The first distinctive characteristic of this new corporatist model is the existence of officially tolerated social pluralism. Unlike the corporatist model described by Jean Oi, groups no longer serve as appendages to the state, but possess independent staff, resources and projects.[65] In fact, Jude Howell finds that most groups receive little government funding other than perhaps free office space; the majority of groups were started voluntarily from below, although some also involved officials in activities in order to informally access resources and contacts, enhance the prestige of the organization and gain political protection for activities.[66] Groups are required to register with the ministry of civil affairs and a supervisory agency, but these regulations have not substantially limited the expansion of civil society in China to date. Attempts to restrict the space and range of organizational activity through registration have turned into a "facade of monopoly."[67] For the most part, these groups establish independent projects and strategies, and any cooperation with local government is due to mutual recognition of comparative advantage: "We [the Yunnan Reproductive Health Association] need a government network, like the women's federation, for this makes our work convenient. It helps us to organize a focus group discussion or visit households. So there is a cooperative relationship."[68] Local government often collaborates with unregistered groups, as the SSCA example illustrates. As Wang finds, these groups possess operational autonomy.[69]

Additionally, there is more pluralism in this model than offered under corporatism, with multiple groups competing inside one policy space or region. Under the corporatist model, the state only recognizes one organization, such as the women's federation, as the sole representative of the interests of the individuals or businesses comprising that organization's constituency. It is only through this channel that incorporated organizations may participate in the policy-making process to help implement policy for the government. This former model of corporatism limits the number of actors participating in the policy process and thus controls the actions of the members. However, since the early 2000s, multiple groups representing the same constituency in a region have proliferated, and some groups such as environmental NGOs increasingly link members across the country through online forums and resources.[70] These groups and practices have proliferated to such as extent that the director of one group engaged in linking civil society actors across regions argues that the official federations now view grassroots groups as policy and resource

65 Oi 1992; Chan and Unger 1995.
66 Howell 2004, 157.
67 Howell 2004, 158.
68 Cited in Howell 2004, 159; interview with Federation staff, Yunnan, June 2007.
69 Wang 2006.
70 Ho 2001.

34 The China Quarterly, 213, March 2013, pp. 19–38

competitors.[71] These groups also participate in the whole process of policy making including policy formation, and no longer just in policy implementation as seen with the former federation model.[72]

The second distinctive characteristic of this new model is the type of control mechanisms used by the state. These mechanisms are called "differentiated control" by Kang Xiaoguang 康晓光, who finds that the state increasingly uses more sophisticated and indirect methods to create positive and negative incentives encouraging groups to work toward meeting state goals.[73] The example of a group called 1KG More (*Duobei yi gongjin* 多背一公斤) illustrates the positive incentives used under the consultative authoritarianism framework.[74] The founder of this grassroots group set up an online network on QQ to coordinate between needy rural schools and potential urban donors. Since 2004, thousands of urban citizens have participated in 1KG More's network by carrying a kilogram of books or other school supplies in their luggage to distribute to children in the impoverished rural areas they visit, and at the same time to share information on the website about the condition of rural schools.

This group helps the local government in Beijing and two other provinces address problems with income inequality between rural and urban areas, such as gaps between rural and urban education. According to the group's founder, "By combining travel with doing good, we hope to change the reality of the imbalance of education between rural and urban areas in China. Although enrolment in higher education is increasing, the proportion continuing their studies in rural areas is far lower, and education standards are much poorer."[75] Since 2004, when the network started, ten thousand 1KG More "volun-tourists" have collected detailed data on over 600 rural schools, distributed books and stationery benefitting at least one million people, and developed new sites representing almost all major Chinese cities.

1KG More initially earned its income by offering corporate social responsibility consulting to businesses; however, the Beijing municipal government recently supported this network as a way to encourage a charity approach to help rural schools by using three main positive incentives – social incubators, government grants and new registration laws. The Beijing municipal government funds a privately-run incubator programme, the Non-Profit Incubator (NPI) established by Lü Zhao 吕朝 in 2006, which trained 1KG More staff members in professional project management, auditing and accounting skills and grant writing.[76] Additionally, the municipal government eased registration regulations for selected groups (which now only require registration with the local bureau of civil affairs and no longer require a supervisory agency) and also initiated a grants programme

71 Interview with director of civil society group, Beijing, July 2007.
72 Mertha 2009.
73 Han and Kang 2005; interview with Kang Xiaoguang, Beijing, July 2010.
74 Interview with head of a capacity-building group working with 1KG More, Beijing, June 2010.
75 1KG More website: http://1kg.blogbus.com/.
76 Interview with Fudan University professor, Shanghai, July 2010.

in 2010 of 300 million yuan (US$44 million) to fund groups proposing social innovation projects. The grants and incubation experience allowed 1KG More to expand into physical offices in Beijing and Guangzhou. These positive incentives "guide" groups toward areas in which the local state would like to see them working, such as social innovation to solve welfare-provision problems.

However, this model also uses negative incentives, as evidenced in the example of the INGO Oxfam. Oxfam successfully partnered with many local governments to undertake poverty alleviation programmes; however, when it attempted to link together college student volunteers with migrant workers in Beijing – two sensitive populations, given high unemployment rates – the ministry of education instructed all Beijing universities to stop collaborating with Oxfam.[77] Oxfam was allowed to continue operating its poverty alleviation programmes including those with migrant populations, but *indirect* control mechanisms such as cutting off the supply of student volunteers were used to "guide" the group back onto a more service-oriented path and away from anything potentially disruptive of social order. Oxfam closed down this programme due to lack of student volunteers, which illustrates the more nuanced and indirect tools of state control that local officials use to balance the strategic ideas of meeting development goals and maintaining social order. Unlike the former model of corporatism, autonomous civil society groups are expanding in size, scope and significance; however, government control over these groups, while still present, is increasingly nuanced. As these examples illustrate, competing ideas among local officials in Beijing – about the perceived benefits and dangers of this emergent civil society and about which type of state model to follow – influence the development of this new model of consultative authoritarianism.

Although variation still exists across provinces and over time in the degree of collaboration or confrontation found in local state–civil society relationships, there is increasing evidence of a national convergence on this model as seen in the use of the Beijing model of "social management" to develop new national regulations for civil society by 2012. As the minister of civil affairs recently announced, "The ministry will take Beijing's experiences as reference and promote them, but the steps will not be as wide-ranging as Beijing's."[78] Thus this consultative authoritarianism model might be adopted nationally as early as next year and serve to promote the growth of operationally autonomous groups and further indirect social controls.

Implications of Consultative Authoritarianism: Better Governance under CCP Rule

While this article primarily relied on examples from Beijing, these local officials serve as both a mirror and microcosm of political trends occurring nationally.

77 Interview with Renmin University professor, Beijing, July 2010; interview with Fudan University professor, Shanghai, July 2010.
78 Le 2011.

Across all provinces in China, the decentralization of public welfare to local governments and the linkage of promotion to the delivery of these goods created the motivation for officials to collaborate with an emerging civil society in the 1990s. The "modular" idea of coproduction represented by the Western regulatory-state model supports this idea of collaboration. However, other "strategic" and "modular" ideas, such as the perceived role of civil society in the colour revolutions and a successful state-led development model, undermined this collaborative relationship model.

The interaction between these conflicting ideas influenced the emergence of a new model of state–society relationship in China – "consultative authoritarianism" – which promotes the simultaneous expansion of a fairly autonomous civil society and the development of more sophisticated and indirect tools of state control over this civil society. Li Junru, a leading Party theorist, advocates the use of "consultative democracy," which is a system whereby the CCP builds consensus around policy decisions through deliberation and consultation with relevant constituencies. I argue that this new state–society model in China encourages this type of consultation with civil society; however, this is *not* democratization but rather a sophisticated authoritarianism that uses more indirect tools of social control. The rise of consultative authoritarianism in China demonstrates an alternative to Western models of both civil society and regulatory state – one that balances the expansion of civil society with more sophisticated state control.

In contradistinction to existing literature on civil society, the social management pilot in Beijing provides evidence that an operationally autonomous civil society is emerging in this authoritarian regime; however, the expansion of civil society does not appear to be leading to democratization but rather to a more resilient authoritarianism and better governance. The increased provision of public goods and pluralistic policy-making creates the conditions for better governance under authoritarianism, which challenges our current understanding of civil society in China and should provoke more study of the implications of this new consultative authoritarianism model.

Bibliography

Blyth, Mark. 1997. "Any more bright ideas? The ideational turn of comparative political economy." *Comparative Politics* 29(1), 229–250.

Bo, Zhiyue, and Gang Chen. 2009. "Global financial crisis and the voice of the New Left in China." *East Asian Institute Background Brief* 443.

Cai, Hongbin, and Daniel Treisman. 2002. "State corroding federalism." *Journal of Public Economics* 88, 819–843.

Chamberlain, Heath. 1993. "On the search for civil society in China." *Modern China* 19, 199–215.

Chan, Anita, and Jonathan Unger. 1995. "China, corporatism, and the East Asian model." *The Australian Journal of Chinese Affairs* 33, 29–53

Chen, Qiao. 2011. "Minzheng bu: gongyi cishan lei di san lei shehui zuzhi you wang zhijie dengji" (Ministry of civil affairs: sees potential for three types of social organizations to register directly). *Beijing shibao*. 24 May.

China Daily. 2010. "Beijing's population exceeds 22 million." 26 February.

Diamond, Larry. 1994. "Rethinking civil society: toward democratic consolidation." *Journal of Democracy* 5, 4–18.

Foster, Kenneth. 2001. "Associations in the embrace of an authoritarian state: state domination of society?" *Studies in Comparative International Development* 35: 84–109.

Ford, Peter. 2009. "China's ant tribe: millions of unemployed college grads." *The Christian Science Monitor*, 21 December.

Frazier, Mark W. 2010. *Socialist Insecurity: Pensions and the Politics of Uneven Development in China.* Ithaca, NY: Cornell University Press.

Geisselmann, Joern and Christine Warmer. 2009. "Public participation in China's municipal affairs." *D + C Development and Cooperation Tribune* 294–296.

Han, Heng, and Kang Xiaoguang. 2005. "Fenlei kongzhi: dangqian Zhongguo dalu guojia yu shehui guanxi yanjiu" ("Differentiated control: current state and society relationship research in mainland China"). *Shehuixui yanjiu* 6. http://www.chinareform.net/2010/0116/8243.html.

Ho, Peter. 2001. "Greening without conflict? Environmentalism, NGOs and civil society in China." *Development and Change* 32, 893–921.

Howell, Jude. 1995. "Prospects for NGOs in China." *Development in Practice* 5(1), 12.

Howell, Jude. 2004. "New directions in civil society: organizing around marginalized interests." In Jude Howell, ed. *Governance in China.* Lanham, MD: Rowman and Littlefield, 143–171.

Howell, Jude and Jenny Pearce. 2002. *Civil Society and Development: a Critical Exploration.* Boulder, CO: Lynne Rienner Publishers.

Hsia, Renee Yuen-Jan, and Lynn T. White III. 2002. "Working amid corporatism and confusion: foreign NGOs in China." *Nonprofit and Voluntary Sector Quarterly* 31, 329.

Huang, Yasheng. 2011. "Rethinking the Beijing consensus," *Asia Policy* 11, 1–26.

Jacobs, Andrew. 2011. "Chinese security officials respond to call for protests." *New York Times*, 21 February.

Jing, Yijia, and E.S. Savas. 2009. "Managing collaborative service delivery: comparing China and the United States." *Public Administration Review* 69 (supplement) 101–07.

Landry, Pierre. 2003. "The political management of mayors in post-Deng China." *The Copenhagen Journal of Asian Studies* 17, 31–58.

Le, Zou. 2011. "NGO registration rules to be relaxed nationwide: civil affairs minister." *Global Times*, 25 May.

Lee, Colleen. 2010. "Special political zones," *The Standard*, 7 September.

Li, David D. 2006. "Large domestic non-intermediated investments and government liabilities: challenges facing China's financial sector reform." World Bank working paper.

Li, He. 2010. "Debating China's economic reform: new Leftists vs. liberals." *Journal of Chinese Political Science* 15, 1–23.

Lian, Yuming. 2010. "Shehui zuzhi de ruoshi diwei jidai gaibian" ("The weak position of social organizations must be changed"). *Beijing Ribao.* 20 September.

Lu, Yiyi. 2007. "The autonomy of Chinese NGOs: a new perspective." *China: an International Journal* 5, 173–203.

Ma, Qiusha. 2002. "The governance of NGOs in China since 1978: how much autonomy?" *Nonprofit and Voluntary Sector Quarterly* 31, 305–330.

Mathews, Jessica. 1997. "Power shift: the rise of global civil society." *Foreign Affairs* 76, January/February.

Mertha, Andrew. 2009. "'Fragmented authoritarianism 2.0': political pluralization in the Chinese policy process." *The China Quarterly* 200, 995–1012.

Mishra, Pankaj. 2006. "China's New Leftist." *The New York Times Magazine*, 15 October.

Nathan, Andrew. 2003. "Authoritarian resilience." *Journal of Democracy* 14 (1), 6–17.

New York Times. 2010. "Freedom and Human Rights in China." 1 March.

Oi, Jean. 1992. "Fiscal reform and the economic foundations of local state corporatism in China." *World Politics* 45, 99–126.

38 The China Quarterly, 213, March 2013, pp. 19–38

Park, Albert, Scott Rozelle, Christine Wong and Changqing Ren. 1996. "Distributional consequences of reforming local public finance in China." *The China Quarterly* 147, 751–778.

Qian, Yingyi, and Barry Weingast. 1996. "China's transition to markets: market-preserving federalism, Chinese style." *Journal of Economic Policy Reform* 1, 149–185.

Saich, Tony. 2000. "Negotiating the state: the development of social organizations in China." *The China Quarterly* 161, 124–141.

Saich, Tony. 2007. "Citizens' perceptions of governance in rural and urban China." *Journal of Chinese Political Science* 12, 1–28.

Salamon, Lester. 1994. "The rise of the nonprofit sector." *Foreign Affairs* July/August.

Salamon, Lester, and Helmut K. Anheier. 1996. *The Emerging Not-For-Profit Sector: An Overview.* Manchester and New York: Manchester University Press.

Sanyal, Bishwapriya. 1994. "*Cooperative Autonomy: The Dialectic of State-NGOs Relationship in Developing Countries.*" International Institute for Labour Studies.

Simon, Karla. 2009. "Regulation of civil society in China: necessary changes after the Olympic Games and the Sichuan earthquake." *Fordham International Law Journal* 32 (3).

Tanner, Murray Scot. 2004. "China rethinks unrest." *The Washington Quarterly* 27, 137–156.

TASS. 2005. "Putin, Hu Jintao to say monopoly in international affairs inadmissible." 28 June.

Wang, Hui. 2001. "Contemporary Chinese thought and the question of modernity." In Xudong Zhang (ed.) *Whither China? Intellectual Politics in Contemporary China.* Durham NC: Duke University Press, 161–197.

Wang, Jisi. 2011. "China's search for a grand strategy subtitle: a rising great power finds its way." *Foreign Affairs* March/April.

Wang, Shaoguang. 2006. "Money and autonomy: patterns of civil society finance and their implications." *Studies in Comparative International Development* 40 (4): 3–29.

Wang, Shaoguang, and Jianyu He. 2004. "Associational revolution in China: mapping the landscapes." *Korea Observer* 35 (3), 485–532.

Wang, Sibin. 2011. "Social service innovation and embedded growth of civil society." Paper presented at the *Civil Society and Harmonious Society* conference, Beijing, China, June 2011.

Whiting, Susan. 2001. *Power and Wealth in Rural China: The Political Economy of Institutional Change*. Cambridge: Cambridge University Press.

Wong, Christine. 2007. "Budget reform in China." *OECD Journal on Budgeting* 7(1), 33–56.

Xiong, Wei, and Qin Meng. 2008. "Lun Zhongguo NGO bentu nengli de kunjing he chulu" (An analysis of Chinese NGO's weak capacity and solution to this predicament." Zhongguo sixiang wang, http://admin.sinoth.com/Doc/article/2008/1/24/server/1000010601.htm, accessed 17 June 2008.

Yang, Dali. 2004. *Remaking the Chinese Leviathan.* Stanford, CA: Stanford University Press.

Yin, Deyong. 2009. "China's attitude toward foreign NGOs." *Washington University Global Studies Law Review* 8 (3).

Young, Nick and Tina Qian. 2006. "Listening to the community is the main ingredient in Chinese NGO recipe for city governments." *China Development Brief*, 2 March.

Zhou, Benshun. 2011. "Zou Zhongguo tese shehui guanli chuangxin zhi lu" ("Social management of innovation with Chinese characteristics") *Qiushi* 10.

The Advance of the Party: Transformation or Takeover of Urban Grassroots Society?*

Patricia M. Thornton†

Abstract

While existing scholarship focuses attention on the impact of state control and repression on Chinese civil society, the increasingly independent role of the Communist Party has been largely overlooked. This article reviews the Party's drive to "comprehensively cover" grassroots society over the previous decade against the theoretical debate unfolding among Chinese scholars and Party theoreticians regarding the Party's role with respect to civil society. Focusing on greater Shanghai, frequently cited as a national model of Party-building, I describe the Party's advance and the emergence of Party-organized non-governmental organizations (PONGOs), a new hybrid form of social organization sponsored and supported by local Party committees. I argue that these developments invite a reconsideration of our understandings of the ongoing "associational revolution" and of the Party's relationship to China's flourishing "third realm."

Keywords: civil society; Chinese Communist Party; NGOs; Party building; urban; social policy; Shanghai

---

The crackdown against civil society organizations and activists that coincided with the 60th anniversary of the founding of the PRC brought a fresh reminder of the Party-state's checkered legacy in dealing with social groups. Following the 17th Party Congress, Party leaders claim to be "testing the waters" (*shi shui* 试水), seeking to "develop the positive functions of civil society and religious organizations" in hopes of creating a "modern civil society" by 2020.[1] Yet mounting tales of harassment, arrest and detention of activists evince the continuing suspicion and mistrust with which central leaders regard grassroots social forces.

* An earlier version of this paper was delivered at a University of Oxford Contemporary China Studies Programme conference entitled "Civic Culture, Harmonious Society: Rethinking Civil Society in Greater China Today," held on 27–28 August 2010 at Jesus College. The author gratefully acknowledges the comments and suggestions offered by conference participants Diana Fu, Karl Gerth, Walter Hatch, Jianyu He, Ming-sho Ho, Michael Hsiao, Winnie King, Qiushi Ma, Vivienne Shue, Sun Tao, Jessica Teets, Xibai Xu and Hong Zhang; and two anonymous reviewers.

† University of Oxford. Email: Patricia.Thornton@politics.ox.ac.uk

1 Zhou Tianyong et al. 2008, 311–12.

 doi:10.1017/S0305741013000039

2 *The China Quarterly*, 213, March 2013, pp. 1–18

Scholarly speculation of the early 1990s regarding the "resurgence" or "re-emergence" of a vibrant civil society capable of countering the Party-state[2] has given way to complex theorization regarding the "blurred boundaries" between the two,[3] and the ways civil society organizations "negotiate the state" by "chipping away at the edges" of its restrictive regulatory and legal frameworks.[4] More recently, Andrew Mertha has described how savvy "policy entrepreneurs," often working in and through non-governmental organizations (hereafter NGOs), are entering the political process "within the structural and procedural constraints of the fragmented authoritarianism framework" to carve out new spaces for participation and contestation.[5]

Yet, whereas the literature on civil society in China has focused on state control over social organizations, the role of the Chinese Communist Party (CCP) has been largely overlooked,[6] despite waves of intensive grassroots Party-building targeting civic organizations that began in the 1990s. The 1998 downsizing under the "small government, great society" (*xiao zhengfu da shehui* 小政府大社会) model was followed by an unprecedented advance of the Party to fill the gaps left by the withdrawal of the state. Party membership has expanded over the course of the reform era from 3.8 per cent of the population in 1978 to 5.2 per cent in 2002; by the end of 2008, the CCP claimed some 75.93 million members, making it the single largest political organization in the world.[7] Well over 120,000 private non-enterprise units (*minban feiqiye* 民办非企业) in 2008 boasted internal Party organizations, a number that continues to rise with the Party's effort to "comprehensively cover" (*quan fugai* 全覆盖) society by establishing footholds in so-called "two new" (*liang xin* 两新) organizations – new economic and new social organizations created since market reform.[8] The advance of the Party in the wake of the state's retreat is being heralded by some as a Chinese "theory of limited government" (*youxian zhengfu lilun* 有限政府理论) involving a "big Party, small state, great society" (*da zhengdang, xiao zhengfu, da shehui* 大政党、小政府、大社会).[9]

Nevertheless, Chinese scholars and Party theoreticians remain divided on the nature of the Party's relationship with emerging social groups. On the one hand, many note that more powerful and capable NGOs and non-profit enterprises can provide much-needed services, reduce governing costs, safeguard social stability and bridge gaps in China's fragmented administrative structure. On the other hand, the presence of Party cells in grassroots social organizations restricts their autonomy and may compromise their ability to speak and act on behalf of

2 Gold, 1990; Strand 1990.
3 Shue 1988; Wang Xu. 1999.
4 Saich 2000; Howell 2007.
5 Mertha 2009.
6 Unger 1996.
7 Appleton et al. 2009; Shambaugh 2008; Dickson 2008, 125–131; Dickson 2007.
8 Lu Yuemian 2004.
9 Hu 2007.

vulnerable groups. Viewed from the grassroots, while the Party offers administrative, political and logistical support to struggling social organizations, it does so at a price. Some charge that internal Party branches exercise excessive zeal in monitoring accounts and activities, police strict legal and regulatory compliance, and demand more frequent participation in events that promote the Party's own agenda at the expense of core service tasks. In short, the emerging consensus is that while the expanding "third realm" (*di san bumen* 第三部门) represents a double-edged sword for the Party, the Party's new involvement with social groups may steer the development of Chinese civil society to serve Party ends.

This article evaluates recent Party-building efforts in "two new" organizations specifically targeting private non-enterprise units (*minban feiqiye* or *minjian feiqiye* 民间非企业), private foundations (*jijin hui* 基金会) and social organizations (*shehui tuanti* 社会团体)[10] against the broader theoretical debate among Chinese scholars and Party theoreticians regarding the Party's evolving role with respect to civil society. Reviewing the Party's recent initiative to "comprehensively cover" society in greater Shanghai, frequently cited as a national model for Party-building, I describe the emergence of Party-organized non-government organizations that I refer to as PONGOs, a new hybrid form designed to encourage the formation of civic groups, and particularly professional charitable organizations capable of taking on public welfare provision under the aegis of Party control. Unlike government-organized NGOs (so-called GONGOs or QUANGOs),[11] the new PONGOs not only rely upon the sponsorship and support of local Party committees for the purposes of registration, but also maintain active internal Party cells that carry out recruitment and other Party-directed activities alongside their core tasks, and police popular compliance with the Party line. In Shanghai, furthermore, the new PONGOs encourage public–private partnerships, social entrepreneurship and branded corporate sponsorship of charity and community events, frequently combining such efforts with patriotic education and the mobilization of public demonstrations of support for Party rule.

These recent developments invite a reconsideration of our understanding of civil society development in contemporary China, and suggest the emergence of a new model of social governance in which a more independent Party mediates between the smaller reform-era state and an increasingly mobile and diverse Chinese society. In building flexible "hub-style" Party organizations capable of spanning jurisdictional and sectoral gaps, the Party explicitly aims to alleviate the "matrix muddle" produced by its crosscutting *tiao* 条/*kuai* 块 administrative structure,[12] and to foster a more integrated, cohesive and harmonious society at

10 On "civic organizations" (*minjian zuzhi*) see Yu 2006.

11 Hood (1973) coined the term "QUANGO" (quasi-non-governmental organization) to describe formally private bodies that maintain a significant relationship to the state, and often discharge state functions.

12 The *tiao/kuai* administrative structure describes the internal division of power within the Chinese Party-state: vertical bureaucratic relationships linking central to local organizations are commonly referred to as "lines" (*tiao*), while horizontal bodies coordinating action within given geographic

the urban grassroots. However, the question remains of whether drawing grassroots civic associations and NGOs into the Party's net facilitates their autonomy[13] or signals an early end to the robust heterogeneity of China's "associational revolution." [14]

The Party and the "Third Realm"

The instability introduced by the expansion of market forces during the reform era triggered a scholarly reconsideration of the optimal balance between state, market and social power in the PRC, amid mounting calls for "the state to advance and the popular to recede" (*guojin mintui* 国进民退), particularly in the aftermath of the 2008 global recession. Some see the rise of organized social forces as a buffer between state and society capable of channeling resources to redress social needs. Others argue that the regulatory pressures imposed upon Chinese NGOs render them entirely dependent upon official support and constrain their activities.[15] While most agree that China's flourishing "third realm" offers both challenges and opportunities for the regime, some envision a new relationship between social groups and the Party independent of the state, particularly as the government withdraws from social welfare and public goods provision. Nonetheless, there is disagreement about how the Party should exercise its power, as well as about the likely consequences of the Party's increasing penetration of the social sphere in the era of reform.

Wu Hui and Zhao Xusheng of the Central Party School, for example, argue that social groups represent a "double-edged sword" (*shuangren jian* 双刃剑) for the Party that might improve governance over the long term, but more presently threatens the Party's leadership at the grassroots by crowding out the social space traditionally occupied by party organizations, thereby undermining the Party's capacity and prestige. Thus, they advocate tightening the existing system of controls to maintain the Party's position of power.[16]

Political scientist Lin Shangli agrees that civic organizations challenge the ruling Party's social base, generating tension and mutual suspicion at the grassroots that undermine its ability to integrate new social forces.[17] However, Lin points out that after 1949, the Party's process of social systematization "not only swallowed up the social space in which NGOs exist, but fundamentally 'hollowed out' (*kongdonghua* 空洞化) the non-governmental nature of the various surviving

footnote continued

areas are known as "pieces" (*kuai*), resulting in a crosshatch of political authority characterized as "fragmented authoritarianism" (Lieberthal 2004, 186–88).

13 Lu Yiyi 2007; Lu Yiyi 2009.

14 Wang and He 2004. The term "associational revolution" was coined by Lester M. Salamon (1994).

15 Hu 2007, 15.

16 Wu and Zhao 2009.

17 Lin 2008.

bodies," reshaping them as de facto Party and state organizations and reducing their effectiveness. Li concludes that the Party's ability to define a more rational relationship with such groups will depend upon its capacity to adapt to changing conditions.[18]

Yin Deci of the Guangzhou Municipal Party School finds that the social diversification (*duoyanghua* 多样化) produced by market reform destroyed the Party's absolute control (*juedui kongzhi quan* 绝对控制权) over society, and threatens the Party's core methods of social mobilization, political instruction (*zhengzhi guanshu* 政治灌输), policy-making and operation (*yunxing* 运行). However, he warns that since new social groups lack the capacity for self-governance, if "the Party's leadership cannot be expressed [there], it will constrict the space within which civic organizations can develop, social capital won't be utilized effectively, and the dynamism of the Party's governing methods will likewise be lost."[19]

Luo Feng, an associate professor of public administration in Shanghai, concurs, but nonetheless criticizes the Party's management of social forces. Luo finds that official attempts to rationalize the administrative structure of social groups and incorporate (*naru* 纳入) them restricts their autonomy, delimits their functionality and engenders political conflict between officials and NGO activists. The Party-state's integrative mechanisms (*zhenghe qi* 整合器) create resistance, as groups struggle to maintain their distinctive identities in the face of countervailing pressure. Luo concludes that a more nuanced approach – that will preserve both the existing administrative order of the Party-state and the ability of legitimate social groups to respond to real social needs – has yet to be found.[20]

By contrast, sociologist Hu Bing asserts that as the state downsizes, it should cede the task of managing social groups to the Party. Whereas history has demonstrated that state power is inefficient, Hu asserts, "with the separation of Party and state, the Party is fully capable of …firmly establishing 'comprehensive coverage' in the social sphere." Social organizations in the PRC tend to be either "top-down" state-organized (*guanban* 官办) NGOs (GONGOs, QUANGOs) or grassroots (*caogen* 草根) social groups. The former encounter difficulty in mobilizing local enthusiasm and interest, whereas the latter lack administrative and financial resources. The Party, however, can bridge these divides: as the state downsizes under the "small state, big society" model, the Party should expand, drawing in and redistributing both power and resources from atomized (*zhidianhua* 质点化) enterprises and agents arrayed within the framework of the market. The Party's "comprehensive coverage" of society makes it uniquely capable of transcending the conflicts of interest and jurisdictional disputes arising from

18 Lin 2007.
19 Yin 2004.
20 Luo Feng 2009.

cross-cutting *tiao/kuai* relationships,[21] and the weaknesses inherent in the "fragmented authoritarian" model.

Wu Xinye, an associate professor of public administration and management, argues that contemporary Chinese civil society is plagued by path-dependent (*lishi de lujing yilai yin* 历史的路径依赖因) outcomes that reproduce weak civic consciousness and low rates of volunteerism, problems that only the Party can solve. However, Wu finds the theoretical debate too polarized, with one extreme position advocating that "the Party completely dominate (*han'gai* 涵盖) society… to the point that Party organizations replace (*daiti* 代替) social groups;" and other extreme advocating that the Party "not interfere in the political sphere of NGOs, allowing complete autonomy to be realized."[22] But NGO development independent of the Party creates fragmentation and the splintering of society into myriad interest groups, working at cross-purposes with each other. Instead, Wu advocates the selective "absorption" (*xina* 吸纳) of NGOs, allowing the Party to shape social policy by legitimating the interests, scope and mode of political participation of NGOs, supporting their provision of public services, and ensuring that they continue to meet genuine social needs. She offers the example of the Shanghai municipal Party committee's 2002 project to "engineer radial influence" (*fusheli gongcheng* 辐射力工程) by "fusing" (*ningju* 凝聚) Party members with grassroots sports teams (*tuandui* 团队), organizations (*zuzhi* 组织) and society (*shehui* 社会). Wu points out that the Party now covers and successfully manages more than 90 per cent of Shanghai's NGOs through its policy of selective "absorption."[23]

However, Li Jingpeng at Beijing University asserts, it is unclear whether the Party's sustained expansion into the "third realm" supports or suffocates new social forces. While "the post-totalitarian political framework generally favours civil society development," the question remains "whether the 'retreat of the state and advance of the Party' actually benefits the development of civil society." The answer "lies in the nature of the Party's advance. If the 'advance of the Party' means that the Party extends its grasp of administrative power, then… the space within which civil society can develop shrinks." But if "the 'advance of the Party' means only the expansion of its power to lead (*lingdao quan* 领导权) and not the expansion of administrative power, then, possibly, the 'advance of the Party' will benefit the development of civil society." The crux of the matter is whether the Party can continue to exercise leadership while letting go of administrative control, and whether the Party can delimit the exercise of its own power, and allow civil society to grow.[24]

While the emerging scholarly consensus concedes that the Party will continue to play a decisive role in shaping China's "associational revolution," most

21 Hu 2007, 13–14.
22 Wu 2006.
23 Wu 2006, 50–54; Kang Xiaoguang 2002.
24 Li 2005.

scholars also agree on the need for reform. At stake is the nature and extent of Party leadership to be exercised in the "third realm," as well as the Party's capacity to "selectively absorb," "integrate" or "comprehensively cover" new social forces in a manner that permits their continued development with a degree of autonomy. The Party's earlier "absolute control" of civic associations "hollowed [them] out," reproduced "path dependent" social pathologies, and prevented the representation of genuine social needs. The success of the Party's new efforts to "engineer radial influence" and "fuse" with new social forces, under test in greater Shanghai, may well be determined, as Li Jingpeng trenchantly observes, in part by the Party's capacity to observe the narrow and sometimes uncertain boundary between its "power to lead" and "administrative control."

"Comprehensively Covering" Grassroots Social Organizations

Intensive Party-building in China's "third realm" preceded the state's tightening of the existing regulatory framework for social organizations. In February 1998, several months before the State Council issued its "Regulations on the Registration and Management of Social Organizations," the Central Committee's Organization Department and the Ministry of Civil Affairs jointly called upon Party personnel to establish grassroots Party branches in social organizations under their supervision, and ensure that they fully "implement the Party's line."[25] In July 2000, the organization department reiterated the call for Party-building, asking internal Party branches to ensure that social organizations comply with national laws and regulations, "adhere to a correct political orientation," and "take the lead in building a [socialist] spiritual civilization and political thought work."[26] This drive to "eliminate blank spots, expand comprehensive coverage, increase effectiveness" (*xiaomie kongbai dian, kuoda fugai mian, zengqiang youxiao xing* 消灭空白点, 扩大覆盖面, 增强有效性) resulted, by the end of 2008, in the creation of Party branches in 53.5 per cent of eligible social groups (*shehui tuanti* 社会团体), 55 per cent of eligible private non-enterprise units (*minban feiqiye danwei* 民办非企业单位), and 51 per cent of eligible foundations (*jijin hui* 基金会) nationwide.[27]

In Shanghai, where grassroots Party-building aimed at "comprehensive coverage" (*quan fugai* 全覆盖) of "two new" organizations began as early as 2001,[28] one recent report suggests that the Party's penetration of eligible social groups now approaches 100 per cent.[29] Another notes that in 2008, out of an estimated three million NGOs, 8,659 had formally registered with the Shanghai Ministry of

25 Zhonggong zhongyang zuzhibu, mingzhengbu 1998.
26 Zhonggong zhongyang zuzhibu guanyu yinfa 2000.
27 Sun 2009, 204–05.
28 Hong 2001.
29 Sun 2009, 205.

Civil Affairs, and over 98 per cent of all eligible social organizations had met Party-building targets.[30]

To accomplish this aim, the Shanghai Municipal Party Committee experimented with new organizational forms, including joint branches (*lianhe zhibu* 联合支部) combining different enterprises, and sometimes local residents, in a neighbourhood or district; temporary branches (*linshi zhibu* 临时支部) for seasonal workers or temporary residents; and Party working small groups (*dang xiaozu, dangde gongzuo xiaozu* 党小组, 党的工作小组) to address specific problems at the grassroots level. The Shanghai Municipal Party Committee organization department and social organization office (*shi shetuan ju* 市社团局) oversaw a four-stage process of application, registration, approval and certification with the Shanghai Ministry of Civil Affairs, and carried out annual inspections to guarantee that supervisory relationships are kept up to date.[31]

These new institutional arrangements facilitate an agenda that fuses entrepreneurial and philanthropic aims at the urban grassroots. New Party branches in private firms push their members to participate in public service activities and "corporate social responsibility" (CSR) programs; social organizations are likewise pressed to adopt more entrepreneurial discourses and professional standards of practice. In December 2009, the National Small Leading Group on the Study and Practice of New Social Organizations (*Quanguo xinshehui zuzhi xuexi shijian huodong zhidao xiaozu* 全国新社会组织学习实践活动指导小组) organized a symposium chaired by the Shanghai Ministry of Civil Affairs to urge local social organizations to not only pursue "real results" (*shishi zaizai de xiaoguo* 实实在在的效果), but to "go a step further" by "paying attention to the fostering and creation of their own brands" (*zhuyi peiyang he chuangzao zishen de pinpai* 注意培养和创造自身的品牌): "only once you have a brand can you boost your influence: the benchmark of development is to become a brand leader. We must cultivate sincere and plain-speaking, competent and effective, and useful new social organizations."[32] In Shanghai's Changning 长宁 district, the Party member service centre (*Dangyuan fuwu zhongxin* 党员服务中心) encourages member organizations to "establish a standard, project distinction, and build the brand" (*lizu guifan, tuchu tese, gouzu pinpai* 立足规范, 突出特色, 构筑品牌) of the Party, and raise its profile by marketing the delivery of high quality public services.[33] The Xu Beihong 徐悲鸿 Fine Arts Kindergarten Party branch, working alongside the school principal (whose motto for the staff is "succeed, improve, develop"), organized a series of activities that encourage "striving to achieve brand excellence in education, and opening up the school to a new developmental road" (*chuang youzhi jiaoyu pinpai, tuo yuanben fazhan xin lu* 创优质教育品牌, 拓园本发展新路).[34]

30 Luo 2009, 36.
31 *Zhongguo shehui bao* 2002.
32 Shanghai shi ziqiang shehui fuwu zongshe 2009.
33 Wang and Wang 2006.
34 "Xu Beihong yishu you'eryuan qing sanba xilie huodong" ("March 8 celebratory activities at Xu Beihong Fine Arts Kindergarten roster"). www.shlxhd.gov.cn, 4 April 2009. Accessed at http://tinyurl.com/9npbnoq.

Similarly, in November 2003 the Communist Youth League joined forces with the National Youth Federation, the Prince's Trust Enterprise Leadership Conference, and UK-based Youth Business International (YBI) to establish Youth Business China (YBC). According to its website, under the Party's tutelage, YBC's chief mission involves increasing employment by helping young entrepreneurs build successful businesses; "vitalizing" the economy by helping entrepreneurs shoulder social responsibility; and increasing social harmony by assisting the government in resolving the problem of unemployment. In the aftermath of the devastating Wenchuan earthquake, YBC launched the "rebuild our home entrepreneurship" campaign and the YBC Special Disaster Region Relief Foundation provided funds to 24 youths in the affected areas to attend a week-long seminar of entrepreneurship training and job shadowing in Shanghai. Additional internships were later arranged in Fujian along with a five-day course in the "Start Your Business" method held at the Haixi Youth Entrepreneurship Training School.[35] Closer to its Shanghai base of operations, YBC hosts a local "young entrepreneurs club" that recently, with the help of the enterprise Party branch at Shanghai Allied Investment Advisory Services, convened a "Who Moved my Cheese?" seminar at a smart hotel for interested members.[36]

The Privatization of Public Services and the New PONGOs

The Party's inculcation of entrepreneurial values and corporate culture among grassroots social organizations is designed with a longer term purpose in mind: the contracting out of public service provision to this emerging tier of non-state organizations through a competitive bidding process. The amount currently budgeted by Shanghai municipal and district level administrative bureaus for the purchase of services formerly provided by the state ranges from several million to several billion yuan per year. In 2006 alone, municipal authorities contracted out a staggering 1.5 billion yuan of special operations, budgetary and extrabudgetary funds collected by state offices to the Shanghai Cultural Development Foundation for cultural projects; the municipal and district governments expended another 67.79 million yuan on political and legal services, community crime prevention, youth services and care for drug addicts. In 2007, Huangpu district purchased services worth over 22.19 million yuan from various community service organizations and enterprises; and in Pudong New Area, the cost of services purchased more than doubled in three years, from 22.282 million in 2003 to 59.55 million yuan in 2006.

Pudong New Area has been designated a "national comprehensive reform municipal city" experimenting with the "service purchase model" (*goumai fuwu*

35 Zhu 2009.

36 "'Nailao zai nali?' YBC (Shanghai) chuangyezhe julebu tebie huodong" ("'Who Moved my Cheese? Special activity of the YBC (Shanghai) entrepreneur club"). http://www.ybc.org.cn/news/newsdetail.jsp?newspid=4577, 21 April 2009. Spencer Johnson's 1998 *Who Moved My Cheese?* is a best-selling motivational book designed to help people cope with change, particularly in the business world.

10 The China Quarterly, 213, March 2013, pp. 1–18

moshi 购买服务模式) in which the district government "jump-started" 26 community service organizations (CSOs) capable of providing social services on a contractual basis through subsidies, loans and other inducements. In order to qualify, CSOs must observe "six divisions" from the state: no sharing of administration, organizational structure, functions, staff, property or physical facilities; during the course of the contract there must be no subordination of the CSO to the district, no exchange of personnel or employees between the two, and no shared property or capital between them.[37]

The "six divisions" observed between the state and non-state service providers, however, do not apply to the Party. Rather, according to the February 1998 notice, Party branches established in registered social organizations "assist [those organizations] in resolving practical problems in their work," and must "be brought into full play in the drive for reform and modernization."[38] In practice, this places social organizations with large and active Party branches at the centre of public service provision within grassroots urban communities, and allows the Party to shape service delivery in a manner tailored to suit Party needs.

In the case of the Putuo District Changshou Road (Street-Level) NGO Service Centre (*Putuoqu Changshoulu jiedao minjian zuzhi fuwu zhongxin* 普陀区长寿路街道民间组织服务中心), established in August 2002 as the first Party-organized NGO clearing house for non-state, civic and non-profit organizations in the PRC, the centre's director concurrently serves as the service centre's branch Party secretary at the behest of the Putuo district joint Party committee. The service centre received 280,000 yuan in operating funds (*jingfei* 经费) from street offices in 2006, which covered approximately 100,000 yuan for the salaries of six full-time employees (the director, a deputy-director, and four staff members), and another 180,000 yuan to support the activities of various social organizations within the district. Its chief function is to coordinate the activities of the 281 registered NGOs and CSOs in the area, advise them regarding existing regulations, and assist and assess their readiness to prepare competitive bids for local public service provision totaling some 1.5 million yuan. The Centre's member organizations – in effect, Party-organized NGOs (PONGOs), with the Centre facilitating the process of registration – employ or represent over 900 Party members, and are in turn represented by nine overlapping Party organizations at the enterprise, street, building or district level, including, as of July 2009: 56 civic non-enterprise units (*minban feiqiye*), 7 social groups (*shehui tuanti*), 25 charitable and philanthropic social organizations, and 193 teams (*qunzhong tuandui* 群众团队).[39] The Centre's constituent organizations span six categories – private non-enterprise units (*minfei danwei* 民非单位), social organizations (*shehui tuanti*), public groups and teams (*qunzhong tuandui*), volunteers (*yigong* 义工), collectively supervised entities (*zonghe guanli* 综合管理), and charity supermarkets (*cishan chaoshi* 慈善超市).

37 Zeng 2008.
38 Zhonggong zhongyang zuzhibu, minzhengbu 1998.
39 Zhou Jiayan 2009.

Hailed as a great success in both local Party- and community-building, the "civic organization service centre" model has also been adopted in the nearby districts of Jing'an 静安 and Minhang 闵行.[40]

In addition to opening up a civic organization service centre to sponsor PONGOs modeled on the one in Putuo, in 2007 the Jing'an district Party committee and district government established a district social organization union (*shehui zuzhi lianhe hui* 社会组织联合会, or *shelianhui* 社联会) capable of mobilizing the district's social organizations to collectively and "conscientiously implement the 'opinions' and 'advice' of the Party committee" while maintaining communication with district street offices. The additional public services provided by member organizations in exchange for registration and support included a series of science lectures that involved the distribution of "anti-cult propaganda materials" aimed at discrediting *falun gong* and other *qigong* sects that boasted a significant following in Jing'an in the mid-1990s; the negotiation of the peaceful resettlement of some 350 district homeowners who had threatened to self-immolate if forced to move; and two social mixers, a "white-collar salon" (*bailing shalong* 白领沙龙) and "salon for middle-aged and elder singles" (*zhonglaonian danshen shalong* 中老年单身沙龙), that drew in 8,000 local residents and purportedly helped a staggering 30 per cent of the middle-aged and older singles find "their other half," thanks to the organization's Party branch.[41] Likewise, in April 2007, Pudong Party and state officials jointly established a "Non-Profit Incubator Centre" (*Shanghai Pudong feiyingli zuzhi fazhan zhongxin* 上海浦东非营利组织发展中心) with the aim of "assisting the creativity of Chinese society and entrepreneurial talent to cultivate public welfare." The incubator provides administrative support, field equipment and registration assistance to social groups, non-enterprise units and foundations within the district, and claims I Study Net (*Wo xue wang* 我学网, www.5xue.com) and 1KG More (*Duo bei yi gongjin* 多背一公斤 www.1kg.org), as successfully "incubated" organizations that are now nationwide non-profit service providers.[42]

Shanghai's new PONGOs include not only the umbrella "service centres" described above, but also a range of smaller Party-sponsored community service organizations and non-profit enterprises throughout greater Shanghai. For example, the Daning Road Street Office Society for the Elderly (*Daninglu jiedao laonian xiehui* 大宁路街道老年协会), established in September 2002 concurrently with its internal Party branch, boasts nearly 200 members. Its mission is the education of neighbourhood senior citizens and retirees, and the creation of a "harmonious, warm, fragrant, and happy home for the elderly," for which they have been recognized with four model civic association awards. According to their Party branch website, the society's specialty is

40 Zhou Yang 2007, 4; Luo Yong 2009, 80–83.
41 Shanghai shi Jing'anqu shehui zuzhi lianhehui 2008.
42 Zhong 2009.

the integration of capital, taking service as the foundation, excelling at doing the Party's work among civic mass organizations (*minjian shetuan* 民间社团), bringing into play the Party's political core, strengthening the organization of the Party's branch among social groups, leading, mediating and serving, and unceasingly simultaneously strengthening both the Party's cohesion and its combat effectiveness (*zhandouli* 战斗力).[43]

The society provides patriotic education lectures on "China's peaceful rise" and the "three represents," helpfully organized by a retired PLA political commissar who is also a district resident. Other activities include outings to revolutionary heritage sites, "nostalgia tours," and the Zhabei 闸北 district "million families learning etiquette" campaign in advance of the Shanghai Expo.[44] In a similar vein, just after National Day 2010, a team of five volunteers from a PONGO in the Changshou road district "braved the rain" to "search out red memories" (*xunzhao hongse jiyi* 寻找红色记忆) from local retirees. Armed with tape recorders, they visited elderly veterans in their homes and exchanged needed items, small gifts and services for their stories.[45]

Shanghai's PONGOs likewise sprang into a high-tide of mobilization to prepare for the 2010 Expo. The Changshou Road (Street-Level) NGO Service Centre organized classes in conversational English and etiquette for civic association staff and volunteers.[46] Party activists within the Shanghai Technical Arts School organized a "Develop Artistic Skill and Grace, Promote the Spirit of the Expo" fashion and make-up show, replete with catwalk, for senior citizens and industry representatives at the local community center.[47] The Putuo District NGO Service Centre organized a "volunteer rescue management team" to crack down on vagrants and beggars congregating in the Jade Buddha Temple area to spruce up the neighbourhood for tourists.[48] The Changshou district cycling team, organized by the Changshou Road (Street-Level) NGO Service Centre, boasts 50 members, 16 of whom also belong to the Party: the group's motto – "Not just a riding team, but a propaganda team, and, moreover, a seed spreader" (*bozhongji* 播种机) – was chosen to highlight the fact that they "are not merely satisfied to pursue their own enjoyment, but moreover in the process wish to support the government's ongoing propaganda efforts, sometimes following the lead of the street committee," and sometimes cooperating with fellow

43 "Zhibu jianjie" ("Introducing our organization"). www.shlxhd.gov.cn. 2007. Accessed 11 August 2011 at http://tinyurl.com/2wwavqyy.

44 "Daning Laoxie chuangping 'wuhao' dang zuzhi de shenbao cailiao" ("Daning Elderly Assistance reviews 'Five Goods' Party organizations information report"). www.shlxhd.gov.cn, 29 August 2007. Accessed at http://tinyurl.com/2fzzaqdk.

45 "Xunzhao hongse jiyi" ("Search for red memories"). http://www.zunlao.org/eventview.asp?id=136, 24 October 2010.

46 Changshou shequ shehui zuzhi jiji canyu ying shibo huodong" ("Changshou district social organizations actively participate in World Expo welcoming activities"). http://www.csjd.gov.cn/cscs/WebFront/sub_news.aspx?cid=35&id=102, 27 March 2009.

47 "Hongyang shibo jingsheng, zhanxian huiyi fengcai" ("Carry forward the World Expo spirit, develop artistry and grace"). http://stj.sh.gov.cn/Info.aspx?ReportId=7335673e-7082-43fd-ab77-706e778dc767, 18 May 2010.

48 "Jianli liang ge gongzuo jizhi—jiuzhu guanli xiaoguo xianzhu" ("Establishing two working mechanisms—notable effect in supporting administration"). http://www.csjd.gov.cn/cscs/WebFront/sub_news.aspx?cid=35&id=67, 16 October 2008.

PONGOs to arrange joint activities. Their efforts and creativity have earned them the grateful recognition of Shanghai municipal authorities, who awarded them "advanced team" status for four consecutive years.[49]

The Shanghai Municipal Party Committee's new "hub-style" network facilitates the exchange of resources and organization of joint activities among various "two new" linked party branch groups. For example, at the behest of their enthusiastic Party branch secretaries, the Xu Beihong Fine Arts Kindergarten and Yixian Garden jointly celebrated International Women's Day with a series of "rich, colourful and varied" activities. In accordance with the theme "I am healthy, bright, happy, and beautiful," representatives of the beauty product line COCO were invited to offer live skincare demonstrations and professional makeovers for members of the staff in the multi-purpose room at Yixian Garden. Their joint report described the event as "novel in form, ground-breaking, and moreover possessing more ideological content, mass character, entertainment value, and broader-ranging" than traditional Party activities. Other recent events have included dominoes tournaments, dance contests and a three-legged race.[50]

Party branches in community and civic associations also engage in monitoring activities, acting either as "barometers" (*qingyubiao* 晴雨表) of grassroots popular sentiment,[51] or "early warning" (*yujing* 预警) nodes that portend social discontent or threats to system stability. In 2003, grassroots NGO branch Party cadres in Xigong uncovered an underground cell of *tian gong* 天功 (heavenly *gong*) practitioners; and the following year, broke up two practice sites for other banned *qigong* groups in their area.[52] In 2008, the Changshou NGO Service Centre organized a volunteer "early warning" information network that quickly unearthed 12 illegal and unregistered grassroots societies, and uncovered plans for no fewer than 20 illegal collective activities, all of which were duly reported to Party and municipal authorities.[53]

Internal Party members in social organizations are required to report to higher levels any activities that deviate (*pianli* 偏离) from the Party line, violations of national or local regulations, and irregularities in financial matters, as well as the involvement of organization members in any "significant political plots" (*zhongda zhengzhi tumou* 重大政治图谋).[54] Not surprisingly, concern about increased surveillance, additional financial obligations and potential meddling by Party members has posed a barrier to Party-building in social groups. The

49 Zhou Hongyun, 2009.
50 "Xu Beihong yishu you'eryuan 'qing san ba' xilie huodong" ("March 8 celebratory activities at Xu Beihong Fine Arts Kindergarten roster"). www.shlxhd.gov.cn, 22 April 2009. Accessed at http://tinyurl.com/9npbnoq.
51 Hu 2007, 14.
52 Zhou Jiayan, 2009.
53 "Shequ shehui zuzhi shuniushi guanli de tansuo yu shijian—Changshou lu jiedao minjian zuzhi fuwu zhongxin" ("Exploring and practicing community social organization hub-style administration—Changshou Street Civic Organization Service Centere") www.shlxhd.gov.cn, 3 September 2009. Accessed at http://tinyurl.com/b77c4me. See also Meng 2009.
54 Ma 2009.

widespread perception that state- and Party-organized social groups are merely an extension of the government persists, despite official insistence to the contrary: "some take government-established civic associations that are neither wholly independent nor autonomous, known as GONGOs, and go so far as to disparagingly refer to them as the 'second government' (*er zhengfu* 二政府)… [implying] that they function as government lackeys and mouthpieces."[55] Deng Guosheng of the Tsinghua NGO Research Centre observes that grassroots charitable associations organized "from above" (*guanban* 官办) are plagued by fears that donations of time and money to such organizations are the result of psychological pressure or implicit coercion, and current sponsorship of charitable organizations is "overkill" (*jiaowang guozheng* 矫枉过正). By including support for developing charities in the cadre performance evaluation, "it is entirely possible to set off a rash of impetuous activity leading to a 'Great Leap Forward' in philanthropy, wasting scarce resources and warping popular understandings of charity."[56] Try as they might to assure the public of their independence from official control, Chinese NGOs established by official agents are still widely regarded as arms of the Party and state structure.

Conclusion: Transformation or Takeover at the Grassroots?

While the state's "dual management system" has discouraged many social groups from formalizing their presence in grassroots society, the Party's recent expansion into the third realm is quickly altering the associational landscape. In many of the urban and periurban areas most deeply affected by market reform, the Party is busily recreating itself as both a service hub and a social network in realms which are "difficult for the state to access and manage,"[57] by selectively encouraging social groups to operate under the watchful eye of local Party officials. The benefits of Party support are by no means lost on NGO activists: according to one author, the presence of an internal Party branch can increase effectiveness and attract talented volunteers and employees, and reverse the popular perception that a group's activities are either mere "child's play" (*xiao'er ke* 小儿科) or "irregular" (*bu zhenggui* 不正规), and "can help dissipate the wariness of potential clients and society at large."[58] Such lures may tempt struggling groups otherwise sceptical of the Party and its agenda, although whether they succeed in winning the "hearts and minds" of either activists or the general public remains to be seen. It is also worth considering the impact of these new strategies on the Party itself: the new focus on facilitating grassroots public service delivery potentially dilutes the Party's effectiveness as a vanguard organization, [59] and the

55 Zhou Hongyun 2009, 12–13.
56 Shen 2010.
57 Zhou Yang 2007, 4.
58 Liu 2009.
59 On the Party's redefinition of its vanguard role, see Lewis and Xue 2003. I wish to thank one anonymous reviewer for pointing out these potential pitfalls.

heterogeneity of fledgling grassroots members may import contradictions from society and divergent interests into the Party.

Nonetheless, internal Party branches clearly exert influence on the NGOs and civic groups that house them, pressing them to adopt more professional and corporate-friendly management, and at least periodically diverting their manpower and resources to pursue the Party's recruitment and mobilizational agendas. While internal Party branches may provide stability, organizational resources and social capital, they also subject groups to increased surveillance and the obligation to participate in Party activities. To the extent that these are mutually supportive of an organization's core interests, the Party's presence is likely to be regarded as beneficial and desirable; but, for others, perceived "conflicts of interest" have already proved problematic, particularly within state-organized NGOs designed to advance the interests of their supervising government units, some of which have actually repelled Party-building efforts. In other cases, grassroots NGOs and non-profit enterprises with "a high degree of autonomy, public welfarism (*gongyi xing* 公益性), volunteerism, a non-profit orientation, and democratic governance" have "shown little interest in Party-building, worrying that the Party is seeking to influence their original organizational arrangements." The new professional associations established for legal personnel have proved unusually difficult for the Party to penetrate for the aforementioned reasons,[60] as well as because, as one Party journal complained, of the generally high "degree of specialization and strength of independence of the legal profession."[61] Likewise, private schools and research institutes established as alternatives to the traditional Party branch-dominated model have doggedly repelled the Party's forays.[62] Striking a satisfactory balance between the interests of the Party and the original mission of a social group requires both "first-rate management skills" and the willingness to negotiate with both state and Party authorities, qualities that not all activists possess.[63] Indeed, civic organizations and voluntary groups today arguably steer an almost impossibly narrow course between the Scylla of state repression and the Charybdis of Party capture, with highly skilled helmsmen apparently in short supply.

Yet as sociologist Kang Xiaoqiang notes, the presumed opposition between state and social forces may be a by-product of Western historical models open to challenge and revision by China's unique developmental trajectory: it is a "long-standing misconception that a simplistic, unilateral opposition arises…pitting the work of Party-building against the autonomy of civic organizations."[64] However, in the absence of clear evidence that such groups retain the power to determine for themselves the nature and extent of their engagement with the

60 Liu 2009, 59.
61 Pan 2004.
62 Yan 2009.
63 Liu 2009, 59.
64 Kang Xiaoqiang. 2008.

Party, it is difficult to predict whether the Party's advance will result in the rise of a more genuinely robust "third realm" in China, or simply strengthen the existing chains of power and control.

References

Appleton, Simon, John Knight, Lina Song and Qingjie Xia. 2009. "The economics of Communist Party membership." *Journal of Development Studies* 45 (2), 256–275.

Dickson, Bruce J. 2007. "Integrating wealth and power in China: the Communist Party's embrace of the private sector." *The China Quarterly* 192, 827–854.

Dickson, Bruce J. 2008. *Wealth Into Power: The Communist Party's Embrace of China's Private Sector*. Cambridge: Cambridge University Press.

Gold, Thomas B. 1990. "The Resurgence of Civil Society in China." *Journal of Democracy* 1 (1), 18–31

Hong, Meifen. 2001. "Shanghai jiceng dangjian shuoguo leilei" ("Innumerable great achievements of Shanghai's grassroots Party-building"). *Jiefang ribao*, 23 June.

Hood, Christopher. 1973. "The rise and rise of the British QUANGO." *New Society* 25, 386–88.

Howell, Jude. 2007. "Civil society in China: chipping away at the edges." *Development* 50(3), 17–23.

Hu, Bing. 2007. "Tansuo minjian zuzhi zuijia shengcun huanjing—zhengdang zuzhi dui minjian zuzhi de yingxiang" ("Exploring the optimal environment for grassroots organizations: the influence of the Party organizations on civic organizations"). *Xuehui* 226 (9), 15.

Kang, Xiaoqiang. 2008. "Minjian zuzhi dangjian de shuangzhong fazhan lujing" ("Two-fold developmental path in Party-building in civic organizations"). *Dangzheng luntan* 4, 16–17.

Kang, Xiaoguang. 2002. "Zailun 'xingzheng xina zhengzhi'—90 niandai Zhongguo dalu zhengzhi fazhan yu zhengzhi wending yanjiu" ("Revisiting 'administrative absorption': research into the development of mainland Chinese politics in the '90s and political stability"). *Ershiyi shiji* (August), 14–30.

Lester, M. Salamon. 1994. "The rise of the nonprofit sector." *Foreign Affairs* 73 (4), 109–122.

Lewis, John W., and Xue Litai. 2003. "Social change and political reform in China: meeting the challenge of success." *The China Quarterly* 176, 926–942.

Li, Jingpeng. 2005. "Hou quanneng zhuyi shidai de gongmin shehui" ("Civil society in the post-totalitarian age"). *Zhongguo gaige* 11, 37.

Lieberthal, Kenneth. 2004. *Governing China, From Revolution through Reform*. New York: W.W. Norton.

Lin, Shangli. 2007. "Liangzhong shehui jiangou: Zhongguo gongchandang yu feizhengfu zuzhi" ("Two types of social construction: the Chinese Communist Party and NGOs"). *Zhongguo feiyingli* 1, 4.

Lin, Shangli. 2008. "Minjian zuzhi yu zhengzhi gaige: Zhongguo de luoji" ("Grassroots organizations and political reform: China's logic"). In Wang Ming (ed.), *Zhonggguo minjian zuzhi 30 nian—zouxiang gongmin shehui* (*Thirty Years of Chinese Grassroots Organizations: Moving toward Civil Society*). Beijing: Shehui kexue wenxian chubanshe, 270–73.

Liu, Li. 2009. "Jiaqiang minban feiqiye danwei dangjian gongzuo yanjiu" ("Research into strengthening Party-building work among private non-enterprise units"). *Lilun daokan* 11, 58.

Lu, Yiyi. 2007. "The autonomy of Chinese NGOs: a new perspective." *China: An International Journal* 5 (2), 173–203.

Lu, Yiyi. 2009. *Nongovernmental Organizations in China*. London: Taylor and Francis.

Lu, Yuemian. 2004. "'Liangxin' lingyu dangzuzhi shezhi moshi chuangxin tanxi" ("Exploring new models of establishing Party organizations in the 'Two News' domain"). *Shanghai dangshi yu dangjian* (August), 49–51.

Luo, Feng. 2009. "Shehui zuzhi de fazhan yu zhizheng dang de zuzhi qianru: zhengdang quanwei chongsu de shehui shijiao" ("Social organization development and embedding the ruling Party's organizations within them: remolding society's perspective of the Party-state's authority"). *Zhonggong Zhejiang shengwei dangxiao xuebao* 4, 31–37.

Luo, Yong. 2009. "Gongyixing minjian zuzhi yu shequ zhili de xianzhuang, kunjing yu zhengce ganyu" ("The current state of public welfare civic groups and community governance, difficulties and policy interventions"). *Gaige yu fazhan* 4, 80–83.

Ma, Xiheng. 2009. "Minjian zuzhi fazhan yu zhizheng dang jianshe—duiyu Shanghai shi minjian zuzhi dangjian shilu de sikao" ("Developing civic organizations and constructing the ruling party—a reflection on the practice of Party-building in grassroots organizations in Shanghai"). *Qiushi* 1, 29.

Meng, Qian. 2009. "Changshou moshi: 'minjian zuzhi fuwu zhongxin' de shequ chuangxin" ("The Changshou model: creating a resident association's 'civic organization service centre'"). *Shequ* 2, 10.

Mertha, Andrew. 2009. "'Fragmented authoritarianism 2.0': political pluralization in the Chinese policy process." *The China Quarterly* 200, 995–1012.

Pan, Weike. 2004. "Zhongjie zuzhi dangjian gongzuo bu gua 'kong dang'" ("Party-building work in intermediary organizations is not hanging 'empty shelves'"). *Gongchan dangyuan* 12, 22.

Saich, Tony. 2000. "Negotiating the state: the development of social organizations in China." *The China Quarterly* 161, 124–141.

Shambaugh, David. 2008. *China's Communist Party: Atrophy and Adaptation.* Berkeley: University of California Press.

Shanghai shi Jing'anqu shehui zuzhi lianhehui. 2008. "Jing'anqu shehui zuzhi fazhan zhuangkuang" ("Condition of developing social organizations in Jing'an District"). Original at http://www.shlxhd.gov.cn, 25 November. Accessed 11 August 2011 at http://tinyurl.com/c2uy3tx.

Shanghai shi ziqiang shehui fuwu zongshe. 2009. "Minzhengbu lingdao tingqu ziqiang deng xin shehui zuzhi 'xueshi huodong' huibao" ("Ministry of Civil Affair's reception of a report on the self-strengthening, etc., of the 'study activities' of new social groups"). 17 December. Accessed at http://tinyurl.com/3yhyp8f.

Shen, Zhenli. 2010. "Guanban cishan" ("State organized charity"). *21 Shiji jingji baodao*, 30 April.

Shue, Vivienne. 1988. *The Reach of the State: Sketches of the Chinese Body Politic.* Stanford, CA: Stanford University Press.

Strand, David. 1990. "Protest in Beijing: civil society and public sphere in China." *Problems of Communism* 39 (3), 1–19.

Sun, Weilin (ed.). 2009. *Shehui zuzhi guanli (Managing Social Organizations)*. Beijing: Zhongguo shehui chubanshe.

Unger, Jonathan. 1996. "'Bridges': private business, the Chinese government and the rise of new associations." *The China Quarterly* 174, 795–819.

Wang, Xu. 1999. "Mutual empowerment of state and society: its nature, conditions, mechanisms, and limits." *Comparative Politics* 31 (2), 231–249.

Wang, Guoliang, and Wang Jiaohui. 2006. "Guanyu jiaqiang dangyuan fuwu zhongxin gongneng jianshe de duice yu jianyi" ("Countermeasures and suggestions on building and strengthening the Party members service centre's functions"). *Shanghai dangshi yu dangjian* 1, 37–38.

Wang, Shaoguang, and He Jianyu. 2004. "Zhongguo de shetuan geming – Zhongguo ren de jieshe bantu" ("China's associational revolution: mapping the associational realm of Chinese citizens"). *Zheijang xuekan* 6, 71–77.

Wu, Hui, and Zhao, Xusheng. 2009. "Jiaqiang dang dui shehui zuzhide lingdao, fahui shehui zuzhi de jiji zuoyong" ("Strengthening the Party's leadership in social organizations, developing their positive functions"). In Guojia minjian zuzhi guanliju, ed., *2008 nian Zhongguo shehui zuzhi lilun yanjiu wenji* (Research Essays on the Theory of Social Organizations in China 2008). Beijing: Zhongguo shehui chubanshe, 8–10.

Wu, Xinye. 2006. "Zhizhengdang yu feizhengfu zuzhi: lilun de chaoyue yu xianshi de lujing—yi chaoyue guojia-shehui fanshi de shijiao" ("The ruling Party and NGOs: beyond theory and real means – the view from beyond the state/society dichotomy"). *Xueshu luntan* 191 (12), 52.

Yan, Hong. 2009. "Jinnian xinshehui zuzhi dangjian yanjiu shuping" ("Review of research on Party-building in new social organizations in recent years"). *Xuexi luntan* 25 (11), 25.

Yin, Deci. 2004. "Zhongguo minjian zuzhi fazhan yu dang de zhizheng fangshi yanjiu" ("Research into the development of grassroots organizations in China and the Party's governing style"). *Tanqiu* 150 (3), 9–16.

Yu, Keping. 2006. "Zhongguo gongmin shehui: guainian, fenlei yu zhidu huangjing" ("Chinese civil society: concepts, typology, and system environment"). *Zhongguo shehui kexue* 1, 14–15.

Zeng, Yonghe. 2008. "Chengshi zhengfu goumai fuwu yu xinxing zhengshe guanxi de goujian" ("The purchase of services by municipal governments and the structure of a new type of state–society relationship"). *Tansuo chuangxin* 1, A41–43.

Zhong, Zhilei. 2009. "NGO zhuce guanli moshide xin tansuo—yi NPI moshi weili" ("New explorations of the registration and management of NGO model: the NPI model example"). *Zhishi jingji* 13, 34–35.

Zhonggong zhongyang zuzhibu guanyu yinfa. 2000. "Guanyu 'Jiaqiang shehui tuanti dang de jianshe gongzuo de yijian' de tongzhi" ("Notice concerning 'Opinion on the work of strengthening Party organizations established in social groups'"). http://www.law-lib.com/law/law_view.asp?id=120475, 21 July.

Zhonggong zhongyang zuzhibu, mingzhengbu. 1998. "Guanyu shehui tuanti zhong jianli dangzuzhi youguan wentide tongzhi" ("Notice concerning the problems of building Party organizations in social groups"). http://www.lawlib.com/law/law_view.asp?id=120476, 16 February.

Zhongguo shehui bao 2002. "Shanghai minjian zuzhi dangjian gongzuo xiansheng duoren" ("Overwhelming strength of Party-building in Shanghai's civic organizations"). 25 June. 2.

Zhou Hongyun. 2009. "Minjian zuzhi fuwu zhongxin bu shi 'er zhengfu'" ("CSO service centre isn't a "second government"). *Shequ* 2, 13.

Zhou Jiayan, ed. 2009. "Hangshi minjian zuzhi dangjian, zujin hexie shehui shequ jianshe" ("Solidify Party-building in civic associations, promote the building of harmonious resident associations"). http://stj.sh.gov.cn/Info.aspx?ReportId=c915ef27-e978-4c2d-8bea-d0a3ff31ec6e, 31 July.

Zhou, Tianyong, *et al.* 2008. *Gongjian: shiqi da hou zhongguo zhengzhi tizhi gaige yanjiu baogao* (*Storming the Fortress: A Report on post-17th Party Congress Reforms of the Chinese Political System*). Xinjiang shengchan jianshe bingtuan chubanshe, 311–12.

Zhou, Yang. 2007. "Jiceng zhengfu zhineng zhuanyi–Shanghai NGO zhili shequ" ("Shifting functions of basic-level government: Shanghai NGO governs resident associations"). *Ershiyi shiji jingji baodao* 21 (23 November), 4.

Zhu, Xiaohong, 2009. "Analysis of YBC's 'Rebuild our home entrepreneurship campaign' – A social enterprise perspective." *The China Nonprofit Review* 1, 263–283.

[23]

Comparative Political Studies
Volume 39 Number 3
April 2006 301-324
© 2006 Sage Publications
10.1177/0010414005280852
http://cps.sagepub.com
hosted at
http://online.sagepub.com

Democracy, Community, Trust

The Impact of Elections in Rural China

Melanie Manion
University of Wisconsin–Madison

This article systematically investigates the impact of elections in rural China on a basic element of the elite-mass relationship: beliefs of ordinary citizens that their leaders are trustworthy. It analyzes data from two surveys of randomly sampled villagers in the same 57 villages in 1990 and 1996, merged with a set of separately collected data detailing features of elections in these villages during the same period of time. The analyses take advantage of uneven progress in grassroots democratization and ask how variation in democratic electoral quality across villages is associated with variation in changed views about the probity (or venality) of local leaders. Results strongly suggest that formal institutions of electoral democracy matter: Designs that feature contestation and encourage voter participation do better at promoting beliefs that leaders are trustworthy. At the same time, results point to the importance of informal community institutions of lineage relationships.

Keywords: *corruption; trust; democratization; elections; clans; China*

A few years before the cascade of revolutions toppled most communist one-party states, Chinese leaders adopted a modest program of electoral democracy to strengthen communist party rule. The provisional law passed by the Chinese legislature in 1987 was restricted in scope to the coun-

Author's Note: This article analyzes data from collaborative surveys conducted by mainland Chinese and American researchers with the support of the Luce Foundation, National Science Foundation, University of Michigan, Smith Richardson Foundation, and State Education Commission of the People's Republic of China. 1990 mass survey data have been deposited at the Inter-University Consortium for Political and Social Research at the University of Michigan. For helpful comments on earlier drafts, the author thanks Michael Bratton, Kent Jennings, Mingming Shen, Wenfang Tang, Lily Tsai, David Weimer, and participants in seminars at the George Washington University, University of South Carolina, and Institute of Political Science, Academia Sinica. Please address all correspondence to Melanie Manion at manion@lafollette.wisc.edu

tryside but was nonetheless of historic significance: It established popularly elected village committees as autonomous bodies of self-government, empowering ordinary Chinese villagers to choose and monitor their own leaders. The law was designed to build public confidence at the rural grassroots in the wake of decollectivization and the atrophy of organizations and leadership (Li & O'Brien, 1999; Thurston, 1998; X. Wang, 1997; White, 1992). Leaders in Beijing pointed to widespread tensions and sporadic violence in the countryside and argued that elections could transform the situation by imposing accountability and replacing coercive and corrupt "local emperors" with trusted, responsive, capable leaders (Li & O'Brien, 1999; O'Brien, 1994; O'Brien & Li, 2000; Shi, 1999; X. Wang, 1997). The Ministry of Civil Affairs (MCA), charged with implementing the law, worked to promote electoral contestation, secret ballots, voting booths, and citizen participation in the processes by which candidates emerge. Progress in implementation was highly uneven (O'Brien & Li, 2000; Thurston, 1998; Z. Wang, 1998). In 1998, the Chinese legislature passed a revised version of the law, no longer provisional, containing many measures of electoral democracy advanced by the MCA. Today, with several rounds of village elections completed, a substantial empirical record has accumulated, enabling systematic study of the effect of these institutional changes. This article investigates the impact of grassroots electoral democracy on a basic element of the elite-mass relationship—the belief of ordinary citizens that their leaders are trustworthy.

The data analyzed here are from two surveys of randomly sampled villagers in the same 57 villages in 1990 and 1996, merged with a set of separately collected data detailing features of elections in these villages during the same period of time (see Appendix 1). The analyses take advantage of uneven progress in grassroots democratization and ask how variation in democratic electoral quality across villages is associated with variation in changed views about the probity (or venality) of local leaders. Not least of all, the analyses also take account of informal institutions that make up the community context in which village elections were introduced—in particular, variation across villages in lineage structure.

In most previous studies, Chinese grassroots democratization features mainly as a dependent variable and only secondarily as an explanatory variable. Studies based on qualitative fieldwork suggest that electoral contestation may have improved governance and given villagers a sense of increased voice in local politics, but it may have intensified lineage conflict too (Li & O'Brien, 1999; O'Brien, 1994; White, 1992). The law appears to have changed political discourse for villagers, providing them with a resource they employ in appeals to authorities at higher levels (Li & O'Brien,

1996; O'Brien, 1996). It has also prompted, in some localities, a greater role for ordinary villagers and village committees in supervising village communist party leaders (Guo & Bernstein, 2004; Lawrence, 1994; Li, 1999). In analyses of survey data, Manion (1996) finds a positive relationship between electoral contestation and congruence in views between villagers and their leaders. A survey by Li (2002) finds a positive relationship between democratic electoral quality and the likelihood of villagers to appeal to their leaders to represent themselves against predatory exactions by higher authorities. In Li (2003), the introduction of free and fair village elections increases political efficacy.

This article contributes to a growing literature on Chinese grassroots democratization and, more generally, to an evaluation of ongoing political institutional change in China. In the broadest sense, the analyses here also add to our knowledge about the effects of new electoral democracy and the relationship between formal electoral institutions and informal networks. The evidence suggests that two essential dimensions of democracy have a significant impact: Beliefs that leaders are "clean" and not corrupt have grown in villages where elections feature more contestation and voting methods promote more participation. At the same time, informal community influences of lineage relationships are also important. This cautions against naive determinism when considering the possibilities or time frame for change induced by formal institutions alone.

Perceived Corruption As a Proxy for Trust

Taking advantage of a new abundance of subjective corruption measures, many quantitative analyses treat perceived corruption as a rough proxy for actual abuses by officials of the public trust.[1] Certainly, where trust in officials is low, a likely reason is indeed low trustworthiness (Hardin, 1999). Yet the illegality of corruption and the obvious biases against reporting it, compared to many other crimes, pose an information problem—described by Myrdal (1968) more than 3 decades ago as a "folklore of corruption" and by Miller, Grodeland, and Koshechkina (2001) recently as a "culture of corruption." Shared beliefs about the ubiquity of corrupt practices may be highly

1. Transparency International has produced a Corruption Perceptions Index (CPI) annually since 1995, ranking 90 or more countries in recent years. Studies based on the CPI include Goldsmith (1999), Treisman (2000), Sandholtz and Koetzle (2000), and Anderson and Tverdova (2003). Other studies use the International Country Risk Guide, one of the sources for compilation of the CPI. For examples of studies using objective measures, see Golden and Chang (2001) and Seligson (2002).

exaggerated but can nonetheless persist in a community and influence how ordinary citizens act in encounters with officials (Manion, 2004).

Without rejecting the possibility that perceptions may reflect practices reasonably well, this article treats perceptions of the probity (or venality) of leaders as intrinsically important. Popular views about corruption among local leaders may imperfectly reflect local practices, but they surely reflect well the quality of elite-mass relationships. They reflect the breadth of trust within the community that leaders are working in the legitimate collective interest, not their own illicit private interest.

In the context examined here, perceived corruption is a particularly apt proxy for trust in local leaders. Corruption is highly salient in China. Since the mid-1980s, it has ranked at or near the top of every public opinion poll as the most urgent problem confronting the country. It is a volatile social issue; it was perhaps the major issue in the 1989 protests in Beijing and other cities in China (Manion, 1990; Mason, 1994; Ostergaard & Petersen, 1991; Sun, 1991). Increasing income inequality has exacerbated the volatility because of a perception that the wealthy have attained their status corruptly (He, 1997). The salience of corruption reflects its more or less unabated growth (Gong, 1994; Manion, 2004; Ostergaard, 1986) and the broadly propagandized official attention to it. In sum, corruption in China is not an abstraction but a real problem of great salience. Chinese leaders (probably correctly) view it as the greatest threat to communist party rule today. Perceived corruption may or may not be a good measure of actual abuses of the public trust, but it does reflect popular views about official trustworthiness in a straightforward way that is easily understood by ordinary Chinese villagers.[2] It is also a particularly interesting measure for the analyses here because Chinese village elections were introduced in part to curb local abuses of power.

Electoral Democracy

The presumed effect of electoral democracy on abuses of power makes sense. Studies appearing in recent years find a fairly consistent empirical association of democracy with less perceived corruption, although scholars disagree on the strength of the relationship and whether long experience of democracy is required for any significant impact (Goldsmith, 1999; Knack &

2. Li (2004) asks villagers to assess the prestige or popular trust [weixin] in the countryside of communist party organizations at different levels, but he treats villagers as informants reporting on the local situation rather than respondents reporting on their own trust in party organizations. In qualitative interviews cited in the article, villagers raise the issue of corruption to express their own individual distrust of party organizations.

Azfar, 2001; Sandholtz & Koetzle, 2000; Treisman, 2000).[3] Theoretically, for a number of reasons, electoral democracy can be expected to enhance collective beliefs, accurate or not, that leaders are generally clean and not corrupt.

First, by design at least, electoral democracy promotes probity of elected leaders. Democratic elections align interests of leaders with interests of voters through two mechanisms: choice and monitoring. Electoral choice means that voters can choose leaders they believe are less likely to abuse public office. The prospect of reelection also affects the conduct of elected leaders; in this way, elections act through the monitoring mechanism. In rural China, where villages average about 1,200 residents, electoral choice can be based on personal knowledge, accumulated through decades, and updated continuously. Compared to elections in contexts of larger scale in which gathering information requires more resources, village elections have the potential to check improper conduct more effectively. An institutional design that subjects leaders to voter choice and rejection at regular intervals can be expected to constrain leaders—who are chosen through a process in which ordinary villagers have a voice—to act in the collective interest rather than in their private interest.[4] The main point here is not, however, that electoral democracy always or necessarily constrains venal officials but that ordinary citizens can expect it generally to have this constraining effect, especially in the small village context and in comparison with the decades-old system of appointments.

Second, to the extent that electoral quality covaries with other qualities of governance, we can expect to see an association with popular beliefs that reflects this. That is, democratic electoral quality may be a proxy for a bundle of institutional features that promote beliefs about trustworthiness of local leaders. The empirical association of democracy with perceived clean government across countries, noted above, has much to do with attendant nonelectoral mechanisms (press freedoms and rule of law, for example) that enhance transparency and accountability. In rural China, elections are only one element of grassroots democratization—increased financial transparency and villagers' participation in decision making are others. Village electoral quality may be associated with beliefs in the probity of local leaders because elections are of a piece with other institutional features that also promote such beliefs.

3. At the same time, Weyland (1998) links democratization with increased corruption in Latin America, pointing to the role of economic liberalization and political power dispersal in increasing the number of opportunities for bribery and veto players requiring bribes.

4. The evidence here does in fact suggest a relationship between actual official probity and democratic quality of village elections. See the discussion of corrupt encounters in the conclusion.

Community Context

Formal institutions are never the whole story, of course. The introduction of electoral democracy in rural China, as in the liberal democracies that replaced communist rule, has taken place in particular contexts that have different implications for how ordinary citizens perceive their leaders. These contexts are defined by existing patterns of vertical and horizontal linkages. Here, I consider a key feature of community context that can be expected to affect the quality of elite-mass relationships in rural China: lineage structure.

Responding to Putnam's (1993) work linking social trust and democratic vitality, Levi (1996) cautions that social networks are a source of both trust and distrust (they promote trust of those inside the network and distrust of those outside it). Warren (1999) extends this argument into the political sphere, noting that competitive electoral campaigns are typically divisive: They manufacture particularized trust by cultivating the distrust of other communities of interest. Chinese village elections do not feature campaigns as such, but these issues are relevant to the effect of informal institutions, such as lineage relationships that confer social identity, on popular beliefs about local corruption. Chinese sociologist Xiao (2001b, p. 87) concludes, on the basis of fieldwork in the late 1990s, that village elections are a powerful catalyst for clan activity: "Elections increase [both] clan trust and clan suspicions; they temporarily moderate conflict within clans and intensify conflict between clans."[5] Xiao and his collaborators find clan influence in elections reflected in a higher likelihood of winning leadership positions for candidates from big clans, the use by candidates of clan affiliation as a credential to win votes, and the practice by a majority of villagers of voting for their own clan.

The notion that the mere introduction of village elections unleashes clan distrust and formalizes the structure of clan influence was argued by Chinese opponents of rural grassroots democratization in the 1980s (see Kelliher, 1997; X. Wang, 1997). They warned of the potential for extreme strife in villages where evenly matched lineages compete for power. As this suggests, the implications of clan influence for elite-mass linkages depend partly on clan structure. For example, in case studies of four villages in southern China, Tsai (2002) finds relations between villagers and village officials in multiple-surname villages are characterized by conflict and distrust. In single-surname villages, however, dense community networks allow villagers to sanction officials who are sensitive to wide social disapproval and, therefore, rarely act so as to incur actual sanctions. Similarly, Kennedy (2002), investigating villager satisfaction with the electoral process, finds

5. See also Xiao et al. (2001a).

that "the interests of the lineage organization and the village as a whole are linked" (p. 479) in single-surname villages and that the situation breeding greatest dissatisfaction is one in which villages have two or three large clans.

In sum, theoretical reasons and empirical evidence suggest that lineage relationships matter. If, as Xiao and others have argued, elections stimulate clan salience and activity, then social distrust among villagers of different lineages may increase and, among villagers, distrust of leaders from different lineages may increase—reflected in perceptions that leaders are corrupt. This is to be expected most in elections that feature a few clans vying for village rule. In single-surname villages or villages with a highly fragmented clan structure, however, we do not expect to observe this sort of increased distrust with village electoral democracy.

Dependent Variable

The discussion above frames the research question for the analyses below. How and how much is variation across villages in democratic electoral quality and lineage structure associated with variation in changed views of ordinary villagers about the probity of their leaders? The dependent variable is a measure of change in trust in local leaders, based on 1990 and 1996 survey responses to questions about perceived local corruption. Questions and response frequencies are summarized in Table 1.

Overall, responses suggest a change in the direction of broader trust: Fifty-one percent of respondents in 1996 considered most officials in their locality clean and not corrupt, compared to 35% in 1990. Some part of the apparent increase in trust may be attributable to changed wording of the question. In the earlier survey, conducted 6 to 8 months after the 1989 urban protests and subsequent crackdown, we judged questions about corruption as too sensitive to ask directly. Instead, we asked about clean government and honest and upright officials. In the less politically charged climate of 1996, we asked about corruption directly. The political environment in 1990 and the more direct wording in 1996 probably also account for the relatively high (and higher in 1996) proportion of missing data. These differences pose a problem for a descriptive measure of trust, but not for the village-level inferential analyses below. This is because systematic biases that can reasonably be presumed to arise from differences across time (including differences in wording) can also reasonably be presumed to operate similarly across villages.[6] The surveys were also conducted in very different economic environ-

6. That is, although the dependent variable may reflect more or less than exact change in villages, it is a valid measure of change to use in the statistical analyses below that estimate the effects of variables on change. It is reasonable to assume that, at most, the difference in question

Table 1
Changing Perceptions of Probity (Venality) of Local Leaders

	Percentage responding in	
How Many Officials are Clean, Not Corrupt?	1990 [a] $N = 1{,}115$	1996 [b] $N = 1{,}216$
Overwhelming majority	6.3	11.8
Majority	28.7	39.0
Minority	37.3	18.4
Hardly any	12.3	7.5
Do not know, no response, or evasive response	15.4	23.3

Note: Coding has been reversed in presentation above, to facilitate comparison.
a. In 1990, the question was, "There has been a lot of talk recently about the issue of 'clean government' [wei zheng qinglian wenti]. How many of the officials around here would you say are 'clean' [wei zheng qinglian], that is, how many are honest and upright officials [qing guan]? Would you say it is the overwhelming majority, the majority, a minority, or hardly any?"
b. In 1996, the question was, "There has been a lot of talk recently about the issue of official corruption [ganbu fubai wenti]. How many of the officials around here would you say are corrupt [fubai]? Would you say it is the overwhelming majority, the majority, a minority, or hardly any?"

ments: an economic slowdown in 1990 and the tail end of a major economic boom in 1996. These macroeconomic changes likely affected villages differently and so must be taken into account in the analyses.

The most straightforward dependent variable for the question of interest here is village-level change in proportions of respondents reporting that most local officials are clean, not corrupt. Unfortunately, as percentages are constrained between 0 and 100, this formulation is also incorrect. The correction here is a logarithmic transformation of the dependent variable to permit estimation of a linear model.[7] Results with the correction are essentially the same as those for the more easily interpretable dependent variable, however. For this reason, I focus discussion on estimation of effects on the latter (although I present both models). Positive numbers indicate a more widely held perception in 1996 that most local leaders are clean and not corrupt, interpreted here as a change in the direction of broader trust.

wording results in the second construct differing from the first by a constant. Then, although the exact change with time is $v_{i2} - v_{i1}$, the measured difference will be $v_{i2} + \propto - v_{i1}$. This is equivalent to subtracting a constant from the dependent variable, which will only affect the estimate of the constant in the estimated equation.

7. I thank Langche Zeng for suggesting the following transformation: log [1996 fraction ÷ (1–1996 fraction)] – log [1990 fraction ÷ (1–1990 fraction)], in which 1990 and 1996 fractions are proportions of village respondents reporting most officials are clean in 1990 and not corrupt in 1996, respectively. With the logarithmic transformation of the dependent variable, two cases drop out of the sample because percentages for 1 year are 100.

Explanatory Variables: Democratic Electoral Quality

Democratic electoral quality is measured as openness of nomination and selection of candidates, degree of electoral contestation, and inclusiveness of voting procedures. Measures are borrowed from Pastor and Tan (2000), who employ a perspective developed from observing elections in many countries, including elections in rural China.[8] The explanatory variables in the analyses below here are village-level averages for all elections held in the 1990 to 1996 period.[9]

Openness of Candidate Nomination and Selection

Villages across China use a variety of methods to generate initial nominations of candidates for village committee positions (see Elklit, 1997; Howell, 1998; Kennedy, 2002; Pastor & Tan 2000). Typically, nominations originate from more than one source. Processes in which ordinary Chinese participate include nominations by groups of individual voters, village small groups, household representatives, and village representative assemblies.[10] Processes in which ordinary Chinese are not involved include nominations by the village election leading small group, the village communist party branch, and township government. Obviously, even the former processes can be manipulated by leaders. Whether this occurs, or the extent to which it influences electoral outcomes, is difficult to discover for a large number of villages.

8. Pastor and Tan (2000) also emphasize the importance of the secret ballot. Chinese village elections do not yet commonly feature secret ballots, in the privacy of voting booths. Voting often takes place at village meetings, and ballots are marked in the open. These practices are relatively private, compared to overtly public voting (such as by applause or show of hands). In our sample, data on ballot privacy are incomplete for 3 villages. In 51 villages, ballots are completed in relative privacy, that is, voting is overtly public in only 3 villages. To avoid dropping observations, the analyses here do not include ballot privacy. Results of all the analyses are substantively and statistically the same when the ballot privacy variable is included, however. Ballot privacy is not significant in any of the analyses, but of course there is little variation on this variable.

9. For most villages, these measures average electoral quality across two elections. In computing the mean values for the analyses here, I eliminated 1996 elections in 6 villages because they were held after the 1996 survey was conducted. To include them would confound the analysis of the impact of electoral quality on the dependent variable here.

10. Village small groups are the former production teams under collectivized agriculture, and they often coincide with natural villages. Village representative assemblies are elected in many villages, especially large villages, to monitor village committee financial decisions and contribute to decisions relating to village economic management. See Lawrence (1994) and Thurston (1998).

However, manipulated or not, the former processes operate through the villagers and can be expected to affect views about the fairness of elections and electoral outcomes. In this sense, they differ fundamentally from the processes monopolized by leaders.

Not all candidates initially nominated are selected to appear on the ballot. The formal candidate list may be reduced through various processes, sometimes depending on how many initial candidates are nominated. If initial nominations yield no more candidates than positions, selection may nonetheless involve candidate vetting. Again, these processes may or may not involve villagers' participation.

For each election in 1990 to 1996, nomination and selection are coded here as three-level ordinal variables, with higher values indicating greater openness of the process to villagers.[11] The analyses below consider openness of nomination and selection independently, with variables that average values for each across elections in each village.[12]

Electoral Contestation

A more obvious component of electoral choice is the degree of electoral contestation. Pastor and Tan (2000) posit an ideal of two candidates for each position, but many Chinese village elections do not meet this criterion. Despite efforts through the years by the MCA and its subordinate bureaus, a number of village elections offer no choice among candidates (although the 1998 law requires it). To be sure, even in elections without choice, villagers can reject candidates and produce a "failed election," as successful candidates must receive a majority of votes cast. Nonetheless, choice among candidates is unequivocally an important component of democratic electoral quality.

Electoral contestation in the analyses here is the mean of the ratio of candidates to positions on the village committee. More than 40% of villages in the sample consistently feature elections with choice, and more than 65% feature at least one election with choice. Electoral contestation in the sample often takes on a mean value of about 1.3, with one third more candidates than positions.

11. Villagers' monopoly of the process takes on the value of 3, monopoly by leaders the value of 1, and participation by both villagers and leaders the value of 2.

12. I have constructed different versions of these variables—with the underlying idea that there are tradeoffs, that openness in selection may be of little import if, for example, the communist party branch monopolizes initial nominations. The different constructions do not yield different results in the analyses here. Without a clear theoretical or empirical basis for choosing one version over another, I present the most straightforward construction.

Inclusiveness of Voting Procedures

The 1998 law mandates direct individual voting by secret ballot in voting booths. In most villages, individual villagers do vote by marking ballots themselves, although frequently in public village meetings. Household representatives usually vote in place of others in their household who are working outside the village. In some villages, heads of households vote by proxy for all household members. In other villages, the village representative assembly determines the final outcome of the village election. Data on voting procedures in our sample of 57 villages are incomplete, but among the 47 for which complete data exist, most permit only direct individual voting and few changed the voting procedures in the 1990 to 1996 period.[13]

What is of interest here is the breadth of participation of villagers as individual voters. This is not necessarily reflected well in figures on voter turnout, probably because turnout is a key performance measure for which local officials mobilize greatly, even if they ignore other features of electoral quality. In our 1996 survey, we asked respondents if they had voted in an election for the village committee. Overall, 56% of villagers report not having voted. It is certainly possible that some villagers who voted failed to recall it, but reported voting clearly reflects village-level features; variation across villages is huge,[14] and the proportion who report having voted is highly correlated with the degree to which procedures promote direct individual voting.[15] As respondents are a random sample of the village population, and as variation across villages in individual-level characteristics is trivial, it is reasonable to suppose that village-level variation in reported voting is related to village-level features.[16]

13. Sixty-two percent permit only direct individual voting: In 6 villages, household representatives decide the election outcome, and in 9 villages, the village representative assembly decides.

14. In the top quarter of villages in the sample, more than 77% of villagers report having voted, but in the bottom quarter, less than 13% report having voted.

15. Correlation is .654, significant at .01. Voting procedure is coded as a four-level ordinal to reflect inclusiveness, with greater inclusiveness taking on higher values. For example, direct individual voting takes on a value of 4, and voting by the village representative assembly a value of 1.

16. Zhong and Chen (2002) explain reported voting in village elections as a function of individual democratic orientation, but their model includes no village-level variables—so the impact of institutional features such as inclusiveness of voting procedures is unknowable. At the same time, the adoption of voting procedures may be somewhat endogenous, a point taken up in the discussion of village democratic culture below. Zhong and Chen also consider evasive responses (in the analyses here, a component of missing data) as substantive neutral responses on a 5-point scale, which makes their results difficult to evaluate.

To be sure, reported voting reflects more than actual voting or inclusiveness of voting procedures. It reflects the salience of elections—related not only to voting procedures but also to the recentness of elections.[17] To avoid dropping observations because of missing data, the analyses we use here are village-level reported voting percentages as a proxy for inclusiveness of voting procedures. To take account of voting salience related to recentness of elections, I include as a control variable the number of months between the 1996 survey and the most recent election. That reported voting reflects the salience of elections beyond voting procedures and distance in time is, however, an important consideration. We can think of reported voting as capturing features of electoral quality that prominently include the inclusiveness of voting procedures and the recentness of elections but also include other village-level features that go unmeasured in the model.

Explanatory Variables: Lineage Relationships and Economic Change

The introduction of elections, however badly or well implemented, offers an opportunity for exclusive groups with different identities to manufacture distrust. Villages with lineage relationships that do not divide the community into a few exclusive groups may have a "leg up": Elections are unlikely to foment increased social and political distrust. Additionally, economic change offers new opportunities for local leaders. Changes in trust may be due to changes in administrative performance related to the local economy, not to electoral quality.

Lineage Relationships

Without extensive fieldwork, which is practical only for a rather small sample, it may be impossible to know the degree to which lineage is an important influence in any particular village. Potential importance can be measured approximately, however, by considering village surname diversity. To be sure, the same surname does not always connote the same lineage or a close horizontal association within the lineage, even in rural context. Within a village, different lineages may have a common surname but trace descent from different founding ancestors, and a single lineage can be divided into different lineage branches (for examples, see Cohen, 1990). That is, although surname diversity is a good indicator of lineage diversity, it is possible for a

17. Reported voting is strongly and significantly correlated with the number of months between the most recent election and the 1996 survey (–.470, significant at .01).

single-surname village to be characterized by many lineage branches and even lineages. Fortuitously, however, none of the 57 villages in our sample approximates a single-surname village.[18]

A proxy measure for the potential importance of lineage relationships can be computed from a random sample of surnames in the village. The lineage measure in the analyses below is computed using such samples for each village and applying to each the standard formula for effective number of parties (typically used to describe the distribution of seats in parliamentary democracies).[19] Lower values reflect greater surname concentration and higher values reflect greater surname diversity.[20] As there are no single-surname villages, small values suggest the possibility of manufactured distrust in elections—two or three lineages vying for dominance or a strong but not predominant lineage in a village with many lineages—rather than village harmony. As smaller values here suggest distrust, not harmony, and larger values suggest weakness (or irrelevance) of lineage influences in politics, the predicted relationship to change in trust in local leaders is positive.

Economic Change

Economic change related to the quality of administrative performance may also explain variation in changes in trust. Improvement (or deterioration) in incomes and income distribution can reflect variation in local leadership in the context of new opportunities presented by economic decentralization. Consider income change first. As improving prosperity is one of the most important roles of local leaders, villagers may credit (or blame) local leaders for changes in local wealth—and may conflate economic success with trustworthiness. Additionally, localities that flourished in the 1980s and 1990s, typically through the growth of rural industry or private entrepreneurship, provided local leaders with comparatively stronger revenue bases on which to draw to support a bloated administration and meet unfunded central mandates that promote predatory exactions from villagers (see Bernstein &

18. Here, village refers to administrative village, which contains within it some number of natural villages. It is certainly possible (and not unlikely) that some natural villages in the 57 administrative villages are single-surname villages—but this poses no problem for the measure described here. Basically, village committees are elected for administrative villages, not for natural villages.

19. Adapted for the analyses here, the formula is $1 \div \Sigma$ (percentage village sample for each surname^2), in which village sample refers to the random sample of surnames in the village.

20. A single-surname village takes on a value of 1 and a village equally divided between three surnames takes on a value of 3. Here, large values reflect fragmentation and probably the weakness of lineage relationships as influences. For example, the unusually high value of 23.12 in one village comes from a random sample of 34 surnames in a village where the most common surname is shared by less than 9% of villagers sampled.

Lu, 2003; Wedeman, 2000). Even if improved prosperity is associated with fewer actual predatory exactions, it can reasonably be expected to affect beliefs about the predatory takings of local leaders. As to the change in income inequality, against an historical background of Maoist egalitarianism, many ordinary Chinese associate growing inequality with low moral scruples of those with wealth and power (He, 1997). Where inequality has increased, villagers may blame local officials, attributing the change to poor administrative performance, or view widening disparity as evidence that those in positions of leadership are not impartial in the distribution of opportunities. In short, increased inequality may promote beliefs that leaders are unworthy of the popular trust for some (but not all) of the same reasons that increased incomes promote beliefs in their trustworthiness.

In the analyses below, village-level change in income is measured by subtracting 1990 per capita income from that of 1996. As positive values indicate increases in per capita income, the predicted relationship to the dependent variable is positive. Village-level change in income inequality is derived from reported household income in the 1990 and 1996 surveys. The measure subtracts the 1990 standard deviation from the 1996 village standard deviation of reported household income.[21] As positive values reflect increases in income inequality, a negative relationship to the dependent variable is predicted; that is, greater increases in income inequality should be associated with greater decreased trust in local leaders.

Control Variables

Electoral democracy may matter little if elections essentially put a formal institutional face on widely shared practices and accompanying expectations about elite-mass relations. The analyses below attempt to control for different points of departure in democratic culture by monitoring the orientation of villagers toward local leaders before electoral democracy can be expected to have an impact on trust.[22] The variable reflecting the scope and intensity of monitoring orientations is based on a simple additive index of responses to

21. To encourage valid reports of income, we asked respondents in both surveys to report household income by choosing from among 15 income ranges, beginning with under 500 yuan and extending up to more than 10,000 yuan. To compute standard deviations, I transformed reported ranges into range midpoints. The standard deviation resulting from this transformation is a reasonable approximation of income distribution in the village, given the structure of available data.

22. The variable is based on responses to the first survey, largely reflecting orientations in 1990, 1 1/2 years after the provisional law went into effect. This problem, to the extent that it is a problem, is mitigated somewhat because orientation is measured with question items on relevant past behaviors, not only attitudes and opinions.

six items asked in the 1990 survey: questions about interest in village elections, attention to public affairs, actions communicating this attention to local officials, and beliefs about the efficacy of such actions.[23] The analyses below use village means of sums of individual-level positive responses.

Although surely inadequate, monitoring orientation is by no means unsuitable as a reflection of a village's democratic culture. Such a culture is likely to be resistant, although not impervious, to change. Not surprisingly, village-level monitoring orientation computed from responses to the 1990 survey is strongly correlated with that computed from responses to the same questions asked in 1996.[24] Also, democratic culture may help explain variation across villages in inclusiveness of voting procedures: In the situation that villagers are interested, attentive, and already communicate effectively with local elites, less inclusive voting is probably not needed to boost voter turnout—and is probably less acceptable to villagers too. This endogeneity of culture and institutions is indeed suggested in a strong and significant correlation between voting procedures and 1990 monitoring orientation.[25]

The analyses also include as control variables village size (1990 population) and village wealth (1990 per capita income).

Analyses and Discussion

Table 2 summarizes the hypothesized direction of relationships for variables of analytic interest. Table 3 presents results from weighted least squares multivariate regression estimations for the most easily interpretable dependent variable.[26] Model I includes all variables, and Model II includes only the analytic variables of significance and control variables. Appendix 2 presents the same estimations yielding essentially the same results using logarithmic transformations of the 1990 and 1996 village percentages.[27] Appendix 3 presents summary statistics for variables used in the analyses.

The results presented in Table 3 suggest that the obvious and elemental features of electoral democracy matter. Other things equal, two electoral variables increase the breadth of trust in local leaders: The extent to which

23. Responses to the six items tend to be highly correlated at the individual level (all significant at .01). Expressed as village population percentages, they tend to be highly correlated at the village level too (significant at .05 or .01).

24. The correlation is .768, significant at .01

25. The correlation is .561, significant at .01.

26. Weighted least squares estimations take into account different numbers of respondents in each village. The range is from 12 to 30 respondents. See Appendix 1.

27. I conducted tests for multicollinearity for all models, with both the untransformed and transformed dependent variable: in no model does the mean variation inflation factor exceed 2, and the largest variance inflation factor for any single variable is 3.13.

Table 2
Hypothesized Relationships: Explanatory Variables and Change in Trust in Local Leaders

Explanatory Variable	Relationship
Electoral contestation	+
Reported voting	+
Openness of candidate nominations	+
Openness of candidate selection	+
Surname diversity	+
Per capita income change	+
Income inequality change	–

Table 3
Impact of Elections and Context on Change in Trust in Local Leaders

Independent Variable	Model I	*SE*	Model II	*SE*
Electoral contestation	17.07502*	8.758429	17.0912*	7.825397
Openness of candidate nominations	–.6473897	3.059035		
Openness of candidate selection	–1.534766	2.516208		
Reported voting	.3760728**	.1185668	.3791136***	.1153367
Surname diversity	1.364633**	.4845797	1.445781***	.4330493
Per capita income change	.0140168*	.0060236	.014512**	.005831
Income inequality change	–.0011717	.0036461		
Control variables				
Monitoring orientation	6.745625	4.317	6.718715	4.164209
1990 population	.0022643	.003501	.0024416	.0033578
1990 per capita income	.0167176	.0115448	.0142982	.0108224
Months since most recent election	.0070349	.1519062	.0081604	.1478434
Intercept	–64.98389**	23.87792	–69.35094***	20.9239
Adjusted R^2	.494		.518	

Note: Observations are from 57 villages. Dependent variable is 1996 percentage village population reporting minority of local officials are corrupt minus 1990 percentage reporting majority of local officials are "clean." Models are weighted least squares estimations, coefficients are unstandardized, significance tests are one-tailed.
$*p < .05$. $**p < .01$, $***p < .001$.

ballots offer choice and procedures encourage individual voting participation. That is, greater electoral contestation and more inclusive voting procedures matter, as predicted. Electoral features reflecting openness of the process to villagers' participation before the election, in nomination and selection of candidates, are not statistically significant in the analyses presented in Table 3. This is at odds with stories in the Chinese press and observations of village elections by Americans through the years. One possible explanation is that the measures themselves are too crude to capture actual villagers' participation or leadership and manipulation in these processes. There may also be insufficient variation in the 57 villages sampled here. Anecdotal evidence about the importance of villager participation in nomination and selection of candidates often points to localities where elections feature successive series of primaries that often begin with many dozens of candidates nominated directly by villagers. More subtle variation in these processes may simply not make enough difference to beliefs about the trustworthiness of local leaders, although it may matter to outcomes not examined here.[28]

The association of electoral contestation and inclusiveness of voting procedures with increased local trust does not, of course, rule out a hypothesis about a different causal mechanism and direction than described above. Electoral quality may itself reflect trustworthiness. The implementation of electoral democracy implies a willingness to practice methods by which ordinary citizens can hold leaders accountable. Local officials who fear an honest electoral verdict because they have abused the popular trust are unlikely to put into place mechanisms that allow citizens to sanction them through the ballot box. That is, greater trustworthiness may produce elections of higher democratic quality. Of course, the leaders who set guidelines for local electoral practices are not the vote seekers in Chinese village elections but officials at the higher township or county levels—and this offers some reassurance about the greater plausibility of the explanation proposed above.[29]

The results presented in Table 3 also point to the importance of basic economic features. Other things equal, and regardless of starting point, increases

28. See Kennedy (2002) for a systematic investigation of recent village elections that demonstrates the importance of nomination procedures.

29. That village committee leaders probably feature prominently (if not exclusively) as the referent for our respondents is suggested by a strong negative correlation between perceptions of the scope of local corruption and assessments of the performance of the village committee head, a question asked in 1996 (–.419, significant at .01, with 864 observations). An interesting finding was that villagers surveyed by Li (2004) report the level of prestige or popular trust of communist party organizations at the township and village levels as practically identical, compared to higher levels of prestige reported for higher levels of organization.

in village prosperity, measured here as per capita income change, are associated with increases in trust. This may be due to a conflation of administrative performance, economic success, and trustworthiness of local leaders in the eyes of ordinary Chinese. Alternatively, if villagers equate corruption with predatory exactions, it may be due to the stronger revenue bases associated with village wealth, which reduce the need to "squeeze" villagers to support local government. That is, improved village prosperity may permit local leaders to be more widely trusted because they are more trustworthy. A less benign possibility is that village prosperity may increase villagers' tolerance of corrupt practices. These causal processes are not mutually exclusive. Any or all may be at work.

Perhaps the most intriguing finding reported in Table 3 has nothing to do with electoral institutions or economic change but with lineage relationships. Clans clearly matter. Other things equal, in villages where lineage structure lends itself most to clan conflict, that is, where villagers can identify with one of only a few clans, clan influence in the new context of village elections promotes distrust. This contrasts with villages where clans are more numerous and, therefore, not a salient feature dividing villagers into distinct categories. Although the sample of 57 villages does not present an opportunity to test clan influence in single-surname villages (where clan identity promotes village harmony), the presumption is that the association of surname concentration with decreased trust would not hold in villages with this lineage structure.

Conclusion

Five years after the introduction of electoral democracy in Poland, Sztompka (1996) observes a culture of endemic social and political distrust, partly a legacy of socialism. It is perhaps naive to expect to find an impact of elections on trust in leaders with less than a decade of accumulated experience. Yet the analyses presented here strongly suggest that the formal institutions of electoral democracy matter: Designs that encourage electoral contestation and voting participation do better at promoting the trust of ordinary citizens in their leaders than do designs that restrict competition and exclude voters. At the same time, community context matters: As elections are opportunities for open conflict, they are also opportunities for the manufacture of distrust in which the structure of relationships is most conducive to distrust rooted in identities (here, clans) rather than in issues. In sum, although formal institutions of elections matter, informal institutions of community matter too.

Of course, arguments presented here are about changes in trust, which does not necessarily reflect trustworthiness. There is some evidence, however, to support the conjecture that the views about probity measured here are not unrelated to actual probity. In 1996, we asked respondents whether they had personally experienced corruption. A much higher proportion of respondents who report an encounter with corruption also believe most local officials are corrupt, compared to those who report no such encounter—63% compared to 28%.[30] This finding suggests that democratic quality of Chinese village elections may, as theory leads us to expect, promote real trustworthiness as well as trust.

It is nonetheless useful to place village electoral democracy in perspective. There is a growing scholarly consensus that, despite great variation, grassroots electoral democracy has progressed and is flourishing, affecting the lives of ordinary Chinese villagers in important ways, for the better. Elections of leaders at higher levels share none of the features of democracy described here, however. Between village and nation are townships, counties, municipalities, and provinces. Although a few townships have seen a few bold electoral experiments, democratic electoral quality is most evident at the lowest level, where it matters greatly for governance and stability but least of all for policy making.

Appendix 1
Data Collection

Survey data analyzed in this article are from two surveys, conducted in 1990 and 1996, in 4 counties, 20 townships, and 57 villages as part of a collaborative project begun by political scientists at Peking University and the University of Michigan. Located in Hebei, Hunan, Anhui, and Tianjin, the counties are a nonprobability sample selected to exhibit some regional variation from a sampling frame of about 20 counties in which, based on the experience of our Chinese colleagues, we could reasonably expect agreement from local authorities to facilitate fieldwork. The townships and villages surveyed are probability samples, selected according to a nested sampling design. In each of the 4 counties, we drew a stratified probability sample of 5 townships, selected with probability proportionate to size and stratified by per capita income. In each selected township, we drew a sample of 3 administrative villages selected with probability proportionate to size. Three villages in one of the Hunan

30. The three most common responses, accounting for nearly three quarters of all responses, describe the use of public office for excessive exactions from ordinary villagers, the use of public office to appropriate public goods, and the use of public funds for feasting and banqueting. Missing data are 254 respondents (21%). The Pearson chi-square for the cross-tabulation is 72.96, significant at .01 (with 864 observations). There is also a fairly strong and statistically significant correlation between reported personal experience with corruption and reported opinions about the prevalence of corrupt officials in the locality (.319, significant at .01).

townships are excluded from this analysis, because of lack of data on village elections.

The sample of villagers is a systematic random sample using interval sampling of individuals drawn from official household registration lists (aggregated at the village level) after first eliminating from the lists individuals below age 18 and above age 80. In the 1996 survey, we attempted to interview again, if they could be found, the respondents interviewed in 1990, but also added respondents to fill out the village sample, with the same sampling method used in 1990. The analyses presented here use the 1990 and 1996 surveys as representative samples of the populations in 57 villages. For the 1990 survey, there are 1,115 respondents; for the 1996 survey, 1,216 respondents; on average, 20 and 21 respondents per village, respectively. Panel data for key variables are insufficient to conduct the analyses here at the individual level.

Data on village elections were collected in summer 1997 by researchers at the Research Center on Contemporary China at Peking University. Demographic and economic data were gathered at the same time using a structured data collection schedule. Questions on elections asked about the most recent three village elections, beginning in 1996 and extending as far back as 1988. All electoral data were obtained from village Communist party branch secretaries and heads of village committees, relying on memory and such records as existed at the village level. Visiting villages myself in fall 1997, I found that information provided by village leaders about the electoral process generally accorded with that provided by villagers but was sometimes different from that provided by township officials. In one Hunan township, researchers could not locate knowledgeable former leaders of the three villages surveyed to report on past elections because of an administrative merger that changed the status of these villages.

Appendix 2
Impact of Elections and Context on Change in Trust in Local Leaders

Independent Variable	Model I	*SE*	Model II	*SE*
Electoral contestation	.8680442*	.4441221	.8364866*	.3970052
Openness of candidate nominations	–.0259062	.1534788		
Openness of candidate selection	–.0973594	.1274416		
Reported voting	.0189653**	.006048	.0188902***	.0058947
Surname diversity	.0622769**	.0242864	.0663529**	.0216609
Per capita income change	.0007351*	.0003026	.0007499**	.0002942
Income inequality change	–.0000636	.0001879		
Monitoring orientation	.3279702	.2180428	.3200787	.2105036
1990 population	.0000655	.0001773	.0000634	.0001713
1990 per capita income	.0008046	.0005807	.0006681	.000543

(continued)

Appendix 2 (continued)

Independent Variable	Model I	*SE*	Model II	*SE*
Months since most recent election	.0032882	.0076647	.0030864	.0074659
Intercept	–3.292884**	1.209545	–3.428687**	1.077485
Adjusted R^2	.445		.470	

Note: Observations are from 55 villages. Dependent variable is computed using logarithmic transformations of 1996 percentage village population reporting minority of local officials are corrupt minus 1990 percentage reporting majority of local officials are "clean." Models are weighted least squares estimations, coefficients are unstandardized, significance tests are one-tailed.
$^*p < .05$. $^{**}p < .01$. $^{***}p < .001$.

Appendix 3
Summary Statistics for Analyses in Table 3 and Appendix 2

Variable	Minimum	Maximum	*M*	*SD*
Change in trust	–47.92	70.59	26.27	21.68
Log change in trust	–2.16	3.04	1.19	1.03
Electoral contestation	0.92	2.00	1.28	0.28
Reported voting	0	92.59	45.06	30.08
Openness of candidate nominations	1.00	3.00	1.93	0.88
Openness of candidate selection	1.00	3.00	1.72	0.88
Surname diversity	1.91	23.12	8.92	5.73
Monitoring orientation	0.80	3.57	1.97	0.71
Per capita income change	412.00	2,254.00	1,237.95	446.60
Income inequality change	–1,139.66	1,734.64	238.18	618.21
1990 population	400.00	3,961.00	1,387.58	700.02
1990 per capita income	277.00	1,469.00	635.89	208.08
Months since last election	1.00	63.00	18.74	16.19

References

Anderson, Christopher J., & Tverdova, Yuliya V. (2003). Corruption, political allegiances, and attitudes toward government in contemporary democracies. *American Journal of Political Science*, *47*(1), 91-109.

Bernstein, Thomas P., & Lu, Xiaobo. (2003). *Taxation without representation in contemporary rural China*. Cambridge, UK: Cambridge University Press.

Cohen, Myron L. (1990). Lineage organization in North China. *Journal of Asian Studies*, *49*(3), 509-534.

Elklit, Jorgen. (1997). The Chinese village committee electoral system. *China Information*, *11*(4), 1-13.

Golden, Miriam, & Chang, Eric C. C. (2001). Competitive corruption: Factional conflict and political malfeasance in postwar Italian Christian democracy. *World Politics*, *53*(4), 588-622.

Goldsmith, Arthur A. (1999). Slapping the grasping hand: Correlates of political corruption in emerging markets. *American Journal of Economics and Sociology*, *58*(4), 865-883.

Gong, Ting. (1994). *The politics of corruption in contemporary China: An analysis of policy outcomes*. Westport, CT: Praeger.

Guo, Zhenglin, & Bernstein, Thomas P. (2004). The impact of elections on the village structure of power: The relations between the village committees and the party branches. *Journal of Contemporary China*, *13*(39), 257-275.

Hardin, Russell. (1999). Do we want trust in government? In Mark E. Warren (Ed.), *Democracy and trust* (pp. 22-41). Cambridge, UK: Cambridge University Press.

He, Qinglian. (1997). *Zhongguo de xianjing* [China's pitfall]. Hong Kong: Mirror Books.

Howell, Jude. (1998). Prospects for village self-governance in China. *Journal of Peasant Studies*, *25*(3), 86-111.

Kelliher, Daniel. (1997). The Chinese debate over village self-government. *China Journal*, *37*, 63-86.

Kennedy, John James. (2002). The face of "grassroots democracy" in rural China: Real versus cosmetic elections. *Asian Survey*, *42*(3), 456-482.

Knack, Stephen, & Azfar, Omar. (2001). Trade intensity, country size, and corruption (Working Paper, No. 243). College Park: University of Maryland, College Park, IRIS Center.

Lawrence, Susan V. (1994). Village representative assemblies: Democracy, Chinese style. *Australian Journal of Chinese Affairs*, *32*, 61-68.

Levi, Margaret. (1996). Social and unsocial capital: A review essay of Robert Putnam's making democracy work. *Politics and Society*, *24*(1), 103-118.

Li, Lianjiang. (1999). The two-ballot system in Shanxi province: Subjecting village party secretaries to a popular vote. *China Journal*, *42*, 103-118.

Li, Lianjiang. (2002). Elections and popular resistance in rural China. *China Information*, *16*(1), 89-107.

Li, Lianjiang. (2003). The empowering effect of village elections in China. *Asian Survey*, *43*(4), 648-662.

Li, Lianjiang. (2004). Political trust in rural China. *Modern China*, *30*(2), 228-258.

Li, Lianjiang, & O'Brien, Kevin J. (1996). Villagers and popular resistance in contemporary China. *Modern China*, *22*(1), 28-61.

Li, Lianjiang, & O'Brien, Kevin J. (1999). The struggle over village elections. In Merle Goldman & Roderick MacFarquhar (Eds.), *The paradox of China's post-Mao reforms* (pp. 129-144). Cambridge, MA: Harvard University Press.

Manion, Melanie. (1990). Reluctant duelists: The logic of the 1989 protests and massacre. In Michel Oksenberg, Lawrence R. Sullivan, & Marc Lambert (Eds.), *Beijing spring, 1989: Confrontation and conflict. The basic documents* (pp. xiii-xlii). Armonk, NY: M. E. Sharpe.

Manion, Melanie. (1996). The electoral connection in the Chinese countryside. *American Political Science Review*, *90*(4), 736-748.

Manion, Melanie. (2004). *Corruption by design: Building clean government in mainland China and Hong Kong*. Cambridge, MA: Harvard University Press.

Mason, T. David. (1994). Modernization and its discontents revisited: The political economy of urban unrest in the People's Republic of China. *Journal of Politics*, *56*(2), 400-424.

Miller, William L., Grodeland, Ase B., & Koshechkina, Tatyona. (2001). *A culture of corruption: Coping with government in post-communist Europe*. Budapest, Hungary: Central European University Press.

Myrdal, Gunnar. (1968). *Asian drama: An inquiry into the poverty of nations*, Vol. 2. New York: Twentieth Century Fund.
O'Brien, Kevin J. (1994). Implementing political reform in China's villages. *Australian Journal of Chinese Affairs*, *32*, 33-59.
O'Brien, Kevin J. (1996). Rightful resistance. *World Politics*, *49*(1), 31-55.
O'Brien, Kevin J., & Li, Lianjiang. (2000). Accommodating "democracy" in a one-party state: Introducing village elections in China. *China Quarterly*, *162*, 465-489.
Ostergaard, Clemens Stubbe. (1986). Explaining China's recent political corruption. *Corruption and Reform*, *1*(1), 209-233.
Ostergaard, Clemens Stubbe, & Petersen, Christina. (1991). Official profiteering and the Tiananmen Square demonstrations in China. *Corruption and Reform*, *6*(2), 87-107.
Pastor, Robert A., & Tan, Qingshan. (2000). The meaning of China's village elections. *China Quarterly*, *162*, 490-512.
Putnam, Robert D. (1993). *Making democracy work*. Princeton, NJ: Princeton University Press.
Sandholtz, Wayne, & Koetzle, William. (2000). Accounting for corruption: Economic structure, democracy, and trade. *International Studies Quarterly*, *44*(1), 31-50.
Seligson, Mitchell A. (2002). The impact of corruption on regime legitimacy: A comparative study of four Latin American countries. *Journal of Politics*, *64*(2), 408-433.
Shi, Tianjian. (1999). Village committee elections in China: Institutionalist tactics for democracy. *World Politics*, *51*(3), 385-412.
Sun, Yan. (1991). The Chinese protests of 1989: The issue of corruption. *Asian Survey*, *31*(8), 762-782.
Sztompka, Piotr. (1996). Trust and emerging democracy: Lessons from Poland. *International Sociology*, *11*(1), 37-62.
Thurston, Anne F. (1998). Muddling toward democracy: Political change in grassroots China (Peaceworks No. 23). Washington, DC: United States Institute of Peace.
Treisman, Daniel. (2000). The causes of corruption: A cross-national study. *Journal of Public Economics*, *76*(3), 399-458.
Tsai, Lily Lee. (2002). Cadres, temple and lineage institutions, and governance in rural China. *China Journal*, *48*, 1-27.
Wang, Xu. (1997). Mutual empowerment of state and peasantry: Grassroots democracy in rural China. *World Development*, *25*(9), 1431-1442.
Wang, Zhenyao. (1998). Village committees: The basis for China's democratization. In Eduard B. Vermeer, Frank N. Pieke, & Woei Lien Chong (Eds.), *Cooperative and collective in China's rural development: Between state and private interests (pp. 239-255). Armonk, NY: M. E. Sharpe.*
Wedeman, Andrew. (2000). Budgets, extra-budgets, and small treasuries: Illegal monies and local autonomy in China. *Journal of Contemporary China*, *9*(25), 489-511.
Weyland, Kurt. (1998). The politics of corruption in Latin America. *Journal of Democracy*, *9*(2), 108-121.
White, Tyrene. (1992). Reforming the countryside. *Current History*, *92*(566), 273-277.
Xiao, Tangbiao (Ed.). (2001a). *Cunzhi zhong de zongzu: Dui jiu ge cun de diaocha yu yanjiu* [Clans in village governance: An investigation of nine villages]. Shanghai, China: Shanghai Bookstore Press.
Xiao, Tangbiao (Ed.). (2001b). *Duo wei shijiao zhong de cunmin zhixuan: Dui 15 ge cunweihui xuanju de guancha yanjiu* [Direct village elections from many perspectives: An investigation of 15 village committee elections]. Beijing, China: Chinese Social Science Press.
Zhong, Yang, & Chen, Jie. (2002). To vote or not to vote: An analysis of peasants' participation in Chinese village elections. *Comparative Political Studies*, *35*(6), 686-712.

[24]

Elections in Rural China: Competition Without Parties

Comparative Political Studies
43(6) 763–790

DOI: 10.1177/0010414009359392
http://cps.sagepub.com
SAGE

Pierre F. Landry[1], Deborah Davis[1], and Shiru Wang[2]

Abstract

Village elections in China present scholars with the case of a single-party regime that allows voters to reject candidates regularly. Using a micro survey of 698 voters in 30 rural election districts, the authors demonstrate that when some candidates can lose, voters participate. A comparison of models of voter turnout and running for office further demonstrates that even when competition is structured to the benefit of party members, the perception of competition as choice between candidates is sufficient to engage voters and increase their perception that the electoral process is fair. These findings hold regardless of a respondent's age, gender, membership in the Communist Party and Youth League, and general knowledge level and access to media. Village wealth and geographical isolation also do not demonstrate a strong substantive impact. One theoretical implication of these findings is that contested elections in authoritarian regimes may simultaneously strengthen demand for accountability and loyalty to the regime.

Keywords

political competition, electoral choice, authoritarianism, China, village elections, participation, voting, candidacy, fairness

[1]Yale University, New Haven, CT
[2]University of Hong Kong, Hong Kong

Corresponding Author:
Pierre F. Landry, Yale University, Department of Political Science, 115 Prospect Street, New Haven, CT 06520-8301
Email: pierre.landry@yale.edu

Political scientists conventionally regard contested elections as essential for democratic politics, and scholarship that articulates explicit definitions of democracy generally requires contested elections whereby incumbents face some risk of defeat (Przeworski, 1988; Przeworski, Alvarez, Cheibub, & Limongi, 2000, chap. 1). Thus recently, there has been scholarly interest in regimes that do not conform to democratic principles but nonetheless hold elections where voters have the power to reject at least some candidates in each round of elections (Diamond, 2002; Geddes, 2005; Hermet, Rose, & Rouquié, 1978; Levitsky & Way, 2002; Magaloni, 2006; Schedler, 2006, pp. 1-23). Perhaps because political parties are so central to the extant literature on elections, elections in regimes that ban parties (or only allow a single one) are not well incorporated into the theoretical literature on authoritarianism. However, using the recent experience of village-level elections in the People's Republic of China, we demonstrate how the opportunity to reject some candidates and choose others for local village councils affects both behavior and attitudes of ordinary citizens. Quite simply we find that (a) when rural voters know that they have the power to eliminate candidates, they are more likely to vote and (b) if they vote in elections, they are more likely to engage in a backward justification of the elections as fair.

To date very few studies have rigorously evaluated the impact of choice on turnout independent of multiparty competition. And even fewer have tested the impact of turnout on popular perceptions of fairness at the individual level. One may argue that choice among candidates all vetted by a single ruling party, the Communist Party in the case of China, is only an illusion of participation. Having more candidates than seats means little if independent candidates cannot emerge. Two candidates may oppose each other on election day for the post of village committee (VC) chairman, but if they do not differ in terms of party affiliation, electoral competition amounts to little more than a random selection between twins. This perspective suggests that elections in one-party states are merely a form of political mobilization that may produce high nominal turnout but leave village elites insulated from even mild electoral pressure.

If the critics of procedural democracy are correct, the existence of limited competition will not by itself be sufficient to elicit voter interest. In the absence of institutional restraints on the ruling party and without multiple parties or democratic culture, authoritarian regimes will tolerate local elections simply because they are able to manipulate them. Voters may be compelled to produce a high turnout, but we should not expect them to engage in such electoral activities as running for office. Nor would we expect them to find the elections fair. By contrast, proponents of minimalist definitions of democracy stress that limited competition is not trivial. As long as a few incumbents can lose, village elections may have a disciplining effect on local political elites. If this view is correct, we would also expect the public to support the institution of elections by turning out voluntarily when it regards races as competitive. We would also expect that election participants are those who report higher levels of satisfaction with the election process.

We evaluate these competing claims using data collected in 2004 in a probability sample of working-age adults in a rural county of southwestern China. After a brief discussion of the history of village elections and recent procedural reforms, we describe the data and research design and then analyze the impact of individual and community characteristics on citizens' behavior and attitudes. We first evaluate voter turn out and show that voters are highly responsive to the provision of even limited competition. We then contrast the impact of the same variables on another mode of electoral participation—running for office—and finally turn to explore how voters evaluate of the degree of electoral fairness. We conclude by discussing the implications of these findings for the theoretical literature on authoritarian regimes. A regime that provides minimally competitive local elections does not necessarily regard such elections as a tool of popular mobilization. Instead, the regime can build the loyalty of its citizenry by providing electoral institutions that can appeal to voters and create a sense that these institutions are fair, even when they do not conform to any conventional interpretation of electoral democracy. One implication of the recent Chinese experience is that contested elections in authoritarian regimes may strengthen both demands for accountability and loyalty to the regime.

The Institution of Village Elections in China

In the high Mao years (1958–1976), the lowest level of state power ended at the people's commune, an administrative unit that supervised and coordinated the economic and political life of up to 50,000 people living in 10 to 20 villages. Villages were subdivided into production teams, usually organized around hamlets or natural villages. Teams were supervised by production brigades, and brigades, which were usually large administrative villages, were supervised by commune governments. County-level officials appointed commune leaders, who in turn appointed leaders in each brigade and production team. Between 1980 and 1983, the post-Mao government decollectivized agriculture and abolished communes with their nested hierarchy of control that reached down into each of China's then nearly one million villages. Township governments replaced communes and villages were to be governed by elected VCs. However, although the 1982 Constitution (Art. 111) indicated that villages would be governed by elected committees, only in 1987 did the Draft Organic Law on Villagers' Self-Governance specify provisions for direct elections, and only in the 1998 Organic Law did village elections become mandatory nationwide.

VCs and their elected leaders have significant power. They oversee the (re)distribution or lease of village land, which remains collectively owned and which since the 1980s has become increasingly valuable. They are also responsible for mediating local civil disputes and for implementing the one-child policy.[1] Each VC consists of at least three members and is headed by a chairperson.[2]

The 1998 Organic Law mandates that candidates be nominated directly by eligible villagers and that all eligible voters can run for office in their own village. Elections must be competitive in the sense that the number of candidates nominated should exceed the number of seats on the VC.[3] Election overseers must count the ballots publicly and announce the results immediately. An election is valid only if a majority of eligible voters cast their ballots, and candidates win if they receive a majority of valid votes. If neither condition is met, new elections must be organized.

Village elections are politically consequential. Based on a two-wave survey of 400 respondents in 20 villages in one county of Jiangxi during the first semicompetitive election in 1999, Li (2003) finds that elections have an empowering effect, in the sense that political efficacy increases once villagers acquire the experience of removing unpopular leaders from office. In addition, multiple studies suggest that the conduct of village elections has improved leadership accountability and the quality of governance as well as the level of popular satisfaction with village governments (Birney, 2007; Kennedy, Rozelle, & Shi, 2004; Manion, 1996, 2006).[4] A high level of electoral participation also empowers the elected VC vis-à-vis the unelected village branches of the Communist Party, particularly when VCs control substantial economic resources (Guo & Bernstein, 2004; Li & O'Brien, 1999; Oi & Rozelle, 2000).

Village elections are more than a plebiscitary exercise because the number of candidates for office must exceed the number of seats available. Hundreds of thousands of candidates lose routinely, and 48% of elected village officials are not Chinese Communist Party (CCP) members (Ministry of Civil Affairs, 2005; Shi, 2000). In sum, Chinese voters make choices and candidates must successfully compete for votes or lose. Indeed, proponents of the Schumpeterian notion that democracy emerges when incumbents lose elections have raised the prospect that village elections may become a training ground for China's future democratization (Horsley, 2001).[5]

Moreover, the institution of the election itself offers a range of possible activities beyond simply casting a ballot. According to the 1998 Organic Law on Villagers' Committees, villagers are expected to monitor electoral proceedings by designating an election commission (Art. 13). They may also nominate candidates (Art. 14) or run for office directly. Finally, between rounds of elections, villagers' representative assemblies are to meet regularly and monitor village leaders (Art. 17-19).[6]

Mandatory elections have been introduced in the context of two decades of reforms that decisively eliminated the economic institutions of the socialist era. However, these economic reforms have left untouched the political monopolies of the CCP (Oi & Rozelle, 2000). Only the posts of village head and VC members are open to popular vote, and non-CCP members who run are not allowed to organize as a political party.[7] Village elections therefore provide a channel that allows villagers to select some of their leaders and reject others, but they are not intended to displace the CCP as the single ruling party.

Data

During the summer of 2004, we conducted a household survey in 30 administrative villages in a rural county of Yunnan Province here identified by the pseudonym of Gaoyuan, a county where 90% of adults work in agriculture.[8]

In the national context, Gaoyuan is typical of noncoastal agricultural counties. All of its major socioeconomic indicators lie within one standard deviation of either the provincial or the national mean (see Table A1). The county is slightly richer than average for Yunnan and therefore approaches the national averages for per capita GDP and fiscal revenue. Thus, although we do not claim that our sample is representative of China or Yunnan in a strict statistical sense, we believe that patterns in Gaoyuan speak directly to the general situation of inland rural counties.

Although Gaoyuan County was purposefully selected, our respondents constitute an equal probability sample of working age adults in the county. To guarantee that we captured both economic and ethnic diversity of the county, we first stratified the 15 townships into two groups: those where the majority of the population belongs to one of China's 55 ethnic minorities and those where the majority are not ethnic minorities. We then randomly selected by two townships (*xiang*) from the first group and three townships from the second. Within each township, we selected a number of administrative villages proportional to the number of households in the township.[9] In total, we drew 30 administrative villages (*xingzhen cun*). Within each administrative village, we randomly selected two natural villages (*ziran cun*).[10]

Because this survey initially focused on understanding current school enrollment, the final respondents in the sample were adults (mostly parents) who were raising children of school age as of July 2004. In each natural village, we established a list of households with such children and drew 12 of those at random. Within households, the gender of the parent to be interviewed was also randomized. The procedure yielded a sample of 698 adults clustered in 30 electoral districts (administrative villages) where elections had been held several weeks before fieldwork was conducted. Because our respondents are primarily parents, our sample captures the set of villagers who are in the labor force and are active members of their communities. Elderly and younger respondents are underrepresented because they were captured only if they effectively raised children because of unusual circumstances in their household. The oldest respondent is 71 and the youngest is 22, with an average age of 38.[11] The Gaoyuan sample does not allow point predictions over the entire adult population of the county, but it is appropriate for multivariable analysis of a wide range of individual- and community-level variables relevant to the study of election participation.

The Gaoyuan sample is one of a handful of samples that analyzes voting behavior since the implementation of the 1998 Organic Law on Villagers' Self-Government and is the only one to our knowledge that has extensive information on both the individual voter and the local community.[12] It has particularly high-quality and rich data because fieldwork was executed only a few weeks after the second round of village elections in Yunnan Province and systematically gathered data on the economic, social, and political life at both individual and village levels. While interviewing village leaders in VC offices, we were often able to directly observe that election results were still prominently displayed, including in some cases lists of candidates and the number of votes they had received. Clearly, the election exercise was still fresh in most respondents' minds, which leads us to believe that data were less prone to measurement error than those in earlier studies that primarily relied on interviews conducted many months or even years after elections had been held.

Estimating Turnout and Degree of Competition

Officials who run authoritarian elections have strong political incentives to maximize turnout, and variation in turnout reflects not individual-level decisions but instead the performance of local officials as election organizers. In the case of Chinese VC elections, officials who face the risk of low turnout can resort to many measures to ensure a high reported turnout. At the end of the voting period on the village square, team leaders can carry roving boxes to the doorstep of the household that did not appear on the square and ask one (or more) member of the household to cast a ballot. This person is ordinarily expected to vote on behalf of the other members of the household if they are not present, whether a formal proxy has been signed or not.[13]

Given the regime's incentives to inflate turnout rates, Zhong and Chen (2002) propose a strict definition of voluntary participation in the election process. By counting as voters only the villagers who personally cast their own ballot, their approach is useful if one is interested in voters who engage in particularly assertive forms of political participation, but it does not conform to standard definitions of turnout.[14] Our benchmark is less restrictive than theirs but differs from the maximalist measure of official turnout reports: We chose instead to simply ask respondents whether or not they voted during the 2004 round of village elections. Thus, voters who filled formal proxies, asked a family member to vote on their behalf, or voted at a roving ballot box are coded as having voted.[15]

To gauge perceptions of competition at the village level, we rely on our respondents' assessments of the election held approximately 2 months before the interviews. Because our respondents were selected at random from two natural villages in each electoral district (also randomly selected), we are confident that estimating the share of respondents who perceive that the election was competitive is a reasonable indicator of the underlying nature of competition in the village. By this yardstick, we find that village elections are significantly less competitive than official reports indicate. We obtain instead a continuum of competition, ranging from the worst case where a bare majority reported competition to a village where all 24 interviewees were unanimous about the existence of competition.

We also find a strong correlation between the perception competition and turnout, a sign that elections are more than a mere plebiscitary exercise in mass mobilization (see Figure 1). Villagers do not simply turn out because they were told to do so. They seem instead to respond to the extent of political competition.

Explaining Voter Participation

Why do Chinese villagers choose to go to the polls? The mobilizational view of elections in authoritarian regimes generally ignores individual voter preferences or characteristics. But in the 1960s and 1970s, scholars of Soviet politics argued that nonvoting was a form of protest against the lack of meaningful competition in Soviet elections and individual attributes could be decisive (Gilison, 1968; Jacobs, 1970; Nelson & Amonashvili, 1992; Swearer, 1961;

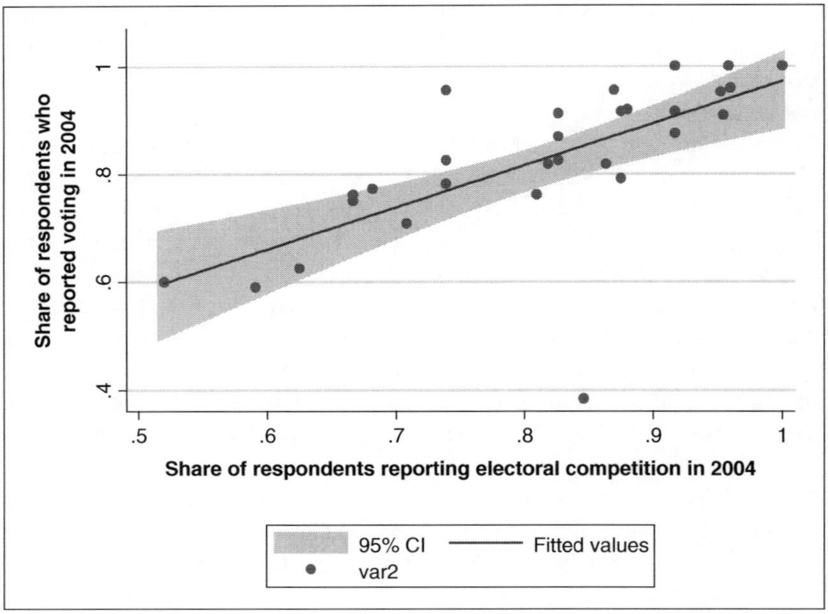

Figure 1. Estimates of perceived electoral competition and voter turnout in 30 Gaoyuan villages

Zaslavsky & Brym, 1978). Several recent studies of Chinese elections similarly confirm a role for individual-level characteristics. Shi (1999b), Chen and Zhong (2002), Zhong and Chen (2002) agree that subjective motivations drive voting behavior, though they disagree about the specific causal mechanisms behind turnout. Shi concludes that people with greater political attentiveness and internal efficacy vote in semicompetitive local elections to fight corruption and abstain from uncompetitive elections as a form of protest. By contrast, Chen and Zhong contend that only those who identify with the regime will vote.

In our study, we assume that political orientation of potential voters affects their response and that that some voters will be more responsive than others to the exhortation of village and township officials to go to the polls. Given the prestige, power, and monopoly power of the CCP, we hypothesize that party members will be more likely to vote than nonparty members and that long-time members will be most likely to vote.[16]

Other individuals who may be more likely than others to vote are current or former members of the Communist Youth League (CYL). Although CCP

Table 1. Education and League Membership

Educational attainment	Percentage among respondents	Percentage of Communist Youth League (CYL) members by education level
Illiterate	10.0	2.1
Some primary	14.8	8.3
Primary	30.5	15.7
Lower middle	38.8	29.7
Vocational secondary	0.4	62.8
High school	5.2	70.6
Some tertiary	0.4	63.9

Note: Test of association between level of education and CYL membership: design-based $F(5.12, 143.35) = 15.10, p = .000$.

membership is rare in rural areas, membership in the league is widespread and is seen as a means to socialize the best educated youth (see Table 1) to perform a range of civic duties and participate in collective activities. The most promising league members are expected to eventually join the Communist Party (Bian, Shu, & Logan, 2001).

The interaction between league membership and education has important implications for the range and intensity of current political activities in the villages. Not only are former league activists and educated villagers personally likely to turn out, but also village leaders can count on them to mobilize other community members on election day.[17] Because 21% of the sample reported having joined the CYL, the mobilizational capacity of this group is likely to have a measurable impact on turnout.

Given the power of village officials to oversee land allocation and supervise economic development, those with the most assets might also be more likely to vote than those with less. Thus, one might predict that voting is tied to one's economic and political interests in village affairs. Shi (1999a) argues that the reform process that turned farmers into key resource providers of local governments has made them more assertive in the face of official predation. This type of activism dovetails with the expectations of reformers in Beijing—specifically the Ministry of Civil Affairs—who conceived of elections as an instrument of good governance (Shi, 1999b).

In previous analyses, political economic models of voting in China have taken the village as the unit of analysis. The implicit assumption in this approach is that village-level politics is best explained by village-level variables because economic variability is greater across rather than within villages. Both Lawrence (1994) and Oi and Rozelle (2000) contend that elections are less likely to develop in economically advanced regions because local elites have few incentives to experiment with alternative political institutions when they are successful. Shi (1999, p. 436), by contrast, reported that the relationship is nonlinear.

It also is true that there have been very few unofficial (nongovernment) surveys prior to ours that collected voter-specific data. For example, in their study of 1996 village elections, Oi and Rozelle (2000) demonstrate that the power of officials was closely linked to the nature of the village economy. However, because they did not collect data at the voter level, the link between the nature of the village economy and turnout is indeterminate. A focus on the village level was valid in an era when the central legislative apparatus did not mandate the provision of competitive elections, and it is not surprising that voter turnout and the overall quality of elections varied by village economic or political characteristics. However, Article 14 of the 1998 Organic Law requires all villages to hold elections in which there are more candidates than seats.[18] This does not mean that all villages implement the law faithfully or that the degree of competition is uniform but rather that the incentives for local official have clearly changed since village elections became mandatory. Regardless of economic circumstances, the civil affairs bureaucracy ensures that elections are held, and township officials are dispatched to monitor their implementation. Furthermore, propaganda through the media has increased public awareness of proper elections procedures. In fact, courts have intervened in election disputes when villagers have challenged incompetence or outright fraud.[19] Townships officials also insist that turnout should be as high as possible because clear documentation of turnout is now one of the regular benchmarks that must be reported upward within the civil affairs bureaucracy. This combination of greater voter awareness with the institutionalization of election procedures suggests that turnout in village elections may vary significantly by individual characteristics of voters.

Multivariate Models of Voting and Running

To test these predictions, we turn to a multivariate probit regression of voting behavior in which we estimate the impact of a wide range of individual and village characteristics. Building on previous work on voter turnout in both democratic and authoritarian regimes, we assess economic, political, and educational background of individual voters controlling for their age, gender, and ethnicity. Economic status is captured by ownership of 20 consumer durables,[20] education by years of formal schooling, and political position by membership in the CCP and Communist League. In addition, we use frequency of newspaper reading and score on a short general knowledge quiz to assess their active knowledge as opposed to educational credentials.[21] To capture the relative economic standing of respondents' households relative to that of other respondents in their village, we use the deviation of a household's score on the possession index from the village mean on the possession index. This measure of deviation from village means provides a more accurate measure of within village inequality than Hu's (2005) self-reported assessment of economic standing. It also allows us to test whether those with the greatest economic stake will be more likely to vote or run for election than poorer villagers (see Table A2 in the appendix for a summary of all independent and dependent variables).

Voting

As one can see in the models that estimate the decision to vote and the decision to run for a position on the VC in 2004, both individual and village characteristics had a statistically significant impact on the political behavior of villagers (see Table 2). But the results did not perfectly confirm our initial expectations. For example, we find that neither Communist Party nor Youth League membership increases turnout. However, we detect a nonlinear relationship between wealth (measured by the possession index of the household) and turnout: The negative (and significant) coefficient for the wealth squared variable suggests that both the poorest and the most economically successful families either are disengaged from village affairs or see no value in participating.

Although the higher villagers' educational attainment the more likely they are to vote, the impact is only marginally significant ($p < .1$). Similarly, and somewhat contrary to expectations that turnout would vary by the age gender, and reading habits, we found no significant impact of being older, being male, or reading a newspaper daily. Even more surprising given past research that shows minority members to be politically marginalized, we found that in this county ethnic minorities were more likely to vote, a pattern that we attribute to the pre-1949 incorporation of ethnic minority Yi leaders into the communist guerilla forces and the active recruitment and promotion of Yi leaders into the county leadership since the early 1950s. Thus, although in some parts of China minorities are isolated from or resistant to mainstream political life, in a county where the minority is almost the majority and where for more than 50 years they have merged community leadership and party

Table 2. Electoral Participation in 2004

Number of observations	689		689	
Number of strata	2		2	
Number of PSUs (villages)	30		30	
Design *df*	28		28	
$F(15, 14)$	6.28		9.32	
Prob > F	.001		.000	
	Voting in 2004 election		Running for office in 2004	
Nominated candidates	0.237	0.422	1.236	0.348***
Communist Party membership	−0.188	0.221	1.379	0.333***
Male	−0.058	0.166	0.282	0.466
Age	−0.028	0.076	−0.234	0.148
Age squared	0.000	0.001	0.002	0.002
Wealth	0.044	0.074	0.008	0.137*
Wealth squared	−0.005	0.004	−0.002	0.006
Wealth deviation from village mean	0.026	0.089	0.184	0.264
Ethnicity (Han majority)	−0.273	0.134**	0.167	0.435
Knowledge	−0.020	0.019	0.024	0.057
Communist Youth League (CYL) membership	−0.014	0.427	−2.029	1.210
Education	0.071	0.033**	0.143	0.064**
Education × CYL	0.002	0.068	0.134	0.142
Newspaper reading	0.312	0.454	−0.003	0.232
Electoral competition (village level)	2.852	0.597***	0.438	1.167
Constant	−0.959	1.801	1.011	2.840

Note: PSU = Primary Sampling Unit. Standard errors corrected for survey design effect.
$^*p \leq .1$ $^{**}p \leq .05$. $^{***}p \leq .01$.

membership, minorities are well integrated into official positions and the party eagerly reaches out to recruit them.[22]

Turning to village characteristics, we find that the degree to which the election was competitive is most decisive. In sum, in the 2004 village elections, although family wealth, individual education, and ethnicity significantly affected participation rates, it was the institutional character of the election process, in particular the perception of choice and competition, that was the single most important factor behind voter turnout.

Running for Village Office

Chinese village elections should not be confused with municipal elections in democratic systems. Formal candidates emerge from a process that resembles straw polls in which villagers are expected to openly nominate peers for the posts of village chair, deputy chair, and ordinary committee members. But in most cases, the Communist Party Branch, the outgoing VC, and township authorities have favorite candidates and have ample formal and informal means of making their preferences known to the villagers, although the voters can theoretically override these preferences in the open nomination process. The top two vote getters in the straw poll usually compete against each other for the post of chairman, whereas the remaining nominees—ranked in decreasing order of votes received—run for the post of ordinary committee member. For example, if a VC has one chairman and three ordinary members, two candidates will be on the ballot for chairman whereas four others will compete for the remaining three seats on the VC. By design, the odds of defeat are far lower among candidates for committee membership than for those seeking the chairmanship of the village.

In Gaoyuan, 12 of our respondents claimed that they were candidates in 2004. Among these we found 5 party members, including 1 of the 2 female candidates. Although one sixth of all CCP members in the sample ended up on a ballot, CCP membership was not an absolute requirement for final candidacy, and the majority of candidates were not party members. Nor is there clear evidence that other political filtering mechanisms prevented ordinary villagers from reaching candidacy. One may argue that the party indirectly filters candidates by allowing nonparty nominees to run formally as long as their spouses are party members. This hypothesis is easily rejected: In the Gaoyuan sample, not a single candidate's spouse was a CCP member.

Because party membership is rare in rural areas, one may also hypothesize that the regime's second best solution is to rely instead on the much larger group of past (or even current) members of the CYL. Because league membership is still a marker of political reliability, officials bent on controlling elections should favor league members over ordinary villagers. Youth League members can easily be asked to join the Communist Party once they are elected to village offices, in contrast to nonleague members, who often lack the educational credentials required to join the party. Even if they do not join, the fact that league members have been politically mobilized and socialized during their youth is likely to increase the odds that they will follow the CCP's lead in the village rather than use their elected office as a platform to challenge the authority of party leaders. Yet we find that none of the seven nonparty candidates were admitted into the Youth League. It is also striking that their educational attainment was far lower than that of party candidates, and they were also considerably younger. We can confidently conclude that in practice both party and nonparty members were allowed in run the Gaoyuan 2004 village elections and that nonparty candidates emerged from strata of villagers that are unlikely to be incorporated in the formal, nonelectoral political institutions that dominated village life before the introduction of elections.

Despite the apparent heterogeneity of candidates, once we control for individual- and village-level characteristics that we used to predict turnout, the multivariate analysis identifies one dominant pathway to candidacy: party membership. When we fit a probit model of candidacy in 2004, party membership has a large impact and is statistically significant at the .01 level (Table 2, "running for office" model). On the other hand, party membership did not guarantee electoral success: Only 2 out of 12 respondents who stood for election were victorious, and neither was a party member. We also find that villagers who nominate candidates were also more likely to run, probably because self-nominations are allowed. It is striking that apart from education (which is also only marginally significant), none of the remaining key factors that would ordinarily be associated with elite political status approach statistical significance: Household wealth does not explain candidacy, nor does political awareness (captured in terms of substantive political knowledge) or frequent reading of newspapers. The ethnic variation we found in voting also disappears. Nor do we detect any evidence that the nature of the community has any impact on candidacy.

In conclusion, if we take the villagers' account of the degree of electoral competition at face value, elections were competitive in most villages and voter participation was directly related to the competitiveness of the election process. Voters reported not only that there were more candidates than seats to be filled (as mandated by law) but also that the CCP allowed some ordinary villagers to emerge from the nomination process who would otherwise be excluded from the historical institutions of Chinese communism: They were not party members, had never joined the CYL, and (with a single exception) had never held political posts in the villages. At the same time, the party plays a decisive role in the grooming of candidates who ended up on the ballot: Party members were far more likely to run than nonmembers. Given our small sample of candidates, we cannot estimate the odds of victory reliably, but we did show without a doubt that nonparty members both ran and won in these contested village elections.

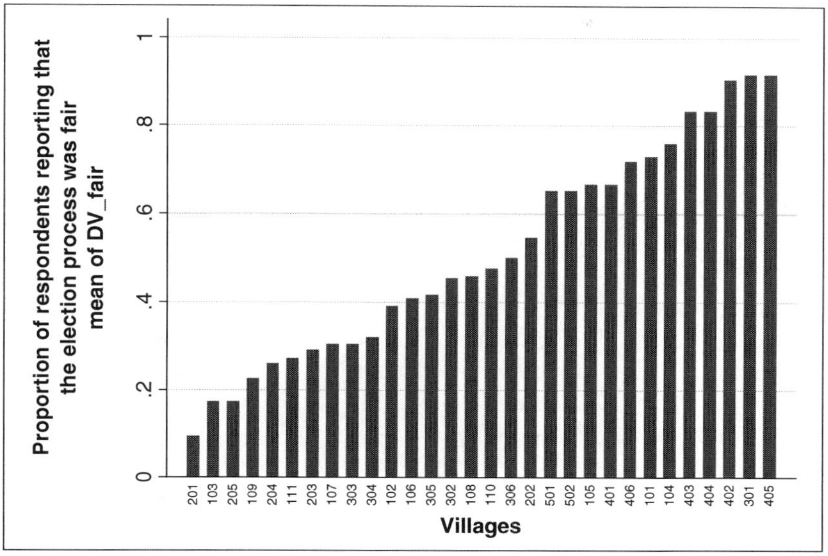

Figure 2. Level of election fairness, aggregated by village
Note: Bars represent village means by aggregating the respondents' answer to the following question: "Do you think that the way of counting ballots in the last election was fair?"

Were Elections Fair?

In addition to the dimension of electoral participation, the quality of election procedures is an important benchmark of the credibility of electoral institutions. Previous studies of Chinese village elections show that free(er) and fair(er) elections improve the responsiveness of leaders and the quality of village governance (Brandt & Turner, 2007; Kennedy et al., 2004; Li & O'Brien, 1999). Lianjiang Li (2003) argues that more villagers participate in politics after they experience "free and fair election" (p. 652). An increased sense of political efficacy encourages voters to press elected village leaders to constrain (and even confront) village Party Branch leaders or abusive township officials, thus making local leaders more accountable to voters.[23]

In the 2004 survey, we asked voters whether they believed that procedures for counting ballots in their village were fair or not. The villagers of Gaoyuan County held sharply different views about the fairness of the election in which they participated. Because we were concerned that some villagers may not have dared report that the election was unfair and would have claimed instead that they did not know or refused to answer the question, we coded as 1 all respondents who affirmed that the process was fair, and all other answers were recoded as 0. Using this benchmark, only 47% of the respondents reported that their village election was fair, and such assessments systematically vary across electoral districts (Figure 2). Given that the politically correct answer was to reply that elections were fair, we take this variation as a sign that respondents were truthful when answering the question.

Electoral participation—especially voting—is probably correlated with individual perceptions of fairness, but the direction of the causal link is contested. Although Birch (2005) contends that satisfaction with electoral procedures encourages turnout, in the context of noninstitutionalized elections where voters have little experience with voting, it is far more likely that individual experience with casting a ballot, observing how ballots are counted, and seeing whether the most vote getters are actually confirmed as election winners all shape individual perceptions of electoral fairness decisively. Furthermore, researchers must live with the constraint that existing data generation efforts allow testing only the impact of elections on attitudes but not whether attitudes measured via surveys after elections have taken place affected voting behavior. Several analyses ignore this temporal sequencing difficulty. For instance, Chen and Zhong (2002, pp. 185-190) use villagers' "support for the regime" and "internal efficacy" or "democratic orientation" measured during postelection interviews as predictors of turnout. Similarly, Shi (1999, p. 1129) used measures of democratic orientation and interest in politics collected after the voters' encounter with elections as predictors of turnout. We agree with Lianjiang Li's conclusion that voters' experience with elections has important psychological consequences. The experience of elections should not only affect voter efficacy but also increase the sense of fairness among the subset of voters who were exposed to "better" elections. Without panel data at the voter level, we contend that only factual or behavioral variables should be used as predictors in cross-sectional designs.[24] Such variables as age, gender, ethnicity, party membership, and number of candidates may be collected following elections, and because they are not influenced by the respondent's voting experience, these variables can be used legitimately as predictors of multivariate models based on cross-section data.

Because we detected a strong positive impact of competition on voting, estimates of the impact of experience with voting on the perception of electoral fairness require an empirical strategy that accounts for the possible endogeneity of our key variable, voting. Y^*_{Vote} and Y^*_{Fair} are latent variables, for which we obverse dichotomous indicators of voting and finding the election was held fairly.

$$Y^*_{Fair} = \beta'\mathbf{X}_1 + u_1 \text{ (where } Y_{Fair} = 1 \text{ if } Y^*_{Fair} > 0, 0 \text{ otherwise)}$$
$$Y^*_{Vote} = \delta_2 Y_{Vote} + \beta'\mathbf{X}_2 + u_2 \text{ (where } Y_{Vote} = 1 \text{ if } Y^*_{Fair} > 0, 0 \text{ otherwise)}$$

This specification closely resembles Maddala's (1983, p. 122) classic exposition.

However, Wilde (2000, p. 311) has since shown that the identification strategy needed to estimate such a model is not as intractable as Maddala suggested, provided that at least one varying exogenous regressor is present in each equation. Altonji, Elder, and Taber (2005) also suggest that bivariate probits may be more appropriate than the traditional instrumental variable approach, which is unworkable with dichotomous endogenous regressors.[25] Jaenicke (2008) has performed Monte Carlo experiments that confirm that bivariate probits with endogenous dummy repressors perform well if the sample size is sufficiently large.[26] We estimated such a *biprobit* model, and because the error terms are not correlated across equations (rho is not significant), we also report the simpler probit specification (Table 3).

In addition to voting, we also account for the experience of deeper electoral engagement, namely, nominating candidates for village office. In this case, the nominated candidates variable is coded 1 if one has ever nominated a candidate in a village election, 0 otherwise. This variable can help adjudicate between those who contend that voting is central to the election experience and those—such as Baogang He (2006) and Kennedy et al. (2004)—who emphasize the importance of more active forms of participation.

We also control for membership in the village political elite, in the sense that Communist Party members, and to a lesser extent Youth League members, were identified as regime supporters in the process of joining these institutions at an earlier point. These individuals are more likely to perceive that elections are fair even if they are not, quite simply because they hold some political clout in their village. Finally, we account for the ethnicity of the respondent because of nature of the research site. In Gaoyuan, the Yi ethnicity was critical to the development of Communist Party as early as the 1930s. Thus, members of the group are more likely to support electoral institutions in a region where they have played a major political role since the foundation of the regime, in contrast to the Han ethnic majority that dominates national but not county politics.

What accounts for the variation of the sense of fairness among villagers? The results are suggestive of a causal chain linking competition to voting,

Table 3. Were Elections Fair?

	Bivariate probit with binary endogenous regressor		Probit	
Number of strata	2		2	
Number of PSUs (villages)	30		30	
Number of observations	689		696	
Population size	902.9		910.3	
Design *df*	28		28	
F	7.78		4.92	
Prob > *F*	.003		.002	
	Fair equation		Fair	
	β	*SE*	β	*SE*
Voted in 2004 election	1.638	0.769**	1.013	0.285***
Nominated candidates	–0.030	0.136	0.001	0.117
Communist Party membership	0.449	0.282	0.355	0.198*
Ethnicity (Han majority)	–0.270	0.196	–0.294	0.167*
Newspaper reading	0.336	0.279	0.413	0.323
Electoral competition (village level)	0.914	1.022	1.430	0.747*
Constant	–1.997	0.493***	–1.907	0.507***
Voted in 2004 equation				
Nominated candidates	0.230	0.432	—	—
Communist Party membership	–0.143	0.262	—	—
Male	–0.099	0.182	—	—
Age	–0.034	0.071	—	—
Age squared	0.000	0.001	—	—
Wealth	0.064	0.097	—	—
Wealth squared	–0.007	0.005	—	—
Wealth deviation from village mean	0.037	0.099	—	—
Ethnicity (Han majority)	–0.219	0.157	—	—
Knowledge	–0.017	0.018	—	—
Communist Youth League (CYL) membership	–0.007	0.415	—	—
Education	0.073	0.035**	—	—
Education × CYL	0.002	0.069	—	—
Newspaper reading	0.361	0.463	—	—
Electoral competition (village level)	2.774	0.524***	—	—
Constant	–0.908	1.612	—	—
Rho	–.411	.431		—

Note: PSU = Primary Sampling Unit. Standard errors corrected for survey design effect.
$^{**}p \leq .05$. $^{***}p \leq .01$.

and in turn voting to fairness. As we found in Table 2, electoral competition is the strongest predictor of turnout. Turning to the fairness equation, we find a large substantive impact of voting (though not as strongly significant as in the simple probit version). The findings are strongly consistent with the hypothesis that villagers' experience with electoral institutions clearly affects their sense of fairness. Villagers who voted were more likely to claim that the elections were fair. These results hold regardless of the respondents' political standing in the village or their ethnicity. In contrast to Kennedy's (2002) findings, we find no evidence of a link between the process of nominating candidates and the individual assessment of electoral fairness, which suggests that villagers who are engaged in complex acts of political participation (e.g., nominating candidates) are not necessarily self-selected regime supporters. We conjecture that the 1998 law may have the effect of preventing the type of blatant interference by higher-level officials that he documents in earlier rounds of elections in Shaanxi Province. Thus, we find no evidence to support the argument that ordinary villagers are routinely disengaged from elections controlled by village elites.

These findings also extend to Communist Party members. Because the party is so influential, one may anticipate that CCP members who benefit from their ties to the party would be more likely to state that the election was fair than nonmembers. But in fact this prediction was not confirmed. Instead, villagers strongly subscribe to the notion that a fair election is an election in which voters have the power to reject some candidates despite the single party's critical role in structuring competition among candidates, and this opinion holds regardless of political status, media usage, and ethnicity.

Conclusions

Gandhi and Przeworski (2006, p. 21) claim that "regimes that exhibit seemingly democratic institutions" are not democracies because "in spite of the celebrating event they call 'elections,' [they] do not allow for the possibility that incumbent rulers could be forced to abandon power as a result of the people's vote." We obviously do not claim that village elections in China are evidence of democratization in a single-party system, but we do stress that villagers' response to the incentives of greater competition makes incumbents frequently lose elections and that being allowed to choose between multiple candidates drives the perception of electoral fairness. Therefore, the experience of Chinese village elections encourages political science to scrutinize the vitality of electoral experiments in authoritarian regimes to consider the impact of choice on individual voter behavior.

Two chains of events are especially noteworthy in the Chinese case. First, voters seem highly responsive to the competitiveness of elections. When candidates must compete for votes or lose office, voters participate and perceive elections as fair. Villagers who lack choice tend not to vote and find elections unfair. The contrast between models of voting and running further demonstrate that even when competition is structured to the benefit of party members, competition defined as choice between candidates still is sufficient to engage voters.

The second chain of events is seemingly less positive for the evolution of the Chinese political system but helps illuminate the logic behind a single party's decision to hold competitive elections: The ruling party disproportionately recruits from the well-educated and those who have been socialized in long-standing institutions of the regime such as the Youth League, and party members are in turn highly likely to appear on the roster of candidates. These candidates do not always win, but the selection mechanism minimizes the risk that elections will be hijacked by political entrepreneurs whose loyalty to the regime has not been tested. The crucial point is that voters seem to be satisfied even with elections that are heavily controlled and offer only a limited degree of choice. This suggests that elections are not only a means to increase accountability but also an instrument that with little political risk the regime can use to bolster popular confidence in the fairness of political institutions.

The mechanisms that we highlight in this article have implications beyond one-party Leninist regimes. An increasing number of authoritarian regimes hold local elections without party competition, even when they do not always do so at the national level. Political scientists should not assume that these local contests are pure window dressing without implications for the nature and durability of the regimes that sponsor them. We suggest that the connections among minimal competition, turnout, and perceived fairness that we found in Chinese village elections should be investigated in the wider set of regimes where multiparty elections are not allowed but where voters nevertheless have some capacity to reject incumbents or proregime candidates.

Appendix

Table A1. Comparison of Gaoyuan County With Yunnan and the Rest of China (1999)

	Gaoyuan	Deviation from Yunnan M	Deviation from China M
Total population	480,000	−0.58	0.05
Rural population	424,000	−0.36	0.11
Rural labor force	257,000	0.22	0.34
Total GDP at current prices (yuan)	292,923	−0.26	0.14
Total value of primary sector (yuan)	40,791	−0.92	−0.47
Total value of secondary sector (yuan)	216,811	0.61	0.66
GDP per capita (yuan)	6,103	0.40	0.29
Local financial revenue (yuan)	11,480	−0.24	0.25
Local financial revenue per capita (yuan)	240	0.48	0.22
Financial expenditures (yuan)	17,202	−0.20	0.21
Number of students in school per 10,000 people	1,713	−0.34	−0.05
Number of doctors per 10,000 people	23.6	0.93	0.26

Source: Data computed from National Bureau of Statistics (2001).
Note: Deviation is defined as $(x_{gaoyuan} - \overline{x}_{ref})$ / (standard deviation (x_{ref})) where $\overline{x}_{ref}$ is the mean value of variable x, either in Yunnan or in the entire dataset. Data include all counties and county-level cities but not urban districts.

Table A2. Summary of All Variables

Number of strata	2
Number of PSUs	30
Design-based degrees of freedom	28
Number of observations	689

	M	Linearized SE	95% confidence interval	
Dependent variables				
Voted in 2004 election	0.817	0.024	0.768	0.866
Ran for office in 2004 election	0.015	0.005	0.004	0.026
Election was fair	0.475	0.036	0.401	0.549
Individual-level independent variables				
Ever nominated a candidate	0.270	0.034	0.200	0.339
Communist Party membership	0.061	0.023	0.014	0.108

(continued)

Table A2. (continued)

	M	Linearized *SE*	95% confidence interval	
Gender (*male* = 1)	0.518	0.046	0.424	0.611
Wealth (possession index)	7.444	0.293	6.844	8.043
Wealth relative to village mean	0.030	0.026	–0.023	0.083
Age	38.499	0.269	37.948	39.050
Ethnicity (Han majority)	0.771	0.042	0.684	0.857
Knowledge	3.069	0.122	2.820	3.319
Communist Youth League member	0.217	0.029	0.157	0.278
Education (years)	5.587	0.199	5.179	5.994
Newspaper reader	0.073	0.008	0.056	0.089
Village-level independent variables				
Per capita income (yuan)	1339.67	38.51	1260.79	1418.56
Time to nearest bus stop (walking minutes)	24.206	7.257	9.339	39.072
Electoral competition	0.815	0.021	0.772	0.857

Note: PSU = Primary Sampling Unit. All estimates account for design effect.

Declaration of Conflicting Interests

The authors declared no potential conflicts of interest with respect to the authorship and/or publication of this article.

Financial Disclosure/Funding

The authors wish to thank the Cheng-Lee endowment at Yale University for research support, the interview team from Gaoyuan county as well as co-investigators Jin XIAO and Yusheng PENG.

Notes

1. Article 2 of the 1998 Organic Law specifies that village committees handle public matters (*gonggong shiwu*) and the provision of public goods (*gongyi shiye*), mediate civil disputes, assist and protect public order, and inform people's governments about the opinions, demands, and proposals of villagers (National People's Congress [NPC], 1998).
2. This information comes from the Organic Law. The Yunnan Provincial Regulations on Implementing the Organic Law allow a Village Committee consisting of between five and nine members.
3. Initial candidates can be nominated by individual voters as well as by groups of villagers. Individual voters may nominate others or themselves. Candidates

who emerge from this initial process can reject or accept the nomination. Once a formal list of nominees is finalized, candidates are elected by popular vote.

4. Su and Yang (2005) also argue that elections help improve governance, but they do not base these claims on survey data or large-*N* cross-village comparisons.
5. Throughout this article, we call an election competitive when some candidates must lose because the number of candidates is greater than the number of contested seats. This conforms to the narrow provisions of the Chinese 1998 Organic Law on village self-government. We cannot take into account the degree to which races are competitive in the sense that the spread between winners and losers is small because electoral data on village elections are exceedingly difficult to obtain unless researchers are physically present in the village on election day.
6. The villagers' representative assemblies can also decide on and amend the village compact.
7. Village elections fall in the category of elections that reveal information about the performance of local officials to their political principals (Geddes, 2005).
8. In 2003 it had a population of nearly a half million residents, of whom 40% were ethnic minorities, primarily Yi.
9. Because of rounding, our sample slightly overdraws the minority stratum. Probability weights were adjusted to account for this small discrepancy in our statistical analyses.
10. At each stage (township, administrative village, and natural village) the sampled units were selected with probability proportional measures of size, which ensures that any household in the sample has the same probability of being selected as any other household in the sample. Because the number of sampled villages varies by townships, the sample is naturally self-weighting at the administrative village level. By selecting two natural villages in each administrative village, we were able to limit clustering to groups of about 12 households per natural village.
11. Throughout our analysis, we also leverage against possible bias by including the respondent age (and its squared value) as a control variable. Nevertheless, the coefficients associated with age should be interpreted with caution. Because our distribution is truncated on the left and on the right, our estimates of the impact of age may be biased downward.
12. Empirical studies of elections that preceded the 1998 law include the work of Manion (1996), Shi (1999b), and Oi and Rozelle (2000). By contrast, Zhong and Chen (2002) conducted their survey work in Jiangsu in 2000.
13. Election observers in China have noted that formal proxies are rarely used among family members: In practice, whoever has access to the voter's registration at the time when the roving box arrives will cast as many votes as there are cards in the household.

14. For instance, absentee ballots or vote by mail are lawful and routine methods of voting in many democracies, and in some American states (e.g., Oregon) they are now the only legal way of casting ballots. Such voters would be excluded under Zhong and Chen's (2002) definition.
15. We accept the possibility that some respondents who claim not to have voted may unknowingly have been counted by the authorities, but we regard such "voters" as nonparticipants.
16. Among 698 interviewees, 30 (or 4.3%) reported being Communist Party members. Probability weights account for the slightly higher estimate (6.0%) when the survey design is taken in account. The 95% confidence interval is [.01, .11].
17. Communist Youth League Membership lapses at the age of 28, though it is possible to join the Communist Party at the age of 18.
18. Article 14 of the Organic Law states that "the village committee is elected from candidates who are nominated directly by eligible voters in the village. The number of candidates must exceed the number of positions" (NPC, 1998).
19. See, for example, People's Court of Tianhe District, Guangzhou municipality, May 10, 2002: "Demand by Wen Zhijian to be reinstated on the list of eligible voters of Lingtong Village following his exclusion by the Lingtong Village Election Committee for failing to meet the rules about the timing of returning residents to the village."
20. The percentage of households that owned each of the 21 items was table (98.0%), electric rice cooker (70.0%), color television (65.0%), bicycle (56.0%), sewing machine (53.0%), DVD (45.0%), desk (29.0%), washing machine (27.0%), telephone (26.0%), motorcycle (23.0%), radio (19.0%), electric fan (18.0%), VCR (9.0%), electric water heater (8.0%), pressure cooker (8.0%), bookshelf (6.0%), camera (6.0%), refrigerator (6.0%), microwave oven (1.0%), computer (0.3%), and air conditioner (0.0%). We excluded beds from the computations because all households reported owning at least one bed. The mean household possession index is 6.97, with a standard deviation of 3.23.
21. We compute an index ranging from 0 to 10 from the number of correct answers to the following questions: "In which city is the seat of [this] prefecture located?" (49% correct answers), "Who is the President of the People's Republic of China?" (40%), "Who is the President of the United States?" (12%), "What is the world's highest mountain?" (51%), "In which year will China host the Olympics?" (23%), "Of which country is Hanoi the capital?" (26%), "Which city is the capital of Iraq?" (8%), "What is the name of China's longest river?" (29%), "In which year was the PRC founded? (39%), and "What is the value of Pi?" (15%). As for the question "Who is the President of the United States?" any reference to President "Bush" or "George Bush" (*bushi, xiao bushi*) is coded as correct. For the value of Pi, the correct integer is sufficient to be considered a valid answer (therefore 3.5 is coded as correct). The combined knowledge score has a mean of 2.9 and a standard deviation of 2.7, with an actual range from 0 to 10.

22. Also because non-Han tend to live in smaller villages than Han but each village must have a party branch with three members, we hypothesize that the likelihood for admission will be higher for minorities.
23. Other sources of leadership accountability can exist beside elections. Solidarity groups can be an efficient pathway to elite responsiveness, as Tsai (2007) contends. But we believe that the conduct of village properly run elections encourages local officials to be responsive to villagers' needs (Birney, 2007; Manion, 1996).
24. Li (2003) is a rare exception to the lack of panel data collected both before and after a round of elections.
25. The reliability of instrumental variable models (and especially their probit specification) has been widely debated in the recent methodological literature. The trade-off between the efficiency and the erogeneity of instrumental variables has plagued their estimation (Bartels, 1991). Dunning (2008) cautions that a focus on the usual discussion of the exclusion restriction alone is not sufficient to guarantee a successful estimation. Altonji, Elder, and Taber (2005) suggest that bivariate probits may be more appropriate, but their approach is not suitable in our case. We thus caution that our IV-probit results are only suggestive of the plausibility of our theoretical mechanism linking competition, turnout, and fairness.
26. Arendt and Larsen (2006) have applied this technique to the relationship between trust and vote in bivariate and trivariate specifications.

References

Altonji, Joseph, Elder, Todd, & Taber, Christopher. (2005). An evaluation of instrumental variable strategies for estimating the effects of Catholic schooling (NBER Working Paper 9358). Cambridge, MA: National Bureau of Economic Research.

Arendt, Jacob Nielsen, & Larsen, Holm Anders. (2006). Probit models with dummy endogenous regressors (Business and Economics Discussion Paper 4/2006). Odense: University of Southern Denmark.

Bartels, Larry M. (1991). Instrumental and "quasi-instrumental" variables. *American Journal of Political Science*, *35*(3), 777-800.

Bian, Yanjie, Shu, Xiaoling, & Logan, John R. (2001). Communist Party membership and regime dynamics in China. *Social Forces*, *79*(3), 805-841.

Birch, Sarah. (2005, September). *Perceptions of electoral fairness and voter turnout*. Paper presented at the annual meeting of the American Political Science Association, Washington, DC.

Birney, Mayling. (2007). *Can local elections contribute to democratic progress in authoritarian regimes? Exploring the political ramifications of China's village elections*. Unpublished doctoral dissertation, Yale University, New Haven, CT.

Brandt, Loren, & Turner, Matthew A. (2007). The usefulness of imperfect elections: The case of village elections in rural China. *Economics and Politics, 19*(3), 453-480.

Chen, Jie, & Zhong, Yang. (2002). Why do people vote in semicompetitive elections in China? *Journal of Politics, 64*(1), 178-197.

Diamond, Larry Jay. (2002). Thinking about hybrid regimes. *Journal of Democracy, 13*(2), 21-35.

Dunning, Thad. (2008). Model specification in instrumental-variables regression. *Political Analysis, 16*, 290-302.

Gandhi, Jennifer, & Przeworski, Adam. (2006). Cooperation, cooptation, and rebellion under dictatorship and politics. *Economics and Politics, 18*(1), 1-26.

Geddes, Barbara. (2005, September). *The role of elections in authoritarian regimes.* Paper presented at the annual meeting of the American Political Science Association, Washington, DC. Retrieved February 20, 2010, from http://www.allacademic.com/meta/p41799_index.html

Gilison, Jerome M. (1968). Soviet elections as a measure of dissent: The missing one percent. *American Political Science Review, 62*(3), 814-826.

Guo, Zhenglin, & Bernstein, Thomas P. (2004). The impact of elections on the village structure of power: The relations between the village committees and the party branches. *Journal of Contemporary China, 13*(39), 257-275.

He, Baogang. (2006). A survey study of voting behavior and political participation in Zhejiang. *Japanese Journal of Political Science, 7*(3), 225-250.

Hermet, Guy, Rose, Richard, & Rouquié, Alain. (1978). *Elections without choice.* New York: John Wiley.

Horsley, Jamie P. (2001). Village elections: Training ground for democratization. *China Business Review, 28*(2), 44-52.

Hu, Rong. (2005). Economic development and the implementation of village elections in rural China. *Journal of Contemporary China, 14*(44), 427-444.

Jacobs, Everett M. (1970). Soviet local elections: What they are, and what they are not. *Soviet Studies, 22*(1), 61-76.

Jaenicke, Johannes. (2008). *Detecting social interactions in bivariate probit models: Some simulation results.* Erfurt, Germany: University of Erfurt, Faculty of Economics, Law and Social Sciences.

Kennedy, John James. (2002). The face of "grassroots democracy": The substantive difference between real and cosmetic elections in rural China. *Asian Survey, 42*(3).

Kennedy, John James, Rozelle, Scott, & Shi, Yaojiang. (2004). Elected leaders and collective land: Farmers' evaluation of village leaders' performance in rural China. *Journal of Chinese Political Science, 9*(1), 1-22.

Lawrence, Susan V. (1994). Democracy, Chinese style. *Australian Journal of Chinese Affairs, 32*, 61-68.

Levitsky, Steven, & Way, Lucan. (2002). The rise of competitive authoritarianism. *Journal of Democracy*, *12*(2), 51-66.

Li, Lianjiang. (2003). The empowering effect of village elections in China. *Asian Survey*, *43*(4), 648-663.

Li, Lianjiang, & O'Brien, Kevin J. (1999). The struggle over village elections. In M. Goldman & R. MacFarquhar (Eds.), *The paradox of China's post-Mao reform* (pp. 129-144). Cambridge, MA: Harvard University Press.

Maddala, G. (1983). *Limited-dependent and qualitative variables in econometrics*. Cambridge, UK: Cambridge University Press.

Magaloni, Beatriz. (2006). *Voting for autocracy: Hegemonic party survival and its demise in Mexico*. Cambridge, UK: Cambridge University Press.

Manion, Melanie F. (1996). The electoral connection in the Chinese countryside. *American Political Science Review, 90*(4), 736-748.

Manion, Melanie. (2006). Democracy, community, trust: The impact of elections in rural China. *Comparative Political Studies*, *39*, 301-324.

Ministry of Civil Affairs. (2005). *Statistical yearbook of Chinese civil affairs*. Retrieved February 20, 2010, from http://www.chinainfobank.com

National Bureau of Statistics. (2001). *Abstract of Chinese county social and economic statistics 2000*. Beijing: Author.

National People's Congress. (1998). *Organic Law on Villagers' Committees of the People's Republic of China*. Retrieved February 1, 2007, from http://www.law-lib.com/law/law_view.asp?id=402

Nelson, Lynn D., & Amonashvili, Paata. (1992). Voting and political attitudes in Soviet Georgia. *Soviet Studies*, *44*(4), 687-698.

Oi, Jean C., & Rozelle, S. (2000). Elections and power: The locus of decision-making in Chinese villages. *China Quarterly*, *162*, 513-539.

Przeworski, Adam. (1988). Democracy as the contingent outcome of conflicts. In J. Elster & R. Slagstad (Eds.), *Constitutionalism and democracy* (pp. 59-80). Cambridge, UK: Cambridge University Press.

Przeworski, Adam, Alvarez, Michael E., Cheibub, Jose Antonio, & Limongi, Fernando. (2000). *Democracy and development: Political institutions and well-being in the world, 1950-1990. Cambridge studies in the theory of democracy*. Cambridge, UK: Cambridge University Press.

Schedler, Andreas. (2006). *Electoral authoritarianism: The dynamics of unfree competition*. Boulder, CO: Lynne Rienner.

Shi, Tianjian. (1999a). Village committee elections in China: Institutionalist tactics for democracy. *World Politics*, *51*, 385-412.

Shi, Tianjian. (1999b). Voting and nonvoting in China: Voting behavior in plebiscitary and limited-choice elections. *Journal of Politics, 61*(4), 1115-1139.

Shi, Tianjian. (2000). Cultural values and democracy in the People's Republic of China. *China Quarterly*, *162*, 540-559.

Su, Fubing, & Yang, Dali. (2005). Elections, governance and accountability in China. *Asian Perspective*, *29*(4), 125-157.

Swearer, Howard R. (1961). The functions of Soviet local elections. *Midwest Journal of Political Science*, *5*(2), 129-149.

Tsai, Lily. (2007). *Accountability without democracy: Solidarity groups and public goods provision in rural China*. Cambridge, UK: Cambridge University Press.

Wilde, Johachim. (2000, December), Identification of multiple equation probit models with endogenous dummy regressors. *Economics Letters, 69*, 309-312.

Zaslavsky, Victor, & Brym, Robert J. (1978). The functions of elections in the USSR. *Soviet Studies*, *30*(3), 362-371.

Zhong, Yang, & Chen, Jie. (2002). To vote or not to vote—An analysis of peasants' participation in Chinese village elections. *Comparative Political Studies, 35*, 686-712.

Bios

Pierre F. Landry is an associate professor of political science at Yale University in New Haven, CT.

Deborah Davis is a professor of sociology at Yale University in New Haven, CT.

Shiru Wang is a postdoctoral fellow in the Division of Policy, Administration and Social Sciences in the Faculty of Education at the University of Hong Kong in Hong Kong.

Journal of Contemporary China (2009), **18**(60), June, 359–378

Routledge
Taylor & Francis Group

Path to Democracy? Assessing village elections in China

KEVIN J. O'BRIEN and RONGBIN HAN*

Election procedures in rural China have improved greatly over the last 20 years and a good number of reasonably free and fair elections have been held. But changes in the 'exercise of power' have not kept up with changes in the 'access to power'. In many communities, township authorities, Party branches, and social forces (such as clans, religious groups, and underworld elements) continue to impede democratic rule. This suggests that a purely procedural definition of democracy is problematic and that democratization depends on the power configuration in which elected bodies are embedded. Putting grassroots democracy into place goes well beyond getting the procedures right, and 'high quality' democracy rests on much more than convening good village elections every three years.

The launch of village elections in China has passed its twentieth anniversary. Elections officially began with the enactment of the *Organic Law of Village Committees* (1987, amended 1998). This law promised 'self-governance' (*zizhi*) via self-management, self-education, and self-service, which were soon reconceived as democratic election, decision making, management, and supervision. Since then, 'grassroots democracy' has become a term freighted with controversy for those who study Chinese politics, and elections have attracted a great deal of attention both domestically and abroad.[1]

Judging by procedures alone, village elections have achieved much. Balloting has been carried out in every province, with Guangdong, Hainan, and Yunnan finally conducting their first elections in 1999, and Tibet its first in 2002. Turnout rates have

*Kevin J. O'Brien is Alann P. Bedford Professor of Asian Studies and Professor of Political Science at the University of California, Berkeley. His books include *Engaging the Law in China: State, Society and Possibilities for Justice* (Stanford, 2005), *Rightful Resistance in Rural China* (Cambridge, 2006), and *Popular Protest in China* (Harvard, 2008). Rongbin Han is a Ph.D. student in the Department of Political Science at the University of California, Berkeley.

1. For review essays, see Gunter Schubert, 'Village elections in the PRC: a Trojan horse of democracy?', Project Discussion Paper No. 19, (2002), available at: http://www.uni-duisburg.de/Institute/OAWISS/neu/downloads/pdf/orange/discuss19.pdf (accessed 25 July 2007); Björn Alpermann, 'An assessment of research on village governance in China and suggestions for future applied research', prepared for the China–EU Training Programme of Village Governance, Beijing, (2003), available at: http://www.china.uni-koeln.de/papers/No%202003-1.pdf, (accessed 28 July 2007).

ISSN 1067-0564 print/ 1469-9400 online/09/600359-20 © 2009 Taylor & Francis
DOI: 10.1080/10670560902770206

generally been high, in many locations reportedly over 90%.[2] Surveys and direct observation by international monitors also show that the conduct of elections (including nomination procedures, competitiveness, and secret balloting) has improved over time.[3]

By many indicators, the future of grassroots democracy in China is bright, much as Tianjian Shi foresaw some years ago.[4] When tracing the introduction of village elections, Shi highlighted the role of democratically committed midlevel officials in the Ministry of Civil Affairs who employed an incremental approach that focused on extent first and quality later. This explanation accords nicely with most theories of democratization and its diffusion, and their emphasis on the role of leaders and their decisions.[5]

Is rural China on the path to democracy that Shi and others have suggested?[6] How should we assess the prospects for grassroots democracy in China? Viewing the mountain of evidence now available in light of the literature on democratization, we re-examine the practice of self-governance and suggest that the working definition of democracy adopted by most observers, which underscores its procedural components, is incomplete. This definition, in a word, leads analysts to over emphasize form at the expense of content. Instead, we follow Sebastian Mazzuca[7] and suggest a distinction between two dimensions of democratization, namely access to power and exercise of power. The introduction of elections has indeed begun to change the way in which village authorities gain power, but this has not necessarily transformed the way they exercise that power. Reducing rural democracy to well-run

2. Tong Zhihui, 'Cunji Xuanju de Lishi Fazhan he Xueshu Yanjiu' ['Historical development and academic research on village elections'], in Liu Yawei, ed., *Wusheng de Geming: Cunmin Zhixuan de Lishi Xianshi he Weilai* [*Silent Revolution: The History, Reality and Future of Village Elections*] (Xi'an: Xibei Daxue Chubanshe, 2002), p. 18; He Xuefeng, 'Cunweihui Xuanju Zhuhuanjie de Diaocha yu Fenxi: Hunansheng Sishigexian Cunweihui Xuanju Xinxi Huifang Huodong Baogao' ['An investigation and analysis of procedures of village committee elections: a report on the data verification of the village committee election in 40 counties in Hunan Province'], available at: http://www.chinarural.org/news_show.aspx?cols=1812&ID=11780 (accessed 1 December 2006). On an 86% turnout rate in 120 villages in Heilongjiang and Anhui, see David Zweig and Chung Siu Fung, 'Elections, democratic values, economic development in rural China', *Journal of Contemporary China* 16(50), (February 2007), pp. 25–26. On 71% turnout in 12 Anhui villages, see Qingshan Tan and Xin Qiushui, 'Village election and governance: do villagers care?', *Journal of Contemporary China* 16(53), (November 2007), p. 585. For 48% turnout (excluding proxy votes) in 12 Jiangsu counties, see Yang Zhong and Jie Chen, 'To vote or not to vote: an analysis of peasants' participation in Chinese village elections', *Comparative Political Studies* 35(6), (August 2002), pp. 692–693.

3. See Qingshan Tan, 'Building institutional rules and procedures: village election in China', *Policy Sciences* 37(1), (March 2004), pp. 1–22; Baogang He, *Rural Democracy in China: The Role of Village Elections* (New York: Palgrave, 2007), pp. 24, 39; Sun Long and Tong Zhihui, 'The standardization of villager committee election procedures', available at: http://www.cartercenter.org/documents/1096.pdf (accessed 29 March 2007). 'Election observation report: Fujian Province village elections, People's Republic of China' (Washington, DC: International Republican Institute, 2003); Melanie Manion, 'How to assess village elections in China', *Journal of Contemporary China* 18(60), (June 2009).

4. Tianjian Shi, 'Village committee elections in China: institutionalist tactics for democracy', *World Politics* 51(3), (April 1999), pp. 385–412.

5. See Guillermo O'Donnell, Philippe Schmitter and Lawrence Whitehead, *Transitions from Authoritarian Rule: Tentative Conclusions about Uncertain Democracies* (Baltimore, MD: Johns Hopkins University Press, 1986), pp. ix–x, also ch. 3; Alfred Stepan, *Arguing Comparative Politics* (Oxford: Oxford University Press, 2001), chs 5 and 8.

6. See also Qingshan Tan, *Village Elections in China: Democratizing the Countryside* (Lewiston, NY: Edward Mellen, 2006); He, *Rural Democracy in China*; Jamie P. Horsley, 'Village elections: training ground for democracy', *China Business Review* 28(2), (March–April 2001), pp. 44–52.

7. Sebastian L. Mazzuca, 'Reconceptualizing democratization: access to power versus excercise of power', in Gerardo L. Munck, ed., *Regimes and Democracy in Latin America* (New York: Oxford University Press, 2007).

elections oversimplifies the complexity of the local power configuration and turns village governance into much less than it is.[8]

Conceptualizing democracy and democratization

Though many observers speak of democracy when they examine self-governance in China, few of them have stopped to define the term. One reason for this may be that they seek to avoid courting controversy, as democracy is at root an 'essentially contested concept'.[9] Still, some efforts have been made by political theorists to standardize usage. For instance, many have taken Robert Dahl's definition of polyarchy as the first, most straightforward characterization of democracy.[10] Following Dahl and Schumpeter, they adopt a 'procedural minimum' understanding of democracy, which 'presumes fully contested elections with full suffrage and the absence of massive fraud, combined with effective guarantees of civil liberties, including freedom of speech, assembly, and association'.[11] Some analysts also add that elected governments must have the power to govern.[12]

The advantages of such a definition are clear. Above all, it facilitates measurement. But on the other hand, understanding democracy in a purely procedural fashion is problematic because it neglects the content of democracy. It does not answer the question of what democratic politics is, and instead focuses on how we might get it. Though choosing leaders through certain methods is an essential element of democracy, impeccable procedures do not guarantee democratic governance. This point is especially important because democracy does not simply denote majority rule,[13] but instead is usually seen to be a congeries of institutions that guarantees rule of law, separation of powers, protection of minorities, and protection of civil liberties.

Analytically, there are also at least two drawbacks to the procedural definition. First, it impedes classification because it fails to capture diverse forms of democratic practice. Democratization waves have produced a striking variety of regimes, many of which share important attributes but differ from each other and from democracies in advanced industrial countries. The simple procedural minimum definition cannot

8. On the relationship of village elections to temple associations, the tax-for-fee reform, and anti-corruption efforts, see Lily L. Tsai, 'The struggle for village public goods provision: informal institutions of accountability in rural China', John James Kennedy, 'The implementation of village elections and tax-for-fee reform in rural northwest China', and Richard Levy, 'Village elections, transparency, and anticorruption: Henan and Guangdong Provinces', all in Elizabeth J. Perry and Merle Goldman, eds, *Grassroots Political Reform in Contemporary China* (Cambridge, MA: Harvard University Press, 2007). For a discussion of the grassroots 'public sphere' and the role village elections play in it, see Mao Dan and Ren Qiang, *Zhongguo Nongcun Gonggong Lingyu de Shengzhang: Zhengzhi Shehuixue Shiye li de Cunmin Zizhi zhu Wenti* [*The Growth of Public Sphere in Rural China: Village Self-Governance from the Perspective of Political Sociology*] (Beijing: Zhongguo Shehui Kexue Chubanshe, 2006).

9. David Collier, Fernando Daniel Hidalgo and Andra Olivia Maciuceanu, 'Essentially contested concepts: debates and applications', *Journal of Political Ideologies* 11(3), (October 2006).

10. Mazzuca, 'Reconceptualizing democratization'.

11. David Collier and Steven Levitsky, 'Democracy with adjectives: conceptual innovation in comparative research', *World Politics* 49(3), (April 1997), p. 434; also Aurel Croissant and Wolfgang Merkel, 'Introduction: democratization in the early twenty-first century', Wolfgang Merkel, 'Embedded and defective democracies', and Leonardo Morlino, 'What is a "good" democracy?', all in *Democratization* 11(5), (2004).

12. Collier and Levitsky, 'Democracy with adjectives'.

13. Nowadays, few would say that democracy can be reduced to majority rule. However, a procedural minimum definition can encourage such a view.

comfortably embrace all these possibilities.[14] Second, this definition encourages prioritizing easily observable dimensions of elections, and downplaying other important attributes of democracy which are not covered in a definition that, most notably, excludes what happens after the voting ends. Attaching so much importance to forms and procedures, especially elections, leads analysts to overlook the substance of democracy and to treat it solely as a way to access power while neglecting how that power is exercised.

Researchers have, of course, noticed the first drawback and a number of techniques have been adopted to address it. For instance, David Collier and Steven Levitsky, among others, have developed a tool called 'diminished subtypes' to distinguish different types of democracy while avoiding concept-stretching.[15] The second drawback—emphasizing readily-measurable election procedures—has received less attention, and this is one reason why the first two generations of democratization studies, which focus on transition and consolidation, have had difficulty explaining the 'low quality' of new democratic regimes beset with corruption, cronyism, and weak accountability.[16]

Democracy, in our way of thinking, not only sets the rules for social forces to compete for political power; it also prescribes how power will be exerted to regulate those forces. Altering the way in which leaders are selected alone does not result in democratic rule, even with the presence of civil liberties. The mode in which political actors behave must also be democratized. And during the whole process, the citizenry must take up new responsibilities and play their role as well. Only with active participation can effective checks and balances be established that ensure the democratic operation of political power.[17]

Consider China's *Organic Law of Village Committees* (1998). The Law promised four democracies: election, decision making, management, and supervision. Whereas grassroots elections alter access to power, the latter three elements change the way power is exercised. However, of the four, access to power has attracted the bulk of the attention. Most studies have centered on the introduction of elections, how elections have been conducted, how the quality of elections can be enhanced, and voting behavior of villagers.[18] Of course, this research has taught us much, but might it be

14. Collier and Levitsky, 'Democracy with adjectives'.

15. *Ibid.* For other research on 'democracy with adjectives', see Croissant and Merkel, 'Introduction'; Merkel, 'Embedded and defective democracies'; and Morlino, 'What is a "good" democracy?'.

16. Mazzuca, 'Reconceptualizing democratization', p. 1. We depart from Mazzuca, however, and follow 'third generation' theorists, by treating improvements in the 'quality of democracy' as an element of democratization.

17. For similar 'third generation' understandings of democratization, see Larry Diamond and Leonardo Morlino, eds, *Assessing the Quality of Democracy* (Baltimore, MD: Johns Hopkins University Press, 2005); and Guillermo O'Donnell, Jorge Vargas Cullell and Osvaldo M. Iazzetta, eds, *The Quality of Democracy: Theory and Applications* (Notre Dame, IN: University of Notre Dame Press, 2004).

18. On the introduction of elections, see Schubert, 'Village elections in the PRC'; Shi, 'Village committee elections in China'; Daniel Kelliher, 'The Chinese debate over village self-government', *China Journal* 37, (January 1997); Kevin J. O'Brien and Lianjiang Li, 'Accommodating "democracy" in a one-party state: introducing village elections in China', *China Quarterly* 162, (June 2000). On voting behavior, see Zhong and Chen, 'To vote or not to vote'; Baogang He, 'A survey study of voting behavior and political participation in Zhejiang', *Japanese Journal of Political Science* 7(3), (2006). Attempts have begun to explore the three other components of village self-governance. In his report to the EU–China Training Programme on Village Governance, Björn Alpermann suggested that more attention be paid to post-election administration, decision-making, and control: Alpermann, 'An assessment of research on village governance in China'. On the effects of elections, more generally, see Guo Zhenglin and Thomas Bernstein, 'The impact of elections on the village

useful to assess grassroots political reform in China from a different perspective? In the next two sections, we evaluate the configuration of power in rural China using an approach that always keeps in mind the difference between accessing power and exercising power.

Accessing power in Chinese villages

Election implementation in rural China has improved both in terms of coverage and procedures. According to the Ministry of Civil Affairs, balloting is now held every three years in over 600,000 villages in all 31 provinces, with nearly 600 million voters taking part.[19] Since the revised *Organic Law* came into force in 1998, election procedures have also been spelled out by authorities at lower levels. By the mid 2000s, nearly every province had issued electoral regulations that matched, or went beyond, the national law, and detailed implementation guidelines had also been formulated by many prefectures, counties, and townships.[20]

Electoral procedures, touching on issues as varied as setting up steering committees and limiting proxy voting, have been clarified both on paper and in practice. During the first decade after the provisional *Organic Law* was passed, the absence of regulations concerning 'election steering committees' (*xuanju lingdao xiaozu*) drew much criticism.[21] Since 1998, both the *Organic Law* and most provincial regulations have come to include stipulations about how new, more circumscribed committees are to be organized and what functions they are to perform.[22] Of perhaps greatest importance, election committee members in the majority of villages are now selected by village assemblies, village groups, or village representative assemblies.[23] This should make them more independent and

Footnote 18 continued
structure of power: the relations between village committees and village Party branches', *Journal of Contemporary China* 13(39), (May 2004); Björn Alpermann, 'The post-election administration of Chinese villages', *China Journal* 46, (July 2001); John James Kennedy, 'The face of "grassroots democracy" in rural China: real versus cosmetic elections', *Asian Survey* 42(3), (May/June 2002); Lianjiang Li, 'The empowering effect of village elections in China', *Asian Survey* 43(4), (July/August 2003); Loren Brandt and Matthew A. Turner, 'The usefulness of corruptible elections', *Economics and Society* 19(3), (November 2007); Melanie Manion, 'Democracy, community, trust: the impact of elections in rural China', *Comparative Political Studies* 39(3), (April 2006).

19. 'Zuohao Minzheng Gongzuo, Qieshi Weihu Renmin Hefa Quanyi: Fang Minzhengbu Buzhang Li Xueju' ['Improve civil affairs work and earnestly defend people's legal rights: interview with the Minister of Civil Affairs Li Xueju'], *Renquan* [*Human Rights*] no. 5, (2004), p. 6.

20. Björn Alpermann, 'Provincial legislation on village elections', *Zeitschrift für Chinesisches Recht* no. 1, (2007); also Yuan Dayi, 'Cunmin Zizhi de Xianzai' ['The current situation of village self-governance'], paper prepared for EU–China Training Programme on Village Governance Conference, Beijing, 5–7 April 2006, available at: http://www.chinaelections.org/NewsInfo.asp?NewsID=92565 (accessed 2 August 2007).

21. See Jorgen Elklit, 'The Chinese village committee electoral system', *China Information* 11(4), (1997), pp. 4–5; Kevin J. O'Brien, 'Villagers, elections, and citizenship in contemporary China', *Modern China* 27(4), (October 2001), p. 420.

22. Alpermann, 'Provincial legislation on village elections'.

23. For data on election committees in 116 villages in six provinces, see Xu Zhigang, Liu Mingxing and Tao Ran, 'Cunzhuang Xuanju Zuiyou Guize de Fei Yizhixing' ['Incongruence in optimal rules for village elections'], *Zhongguo Nongcun Guancha* [*China Rural Survey*] no. 6, (2006), pp. 62–71. In the 2002 elections, village assemblies, village groups, or village representative assemblies selected election committee members in 98% of Shaanxi's villages. See 'Table of 2002 village elections in Shaanxi', available at: http://www.chinarural.org/news_show.aspx?cols=1810&ID=35295 (accessed 5 August 2007).

responsive, even though committees in most locations continue to be presided over by village Party secretaries or sitting committee directors.[24]

Voter registration helps ensure voting rights and the validity of elections. Though both the *Organic Law* and provincial legislation remain murky about precisely who can vote, stipulations that require publication of a voters' list 20 days before an election offer an opportunity to raise objections, and in some cases have led to lawsuits by those who felt they were excluded illegally.[25] In the 2002 Shaanxi elections, for example, voter lists were disputed in 7% of the province's villages, and although only 23% of villages published their list a full 20 days prior to the election, most villages issued theirs well before election day, as sometimes had occurred in the past.[26]

Candidate nomination has received much attention because it is crucial to an election's competitiveness and fairness. Control over the nominating process has been gradually loosened over the last two decades. In particular, selection through 'sea-elections' (*haixuan*), which entitles every voter to nominate primary candidates, has now spread to 26 provinces. Other forms of open nomination, such as joint or self-nomination, are also permitted in seven provinces.[27] At least four counties in Zhejiang, Jiangsu, Jiangxi and rural Chongqing went to new lengths in 2004 and 2005 and held direct elections without primaries or any prior selection of formal candidates.[28]

24. In Shaanxi's 2002 elections, for example, 79% of election committees were chaired by the Party secretary and 7% were chaired by the village committee director. See 'Table of 2002 village elections in Shaanxi'. Similar rates were found in other provinces: 87% and 6% in Fujian's 2003 elections, 91% and 7% in Chongqing's 2004 elections. See 'Table of 2003 village elections in Fujian', available at: http://www.chinarural.org/news_show.aspx?cols=1810&ID=35282 (accessed 11 August 2007); 'Table of 2004 village elections in Chongqing', available at: http://www.chinarural.org/news_show.aspx?cols=1811&ID=35745 (accessed 11 August 2007). On election committees in Jiangsu that are 'usually' led by village Party secretaries, see Zhong and Chen, 'To vote or not to vote', p. 696. In some places, local leaders continue to impede election committees. For examples from Shaanxi and Jiangxi, see Mu Ge, 'Xuanweihui he Cunweihui de Jiaoliang' ['The struggle between an election committee and the village committee'], available at: http://www.96990.cn/Blog/3/11206.shtml (accessed 6 August 2007); Xiao Tangbiao and Qiu Xinyou, 'Cunweihui Xuanju Zhong de Xuanju Weiyuanhui' ['Election committees in village elections'], *Qiushi* [*Seeking Truth*] no. 2, (2002), pp. 60–62.

25. For disputes that resulted in lawsuits, see 'Wu Shaohui Bufu Xuanmin Zige Chuli Jueding An' ['The case of Wu Shaohui disagreeing with a voter eligibility decision'], *Zhonghua Renmin Gongheguo Zuigao Renmin Fayuan Gongbao* [*Bulletin of People's Supreme Court, PRC*] no. 6, (2003), p. 29; Zhang Xinguo and Chen Junxian, 'Nongjiafei Jiafei le Xuanjuquan' ['Losing voter eligibility owing to marriage to a non-rural resident'], *Jiangsu Nongcun Jingji* [*Jiangsu Rural Economy*] no. 10, (2002), p. 34; 'Chen Chencai Xuanmin Zige An' ['The case of Chen Chencai's voter eligibility'], available at: http://www.gdcourts.gov.cn/alxc/ms/t20031225_2684.htm (accessed 4 August 2007).

26. 'Table of 2002 village elections in Shaanxi'.

27. Alpermann, 'Provincial legislation on village elections', p. 5. On opening the candidate selection process, see Kennedy, 'The implementation of village elections', pp. 63–64.

28. Ma Fuyun, 'Cunweihui Zhijie Xuanju de Moshi Yanjiu' ['Research on the election system of village committees'], *Zhongguo Nongcun Guancha* [*China Rural Survey*] no. 4, (2006), pp. 65–72; 'Zhejiang Jinhua Wu Houxuanren Xuanju Jiang Quanmian Tuiguang' ['Elections in Jinhua, Zhejiang without pre-selected candidates will be popularized'], *Lingdao Juece Xinxi* [*Information on Leadership Policy*] no. 15, (April 2005), p. 22; Xiao Mei, 'Tongzhou: Cunweihui Xuanju Jiang Changshi Wu Houxuanren Yicixing Zhijie Toupiao Xuanju' ['Tongzhou: one time ballot without pre-selected candidates will be tried in village committee elections'], available at: http://www.tz.gov.cn/tzdz/showinfo/showInfo.aspx?InfoID=2edb6a04-178d-4553-95ad-5aeb18f0f8f8 (accessed 6 August 2007); Huang Hui and Li Qing, 'Jiangxi Xuanchu Shoupi Zijian Haixuan Cunguan' ['The first village officials by self-nominated sea election are elected in Jiangxi'], *Fazhi Ribao* [*Legal Daily*], (31 October 2005). In the 28 provinces in which it is allowed, write-in candidates have on occasion been elected. Pan Jia'en and Jiang Yunxiang, 'Yuecun Beihou de Gushi' ['Inside story of Yue village'], *Zhongguo Gaige Nongcun Ban* [*China Reform Rural Edition*] no. 3, (2003), pp. 39–41.

Number of candidates is another indicator of competitiveness. When village elections were first introduced, non-competitive elections (*deng'e xuanju*) were common.[29] Today, multi-candidate elections have become the rule. Most provincial regulations prescribe that there be two candidates for village committee director and vice-director, and that the number of candidates for ordinary committee members should outnumber the positions available by at least one. Though this permits minimal competition for ordinary committee spots, 'sea-elections' and self-nomination can increase the number of primary and final candidates greatly.[30] In one southern village where only two formal candidates for director were put up, 25 additional individuals were nominated by villagers, and two of them made it to the list of final candidates. In the same election, villagers proposed 38 nominees for vice director and 66 for the four other seats on the village committee.[31]

Once nominees are set, campaigning, ballot secrecy, and the use of roving ballot boxes and proxy-voting are all important factors that affect whether villagers can express their preferences on election day. Elklit's early study found that campaigning amounted to little more than informal discussion among villagers because many local regulations failed to mention campaigning.[32] This has changed. Despite continuing anxiety about candidates 'pulling votes' (*lapiao*), candidates in most places are now given opportunities to deliver speeches or engage in other forms of campaigning. According to a 2000 survey conducted in 77 counties across Fujian, 90% of respondents said that candidates addressed either a village assembly or village representative assembly, and 27% reported that other campaign activities, including home visits and introductions by supporters, took place.[33] A similar survey in 40 Hunan counties showed that over 80% of voters reported that candidates spoke to village assemblies, village representative assemblies, or voters, either on election day or before.[34]

Enhanced ballot secrecy and security is also evident. Secret balloting was not a common practice when elections were first introduced, but this is no longer the case. In Fujian, a national pacesetter, none of the 1989 elections employed a secret

29. Elklit, 'The Chinese village committee electoral system'; O'Brien, 'Villagers, elections, and citizenship in contemporary China'; Ma Wenquan, 'Guanyu Cunmin Zizhi de Shijian yu Sikao' ['Practice and reflection on village self-governance'], available at: http://www.chinaelections.org/NewsInfo.asp?NewsID=23806 (accessed 6 August 2007).

30. Final candidates are usually chosen according to the number of nominating votes received, by a second round of voting, or by the village representative assembly or election committee. Xu Zhigang *et al.*, 'Cunzhuang Xuanju Zuiyou Guize de Fei Yizhixing', p. 68.

31. Dai Lichao, 'Gaopingcun Xuanju Guancha' ['Observation of Gaoping village election'], in Lianjiang Li, Guo Zhenglin and Xiao Tangbiao, eds, *Cunweihui Xuanju Guancha* [*Observation of Village Elections*] (Tianjin: Tianjin Renmin Chubanshe, 2001), pp. 44–112.

32. Elklit, 'The Chinese village committee electoral system', p. 9.

33. Song Yuehong, 'Fujiansheng 2000 Niandu Cunweihui Xuanju Tongji yu Huifang Diaocha Shuju Bijiao' ['Comparison of statistics and data verification of 2000 village elections in Fujian Province'], available at: http://www.chinarural.org/news_show.aspx?cols=1812&ID=11774 (accessed 6 August 2007).

34. He Xuefeng, 'Cunweihui Xuanju Zhuhuanjie de Diaocha yu Fenxi'. Campaign speeches have been encouraged by some local officials to combat unlawful campaign activities, such as attracting votes via coercion or buying votes with cash, gifts, or banquets. The logic is that institutionalizing campaigning will make elections less dependent on personal resources and also offer candidates regular channels to present themselves. Zhang Rongmin, 'Qiantan Guifan he Zhili Cunweihui Xuanju zhong de Jingzheng Xingwei' ['A preliminary discussion of regulating and managing campaign activities in village elections'], paper prepared for EU–China Training Programme on Village Governance Conference, Beijing, 5–7 April 2006, available at: http://www.chinaelections.com/NewsInfo.asp?NewsID=91176 (accessed 6 August 2007).

ballot, but by 1997 95% did.[35] The use of voting booths has been written into the *Organic Law* and efforts have been made to implement ballot secrecy nationwide, though with less than complete success.[36] A national survey conducted by the Ministry of Civil Affairs in 2005 found that 49% of villages made secret voting cubicles available.[37] Since many villagers are not accustomed to filling out votes in private or feel pressure from fellow voters not to do so, some localities have started to make use of a secret voting space mandatory. In Shaanxi's 2002 elections, for example, 96% of villages made such a space available and 5% made it compulsory.[38]

Two more aspects of voting, namely the use of proxies and 'roving ballot boxes' (*liudong piaoxiang*) deserve mention. As outside observers have long complained, these practices may have been designed to make elections more inclusive, but they also threaten ballot secrecy and are open to abuse.[39] Though neither practice has been banned nationwide, local regulations have limited both. For instance, in 2000 Fujian eliminated proxy-voting and introduced absentee balloting.[40] More recently, Chongqing and Gansu also banned proxy-voting.[41] In the 28 provinces that still permit it, restrictions are now in place: all have limited the number of votes proxies can cast, five provinces require written authorizations, and 15 require prior consent by the village election committee.[42] And there is evidence that implementation has followed the law. Whereas in Fujian 15% of villages allowed proxy voting before 1998, now only 3% do. In Jilin and Hunan, far less than 1% of villages prohibited proxy voting before 1998; now, 18% and 8%, respectively, do.[43]

Like proxy-voting, controls over roving ballot boxes are becoming stricter. Roving boxes are no longer an option in seven provinces including Hebei, Jilin, Jiangsu, Shanxi, Sichuan, and rural Shanghai and Chongqing. In Anhui and Hunan, voters using boxes must be registered with the election committee and a list of their names published. In Guangdong, consent from township authorities must be obtained before deploying roving boxes.[44] Reform here is evident even in provinces, such

35. The Carter Center, 'Report of the Fifth Mission on Chinese village elections', (20 June–3 July 1998), p. 4.

36. Alpermann, 'Provincial legislation on village elections', p. 6. One source claimed that over 90% of villages in 11 provinces used secret ballot booths. Shi Weimin, 'Zhongguo Cunmin Zizhi Zouxiang Weilai' ['China village self-governance in the future'], paper prepared for EU–China Training Programme on Village Governance Conference, Beijing, 5–7 April 2006, available at: http://www.chinaelections.org/NewsInfo.asp?NewsID=92552 (accessed 6 August 2007). See also Fan Yu, 'Cunweihui Xuanju Zhidu de Yanjin ji Tedian' ['Evolution and characteristics of the village committee electoral system'], *Zhongguo Nongcun Guancha* [*China Rural Survey*] no. 1, (2006), p. 63.

37. He, *Rural Democracy in China*, p. 33.

38. 'Table of 2002 village elections in Shaanxi'.

39. O'Brien, 'Villagers, elections, and citizenship in contemporary China', pp. 421–422; The Carter Center, 'The Carter Center delegation to observe village elections in China', (4–16 March 1997), p. 15; The Carter Center, 'Carter Center delegation report: village elections in China and agreement on cooperation with the Ministry of Civil Affairs, People's Republic of China', (2–15 March 1998), pp. 11–12; International Republican Institute, 'Election observation report: Sichuan, People's Republic of China', (November 1998), p. 11.

40. The Carter Center, 'Observation of village elections in Fujian and the conference to revise the national procedures on villager committee elections', (1–7 August 2000), p. 22.

41. Alpermann, 'Provincial legislation on village elections', p. 8.

42. *Ibid.*

43. Tan, *Village Elections in China*, pp. 234–250.

44. Yu Weiliang, ed., *Cunmin Weiyuanhui Xuanju Guicheng Jiaopian Shuoming* [*Overhead Transparencies on Village Elections: A Handbook*], EU–China Training Programme on Village Governance, (2003), p. 58; Alpermann, 'Provincial legislation on village elections', p. 8.

as Jiangxi, which have villages that often sprawl over many square kilometers. In a survey of 40 Jiangxi communities following the 1999 elections, 40% of elections relied entirely on roving boxes, 53% used roving boxes in combination with other methods, and only 8% did not use them.[45] Province-wide statistics had changed significantly by 2002, with 29% of villages not employing roving boxes, and those only using them falling to less than 10%.[46]

Village elections in China remain far from perfect. Many procedural failings identified by Chinese and international observers, including the Ministry of Civil Affairs, the Carter Center, the International Republican Institute, and the European Union, have not been fully addressed. New problems are also emerging, such as vote-buying, literacy tests for candidates, interference in recall efforts, and 'hoodlum elections', where local toughs secure votes (or influence ballot-counting) through threats and intimidation.[47] Still, electoral procedures have improved greatly in the last two decades and a good number of competitive and reasonably fair elections have been held. Access to power, in other words, has expanded. But have similar changes in the exercise of power occurred?

Exercising power in Chinese villages

Observers have rightly noted that village elections exert some influence over political life in the Chinese countryside. Lianjiang Li, among others, has found that balloting has an empowering effect: free and fair elections can produce more responsive leaders and make them more impartial when enforcing state policies; it also provides an opportunity to dislodge cadres whom villagers like least.[48] John Kennedy and his coauthors, based on a 2000–2001 survey of 34 villages, likewise discovered that freely elected leaders were more accountable to villagers and that their land

45. Xiao Tangbiao, Qiu Xinyou, Tang Xiaoteng *et al.*, *Duowei Shijiao zhong de Cunmin Zhixuan* [*Direct Village Elections from Multiple Perspectives*] (Beijing: Zhongguo Shehuikexue Chubanshe, 2001), p. 27.

46. Out of 19,320 villages, 91% had election assemblies, 60% set up voting stations, 92% provided secret ballot booths and 71% used roving boxes. 'Table of 2002 village elections in Jiangxi', available at: http://www.chinarural.org/news_show.aspx?cols=1810&ID=35270 (accessed 9 August 2007).

47. He, *Rural Democracy in China*, pp. 59, 150, 214. On screening candidates and circumscribed rights of recall, see Alpermann, 'Provincial legislation on village elections', pp. 4–5, 10. For more on problematic recall efforts, see Xin Wang and Du Ke, 'Bamian Nan, Nan Zai Hechu?' ['Difficult to recall: where the difficulties lie?'], *Zhongguo Gaige Nongcun Ban* [*China Reform Rural Edition*] no. 10, (2004), pp. 26–27; Li Shan, 'Minxuan Cunguan: Feifa Bamian Shifei Duo' ['Elected village officials: illegally recalling them causes many problems'], *Jiangsu Nongcun Jingji* [*Jiangsu Rural Economy*] no. 1, (2003), pp. 42–43; 'Cunmin Bamian Buliao Cunzhuren: Wenti Chuzai Nali?' ['Villages cannot recall village committee chairs: where are the problems?'], *Lingdao Juece Xinxi* [*Information on Leadership Policy*] no. 13, (April 2007), p. 22. On a 'hoodlum election' in Shaanxi, see Kennedy, 'The face of "grassroots democracy" in rural China', p. 479. The Ministry of Civil Affairs has acknowledged many of these problems. See Guan Xiaofeng, 'Progress and problems mark elections', available at: http://www.chinadaily.com.cn/china/2007-07/10/content_6142535.htm (accessed 20 December 2007); also Kevin J. O'Brien, 'Improving election procedures: some modest proposals', unpublished paper, (23 April 2006), available at: http://papers.ssrn.com/sol3/papers.cfm?abstract_id=1157092; Qingshan Tan, 'Building democratic infrastructure: village electoral institutions', *Journal of Contemporary China* 18(60), (June 2009). On vote-buying suggesting that votes have value and interference by townships may be declining, see John James Kennedy, 'Legitimacy with Chinese characteristics: "two increases, one reduction"', *Journal of Contemporary China* 18(60), (June 2009).

48. Li, 'The empowering effect of village elections in China'; also Lianjiang Li and Kevin J. O'Brien, 'The struggle over village elections', in Merle Goldman and Roderick MacFarquhar, eds, *The Paradox of China's Post-Mao Reform* (Cambridge, MA: Harvard University Press, 1999), pp. 140–143; and Lianjiang Li, 'Elections and popular resistance in rural China', *China Information* 15(2), (2001), pp. 10–18.

management decisions reflected popular preferences for fair reallocation.[49] Along similar lines, Brandt and Turner have demonstrated that even corruptible elections can help curtail rent-seeking by local leaders,[50] while Baogang He has concluded that elections often lead village committee directors to place voters' interests over those of townships and Party branches.[51]

Grassroots balloting has also had a perceptible effect on villagers' attitudes and citizenship consciousness.[52] Kevin O'Brien has argued that elections are not only efforts to draw rural people into the local polity, but they are also an avenue through which citizenship practices may emerge before full citizenship is recognized.[53] Lianjiang Li has shown that free and fair elections enhance feelings of political efficacy and can help implant the idea that political power derives from the consent of the people.[54] And in a recent study of a long-time 'demonstration' (*shifan*) area, Gunter Schubert and Chen Xuelian suggest that elections can boost regime legitimacy, owing to a 'rational trust' that villagers come to have in their leaders, in which elections assure voters that this trust will be honored.[55] Melanie Manion, based on two surveys and other data collected between 1990 and 1996 from 57 villages in Hebei, Hunan, Anhui, and Tianjin, has also found that there is a positive correlation between electoral quality and villagers' beliefs that leaders are trustworthy.[56]

The impact of village elections cannot be denied. Elections, however, have not done away with several constraints that continue to impede democratic rule. Members of village committees may win their position through the ballot box, but once they gain office they still must take into account (and often compete with) township governments, village Party branches, and social forces, such as clans, religious organizations, and criminal gangs. In an ongoing struggle for power and legitimacy, tensions often arise between village committees and officials at the lowest rung of the state hierarchy, Party organs that remain the locus of power in a village, and societal groupings that possess their own sources of authority.[57] In many

49. John James Kennedy, Scott Rozelle and Yaojiang Shi, 'Elected leaders and collective land: farmers' evaluation of village leaders' performance in rural China', *Journal of Chinese Political Science* 9(1), (Spring 2004).

50. Brandt and Turner, 'The usefulness of corruptible elections'. On elections, both competitive and non-competitive, increasing the share of public expenditure in a village's budget, see Shuna Wang and Yang Yao, 'Grassroots democracy and local governance: evidence from rural China', *World Development* 35(10), (October 2007).

51. He, *Rural Democracy in China*, pp. 109–111.

52. Kennedy, 'The face of "grassroots democracy" in rural China'; Jie Chen, 'Popular support for village self-government in China: intensity and sources', *Asian Survey* 45(6), (November/December 2005); Manion, 'Democracy, community, trust'; Kennedy, 'Legitimacy with Chinese characteristics'.

53. O'Brien, 'Villagers, elections, and citizenship in contemporary China'. See also, Susanne Brandstädter and Gunter Schubert, 'Democratic thought and practice in rural China', *Democratization* 12(5), (December 2005), pp. 810–813; He, *Rural Democracy in China*, p. 50. On, however, villages with well-run elections in which civic consciousness has not noticeably increased, see Lily Tsai, *Accountability without Democracy: Solidarity Groups and Public Goods Provision in Rural China* (New York: Cambridge University Press, 2007), pp. 198, 223–226.

54. Li, 'The empowering effect of village elections in China'.

55. Gunter Schubert and Chen Xuelian, 'Village elections in contemporary China: new spaces for generating regime legitimacy? Experiences from Lishu County', *China Perspectives*, no. 3 (2007), pp. 12–27.

56. Manion, 'Democracy, community, trust'.

57. See Mao Dan and Ren Qiang, *Zhongguo Nongcun Gonggong Lingyu de Shengzhang*, pp. 53–68. Thomas P. Bernstein ['Village democracy and its limits', *ASIEN* 99, (April 2006), p. 30] writes: 'even when village elections work well, the power of elected village committees is limited because they necessarily function within an authoritarian political environment that is not structured to respond to the demands of constituents'. On data that suggest that village committees 'are still in the long shadow of township governments and village Party secretaries', see Tan and Xin, 'Village election and governance', p. 596; also Wang and Yao, 'Grassroots democracy and local governance', pp. 1635–1636.

communities, village committees have failed to achieve their potential, and in some they control few resources and are close to insignificant.[58]

Townships and village committees

Township governments, representing the formal state apparatus, are especially heavily implicated in efforts by village cadres to exercise power.[59] Björn Alpermann was among the first to note that 'the Chinese Party-state has been using self-government as another way to control rural politics'.[60] Indeed, the *Organic Law* (Arts. 4, 6) states that village committee members not only manage village affairs; they also fulfill tasks assigned by higher levels. Although the Law (Art. 4) stipulates that townships only 'guide' (*zhidao*) rather than 'lead' (*lingdao*) village committees, in practice, committees are often treated as line-organs of a township in high-priority policy areas.[61] Clashes, in these circumstances, become nearly inevitable when committee members dare to resist unpopular assignments, such as collecting levies, implementing costly 'target-hitting' (*dabiao*) programs, or completing other delegated tasks.[62] More often than not, when townships and village committees disagree, it is the village cadres who come out on the losing side.

Consider assessing levies, a recurring source of conflict between townships and villages in the 1990s.[63] This thankless task put elected cadres in a difficult position, insofar as they had to choose between fulfilling orders from above and keeping financial burdens down for fellow villagers. This dilemma, combined with perennially low compensation, made office-holding in some villages so unattractive that some cadres refused to complete their terms. In one study of 29 Hubei villages, He Xuefeng and Wang Ximing learned that committee directors in seven villages, frustrated by difficulties surrounding revenue collection, resigned within one year of their election in 1999.[64]

58. In a suburban village outside Tianjin that O'Brien visited in 1999, it was clear that the Muslim elders who managed the mosque dominated community decision making. Much younger village committee members appeared to be little more than their errand boys.

59. For a summary of reasons why local governments interfere in village affairs, see Alpermann, 'An assessment of research on village governance in China'; also, Bernstein, 'Village democracy and its limits', p. 33. On ways, however, that townships support free and fair elections, see He, *Rural Democracy in China*, pp. 142–146.

60. Alpermann, 'The post-election administration of Chinese villages', p. 47.

61. *Ibid*., p. 46; also Xu Wang, *Mutual Empowerment of State and Peasantry: Village Self-Government in Rural China* (New York: Nova Science, 2003), p. 67. Björn Alpermann, 'Institutionalizing village governance in China', *Journal of Contemporary China* 18(60), (June 2009).

62. See Mao Dan and Ren Qiang, *Zhongguo Nongcun Gonggong Lingyu de Shengzhang*, p. 52. For a collection of such cases, see Xu Yong and Xiang Jiquan, eds, *Cunmin Zizhi Jincheng zhong de Xiangcun Guanxi* [*Township and Village Relations in the Process of Village Self-Governance*] (*Wuhan: Huazhong Shifan Daxue Chubanshe*, 2003). For case studies and statistical analysis of weak village committees, and a conclusion that 'even in villages with extremely good implementation of democratic reforms, citizens do not necessarily have a great deal of leverage over officials, accurate information about their activities, or a particularly strong sense of public duty', see Tsai, Accountability without Democracy, ch. 7, quoted text on p. 190.

63. Xu Liming, Zhang Linsheng and Wang Zhiheng, *Nongcun Shuifei Gaige Chuyi* [*Opinions on Rural Tax-for-Fee Reform*] (Beijing: Zhongguo Nongye Kexue Jishu Chubanshe, 2002), p. 158; also Xu Yong, 'Cunmin Zizhi, Zhengfu Renwu ji Shuifei Gaige' ['Village self-governance, government tasks and tax-for-fee reform'], *Zhongguo Nongcun Jingji* [*Chinese Rural Economy*] no. 11, (2001).

64. He Xuefeng and Wang Ximing, 'Cunzu de Guimo yu Ganbu' ['Scale of village groups and their cadres'], in Xu Yong and Xiang Jiquan, eds, *Cunmin Zizhi Jincheng zhong de Xiangcun Guanxi*, p. 502.

Unpopular target-hitting programs are another source of discord. Overly ambitious development schemes, image-building efforts, and fancifully high targets are often imposed on village committees.[65] Though the tax-for-fee reform and abolition of the agricultural tax simplified revenue collection, it did not free committee members from other duties assigned from above. Evidence from many locations suggests that to maintain and strengthen control over villages, some townships are turning 'soft targets' (*ruan zhibiao*) into 'hard tasks' (*ying renwu*) that cannot be downplayed or ignored. In Henan, for example, in the face of strong community opposition, villages have been saddled with target-hitting projects, such as building 40 methane-generating pits or 200 *mu* of vegetable sheds.[66] In another Henan county, higher-ups ordered that at least one collective enterprise be set up in every village within a year. Over 100 paper mills were built, all of which went bankrupt, causing enormous losses, a chorus of popular complaint, and lasting environmental damage.[67]

Unpopular tasks may also be foisted on villages by townships that encounter unexpected problems. For example, in order to develop the local economy, higher-ups sometimes compel villages to supply raw materials to or buy products from local enterprises. One committee director in Jiangxi explained how he felt 'pressure from both sides' (*liangtou shouqi*): township authorities assigned him a high procurement quota to prop up a bamboo ware plant that was desperately short of cash, but villagers were unwilling to sell their bamboo unless they received timely and sufficient payment. The director felt trapped and could not satisfy both the township and voters who had elected him.[68]

Townships often treat elected committees as if they were subordinates, and village leaders may find themselves squeezed, like the meat in an overstuffed sandwich, or as the Jiangxi director quoted above put it: 'like a rat caught in the bellows' (*laoshu jin le fengxiang*). Sometimes, it does not even take much pressure to coax committee members to 'voluntarily be responsible to higher levels' (*zijue duishang fuze*).[69] Fiscal realities and features of the cadre management system make it difficult to refuse jobs imposed by townships, whatever the views of voters.

To fulfill many of their responsibilities, such as providing public goods, committees often must rely on townships for help. The tax-for-fee reform deepened a

65. Cho Soo-sung, 'On the relationship between Chinese township/town governments and villager committees', Zhang Guangxiu, 'A study of the relationship between villager self-government and basic-level government', and Cheng Tongshun, 'The relationship between the township/town government and the village in the context of villager self-government in China', papers all prepared for the *International Symposium on Villager Self-Government and the Development of Rural Society in China*, sponsored by the Carter Center and the Ministry of Civil Affairs, Beijing, 2–5 September 2001.

66. Liu Tao, 'Shuifei Gaige hou de Zhibiaohua: Chongxin Jiedu Xiang, Cun, Zu, Min Guanxi' ['Target-setting after tax-for-fee reform: rethinking relations among townships, villages, small groups, and villagers'], available at: http://www.snzg.cn/article/show.php?itemid-6758/page-1.html (accessed 2 October 2007).

67. For this incident and county pressures placed on townships, which are then transmitted to villages, see Kevin J. O'Brien and Lianjiang Li, 'Selective policy implementation in rural China', *Comparative Politics* 31(2), (January 1999), p. 176.

68. Lan Yuanjun, 'Liangtou Shouqi hou Mo Chulai de Luzi' ['A way out of pressure from both sides'], *Xiangzhen Luntan* [*Township Forum*] no. 11, (2001), p. 14.

69. Mao Dan and Ren Qiang, *Zhongguo Nongcun Gonggong Lingyu de Shengzhang*, p. 53.

fiscal crisis in many villages (and townships), as local leaders lost the ability to raise funds they had previously depended upon. Constructing and repairing roads, maintaining irrigation systems, and supporting the elderly and disabled, all have become more difficult, especially in agricultural areas and communities where other social institutions cannot pick up the slack.[70] In order to obtain needed resources, village cadres tend to be cooperative when townships assign them even highly unpopular tasks.

Personnel management regulations have also created incentives that spur cadres to respond to demands received from above. The 'cadre responsibility system' (*ganbu guanli zerenzhi*) links bonuses and punishment to higher level assessments of performance. In many locations, the salary and bonuses of village committee members are determined by township authorities, and levels are set in accord with how well important assignments are carried out.[71] Some localities, in the wake of the tax-for-fee reform, have gone so far as to list village cadres on the township or county level payroll. This further empowers townships, and makes committee members more pliable in the face of demands from above.[72]

Finally, some committees do not control their own budgets. Entrusting village accounts to township management has become a common means to strengthen supervision of rural finances. This has created opportunities for townships to appropriate village funds and may leave elected bodies with virtually nothing to manage.[73] Although this need not enhance compliance, it does diminish the role of committee members, and makes how democratically they were elected somewhat beside the point.

Party branches and village committees

Village-level Party organizations are another obstacle to grassroots democratization. Though the *Organic Law* (Art. 3) states that Party branches should 'support villagers in developing self-governance and exercising their democratic rights', it also insists

70. See Tsai, *Accountability without Democracy*, ch. 7; also, Yuan Song, 'Gonggongpin Gongji Zhikun: Fucun Diaocha Lianzai (9)' ['Difficulties in public goods provision: ninth in a series of reports from the investigation of Fu village'], available at: http://www.snzg.cn/article/show.php?itemid-7233/page-1.html (accessed 2 October 2007).

71. One counter-trend, which should make elected cadres more accountable to voters, is that 'villagers' evaluations' (*minzhu pingchou*) are now sometimes consulted when township authorities decide on a village cadres' salary. But even in these cases, baseline salary is usually set by the township according to its own criteria. Cheng Sinian, 'Rang Cunmin Gei Cunguan Ping Gongzi de Banfa Hao' ['It is a good method to let villagers grade village cadres' salary'], *Nongcun Fazhan Luncong* [*Rural Development Forum*] no. 10, (2000), p. 45. Tian Yuanxin, Qu Xuan and Li Dao, 'Cunmin Gei Cun Ganbu Ding Baochou' ['Villagers assess how much village cadres should earn'], *Xiangzhen Luntan* [*Township Forum*] no. 3, (2005), p. 13; also Alpermann, 'The post-election administration of Chinese villages', p. 68.

72. This is not a nationwide practice, though it has been implemented widely. For details, see Ning Zekui, Liu Hailiang, Wang Zhengbing and Chai Haofang, 'Cunganbu Xiang Hechu Qu' ['Where village cadres are heading'], *Zhongguo Nongcun Guancha* [*China Rural Survey*] no. 1, (2005), p. 60; also Zhong and Chen, 'To vote or not to vote', p. 698.

73. Fubing Su and Dali Yang, 'Elections, governance, and accountability in rural China', *Asian Perspective* 29(4), (2005). On township supervision of village finances in five provinces, see Alpermann, 'Institutionalizing village governance in China'.

that branches are a village's 'leadership core' (*lingdao hexin*). This means that Party leaders play a dominant role in most locations, with the Party secretary usually considered the village 'number one' (*yi ba shou*), and the committee director the village 'number two' (*er ba shou*).[74]

Fieldwork and surveys of grassroots cadres have confirmed the pre-eminence of Party secretaries. In 1999, Liang Kaijin and He Xuefeng estimated that 80% of secretaries nationwide were their village's top power holder, whereas an in-depth study of eight communities in 2002–2003 concluded that Party secretaries had the final word in seven of them.[75] Baogang He likewise found that dominance of elected committees 'only takes place in a limited number of cases'.[76] In a survey of 111 committee directors in four Zhejiang prefectures, 15% of He's respondents said they had more power than the village Party secretary, while 71% reported that the secretary had more power.[77]

Given the Party branch's status as 'leadership core', it is often unclear what a village committee should take charge of: in what areas must the branch follow the committee's lead? The *Organic Law* and implementing regulations that we have seen fail to specify a clear division of responsibilities between the two bodies. This often leads to clashes over, for instance, collective resources, as committees and branches struggle to secure final say over enterprises, economic cooperatives, and land.[78] When elected cadres lose these skirmishes, as they often do, some have become so frustrated that they have withdrawn from political life. In 2001, *People's Daily* reported that 57 committee members from four townships in Qixia Prefecture, Shandong, resigned in protest against Party branches that monopolized village politics. They charged that a full year after being elected, branches still refused to give them access to the account books and the official seal that

74. Song Yuehong, 'Cunmin Zizhi Zhong de Liangwei Guanxi' ['Relations between village Party branches and village committees in village self-governance'], *Zhongguo Gaige Nongcun Ban* [*China Reform Rural Edition*] no. 7, (2002), p. 47; Yang Jirong, 'Lun Nongcun Jiceng Dangnei Minzhu yu Cunmin Zizhi de Xianjie yu Hudong' ['On grassroots democracy within the Party and its connection and interaction with village self-governance'], *Lilun yu Gaige* [*Theory and Reform*] no. 6, (2003), pp. 33–36; Chu Zhi, 'Cunzhishu Zenyang Danghao Yibashou' ['How can village Party secretaries perform well as number one'], *Dangyuan Ganbu Zhiyou* [*Party Members' and Cadres' Friend*] no. 9, (2002), pp. 12–13; also Zhong and Chen, 'To vote or not to vote', p. 697; Schubert and Chen, 'Village elections in contemporary China', p. 19; He, *Rural Democracy in China*, p. 114. On the growing power of village committees, but their continuing secondary status, see Tan and Xin, 'Village election and governance', pp. 588–593; also Wang, *Mutual Empowerment of State and Peasantry*, pp. 143–147.

75. Liang Kaijin and He Xuefeng, *Cunji Zuzhi Zhidu Anpai yu Chuangzhi* [*Institutional Arrangements and Innovations in Village-Level Organizations*] (Beijing: Hongqi Chubanshe, 1999), p. 118; Dong Jiang'ai, 'Cunji Xuanju zhong Xingcheng de Liangwei Guanxi Duili ji Chulu' ['Outbreak of rivalry between Party branches and village committees in village elections and its solution'], *Huazhong Shifan Daxue Xuebao, Sheke Ban* [*Journal of Huazhong Normal University, Social Sciences Edition*] 44(1), (January 2005), p. 56.

76. Baogang He, 'The theory and practice of Chinese grassroots governance: five models', *Japanese Journal of Political Science* 4(2), (2003), pp. 308–310.

77. He, *Rural Democracy in China*, pp. 112–113. On the relative power of Party secretaries and committee directors hinging on control over income-producing enterprises and land, see Jean C. Oi and Scott Rozelle, 'Elections and power: the locus of decision-making in Chinese villages', *China Quarterly* 162, (June 2000), pp. 513–539.

78. See Pan Jiawei and Zhou Xianri, *Cunmin Zizhi yu Xingzhengquan de Chongtu* [*Conflicts between Village Self-Governance and Administrative Power*] (Beijing: Zhongguo Renmin Daxue Chubanshe, 2004), pp. 145–146; also Xu Zhiyong, 'Xuanju Zhihou: Lijicun Cunmin Zizhi Diaocha' ['Post-election: investigation of village self-governance in Liji'], *Zhongguo Gaige Nongcun Ban* [*China Reform: Rural Edition*] no. 2, (2003), pp. 10–14; Bernstein, 'Village democracy and its limits', p. 36; Zhang Jingping, 'Jingxuan Cunguan de Jiaoliang' ['Struggle in the village election'], *Nanfeng Chuang* [*Southern Exposure*] no. 9, (May 2005), pp. 30–35.

symbolizes public power.[79] Such incidents are not rare. Guo Zhenglin found that in the two years after Guangdong introduced elections in 1998, over 800 committee members resigned, most often because they had been frozen out of decision making by Party branches.[80]

Even fairly powerful village committees are vulnerable to Party influence, through personnel overlap. Surveys have shown that a large number of committee members, and directors in particular, belong to the Communist Party. For instance, following Jiangsu's balloting in 2006, almost 90% (15,649 out of 17,411) of committee directors were Party members.[81] Figures for earlier rounds of voting in rural Shanghai (2002), Fujian (2003), and Shaanxi (2002) were 89%, 66%, and 66%, respectively.[82] Party penetration is important because, unlike elected cadres, whose legitimacy is based on popular votes, Party members who sit on village committees derive some of their authority from being agents of the Party-state.[83] This raises an obvious question: even when Party members have won a spot on a village committee in a free and fair election, will they stand with villagers when Party superiors instruct them to do otherwise?

Since the turn of the century, Party penetration of committees has taken a new, more institutionalized form, which, according to Sylvia Chan, strengthens over-representation of Party members and is a sign of the Party's intention 'to re-concentrate its power in rural areas'.[84] In July 2002, the Central Committee and State Council jointly issued a circular that endorsed 'concurrent office-holding by village chiefs and Party secretaries' (*yijiantiao*) and 'merging the Party branch and the village committee' (*liangwei heyi*).[85] This policy sometimes takes the form of village committees being elected first, and some of their members being placed on Party branches later (*xianzheng houdang*); at other times, it means the Party secretary and other Party branch members are encouraged to run in village committee elections at the first opportunity (*xiandang houzheng*). As a sure-fire way to reduce the size of the village payroll and mitigate tension between branches and committees, this

79. Cui Shixin, 'Cunguan Weihe Yao Cizhi' ['Why village heads want to resign'], *Renmin Ribao* [*People's Daily*], (21 March 2001); also Xu Zhiyong, 'Xuanju Zhihou'. For regulations concerning control of the village seal, see He, *Rural Democracy in China*, p. 112.

80. Guo Zhenglin, 'Cunmin Xuanju hou de Nongcun Dangzheng Eryuan Quanli Jiegou' ['The bicameral power structure of the rural Party apparatus and its administration in the wake of villagers' elections'], paper prepared for the *International Symposium on Villagers' Self-Government and the Development of Rural Society in China*, sponsored by the Carter Center and the Ministry of Civil Affairs, Beijing, 2–5 September 2001, p. 253.

81. 'Summarizing table of seventh round village elections in Jiangsu Province', available at: http://www.chinarural.org/news_show.aspx?cols=1810&ID=35289 (accessed 12 December 2006).

82. Percentages are calculated from the following tables: 'Table of 2002 village elections in Shaanxi'; 'Table of 2002 village elections in Shanghai', available at: http://www.chinarural.org/news_show.aspx?cols=1810&ID=35331; 'Table of 2003 village elections in Fujian'; all accessed 12 December 2006. For similar statistics on earlier elections in a number of provinces, see Pastor and Tan, 'The meaning of China's village elections', p. 140. For data, mostly from the 1990s, that show an increasing number on non-communists on village committees, see He, *Rural Democracy in China*, pp. 107–108.

83. Guo and Bernstein, 'The impact of elections on the village structure of power'.

84. Sylvia Chan, 'Villagers' representative assemblies: towards democracy or centralism?', *China: An International Journal* 1(2), (2003), p. 192. Baogang He, ('The theory and practice of Chinese grassroots governance', p. 309) also speaks of 'a deliberate attempt to strengthen the Party branch'.

85. 'Zhonggong Zhongyang Bangongting Guowuyuan Bangongting Guanyu Jinyibu Zuohao Cunmin Weiyuanhui Huanjie Xuanju Gongzuo de Tongzhi' ['Circular by General Offices of Party Central Committee and State Council on further improving the work of next round village committee elections), (14 July 2002), available at: http://www.gov.cn/gongbao/content/2002/content_61679.htm (accessed 1 December 2007); also Bernstein, 'Village democracy and its limits', p. 37; Guo and Bernstein, 'The impact of elections on the village structure of power', pp. 272, 275; He, *Rural Democracy in China*, p. 119.

initiative has been implemented widely.[86] In Shandong, authorities even prescribed that the overlap rate of the two top positions should exceed 80% and that of the full branch and village committee should reach 70%.[87] Having to face voters could make Party branch members more accountable,[88] but influence often flows the other way.[89] Overlapping membership, along with joint or consecutive meetings of the two organizations, can blur whether concurrent office-holders are responsible to their constituents or their Party masters.[90] Some Chinese researchers have even begun to wonder whether overlapping membership might lead to a return of unfettered rule by Party branches, especially Party secretaries, thus making village elections close to meaningless.[91]

Social forces and village committees

In addition to Party branches and townships, lineage groups, religious organizations, and criminal elements play a role in some villages. These social forces may gain access to public power through elections, or have other means to become involved with decision making and policy implementation. Although informal institutions may enhance accountability and promote public goods provision,[92] they also operate according to their own customs, norms, and rules, many of which have little to do with democracy.

86. For Shandong, see *Dazhong Ribao* [*The Masses Daily*], (25 September 2004); for Henan, see http://news.sohu.com/20050715/n226325095.shtml; for Hunan, see http://www.chinanews.com.cn/news/2004year/2004-06-01/26/443107.shtml; for Anhui, see http://www.chinanews.com.cn/news/2004/2004-11-07/26/503213.shtml; for Hainan, see http://www.chinanews.com.cn/news/2004year/2004-07-23/26/463605.shtml; for Guangdong, see http://www.southcn.com/news/gdnews/gdtodayimportant/200501250071.htm; for Shanxi, see http://cpc.people.com.cn/GB/64093/64100/5946051.html (all accessed 30 November 2007).

87. Wang Kequn, 'Nongyeshui Quxiao hou Xiangzhen Guanli Tizhi Yudao de Wenti' ['Problems encountered in the township management system after abolishing the agricultural tax'], *Zhongguo Fazhan Guancha* [*China Development Observation*] no. 5, (2005), pp. 38–40. Guangdong also advocates 70% overlap of branches and committees. See Richard Levy, 'The village self-government movement', *China Information* 17(1), (2003), p. 34.

88. Dang Guoying, 'Liangwei Heyi Shige Hao Banfa' ['Concurrent holding of offices is a good solution'], *Zhongguo Gaige (Nongcun Ban)* [*China Reform (Rural Edition)*] no. 2, (2004), p. 28.

89. Party members remain subject to Party discipline, and they may also be more accommodating to township leaders. Lu Fuxing, 'Yijiantiao de Shixiao yu Lilun zhi Chayi' ['Gaps between real effects and theoretical implications of concurrent office-holding'], *Hunan Gong'an Gaodeng Zhuanke Xuexiao Xuebao* [*Journal of Hunan Public Security College*] 16(5), (October 2004), p. 17. Some researchers (Lianjiang Li, personal communication, November 2007) argue that what really matters is not who serves as both the secretary and director, but how one gets the two positions.

90. Zhang Yuanhong, 'Liangwei Heyi Qineng Tuiguang' ['Concurrent office-holding should not be promoted'], *Zhongguo Gaige* [*China Reform*] no. 8, (2001), pp. 56–57; Chang Zizhong, 'Cunliangwei Yijiantiao Wenti Baicun Tiaocha' ['One-hundred-village survey on concurrent office-holding in village committees and party branches'], *Xiangzhen Luntan* [*Township Forum*] no. 7, (2007), pp. 9–10; Qin Junbo, 'Cunzhishu Jianren Cunzhuren Ying Huanxing' ['Concurrent-holding of Party secretary and village head positions should be deferred'], *Xiangzhen Luntan* [*Township Forum*] no. 3, (2002), p. 12.

91. Chang Zizhong, 'Cunliangwei Yijiantiao Wenti Baicun Tiaocha'; Qin Junbo, 'Cunzhishu Jianren Cunzhuren Ying Huanxing'. Some authors argue that concurrent office-holding will help resolve personal conflicts between party secretaries and village committee directors, but cannot remedy organizational conflicts or reduce disputes over authority. Xu Zengyang and Ren Baoyu, 'Yijiantiao Zhenneng Jiejue Liangwei Chongtu Ma: Cunzhibu yu Cunweihui Chongtu de Sanzhong Leixing ji Jiejue Silu' ['Will concurrent office-holding resolve conflicts between the two organizations? Three types of conflict between village committees and Party branches and one possible resolution'], *Zhongguo Nongcun Guancha* [*China Rural Survey*] no. 1, (2002), pp. 69–74.

92. Lily L. Tsai, 'Solidarity groups, informal accountability, and local public goods provision in rural China', *American Political Science Review* 101(2), (May 2007); Lily L. Tsai, 'Cadres, temple and lineage institutions, and governance in rural China', *China Journal* no. 48, (July 2002).

Clans (*zongzu*), in particular, have experienced a resurgence in the reform era, and in some locations 'are once again sources of power and authority'.[93] While kinship ties need not always have a baleful effect on democratic rule, strong lineage attachments can become a mechanism through which individual rights and minority protections are infringed.[94] Majority rule sometimes produces dominance of one clan, or disruptive, ongoing struggle between several clans, which leads to fierce conflict and makes governance nearly impossible. For example, the Li lineage in one Hunan community used elections to usurp the power of a village committee and transformed grassroots government into an armed tool of clan power.[95] In another 'extreme case' focusing on disputed land adjustments in Shaanxi, open elections heightened clan tensions, turned a Party secretary against a committee director, and brought governance almost to a standstill.[96] Much more research is needed to learn how and when lineage ties affect village committees and the quality of democracy.

Religious organizations can also be obstacles to grassroots democratization when they compete with village committees for resources or leadership in community affairs. In one Shaanxi village, shortly after a committee and a Catholic church joined forces to build a primary school, wrangling over control of the school broke out. Instead of seeking a compromise, the church leaders publicized the conflict and mobilized their followers to challenge the elected cadres, resulting in a deep division in the village.[97]

Local strongmen and gangsters pose a far more direct threat to democracy. Stories of 'evil forces' (*hei'e shili*) undermining rural governance are increasingly common. Though some observers argue that imperfect election procedures make villages vulnerable to takeover by bullies and thugs,[98] others note that in some places representatives of 'black society' have obtained power by soliciting support from fellow lineage members, intimidating villagers, and promising decisive action.[99] Even when they fail to subvert a village committee, underworld forces can exert an

93. Bernstein, 'Village democracy and its limits', p. 38. In Lishu County, Jilin, like much of the Northeast, clans are not important power-brokers. See Schubert and Chen, 'Village elections in contemporary China', p. 20.

94. Xu Yong, *Zhongguo Nongcun Cunmin Zizhi* [*Village Self-Government in Rural China*] (Wuhan: Huazhong Shifan Daxue Chubanshe, 1997), pp. 354–366.

95. Yu Jianrong, 'Yao Jingti Zongzu Shili dui Nongcun Jiceng Zhengquan de Yingxiang' ['Be alert to clan influences on rural grassroots government'], *Jiangsu Shehui Kexue* [*Jiangsu Social Sciences*] no. 4, (2004), pp. 7–8.

96. Kennedy, 'The face of "grassroots democracy" in rural China', pp. 480–481. For evidence, however, that elections can also produce balanced village committees and mitigate lineage conflict, see Kennedy, 'The implementation of village elections', pp. 67–68. On declining clan influence overall, but continuing relevance especially in poorer, agricultural, and single surname dominant villages, see He, *Rural Democracy in China*, pp. 177–194.

97. Villagers claimed that this confrontation was even more intense than those that occurred during the Cultural Revolution. Miao Yuexia, 'Xiangcun Minjian Zongjiao yu Cunmin Zizhi: Yixiang Shehui Ziben Yanjiu' ['Rural religion and village self-governance: research on social capital'], *Zhejiang Shehui Kexue* [*Zhejiang Social Sciences*] no. 6, (November 2006), pp. 99–104. In some locations, temples and churches provide an alternative form of public accountability. Tsai, *Accountability without Democracy*.

98. He Xuefeng, 'Dangqian Cunmin Zizhi Yanjiu Zhong Xuyao Chengqing de Ruogan Wenti' ['Some problems in current studies of villagers' self-government'], *Zhongguo Nongcun Guancha* [*China Rural Survey*] no. 2, (2002), pp. 66–67.

99. Yu Jianrong, 'Jingti Hei'e Shili Dui Nongcun Jiceng Zhengquan de Qinru' ['Be alert to the invasion of evil forces into rural grassroots government'], *Juece Zixun* [*Policy Making Consultation*] no. 8, (2003), pp. 34–35; Sun Chunlong, 'Ruci Cunmin Zizhi' ['What village self-governance is like'], *Xin Xibu* [*New West*] no. 9, (2004), pp. 8–11.

influence by challenging, marginalizing or sidelining elected leaders.[100] Some gangs have gone so far as to set up 'private police stations' (*minban paichusuo*) and 'underground courts' (*dixia fating*) to handle disputes over land, debt, and other conflicts.[101]

The township, the Party branch, and an array of social forces constitute the local power configuration in which village committees are embedded. We have underscored the independent effect of each of these factors, but they can also work together to impede democratic governance. Strong clan ties combined with a powerful criminal sector can contribute to conflicts between a Party branch and a village committee;[102] Party cadres, after losing a village committee election, may turn to township allies or the underworld to maintain their position as top person in the village.[103] Improved electoral procedures have enhanced access to power, but elected cadres cannot escape the broader political and social context in which they operate.

Conclusion

In a country like China, grassroots democratization is a multi-faceted process that involves much more than holding a good election every three years. Two decades after the *Organic Law* first came into force, election procedures have improved significantly, both on paper and on the ground. Meaningful changes touching on steering committees, voter registration, candidate nomination, campaigning, secret balloting, and proxy-voting have taken hold and begun to expand access to power. Yet the quality of democracy in much of the countryside remains stubbornly low, mainly because village committees, once an election is over, are situated in a socio-political environment that has changed surprisingly little.

Village committees are surrounded on all sides. First, the state, represented by township authorities, has many opportunities to influence grassroots governance. Elected cadres are expected to complete tasks assigned by higher levels, much as their appointed predecessors were. Unwelcome duties, such as collecting levies or meeting unreasonable targets, regularly force committee members to choose between fealty to the township and responsiveness to fellow villagers. Financial reliance on townships and the role that higher levels play in cadre assessment inclines even the most democratically minded committee members to side with township superiors. Village committee members, in the end, are still subordinates—the place where state meets society—as much as they are the voice of voters who elected them.

100. Liu Lixin, Pao Jinxuan and Zhang Lingzhi, 'Hei'e Shili Ranzhi Nongcun Jiceng Zhengquan Toushi' ['Investigation of evil forces encroaching on rural grassroots governance'], *Sanyue Feng* [*March Wind*] no. 4, (2004), pp. 7–9.

101. Xu Liming, 'Cunmin Zizhi de Shehui Kunjing' ['Social predicament of village self-governance'], *Zhonggong Zhengzhou Shiwei Dangxiao Xuebao* [*Journal of the Party School of Zhengzhou Municipal Committee*] no. 3, (2005), p. 52.

102. Wang Jinhong, 'Liangwei Maodun: Jingyan Fenxi yu Lilun Piping' ['Conflict between Party branches and village committees: empirical analysis and theoretical critique'], *Huazhong Shifan Daxue Xuebao, Sheke Ban* [*Journal of Huazhong Normal University, Social Sciences Edition*] 44(5), (September 2005), pp. 18–24.

103. For an example, see 'Nongcun Queshao Shenme?' ['What is lacking in rural areas?'], available at: http://www.lwjx.com.cn/bbs/dv_rss.asp?s=xhtml&boardid=6&id=3210&page=15 (accessed 15 December 2007).

Second, village Party branches have no small say in decision making and policy implementation. In most communities, Party branches remain the dominant force and village committees play a distinctly secondary role. The Party branch's status as 'leadership core' is often evident in control over collective resources, such as land, economic cooperatives and enterprises, and also in overlapping membership on village committees. Despite efforts by many committee directors to assert their independence and exploit the legitimacy that elections confer, recent reforms that encourage concurrent office-holding may dilute the 'electoral connection'[104] by blurring whether committee members are responsible to their constituents or their Party superiors.[105]

Finally, informal institutions, including lineage groups, religious organizations, and criminal gangs, can interfere with democratic governance. Clans, churches or temples, and Mafia-like groups, can be alternative sources of authority and competitors for control over community affairs. In some villages, this has resulted in serious splits that bring governance to a halt. In others, elected cadres have been pushed aside, or turned into figureheads. In still others, sectarian interests have deeply penetrated village committees, sometimes leading to a trampling of minority rights.

Village elections alone are clearly not enough to ensure democratic governance. To understand democratization in rural China, we need ask not only how procedures are introduced and improved, but also how the village committees interact with other actors in the local power configuration. Though improving elections is a critical aspect of democratization, good procedures alone cannot guarantee high quality democratic rule. Long-time students of democratization have recognized this, too, with Larry Diamond and Leonardo Morlino, for example, arguing that a fully democratic regime not only satisfies popular expectations regarding 'procedural quality', but also allows citizens to enjoy 'quality of content' and 'quality of results'.[106]

This suggests some limits of this study and an agenda for the future. Examining constraints that impede democratization is not the same as assessing post-election governance, or how power is exercised in villages. In other words, obstacles notwithstanding, increased responsiveness is appearing in some places. For every analyst who concludes 'except in a few localities, elections have little positive impact on preventing rural authorities from abusing power',[107] another finds that elections have empowered villagers or enhanced accountability.[108] Beyond specifying the obstacles to democratization, we need more studies that explain how, when, and where elections have changed the relationship between cadres and voters.

104. The term was first made popular by David Mayhew and was brought to the China field by Melanie Manion. See David R. Mayhew, *Congress: The Electoral Connection* (New Haven: Yale University Press, 1974); Melanie Manion, 'The electoral connection in the Chinese countryside', *American Political Science Review* 90(4), (December 1996).

105. As we discuss above, it is also possible that these reforms will help democratize Party branches. For experiments with subjecting Party branch members to a village-wide vote of confidence, see Lianjiang Li, 'The two-ballot system in Shanxi Province: subjecting village Party secretaries to a popular vote', *China Journal* 42, (July 1999).

106. Larry Diamond and Leonardo Morlino, 'The quality of democracy: an overview', *Journal of Democracy* 15(4), (1994), p. 22.

107. Zhang Jing, *Jiceng Zhengquan: Xiangcun Zhidu Zhu Wenti* [*Problems of Rural Level Governance in China*] (Hangzhou: Zhejiang Renmin Chubanshe, 2000), p. 208.

108. For examples, see the sources listed in footnotes 48–56.

At the same, we also need more research on whether elections deter power holders from seeking personal gain above all else. The issue in some villages is not committee members who are pushed around by townships, Party branches, and social forces, but elected cadres who free themselves of all constraints and act only for themselves. Where does this occur? Why, in some places, are the constraints that we have emphasized and the ones that elections create both ineffective in preventing self-serving behavior? Are limited changes in governance after several rounds of elections a cause of increasing voter apathy,[109] as villagers conclude that whomever is in office will be corrupt and abusive, because 'all crows under heaven are equally black'[110] or 'it makes no sense to replace a full tiger with a hungry wolf?'[111]

As Norbert Bobbio reminds us, democracy is subversive in a highly radical sense because it subverts the traditional and natural notion that power flows downward.[112] Without denying the achievements of the last two decades, we have suggested that the process of putting democracy in place goes well beyond 'getting the procedures right', especially in an authoritarian setting where democracy is not the only game in town. Much as a one-day trip to observe an election reveals something, but not everything, about what the next three years will bring, changes in access to power can be trumped by a non-democratic environment that encircles an election victor.[113] Governance, even in a single village, has many components and expanded access to power conditions, but does not determine how power is exercised. 'High quality democracy' in rural China, let alone the whole nation, rests on much more than good village elections.

109. Wei Xinghe and Guo Yunhua, 'Zhengzhi Lengmo: Nongmin dui Cunweihui Xuanju de Yizhong Xingwei' ['Political apathy: one kind of villagers' attitude towards village committee elections'], *Qiushi* [*Seeking Facts*] no. 10, (2003), pp. 60–62; Wang Xiaojun, 'Zhixuan Lilian Zhihou de Cunweihui Xuanju Yanjiu: Yi Jiangxisheng T Xian 20 ge Cun Weili' ['Study of elections in 20 Jiangxi villages in T County which have experienced direct elections'], *Yunnan Xingzheng Xueyuan Yuanbao* [*Journal of Yunnan Public Administration College*] no. 1, (2007), pp. 82–85. But compare, Tan and Xin, 'Village election and governance', p. 597.

110. See Xie Meili, 'Wanshan Cunweihui Xuanju Zhidu, Cujin Xinnongcun Hexie Fazhan' ['Improve village committee electoral institutions and promote harmonious development of new rural areas'], *Zhongguo Xingzheng Guanli* [*Chinese Public Administration*] no. 11, (2006), p. 57; also see Kevin J. O'Brien and Lianjiang Li, *Rightful Resistance in Rural China* (New York: Cambridge University Press, 2006), p. 125.

111. For this remark, see Lianjiang Li and Kevin J. O'Brien, 'Villagers and popular resistance in contemporary China', *Modern China* 22(1), (January 1996), p. 34. For similar sayings involving famished wolves or tigers, see Xu Yong, 'Qianghua Minzhu Jiandu, Cujin Zhili Zhuanxing' ['Strengthen democratic supervision and promote governance transition'], *Xiangzhen Luntan* [*Township Forum*] no. 4, (2001), p. 10; He Xuefeng, 'Guanyu Cunzhuang Quanli Kuozhanxing de Taolun' ['Discussion on the expansion of village power structure'], *Yunnan Shehui Kexue* [*Yunnan Social Sciences*] no. 6, (2000), p. 39.

112. Norberto Bobbio, *Which Socialism? Marxism, Socialism, and Democracy* (Minneapolis: University of Minnesota Press, 1987), p. 74.

113. On placing elections in a comprehensive framework that goes beyond the village and also considers cadre behavior, villager awareness, and cultural context, see Gunter Schubert, 'Studying "democratic" governance in contemporary China: looking at the village is not enough', *Journal of Contemporary China* 18(60), (June 2009).

[26]

Innovation in China's Local Governance: 'Open Recommendation and Selection'*

Tony Saich and Xuedong Yang

Following the Fifteenth Party Congress (1997), there was not only the consolidation of the villagers' election program but also an increased interest in reforming township government. A small number of localities took General Secretary, Jiang Zemin's comments to extend the "scope of democracy" at the grassroots level and to establish a "sound system of democratic elections" for grassroots organs of power as a green light to experiment with township elections.[1] Subsequent reports of the first direct election of a township head in Buyun, Sichuan Province in December 1998, stirred great interest within China and abroad that this might mark the extension of direct elections from the village to the township level.[2] However, the Buyun model was rejected as unconstitutional and, to date, higher-level party and state leaders have not sanctioned the direct election of township leaders.[3] The

---

* Xuedong Yang conducted the fieldwork for this article in Suining in September 2001. The authors would like to thank Zhang Jinming (former district party secretary, currently vice-mayor of Suining), Yang Huadi (deputy party secretary of Shizhong District), Ma Shengkang (director of the organization department of Shizhong District), Liu Hui (deputy-director of the organization department), Xiang Daoquan (former head of Baoshi Township, currently party secretary of Hengshan Township), Tang Kunlong (party secretary of Dongchan Township) and other local officials. They provided much information about the direct election in Buyun and about the process of "open recommendation and selection" (*gongtui gongxuan*). Unless otherwise noted, the information in this article is drawn from discussions with them. We would also like to thank Li Fan, who provided much useful information on the specifics of the Buyun election. Finally, we would like to thank editor Tim Cheek and three anonymous reviewers for their comments on an earlier draft. However, the authors alone are responsible for the ideas expressed here.

1 Jiang Zemin, "Hold High the Great Banner of Deng Xiaoping Theory for an All-Round Advancement of the Cause of Building Socialism with Chinese Characteristics into the 21st Century", *Beijing Review*, vol. 40, no. 40 (October 6-12, 1997).

2 The election was widely covered by the international press (see articles in *New York Times, South China Morning Post,* and *Washington Post*) following a report in China's adventurous newspaper *Nanfang zhoumo* (Southern Weekly) on January 15, 1999. The most complete overview is the three-part series by Li Fan in *Ming bao* (February 11, 12, and 13, 1999). The Li Fan articles are translated in Foreign Broadcast Information Service, *Daily Report: China,* February 16, 1999. See also Li Fan, et al, *Chuangxin yu fazhan—xiangzhenzhang xuanju zhidu gaige* (Innovation and Reform: Reform of the System for Election of Township and Town Heads) (Beijing: Dongfang chubanshe, 2000).

3 The election was first criticized as unconstitutional in an article by Zha Qingjiu that appeared in the authoritative *Fazhi ribao* (Legal Daily), January 19, 1999 (Minzhu bu neng chaoyue falu [Democracy Must Not Overstep the Law]). The direct election of township heads should not be confused with the direct election of representatives to the local people's congress. Up to the county level, delegates to the people's congress have been elected directly since the system was restored in 1980.

Pacific Affairs: Volume 76, No. 2 – Summer 2003

focus on the direct township election has also obscured a significant and apparently more enduring innovation in widening the process for selection of township leaders, Open Recommendation and Selection (ORS—*gongtui gongxuan*).[4] This experiment is significant as an example of how innovation may proceed in other townships in China. It also raises a more general question about the relationship between economic development and political innovation. It is generally accepted that innovation is more likely to occur once a certain level of economic development or marketization has taken place. Yet, Buyun is in the West China, an area less developed economically, and appears initially to be an unlikely source for political innovation. In this case, crisis caused innovation but a number of key institutional reforms have occurred in the poorer areas rather than in those that have become affluent under the reforms.

While it is now generally accepted that village elections are legitimate and necessary,[5] how to deal with township government is a more complex and deeply contested topic. Most importantly, the township forms the lowest level of state administration and thus its officials are state cadres. Their appointment, evaluation and approval procedures are decided within the set of relations between the township people's congress and the county congress, the party committee for the township and that at the county level. Township leaders come under the party's *nomenclature* list, meaning that the party must oversee and sanction even those leaders who are to be elected through one means or another.[6] The township is thus nested within the party and state networks and is the key interface between state and society. By contrast, villages are not part of the state structure and directly elected villagers' committees were established in an attempt to fill the administrative vacuum caused by the dismantling of the commune and brigade structures in the countryside. In the early to mid-1980s, village management had collapsed in many parts of rural China, or they operated policies that were at variance with state demands on villagers. As Daniel Kelliher has pointed out, the starting point for gaining acceptance for villagers' committees was to accept that there was a political crisis in the countryside that probably

4 Recent articles on the issue of township elections include Lianjiang Li, "The Politics of Introducing Direct Township Elections in China", in *The China Quarterly*, September 2002, no. 171, pp. 704-23; Joseph Y.S. Cheng, "Direct Elections of Town and Township Heads in China: The Dapeng and Buyun Experiments", in *China Information*, vol. No. 1, 2001, pp. 104-37; Baogang He, "From Village to Township: Will China Move Elections One Level Up", East Asian Institute, National University of Singapore, Background Brief, No. 126; and Baogang He and Youxing Lang, "China's First Direct Election of the Township Head: A Case Study of Buyun", *Japanese Journal of Political Science*, vol. 2, no. 1, May 2001, pp. 1-22.

5 This was confirmed in November 1998 with the passage of the Villager Committees Organization Law of the People's Republic of China, see *Renmin ribao* (People's Daily), November 5, 1998.

6 For the nature of this process related to the people's congress at the township level see Melanie Manion, "Chinese Democratization in Perspective: Electorates and Selectorates at the Township Level," *The China Quarterly*, no. 163 (September 2000), pp. 764-82.

could only be resolved by allowing the villagers enhanced capacity for self-government.[7]

Despite reformers' hopes that the level of direct election would be raised to the township, the same logic does not apply and the vested institutional interests opposing change are stronger.[8] Support has come from within the people's consultative conference system and the Ministry of Civil Affairs (MOCA) that oversees the village elections. In March 1998, the MOCA official in charge of elections drafted a document suggesting that township elections might be carried out if conditions were ripe. This was rejected by the Politburo, although Wen Jiabao, among others, was said to have supported the idea during discussions at Beidaihe.[9] This did not kill the issue, however, and at the March 1999 Chinese People's Political Consultative Conference session, 35 members of an agricultural subcommittee proposed that the Legal Work Committee of the National People's Congress should study and introduce a law to promote the direct election of township leaders.[10] The request went unanswered and in April 1999, Zhang Mingliang, then the official in charge of village elections at the Ministry of Civil Affairs, stated that once uniform conditions were in place in the villages, direct elections could be initiated for the townships. However, as he acknowledged, since elections were not functioning properly in 40 percent of villages it could be a long wait. Even Premier Zhu Rongji suggested support for this initiative at a news conference in March 2000.[11]

One major institutional barrier to raising the level is that township elections would not, presumably, fall under the domain of MOCA but more likely the people's congress system. This would require establishing principles and understanding within an entirely different administrative system. Apart from contravening current legal provisions for the township people's congress to appoint the township head, it would fundamentally challenge the control of the local party apparatus. It is perhaps unsurprising that to date neither township leaders nor the people's congress system have expressed enthusiasm for direct township leader elections. Baogang He's survey of 115 township leaders in Zhejiang found that over 77 percent found direct elections premature, while a survey of 536 township leaders found 55 percent declaring them premature, with a further 19.8 percent considering them not suitable.[12] However, given the lack of any official promotion, it may also be considered surprising that one in five township leaders would support elections.

7 Daniel Kelliher, "The Chinese Debate over Village Self-Government," *The China Journal*, no. 37 (January 1997), pp. 31-62.

8 On institutional opposition from the people's congress system and the party's organization bureau see He, "From Village to Township," pp. 10-11.

9 He, "From Village to Township," pp. 11-12.

10 *South China Morning Post*, March 9, 1999.

11 *Renmin ribao*, March 16, 2000, p. 1.

12 He, "From Village to Township," pp. 7-8.

Pacific Affairs: Volume 76, No. 2 – Summer 2003

The National People's Congress (NPC) under Li Peng's leadership was not a supporter of expanding the scope of direct elections. A number of provinces, including Guangdong, sent requests to the NPC to conduct elections but all were rejected.[13] Shenzhen, in particular, was keen in late – 1997, early 1998 to push ahead with direct township elections. It hoped to experiment with two townships in 1998 as a prelude to subsequently electing all township heads. Shenzhen has been keen to maintain its place as a pacesetter and its officials have sought to claim that it would be right for it to be at the forefront of political reform, having led in economic reform through the 1980s and early 1990s. However, the senior leadership in Beijing was not so supportive and the General Office of the NPC put the brake on reform attempts in Shenzhen.[14]

It appears that not only Li Peng but also Jiang Zemin is no supporter of direct township head elections[15] and in July 2001 a Central Committee document tried to call a halt to experimentation by declaring that the direct election of township heads was unconstitutional and contrary to the organic law on local people's congresses and people's governments.[16]

To date, party preference has been to deal with issues of government transparency rather than accountability at the township level. Thus, in June 1998 a joint Central Committee and State Council Circular recognized that government reform should be encouraged for the 45,000 towns and townships, and stated that the party should "seek proper ways to introduce the practice of open administration in government bodies at the township level." This has become increasingly common practice, with provinces such as Fujian, Hunan and Shanxi at the forefront of making township revenue and expenditures public and having an open system for government construction contracts. In Guangxi, townships have established supervisory groups to oversee administration. Such groups include members of the people's congress, delegates from the party committee, the disciplinary and control commission, retired cadres and villagers' delegates.[17]

The Sixteenth Party Congress (2002) did not offer hope for progress on the direct election of township heads but rather stressed the need to tighten party control to maintain social stability. In fact, the sections in Jiang's report

---

13 *Yazhou zhoukan* (Asia Week), February 8-14, 1999.

14 Interviews with Shenzhen party leaders, July 2001.

15 According to Lianjiang Li, Jiang told Anhui delegates at the 2001 NPC session that the villagers' committee elections should not be extended upwards. Li, "The Politics of," p. 704.

16 Document no. 12 July 2001, "Zhonggong zhongyang guanyu zhuanfa 'Zhonggong quanguo renda changweihui dangzu guanyu quanguo xiangji renmin daibiao dahui huanjie xuanju gongzuo youguan wenti de yijian' de tongzhi" (Notice of the Central Committee of the Chinese Communist party on Transmitting 'Suggestions of the Party group of the Standing Committee of the NPC on Certain Questions Concerning the Election of Township Level People's Congresses').

17 See Liu Xitang, "Guanyu xiangji minzhu fazhan de diaocha yu sikao" (An Investigation of and Thoughts on the Development of Township Democracy), *Jingji shehui tizhi bijiao* (Comparative Economic and Social Systems), no. 2 (2000), p. 72.

to the congress on political restructuring dealt only with regularizing the party's relationship with various state institutions and mass organizations. Jiang stressed that the "party commands the overall situation" and, on the people's congress specifically, noted that they were to ensure that party views become the "will of the state" and that "candidates recommended by party organizations become leading cadres of the organs of state power through legal procedures."[18] Such an emphasis is not likely to accommodate elections in which candidate choice and selection are taken out of the control of party organization departments. It seems likely that Jiang's view was influenced by both the attempts of the China Democratic Party to register in various provinces and the fear that campaigning may be taken advantage of by *Falungong* members.[19]

This has not resolved, however, how the party deals with enhancing legitimacy at the township level and finding candidates that will enjoy a modicum of local support. In 1998, before the Circular was issued, three townships experimented with the direct election of township heads, all of them wishing to be the first in China to stage such an election. These were Buyun and Nanchang in Sichuan and Dapeng in Shenzhen. The Dapeng election was deemed to fall within the current regulatory framework and the provincial organization department closely controlled the Nancheng election, but Buyun was deemed unconstitutional.[20] However, this has not marked the end of experimentation, more broadly or within the Suining Municipality where Buyun is located. In addition to the direct election in Buyun, Suining's Shizhong (Central) District has experimented with other innovative measures to broaden civic engagement and increase competition in selecting township leaders, including the party secretary and township head. In particular, Shizhong was praised for developing a process within existing regulations that "increased transparency and competition in promoting cadres."[21] The term used by the local organization department

---

18 Jiang Zemin, "Build a Well-Off Society in an All-Round Way and Create a New Situation in Building Socialism with Chinese Characteristics," http://english.peopledaily.com.cn, November 8, 2002.

19 He, "From Village to Township," p. 2.

20 The Nancheng election was held on December 5, 1998 while that in Buyun was held on December 31. Thus, while Nancheng may claim the title of the first such election since 1949, the moral high ground lies with Buyun. As Lianjiang Li notes "it was freer, fairer and more competitive in almost all aspects than the earlier Nancheng election." Li, "The Politics of," pp. 714-15. For an extensive account of the Nancheng election see Li Fan, *Zhongguo jiceng minzhu fazhan baogao, 2000-2001* (2000-2001 Report on the Development of Grassroots Democracy in China) (Beijing: Dongfang chubanshe, 2002), pp. 376-88.

21 Yu Keping (ed.), *Zhongguo difang zhengfu chuangxin 2002* (Innovations in Chinese Local Government) (Beijing: Shehui kexue wenxian chubanshe, 2002), p. 16. This programme is organized jointly by the China Center for Comparative Politics and Economics under the Translation Bureau of the Central Committee and the Comparative Research Center for the Party under the Central Party School. Among other winners that were related to elections were: Qianxi County in Hebei Province for its direct election of delegates to Women's Associations and Guangshui Municipality (Hubei) for its "Two-ballot" election for party secretaries at the village level.

Pacific Affairs: Volume 76, No. 2 – Summer 2003

is "open recommendation and selection" (*gongtui gongxuan*).[22] Unlike the direct Buyun election, this process does not contravene existing regulations and is more acceptable as it ensures a strong role for the local party and state institutions.[23] ORS is also used for the selection of party secretaries, thus opening up the process to ordinary party members rather than restricting appointment to higher-level party officials. A degree of competition replaces secretive appointment from above.

In the following sections we discuss briefly three well-documented approaches for the selection of township leaders before concentrating on a fourth, "open recommendation and selection." In the conclusions we make some tentative observations about how the experiments impact on China's on-going institutional transformation and the tension between maintaining a Leninist organizational framework while seeking to broaden participation to enhance legitimacy.[24]

New Methods of Township Leadership Selection

As noted above, the situation of the township is completely different from that of the villages, where direct elections, with the exception of party leaders, have been institutionalized. Township cadres working on the lowest rung of the state ladder are recruited and paid by the state and are in its full-time employ. Village leaders work on a part-time basis and are compensated for their work out of the village's own finances. The social structure of the township is naturally more diverse than that of the village; community-based politics are more complex when population size, geographic spread, and employment mix make the construction of participatory politics within the existing framework difficult. This means that township elections will require a more careful institutional design, as well as greater political and financial support.

During the 1990s, it is clear that in many areas problems have arisen between local administrations and society, and the township has been the focal point for unrest and conflict. The townships have many demands placed on them by higher-level authorities and unless they are able to establish an

---

22 Nanbu County in Sichuan Province has also used this system but only for deputy heads. See Li, "An Investigation of and Thoughts on," p. 73.

23 The Buyun election breaches Article 101 of the State Constitution that states "Local people's congresses at the different levels elect and have the power to recall, at the corresponding level, governors and deputy governors, mayors and deputy mayors, heads and deputy heads of counties, districts, townships, and towns." Further the Organic Law for Local People's Congresses and Local People's Governments reiterates these powers of appointment and removal of personnel.

24 While the account by Joseph Cheng on the Buyun and Dapeng elections is essentially descriptive, Lianjiang Li's analysis takes the optimistic view that the new leadership may be more amenable to acceptance and that the international community can play a role in protecting grassroots experiments. We are more circumspect and view ORS as a viable way of broadening participation while resisting direct elections.

independent financial base (witness the rush to establish township enterprises in certain parts of China) it is harder for them to carry out extensive programmes to benefit local society. Government agencies at the township level fall under the dual leadership of the township and county governments. Real power and influence resides at the county level that sets targets and quotas for the township officials and can provide rewards (promotion or money) and mete out discipline (demotion or fines).[25] This can even take the form of more formal contracts between the county government and its agencies at the township level. Apart from distorting incentives for township officials, the system weakens the capacity for comprehensive development by township governments. One set of Chinese researchers has even referred to the responsibilities of the townships as being "dismembered" by the county.[26] Failure to meet one of the priority targets set by the county will negate good performance in all other areas, referred to as "one ticket override" (*yipiao foujue*).[27] However, many townships do not have adequate financial resources to carry out their mandated obligations. Their financial relationship to the county is not defined sufficiently clearly after the 1993-94 tax reforms. Thus the township position is weakened even further, lacking not only power but also the necessary finances to carry out its mandate .

This system produces a number of problems. First, the townships' burden of debt has a tendency to increase. This has been compounded in recent years in some areas by the problems that the township and village enterprises have run into. Most townships cannot support the provision of an adequate level of public goods and services. Indeed, in many townships revenues are insufficient to cover the salaries and expenses of officials. Despite the unreliable financing, most township governments are overstaffed, as a government position still represents one of the best alternatives for employment and it does offer the opportunity for turning appointment into financial gain, both legally and illegally obtained.

Last but not least, these factors have created friction between local officials and farmers. The burden of revenue collection is passed onto the farmers in the form of illegal fines and levies, commonly referred to as the "three arbitraries"—*san luan*—*luan shoufei* (arbitrary taxation), *luan fakuan*

25 It is rare to use financial penalties for officials at the township level, as their salaries are considered too low.

26 Li Xueju, Wang Zhenyao and Tang Jinsu (eds.), *Zhongguo xiangzhen zhengquan de xianzhuang yu gaige* (The Current Situation and Reform of Power in Chinese Villages and Townships) (Beijing: Zhongguo shehui chubanshe, 1994) p. 5.

27 For more on this system see Maria Edin, *Market Forces and Communist Power: Local Political Institutions and Economic Development in China* (Uppsala: Uppsala University Press, 2000); Rong Jingben et al., *Cong yalixing tizhi xiang minzhu hezuo tizhi de zhuanbian* (The Transformation from a Pressurized System to a Democratic Cooperative System) (Beijing: Zhongyang bianyi chubanshe, 1998); Tony Saich, "The Blind Man and the Elephant: Analysing the Local State in China," in Luigi Tomba (ed.); and Susan H. Whiting, *Power and Wealth in Rural China: The Political Economy of Institutional Change* (New York: Cambridge University Press, 2001).

Pacific Affairs: Volume 76, No. 2 – Summer 2003

(arbitrary fines) and *luan tanpei* (arbitrary expropriation).[28] At the same time that they are confronted with the inadequacies of the local administration, many farmers have become more aware of their rights through the mass media, the popularization of laws and regulations, and from the migration to the cities. With the existing system not providing any formal effective channels for redress of grievance, the end result has often been violence, blockading townships or attacking township officials.[29]

The recognition that township governing structures are failing them seems to be behind party leaders' willingness to allow limited institutional experimentation to improve transparency and accountability and to restore authority and legitimacy. Thus, there is the recognition of the need for institutional innovation to deal with these problems and this might even provide the possibility for a further political restructuring of local government. However, this process will not be allowed to proceed without strong oversight and thus the capacity for far-reaching change remains circumscribed.

A few innovators have focused on the process of the selection of township heads. Yet the options within the current administrative framework remain limited as the power of appointment of the township head lies with the people's congress. In fact, the reality is that the party committee at the next highest level (county or municipality) must first nominate the candidate. The process is not multi-candidate. Given the lack of transparency, this places enormous discretionary power in the hands of the party committee and often in those of the party secretary at the higher level. This places the selection procedure in a black box and distorts the incentives for one to become a township head. It is common for prospective candidates to spend most of their time catering to the whims of their superiors, with little incentive to work for the people as they have no say in the process of selection. This has been behind the increasingly commonplace practice of "selling and purchase of official posts" (*maiguan maiguan*).

Yet county party authorities also have a stake in ensuring that their choice for candidate will be popular and will enjoy some semblance of a popular mandate. This would help strengthen the party's legitimacy at the local level and would help it to rejuvenate itself by incorporating members who enjoy local credibility. In addition, as is the case in the villages, it is expected that this will help with better implementation of unpopular policies. This train of thinking has legitimated experimentation with the selection of township heads. To date, there have been four main methods, outlined below.

---

28 See also Andrew Wedeman, "Budgets, Extra-Budgets, and Small Treasuries: Illegal Monies and Local Autonomy in China," *Journal of Contemporary China*, vol. 9, no. 25 (November 2000), p. 400.

29 On the rural unrest see Thomas P. Bernstein and Xiaobo Lu, "Taxation Without Representation: Peasants, the Central and the Local States in Reform China," *The China Quarterly*, no. 163 (September 2000), pp. 742-63.

1) Direct Election of Township Head

According to current regulations, direct election of a township head by the local residents is illegal. Despite this, a few townships have held direct elections, the most widely publicized example being Buyun Township in Suining Municipality, Sichuan.[30] The entire process in Buyun took about two months from preparation to the actual voting and while it broadened the process for candidate nomination, the party retained control over the selection mechanism.[31] Initially some 15 candidates were nominated, including non-party members; nominations could be put forward either by a recognized organization or by a group of 30 voters. These 15 candidates were then considered by a joint electoral committee consisting of 162 members,[32] who would make a final selection of two candidates. The candidates had 20 minutes to make a campaign speech and a further 10 minutes for questions and answers. To ensure that the district authorities were not entirely bypassed, they used their constitutional right of nomination to propose that the Buyun Party Committee deputy secretary, Tan Xiaoqiu, be added to the list of final candidates. The final vote was fixed for December 31, 1998, giving the candidates about a week to visit and campaign in the 10 villages and the central marketplace.[33] The official nominee, Mr. Tan, won, but the results were close, with 50.19 percent (3130) of the votes cast. Tan Xiaoqiu thus became the first directly elected township head to take office. He took his oath of office on January 4, 1999 after the township congress had approved the voting. As noted above, the election became a focal point of brief discussion before it was declared unconstitutional. This method has not been used since.

2) "Three-Ballot" Election for Township Head

While Buyun was carrying out its election, Dapeng Township in the Longgang District of Shenzhen was preparing its own election for a township head.[34]

30 A few weeks earlier, Nancheng Township in Qingshen County, Sichuan also held a direct election for the township head and deputy. For further details of the Buyun election readers are referred to Cheng, "Direct Elections," pp. 118-30 and Li, "The Politics of," pp. 710-19. We shall just highlight the key aspects here.

31 Buyun has a population of around 16,000 living in an area of 32 square kilometres. Another 4000 people work outside of its jurisdiction. The average per capita income is 1636 *yuan*. It is less developed than other townships in the district. There are 10 villagers' committees in the township.

32 The committee was drawn from village heads, village party secretaries, and three village representatives from each of the 10 villages, members of the township party committee and other leaders from the township party and government organizations.

33 It is estimated that almost all of the inhabitants heard the various speeches and 650 raised questions. The questions ranged across topics such as agricultural production, farmers' burdens, taxation, market building, environmental protection, family planning, social security and the construction of village roads and education.

34 Dapeng has a population of around 50,000 spread out over 82.81 square kilometres. The per capita income is 4900 *yuan*. There are six village committees and two residents' committees. For a detailed account see Cheng, "Direct Elections," pp. 113-17 and Li Fan, *Chuangxin yu fazhan*, pp. 91-95.

Pacific Affairs: Volume 76, No. 2 – Summer 2003

The method chosen resembles the *haixuan* principle (literally meaning from the sea) used in village elections, which allows candidates to be put forward by local organizations or groups of individuals. The method is also based on that of the "two ballot system" that has been experimented with for the election of village party secretaries.[35] In this process, party members and villagers or villagers' representatives vote in the first round to decide who will be candidates for a second ballot within the party itself. All party members vote to elect the party secretary from the candidates presented. This process is often referred to as a "poll test" or "democratic recommendation." It provides a chance to test the credibility of candidates among the broader populace while ensuring that the party itself keeps control over the final outcome. When this process is moved to the township level it becomes a "three-ballot" process. The main reason for this is that the township head must be "elected" by the people's congress after a two-round process of recommendation. Thus, a third ballot is necessary.

In Dapeng this election process lasted around four months. The incumbent township head, Li Weiwen, won 76 percent (813) of the votes of the representative group that listened to campaign speeches and questioned the five candidates. Mr. Li received unanimous support (45 votes) from the representatives of the township congress. The election was widely promoted by the Shenzhen authorities as an institutional breakthrough that was consistent with current regulation. Shenzhen also held a national meeting to disseminate the experience of Dapeng as a model for others to follow. However, it seems that the experiment will not be continued.[36] From a participatory viewpoint, there are clear drawbacks in this process. First, the representative group clearly does not select the township head and furthermore it cannot represent all of the voters. The fact that there is only one candidate provided to the congress rather than multiple candidates weakens the competitiveness of the final election. Last but not least, the desire to remain within the existing regulations seriously circumscribes the extent to which the election can be considered genuinely democratic.

3) "Two-Ballot" Election of Township Head

This method was adopted in Zhuoli Township, Linyi County in Shanxi province in 1999,[37] an area that is well-known for its two-ballot village party

35 For details see Lianjiang Li, "The Two-Ballot System in Shanxi Province: Subjecting Village Party Secretaries to a Popular Vote," *The China Journal*, no. 42 (July 1999), pp. 103-18.

36 According to information provided to a colleague of ours from a leader of the organization department of Longgang District, August 2001.

37 Zhouli has a population of 13,228 spread over an area of 48.05 square kilometers. There are eight villagers' committees and the average per capita income is 2450 *yuan*. See also Li Fan, *Chuangxin yu fazhan*, pp. 71-78.

election.[38] As in Longgang, the Zhuoli method derives from the two-ballot village model, but in addition to voting for the township head it was also used for the party secretary and the chair of the people's congress. On April 16, the incumbent party secretary, the township head and the chair of the presidium of the people's congress presented their work to 500 representatives at a work report conference.[39] There was no opportunity to raise questions. Two days later (April 18) a vote was held with some 9000 people voting at 17 different polling booths. Voters were presented with three choices for each candidate: have confidence in (*xinren*), have basic confidence in (*jiben xinren*), or no confidence in (*bu xinren*). Any candidate who received less than a 50 percent level of support in the first two categories was not to be recommended by the township as a candidate for the next party and people's congress elections. In fact, all three gained sufficient support.

Although this system is commonly referred to as a "two ballot" system, the second ballot is not public.[40] The township election does not directly follow the first vote. The result of the first vote is only used as a reference for the county leaders to consider when appointing the new leadership at the township level. It is also difficult to know the role the work report meeting actually plays in the first ballot. While all eligible voters are entitled to vote to evaluate the township leaders, they were not entitled to listen to their presentations.

These three selection methods try to broaden the scope of participation in the selection of township leadership and to provide some feedback on the views of villagers. The direct election method in Buyun and Nancheng is the most open and competitive, with the party guiding the process rather than being the decision maker. The latter two methods that fall within the current regulations are weaker in providing a direct link between voter preferences and outcomes. Both rely on a system in which a few choose on behalf of the whole. This may lead to disillusionment with the process of feedback. Essentially people are mobilized to vote for a process that boils down choice to a single candidate and that is in any case only in the form of a recommendation. In this context, it is interesting to look at the fourth method ("open recommendation and selection") as a way to provide better input within the framework of existing regulations.

38 See Li, "The Two-Ballot System in Shanxi province."

39 These included township government cadres, village party cadres and members of villagers' committees and some village delegates. The Linyi Party Committee also invited a number of other guests to listen to the meeting and to disseminate its ideas. These included cadres from higher levels, some scholars and some reporters.

40 Shi Weimin, *Gongxuan yu zhixuan: xiangzhen renda xuanju zhidu fazhan* (Public Elections and Direct Elections: Studies of the Electoral System of Township Congresses) (Zhongguo shehui kexue chubanshe, 2000).

Pacific Affairs: Volume 76, No. 2 – Summer 2003

4) Open Recommendation and Selection

The precise origins of this method are unclear.[41] As far as we are aware, however, the Shizhong District of Suining Municipality in Sichuan first implemented it on a systematic basis. The Shizhong District organized its ORS during the first half of 1998 and in addition to the township head, the process also involved the selection of the party secretary.[42]

Clearly ORS is not an election but rather a process that uses some electoral procedures to enable a representative group broader than that of the township people's congress to have a strong role in the selection of the candidates. It is different from the traditional *nomenclature* method by which the party selects its officials since it entails a higher degree of openness and competition. However, it is clearly more open than it is competitive. Consequently the ORS method can be viewed as a transitional institutional process situated between the conventional process of party nomination and congress ratification, and a direct election. In terms of public participation, it is more open and competitive than traditional practice but less so than a direct election.

In late 1997, the Shizhong District Party Committee launched a plan to accelerate the reform of its cadre system, recognizing that the current system did not meet the demands of the more complex environment. They decided that the reforms should ensure the recruitment of more highly qualified officials and encourage more participation. In January 1998, the fourth party plenum of Shizhong District presented its work report that included an outline of the ORS method. Initially, it was the party's intention only to use the "open recommendation and selection" method for a limited number of appointments to its functional bureaus and it did not include township heads.

In May 1998, an event occurred in Baoshi Township that changed the minds of the district party leaders. Both the party secretary and the township head were removed from office because of corruption and it appeared that a further 20 township officials were involved, including the chair of the township congress.[43] Given the strong economic growth in the township, the leadership had been regarded highly by the district authorities. This judgment was now called into question and district leaders began to see that

---

41 In part this derives from the fact that local officials often lack the resources to promote innovation. However, it also stems from the fact that some local officials do not wish to disseminate such experimentation widely to prevent undue attention and pressure from higher levels.

42 The case mentioned by Liu Xitang in Nanbu County, Sichuan occurred four months after that in Shizhong. In addition it only covered the position of township deputy-head. However, the process was extensive, involving the selection of 178 deputy heads for 79 townships, although the final number selected was 175. Liu, "An Investigation of and thoughts on," p. 73.Liu is an employee of the Ministry of Civil Affairs. While both Cheng and Li mention this process (pp. 710-11 and 118-19 respectively), they do so only as a prelude to the Buyun election and do not discuss it as an independent, on-going process.

43 For an account see Hu Shubao, "Buyun zhixuan diaocha baogao," (An Investigation Report on the Buyun Direct Election), in *Beijing yu fenxi* (Background and Analysis), no. 25 (January 2001), p. 2.

there were problems with the traditional closed system of appointment. In addition, because of the host of problems left behind by the disgraced leadership, they had trouble finding a suitable candidate who was willing to work in Baoshi.[44] Consequently, the Shizhong District Party Committee decided to extend the ORS method to the position of Baoshi township head.[45]

Not surprisingly, such a decision was contentious. Some district leaders felt that as the use of "open recommendation and selection" to select a township head in Sichuan was unprecedented it would be risky and might lead to unforeseen problems and failure. The organization department that was to oversee the process lacked experience and the necessary skills to operate the selection. It had to try to learn quickly from others while, at the same time, developing some new measures to deal with problems as they emerged. There was also suspicion among the general public that the process might not be as open and competitive as was suggested and that the party might have already secretly decided upon the candidate, in line with usual practice. Some of the remaining township officials were also unhappy with the turn of events, as they had anticipated automatic promotion, something that would now be challenged by the implementation of ORS. Despite this opposition and uncertainty, at the end of May the decision was made to move forward.

On May 12, 1998 the District Party Committee adopted a formal decision to hold the ORS and a leading group was established to oversee the process. Although the district organization department implemented the selection process, others were represented in the leading group and did participate in the process. Members of the leading group were drawn from the discipline and inspection committee, the propaganda department, the standing committee of the people's congress, the people's political consultative conference and the district government. This helped build an initial consensus and reduce opposition to the process.

The formal procedure began on May 25 with a process of public application. In addition to nominated cadres, party secretaries and village heads in certain townships were allowed to apply if they met basic criteria.[46]

44 As noted below, there were plenty willing to fill the post but the district leaders were concerned about their suitability and credibility.

45 Such a shift can be deciphered from the decision issued by the party in May. In addition to the township head (*zhengke*), the other eight positions are all at the deputy level (*fuke*). Interviews with local leaders in Shizhong in September 2001 confirmed this. See also Shizhong District Party Committee "Guanyu gongkai tuixuan Baoshi zhen renmin zhengfu zhenzhang houxuanren de jueding" (Decision on the Open Election of the Deputy Township Head of the Baoshi People's Government), May 12, 1998. The same day the Shizhong District Open Election Work Leading Small Group Office issued "Suining shi Shizhongqu gongkai tuixuan Baoshizhen renmin zhengfu zhenzhang houxuanren jianchang" (Suining Municipality Shizhong District General Guidelines for the Selection of the Deputy Township Head of the Baoshi People's Government). See Li Fan, *Chuangxin yu fazhan*, p. 80.

46 The most important were that they had to be born after June 1, 1960, have graduated from high school and be in good health. There was no requirement concerning official position.

Pacific Affairs: Volume 76, No. 2 – Summer 2003

Of the 69 who applied, 67 were considered to be qualified and in June they took a three-hour written exam. This more open process resulted in about half the candidates not being on the state's payroll.[47] The top six candidates from the written exam then had an oral exam on June 22. The oral exam was held in front of a group of 149 Baoshi representatives who whittled the list down to two after all six had finished the question and answer session.[48] The two remaining candidates were then recommended to the township congress for final selection. This selection was held on the same day. Xiang Daoquan, who was only 29 years old at the time, was elected with 46 of the 49 votes of the township congress delegates.[49]

The district leadership was pleased with the outcome of this experiment and felt it had both the confidence and the experience to extend its application. Importantly, higher-level authorities did not criticize "open recommendation and selection" and the provincial organization department invited representatives from Shizhong to present their experience at a provincial conference.[50] The ORS method was also reported on in detail by the *Sichuan Daily* and on Sichuan television. The District Party Committee then decided to extend ORS to the township party secretary and this process began in September 1998. Dongchan and Lianhua townships were chosen as the trial sites. In addition, they also organized the open selection of the township head in Hengshan.

The basic procedures for the selection of the township head and the party secretary are essentially the same. Here we shall describe the four-stage process for ORS for the township party secretary. ***Stage one: application and qualifications.*** A set of criteria were established for all potential applicants of which the most important were that they should have at least a college degree, an administrative rank of at least deputy section head (*fuke*) and be born after September 30, 1958 (thus, under 40). The requirements for party secretary were more stringent than those for township head as village officials were allowed to participate even though they do not enjoy a formal bureaucratic rank. Despite seemingly strict criteria, there were 99 applicants for the two positions revealing a relatively large pool of candidates.[51]

Stage two: written examination. This was considered the most objective phase of the selection process. A special group established by the organization department was responsible for designing the examination, and it made

47 See also, Lianjiang Li, "The Politics of," p. 711.

48 This group included all 49 township congress delegates, 68 officials from the villages and the township and 32 officials from the district level.

49 Xiang was actually fourth after the written exam. The person who was first after the written exam was placed last after the oral exam.

50 This was at a meeting on organizational work in the countryside held in September 1998. The Shizhong Party Secretary talked to the meeting about the ORS method.

51 There were 69 candidates for the township head positions, of whom two were considered unsuitable. There were 76 candidates for the Hengshan township head election, of whom four were deemed unsuitable. Li Fan, *Chuangxin yu fazhan*, p. 82.

secret visits to other counties for this purpose. All the questions were kept confidential until the exam and covered areas such as Deng Xiaoping Theory, market economy theory, public administration, leadership, laws, science and technology, history, official documents, contemporary politics, essential agricultural work and agricultural production. The highest possible score was 150 points. The questions were structured in different ways. For some questions it was necessary to fill in the blank spaces, others were multiple choice, while yet others required short reasoned judgments. The case method was also stressed with two cases presented. One case involved investigation by the leader into flood prevention work while the other concerned a case of the villagers suing the government. These were realistic cases for the aspiring leaders to grapple with. In 1998, the Yangtze River area suffered from serious flooding and Sichuan constitutes the vital up-stream area. Thus, flood prevention is an important part of local government work, touching on questions of security, development and livelihood. Sichuan has also become well-known for the severity of its rural disturbances in recent years, with numerous cases of conflict between the farmers and the local government. Thus, we can see that the written examination did contain some substantive issues that were based on possible real-life situations. Review of the written examination led to the selection of the top six candidates, who then participated in the oral examination. The organization department also set up a two-day visit and investigation of the relevant township for them.[52]

Stage Three: Oral Examination. This phase more or less resembled campaign speech making, with a representative group voting to make a final selection of candidates after listening to speeches and raising questions. Naming this group proved difficult under the existing institutional arrangements and the local organization department simply decided to call it a defense meeting.[53] The voting process was called "democratic recommendation" (*minzhu tuijian*). The representative groups, of course, widened participation from traditional methods and comprised: heads of the district party committee, the district government, the people's congress and people's political consultative conference, the heads of various government entities, township-level cadres (party members), village officials (party members),

52 Obviously two days is too short a time period for the candidates to get to know the township where they might work. It is also too short a period of time for the township residents to interact with the candidates. This was later recognized by the district authorities, who stipulated in the "Interim Provisions for the ORS for Township Heads of the Shizhong District of Suining Municipality" that the time for investigation in the township should not be less than seven days. This was drafted on the basis of the first three experiments. The original regulations requiring two to three days can be found in Li Fan, *Chuangxin yu fazhan*, pp. 86-91.

53 In the three experiments there was no definitive process for stipulating how the representative group should be formed and what its composition should be. The "Interim Provisions" state clearly that the total number of representatives must exceed 1 percent of the township population (it was to exceed 1percent in large and medium townships and 2 percent in small townships). The total number of cadres from the district level was not to exceed 10 percent of the representatives.

village party members, and heads of district-level sectors. In the Lianhua township, the number of members in the representative group totaled 278.

There were four questions, of which one was known and could be prepared ahead of time. The other three questions were not made known. Voting took place following the oral examination, with the two candidates who received the highest number of votes recommended to an expanded meeting of the standing committee of the district party committee.

Stage four: nomination and announcement. The expanded meeting respected the results of the vote and thus the candidate who had the highest number of votes was nominated as township party secretary and was announced on the spot. However, the process for confirmation of the party secretary and township head is different. The party secretary needs to be approved by the higher-level party committee while the township head needs to be "elected" by the people's congress. Eventually Xia Xiandong and Tang Kunlun were elected party secretaries of Lianhua and Dongchan townships, with 122 and 321 votes respectively.

Open Recommendation and Selection as a Mechanism for Broader but Controlled Participation

Clearly ORS broadens the scope of participation in the selection of local leaders in contrast with traditional methods, but it retains the Leninist concern for control of the process should anything deemed untoward happen. Two institutional adjustments are made to broaden participation. First, the criteria for application are lowered. In the case of township head, village officials and lower-ranked cadres (below deputy section chief, *fuke*) are permitted to participate. Having the status of farmer is not a barrier to being able to compete for a formal bureaucratic position that is financed out of the state's budget and which oversees a larger geographic terrain than the village. More younger officials can participate because the requirement for level of bureaucratic rank is lower than usual.[54] For example, among 67 applicants in Baoshi, there were 20 (30 percent) cadres ranked just below that of deputy section chief, namely at *gu* level, with another 28 (41 percent) who were ordinary cadres or village officials. In terms of age, the number of applicants under 33 years formed the majority (41 or 61 percent).

The second institutional innovation is that the voting by the representative group is decisive. This modifies the party's dominance of the entire selection procedure for the township head. Under the old process, the organization department would provide a name list for the party standing committee should positions in a township become vacant. The standing committee—

54 In county-level politics, it normally takes five or more years to be promoted from *fuke* rank to *zhengke* (i.e., township head). This means that it is very difficult for an official ranked below *fuke* to be able to jump up to the *zhengke* level.

usually made up of seven to nine members—would then convene to discuss the recommended candidates. A meeting of the party secretaries would usually precede this meeting.[55] This meeting is the quintessential bargaining and deal-making session, where a basic consensus is formed after people horse-trade their favourite candidates. The decision is then presented to the standing committee, which is highly unlikely to raise criticism of the proposed choices. The final decision is approved and issued in the name of the standing committee. The process is then shifted from the district to the township level. The candidate for party secretary is elected by the township's party congress while the township head is elected by the people's congress.

Beginning in the 1990s, this traditional process began to be modified through the adoption of the "democratic recommendation" process. This meant, in practice, that the organization department called together some staff from a work unit to request an evaluation of their head. However, this process was more one of form than content, as the evaluation did not necessarily have an impact on the decision made at the higher level. The work of a township head had the potential to affect all residents in the township but virtually none had input regarding an appointment. This is also the case with "democratic recommendation," as it is an internal process and excludes the villagers themselves.

A different procedure is followed with the recommendation group in the "open recommendation and selection" process, even though the old name of "democratic recommendation" is retained. First, it is the representative group not the standing committee that makes the final decision on the candidates. Second, more ordinary cadres participate in the group, rather than just the district's leading cadres. For example, in Baoshi ordinary cadres comprised 68 of the 149 representatives (45.6 percent). If we include the number of ordinary cadres who were township congress delegates then the total would top 50 percent. This is the same with ORS voting for the party secretary. Village officials play a decisive role in the final selection because they dominate the representative group. In Lianhua there are 198 village officials (about 71 percent) out of a group total of 278.[56] In Dongchan there were 237 (about 61 percent) village officials out of a total of 388 in the group.[57] This means that any person who wishes to win the election must gain the support of the village level officials. Without this support, no candidate could emerge as a winner even if she/he did well on the written examination and was the preferred choice of the higher-level authorities.

55 The Party statutes do not stipulate that such a meeting be held but it has become common practice. It provides a strong institutional mechanism for the party secretary to monopolize the power of decision making.

56 There were 48 township and 32 district votes but each selector could vote for two candidates if they so wished.

57 There were 107 township and 44 district votes but each selector could vote for two candidates if they so wished.

Pacific Affairs: Volume 76, No. 2 – Summer 2003

The size and structure of the representative group makes it hard for the party to influence the voting. This can be seen by analyzing the voting behaviour of the representative group. The distribution of the votes is interesting, with an obvious divergence between the district-level and the village-level officials in terms of their choice of candidate. We should keep in mind that all members of the standing committee of the party are district-level cadres. In Lianhua, almost half of the 32 district-level cadres voted for Yuan Jie (15 votes) but Yuan received only 8 votes from the village-level officials. By contrast, Xia Xiandong received a total of 87 votes even though he received only 7 district-level votes. He still won in Lianhua township. In Dongchan the contrast is even clearer. The eventual winner, Tang Kunlun, won 164 of the 237 village-level official votes (over 60 percent), while only 23 of the 44 district-level cadres voted for him. The third-place candidate, Zhang Jiwu, received 32 votes from the district-level cadres but only 46 votes from the village level. Given this situation, it is difficult for the party to manipulate the results of the election.

When we compare the voting behaviour of the village-level officials and the township cadres, we find much greater congruence. In Lianhua, Xia Xiandong polled the highest vote among both the village and the township officials, while in Dongchan, Tang Kunlun received the highest village vote and was second to Yi Pengfei for the township votes (44:57). Two cases are not sufficient to make any robust conclusions but we can make one tentative suggestion about these voting outcomes. The main reason for the convergence is probably that township cadres maintain close working relationships and interact frequently with village officials. This means that a consensus on the candidates is more likely than between the district and the village. In the villages, the candidate's practical capabilities rather than their speech-making capacity is considered more important. By contrast, district-level cadres might pay more attention to a candidate's rhetoric and their alignment with the policies of the party and the Shizhong District in particular. Some villagers commented that they preferred a person they saw as honest, credible and modest even if they were not a good public speaker. They felt that it was easier to communicate with such a person.

However, this does not mean that the party has foregone its control; its Leninist predisposition is still apparent. We are not dealing with open representation but rather with the creation of a controlled opening through which to gauge public receptivity to proposed candidates. The last thing the party wants is to put forward a slate of candidates that will be rejected by those they will be overseeing.[58] The representative group is much smaller

58 As Manion notes when looking at the process for electing people's congress delegates, the system is designed to align preferences of selectorates and electorates. The party wants to select candidates that can win an election and thus enhance the party's own legitimacy. Manion, "Chinese Democratization in Perspective," pp. 780-81.

than the potential voter pool. It enables elite rather than popular participation. It is limited within the system and is not inclusive, with most representatives being drawn from among officialdom at different levels.

It should also be remembered that the party controls the selection of the township heads even though it cannot decide directly who the candidates are, let alone which candidate will win. The party exerts its influence in at least three ways. First, it is the only rule maker for ORS and monopolizes the privilege of setting the criteria for application, reviewing the applicants, designing the exams and drafting the voting procedures. The party can manipulate the criteria on age, education level and years of work to limit the scope of applicants and help it find those potential officials who fit its defined needs. In this case, there was a need to provide younger and better-educated officials. As the rules were institutionalized, in fact, the criteria for application were tightened. Thus, in Baoshi township the party allowed all cadres below the *fuke* level to participate but this was limited in the "Interim Provisions" of November 3, 1998. The provisions raised the years of necessary work experience as well as the level of administrative experience. It was deemed that the candidate should hold a *guji* position and have a college diploma and at least five years' work experience. If the applicant was a farmer, he or she should have worked as a party secretary or village head for more than three years.

Second, the party could still move the township officials elected by ORS at will. Xiang Daoquan, the township head elected in Baoshi was moved to Hengshan Township to be party secretary after just one year in office. This showed that the party was not bound by the desire of the representative group, especially not that of its local participants. Clearly, the ORS process is not a means of promoting democracy. Its primary role is to increase the talent pool and vet effective cadres. This could undermine the longer-term effectiveness of the process. In fact, some cadres in the organization department were also concerned about the speed with which Xiang was moved. They felt that local residents would not believe that ORS was effective and that township heads might not devote themselves to their work sufficiently if they thought that they could still be moved at will. Some villagers—as well as Xiang himself—thought that it would have been better for him to work longer in Baoshi as he had been "elected" to the job and had become familiar with the township.

Last but not least, most officials are still party members, meaning that their ties of loyalty are still to the party organization rather than to the local community. Most applicants are party members. For example, in Baoshi, 52 of the 67 applicants (78 percent) were party members while only two applicants came from the other ("democratic") political parties.

Pacific Affairs: Volume 76, No. 2 – Summer 2003

Concluding Comments: Institutional Innovation and Economic Development

At first glance it may seem strange that these innovations have taken place in Suining, a small municipality in the west of China that lags economically behind the more developed areas of the east. More conventional wisdom on the relationship between economic development and political reform would suggest that Suining is an unlikely candidate to be a pioneer of political reform.

Of course we are dealing with institutional innovation rather than democratization but still it is interesting to note that a number of key innovations in China since the 1970s have occurred in less economically developed areas. Two prominent examples from rural China are the household responsibility system and the villagers' committee elections. The former was initiated in a poor village in Anhui province in 1978. The village election programme began in two Guangxi counties in late 1980 and early 1981. Both these experiments led to the development of national policy and made a decisive contribution to change in rural China.

In poorer areas, the impact of a crisis is likely to be felt first and can result in innovation by the local government. This was the case with Suining. Both general factors and some specific causes explain Suining's decision to undertake institutional innovation. First, local governments in many poor areas lack the revenue to meet basic public needs or to respond to crises. This can create the need to innovate with existing institutions. Opening up the political system or broadening public participation is, however, only likely to be a measure of last resort. Second, local communities in poorer areas may be less riven by interest groups and the forces of pluralism. This may facilitate consensus building about alternative solutions. Third, innovation initiated by government might be accepted more readily. Local societies might not have much information about alternatives, especially if migration is not particularly significant. Under these circumstances the combination of remoteness would allow for more experimentation, as it does not fall under such strict scrutiny from the political centre. At the same time, the innovation is liable to be within existing institutional frameworks as access to information on alternatives will be limited.

In the specific case of Suining, the economic scandal caused by the corruption of local cadres pushed the district leadership to reconsider the method through which they selected township officials. The fact that "open recommendation and selection" appeared successful in Baoshi led them to broaden the process to other townships and to the selection of the party secretary. The use of ORS for the selection of the party secretary is more significant than that of township head because it opens up the internal operations of the party to a broader, albeit limited, public. Even though participation was limited, the oral examination and the structure of the recommendation group would result in most inhabitants knowing a lot more about prospective candidates than would normally be the case.

Innovation in China's Local Governance

Leadership is also important in promoting or resisting change.[59] In many localities, an insightful and strong-willed individual leader can play a crucial role in initiating and implementing reform. This was clearly the case in Shizhong with Zhang Jinming, the former party secretary who has now been promoted to vice-mayor of Suining Municipality. She played a key role in initiating and sustaining momentum for ORS. Importantly, she had experience outside of Suining, having worked in the Sichuan provincial committee of the Youth League and as an intern in the Ministry of Foreign Trade and Economic Cooperation in Beijing. She was enthusiastic about reforming the traditional cadre system and persisted over the objections of some members of the party standing committee. Her continued support enabled the trial sites to complete the work and the success in these areas, and gave confidence to other district leaders to persist with the reform.[60]

Regional competition also played a role in pushing ahead innovation. Some scholars have argued that competition among local governments wishing to improve economic growth has been a major force promoting fast economic growth.[61] While political innovation is much riskier than economic changes, competition also exists in this area. Localities can be willing to act as trial sites for experimentation because of the potential for recognition and benefits from higher levels of party leadership. If experimentation is successful, local leaders might be promoted more quickly. In Suining, the ORS process attracted attention from the Sichuan provincial party committee and also from some scholars based in Beijing. Zhang Jinming, as noted above, made a presentation to the provincial organization department in September 1998 that promoted the experiment. Through discussions with the scholars present at the meeting, she became aware that Dapeng in Shenzhen was planning to hold a direct election for township head. As a result, she decided to speed up the process for the direct election in Buyun to ensure that it would be the first in China. Cadres in Suining were very proud to be known

59 For more on this see Xuedong Yang, "Diyu, geren yu zhidu chuangxin—dui Shaanxi sheng Xianyangshi Qindu qu gaige de gean fenxi" (Region, Individuals and Institutional Innovation: A Case Study of Qindu District, Xianyang City in Shaanxi Province) in Rong Jingben et al., *Zailun cong yalixing tizhi xiang minzhu hezuo tizhi de zhuanbian* (Further Discussion of the Transformation from the Pressurized System to the Democratic System of Cooperation) (Beijing: Zhongyang bianyi ju chubanshe , 2001), pp. 189-245.

60 Others confirm this in their analysis of the Buyun election. He Baogang and Lang Youxing noted, "In the course of making the decision, Zhang Jinming, the party secretary of Shizhong District, played a key role. She not only has a pioneering spirit but also is also open-minded and is good at theoretical analysis. Her determination finally promoted the direct election in Shizhong District. See "Predicament in Buyun: A Study of the First Direct Election of a Township Head in China), *Ershiyi shijie* (The Twenty-First Century), No. 64 (April 2000), pp. 125-36.

61 See Steven M. Goldstein, "China in Transition: The Political Foundations of Incremental Reform," *The China Quarterly*, no. 144 (December 1995), pp. 1105-31 and Thomas G. Rawski, "Implications of China's Reform Experience", *The China Quarterly*, no. 144 (December 1995), pp. 1150-73.

Pacific Affairs: Volume 76, No. 2 – Summer 2003

as the first to hold a direct election while those in Shenzhen were disappointed by the news that they had been beaten.

While a crisis might produce a one-time experiment, it is more difficult to ensure the sustainability of a new institutional innovation. Once the perceived crisis is past there is a tendency to set aside the innovation. However, in the case of ORS, momentum has been maintained. A September 2001 document issued by the Sichuan Provincial Organization Bureau required all counties, with the exception of those in minority autonomous regions, to carry out the ORS method of selection in at least one-third of the townships by the end of that year.[62] While this process has been accepted at the provincial level (and even at this level there is uncertainty about institutionalizing the representative group), it has not been adopted as national policy. National policy has favoured a similar process called "open selection" (*gongkai xuanba*). However there are two principle differences. First, in general "open selection" is only used for the position of deputy. Second, if some head positions are selected through this process, it is within functional sectors and not within the administrative organs.

"Open recommendation and selection" is just one of the innovations that have been introduced to reform the cadre system since the 15th Party Congress (September 1997) and we can expect more with the rising concern about corruption within party ranks. Party leaders are worried about a drift of qualified party members out of leading party and state positions to the foreign and private sector, where not only is the pay higher but where promotion can be more rapid. Within this context, the use of selection methods such as ORS is seen as a way of improving promotion chances for younger people. Under the traditional system, it is difficult for a person under 40 or 45 years of age to head a township. In Suining, many township heads are below the age of 30 and the youngest head was only 26 years old at the time of selection. However, some older cadres have not been so pleased with the outcomes of ORS and have tried to obstruct its implementation. Many cadres working in the county-level administration who are around 45 years old can now find it difficult to gain promotion to head a township and as a result some have to retire early.

This novel system offers new opportunities to the individual while providing the party with the chance to unearth good local talent. Individuals can make a case for selection without having to rely solely on currying favour with existing leaders. One deputy party secretary of Shizhong commented that he was surprised to find so many talented people in the district. It has allowed the organization department to have a better sense of which qualified

62 Organization Bureau of Sichuan Province, "Zhonggong Sichuan shengwei zuzhibu guanyu zuohao xiang (zhen) cun huanjie xuanju gongzuo de tongzhi (Announcement of the Organization Bureau of Sichuan Provincial CCP Committee Concerning Implementing Smoothly Elections for Change of Leadership in Towns [Townships] and Villages), September 6, 2001.

candidates enjoy a broader credibility. Some of those who did not win in the final vote have subsequently been considered good enough for promotion elsewhere.

However, in terms of institutional design, ORS has a number of shortcomings. First, the application criteria are still restrictive, imposing age, education and administrative ranking requirements that limit the scope of applicants. Second, there are problems with the technical implementation of the voting. For example, there are no voting booths that provide privacy and there is no open count of the vote. Third, higher levels can still remove those elected during their term of office.

The development of a process such as ORS represents a local attempt by the party to deal with what a number of observers see as a process of institutional decline resulting from economic reforms.[63] It is an attempt to address the evolving realities of local-level politics and to improve the quality of the officials that are appointed to key posts. Certainly, there was a demand for these jobs, with over 60 applicants for each position, revealing that in a poorer area such as Suining a job in the bureaucracy is considered a good thing.[64] It also provides the party with feedback from society about the kinds of individuals that it is selecting and in this sense provides a modicum of democratization within the local party apparatus. ORS allows more party members at the grass-roots level to participate in the choice of party secretaries at the next level. In fact, they dominate the representative group. This process can help broaden the base of the party's legitimacy at the local level.

This does not mean that the party's Leninist predilections have been abandoned nor is there any indication that processes such as ORS are seen as a stepping stone to direct elections at the township level. The organization department remains in control of reforming the cadre system, and the relationship between the representative groups, the people's congress and the party committee remains unclear. The party will still guide the process of selection and, as we have seen, can still remove or transfer those selected whenever they choose to do so. Senior party leaders have vacillated on the question as to whether direct elections at the township level would be a good thing or not. On balance they have tended to resist this move. The Central Secretariat of the CCP issued a document in September 2001 that called for experimentation with township elections to be postponed, as the

---

63 See, for example, Minxin Pei, "Racing Against Time: Institutional Decay and Renewal in China," in William A. Joseph, *China Briefing 1995-95* (Armonk, NY: M.E. Sharpe inc., 1997), pp. 11-49; and Andrew Walder, "The Quiet Revolution from Within: Economic Reform as a Source of Political Decline," in Andrew Walder (ed.), *The Waning of the Communist State: Economic Origins of Political Decline in China and Hungary* (Berkeley: University of California Press, 1995), pp. 1-24.

64 In part this highlights the fact that the local state is too large in most localities. It might also point to the fact that many feel that not only are the official benefits of office holding good, but the unofficial perks are attractive as well.

Pacific Affairs: Volume 76, No. 2 – Summer 2003

existing legal framework did not provide adequate legitimacy for this.[65] However, while the centre vacillates, local governments and party institutions have to find real solutions to the problems that confront them. Perhaps the biggest problem is that of legitimacy in regard to the governing organs themselves. This would suggest that we might see more local institutional innovation that tries to walk the fine line of broadening civic participation while retaining Leninist organizational control.[66] This may seem a contradiction in terms but without any clear direction from the centre, the only solutions for localities are those that operate within existing institutional guidelines and effectively exploit the grey areas of party command to enhance local representation.

Harvard University, Cambridge, U.S.A.,
and China Center for Comparative Politics and Economics,
Beijing, China, June 2003

65 There seems to be some confusion about this document and its status. Officials who are familiar with the document said that while the document had been issued in the name of the Central Secretariat, it had not been drafted by the Secretariat but rather by officials in the National People's Congress. They claimed that it did not necessarily reflect the intention of the party as the drafters were not familiar with the process of the elections at the township level and had just heard a number of complaints about the process. The complaints had formed the basis for their draft.

66 As Baogang He has noted recently, experiments have continued in provinces such as Henan, Guangdong, and Shaanxi, where they use less politically contentious terms such as "confidence votes" or "extensive opinion polls." He, "From Village to Township," p. 5.

B.J.Pol.S. **38,** 411–432 *Copyright © 2008 Cambridge University Press*
doi:10.1017/S0007123408000215 *Printed in the United Kingdom*

Power Structure and Regime Resilience: Contentious Politics in China

YONGSHUN CAI*

Authoritarian governments may face serious uncertainties when dealing with popular resistance because of the unpredictable consequences of making concessions or repressing opposition. However, a political system with multiple levels of authority can help reduce the uncertainties by granting conditional autonomy to lower-level authorities. Such a power structure prevents excessive repression and unconditional concessions when the priorities of different levels of authority do not match. Under this political arrangement, the central authority can avoid blame when local authorities use repression. The divided power also helps reduce the uncertainties faced by the central authority because it will then have to deal with only a very limited number of instances of resistance. Using the case of China, this article shows that divided state power has allowed the party-state to maintain social stability amid numerous instances of social unrest during the reform era.

Authoritarian governments may face serious uncertainties in dealing with popular resistance. Making concessions tends to trigger more resistance or even the collapse of the regime, but reliance on repression damages the regime's legitimacy and makes it less sensitive to popular demands.[1] How can authoritarian governments reduce these uncertainties? This article suggests that certain political arrangements can help address this dilemma. More specifically, in a political system with multiple-level authorities, the regime's resilience will be enhanced if the top-level authority assigns the responsibility for dealing with popular resistance to lower-level authorities and grants them conditional autonomy. This arrangement places constraints on both resisters and lower-level authorities, and it therefore addresses the concession–repression dilemma by discouraging both unconditional concessions and excessive repression. Moreover, the arrangement also protects the top-level authority's image by allowing it to distance itself from lower-level authorities that use repressive measures.

Authoritarian regimes are characterized by the lack of political opportunities for collective action, but this does not mean that popular resistance is absent in such regimes.[2] In China, for example, there have been numerous instances of collective resistance in recent years.[3] Reportedly, the number of such occurrences increased ten times from 8,700 in 1993 to 87,000 in 2005.[4] Whilst not all of these instances were disruptive, many were. In 2003,

* Division of Social Science, Hong Kong University of Science and Technology. The author wishes to thank the anonymous reviewers and the Editor, Sarah Birch, for their suggestions.

[1] Jack Goldstone and Charles Tilly, 'Threat (and Opportunity): Popular Action and State Response in the Dynamics of Contentious Action', in Ronald R. Aminzade, Jack A. Goldstone, Doug McAdam, Elizabeth J. Perry, William H. Sewell Jr, Sidney Tarrow and Charles Tilley, eds, *Silence and Voice in the Study of Contentious Politics* (New York: Cambridge University Press, 2001), pp. 179–94.

[2] See, for example, Kurt Schock, *Unarmed Insurrections: People Power Movements in Non-democracies* (Minneapolis: University of Minnesota Press, 2005).

[3] These incidents include demonstrations, protests, strikes, disruptive collective petitions, sit-in demonstrations, fasting, posting slogans, attacking state agencies, surrounding leaders, blocking traffic, looting and damaging property (Chen Zhaxu, 'Actively Preventing and Appropriately Dealing with Instances of Collective Action', *Research on Public Security*, 5 (2001), 16–19).

[4] Jae Ho Chung, Hongyi Lai and Ming Xia, 'Mounting Challenges to Governance in China: Surveying Collective Protestors, Religious Sects and Criminal Organizations', *China Journal*, 56 (2006), 1–31.

there were 3,100 instances of highways, roads or railways being blocked and 3,900 attacks on state agencies.[5] Citizens' resistance has become a serious concern for the central party-state, and it is against this background that building a so-called 'harmonious society' has recently become a top priority of the central party-state.[6]

In some other transitional economies, a large increase in collective actions, such as strikes, occurred only after the regime collapsed, which relaxed the political constraints on resistance. In Poland the number of strikes in 1989 was 894, whereas it was 7,443 in 1993 (or 8.3 times more); in the former Soviet Union, the number of strikes was 1,771 in 1990, and this number rose to 6,273 in 1992 (or 3.5 times more).[7] In comparison, the large increase in popular resistance in China has occurred without regime change. The frequency and magnitude of collective actions in China appear puzzling: why are so many instances of resistance possible given the political system and state power? However, the many cases of resistance have not posed an insurmountable challenge to social and political order in a country that is undergoing tremendous socio-economic change. The coexistence of social disturbance and political stability in China reveals the state's resilience.[8] This article provides an explanation for this resilience by highlighting the importance of political arrangements. It shows that the Chinese party-state has been able to maintain social stability amid numerous social conflicts and prevent the unpredictable consequences of making concessions or repressing resistance because the political arrangements grant conditional autonomy to local governments.

AUTHORITARIAN GOVERNMENTS AND THE CONCESSION–REPRESSION DILEMMA

A state can respond to popular resistance with repression, tolerance or concessions.[9] Its choice has to do with, among other things,[10] the type of political regime, which shapes political leaders' calculations.[11] In democracies, politicians face the pressure of elections and have to be cautious when using repression, and democratic systems are thus more likely to tolerate certain types of dissident behaviour and may use a mix of concessions and repression or more concessions.[12] By comparison, political leaders in authoritarian regimes do not face the pressure of elections, but they are more sensitive to popular resistance.[13] The occurrence of citizens' resistance signals problems with social control or the weakness of the government because such resistance is not supposed to occur in a regime where

[5] He Zuowen, 'Properly Handling Conflicts in Our Country', *Scientific Socialism*, 2 (2005), 8–11.

[6] On 28 July 2005, *The People's Daily*, the Chinese Communist Party's mouthpiece, published a front-page commentary entitled 'Maintaining Stability, Promoting Development', urging citizens to obey the law and warning that any threats to social stability would not be tolerated by the authorities.

[7] Zhang Sai, *World Statistics 1995* (Beijing: China Statistics Press, 1996), pp. 347–9.

[8] Jean Oi, 'Realms of Freedom in Post-Mao China', in William Kirby, ed., *Realms of Freedom in Modern China* (Palo Alto, Calif.: Stanford University Press, 2003), pp. 264–84.

[9] Frances Fox Piven and Richard Cloward, *Poor People's Movements: Why They Succeeded, How They Fail* (New York: Vintage, 1977), p. 27.

[10] One important factor that affects the state's response is the power of the resisters. See, among others, William Gamson, *The Strategy of Social Protest* (Homewood, Ill.: Dorsey, 1990), pp. 81–2; McAdam, *Political Process and the Development of Black Insurgency*, p. 56.

[11] Goldstone and Tilly, 'Threat (and Opportunity)', pp. 192–3.

[12] Frances Piven and Richard Cloward, *Regulating the Poor: The Functions of Public Welfare* (New York: Vintage, 1993), p. 172.

[13] Goldstone and Tilly, 'Threat (and Opportunity)', p. 192.

citizens are denied the right to challenge the state.[14] Repression is thus commonly used to show the state's power and determination to protect the political system.[15]

However, authoritarian governments do not rely exclusively on repression; they may also make concessions. Excessively strong repression not only causes the opposition to gain allies: it may also 'leave the opposition little alternative but to revolt'[16] or it 'can produce a radicalization of collective action and a more effective organization of opponents'.[17] In addition, repression undermines the regime's legitimacy. Although authoritarian regimes are less reliant on legitimacy for survival than their democratic counterparts, they certainly have incentives to build and strengthen their legitimacy.[18] Authoritarian states with a higher-level of legitimacy not only have a better chance of surviving crises but also save on the costs of imposing strict and constant control over the society.[19]

Nevertheless, authoritarian governments do face serious uncertainties in making concessions. Goldstone and Tilly suggest that modest concessions made by the government can be fatal to the regime; one reason for this is the 'de Tocqueville effect': minor changes made by the regime indicate its illegitimacy but do not fully address the causes of the illegitimacy, and thus lead to greater demands for elimination or transformation of the regime. Secondly, concessions may increase perceptions of state weaknesses, making others believe that they too can extract more from the regime.[20] Therefore, the state's failure to demonstrate its actual power or credible threats may trigger regime-threatening actions.[21]

Although authoritarian states do not always face such life-or-death crises from social unrest, small-scale resistance, if unchecked, chips away at state power. The emergence of Solidarity in Poland, for instance, originated from economic demands. The government's ineffective repression of the movement made it into a testing ground of various modes of resistance that contributed to the subsequent better-organized and forceful resistance

[14] Susanne Lohmann, 'The Dynamics of Information Cascades: The Monday Demonstration in Leipzeig East Germany, 1989–1991', *World Politics*, 47 (1994), 42–101; Charles Kurzman, 'Structural Opportunities and Perceived Opportunity in Social-Movement Theory: The Iranian Revolution of 1979', *American Sociological Review*, 61 (1996), 153–70.

[15] Christian Davenport, 'Multi-Dimensional Threat Perception and State Repression: An Inquiry into Why States Apply Negative Sanctions', *American Journal of Political Science*, 39 (1995), 683–713; Goldstone and Tilly, 'Threat (and Opportunity)', pp. 192–3.

[16] Scott Gartner and Patrick Regan, 'Threat and Repression: The Non-Liner Relationship between Government and Opposition Violence', *Journal of Peace Research*, 33 (1996), 273–88, at p. 285; Paul Almeida, 'Opportunity Organizations and Threat-Induced Contention: Protest Waves in Authoritarian Settings', *American Journal of Sociology*, 109 (2003), 345–400.

[17] Sidney Tarrow, *Power in Movement* (New York: Cambridge University Press, 1998), p. 93; Will Moore, 'Repression and Dissent: Substitution, Context, and Timing,' *American Journal of Political Science*, 42 (1998), 851–73.

[18] Saxonberg writes, 'even if the Soviet-type regimes never gained complete legitimacy in the sense of gaining popular support for the system, they certainly tried' (Steven Saxonberg, *The Fall: A Comparative Study of the End of Communism in Czechoslovakia, East German, Hungary and Poland* (Amsterdam: Harwood Academic, 2001), p. 147).

[19] Anthony Oberschall, 'Opportunities and Framing in the Eastern Europe Revolts of 1989', in Doug McAdam, John D. McCarthy and Mayer N. Zald, eds, *Comparative Perspectives on Social Movements* (Cambridge: Cambridge University Press, 1996), pp. 172–99.

[20] Goldstone and Tilly, 'Threat (and Opportunity)', p. 188.

[21] Lohmann, 'The Dynamics of Information Cascades'; Kurzman, 'Structural Opportunities and Perceived Opportunity in Social-Movement Theory'; Timur Kuran, 'Now Out of Never: The Element of Surprise in the East European Revolution of 1989', *World Politics*, 44 (1991), 7–48.

which was fatal to the regime.[22] This process of testing the boundary of state tolerance is, to a great extent, what Scott describes as the weak resisting the powerful through the 'hidden transcript' (i.e., discourse taking place 'offstage'): 'The hidden transcript is continually pressing against the limit of what is permitted on stage, much as a body of water might press against a dam'. If the act of insubordination is not rebuked or punished, then others will exploit that breach and expand the territory: 'A small success is likely to encourage others to venture further, and the process can escalate rapidly'.[23]

The balance between concessions and repression is thus a serious issue faced by authoritarian governments. In China, unprecedented socio-economic changes have given rise to numerous conflicts in the society.[24] Tolerating certain modes of resistance (such as disruptive action) will certainly lead to more resistance, which threatens economic reforms and social stability. However, reliance on repression will only fuel the resentment, seriously damage the regime's legitimacy, and produce backlashes that threaten the regime's survival in crises, as reflected in the 1989 Tiananmen incident.[25] While a regime with strong resilience is better able to address the concession–repression dilemma, the question is how the state can balance the two options.

Divided State Power and Regime Resilience

It is a reasonable assumption that the state's response to popular resistance depends on its perception of the costs and benefits associated with the choice of a particular response. However, as Goldstone and Tilly show, the state's calculations, regardless of how sophisticated they are, may still fail to reduce the uncertainties.[26] This article suggests that the state's response is shaped by the political arrangements, and certain arrangements can help the state address the concession–repression dilemma and enhance the regime's resilience.

In dealing with a large number of instances of resistance, it is essentially impossible for authoritarian governments to give up repression. The issue becomes what type of repression can be used and, more importantly, who carries out the repression and takes the blame. A political system will help maintain social stability if the political arrangements allow the state to adopt repression whilst reducing the damage to the regime's legitimacy and to prevent concessions from being interpreted as signs of weakness. This is possible when there is more than one authority which deals with popular resistance. The existence

[22] Roman Laba, *The Roots of Solidarity: A Political Sociology of Poland's Working-Class Democratization* (Princeton, N.J.: Princeton University Press, 1991).

[23] James Scott, *Domination and the Arts of Resistance: Hidden Transcript* (New Haven, Conn.: Yale University Press, 1990), p. 196.

[24] Dali Yang, 'Economic Transformation and Its Political Discontents in China: Authoritarianism, Unequal Growth, and the Dilemmas of Political Development', *Annual Review of Political Science*, 9 (2006), 143–64.

[25] The 1989 Tiananmen incident not only showed the consequence of a divided ruling elite but also revealed the serious impact of the lack of legitimacy on regime survival. Central leaders acknowledged that many people protested in the incident because of their resentment against corruption. What was more astonishing was the participation of state agents. Between 15 and 19 May 1989, about 700 work units had employees who held demonstrations in Beijing, including about seventy party and government agencies. Fifty of the seventy agencies, including the State Council, belonged to the central party committee and the central government (State Education Commission, *The Soul-Stirring 56 Days* (Beijing: Land Press, 1989), p. 138).

[26] Goldstone and Tilly describe how there can be a variety of undesirable scenarios that the state encounters in using repression or concessions because of the unknown consequences of a response (Goldstone and Tilly, 'Threat (and Opportunity)', pp. 188–92).

of multiple authorities integrated into a political hierarchy provides significant space for the top-level authority to deal with popular resistance when it grants conditional autonomy to a lower-level authority. Conditional autonomy means that the lower-level authority or the local government has considerable autonomy in dealing with popular resistance while facing constraints imposed by the top-level authority or the central government.

Therefore, while it is commonly suggested that a government with strong power is better able to deal with resistance,[27] this article shows that in an authoritarian state with a number of lower-level authorities, the central government can be better positioned by giving up part of its power to local governments.[28] This structure of divided state power assists the central government in dealing with resistance in several important ways. First, the divided power creates space for the central government to avoid blame. Authoritarian states are said to be less able to avoid blame because the concentration of power in the hands of the government also means the concentration of responsibility and blame.[29] By delegating the power to deal with popular resistance to lower-level authorities, the central government shifts the responsibility to those lower-level authorities, thereby avoiding being in blame-generating situations itself.

Secondly, while tolerating resistance which does not threaten the regime, this structure places constraints on both resisters and local governments. Unlike the situation where there is only a single authority, the existence of multiple authorities implies that the state's policies towards protesters are inconsistent when the interests of those state authorities differ. These inconsistencies not only create political space for resistance but also prevent local authorities from adopting certain modes of response (for example, violent repression). However, resisters face more serious constraints. The local authorities' autonomy, though conditional, still allows them to adopt a range of responses to deal with most of the instances of resistance in the light of their own interests, which implies that concessions to resisters are conditional. Therefore, the divided state power prevents both excessive repression that damages the regime's legitimacy and unconditional concessions that lead to the 'lack of discipline'.[30]

Thirdly, this structure reduces the uncertainties for the central government. Goldstone and Tilly suggest that the state faces 'considerable hazards' in dealing with popular resistance largely because 'the state, in general, will have a hard time picking the right level of concessions and repression to respond to a group'.[31] In other words, concessions or repression at the wrong time may prove costly or fatal.[32] A power structure with multiple authorities reduces the hazards for the central government because only a very limited number of instances of social discord will need to be addressed by the central government itself. The uncertainty is further reduced because those limited instances have already been

[27] Doug McAdam, *Political Process and the Development of Black Insurgency, 1930–1970*, 2nd edn (Chicago: University of Chicago Press, 1999), pp. 44–7; Charles Tilly, *From Mobilization to Revolution* (New York: Random House, 1978), pp. 114–15.

[28] Authoritarian regimes can be fragmented. The 'fragmented authoritarianism' model, for example, has been used to describe policy making in China. However, the 'fragmented authoritarianism' model focuses more on the horizontal divide among state agencies, whereas this article focuses on the vertical divide between the central and local governments. See Kenneth Lieberthal and David Lampton, eds, *Bureaucracy, Politics, and Decision Making in Post-Mao China* (Berkeley: University of California Press, 1992).

[29] Kent Weaver, 'The Politics of Blame Avoidance', *Journal of Public Policy*, 6 (1986), 371–98.

[30] Federick Barghoon, *Politics in Russia* (Boston, Mass.: Little, Brown, 1972), p. 308.

[31] Goldstone and Tilly, 'Threat (and Opportunity)', p. 187.

[32] Lohmann, 'The Dynamics of Informational Cascades'.

(mis)handled by the local government, which gives the central government more time and information to work on solutions. As discussed below, the divided state power is crucial to the regime's resilience in dealing with popular resistance in China today.

THE POWER STRUCTURE IN CHINA AND ITS IMPLICATIONS

China's political hierarchy has multiple levels of government.[33] For analytical convenience, the political structure can be seen as consisting of the central government and local governments. Decentralization in China has granted considerable power and autonomy to local governments. Indeed, they enjoy more autonomy than their counterparts in some former socialist countries (for example, the Soviet Union) or even democracies (for instance, India).[34] The autonomy assumed by local governments in China has been consolidated or strengthened because of their role in economic development, which has led some scholars to conclude that there is a Chinese style of federalism.[35] Given their power, local governments in China are doomed to play a crucial role in managing local affairs, which is also the reason for their abuse of power.[36]

The delegation of power, however, also means the delegation of responsibility (and blame). Decentralization shifts most of the responsibility of dealing with citizens' resistance to local governments, and the central government holds local governments accountable by assigning the responsibility directly to local leaders. The Chinese political system is different from the federal system in a democracy because local officials in China are appointed by the upper-level authorities and have to fulfil assigned responsibilities.[37] During the reform period, maintaining social stability has been one of the most important responsibilities assigned to local governments. In the Chinese political system, top leaders (i.e., the party secretary and the head of the government) at each local level assume the most power. Also, because dealing with citizens' resistance is often an urgent matter, local leaders, especially the party secretary, assume the most decision-making power and thereby the most responsibility in maintaining social stability.[38] Their performance or even political careers are closely linked to their fulfilment of this responsibility.[39] Top local leaders are expected to handle large-scale resistance in person. For example, in Anhui province in 2005, the party secretary of a city, who was also promoted to hold another

[33] Kenneth Lieberthal, *Governing China: From Revolution through Reform* (New York: W.W. Norton, 1995).

[34] Pradeep Chhibber and Samuel Eldersveld, 'Local Elites and Popular Support for Economic Reform in China and India', *Comparative Political Studies*, 33 (2000), 350–73.

[35] Gabriella Montinola, Yingyi Qian and Barry Weingast, 'Federalism, Chinese Style: The Political Basis for Economic Success', *World Politics*, 41 (1996), 50–81.

[36] Kevin O'Brien and Lianjiang Li, 'Selective Policy Implementation in Rural China', *Comparative Politics*, 31 (1999), 167–86.

[37] Yasheng Huang, *Inflation and Investment Controls in China: The Political Economy of Central–Local Relations during the Reform Era* (New York: Cambridge University Press, 1996).

[38] At the county and township levels, it is common for the party secretary to sign the so-called responsibility contract with upper-level authorities to ensure the fulfilment of assigned tasks, including achieving social stability. City-level party secretaries may not be required to sign such contracts, but they are certainly assessed for this responsibility (Dong Xueqing, Zhang Heping and Zhang Zeyuan, 'The Life of County Party Secretaries', *Perspectives*, 9 November 2005, pp. 21–4; Maria Edin, 'State Capacity and Local Agent Control in China: CCP Cadre Management from a Township Perspective', *China Quarterly*, 173 (2003), 35–72.

[39] Kevin O'Brien and Lianjiang Li, *Rightful Resistance in Rural China* (New York: Cambridge University Press, 2006); Edin, 'State Capacity and Local Agent Control in China'.

important position of vice provincial governor, was removed because he was absent without justifiable reasons when a riot involving 10,000 people occurred in his city.[40]

The Choice of the Mode of Response

While local leaders are strongly motivated to prevent and stop citizens' resistance, especially large-scale resistance, they face constraints in choosing the mode of response because of the different priorities between the central and local governments when they deal with citizens' 'non-political' resistance.[41] Both levels of government may adopt one of the following modes of response: (1) concessions (i.e., citizens' demands are met); (2) concessions with discipline (i.e., citizens' demands are met, but some or all participants are punished); (3) tolerance (i.e., citizens' demands are ignored, but the government also tolerates their resistance); and (4) repression (i.e., citizens' demands are ignored, and some or all participants are punished).

A crucial factor that makes the central government behave differently from local governments is its greater interest in protecting the regime's legitimacy.[42] Legitimacy is about the political system's worthiness of being recognized.[43] Given that the central government is more responsible for the operation of the political system or it largely represents the regime, it has a greater interest in protecting the regime's legitimacy. In contrast, local officials in China are more concerned with policy implementation or task fulfilment (such as maintaining social stability) and local issues, and thus legitimacy is not their main concern.[44] A simple comparison of the incentive structures faced by the two levels of government reveals that the central government's more serious concern over legitimacy helps to make it more tolerant towards popular resistance than the local government.

The central and local governments incur two types of costs when concessions are made: (1) economic and/or political costs; and (2) signs of weakness (see Table 1). Addressing citizens' complaints may require the expenditure of financial resources (economic costs). It may also require the government to correct its practices or policies or discipline state agents deemed responsible for the grievances or resistance (political costs). The cost of showing weakness is that making concessions may trigger more demands or actions. If the

[40] In the riot, police cars were torched, six police officers were wounded and a nearby department store was looted. It was later discovered that the party secretary was with his mistress in another city for relaxation, and he was annoyed by the phone calls and turned off his cell phone. He was later arrested for corruption (Xiao Zhong, 'An Investigation of the Removal of He Minxu, a Vice Governor of Anhui Province', *Inspections*, 20 (2006), 21–2).

[41] By non-political resistance, I mean that participants do not raise political demands that challenge the political authority of the party or the government. Such actions are normally based on legitimate or lawful claims or, as the government claims, are 'internal conflicts within the people'. To be sure, non-political resistance may be 'boundary-spanning' or illegal according to the Chinese law. The government treats actions that aim to overthrow the party or the government or attack important facilities as unacceptable (see Long Xianlei, 'Sticking to Rule by Law and Appropriately Handling Instances of Collective Action', *Public Security Research*, 12 (2001), 50–3; Fan Fuming, 'Characteristics of Collective Action in Blocking Railways and Some Countermeasures', *Journal of Shanghai Public Security Academy*, 3 (2001), 30–4; Kevin O'Brien, 'Neither Transgressive Nor Contained: Boundary-Spanning Contention in China', *Mobilization*, 8 (2003), 51–64).

[42] Ethan Michelson, 'Peasants' Burdens and State Response: Exploring State Concession to Popular Tax Resistance in Rural China' (unpublished, 2005).

[43] Frank Michelman, 'Ida's Way: Constructing the Respect-Worthy Governmental System', *Fordham Law Review*, 72 (2003), 345–62.

[44] O'Brien and Li, 'Selective Policy Implementation in Rural China'; Thomas Bernstein and Xiaobo Lu, *Taxation without Representation in Contemporary Rural China* (New York: Cambridge University Press, 2003).

TABLE 1 *Costs and Benefits in Concessions and Repression*

	Benefits	Costs
Concessions	a. Stopping resistance b. Gaining legitimacy	a. Economic and/or political costs b. Signs of weakness
Repression	Deterring resistance	a. Loss of legitimacy b. Risks in repressive measures

cost of showing weakness is considered to be the same for the two levels of government, the central government incurs a smaller cost than the local government does when making concessions. First, when the central government intervenes in a dispute and makes concessions, it often requires the local government to address citizen grievances with local financial resources. Secondly, when malfeasant local officials are disciplined, the local government incurs a heavier loss because it relies more directly on these officials for local governance than does the central government. As far as the benefits are concerned, if stopping resistance is equally desirable to the two levels of government, the central government gains more because legitimacy is more important to the central government than to the local government.

In the case of repression, the two levels of government also incur two types of costs: (1) loss of legitimacy; and (2) risk from repression (Table 1). Repressing citizens' resistance with legitimate claims damages the regime's legitimacy. For the reasons discussed above, the central government faces a higher cost of losing legitimacy than the local government when repression is used.

The other type of cost incurred from repression is the risk arising from ineffective or failed repressive measures. For the central government, the risk means ineffective repression leading to more serious or regime-threatening resistance. This possibility (or the risk) is rather small given the power of the central party-state in China. In contrast, the local government faces a more serious risk in repressing resistance. For one, ineffective repression may cause the escalation of resistance, which signals the local government's failure in maintaining social stability. For another, forceful repression which causes serious casualties will damage regime legitimacy.[45] In either situation, the central government will intervene, and local officials may be punished. However, the local government will face a small cost from repression if it is able to use the modes of repression that carry little risk (i.e., legitimacy is not its serious concern). Hence, when the risk from repression is low for both levels of government, the local government is more likely to use repression than the central government.

[45] The central government prohibits the use of force in dealing with peaceful resistance. According to the 1998 directive issued by the central government, state authorities are required to settle instances of social unrest based on considerations of whether or not participants' demands are political, there is organized violence, there is intentional confrontation, and there is support for the resistance from overseas. In dealing with organized attacks that are consciously directed at party and government agencies and other important facilities, force can be used, but it should not be used to deal with non-political and peaceful action by citizens with legitimate demands. Police officers who directly face participants can bring equipment but not weapons with them, while back-up officers can bring weapons with them if necessary (see Long, 'Sticking to Rule by Law and Appropriately Handling Instances of Collective Action').

Yet, although the central government is more tolerant of citizens' resistance, its concessions are conditional. When the central government decides to make concessions to citizens, it often means that it will intervene in the conflict between citizens and a local government. This is likely when the central government feels the pressure to stop the resistance and to protect regime legitimacy. In collective resistance, a few factors often make the central government regard intervention as necessary: (1) casualties from the resistance, (2) media exposure, and (3) the number of participants in the resistance. Casualties and media exposure can generate serious pressure on legitimacy, while the large number of people indicates the scope of resentment and the potential disruptive consequences. Hence, a combination of casualties with media exposure or with a large number of participants is very likely to invite intervention from the central government.

Conversely, the central government is very unlikely to intervene in disputes that are peaceful and small scale simply because the pressure for intervention is small. The central government may also fail to intervene in some large-scale incidents because of the political costs incurred from the necessity of disciplining local governments or their officials. Punishing local officials, especially high-ranking ones, can be a complex political issue. Specifically, the central government is less willing to intervene in cases that involve high-ranking local officials (for example, at the provincial level), as opposed to low-ranking local officials (for example, at the township or county levels).[46]

These conditions for the central government's intervention affect the local governments' responses. When facing intervention or a threat of intervention from the central government, local governments will have to use concessions or concessions with discipline to stop citizens' resistance quickly. However, in the absence of intervention or when the likelihood of intervention is negligibly small, local governments assume considerable autonomy in choosing the mode of response. Concessions will be difficult if (1) the local government faces high economic or political costs; and (2) partial concessions or tolerance results in persistent resistance which threatens social stability or local leaders' images. In these circumstances, repression is a low-cost option, but the local government will also take the blame for repression.

DEALING WITH POPULAR RESISTANCE IN CHINA

To examine how the government deals with popular resistance is largely to examine the outcomes of the resistance. Popular resistance in China has received much academic attention in recent years,[47] but how the government at each level responds to it has not been adequately examined. This is largely because cases of collective resistance are rarely reported in a way that makes systematic comparisons feasible. To reduce this problem, this research tries to tap as many sources as possible, which is achievable due to the increase of reports in and outside China. This study is based on a collection of seventy-eight cases (see Table 2). A basic criterion for including a case is that there should be information about the outcome (i.e., whether or not the protesters' demands were met and how the

[46] Li Zhilun, 'Strengthening the Discipline of Party Members and Governance and Doing a Good Job of Enforcing Anticorruption Measures', *China Discipline Inspection*, 4 (2000), 5–7.

[47] See, among others, O'Brien and Li, *Rightful Resistance in Rural China*, chap. 2; Yongshun Cai, *State and Laid-Off Workers in Reform China: The Silence and Collective Action of the Retrenched* (London: Routledge, 2006), chap. 7; Bernstein and Lu, *Taxation without Representation in Contemporary Rural China*, chap. 5; Elizabeth Perry and Mark Seldon, eds, *Chinese Society: Change, Conflict and Resistance*, 2nd edn (New York: Routledge, 2003).

TABLE 2 *Number of Cases Collected*

	Number		Number
Modes of action		*Results of action*	
Petitions	29	Concessions	10
Protests/demonstration	17	Concessions with discipline	10
Confrontations	17	Repression	54
Attacks on state agencies	15	Tolerance	4
Total	78	Total	78
Intervention by		*Punishment (people)*	
The central government	5	Detained	308
Provincial authority only	10	Arrested	21
None	63	Sentenced to jail	255
Total	78	Total	584

Source: Author's collection.

government dealt with the participants, see Appendix).[48] Certainly, this number does not allow us to draw conclusions on the frequency of successful resistance or the frequency of repression in China. Nonetheless, our collection includes cases that occurred in twenty-one provinces between 1995 and 2006, and they do shed light on the state's response to popular resistance.

Our data provide evidence for the rationale behind government response analysed in the earlier section. They show that the outcome of popular resistance is largely determined by the cost of concessions and the forcefulness of resistance. For analytical convenience, we divide participants' claims into high-cost demands and low-cost demands. A demand is seen as costly to meet if it creates a zero-sum game between the government and protesters in the sense that the protesters' gain is the government's loss (i.e., economic or political cost); otherwise, a demand is seen as less costly to meet (for example, addressing citizen grievances caused by a third party). The political hierarchy in China implies that intervention or the threat of intervention from the central authorities remains the most serious constraint on local governments or a crucial condition for successful resistance.[49] Based on the three conditions for intervention discussed earlier, we see an action as forceful if it has more than 500 participants, involves casualties or receives media coverage; otherwise, an action is seen as less forceful.[50]

As Figure 1 shows, repression is most likely to be used when the demands are costly while the resistance is not forceful. Of the forty-two cases of less forceful resistance with high-cost demands, forty were repressed. By comparison, concessions or concessions with discipline are commonly used to deal with forceful resistance. Only three of the twenty instances of forceful resistance were repressed. Yet, success in resistance with high-cost

[48] It must be acknowledged that this criterion for case collection has a limitation because cases whose results were not reported were excluded. This is also the reason why our collection only includes four cases that were tolerated or ignored by local governments.

[49] O'Brien and Li, *Rightful Resistance in Rural China*, chap. 2; Bernstein and Lu, *Taxation without Representation in Contemporary Rural China*, chap. 5.

[50] According to the police department, a collective action involving more than 500 is seen as a large-scale action, and an action involving more than 1,000 participants is seen as an especially large-scale action (see Chen Jinsheng, *Research Report on Instances of Collective Action* (Beijing: Mass Press, 2004), p. 32).

Cost of concessions	Forcefulness of Action: Forceful	Forcefulness of Action: Not Forceful
Low	a. Concessions (5)* b. Repression c. Tolerance	a. Concessions (2) b. Repression (6) c. Tolerance (3)
High	a. Concessions (12)† b. Repression (3) c. Tolerance	a. Concessions (1) b. Repression (40) c. Tolerance (1)

Fig. 1. State response to popular resistance

Notes: *Including two cases of concessions with discipline; †Including eight cases of concessions with discipline; $N = 73$; five cases were excluded because they did not have clear demands.

demands can be costly because the local government commonly uses concessions with discipline to deal with such incidents. Our data thus reveal local governments' constraints and autonomy in dealing with popular resistance. By demonstrating the circumstances under which concessions and repression are used by local governments, the remainder of this section examines how the political arrangement has helped to maintain social stability in China while protecting the central government's legitimacy.

Intervention from the Central Government and Concessions

Among the seventy-eight cases we collected, local governments made concessions or concessions with discipline in eleven of the twenty successful cases because of the intervention from the central government (five cases) or provincial governments (six cases). Those cases also show that the intervention is highly conditional or selective. Usually, once the central government has decided to intervene, it has to make concessions to citizens and sometimes punish malfeasant agents to show 'how your sins have provoked the wrath of the fanatics and have brought this punishment upon yourselves'.[51] The central government tends to intervene when the pressure of regime legitimacy mounts, especially after media exposure.

For example, in Jiahe county in Hunan province, the local governments carried out housing demolition in 2003 without providing reasonable compensation to the homeowners and arrested three people who resisted. After Chinese Central Television disclosed the case, the central government sent a team to the county. In the end, the homeowners received more compensation and the three people were released. Four officials, including the county party secretary and the county magistrate, were removed and a fifth was given party discipline.[52]

At other times, popular resistance invites intervention when protesters pressure the legitimacy of the central government with innovative tactics. In Linquan county in Anhui province, the government imposed heavy taxes and fees on the already poor peasants by ignoring the central government's regulations.[53] From 1992 to 1995, peasants from a village made repeated but fruitless appeals to state authorities at the central and local levels.

[51] Gamson, *The Strategy of Social Protest*, p. 82.
[52] *Southern Urban News*, 6 June 2004, p. 2.
[53] Chen Guidi and Chun Tao, *Survey of Chinese Peasants* (Beijing: People's Literature Press, 2003), pp. 82–120.

Two peasant leaders were sentenced to jail for the petitions. Under the leadership of one peasant who was released from the prison, seventy-four peasants went to Beijing to make another desperate appeal. On Sunday 29 October 1995, the seventy-four peasants went to Tiananmen Square one after another to avoid being noticed as a group. After all of them had arrived, they suddenly knelt down. Their action immediately attracted attention from the central government, which required the local officials from Anhui to travel to Beijing that night. The peasants' problems were addressed and the county party secretary was transferred.

The central government may also intervene because the scale of resistance is too large to ignore and the resistance involves casualties. In October 2004, about 100,000 peasants in Hanyuan, a county in Sichuan province, protested against low compensation for the loss of farmland and homes due to the construction of a dam. After repeated but fruitless petitions to higher-level authorities, tens of thousands of peasants approached the construction site on the night of 27 October 2004 to stop the construction. The government sent about 1,500 police officers to maintain order. Violent confrontations occurred between the peasants and the police officers, resulting in the deaths of both citizens and police officers. Given the vast number of peasants, the local government sent more than 10,000 militiamen to help establish order. Reportedly, the provincial party secretary who went to the site to address the problem was surrounded by the peasants for hours. When the central government learned of the news, it sent a work team headed by a leader of the State Council to the county. The team announced the central government's decision that the event was a 'large-scale gathering of migrants who did not know the truth about the cause of confrontation' (i.e., exempting the responsibility of most participants). Meanwhile, the provincial government promised to increase the compensation and to have their homes relocated. A deputy city mayor who had been promoted from being the county's party secretary, together with at least seven senior county officials, was detained on charges of corruption. The county's party secretary was also removed.[54]

These cases show that local officials who abuse power may face serious consequences. An intervention by the central government can both enhance regime legitimacy and warn local officials against the abuse of power. Such concessions are, however, conditional. The central government faces costs when the intervention leads to the punishment of local officials. In the above cases in Jiahe, Linquan and Hanyuan, the highest-level officials who were disciplined were county-level officials who were in the low rungs of the political hierarchy. When high-ranking local officials are involved in a dispute or its settlement, the central government is less willing to intervene.[55] In these circumstances, the central government would reduce the damage to its image and regime legitimacy by prohibiting the media from covering the cases.

In December 2005, a bloody confrontation occurred in Dongzhou, a village in Shanwei city in Guangdong province. In this village, the city government built a power plant that occupied a plot of land. The villagers complained about inadequate compensation for the land and pollution of their water. A deadly confrontation between villagers and police officers occurred on 6 December during which, according to the official account, three peasants were killed and eight were wounded. Shooting unarmed citizens has been very

[54] *South China Morning Post*, 4 January 2005, p. 4.

[55] In several legal cases, the central government knew the problems but refused to intervene because those cases involved some provincial leaders (*21st Century Global Report*, 2 March 2003, p. 1).

rare in China since 1989, but only the deputy head of the city public security bureau was given administrative discipline. The central government kept a very low profile in this case. It was not until 10 December that the Xinhua News Agency released a short news piece on this event, accusing a few peasants of inciting the riot. The central government sent a team to the province (but not to the village), and it apparently accepted the explanation of the local government, which blamed a few peasants for the confrontation. It is not very clear why the central government did not punish any other local official in this case. One very likely reason is that provincial leaders in Guangdong had directly intervened in the settlement of this case. The shooting occurred on 6 December. The provincial party secretary went to the village the next day. The provincial party secretary was a member of the politburo, the paramount party body in China, and his views might have had to be respected even by the central authorities. The brief news released by the Xinhua News Agency on 10 December was provided by the local government. Hence, even if the central government found that the released report was flawed, it would be almost impossible for it to change the statement later.[56]

The central government's intervention is not only conditional but also limited in that it does not intervene in local governments' punishment of some participants, especially in drastic actions, after concessions are made. This is understandable because unconditional concessions will make the local government vulnerable. Tarrow writes, 'One of the most remarkable characteristics of collective action is that it expands the opportunities of others. Protesting groups put issues on the agenda with which other people identify and demonstrate the utility of collective action that others can copy or innovate upon.'[57] By punishing certain participants, the local government shows that a victory can be very costly, thereby reducing the encouraging effect. In the Hanyuan case, the county and city government imposed serious punishment on some participants *ex post*. In 2005, twenty-eight participants were tried in local courts and found guilty, and one was executed on the charge of killing a police officer.[58] In the Linquan and Jiahe cases, participants were jailed before intervention from the central government.

Intervention from the Provincial Authority and Concessions

The above discussion does not mean that citizens will always fail without intervention from the central government. The local government's worry about a possible intervention from the central government may also lead to concessions. Most conflicts between citizens and the government in China have been caused by grassroots governments or their agencies, especially at the county level.[59] The highest-level local authority in a place is the provincial-level authority. Hence, an intervention from the provincial government is the most important way for citizens to have their voices heard in the absence of attention

[56] After the bloody confrontation, the city government exercised strict control over the village, preventing a free flow of information between villagers and external parties for months. Police searched for and arrested those who had participated in the riots. Not surprisingly, this incident was not allowed to be reported in the country (*South China Morning Post*, 12 December 2005, p. 4; *South China Morning Post*, 3 March 2006, p. 6).

[57] Tarrow, *Power in Movement*, p. 97.

[58] *Yan'an Daily*, 27 March 2006, p. 4

[59] Xie Li, 'An Analysis of Administrative Reconsiderations in the Country in 2000', *Administration and Law*, 6 (2001), 18–19.

from the central government.[60] Those factors (i.e., casualties, media exposure and number of participants) that affect the central government's intervention also shape the provincial authority's reaction. When a serious confrontation occurs in a place, the provincial government will naturally react because its response is likely to be interpreted by the central government as the local leaders' ability to govern. In addition, as regulated, serious confrontations should be reported to the pertinent central authorities within a regulated period of time (for example, two hours).[61] If such cases are disclosed in the media or are reported to the central government, provincial leaders will be under pressure to solve the conflict as soon as possible. They may, therefore, punish those officials deemed responsible for the confrontation in order not to disappoint the central government.

In one case in Dingzhou city (i.e., at the county administrative level) in Hebei province, the local government constructed a power plant, and the plant needed a piece of land from a village to store the coal ash from it.[62] The construction of the ash-storage facility was contracted to a businessman who received strong support from the local government. In March 2004, when villagers learned that they had been seriously under-compensated, they began to make petitions to different levels of authorities but were ignored. A few villagers were sentenced to jail for their resistance. Before July 2004, the city government and the contractor made more than ten attempts to construct the ash-storage facility with force by sending police officers to the site, but they met the strong resistance of the peasants. The peasants then built dozens of tents on the land to prevent the construction, with 100 to 200 villagers on duty each night. Such peasant resistance upset the local government and the contractor. In the early morning of 11 June 2005, more than 300 thugs suddenly attacked the peasants who were sleeping in the tents, killing six peasants and wounding another forty-eight. One peasant managed to videotape the fighting at the cost of a broken arm. The five-minute footage was later shown on the internet as well as by foreign television networks.

The casualties and media coverage generated serious pressure on the local authorities, including the provincial government. The provincial public security bureau immediately formed a taskforce to solve the case, and it found that the contractor had hired the thugs. On 13 June 2005, two days after the event, the provincial authority in Hebei removed the city party secretary and the mayor. In December, twenty-seven suspects were tried. Four suspects who organized the attack were sentenced to death, three were sentenced to the death penalty with a reprieve, and another six, including the party secretary and the contractor, were sentenced to life imprisonment. The party secretary was accused of participating in the planning of the attack (their plan was not to inflict fatal injuries on the villagers). The provincial government also decided not to use the village's land for the project.[63]

Nevertheless, whether or not the provincial authority will intervene and how it will intervene in a confrontation are also conditional. The provincial authority may not intervene or only intervene in a symbolic way if it believes that doing this will not draw blame from the central authorities as in the Shanwei case. In addition, as provincial leaders punish malfeasant officials mainly because they want to distance themselves from those

[60] In addition, because the top leaders (i.e., the party secretary and the magistrate) in a county are directly under the management of the provincial authority, these leaders will not be effectively disciplined without intervention from the provincial authority.

[61] Chen, *Research Report on Instances of Collective Action*, pp. 275–97.

[62] *China Economic Times*, 20 June 2005, p. 3.

[63] *Overseas Chinese News*, 16 December 2005, p. 2.

officials, they do not have an incentive to prevent lower-level officials from punishing certain participants who are believed to have damaged the image of local authorities, including the provincial government. The provincial government may even require local governments to punish certain participants. Therefore, it is common for both local officials and some participants to be punished when serious confrontations occur. Of the seventy-eight cases we collected, the provincial authorities intervened in ten cases, and participants were detained, arrested or put in jail in eight of them.

In a high-profile case in Zhejiang province, peasants succeeded in forcing local governments to accept their demands but paid a high cost. The government in Dongyang, a county-level city, set up an industrial park in one of its townships in 2001. The chemical factories in the park produced serious pollutants that threatened the villagers' health and damaged their farmland. The villagers appealed to the local and central authorities repeatedly, but to no effect. In 2001, more than ten villagers were arrested by the local government for their assault on the factories in the park. After four years of fruitless efforts, the villagers built tents at the industrial park's entrance in 2005. For two weeks in March and April 2005, about 200 elderly villagers lived in the tents to keep a 24-hour vigil to block the entrance to the industrial park. In the early morning of 10 April 2005, the city government organized about 3,500 police officers and government officials to disperse the villagers and dismantle the tents. With a rumour flying around that two elderly women had been killed in the confrontation (reportedly, nobody was killed), thousands of angry villagers clashed with the police and government officials, beating them and smashing dozens of cars and buses that had ferried the police officers and officials. Local officials and police did not dare to use more force and ran away.[64]

After the confrontation, the local government was eager to end the situation, and six of the thirteen factories were ordered to move out of the township for good. The provincial authority imposed serious punishment on the major local officials deemed responsible for the event. The former city party secretary, who had been promoted as the head of the propaganda department of the higher-level city party committee, was removed from his position. The deputy city party secretary, who was also the mayor, was removed from both positions, and the township party secretary was also removed. Another five officials, including a deputy mayor, were given administrative discipline.[65] The peasants, however, also paid a high price. Eight peasants were given sentences of between eight months and five years in jail. One official said to them, 'If you're not guilty, then the government is. And the government cannot be guilty'. As a result, the case of Huaxi illustrates that 'even when farmers win, they lose'.[66]

Local Governments' Autonomy and Repression

While intervention from above does not always entirely favour citizens who stage resistance, their chance of success is significantly reduced if there is no such intervention at all. Given the conditions for intervention from above discussed earlier, most cases of citizens' resistance will not trigger intervention from above. First, most instances of

[64] In the end, more than 140 people were sent to hospitals, a majority of them police officers and government officials, including a deputy city mayor (*South China Morning Post*, 3 March 2006, p. 2).

[65] The other four were the head and two deputy heads of the environmental protection bureau and the township head (*Jinhua Daily*, 1 January 2006, p. 1).

[66] *South China Morning Post*, 3 March 2006, p. 2.

resistance tend to be peaceful and do not involve serious casualties because the use of violence is not a common option on the part of citizens.[67] What Tarrow writes is also true in China: 'Where violence occurs or is even likely, this gives authorities a mandate for repression and turns non-violent sympathizers away.'[68] As discussed below, citizens' use of violence justifies local governments' repression and increases the risks for themselves.

Secondly, citizens' disruptive actions make sensitive news, and such stories are rarely reported in the media within China before they end. Thirdly, most instances are relatively small scale. The numbers of participants in disruptive actions range from dozens to tens of thousands in China. An account of about 3,600 instances that occurred in six provinces shows that the average number of participants was eighty-one.[69] Nationwide, about 730,000 people participated in 8,700 instances of collective action in 1993, or on average eighty-four in each; in 2004, about 3.76 million people participated in 74,000 instances of collective action, or an average of fifty-one in each.[70]

According to the police department, an action with more than 500 participants is regarded as a large-scale action, and an action with more than 1,000 participants is an especially large-scale one.[71] If this criterion is used, most instances of collective action in China are small scale. Since 1994, collective actions with 100 or more participants have not exceeded 16 per cent of the total number of instances, and it was 12 per cent out of 58,500 in 2003.[72] An account of 1,117 instances of social unrest shows that cases with more than 500 participants accounted for 7 per cent, and those cases with more than 1,000 participants accounted for 2.2 per cent, whereas those cases involving less than 100 participants accounted for 76 per cent.[73] Despite these facts, the actual number of large-scale actions is not small. Nationwide, the number of instances with 100 or more participants in each increased from 1,400 in 1994 to 7,000 in 2003.[74] However, it is impossible for the central and provincial governments to intervene in most of these cases. Therefore, local governments at the county and city levels, which handle the most incidents of resistance, assume significant autonomy.

The Rationale Behind Repression

As mentioned earlier, local governments in China do not have to use repression if concessions are not costly. For example, existing research on worker resistance to economic restructuring finds that some unpaid workers succeeded in receiving some allowance by approaching the government.[75] Nevertheless, repression does remain an important option, which suggests that popular resistance can be costly. In the seventy-eight cases we collected, 255 people were sentenced to jail for up to fifteen years, and one was

[67] Cai, *State and Laid-Off Workers in Reform China*, p. 95.

[68] Tarrow, *Power in Movement*, p. 104.

[69] Chen, *Research Report on Instances of Collective Action*, pp. 63–4.

[70] He, 'Properly Handling Conflicts in Our Country', p. 9.

[71] Chen, *Research Report on Instances of Collective Action*, p. 32.

[72] It was 13.6 per cent (out of 10,000) in 1994 and 14.5 per cent (out of 30,000) in 2000 (He, 'Properly Handling Conflicts in Our Country', p. 10).

[73] Chen, *Research Report on Instances of Collective Action*, p. 62.

[74] He, 'Properly Handling Conflicts in Our Country', p. 9.

[75] Ching Kwan Lee, 'The "Revenge of History": Collective Memories and Labor Protests in Northeastern China', *Ethnography*, 1 (2000), 217–37.

sentenced to death. Another 308 were detained, and twenty-one were arrested, some of whom were later tried in courts and were likely to be sentenced to jail.

The cases we collected suggest several reasons for the use of repression. One is the cost of concessions. Popular resistance is likely to be suppressed when the participants' demands are regarded as difficult to meet (see Figure 1). In our collection, forty-two of the seventy-eight cases concerned economic demands. However, not all economic demands are easy to meet. For example, twenty of the forty-two cases concerned disputes over land use in rural China, predominantly, the non-agricultural use of farmland. An official in the Ministry of Land and Resources said in 2006, 'Almost all the serious law violations in land use involve the government or leaders'.[76] As local governments tend to reap benefits using farmland for non-agricultural activities, they are reluctant to pay peasants adequately. Repression becomes their common option when farmers resist.

Secondly, repression is used because citizens' resistance threatens the image or authority of local governments or local leaders. Take collective petitions as an example. Participants were punished in nineteen of the twenty-nine petition cases we collected. In one case in Gansu province in 2005, more than 200 villagers appealed to the county government for the release of a person who provided legal advice to the villagers in a land dispute. However, the petitioners were accused of attacking state agencies, though they did not even enter the office compound. Eleven petitioners were sentenced to jail for up to five and a half years.[77]

Sometimes, petitioners who have a high stake in their action refuse to give up their resistance easily. Yet, when their resistance becomes persistent, local governments are upset because such resistance may escalate into more disruptive actions or be directed to upper-level authorities. In twelve of the nineteen cases, citizens were punished because they made repeated petitions. In one case in Hebei province in 2000, three villagers were sentenced to jail for up to five years because they led villagers to appeal to the city government repeatedly for a solution to a land dispute.[78] Local governments are especially reluctant to see their local people present petitions to provincial or central authorities. In five cases, the participants were punished because they appealed to the central and provincial authorities in an 'unacceptable' way. In one case, five petitioners from Shanxi province went to the central authorities in Beijing in 2005 but were accused of violating the rules. All of them were ruled guilty in the local court in Shanxi and were sentenced to jail for three to five and a half years.[79] A provincial-level official thus said, 'Protection of and sympathy for petitioners is possible only to a limited extent. Arresting petitioners often reflects the will of the major party and government leaders'.[80]

Thirdly, repression is used because the political risk is small. Most incidents of resistance are not forceful enough to deter repression. While intervention from above is an important condition for successful resistance, it was absent in sixty-three of the seventy-eight cases we collected. Nationwide, the percentage of the cases ignored by the central and provincial governments could be much larger. The lack of intervention has to do with the scale of resistance, which partly indicates its forcefulness. In the fifty-six failed cases (excluding two riots) we collected, only in two cases did the number of participants reach 1,000. Local

[76] *New Beijing Post*, 16 April 2006, p. 2.
[77] *Western Business News*, 9 February 2006, p. 2.
[78] *China Youth Daily*, 31 August 2001, p. 3.
[79] *Shanxi Daily*, 13 September 2005, p. 1.
[80] Li Junde, 'Is Petitioning A Crime?' *Perspective*, 7 April 2003, pp. 25–6.

governments made concessions without intervention from above in nine of the twenty successful cases. In four of the nine cases, the number of participants exceeded 5,000. In another four cases, the number of participants ranged from 1,000 to more than 3,000. The final case was a small-scale one in which more than 200 villagers appealed to the city government, complaining about the corruption of their village party secretary. These cases do not mean that small-scale resistance never succeeds, but its chance is much smaller because both the central and local governments feel less pressure.[81]

The risks from repression are reduced also because pertinent laws provide convenient bases for local governments to punish certain participants who are commonly accused of 'holding illegal assemblies and demonstrations', 'inciting the masses to attack a government agency', 'inciting the masses to disrupt social order', or 'assembling a crowd to disrupt traffic'. For example, according to criminal law, those who organize the masses to attack state agencies can be sentenced to up to ten years in prison. In addition, a collective petition to the government with more than five participants is also illegal. Participants who intend to form independent organizations or have connections with overseas organizations may be accused of 'subverting the government', which is a political crime. Whether or not popular resistance violates the law can be subject to the interpretation of the local government.

Certainly, some participants have been punished because their behaviour seriously violated the law and caused damage. In a district in Guangdong province, a few villagers who had conflicts with the township government, together with students who were resentful about the high tuition fees, held a demonstration in February 2001, which also attracted other participants. After they had marched to the township government, the demonstration turned into a riot. The participants attacked the township government, burned down 107 rooms and took more than twenty motorcycles and other property belonging to government employees. As a result, twenty-three participants were punished, with one sentenced to jail for ten years, two sentenced to six years and another two sentenced to five years.[82] Repression is commonly used to deal with such riots.

Given local governments' autonomy, participants have to be cautious in choosing the mode of resistance in order to reduce the risks. As elsewhere, 'the non-violent demonstrators need more courage; the militants have to be wiser'.[83] In China, when violence occurs, it is rarely planned; instead, it is often triggered by factors that are not anticipated by the participants or the government. All the same, as mentioned earlier, many participants may still be punished for peaceful resistance because local governments have discretion to interpret their actions, especially when some actions are 'boundary-spanning'.[84]

In forty-nine of seventy-eight cases, participants resorted to protests, demonstrations, confrontations with officials or police officers or attacks on state agencies (as claimed by the government). In thirty-six cases (excluding the cases of concessions with discipline), the participants were punished. In one case in a county in the Guangxi Autonomous Region in 2005, more than 200 villagers approached the county authorities because of a dispute

[81] Xi Chen, 'Chinese Petitioners' Tactics and Their Efficacy' (paper presented at the Conference on Grassroots Political Reform in Contemporary China, Fairbank Center, Harvard University, October 2004).

[82] *Pingdingshan Daily*, 2 January 2002, p. 3.

[83] Donatella della Porta, 'Protest, Protesters, and Protest Policing: Public Discourses in Italy and Germany from the 1960s to the 1980s', in Marco Giugni, Doug McAdam and Charles Tilly, eds, *How Social Movements Matter* (Minneapolis: University of Minnesota Press, 1999), pp. 66–96, at p. 82.

[84] O'Brien, 'Neither Transgressive Nor Contained'.

over land ownership. They were accused of disrupting the social order and about 110 peasants were detained although they had not caused any damage. Eighty-two were released after each had paid between 2,000 to 8,000 yuan in bail, and ten were sent to labour camps for up to two years. Another seventeen were sentenced to jail for up to eight years. This case may not be typical, but it indicates the degree to which the local government can abuse its power.[85]

Such cases of repression have no doubt damaged the image of the local government. Nevertheless, the people may not blame the central or even the provincial government as much as they blame the local government because the former governments are not involved in the repression.[86] In forty-three of the seventy-eight cases in which some participants were put in jail, only in one case was the first trial conducted in a city court (i.e., two worker leaders in Liaoyang were accused of subverting the government), whereas all the other cases were tried in county-level courts. This implies that almost all the lawsuits (i.e., forty-two cases) against the participants were filed by state authorities at the county level or lower. Hence, it may not be an exaggeration to state that the repression in most instances has been carried out without the knowledge of the central government. Although Chinese citizens' trust in the central government easily tends to disappear after they have made fruitless appeals to the central authorities,[87] it is very likely that participants in most of the tens of thousands of cases have not appealed to the central government before they fail or are repressed. Yet, the central government will face a serious problem if an increasingly large number of citizens realize that it is unwilling or unable to address their grievances.

CONCLUSION

Unlike most transitional economies, China is simultaneously undergoing market reforms, socio-economic transformation and urbanization. The society is replete with conflicts and citizens' resistance. In the pre-reform period, mass movements (such as the Cultural Revolution) were initiated by the party-state or top leaders, and they could be stopped when the elite decided to do so. In comparison, during the reform period, citizens undertake incidents of resistance based on their own interests. Therefore, how to manage social conflict is a serious issue faced by the Chinese party-state. Economic development can be a solution to some of the problems that have triggered resistance, but it is far from adequate. As some of the cases presented in this article have shown, certain modes of development (such as the occupation of farmland, privatization and pollution) have caused conflicts directly.

This article demonstrates that the power structure within the Chinese political system adds significant resilience to the regime in addressing social conflicts by granting conditional autonomy to local governments. Decentralization in China has institutionalized the strong power of local governments, but local officials also have to fulfil assigned responsibilities. This political arrangement has important implications for the management of citizen resistance. One is that it affects the regime's legitimacy. Kuran shows that the sudden collapse of socialist regimes in Eastern Europe has to do with citizens who chose to pursue their true preferences when opportunities (for example, crises) arose, with these

85 *Takungbao*, 20 January 2006, p. 4.
86 Lianjiang Li, 'Political Trust in Rural China', *Modern China*, 30 (2003), 228–58.
87 Yu Jianrong, 'Criticisms of the Petition System in China', *China Reform*, 2 (2005), 26–8.

true preferences differing from what the governments desired because the regimes had lost legitimacy.[88]

In China, decentralization helps to protect the legitimacy of the central government and the regime in two ways. First, the decentralized power structure allows the central government to distance itself from blame-generating situations when local governments use repression, which is a basic method of avoiding blame or protecting legitimacy.[89] Moreover, when large-scale incidents or incidents involving casualties occur, the central government's intervention shifts the responsibility and blame to local governments. This arrangement also allows the central government to '*pretend*' not to know of the repression when it does not want to intervene. Secondly, given that local governments assume considerable power and autonomy, there can be variation in their attitudes towards disgruntled citizens. Such variation may reduce citizens' blame of the political system (i.e., they attribute the problems to their local governments), and citizens' perceptions of the regime's legitimacy may vary across the country.[90]

Divided state power also promotes the regime's resilience by improving information flow. Reliance on repression makes the government less sensitive to citizens' problems and complaints, which further damages the regime's legitimacy.[91] In China, by tolerating resistance from citizens that does not threaten the regime, the central government is better informed about the social situation and the sources of citizens' grievances,[92] which allows the party-state to address some of the problems to protect its legitimacy. Therefore, popular resistance in China has not only helped to force the central government to strengthen the implementation of policies favouring citizens but has also contributed to the adjustment of national policies disfavouring citizens.[93]

However, local governments' autonomy and power also prevents what can be called 'flabby flexibility' or 'lack of discipline'.[94] Local governments' power determines that citizens' resistance in China is short lived, often isolated and does not challenge the regime. Unlike the communist government in Poland, both the central and local governments in China are intolerant of organized resistance. Therefore, the many instances of resistance by different groups of people who have been affected by the reform or socio-economic changes remain largely unconnected in China.[95] If effective challenges to a regime are made possible often by the presence of organizational networks that can mobilize participants,[96] what happened in communist Poland (i.e., regime-threatening resistance)

[88] Kuran, 'Now Out of Never'.

[89] Weaver, 'The Politics of Blame Avoidance'.

[90] See, for example, Jie Chen, *Popular Political Support in Urban China* (Palo Alto, Calif.: Stanford University Press, 2004).

[91] In the former East Germany, the populace was by and large discontented with its standard of living and lack of political freedom, and it grew increasingly so in the period 1975–89. However, there had been little action taken until 1989 because the violent suppression of the 1953 mass uprising with the help of Soviet military forces rendered the cost of anti-regime protest prohibitive for all but a small minority. Nonetheless, repression also led the people to lose confidence in the communist system. See Lohmann, 'The Dynamics of Information Cascades'.

[92] O'Brien and Li, *Rightful Resistance in Rural China*, chap. 2.

[93] Chen and Chun, *Survey of Chinese Peasants*; Bernstein and Lu, *Taxation without Representation in Contemporary Rural China*.

[94] Barghoon, *Politics in Russia*, p. 308.

[95] Bernstein and Lu, *Taxation without Representation in Contemporary Rural China*, chap. 5.

[96] McAdam, *Political Process and the Development of Black Insurgency, 1930–70*; Tilly, *From Mobilization to Revolution*.

is unlikely to take place in China at least in the near future. The reason is simple: 'when threats [from the government] occur without a preexisting organizational infrastructure, they will likely deter challengers from sustained contention'.[97]

Nevertheless, given the multiple levels of authority in China, resistance is likely to persist as long as citizen rights are violated, and the central government is constrained by regime legitimacy. Tensions between citizens' intentions to protect their rights and the limited political space will continue to serve as an important driving force for the party-state to institutionalize state–citizen interactions by restraining its power and getting 'the struggle off the streets and into the courts'.[98]

APPENDIX: DATA COLLECTION

The data used in this study were collected from several sources. Forty-nine of the seventy-eight cases were collected from formal publications (i.e., permitted by the government) in China, and sixteen were collected from government websites or government-permitted sources. The remaining thirteen cases were collected from the author's fieldwork in China and overseas media.

Sources

Petitions (twenty-nine cases). Chen Guidi and Chun Tao, *Zhongguo nonmin diaocha* (Beijing: Renmin wenxu chubanshe, 2004), pp. 82–120; *Shenzhen Yearbook 1998*, p. 209; *Fazhi ribao*, 2 December 2000; *Zhongguo qingnian bao*, 31 August 2001; *Fazhi ribao*, 3 July 2000; Lian Xinqiao, 'Miandui baimin jifang qunzhong', *Minqing yu xinfang*, no. 5 (2001), p. 24; The Research Group, *Zhongguo zhuanxingqi quntixing tufashijian duice yanjiu* (Research on measures to deal with mass incidents) (Beijing: Xueyuan chubanshe, 2003), p. 316; <http://news3.xinhuanet.com/focus/2003–04/16/content_833579.htm>, accessed 21 March 2006; *Zhongguo jingji shibao*, 2 January 2003; *Beijng yule xinbao*, 7 January 2004; Philip P. Pan, *Washington Post*, 7 August 2004; Li Li, 'Baimin qunzhong jifang, fasheng zai huanjie xuanju hou', *Minqing yu xinfang*, no. 11 (2003), pp. 16–17; *Shengyang wanbao*, 22 October 2004; <http://www.sd. xinhuanet.com/news/2005–08/17/content_4902146.htm>, accessed 21 March 2006; *Shaanxi ribao*, 13 September 2005; *Huashangbao*, 19 January 2006; *Jinhua ribao*, 14 March 2006; *Huashangbao*, 19 January 2006; *Lanzhou chenbao*, 31 December 2005; *Shanxi fazhibao*, 24 November 2004; <http://www.pingyin.cn/2006/4–12/100111 755 72.html>, accessed 22 April 2006; <http://www.yinzi.cn/sx/ShangLuo/news/2006/03/1910031421.html>, accessed 25 March 2006; *Nanyang ribao*, 20 April 2006; *Jinghua shibao* (Jinghua Times), 9 March 2005; Yongshun Cai, *State and Laid-off Workers in Reform China: The Silence and Collective Action of the Retrenched* (London: Routledge, 2006), pp. 96–9; *Mingpao*, 7 March 2001; interviews with the author held in China in November 2005.

Protests (seventeen cases). 'We want to eat', *Far Eastern Economic Review*, 160 (26 June 1997); <http://dailynews.sina.com.cn/s/143443.html>, accessed 4 February 2006; *Nanfang ribao*, 27 July 2000; *Jinhua ribao*, 12 June 2001; <http://jcy.bjtzh.gov.cn/gzdt/jcyw/jcyw (03) 09.htm>, accessed 2 April 2006; Eric Eckholm, 'Where workers, too, rust, bitterness boils', *New York Times*, 20 March 2002; *Beijng yule xinbao*, 7 January 2004; *Nanfang duoshi bao*, 18 May 2004; *Nanfang duoshi bao*, 18 May 2004; <http://www.cq. chinanews. com.cn/newsview.asp? nid = 52739>, accessed 2 April 2006; *Fazhi ribao*, 5 September 2004; Kathy Chen, 'Chinese protests grow more frequent, violent', *Wall Street Journal*, 5 November 2004; *Yin zhoukan*, 14 October 2004; Tang Jianguang, 'Ningxia Yinchuan chuzuche tingyun fengbo' (The incident of the taxi drivers' strike in Yinchuan of Ningxia), *Xinwen zhoukan* (Newsweekly), 8 September 2004, pp. 11–13; <http://www.lawyer-china.com/comhom/stilaw/791.asp>, accessed 5 March 2006; <http://news.sdinfo.net/72340168526266368/20010430/18722.shtml>, accessed 22 March 2006; *Shenzhen shangbao*, 5 April 2006.

[97] Almeida, 'Opportunity Organizations and Threat-Induced Contention', pp. 387–8.

[98] Samuel Huntington, *Political Order in Changing Societies* (New Haven, Conn.: Yale University Press, 1968), p. 359.

Confrontations (seventeen cases). Qin Guolin, Chen Hong and Shi Dezhou, 'Qian ren jifang', *Minqing yu xinfang*, no. 3 (2002), pp. 40–1; Dai Gang, 'Hongjiang quntixing shijian chuzhi yinfa de xikao', *Gongan yanjiu*, no. 7 (2001), pp. 65–8; < http://www.qtfy.gov.cn/show.asp?id = 320 >, accessed 3 March 2006; < http://www.bbzy.org/detail.jsp?title >, accessed 2 April 2006; *Jinghua shibao*, 2 April 2006; Shi Jiangtao, 'Peasants in upstream fight to halt dam', *South China Morning Post*, 4 January 2005; Joseph Kahn, 'For China masses, an increasingly short fuse', *International Herald Tribune*, 31 December 2004; *Chizhou ribao*, 27 June 2005; < http://www. Longhui. net/news/local/200 405/14458.htm >, accessed 21 March 2006; < http://www.sjw.gov.cn/common/Show Info. aspx?id = 145942 >, accessed 2 March 2006; Edward Cody, 'For Chinese, peasant revolt is rare victory', *Washington Post*, 13 June 2005; *Takungpao*, 19 January 2006; Wang Keqin and Qiao Guodong, 'Hebei Dingzhou cunmin canlie duikang buming wuzhuang xiji an diaocha' (An investigation of the armed attack on the villagers in Dingzhou in Hebei province), *Zhongguo Jingji shibao* (China Economic Times), 20 June 2005; Minnie Chan, 'Shanwei villagers seethe at ill-treatment in land grab', *South China Morning Post*, 3 March 2006; *Mingpo*, 13 October 2006; Howard French, 'Anger in China rises over threat to environment', *New York Times*, 19 July 2005; Yu Jianrong, 'Nongmin youzuzhi kangzhen jiqi fenxian', *Zhanlu yu guanli*, 3 (2003), 1–16; reports from district courts.

Attacks (fifteen cases). Nanfang ribao, 28 August 2000; *Nanfang dushi bao*, 24 November 1999; *Jiancha ribao*, 11 June 2001; *Beijing wanbao*, 5 January 2003; *Beijng yule xinbao*, 17 January 2005; *Chengdu shangbao*, 2 November 2004; *Sanqin dushi bao*, 29 October 2004; *Yangzhi wanbao*, 10 May 2005; *Wuhan Wanbao*, 27 September 2005; *Xibu shangbao*, 9 February 2006; < http://www.investchina.com.cn/chinese/law/92993.htm >, accessed 15 April 2006; *Chende ribao*, 21 October 2003; < http://hnfy.chinacourt.org/public/detail.php?id = 50328 >, accessed 27 March 2006; *Jiancha ribao*, 19 December 2005; < http://www.lz160.net/show news.asp?new_id = 3905 >, accessed 10 April 2006.

[28]

RIGHTS CONSCIOUSNESS AND RULES CONSCIOUSNESS IN CONTEMPORARY CHINA

Lianjiang Li*

Rights claims by ordinary people in reform-era China have taken many different forms. Workers claim a right to "labor and subsistence", pensioners claim the "sacred right not to have to labor", and migrant workers claim the right to organize unions.[1] Farmers assert a right to refuse to pay the grain tax when a township breaches its responsibilities, a right to reject excessive fees and a right to elect village leaders.[2] Moreover, rights talk is not simply empty. In numerous cases, efforts to claim lawful rights have spurred disruptive protests. By 2003 "rights-defense activities" (*weiquan huodong* 维权活动), such as petitioning and demonstrating, had become so widespread that a Chinese commentator dubbed it "the Year of Citizenship Rights".[3]

Scholars, however, disagree about how to understand popular rights claims and the contention associated with them. Kevin O'Brien and Lianjiang Li suggest that farmers' claims about rights represent a nascent rights consciousness and that rightful resistance

---

* For helpful comments on earlier drafts, I would like to thank Susanne Brandstädter, Timothy Cheek, David Kelly, Andrew Kipnis, Pierre Landry, Melanie Manion, Andrew Mertha, Luigi Tomba, Linda Wong, two anonymous reviewers and especially Kevin O'Brien. Financial support for survey and post-survey fieldwork was provided by the Research Council of the Hong Kong Government and the South China Program of the Chinese University of Hong Kong.

1 Ching Kwan Lee, "From the Specter of Mao to the Spirit of the Law: Labor Insurgency in China", *Theory and Society*, Vol. 31, No. 2 (April 2002), p. 207; William Hurst and Kevin J. O'Brien, "China's Contentious Pensioners", *The China Quarterly*, No. 170 (June 2002), p. 351; Feng Chen, "Individual Rights and Collective Rights: Labor's Predicament in China", *Communist and Post-Communist Studies*, Vol. 40, No. 1 (March 2007), pp. 67-69.

2 Lianjiang Li and Kevin J. O'Brien, "Villagers and Popular Resistance in Contemporary China", *Modern China*, Vol. 22, No. 1 (January 1996), p. 41; Thomas P. Bernstein and Xiaobo Lü, *Taxation without Representation in Contemporary Rural China* (New York: Cambridge University Press, 2003); Kevin J. O'Brien, "Villagers, Elections, and Citizenship in Contemporary China", *Modern China*, Vol. 27, No. 4 (October 2001), pp. 407-35.

3 Wang Yi, "2003: gongmin quanli nian" (2003: The Year of Citizenship Rights), *Xinwen zhoukan* (China Newsweek), No. 47 (22 December 2003), pp. 20-21.

could "evolve into a more far-reaching counterhegemonic project".[4] Similarly, Merle Goldman argues that demands for popular rights "indicate a bottom-up claim to citizenship" which may precipitate "a fundamental breakthrough in state–society relations".[5] Elizabeth Perry, on the other hand, believes that what appears to be rights consciousness is instead a historically-familiar "rules consciousness". As Perry sees it, popular contention driven by rules consciousness implies no major challenge to the Party-state and can "undergird rather than undermine" the political system by providing "an effective check on the misbehavior of state authorities".[6]

This debate, which came to a head in two panels at the 2009 Association of Asian Studies meeting,[7] calls for a clearer definition of rules and rights consciousness along with tests that allow us to distinguish between the two. What is rules consciousness? What is rights consciousness? How can we tell one from the other? This paper conducts an analysis of claims about rights made by aggrieved workers and farmers to define rules consciousness. It then refines existing definitions of rights consciousness in light of Chinese political practice. To distinguish rules consciousness from rights consciousness, this paper uses survey data to illustrate how four types of claims by members of one social group—farmers—are related to trust in central and township leaders.

Rules Consciousness

Perry argues that the following statement by retired workers from Anyuan reflects rules consciousness:

---

4 Lianjiang Li and Kevin J. O'Brien, "Villagers and Popular Resistance", p. 55; Kevin J. O'Brien and Lianjiang Li, *Rightful Resistance in Rural China* (New York: Cambridge University Press, 2006), pp. 121-26.

5 Merle Goldman, *Political Rights in Post-Mao China* (Ann Arbor: Association for Asian Studies, 2007), pp. 71ff. For similar arguments, see Benjamin L. Liebman, "Class Action Litigation in China", *Harvard Law Review*, Vol. 111, No. 6 (April 1998), pp. 1523-41; David Zweig, "The Externalities of Development: Can New Political Institutions Manage Rural Conflicts?", in Elizabeth J. Perry and Mark Selden (eds), *Chinese Society: Change, Conflict and Resistance* (London: Routledge, 2000), p. 132; Guobin Yang, "Civil Society in China: A Dynamic Field of Study", *China Review International*, Vol. 9, No. 1 (Spring 2002), p. 11; Mary E. Gallagher, "Mobilizing the Law in China: 'Informed Disenchantment' and the Development of Legal Consciousness", *Law and Society Review*, Vol. 40, No. 4 (December 2006), p. 785; Ching Kwan Lee, *Against the Law: Labor Protests in China's Rustbelt and Sunbelt* (Berkeley: University of California Press, 2007), p. 27.

6 Elizabeth J. Perry, "Studying Chinese Politics: Farewell to Revolution?", *The China Journal*, No. 57 (January 2007), p. 21; Elizabeth J. Perry, "Chinese Conceptions of 'Rights': From Mencius to Mao—and Now", *Perspectives on Politics*, Vol. 6, No. 1 (March 2008), p. 37, pp. 45-47; Elizabeth J. Perry, "A New Rights Consciousness?", *Journal of Democracy*, Vol. 20, No. 3 (July 2009), pp. 17-20.

7 The panel on "Rights Consciousness vs. Rules Consciousness in Chinese Society: Data and Debate on Farmers, Migrant Workers, and Intellectuals"; and Perry's contribution to the roundtable on "The Chinese Student Movement Twenty Years After: Continuities and Changes in Popular Contention since 1989". The Annual Meeting of the Association for Asian Studies, Chicago, 26–29 March 2009.

> Please permit us, along with the mass of retired workers across the country, to enjoy the newly designated wage standards. If you ignore this, and refuse to resolve the issue of our legitimate rights and interests, we will [after obtaining the city government's permission and protection], at an appropriate time, in accordance with our constitutionally given rights, organize a large-scale protest demonstration. We will enlist the assistance of the media in upholding justice, or we may ask relevant government agencies to investigate the internal economic operations of the company. This is the democratic and legitimate supervisory authority given to us by the Chinese Communist Party. Of course a confrontation is not our first choice; our choice is a peaceful livelihood.[8]

In this statement, from an open letter to the Party secretary and the chairman of the board of trustees of the Ping mining company in Anyuan, a group of retirees asserted three rights: the economic right to enjoy wage standards set by the central government, the legal and constitutional right to organize demonstrations, and the Party-granted right to supervise the management of a state-owned enterprise. The claims are clearly rules-based: the substance of the claimed entitlement is enforcement of existing rules; existing rules form the basis for the claim; and the purpose of the claim is to ensure that local rule-enforcement authorities comply with existing central policies and state laws.[9]

The retirees' claims seem to be framed in five different steps.[10] First, upon learning about new wage standards the retirees realized that the company had denied them pension increases in spite of government wage policies. Such awareness generated or reinforced skepticism toward company authorities, who, the retirees believed, "think nothing of [government] documents and do not care whether we live or die". Second, the retirees perceived the vulnerability of company leaders who, they argued, had violated rules made by the Center. Third, the retirees believed that they were on equal footing with company decision-makers in relation to rules made by the central government: "We hope that company leaders understand our good intentions and deal with the victims—retirees of the Ping Mine—*on equal standing*" [italics added]. Fourth, the retirees located an institutional opening to pursue their claims without breaking the law. Lastly, they

8 Elizabeth J. Perry, "Chinese Conceptions of 'Rights'", p. 47. In brackets is an omitted clause. For the Chinese original, see Yu Jianrong, *Zhongguo gongren jieji zhuangkuang: Anyuan shilu* (The Plight of China's Working Class: Annals of Anyuan) (Hong Kong: Mirror Book, 2006), p. 372.

9 For the analytical framework, see Ian Shapiro, *The Evolution of Rights in Liberal Theory* (New York: Cambridge University Press, 1986), p. 14.

10 On framing, see David A. Snow, E. Burke Rochford, Jr., Steven K. Worden and Robert D. Benford, "Frame Alignment Processes, Micromobilization, and Movement Participation", *American Sociological Review*, Vol. 51, No. 4 (August 1986), pp. 464-81. For analyses of framing in contentious politics of contemporary China, see William Hurst, "Mass Frames and Worker Protest"; Feng Chen, "Worker Leaders and Framing Factory-based Resistance", in Kevin J. O'Brien (ed.), *Popular Protest in China* (Cambridge MA: Harvard University Press, 2008), pp. 71-87, 88-107; Patricia M. Thornton, "Framing Dissent in Contemporary China", *The China Quarterly*, No. 171 (September 2002), pp. 661-80.

seemed to have derived a feeling of empowerment from their faith in the Center, which they believed would not countenance abusive actions by the company: "The Center's policies are good and welcomed by ordinary people. The main problem is that the policies are not implemented down below, and the Center must not know about it".[11] Viewed from such a perspective, fighting for protection from abusive local authorities is not overly risky and stands a reasonable chance of succeeding.

Taking into account how it is expressed and framed, rules consciousness can be defined as a combination of awareness of the necessity for protection from *local* rule-enforcement authorities and eagerness to obtain such protection through direct or indirect participation in rule-enforcement.[12] Rules consciousness presumes skepticism toward local rule-enforcement authorities and a sense of equality with them before the rules. In its simplest sense, rules consciousness implies a demand to preempt or halt abusive rule-enforcement, but it involves no challenge to the legitimacy of existing rules, no demand for rule change or new rules, and no demand for participation in rule-making. As Perry points out, the mobilization of rules consciousness can be a force that serves political and regime stability.[13]

Public pronouncements by the powerless under authoritarian rule, however, cannot simply be taken at face value. In fact, once we look at their hidden discourse and their actions, it is clear that the Anyuan retirees possessed something more than rules consciousness. In their "public transcripts",[14] the retirees sounded as though they had faith in the city government, pledging to organize a demonstration "after obtaining the city government's permission and protection". In fact, they had no illusions about city officials. As they explained to a trusted observer: "Workers' representatives have analyzed [the situation] and concluded that it is impossible for the public security bureau to approve the application. Although China has a *Law on Processions and Demonstrations*, when has any application under it been approved?" The Anyuan retirees submitted an application simply to "apply pressure" on the company and to demonstrate their good will in intending to "take strong measures only after courteous ones failed". They did not care much if the public security bureau turned down their application. What they pledged not to do was in fact exactly what they planned to do.[15]

The plan which the Anyuan retirees hatched was to repeat what they had done in 2004, when they had staged a mass demonstration without permission. As one participant proudly recounted:

> On August 26 [2004], we retired workers finally took action ... It was a great event. Thousands of workers went to Pingxiang City from all directions and gathered at

---

[11] Yu Jianrong, *Zhongguo gongren jieji zhuangkuang*, p. 352, see also pp. 114, 356, 330-31, 331, 372.

[12] Contrast p. 54, below, and its accompanying note 30, on rights consciousness.

[13] Elizabeth J. Perry, "Chinese Conceptions of 'Rights'", p. 45.

[14] On the distinction between public and hidden transcripts, see James C. Scott, *Domination and the Arts of Resistance: Hidden Transcripts* (New Haven: Yale University Press, 1990).

[15] Yu Jianrong, *Zhongguo gongren jieji zhuangkuang*, pp. 372, 366-67.

> the Mining Bureau. The whole city was shocked, and traffic on several streets was blocked. The Pingxiang city government dispatched many policemen, but the police could do nothing about us. We didn't shout any slogans, raise any banners, beat anybody, nor did we occupy any public spaces. We just walked toward the Mining Bureau as if we were going shopping, and then we just stood in the square in front of the Mining Bureau. Nobody can forbid us to walk; neither can anybody forbid us just to stand there. Our action truly terrified the officials. They begged us to send in representatives for negotiation and ordered the mining companies to pick up the workers. In the end, we sent in representatives to negotiate with them, and they received our petition.[16]

When taking this action, the Anyuan retirees went significantly beyond a demonstration of the rules consciousness that they had articulated in the open letter. They knew there was a law on demonstrations, yet they deliberately sidestepped it. They insisted that they were just walking on the street and standing in the square rather than staging a parade or demonstration, yet they dispatched representatives to negotiate with the authorities. Moreover, they showed no unease about having broken the law. Instead, they seemed to take great pride in what they did.

In the course of transcending rules consciousness, the Anyuan retirees also made claims that were seemingly "contained" but in fact were "boundary-spanning" or even "transgressive".[17] In their open letters to top managers of the mining company, Anyuan retirees invoked two kinds of rules to justify their claims. They cited "primary rules", namely, enforceable laws and regulations such as the national wage policy, the Labor Law, the Trade Union Law and the Law on State-owned Enterprises. They also cited "secondary rules" that govern rule-making,[18] for example, the Constitution, the principle of "creating a party that promotes justice and rules for the people", Jiang Zemin's notion of "the three-represents", and "Deng Xiaoping's theory that the objective of developing the economy is to improve people's livelihood".[19] More importantly, the retirees cited soft, secondary principles as if they were enforceable primary rules. Although the retirees did not explicitly demand that central leaders comply with the Constitution and the ruling party's legitimating formulas, some of them had a reason to do so. These workers expressed grave doubts about the Center itself, complaining that the Communist Party was "no longer a party of workers".[20]

---

16 *Ibid.*, p. 359.

17 See Douglas McAdam, Charles Tilly and Sidney G. Tarrow, *Dynamics of Contention* (New York: Cambridge University Press, 2001), p. 7; Kevin J. O'Brien, "Neither Transgressive nor Contained: Boundary-Spanning Contention in China", *Mobilization*, Vol. 8, No. 1 (February 2003), pp. 51-64.

18 On the distinction between "primary" and "secondary" rules, see Herbert L. A. Hart, *The Concept of Law* (Oxford: Oxford University Press, 1960), pp. 89-96; Ronald Dworkin, *Taking Rights Seriously* (Cambridge MA: Harvard University Press, 1977), pp. 19-31.

19 Yu Jianrong, *Zhongguo gongren jieji zhuangkuang*, pp. 330-31.

20 *Ibid.*, pp. 62-63, pp. 112-14, p. 222, p. 241, p. 262.

That Anyuan retirees moved beyond rules consciousness in action and in their hidden discourse is open to two interpretations. One is that they believed, as many Chinese have done for centuries, that "it is right to rebel" against abusive local authorities without challenging the top ruler.[21] The other is that they had rights consciousness. I argue that if the Anyuan retirees' distrust in the Party is associated with an explicit demand that the Party abide by its own ruling principles, that claim is best understood as rights consciousness.[22]

Like workers in many cities,[23] some Chinese farmers share the rules consciousness articulated by Anyuan retirees. These farmers carefully frame their claims within existing rules in their public announcements. They share workers' skepticism toward local rule-enforcement authorities as well as their sense of equality with local officials before the rules made by the central government. Typical public statements of rules consciousness made by farmers include:

> Failing to carry out the "three-linkage-policy" amounts to unilaterally breaking a contract. I have the right not to pay the grain tax.
>
> If you [local officials] don't listen to the Center, then we won't listen to you.[24]

Also like the Anyuan retirees, many farmers often transcend rules consciousness both in action and in what they say behind closed doors. First, some farmers pledge to follow certain rules but then bypass them when popular action begins. For instance, a Hunan villager pledged to lodge petitions according to the *Regulations Concerning Works of Letters and Visits* (1995) but ignored its restriction on collective visits by dividing a large group into small teams; other villagers in Hunan held demonstrations without seeking permission and insisted that they were publicizing policies rather than staging a protest parade. Second, some farmers argue that they are in the right when they break the law if they are impelled to do so by abusive local authorities. A protest leader in Hengyang, Hunan, for instance, admitted that he organized a traffic blockade in the county seat but insisted that he was driven to adopt a "forceful" measure after the county government turned a deaf ear to his rightful demands. Finally, some farmers cite both primary and secondary rules to justify their claims. Several farmers from Hengyang County, for instance, insisted in 2003 that they had

---

21 Elizabeth J. Perry, "Chinese Conceptions of 'Rights'", p. 45.

22 A favorite strategy of dissidents in the former socialist countries in Eastern Europe was to demand that Communist regimes comply with their own constitutions, see Jeremy Brooke Straughn, "Taking the State at its Word: The Arts of Consentful Contention in the German Democratic Republic", *American Journal of Sociology*, Vol. 110, No. 6 (May 2005), pp. 1598-650; Adam Przeworski, *Democracy and the Market: Political and Economic Reforms in Eastern Europe and Latin America* (New York: Cambridge University Press, 1991), p. 2.

23 See Mary E. Gallagher, "Mobilizing the Law in China", p. 785; William Hurst and Kevin J. O'Brien, "China's Contentious Pensioners", p. 351; Feng Chen, "Individual Rights and Collective Rights", pp. 67-69; Ching Kwan Lee and Yuan Shen, "The Paradox and Possibility of a Public Sociology of Labor", *Work and Occupations*, Vol. 36, No. 2 (May 2009), p. 120.

24 Lianjiang Li and Kevin J. O'Brien, "Villagers and Popular Resistance", pp. 41, 47.

a right to establish a farmers' association because the Constitution granted citizens the freedom of association.[25]

Unlike the Anyuan retirees, at least as reported by Perry and by Yu, some farmers have also made claims that unambiguously represent rights consciousness.

Rights Consciousness

Scholars have defined rights consciousness as the awareness of existing rights, the willingness to assert rights, and the understanding of social relations in terms of rights.[26] Rights, in turn, are commonly defined as individual claims against the state. Negative rights prescribe what the state must not do to its citizens: "If someone has a right to something, then it is wrong for the government to deny it to him even though it would be in the general interest to do so". Positive rights, on the other hand, prescribe what the state is obliged to provide its citizens.[27]

Existing definitions of rights consciousness do not apply fully to China because they presuppose a tradition of rights and politically independent rights-enforcement institutions, which are largely absent.[28] The absence of institutionalized rights, however,

---

25 Yu Jianrong, *Dangdai Zhongguo nongmin de weiquan kangzheng: Hunan Hengyang kaocha* (Organized Peasant Resistance in Contemporary China: An Investigation of Hengyang County of Hunan Province) (Beijing: Zhongguo Wenhua Chubanshe, 2007), pp. 80-81, 115, 307-09, 356.

26 For definitions of rights consciousness, see Stephen L. Wasby, "History of the Court: Rights Consciousness in Contemporary Society", in Kermit L. Hall, James W. Ely, Jr., Joel B. Grossman and William M. Wiecek (eds), *The Oxford Companion to the Supreme Court of the United States* (Oxford: Oxford University Press, 1992), p. 398; Austin Sarat, "Studying American Legal Culture: An Assessment of Survey Evidence", *Law and Society Review*, Vol. 11, No. 3 (September 1977), p. 450; James L. Gibson, Raymond M. Duch and Kent L. Tedin, "Democratic Values and the Transformation of the Soviet Union", *Journal of Politics*, Vol. 54, No. 2 (May 1992), p. 343; James L. Gibson and Raymond M. Duch, "Support for Rights in Western Europe and the Soviet Union: An Analysis of the Beliefs of Mass Publics", in Frederick D. Weil, Jeffrey Huffman and Mary Gautier (eds), *Research on Democracy: Democratization in Eastern and Western Europe* (Greenwich: JAI Press, 1993), p. 242; Michael W. McCann, *Rights at Work: Pay Equity Reform and the Politics of Legal Mobilization* (Chicago: University of Chicago Press, 1994), p. 7; Michael McCann, "Law and Social Movements: Contemporary Perspectives", *Annual Review of Law and Social Science*, Vol. 2 (2006), p. 22.

27 Ronald Dworkin, *Taking Rights Seriously*, p. 269. On the evolution of rights in Western Europe, see Thomas H. Marshall, *Class, Citizenship, and Social Development* (Westport: Greenwood Press, 1976).

28 On conceptions of rights advocated by Chinese authorities and intellectuals, see Gungwu Wang, "Power, Rights and Duties in Chinese History", *Australian Journal of Chinese Affairs*, No. 3 (January 1980), pp. 1-26; Andrew J. Nathan, *Chinese Democracy* (Berkeley: University of California Press, 1985); Edwards R. Randle, Louis Henkin and Andrew J. Nathan, *Human Rights in Contemporary China* (New York: Columbia University Press, 1986); Stephen C. Angle, *Human Rights and Chinese Thought* (New York: Cambridge University Press, 2002); Randall P. Peerenboom, "What's Wrong with Chinese Rights: Towards a Theory of Rights with Chinese Characteristics", *Harvard Human Rights*

is not a barrier to appreciating the necessity of having rights, nor is it an obstacle to asserting rights as if one had them. Quite a number of Chinese farmers, as Kevin O'Brien has observed, "are acting like citizens before they are citizens".[29] Based on these considerations, this study defines rights consciousness as a combination of awareness of the necessity for protection from *central* rule-making authorities and eagerness to acquire such protection through direct or indirect participation in rule-making.[30] Rights consciousness so defined presumes skepticism toward central rule-making authorities and an understanding that the ruled are equal with the ruler in relation to general constitutional principles that govern rule-making and/or antecedent principles that are, in Perry's words, "both prior—and superior—to" political rules.[31] Doubt about central leaders' commitment to rule in the interests of the ruled, in particular, is a necessary condition for the birth of rights consciousness.

Some Chinese farmers have explicitly expressed their doubts about central rule-making authorities. A Hunan villager, for instance, argued that "the lawmakers are not quite fair to us, so the laws themselves are unfair". He compared Mao Zedong and Deng Xiaoping to two generations of shepherds. The father drove his herds to poor grasslands and kept them half-starved and weak out of fear of rebellion; the son drove his herds to greener grasslands but allowed his dogs and hawks to fatten themselves on the cattle.[32] Another Hunan farmer argued that farmers had been treated like "modern slaves" (*xiandai nongnu* 现代农奴) for much of the time since 1949.[33] He challenged

Journal, Vol. 6 (Spring 1993), pp. 29-58; Randall P. Peerenboom, "Human Rights, China, and Cross-Cultural Inquiry: Philosophy, History, and Power Politics", *Philosophy East and West*, Vol. 55, No. 2 (April 2005), pp. 283-320; Elizabeth J. Perry, "Chinese Conceptions of 'Rights'"; Peter Zarrow, "Anti-Despotism and 'Rights Talk': The Intellectual Origins of Modern Human Rights Thinking in the Late Qing", *Modern China*, Vol. 34, No. 2 (April 2008), pp. 179-209.

29 Kevin J. O'Brien, "Villagers, Elections, and Citizenship in Contemporary China", p. 425.

30 The distinction between rule-making and rule-enforcement authority is relative. When they face a dictator, who holds both ultimate rule-making and rule-enforcement powers, individuals who are aware of the necessity of having protection from rule-enforcement power and are eager to obtain such protection have rights rather than rules consciousness. As Georg Simmel points out: "If the absolute despot accompanies his orders by the threat of punishment or the promise of reward, this implies that he himself wishes to be bound by the decrees he issues. The subordinate is expected to have the *right* [italics added] to request something of him; and by establishing the punishment, no matter how horrible, the despot commits himself not to impose a more severe one" (Georg Simmel, *The Sociology of Georg Simmel*, translated, edited and with an introduction by Kurt H. Wolff [Glencoe: Free Press, 1950], pp. 186-87). Moreover, provincial-level people's congresses in China have the authority to enact local regulations, see Young Nam Cho, *Local People's Congresses in China: Development and Transition* (New York: Cambridge University Press, 2008) and Ming Xia, *The People's Congresses and Governance in China: Toward a Network Model of Governance* (London: Routledge, 2007).

31 Elizabeth J. Perry, "Chinese Conceptions of 'Rights'", p. 39.

32 Yu Jianrong, *Dangdai Zhongguo nongmin de weiquan kangzheng*, pp. 510, 515-17.

33 *Ibid.*, pp. 477-79.

the legitimacy of current laws and policies and questioned the rulers' commitment to rule in the interests of farmers with a barrage of questions, including:

> Why does the state make policies? What are policies for?
>
> Why does the state make laws? What are laws for?
>
> Do policies and laws of the state serve the public interest, private interest, or the interest of the powerful?
>
> Are policies and laws weapons made exclusively to control ordinary folks?
>
> Are policies and laws regulations that endow powerholders with the highest status and particularly high-end entertainment?
>
> Are policies and laws thunder and lightning that powerholders use to decide the life and death of common people? Are they tools of dictatorship?[34]

Since rights consciousness is directed against central rule-making authorities, claims that embody it should have the following features: the substance of the claimed entitlement should be rule changes, which involve the abolition of existing rules and/or the making of new rules; the basis of the entitlement should be antecedent principles and/or general constitutional rules that govern rule-making; and the purpose of the entitlement should be to stop or prevent central leaders from ruling arbitrarily.

Chinese farmers have made claims with precisely these features. First, some of them, often and loudly, demand rule changes. In the last two decades, for instance, many villagers have demanded that the discriminatory household registration system be abolished. When asked to comply with birth control policy, a farmer in Beijing suburb responded: "Give me an [urban] household registration, give me labor insurance, then I agree to be sterilized immediately".[35] Similarly, tens of thousands of farmers in Hanyuan County, Sichuan Province, who were forced to relocate owing to dam construction, demanded in 2004 that they be compensated at the same level as urban residents.[36] Some farmers have even insisted on popular election of top national leaders. A Hebei villager, for instance, argued that "all government leaders, including the state chairman, should be directly elected by the masses rather than appointed by higher levels".[37]

Chinese farmers also justify their demand for rule changes by invoking antecedent principles. A Hunan villager, for instance, argued that farmers should have the right to own contracted land because "the land of China was cultivated

---

34 *Ibid.*, pp. 488-89.

35 Li Kang, "Jiceng zhengquan yu jiceng shequ" (Grassroots Government and Grassroots Community), in Li Xueju, Wang Zhenyao and Tang Jinsu (eds), *Zhongguo xiangzhen zhengquan de xianzhuang yu gaige* (Current Situation and Reform of Chinese Township Government) (Beijing: Zhongguo Shehui Chubanshe, 1994), p. 267.

36 Personal correspondence with a researcher at the Chinese Academy of Social Sciences, October 2007.

37 Author's interview, Hebei, September 1993.

by ancestors of the Chinese nation and belongs to all descendants of Emperors Yan and Huang. The people are the landlord and should have the sovereign right to use and manage the land".[38]

Lastly, some Chinese farmers have demanded that central leaders be held accountable to the popular will. A farmer from Anhui, for instance, argued in 1998 that "taxpayers pay taxes to their own government so that the government can more effectively fulfill its legal obligations to taxpayers. If the government fails to perform its duties, then taxpayers do not have to pay taxes".[39] Some farmers have also made more pointed claims against unaccountable central leaders. A villager from Hunan, for instance, stated that "the state's revenue is tax money, which comes from the people, so the people should have the right to supervise and audit [its use]". He further argued that farmers should have the right to elect and dismiss all "people's servants":

> When so-called people's servants are rogues and ignore their duties, why don't the people have the right to elect and dismiss their servants? ... The people should be the master. Popular sovereignty is above everything else and it is greater than everything else. The people should have the right to manage and supervise everything.[40]

Another Hunan farmer, Ling Chunwei, put forth a similar claim for accountability. According to him, the Constitution is an agreement reached between the rulers and the ruled through consultation, and it is binding on both parties:

> The Constitution and the law are documents agreed to by the top ruling group and the ruled through communication, consultation and compromise under a given historical condition in a country. They require compliance from both sides and are binding for both sides ... If the government is faithful to the law and the people, the people will believe that it is a good government and rally closely around it. With the people rallying around it, the government will be an invincible force and will sweep all die-hard and corrupt elements onto the rubbish heap of history. Otherwise the government will be cast aside by the people and eliminated by history.[41]

As politically savvy as he was, Ling must have appreciated that he was not describing how the Constitution and related laws were agreed to in China. In his ever-so-reasonable language he was in fact prescribing how the Constitution and laws should be made and arguing why they should bind both ruler and ruled. He wrote as if the people already had a right to participate in Constitution-making as well as a right to retract their consent if the "top ruling group" failed to honor its responsibilities. Like many other farmers, he was, as Kevin O'Brien has put it, "cloaking a daring

[38] Yu Jianrong, *Dangdai Zhongguo nongmin de weiquan kangzheng*, p. 496.

[39] Remark written by a survey correspondent from Anhui Province in 1998.

[40] Yu Jianrong, *Dangdai Zhongguo nongmin de weiquan kangzheng*, pp. 497, 487.

[41] *Ibid.*, p. 111.

proactive claim in reactive terms, demanding citizenship rights they had never enjoyed, while making it appear they had just been deprived of them".[42]

An Empirical Test

Admittedly, the farmers quoted above were exceptionally thoughtful and articulate. To see whether rights consciousness is also found among ordinary villagers, this section uses survey data to examine how farmers' claims are related to trust in central rule-making and local rule-enforcement authorities.

Data and Methods of Analysis

The survey was conducted in 2007. The field sites were D County and W County in Fujian Province, S County in Jiangxi Province, and Y County in Zhejiang Province. The four counties were selected by convenience. Sampling in each county was conducted in three stages. First, five townships were selected with probability proportionate to size (PPS). Second, four villages were selected from each township with PPS. Lastly, within each selected village around 20 randomly chosen individuals over the age of 18 were interviewed.[43] Altogether 1,600 farmers were interviewed. Cases were weighted according to the rural population size of the county.[44] To adjust for survey design effects, each township was treated as a stratum and each village a cluster.

Unobservable factors such as claims against government authorities and trust in government leaders were tapped with multiple indicators to improve measurement reliability. Data analysis proceeded in two steps. First, confirmatory factor analysis was used to assure that multiple measures of latent theoretical constructs were reliable. A path model was then estimated to examine the relationship between claims, trust in government leaders, and other factors that might affect an individual's rights and rules consciousness. Ordinal indicators of latent constructs were treated as crude measurements of latent continuous factors. The WLSMV (weighted least squares mean and variance adjusted) estimator was used to correct for the bias that results from having ordinal endogenous variables in the model.[45] Since it relies on a local probability sample, the research focuses on exploring relationships between variables.[46]

---

[42] Kevin J. O'Brien, "Villagers, Elections, and Citizenship", p. 429.

[43] Interviews were administered by advanced undergraduate students in the Department of Sociology at a leading university in South China under the supervision of their professor.

[44] On weighting procedure and formulas, see Pierre Foy, "Calculation of Sampling Weights", in Michael O. Martin and Dano L. Kelly (eds), *Technical Report Volume II: Implementation and Analysis* (Chestnut Hill: Boston College, 1997), pp. 71-80.

[45] Linda K. Muthén and Bengt O. Muthén, *Mplus User's Guide*, 4th Edition (Los Angeles: Muthén and Muthén, 2006).

[46] See Melanie Manion, "Survey Research in the Study of Contemporary China: Learning from Local Samples", *The China Quarterly*, No. 139 (September 1994), pp. 741-65.

Four Types of Claims

One difficulty with analyzing the Chinese discourse on rights is that the word for "rights" (*quanli* 权利) and the word for "power" or "authority" (*quanli* 权力) are homonyms.[47] Even fairly educated people often use the word for "power" or "authority" when they mean "rights". For instance, when the Anyuan retirees wrote in their open letter "this is the democratic and legitimate supervisory authority (权力) given to us by the Chinese Communist Party", they must have meant "right" (权利) because they insisted that they were striving for "lawful rights and interests" (*hefa quanyi* 合法权益), not "power" (权).[48] Compounding these linguistic complexities, claims about rights are often made with reference to both primary and secondary rules and even in the form of value judgments, which reference abstract "principles" (*li* 理). For instance, when farmers argued that in principle the village Party secretary should be elected by all villagers because he managed the affairs of the whole village rather than those of Party members, they made a claim about rights.[49] A third difficulty is that farmers often make rights claims without specifying which level of government they are targeting. They talk generally about "the government" (*zhengfu* 政府), which they use to refer to both the Center and various levels of sub-national government.[50] Owing to these complications, claims are classified along two dimensions. First, a claim may be made against either local rule-enforcement authorities or central rule-making authorities. Second, a claim is reactive if the claimed entitlement is at least arguably based on existing political rules; it is proactive if the claimed entitlement requires fundamental rule changes or new rules.[51]

The survey showed that Chinese farmers had four types of claims. First, most issued a strong reactive claim against local rule-enforcement authorities. Over 80 per cent of 1,600 respondents agreed that farmers should have the right to demand that higher levels dismiss corrupt township officials, and over 70 per cent of the respondents agreed that farmers should have the right to disobey local policies that run against the law and central policies (see Appendix for variable descriptions). Both claims were directed against local authorities, and they were arguably based on existing rules. The State Council's Regulation on Peasant Burdens and Labor (1991) and the Agriculture Law (1993), for instance, granted farmers the right to reject excessive fees. This type of claim is indicative of the rules consciousness that Perry discusses, if it is associated with distrust in local rule-enforcement authorities.

47 See Deborah Cao, *Chinese Law: A Language Perspective* (Burlinton: Ashgate, 2004), pp. 71-75.

48 Yu Jianrong, *Zhongguo gongren jieji zhuangkuang*, pp. 363, 372.

49 Lianjiang Li, "The Two-Ballot System in Shanxi Province: Subjecting Village Party Secretaries to a Popular Vote", *The China Journal*, No. 42 (July 1999), p. 104.

50 See, for instance, Yu Jianrong, *Dangdai Zhongguo nongmin de weiquan kangzheng*, pp. 187-425.

51 On the distinction between "reactive" and "proactive" claims, see Charles Tilly, "Contentious Repertoires in Great Britain, 1758–1834", *Social Science History*, Vol. 17, No. 2 (Summer 1993), pp. 253-80.

Second, a large majority of farmers had a strong proactive claim against both local rule-enforcement and central rule-making authorities. Over 85 per cent of the respondents agreed that, in principle, the township head should be elected by ordinary people through voting, and nearly 40 per cent thought that the township head should be popularly elected with one-man one-vote and that such elections could be held right away. These claims were proactive because the claimed entitlement had no grounding in current rules. In fact, introducing popular election of township heads would require a constitutional amendment, and experimental township elections have been repudiated several times over the last decade by central leaders.[52] This type of claim reflects rights consciousness, if it is associated with skepticism toward central rule-makers.

Third, a good number of farmers issued a fairly strong reactive claim against central leaders. Over 65 per cent of the respondents agreed that ordinary people should have the right to criticize decisions made by the Center, and 64 per cent of the respondents agreed that farmers should have the right to demand the recall of central leaders who do not care about farmers. The claims were reactive because the claimed entitlement was arguably based on current rules, such as the Constitution (Art. 41) and the Communist Party's pledge to "serve the people". This type of claim is indicative of rights consciousness if it is associated with skepticism toward central rule-making authorities.

Lastly, a significant number of farmers had a proactive claim against central leaders. Over 65 per cent of the respondents agreed that, in principle, the state chairman should be elected by ordinary people through voting, and over 15 per cent thought that the state chairman should be popularly elected with one-man one-vote and that such elections could be held right away. Like the claims about the right to elect the township government head by popular vote, these claims were proactive because the claimed entitlement had no grounding in current rules. Furthermore, these claims targeted the state chairman—the top ruling authority in China. This type of claim embodies rights consciousness, if it is associated with skepticism toward central rule-making authorities.

Trust in Government Leaders as a Criterion

The crucial distinction between rules and rights consciousness, it will be recalled, is that the former presumes skepticism toward local rule-enforcement authorities while the latter presumes skepticism toward central rule-making authorities. To explore whether the four types of claims represent rights or rules consciousness, this study uses multiple regressions to examine how they correlate with confidence in central and local authorities. Trust in central leaders is used as a proxy for trust in central

---

[52] For discussions of the constitutionality of township elections, see Lianjiang Li, "The Politics of Introducing Direct Township Elections in China", *The China Quarterly*, No. 171 (September 2002), pp. 704-23; Tony Saich and Xuedong Yang, "Innovation in China Local Governance: 'Open Recommendation and Selection'", *Pacific Affairs*, Vol. 76, No. 2 (Summer 2003), pp. 185-208.

rule-making authorities, and trust in township leaders is used as a proxy for trust in local rule-enforcement authorities.

Trust in political leaders is multi-dimensional, as its objects include leaders' commitment, competence, character, equity, honesty and responsiveness.[53] This study focuses on trust in the government leaders' commitment to rule in the interests of the governed,[54] because skepticism in this regard is most likely to enhance appreciation of the necessity of having protection from government authorities. To measure trust in commitment to rule in the interests of the governed, respondents were asked if they believed that the township and central leaders: (1) put their own interests before those of farmers; (2) do not care whether farmers will agree when they make policies/decisions; and (3) care primarily about the powerful and rich and neglect the interests of ordinary people. Trust in township leaders was significantly weaker than that in central leaders. Over 22 per cent of the respondents had no confidence in township leaders in all three aspects, while 15 per cent had no trust in central leaders. Conversely, over 35 per cent of the respondents were confident about central leaders in all three aspects, while less than 20 per cent had full confidence in township leaders. The observation corroborates a previous finding that the Chinese people have less trust in lower levels of government than in higher levels.[55]

To make sure that the observed correlation between a claim about rights and trust in leaders was not spurious, eight factors that might affect a farmer's attitude toward central and local authorities were controlled. First, internal political efficacy, which refers to the sense of competence in understanding public affairs and participating in politics,[56] was controlled, since more efficacious individuals were expected to have stronger claims. Second, personal assertiveness was controlled, as more assertive individuals might make stronger claims against government authorities. The third control variable was knowledge about potentially beneficial central policies and laws, because more knowledgeable individuals might have stronger rules consciousness but weaker rights consciousness. In addition, four demographic features, namely, gender, age, education, and membership in the Chinese Communist Party (CCP), were also controlled. Lastly, three county dummies, W County in Fujian Province, S County in Jiangxi Province and Y County in Zhejiang Province, were included in the analyses to control for the effect of

---

[53] See Jack Citrin and Christopher Muste, "Trust in Government", in John P. Robinson, Phillip R. Shaver and Lawrence S. Wrightsman (eds), *Measures of Political Attitudes* (San Diego: Academic Press, 1999), pp. 466-69.

[54] Margaret Levi and Laura Stoker, "Political Trust and Trustworthiness", *Annual Review of Political Science*, Vol. 3 (2000), p. 476.

[55] See Tianjian Shi, "Cultural Values and Political Trust: A Comparison of the People's Republic of China and Taiwan", *Comparative Politics*, Vol. 33, No. 4 (July 2001), pp. 401-19; Lianjiang Li, "Political Trust in Rural China", *Modern China*, Vol. 30, No. 2 (April 2004), pp. 228-58.

[56] See George I. Balch, "Multiple Indicators in Survey Research: The Concept 'Sense of Political Efficacy'", *Political Methodology*, Vol. 1 (1974), pp. 1-43; Stephen C. Craig and Michael A. Maggiotto, "Measuring Political Efficacy", *Political Methodology*, Vol. 8 (1982), pp. 89-110.

unobserved differences between the four selected counties. D County in Fujian was used as the reference (see Appendix for variable descriptions).

Model and Results

A path model was constructed based on the theoretical considerations discussed above. Exogenous variables listed in the rectangular box on the left-hand side of Figure 1 were allowed to influence all endogenous variables on the right-hand side of the bracket. The model held that trust in the central and township leaders affected claims about rights. Trust in township leaders was assumed to affect trust in central leaders. Internal efficacy, personal assertiveness, and legal knowledge were allowed to influence claims about rights. The model has four versions, which are identical except that they estimate, respectively, the relationship between trust in central and township leaders and the four different types of claims.[57]

Figure 1. Path model

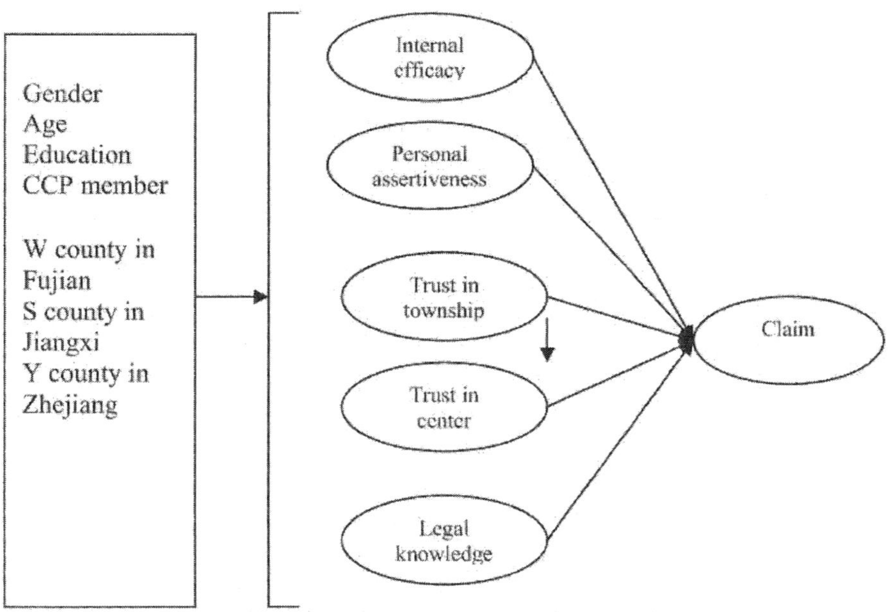

Note: Exogenous variables listed in the rectangular box are allowed to affect all endogenous ones on the right side of the bracket. Indicators of latent constructs and error/residual terms of endogenous variables are suppressed for the sake of clarity.

---

[57] Missing cases were deleted listwise. For comparative purpose, the model was also fitted to a singly imputed dataset generated with the Expectation Maximization (EM) algorithm and five multiply imputed datasets generated using the Markov Chain Monte Carlo (MCMC) method. Results obtained from the three alternative treatments of missing values are highly consistent with each other.

The results appearing in Table 1 can be grouped into four general findings.[58] First, the reactive claim against local rule-enforcement authorities represented rules consciousness, as it was associated with skepticism toward township leaders. All else being equal, individuals with stronger doubts about township leaders had a stronger claim about the right to protest against abusive rule-enforcement authorities and the right to resist illicit local policies. The fact that confidence in central leaders had a positive effect on this claim also suggested that it represented rules consciousness. In theory, rules consciousness presumes neither trust nor distrust in central rule-makers, because it can be entirely strategic. In reality, however, rules consciousness in authoritarian China may presume some confidence in rule-making authorities, because asserting rights against local authorities is too risky if one does not believe that central leaders want faithful rule enforcement. The finding corroborates an earlier observation that farmers with more trust in central leaders are more likely to petition.[59]

Table 1: Correlation of Claims against Government Authorities and Trust in Government Leaders' Commitment to the Interests of the Governed

	Reactive claim against local rule-enforcement authorities	Proactive claim against local rule-enforcement authorities	Reactive claim against central rule-making authorities	Proactive claim against central rule-making authorities
Trust in township leaders (low to high)	-.170** (.058)	-.221*** (.046)	-.270*** (.044)	.035 (.051)
Trust in central leaders (low to high)	.187*** (.057)	.176** (.058)	-.004 (.041)	-.188*** (.033)
Internal efficacy (low to high)	.069† (.036)	.225*** (.027)	.051† (.028)	.109 (.068)
Personal assertiveness (weak to strong)	.105* (.050)	.180** (.069)	.089† (.050)	.183*** (.053)

58 Table 1 presents a variety of goodness-of-fit statistics for the model. These statistics indicate overall that the model fits the data very well. The model is not an exact fit ($p < .001$). However, three widely-accepted close fit indexes, namely, Comparative Fit Index (CFI), Tucker-Lewis Index (TLI, also called Non-Normed Fit Index (NNFI)), and Root Mean Squared Error of Approximation (RMSEA), meet conventional cut-off criteria, which are, respectively, CFI >.950, TLI > 950, and RMSEA <.060 (see Li-Tze Hu and Peter M. Bentler, "Cutoff Criteria for Fit Indices in Covariance Structure Analysis: Conventional Criteria versus New Alternatives", *Structural Equation Modeling*, Vol. 6, No. 1 [March 1999], pp. 1-55). Also see Herbert W. Marsh, Kit-Tai Hau and Zhonglin Wen, "In Search of Golden Rules: Comment on Hypothesis-Testing Approaches to Setting Cutoff Values for Fit Indexes and Dangers in Overgeneralizing Hu and Bentler's (1999) Findings", *Structural Equation Modeling*, Vol. 11, No. 3 (September 2004), pp. 320-41). The goodness-of-fit test results assure us that the estimated coefficients are acceptable descriptions of the data and can be used to test hypotheses.

59 Lianjiang Li, "Political Trust and Petitioning in the Chinese Countryside", *Comparative Politics*, Vol. 40, No. 2 (January 2008), p. 214.

Legal knowledge (low to high)	.061 (.058)	-.234** (.079)	.085 (.071)	.005 (.043)
Gender (0= female; 1=male)	.094 (.072)	.057 (.073)	.054 (.065)	-.057 (.061)
Age (18-88 years)	.004 (.004)	-.002 (.004)	.000 (.002)	.001 (.003)
Education (0-21 years)	.010 (.013)	.009 (.014)	.016 (.012)	-.009 (.015)
CCP membership (0=non-member, 1=member)	.039 (.096)	-.189* (.091)	-.108 (.076)	-.214* (.104)
W County in Fujian (0=no; 1=yes)	.051 (.110)	.200* (.097)	.024 (.093)	.129† (.075)
S County in Jiangxi (0=no; 1=yes)	-.376** (.134)	.127 (.145)	-.164 (.109)	.126 (.121)
Y County in Zhejiang (0=no; 1=yes)	.076 (.113)	.497*** (.102)	.223* (.096)	.391*** (.109)
R2	.113	.285	.273	.107
Model fit indexes				
χ^2	42.872	40.525	44.645	45.563
DF	14	14	15	15
P value	.000	.000	.000	.000
CFI	.985	.986	.985	.984
TLI	.980	.982	.980	.980
RMSEA	.037	.036	.036	.037
Observations	1,498	1,488	1,492	1,489

Notes: Entries are unstandardized OLS coefficients, with standard errors in parenthesis beneath them.

† p ? .05 one-sided; * p ? .05 two-sided; ** p ? .01 two-sided; *** p ? .001 two sided. Data are weighted.

Second, the proactive claim against township leaders was expected to represent rights consciousness in that it required a major rule change which central leaders had repeatedly refused to make. The empirical result, however, was ambiguous. On one hand, the claim about a right to elect township heads by popular vote was associated with skepticism toward township leaders, which suggested that farmers who made the claim sought to hold township authorities accountable. On the other hand, this proactive claim was positively associated with trust in central leaders, which suggested that farmers who demand township elections did not aim to use such elections to constrain the power of central leaders, nor did they believe that central leaders opposed such elections. One may regard this claim as a tentative expression of rights consciousness, in that it asserts a new right that central rule-makers have repeatedly refused to grant. This claim, however, falls short of unambiguously representing rights consciousness, in that farmers who made it seemed to believe that central rule-making authorities would not deny them the right to elect township heads, probably because they did not know that the top leaders criticized and banned experimental township elections.

Third, the reactive claim against central leaders might represent rights consciousness. Regardless of level of confidence in central leaders, farmers made a fairly strong claim to a right to criticize central policies and the right to demand dismissal of unresponsive central leaders. The claim bespoke rights consciousness because 1) the rules invoked were general constitutional principles and legitimating formulas, which govern rule-making; 2) the claim was associated with a neutral judgment about the trustworthiness of central leaders, which in China likely indicated lack of confidence; and 3) the purpose of the claimed entitlement was to hold central leaders accountable.

Lastly, the proactive claim against rule-making authorities unambiguously represented rights consciousness, since it was associated with distrust in central leaders. All else being equal, individuals with stronger doubts about central leaders' commitment to rule in the interests of farmers were more eager to claim a right to elect the state chairman by popular vote. The finding suggested that a significant number of farmers were aware of the necessity of having protection from central rule-makers and had a real desire to obtain that protection through popular election of the country's top ruler. This observation provided definitive evidence that at least some farmers had rights consciousness.[60]

Conclusions

Rules and rights consciousness in contemporary China share the common goal of stopping or preventing the arbitrary exercise of power, but they have different objects, ideational foundations and behavioral implications. Rules consciousness targets rule-enforcement authorities, presumes skepticism toward them and a sense of equality with them before central policies and state laws, and implies a demand for direct or indirect participation in rule-enforcement. Rights consciousness, on the other hand, targets rule-making authorities, presumes skepticism toward them and a sense of equality with them before antecedent principles and/or constitutional principles, and implies a demand for direct or indirect participation in rule-making. Chinese workers in Anyuan, as we can see in the research by Perry and Yu, certainly have rules consciousness, but they have also moved beyond it in action and in their closed-door discussions. Chinese farmers likewise display rules consciousness, and they too have transcended rules consciousness in rhetoric and action. Some Chinese farmers, moreover, have also unambiguously shown evidence of rights consciousness. In sum,

---

[60] It is worth noting that, due to the lack of longitudinal data, this research cannot establish causal relationships between trust in central and township leaders and claims against government authorities. In fact, alternative models that posit different relations between trust and claims would fit the data equally well, see Ingeborg Stelzl, "Changing a Causal Hypothesis without Changing the Fit: Some Rules for Generating Equivalent Path Models", *Multivariate Behavioral Research*, Vol. 21, No. 3 (July 1986), pp. 309-31.

ordinary Chinese people do have rules consciousness, but it is problematic to conclude that they only have rules consciousness and no rights consciousness.[61]

Both rules and rights consciousness represent a significant break from what Wei-ming Tu calls "duty consciousness", which presumes a hierarchical order in which ordinary people are obliged to obey all political authorities.[62] Popular protests driven by rules consciousness may help pave the way for building the rule by law or even the rule of law. Moreover, the mobilization of rules consciousness can contribute to the growth of rights consciousness by encouraging popular protests against local authorities, because such contention often weakens popular trust in central leaders, which in turn may foster rights consciousness. Rights and rules consciousness are not mutually exclusive. Individuals may express strong skepticism toward local rule-enforcement without losing confidence in central rule-making authorities, but they may also have strong skepticism toward both central and local authorities. Accordingly, individuals may have a combination of strong rules consciousness and weak rights consciousness, but they may also have strong rules consciousness and strong rights consciousness.

The growth of rights consciousness among China's rural population is a significant political development. Perry is right that rules consciousness is an old story in China, but important changes have occurred, too. China has undergone unprecedented changes in its economy, educational system, social life, and legal infrastructure since 1949, particularly in the last three decades. The fact that the political system continues to be authoritarian undoubtedly inhibits the growth and manifestation of rights consciousness, but the regime's suppression of popular demands for rights may also enhance rights consciousness, especially when popular contention occurs over issues that impinge on people's economic interests. In recent years, corruption-ridden market reforms, forced urbanization, unfair social welfare policies and predatory development projects have dramatically increased the number of confrontations between ordinary people and various levels of government authorities. More and more Chinese people attempt to assert their rights—either legally-endowed or not—within the existing political and legal system. When their efforts are frustrated, those individuals may become more distrustful about the legitimacy of existing laws and regulations, as well as about central rule-making authorities, and may thereby develop stronger rights consciousness.

Analytically distinct types of political consciousness often co-exist in the mind of the same individual. Conceptual dichotomies such as rules and rights consciousness are a useful tool for classification, but a typology is always an abstraction rather than a description of reality. As we see in this study, many ordinary farmers have both rules and rights consciousness rather than only one or the other of them.

---

[61] Further empirical work is needed to discover if Chinese workers in Anyuan and elsewhere also have rights consciousness; ongoing research by Feng Chen, Mary Gallagher, William Hurst, Ching Kwan Lee and others suggests they are quite likely to do so.

[62] Wei-ming Tu, "Li as Process of Humanization", *Philosophy East and West*, Vol. 22, No. 2 (April 1972), p. 196.

The formation of two distinct ways of approaching state power may depend on whether there are national laws or central policies that ordinary people can strategically invoke to justify their claims against government authorities. On issues such as excessive local taxation, which was explicitly prohibited, Chinese farmers are more likely to develop rules consciousness. By contrast, on topics such as land appropriation, where existing laws and regulations provide at best a tenuous basis for claims, farmers are more likely to develop rights consciousness. In addition, how rights and rules consciousness are manifested may depend on the perceived risk of doing so. If people assert their rules-based claims using the politically accepted language of rights, they may also disguise their claims about rights using the even safer language of rules.

To figure out the extent to which ordinary Chinese people have rights consciousness, rules consciousness and/or a combination of both, it is critical to analyze both their public claims and more hidden discourses and to examine what they pledge to do, what they actually do, and how they interpret what they have done. The fact that rules consciousness and rights consciousness often co-exist in the mind of the same individual is exactly why it is important to distinguish them from each other. Compared to those who only have rules consciousness, individuals who also have rights consciousness are more likely to press for institutional changes in the hope of converting revocable "state-endowed rights" into inalienable rights. If rights consciousness keeps a democracy healthy by turning citizens into active participants in governance,[63] the mobilization of rights consciousness may help chart a course toward a more participatory political system in China.

Appendix: Description of Variables

	Mean	SD	Std. Factor Loading
DEPENDENT VARIABLES			
Latent REACTIVE CLAIM AGAINST LOCAL RULE-ENFORCEMENT AUTHORITIES			
Farmers should have the right to demand higher levels to dismiss corrupt township officials.	2.928	.630	.781
Farmers should have the right to disobey local policies that run against the law and central policies.	2.784	.692	.801
1=strongly disagree; 2=disagree; 3=agree; 4=strongly agree			

[63] James L. Gibson, Raymond M. Duch and Kent L. Tedin, "Democratic Values and the Transformation of the Soviet Union", p. 345.

Latent PROACTIVE CLAIM AGAINST LOCAL RULE-ENFORCEMENT AUTHORITIES			
In principle the township head should be elected by ordinary people through voting. 1=strongly disagree; 2=disagree; 3=agree; 4=strongly agree	3.002	.564	.573
Do you think that the township head should be elected by popular vote with one-man one-vote? 1=no; 2=yes but conditions are not ripe; 3=yes and can be held now	2.271	.666	.581
Latent REACTIVE CLAIM AGAINST CENTRAL RULE-MAKING AUTHORITIES			
Ordinary people should have the right to criticize decisions made by the Center.	2.687	.688	.535
Farmers should have the right to demand the recall of central leaders who do not care about them.	2.718	.687	.541
1=strongly agree; 2=agree; 3=disagree; 4=strongly disagree			
Latent PROACTIVE CLAIM AGAINST CENTRAL RULE-MAKING AUTHORITIES			
In principle the state chairman should be elected by ordinary people through voting. 1=strongly disagree; 2=disagree; 3=agree; 4=strongly agree	2.758	.711	.666
Do you think that the state chairman should be directly elected by the people through one-man one-vote? 1=no; 2=yes but conditions are not ripe; 3=yes and can be held now.	1.874	.664	.679
EXPLANATORY VARIABLES			
Latent TRUST IN CENTRAL LEADERS' COMMITMENT TO RULE IN THE INTERESTS OF THE GOVERNED Do you believe the following statements about central leaders?			
They put their own interests before those of farmers.	3.307	1.233	.776
They do not care if farmers agree when they make policies.	3.261	1.212	.832
They care primarily about the powerful and rich and neglect the interests of ordinary people.	3.409	1.232	.899
1=fully believe; 2=believe; 3=half believe and half doubt; 4=disbelieve; 5=fully disbelieve			
Latent TRUST IN TOWNSHIP LEADERS' COMMITMENT TO THE PUBLIC INTEREST Do you believe that the following statement about township government leaders?			
They put their own interests before those of farmers.	2.770	1.108	.767
They do not care if farmers agree when they make decisions.	2.895	1.086	.790

(*continued overleaf*)

(*continued*)

They care primarily about the powerful and rich and neglect the interests of ordinary people.	3.006	1.116	.862
1=fully believe; 2=believe; 3=half believe and half doubt; 4=disbelieve; 5=fully disbelieve			
CONTROL VARIABLES			
Latent POLITICAL EFFICACY Do you think you can do the following?			
Judge a county head's performance after listening to his/her work report.	3.170	.922	.857
Judge which one is better if two county head candidates debate each other.	3.177	.939	.960
Judge if a county head's decisions benefit or harm self-interests.	3.285	.959	.859
1=definitely can't; 2=can't; 3=unsure; 4=can; 5=definitely can			
Latent LEGAL KNOWLEDGE			
What law allows ordinary people to sue the government?	.133	.340	.928
What law stipulates that villagers' committee director must be democratically elected by villagers?	.158	.364	.917
What legal regulation allows ordinary people to petition?	.133	.340	.928
0=don't know or wrong answer; 1=correct answer			
Latent PERSONAL ASSERTIVENESS Do the following descriptions fit your character?			
I'm not fearful of officials and I don't hesitate to object to any official who has done something wrong.	.483	.500	.788
I'm competitive and eager to win and I'm not fearful of strong and bullheaded people.	.450	.498	.874
I can't stand the powerful and influential bullying the powerless and weak and I like to stand up for the weak.	.597	.491	.958
I'm not afraid of suffering a beating, arrest, or death in the course of upholding justice.	.487	.500	.898
I can't stand unfairness in society and I like to poke into it even when it is not my own business.	.551	.498	.777
0=no; 1 = yes			
DEMOGRAPHIC VARIABLES			
Gender (0 = female; 1 = male)	.516	.500	
Age (range 18—88)	41.27	13.602	
Education (0—21 years)	8.024	3.490	
CCP membership (0 = non-member; 1 = member)	.176	.381	
Notes: Row entries are means, standard deviations, and standardized factor loadings.			

[29]

Articles

Chinese Conceptions of "Rights": From Mencius to Mao—and Now

Elizabeth J. Perry

The recent explosion of popular protest in China, often framed as a demand for the fulfillment of "rights," has captured widespread attention. Some observers interpret the protests as signs of a "moral vacuum." Others see the unrest as signaling a powerful new "rights consciousness." In either case, the protests are often regarded as a major challenge to the stability of the political system. In this article, an examination of Chinese conceptions of "rights," as reflected in the ethical discourses of philosophers, political leaders, and protesters (and as contrasted with American understandings of rights), provides the basis for questioning prevailing assumptions about the fragility of the Chinese political order. For over two millennia, Chinese political thought, policy, and protest have assigned central priority to the attainment of socioeconomic security. As a result, the meaning of "rights" in Chinese political discourse differs significantly from the Anglo-American tradition. Viewed in historical context, China's contemporary "rights" protests seem less politically threatening. The Chinese polity appears neither as vacuous nor as vulnerable as it is sometimes assumed to be.

In recent years, U.S. newspapers and magazines have been filled with dramatic stories about all manner of popular protest in China: tax riots by aggrieved peasants in the agrarian countryside, strikes by disgruntled workers in the industrial rustbelt, petitions by feisty retirees whose pensions fall short of expectations, resistance by irate villagers to the illegal sale of their collective lands, and so forth. Journalists are not the only people writing about this issue. The study of contentious politics in contemporary China has of late become a rapid-growth industry among American social scientists.[1]

Elizabeth J. Perry is Henry Rosovsky Professor of Government at Harvard University and is the current President of the Association for Asian Studies (eperry@latte.harvard.edu).
A preliminary draft of this paper was delivered as a keynote address at the conference on Socioeconomic Rights and Justice in China held at Dickinson College in April 2004. The author is grateful to the conference organizer, Neil Diamant, for the invitation to consider these issues and to the other conference participants (especially David Strand and Jerome Cohen) for their challenging comments and questions. A substantially revised version was presented at the conference in memory of Benjamin Schwartz, held in Shanghai at East China Normal University in December 2006. Thanks are due to the conference organizers and participants (particularly Zhu Zhenghui, Xu Jilin, Zhang Jishun, Tong Shijun, and Roderick MacFarquhar) for their stimulating suggestions. Appreciation is also extended to Stephen Angle, Nara Dillon, Mary Gallagher, and Kevin O'Brien for their critical reading of an earlier draft.

A distinctly normative tone, inflected with an Anglo-American language of human rights, can be seen in many of the recent writings on this issue. On the one hand, some journalists (and more than a few scholars as well) describe the contemporary protests as symptoms of a pervasive "moral vacuum" in which Chinese supposedly find themselves. Post-Mao China is depicted as a society where Marxism has been discredited, but—absent a Western appreciation of individual natural rights—Chinese have no moral compass to guide their changing and confused lives.[2] Because of this alleged ethical and spiritual vacuum, we are told, millions of Chinese have turned to other forms of solace (e.g., Falun Gong, underground Christianity, and so forth) that often result in the trampling of their unprotected human rights by the state. On the other hand, many scholars (and some journalists as well) have detected in the surge of popular protest in post-Mao China an emergent "rights consciousness"—indicating a supposed bottom-up claim to citizenship and auguring a fundamental breakthrough in state-society relations.[3] In the judgment of these American analysts, "rights talk" among Chinese protesters represents a powerful new social phenomenon, posing a potential challenge to the survival of the Communist state.

The Chinese government paints a very different picture, of course. In a State Council White Paper, issued in the year 2000 and entitled "Fifty Years of Progress in China's Human Rights," the government credits the People's Republic with having bestowed upon the Chinese people an unprecedented enjoyment of human rights—most notably in the form of socioeconomic justice. Interestingly, this official Chinese White Paper does not suggest that

DOI: 10.1017/S1537592708080055

such rights were entirely absent before the Communist revolution. Rather, the State Council report contends that—prior to the advent of Western imperialism—the Chinese people had experienced some minimal fulfillment of rights, but that this safety net was demolished by the foreign assaults of the mid-nineteenth century. To quote directly from the 2000 White Paper:

> Invaded and enslaved by various foreign powers, old China lost its state sovereignty, and *its people's human rights lost their minimum guarantee.* The first important achievement of the Chinese Communist Party . . . was to drive the imperialist invaders out of China, paving the way for China to realize real independence. . . . The genuine and complete independence of China has created the fundamental premise for the Chinese people's selection of their own social and political systems . . . and for the uninterrupted improvement of human rights in China.[4]

Beyond its obvious propagandistic flavor, this passage is revealing in several respects. First, it suggests that before the opium wars of the mid-nineteenth century, imperial Chinese regimes did have some commitment to a minimum guarantee of "human rights" for their people. And second, it makes clear that—in the eyes of the contemporary Chinese government—the West was responsible not for bringing to China a newfound appreciation of human rights, but rather for depriving the Chinese of rights that they had previously enjoyed. State sovereignty and national independence are seen as the basic prerequisites for a further improvement in human rights, an improvement that must after all be founded in a political and social system of China's own choosing.

Amnesty International and other human rights groups immediately labeled this Chinese White Paper a "whitewash" and denounced the PRC's failure to live up to its own claims.[5] The U.S. State Department chided China for a "poor" human rights record marred by "numerous and serious abuses."[6] The Chinese government responded with an equally unflattering assessment of America's human rights record, pointing to flagrant racial discrimination, callous neglect of the poor and homeless, and so on.[7] This war of words continued, and even escalated, in subsequent years.[8]

My purpose in this article is *not* to evaluate the actual human rights record of either America or China—whether at present or in the past. My purview is limited to *conceptions* of rights, as reflected in the ethical discourses of Chinese philosophers, political leaders, and protesters (and as contrasted with American understandings of rights). In examining these normative claims, I will question both the "moral vacuum" and the "rights-based challenge" perspectives that infuse much of the Western literature on contemporary China. Arguing that an enduring emphasis on collective socioeconomic justice distinguishes mainstream Chinese political thought from an Anglo-American focus on individual rights, I conclude that the contemporary Chinese political order is neither as vacuous nor as vulnerable as sometimes depicted.

The 2000 White Paper makes crystal clear, as have numerous other publications by the Chinese government before and since, that—when it comes to human rights—socioeconomic considerations rank first among its priorities. The recent amendment of the Chinese Constitution to include a provision respecting and protecting human rights does not change this basic conception of human rights. The 2004 Chinese White Paper on human rights progress, issued two weeks after the amendment of the Constitution, states the following: "The Chinese government continues to put the safeguarding and promotion of the *people's rights to subsistence and development* on the top of its agenda."[9]

The government asserts, in other words, that its people have a right to some minimum standard of living ("subsistence" or *shengcun*)—and, moreover, they have a right to expect an improvement in that standard ("development" or *fazhan*). The first idea—that people have a just claim to a decent livelihood and that a state's legitimacy depends upon satisfying this claim—goes very far back in Chinese political thought. It has roots in the teachings of Confucius (sixth–fifth century BC) and was elaborated by the influential Confucian philosopher Mencius (fourth–third century BC). Although Mencius never framed his arguments in a language of "rights," he did emphasize the links between economic welfare and legitimate rule. The second idea—that the state should promote socioeconomic development—is a more recent notion, advanced by Chinese political leaders since the late nineteenth century and articulated with particular force by Mao Zedong during his revolutionary drive to power and afterwards.[10] Both of these concepts, subsistence and development, are not simply abstract mantras uttered by Chinese philosophers and statesmen; they are also central to the ways in which ordinary people in China think and act politically.

Concerns about socioeconomic justice are not peculiarly Chinese, of course. T.H. Marshall, in his classic work on the rise of citizenship in Western Europe, pointed to "social citizenship"—or the collective right to economic welfare and social security—as the highest expression of citizenship. In Marshall's evolutionary account, a minimalist *civil citizenship*—or the guarantee of individual rights to property, personal liberty, and legal justice—appeared in eighteenth-century Europe, while the nineteenth century saw the emergence of a more developed sense of *political citizenship*—or the right to participate in the exercise of government power. Only in the twentieth century, however, did a claim to full *social citizenship* (as embodied in the modern welfare state) become widespread across Europe.[11]

Samuel Fleischacker, in his recent history of distributive justice, traces the acknowledgment of "a right of all people to a certain socioeconomic status" back to the eighteenth century, to the writings of Rousseau, Smith, Kant, and Babeuf.[12] According to Fleischacker, however, "for most of human history practically no one held, even as an ideal, the view that everyone should have their basic needs satisfied."[13] While Fleischacker may well be correct in his critique of early Western thought, his argument entirely overlooks the Confucian tradition. An abiding concern with distributive justice has marked Chinese political thought for more than two millennia.[14] Contrary to the scenario that Marshall outlines for Western Europe, in China an appreciation of "social citizenship" predated political citizenship by many centuries.[15]

In the U.S., by comparison with both ancient China and modern Europe, a commitment to social citizenship has been notably weak. American political philosophers, in pondering the primary function of government, have historically emphasized the protection of individual freedoms (or what Marshall regarded as the lowest form of citizenship). This view, which prizes strict limits on state intervention, has pervaded popular political sentiment in the U.S. as well. The political theorist Louis Hartz characterized the American Way of Life as "a nationalist articulation of Locke which usually does not know that Locke himself is involved."[16] Fundamental to Locke's political philosophy was an emphasis upon natural rights as both prior—and superior—to laws enacted by the state. Locke's understanding of natural law stressed individual inalienable rights (to life, liberty, and property). In his conception, the role of government was a limited one; the state simply guaranteed the social order necessary to permit the exercise of individuals' natural rights. Rebellion was justifiable, but only if government violated the "social contract" either by failing to ensure public order or by aggrandizing its powers vis-à-vis society.[17] Locke's views were consistent with mainstream European political thought in his day, which saw the state's responsibilities as highly circumscribed.

By contrast, Chinese statecraft since the times of Mencius has envisioned a more proactive role for government—which was expected to promote economic welfare and security. Such expectations carried important practical consequences. As R. Bin Wong observes in his comparison of European and Chinese state formation, "When we turn to issues of material welfare, we find a [Chinese] tradition of intervention in subsistence issues that dwarfs European government efforts to address the insecurities of agrarian economies."[18] The idea that good governance rests upon guaranteeing the livelihood of ordinary people has been a hallmark of Chinese political philosophy and practice from Mencius to Mao—and beyond. It is reflected not only in government pronouncements and policies, but also in grassroots protests—an issue to which I shall return later in this paper.

Another thing that the ancient philosopher Mencius and the modern revolutionary Mao shared in common, besides an expressed concern for collective welfare, was an explanation—and in Mao's case even a celebration—of popular uprisings as a legitimate response to a government's failure to fulfill its social responsibilities. When Mencius was asked by one anxious king what he should do in order to hold onto the throne, Mencius answered simply: "Protect the people."[19] He continued, "An intelligent ruler will regulate the livelihood of the people, so as to make sure that . . . in good years they shall always be abundantly satisfied, and that in bad years they shall escape the danger of perishing."[20] Here then was a crisply stated Confucian "moral economy" that made protecting and promoting the people's livelihood the cornerstone of statecraft.

The Book of History (*Shujing*), an ancient Chinese philosophical text from which Mencius—like Confucius—drew many of his central ideas, contained the notion of the Mandate of Heaven (*tianming*) which treated rebellion as Heaven's way of removing the mantle of leadership from immoral rulers and bestowing it instead upon those who were virtuous enough to replace them. The concept of the Mandate of Heaven as a rationale for rebellion first appeared in China around the founding of the Zhou dynasty in the eleventh century BC. Seven hundred years later, Mencius expanded upon this idea by linking the authority of Heaven (*tian*) with the support of the people (*ren*). When asked by one of his disciples how a ruler had gained the realm, Mencius replied, "Heaven gave the empire to him; the people gave it to him" (*tian yu zhi, ren yu zhi*).[21] He went on to explain, "The people are the most important element . . . Therefore to gain the support of the ordinary people is to become emperor."[22] Mencius' idea of anchoring political legitimacy in the assent of the people may not seem particularly noteworthy today; after all, since the American and French revolutions most modern states have advanced far bolder claims to popular sovereignty. But considering the time in which it was proposed, more than two millennia ago, this stress on popular support was truly extraordinary.

When we compare the Mencian Mandate of Heaven with a European divine right of kings or a Japanese belief in an unbroken imperial line descending from the Sun Goddess, the contrast is stark. In Mencius, royal blood did not constitute a continuing basis of political legitimacy. The Mandate of Heaven was subject to change (*tianming feichang*),[23] and required constant renewal through popular support. How did one garner such backing? By behaving benevolently and providing for the people's livelihood. The ancient emperors, Mencius noted with nostalgic approval, undertook frequent "tours of inspection" for the purpose of ensuring a bountiful harvest: "In the spring they examined the plowing, and supplied any deficiency of seed; in the autumn they examined the reaping, and supplied any deficiency of yield."[24] Only when the harvest was secure and the peasantry was satisfied did a ruler enjoy the Mandate of Heaven. To neglect the people's livelihood was to invite rebellion: "When the hungry go without food . . . the people become unruly."[25] The most important virtue of a ruler was benevolence (*ren*) or sympathy with the plight of the people. If a sovereign failed to provide for the well-being of his people, rebellion was the natural reaction. As Benjamin Schwartz noted, "It is made amply clear in the *Analects* and particularly in the *Mencius,* that the moral behavior of the masses is dependent upon their economic welfare."[26]

The differences between the Chinese and other imperial systems (European as well as Japanese) were significant, but so too were the differences with many modern republican political systems. Compare Mencius' view of rebellion with that of Thomas Jefferson, for example. Both Mencius and Jefferson stress the granting or withholding of popular support, but to very different ends. Jefferson's understanding of revolution drew not on the Book of History but on Locke's *Second Treatise.*[27] In Jefferson's stirring speeches, rebellion was both natural and justifiable—but as a check on political tyranny, not as a reaction to socioeconomic injustice. A child of the Enlightenment, Jefferson viewed periodic armed rebellion as essential in sustaining democratic freedoms. As he put it, "God forbid we should ever be twenty years without such a rebellion. . . . What country can preserve its liberties if the rulers are not warned from time to time that their people preserve the spirit of resistance? Let them take up arms. . . . The tree of liberty must be refreshed from time to time with the blood of patriots and tyrants. It is its natural manure."[28] For Thomas Jefferson, tyranny, not poverty, was the root cause of periodic rightful rebellion.

Mao Zedong, who came of age more than a century after Jefferson, was of course deeply influenced by Western political philosophies—first anarchism and then Marxism. But many of Mao's ideas were congruent with his own cultural traditions as well. As Schwartz stresses, although a principal source of the Maoist vision was Marxist-Leninist ideology, "this does not preclude the fact that in some of its aspects it coincides with certain traditional Chinese habits of thought and behavior."[29] Indeed, there are more than a few points of commonality between Confucianism and Marxism. The belief that human nature is inherently social, and that conflict between the individual and the larger community is unnatural and unnecessary, is certainly central to both.[30]

Here I would like to highlight two affinities between Mao and Mencius: the importance of popular—in particular *peasant*—support in establishing political legitimacy, and relatedly, the natural propensity of those who are hard pressed economically to rebel against rapacious officials.[31] Nowhere did Mao express these views more passionately or eloquently than in his famous "Report on an Investigation of the Peasant Movement in Hunan," published in March of 1927 at a time when most of his comrades in the Chinese Communist Party were still focusing on workers in the cities rather than on the rural peasantry. Based upon a 32-day investigation of five counties in his home province of Hunan, Mao described his awakening to the importance of the peasantry. As he wrote:

> In a very short time, in China's central, southern and northern provinces, several hundred million peasants will rise like a mighty storm, like a hurricane, a force so swift and violent that no power, however great, will be able to hold it back. They will smash all the trammels that bind them and rush forward along the road to liberation. They will sweep all the imperialists, warlords, corrupt officials, local bullies and evil gentry into their graves. Every revolutionary party and every revolutionary comrade will be put to the test, to be accepted or rejected as they decide. There are three alternatives. To march at their head and lead them? To trail behind them, gesticulating and criticizing? Or to stand in their way and oppose them? Every Chinese is free to choose, but events will force you to make the choice quickly.[32]

Here Mao depicts the peasantry as a force of nature—"a mighty storm," "a hurricane"—and argues that revolutionary success hinges upon acknowledging and accepting the natural inclinations of the peasants, rough and violent as they may be.

> The peasants are clear-sighted. Who is bad and who is not, who is the worst and who is not quite so vicious, who deserves severe punishment and who deserves to be let off lightly—the peasants keep clear accounts and very seldom has the punishment exceeded the crime . . . A revolution is not a dinner party, or writing an essay, or painting a picture or doing embroidery; it cannot be so refined, so leisurely and gentle, so temperate, kind courteous, restrained and magnanimous. . . . The rural areas need a mighty revolutionary upsurge, for it alone can rouse the people in their millions to become a powerful force.[33]

In Mao's view the revolutionary instincts of the peasantry derive from their poverty. Hence it is the poorest peasants, those with the least to lose, who are naturally the most revolutionary.

> Leadership by the poor peasants is absolutely necessary. Without the poor peasants there would be no revolution. To deny their role is to deny the revolution. To attack them is to attack the revolution. They have never been wrong on the general direction of the revolution.[34]

In these stirring passages, Mao puts forth a view of revolution quite different from that of Marx and Lenin; whereas for Marx the urban proletariat served as the revolutionary vanguard and for Lenin the Communist Party fulfilled that purpose, Mao is here assigning the role of revolutionary vanguard to the poor peasants who, as he described them "are not afraid of losing anything."

Although Mao's Marxian celebration of class struggle put him at odds with a Confucian preference for social harmony, he nevertheless shared with Mencius a stress on the peasantry as the decisive political force—and a belief that peasant poverty was the root cause of revolution (the modern Chinese term for which, *geming,* carries the meaning of "to change the mandate").[35] After the establishment of a

Communist regime in China, when Mao's thoughts turned to developmental issues, he continued to emphasize the pivotal and dynamic role of the peasantry. In late 1955, Mao wrote of agricultural collectivization much as he had written of rural revolution thirty years before:

> A new upsurge in the socialist mass movement is imminent throughout the countryside. But some of our comrades are tottering along like a woman with bound feet and constantly complaining, "you're going too fast" . . . The high tide of socialist transformation in the countryside . . . will soon sweep over the whole country. It is a vast socialist revolutionary movement involving a rural population of more than 500 million and it has extremely great and world-wide significance . . . . The leadership should never lag behind the mass movement, but the present situation is one in which the mass movement is running ahead of the leadership . . .[36]

Again it was the peasantry, rather than the cadres, who were naturally attuned to the demands of revolutionary progress. And again it was poverty that generated their insight and enthusiasm:

> Both the poor peasants and the lower strata of the new and old middle peasants are enthusiastic about the socialist road . . . because the poor peasants are in a difficult economic position and because the lower middle peasants are still not well off, although their economic position is better than before liberation.[37]

Those who were materially well off, by contrast, failed to appreciate the latent power of the masses. They failed, in other words, to grasp the "Mandate of Heaven."

> The well-to-do jeered: "Those ragamuffins think they can set up a cooperative. Never heard of a chicken feather flying up to Heaven." But that is just what this chicken feather has done . . . The poor want to remake their lives. The old system is dying and a new system is being born. Chicken feathers really are flying up to Heaven.[38]

Here, six years after the founding of a new Communist government, Mao was again identifying peasant poverty as the motor propelling historic transformation—now not political revolution but economic development in the form of agricultural collectivization.

We can certainly question the degree to which collectivization benefited the Chinese peasantry, but regardless of how we evaluate China's actual record of collectivized agriculture, it is worth recalling the political rationale that lay behind it. As Mao presented the situation to his skeptical colleagues, collectivization was being driven by the irrepressible yearning of the poor peasants for a better life. Once again, as had been true twenty years before when he investigated the peasant movement in Hunan, Mao insisted that the peasants were out in front of the Communist party—and party cadres would have to catch up quickly unless they were to be trampled underfoot by a restless populace rushing forward along the road toward socialism. The impoverished peasants, he exclaimed, were performing what had once seemed impossible: chicken feathers were flying up to Heaven. As in Mencius, cosmic authority (Heaven) was linked to the well-being of the peasantry—and political leaders, if they were to retain their legitimacy, would have to get in step with peasant demands to protect and promote their livelihood.

For Mencius, peasant demands had been limited to *subsistence*. By Mao's time, the peasantry was seen as demanding not only subsistence, but *development* as well. Central to Marxism-Leninism is of course an appreciation of the dynamism of economic transformation. Peasants now rightfully expected to see an improvement in their livelihood—and held government officials accountable to this higher standard. Mao cautioned that cadres would have to stop tottering along like women with bound feet if they were going to satisfy the peasants' escalating aspirations.

Today, more than thirty years after Mao's death, his ideas—not to mention those of the ancient Mencius—may appear somewhat dated. I have revisited these ideas because I believe that they offer some telling clues about contemporary Chinese politics. Chairman Mao's successors—Deng Xiaoping, Jiang Zemin, Hu Jintao, and Wen Jiabao—have all emphasized economic development, and specifically poverty alleviation for the hard-pressed peasantry, as a cornerstone of their claim to political legitimacy. This was the rationale with which Deng Xiaoping launched his historic economic reforms in December 1978—spearheaded by the household responsibility system for peasants in poorer parts of the countryside. When rural incomes soared in the early 1980s, Deng rejoiced that his reforms were off to a promising start.

Although Western observers have often faulted the post-Mao leadership for a failure to promote democratization and the enlargement of political rights, Chinese leaders themselves appear far more concerned about aggressively pursuing socioeconomic objectives—especially the goal of ensuring that poor peasants enjoy a decent and improving livelihood. When Deng Xiaoping initiated his reforms, in sharp contrast to Gorbachev in the Soviet Union, he talked not of *glastnost* (political openness) or of *perestroika* (restructuring) but of *xiaokang* (economic comfort).

In December 1979 Deng Xiaoping was asked by the Prime Minister of Japan about the meaning of China's so-called Four Modernizations, the catchy phrase that summed up the post-Mao reform effort. The Four Modernizations, as articulated by the late Premier Zhou Enlai, called for developing China's agriculture, industry, science and technology, and national defense. Some Chinese dissidents, such as Wei Jingsheng, criticized the Chinese leadership for not including a fifth modernization in its recipe for development: democratization. But Deng Xiaoping, in responding to the inquiry of the Japanese Prime Minister, mentioned none of these things. Instead, he replied this way: "The Four Modernizations that we want to implement are a Chinese-style of Modernization. Our concept of Four Modernizations is not the same as your concept of modernization. What we seek to realize is an economically comfortable family (*xiaokang zhi jia*)."[39]

The term *xiaokang* has an ancient lineage. It appears repeatedly in the Confucian classics. In both the Book of Rites (*Liji*) and the Book of Songs (*Shijing*), the term *xiaokang* refers to a type of society which, although not as perfect as the utopian Great Harmony (*datong*)—the ideal society that both Confucius and Mao were prone to invoke—is nevertheless the next best thing because it provides everyone with economic comfort.[40] In the Book of Songs the "economically comfortable family" (*xiaokang zhi jia*) is described as a household whose labors afford it a decent level of subsistence.

In January 1980, Deng gave concrete meaning to this concept. He explained his economically comfortable (*xiaokang*) standard as a per capita GDP for China of $1,000 (U.S.) dollars by the end of the twentieth century. Four years later, Deng backpedaled a bit, shaving a couple hundred dollars off his target. As he put it in October 1984: "We have established a clear political goal: to reach a per capita GDP of $800 (U.S.) by the end of this century, so that the people's livelihood reaches an economically comfortable standard (*renmin shenghuo dadao xiaokang shuiping*)." In June of 1986, he explained further: "By the year 2000 we plan to establish an economically comfortable society (*xiaokang shehui*). To be too ambitious won't work. We must seek truth from facts. A so-called economically comfortable society, although not wealthy, is able to make do. We are a socialist country. Our national income should be distributed fairly so as to allow all the people to benefit—without some people becoming too rich and others too poor."

A similar rationale was embraced by Deng's successor, Jiang Zemin, when he announced his Great Western Development Strategy in June of 1999. Jiang's "Great Leap West" called for massive state investment, foreign loans, and private capital to be diverted from the rich coastal areas to the more remote regions of the interior countryside. The stated goals of Jiang's ambitious policy were to "increase the income of the population" and "bring prosperity to all nationalities."[41] In his final speech as General Secretary of the Chinese Communist Party, Jiang updated Deng's *xiaokang* target, pledging to turn China into an "economically comfortable society" with a GDP of $ 4 trillion (U.S.) by the year 2020.[42]

In the run-up to the 16th Party Congress in the fall of 2002, an article in the Communist Party newspaper, *People's Daily*, announced that "the ancient Chinese ideal of an economically comfortable society (*xiaokang shehui*), revitalized by the country's late leader Deng Xiaoping, is likely to be a hot topic at the 16th National Congress of the Communist Party of China."[43] At the 16th Party Congress the new Chinese leadership, in keeping with Jiang Zemin's parting pledge, set forth the goal of establishing an "economically comfortable society" by the year 2020. Appropriately enough for a 16th Party Congress, sixteen targets were announced. For example, whereas in 2002, China's per capita GDP stood at 8,000 yuan, by 2020 it is supposed to soar to 24,000 yuan.[44] While in 2002, per capita peasant income was a mere 2,476 yuan, by 2020 it is projected to reach 6,860 yuan. And so on. Still, compared to Jiang's paramount interest in economic growth, his successors have put greater emphasis upon socioeconomic well-being. At the last party congress, several central leaders pointed out that peasants lag behind city dwellers not only in terms of income, but also in access to medical care, education, and other key indicators of human welfare.

The aim of an economically comfortable society is considerably less ambitious than the utopian Confucian (or Communist) vision of a "Great Harmony," but the current Chinese leadership in directing attention to the plight of the peasantry draws inspiration from Mao Zedong as well as from Mencius. Both Premier Wen Jiabao and President Hu Jintao have made highly publicized trips to poor rural areas that once served as Mao's revolutionary bases—underscoring the central government's deep concern for the livelihood of the struggling peasantry and its avowed commitment to socioeconomic justice. On a visit to the site of the former Jiangxi Soviet in the summer of 2003, Hu Jintao enjoined officials at all levels of the party to "carry on the revolutionary tradition." As Hu put it, "Comrade Mao Zedong and other revolutionaries of the elder generation not only made historical achievements by realizing national independence and liberation, but also bequeathed to us precious spiritual wealth." A front page article in *People's Daily* elaborated on Hu's remarks: "such revolutionary spirit and tradition, which were fostered through arduous struggles, provide strength for overcoming difficulties and risks of all kinds in our way forward."[45]

The current leaders of China are acutely mindful of the decisive role of the peasantry in facilitating—or forestalling—overall national progress. At the 10th National People's Congress in March 2006, Premier Wen Jiabao set forth the guiding policy of "building a new socialist countryside." In an international press conference held at the conclusion of the NPC, the Premier explained:

> The issues concerning agriculture, rural areas and farmers are fundamental ones bearing on the overall interests of China's modernization drive . . . The development of rural areas . . . will facilitate our efforts to build an economically comfortable society (*xiaokang shehui*) in the countryside and modernize China's agricultural sector. This is a significant step in terms of the overall modernization of the country. . . To build a new socialist countryside . . . we need to respect . . . the will of the people in rural areas . . . We need to . . . deliver tangible benefits to farmers. . . And we need to use this as a yardstick to measure our progress and performance."[46]

A year later, Wen's two-hour keynote speech at the March 2007 National People's Congress struck a similar theme, repeatedly emphasizing the central government's concern for the "three rurals" (*sannong*)—i.e., peasants (*nongmin*), agriculture (*nongye*), and countryside (*nongcun*): "We will focus on rural economic development and make substantial progress in building a new socialist countryside. We need to consolidate, improve and strengthen policies for supporting agriculture and giving favorable treatment to farmers, provide more support for agriculture, rural areas and farmers, and promote restructuring of agriculture and the rural economy."[47]

The central leadership is not shy about touting the Maoist *bona fides* of its "new socialist countryside" campaign. As one government report lauded the benefits of the program:

> By the side of the Red Well in Shazhoubei Village in Ruijin City, an old villager named Yang Qingpo could scarcely believe his eyes when he strolled around the newly built cement roads of the village. How could a village where he'd lived for over 60 years change overnight? The old toilets and dilapidated pigpens had been torn down and the garbage that had been piled high around all the houses was gone. Newly built houses were neat and clean . . . 'The new socialist village construction has brought us old folks great benefit. Thanks be to the Communist Party!' He touched the stone tablet next to the Red Well which read, 'When drinking the water, don't forget the one who dug the well. Think often of Chairman Mao.' He felt that it expressed his own deepest sentiments.[48]

In practice, the new socialist countryside initiative—which is often coercively implemented—replicates some of the excesses and insensitivities toward the peasantry for which Mao's own campaigns were known.[49] Yet, conceptually, it shares with Maoism an overriding concern for peasant livelihood.

While Western critics express disappointment that China's leaders seem reluctant to devote the same attention to political reform that they lavish upon precise indicators of socioeconomic goals, those who are most affected by these policies—the ordinary Chinese people—may feel somewhat differently. If we examine the recent protests that have erupted in China, we generally find them framed in a language more reminiscent of Mencius or Mao than of Locke or Jefferson.

In many rural protests, the symbolism of the Mandate of Heaven remains salient. Just a few years ago, peasant protesters in Hunan—in the manner of third century BC rebels Chen Sheng and Wu Guang, who led the first peasant revolt recorded in Chinese history—swore an oath to Heaven and marched behind banners proclaiming "Prepare the Way for Heaven" as they pressed their demands for lower taxes on township and county offices. Their rhetoric was replete with Mencian resonance: "The people's anger overwhelms Heaven;" "If the people are impoverished, the realm should be anxious; if the people complain, the realm should be afraid." Equally interesting is the manner in which local officials responded to these challenges. In one Hunan county, authorities posted a sign outside the tax office saying: "Like the imperial grain tax, the state tax cannot be resisted."[50] But of course much has in fact changed since imperial days, and contemporary peasant protesters have other, more recent rhetorical weapons with which to fight their battles. In phrases redolent of Mao Zedong, today's protesters proclaim, "It is right to rebel," "All Power to the Peasants," "The Peasants are Clear Sighted," "Down with the new landlords!"[51]

Peasants are not the only protesters to draw inspiration from the Chinese tradition of distributive justice. A protest by displaced workers at a knitting mill in Chongqing was one of many such incidents that have erupted in depressed industrial centers around the country in recent years. The factory announced in November 1992 that it was declaring bankruptcy and that its 3,000 workers would have to seek alternative employment on their own. Moreover, retired workers were to be reduced to monthly stipends of only 50 yuan, in contrast to original levels of 150 to 250 yuan. To protest these reversals, a petition movement was launched:

> The retired workers who led the demonstration procession knelt down before the armed policemen, pleading tearfully that they only wanted to lodge a petition to be able to receive their original pensions and only hoped for *the right of subsistence*. . . The retired workers said that the pensions represented the work accumulation that they had made in the past decades and belonged to part of the surplus value they had created . . . Workers on the job said: We just worked according to orders, and business losses were caused by mistakes in the economic plan for guiding production; the blame should not be placed on the workers. The state should be responsible for the future of the workers and should provide them with jobs and training, thus guaranteeing workers' *basic right of survival*.[52]

While arguments about surplus value and the economic plan reflect the influence of Marxism and Communism, demands claiming a fundamental right to subsistence—presented on bended knee—have a much older pedigree.

We find numerous expressions of this Mencian claim in urban as well as rural protests. A report in 1995, for example, noted that "workers in Liaoning and Sichuan often took to the streets and staged demonstrations to express their resentment. They called for 'being able to get food for survival.'"[53] Sociologist Ching Kwan Lee concludes in a recent survey of labor unrest in China that "subsistence rights occupied top priority in the slogans."[54] In foregrounding subsistence demands, today's workers are echoing long established protest frames. In the first major industrial strike instigated by Mao and his comrades—the Anyuan coal miners' strike of 1922—the strikers (who were among the best compensated workers of their day) issued a manifesto that proclaimed: "We want to live! We want to eat! Now we are starving! Our lives are in danger! Seeking life in the midst of death, we have no choice but to take up the weapon of last resort—to strike."[55] During recent pension protests at the Anyuan mine, retired miners demanding higher compensation highlighted the gap between the image of *xiaokang* prosperity put forth by the Communist Party leadership and their own dismal circumstances.[56]

In contemporary Chinese labor protests, moral economy claims to subsistence are often laced with Marxist rhetoric: "Workers are the masters of the country," "Yes to socialism, no to capitalism," "Long live the working class."[57] Frequently the catchwords of the central leadership are invoked, as in the recent Anyuan pensioners' demonstration: "Strengthen the Three Represents! We want to eat, and we also want to move toward economic comfort (*xiaokang*)!"[58] The slogans that appear to resonate most strongly with officials, however, are those that avow an age-old claim to a basic livelihood. A newspaper report on a series of labor protests in the northern industrial city of Shenyang gave the following account:

> Workers have marched on government offices to protest against their wretched living conditions. . . Soft-hearted officials could not turn away the request for subsidies and wages . . . The mayor of Shenyang declared, "The people are ours. They must at least be able to eat."[59]

To be sure, the protests sweeping both urban and rural China today spring from multiple causes and are manifested in many different ways. In the countryside, with the recent abolition of the state agricultural tax, land disputes have replaced tax protests as the primary trigger of collective violence. Even so, the insistent demand for socioeconomic justice—framed as a moral claim to subsistence—is a thread that binds many of these otherwise disparate incidents together. Although the land disputes concern property rights, they tend to be presented in moral economy terms. In a recent protest against the seizure of collective land in Guangdong's Shunde county, for example, villagers complained to higher-level officials that local cadres "don't care if the peasants are without land and livelihood."[60] In a land dispute near Shenzhen, a protester explained to a foreign journalist, "I have no choice. I have an obligation to fight for our land, along with my fellow villagers. We have to keep fighting until we get our land back. This is the root of our life."[61] In response to the spate of land conflicts, Premier Wen Jiabao declared that "some locales are unlawfully occupying farmers' land and not offering reasonable economic compensation and arrangements for livelihood, and this is sparking mass incidents in the countryside . . . We absolutely cannot commit a historic error over land problems."[62] Wen's speech was followed by a deluge of state-issued pledges for the construction of a new, more just "socialist countryside." The articulation of a well-recognized right to a decent livelihood indicates that, despite the Chinese government's apparent lack of concern for human rights as Americans may define them, the country is not necessarily suffering from a moral vacuum.[63]

Despite America's own persistent problems of poverty and homelessness, we do not see many social movements in the contemporary United States focused on a demand for economic justice. Instead, collective actions generally center on claims of individual civil rights. Take, for example, the numerous—and sometimes violent—confrontations surrounding the question of abortion. "Pro-life" advocates put forth claims on behalf of an unborn child's "natural right" to life, whereas "pro-choice" advocates advance claims on behalf of "reproductive rights"—or a woman's "natural right" to control her own body. Fierce as the conflict is, both sides agree that the proper role of government in this bitter controversy is to protect inalienable individual rights (whether by upholding or by overturning the *Roe v. Wade* Supreme Court decision of 1973).

Consider another persistent source of unrest in contemporary America—the extremist militia groups which have mushroomed across the land in recent years. Armed militias claiming Jeffersonian roots have been linked to a string of terrorist attacks against the U.S. federal government.[64] Insisting that their activities conform to the spirit of the American Revolution, these groups honor an individual's right to bear arms in defense of freedom (enshrined in the Second Amendment) as the central cause and lasting legacy of the Revolution.[65] As a member of the Missouri Fifty-First Militia puts it, "the primary trigger for the Revolution was the same as it is today: you don't mess with a free man's right to keep and bear arms."[66] In the eyes of their militant members, these maverick militias stand as guardians of a natural right to personal liberty against an oppressive federal government. The literature produced by such groups makes frequent reference to an eighteenth-century republican ideology that saw the armed citizen as a people's best protection against despotism. Thomas Jefferson's call to arms is quoted with particular fervor.[67]

In America, even fundamentally economic protests are framed as a question of civil rights. Take the case of the "California Tax Revolt," whose successful challenge to escalating property taxes (with the passage of Proposition 13 in 1978) ignited similar protests across much of the U.S.[68] The leader of the movement, Howard Jarvis, justified his activities not with socioeconomic arguments, but in terms of a struggle by rights-bearing citizens against despotism: "The entire basis of free government in America was being destroyed by virtually unlimited taxation, which can only lead to . . . dictatorship."[69] Tyranny, not poverty, was offered as the reason for rightful rebellion. To Americans, *liberty* rather than *livelihood* is the foundation of political morality.

In arguing for a significant difference between mainstream Chinese and American conceptions of rights, and their implications for popular protest, I do not mean to suggest that all (or even any) Chinese think only about socioeconomic security, to the exclusion of all other concerns. That would be just as silly as to suggest that Americans care only about political freedom and eschew all material interests. The example of China's Tiananmen

Uprising (led by students demanding democracy) or of America's pay equity campaign (led by women demanding equal pay for equal work) is enough to dispel any such misunderstanding.[70] But there is nonetheless, I believe, an important difference in emphasis between the two political cultures—manifested not only in abstract philosophical discourse but in political rhetoric and popular protest as well.

For that reason, I am skeptical of a central theme in much of the recent American social science scholarship on China, suggesting that the popular discourse of "rights" observable in recent protests indicates a newfound claim to citizenship that poses a fundamental challenge to state authority.[71] Such arguments, I believe, overstate both the novelty and the political threat posed by such protests. Kevin O'Brien and Li Lianjiang, in their study of rural protest in contemporary China, note that "the notion of being a citizen is seeping into popular discourse" and urge that "we should not underestimate the implications of rising rights consciousness and a growing fluency in 'rights talk' in a nation where rights have traditionally been weakly protected"—on grounds that "today's rightful resistance could . . . evolve into a more far-reaching counterhegemonic project."[72] David Zweig attributes China's "current political and social dilemma" to "the confrontation between an emerging 'rights conscious peasantry' and rapacious or entrepreneurial bureaucrats."[73] Maria Heimer highlights the possibility that "growing rights consciousness in the Chinese countryside may contribute to significant political changes."[74] Merle Goldman argues in her book *From Comrade to Citizen* that "one of the major changes in the last two decades of the twentieth century was a growing sense of rights consciousness, particularly of political rights" among the Chinese population at large. The rapid and widespread development of citizenship and civil society, she contends, has the potential "to produce in China changes as profound as those that occurred earlier in Eastern Europe."[75]

The impact of China's 1995 Labor Law on the swelling tide of labor disputes has attracted particular attention from observers in this country.[76] Mary Gallagher sees the new law, and related legal institutions as helping to generate "increased societal conflict and rising rights-consciousness among Chinese workers . . . .[W]orkers are increasingly likely to use these new institutions to press for the protection of their rights and interests."[77] Bolder claims appear in journalistic reporting on China; a recent *Business Week* article, mindful of the precedent of Solidarity in Poland, speaks glowingly of "a new labor-rights revolution sweeping China."[78]

There is no doubt that the terms "rights" (*quanli*) and "citizen" (*gongmin*) suffuse both official and popular discourse in contemporary China. But workers who demand that as "citizens" they have a "right" to eat would seem to be following more in the moral economy footsteps of Mencius and Mao than in the liberal tradition of Locke or Jefferson. In a series of newspaper articles that Mao Zedong published in 1922 to promote the idea of a national labor law, Mao (drawing upon the international socialist discourse of his day) identified three "rights" (*quan*) that such a law would guarantee: (1) the right to subsistence (*shengcun quan*); (2) the right to work (*laodong quan*); and (3) the right to the entire proceeds of one's labor (*laodong quanshou quan*).[79] Surely, then, we should not impute to the discussion surrounding China's latest labor law some new sense of citizenship rights heralding a democratic revolution-from-below. Indeed, when Sociologist Ching Kwan Lee, impressed by the "constant invocation of law and legal rights in workers' interaction with local officials," suggested to some protest leaders that they were fighting for citizens' legal rights, she was greeted with ridicule: "Workers' thinking is not that advanced," "Legal rights? What is legal, where is the law?"[80] The 1995 Labor Law makes clear that its provisions are designed to facilitate state goals: "This Law is hereby formulated in accordance with the Constitution in order to protect the legitimate rights and interests of laborers, readjust the labor relationship, establish and safeguard the labor system to suit the socialist market economy, and promote economic development and social progress."[81]

China's pervasive moral economy protests, framed in a language of "rights," have often demanded (sometimes successfully) the removal of unpopular lower-level officials. Rarely, however, have they questioned the ruling authority of either the Communist Party or its ideology. In this respect, contemporary protesters bear some resemblance to imperial-era rebels. The endemic unrest that punctuated the history of imperial China often led to the replacement of particular officials (and very occasionally even of dynasties), while at the same time retaining and reinforcing certain basic principles of the Confucian order. Writing in the middle of the nineteenth century, the English Sinologist Thomas Meadows offered the following explanation for the remarkable longevity of the imperial Chinese system: "In China . . . it is precisely the right to rebel that has been a chief element of a national stability, unparalleled in the world's history."[82] While one would be foolhardy to forecast for the current political order anything approaching the lengthy lifespan enjoyed by the imperial system, it does nonetheless appear that today's patterns of protest—still animated by a widespread appreciation of "the right to rebel"[83]—may prove more system-supportive than system-subversive. In an authoritarian polity, where elections do not provide an effective check on the misbehavior of state authorities, protests can help to serve that function—thereby undergirding rather than undermining the political system.[84] Moreover, the current central government's willingness to respond to some of the protesters' key grievances, witnessed most dramatically in the 2006 abolition of the age-old agricultural tax followed by the promulgation of a new property rights law, points more toward political flexibility than toward fragility.

The Chinese state itself actively encourages a conceptual linkage between "livelihood" and "rights." At a government-sponsored art exhibition held in Beijing in February, 2003, to celebrate the first anniversary of the founding of the officially-authorized Chinese journal, *Human Rights,* the editor-in-chief (speaking beneath portraits of Mao, Deng, and Jiang) praised the exhibits for portraying "stories in which the Chinese government and the Chinese people fight for human rights (*renquan*). Graphically, they reflect the spirit of the Chinese people in striving for a *xiaokang,* or economically comfortable standard of living, and a vigorous development of the human rights under-taking in China."[85]

This is not to deny that the pervasive "rights talk" in contemporary China, officially encouraged though it is, may serve to stimulate even further popular protest. Indeed the Chinese term for "human rights" (*renquan*) also carries the possible meaning of "people's power." However, expectations of welfare provision *from* the state (i.e., what T.H. Marshall called "social citizenship") clearly cannot be equated with demands for legal protections *against* the state ("civil citizenship")—nor with demands for participation *in* the state ("political citizenship"). Moreover, in China even political citizenship (e.g., the right to vote, to file petitions, to stage protests, to establish associations, etc.) is generally understood as a state-conferred privilege rather than as a natural or inalienable prerogative. Andrew Nathan points out that "political rights in China were consistently regarded as a grant given by the state to the citizens, to enable them to contribute their energies to the needs of the nation."[86]

The Chinese term for "citizen" (*gongmin*)—literally a "public person"—connotes collective membership in the polity, rather than a claim to individual or inalienable rights *vis-à-vis* the state. Although the term "rights" (*quan* or *quanli*) did not figure centrally in Mencius, it has played an important role in Chinese political discourse since its introduction in the mid-nineteenth century by the American missionary, W.A.P. Martin.[87] But the meaning of the term *quan* (as is also true of the term "rights" in Western philosophical discourse) was from the start inconsistent.[88] Even Martin sometimes used the character *quan* to translate the English word "authority" as well as "rights."[89] And Chinese thinkers who contributed to what Marina Svensson has characterized as "a rich and internally contested debate on human rights since the late Qing dynasty,"[90] often did so within a Confucian—specifically Mencian—framework.

Liang Qichao, modern China's most influential proponent of "rights consciousness" explicitly linked his concept to Mencius' understanding of human morality.[91] Liang's notion of rights implied an ethical responsibility toward the collective good, rather than a protection of individual freedoms: "As rights consciousness gets increasingly developed, people's duties become increasingly strong."[92] This understanding of rights as an expression of group unity, rather than of personal liberty, can be seen in Republican-period popular discourse as well. The Anyuan coal miners, whose 1922 Communist-inspired strike manifesto had highlighted subsistence claims, savored their historic victory with a return-to-work manifesto which pledged a continuing struggle for collective rights: "Starting today, let us tighten our group unity, a multitude with but a single mind, to struggle for our own rights!"[93]

Liang Qichao was certainly not the only modern Chinese thinker to develop a conception of rights as a cornerstone of his philosophy. But regardless of variations in partisan leanings, and despite the growing influence of Western ideas on this discussion, political rights in modern China were consistently regarded as bound up with a moral responsibility to the larger political community. The anarchist Liu Shipei credited Mencius (via Wang Yangming) with an ethical understanding of human nature that underpinned his own views of rights as inextricably tied to mutual and collective responsibilities on the part of rulers and ruled alike.[94] The co-founder of the Chinese Communist Party, Chen Duxiu, concluded that it was necessary for the sake of the nation to "sacrifice a part of the rights of individuals, in order to protect the rights of the whole citizenry."[95] A similar perspective, in which the state is both the benefactor and the beneficiary of citizen rights, permeates official Chinese state discourse. Examining China's national constitutions from the late Qing (1908) through the PRC, Nathan observes that "in none of the constitutions were rights considered to be derived from human personhood; they were derived from citizenship in the state . . ."[96]

Stephen Angle's careful study of the philosophical origins and implications of Chinese conceptions of human rights since the Song Neo-Confucianists argues persuasively that "Chinese rights discourse is not merely an imperfect attempt to mirror Western ideals . . . it has a coherent history and is made up of Chinese concepts and concerns . . . China has a rich and distinctive rights discourse."[97] This is of course not to suggest that Chinese conceptions of rights are consistent, unchanging, or impervious to foreign influence. However, rather than assume that the invocation of "rights" in contemporary China bears a close affinity to Anglo-American conceptions of human rights and civil society, which *ipso facto* imply a liberal critique of overweening state power, we should be alert to the distinctive origins and implications of "rights talk" in other cultural and political contexts.

In a country where rights are seen more as state-authorized channels to enhance national unity and prosperity than as naturally endowed protections against state intrusion, popular demands for the exercise of political rights are perhaps better seen as an affirmation of—rather than an affront to—state power. For this reason, I prefer to characterize the framing of protest in contemporary China as "rules consciousness" rather than "rights consciousness."[98] In 2004, the Anyuan protesters presented a petition to the Pingxiang Mining Company and its Communist Party Committee:

> Please permit us, along with the majority of retired workers across the country, to enjoy the newly designated wage standards. If you ignore this, and refuse to resolve the issue of our legitimate rights and interests . . . at an appropriate time, in accordance with our constitutionally given rights, we will organize a large-scale protest demonstration. We will enlist the assistance of the media in upholding justice. And we may ask relevant government agencies to investigate the insider economic machinations of the Company. This is the democratic and legitimate supervisory authority given to us by the Chinese Communist Party. Of course a confrontation is not our first choice; our first choice is a peaceful livelihood."[99]

In their various manifestos, the Anyuan retirees stressed that their protest was purely a demand for economic justice, as promised by the state; it therefore posed no threat to political stability. An activist explained, "We're seeking wages and welfare, not power (*quan*) or politics. We are asking for permission to stage a demonstration. We may not receive it, but the right to request it is stipulated in the national constitution."[100]

It is of course entirely possible, indeed probable, that Chinese protesters—like their counterparts around the world—often parrot the language of the state in order to maximize the chances for a favorable outcome and minimize the likelihood of repression from otherwise hostile officials. Even so, it would seem unwarranted (and quite misleading) to read into their impassioned pronouncements something resembling an Anglo-American "rights revolution." Taken seriously on its own terms, widespread popular protest in China points neither to an indigenous moral vacuum nor toward an epochal clash with state authority.

Notes

1 For a small sampling of this large literature, see Perry and Selden 2003; Gries and Rosen 2004; and O'Brien and Stern forthcoming.
2 See, for example, Gilley 2004, 45 ff.
3 See, among many others, Goldman 2007, 71ff.
4 Information Office of the State Council of the People's Republic of China. 2000; emphasis added.
5 See, for example, the reaction by Human Rights Watch, http://hrw.org/english/docs/2001/04/10/china242.htm.
6 U.S. Department of State, 2002.
7 Information Office of the State Council of the People's Republic of China, 2002.
8 In March 2006, Condoleezza Rice issued the 2005 State Department report branding China as one of the world's worst human rights offenders. The Chinese response painted America as a nation riddled with violent crime and racial discrimination, embroiled in a scandal over the presidential authorization of the wiretapping of some domestic phone calls, and patrolled by brutal policemen who shoot dead infants, bash retired teachers, and abandon prison inmates (in New Orleans) as flood waters rise. As journalist John Taylor put it, "You can almost say 'one report deserves another.'" See "Correspondents Report" (March 12, 2006) in http://www.abc.net.au/correspondents/content/2006/s1589404.htm.
9 Information Office of the State Council of the People's Republic of China, 2004. Emphasis added.
10 On the nineteenth-century formulation, see Schwartz 1964. On Mao's drive to power, see Schwartz 1951.
11 Marshall 1964.
12 Fleischacker 2004, ch. 2.
13 Fleischacker 2004, 2.
14 Munro 2001.
15 Wong 1999, 97–122.
16 Hartz 1955, 11.
17 Locke 1960.
18 Wong 1997, 97.
19 Mencius, Book I, Part I, ch. 7, verse 3.
20 Mencius, Book I, Part I, ch. 7, verse 21.
21 Mencius, Book V, Part I, ch. 5, verse 6.
22 Mencius, Book VII, Part II, ch. 14, verses 1–2.
23 Mencius, Book IV, Part I, ch. 7, verse 5.
24 Mencius, Book I, Part II, ch. IV, verse 5.
25 Mencius, Book I, Part II, ch. 4, verse 6.
26 Schwartz 1964, 11.
27 In fact, "so close is the Declaration of Independence to Locke in form, phraseology, and content, that Jefferson was accused of copying the *Second Treatise.*" Peardon 1952, xx.
28 Jefferson 1787.
29 Schwartz 1968, 172.
30 Munro 2000.
31 Again it is important to note that Mencius did not employ the term "rights" (*quanli*); nonetheless he viewed peasant rebellion in the face of poverty as a natural occurrence. Mao held a considerably more positive view of rebellion; as he put it, "Marxism has hundreds and thousands of principles, but they can be summed up in one sentence: 'it is right to rebel' (*zaofan youli*)!"
32 Mao 1971, 23–24.
33 Mao 1971, 29–30.
34 Mao 1971, 34–35.
35 Schwartz 1951, 188–204 emphasized Mao's embrace of a "purely peasant mass base" as the heart of his distinctive revolutionary approach.
36 Mao 1971, 389–90.

37 Mao 1971, 394.
38 Mao 1971, 422–24.
39 *Beijing Times* (November 10, 2002).
40 On Mao's invocation of the concept of "Great Harmony," see Wakeman 1973.
41 *People's Daily Online* (September 16, 2000; May 21, 2002); *China Development Brief* (October 1, 2000).
42 *People's Daily Online* (November 8, 2002).
43 *People's Daily Online* (November 6, 2002).
44 In 2002, 8,000 yuan was equivalent to $960 (U.S.).
45 *Renmin ribao* [People's Daily] (September 3, 2003).
46 *People's Daily Online* (March 15, 2006).
47 *China Daily Online* (March 19, 2007).
48 Zhang, Luo and Gong 2005, 8.
49 Han 2006, 36–38.
50 Yu 2003.
51 Ouyang 1991, 55; Shih 1993, 40.
52 Niu 1993, 67; emphasis added.
53 "Dispatch from Beijing: 'Labor Unrest Reportedly Occurs in Liaoning and Sichuan'". 1995. In *Lianhe bao* (Hong Kong), translated in *Foreign Broadcast Information Service* (May 8), 42–43.
54 Lee 2003, 80.
55 Pingxiang City Chinese Communist Party Editorial Group. 1990. Vol. 1, 41.
56 *Qunzhong liyi wuxiaoshi* [The prerogatives of the masses are no trifling matter], unpublished protest manifesto (Anyuan: June 2004).
57 Lee 2003, 81.
58 Yu 2006, 365.
59 Sun and Ma 1995, 24.
60 *Radio Free Asia,* November 9, 2006.
61 Luis Ramirez, *Voice of America,* August 13, 2006.
62 Buckley 2006.
63 Edmund Fung observes that "while Marxism is a dead letter in the PRC, democratic socialist values are not." Fung 2006, 479.
64 Crothers 2003.
65 In fact, the Second Amendment to the U.S. Constitution guarantees a collective, not an individual, right to bear arms: "A well regulated Militia being necessary to the security of a free State, the right of the people to keep and bear Arms shall not be infringed."
66 Mulloy 2004, 47.
67 Hamilton 1996, 1.
68 Sears and Citrin 1985, 226–235.
69 Jarvis 1979, 7.
70 Calhoun 1994; McCann 1994. But it is important to note that pay equity was also presented as an individual right to equal treatment under the law, rather than as a collective economic right. See Weir 1992 for an analysis of the persistent failure of a general "right to work" movement to take hold in the United States.
71 Of course this argument is not made in precisely the same way, or to the same degree, by every author. Still, Merle Goldman's conclusion that "a growing consciousness of citizenship and organized efforts to assert political rights . . . . signify the beginnings of a genuine change in the relationship between China's population at large and the state at the beginning of the twenty-first century" is shared by much of the mainstream scholarly literature. Goldman 2007, 74.
72 O'Brien and Li 2006, 126–127. In a thoughtful footnote at 117–118, O'Brien and Li provide a discussion of the meaning of rights in a Chinese context that is quite compatible with central arguments in this paper.
73 Zweig 2003, 132.
74 Heimer and Thogersen 2006, 68.
75 Goldman 2005, 2, 24.
76 Lee 2002.
77 Gallagher 2005, 121, 158.
78 Roberts 2005.
79 Hunan Federation of Trade Unions, ed., *Hunan yundong shiliao xuanbian* [Selected historical materials on the Hunan labor movement] (Changsha: 1984), vol. 1: 148–149.
80 Lee 2007, 116.
81 *Labor Law of the People's Republic of China,* promulgated on January 1, 1995.
82 Meadows 1856, 27.
83 The classical phrase "It is right to rebel" (*zaofan youli*)—sometimes translated as "to rebel is justified"—was deployed by Mao Zedong at the start of his Cultural Revolution to encourage student Red Guards to attack "capitalist roaders." For a recent history of the Cultural Revolution, see MacFarquhar and Schoenhals 2006.
84 The much-ballyhooed village elections, it should be noted, are seldom fully democratic procedurally, and in any case do not extend beyond the village committee—which is not part of the formal state structure (the lowest rung of which is the township government).
85 http://www.humanrights-china.org.
86 Nathan 1985, 107.
87 Angle 2002, 3.
88 Huang 1994.
89 Angle and Svensson 2001, xv.
90 Svensson 2002, 2.
91 Angle 2002, 153–154.
92 Liang Qichao, "On Rights Consciousness;" quoted in Angle, 2002: 159.
93 Pingxiang City Chinese Communist Party Editorial Group 1990, volume 1, 45.
94 Liu Shipei, "The Essentials of the Chinese Social Contract" and "Textbook on Ethics," quoted in Angle 2002, 172–175.

95 Chen Duxiu, "The Direction of Contemporary Education;" quoted in Angle 2002, 186.
96 Nathan 1985, 111.
97 Angle 2002, 206–207; 250–251.
98 Perry 2007, 20–21.
99 Yu 2006, 372.
100 Yu 2006, 417.

References

Angle, Stephen C. 2002. *Human Rights and Chinese Thought: A Cross-Cultural Inquiry.* New York: Cambridge University Press.

Angle, Stephen C., and Marina Svensson, eds. 2001. *The Chinese Human Rights Reader.* Armonk, NY: M.E. Sharpe.

Buckley, Chris. 2006. "China's land grabs fueling unrest, says Premier." *Reuters*, January 20.

Calhoun, Craig. 1994. *Neither Gods nor Emperors: Students and the Struggle for Democracy in China.* Berkeley: University of California Press.

Crothers, Lane. 2003. *Rage on the Right: The American Militia Movement from Ruby Ridge to Homeland Security.* Lanham, MD: Rowman and Littlefield.

Fleischacker, Samuel. 2004. *A Short History of Distributive Justice.* Cambridge: Harvard University Press.

Fung, Edmund S.K. 2006. The idea of freedom in modern China revisited. *Modern China,* no. 33.

Gallagher, Mary. 2005. *Contagious Capitalism: Globalization and the Politics of Labor in China.* Princeton: Princeton University Press.

Gilley, Bruce. 2004. *China's Democratic Future.* New York: Columbia University Press.

Goldman, Merle. 2005. *From Comrade to Citizen: The Struggle for Political Rights in China.* Cambridge: Harvard University Press.

———. 2007. *Political Rights in Post-Mao China.* Ann Arbor: Association for Asian Studies.

Gries, Peter Hays, and Stanley Rosen, eds. 2004. *State and Society in 21st Century China: Crisis, Contention and Legitimation.* New York: Routledge.

Hamilton, Neil A. 1996. *Militias in America.* Santa Barbara: ABC-Clio.

Han Jun. 2006. "Zouchu xin nongcun jianshe de wuqu" [Escaping the mistakes in new socialist countryside construction]. *Xin nongcun jianshe,* October 2006.

Hartz, Louis. 1955. *The Liberal Tradition in America: An Interpretation of American Political Thought since the Revolution.* New York: Harcourt, Brace and World.

Heimer, Maria, and Stig Thogersen, eds. 2006. *Doing Fieldwork in China.* Honolulu: University of Hawaii Press.

Huang Kewu. 1994. *Yige bei fangqi de xuanze: Liang Qichao tiaoshi sixiang zhi yanjiu* [The rejected path: a study of Liang Qichao's accommodative thinking]. Taipei: Academia Sinica Modern History Institute.

Information Office of the State Council of the People's Republic of China. 2000. "Fifty Years of Progress in China's Human Rights." Beijing.

———. 2002. "Human Rights Record of the United States in 2001." Beijing.

———. 2004. "China's Progress in Human Rights in 2004." Beijing.

Jarvis, Harold. 1979. *I'm Mad as Hell: The Exclusive Story of the Tax Revolt and Its Leader.* New York: Times Books.

Jefferson, Thomas. 1787. *Letter to William S. Smith.* Paris: November 13, 1787.

Lee, Ching Kwan Lee. 2002. From the specter of Mao to the spirit of the law: Labor insurgency in China. *Theory and Society* 31 (April): 189–228.

———. 2003. "Pathways of Labour Insurgency." In *Chinese Society: Change, Conflict and Resistance,* ed. Elizabeth J.Perry and Mark Selden. New York: Routledge.

———. 2007. *Against the Law: Labor Protests in China's Rustbelt and Sunbelt.* Berkeley: University of California Press.

Locke, John. 1960. *Two Treatises of Government.* New York: Cambridge University Press.

MacFarquhar, Roderick, and Michael Schoenhals. 2006. *Mao's Last Revolution.* Cambridge: Harvard University Press.

Mao Zedong. 1971. *Selected Readings from the Works of Mao Tsetung.* Beijing: Foreign Languages Press.

Marshall, T.H. 1964. *Class, Citizenship and Social Development.* Garden City: Doubleday.

McCann, Michael W. 1994. *Rights at Work: Pay Equity Reform and the Politics of Legal Mobilization.* Chicago: University of Chicago Press.

Meadows, Thomas Taylor. 1856. *The Chinese and their Rebellions.* London: Smith, Elder, and Company.

Mencius. 1970. *The Works of Mencius [Chinese and English].* Trans. James Legge. New York: Dover Publications.

Mulloy, D.J. 2004. *American Extremism: History, Politics and the Militia Movement.* New York: Routledge.

Munro, Donald J. 2000. *The Concept of Man in Contemporary China.* Ann Arbor: University of Michigan Press.

———. 2001. *The Concept of Man in Early China.* Ann Arbor: University of Michigan Press.

Nathan, Andrew J. 1985. *Chinese Democracy.* Berkeley: University of California Press.

Niu A. 1993. "A Strike Takes Place in Chongqing Knitting Mill." In *Zheng Ming* (no. 186), translated in *Foreign Broadcast Information Service* (April 6).

O'Brien, Kevin J., and Li Lianjiang. 2006. *Rightful Resistance in Rural China.* Cambridge: Cambridge University Press.

O'Brien, Kevin J., and Rachel E. Stern, eds. Forthcoming. *Popular Contention in China.* Cambridge: Harvard University Press.
Ouyang Wei. 1991. "Peasants in Yintao Township, Shuyang County, Jiangsu Province Rise Up Against Tax Collections," in *Bai Xing* (no. 250), translated in *Foreign Broadcast Information Service* (October 28).
Peardon, Thomas P., ed. 1952. John Locke, *The Second Treatise of Government.* New York: Bobbs-Merrill.
Perry, Elizabeth J. 2007. Studying Chinese politics: Farewell to revolution? *China Journal* 57 (January): 1–22.
Perry, Elizabeth J., and Mark Selden, eds. 2003. *Chinese Society: Change, Conflict and Resistance.* New York: Routledge.
Pingxiang City Chinese Communist Party Editorial Group, ed, 1990. *Anyuan lukuang gongren yundong* [The Anyuan railway and mine workers' movement]. Beijing: Chinese Communist Party History Documents Press, 2 volumes.
Roberts, Dexter. 2005. "Waking Up to Their Rights." *Business Week,* August 22/29: 123.
Schwartz, Benjamin I. 1951. *Chinese Communism and the Rise of Mao.* Cambridge: Harvard University Press.
———. 1964. *In Search of Wealth and Power: Yen Fu and the West.* Cambridge: Harvard University Press.
———. 1968. *Communism and China: Ideology in Flux.* Cambridge: Harvard University Press.
Sears, David O., and Jack Citrin. 1985. *Tax Revolt: Something for Nothing in California.* Cambridge: Harvard University Press.
Shih Men. 1993. "Reference News." In *Zheng Ming* (no. 191), translated in *Foreign Broadcast Information Service* (September 10).
Sun Yupeng and Ma Guang. 1995. "Replacing Concepts, Taking Part in Reform-Dialogue on Problems of Industrial Workers." In *Liaoning ribao* (Nov. 22 and Dec. 6, 1994), translated in *Foreign Broadcast Information Service* (March 16, 1995).
Svensson, Marina. 2002. *Debating Human Rights in China.* Lanham: Rowman and Littlefield.
U.S. Department of State. 2002. "Country Reports on Human Rights Practices: China, 2001." (Released by the Bureau of Democracy, Human Rights and Labor, March 4, 2002).
Wakeman, Frederic Jr. 1973. *History and Will: Philosophical Perspectives on Mao Tse-tung's Thought.* Berkeley: University of California Press.
Weir, Margaret. 1992. *Politics and Jobs: The Boundaries of Employment Policy in the United States.* Princeton: Princeton University Press.
Wong, R. Bin. 1997. *China Transformed: Historical Change and the Limits of European Experience.* Ithaca: Cornell University Press.
———. 1999. Citizenship in Chinese history. In *Extending Citizenship, Reconfiguring States* ed. Michael Hanagan and Charles Tilly. Lanham: Rowman and Littlefield.
Yu Jianrong. 2003. "Nongmin you zuzhi kangzheng ji qi zhengshi fengxian: Hunansheng Hxian diaocha" [Organized peasant resistance and its political risks: An investigation of H County in Hunan Province]. *Zhanlue yu guanli,* no. 3: 1–16.
———. 2006. *Zhongguo gongren jieji zhuangkuang: Anyuan shilu* [The plight of China's working class: annals of Anyuan]. Hong Kong and New York: Mirror Books.
Zhang Xiufeng, Luo Lin, and Gong Wenrui. 2005. "Goujian hexie xin nongcun—Ganzhou yinxiangji" [Constructing a harmonious new countryside—impressions of Ganzhou]. *Fukan,* July 9.
Zweig, David. 2003. To the courts or to the barricades: Can new political institutions manage rural conflict? In *Chinese Society: Change, Conflict and Resistance,* ed. Elizabeth J. Perry and Mark Selden. New York: Routledge.

Part VI
Authoritarian Resilience or Democratization

[30]

China's Changing of the Guard

AUTHORITARIAN RESILIENCE

Andrew J. Nathan

Andrew J. Nathan *is Class of 1919 Professor of Political Science at Columbia University. He is co-editor with Perry Link of* The Tiananmen Papers *(2001) and co-author with Bruce Gilley of* China's New Rulers: The Secret Files *(2002).*

After the Tiananmen crisis in June, 1989, many observers thought that the rule of the Chinese Communist Party (CCP) would collapse. Instead, the regime brought inflation under control, restarted economic growth, expanded foreign trade, and increased its absorption of foreign direct investment. It restored normal relations with the G-7 countries that had imposed sanctions, resumed the exchange of summits with the United States, presided over the retrocession of Hong Kong to Chinese sovereignty, and won the right to hold the 2008 Olympics in Beijing. It arrested or exiled political dissidents, crushed the fledgling China Democratic Party, and seems to have largely suppressed the Falun Gong spiritual movement.

Many China specialists and democracy theorists—myself among them—expected the regime to fall to democratization's "third wave."[1] Instead, the regime has reconsolidated itself.[2] Regime theory holds that authoritarian systems are inherently fragile because of weak legitimacy, overreliance on coercion, overcentralization of decision making, and the predominance of personal power over institutional norms. This particular authoritarian system, however, has proven resilient.

The causes of its resilience are complex. But many of them can be summed up in the concept of institutionalization—understood either in the currently fashionable sense of behavior that is constrained by formal and informal rules, or in the older sense summarized by Samuel P. Huntington as consisting of the adaptability, complexity, autonomy, and coherence of state organizations.[3] This article focuses on four aspects of the CCP regime's institutionalization: 1) the increasingly norm-bound nature of its succession politics; 2) the increase in meritocratic as opposed to factional considerations in the promotion of political elites; 3) the differentiation and functional specialization of institutions within the regime; and 4) the establishment of institutions for political participation and appeal that strengthen the CCP's legitimacy among the public at large. While these developments do not guarantee that the regime will be able to solve all the challenges that it faces, they do caution against too-hasty arguments that it cannot adapt and survive.

Norm-Bound Succession Politics

As this article is published, the Chinese regime is in the middle of a historic demonstration of institutional stability: its peaceful, orderly transition from the so-called third generation of leadership, headed by Jiang Zemin, to the fourth, headed by Hu Jintao. Few authoritarian regimes—be they communist, fascist, corporatist, or personalist—have managed to conduct orderly, peaceful, timely, and stable successions. Instead, the moment of transfer has almost always been a moment of crisis—breaking out ahead of or behind the nominal schedule, involving purges or arrests, factionalism, sometimes violence, and opening the door to the chaotic intrusion into the political process of the masses or the military. China's current succession displays attributes of institutionalization unusual in the history of authoritarianism and unprecedented in the history of the PRC. It is the most orderly, peaceful, deliberate, and rule-bound succession in the history of modern China outside of the recent institutionalization of electoral democracy in Taiwan.[4]

Hu Jintao, the new general secretary of the CCP as of the Sixteenth Party Congress in November 2002, has held the position of successor-apparent for ten years. Four of the other eight top-ranking appointments (Wu Bangguo, Wen Jiabao, Zeng Qinghong, and Luo Gan) had been decided a year or two in advance. The remaining four members of the Politburo Standing Committee (PBSC) were simply elevated from the outgoing Politburo. Barring a major crisis, the transition will continue to an orderly conclusion in March 2003, leading to the election of Hu Jintao as state president and chairman of the Central Military Commission, Wu Bangguo as chair of the National People's Congress (NPC), and Wen Jiabao as premier. Outgoing officials President Jiang Zemin, NPC Chair Li Peng, and Premier Zhu Rongji will leave their state offices, having already left their Party offices in the fall, and will cease to have any direct role in politics.

It takes some historical perspective to appreciate this outcome for the achievement that it is. During the Mao years, Party congresses and National People's Congresses seldom met, and when they did it was rarely on schedule. There have never before been effective terms of office or age limits for persons holding the rank of "central leader"; Mao and Deng each exercised supreme authority until the end of his life. Nor has there ever been an orderly assumption of office by a designated successor:

Mao purged Liu Shaoqi, the president of the PRC, by having Red Guards seize him and put him in prison, where he died. Mao's officially designated successor, Lin Biao, allegedly tried to seize power from Mao, was discovered, and died in a plane crash while fleeing. Mao appointed Hua Guofeng as his successor simply by stating that Hua was his choice. Hua was removed from office at Deng Xiaoping's behest before Hua's term of office was over. Deng removed from power both of his own chosen successors, Hu Yaobang and Zhao Ziyang. Deng and the other elders overrode the Politburo in 1989 to impose Jiang Zemin as successor to the Party leadership.

Measured against these historical precedents, the current succession displays many firsts, all indicative of institutionalization:

• Jiang Zemin survived his full allotted time in office. He was installed as general secretary in 1989, and was reelected in 1992 and 1997, serving two-and-a-half terms (he assumed the Central Military Commission chairmanship in 1989 and the state presidency in 1992). His patron, Deng, did not remove him from office (although Deng considered doing so in 1992). Although Jiang was called to the top post in Beijing over the heads of Li Peng and Li Ruihuan, and had at times adversarial relations with both of them, neither tried to replace him. In consolidating his authority, Jiang engineered the fall from power of Yang Shangkun in 1992 and Qiao Shi in 1997, but neither of these men tried to unseat him.

• Jiang did not stay in office past the time when, according to the rules, he should have left office. In 1997, the Politburo established by consensus a new, informal rule that senior leaders should not be reappointed to another term after they reach the age of 70. When this rule was established, Jiang was 71, but he had himself declared a one-time exception to it, promising to retire in 2002. This promise, along with the fact that he would be 76 in 2002, were the main reasons why no serious consideration was given to his remaining in office, even though there was much speculation in the international press that he was trying to stay. The age-70 rule will also make it necessary for Jiang to retire from the post of Central Military Commission chairman, a post for which there have never been either term or age limits, and to which the 1997 decision did not explicitly apply. Jiang's third post, the state presidency, is limited by the Constitution to two terms, which he has already served.

• Jiang Zemin was the first leader in the history of the People's Republic of China (PRC) not to select his own successor. Mao chose several successors for himself (Liu Shaoqi, Lin Biao, and Hua Guofeng). So did Deng (Hu Yaobang, Zhao Ziyang, and Jiang Zemin). By contrast, Deng Xiaoping made Hu Jintao the PBSC's youngest member in 1992, and for the entire ten years of Hu's incumbency as informal successor-designate, Jiang Zemin did not challenge Hu's position. The incoming premier, Wen Jiabao, was recommended by Zhu Rongji over Jiang's choices, Wu Bangguo and Li Changchun.

• The retired elders (consisting after 1997 of Wan Li, Qiao Shi, Song Ping, Liu Huaqing, and several others) did not attempt to intervene in the succession or, indeed, in any decision. The right of three earlier elders (Deng Xiaoping, Chen Yun, and Li Xiannian) to intervene had been established by a secret Politburo resolution in 1987 and was reinforced by Deng's chairmanship of the Central Military Commission. This right was exercised to decisive effect during the 1989 Tiananmen crisis.[5] In 1997, Deng Xiaoping, the last of the three elders, died. A new group of elders was created by the retirements of Qiao Shi and others from the PBSC. The 1987 Politburo resolution was not renewed for them, nor did any of them sit on the CMC. These new elders received intra-Party documents and occasionally expressed their views,[6] but they did not attend Politburo meetings or exercise any decision-making power.

• The military exercised no influence over the succession. Although some senior military officers spoke in favor of Jiang's staying on in the position of CMC chair, they were ignored. They expressed no views on any other issue relating to the transfer of power. The succession of uniformed officers within the CMC echoes that in the civilian hierarchy: Senior officers associated with Jiang Zemin and over the age of 70—Fu Quanyou and Yu Yongbo—have retired, to be replaced by a younger generation of officers. Following a tradition set in place in 1997, no uniformed officer was elected to the PBSC; the military representatives in Party Center were seated in the Politburo.

• The selection of the new Politburo was made by consensus within the old Politburo. The process was, to be sure, dominated by the senior members, and each of them tried and succeeded in placing associates in the successor body. But these factional considerations were played out within limits imposed by the need for a leadership consensus. None of the top leaders—Jiang, Li Peng, or Zhu Rongji—was powerful enough to force a nominee on his colleagues against their wills.

Never before in PRC history has there been a succession whose arrangements were fixed this far in advance, remained so stable to the end, and whose results so unambiguously transferred power from one generation of leaders to another. It is not that factions no longer exist, but that their powers are now in a state of mutual balance and that they have all learned a thing or two from the PRC's history. Political factions today have neither the power nor, perhaps more importantly, the will to upset rules that have been painfully arrived at. The absence of anyone with supreme power to upset these rules helps make them self-reinforcing.

Meritocracy Modifies Factionalism

Factional considerations played a role in the succession process. But they were constrained by a twenty-year process of meritocratic winnowing that limited the list of candidates who could be considered in the final jockeying for position. Certainly, except for the period of the Cultural Revolution (1966–76), there have always been both meritocratic and factional elements in promotions within the Chinese party-state. But until now, even at the most meritocratic times, the major criteria for promotion at the top were the ability to shift with changing political lines and personal loyalty to the top leader—first Mao Zedong, then Deng Xiaoping. While those among the new leading group are ideologically alert and politically savvy, and have mostly allied themselves with one senior leader or another, they rose to the top predominantly because of administrative skill, technical knowledge, educational background, and Party, rather than personal loyalty.

Political factions today have neither the power nor the will to upset rules that have been painfully arrived at. The absence of anyone with supreme power to upset these rules helps make them self-reinforcing.

The start of this process was Deng Xiaoping's 1980 instruction to senior Party leaders to undertake a "four-way transformation" *(sihua)* of the cadre corps by finding and promoting cadres around the age of 40 who were "revolutionary, younger, more educated, and more technically specialized" *(geminghua, nianqinghua, zhishihua, zhuanyehua)*. In this way, Hu Jintao was promoted several levels by the CCP first secretary of Gansu Province, where he was then working; Wu Bangguo was promoted to party secretary of Shanghai's science and technology commission; and Wen Jiabao became deputy head of the provincial geology bureau in Gansu. The story was more or less the same for each member of the new Politburo.

In 1983, the CCP's Organization Department created a list of the most promising cadres of the "four transformations" generation, which it turned to whenever it needed to recommend a younger cadre for a post carrying ministerial rank. Hu Jintao was selected from this list to become Party secretary of Guizhou, Wen Jiabao to become deputy head of the powerful Central Party Office, and so on. The same cadre-rejuvenation policy led Deng to order that someone younger than 50 be appointed to the Fourteenth Politburo Standing Committee in 1992. That choice fell upon Hu Jintao, so that his current accession to the position of General Secretary marks the orderly working out of the same process set in motion twenty years earlier.

Five of the nine members of today's new PBSC were members or alternate members of the Central Committee in 1982. This indicates the deliberateness and regularity of the succession process. The need to select PBSC members from the relatively small pool of candidates who survived the twenty-year selection process constrained the way in which factionalism worked between 2000 and 2002. Jiang Zemin could make the case for Zeng Qinghong or Zeng Peiyan, Li Peng for Luo Gan, and Zhu Rongji for Wen Jiabao, only on the basis of each person's excellent performance over the course of two decades in technically and administratively challenging jobs, and not because of symbolic importance (for example, Mao's promotion of Chen Yonggui) or ideological correctness (Mao's promotion of the so-called Gang of Four).

A norm of staff neutrality has become to some degree accepted at high levels within the Party Center, the State Council, and the Central Military Commission, so that the careers of rising stars have been relatively unperturbed by factional turmoil at the top. When Zhao Ziyang was purged in 1989, a few of his associates were immediately purged, but most of them were gradually moved into secondary bureaucratic posts over the course of the next couple of years. Some even continued to advance in their careers. Wen Jiabao, for example, served eight consecutive years as director of the powerful Party Central Office under three different general secretaries (Hu Yaobang, Zhao Ziyang, and Jiang Zemin). In contrast to the old spoils-like practices in which a leader's purge led quickly to the rooting-out of his followers several levels down the political system, the new system limits the damage that factional strife does to the orderly careers of the rising generation of leaders.

The product of this less factionalized, more regularized process is a competent leadership group that has high morale; that is politically balanced in representing different factions in the Party; that lacks one or two dominant figures, and is thus structurally constrained to make decisions collectively; and that is probably as collegial as any political leadership can be, because all the members came to the top through the same process, which they all view as having been broadly fair.[7]

Whether this event sets the template for future successions remains uncertain, but the chances of that happening are increased insofar as the current succession entrenches—as it does—rules that have elite support (for example, the age-70 rule), historical depth (the rules governing the meritocratic promotion system), and structural reinforcement from the informal political structure of balanced factional power.

Institutional Differentiation within the Regime

At the high point of political reform in 1987, Zhao Ziyang proposed the "separation of Party and government" and the "separation of Party and enterprise." With Zhao's fall from power in 1989, these ideas were abandoned. Yet in the intervening 14 years, much of what he proposed has happened by evolution, as the separation of responsibilities and spheres of authority—which Max Weber saw as definitive characteristics of the modern state—has gradually increased. What belongs to a given agency to handle is usually handled by that agency not only without interference, but with a growing sense that interference would be illegitimate.

One group of specialists, located in the Party Center, manages ideology, mobilization, and propaganda (in the outgoing regime, it included people like Jiang Zemin, Li Ruihuan, Hu Jintao, and Zeng Qinghong). Another group, located in the State Council, makes economic policy (including Premier Zhu Rongji, vice-premiers Wen Jiabao and Wu Bangguo, most State Council members, and most provincial governors and Party secretaries). Provincial-level governors and Party secretaries have an increasingly wide scope to set local policy in such areas as education, health, welfare, the environment, foreign investment, and economic development. Many large state enterprises have now been removed from state ownership or placed under joint state-private ownership. Enterprise-management decisions are made on predominantly economic rather than political bases. State Council members, provincial-level officials, and enterprise managers are selected increasingly for their policy-relevant expertise. And economic policy makers at all levels suffer less and less frequently from intervention by the ideology-and-mobilization specialists.

The NPC has become progressively more autonomous, initiating legislation and actively reviewing and altering the proposals for legislation presented to it.[8] The police and courts remain highly politicized, but in the case of the courts, at least, a norm of judicial independence has been declared (in the 1994 Judges' Law and elsewhere) and judges are applying it more often in economic and criminal cases that are not sensitive enough to draw interference from Party authorities.

The military is still a "Party army," but it has also become smaller, more technically competent, and more professional. The officers being promoted to the CMC in the current succession are, as a group, distinguished more for their professional accomplishments and less for their political loyalties than was the case with previous CMC cohorts.[9] Calls have come, apparently from the younger members of the officer corps, to make the army a nonpartisan national force without the obligation to defend a particular ruling party. And although the incoming leader, Hu Jintao, has rejected these calls, the fact that they were voiced at all is a sign of a growing professional ethos wihin military ranks.[10]

All Chinese media are owned (at least formally, and for the most part actually) by Party and state agencies. But the media have become more commercialized and therefore less politicized. A handful of important outlets remain under variously direct control by the Party's propaganda department—for instance, *People's Daily,* the New China News Agency, China Central Television, provincial-level Party newspapers, the army newspaper, and so on. But to some extent, these media—and even more so, other newspapers, magazines, and radio or television stations around the country—fight for market share by covering movie and pop stars, sports, and scandals. In the political domain, they often push the envelope of what the regime considers off-limits by investigating stories about local corruption and abuses of power.

To be sure, the Chinese regime is still a party-state, in which the Party penetrates all other institutions and makes policy for all realms of action. And it is still a centralized, unitary system in which power at lower levels derives from grants by the center. But neither the top leader nor the central Party organs interfere as much in the work of other agencies as was the case under Mao and (less so) Deng. Ideological considerations have only marginal, if any, influence on most policy decisions. And staff members are promoted increasingly on the basis of their professional expertise in a relevant area.

All of this is partly to say, as has often been said before, that the regime is pragmatic. But behind the attitude of pragmatism lie increased institutional complexity, autonomy, and coherence—attributes that according to Huntington's theory should equip the regime to adapt more successfully to the challenges it faces.

Input Institutions and Political Legitimacy

One of the puzzles of the post-Tiananmen period has been the regime's apparent ability to rehabilitate its legitimacy (defined as the public's belief that the regime is lawful and should be obeyed) from the low point of 1989, when vast, nationwide prodemocracy demonstrations revealed the disaffection of a large segment of the urban population.

General theories of authoritarian regimes, along with empirical impressions of the current situation in China, might lead one to expect that the regime would now be decidedly low on legitimacy: Although authoritarian regimes often enjoy high legitimacy when they come to power, that legitimacy usually deteriorates for want of democratic procedures to cultivate ongoing consent. In the case of contemporary China, the regime's ideology is bankrupt. The transition from a socialist to a quasi-market economy has created a great deal of social unrest. And the regime relies heavily on coercion to repress political and religious dissent.

Direct evidence about attitudes, however, shows the contrary. In a 1993 nationwide random-sample survey conducted by Tianjian Shi, 94.1 percent of respondents agreed or strongly agreed with the statement that, "We should trust and obey the government, for in the last analysis it serves our interests." A 2002 survey by Shi found high percentages of respondents who answered similarly regarding both the central and local governments.[11] There is much other evidence from both quantitative and qualitative studies to suggest that expressions of dissatisfaction, including widely reported worker and peasant demonstrations, are usually directed at lower-level authorities, while the regime as a whole continues to enjoy high levels of acceptance.

A number of explanations can be offered for this pattern. Among them:

• Most people's living standards have risen during two decades of economic growth.

• The Party has coopted elites by offering Party membership to able persons from all walks of life and by granting the informal protection of property rights to private entrepreneurs. This new direction in Party policy has been given ideological grounding in Jiang Zemin's theory of the "Three Represents," which says that the Party should represent advanced productive forces, advanced culture, and the basic interests of all the Chinese working people—that is, that it should stand for the middle classes as much as or more than the workers and peasants.

• The Chinese display relatively high interpersonal trust, an attitude that precedes and fosters regime legitimacy.[12]

• The Chinese population favors stability and fears political disorder. By pointing to the example of postcommunist chaos in Russia, the CCP has persuaded most Chinese, including intellectuals—from whom criticism might be particularly expected—that political reform is dangerous to their welfare.

• Thanks to the success of political repression, there is no organized alternative to the regime.

• Coercive repression—in 1989 and after—may itself have generated legitimacy by persuading the public that the regime's grip on power is unshakeable. Effective repression may generate only resigned obedience at first, but to maintain cognitive consonance, citizens who have no choice but to obey a regime may come to evaluate its performance and responsiveness (themselves components of legitimacy) relatively highly.[13] In seeking psychological coherence, citizens may convince themselves that their acceptance of the regime is voluntary—precisely because of, not despite, the fact that they have no alternative.

All these explanations may have value. Here, though, I would like to develop another explanation, more directly related to this essay's theme of institutionalization: The regime has developed a series of input institutions (that is, institutions that people can use to apprise the state of their concerns) that allow Chinese to believe that they have some influence on policy decisions and personnel choices at the local level.

The most thorough account of these institutions is Tianjian Shi's *Political Participation in Beijing*, which, although researched before 1989, describes institutions that are still in place. According to Shi, Chinese participate at the local and work-unit levels in a variety of ways. These include voting, assisting candidates in local-level elections, and lobbying unit leaders. Participation is frequent, and activism is correlated with a sense of political efficacy (defined as an individual's belief that he or she is capable of having some effect on the political system). Shi's argument is supported by the work of Melanie Manion, who has shown that in localities with competitive village elections, leaders' policy positions are closer to those of their constituents than in villages with noncompetitive voting.[14]

In addition to the institutions discussed by Shi and Manion, there are at least four other sets of input institutions that may help to create regime legitimacy at the mass level:

- The Administrative Litigation Act of 1989 allows citizens to sue government agencies for alleged violations of government policy. According to Minxin Pei, the number of suits stood in 1999 at 98,600. The success rate (determined by court victories plus favorable settlements) has ranged from 27 percent to around 40 percent. In at least one province, government financial support is now offered through a legal aid program to enable poor citizens to take advantage of the program.[15]
- Party and government agencies maintain offices for citizen complaints—letters-and-visits departments *(xinfangju)*—which can be delivered in person or by letter. Little research has been done on this process, but the offices are common and their ability to deal with individual citizen complaints may be considerable.
- As people's congresses at all levels have grown more independent—along with people's political consultative conferences, United Front structures that meet at each level just prior to the meeting of the people's congress—they have become an increasingly important channel by which citizen complaints may be aired through representatives.
- As the mass media have become more independent and market-driven, so too have they increasingly positioned themselves as tribunes of the people, exposing complaints against wrong-doing by local-level officials.

These channels of demand- and complaint-making have two common features. One is that they encourage individual rather than group-based inputs, the latter of which are viewed as threatening by the regime. The other is that they focus complaints against specific local-level agencies or officials, diffusing possible aggression against the Chinese party-state generally. Accordingly, they enable citizens to pursue grievances without creating the potential to threaten the regime as a whole.

An Authoritarian Transition?

Despite the institutionalization of orderly succession processes, meritocratic promotions, bureaucratic differentiation, and channels of mass participation and appeal, the regime still faces massive challenges to its survival. This essay does not attempt to predict whether the regime will surmount them. What we can say on available evidence is that the regime is not supine, weak, or bereft of policy options. In contrast with the Soviet and Eastern European ruling groups in the late 1980s and early 1990s, the new Chinese leaders do not feel that they are at the end of history. The policy-statement excerpts contained in their investigation reports show that these leaders think they can solve China's problems.[16] They intend to fight corruption; reform the state-owned enterprises; ameliorate the lot of the peasants; improve the environment;

comply with World Trade Organization rules while using transitional privileges to ease China's entry into full compliance; suppress political opposition; meet the challenge of U.S. containment; and, above all, stay in power and direct China's modernization. The argument that democratization, freedom, and human rights would lead to a truer kind of stability—as convincing as it may be to the democrats of the world—holds no appeal for these men.

The theoretical implications of China's authoritarian resilience are complex. For the last half-century, scholars have debated whether totalitarian regimes can adapt to modernity. The implications of the Chinese case for this discussion are two: First, in order to adapt and survive, the regime has had to do many of the things predicted by Talcott Parsons and those who elaborated his theory: The regime has had to 1) abandon utopian ideology and charismatic styles of leadership; 2) empower a technocratic elite; 3) introduce bureaucratic regularization, complexity, and specialization; and 4) reduce control over private speech and action. Second, contrary to the Parsonian prediction, these adaptations have not led to regime change. In Richard Lowenthal's terms, the regime has moved "from utopia to development."[17] But the Party has been able to do all these things without triggering a transition to democracy.

Although such a transition might still lie somewhere in the future, the experience of the past two decades suggests that it is not inevitable. Under conditions that elsewhere have led to democratic transition, China has made a transition instead from totalitarianism to a classic authoritarian regime, and one that appears increasingly stable.

Of course, neither society-centered nor actor-centered theories of democratic transition predict any particular outcome to be inevitable in any particular time frame. The Chinese case may, accordingly, merely reinforce the lesson that the outcome depends on politicians and their will to power. Alternatively, it may end up reminding us that democratic transition can take a long time. But it may also suggest a more disturbing possibility: that authoritarianism is a viable regime form even under conditions of advanced modernization and integration with the global economy.

NOTES

1. As an example, see the multi-author symposium on Chinese democracy in *Journal of Democracy* 9 (January 1998).

2. In other words, to adapt a concept from democratic consolidation theory, the CCP has once again made itself the only game in town and is in the process of carrying out a successful transfer of power.

3. Samuel P. Huntington, *Political Order in Changing Societies* (New Haven: Yale University Press, 1968), 12–24.

4. The factual base for this discussion is contained in Andrew J. Nathan and Bruce Gilley, *China's New Rulers: The Secret Files* (New York: New York Review Books,

2002), and is summarized in two articles in the *New York Review of Books,* 26 September and 10 October 2002. These publications are in turn based on Zong Hairen, *Disidai* (The Fourth Generation) (Carle Place, N.Y.: Mirror Books, 2002). Zong Hairen's account of the new generation of Chinese leaders is based on material contained in internal investigation reports on candidates for the new Politburo compiled by the Chinese Communist Party's Organization Department.

5. *The Tiananmen Papers: The Chinese Leadership's Decision to Use Force Against Their Own People—In Their Own Words,* Zhang Liang, comp., Andrew J. Nathan and Perry Link, eds. (New York: PublicAffairs Books, 2001), 102, n. 1, and passim.

6. Zong Hairen, *Zhu Rongji zai 1999* (Zhu Rongji in 1999) (Carle Place, N.Y.: Mingjing Chubanshe, 2001); English translation edited by Andrew J. Nathan in *Chinese Law and Government* (January–February and March–April 2002).

7. Like any meritocratic process, of course, this one had elements of contingency. Hu Jintao's career is a good example, in particular his 1992 selection from among four candidates as the representative of the Fourth Generation to join the PBSC.

8. Michael Dowdle, "The Constitutional Development and Operations of the National People's Congress," *Columbia Journal of Asian Law* 12 (Spring 1997): 1–125.

9. *Disidai,* ch. 11.

10. *Disidai,* ch. 1.

11. The 1993 survey was conducted for the project on "Political Culture and Political Participation in Mainland China, Taiwan, and Hong Kong." The 2002 survey was conducted for the project on "East Asia Barometer: Comparative Survey of Democratization and Value Changes." Data courtesy of Tianjian Shi.

12. Ronald Inglehart, *Modernization and Postmodernization: Cultural, Economic, and Political Change in 43 Societies* (Princeton: Princeton University Press, 1997), 173, n. 2. Also Tianjian Shi, "Cultural Impacts on Political Trust: A Comparision of Mainland China and Taiwan," *Comparative Politics* 33 (July 2001): 401–19.

13. On components of legitimacy, see M. Stephen Weatherford, "Measuring Political Legitimacy," *American Political Science Review* 86 (March 1992): 149–66. The relationship I am proposing between successful coercion and legitimacy is hypothetical; so far as I know it has not been empirically established.

14. Tianjian Shi, *Political Participation in Beijing* (Cambridge: Harvard University Press, 1997); Melanie Manion, "The Electoral Connection in the Chinese Countryside," *American Political Science Review* 90 (December 1996): 736–48.

15. Minxin Pei, "Citizens v. Mandarins: Administrative Litigation in China," *China Quarterly* (December 1997): 832–62, and personal communication. On legal aid, see *Disidai,* ch. 7; the province is Guangdong.

16. See Andrew J. Nathan and Bruce Gilley, *New Rulers,* chs. 7, 8.

17. Talcott Parsons, *The Social System* (New York: Free Press, 1951), 525–35; Richard Lowenthal, "Development vs. Utopia in Communist Policy," in Chalmers Johnson, ed., *Change in Communist Systems* (Stanford: Stanford University Press, 1970), 33–116.

[31]

4

Cooptation and Corporatism in China

The Logic of Party Adaptation

Bruce J. Dickson

The political implications of China's economic reforms center on the adaptability of the Chinese Communist Party (CCP). Can it successfully adapt to the new economic and social environment its reforms are creating? Or is its ability to cope being undermined by these changes? In the midst of rapid economic change, scholars have identified trends that may be evidence of potential political transformation. On the one hand, entrepreneurs and skilled expertise are being recruited into the party. Cooptation facilitates adaptation by bringing into the party new elites who may invigorate it with new ideas and new goals. In addition, local party and government officials are developing corporatist arrangements to promote economic change. These trends give hope to some that economic reform will eventually lead to gradual political change, allowing China's transition from communism to be more like Hungary or Poland (or even Taiwan) and thereby avoid the turmoil that accompanied political change in the rest of Eastern Europe and the former Soviet Union. Along with these promising signs of rejuvenation are contrary signs of disintegration. Large numbers of party members are abandoning their party responsibilities to pursue economic opportunities. The nonstate sector of the economy is growing so fast that most enterprises do not have party organizations within them and few new members are being recruited from their workforce. In some rural areas, party organizations are paralyzed, recruitment of new members is difficult, and lineage-based clans are competing with the party for influence. These are warning signs of disintegration, of a party unable to manage its members, to have direct institutional links with the most dynamic sectors of the economy, or to control its society.

Although we cannot predict the ultimate fate of the CCP, comparing the experiences of other Leninist parties can at least clarify the kinds of questions we need to be asking. The challenges faced by the CCP—how to liberalize its economy without destabilizing the political system, how to change its organization and attract new members in order to carry out new tasks, how to balance the need to adapt with the need to uphold party traditions—are not unique. Nor are the strategies it has adopted to meet these challenges. Whether it will be successful, however, will depend largely on the peculiarities of the Chinese context: the legacies of the Maoist era, past decisions by party leaders regarding the scope and pace of economic and political reform, the continued influence of orthodox voices at the apex of the political system, and the evolving relationship between state and society.

Much of the recent scholarship on China has focused on the political system as a whole, and in particular the extent of central state power relative to local governments and society.[1] The impact of economic reform on the CCP itself, as opposed to the state as a whole, has received less extensive attention.[2] This chapter will consider the implications of ongoing economic reforms for the CCP by focusing on the two key elements of organizational adaptation: the cooptation of new members and the creation of new links with outside organizations. It will compare the kinds of elites being coopted into the CCP with those coopted into the ruling parties of Hungary and Taiwan, the best examples of successful transformation of Leninist parties, and therefore consider whether a similar transformation is possible in China. It will then consider the utility of the growing literature on corporatism in China for understanding its changing political economy and its consequent impact on the political system. Both cooptation and corporatism are having positive impacts on China's economy and the CCP, but as I will argue, neither is likely to lead to the transformation of China's political system. The evolutionary forces now at work are likely to be incompatible with the Leninist political system in China and will serve to undermine the foundations of that system, rather than prop it up. The expectation of incremental change, while reassuring in its depiction of political change without turmoil and instability, may therefore be misplaced.

THE ONSET OF ADAPTATION AND THE LOGIC OF INCLUSION

The CCP's decision at the Third Plenum in December 1978 to abandon class struggle and to pursue economic modernization announced the beginning of the post-Mao reform era and the onset of the CCP's adaptation. These reforms led to profound changes in China's economy and society and consequently its politics. But it also set up a debate within the CCP between those who sought to protect party traditions and preserve their own positions on the one hand, and those who sought the party's adaptation to facilitate economic change, on the other.

Organizations have two main strategies for coping with environmental change: cooptation of new personnel and creation of new links with other organizations. These strategies allow the organization to be better integrated with its environment and better informed of changes occurring therein. Cooptation allows the organization to add new skills, experiences, and resources (such as political support) that may enhance its performance and increase its chance of survival. But cooptation can also threaten the organization if these coopted actors do not share its goals. The organization may receive needed support but as a consequence be diverted from its original mission.[3] Therefore, the cooptation decision may be contested within the organization. Other organizational goals, such as self-preservation and self-replication, can become paramount, limiting the organization's ability to adapt successfully to new challenges. Opponents of adaptation may point to party traditions and established norms as more legitimate grounds for resisting change than sheer self-interest.[4]

The experience of authoritarian parties, and Leninist parties in particular, is consistent with this dilemma posed by cooptation. As they abandon class struggle for the sake of economic modernization, these parties typically switch from an exclusionary to an inclusionary, or cooptive, recruitment policy.[5] Organizations coopt those they depend on, who possess resources they require, or who pose a threat to the organization. In the post-Mao period, the switch from class struggle to economic modernization as the key task of the party has made the party dependent on the technocrats and entrepreneurs who make the economy grow. Former class enemies and counterrevolutionaries are now brought into the party because they have the skills desired by party leaders to accomplish their new policy agenda. This may lead to the rejuvenation of the party, but may also lead to long-term degradation if the interests of these new members conflict with party traditions. As the party tries to adapt by coopting new members, supporters of party traditions resist "assimilating new actors whose loyalty to the organization (as opposed to its ostensible goals) is in doubt."[6] This is precisely the dilemma posed by admitting technocrats and entrepreneurs into the CCP: they are committed to economic growth, but more orthodox leaders question their support of communism and loyalty to the CCP. Those who are more concerned with self-preservation than adaptation resist the arrival of former enemies into their midst.

But the concerns of defenders of party traditions about the potential threat posed by entrepreneurs are not totally self-interested. The main threat to an authoritarian regime is the "diversification of the elite resulting from the rise of new groups controlling autonomous sources of economic power, that is, from the development of an independently wealthy business and industrial middle class."[7] The creation of autonomous sources of wealth weakens one of the key institutional pillars of a communist system: state control over the economy, resulting in organized dependence—the dependence of society on the state for economic security (jobs, housing, food, etc.) as well as political protection.[8] As economic reform creates alternative paths toward career mobility and acquisition of wealth (through education and entrepreneurship), dependence on the state is reduced, and the power of the state and its ruling party is similarly diminished. Thus the fears of party conservatives are not totally self-serving or illusory.

The second key strategy for an organization to cope with environmental change is to create links with other organizations in its environment. These links with other organizations allow information (and potentially influence) to flow between the organizations, elicit support for the organization, and may enhance its legitimacy.[9] Similarly, as a Leninist party enters the period of adaptation (or what Ken Jowitt calls inclusion), it substitutes the manipulation of symbols with the manipulation of organizations.[10] In other words, the party relies less on coercion and propaganda to control society and develops links with other organizations, either new ones that it sanctions or old ones it revives, such as united front organizations, labor unions, or professional associations. These corporate groups allow the party to organize interests emerging in the course of reform. Links between the party and the organizations allow both the articulation of those interests and the preservation of the party's role as the arbiter of competing interests.[11] In China, the state has created a dense web of economic and social organizations in order to channel interest articulation, regularize the flow of information between the state and key groups in society, replace direct state controls over the economy and society with at least partial social regulation, and screen out unwanted groups. Thus official recognition of social organizations serves the dual purpose of incorporating interests and viewpoints the state finds acceptable and repressing those it finds unacceptable or threatening.[12]

As with cooptation, however, the manipulation of organizations carries potential risks. An organization that previously enjoyed extreme autonomy (as is the case for most Leninist parties prior to inclusion) may be "unable to cope with a world in which it does not have arbitrary control."[13] Creating links with other organizations may strengthen those organizations at the expense of the party. These organizations may develop an identity separate from the party and eventually seek to represent the interests of their members and resist acting as agents of the party. What begins with the party's manipulation of organizations may lead to those organizations' manipulation of the party. Such an arrangement is incompatible with a Leninist political system. Cooptation and organizational links with nonparty organizations are key elements of inclusion, but they both come with risks attached. While they are necessary for the party's adaptation, they are not guarantors of the party's survival and may in fact contribute to its demise.

For one-party authoritarian regimes and complex organizations, the period of adaptation may be open-ended as the regime or organization makes repeated adjustments to its ever-changing environment. For Leninist parties, however, there is a tension between policies of inclusion and the party's mobilizational needs. Jowitt's original model of inclusion for Leninist parties implied it was a long-term and presumably open-ended strategy of survival, but later suggested it was simply the phase preceding the "Leninist extinction" because the liberalization that accompanied inclusion weakened the foundations of Leninist parties in Eastern Europe and the Soviet Union.[14] China's leaders have been wary of making a similar mistake and have tried to limit the extent of inclusion in order to achieve "reform without liberalization," but have had a difficult time balancing the two elements of this dichotomy.[15] As the CCP adopted economic modernization as its key task, it confronted precisely the same mobilizational challenges that are inherent to the period of inclusion for Leninist parties identified by Jowitt: increased social heterogeneity as the working classes developed a clearer identity independent of the state;[16] increased occupational and geographic mobility, which challenged the party's ability to monitor and control society;[17] the displacement of the traditional "revolutionary" classes by new elites with professional and technical skills;[18] the cynicism of youth, in particular the changing attitudes toward the party.[19] But the biggest challenge concerns the party's own identity. How can it reconcile its cooptation of wealthy businessmen and the promotion of entrepreneurial skills with its traditional status as a vanguard party representing the interests of workers, peasants, and soldiers? How can the party balance its desire to integrate with society to promote economic modernization with its desire to maintain its monopoly on legitimate political organization and its ability to mobilize society on behalf of political and social goals? To examine these key questions, the following sections will focus on the two key dimensions of inclusion: cooptation of new personnel and creation of new organizational links.

COOPTATION

Since its arrival as the ruling party of China in 1949, a key and divisive issue confronting the CCP has been the appropriate skills and political backgrounds of potential party members. As the party alternated between periods of radicalist upsurges designed to transform the economy and society and periods of restoration designed to resume economic production and social order, criteria for recruitment also changed.[20] During periods of radicalism, when the party pursued utopian goals in its economic and social policies and promoted class struggle in its relations with society, the party rewarded political reliability and ideological fervor, while downgrading—and in some cases persecuting—technical expertise and intellectual freedom. In contrast, when the party emphasized economic development during periods of recovery from radical policies, the party targeted for advancement those with the experience and skills needed to manage the economy and impose order.

Rather than evolving in a linear fashion, therefore, the CCP remained stuck in recurring cycles of transformation and consolidation largely because Mao resisted the institutionalization of the party required by consolidation. As a result, the debate over the proper qualities of party members and cadres was never decisively resolved in favor of either "redness" or expertise. The alleged presence of class enemies and the consequent ongoing need for class struggle meant that some people were excluded from the political system and from the CCP in particular. This is the essence of an exclusionary recruitment policy, appropriate for both the periods of transformation and consolidation.

The transition to economic modernization in the post-Mao period necessitated changes in the definition of the party's work and also in the state–society relationship. Victims of previous political campaigns were released from prison and exonerated; former "class enemies" had their political labels removed and were welcomed into the definition of the "people." In China as in Hungary, reconciliation policies included the end of persecution of alleged class enemies, the release of political enemies from prison camps, expanded exposure to foreign media, greater travel and education opportunities, and enhanced artistic creativity and labor mobility.[21] The party also changed its recruitment policies. It first targeted the people with the types of technical skills needed for economic modernization and then began to coopt new social and economic elites in recognition of their prestige and accomplishments. The cooptation of experts and entrepreneurs prompted a debate within the CCP between those who argued the party had to adapt to survive and those who felt this particular form of adaptation undermined party traditions and thereby reduced its long-term survivability rather than enhanced it.

The Renewed Emphasis on Expertise

As the CCP abandoned class struggle as its core task and shifted to economic modernization, it first weeded out those whose radical tendencies made them unlikely supporters of reform and also rehabilitated the victims of past political campaigns, especially the antirightist movement of 1956–1957 and the Cultural Revolution of 1966–1976. These victims were generally too old and poorly educated to guarantee the success of reform, so the CCP also recruited those who were "more revolutionary, younger, better educated, and more professionally competent." The emphasis on education was particularly apparent. Whereas less than 13 percent of party members had a high school or better education in the late 1970s, by the time of the Sixteenth Party Congress in November 2002 the figure had risen to 53 percent. Improvements in the education qualifications of local officials from the provincial to the county level were even more dramatic: in 1981, only 16 percent had a college education; twenty years later in 2001, 88 percent did. Within the Central Committee (CC), the proportion of those with a college degree rose from 55 percent in 1982 to 99 percent in 2002. The current fourth generation of leaders is characterized by its technocratic credentials (i.e., education and professional experience in science, engineering, or management). All nine members of the Standing Committee of the Politburo and eight of the ten members of the State Council are technocrats. Below this top level, however, the predominance of technocrats has begun to wane. Research by Li Cheng reveals that the percentage of technocrats on the CC fell from 52 percent in 1997 to 46 percent in 2002. At the provincial level, the percentage of technocrats fell even farther, from 75 percent in 1997 to only 42 percent in 2003, and none of the provincial leaders appointed after March 2003 are engineers.

Instead, the new provincial leadership, the likely source of central leaders in the fifth generation, are notable for their backgrounds in the social sciences, the humanities, and the law.[22]

In contrast to the improving educational qualifications, the CCP was less successful recruiting youth and therefore in the mid-1980s adopted the standard that two-thirds of new recruits had to be less than thirty-five years old. During 1997–2002, over 75 percent of new recruits were under the age of thirty-five. However, the party as a whole continued to age and the percentage of all party members under thirty-five actually fell from 27.3 percent in 1987 to 23.3 percent in 2002.[23]

Renewed efforts to recruit frontline workers revealed the tension between inclusion and mobilization. By the late 1980s, more orthodox leaders began to argue that the exclusive reliance on expertise had pushed aside political reliability as a criterion for recruitment and promotion.[24] From their perspective, the proletariat was being squeezed out by economic and technical elites: "progressive" forces (i.e., workers and peasants) were declining in numbers and influence, while those who until recently had been persecuted as "reactionary" forces (intellectuals and entrepreneurs) were on the rise. Although these latter groups had contributed immeasurably to the success of the post-Mao economic reforms, they also threatened the traditional base of the party. The emphasis on workers did not replace the need for expertise, but simply restored the proletariat to its previous position of status in the party.

Concerns about emphasizing expertise over political reliability became especially prominent after the Tiananmen demonstrations of 1989, in which large numbers of party members and cadres openly participated, demonstrating that the party was losing not only its external support but more importantly its internal cohesion. In a December 1989 speech at the Central Party School, CCP general secretary Jiang Zemin said, "We must make sure that the leading authority of all party and state organs is in the hands *of loyal Marxists*."[25] A commentator's article in *People's Daily*, the CCP's official paper, criticized two errors in recruiting cadres: first, focusing on education and professional competence at the expense of being more revolutionary and, second, giving exclusive priority to intellectuals and ignoring workers, peasants, and others at the grassroots level.[26]

After the imposition of martial law in June 1989, the CCP changed its recruitment policies to match its orthodox rhetoric. The CCP paid new interest to recruiting "workers at the forefront of production." Age and education remained key criteria for new recruits, but now the party also sought out those directly involved in agricultural and industrial production and deemphasized those engaged in administrative or intellectual pursuits. For instance, although 69.2 percent of the 1.87 million new party members recruited in 1994 reportedly were under thirty-five and 70.8 percent had a senior high school education or better, 854,000 (45.7 percent) were "forefront" farmers and workers, and only 328,000 (17.6 percent) were technical experts.[27] The emphasis on recruiting from among frontline workers was meant to reduce the influence of "nonproductive" trades, especially intellectuals and teachers, who were blamed for contributing to the 1989 demonstrations. This did not end the CCP's efforts to coopt expertise, but reflected its desire to mobilize its traditional supporters to balance the new elites in the organization. In fact, beginning in the mid-1990s, as the pace of economic reform began to accelerate again, the CCP reemphasized the value of entrepreneurial skills, especially for cadres. This strategy of relying on technical and economic elites had a dramatic impact on the composition of the CCP's membership: between 1994 and 2003, the share of workers and farmers in the CCP dropped from 63 to 44 percent.

The Debate over Coopting Entrepreneurs

Beginning in the mid-1980s, entrepreneurs were coopted into the party in large numbers. The State Industrial and Commercial Administrative and Management Bureau reported that 15 percent of owners of private firms were party members.[28] A 1989 survey of private *(siying)* entrepreneurs in Wenzhou found that 31.7 percent were party members, of whom two-thirds had at least a senior high school education and 17 percent were former state cadres. In addition, one-quarter of members in Wenzhou's people-run business associations *(minying gonghui)* were party members.[29] At the end of 1991, over 200,000 party members reportedly registered as private entrepreneurs, representing 4 percent of party members and 8 percent of entrepreneurs.[30] A nationwide survey in 1995 found that 17.1 percent of private entrepreneurs were party members, and by 2004, 30 percent of entrepreneurs were "red capitalists."[31]

The presence of newly wealthy entrepreneurs in the party irritated some party veterans, who felt their contributions to the revolution were being betrayed by the party's new commitment to economic growth. Fearing that bourgeois influences were spreading into the party, the CCP banned the new recruitment of private entrepreneurs into the party after the imposition of martial law in 1989; entrepreneurs already in the party could no longer hold official positions.[32] In September 1995, the organization department repeated that the party would not admit private entrepreneurs "because they are capitalists bent on exploiting the labor force."[33]

Criticism of this trend was especially prominent in the journals representing the party's orthodox positions, such as *Zhenli de zhuiqiu* (The pursuit of truth). These journals published exposé-style articles that criticized the practice of recruiting entrepreneurs into the party and appointing them to official positions (which violated official party policy) and the policy of encouraging party members to take the lead in getting rich *(daitou zhifu)*. These articles argued that the presence of wealthy people in the CCP contradicted the allegedly proletarian nature of the party, creating confusion regarding the party's identity and policies.[34] From this perspective, the trend of coopting entrepreneurs undermined the party and threatened its survival.

Despite the consistency of central policy on this issue in the 1990s, local party committees circumvented these restrictions. Some local party committees classified private enterprises as collective or joint stock enterprises, thereby allowing them to recruit their leaders while remaining in technical compliance with the central ban.[35]

The head of the organization department in an unspecified city in Shandong defended the practice of recruiting entrepreneurs, who had proven their innovativeness, administrative skills, and ability to produce wealth, which he claimed were the main criteria for party membership. "While maintaining party member standards, active recruitment into the party of outstanding people from among the owners of private enterprises can highlight the timeliness of the socialist market economy, and can make full use of the role of party members as vanguards and models in leading the masses along the path of common prosperity."[36] These trends were repeatedly criticized by the center. Orthodox leaders contended that the ability to innovate, manage, and create wealth could not substitute for the political standards also required of party members. In September 1995, Yu Yunyao, deputy director of the CCP's organization department, said even debating the advantages and disadvantages of recruiting entrepreneurs was irresponsible.[37]

Finally, CCP general secretary Jiang Zemin recommended lifting the ban on recruiting entrepreneurs and other new elites into the party in his Party Day speech of July 1, 2001. This recommendation was contained within his advocacy of the "three represents" policy, in which the CCP no longer simply represented the proletarian vanguard but also represented the advanced productive forces, advanced culture, and the general interests of the vast majority of the Chinese people.[38] This was a dramatic shift in the party ideological orientation and its relations with society, but was more importantly an effort to make party policy fit with China's new reality by welcoming into the party the new urban elites ("advanced productive forces") who were most responsible for China's economic and social development.

Why was the ban on private entrepreneurs so ineffective while it was still in place? For one thing, there was little indication it was seriously enforced. More importantly, recruiting entrepreneurs into the party was advantageous for both local officials and entrepreneurs. For officials, it allowed them to coopt potential opposition, to establish links with the private sector and promote growth, and to create personal ties to wealthy and successful entrepreneurs. Why did entrepreneurs want to get into the CCP? Party membership gave them easier access to loans, official discretion, and protection from competition and unfair policy implementation. Moreover, the desire to be "within the system" is stronger than the desire for autonomy in China, where autonomy from the state has major disadvantages. As elsewhere in Asia, entrepreneurs are partners with the state, not adversaries of it. Finally, there is a strong belief that CCP members have advantages in business. The result is a symbiotic relationship that benefits both sides. Local and individual interests outweighed the negligible risk of punishment for violating the formal ban. In fact, the state constitution was revised in spring 1999 to protect the rights of the private sector, and again in 2003 to better protect private property.

Despite the party's steady embrace of the private sector and the lifting of the ban on recruiting private entrepreneurs, the practice of coopting entrepreneurs into the party has virtually stopped, although the reasons are not clear. The growth in the number of "red capitalists" from less than 20 percent before Jiang's July 1 speech to

30 percent in 2004 came not from new recruitment but from the ongoing privatization of state-owned enterprises. Former SOE managers, almost all of whom were party members, instantly became red capitalists once they became owners and managers of newly privatized firms. But other private entrepreneurs did not seek admission into the party. Some felt local party officials were still not sufficiently supportive of the private sector, despite central policy; others felt that party membership would constrain or expose their business practices to closer scrutiny and limit their flexibility; others complained about the rampant corruption within the party. Oddly enough, the cooptation of entrepreneurs into the party was more common when the practice was officially banned than after it became formal party policy.

The Political Implications of Cooptation

What are the political consequences of these policies of cooptation? Will they lead to rejuvenation of the party by drawing in new elites, or will they undermine the foundations of the Leninist system in China? Scholars have generally seen the inclusion of new elites into the party as a positive development. According to Hong Yung Lee, the presence of technocrats in the party and government bureaucracies better balances "the political needs of the Leninist party and the structural prerequisites of economic development."[39] Similarly, Kristen Parris sees entrepreneurs as a "force for change within the party rank and file."[40] While cooptive parties tend to be more adaptable than those with exclusive recruitment policies, *who* is being coopted has important implications for *how* the party adapts. To show why this is so, it is best to distinguish different types of elites.

Yanqi Tong makes a useful distinction between a civil society organized to regulate the supply of goods and services (a "noncritical realm" that does not pose a direct challenge to the regime, and may even be welcomed by it) and a political society designed to "influence state decisions or to obtain a share of state power" (a "critical realm" that does threaten the regime's monopoly on power and therefore becomes the target of repression). The success of the critical realm depends on the existence and support of the noncritical realm. They are complementary, though not equal, and "the development of non-critical and critical realms often represent different stages in the emergence of an autonomous civil society and, in the process, of political change."[41]

In a Leninist system, the presence of this noncritical realm is the result of political liberalization, not its cause. Party leaders, who need allies in their inner-party battles and social organizations to take over social and economic self-regulatory functions as the state liberalizes its control over society, support the emergence of this realm of civil society. The rise of a critical realm, in contrast, is the product of its own leaders and is rarely welcomed by the regime, even by party reformers. The noncritical realm of civil society reinforces the regime's decision to liberalize (reduced state interference in the economy and the daily lives of the citizenry), but it is the critical realm of political society that pressures the regime to democratize (public involvement in the selection of state leaders and accountability over their actions).

The implications of this distinction between critical and noncritical realms are best seen by comparing the experience of Leninist parties in Hungary, Taiwan, and China.

In Hungary, the policy of cooptation focused on the critical intelligentsia. Leaders of the Hungarian Socialist Workers Party decided in the early 1960s to coopt nonmanual workers into the party, including not only clerical and managerial staff but also young intelligentsia. Other Eastern European communist parties responded to demands for political reform by purging party ranks of intellectuals and thereby created an external social opposition. The Hungarian party instead eliminated the potential threat of external dissent by drawing critical intelligentsia into the party. In so doing, "the party [in Hungary] both perpetuated its rule and created the means of its eventual downfall."[42] At the central level, intellectuals were channeled into government positions, leaving party loyalists in control of all key party posts. In rural areas, however, conservative party secretaries with extensive patronage networks shut intellectuals out of influential positions.

Frustrated by the lack of upward mobility and by their exclusion from decision-making arenas, local intellectuals organized informal networks which in the 1980s became the basis for the "party reform circles." These party reform circles took shape as political circles outside the party were growing and as the reformist coalition in the party elite, which had forced hard-liner Janos Kadar's resignation as party chief in 1988, was itself splitting, creating more space for political activity.[43] In May 1989, the party reform circles held their first national conference, attended by 440 delegates representing over 10,000 members of 110 reform circles.[44] In alliance with central party reformers, the reform circles achieved the dissolution of the Socialist Workers Party and its reformation as the Hungarian Socialist Party in October 1989. Originally formed as an antiestablishment movement against the official party structure, the circles refused to institutionalize themselves and quickly lost the initiative to older party leaders. The circles broke up shortly after the creation of the Socialist Party. Although they contributed immeasurably to the transformation of the Hungarian party and the democratization of the Hungarian political system, reform circle members were unable to benefit from the changes they brought about.

Cooptation was also a major factor of the transformation of the Kuomintang (KMT), the ruling party in Taiwan.[45] In the early 1970s, the central leaders of the KMT, principally Chiang Ching-kuo and Li Huan, sponsored the Taiwanization policy, which brought large numbers of youth with political ambitions into the party. The policy had two main goals. First, Taiwanization was designed to change the reputation of the KMT. Before Taiwanization, all key positions were held by émigrés from the mainland; beginning in the early 1970s, the KMT gradually shed its mainlander reputation and came to represent a broader spectrum of Taiwan's society. Second, Taiwanization was intended to improve the effectiveness of the ruling party by attracting young people with talent rather than simply political connections. Most new members were recruited when they were still in college, and some were given scholarships for foreign graduate study, mostly in the United States, where they were exposed to the workings of a democratic political system. The KMT coopted these educated youth in order to channel their political ambitions into the KMT and preempt their joining the opposition. The KMT also used the promise of elected office to attract these young elites. With opposition parties banned, an official nomination by the KMT virtually guaranteed electoral victory. At the same time that it coopted some youth, it continued to repress the political opposition that was excluded from the party and made it difficult for them to compete in elections.

The centrally sponsored policy of cooptation known as Taiwanization led to the adaptation of the political system in several ways. First, many of those who played key roles in the transformation of the KMT and the gradual democratization of Taiwan's political system during the 1980s were recruited under the Taiwanization program of the 1970s. Young elites with political ambitions created pressure within the KMT for democratization. They sought more open, competitive elections to advance their careers. Second, their experience in the United States and other foreign countries exposed them to more liberal political systems, further fueling their desire for democratization. These internal pressures in combination with the growing support for democratization outside the party eventually led to the democratic breakthrough of 1986–1987. Third, Taiwanization also led to a basic change in the key task of the KMT: from achieving reunification with the mainland to the economic and political development of Taiwan itself.[46]

In Hungary and Taiwan, the ruling parties reduced the potential threat of external dissent by coopting critical intelligentsia and politically ambitious youth (i.e., those from the critical realm of political society) into the party. In contrast, the CCP continues to exclude critical intelligentsia from the political system in general and the party in particular. Instead, it targets experts and entrepreneurs from the noncritical realm of civil society, but even the entrepreneurs are excluded from holding official posts. The ultimate consequences of the CCP policy of inclusion is not yet clear; indeed, in Hungary and Taiwan there were lengthy gaps between the initial cooptation and the subsequent political effects. But there is little reason to assume that technocrats and entrepreneurs will make similar demands on the CCP that critical intelligentsia did in Hungary and Taiwan. Technocrats and entrepreneurs may indeed prove to be a force for change within the CCP, but more time—and more research—is needed to determine what types of change they will promote.

As members of the noncritical sphere, technocrats and entrepreneurs could play a supporting role in the course of political change. Some have argued that technocrats are more likely to favor democratization than the revolutionaries they replaced; others have argued that technocracy will only lead to a more efficient form of authoritarianism.[47] For my purposes, the key point is that technocrats belong to the noncritical realm. They are primarily concerned with promoting economic growth and to that end limiting the influence of ideology in policy making. But technocrats may also be essential allies of democrats. A key element of Hungary's democratization was the informal alliance of technocrats who desired less party interference in the economy, party reformers who wanted to be rid of conservatives, and democrats outside the party.[48] But in China, "bureaucratic technocrats are not enthusiastic about political democratization."[49] Moreover, most technocrats were trained in China, the former Soviet Union, or Eastern Europe. Unlike KMT elites, many of whom received college degrees in the United States and other Western countries, CCP technocrats lack exposure to alternative political values and institutional arrangements.[50] Although younger technocrats have been acquiring more exposure to the West and in the future may be more open to adaptation, it will be many years before they are the decisive force within the party. Moreover, as noted above, the prevalence of technocrats among central committee members and provincial leaders is already declining in favor of those educated in the social sciences, law, and humanities.

Could entrepreneurs be allies of democrats in China? The evidence so far has been mixed. Margaret Pearson argues that they are not likely to initiate demands for systemic change but could be "available to lend support if others take the lead in pressuring for economic and political change."[51] During the 1989 demonstrations, the Beijing Stone Group provided ample and visible support for student demonstrators, but elsewhere in China entrepreneurs withheld their support. In Xiamen, one of the special economic zones in southern China, entrepreneurs disapproved of students' demands for rapid reform, preferring state-sponsored reform to bottom-up pressures that could result in instability.[52] Entrepreneurs may favor liberalization in order to promote economic growth, but there is little evidence that these same people favor democratization. The growing alignment between local political and economic elites may in fact reinforce the status quo because both sets of actors benefit from its preservation. The party retains its monopoly over political participation and takes credit for the economic growth created by the entrepreneurs. Entrepreneurs may be unwilling to risk the certain benefits of the existing system, despite its many irrationalities, for the uncertainties of an alternative arrangement. Indeed, Jonathan Unger and Anita Chan note that entrepreneurs and even intellectuals who belong to the Chinese People's Political Consultative Congress "support further economic and political reforms—but they are usually *not* pro-democracy."[53]

The reforms in Hungary and Taiwan also had an element of indigenization that is wholly lacking in China. In Hungary, the Communist Party was seen as the creation of the Soviet Union, especially after the repression of the 1956 uprising, and therefore lacked domestic legitimacy. The party used its policy of cooptation and tolerance of pluralism within the party to soften its image as an alien force and to legitimize its rule.[54] In Taiwan, the policy of cooptation was motivated by a desire to change the KMT's image as an unwanted occupying force. The very name of the program, Taiwanization (in Chinese, *bentuhua*, literally indigenization) announces its goal. In so doing, the KMT tried to sink roots in local society, not just to control it, but also to appear more responsive to it. The CCP lacks these motivations for adaptation. One of its primary bases of legitimacy is its victory in the Chinese civil war. It is not motivated by the search for domestic sources of legitimacy nor by the type of ethnic conflict that prompted Taiwanization.

Technocrats and entrepreneurs have had an important impact on the progress of reform and the performance of the CCP. They have been strong supporters of liberalization and have contributed to the rapid pace of economic growth. But their overt support for liberalization must be distinguished from their muted support for democratization. As the comparison with Hungary and Taiwan show, cooptation enhances the adaptability of Leninist parties, but not all coopted elites favor the same types of adaptation. China's technocrats and entrepreneurs, drawn from the noncritical realm of civil society, are unlikely to initiate democratizing reforms, although they may prove to be indispensable allies of those who do favor such reforms.

ORGANIZATIONAL LINKS BETWEEN THE CCP AND SOCIETY: A CORPORATIST SOLUTION?

The second element of party adaptation concerns organizational arrangements. The party may rejuvenate united front groups or create new organizations to incorporate new groups into the political system. Recent scholarship on China has found extensive evidence of this type of inclusion and has defined it as corporatism.[55] The concept of corporatism is a familiar one in comparative politics, and describes a system of representation in which interests are vertically organized into peak associations to limit and institutionalize the participation of key groups in the policy process.[56] Corporatist arrangements may be dominated by the state in an authoritarian political system, a variant known as state corporatism, or they may provide greater autonomy and influence for the groups themselves in a more democratic setting, a variant known as societal corporatism.

The emerging corporatist elements in China's political system provide a rationale for the more harmonious relations between state and society characteristic of inclusion. The corporatist model points out that the state and society relationship is based on achieving consensus and common goals, not a zero-sum struggle for power. As Douglas Chalmers notes, "Corporatism has much in common with socialism's understanding of society after the end of class conflict." A harmony of interests is possible without the total transformation of society.[57] Similarly, Alfred Stepan identified the universal appeal of corporatism to elites facing "a perceived threat of fragmentation" and who reject both the liberal ideals of individualism and checks and balances and the Marxist ideals of class conflict "because they are seen as legitimizing conflict."[58]

Corporatist structures are consequently emerging in China as a substitute for coercion, propaganda, and central planning to maintain party hegemony. As Unger and Chan argue, corporatism is "a mechanism through which the state's grip could be lessened" but not released altogether. "The more the economy decentralizes, the more corporatist associations get established as substitute control mechanisms."[59] This is a perfect illustration of the logic of inclusion: because the CCP is no longer able to manipulate the nation with symbols and propaganda, it therefore tries to manipulate the organizations through which society interacts with the state.

While drawing attention to the evolving corporatist structures, some scholars also allude to another consequence of economic reform. For instance, Unger and Chan assert that "yet at the very same time that these new corporatist structures get erected and firmed up by the Chinese state, forces are simultaneously at work that undermine and weaken the central state's power over them."[60] They believe that at least some of China's groups operating in the current state corporatist mold are "shifting gradually but perceptibly in a 'societal-corporatist' direction," in which organized groups will assert the interests of the people they nominally represent.[61] Gordon White, Jude Howell, and Shang Xiaoyuan also repeatedly allude to the potential of civic associations evolving from a corporatist logic to constitute a civil society, with a dense mix of organizations largely autonomous from constraints imposed by local officials, but still embedded in the state.[62]

This points to a more provocative question, Are corporatist arrangements compatible with a Leninist system? Or will the emergence and evolution of corporatism lead to the decay of Leninist institutions? To answer these questions, it is necessary to explore the implications of the corporatist model.

How useful is corporatism for understanding Chinese politics? In his critique of the interest group model of Soviet politics, William Odom listed three criteria for evaluating a model: it must capture the core elements of the political system; it must be comparative in nature; and it must account for change.[63] According to Odom, the interest group model failed on two accounts: first, it focused most of its attention on peripheral elements of the system (institutional pluralism) and second, it therefore misinterpreted signs of political decay for political development. The advocates of the corporatist model in China are not so ambitious in their claims for political change, but generally limit themselves to analysis of the evolving institutional arrangements that govern China's political economy. Still, they do include allusions of political transformation that deserve greater scrutiny. Like the proponents of the Soviet interest group model, advocates of Chinese corporatism may be misleading us in terms of the expected future course of Chinese politics.

Is China a corporatist system? Most scholars do not argue that China has a full-blown corporatist system, only that there are corporatist elements emerging in the course of economic reform. Corporatism is an ideal type; it does not define a political system, but corporatist elements are present in a variety of contexts. Democratic countries such as Britain and the Netherlands, bureaucratic authoritarian countries such as Brazil and Argentina, military regimes such as Peru and South Korea, one-party regimes such as Mexico and Taiwan, and communist countries such as Poland, the Soviet Union, and most recently China have been described as corporatist. The corporatist model does capture core elements of the China's political system, especially concerning its political economy. The state has created or licensed associations for independent entrepreneurs, owners of private enterprises, enterprises with foreign investment, organized labor, Catholic and Protestant churches, writers, scientists, and other functional interests. These associations are noncompetitive and when two or more exist the state forces them to merge or one or more to disband. Membership is compulsory, and members in business associations are often enrolled when they receive their business license. The leaders of these associations are often officials from the party or government offices responsible for regulating or managing them, and association offices are often in government compounds.[64]

These corporatist elements have very much in common with the key aspects of a Leninist system. A Leninist system is based on the ruling party's monopoly on legitimate political organization. The state may create mass organizations to link state and society, and these organizations are typically staffed and budgeted in large part by the state. A Leninist party also prevents the spontaneous formation of new organizations, especially where an official one already exists, and the presence of organizations outside of its control is a challenge to its authority. During periods of transformation and consolidation, the state uses these organizations as "transmission belts" to send authoritative decisions to lower levels of the organizations. The state grants leaders of these organizations a degree of leeway to manage their organizations and the people they nominally represent, but prevents interests and preferences from working their way back up through the organization to influence state policy. During the period of inclusion, these same organizations become channels for interest representation so that these interests can be incorporated into the state. As the party loses its ability to monitor the activities of these organizations and sanction the behavior of its members, and society more generally, one of the institutional pillars of a Leninist system is weakened.[65] This points out the contradictions in the competing goals of inclusion and mobilization for a Leninist party.

To portray the potential evolution of corporatism, advocates of the corporatist model in China highlight examples of leaders who change from being agents of the state to become advocates for their associations. But the corporatist model considers the state as a "'naturally' divided entity" with different interests derived from its relations with economic and professional groups. According to Chalmers, "One cannot talk of state interests as opposed to those of society when the state is in fact made up of ties with interests in society."[66] Interest representation is not the defining difference between state and societal corporatism. Rather, the power relationship between the state and corporate groups distinguishes the two subtypes, and that relationship is dependent on whether the political system is authoritarian or democratic in nature. Unger found that the federation for large-scale business "is still too tightly bound to the party-state in its structure and staffing" to be described as societal corporatist although it was "gravitating" in that direction due to "a growing desire even on the part of some of its minders for it to play such a societal corporatist role."[67] The desire for increased autonomy for organized interests undoubtedly continues to exist in China, but those wishes are not compatible with the CCP's desire to preserve its power.

Despite its policies of inclusion, the central fact of China's political system remains that it is ruled by a Leninist party. The party enjoys and protects its monopoly on political organization. In his case study of Xiaoshan city, Gordon White found that only the most politically inconsequential of social organizations (sports, arts and culture, retired teachers, and female factory managers) were autonomous, in that there was no overlapping of personnel with the sponsoring government bureau and no financial subsidies.[68] At the same time, bottom-up demands for new and autonomous social organizations (for labor, entrepreneurs, students, etc.) were rejected and repressed. Unger and Chan argue that some of the key demands during the 1989 protests involved gaining state approval for autonomous unions for students and workers in Beijing. "To the extent that they were demanding a *structural* change in the political system, it was to effect a shift to a societal corporatism in which they could choose their own leadership and set their own agendas."[69] But the CCP's rejection of this demand and its violent repression of protestors shows that Leninism, not corporatism, still defines China's political system. Beginning in 1998, the CCP severely and successfully suppressed efforts to create China's first opposition party, the China Democracy Party, showing that a Leninist logic still prevails in China.[70] If the party's monopoly is undermined, we will witness not simply an incremental and gradual evolution from state to societal corporatism, but increased political decay of the communist system itself.

Corporatist trends are nevertheless affecting several key factors of China's political system. An important variation on corporatism as practiced in China is that corporatist groups are usually sanctioned and controlled by local party and government authorities and not always vertically organized into peak associations whose primary interaction is with the central state. This has exacerbated the decentralization of political and economic authority. Just as corporate associations no longer act as transmission belts, local governments no longer act as loyal agents of the center.[71] This is a potential sign of disintegration, not just for the CCP but the political system as a whole. Relatedly, as a result of these newly created institutional links, the party's traditional concern with party building as a means of linking state and society and monitoring compliance with party policy has atrophied.

The creation of a market economy has created new opportunities for pursuing personal goals that do not require joining the party. Indeed, party membership is now seen by many as detrimental to fulfilling individual interests. The new collectively and privately owned and foreign funded enterprises are being created so fast that the party cannot create party organizations within most of them, and many do not even have party members. Party organizations in the countryside have weakened, and recruiting new members has become increasingly difficult. Moreover, many party members in rural areas have become migrant workers seeking jobs in coastal cities, further reducing the party's presence in the countryside. In more prosperous areas, up to 10 percent of migrant workers are party members. Most of them are young and middle-aged and either business oriented or "backbone workers," precisely the kinds of people the party would like to utilize. Once they join the migrant population, these party members lose touch with their original party unit and do not register with the party committee in their new location. Consequently, they no longer fulfill their responsibilities to the party or fulfill their "vanguard role."[72]

The second criterion for a model is that it allows comparisons to be drawn with other countries, and the corporatist model is clearly comparative in nature. But because corporatism is present in so many contexts, it is important to clearly identify the subtypes of the concept so that comparisons are drawn with the right countries. Both state and societal corporatism are monopolistic forms of group politics and therefore are structurally similar. Yet their origins and dynamics are fundamentally different. State corporatism is generally associated with authoritarian regimes, whereas societal corporatism is "more an evolution—perhaps a corruption—of liberalism."[73] Societal corporatism is not compatible with a Leninist system because the former requires the types of autonomous and politically active groups that the latter refuses to tolerate. The notion of state corporatism is less threatening to the regime: instead of autonomy, corporate groups are embedded in the state, where they can be manipulated, their leaders replaced, and their finances controlled. Leninist parties seek to prevent autonomous groups, and for good reason. The Eastern European experience shows that the rise of civil society has a significant—and in some cases decisive—impact on the collapse of communism.[74]

The third criterion of a model's utility is its ability to account for change, and this is where the corporatist model as applied to China most falls short. The depiction of a gradual and incremental evolution from state to societal corporatism is not consistent with the wider literature. According to Philippe Schmitter, state corporatism is unlikely to transform itself continuously toward societal corporatism; instead, it must "degenerate into openly conflictual, multifaceted, uncontrolled interest politics—pluralism in other words."[75] This is exactly what Leninism is designed to prevent. We should not expect that the transition from state to societal corporatism will occur amid regime continuity.

The incremental transformation depicted by the advocates of the corporatist model is based not only on faulty logic but also problematic analogies. Unger and Chan suggest that Japan, South Korea, and Taiwan all made smooth transitions from state to societal corporatism and conclude that a similar transformation in China is possible. But in all three cases the transition from state to societal corporatism was epiphenomenal to changes taking place in the larger political system. In each case, societal corporatism was the consequence of democratization, but the modes of democratization were fundamentally different in each country. Despite the near ubiquity of corporatism in all sorts of political systems, we should be wary of drawing comparisons across different types of political systems. Unger and Chan further suggest that as political liberalization continues in China, "it is far more likely to involve such incremental shifts into societal corporatism rather than the introduction of any form of political democracy." But societal corporatism and democracy are not independent of one another. The emergence of societal corporatism was the consequence of democratization elsewhere in East Asia, not an alternative to it. In other countries, societal corporatism developed in an already pluralist setting. The combination of societal corporatism and rule by a Leninist party would therefore not likely be a stable one.

Corporatism may survive the transition from communism in China, but communism is unlikely to survive the transition to corporatism. Chan cites the relegalization of Solidarity in spring 1989 as a possible model for increased autonomy of China's labor organizations.[76] But within a few months of this step, the communist government in Poland negotiated its way out of existence. This example of "socialist societal corporatism" existed only for the short period of time between the relegalization of Solidarity in April 1989 and the appointment of the first noncommunist prime minister, Solidarity adviser Tadeusz Mazowiecki, in September 1989.[77] This is a poor precedent, either for theory building or for party policy.

A more promising approach may be to apply Stepan's typology of exclusionary and inclusionary poles within state corporatism.[78] A regime can shift between exclusionary and inclusionary policies over time, and even practice them simultaneously. For instance, the CCP has allowed the All-China Federation of Trade Unions in recent years to advocate strongly the interest of labor in the policy and legislative process, but also imprisoned those who advocate the formation of independent trade unions. Stepan's typology may account for trends that scholars are finding without stretching the concept of societal corporatism beyond recognition.

Corporatist features are clearly emerging in China as a substitute for the CCP's totalitarian impulse to control state and society in the Maoist years. But the ultimate political implications of this trend are still uncertain. Whereas some scholars see the promise of societal corporatism coming into view, others see signs of disintegration. The creation of corporatist organizations to link state and society was part of the CCP's strategy of inclusion and it remains dedicated to preventing the rise of autonomous organizations. Before societal corporatism replaces Leninism as the defining feature of China's political system, the party would have to abandon its monopoly on political organization. This is a fundamental change that the CCP has steadfastly opposed. If the party's control over key organizations erodes to such an extent that state corporatism begins to transform into societal corporatism, the real story will not be about the rise of corporatism but more fundamental political change in China.

CONCLUSION

The logic of inclusion offers a useful framework for analyzing the CCP's policies of coopting new elites and forging links with nonparty organizations, as well as understanding the problems that have arisen as a consequence. Although inclusion seems to be a natural phase in the evolution of Leninist parties, the tension between inclusion and mobilization also indicates why adaptation is so difficult, and why the transformation of Leninist parties is so rare. While cooptation and the creation of organizational links seem necessary to promote economic modernization, neither is sufficient to guarantee the party's survival. Instead of leading to rejuvenation, inclusion may contribute to a Leninist party's disintegration.

The cooptation of new elites is a classic strategy of adaptation for Leninist parties and for organizations in general, but it is a risky strategy. As the case of the CCP shows, coopted elites may not support or even sympathize with party traditions—indeed, the technocrats and entrepreneurs who are now being courted were previously targeted as class enemies. Even though the newly coopted technocrats and entrepreneurs are unlikely to initiate pressures for democratizing reforms, they may be powerful allies if others inside and outside the party do so. The attention given to coopting new elites and promoting economic reforms has also led to deterioration of traditional party building, leaving the party less able to mobilize and control society and its own members at a time of increasing political, economic, and social change.

Proponents of corporatism in China may be doing us a disservice. They are uncovering important changes in China's political economy that may have profound implications for its political system. But in their quest for a comparative concept to analyze changes in China, they have latched onto a concept that does not give sufficient emphasis to the central fact of China's political system—the continued rule of a Leninist party. The corporatist approach also does not give adequate attention to the experience of other Leninist parties for whom political change was tumultuous, not gradual. Hungary and Taiwan are exceptions to this general rule, but as noted above the CCP lacks the key features that prompted their transformation, and corporatism was not a key factor in their democratization. By implying a possible path of incremental political change that is not consistent with either the general literature or the political experience of other countries, advocates of the corporatist approach may mislead us.

The CCP is pursuing policies of inclusion, both by coopting new elites and creating links with nonparty organizations, while at the same time lamenting the loss of its mobilizational capacity. Some local party officials, and many scholars, argue that the solution to this dilemma is to deemphasize mobilizational goals for the sake of greater economic growth. From this perspective, party organs should not be present in the nonstate sectors of the economy specifically because they tend to retard growth and frighten off potential investors. Cooptation and new organizational links offer alternatives to traditional party building as means to link the party with society. From the perspective of the party, however, its organizational interests are being challenged by these policies of inclusion. As its capacity to monitor compliance with its policies, enforce norms of behavior, and mobilize society on behalf of regime goals deteriorates, the Leninist attributes of the CCP and its viability as the ruling party are also undermined. As Samuel Huntington noted, the strength of an authoritarian regime depends in large part on the strength of its party; as the party weakens, so too does the regime it governs.[79] While noting the positive trends of cooptation and corporatism, we should not lose sight of the negative consequences for the CCP and the implications for the political system as a whole.

NOTES

I would like to acknowledge the financial support of the Smith Richardson Foundation and the U.S. Institute of Peace, and the comments and suggestions of Scott Kennedy, Jason Kindopp, Kevin O'Brien, Maria Rost Rublee, Traci Swanson, Martin King Whyte, Yang Zhong, and several anonymous reviewers.

1. See, for instance, Joseph Fewsmith, *China since Tiananmen: The Politics of Transition* (New York: Cambridge University Press, 2001); Murray Scot Tanner, *The Politics of Law Making in Post-Mao China: Institutions, Processes, and Democratic Prospects* (Oxford: Oxford University Press, 1998); Andrew G. Walder, ed., *The Waning of the Communist State: Economic Origins of Political Decline in China and Hungary* (Berkeley: University of California Press, 1995); Susan Shirk, *The Political Logic of Reform in China* (Berkeley: University of California Press, 1993).

2. Some scholars have looked at different facets of this issue: Minxin Pei, *China's Trapped Transition: The Limits of Developmental Autocracy* (Cambridge, MA: Harvard University Press, 2006); Kjeld Erik Brodsgaard and Zheng Yongnian, eds., *Bringing the Party Back In: How China Is Governed* (Singapore: Eastern Universities Press, 2004); Yanqi Tong, *Transitions from State Socialism: Economic and Political Change in Hungary and China* (Lanham, MD: Rowman & Littlefield, 1997).

3. Philip P. Selznick, *TVA and the Grass Roots* (Berkeley: University of California Press, 1949); Jeffrey Pfeffer and Gerald B. Salancik, *The External Control of Organizations: A Resource Dependence Perspective* (New York: Harper & Row, 1978), 164–165.

4. Michael T. Hannan and John Freeman, *Organizational Ecology* (Cambridge, MA: Harvard University Press, 1991), 67–68; Pfeffer and Salancik, *External Control*, 82.

5. Samuel P. Huntington, "Social and Institutional Dynamics of One-Party Systems," in Samuel P. Huntington and Clement H. Moore, eds., *Authoritarian Politics in Modern Society: The Dynamics of Established One-Party Systems* (New York: Basic, 1970); Ken Jowitt, "Inclusion," in *New World Disorder* (Berkeley: University of California Press, 1992).

6. Patrick H. O'Neil, "Revolution from Within: Institutional Analysis, Transitions from Authoritarianism, and the Case of Hungary," *World Politics*, July 1996, 579–603, quote from 585.

7. Huntington, "Social and Institutional Dynamics," 20.

8. Andrew G. Walder, "The Quiet Revolution from Within: Economic Reform as a Source of Political Decline," in Walder, ed., *Waning of the Communist State.*

9. Pfeffer and Salancik, *External Control of Organizations*, 143–147.

10. Jowitt, "Inclusion," 101–102.

11. Huntington, "Social and Institutional Dynamics," 34–36.

12. See Gordon White, Jude Howell, and Shang Xiaoyuan, *In Search of Civil Society: Market Reform and Social Change in Contemporary China* (Oxford: Oxford University Press, 1996).

13. James G. March and Johan P. Olsen, *Rediscovering Institutions: The Organizational Basis for Politics* (New York: Free Press, 1989), 47.

14. Jowitt, "The Leninist Extinction," in *New World Disorder.*

15. Kevin O'Brien, *Reform without Liberalization: China's National People's Congress and the Politics of Institutional Change* (New York: Cambridge University Press, 1990), esp. 6–8; 174–178.

16. Andrew G. Walder, "Industrial Workers: Some Observations on the 1980s," in Arthur Lewis Rosenbaum, ed., *State and Society in China: The Consequences of Reform* (Boulder, CO: Westview, 1992); Ching Kwan Lee, "Pathways of Labor Insurgency," in Elizabeth J. Perry and Mark Selden, eds., *Chinese Society: Change, Conflict, and Resistance*, 2nd ed. (London: Routledge, 2003), 71–92.

17. Dorothy Solinger, "China's Urban Transients in the Transition from Socialism and the Collapse of the Communist 'Urban Public Goods Regime,'" *Comparative Politics*, January 1995, 127–146.

18. Li Cheng and Lynn White, "Elite Transformation and Modern Change in Mainland China and Taiwan: Empirical Data and the Theory of Technocracy," *China Quarterly*, March 1990, 1–35; Hans Hendrischke, "Expertocracy and Professionalism," in David S. G. Goodman and Beverly Hooper, eds., *China's Quiet Revolution: New Interactions between State and Society* (New York: St. Martin's, 1994).

19. Stanley Rosen, "The Victory of Materialism: Aspirations to Join China's Urban Moneyed Classes and the Commercialization of Education," *China Journal*, January 2004, 27–52.

20. Zhao Shenghui, ed., *Zhongguo gongchandang zuzhi shi gangyao* [History of CCP organization] (Anhui: Anhui renmin chubanshe, 1987), chaps. 5–7; Chen Zhili, ed., *Zhongguo gongchandang jianshe shi* [History of CCP party building] (Shanghai: Shanghai renmin chubanshe, 1991), chaps. 5–7. Variations in criteria for party recruitment fit the general pattern of policy cycles described in G. William Skinner and Edwin A. Winckler, "Compliance Succession in Rural China: A Cyclical Theory," in Amitai Etzioni, ed., *A Sociological Reader on Complex Organizations* (New York: Holt, Rinehart & Winston, 1969).

21. Yanqi Tong, "State, Society, and Political Change in China and Hungary," *Comparative Politics*, April 1994, 333–353.

22. Li Cheng, "Hu's New Deal and the New Provincial Chiefs," *China Leadership Monitor*, Spring 2004.

23. *Xinhua*, June 22, 1988, in Foreign Broadcast Information Service: Daily Report—China (hereafter FBIS), June 24, 1988, 19; *Xinhua*, October 6, 1992, in FBIS, October 6, 1992, 29; *Xinhua*, July 7, 1997, in FBIS (online service), July 7, 1997; *Xinhua*, September 1, 2002, in FBIS, September 1, 2002.

24. For instance, see Li Yanxi, "Shelun dangyuan duiwu de shuliang kongzhi" [Limit the number of CCP members], *Xuexi yu shixian* [Wuchang], January 1989, 49–51, in *Fuyin baokan ziliao, D2: Zhongguo gongchandang* [hereafter FBZ], February 1989, 136–138; Zhou Peng, "Shinian lai fazhan dangyuan gongzuo de huigu" [Review of the past ten years of party recruitment], *Dangzheng wenhui*, January 1989, 12, in FBZ, March 1989, 133; Dong Wanmin, "Yange anzhao biaozhun fazhang dangyuan" [Recruit party members strictly according to standards], *Henan ribao*, January 7, 1991, in FBZ, January 1991, 127–128.

25. *Xinhua*, December 29, 1989, in FBIS, January 10, 1990, 17–19 (emphasis added).

26. *Renmin ribao*, March 11, 1990, 1, in FBIS, April 5, 1990, 29.

27. *Xinhua*, June 29, 1995, in FBIS, June 30, 1995, 12–13.

28. Reported in *Jingji cankao*, November 4, 1988, in FBIS, December 7, 1988, 36.

29. Kristen Parris, "Local Initiative and National Reform: The Wenzhou Model of Development," *China Quarterly*, June 1993, 259, 261.

30. From a *Xinwen wenzhai* report cited in *Ming Pao*, August 4, 1992, in FBIS, August 14, 1992, 20.

31. *Zhongguo siying jingji nianjian, 1996* [China's private economy yearbook, 1996] (Beijing: Zhongguo gongshang lianhe chubanshe, 1996), 162.

32. This was first reported in *South China Morning Post*, August 29, 1989, in FBIS, August 29, 1989, and later confirmed in *Zhenli de zhuiqiu*, November 11, 1994, in FBIS, January 12, 1995.

33. Press Digest of the central organization department, as reported in *China News Digest*, September 17, 1995.

34. See, for instance, "Lun dangyuan daitou zhifu yu dailing qunzhong gongtong zhifu," *Zhenli de zhuiqiu*, July 1998, 13–20.

35. Interviews in Zhejiang, summer 1997. Classifying private enterprises as collectives (known as red-hat enterprises) is not done solely, or even primarily, to allow party recruitment; rather it is done for the mutual benefit of entrepreneurs and local officials. See Kristen Parris, "Private Entrepreneurs as Citizens: From Leninism to Corporatism," *China Information*, Winter 1995–Spring 1996, 1–28.

36. Quoted in *Zhenli de zhuiqiu*, November 11, 1994, in FBIS, January 12, 1995, 24–25; the article went on to criticize this viewpoint.

37. *Zhongguo xinwenshe*, September 6, 1995, in FBIS, September 8, 1995, 16.

38. For an elaboration of the rationale and implications of the "three represents" policy, see Bruce Dickson, "Dilemmas of Party Adaptation: The CCP's Strategies for Survival," in Peter Hays Gries and Stanley Rosen, eds., *State and Society in Twenty-first Century China: Crisis, Contention, and Legitimation* (New York: Routledge, 2004).

39. Hong Yung Lee, *From Revolutionary Cadres to Party Technocrats in Socialist China* (Berkeley: University of California Press, 1991), 2. Lee believes that markets and Leninism are incompatible, leading eventually to an authoritarian development state in China.

40. Parris, "Local Initiative and National Reform," 261.

41. Tong, "State, Society, and Political Change," 334. Gordon White and his collaborators make a similar point regarding the separate but potentially reinforcing market and political dynamics of China's emerging civil society; see White, Howell, and Shang, *In Search of Civil Society*, especially 7–10.

42. O'Neil, "Revolution from Within," 587.

43. Tong, "State, Society, and Political Change," 346–347.

44. O'Neil, "Revolution from Within," 594.

45. Bruce J. Dickson, *Democratization in China and Taiwan: The Adaptability of Leninist Parties* (Oxford: Oxford University Press, 1997), 122–130.

46. Dickson, *Democratization*, 204–216.

47. Li and White, "Elite Transformation and Modern Change in Mainland China and Taiwan"; Hendrischke, "Expertocracy and Professionalism."

48. Tong, "State, Society, and Political Change," 347.

49. Hong Yung Lee, "China's New Bureaucracy," in Rosenbaum, ed., *State and Society in China*, 71.

50. Dickson, *Democratization in China and Taiwan*, 134–135.

51. Margaret M. Pearson, "The Janus Face of Business Associations in China: Socialist Corporatism in Foreign Enterprises," *Australian Journal of Chinese Affairs*, January 1994, 25–46; "China's Emerging Business Class: Democracy's Harbinger?" *Current History*, September 1998, 268–272.

52. David L. Wank, "Private Business, Bureaucracy, and Political Alliance in a Chinese City," *Australian Journal of Chinese Affairs*, January 1995, 63–65.

53. Jonathan Unger and Anita Chan, "Corporatism in China: A Developmental State in an East Asian Context," in Barrett L. McCormick and Jonathan Unger, eds., *China after Socialism: In the Footsteps of Eastern Europe or East Asia?* (Armonk, NY: Sharpe, 1995), 111; emphasis in original.

54. John Ishiyama, "Communist Parties in Transition: Structures, Leaders, and Processes of Democratization in Eastern Europe," *Comparative Politics*, January 1995, 158–159.

55. Pearson, "Janus Face of Business Associations"; Unger and Chan, "Corporatism in China"; Chan, "Revolution or Corporatism?"; White et al., *In Search of Civil Society*; Jonathan Unger, "'Bridges': Private Business, the Chinese Government and the Rise of New Associations," *China Quarterly*, September 1996, 795–819; Christopher Earle Nevitt, "Private Business Associations in China: Evidence of Civil Society or Local State Power," *China Journal*, July 1997, 25–43.

56. Philippe C. Schmitter, "Still the Century of Corporatism?" in Schmitter and Gerhard Lehmbruch, eds., *Trends towards Corporatist Intermediation* (Beverly Hills, CA: Sage, 1979).

57. Douglas A. Chalmers, "Corporatism and Comparative Politics," in Howard J. Wiarda, ed., *New Directions in Comparative Politics* (Boulder, CO: Westview, 1985), 62.

58. Alfred C. Stepan, *The State and Society: Peru in Comparative Perspective* (Princeton, NJ: Princeton University Press, 1978), 58.

59. Unger and Chan, "Corporatism in China," 105, 107.

60. Unger and Chan, "Corporatism in China," 107.

61. Unger and Chan, "Corporatism in China," 129. Unger and Chan make the same point in their separate writings; see, for instance, Unger, "'Bridges': Private Business, the Chinese Government and the Rise of New Associations"; Chan, "Revolution or Corporatism? Workers in Search of a Solution," in Goodman and Hooper, eds., *China's Quiet Revolution*. Not all advocates of corporatism are so optimistic. Pearson notes "the absence of a compulsion to resolve the tension between autonomy and state dominance"; see "Janus Face of Business Associations," 446.

62. White et al., *In Search of Civil Society*. This is the mirror image of Peter Evans's notion of embedded autonomy: here it is the civil associations that seek connections with the state in order to be effective.

63. William G. Odom, "Soviet Politics and After: Old and New Concepts," *World Politics*, October 1992, 66–98. Odom borrowed these criteria from Huntington's "Paradigms of American Politics: Beyond the One, the Two, and the Many," *Political Science Quarterly*, March 1974, 7.

64. Recent research by Scott Kennedy has found even less corporatist influence in China's business associations. Instead, business has begun to lobby the government on a variety of issues, such as setting industrial standards. This type of collective action by China's private entrepreneurs is more indicative of growing competition and pluralism, at least in the industrial and commercial sectors. See Kennedy, *The Business of Lobbying in China* (Cambridge, MA: Harvard University Press, 2005).

65. Walder makes a similar point in "Quiet Revolution from Within."

66. Chalmers, "Corporatism and Comparative Politics," 67–68.

67. Unger, "'Bridges,'" 818.

68. White, "Prospects for Civil Society."

69. Unger and Chan, "Corporatism in China," 112.

70. Teresa Wright, "The China Democracy Party and the Politics of Protest in the 1980s–1990s," *China Quarterly*, December 2002, 906–926.

71. See Wang Shaoguang, "The Rise of the Regions: Fiscal Reform and the Decline of Central State Capacity in China," in Walder, ed., *Waning of the Communist State*; and Jia Hao and Lin Zhimin, eds., *Changing Central-Local Relations in China* (Boulder, CO: Westview, 1994); for a contrary view, see Huang Yasheng, *Inflation and Investment Controls in China: The Political Economy of Central-Local Relations during the Reform Era* (New York: Cambridge University Press, 1996).

72. Liang Yanjia and Li Kaisheng, "Jiguan qishiye danwei dangyuan liudong de diaocha he sikao" [Investigation and reflection on floating party members in administrative and enterprise units], *Lingnan xuekan* (Guangzhou), January 1994, 3–56, in FBZ, February 1994, 144–147; *Hong Kong Standard*, December 29, 1994, in FBIS, December 29, 1994, 33–34; *Ming Pao* (Hong Kong), February 3, 1995, in FBIS, February 6, 1995, 24.

73. Chalmers, "Corporatism and Comparative Politics," 60; see also Schmitter, "Still the Century of Corporatism?" 22–25.

74. Marcia A. Wiegle and Jim Butterfield, "Civil Society in Reforming Communist Regimes: The Logic of Emergence," *Comparative Politics*, October 1992, 1–24; Vladimir Tismaneanu, *Reinventing Politics: Eastern Europe from Stalin to Havel* (New York: Free Press, 1992).

75. Schmitter, "Still the Century of Corporatism?" 41.

76. Chan, "Revolution or Corporatism?" 83.

77. Tismaneanu, *Reinventing Politics*, 192–194.

78. Stepan, *State and Society*, 73–81.

79. Huntington, "Social and Institutional Dynamics," 9.

[32]

WHEN WILL THE CHINESE PEOPLE BE FREE?

Henry S. Rowen

***Henry S. Rowen** is director emeritus of the Asia-Pacific Research Center at the Freeman Spogli Institute for International Studies and professor emeritus in the Graduate School of Business at Stanford University. He is also a senior fellow at the Hoover Institution on War, Revolution, and Peace.*

Little more than a decade ago, my answer to the question posed by this essay's title was the year 2015.[1] My assessment, published in the Fall 1996 issue of *The National Interest,* began by observing that all countries (leaving aside states that make nearly all their money from oil exports) which had attained a Gross Domestic Product per capita (GDPpc) of at least US$8,000 per year (as measured by the Purchasing-Power Parity or PPP standard for the year 1995) stood no worse than Partly Free in the ratings of political rights and civil liberties published annually by Freedom House (FH).

As China's economy was growing at a rate that promised to carry it to a level near or beyond that GDPpc benchmark by 2015, I reasoned that this, the world's largest country, was a good bet to move into the Partly Free category as well. Since then, China has remained deep in Not Free territory even though its civil-liberties score has improved a bit—from an absolutely abysmal 7 to a still-sorry 6 on the 7-point FH scale—while its political-rights score has remained stuck at the worst level.

Yet today, as I survey matters from a point slightly more than midway between 1996 and 2015, I stand by my main conclusion: China will in the short term continue to warrant a Not Free classification, but by 2015 it should edge into the Partly Free category. Indeed, I will go further and predict that, should China's economy and the educational attainments of its population continue to grow as they have in recent years, the more than one-sixth of the world's people who live in China will by 2025 be citizens of a country correctly classed as belonging to the Free nations of the earth.

Journal of Democracy Volume 18, Number 3 July 2007

In order to flesh out my analysis, I shall examine four questions. The first asks about the prospects for sustained economic growth. The second inquires into what recent scholarship tells us about the nexus between economic development and political freedom. The third estimates when a relatively free China is likely to emerge. And the fourth ponders the implications for war and peace that are likely to flow from this momentous change.

Let us take the question of the economy first. China's per-capita growth over the last decade has averaged a highly impressive 8.5 percent annually (reaching a GDPpc of $6,000 in 2006 international-PPP dollars).[2] Serious challenges lie ahead, yet given China's competent economic-policy makers, a supportable projection is an average per-capita growth rate of 7 percent a year, enough to raise GDPpc to $10,000 PPP by 2015. After that, slower workforce expansion (a product of changing demographics) plus China's expected approach toward convergence with the world's leading developed economies suggest that the growth rate will climb less steeply. Annual growth of 5 percent in GDPpc starting in 2015 will bring China to roughly $14,000 PPP (in 2006 dollars) by 2025, or about where Argentina is today.

Short-term disruptions would do little to disturb this projection. There was such a hitch after the Tiananmen Square massacre in 1989, but the growth rate subsequently recovered so robustly that the slow period was soon offset with no lasting economic effects. The prospect for sustained growth over at least the next decade appears strong.

Does Prosperity Breed Liberty?

The next question to be explored is the relation between economic development and democratic freedom. There are three possibilities: 1) Development might lead to democracy; 2) democracy might foster development; or 3) there might be a common cause driving both.

My 1996 projection was based on the first direction. This is the hypothesis, associated with Seymour Martin Lipset, that only a society with educated, wealthy people can resist the appeal of demagogues.[3] Stable democracy presupposes a certain level of accumulated human, social, and physical capital. A related view is that institutions which promote limited government (particularly via constraints placed on executive power) support growth.[4]

Education promotes growth, and might also independently promote political pluralization by reducing the costs of political action in support of relatively democratic regimes.[5] Schooling makes democratic revolutions against dictatorships more probable and successful antidemocratic coups less probable. After analyzing more than a hundred countries, Robert J. Barro found that higher incomes and higher levels of (primary) education predict higher freedoms.[6] He also found significant time lags between the appearance of a factor positive for electoral rights and its expression in politics. He interpreted such lags as tokens of inertia in institutions affected by changes in economic and social variables, and noted that after about two decades "the level of democracy is nearly fully determined by the economic and social variables."[7] This observation helps one to understand why a rapidly growing country such as China has a freedom rating today well below the level that its current income would predict.

Adam Przeworski and his coauthors also find that levels of economic development best predict the incidence of various types of political regimes. To explain this, however, they point to the superior survival capacity of wealthier democracies rather than to transitions from dictatorship to democracy at higher levels of wealth. The higher the level of income that a given country enjoys, these researchers note, the better are the odds that a democratic regime in that country will endure. They estimate the probability that a democracy will die in a country where annual GDPpc is $6,000 (in 2006 PPP dollars) as close to zero. In contrast, Carles Boix and Susan Stokes attribute transitions to democracy in wealthier countries to incomes becoming more equally distributed as development progresses: "[T]he rich find a democratic tax structure to be less expensive for them as their country gets wealthier and they are more willing to countenance democratization."[8]

The second possibility is realized if the rules of electoral democracy turn out to be better on average for development than are those of dictatorships. Democracies tend to foster governmental transparency and the production of public goods while placing some limits on what rulers can steal. Yet a democracy with a populist bent can insist on economically damaging schemes for redistributing income and wealth. Barro and Prezworski are among those who find that democracy does not lead directly to higher growth. According to Torsten Persson and Guido Tabellini, the evidence that democratizations yield economic growth is weak. They also write that "democracy" is too blunt a concept and that institutional details matter greatly.[9] The theoretical picture remains unclear and the literature is divided.

The third possibility, that democracy and development have a common cause, finds support from Daron Acemoglu and his coauthors, who argue that "though income and democracy are positively correlated, there is no evidence of a causal effect. Instead . . . historical factors appear to have shaped the divergent political and economic development paths of various societies, leading to the positive association between democracy and economic performance."[10] These scholars see political and economic development paths as interwoven. Some countries embarked on development paths associated with democracy and economic growth, while others followed paths based on dictatorship, repression, and more limited growth.

Might there be a regional, specifically Sinitic, effect involving the polities influenced by Chinese civilization? These also include Japan, the two Koreas, Vietnam, Singapore, and Taiwan. Today they present a mixed picture. Japan, South Korea, and Taiwan are rated Free; Singapore is Partly Free; and North Korea, Vietnam, and China are Not Free. Nonetheless, the paths carved out by Japan, South Korea, and Taiwan show that Western-style democracy can take root in Sinitic societies.

Growth-friendly policies, if consistently pursued, lead to the accumulation of human and physical capital and the rise of limited government.

Education is crucial, and here China does not impress. In 2000, the country's entire over-25 population had only an average of 5.74 years of schooling (between all developing countries at 4.89 years and the East Asia and Pacific country average of 6.50 years).[11] Yet large educational-improvement efforts are underway, especially in rural areas and the rapidly expanding postsecondary sector. My projection is that by 2025 the average Chinese person over 25 will have had almost eight years of formal schooling.

Between 1999 and 2005, postsecondary admissions tripled, reaching five million during the latter year. Currently China has about twenty million people with higher degrees; by 2020 there will be more than a hundred million. Although there are problems of educational quality and jobs, China's rising educational indicators bode well for both economic development and democracy.

What conclusion should we draw from the scholarship so far on democracy and development? I think it is that growth-friendly policies, if consistently pursued (historically determined institutions may prevent this), lead to the accumulation of human and physical capital and the rise of limited government. Autocratic regimes in economically growing countries can delay but not ultimately stop this from happening.

China's so-far slight improvement in the FH rankings has been in the Civil Liberties category, where it has gone from a 7 (the absolute worst score) to a 6. Looking behind the FH numbers, we can identify several factors that have led to a substantial growth in personal liberties and promise more freedom to come.

The first is that a modern economy is simply not compatible with the Leninist requirement of comprehensive party and state control over society. The Chinese Communist Party (CCP) has faced a hard choice: Maintain control and risk economic stagnation and political disaffection, or let go and risk eventually losing dominance. The CCP has chosen to pull back in several domains. Most notably, it allows markets to function. It also has accorded certain legal institutions and media outlets a degree of autonomy. The CCP has become Marxist-Leninist in name only. In reality, it seeks to rule a system that might be called party-state capitalism, setting broad rules while leaving much authority to local Party figures and various private actors. Central authorities can intervene, but they ration their energies.

One might think that a party which promotes markets, has formally enrolled "capitalists," and has allowed the state sector's share of the economy to shrink has lost any plausible claim to be called communist or socialist. Phrases such as "capitalism with Chinese characteristics" and "democratic socialism" do not disguise the reality of the CCP's massive but mostly unacknowledged ideological shift. Not that there is much nostalgia for socialism—or even a Confucian contempt for profit: In a 2005 survey of twenty countries, China featured the highest share of respondents (74 percent) who agreed with the proposition that the best economic system is "the free-market economy."[12]

The regime's legitimacy seems to rest on three main pillars: 1) It has brought social order after a century and a half of upheavals;[13] 2) people's incomes are growing rapidly (even if the growth is unevenly distributed); and 3) Chinese enjoy a sense that the Beijing government is restoring China to its rightful place of prominence in the world.

Surveys show that confidence in the government is high, and people seem satisfied with the way that "democracy" is unfolding.[14] Yet sources of discontent such as corruption, environmental damage, and sharp income inequality remain. In a departure from Chinese tradition, there is a developing attitude that individuals have rights.

Local elections, along with the aforementioned rise of certain relatively autonomous legal and media institutions, are helping to expand personal liberties and may have the potential to transform Chinese society.

Legal Institutions, Social Groups, and the Media

Legal reform began in 1979 when the CCP under its leader Deng Xiaoping decided that a modern economy required clear, predictable rules rather than obscure, arbitrary decisions. Although China remains a long way from being under the rule of law, the country has made considerable progress.[15] The main questions have to do with the extent of legal institutions' de facto independence today and the advances they might make tomorrow, together with the closely related issue of which, if any, claims to authority the Party will choose to defend to the end.

Almost three decades after Deng started the reform process, the National People's Congress (NPC) has passed many laws—determined by the State Council—and established a nationwide judiciary. Laws now provide for judicial review of the acts of state agents, compensation for damages from unlawful state actions, protection for people subject to noncriminal administrative sanctions, and rights to counsel and procedures for the conduct of criminal trials. Business transactions increasingly conform to legal rules. Important international commitments flow from China's membership in the World Trade Organization.

Many laws are ambiguous and contradictory, giving the Party ample opportunities to maintain its authority while also allowing changes to occur. Thus the Organic Law on Villager Committees recognizes the authority of the elected village head but requires committee conformance with "state policies" (thereby allowing the local Party secretary to overrule the locally elected leader). One consequence of these ambiguities is that local officials often are able to pick or interpret the laws that they prefer to follow.

With the number of lawyers at 150,000 and climbing, more people are seeking legal representation. The 4.3 million civil cases that China's courts heard in 2004 marked a 30 percent increase over the 1999 figure. People are suing not only one another but also state officials and enterprises with links to the Party-state establishment. Such suits can serve the Party-state's overall goal of "curbing administrative wrongdoing."[16]

The legal system remains firmly under CCP control. Party members often determine court decisions, officials press judges to throw out suits over property rights, and citizens' legal rights to counsel are ignored when the Party or local officials have already decided the case. Yet the system is evolving. The Supreme People's Court has begun to make interpretations and decisions—a role contrary to communist dogma. An anticorruption guideline dating from 2000 requires judges to stand aside from civil cases if they have taken money or gifts from a litigant. Judges are also banned from taking lucrative positions at law firms until at least two years after leaving the bench.

Many shocking abuses of the law occur. Nonetheless, a better-educated population and a more complex economy demand the rise of improved legal institutions. Rural unrest and pervasive corruption pressure leaders to take more steps toward the rule of law even if this means having to relax the Party's control over society. Thus developments in the legal arena, halting though they are, signal something positive about China's economic and political future.

Any Leninist regime must be suspicious of organizations—particularly social organizations cutting across class or regional lines—that it does not control. So far, the groups most worrisome to the powers that be have been religious in nature, such as the Falun Gong meditation movement. Nongovernmental organizations (NGOs) in general have been proliferating. More than 280,000 were officially registered as of 2005; unofficial estimates put the number of unregistered NGOs as high as two million. The regime monitors their activities, but accords them de facto leeway because of the benefits they bring. Many seek improvements in health, education, environmental protection, and services for the disabled, all to the sound of government toleration or even approval. By contrast, groups that focus on human rights and cultivate foreign ties have suffered increasing official harassment over the past two years.

The jailing of journalists, the closing of newspapers, and the censoring of websites reveal the CCP's determination to limit information and the independent organizing that it may spur. Nonetheless, information access and the ease of communication have both been on the rise. The media enjoy the freest hand they have had over their own content since 1949.[17]

The last three decades have seen the appearance of many new magazines and newspapers as well as talk radio, the Internet, and cell phones. The media cover a far wider range of topics than earlier, including official malfeasance and social problems as well as everyday concerns. More than a hundred million Chinese enjoy Internet access, and 450 million people—more than a third of the population—use cell phones. The government was able to block news of the Severe Acute Respiratory Syndrome (SARS) outbreak in late 2002 and early 2003—risking a global pandemic—but with half a billion text messages now beaming back and forth daily, the censors' task is hard and growing harder. What the regime ought to fear more than the spread of "unpatriotic" messages is the usefulness of devices such as the cheap, ubiquitous cell phone in organizing protests, exposing cover-ups, and even exacerbating situations that sometimes become riotous.

A conflict of goals besets the CCP. It wants economic information to flow freely, and the media can help to ferret out local corruption. Yet communications with any political coloration worry the Party greatly. The imperatives pull in opposite directions, giving rise to cycles of relaxation (the late 1980s before Tiananmen) and repression (the years after Tiananmen as well as the period since 2004). Backslidings toward restriction are almost certainly in store from time to time. Yet the underlying choice to accept markets is boosting people's access to information and their ability to reach each other, even if the right to free speech has yet to be recognized.

Village Elections Today, Township Elections Tomorrow?

The 1988 Organic Law on Villager Committees required that they be popularly elected and charged with responsibility and hence authority in such areas as fiscal management, land allocation, and education. By the mid-1990s, 90 percent of committee heads held their posts by virtue of the ballot. The degree to which elections are fair, open, and competitive varies. Such requirements as direct nomination by individuals, multiple candidates, secret ballots, public counting of all votes, immediate announcement of results, and regular recall procedures are not always followed, and the CCP's influence can decide outcomes.

As people come to enjoy more personal freedom, demand a larger say in matters that touch them directly, and feel fewer inhibitions about manifesting their discontents, the governance problems facing the CCP mount. If denied regular ways of dealing with their grievances and desires, people will increasingly choose irregular ways. The CCP might decide that the best way to fend off disorder is to empower people more. Township elections could be next.

The authorities in Beijing keep track of what they call "mass incidents." In 1995, about ten thousand were reported; a decade later the official figure had increased almost ninefold. Grievances are not in short supply. Although rural incomes have slowly grown, health and educational services have deteriorated in many places and the income gap between city and countryside is growing. The urban-rural Gini coefficient went from 0.28 in 1991 to 0.46 in 2000. (A higher number means less equal; it is 0.30 on average in Europe and 0.45 in the United States.) Income differences have also widened within urban areas, symbolized by reports of (dollar) billionaires.

Although taxes on peasants have been abolished, local officials still find ways to cheat them, often by colluding with developers to seize peasant lands with little compensation. With legal channels clogged and inadequate, mass protests become vehicles for voicing discontent and seeking change. The police report that many protests have elaborate organizations, complete with designated leaders, "public spokespersons," "activists," and "underground core groups." The protesters typically steer away from anything that looks like a direct challenge to Party authority, preferring to cite rights listed in party documents, laws, State Council regulations, and speeches by CCP leaders. Protests also tend to be carefully limited to local matters.

Informal protocols have evolved. The resisters seek redress by publicizing local officials' violations of national laws and norms. Local officials sometimes ignore the protesters or go through endless procedures without fixing the problems. If demonstrations persist or get too large, authorities may call in the police, arrest ringleaders, and then provide some compensation to the protesters. One scholar claims that "the state has made a conscious decision not to use its full coercive power to stop demonstrations. The airing of peasant grievances has become an accepted part of local politics. Workers and peasants now take to the streets feeling that it is now within bounds."[18]

Here as elsewhere, the government faces cross-pressures. Protests help to reveal the locations of abusive (and hence trouble-creating) local officials in need of removal, but an authoritarian party-state can hardly welcome frequent spontaneous demonstrations. The regime's solution so far has been to spend more on infrastructure, pollution control, health care, and education in rural areas while also campaigning against trouble-makers, with a focus on abusive and corrupt officials. Whether such efforts will contain the problem, however, remains unclear.

One should not assume that wildcat protests in the countryside mean the regime is seriously threatened. People know the role of protests—and of leaders sometimes encouraging them—in their history. Yet while such unrest is not a sign that the Party is tottering, neither is it a sign of Party legitimacy.

More wealth means more freedom. People have assets, more choices among goods, and a greater ability to decide where to work, live, and travel. Private ownership of housing, automobiles, and businesses is becoming widespread in China, and many small enterprises have gone from state to private hands.

Not so long ago, a typical city-dweller depended directly on the state for schooling, health care, and housing. Reforms reduced these services but made many more goods available. And there are better jobs. The labor market is not fully free, and there is unemployment, including among new university graduates, but one of a citizen's major life choices—work—is no longer dictated by government.

A residency permit, long needed to gain access to state-enterprise jobs as well as housing, education, and various subsidies, is less vital than before. Economic liberalization, labor surpluses in the modernizing agricultural sector, and the shrinking of the state sector have led more than a hundred million people without permits to move to cities. There they often lack services but stay on anyway, evidently preferring freer urban air to the straitened life prospects that faced them in the countryside.

As literacy, urbanization, and mass-media exposure rise, modernizing societies experience characteristic shifts in values. The grip of tradition and hierarchy loosens as women begin working outside the home, the nuclear family replaces the extended one, marriage becomes more an individual choice than a family decision, and women bear children later in life. Such changes are occurring in China. Alex Inkeles writes that although not everything is changing, least of all the Chinese commitment to filial piety, "[m]any fundamental values are being challenged and reformulated, basic human relationships are redefined and reordered, and numerous traditional ways of thinking and behaving are undergoing a great transformation."[19] Overall, investigators find the rejection of values that have long been near the core of Chinese culture to be "nothing short of phenomenal."[20]

One interpretation of the above is that civil liberties have outrun political rights. The state might seek to close this gap by taking away people's recently acquired personal liberties, but such a course would cause so much trouble that officials are unlikely to pursue it. The gap might also portend coming political instability. Here, what matters is that coming events not interfere with long-term growth in education and income. One can, of course, postulate long-lasting political instability, or slower long-term growth, but my projection assumes that neither of these will happen.

China's long-term prospects for achieving stable liberal democracy will be best if the liberal part comes first as a groundwork for the democratic part.

China's long-term prospects for achieving a stable form of liberal-democratic government will in all likelihood be best if the liberal part comes first as a groundwork for the democratic part. For that groundwork to be securely laid, education needs to continue spreading and improving, property rights need to receive increasing protection, transparent legal and financial institutions need to grow along with a robust private sector, personal liberties need to keep expanding, and income distribution needs to avoid extremes of inequality. The general idea, as Persson and Tabellini put it, is that "the sequence of reforms is crucial; countries liberalizing their economies before extending political rights do better."[21]

Former U.S. secretary of state George Schultz once related to me how Deng Xiaoping addressed the matter in July 1988, when the two men were discussing Mikhail Gorbachev's reforms in the Soviet Union: "He's got it backwards," said Deng. "He opened up the political system without a clue about the economy. The result is chaos. I did it the other way around, starting in agriculture and small businesses, where opening up worked, so now I have a demand for more of what succeeds." When Schultz asked when political opening would occur, Deng said: "That will come later and will start small, just as in the economy. You have to be patient but you have to get the sequence right."

Scholar He Baogang suggests that the CCP might become the seedbed of a multiparty system, or at least its functional equivalent.[22] The CCP is home to factions that represent different interests, it holds internal contests for posts, and it is increasingly eager to monitor its members' performance, all of which might help to limit its tendencies toward tyranny and corruption. Taking another tack, Gang Lin argues that democracy (at least within the Party), rather than arising as a side-effect of ruling-party splits, could become a tool in the CCP's campaign to prop up its own authority.[23]

How will events unfold? No one can convincingly claim to know. There are many possible paths—rough, smooth, or in-between—that can lead to democracy. One way to gauge the route that may lie before China would be to estimate how freedoms might evolve as the country works its way through the lag between rapidly changing socioeconomic realities and the political modes and orders that come under

Table—Predictions for China's Future

Year	Per Capita GDP (2006 PPP)	Average Years of Schooling (>25)	Predicted Electoral Rights	Predicted Freedom House Rating
2010	$8,500	6.3	22	Not Free
2015	$10,000	6.7	43	Partly Free
2020	$11,800	7.2	61	Partly Free
2025	$14,000	7.7	76	Free

pressure to keep up despite the drag exerted by the force of institutional inertia.

Robert J. Barro's model generates quantitative predictions for electoral rights (corresponding to FH's "Political Rghts" category). He found that the level of democracy, so measured, that is present in a given earlier period allows one to forecast the level of democracy found in a later period, albeit with decreasing certainty as the interval between periods widens. Barro also found several social variables to be predictors of democracy. These rising (in the case of China) variables include GDPpc and the educational level of the populace. Another positive predictor of democracy is a shrinking gap between the proportions of males and females who have been to primary school. Thus the extent of democracy in a country converges gradually toward a (moving) target determined by the social variables.

On a scale of zero to a hundred, entering my predicted social inputs (economic and educational inputs plus others) yields the predictions about electoral rights shown in the Table above for successive five-year periods to 2025. For 2010, China is still Not Free but by 2015 it edges into the Partly Free category and gets into the Free one by 2025. Evidence from around the world suggests that over almost two decades, a well-educated people whose average income is rising toward a figure of perhaps $14,000 (PPP) by 2025 will almost certainly see its freedoms—including its electoral freedoms—expand. In 2005, every country in the world (oil states excepted) with GDPpc topping $8,000 (PPP) was at least Partly Free; indeed, all ranked as Free except the tiny island city-state of Singapore.[24]

And yet—several things could go wrong. I have mentioned some of them.[25] The Barro parameters are based on the experiences of many countries and China is but one. In any case, I do not argue that China will ever be a Sweden or New Zealand; its democracy will probably have some "Chinese characteristics." Nearby there is Taiwan, whose democratization took almost forty years to complete beginning with local elections in the early 1950s; counting the same number of years from China's 1988 Organic Law on Villager Committees yields about 2025. The technocratic authoritarianism of Singapore offers a model that some CCP leaders must prefer to Taiwan's. Or Chinese politicians might come up with a novel political arrangement that falls short of true liberal democracy but nonetheless offers the Chinese people more liberty and a bigger say in how they are ruled than they currently enjoy.

Implications for Peace

I observed in 1996 that a democratic China in a region with many democracies would be good for peace because democracies do not fight each other (which does not imply that democracies are inherently peaceable).

Yet all is not necessarily well. Edward D. Mansfield and Jack Snyder find that countries making the transition from authoritarian to democratic governance are more likely to start foreign broils than are consolidated democracies because internal contests for power can cause a faction to identify, or to conjure up, a foreign enemy as a means of rallying mass support.[26] Mansfield and Snyder hold that this is most likely where elections are held in countries with a weak sense of nationhood, a shaky rule of law, feeble bureaucracies, poor civilian control of the military, a winner-take-all attitude among contending parties, and few safeguards for press freedom. This leads them to recommend that, where possible, elections should come on the heels and not ahead of institution-building, with a competent central government and legal system needed most urgently of all.

If these premises are correct, China's prospects are not bad. The Chinese today possess a strong sense of nationhood, a legal system that is moving in the right direction, a military that seems firmly under civilian control, increased professionalism in many organizations, and nothing like the shadow of "premature" elections on the horizon. Other positives for peace are China's high trade-to-GDP ratio and membership in several international organizations.

On the negative side, the country's experience with competing political parties was brief and long ago, and it turned out poorly. Corruption is pervasive, and the Communist Party shows no sign of a being ready to put up with having to run against anyone, much less lose to them. Most worrisome of all is the flashpoint for nationalist conflagration that sits just off China's coast on the other side of the Taiwan Strait.

To Beijing, Taiwan is but a renegade province, and the use of force against it would count not as a foreign war but as a domestic police action. If the disaster of an armed conflict between Beijing and Taipei (whose supporters are Japan and the United States) can be averted long enough for the mainland to become a democracy, the prospect of a peaceful solution will gather strength. Indeed, a more democratic mainland China is probably necessary for a peaceful resolution of this dispute. Yet a power struggle within China that drove some faction or factions to rouse popular nationalist sentiment could be one way in which rising political pluralism might lead to big trouble. Another way would be for Taiwan to declare itself an independent country.

Should the hazards that come with transition be skirted, the democratic-peace thesis leads to a prediction that relations between China on the one hand and Japan and the United States on the other will remain pacific. Nonetheless, China's burgeoning economic and military clout will have consequences. In twenty years, the PRC's annual defense budget might exceed $200 billion, and its military forces will have high-technology weapons. Its power will cause many small states to align themselves with Beijing like iron filings near a powerful magnet. There would remain the chance that China could use force against nondemocracies, but a China that navigates the transition to democracy without taking up the sword should on the whole improve the prospects for peace in the region and beyond.

Returning to the four questions posed at the beginning of this essay: 1) The economy looks likely to stay on a high growth path, albeit slowing as China's demography changes and its economy's performance converges on that of the world leaders. It is not immune to serious disruption. 2) Seymour Martin Lipset's hypothesis that development leads to freedoms is better supported than any current rival explanation. 3) By 2015, there is a good chance that China will have made its way into Freedom House's middling or Partly Free group, with a ranking as Free following by 2025. 4) Although the period of transition to free government could hold dangers, a democratic China will be a China that is less likely to fight with its democratic neighbors.

Sometimes events move fast. As late as the mid-1980s, few even among the experts anticipated that the Soviet Union would soon be gone. I am not suggesting that the CCP will be gone in one or two decades, but I do think that if it survives, it will be because it has learned to adapt and adjust to a much transformed—meaning a much freer—political landscape.

NOTES

I owe thanks to many people, especially Robert Barro, Tricia Bolle, Peter Lorentzen, Alex Inkeles, John Lewis, Stanley Lubman, and Andrew Walder, none of whom bears any responsibility for the results.

1. Henry S. Rowen, "The Short March: China's Road to Democracy," *National Interest* 45 (Fall 1996): 61–70.

2. The widely used *CIA World Factbook* (*www.cia.gov/cia/publications/factbook/index.html*) estimates China's GDPpc for 2006 as $7,600 rather than the $6,000 figure that I deem more accurate. Estimating PPP values is an imperfect art and the *Factbook* value seems too high for a country whose exchange-rate GDPpc is only $1,900 per annum. This last number, based on data from China's National Statistical Bureau, is much less controversial than the PPP figure.

3. Seymour Martin Lipset, "Some Social Requisites of Democracy: Economic

Development and Political Legitimacy," *American Political Science Review* 53 (March 1959): 69–105.

4. Edward L. Glaeser et al., "Do Institutions Cause Growth?" National Bureau of Economic Research Working Paper No. 10568, 2004.

5. Edward L. Glaeser, Giacomo Ponzetto, and Andrei Schleifer, "Why Does Democracy Need Education?" National Bureau of Economic Research Working Paper No. 12128, 2006.

6. Robert J. Barro, "Determinants of Democracy," *Journal of Political Economy* 107 (December 1999): S158–83.

7. Robert J. Barro, "Rule of Law, Democracy, and Economic Performance," *2000 Index of Economic Freedom* (Washington, D.C.: Heritage Foundation, 2000).

8. Adam Przeworski et al., *Democracy and Development: Political Institutions and Material Well-Being in the World, 1950–1990* (Cambridge: Cambridge University Press, 2000); Carles Boix and Susan C. Stokes, "Endogenous Democratization," *World Politics* 55 (July 2003): 517–49.

9. Torsten Persson and Guido Tabellini, "Democracy and Development: The Devil in the Details," National Bureau of Economic Research, Working Paper No. 11993, 2006.

10. Daron Acemoglu, Simon Johnson, and James A. Robinson, "The Colonial Origins of Comparative Development: An Empirical Investigation," *American Economic Review* 91 (December 2001): 1369–1401.

11. Robert J. Barro and Jong-Wha Lee, "International Data on Educational Attainment: Updates and Implications," *Oxford Economic Papers* 53 (2001): 541–63.

12. See *www.globescan.com/news_archives/pipa_market.html.*

13. When asked in a 2003 Roper Survey where stability ranked as a social value, Chinese ranked it second. Its average ranking by other nations' citizens was twenty-third. Joshua Cooper Ramo, "The Beijing Consensus," at *http://fpc.org.uk/publications/123.*

14. Zhengxu Wang, "Before the Emergence of Critical Citizens: Economic Devlopment and Political Trust in China," *International Review of Sociology* 15 (March 2005): 155–71.

15. "[T]he progress in legal reform since the end of the Mao era has been unprecedented in Chinese history, as reflected in the passage of a large number of new laws, the increasing use of the courts to resolve economic disputes, social and state-society conflicts, the development of a professional legal community, and improvements in judicial procedures. . . . Chinese courts have assumed an indispensable role in resolving economic, social and, to a limited extent—political—conflicts." Minxin Pei, "Statement to the Senate Foreign Relations Committee, June 7, 2005," at *http://www.senate.gov/foreign/testimony/2005/PeiTestimony050607.pdf.*

16. Benjamin L. Liebman, "Watchdog or Demagogue? The Media in the Chinese Legal System," *Columbia Law Review* 105 (January 2005): 64.

17. Liebman, "Watchdog or Demagogue?" 56.

18. Jean Oi, "Bending Without Breaking: The Adaptability of Chinese Political

Institutions," in Nicholas C. Hope, Dennis Tao Yang, and Mu Yang Li, eds., *How Far Across the River? Chinese Policy Reform at the Millennium* (Stanford: Stanford University Press, 2003), 450–68.

19. Alex Inkeles, "The Generalist Meets the China Specialist," in *One World Emerging? Convergence and Divergence in Industrial Societies* (Boulder, Colo.: Westview, 1998), 96–113.

20. Goodwin C. Chu and Yanan Ju, *The Great Wall in Ruins: Communication and Cultural Change in China* (Albany: State University of New York Press, 1993).

21. Persson and Tabellini, "Democracy and Development," 2.

22. He Baogang, "Intra-Party Democracy: A Revisionist Perspective from Below," in Kjeld Erik Broedsgaard and Yongnian Zheng, eds., *The Chinese Communist Party in a New Era: Renewal and Reform* (London: Routledge, 2005), 192–209.

23. Gang Lin, "Ideology and Political Institutions for a New Era," in Gang Lin and Xiaobo Hu, eds., *China After Jiang* (Stanford: Stanford University Press, 2003).

24. The 2006 coup in Thailand has caused that country to drop from Free all the way to Not Free in the FH rankings. Thailand's 2006 PPP level of $9,100 makes this a rare event. Russia, where per-capita income was $12,100 PPP in 2006, was recently downgraded from Partly Free to Not Free. Yet Russia earns more than 60 percent of its export revenues from oil and natural gas, which puts it in the (politically unfortunate) category of petroleum states and hence outside the relevant comparison set for this essay.

25. Assuming a future growth rate 1 percentage point lower than in the case shown in the text would put China in the Partly Free rather than the Free FH category as of 2025.

26. Edward D. Mansfield and Jack Snyder, *Electing to Fight: Why Emerging Democracies Go to War* (Cambridge: MIT Press, 2005). For critiques of this line of thinking, see Michael McFaul, "Are New Democracies War-Prone?" *Journal of Democracy* 18 (April 2007): 160–67; and John R. Oneal, Bruce Russett, and Michael L. Berbaum, "Causes of Peace: Democracy, Interdependence, and International Organizations, 1885–1992," *International Studies Quarterly* 47 (September 2003): 371–93.

[33]

The End of the CCP's Resilient Authoritarianism? A Tripartite Assessment of Shifting Power in China*

Cheng Li†

Abstract

This essay challenges the widely held view of the CCP's purported "resilient authoritarianism," which asserts that China's one-party political system is able to enhance the state capacity to govern effectively through institutional adaptations and policy adjustments. An analysis of the recent and still unfolding Bo Xilai crisis reveals the flaws in China's political system, including nepotism and patron–client ties in the selection of leaders, rampant corruption, the growing oligarchic power of state-owned enterprises, elites' contempt for the law and the potential failure to broker deals between competing factions in the Party leadership. The essay argues that the CCP's "authoritarian resilience" is a stagnant system, both conceptually and empirically, because it resists much-needed democratic changes in the country. The problems of the resilient authoritarianism thesis is traceable to the monolithic conceptualizing of China – the failure to appreciate seemingly paradoxical transformative trends in the country, which this essay characterizes as three paralleled developments, namely, 1) weak leaders, strong factions; 2) weak government, strong interest groups; and 3) weak Party, strong country. One should not confuse China's national resilience (in terms of the emerging middle class, new interest group politics, and dynamic society) with the CCP's capacity and legitimacy to rule the country. The essay concludes that if the CCP intends to regain the public's confidence and avoid a bottom-up revolution, it must abandon the notion of "authoritarian resilience" and embrace a systematic democratic transition with bold steps towards intra-Party elections, judicial independence and a gradual opening of the mainstream media.

Keywords: Chinese Communist Party; resilient authoritarianism; factional politics; intra-Party democracy; leadership transition; corruption; fifth generation

---

* The author thanks Chris Bramall, Eve Cary, Jordan Lee and John Langdon for suggesting ways in which to clarify the article.

† Brookings. Email: cli@brookings.edu

 doi:10.1017/S0305741012000902

596 The China Quarterly, 211, September 2012, pp. 595–623

If there is one recurring mistake that the international community makes when analysing present-day China, it is to describe the world's most populous and rapidly changing country in monolithic terms. Many commentators fail to draw a distinction between China's ruling elite and Chinese society when they assess the current status and future trajectory of Chinese politics.[1] Given that China has become increasingly pluralistic, with the arrival of many new socio-political players and an increasingly complicated decision-making process, inaccurate generalizations are more problematic today than ever before.

Over the past decade, overseas China analysts have tended to characterize the Chinese authoritarian political system as "resilient" and "strong."[2] According to their logic, the Chinese Communist Party (CCP) seems to have found a sustainable way to maintain its rule over its fast-growing economy. In the view of these foreign observers, China's increasing national strength, growing societal diversity, and emerging intra-Party checks and balances are factors that strengthen rather than undermine CCP rule.[3] In general, this perspective tends to underestimate the vulnerability of the authoritarian one-party system. New socio-economic forces in the country pose serious challenges to the CCP's resilient authoritarianism. Meanwhile, competing factions within the Party leadership may fail to broker the necessary deals to preserve Party unity.

Some of the fundamental flaws of the Chinese political system were on display in the spring 2012 political crisis concerning Bo Xilai 薄熙来, one of the Party's rising stars and chief of China's largest city, Chongqing. Official corruption, for example, is unprecedented in scope and scale in contemporary China. Ironically, Bo had been a leader known for his tough stance on corruption, having spearheaded a "smashing mafia" (*dahei* 打黑) campaign, but now most consider him to be a kind of "head of the mafia." Consequently, public trust in the CCP's leadership has perhaps fallen to its lowest point in the post-Mao era. The Party has lost the moral high ground. If the allegations are shown to be true, it seems that absolutely no moral constraints were at play in the cases of Gu Kailai 谷開來 (Bo's wife), former Chongqing Police Chief

1 Perry Link, a long-time critic of the Chinese authorities, recently made a strong and valid critique of some American experts on China for their use of the terms "China" or "the Chinese" to "refer exclusively to elite circles" of the Chinese Communist Party. Link warned that allowing "China" to represent only a small elite "is dangerous in that it adumbrates nearly a fifth of the world's population. It also prevents a square consideration of how long the regime will last" (2012, 27). Interestingly, Gordon Chang, another well-known critic of the CCP leadership, has continued to predict "the coming collapse of China," while primarily referring to the potential fall of the CCP (2011). For an earlier version of his thesis, see Chang 2001.

2 David Shambaugh, for example, observed that the CCP is a "reasonably strong and resilient institution" (2008, 176). See also Nathan 2003; Miller 2008b; Miller 2009.

3 According to Andrew Nathan, "the regime's institutional changes have so far served to consolidate rather than weaken authoritarianism" (2006, 3); see also Fewsmith 2006; Brown 2009; Dickson 2003; Dickson 2008; Tsai 2007; Yang 2004.

Wang Lijun 王立军 and Bo himself, which allegedly involved murder, assassination, torture and other abuses of power.[4]

Despite efforts on the part of the CCP leadership to earmark these incidents as "isolated and exceptional phenomena," many PRC public intellectuals openly argue that rampant official corruption, especially when involving top CCP leaders' families, exemplifies a decadent form of crony capitalism (*quangui zibenzhuyi* 权贵资本主义) that is more the rule than the exception in the Chinese political system.[5] The Bo imbroglio is certainly not solely a reflection of his notorious egotism.[6] The scandal is arguably the most serious political crisis since the 1989 Tiananmen incident and constitutes a major challenge to the legitimacy of the CCP leadership as a whole.

For the overseas China studies community, it is essential to go beyond superficial discussions of these Hollywood-like political spectacles, which in fact may obscure broader power shifts occurring behind these ostensibly unrelated events. In stark contrast to the 1989 Tiananmen crisis, China's economy and society have, at least until now, seen little disruption in the wake of the Bo Xilai crisis, illustrating a scenario in which the country can remain largely intact despite a series of vicious power struggles in Zhongnanhai 中南海. Some American China analysts, however, have mistaken China's national resilience for evidence of the CCP's governing capacity and political legitimacy. Recent debates on "why China won't collapse" are highly misleading because one can reasonably argue that the issue of the day is whether or not the Party will survive, not the country.[7]

China's political future, especially the survival of its one-party system, is a controversial issue that should be subject to more rigorous intellectual and policy debates. The notion of resilient authoritarianism, the prevailing analytical framework with which many academics in the West have studied the Chinese political system in the last decade or so, must be re-examined in the light of recent political phenomena. An empirically well-grounded and balanced assessment of the unfolding political crisis is particularly valuable today, not only because China is at a crossroads in terms of domestic development, but also because it now has more influence on the world economy and regional security than at any other time in modern history. Misperception of China's socio-economic

4 It was widely reported in overseas Chinese media that Jiang Zemin, former general secretary of the CCP, recently commented on the Bo Xilai scandal that "Bo has crossed the bottom line of human civilization." *Sing Tao Daily*, 28 May 2012.

5 For example, Zhang Ming (2012) launched a strong critique of the rampancy of official corruption by dozens of CCP top leaders in March, a few months before the foreign media began to trace "family trees" of crony capitalism among the Chinese leadership. For the CCP authorities' effort to make the Bo case "isolated and exceptional," see Sina News, posted on 25 May 2012, http://news.sina.com.hk/news/1617/3/1/2673095/1.html.

6 Bo has been long famous for his political ambition (see Li 2001, 165–66). In the months preceding the crisis, Su Wei, a scholar close to Bo at the Chongqing Party School, compared Bo Xilai and Chongqing mayor Huang Qifan to former leaders Mao Zedong and Zhou Enlai in comments circulated in both the Chongqing and national media. See Sina Global Newsnet, posted online on 20 September 2011 http://dailynews.sina.com/bg/chn/chnnews/ausdaily/20110920/18402783790.html.

7 For example, see Bell 2012.

conditions carries with it the risk of implementing ineffective government policies toward the PRC.

This article first presents a critical review of the main arguments for resilient authoritarianism and explains why they are inadequate in understanding Chinese politics today. It then identifies three transformative trends in the PRC. For the sake of clarity, these three developments are summarized in the form of three parallel phrases: 1) weak leaders, strong factions; 2) weak government, strong interest groups; and 3) weak Party, strong country.[8] The shifting power of various constituencies in China reflects the multi-dimensional and dynamic changes underway in the country.

Resilient Authoritarianism: A Critical Review

Western scholarship on the Chinese state's resilient authoritarianism began to emerge in the mid-1990s and has become the mainstream position over the last decade. When the CCP survived the political turmoil of the 1989 Tiananmen incident, which had posed a serious legitimacy crisis, many China analysts began to appreciate the endurance and adaptability with which the Chinese leadership handled daunting challenges both at home and abroad. The political succession from Jiang Zemin 江泽民's third generation of leadership to Hu Jintao 胡锦涛's fourth generation, which took place at the 16th National Congress of the CCP in 2002, was remarkable for being the first time in PRC history that the CCP leadership conducted a peaceful, orderly and institutionalized transfer of power. It is quite common for overseas China analysts to view the CCP as being limber and adaptable enough to respond quickly to changes to their environment and to become better qualified and more competent with time. "The result," as some scholars have observed, "has been to create a power system characterized by 'authoritarian resilience.'"[9]

By definition, the CCP's resilient authoritarianism refers to a one-party political system that is able to "enhance the capacity of the state to govern effectively" through institutional adaptations and policy adjustments.[10] According to some analysts, the CCP's resilient authoritarian system can successfully resist or prevent democratic demand. Not surprisingly, Party conservatives seek to reinforce the belief that "democracy is not appropriate for China," but that a resilient authoritarian system is.[11] This is evident, for example, in Chairman of the National People's Congress Wu Bangguo 吴邦国's recent pronouncement of the 'five nos' for China."[12]

8 Some of this discussion about the tripartite assessment of power shifts in China also previously appeared in my short opinion piece presented at the first annual conference of the Johnson Center for the Study of American Diplomacy, held in honour of Henry Kissinger at Yale University in March 2012. See Li 2012b.

9 Brodsgaard and Zheng 2006, 2.

10 Dickson 2005, 1.

11 *Ibid.*, 11.

12 Wu Bangguo's famous "five nos" refer to 1) no multiple party system; 2) no pluralism in ideology; 3) no checks and balances in power or bicameral parliament; 4) no federal system; and 5) no privatization. He

The authoritarian resilience thesis seems to hold up if one examines the change and continuity of the broad policy framework that each generation of CCP leaders has embraced over the past two decades. In his famous "southern tour" in 1992, Deng Xiaoping 邓小平 called for greater market reform and economic privatization while continuing to crackdown on political dissent. Jiang Zemin broadened the power base of the CCP by recruiting entrepreneurs and other new socio-economic players (a formulation known as the "three represents"), while launching a harsh political campaign against the Falun Gong, an emerging group of religious believers. Hu Jintao's populist appeal for a "harmonious society" sought to reduce economic disparities and social tensions while tightening censorship over the media and police control in society, especially in ethnic minority regions. In all of these major socio-economic and political developments, the CCP's top leaders made a calculated but far-reaching ideological and policy move in one area, but resisted political pressure in another.

Some of the CCP adaptations were also the result of lessons learned from other authoritarian regimes. As David Shambaugh has observed, some of the CCP's new policies and procedures were developed in response to systematic study of post-communist and non-communist Party states. The CCP proactively attempted to "reform and rebuild itself institutionally – thereby sustaining its political legitimacy and power."[13] According to Alice Miller, "the pattern of Hu Jintao's leadership as first among equals suggests that they have managed to avoid a dictatorship as well as prevent the gerontocratic stagnation that the Soviet leadership suffered by the early 1980s because it failed to address the same issue."[14]

Is the Chinese authoritarian system resilient? Insights from liberal PRC thinkers

To assume that the CCP's resilient authoritarianism will allow the Party leadership to weather political storms in the years and decades to come, however, is to take the authoritarian resilience thesis too far. Richard McGregor, former Beijing bureau chief of the *Financial Times* and the author of the oft-cited book *The Party*, regarded the perception that "the Party can't rule forever" as one of the "five myths about the Chinese Communist Party."[15] In his words, "Yes it can. Or at least for the foreseeable future."[16]

Ironically, CCP official directives are often less optimistic about the Party's capacity to govern and its non-democratic resilience. In September 2009, the

---

footnote continued

made this statement at the fourth plenary session of the 11th National People's Congress held in Beijing on 11 March 2011. See *Zhongguo xinwen wang*, posted on 11 March 2011. http://www.china.com.cn/2011/2011-03/11/content_22114099.htm.

13 Shambaugh 2008, 9.

14 Miller 2008b, 77.

15 McGregor 2011. For the mentioned book, see McGregor 2010.

16 McGregor 2011.

600 The China Quarterly, 211, September 2012, pp. 595–623

Fourth Plenary Session of the 17th Central Committee of the CCP called for the promotion of democracy within the Party and an intensification of the anti-corruption drive within the leadership. According to the directives adopted at the meeting, many problems internal to the CCP were exacerbated by new domestic and international circumstances and "are severely weakening the Party's creativity, unity and effectiveness in dealing with these problems."[17] Therefore, careful management of the Party "has never been so arduous and urgent."[18] The directives particularly stress the importance of intra-Party democracy, describing it as the "lifeblood of the Party" (*dang de shengming* 党的生命).[19] More recently, the *People's Daily*, the Chinese official propaganda organ, issued an editorial on the 91st anniversary of the founding of the CCP that called for greater efforts to overcome four main crises confronting the Party, namely, "slacking spirit, lack of capacity, distance from the masses, and rampant corruption."[20]

It should be noted that for liberal CCP leaders like Wen Jiabao 温家宝, Li Yuanchao 李源潮, Wang Yang 汪洋 and their advisors, intra-Party democracy is only a means, not the end, of fulfilling China's democratic aspirations. On many occasions, Wen, Li and Wang have argued explicitly that democracy reflects universal values and should be the shared aspiration of the Chinese people. In an interview with the Chinese media, Yu Keping 俞可平, a distinguished CCP theoretician, argued that it would be a grave mistake to assume that China only needs intra-Party democracy, instead of a truer people's democracy (*renmin minzhu* 人民民主) or social democracy (*shehui minzhu* 社会民主), both of which would include grassroots and general democratic elections.[21] For Yu, intra-Party democracy and people's democracy are complementary. The former is top-down or inside-out and the latter is bottom-up, but ideally the two can meet in the middle. In a strategic sense, Yu Keping and his like-minded colleagues place great importance on intra-Party democracy with the objective that it will pave the way for Chinese democracy in a broader sense. Yu believes that China's quest for democracy should, and eventually will, have a qualitative "breakthrough" of some sort.[22]

Similarly, Wang Changjiang 王长江, professor and chairman of the department of Party building at the Central Party School (CPS), recently argued that the promotion of intra-Party democracy need not be at the expense of social democracy. He cited major recent crises, such as the ethnic tensions in Tibet and

17 See *People's Daily* online, 19 September 2009: http://english.people.com.cn/90001/90776/90785/6761990.html.

18 *Ibid.*

19 For the communiqué on the directives of the Fourth Plenary Session of the 17th Central Committee of the Chinese Communist Party, see http://cpc.people.com.cn/GB/64093/64094/10080626.html.

20 "Jingshen xiedai, nengli bu zu, tuoli qunzhong, xiaoji fubai." *Renmin ribao*, 1 July 2012, 1. Also see *Shijie ribao*, 1 July 2012, A5.

21 Yu 2009b.

22 See http://www.hi.chinanews.com.cn/hnnew/2005-10-20/29705.html, 20 August 2008; and also Yu 2009a, 1–6.

Xinjiang and social unrest elsewhere, to highlight the urgency of developing democracy in China. In Wang's words, "social democracy should not wait."[23] These views, expressed by the liberal scholars in the CCP establishment, differ profoundly from Richard McGregor's generalization that the Chinese people and leaders have no interest in democracy. McGregor recently stated: "The idea that China would one day become a democracy was always a Western notion, born of our theories about how political systems evolve. Yet all evidence so far suggests these theories are wrong."[24] McGregor's view is also incompatible with recent public opinion surveys in China. The English edition of *Global Times* (a branch of the official *People's Daily*) reported that its research centre recently conducted a survey of 1,010 people in seven Chinese cities and found that 63.6 per cent of respondents did not oppose adopting Western-style democracy in China.[25]

Zi Zhongyun 资中筠, a distinguished scholar and former director of the Institute of American Studies at the Chinese Academy of Social Science (CASS), apparently disagreed with both McGregor and conservative hardliners in the CCP leadership. In her recently edited book, she bluntly challenged CCP officials who have spread the false notions that democracy is not suitable for the Chinese people and that universal values are nothing but a Western conspiracy against China.[26] She used the term "obscurantism" (*mengmeizhuyi* 蒙昧注义) to describe the efforts on the part of those opposed to democratic change to mislead the Chinese public. She particularly warned of the danger of nationalism – the tendency to excuse injustice in society in the name of the state interests.[27] Zi observed that in every crucial moment of the century-long Chinese movement for democracy and constitutionalism, conservatives have always drawn on the so-called "Chinese essence" and patriotism to resist Western influence and China's political transformation.[28]

One should note that Yu Keping, Wang Changjiang, and Zi Zhongyun are all CCP members who are part of the Chinese political establishment. None of them is a political dissident or someone who favours a radical bottom-up political uprising, although all three seem to be concerned about the lack of real political reform in recent years. Yet even these liberal thinkers within the Party have been pushing hard for democracy, the rule of law and human rights in China, which they regard as universal values rather than as mere Western ideas. They are no admirers of authoritarian resilience.

One can argue that if a political system is really resilient, it should always be open to new ideas and new experiments, as one change will lead to another.

23 Wang 2009.

24 McGregor 2011.

25 Also 49.4 % of people expected that China would have a revolution if the leadership fails to pursue real political reforms and only 8.5 % believed that revolution is impossible. Quoted from *Shijie ribao*, 15 March 2012, A12.

26 Zi 2011, 171.

27 *Ibid.*, 173.

28 *Ibid.*, 22.

602 The China Quarterly, 211, September 2012, pp. 595–623

Otherwise, it should be considered a stagnant system. Some Western scholars have also rejected the authoritarian resilience thesis. Richard Baum, for example, has argued that democracy is the political system most responsive to emergent social forces, and thus will emerge victorious in China as well as in many other parts of the world.[29]

Is Chinese political institutionalization effective and sustainable?

More specifically, the authoritarian resilience thesis has apparently become increasingly problematic in the Chinese context. In his analysis of why the CCP has been able to remain in power since the 1989 Tiananmen incident, Andrew Nathan outlined four important institutional developments in the Chinese political system:

1) the increasingly norm-bound nature of its succession politics;
2) the increase in meritocratic, as opposed to factional, considerations in the promotion of political elites;
3) the differentiation and functional specialization of institutions within the regime; and
4) the establishment of institutions for political participation that strengthen the CCP's legitimacy among the public at large.[30]

All of these institutional mechanisms have been on the agenda of the CCP leadership. Some have already affected the political behaviour of leaders and changed the game of Chinese elite politics over the past decade or so. But one can also argue that for now none of them has been very effective in making the system more resilient.

Regarding Nathan's first point, it is true that some institutional rules and norms have developed over the past two decades, such as term limits and age requirements for retirement. They not only generate a sense of increased consistency and fairness in the selection of leaders, but also speed up the circulation of the Chinese political elite. Some of yesterday's solutions, however, are becoming today's problems. One of the most important phenomena in present-day China is the fact that many retired leaders have become increasingly outspoken when it comes to criticizing the policies adopted by the current leadership. This is a healthy political development that has led Chinese politics to become more transparent and more pluralistic, but it is also very politically sensitive for a country that has placed such a high priority on harmony and stability. While retired leaders' criticisms may reflect their genuine consciousness about the need for sound policies at this crucial moment in China's development, they can also be seen as a way that retired leaders express their personal dissatisfaction and anger.

29 Baum 2007. For other strong criticisms of CCP resilient authoritarianism, see Pei 2008; Shirk 2007; Lü 2000.

30 Nathan 2003, 6–7.

Due to term and age limits, many capable leaders in good health have had to step down in their late 50s. Some of them later pursued business activities (*xiahai* 下海) after retirement, and some seized this "last opportunity" to use political power for personal gain or other malfeasance, known in China as "the age 59 phenomenon" (*wushijiu sui xianxiang* 五十九岁现象).[31] As a result of the strict implementation of institutional regulations and norms over the past two decades, there has been a significant increase in the number of retired leaders, and they have become an important political force in their own right. Unless the CCP authorities adopt more electoral mechanisms in the selection of senior leaders, the issues of age discrimination and the political resentment of retired leaders will likely become increasingly acute.

Prior to the Bo Xilai crisis, many analysts believed that Chinese political institutionalization had developed well enough to make the upcoming leadership succession at the 18th Party Congress as smooth and orderly as the one in 2002. The most notable recent example is a book published by Robert Lawrence Kuhn, a businessman who has since become a biographer of the PRC's senior leaders. Through extensive interviews with many rising stars of the so-called fifth generation of PRC leaders, Kuhn offered nothing but praise for their talents, wisdom and vision.[32] Kuhn and other like-minded overseas analysts have overlooked the CCP's deficiencies – or more precisely, the stagnancy of the authoritarian system – when it comes to selecting its national leaders. The importance of the Bo Xilai episode was, to a great extent, the fact that he aggressively and unprecedentedly campaigned to obtain a seat in the next Politburo Standing Committee. While Bo has been purged possibly for his alleged crimes and his "violation of party rules," until a more legitimate mechanism to select leaders is implemented these problems will continue to undermine the leadership unity and the Party's governance capacity.

With respect to intra-Party checks and balances as a whole, Chinese leadership politics has indeed undergone a process of increasing institutionalization over the past decade, as Alice Miller has observed.[33] My study of the possible emergence of bipartisanship within the upper echelons of the CCP also focused on new norms and practices in Chinese elite politics.[34] It is important to recognize, however, that newly developed institutional experiments can either fail or lead to further and greater changes if the system is genuinely resilient.

Nathan's second point about meritocracy in the formation of the Chinese leadership might resonate well in the West. In many cases, political leaders in Western democracies are not well prepared, educationally or professionally, before being elected to office. Relatively speaking, Chinese leaders have been well educated, which was especially true in the case of the third generation of

31 Many of the senior level leaders who were purged on corruption charges had begun to engage in bribery, embezzlement, and other illegal activities at the age of 59 – the year before their retirement.

32 Kuhn 2010.

33 Miller 2008a.

34 For a detailed discussion of the origin of the new norms and practices, see Li 2005.

604 The China Quarterly, 211, September 2012, pp. 595–623

leadership led by Jiang Zemin – many of whom studied overseas (in the Soviet Union and the East European countries in the 1950s) – as well as Hu Jintao's fourth generation, in which a majority were engineers by training.[35] In a sense, these leaders could be seen as technocrats. As for the upcoming fifth generation of leaders, although they are less technocratic than the last two generations, some have studied in the West or Japan as visiting scholars. Generally speaking, they seem more informed about world affairs than their counterparts in other countries. According to some foreign observers, a majority of Chinese national leaders have previously served as municipal and provincial leaders for many years or even decades, and are thus well prepared for the national stage.

However, in the eyes of the Chinese public, especially critics of the Party, the current method of selecting PRC leaders is anything but meritocratic. In the absence of democratic competition, nepotism in various forms (such as blood ties, school ties, regional identities, *mishu* 秘书 or personal assistant experiences and patron–client ties) continues to play a crucial role. Three new phenomena deserve special attention.

First, all of the leading candidates for the next Politburo, and especially the Standing Committee that will be formed during the 18th Party Congress in the autumn of 2012, are well known for their strong family backgrounds, factional affiliations or other patron–client ties. One can reasonably argue, as many in China do, that their rise to the pinnacle of power in the most populous country in the world has had more to do with heavyweight patrons than with their own leadership credentials and administrative achievements.

Second, a large number of the fifth and sixth generation leaders hold post-graduate degrees. For example, among the 402 newly appointed Standing Committee members of China's 31 provincial-level Party committees, 298 (74 per cent) hold post-graduate degrees and 92 (22.8 per cent) have PhD degrees.[36] However, a closer look at these leaders reveals that an overwhelming majority of them attended these degree programmes on a part-time basis, often in recent years while they served as senior leaders in municipal and provincial governments.

These advanced degrees have even become a liability for these leaders. Minxin Pei, a prominent US-based scholar of Chinese elite politics, has called this phenomenon of inflated advanced degrees among Chinese officials a sign of "systemic cheating."[37]As Pei puts it, "many Chinese officials use fake or dubiously acquired academic credentials to burnish their resumes … in order to gain an advantage in the competition for power."[38] Along the same lines, Wang Yukai 汪玉凯, professor in the Chinese Academy of Governance, recently pointed

35 For a more detailed discussion of the educational backgrounds of the third and fourth generations, see Li 2001.
36 *Nanfang dushi bao*, 4 July 2012. Also see http://nf.nfdaily.cn/nfdsb/content/2012-07/04/content_49948516.htm.
37 Pei 2012.
38 *Ibid.*

out, "When you see these part-time degrees obtained by senior leaders, you cannot rule out the possibility that they are fraudulent."[39]

The third phenomenon is undoubtedly the most troubling. It has been widely reported even in official Chinese media that in order to get appointments and promotions, some officials, especially those who do not have strong family backgrounds or political connections (*guanxi* 关系), have routinely used bribes to "purchase office" (*maiguan* 买官).[40] According to the Hong Kong and Singapore media (though not verified), Liu Zhijun 刘志军, a former minister of railways, intended to use two billion yuan to "purchase" the post of vice premiership, and even a seat in the 2012 Politburo, before he was arrested on corruption charges in February 2011.[41] These three phenomena have understandably tarnished the CCP's reputation for meritocracy among the Chinese public.

Regarding the separation of power in the Chinese political system, since the 1989 purge of Zhao Ziyang 赵紫阳 the CCP has explicitly stated that it is not interested in pursuing a Western-style tripartite division of government. Instead, the leadership has proposed institutional separation of the Party into three divisions, namely: decision-making, policy implementation, and supervision. Given that CCP power remains unchecked, however, what Andrew Nathan has described as the "functional specialization of institutions within the regime" has largely consisted of empty words on the part of the Party leadership.

For example, judicial power has been increasingly marginalized in the PRC political structure over the past decade, as the Party has strongly resisted judicial independence and given infinite power to the Central Commission of Politics and Law (CCPL) of the CCP. The Central Commission of Politics and Law, known as *zhengfawei* 政法委, oversees all law enforcement authorities, including the Supreme People's Court, Supreme People's Procuratorate, Ministry of Justice, Ministry of Public Security, and Ministry of State Security, making it a very powerful organ.[42]

This absence of functional specialization between Chinese governmental institutions undermines arguments that channels for political participation have broadened – the fourth area of Chinese institutional development that Nathan describes. According to Bruce Dickson, the CCP has created new political institutions "to channel political participation and to provide a bridge between state and society," such as village elections and government offices for petition letters and complaint visits (known as the *xinfang* 信访 system).[43] Some Western observers argue that "in China, protests, corruption probes and village elections

39 Xinhua News Net, 4 July 2012, http://news.xinhuanet.com/politics/2012-07/04/c_123366738.htm.

40 Pei 2012.

41 *Lianhe zaobao*, 27 February 2011. Also see http://www.zaobao.com/wencui/2011/02/hongkong110227c.shtml.

42 All the Party committees of provinces, municipalities and counties establish respective politics and law commissions.

43 Dickson 2005, 4.

provide a certain degree of accountability without democracy."[44] The number and scale of group protests, however, have increased in recent years and some have become increasingly violent. In response, the Chinese leadership has lately adopted what Mary Gallagher calls "a mixture of carrots and sticks" – political repression on one hand and growth-producing public goods on the other."[45] The fact that the CCP leadership has been paranoid about the need to maintain social stability shows the serious limitations of institutionalized public participation.

Will today's ally become tomorrow's challenger? The role of the middle class

One of the central arguments of the "authoritarian resilience" thesis is that the CCP has relied on economic development and material incentives to prevent grassroots demand for socio-political challenges. "The main reason why the CCP is so strong," a foreign journalist has observed, "is that the Chinese are aware of the improvements that have been made in such a short period of time."[46] New socio-economic forces, especially entrepreneurs and the emerging middle class, are understood to be political allies of the CCP regime.[47]

But this assumption should be subject to greater scrutiny. Just as yesterday's political target could be today's political ally, so too could today's political ally become tomorrow's political rabble-rouser. Recent studies conducted in China have found that the Chinese middle class, more than other social groups, tends to be cynical about the policy promises made by authorities, more demanding of policy implementation and more sensitive when it comes to official corruption.[48] If middle-class Chinese begin to feel that their voices are being suppressed, that their access to information is unjustly being blocked or that their space for social action is being unduly confined, increased political dissent may begin to take shape.[49]

The Chinese middle class's grievances over government policy have become increasingly evident, partly because the expansion of the middle class has slowed and economic disparity has increased in recent years. The high unemployment rate among recent college graduates (who usually come from middle-class families and are presumed to be members of China's future middle class) should send an alarming signal to the Chinese government. In a recent forum on China's response to the global financial crisis held by the Academy of Chinese Reform and Development in Beijing, Chinese scholars argued that the government should pay much greater attention to the needs and concerns of the middle

44 Dimitrov 2008, 27.
45 Gallagher 2009.
46 Vela 2009.
47 The definition of the Chinese middle class is often based on sets of combined criteria including occupation, income, consumption and self-identification. See Li Chunling 2010.
48 Zhang 2008.
49 For a more detailed discussion of the complicated and changing role of the middle class in Chinese politics, see Li Chunling 2010.

class – otherwise, they argued, the "sensitive" Chinese middle class could become the "angry" middle class.[50]

Members of the Chinese middle class have indeed been up in arms over official corruption and the CCP leadership's lack of accountability and transparency in cases such as food safety, environmental pollution and the 2011 Wenzhou bullet train incident that killed 40 passengers. Like their counterparts elsewhere, the Chinese middle class is also interested in media freedom and resents government censorship.

The Chinese middle class is particularly concerned about the increasingly obvious oligarchic power of state-owned enterprises (SOEs), a trend working at the expense of the private sector. A study conducted by Chinese scholars shows that the total profits made by China's 500 largest private companies in 2009 were less than the total revenues of two SOE companies, China Mobile and Sinopec.[51] Ironically, the private sector's net return on investment in 2009 was 8.2 per cent, compared to the 3.1 per cent for SOEs.[52] The impressive growth of China Mobile has been attributed, at least partially, to the company's monopoly on China's domestic telecommunications market. With large SOEs monopolizing the telecommunications sector, there is no incentive for these flagship companies to pursue technological innovation.

Xu Xiaonian 许小年, a professor of economics and finance at the China Europe International Business School in Shanghai, uses the term "crony capitalism" or "state capitalism," to express his reservations about this growing trend toward state monopoly.[53] He believes that, with the rapid expansion of SOEs in the past few years, China has in fact begun to reverse Deng Xiaoping's plan for the country's development. In Xu's view, China is drawing the wrong lessons from the recent global financial crisis and heading in the wrong direction. According to Xu, the main beneficiaries of SOE growth are corrupt officials, not the Chinese public. He believes that in today's China, entrepreneurs only exist in the private sector and not in SOEs, because SOE managers have neither an entrepreneurial spirit nor a sense of responsibility for their companies' losses.[54] Generally speaking, private entrepreneurs have always been denied bank loans and preferential policies.

Echoing Xu's critique, Chen Zhiwu, an economist at Yale University, observes that 25.5 per cent of fiscal expenditures in China in 2011 were used for social welfare, public health, education and other public goods, while 38 per cent of fiscal expenditures were spent as administrative expenses. By contrast, in the

50 Hu Xiao 2009, 1.

51 *Beijing shangbao*, 30 August 2010. See also http://news.xinhuanet.com/fortune/2010-08/30/c_12496387.htm.

52 See http://xuxiaonian.blog.sohu.com/160724498.html.

53 For Xu Xiaonian's views, see http://xuxiaonian.blog.sohu.com/158818651.html. And *Lianhe zaobao*, 1 August 2010, http://finance.ifeng.com/opinion/zjgc/20100830/2567934.shtml. Also see Bremmer 2010; Huang 2008.

54 See http://finance.ifeng.com/news/20101205/3005151.shtml.

608 The China Quarterly, 211, September 2012, pp. 595–623

United States the fiscal expenditures on these two categories were 73 and 10 per cent, respectively.[55] He called for a reallocation of resources, through democratic reforms in the Chinese political system, to help the country's middle and lower classes.

Three Transformative Trends

This review of the resilient authoritarianism thesis suggests that thinking of the Chinese political system in monolithic terms tends to lead to dogmatic cynicism, on the one hand, or wishful thinking on the other. While the CCP's omnipresence and its future should be a central concern, we need to explore the internal dynamics and tensions within the Party in greater detail. At the same time, transformative trends in broader contexts – the shifting power and relative strength and weakness of other factors besides the Party– deserve greater attention. Altogether, they can help us reconcile in a more holistic way the widely divergent phenomena and contrasting analyses discussed above.

Trend one: weak leaders, strong factions

Over the past three decades, China has been gradually moving away from rule by a single, charismatic all-powerful leader such as Mao Zedong and Deng Xiaoping toward a collective form of leadership. This transformation has ended the era of strongman politics and, to a certain extent, China's long history of arbitrary decision-making by a lone individual. This transition, of course, has been a gradual process. Mao Zedong 毛泽东, a god-like figure, wielded almost limitless power, especially during the Cultural Revolution. Mao routinely made major policy decisions alone, such as the devastating Great Leap Forward and the Cultural Revolution.[56] During the Deng era, as a result of his legendary political career and formidable patron-client ties, a set of reform initiatives – including establishing special economic zones and sending students to study in the West – were carried out with little resistance. Following the Tiananmen incident Deng maintained his role as China's paramount leader even while he held no important leadership position.[57]

Both Jiang Zemin of the third generation and Hu Jintao of the fourth are technocrats who lack the charisma and revolutionary credentials of Deng, but both had broad administrative experience and were good at coalition-building and reaching political compromises. They were, to a great extent, no more than "first among equals" in their respective generations of collective leadership. They could hardly put to use the sort of power enjoyed by Deng, especially when it came to commanding the People's Liberation Army (PLA).

55 Chen 2012.
56 Teiwes and Sun 1998; MacFarquhar and Schoenhals 2008; Hu Angang 2009.
57 Vogel 2011.

Nevertheless, both Jiang and Hu owed much of their power to Deng's endorsement.

As the Hu Jintao era comes to an end, Chinese elites have started to review his administration, and a central theme is a profound sense of disappointment. Hu has been criticized – fairly or not – for his "inaction" (*wuwei* 无为) – a popular term in both Chinese blogs and everyday conversations. Some prominent Chinese public intellectuals have openly called the two five-year terms of the Hu leadership "the lost decade."[58] Premier Wen Jiabao has also been regarded as "weak" and "ineffective."

These criticisms of Hu and Wen may only reflect the views of some interest groups and opinion leaders, and not necessarily the general public. China's vast population of farmers and migrant workers may still see Hu and Wen as leaders who have worked to protect and advance their interests, and many liberal intellectuals in China still seem to consider Wen their best hope for arriving at real political reform. But these widely held negative sentiments nevertheless serve to undermine the power and authority of the Hu–Wen administration.

The profound shift in the source and legitimacy of the leadership is even more salient for the emerging fifth generation of leaders. At the start of their tenure, the upcoming generation of leaders, led by the dual-successor pair Xi Jinping 习近平 and Li Keqiang 李克强, are likely even weaker than their predecessors due to their lack of previous achievements, their need to share power and the growing competitive pressure among their peers. They thus will have to rely even more on collective leadership when making major decisions. In line with this development, Chinese authorities have placed increasing emphasis on "collective leadership," which the 2007 Party Congress Communiqué defines as "a system with division of responsibilities among individual leaders in an effort to prevent arbitrary decision making by a single top leader."[59]

Collective leadership naturally makes factional politics all the more essential. The CCP leadership is now structured around two informal coalitions or factions that check and balance each other's power. The two groups can be labelled the "populist coalition" (*mincui tongmeng* 民粹同盟) led by President Hu Jintao, and the "elitist coalition" (*jingying tongmeng* 精英同盟) which emerged in the Jiang era and is currently led by Wu Bangguo, chairman of the national legislature (and currently the second highest ranking leader in the CCP). The two most likely top leaders after the 18th Party Congress, elitist Xi and populist Li, each represent one of these coalitions. This division of power can be referred to as the "one Party, two coalitions" (*yi dang, liang pai* 一党两派) political mechanism.[60]

The elitist coalition consists mainly of princelings (leaders whose parents are high-ranking officials) and the Shanghai gang (leaders who advanced their political careers in Shanghai when Jiang was the Party chief there in the 1980s), while

58 Li and Cary 2011.
59 Xinhua News Net, 15 October 2011, http://news.sina.com.cn/c/2007-10-15/113314089759.shtml.
60 Li 2005.

the populist coalition consists primarily of former Chinese Communist Youth league officials (known as *tuanpai* 团派), which is Hu Jintao's power base. These two coalitions have contrasting policy initiatives and priorities. The elitist coalition emphasizes GDP growth while the populist coalition advocates social justice and social cohesion. In general, the elitist group dominates the economic and financial sectors and represents the interests of the coastal region while the populist coalition prevails in Party organizations and often claims to voice the concerns of the inland region. In terms of political reforms, leaders of the populist coalition are more interested in promoting intra-Party elections than their counterparts in the elitist coalition, because even members of the political establishment, such as delegates to the Party Congress, often vote against well-known princelings. For example, Bo Xilai was eliminated twice in the elections for the Central Committee at the Party Congress in the 1990s.

Factional politics is, of course, not a new development in the PRC. Major events during the Mao era, such as the Anti-Rightist campaign, the Cultural Revolution and the 1989 Tiananmen crisis, were all related to factional infighting within the CCP leadership. But factional politics in present-day China is no longer a winner-takes-all zero-sum game. This is largely because these two political camps have almost equal power. They have divided the number of seats in the top leadership organizations into a near-perfect balance.

Table 1 shows that in every important leadership body in 2011 (prior to Bo Xilai's downfall), the elitist coalition and populist coalition have had an equal

Table 1: **Equal Allocation of Seats between Two Coalitions (2011)**

	Elitist Coalition (Jiang's Camp)	**Populist Coalition (Hu's Camp)**
Politburo Standing Committee (fifth Generation)	Xi Jinping 习近平 (princeling)	Li Keqiang 李克强 (*tuanpai*)
Politburo (fifth Generation)	Xi Jinping (princeling) Wang Qishan 王岐山 (princeling) Bo Xilai 薄熙来(princeling)	Li Keqiang (*tuanpai*) Li Yuanchao 李源潮 (*tuanpai*) Wang Yang 汪洋 (*tuanpai*)
Secretariat (fifth Generation)	Xi Jinping (princeling) Wang Huning 王沪宁 (Shanghai gang)	Li Yuanchao (*tuanpai*) Ling Jihua 令计划 (*tuanpai*)
Vice Premier	Wang Qishan (princeling) Zhang Dejiang 张德江 (princeling)	Li Keqiang (*tuanpai*) Hui Liangyu 回良玉 (Hu protégé)
State Councillor (civilian)	Ma Kai 马凯 (princeling) Meng Jianzhu 孟建柱 (Shanghai gang)	Liu Yandong 刘延东 (*tuanpai*) Dai Bingguo 戴秉国 (Hu protégé)

Notes and sources:
For the definition of the fifth generation of CCP leaders and the formation of the two coalitions, see Li 2008b; Li 2012a.

allocation of seats in terms of either the representation of fifth-generation leaders or general composition. The two coalitions have managed to arrange a perfect balance of power among the fifth generation of rising stars (one of each in the PSC, three of each in the Politburo and two of each in the six-member Secretariat, an important leadership body that handles the Party's routine business and administrative matters. This balance was also evident in the composition of the four vice premiers and four state councillors (civilian members) in the State Council, including both the fourth and fifth generations.[61]

These two camps have different leadership skills and expertise, as well as access to different socio-economic and political resources. The remarkably meteoric falls of two "heavyweight rising stars" in the Politburo – Shanghai Party Chief Chen Liangyu 陈良宇 (a member of the Shanghai gang) in 2006 and Chongqing Party Chief Bo Xilai (a princeling) in 2012 – are testimony to the phenomenon of "weak leaders, strong factions." Faction leaders involved in serious scandals can be easily dismissed, but factions or coalitions are too strong to be dismantled. The leaders who replaced Chen and Bo, Xi Jinping and Zhang Dejiang, came from the same respective coalitions. Deals have to be made in the shared interest of the CCP's survival. Checks and balances of power between these two coalitions have remained intact in the wake of both crises.

Neither the elitist coalition nor the populist coalition can, or even wants to, totally defeat the other. Each coalition has its own strengths, including representing different constituencies, which the other does not possess. Their relationship, when it comes to policy-making, is one of both competition and cooperation. For example, the Party leadership will be extremely cautious and will avoid expanding the scope of the Bo Xilai case to other senior leaders. Purges will be relatively limited. The fact that certain leaders closely affiliated with Bo, such as Chongqing Mayor Huang Qifan 黄奇帆, have remained in their leadership posts implies that the top leadership does not intend to punish too many people. The fact that the country is facing so many destabilizing factors on the eve of the 18th Party Congress will also impel the leadership to limit the scope of recrimination.

Therefore, though the Bo case is a victory for Hu's camp, this victory will not necessarily translate into additional populist seats on the Politburo Standing Committee. The makeup of the future Standing Committee will largely be determined through compromises between the two coalitions. The balance of power within this system will not be easily changed. If the princeling faction were to collapse, this would constitute an unimaginable revolution. Thus, at the moment, there is a tremendous incentive for the Party's top leadership to preserve the current structure of "one Party, two coalitions," and display unity and solidarity.

Because factional politics play such as an important role in present-day China, understanding the composition of the next Politburo Standing Committee (PSC)

61 Two *tuanpai* leaders, Li Yuanchao and Liu Yandong, are also princelings in terms of their family backgrounds, but their career experiences and close political association with Hu Jintao (who played a direct role in their promotion to the Politburo) make them more loyal to Hu and the populist coalition.

612 The China Quarterly, 211, September 2012, pp. 595–623

Table 2: **Factional Identities of the Leading Candidates for the Post-2012 Politburo Standing Committee**

Elitist Coalition (Jiang's Camp)			Populist Coalition (Hu's Camp)		
Name	***Current Position***	***Factional Identity***	***Name***	***Current Position***	***Factional Identity***
Xi Jinping 习近平	Vice President	princeling	Li Keqiang 李克强	Executive Vice Premier	*tuanpai*
Wang Qishan 王岐山	Vice Premier	princeling	Li Yuanchao 李源潮	Head, Organization Department	*tuanpai*
Zhang Dejiang 张德江	Vice Premier	princeling	Liu Yunshan 刘云山	Head, Propaganda Department	*tuanpai*
Zhang Gaoli 张高丽	Tianjin Party Secretary	Jiang's protégé	Wang Yang 汪洋	Guangdong Party Secretary	*tuanpai*
Yu Zhengsheng 俞正声	Shanghai Party Secretary	princeling	Liu Yandong 刘延东	State Councillor	*tuanpai*
Meng Jianzhu 孟建柱	Minister of Public Security	Shanghai gang	Ling Jihua 令计划	Head, CCP General Office	*tuanpai*
Zhang Chunxian 张春贤	Xinjiang Party Secretary	Jiang's protégé	Hu Chunhua 胡春华	Hebei Party Secretary	*tuanpai*

Source:
Li 2012a.

tends to attract the greatest attention in the study of Chinese politics. While no one knows which seven or nine leaders will eventually reach this pivotal body of power, 14 leaders stand out among their peers as leading candidates (see Table 2). This list is based on a combination of factors such as the leaders' current positions, ages, term limits on the Politburo, tenures on the CCP Central Committee, and previous leadership experiences.[62]

Among the 14 candidates listed, ten currently serve on the 25-member Politburo and two (Xi Jinping and Li Keqiang) are already on the current PSC. It is interesting to note that these leading candidates are equally divided by political coalition – seven elitists and seven populists. Within the elitist coalition, four leaders are princelings, two are the protégés of Jiang Zemin and one is a prominent member of the Shanghai Gang. Within the populist coalition, all seven are *tuanpai* leaders who have strong patron–client ties to Hu Jintao.

These two coalitions share an interest in domestic social stability and aspire to continue China's rise on the world stage, and these common goals often lead the

62 For a detailed discussion of the credentials of these candidates, see Li 2012a.

two coalitions to compromise and cooperate with each other. Yet, as Chinese society becomes increasingly pluralistic in views and values – and as the Chinese leadership confronts a variety of daunting policy challenges – policy differences within the leadership are likely to become more transparent to the public.

Trend two: weak government, strong interest groups

Compared with many other countries in the world, the PRC government has tremendous financial and political resources, largely as a result of both its rapid economic growth and its authoritarian political system. Yet the Chinese government faces a multitude of daunting problems, such as economic disparities, inflation, a possible property bubble, growing local debt, rampant official corruption, frequent instances of social unrest, environmental degradation, resource scarcity, food safety and public health security issues, the lack of a social safety net, and ethnic tensions in Xinjiang and Tibet.

It has been widely noted that the State Council has become less effective at controlling China's provinces, major cities and even key SOEs with regards to economic policies. A recent, popular barb, that "the premier cannot control a general manager" (*zongli guanbuliao zong jingli* 总理管不了总经理), reflects serious problems with the administrative capacity of the central government. The tension and competition between the two competing coalitions discussed earlier also tend to make the decision-making process lengthier and more complicated, which could even result in deadlock one day. China is no democracy, but in this regard might develop some problems characteristic of democracies. Purged local chiefs, most noticeably Bo Xilai and Chen Liangyu, were also known for their explicit challenges to the authority and the policy initiatives of Premier Wen and the central government.

More importantly, never in the six-decade history of the PRC have interest groups been as powerful and influential as they have been in recent years. Like elsewhere in the world, Chinese interest groups are a diverse lot. They include, for example, geographic regions, bureaucratic institutions, the military, the increasingly commercialized media, non-governmental organizations (NGOs) and local governments.

Local governments in the coastal and inland regions are political interest groups that exert strong influence in Beijing and work to ensure that the central government adopts socio-economic policies that advance their regional interests.[63] By way of background: in 2010 among China's 100 wealthiest counties 93, including the top 40, were located in coastal provinces.[64] According to one recent study, nearly 90 per cent of China's exports still come from the coastal

63 For the local factors in sociopolitical changes in China and other East and Southeast Asian countries, see White, Zhou and Rigger 2013 forthcoming.

64 See http://bbs.nhzj.com/viewthread.php?tid=377464.

provinces.[65] In the past few years, provincial and local governments' "liaison offices in Beijing" (*zhujingban* 驻京办), the region-based Chinese lobbying groups, have rapidly increased in number. In January 2010, the central government had to issue new regulations to substantially reduce the permitted number of these offices representing local interests and to require financial auditing of the remaining lobbying groups at the provincial and municipality levels.[66]

In terms of social strata, Chinese interest groups can be categorized into three major groups: corporate and industrial interest groups (known as the "black collar" stratum), the previously discussed emerging middle class ("white collar" professionals), and vulnerable social groups such as migrants ("blue collar" workers). The term "black collar" was recently created in China to refer to the increasing number of the rich and powerful who dress in black, drive black cars, have hidden incomes, live secret lives with concubines, have ties to the criminal underground (*heishehui* 黑社会, or black society) and, most importantly, operate their businesses and wield their economic power in an opaque manner.[67] China's most active corporate and industrial interest groups consist mainly of two clusters. The first includes business elites who work in state monopolized industries such as banking, oil, electricity, coal, telecommunications, aviation, railway, tobacco and shipping; and the second consists of the lobby groups who work for state, foreign or private firms in sectors such as real estate. It has been widely reported in the Chinese media that business interest groups have routinely bribed local officials and formed a "wicked coalition" with local governments.[68]

For example, the various players associated with property development have emerged as one of the most powerful special interest groups in present-day China. The strong power of this group explains why it took 13 years for China to pass the anti-monopoly law, why the macroeconomic control policy of the last decade was largely ineffective and why the widely acknowledged property bubble has continued to grow. In each of these cases, corporate and industrial interest groups have encroached upon the governmental decision-making process, either by creating government policy deadlock or manipulating policies in their own favour.

According to the official state account, more than 70 per cent of the total 120 companies under the State-owned Assets Supervision and Administration Commission (SASAC) were engaged in the real estate business and property

65 Yao 2010. Also see http://www.foreignaffairs.com/articles/65947/the-end-of-the-beijing-consensus?page=show.

66 *Liaowang xinwen zhoukan*, 23 January 2010.

67 It is unclear who first coined the term black-collar stratum. Most online postings in China attribute the label to US-educated economist Lang Xianping (Larry Lang), but Lang has publically denied that he wrote the widely circulated article that popularized the term. See "The Black-Collar Class" (www.chinatranslated.com/?p=407). Translated: "Commentary and Analysis on China's Economic and Political Situation," June 12, 2009.

68 *Zhongguo xinwen zhoukan*, 13 January 2006, *Liaowang*, 5 December 2005, and also see http://www.chinesenewsnet.com, 12 December 2005.

development in 2010.[69] In response, the State Council ordered 78 SASAC companies to withdraw their investments in the real estate business.[70] But resistance from these companies made the government order largely ineffective. Some have speculated that a significant portion of the stimulus package (4 trillion yuan or US$586 billion) implemented in the wake of the 2008 global financial crisis was misdirected to property development. According to a senior researcher of the Ministry of Housing and Urban-Rural Development, about 32 per cent of the stimulus package was invested in real estate.[71]

As for the lower social strata, a manual labour shortage in some coastal cities in recent years reflects the growing political consciousness of these so-called vulnerable social groups (*ruoshi qunti* 弱势群体), especially among the younger generation of migrant workers, to protect their own rights. They have become increasingly resentful over all sorts of discriminative policies against migrant workers, farmers and urban poor. They have moved from one job to the next in order to receive a well-deserved, decent salary. At least partly due to their tireless demands, China has recently witnessed a dramatic increase in wages.

Challenges arising from restive social groups and greedy corporate interest groups are not unique to reform-era China. Democracies in the West (and the East) are certainly not immune to these problems. Quite the contrary, public petitions for social justice and protests against governments' domestic or foreign policies are often seen as part of the normal socio-economic and political life of these countries.

As for the corporate and industrial interest groups, they are probably equally, if not more, powerful and influential in some Western countries than they are in China. In the US, for example, hundreds of lobbying groups have flooded into Washington DC and now constitute an essential feature of American politics. From time to time, these business lobbies have been caught manipulating the democratic system for a company's commercial gain. In his classic work on democracy, Robert Dahl argues that the development of Western democracies is a process dominated by many different sets of leaders, each having access to a different combination of political resources and representing the interests of different sectors and groups in the society.[72] The democratic pluralist system disperses power, influence, authority and control away from any single group of power elites sharing the same social background toward a variety of individuals, groups, associations and organizations.[73] In a sense, democracy is a matter of establishing rules for mediating conflicting interests among social groups in a given society. Yao Yang 姚洋, a professor at Peking University, has argued along the same lines: "An open and inclusive political process has generally

69 *Qianjiang wanbao*, 11 February 2010. Also see http://www.chinanews.com.cn/estate/estate-lspl/news/2010/02-11/2121577.shtml.
70 See http://bt.xinhuanet.com/2010-03/19/content_19293215.htm.
71 See http://news.xinhuanet.com/fortune/2009-03/17/content_11024848.htm.
72 Dahl 1961, 68.
73 Dahl 1961, 252 and 270.

checked the power of interest groups in advanced democracies such as the United States. Indeed, this is precisely the mandate of a disinterested government – to balance the demands of different social groups."[74]

Interest group politics should be seen as neither a threat to socio-political stability nor a challenge to the legitimacy of the government, but rather are regarded as necessary components of democratic governance. The key to coordinating interest group politics, both Dahn and Yao argue, is to establish institutional and democratic mechanisms. Various interests groups can exert their influence through elections, bureaucratic decision-making and judicial processes. In response, the independence of the media and the supremacy of the constitution supervise and safeguard the democratic process. Political crises do occur from time to time, but democratic institutions in general and interest group politics in particular (including the important role of the middle class) are not the source of socio-political instability, but rather the foundation of long-term stability. The rapid emergence of various forms of interest groups and resulting new dynamics in Chinese politics has already profoundly changed how the country is governed.

Trend three: weak party, strong country

The Chinese Communist Party is the world's largest ruling party, consisting of 4 million grassroots branches and 82.6 million members, and it continues to grow. In the absence of any organized opposition, the Party seems unchallengeable in the near future. It should be noted that China's political reforms, including intra-Party democracy, have made almost no progress at all since the Fourth Plenary Session of the 17th Central Committee in the autumn of 2009. This may be attributed to two situational factors. First, the 2008 global financial crisis revealed problems in Western democracies and thus led some left-wing Chinese leaders and public intellectuals, especially advocates for resilient authoritarianism, to argue for the vitality and advantages of one-Party rule in China. Second, the Arab Spring presented a disturbing picture to CCP leaders, as they could face the same outcome as the Mubarak regime. As a result, a majority of CCP leaders across the factional dividing line have decided not to pursue further political reforms. Instead, they have exerted tighter control over social gatherings, grassroots elections, the media and civil society.

One can reasonably assume that the paranoid and excessive use of police force in reaction to the so-called "Chinese Jasmine Revolution" in front of the McDonald's near Tiananmen Square in February 2011 was a sign of the Party's weakness.[75] It is also a sign of weakness that the total amount of money used for "maintaining social stability" in 2009 was 514 billion yuan – almost

74 Yao 2010.

75 A widely spread political joke described the composition of the 1,000 people gathered in front of the McDonald's restaurant in Wangfujing, Beijing, that day. Among them, 990 were said to be undercover police, eight were foreign journalists, one was US Ambassador to China Jon Huntsman who "just happened to be there" and one was actually a protestor.

identical to China's total national defence budget (532 billion yuan) that year. The Chinese government's budget for national defence in 2012 was 670.3 billion yuan, but the budget for the police and other public security expenditures was 701.8 billion yuan (an 11.5 per cent increase).[76] It is widely believed that the Chinese authorities spent 60 million yuan annually looking after Chen Guangcheng 陈光诚 alone, mainly by hiring about 100 local police and other cadres.[77]

The large-scale outflow of capital in recent years (presumably by corrupt officials) further indicates Party elites' lack of confidence in the country's socio-political stability. According to a 2011 report released by Washington-based Global Financial Integrity (GFI), from 2000 to 2009 China's illegal capital outflow totalled US$2.74 trillion, five times more than the total amount from the second-ranked country, Mexico.[78] The People's Bank of China reported in 2011 that from the mid-1990s to 2008, thousands of government officials and state-owned enterprise executives moved a total of 800 billion yuan (US$126 billion) overseas.[79]

According to an internal report by the CCP Organization Department, of the 8,370 senior executives in China's 120 companies directly under the leadership of the SASAC, 6,370 have immediate family members who live overseas or hold foreign passports. In Guangzhou, of approximately 1,000 corruption cases under investigation in recent years, half have occurred in SOEs, and of those who escaped overseas with foreign assets, 70 per cent were from SOEs and central financial institutions.[80] Li Chengyan 李成言, director of the Governance Studies Center of Peking University, recently told the Chinese media that "the large scale of capital outflow by corrupt officials shows that these CCP leaders know better than anyone else that the so-called China model (the CCP's resilient authoritarianism) is false – one that is not sustainable.[81]

Despite the fact that the dismissal of Bo Xilai can be seen as an important move in the right direction, this dramatic incident has nevertheless damaged the reputation of the CCP leadership. The troubles within the CCP leadership, however, should not necessarily be viewed as a problem for, or weakness of, the country. In his now well-known speech at the China Reform Forum on December 2011, Zhang Lifan 章立凡, a public intellectual in Beijing, argued that "China is not in danger, but the CCP is."[82] In his view, many CCP members do not care whether the CCP will collapse, but are instead only concerned about the wellbeing of their own families. CCP leaders are also well prepared for their own future. Zhang Lifan stated bluntly: "if the next generation leaders do not

76 *Shijie ribao*, 3 May 2012, A4.
77 *Ibid.*
78 *Shijie ribao*, 20 April 2012, A4.
79 *Shijie ribao*, 7 June 2012, A1.
80 *Shijie ribao*, 14 May 2012, A3.
81 *Shijie ribao*, 4 June 2012, A1.
82 Zhang Lifan's blog, post on 1 February 2012, http://blog.sina.com.cn/s/blog_4b86a2630100zhuv.html.

618 The China Quarterly, 211, September 2012, pp. 595–623

pursue political reforms in their first term, there is no point in doing so in their second term." In his words, "China should witness either reforms in the first five years, or the end of the CCP in ten years."[83]

Recent demand for constitutionalism among liberal intellectuals and calls among some military officers for a "state army" rather than a "Party army" both constitute new challenges to CCP rule. As the CCP becomes weaker, many commentators in China have given more attention to the intriguing role of the PLA. Qian Liqun 钱理群, a distinguished scholar at Peking University, recently warned that "if the civilian leadership cannot form a strong coalition for political reforms, the young officers in the PLA will seize the moment. It would be a tragedy if the military presents the loudest noise for "democratic change" in China. That was the nightmare of 20th-century China, and it was also the grave lesson of the rise of Japanese militarism in the last century."[84] Qian believes that the princelings within the PLA will bolster the army's power in the upcoming Xi era, thereby increasing the risk of military interference in domestic politics.

Qian's worries were reinforced by recent remarks by Zhang Musheng 张木生, a well-known conservative scholar who has close ties with General Liu Yuan 刘源. General Liu is a princeling in the PLA, a controversial rising star in the military's senior leadership who is the son of former PRC president Liu Shaoqi 刘少奇. Zhang made a controversial speech in which he argued that present-day China is ruled by some incompetent and weak leaders who have led the country into a social and political crisis. "The future generation of leaders," in his words, "will not be like that!"[85]

He Pin, a seasoned New York-based analyst of Chinese elite politics, is doubtful of scenarios that predict a military takeover or chaos in the country. He believes that the "possibility for chaos in China is low for four reasons: 1) there are no strong region-based military warlords; 2) with the exception of a few ethnic regions, there is an absence of major regional conflict over resources; 3) the new leadership will most likely promote the economic integration of the country; and 4) in terms of the international environment, foreign powers do not want chaos in China."[86]

The fact that the Bo crisis has hit the CCP leadership more severely than it has affected the Chinese economy reflects the maturity of Chinese society and the strength of the country as a whole. China is not in decline, and is certainly not heading toward a collapse. One should not lose the big picture that China is on a historical rise, although this rise is unlikely to be strictly linear due to all of the daunting challenges – socio-economic, political, environmental, demographic and in the realm of foreign policy.

China's upcoming transition to a more accountable, more representative and less corrupt political system, driven primarily by an on-going legitimacy crisis,

83 *Ibid.*
84 Qian 2012.
85 *Ibid.*
86 He Pin 2012, 186–87.

will not be easy. But the Chinese public's shared perception of China's rise on the world stage and all of the reform-era socio-economic developments that contribute to the country's national resilience (not the CCP's resilient authoritarianism) may make China's political transformation different from the experiences of the former Soviet Union, the Eastern bloc communist states and the "Arab Awakening" countries.

Despite a recent slowdown in China's breakneck economic growth, the country will likely continue to be one of the world's fast-growing economies for the next decade and beyond due to a combination of factors. These include the country's solid industrial foundation, its newly built world-class infrastructure, high rates of investment and savings, the continuing strong input of foreign direct investment, an impressive amount of foreign reserves, a large domestic market, human resource advantages, growing entrepreneurship and last but certainly not least the country's commitment to transitioning toward a domestic, demand-driven, and environmentally friendly mode of economic growth.[87] On top of that, the Chinese people who have created an economic miracle are unlikely to stop just at the gate of political democracy.

Final Thoughts

From a broader perspective, although these three shifts of power are the cause of some tension in the governance of the country and create a sense of uncertainty, they can be considered as very encouraging and positive developments for China. Factional checks and balances within the CCP leadership, dynamic interest groups – especially the increasingly important role of the middle class – and the widely shared perception of a rising power on the world stage and the public confidence this has engendered may all prove to be important factors in an eventual transition to democracy.

For the near future, the focus of China analysts should not only be on whether the CCP leadership uses proper legal procedures to deal with the Bo Xilai case, but also whether the leadership can seize the opportunity to reach a new consensus and seriously pursue political reforms. It is clearer today than perhaps any time during the reform era that the CCP's "authoritarian resilience," both conceptually and empirically, is a stagnant system because of its resistance to a democratic transition.

If the CCP wants to regain the public's confidence and avoid a bottom-up revolution, it must embrace genuine systematic democratic change in the country. The following profound transformations need to be made. First, in addition to handling the Bo case through established legal mechanisms, a call for legal reforms – including judiciary reform, the rule of law and constitutionalism – will become very important.[88] This could be a wonderful opportunity for liberal

87 For more discussion of China's economic forecast, see Hu Angang 2011.

88 For a detailed discussion of recent public and intellectual demand for constitutionalism, see He Weifang 2012. Also see Peerenboom 2002, Li and Jordan 2009; Wishik 2012.

620 The China Quarterly, 211, September 2012, pp. 595–623

leaders, and to a certain extent all leaders, to realize that legal reform is the best way to protect themselves in a country that still lacks the rule of law. It will take many years and even decades for China to fully build a constitutional system, but the ideological, political and legal statement that the Party should be under, rather than above, the constitution should be made sooner.

Second, the CCP should pursue bolder intra-Party elections, which could involve voting as a means of assigning leadership positions. For example, to select the members of the next Politburo Standing Committee, the CCP could put ten or eleven candidates on a ballot and have the Central Committee select nine of them, or have eight or nine candidates if the PSC changes to seven seats. This kind of "more candidates than seats" election (*cha'e xuanju* 差额选举) at the top level of leadership should be institutionalized immediately to bring a much-needed new source of legitimacy to the Party.

Third, media regulation is also in urgent need of reform. China has entered a "season of rumours," and social media has become so powerful that Chinese authorities often shut down domestic micro-blogging services. This is not an effective way to run the country (especially when China is supposed to have an innovation-driven economy). The reason people go to social media for news is that the mainstream media does not tell them much. Thus, the way to avoid the sensationalism produced by social media is to open up the mainstream media. This is not only in the interest of liberal intellectuals, but the Chinese leaders themselves. The more these sensational stories are suppressed, the more powerful they become. Ten years of commercialization of the Chinese media have already prepared Chinese journalists to pursue freedom of press. The on-going revolutionary change in social media and telecommunications will make media freedom a necessity rather than a choice.

It would be intellectually and politically naïve to believe that Bo's downfall will only have positive ramifications and that nothing will go wrong in China. It is worth remembering, however, that the assassination of a Taiwanese writer by agents of Taiwan's Nationalist Party helped trigger the island's transition from authoritarianism to democracy in the mid-1980s. Similarly, the CCP must now either make changes to be on the right side of history or be left behind. From a broader perspective, weak leaders, weak government and weak Party are not trends that are unique to China; they are common challenges in today's world. Welcome, China, to the 21st century!

Bibliography

Baum, Richard. 2007. "The Limits of Authoritarian Resilience." Paper presented in the conference held in the Centre for International Studies and Research, Sciences Po, Paris, 17 January 2007. See also http://www.ceri-sciences-po.org/archive/jan07/art_rb.pdf.

Bell, Daniel. 2012. "Why China won't collapse." *The Christian Science Monitor*, posted online 11 July 2012 http://m.csmonitor.com/Commentary/Opinion/2012/0711/Why-China-won-t-collapse.

Bremmer, Ian. 2010. *The End of the Free Market: Who Wins the War between States and Corporations?* New York: Portfolio.

Brødsgaard, Kjeld Erik and Zheng Yongnian. 2006. "Introduction: Whither the Chinese Communist Party?" In Brødsgaard, Kjeld Erikand Zheng Yongnian (eds.), *The Chinese Communist Party in Reform*. New York: Routledge.

Brown, Kerry. 2009. *Friends and Enemies: The Past, Present and Future of the Communist Party of China*. New York: Anthem Press.

Chang, Gordon. 2001. *The Coming Collapse of China*. New York: Random House.

Chang, Gordon. 2011. "*The Coming Collapse of China*: 2012 Edition." *Foreign Policy*, posted on 29 December 2011. http://www.foreignpolicy.com/articles/2011/12/29/the_coming_collapse_of_china_2012_edition.

Chen, Zhiwu. 2012. "Zhongguo daole fei minzhu buke de shihou" (It is the time when China must make a transition to democracy). *Duowei News*, posted on 2 January 2012. http://china.dwnews.com/news/2012-01-02/58470187.html.

Dickson, Bruce. 2003. *Red Capitalists in China: The Party, Private Entrepreneurs, and Prospects for Political Change*. New York: Cambridge University Press.

Dickson, Bruce. 2005. "Populist Authoritarianism: The Future of the Chinese Communist Party," Occasional Papers. Carnegie Endorsement for International Peace.

Dickson, Bruce. 2008. *Wealth into Power: The Communist Party's Embrace of China's Private Sector*. New York: Cambridge University Press.

Dimitrov, Martin. 2008. "The Resilient Authoritarians." *Current History* 107 (705), 24–29.

Dahl, Robert. 1961. *Who Governs? Democracy and Power in an American City*. New Haven, CT: Yale University Press.

Fewsmith, Joseph. 2006. "Inner-Party democracy: development and limitations." *China Leadership Monitor* 31, 1–11.

Gallagher, Mary. 2009. "Power tool or dull blade? Resilient autocracy and the selectorate theory." Unpublished paper, available at http://faculty.maxwell.syr.edu/johanson/papers/gallagher_hanson07.pdf.

He, Pin. 2012. *Keyi queding de Zhongguo weilai* (China's Future Can Be Determined). New York: Mirror Books, 2012.

He, Weifang. 2012. *In the Name of Justice: Striving for the Rule of Law in China*. Washington DC: The Brookings Institution Press.

Hu, Angang. 2009. *Mao Zedong yu wenge* (Mao Zedong and the Cultural Revolution). Hong Kong: Strong Wind Press.

Hu, Angang. 2011. *China in 2020: A New Type of Superpower*. Washington, DC: Brookings Institution Press.

Hu, Xiao. 2009. "Yi gaige yifu jingji weiji" (Accelerate reforms to respond to the economic crisis). *Zhongguo jingji shibao*, 3 March.

Huang, Yasheng. 2008. *Capitalism with Chinese Characteristics: Entrepreneurship and the State*. New York: Cambridge University Press.

Kuhn, Robert Lawrence. 2010. *How China's Leaders Think*. New York: John Wiley and Sons.

Li, Cheng. 2001. *China's Leaders: The New Generation*. Lanham, MD: Rowman and Littlefield.

Li, Cheng. 2005. "The new bipartisanship within the Chinese Communist Party," *Orbis* 49 (3), 387–400.

Li, Cheng (ed.). 2008. *China's Changing Political Landscape: Prospects for Democracy*, Washington DC: The Brookings Institution Press.

Li, Cheng (ed.). 2010. *China's Emerging Middle Class: Beyond Economic Transformation*. Washington, DC: The Brookings Institution Press.

Li, Cheng. 2012a. "The battle for China's top nine leadership posts." *The Washington Quarterly* 35 (1), 131–145.

Li, Cheng. 2012b. "Power shift in China, Part I." Yale Global online magazine, posted on 16 April 2012, http://yaleglobal.yale.edu/content/power-shift-china-part-i.

Li, Cheng and Eve Cary. 2011. "The last year of Hu's leadership: Hu's to blame?" *China Brief* 11 (23). 20 December.

622 *The China Quarterly*, 211, September 2012, pp. 595–623

Li, Cheng and Jordan Lee. 2009. "China's legal system." *China Review* 48, 1–3.

Li, Chunling. 2010. "Characterizing China's middle classes: heterogeneous composition and multiple identities." In Cheng Li, (ed.) *China's Emerging Middle Class: Beyond Economic Transformation*. Washington, DC: The Brookings Institution Press, 135–156.

Link, Perry. 2012. "America's outdated view of China." *The Washington Post*, 10 May.

Lü, Xiaobo. 2000. *Cadres and Corruption: The Organizational Involution of the Chinese Communist Party*. Stanford, CA: Stanford University Press.

MacFarquhar, Roderick and Michael Schoenhals. 2008. *Mao's Last Revolution*. Cambridge, MA: Harvard University Press.

McGregor, Richard. 2010. *The Party: The Secret World of China's Communist Rulers*. New York: Harper.

McGregor, Richard. 2011. "Five myths about the Chinese Communist Party." *Foreign Policy*, January/February.

Miller, Alice. 2008a. "China's new Party leadership." *China Leadership Monitor* 23.

Miller, Alice. 2008b. "Institutionalization and the changing dynamics of Chinese leadership politics." In Cheng Li (ed.), *China's Changing Political Landscape: Prospects for Democracy*, Washington DC: The Brookings Institution Press, 61–79.

Miller, Alice. 2009. "Leadership sustains public unity amid stress." *China Leadership Monitor* 29.

Nathan, Andrew J. 2003. "Authoritarian resilience," *Journal of Democracy* 14 (1), 6–17.

Nathan, Andrew. 2006. "Debate #1: is Communist Party rule sustainable in China?" Reframing China Policy: The Carnegie Debates, Washington, DC, posted on 5 October 2006, http://www.carnegieendowment.org/files/cds_nathan.pdf.

Peerenboom, Randall. 2002. *China's Long March toward the Rule of Law*. New York: Cambridge University Press.

Pei, Minxin. 2008. *China's Trapped Transition: The Limits of Developmental Autocracy*. Cambridge, MA: Harvard University Press.

Pei, Minxin. 2012. "The myth of Chinese meritocracy." *Project Syndicate*, 15 May, http://www.project-syndicate.org/commentary/the-myth-of-chinese-meritocracy.

Qian, Liqun. 2012. "Lao hongweibing dangzheng de danyou" ("Worries about the rule of the old Red Guards"). *Wenzhai*, 19 February.

Shambaugh, David. 2008. *China's Communist Party: Atrophy and Adaptation*. Berkeley, CA: University of California Press.

Shirk, Susan L. 2007. *China: Fragile Superpower: How China's Internal Politics Could Derail Its Peaceful Rise*. New York: Oxford University Press.

Teiwes, Frederick C. and Warren Sun. 1998. *China's Road to Disaster: Mao, Central Politicians, and Provincial Leaders in the Unfolding of the Great Leap Forward 1955–1959*. New York. M.E. Sharpe.

Tsai, Kellee. 2007. *Capitalism without Democracy: The Private Sector in Contemporary China*. Ithaca, NY: Cornell University Press.

Vela, Justin. 2009. "The secret of the CCP's success." Asia Times Online, posted on 3 October 2009, http://www.atimes.com/atimes/China/KJ03Ad01.html.

Vogel, Ezra F. 2011. *Deng Xiaoping and the Transformation of China*. Cambridge, MA: Harvard University Press.

Wang, Changjiang. 2009. "*Zhuoli tuijin dang zhizheng de gaige chuangxin*" (Promoting reforms and innovation in the Party). *Jiefang ribao*, 28 September.

White, Lynn, Kate Zhou, and Shelley Rigger. 2013 forthcoming. *Democratization in China, Korea, and Southeast Asia? Local and National Perspectives*. New York: Routledge.

Wishik, Anton. 2012. "The Bo Xilai crisis: a curse or a blessing for China? An interview with Cheng Li," posted on 18 April 2012, http://www.nbr.org/research/activity.aspx?id=236.

Yang, Dali L. 2004. *Remaking the Chinese Leviathan: Market Transition and the Politics of Governance in China*. Stanford, CA: Stanford University Press.

Yao, Yang. 2010. "The end of the Beijing consensus: can China's model of authoritarian growth survive?" *Foreign Affairs*, 2 February.

Yu, Keping. 2009a. *Democracy Is a Good Thing: Essays on Politics, Society and Culture in Contemporary China*. Washington DC: The Brookings Institution Press.

Yu, Keping. 2009b. "*Xuyao liqing youguan minzhu de ji ge guanxi*" (The necessity to clarify several conceptual factors concerning democracy). *Beijing ribao*, 16 March. Also at http://theory.people.com.cn/GB/49150/49152/8965735.html.

Zhang, Ming. 2012. "Zhongguo xiang he chuqu?" (Whither China?). *Ershiyi shiji*, 3 March.

Zhang, Yi. 2008. "Dangdai Zhongguo zhongchan jieceng de zhengzhi taidu" ("Political attitudes of the middle stratum in contemporary China"). *Zhongguo shehui kexue* 2, 117–131.

Zhao, Suisheng (ed.). 2006. *Debating Political Reform in China: Rule of Law vs. Democratization*. Armonk, NY: M. E. Sharpe.

Zi, Zhongyun (ed.). 2011. *Qimeng yu Zhongguo shehui zhuanxing* (*The Enlightenment and Transformation of Chinese Society*). Beijing: Shehui kexue wenxian chubanshe.